A MANUAL

OF

ROMAN ANTIQUITIES.

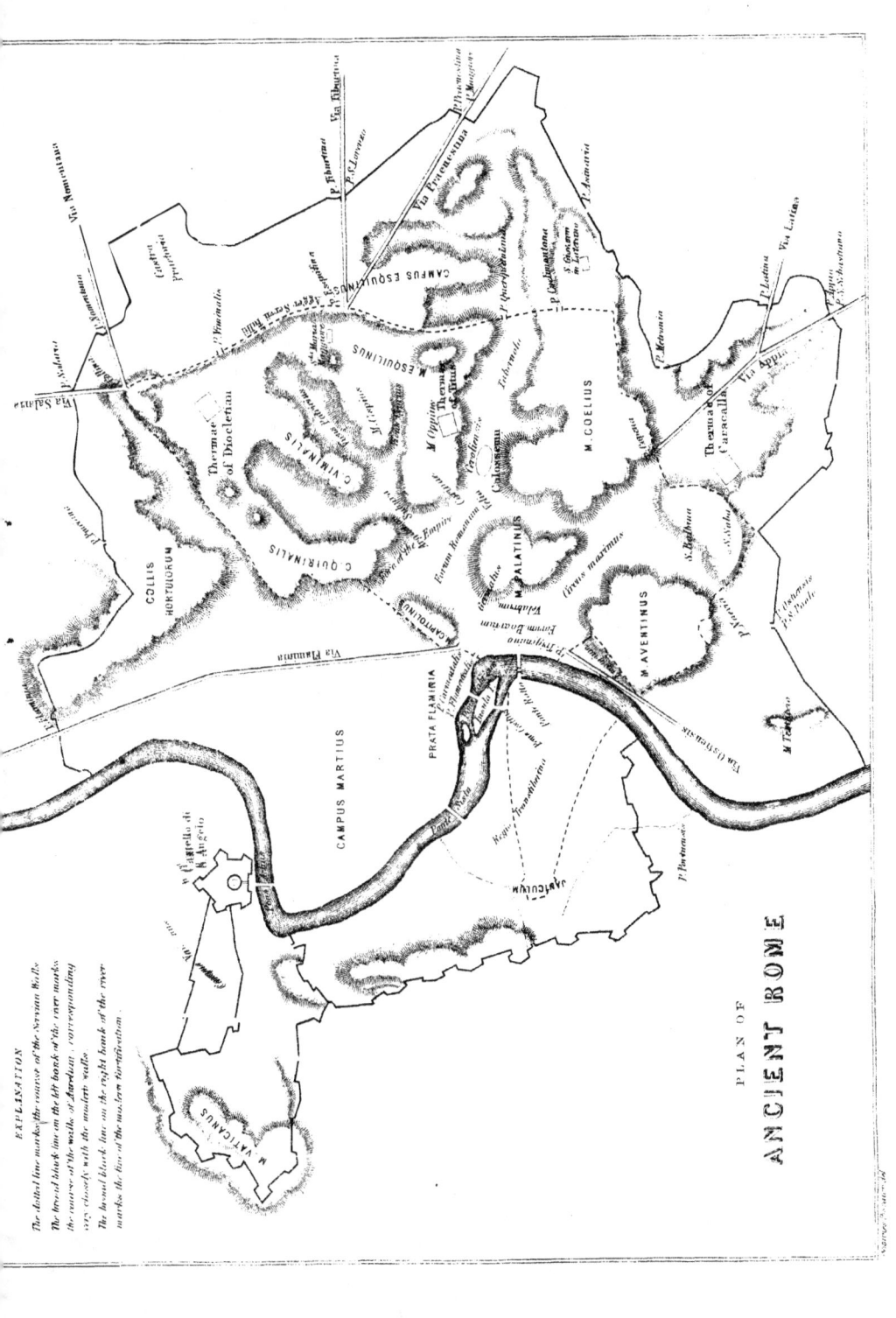

PLAN OF ANCIENT ROME

A MANUAL

OF

ROMAN ANTIQUITIES

BY

WILLIAM RAMSAY, M.A.

PROFESSOR OF HUMANITY IN THE UNIVERSITY OF GLASGOW

WITH NUMEROUS ILLUSTRATIONS

FOURTEENTH EDITION, REVISED AND ENLARGED.

WIPF & STOCK · Eugene, Oregon

Wipf and Stock Publishers
199 W 8th Ave, Suite 3
Eugene, OR 97401

A Manual of Roman Antiquities
Fourteenth Edition, Revised, and Enlarged
By William M. Ramsay
Softcover ISBN-13: 978-1-6667-5614-2
Publication date 8/12/2022
Previously published by Charles Griffin and Company, 1859

This edition is a scanned facsimile of the original edition published in 1859.

PREFACE.

In compiling this Treatise, I have endeavoured to present, in a connected form, such information on the Topography of the Roman City, on the rise and gradual development of the Roman Constitution, and on the social and domestic habits and feelings of the Roman People, as may serve to remove some of the obstacles which impede the progress of those who are desirous of applying themselves to the study of Latin Literature. It must be understood, however, that the inquiries here prosecuted do not extend beyond the latter portion of the first century after the birth of Christ. But, even when thus limited, the subject is so vast and so varied, that while it has been found impossible to dilate upon any topic, it has been necessary to touch very lightly upon several, and to pass over altogether many more which, although highly interesting in themselves, do not bear directly upon the object in view.

It would answer no good purpose to enumerate the long array of treatises and disquisitions which have been consulted in drawing up a work like the present, which ought to exhibit in a condensed shape the results of tedious and intricate researches, but I cannot pass over in silence the great assistance I have received from the "Gallus" and the "Handbuch der Römischen Altherthümer," unfortunately never completed, of the late lamented Wilhelm Adolph Becker.

Those who desire to enlarge their knowledge upon any of the subjects discussed in the following pages, may consult with advantage the excellent "Dictionary of Greek and Roman Antiquities," edited by my accomplished friend Doctor William Smith. I had the honour to contribute a few articles to that book, but I do not feel myself prohibited by that circumstance from speaking of it, as a whole, in terms of the warmest praise.

WILLIAM RAMSAY.

GLASGOW COLLEGE, 28th January, 1851.

ADVERTISEMENT TO THE FOURTH EDITION.

The fact that three large editions of the "Manual of Roman Antiquities" have been sold off within a limited period, is a very gratifying proof that my labours have been approved of by those most competent to form a judgment. At the suggestion of some persons, for whose opinion I entertain great respect, I have added to this edition a chapter upon Roman Agriculture, which will, I trust, be found serviceable.

W. R.

COLLEGE OF GLASGOW,
20th March, 1859.

CONTENTS.

CHAP. I.
TOPOGRAPHY OF ROME, ... 1

CHAP. II.
ON THE ORIGIN OF THE ROMAN PEOPLE, AND THEIR POLITICAL AND
SOCIAL ORGANIZATION, FROM THE EARLIEST TIMES, . . . 60

CHAP. III.
ON THE GENERAL PRINCIPLES OF THE ROMAN CONSTITUTION, AND
THE RIGHTS OF THE DIFFERENT CLASSES OF PERSONS WHO FORMED
THE POPULATION OF THE ROMAN EMPIRE, ... 79

CHAP. IV.
THE COMITIA, ... 104

CHAP. V.
MAGISTRATES OF THE REGAL AND REPUBLICAN PERIODS AND UNDER
THE EARLY EMPERORS, ... 131

CHAP. VI.
THE SENATE, ... 218

CHAP. VII.
ON THE PUBLIC LANDS AND THE AGRARIAN LAWS, . . . 225

CHAP. VIII.
THE ROMAN REVENUES, ... 252

CONTENTS.

CHAP. IX.
ROMAN LAW AND THE ADMINISTRATION OF JUSTICE, . . . 241

CHAP. X.
RELIGION OF ROME, ... 316

CHAP. XI.
THE ROMAN CALENDAR, ... 362

CHAP. XII.
THE MILITARY AND NAVAL AFFAIRS OF THE ROMANS, . . . 377

CHAP. XIII.
ROMAN WEIGHTS AND MEASURES—COINS—COMPUTATION OF MONEY—
INTEREST OF MONEY, ... 408

CHAP. XIV.
PRIVATE LIFE OF THE ROMANS, ... 421

CHAP. XV.
AGRICULTURE, ... 468

Rome seated on the Seven Hills, from a large Brass of Vespasian.

LIST OF ILLUSTRATIONS.

	PAGE
PUTEAL LIBONIS. *Denarius of the Gens Scribonia,*	12
FAUSTULUS, &c. *Denarius of the Gens Pompeia,*	13
TEMPLUM DIVAE FAUSTINAE,	15
AEDES VESTAE. *Denarius of the Gens Cassia,*	15
VENUS CLOACINA. *Denarius of the Gens Mussidia,*	17
THE DIOSCURI. *Denarius of the Gens Postumia,*	18
BASILICA ÆMILIA ET FULVIA. *Denarius of the Gens Æmilia,*	19
TEMPLUM IANI. *Large Brass of Nero,*	20
COLUMNA TRAIANA,	24
BASILICA ULPIA. *Large Brass of Trajan,*	24
ARCUS TRIUMPHALIS. *Large Brass of Trajan,*	24
TEMPLUM DIVI TRAIANI. *Large Brass of Trajan,*	24
CAPITOLIUM. *Denarius of the Gens Petillia,*	26
CAPITOLIUM. *Large Brass of Vespasian,*	26
CAPITOLIUM. *Silver Medallion of Domitian,*	26
ARCUS SEPTIMII SEVERI,	27
TULLIANUM. *Sir W. Gell's Rome,*	28
ARCUS TITI,	31
TEMPLUM PACIS. *Large Brass of Hadrian,*	31
COLOSSEUM,	35
ARCUS CONSTANTINI,	36
ARCUS ARGENTARIUS,	40
TEMPLUM IANI QUADRIFRONTIS,	41
AEDES VESTAE,	41
TEMPLUM FORTUNAE VIRILIS,	42
THEATRUM MARCELLI,	45
PORTICUS OCTAVIAE,	45
VILLA PUBLICA. *Denarius of the Gens Didia,*	46
PANTHEON,	47
SEPULCHRUM HADRIANI, *now the Castello di S. Angelo,*	50
PONS AEMILIUS. *Denarius of Gens Aemilia,*	51
INSULA TIBERINA,	52

LIST OF ILLUSTRATIONS.

	PAGE
AQUA MARCIA. *Denarius of Q. Marcius Philippus,*	56
CLOACA MAXIMA. *Sir W. Gell's Rome,*	59
THE SERVIAN WALL. *Sir W. Gell's Rome,*	59
BALLOTING. *Denarius of the Gens Cassia,*	109
BALLOTING. *Denarius of the Gens Hostilia,*	109
SELLA CURULIS AND FASCES,	137
AEDILES CEREALES. *Denarius of the Gens Calpurnia,*	159
SACERDOTAL INSTRUMENTS. *Denarius of Nero,*	206
AUGUSTUS IN A TRIUMPHAL CAR DRAWN BY ELEPHANTS. *Large Brass of Augustus,*	212
CARPENTUM. *Large Brass of Agrippina,*	212
FUNERAL PYRE, with Legend CONSECRATIO. *Large Brass of Antoninus Pius,*	212
EMPRESS ASCENDING TO HEAVEN ON A PEACOCK. *Large Brass of Julia Domna,*	212
LICTOR WITH THE FASCES, *from an Ancient Bas-relief,*	224
ROMAN LYRES. *Hope's Costumes of the Ancients,*	231
R. CC. (*Remissae Centesimae.*) *Third Brass of Caligula,*	237
R. XL. (*Remissae Quadragesimae.*) *Large Brass of Galba,*	237
SACRED UTENSILS. *Frieze of the Temple of Jupiter Tonans,*	240
PROVOCO. *Denarius of the Gens Porcia,*	286
SACRIFICIAL KNIFE AND AXE. *Frieze of the Temple of Jupiter Tonans,*	315
LITUUS. *Frieze of the Temple of Jupiter Tonans,*	329
ALBOGALERUS. *Frieze of the Temple of Jupiter Tonans,*	333
ANCILIA. *Denarius of Augustus,*	334
SACRED UTENSILS. *Denarius of Cæsar,*	343
SIMPULUM AND LITUUS. *Aureus of Augustus,*	344
SACRED UTENSILS. *Large Brass of M. Aurelius,*	344
ROMAN EMPEROR SACRIFICING. *Large Brass of Caligula,*	344
PLAN OF THE CIRCUS OF CARACALLA,	349
CIRCUS MAXIMUS. *Large Brass of Trajan,*	349
METAE OF THE CIRCUS. *Large Brass of Balbinus,*	349
PLAN OF A ROMAN THEATRE. *According to Vitruvius,*	355
PLAN OF A ROMAN THEATRE. *Pompeii,*	355
COLOSSEUM. *Large Brass of Titus,*	357
AMPHITHEATRE OF POMPEII,	357
JUPITER, JUNO, AND MINERVA. *Bas-relief in the Capitol,*	361
STANDARD BEARER AND LEGIONARIES. *Trajan's Column,*	376
GREEK WARRIOR. *Hope's Costumes of the Ancients,*	382
DACIAN HORSEMAN. *Trajan's Column,*	385
ROMAN STANDARDS. *Denarius of M. Antonius,*	393
TRIUMPHAL ARCH. *Large Brass of Nero,*	394
ROMAN EMPEROR AND SLINGERS. *Trajan's Column,*	402
SHIP. *Tomb at Pompeii,*	404
SHIP. *Large Brass of Commodus,*	405
SHIP. *After Scheffer,*	407
ROMAN COINS. *Various,*	413—417
NUPTIAL COUCH. *Ancient Painting*	424

LIST OF ILLUSTRATIONS.

	PAGE
INTERIOR OF TOMB. *Pompeii*,	427
ROMAN BATH, *from the Baths of Titus*,	435
ROMAN AMPHORAE. *Pompeii*,	439
TIBIA. The Double Flute, *from a Painting at Pompeii*,	448
ISIS WITH SISTRUM. *Ancient Statue*,	450
LYRE AND PECTEN. *From Ancient Paintings*,	450
THE TOGA, *from Ancient Statues*,	452
JUPITER. *Statue in the Gallery of Florence*,	453
STATUE OF A LADY. *Pompeii*,	453
THE PAENULA. *Ancient Statue*,	453
CALCEI AND SOLEAE. *Becker's Gallus*,	454
PLANS OF ROMAN HOUSES,	466, 467
JUPITER WITH STATUE OF VICTORY. *Hope's Costumes of the Ancients*,	497

CHAPTER I.

TOPOGRAPHY OF ROME.[1]

Campagna di Roma.—The district now known as the *Campagna di Roma* extends along the shore of the Mediterranean for sixty miles southward from the mouth of the Tiber, and inland as far as the first slopes of the Apennines, which here begin to rise at a distance of from 25 to 35 miles from the sea. This region presents a very peculiar aspect. In the immediate vicinity of the coast the land is low and swampy, and as we ascend the streams the meadows which border their banks partake of the same character. But the remainder of the country is a vast expanse of table land, rolling in long swells, broken and furrowed in all directions by deep ravines and water-courses, the sides of which are frequently rocky and precipitous. The surface of the table land is, for the most part, perfectly dry, the general elevation above the level of the sea is seldom less than 100 feet, and in some places it rises into ridges of considerable height, while in the midst of the plain the bold, picturesque, isolated mass of the Alban hills (*Mons Albanus*) divides the Campagna proper from the deadly level of the Pomptine marshes (*Paludes Pomptinae.*)

Site of Rome.—*The seven hills.*—About eighteen miles from the mouth of the Tiber, the stream, whose course is south by west, makes a very sudden bend nearly due west; and, as it gradually sweeps back to its former direction, forms an acute angle, in which lies an alluvial meadow, containing upwards of 300 English acres. This is the celebrated *Campus Martius*, and on this flat a great portion of the modern city has been built. The southern extremity of the Campus Martius was known by the name of the *Prata Flaminia.*

A steep bank rises abruptly from the edge of the Campus Martius, and then slopes gradually into the table land, which forms the general surface of the country beyond. This bank presents a very irregular and rugged outline towards the river, the continuous ridge being broken by numerous projecting bluffs, which jut out into the low ground, and, of these, the four which approach most nearly to the river, at the southern extremity of the Campus Martius, being cut off from

---

[1] It is necessary to warn the young scholar that almost every point connected with the topography of ancient Rome, beyond the mere identification of the seven hills, has given rise to animated, complex and interminable controversies, which, in some cases, such as the disputes regarding the position of the Forum, and the determination of the *Arx* and the *Capitolium*, may almost be said to have assumed the aspect of a national quarrel, since nearly all Italian antiquaries adopt one set of opinions, while the most eminent Germans agree in advocating opposite views. We cannot, of course, in a work like the present, attempt to give even an outline of the arguments and illustrations employed by the conflicting parties; but we shall endeavour to state plainly those conclusions which appear most reasonable, following, in a great measure, as our most trustworthy guides, the great work by Platner, Bunsen, Gerhard and Rostell, entitled "Beschreibung der Stadt Rom," and the first part of the "Handbuch der Römischen Alterthümer," by the late lamented Wilhelm Adolph Becker, to which we may add some excellent papers in the Classical Museum by Mr. E. H. Bunbury.

B

the main ridge, and from each other, by intersecting hollows, stand as small isolated hills, with steep rocky escarpments. The smallest of the four, that which lies farthest to the north, is the MONS CAPITOLINUS; next in size, to the south of the Capitoline, is the PALATIUM or MONS PALATINUS; to the south of the Palatine, larger than either of the preceding, and almost touching the river, is the MONS AVENTINUS; to the south-east of the Palatine, and separated both from it and from the Aventine by a deep hollow, is the MONS COELIUS, originally called, we are told, MONS QUERQUETULANUS.

Another deep hollow to the north of the Coelian divides it from a long continuous ridge, which, on the east, slopes gradually into the Campagna, while on the west, or side next the river, it is broken into four tongues, separated from each other by narrow dells. These tongues, taken in succession, are, ESQUILIAE or MONS ESQUILINUS, which comprehends two projections, severally distinguished, in ancient times as the *Mons Oppius* and the *Mons Cispius*,[1] names, however, which, in the Augustan age, were known to the learned only—beyond the Mons Cispius, the COLLIS VIMINALIS—beyond the Viminal, the COLLIS QUIRINALIS—beyond the Quirinal the COLLIS HORTULORUM, called, at a late period, *Mons Pincius*. The *Mons Capitolinus*, *Mons Palatinus*, *Mons Aventinus*, *Mons Coelius*, *Mons Esquilinus*, *Collis Viminalis*, *Collis Quirinalis*, are the far-famed *Seven hills of Rome*. It will be seen from this description, which must be carefully compared with the plan prefixed to this chapter, that the *Mons Capitolinus*, the *Mons Palatinus*, the *Mons Aventinus*, and the *Mons Coelius* can alone be regarded as hills, in the ordinary acceptation of the term, the remainder are mere irregular projections in the table land which constitutes the Campagna.

The broad slope of the Mons Oppius, towards the Palatine, was the *Carinae*;[2] the low ridge which runs from the Palatine towards the Carinae was the *Velia*; the lower slope of the Palatine, towards the Capitoline and the Tiber, was the *Cermalus* or *Germalus*; one of the branches of the Coelian, whose outline, on the eastern side, is not very sharply defined, was the *Coeliolus* or *Minor Coelius*.[3] Lastly, it will be observed that there is a hill behind the Aventine, separated from it by a well marked hollow, the two highest points being now marked by the modern churches of S. Saba and S. Balbina. We can scarcely suppose that it was regarded merely as a part of the Aventine, but we do not find it designated by any separate name, nor, indeed, is it distinctly noticed by any classical author.

It must be remarked, that the hills of Rome do not now present, by any means, the same aspect which they must have borne during the earlier ages of the city. Their summits have been smoothed and levelled to adapt them for the foundations of the edifices by which they were crowned; their steep rocky sides have been, in many places, sloped away in order to afford more easy access, and the enormous accumulation of rubbish around their bases, has raised the surface of the ground below, and thus materially diminished their apparent elevation.

Nearly opposite to the base of the Capitoline, the river, dividing into two branches, forms, as they reunite, a small island, the *Insula Tiberina*.

Crossing over to the right bank of the Tiber, a long continuous ridge extends from the vertex of the acute angle formed by the bend of the river, as far as the Aventine, this is the IANICULUM. To the north-west of the Janiculum, separated from it by a deep depression, and at a greater distance from the river, is the

---

[1] Varro L. L. V. § 50. Fest. s.v. *Septimontio*, p. 348. Aul. Gell. XV. 1.
[2] Liv. XXVI.10. Dionys. III. 22.
[3] Varro L. L. V. § 46.—Orat. de Harusp. Resp. 15. Mart. XII. 18.

MONS VATICANUS. The meadow between the Vatican and the Tiber was the *Ager Vaticanus*, of which the *Prata Quinctia* formed a part, and the slope between the Janiculum and the Tiber, was comprehended under the general designation of *Regio Transtiberina*.

Returning to the left bank and the seven hills, we may now notice the hollows and open spaces, by which the different eminences were separated from each other. The ravine between the Palatine and the Aventine was the *Vallis Murcia*, it was traversed by a small rivulet, the *Aqua Crabra*, and here was laid out the *Circus Maximus*, the great race-course of Rome. In the low ground, extending from the Capitoline towards the Velia lay the *Forum Romanum*; to the north-east of the Forum Romanum the extensive Fora of the Emperors were formed, the *Forum Iulium*, the *Forum Augusti*, the *Forum Nervae*, and, by far the most magnificent of all, the *Forum Traiani*, which lay immediately under the Quirinal, vast masses of the hill itself having been cut away, in order to enlarge the area. Passing over the ridge of the Velia, we descend into the hollow between the Coelian and the Esquiline, of which the western portion seems to have been known anciently by the name *Ceroliensis*,[1] and is now marked by the stupendous ruins of the Coliseum, while farther east we ought, probably, to place the *Tabernola*.[2] In the hollow between the Esquiline and the Quirinal, where the two projecting tongues of these hills almost meet, lay the *Suburra*,[3] one of the most busy and thickly peopled quarters of the city; a street running from the Suburra through the narrow opening between the Mons Cispius and the Mons Oppius, was the *Vicus Cyprius*,[4] the slope which led up from it to the high ground of the Esquiline was the *Clivus Urbius*,[5] and at the extremity of this slope was the *Vicus Sceleratus*,[6] so called because this was the spot where Tullia drove her chariot over the dead body of her murdered father. In the hollow between the Esquiline and the Viminal was the *Vicus Patricius*,[7] and between the Suburra and the Forum was the *Argiletum*, (*i.e.* the clay-field,) a word which the perverse etymologists of Rome chose to consider a compound of *Argi letum*, and to explain it invented a legend about an imaginary hero, Argos, who was represented as having met his death upon this spot.[8] In the neighbourhood of the Argiletum was the district of the *Lautumiae* or stone-quarries, where one of the prisons was situated, hence called *Carcer Lautumiarum*, or simply *Lautumiae*,[9] which must be carefully distinguished from the more ancient prison on the slope of the Capitoline, to be mentioned hereafter.

The whole of the low ground lying between the Tiber, the north point of the Aventine, the south point of the Capitoline, and the west point of the Palatine was, from a very early period, designated as the *Velabrum*. This space, together with the Forum, and the hollow between the Capitoline and the Palatine, which connects them, was a swamp, frequently overflowed by the river until the stagnant waters were carried off by the great drain known as the *Cloaca Maxima*, while, at the same time, the river was confined within its bed by a

---
[1] Varro L.L.V., § 47.
[2] Varro L.L. V. § 47. 50.
[3] Varro L.L. V. § 48. Fest. s.v. *Suburra*, p. 309.
[4] This is the opinion expressed by Urlichs in the Beschreibung der S.R. Bk. III. p. 194; but it is impugned by Becker, Thl. I. p. 526.
[5] Liv. I. 48. Fest. s.v. *Orbius clivus*, p. 182.
[6] Liv. l.c.
[7] Fest. s.v., *Septimontio*, p. 348. Paul. Diac. p. 221. Martial. VII. 73.
[8] Varro L.L. V, § 157. Liv. I. 19. Virg. Æn. VIII. 345 Mart. I 3. 117. II. 17
[9] Liv. XXVII. 27. XXXII. 26. XXXVII. 3. XXXIX. 44.

strong bulwark, faced with hewn stone; this parapet and the cloaca being among the few works of that early period which still remain entire. At the south-west end of the Velabrum, near the opening of the Vallis Murcia, was the *Forum Boarium* or cattle-market; under the Aventine was the *Emporium*, or wharf, where merchant vessels loaded and discharged their cargoes, and the whole of the quarter was connected with the Forum by two great streets, the *Vicus Tuscus* and the *Vicus Iugarius*.

The student having made himself master of the relative position of the different landmarks here enumerated, by a careful comparison of the above remarks with the plan of the city placed at the commencement of this chapter, we shall proceed to give a sketch of the original limits and gradual extension of Rome; but before entering upon this part of the subject, we may briefly advert to the ceremonies observed by the primitive inhabitants of central Italy in founding a new city—ceremonies which, it is said, were chiefly of Etruscan origin.

Founding of a City.—On a day when the omens were favourable, (*die auspicato*,) a hole was dug on the spot which was to be the central point, the Ἑστία or focus, as it were, of the new city. Into this hole was cast a small quantity of corn and of all things necessary for supporting the life of man, each of the new citizens brought a handful of earth from the spot where he had previously dwelt, and this was thrown in above the other objects. The hole was then filled up to a level with the surface of the ground, an altar was erected on the spot, and sacrifice offered. The founder of the new city, (*conditor*,) with his cloak arranged in the Gabian fashion, (*cinctu Gabino*,) that is, with one end of the toga thrown over his head, and the other bound tight round his waist, like a girdle, traced out the circle of the walls with a plough, to which were yoked a bull on the right hand and a cow on the left. The share was made of bronze, it was directed in such a manner that the furrow slice fell inwards, and it was carried over (*suspendere aratrum*) those spots where it was intended to place a gate. The furrow thus formed (*primigenius sulcus*) represented the ditch, and the ridge the walls of the proposed city; the whole circuit being considered holy, except where the plough had been lifted up.[1]

Pomoerium.—The *pomoerium* of an ancient Italian city was, strictly speaking, a space kept clear of buildings and cultivation on both sides of the wall. The necessity for preserving an open area of this kind was evident in a military point of view, and in order to prevent it from being encroached upon, it was consecrated. Although this was the original meaning of the word *Pomoerium*, the term, in practice, was more frequently applied, in a restricted sense, to the outer boundary of the pomoerium, that is, to a line drawn round the walls at some distance outside the city, the course of which was marked by stones set up at intervals, (*cippi—cippi pomoeri—certis spatiis interiecti lapides*,) and this line defined the limit within which the auspices in regard to all matters regarding the welfare of the city itself (*urbana auspicia*) might be taken. When the population of a city received a large increase, and suburbs were formed, it would, of course, become necessary to form a new circle, embracing a wider space, and to unconsecrate (*exangurare*) a portion of the ground previously held sacred, that is, in technical language, *Proferre* s. *augere* s. *ampliare et terminare pomoerium—pomoerio addere—propagare terminos urbis*. According to the Roman constitution, no one was permitted to extend the pomoerium, unless he had

---

[1] Cato quoted by Serv. ad Virg. Æn. V. 755. Varro L.L. V. § 143. Ovid. Fast. IV. 821. Plutarch. Rom. 11. Q. R. 27. Dionys. I. 88. Joann. Lyd. IV. 50. Paul. Diac. a.v. *primigenius*, p. 236. Mü..er die Etrusk. II. p. 145.

extended the dominions of the Roman people; and although many generals under the republic might have claimed the privilege, no such extension took place from the reign of Servius Tullius to the dictatorship of Sulla, by whom, by Augustus, and by Claudius, (and perhaps by Julius Cæsar also,) the pomoerium was successively enlarged. Stones have been found in various places around Rome, which commemorate the extension of the pomoerium by Augustus and Claudius, and we give an inscription copied from one of these, which possesses peculiar interest, from exhibiting one of the new letters added to the Roman alphabet by the last named emperor—TI. CLAUDIUS. DRUSI. F. CÆSAR. AUG. GERMANICUS. PONT. MAX. TRIB. POT. VIIII. IMP. XVI. COS. IIII. CENSOR. P. P. AUCTIS. POPULI. ROMANI. FINIBUS. POMERIUM. AMPLIAƎIT. TERMINAƎITQ.[1]

Ager effatus.—Altogether distinct from the Pomoerium was the *ager effatus*, the name given to a space contained between the outer limit of the pomoerium and a circle drawn round the city, embracing a wider circuit than the pomoerium. Those auspices which were in no way connected with the internal affairs of the city, or with matters transacted within the city itself, such as the auspices which referred to a foreign war, or to those assemblies of the people which could not be held within the pomoerium, were observed in the *ager effatus*, and could be taken nowhere else. Thus, we understand the necessity imposed upon generals of returning to the city, even from a great distance, if circumstances occurred which rendered it imperative to renew the auspices (*auspicia repetere—auspicia renovare.*) From what has been said, it will be perceived that the pomoerium was within the *ager effatus*, but did not form a part of it.[2]

Cities on the Seven Hills, more ancient than Rome.—The advantages presented by the site described above were so numerous and so obvious, that they could not fail to be observed and turned to account by some of the various tribes which, in remote ages, occupied, in succession, the lower valley of the Tiber. Accordingly, we find traditions of an ancient town on the Capitoline named *Saturnia*, the hill itself having been designated *Mons Saturnius*. In like manner, a town *Ænea*, or *Antipolis*, is said to have once existed on the Janiculum, while the poem of Virgil has made every one familiar with the colony planted by the Arcadian Evander on the Palatine – a legend which evidently points to a Pelasgian settlement.[3]

City of Romulus, and its gradual extension until the reign of Servius Tullius.—All ancient writers agree that the original city of Romulus was built upon the Palatine. The name *Roma Quadrata* (Ρώμη τετράγωνος) was evidently derived from its form, the outline of the Palatine being quadrangular. The number of gates was three or four, three being the smallest number allowed by the Etruscan discipline, (Serv. ad Virg. Æn. I. 422.) and of these, the names of two have been preserved, the *Porta Mugionis* s. *Mugonia*, afterwards known as the *Vetus Porta Palatii*, and the *Porta Romanula* s. *Romana*. The former appears to have stood upon the north-east side of the hill, at the point where the Velia branches off, the latter on the north-west side, above the Velabrum. The wall would naturally run along the rocky scarp, while the pomoerium was traced round the base of the hill. The line of this pomoerium is minutely

---

[1] On the subject of the Pomoerium see especially Varro L. L. V. § 143. Liv. I. 44. Tacit. Ann. XII. 23, 24. Aul. Gell. XIII. 14. Dion Cass. XLIII. 50. XLIV. 49. Vopisc. Aurelian. 21. Orell. Corp. Inscrip. Latt. n. 710.
[2] Varro L.L. VI. § 53. Cic. de N.D. II. 4. de Div. I. 17. Epp. ad Q. F. II. 2. Liv. VIII. 30. X. 3. XXIII. 19. Serv. ad Virg. Æn. II. 178. VI. 197.
[3] Varro L.L. V. § 45. Plin. H.N. III. 5. Solin. I. 13. Dionys. I. 73. Festus. s.v. *Saturnia*, p. 322. Serv. Virg. Æn. VIII. 319.

described by Tacitus, (Ann. XII. 23. 24.) who evidently derived his information from some ancient and authentic record.[1]

With regard to the gradual extension of the city, the statements of different writers are somewhat at variance with each other; but the prevailing belief was that the Capitoline, the Forum, and perhaps a portion of the Quirinal, were added upon the union of the people of Romulus with the Sabines; that upon the destruction of Alba Longa and the removal of the inhabitants, the Mons Coelius was occupied; that after the fresh conquests achieved by Ancus Martius, the Aventine was taken in; while the Viminal, the Esquiline, and the Quirinal were annexed by Tarquinius Priscus, and Servius Tullius. To the latter especially is ascribed the completion of the great work commenced by his predecessor, the construction, namely, of a wall which enclosed the whole of the seven hills, and perhaps a portion of the Janiculum beyond the Tiber. All admit that the circuit thus marked out remained unchanged for eight hundred years, that is, until the reign of the Emperor Aurelian, by whom a new and more extensive line of fortifications was constructed.[2] The limits of the city, as defined by Servius Tullius, demand particular attention.

Course of the Servian Wall.—Even in the time of Dionysius, it had become a task of considerable difficulty to trace the exact line of the Servian wall, in consequence of the mass of building by which it was masked on both sides. But although doubts may have been entertained with regard to its position at some particular points, the character of the ground is such, that even in the present day we can, with confidence, determine its course within narrow limits. We are much assisted by the information contained in ancient writers regarding the gates, the position of which can, in several instances, be identified with tolerable certainty. We have, moreover, every reason to believe that the engineers availed themselves at every point of the advantages presented by the natural aspect of the ground, and that while few or no bulwarks would be regarded as necessary on the tops of the crags, so, on the other hand, the openings presented by the hollows and by the plain would be fortified with uncommon care. The side on which Rome was most accessible was on the north-west, for there, as previously remarked, the long ridge which connects the projecting tongues of the Quirinal the Viminal and the Esquiline falls with a very gradual and gentle slope to the level of the table land of the Campagna. Accordingly, an immense rampart of earth, with a deep ditch in front, was formed on the crest of this height, and remains of the *Agger Servii Tullii*, as it was called, can still be distinctly traced. It was about two-thirds of a mile in length, fifty feet broad, crowned by a wall and strengthened by towers, while the ditch in front was one hundred feet broad and thirty feet deep. The general course of the walls, as marked out by the most judicious topographers, will be better understood by examining the plan than by any verbal description. It will be seen that at one point only was the line interrupted, viz., between the Capitoline and the Aventine, and here the river, the bank being faced with a stone parapet, was considered to afford sufficient protection. This, however, it ought to be remarked, is a disputed point; for Niebuhr and Bunsen both maintain that the wall actually ran across the Velabrum at some distance from the Tiber. The whole circuit of the Servian

---

[1] Varro L.L. V. § 164. VI. § 24. ap. Non. XII. s.v. *secundum*, p. 363. ap. Solin. I. 17. Liv. I. 12. Ovid. Trist. III. i. 31. Plin H.N. III 5. Solin. I. 24. Dionys. II. 50. 65. Fest. s.v. *Quadrata*, p. 258. s.v. *Romana porta*, p. 268. Paul. Diac s v. *Mugionia*, p. 144.

[2] On the gradual extension of the city, see Liv. I. 30. 33. 36. 44. III. 67. Dionys II. 36. 37. 50. 62. III. 1. 43.

city, thus defined, is about five miles, which agrees perfectly with the statement of Dionysius, that the portion of Rome within the walls corresponded very nearly in extent with Athens. (Dionys. IV. 13. Thucyd. II. 13.)[1]

Gates of the Servian City.—The number of the gates has been variously estimated, according to the various interpretations assigned to different passages in the classical writers and the grammarians. By some it is carried up to twenty-six, by others it is placed much lower; but Pliny distinctly asserts that in the reign of Vespasian there were thirty-seven. Much confusion has undoubtedly arisen from the fact that, in the course of centuries, many gates would be built up, and new ones broken out; and thus, although we may be able to discover the names of more than twenty, it does not follow that the whole of these were in existence at the same time. We shall notice briefly the most important, that is, those which are most frequently mentioned from being connected with the principal thoroughfares, and those which possess some special interest from historical associations.

1. *Porta Collina*, at the north-west extremity of the Agger, the most northern point of the fortifications. (Liv. II. 11.)

2. *Porta Esquilina*, at the other extremity of the Agger.

3. *Porta Viminalis*, about the centre of the Agger, between the Porta Collina and the Porta Esquilina. It is specially mentioned by Strabo (V. 3. § 7.)

4. *Porta Querquetulana*, s. *Querquetularia*, probably in the hollow which divides the Esquiline from the Coelian. (Plin. H. N. XVI. 10. Fest. s.v. *Querquetulanae*, p. 261.)

5. *Porta Coelimontana*, to the south of the Querquetulana, where the Coelian joins the table land by a gentle declivity. (Liv. XXXV. 9. Cic. in Pis. 23.)

6. *Porta Capena*, in the hollow between the Coelian and the Aventine, but almost touching the base of the former hill. This may be regarded as the most important of all the gates, since at this point the great Via Appia commenced.

7. *Porta Trigemina*, at the north-west corner of the Aventine—the name was probably derived from its having three archways or Iani (*perviae transitiones*.)

Between the Porta Capena and the Porta Trigemina were the *Porta Rauduculana*, the *Porta Naevia*, and the *Porta Lavernalis*, which are of little note. The *Porta Navalis*, in all probability, opened upon the river under the Aventine.

8. *Porta Flumentana*, unquestionably close to the Tiber, and probably in the short line of wall running down from the south-west extremity of the Capitoline to the river. (Liv. XXXV. 9. 21. Paul. Diac. s.v. *Flumentana*, p. 89.)

9. *Porta Carmentalis*, in the same portion of the wall with the preceding. It was named from an altar of Carmentis, whom the popular legend regarded as the prophetic mother of Evander, was situated at the foot of the Capitoline, and opened out upon the Prata Flaminia. The gate had two arched passages, (*Iani*) of which that on the right hand of those quitting the city was regarded as of evil omen, and named *Porta Scelerata*, because the Fabii were said to have passed through it when they marched forth on their ill-fated enterprise. (Liv. II. 49. XXIV. 47. Ovid, Fast. II. 201. Fest. s.v. *Religioni*, p. 285. Dionys. I. 32. Solin. I. 13. Serv. ad Virg. Æn. VIII. 387.)

The *Porta Ratumena* (Fest. s.v. *Ratumena*, p. 274. Plin. H. N. VIII. 42. Plutarch. Popl. 13.) and the *Porta Fontinalis* (Liv. XXXV. 10) appears to have been situated in that part of the wall which ran along the Campus Martius,

---

[1] Dionys. IV. 13. IX. 68. Cic. de Rep. II. 6. By Plin. H.N. III. 5. it is called the Agge of Tarquinius Superbus.

connecting the Capitoline with the Quirinal; the *Porta Sanqualis*, named from the adjoining temple of *Sancus* or *Dius Fidius*, (Liv. VIII. 20. Paul. Diac. s.v. *Sanqualis*, p. 345.) and the *Porta Salutaris*, named from the adjoining temple of *Salus*, (Liv. IX. 43. X. 1. Plin. XXXV. 4. Paul. Diac. s.v. *Salutaris Porta*, p. 327.) were both upon the heights of the Quirinal.

One gate more deserves particular notice—the *Porta Triumphalis*, so called, it would appear, because through it all the triumphal processions entered the city, its use being restricted to these or similar solemnities. It is not often mentioned, and its position has given rise to much controversy among topographers, none of whom have succeeded in demonstrating the truth of their theories. The passages upon which the arguments employed must of necessity rest are, Cic. in Pison. 23. Tacit. Ann. I. 8. Sueton. Octav. 100. Joseph. B. J. VII. 5. § 4. Dion Cass. LVI. 42. Compare also Sueton. Ner. 25. Dion Cass. LXIII. 20.

Regions of the Servian City.—Servius divided the whole space included by his walls, with the exception of the Aventine and the Capitoline, into four districts, (*Regiones*,) which corresponded with his distribution of the four city tribes.

1. *Regio Suburana*, comprising the Coelian, the valley between the Coelian and the Esquiline, (*Ceroliensis*,) the Carinae and the Subura. 2. *Regio Esquilina*, comprising the remainder of the Esquiline and the valley between the Esquiline and the Viminal. 3. *Regio Collina*, comprising the Viminal and the Quirinal, with the valley between them. 4. *Regio Palatina*, comprising the whole of the Palatine with the Velia, the valley between the Palatine and the Coelian, and, probably, the low grounds of the Velabrum. (Varro L.L. V. § 46—53.)

Septimontium.—Connected with the early topography of the city, was the *Septimontium*, or *Septimontiale Sacrum*, a festival celebrated in the month of December by the inhabitants of seven elevated spots in Rome, which kept alive, in later times, the memory of a period when these districts were first united by a common bond; but these were quite distinct from the seven hills of the Servian city. Festus names as the localities, in each of which sacrifice was offered by the inhabitants on this holy day, the following: Palatium, Velia, Fagutal, Subura, Cermalus, Oppius, Coelius Mons, Cispius Mons; the number being here eight, one must have been interpolated, and some critics would reject the Subura, while others exclude the Coelius. The position of all has been already indicated, with the exception of the *Fagutal*, which is usually placed near the *Porta Esquilina*, or in the hollow between the Esquiline and the Coelian. In any case, it will be perceived that the confederacy or league commemorated by the Septimontium was confined to the inhabitants of the Palatine, the Esquiline and the Coelian, to the exclusion of the Capitoline, the Aventine, the Viminal, and the Quirinal. (Varro L.L. V. § 41. VI. § 24. Festus s.v. *Septimontio*, p. 348. Plutarch. Q. R. 69. Sueton. Dom. 4.)

Connection of the Janiculum with the City.—Although the Janiculum was not regarded as forming a part of the city, yet its commanding position must have suggested the expediency,[1] and, indeed, the necessity, of establishing an outwork on it. Accordingly, both Livy[2] and Dionysius[3] agree in asserting that as early as the time of Ancus Martius, it was fortified with a wall, and that a communication was established by means of the *Pons Sublicius*, of which more hereafter. At the same time, it seems unquestionable, that, for some time after

---

[1] Cic. de leg. agr. I. 5. II. 97.   [2] I. 33.   [3] III. 45.

the expulsion of the kings, Rome possessed nothing on the right bank of the Tiber; although, as it gradually recovered its power, the re-occupation of the Janiculum would be one of the first objects of attention. As to the position of affairs towards the close of the republic, see Appian. B. C. I. 68. Cic. l. c.

The City in the age of Augustus.—It is universally admitted that the fortified circuit marked out by Servius Tullius remained unchanged for eight hundred years, until the period when a new and more extensive line of walls was erected by Aurelian and his successor. But although the boundary of the Servian city remained unaltered, it must not be supposed that the city itself did not increase. There can be little doubt that a considerable portion of the ground enclosed by Servius was not built upon at all at that early epoch, but that large spaces remained open for the purpose of affording accommodation to the troops of countrymen, who, with their families and flocks and herds, sought refuge in the city when their lands and property were threatened by the inroads of a hostile tribe. When, however, the fixed population began to increase with great rapidity, and when all danger of invasion had passed away with the discomfiture of Hannibal, not only was the vacant ground gradually covered with dense masses of building, but the sacred character of the pomoerium itself was disregarded, and the walls became so choked up with houses that it was impossible, in some places, to follow their course. In addition to this, large suburbs sprung up outside the walls, and even beyond the Tiber, and stretched in every direction, so that it was not easy to determine precisely the limits of the city, just as is the case with London at the present day. (See Dionys. II. 37. who speaks as an eye witness.)

Regions of Augustus.—Augustus, for the convenience of civil administration, divided the whole of the city proper, together with the suburbs, into fourteen districts, or *Regiones*, named from the most remarkable object or locality in each:—

I. *Porta Capena.* II. *Coelimontana.* III. *Isis et Serapis.* IV. *Templum Pacis.* V. *Esquilina.* VI. *Alta Semita.* VII. *Via Lata.* VIII. *Forum Romanum.* IX. *Circus Flaminius.* X. *Palatium.* XI. *Circus Maximus.* XII. *Piscina Publica.* XIII. *Aventinus.* XIV. *Transtiberina.*

This arrangement does not demand any particular notice, for the division into regions being, in the great majority of cases, purely arbitrary, the boundaries of each cannot be ascertained with any degree of accuracy; and the two works, bearing the names of Victor and Sextus Rufus, which describe Rome according to these regions, and which, for a long period, formed the groundwork of all treatises on the topography of the ancient city, are now recognized as fabrications of a comparatively recent date. In what follows, therefore, we shall fill up the outline already traced, guided chiefly by the natural features of the ground.

We shall first describe the Forum, the centre, the heart, as it were, of the city; we shall next mention the most remarkable objects on each of the seven hills, in succession, and in the valleys which separate these hills, and then discuss the low grounds which they overlook; concluding with an enumeration of the bridges, of the aqueducts, and of the high roads which branched off in different directions. Before entering upon this part of our task, we may say a few words upon—

The Walls of Aurelian.—All apprehensions of foreign invasion had ceased with the close of the second Punic war, and for many centuries the revival of such alarms seemed impossible. Hence, among the various extensive and costly works undertaken by the earlier emperors, for the comfort or embellishment of the city,

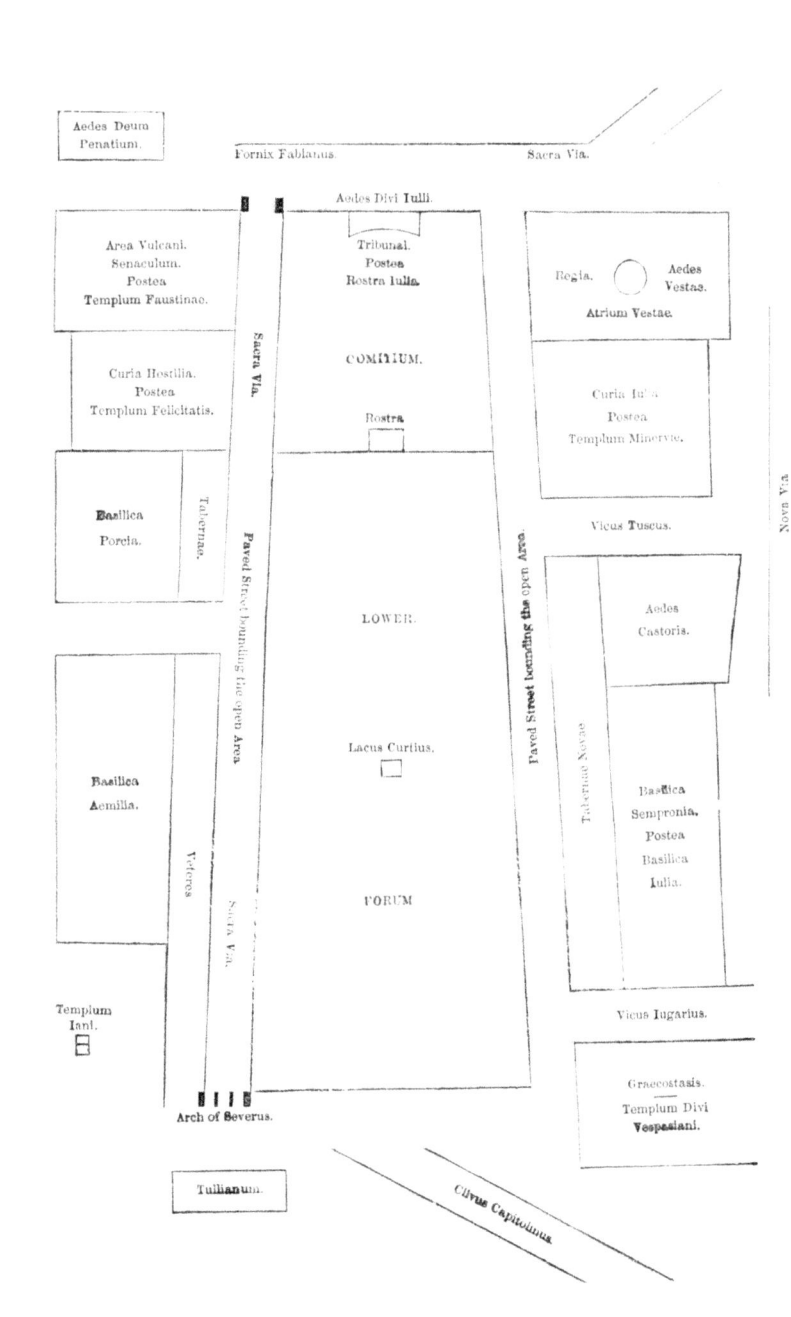

no thought seems ever to have been bestowed upon fortifications. But when hordes of fierce barbarians, on the northern and north-eastern frontiers, began to threaten the soil of Italy itself, the necessity of affording protection to the metropolis, which could not have offered even a show of resistance to an invader, became evident and urgent. Accordingly, the strong-minded and energetic Aurelian formed the design of encircling, with a great wall, the whole of the vast mass of building which had grown up beyond the ancient limits; and the task which he commenced with vigour, but was prevented from finishing by death, was completed by his successor, Probus. Much discussion has arisen with regard to the actual extent of these walls in consequence of an expression in Vopiscus, (Vit. Aurel. 39.) which has been interpreted to signify that their circumference was fifty miles, a statement, not only incredible in itself, but utterly at variance with all that has been brought to light by modern investigations. It is now generally admitted that the walls, as they exist at present, on the left bank of the river, are identical in their course with those of Aurelian, which were subsequently repaired and almost rebuilt by Honorius, and by Belisarius. The actual circuit on the left bank of the Tiber is about eleven Roman miles, which will not differ very widely from the representation of Vopiscus, if we understand his "*quinquaginta prope millia*" to denote 50,000 feet, and not 50,000 paces, although such a form of expression is unquestionably at variance with the ordinary usages of the language. The circumference of Rome in the time of Vespasian was, according to Pliny, (H. N. III. 5.) thirteen Roman miles; but this included the Transtiberina Regio. It does not fall within the limits of the present work to enter into any discussion with regard to the points embraced by the new walls; but their general course will be understood by referring to the plan on which they are laid down, as well as those of Servius. It will be seen that on the left bank they took in the whole of the Collis Hortulorum and of the Campus Martius, while on the right bank they included but a small portion of the Janiculum, the whole of which, as well as of the Vatican, is embraced by the modern wall. According to Procopius, there were fourteen gates (πύλαι,) besides wickets (πυλίδες.)

THE FORUM.

All important towns in ancient Greece and Italy had an open area in some central situation, which served as a place of general resort for the citizens. In the immediate vicinity the courts of justice and the government offices were usually established; here the principal merchants and bankers transacted their business, and here public meetings of every description were held—it was, as it were, the focus of commercial, legal, and political life. This space was termed by the Greeks ἀγορά, by the Italians *Forum*. In regard to Rome we generally speak of the *Forum Romanum* emphatically, in order to distinguish the Forum of the republic from numerous other fora, constructed, chiefly for legal purposes, by different emperors, and from the ordinary *fora*, or bazaars, where goods of a particular description were retailed, such as the *forum olitorium*, or vegetable market, the *forum piscatorium*, or fish market, the *forum boarium*, or cattle market, and others.

Forum Romanum.—This may be regarded as the most interesting locality in Rome, from both the number and the character of the historical events with which it is associated. For a long period much doubt existed as to its precise position and limits; but these have now been ascertained in the most satisfactory manner by recent excavations. It stretched, as we have already indicated, from

TOPOGRAPHY OF ROME.

the base of the Capitoline as far as the bottom of the slope of the Velia. In length it extended about 224 yards; its greatest breadth, at the base of the Capitoline, was about 68 yards, and it gradually diminished in width as it receded from the Capitoline, until, at the opposite extremity, it was reduced to 36 yards. This space must appear extremely confined, when we take into account the immense population of Rome towards the close of the republic, and the vast amount of business transacted within its precincts; but it must be remembered, that when it was first formed the city was little more than a large village—that from a very early period it was surrounded by shops and edifices of all descriptions, the property of private individuals, and that consequently its extension became a matter of great difficulty, although means were eventually taken to increase the amount of accommodation by the erection of porticoes and courthouses, opening off it. The annexed plan is intended to convey a general idea of the relative position of the different objects in and around the forum. The eye is supposed to be looking from the Mons Capitolinus towards the Velia.

The forum consisted essentially of two parts: 1. The *Comitium*, and 2. The *Forum* proper, or lower forum. These two terms are frequently employed as distinct from each other, and each must be examined separately.[1]

COMITIUM.

This name was given to that portion of the Forum which was most remote from the Capitoline, comprising, perhaps, one-fourth of the whole area. It was consecrated by the augurs, while the remainder of the Forum was not, and was set apart for particular purposes.

It was the regular place of meeting for the *Comitia Curiata*, or constitutional assemblies of the patricians, and hence, according to the most reasonable etymology, the name was derived—COMITIUM *ab eo, quod* COIBANT *eo Comitiis Curiatis et litium causa*.[2] In the Comitium public meetings (*conciones*) also of all classes were held; and when games were exhibited in the lower forum, the Comitium was frequently covered over with an awning for the convenience of the senators and other dignified persons who stood there to witness the show.[3]

Tribunal. Puteal.—On the Comitium, at the extremity most remote from the Capitoline, was a raised platform, the original *Tribunal*, where the Praetor Urbanus sat to administer justice. It was used for this purpose down to the very close of the republic, although, from the increase of legal business, both civil and criminal, numerous other tribunalia were established elsewhere. Close to the tribunal was an altar in the shape of a well-cover, (*puteal*,) under which the razor and whetstone of the augur Attus Navius were buried; this was the celebrated *Puteal Libonis* or *Puteal Scribonianum*, so named in consequence

of having been restored and beautified by a certain Scribonius Libo, which became a noted rendezvous for men of business. A representation of this monument as it appears upon a denarius of the Gens Scribonia, is annexed.[4]

---

[1] Cic. in Verr. I. 22. pro. Sest. 35. Liv. V. 55. XXXIV. 45. Dionys. I. 87. II. 29. III. 1. 8.
[2] Varro L. L. V. § 155.
[3] Liv. XXVII. 36.
[4] Cic. de divin. I. 17. Hor. S. II. vi. 35 Epp. I. xix. 8. Pers. S. IV. 49 and the scholiasts upon these passages. Ovid. R.A. 561.

TOPOGRAPHY OF ROME.

Rostra.—On the boundary line, between the Comitium and the lower forum, stood the elevated platform, (*subgestus*,) adorned with naval trophies won (B.C. 338) from the Antiates, and hence called *Rostra*, from which the magistrates and other public speakers were wont to harangue the people. The Rostra, from being consecrated, is frequently spoken of as a *templum*.[1]

Towards the close of Julius Cæsar's career, or in the early part of the reign of Augustus, the position of the Rostra was changed and transferred from the Comitium to the south side of the lower forum.[2]

Rostra Iulia. Aedes divi Iulii.—When the body of Julius Cæsar was in the act of being conveyed to the Campus Martius, the populace siezed the bier, and having raised a funeral pile, burned the corpse at the upper end of the Comitium. An altar and a column were soon after erected on the spot, and eventually a temple, to the deified dictator was raised on an elevated base ($κρηπίς$) immediately facing the capitol, the ancient Tribunal having, in all probability, been removed to make way for it. The front of this elevated base was decorated with the rostra of the ships captured at Actium, and from that time forward was named *Rostra Iulia*, which we must carefully distinguish from the original *Rostra*.[3]

There is reason to believe that a third structure bearing the name *Rostra* was erected, during the empire, at the base of the Capitoline.

Ficus Ruminalis, &c.[4]—On the Comitium were some of the most ancient memorials connected with the legendary history of the city. Here was to be seen, even in the reign of Nero, the *Ficus Ruminalis*, the sacred fig tree under which Romulus and Remus were suckled by the wolf. This originally grew upon that part of the Palatine called *Germalus*, (see above, p. 2;) but was transplanted miraculously to the Comitium, through the instrumentality of Attus Navius, whose statue stood hard by with veiled head (*capite velato*.) In the annexed cut will be seen the wolf, the twins, the fig tree, the woodpecker and the shepherd Faustulus, as rudely represented on a denarius of the Gens Pompeia.

On the Comitium, near the Rostra, was a statue of the Satyr Marsyas, where the pleaders were wont to congregate,[5] and three very ancient statues of the Sibyls, described by Pliny. It must be observed, however, that some of our best modern authorities suppose that the Sibyls, as well as the Marsyas, were in the lower forum; the Rostra, in connection with which they are mentioned, being, according to this view, the Rostra of the republic after it had been removed.[6]

We now proceed to notice the buildings which were ranged along the Comitium upon both sides.

---

[1] Liv. VIII. 14. Plin. XXXIV. 5. Ascon. ad Cic. pro. Mil. 5.
[2] Ascon. l.c. Suet. Octav. 100. Dion Cass. XLIII. 49. L. VI. 34.
[3] Cic. ad Att. XIV. 15. ad Fam. XI. 2. Philipp. I. 2. Liv. Epit. CXVI. Ov. Met. XV. 841. Epp. ex P. II. ii. 85. Appian. B.C. II. 148. III. 2. Dion Cass. XLIV. 51. XLVII. 18. LI. 19. LVI. 34.
[4] Paul. Diac. s.v. *Ruminalis*, p. 271. Fest. s.v. *Navia*, p. 169. Liv. I. 36. Plin. H N. XV 18. Tacit. Ann. XIII. 58. Dionys. III. 71.
[5] Hor. S. I. vi. 120, and Schol. Cruq. Martial. II. 64. Senec. de benef. VI. 32. Plin. H.N. XXI. 3.
[6] Becker, Handbuch, I. Thl., p 321 361.

Curia Hostilia.—Facing the Comitium, on the north side, and immediately opposite to the Rostra, stood the *Curia Hostilia*. It was built originally, we are told, by Tullius Hostilius, after the destruction of Alba Longa, and from that time forward, until the downfal of the republic,[1] was the ordinary place of meeting for the Senate. It was either rebuilt or extensively repaired by Sulla—it was consumed by fire in the tumults which followed the death of Clodius—it was rebuilt by Faustus, the son of Sulla, and soon after demolished by Julius Cæsar, in order to make room for a temple of *Felicitas*. In consequence of the prodigies which followed the death of Cæsar, the Senate passed a vote to restore the Curia; but this resolution does not appear to have been carried into effect.[2]

Vulcanal. Graecostasis. Senaculum.—The remaining space on the north side of the Comitium, seems to have been divided into three compartments; but how these were arranged with regard to each other, it is impossible now to determine. The *Vulcanal* or *Area Vulcani* was an elevated spot where, as tradition told, Tatius and Romulus were wont to meet in conference. By the latter it was dedicated to Vulcanus, and here he placed the brazen chariot brought from Cameria, and planted a lotus tree, the same which Pliny believed to exist when he wrote. To this place also was removed the famous statue of Horatius Cocles, which originally stood on the Comitium; and here a chapel was erected to Concord (*Ædicula Concordiae*) by Cn. Flavius.[3]

The *Graecostasis* was a raised platform on which foreign ambassadors stood when about to be admitted to an audience of the Senate.[4]

The *Senaculum* appears to have been an open vestibule or promenade attached to the senate-house, where the members were wont to meet and converse before proceeding to formal business.[5] Under the empire there seems to have been another Graecostasis bordering on the lower forum, and we read of several senacula.

Templum Divae Faustinae.—The space covered, under the republic, by the Vulcanal, Graecostasis, and Senaculum, was, at a subsequent period, occupied by the temple dedicated by Antoninus Pius to the memory of his wife Faustina. This, having been destroyed by fire, was restored by the senate, and dedicated to Antoninus and Faustina jointly. Of the second edifice ten columns still exist, as represented on the next page, supporting a frieze, with the inscription Divo. Antonino. Et. Divæ. Faustinæ. Ex. S. C., the whole forming part of the modern church of S. Lorenzo in Miranda.

These remains may be regarded as marking the north-east angle of the ancient Comitium.

Aedes Deum Penatium.—At a very short distance from this point, but not included within the limits of the forum, stood the temple of the Public Penates (*Aedes Deum Penatium*) a portion of which is included in the modern church of SS. Cosma et Damiano.

Aedes Vestae. Regia.—Passing to the south side of the Comitium, opposite to the Curia and Vulcanal, stood the temple of Vesta (*Aedes Vestae*) the most holy of all the shrines of Rome, in whose penetralia the Palladium was

---

[1] Liv. I. 30. XXII. 7. 60. Cic. de rep. II. 17. Varro L.L. V. § 155.
[2] Cic. pro Mil. 23. et Ascon ad loc. Plin. H.N. XXXIV. 6. Appian. B.C. II. 21. Dion Cass. XL. 49. 50. XLIV. 5. XLV. 17.
[3] Dionys. II. 50. 54. V. 25. Plut. Rom. 24. Liv. II. 10. IX. 46. Plin. H.N. XVI. 44. Aul. Gell. IV. 5.
[4] Varro L. L. V. § 155.
[5] Varro L. L. V. § 156. Val. Max. II. ii. 6. According to Festus, p. 347, *Senaculum* was another word for a *Curia* or senate-house.

preserved; and connected with it was a considerable pile of building affording accommodation to the Vestal Virgins, who all lived within the hallowed precincts. The shrine itself was immediately under the Palatine, the site being now occupied by the modern church of S. Maria Liberatrice; but it was connected with the Comitium by the building called the *Atrium Vestae*, or frequently *Atrium Regium*, or simply *Regia*, from having been the dwelling of Numa. Under the republic the Regia was the official residence of the Pontifex Maximus.[1] Annexed is a representation of the sanctuary as it appears upon a denarius of the Gens Cassia, exhibiting the round form common to all the temples of this goddess: the other symbols on this interesting coin will be explained hereafter.

Curia Iulia.—When the Curia Hostilia was finally removed by Julius Cæsar, it became necessary to provide a substitute, and accordingly a new hall, the *Curia Iulia*, was commenced and finished by the dictator, but consecrated by Augustus. The precise spot is nowhere specified; but we are expressly told by Pliny[2] and Dion Cassius[3] that it was close to the Comitium, (*in comitio—*

---

[1] Plut. Num. 14. Appian. B.C. II. 148. Hor. C. I. ii. 15. and Schol. Cruq. Ovid. Fast. VI. 263. Trist. III. i. 29. Dion Cass. Fragm. Vales. XX. Serv. ad Virg. Æn. VIII. 363, says, *Quis enim ignorat, Regiam, ubi Numa habitaverit, in radicibus Palatii finibusque Romani fori esse.*
[2] H.N. XXXV. 4.
[3] XLIV. 5. XLVII. 19. LI. 22.

παρά τῷ κομιτίῳ,) and it is equally certain that it did not occupy the site of the *Curia Hostilia*. Hence, it will be difficult to find a space where it could have been placed, except immediately adjoining to the Atrium Vestae.[1] The Curia Iulia was, in all probability, destroyed in the great fire during the reign of Nero; and we have reason to believe that the area was filled by a temple of Minerva, one of the numerous shrines raised in honour of that Goddess by the Emperor Domitian. By him, also, or by one of his successors, a new senate-house, a *Senatus*, as it was termed in the decline of Latinity, was built, not beside the Comitium, but at the foot of the Capitoline.

Fornix Fabianus.—Lastly, at the extremity of the Comitium, probably at the north-east angle, stood the *Fornix Fabianus*, an arch erected by Q. Fabius Maximus, (consul B.C. 121) when censor, as a memorial, it is supposed, of his victory over the Allobroges.[2]

LOWER FORUM.

We now proceed to consider the lower Forum, as distinct from the Comitium. In this open space all ordinary business was transacted; it was the regular place of meeting for the Comitia Tributa, and during the greater portion of the republic gladiatorial shows were exhibited here, and public banquets laid out.[3] We shall notice the most remarkable objects.

Lacus Curtius.—An altar, in the very centre of the Forum, marked the position of the *Lacus Curtius*, concerning which there were three distinct legends: 1. That it was a memorial of the great battle between the Romans and Sabines which followed the seizure of the Sabine maidens, this being the spot where the horse of Curtius, the Roman champion, succeeded in struggling out of the swamp in which it had become entangled.[4] 2. That this was the place where, in the fourth century of the city, a yawning gulf suddenly opened, into which plunged the youthful warrior, M. Curtius, generously devoting himself to destruction in order to secure the welfare of his country.[5] 3. That it was a spot which had been struck by lightning, (*fulguritum*) and, as usual under such circumstances, surrounded by an enclosure and regarded as sacred, the ceremonies having been performed by C. Curtius, who was consul B.C. 310.[6]

Close to the Lacus Curtius grew a fig-tree, an olive, and a vine, which seem to have been regarded with the same reverence by the plebeians of the olden time, as the fig-tree on the Comitium was by the patricians.[7] Close to the Lacus Curtius, Galba sunk under the blows of his murderers, and here a statue was afterwards erected to his memory by the Senate.[8] Finally, beside the Lacus Curtius was erected the equestrian statue of Domitian, so minutely described by Statius, in a passage which ought to prove a valuable guide in determining the position of several of the most remarkable objects in and around the forum.[9]

---

[1] See Varro ap. Aul. Gell. XIV. 7. Propert. IV. iv. 13.
[2] Cic. pro Planc. 7. in Verr. Act. I. 7. and Schol. De Orat. II. 66. Senec. de const. sap. 1. Trebell. Poll. Salonin. 1.
[3] Dionys. VII 59. Liv. XXIII. 30. XXVII. 36. XXXI. 50. XXXIX. 46. Cic. pro Sest. 58. Sueton Tib. 7. Prop. IV. viii. 76. Ovid. A. A. I. 163. Plin. H.N. XV. 18. Dion Cass. XL 49. LV 8.
[4] Liv. I. 13. Dionys. II. 42. Plut. Rom 18. Ovid. Fast. VI. 395. Stat. Silv I. i. 66. 78
[5] Liv VII. 6. Plin. H.N. l c. Val. Max. V. vi. 2.
[6] Varro L. L. V § 148—150, gives all the accounts.
[7] Plin H N XV. 18.
[8] Tacit Hist. II. 55. Suet. Galb. 21.
[9] Stat. Silv I. i.

Columna Rostrata.—In the forum was the celebrated pillar adorned with the Rostra of war-galleys, erected to commemorate the great naval victory gained by Duillius, in the first Punic war, (B.C. 260.)[1] A fragment of the original inscription engraved upon the base of the column, or, rather, of a copy of it made at a later epoch, still exists, and is a most valuable monument for illustrating the history of the Latin language.

Columna Maenia.—This pillar was erected, according to the statement of Pliny, in honour of C. Mænius, who, in B.C. 338, triumphed over the Antiates, while the Scholiast on Cicero asserts that it was named from a certain Mænius, who, having sold the whole of his property to form a part of the site for the Porcian Basilica, (see below,) reserved one column, from which he and his descendants might view the gladiatorial shows, a circumstance which could have no connection with a pillar *in* the forum, although it may serve to explain the term *Maeniana*, which originally denoted scaffoldings or balconies from which spectators viewed the games. We find that the *Columna Maenia* was the place where the *Triumviri Capitales* were wont to hold their courts for the trial of slaves and malefactors of the lowest class.[2]

Iani.—There were three archways or *Iani* in the forum, one at each extremity and one in the middle, severally distinguished as *Ianus Summus—Ianus Medius—Ianus Imus*, of which the *Ianus Medius* was one of the chief resorts of monied men and usurers.[3]

Tribunal Aurelium.—The tribunal of the Praetor Urbanus was, as we have seen, in the Comitium; but as legal business rapidly increased, it was found necessary to multiply the courts; and, in all probability, when criminal trials became frequent, each of the judges had a separate court in some of the Basilicae, which we shall describe below. In Cicero we hear several times of the *Tribunal Aurelium* (also of the *Gradus Aurelii*,) and it is conjectured that it was the same with that which he elsewhere notices as having been *in medio foro*.[4]

Cloacinae Sacrum.—On the north side of the forum was an altar of Venus Cloacina (CLUERE *antiqui* PURGARE *dicebant*,) where the Romans and Sabines were said to have purified themselves after they had been persuaded to lay down their arms by the entreaties of the women. On a denarius of the Gens Mussidia, of which a cut is subjoined, we find a structure represented with the word CLOACIN. below, which we can scarcely doubt was attached to the altar in question. It is supposed to have been employed for some purpose connected with the voting at the Comitia, and hence it is imagined that, of the two figures delineated, one is giving and the other receiving a balloting ticket,[5] but this seems very doubtful.

Statuae.—There were several statues in the forum, among which we find specially noticed that of Mænius, that of L. Camillus, and that of Q. Marcius Tremulus, who triumphed over the Hernici. Close to the latter, in later times, was placed the effigy of L. Antonius, brother of the triumvir.[6]

1 Quintil. I.O. I. 7. Silius VI. 663.
2 Plin. H.N. XXXIV. 5. VII. 60. Cic. divin. in Q. Cæcil. 16. and Schol. pro Sest. 58. Fest. s.v. *Maeniana*, p. 134.
3 Liv. XLI. 27. Hor. S. II. iii. 18. Epp. I. i. 54. Cic. Phil. VI. 5. VII. 6. Ovid. R.A. 561.
4 Cic. pro Sest. 15. in Pison. 5. pro Cluent. 34. Epp. ad Q. F. II. 3.
5 Liv. III. 48. Plin. H.N. XV. 29. Plaut. Curc. IV. i. 9. Eckhel, Doctrin. num. vet. Tom. V. p. 258.
6 Liv. VIII. 13. IX. 43. Cic. Philipp. VI. 5.

Milliarium Aureum.—At the foot of the slope leading up to the Capitoline, but in the forum, (*in capite fori,*) Augustus set up a gilded column, similar in shape to an ordinary mile-stone. This *Milliarium Aureum* was regarded as the *Umbilicus*, or central point of the whole Roman empire, from which all the highways radiated in different directions, and on it were inscribed the distances to the most important points, calculated from the gates at which the respective roads emerged from the city.[1]

Tabula Valeria. Tabula Sestia.—Cicero twice designates a particular part of the forum by the words *Tabula Valeria*,[2] which are fully explained by Pliny,[3] who informs us that M. Valerius Maximus Messala placed upon one side of the Curia Hostilia a picture representing the victory gained by him in Sicily over Hiero and the Carthaginians, B.C. 263. The *Tabula Sestia* spoken of in the speech Pro Quinctio[4] as in the forum, was probably something of the same kind.

We now proceed, as in the case of the Comitium, to mention the buildings which lined the lower forum on both sides.

Tabernae Veteres. Tabernae Novae.—Both sides of the lower forum, from the time of Tarquinius Priscus, were lined with porticoes, to which rows of shops (*tabernae*) were attached; these were at first tenanted by schoolmasters and by ordinary tradesmen, among whom butchers are especially noticed; but in process of time, were occupied almost exclusively by bankers, and hence, are frequently comprehended under the general designation of *Argentariae Tabernae*. The row upon the south side, having been erected first, bore the name of *Veteres Tabernae*, those on the north side of *Novae Tabernae*, while a particular compartment was known as the *Septem Tabernae*, and at a later period as the *Quinque Tabernae*. These localities were so continually in the mouth of every one, that we find them generally spoken of simply as *Veteres—Novae—Argentariae,* the substantive *Tabernae* being dropped for brevity.

Ædes Castoris.—On the south side of the forum, separated from the Delubrum Vestae and the Curia Iulia, by the *Vicus Tuscus,* stood the celebrated temple of the *Dioscuri,* generally mentioned as the *Ædes Castoris.* It was built upon a spot where rose a spring called the *Lacus Iuturnae,* at which the twin brethren watered their steeds after the battle of the Lake Regillus. It was dedicated B.C. 484, on the Ides of Quinctilis, the anniversary of the battle—was repaired by L. Metellus (consul B.C. 119)—was rebuilt by Tiberius in the lifetime of Augustus, and dedicated A.D. 6, and was connected with the palace by Caligula, who placed his own effigy between those of the twin gods.[6] In the cut annexed, taken from a denarius of the Gens Postumia, the Dioscuri are seen watering their steeds at the Lacus Iuturnae on the evening of the battle.

---

[1] Tacit. Hist. I. 27.   Suet. Oth 6.   Plin. H.N. III. 5.   Plut. Galb. 24.   Dion Cass. LIV. 8.
[2] Cic. in Vat. 9. ad Fam. XIV. 2
[3] Plin. H.N. XXXV. 4.
[4] Cic. pro Quinct. 6.
[5] Liv. I. 35. III 44. IX. 40. XXVI. 11. 27. XXVII. 11.   Varro. L.L. VI. § 59. 91.   Varro ap. Non. s.v. *Tabernas*, p. 364.   Cic. Acad. II. 22.   Dionys. XI. 28.
[6] Dionys. VI. 13.   Plut. Coriol. 3.   Val. Max. I. viii. 1.   Ovid. Fast. I. 707.   Cic. pro Scaur 46 in Verr. I. 49. 59. V. 72. and notes of Ascon.   Dion Cass. LV. 8. LIX. 28.   Sueton ul. 22 Monum Ancyran.

Basilicae.—The population of Rome increased so rapidly after the close of the second Punic war, that great inconvenience was experienced from the limited extent of the forum. In order to procure additional accommodation, the property of private individuals, which lay behind the streets bounding the open area, was bought up from time to time, and spacious *Basilicae* were erected communicating with the forum. These structures were covered porticoes, in which persons assembled for the transaction of business; and in these, eventually, most of the proceedings of the law courts were conducted. The name *Basilica* (sc. *aula*) is generally derived from the στοὰ βασίλειος at Athens, where the king archon (ἄρχων βασιλεύς) administered justice. The chief basilicae taken in chronological order, were—

1. *Basilica Porcia*, built by M. Porcius Cato, while censor, B.C. 184. Two private houses in the Lautumiae and four shops were purchased, in order to obtain the site which was immediately adjoining to the Curia Hostilia, along with which it was damaged, if not actually consumed, by fire, in the riot after the death of Clodius, B.C. 52, and from this time we hear nothing more of it. Behind, or on one side, was a fish market (*forum piscarium s. piscatorium*.)[1]

2. *Basilica Æmilia et Fulvia*, erected B.C. 179, by M. Fulvius Nobilior, who was censor in that year along with M. Æmilius Lepidus. It was opposite to the middle of the forum (*in medio foro*,) from which it was separated by the *argentariae novae*, and therefore stood upon the north side. It was thoroughly repaired and apparently greatly enlarged in B.C. 55, by L. Æmilius Paullus, (consul B.C. 50,) and hence, in aftertimes, was frequently termed *Basilica Paulli*, and by Statius *sublimis regia Paulli*. We must, however, mention, that the words of Cicero, which form our authority for this restoration, are so ambiguous, that many topographers have concluded that Paullus not only repaired the ancient Basilica Fulvia, but also constructed upon one side of it another far more magnificent, and that this latter is the true Basilica Paulli.[2] On a denarius of the Gens Aemilia, of which a cut is annexed, we see a building of two stories, supported by pillars, with the legend AIMILIA. M. LEPIDUS. REF. S.C. We can scarcely doubt that this refers to the *Basilica Æmilia*, and to its restoration by a member of the same gens.

3. *Basilica Sempronia*, erected B.C. 169, by Tiberius Sempronius Gracchus, who was censor in that year. It was on the opposite side of the forum from the two already named, being "ponc veteres" at the angle formed by the Vicus Tuscus with the forum, where stood a statue of Vertumnus. The house of P. Africanus together with some shops and butchers' stalls, (*tabernas et lanienas*) were purchased to make room for it. We seldom hear of this basilica, and know not how long it existed; but it is not improbable that a portion of the Basilica Julia, to be described below, may have occupied the same site.[3]

4. *Basilica Opimia*, known solely from a single passage in Varro, by whom it is placed beside the *Senaculum* and the *Ædes Concordiae*. It is recorded

---

[1] Liv. XXVI. 27. XXXIX. 44. Ascon. in Cic. pro Mil. Argum. Pseud. Ascon. in Cic. Div. in Q. Caecil. 16. Plut. Cat. Mai. 19. Cat. Min. 5. Plaut. Curc. IV. i. 9. Capt. IV. ii. 33. Fest. s.v. *Piscatorii ludi*, p. 238.
[2] Liv. XL. 51. Varro L.L. VI. § 4. Cic. ad Att. IV. 16. Stat. Silv. I. l. 29. See also authorities under *Basilica Julia*.
[3] Liv. XLIV. 16. Pseud. Ascon. in Cic. Verr. I. 59.

that L. Opimius, consul B.C. 121, after the death of C. Gracchus, erected in the forum, by order of the Senate, a temple of Concord ; but nothing is said of a basilica. Hence many scholars believe that the text of Varro is corrupt in this place, and the MSS., undoubtedly, vary materially.[1]

5. *Basilica Iulia*, erected with funds supplied by Julius Cæsar and dedicated B.C. 46, although Augustus claimed the merit of having completed it. Twenty years afterwards it was destroyed by fire and rebuilt by Augustus, who dedicated it under the names of his grandsons Caius and Lucius ; but it appears to have been still usually distinguished by its original designation. It was again destroyed by fire in A.D. 282, and was restored by Diocletian. Its position is well ascertained by comparing the statements of the Monumentum Ancyranum with the words of Festus and of the Notitia, from which it is clear that it must have stood between the Ædes Castoris and the point where the Vicus Jugarius entered the forum; and at this angle there was, at one period, an artificial basin or tank, called the *Lacus Servilius*.[2]

Graecostasis Imperii. Templum Divi Vespasiani.—Nearer the Capitoline than the Basilica Iulia, on the same side of the forum, was the *Graecostasis* s. *Graecostadium* of the empire, and between the *Graecostadium* and the Capitoline was the Temple of Vespasian, of which, as restored at a late period, eight columns still remain.

Temple of Ianus.—Not actually in the forum, but in the immediate vicinity, was the celebrated temple of Ianus, built by Numa, which was always closed in time of peace and open during war only, (hence called *indicem pacis bellique*[3] and its gates *geminae belli portae*.)[4] The edifice, as well as the deity, was designated *Ianus Bifrons*[5]—*Ianus Quirinus*[6]—*Ianus Geminus*;[7] and, in all probability, served originally as a gate to the citadel, and may be identical with the *Porta Ianualis* named by Varro.[8] We are told by Livy[9] that it stood at the lower

extremity of the Argiletum (*ad infimum Argiletum*) that is, near the north-east angle of the forum; and it is evident from the words of Ovid,[10] that it was close to the bottom of the Capitoline. But since it was not the only shrine in Rome dedicated to this god, and since all open archways (*perviae transitiones*) were called *Jani*, we must carefully avoid confounding[11] the peace and war temple with that temple of Janus built by Duillius in the Forum Olitorium near the spot where the theatre of Marcellus was afterwards erected,[12] with the three arches or Jani in the Forum Romanum mentioned above, and with the Janus

[1] Varro L.L. V. § 156. comp. Appian. B.C. I. 26. Plut. C. Gracch. 17. Augustin. C.D. III. 25. Cic. pro Sest. 67.
[2] Plut. Caes. 29. Galb. 26. Appian. B.C. II. 26. Dion Cass. XLIX. 42. LIV. 24. Plin. H.N. XXXVI. 15. Tacit. Ann. III. 72. Monum. Ancyran. Hieron. Chron. Euseb. Olymp. CLXXXIII. 3. Suet. Octav. 29. Calig. 37. Plin. Epp. II. 18. Festus s.v. *Lacus Servilius*, p. 290.
[3] Liv. I. 19.
[4] Virg. Æn. VII. 607. Plut. Num. 20.
[5] Virg. Æn. VII. 180. XII. 198.
[6] Hor. C. IV. xv. 8.
[7] Varro. L.L. V. § 156. Plin. H.N. XXXIV. 7.
[8] Varro, L L. V. § 165.
[9] Liv. I. 19.
[10] Fast. I. 295. seqq.
[11] As Servius has done ad Virg. Æn. VII. 607.
[12] Tacit. Ann. II. 49.

Quadrifrons in the Forum Boarium, to be noticed hereafter. Additional embarrassment, with regard to the temple built by Numa, has arisen from a remark by Varro,[1] that the place where it stood was called *Lautolae*, from some hot springs which once existed there, and these hot springs play a conspicuous part in the tale narrated by Ovid.[2] On the other hand, there were certainly, at one period, hot springs called *Lautolae* under the Carinae, and hence some grammarians have transported the temple, with all its legends, to that quarter of the city.[3] We have little or no information in regard to the changes, if any, which the original temple of Numa underwent during successive ages; but we can form some idea of the general appearance of the structure as it existed under Nero from the representations which are found upon numerous coins of that emperor. That which is annexed is from a large brass.

SACRA VIA.

Closely connected with the forum, and associated in the Roman mind with the proudest recollections, was the *Sacra Via*, so called, it would seem, because it was the route followed by triumphal processions and religious pageants, as they defiled through the forum before ascending the Capitoline, although the antiquarians of the Augustan age believed that it received its name from the meeting of Romulus and Tatius when they solemnly pledged their faith to each other.[4] The course of the Sacred Way has given rise to at least as much controversy as any portion of Roman topography; but although all the questions connected with the subject cannot be answered in a satisfactory manner, the recent investigations concerning the forum have cleared away many difficulties. Varro[5] states expressly that the commencement of the Sacred Way (*Caput Sacrae Viae*) was at the chapel of the goddess *Strenia*, and that it extended to the Arx. We, moreover, infer from his words, that the said chapel was in or near the Ceroliensis, which is generally believed to be the hollow between the Coelian and the Esquiline, in which the Coliseum stands, (see above p. 3.) He adds that although this was the real extent of the Sacred Way, the term, in its ordinary acceptation, was limited to that portion which terminated at the first ascent on leaving the forum. The ascent here indicated must be what Horace calls the *Sacer Clivus*,[6] the slope, namely, of the Velia, on the top of which the arch of Titus was built, and this was the highest point (*summa sacra via*.) Festus[7] confirms this account, and fixes two other points, the *Regia*, which agrees with Horace,[8] (*ventum erat ad Vestae*,) and the *Domus Regis Sacrificuli*; but the position of the latter is, unfortunately, quite unknown. We are hence induced to lay down the course of the Sacred Way as follows: Beginning where the arch of Constantine now stands, it passed through the valley of the Coliseum--ascended the Velia--passed under the arch of Titus--descended the Sacer Clivus--skirted the buildings attached to the temple of Vesta--passed over to the opposite side of the forum--under the Fornix Fabianus--in front of the Curia Hostilia--the Basilica Porcia--the Basilica Æmilia, and, finally, under the arch of Severus--up the Clivus Capitolinus.

[1] Varro, L. L. V. § 156.
[2] Ovid. Fast. I. 259. seqq.
[3] e.g. Macrob. S. I 9.
[4] Dionys. II. 46. Appian. fragm. I. 6. Fest. s.v. *Sacram viam*, p. 290. Serv. ad Virg. Æn. VIII. 641. comp. Plut. Rom. 19.
[5] Varro L.L. V. § 47.
[6] Hor. C. IV. ii. 33. Epod. VII. 7. comp. Mart. I. 70.
[7] Fest. s.v. *Sacram viam* p. 290.
[8] Hor. S. I. ix. 35.

On the *Summa Sacra Via* was a fruit market and shops for fancy wares. Here also was the *Sacellum Larum*,[1] and an equestrian statue of the heroic Cloelia.[2]

Nova Via.—A street frequently mentioned in the classics by the name of the *Nova Via* branched off from the Via Sacra, on the summit of the Velia, close to the Porta Mugonia. Descending the slope, it ran behind the shrine of Vesta, skirted the base of the Palatine, and entered the Velabrum, passing under the Porta Romanula, with which it communicated by steps. The windows of the house of Tarquinius Priscus, which stood beside the temple of Jupiter Stator, looked out upon the highest part of the Nova Via, (*summa Nova Via*,) and near the point where it reached the low level of the Forum, (*infima Nova Via*,) an altar was erected to *Aius Locutius*, (or *Aius Loquens*,) the god whose mysterious voice gave warning of the approach of the Gauls.[3]

FORA OF THE EMPIRE.

The Fora of the empire were as much superior in magnificence to the Forum Romanum as they were inferior in historical interest and association. Indeed, the allusions to them in classical writers are, comparatively speaking, so scanty and unimportant that we might almost be content to pass them over, and leave their sites and the arrangement of their constituent parts to local topographers and architectural antiquarians, who have here found ample room for speculation and dispute. Their position in relation to each other, and to the forum Romanum, has been minutely examined and described in the works of Bunsen and Becker, whose views on this subject approach, in all probability, as nearly to the truth as the present state of our knowledge will permit. Nor can we hope speedily to obtain much new information; for little can be effected by means of excavation, in consequence of the mass of modern edifices by which the ground is, in a great measure covered.

These fora were four in number; and it must be remarked that they were devoted entirely to legal, literary, and religious purposes, neither political nor mercantile business being transacted within their precincts.

1. **Forum Iulium.**—Commenced by Julius Cæsar before the outbreak of the civil war, and dedicated B.C. 46, after his quadruple triumph; but not completely finished until after his death. In size it was somewhat smaller than the *Forum Romanum*, which was therefore styled the *Forum Magnum*, but the ground alone, which formed the area, cost one hundred millions of sesterces. Its chief ornament was a temple of *Venus Genetrix*, the great mother of the Julian line, which Cæsar vowed before the battle of Pharsalia. Here the Senate occasionally assembled.[4]

2. **Forum Augustum.**—Augustus, in the war against Brutus and Cassius, vowed a temple to *Mars Ultor*, and in consequence of the rapid increase of the population and of legal business, was induced to connect a forum with it, which he opened to the public even before the dedication of the temple, which took place in B.C. 2. The space required was obtained entirely by the purchase of private property, and was therefore smaller than the prince desired, since he felt unwilling to eject citizens from their dwellings without their free consent. No doubt is entertained that the remains of an arch, now known as the *Arco de'*

---

[1] Varro R.R. I. 2. Ovid. A.A. II. 265. Anthol. Lat. n. 1636 ed. Meyer. Propert. II. xxiv. 11. Ovid. Amorr. I. viii 99. Fast. VI. 783.
[2] Liv. II. 13. Dionys. V. 35. comp. Plut. Popl. 19.
[3] Varro L.L. V. § 164. VI. § 24. 59 ap Aul. Gell. XVI. 17. Liv. I. 41. V. 32 50. 52. Cic. de div. I. 45. II. 32 Solin I. § 24. Ovid. Fast. VI. 395. Plut. Cam. 30. de fort. Rom. 5.
[4] Sueton. Caes. 26. Plin II N. XXXV. 12 XXXVI. 15 Tacit. Ann. XVI. 27. Appian B.C. II. 102. Dion Cass. XLIII. 22. Monum. Ancyran.

Pantini, formed a part of the portico of the temple of Mars Ultor, and hence one fixed point at least is obtained for determining the relative position of the imperial fora. This temple of Mars Ultor must be distinguished from the small shrine on the Capitoline erected by Augustus to the god under the same title. Of this we shall speak in the proper place.[1]

When Ovid refers to *tria fora*,[2] he includes the *Forum Romanum*, the *Forum Iulium*, and the *Forum Augustum*.

3. **Forum Transitorium, s. Pervium, s. Palladium, s. Nervae.**—Vespasian having erected a magnificent temple of peace behind the *Aedes Deum Penatium* (see above, p. 14,) to the north-east of the Comitium, his son Domitian determined to remove the private buildings from the space between this temple and the two last named fora, and to convert the area thus obtained into a new forum. He did not, however, live to witness the completion of this scheme, which was carried out by Nerva. The forum thus formed was called *Forum Nervae*, from the emperor by whom it was dedicated—*Transitorium* or *Pervium*, in consequence, it would seem, of having been traversed by some important thoroughfare—*Palladium*, from a temple of Minerva, which, together with a shrine of Janus Quadrifrons, formed its chief ornament.[3]

4. **Forum Traiani.**—The forum of Trajan, built according to the plan of Apollodorus of Damascus, must be regarded, whether we consider the extent of the area which it embraced, the gigantic operations performed in cutting away the Quirinal to extend this area, or the number and the magnificence of the structures comprehended within its limits, as the most vast and most splendid work of the imperial times.

It consisted of six parts—

(1.) The *Forum* proper, divided into the *Atrium Fori* and the *Area Fori*. In the centre of the former was an equestrian statue of Trajan.

(2.) *Basilica Ulpia*, called by Lampridius *Basilica Traiani*.

(3.) *Columna Traiani*. This celebrated column is still entire. The shaft is covered with a series of most interesting bas reliefs, commemorating the achievements of the emperor, who was interred at its base. It stood in the centre of a small square, surrounded by porticoes.

(4.) *Bibliotheca Ulpia*.

(5.) *Templum Divi Traiani*, dedicated by Hadrian.

(6.) *Arcus Triumphalis*.

Very considerable remains of this gorgeous undertaking can still be traced, and will be found fully described in all the more important works on modern Rome.[4] In the cuts on the following page will be seen the column with the remains of the portico as it exists in the present day—the Basilica Ulpia, the Triumphal Arch, and two temples, or two different views of the same temple, all as represented on large brass coins of Trajan.

---

[1] Suet. Octav. 29. 31. 56. Velleius II. 39. 100. Martial. VII. 51. Macrob. S. II. 4. Dion Cass. LIV. 8. LVI. 27. LXVIII. 10.
[2] Trist. III. xii. 24.
[3] Suet. Dom. 5. Martial. X. 28. Stat. Silv. IV. iii. 9. Lamprid. Alex. Sev. 28. Aur. Vict. Caes. 9. 12 Serv. ad Virg. Æn. VII. 607. Lyd. de Mens. IV. 1.
[4] Dion Cass. LXVIII. 16. 29. LXIX. 2 4. Spartian. Hadr. 7. Capitolin. Antonin. 21. 22. Lamprid. Alex. Sev. 26. Commod. 2. Vopisc. Prob. 2. Aurelian. 1. Tacit. 8. Aurel. Vict. Epit. 13. Ammian. Marcell. XVI. 10. Aul. Gell. XI. 17. XIII. 24.

MONS CAPITOLINUS.

The Capitoline hill, the smallest of the seven, is about three quarters of a mile in circumference at its base, running from north-east to south-west, and approaching, at its southern extremity, within 250 yards of the river. It has two tops, separated by a hollow, which was called *Inter duos lucos*, now the Piazza del Campidoglio, and this hollow tradition declared to be the spot where Romulus formed his *Asylum*.[1] The northern summit is the more lofty, rising to the height of about 160 feet above the sea, or 127 above the ordinary level of the Tiber; while the southern summit is about 10 feet lower. On one of the two summits stood the *Arx* or citadel, on the other the great national temple, the *Capitolium*, dedicated to Jupiter Optimus Maximus conjointly with Juno and Minerva.[2] That one of these summits was the Arx and the other the site of the Capitolium is admitted by nearly all topographers; but whether the Arx stood on the northern and the Capitolium on the southern summit, or *vice versa*, is a question which has given rise to fierce and prolonged controversies. The discussion has, moreover, been rendered more intricate by the loose manner in which the terms *Arx* and *Capitolium* are employed by ancient writers. Thus, since the whole hill was strongly fortified and regarded as the citadel of Rome, *Arx* is frequently used as synonymous with *Mons Capitolinus*; while, in like manner, *Capitolium* has an equal latitude of signification. It would be impossible here to give even an outline of the arguments adduced by the conflicting parties, or of the ingenious inferences which have been drawn from minute circumstances. It is enough to say, that those scholars who have studied the subject most deeply, and are best able to form a sound opinion, agree that the *Arx* or citadel proper must have stood upon the northern and more lofty of the two summits, now occupied by the church of Santa Maria in Araceli, and that the temple of Jupiter stood upon the lower eminence, now the site of the Palazzo Caffarelli. This lower summit presented, in ancient times, a rocky face towards the river, the precipice falling abruptly not less than 80 feet; but it is now considerably less, having, in the course of ages, been cut down and sloped away—this was the *Saxum Tarpeium* or *Rupes Tarpeia*, the whole of the lower summit being the *Mons Tarpeius*, although the latter term, and also *Arx Tarpeia*, is employed, like *Arx* and *Capitolium*, to designate the whole hill.[3]

The *Capitolium* was vowed by Tarquinius Priscus, in the Sabine war,[4] but he lived to lay the foundation only; the work was prosecuted with great vigour by Superbus, who called in the aid of Etruscan workmen, and was nearly finished at the time of the revolution; for we find that it was dedicated in the year of the first consulate.[5] The legends connected with the founding of the temple—the refusal of Terminus and Juventas to remove from the spot—the finding of a human head, from which the name *Capitolium* was said to have been derived, are all recorded by the native and foreign historians of Roman affairs.[6] The edifice contained three *cellae* or shrines—in the central compartment was the statue of Jupiter seated, arrayed in costly robes, with his face painted scarlet; on his right hand was the statue of Minerva, on his left the statue of Juno, both standing. The original structure remained unharmed until B.C. 83, when it was

---
1 Liv. I. 8. Dionys. II. 15. Ovid. Fast. III. 429.
2 *Arx* and *Capitolium* are frequently distinctly opposed to each other, *e.g.* Liv. VI. 20. Dionys. II. 15. Aul. Gell. V. 12.
3 Liv. I. 55. Varro, L.L. V. § 41. Plut. Rom. 18. Tacit. Hist. III. 71.
4 Liv. I. 38. Cic. de R. II. 20. Dionys. III. 69. IV. 59. Tacit. Hist. III. 72.
5 Polyb. III. 22. Liv. II. 8. Plut. Popl. 13. 14.
6 Varro L.L. V. § 41. Liv. I. 55. 56. V. 54. Dionys. IV. 59. seqq.

26   TOPOGRAPHY OF ROME.

consumed by fire. This misfortune happened during the civil wars of **Marius** and Sulla; but does not appear to have been connected with any struggle or tumult.[1] It was restored with great magnificence by Sulla,[2] who did not live to dedicate the new edifice; but this ceremony was performed by Q. Lutatius Catulus, (consul B.C. 78,) and hence the building is called by Cicero *Monumentum Catuli*.[3] This second temple was destroyed in A.D. 69, by the partizans of Vitellius—restored by Vespasian[4]—consumed by fire almost immediately after his death, and rebuilt with great splendour by Domitian.[5] Of the destruction of this fourth edifice we have no distinct record.

The cuts below represent the temple at three of these epochs; the first is from

a denarius of the *Gens Petillia*, which bore the cognomen of Capitolinus, and must be intended to depict the capitol as restored by Sulla, the second is from a large brass of Vespasian, the third from a Greek silver medallion of Domitian; in the two latter the sitting figure of Jupiter between the standing figures of Juno and Minerva is distinctly visible.

In front of the temple was an open space, the *Area Capitolina*, in which public meetings of different kinds were occasionally held,[6] and in the immediate vicinity was the *Curia Kalabra*, where, in ancient times, the priests made proclamation, on the kalends of each month, of the period when the Nones and Ides would fall, and of other matters connected with the Kalendar.[7] The other buildings of note on the lower summit, were the temples—of *Jupiter Feretrius*, founded by Romulus, in which Spolia Opima were deposited[8]—of *Fides*, originally built by Numa, renewed, B.C. 259, by M. Atilius Calatinus, and afterwards by M. Aemilius Scaurus[9]—of *Mens*, and of *Venus Erycina*, both dedicated during the second Punic war[10]—of *Honos et Virtus*, dedicated by C. Marius, and hence

---

1 Appian. B.C. I. 83. Tacit. Hist. III. 72.
2 Tacit. l.c. Plut. Popl 18.
3 Plut l.c. Cic. in Verr. IV. 31. 38. Liv. Epit. **XCVIII**. **Suet. Caes.** Dion Cass. XXXVII. 44. XLIII. 14.
4 Tacit. Hist. IV. 53. Suet. Vesp. 8. Dion. Cass. LXVI. 10.
5 Plut. Popl. 15. Suet. Dom. 5. Dion Cass. LXVI. 24.
6 Liv. XXV. 3. XLIII. 16. XLV. 36.
7 Varro L L. V. § 13. VI. § 27.
8 Liv. I. 10. IV. 20. Dionys. II. 34.
9 Liv. I. 21. Cic. de N D. II. 23. Plut. Num. 16.
10 Liv. **XXII**. 10. **XXIII**. 31. Cic. de N.D. l.c. Plut. de fort. Rom. 10.

styled *Monumentum Marii* [1]—of *Jupiter Tonans*, and of *Mars Ultor*, built by Augustus,[2] and of *Jupiter Custos*, built by Domitian.[3]

On the *Arx* were—the *Auguraculum*, a sacred stone on which the Augur sat with veiled head looking towards the south when taking auspices on behalf of the state—a temple of *Iuno Moneta*, with the *officina* or mint attached, built on the spot where the mansion of king Tatius, and afterwards the house of M. Manlius had stood [4]—and a temple of *Concordia*, built during the second Punic war.[5]

In the hollow between the two summits was a temple of *Veiovis*; but this does not appear to have been the shrine which in earlier times conferred on the spot the character of a sanctuary.[6]

Approaches to the Capitol.—The only approach to the capitol during the kingly and republican periods was by the sloping road called *Clivus Capitolinus*, which led up from the forum; but in the imperial times it was accessible on the opposite or river side, by a hundred steps.[7] The former must be more particularly described.

Clivus Capitolinus.—At the bottom of the Clivus Capitolinus stood, and still stands, as represented in the annexed cut, the triumphal arch erected by Septimius Severus to commemorate his conquests in the East.

Passing through this, the road turned to the left and ascended the slope. On the right hand was the temple of *Concordia*; the open space in front being the *Area Concordiae*. It was founded by M. Furius Camillus about B.C. 366—rebuilt by Tiberius, and contained many remarkable works of art. Here, both

[1] Cic. pro Sest. 54. pro Planc. 32. and schol. de Div. I. 28. Vitruv. II' 9. Fest. s. v *summissiorem* p. 344.
[2] Dion Cass. LIV. 4. 8.
[3] Suet. Dom. 5.
[4] Plut. Rom. 20. Solin. I. 21. Liv. VI. 20. VII. 28.
[5] Liv. XXII. 33.
[6] Liv. II. 1. Dionys. II. 15. Plut. Rom. 9
[7] Tacit. Hist. III. 71.

during the republic and under the empire, the Senate occasionally held their meetings; and here the memorable debate took place during the Catilinarian conspiracy.[1] Near the temple of Concord was the temple of *Saturnus*, three columns of which still remain; and connected with it was a very ancient *Ara Saturni* and a *Sacellum Ditis*. The temple itself was dedicated B.C. 498 or 497; but the building is said to have been commenced by the second Tarquin, or even by Tullus Hostilius. It was rebuilt by L. Munatius Plancus, about B.C. 42, and again renewed by Septimius Severus. During the republic it was employed as the State treasury, (*aerarium*,) and here not only the public money but the military standards also, the decrees of the Senate, and all public documents were deposited,[3] until the erection of the *Tabularium* or record-office, which was built soon after the burning of the capitol, in B.C. 83, and dedicated by Q. Lutatius Catulus, as proved by the inscription now, or lately, legible on the substructions—Q. LUTATIUS Q. F. Q. N. CATULUS COS. SUBSTRUCTIONEM ET TABULARIUM EX S.C. FACIUNDUM COERAVIT.

Tullianum.—On the right hand side of the modern ascent from the forum to the capitol, which does not, however, coincide with the ancient Clivus Capitolinus, we find a very interesting memorial of the earliest ages of the city. This is the prison built according to the Roman writers by Ancus Martius, to which his successor added an underground dungeon, ever after known as the *Tullianum*, and most graphically described by Sallust. The upper and lower cells are still

both entire, and have been converted into chapels. Originally the only access to the under prison was by a hole in the vaulted roof, through which criminals were let down; the steps by which we now descend are modern. The annexed cut taken from the excellent work of Sir William Gell on "The Topography of Rome and its Vicinity," presents an accurate view of the present aspect of this ancient structure, and the remarks upon it in the work itself are well worthy of attention. Here perished Jugurtha—here Lentulus, and others connected with the conspiracy of Catiline; and here, according to the traditions of the Roman Catholic church, St. Peter was confined. The term Mamertine Prison, (*Carcer Mamertinus*,) by which it is now generally distinguished, is to be found in no classic author.[4]

In the immediate vicinity of the prison, were the *Scalae Gemoniae* on which the bodies of criminals who had been put to death were exposed.[5]

PALATIUM, S. MONS PALATINUS.

The Palatine was, as we have already seen, the site of the original city of Romulus. It is elevated 166 feet above the level of the sea, or 133 above the

[1] Plut. Cam. 42. Liv. XXXIX. 56. XL. 19. Cic. Philipp. II. 7. VII. 8. Suet. Tib. 20. Plin. H.N. XXXIV. 8. XXX VII. 1. Ovid Fast. I. 641. Dion Cass. LV. 8.
[2] Dionys. I. 34. VI. 1. Macrob. S. I. 8. 11. Fest. s.v. *Saturnia* p. 322. Suet. Octav. 2º. Orell. C. I. No. 590.
[3] Plut. Popl. 12. Q.R. 42. Liv. III. 69.
[4] Liv. I. 33. XXIX. 22. XXXIV. 44. Varro L.L. V. § 151. Fest. s.v. *Tullianum* p. 356. Sallust Cat. 55. Plut. Mar. 12.
[5] Val. Max. VI. ix. 13. Tacit. Hist. III. 74. Dion Cass. LVIII. 5.

ordinary level of the Tiber; but it probably was at one time considerably higher, its summit, as well as those of the other hills, having been cut down and levelled, in order to afford a greater extent of flat ground for building.

The slope to the north-west, in the direction of the capitol, bore the name of *Germalus* or *Cermalus*;[1] and in this locality were many objects connected with the earliest traditions. Here was the *Lupercal*, or cave of *Lupercus*, who was eventually identified with Arcadian Pan;[2] here grew the *Ficus Ruminalis*, beneath whose shade the twin brothers were suckled by the wolf, and which was afterwards miraculously transplanted to the *Comitium*;[3] here was the *Casa Romuli*,[4] the humble dwelling of the first king; here the sacred cornelian-cherry tree, which sprung from the shaft of a spear hurled by Romulus from the Aventine.[5] Higher up the hill, on the same side, was the shrine of the goddess *Victoria*, which was said to have been in existence before the foundation of Rome, and in which, on account of its peculiar sanctity, was deposited the effigy of the *Magna Mater* when transported from Pessinuns to Rome, B.C. 205, until a separate temple was erected to receive it, which also stood upon the Palatine, facing the east.[6] On the summit was the *Curia Saliorum*, where the Lituus of Romulus and the Ancilia were preserved.[7]

Near the *Porta Mugonia*, overlooking the *Nova Via* and the forum, was the temple of *Iupiter Stator*, vowed by Romulus in his great conflict with the Sabines, and beside it stood the royal dwelling of Tarquinus Priscus and his successors.[8] On the south-east extremity, above the spot where the Arch of Constantine now stands, was the edifice called *Curiae Veteres*, where of old the thirty Curiae were wont to hold their religious assemblies.[9] But the most celebrated temple on the hill was that of *Apollo*, built of Carara marble by Augustus soon after the battle of Actium, and dedicated B.C. 28. It was surrounded by colonnades of African marble, and to it were attached spacious halls, which contained the celebrated library. The open space in front was the *Area Apollinis*; and here, between the pillars of the portico, stood statues of the fifty daughters of Danaus, while opposite to them, if we can trust the scholiast on Persius, in the open air, were ranged the fifty sons of Ægyptus upon horse-back.[10]

On the Palatine, during the republic, many of the noblest and most distinguished citizens had their dwellings. Here was the house of the traitor, Vitruvius Vaccus, which, having been levelled with the ground, (B.C. 311,) the site remained without buildings, under the name of *Vacci prata*,[11]—of M. Fulvius Flaccus, which was demolished during the troubles of the Gracchi, its place being occupied at a subsequent period by a colonnade built by Q. Lutatius Catulus. (*Porticus Catuli*,) and decorated with the spoils won by him in the Cimbric

---

[1] Varro L.L. V. § 54. Plut. Rom. 3. Paul. Diac. s.v. *Cermalus* p. 55. s.v. *Septimontium*, p 341,
[2] Dionys. I. 32. 79.
[3] Dionys. I. 79. Varro, L.L. V. § 54. Paul. Diac. s.v. *Ruminalis* p. 271. Plut. Rom. 4. Ovid. Fast. II. 410. Serv. ad Virg. Æn. VIII. 90.
[4] Varro. Dionys. ll. cc. Plut. Rom. 20.
[5] Plut. l. c.
[6] Dionys. L 32. Liv. X. 33. XXIX. 14. XXXVL 36. Dion Cass. XLVI. 33.
[7] Cic. de divin. I. 17. Dionys. fragmt. Val. Max. I. viii 11.
[8] Liv. I. 12. 41. Dionys. II. 50. Ovid. Trist. III. i. 31. Plut. Cic. 16. Plin. H.N. XXXIV. 6. Solin. I. 24.
[9] Varro L.L. V. § 155. Ovid Fast. III. 139. Macrob. S. I. 12.
[10] Dion Cass. XLIX. 15. LIII. 1. Velleius II. 81. Suet. Octav. 29. Schol. Pers. II. 56. Ovid. Trist. III. i. 59.
[11] Liv. VIII. 19.

war [1]—of M. Livius Drusus, which afterwards belonged to one of the Crassi, then to Cicero, and, upon his banishment, was demolished by Clodius, who extended the Porticus Catuli, and dedicated the remainder of the Area to *Libertas*. [2] On the Palatine lived M. Scaurus, so renowned for his sumptuous extravagance; M. Antonius, whose mansion was made over to Agrippa and Messala; Catiline and Hortensius, whose houses were subsequently occupied by Augustus. [3] With him a new epoch commenced in the history of the hill; the name *Palatium* soon began to mean the imperial residence, and, in process of time, was appropriated to denote the imperial residence not only at Rome, but in any part of the world. Tiberius had a house on the Palatine called the *Domus Tiberiana*, [4] separate from that of Augustus. It retained its name for a considerable period after his accession, and a public library was attached to it. We cannot doubt that during the reign of the second emperor, as well as those of his immediate successors, especially Caligula, [5] considerable changes and extensions must have taken place in the buildings allotted for the reception of the court, in order to accommodate the numerous officers of state and their retainers; but still there were unquestionably many private residences on the hill, especially on the northern side. During the reign of Nero, however, the prince appropriated the whole of the Palatine, of the Velia, of the valley of the Coliseum, and of the south-eastern portion of the Esquiline, including the gardens of Maecenas, and up to the Servian Agger, for his *Domus Transitoria;* but this having been destroyed in the great fire, was succeeded by the still more celebrated *Domus Aurea*, [6] which was to have transcended in magnificence every thing before imagined in imperial Rome. The projector, however, did not live to complete his plan, and the work, continued through the brief reign of Otho, [7] was stopped by Vespasian, who at once restricted its limits to the Palatine itself, which from this time forward, was occupied almost exclusively by the buildings requisite for the court.

At the southern extremity of the Palatine, Septimius Severus erected his *Septizonium*, a building of which remains existed towards the close of the 16th century, but of which the nature and object are quite unknown. [8]

Approaches to the Palatine.—The principal access to the Palatine, at all epochs, was through the *Porta Mugonia*, (see above, p. 5,) which opened out upon the Velia. The only other access known to us was by the *Clivus Victoriae*, through the *Porta Romanula*, which was approached by steps from the point where the *Nova Via* entered the *Velabrum*. [9]

The Velia.—It does not appear that there were any buildings of importance upon the Velia, with the exception of those already mentioned in connection with *Sacra Via*, before the reign of Nero, by whom it was comprehended within the limits of his Domus Aurea; but at a subsequent period its summit and base were adorned by some of the most splendid edifices of the empire.

At the top of the Velia, and the highest point of the Sacred Way, stood, and still stands, as represented in the annexed cut, the Triumphal Arch of Titus,

---

1 Val. Max. VI. iii. 1. Orat. pro dom. 43.
2 Velleius II. 14. Plut. Cic. 8. 33. Cic. in. Pison. 11, and note of Ascon. ad Fam. V. 6. Orat. pro. dom. 44. Dion Cass. XXXVIII. 17.
3 Cic. pro. Scaur. and note of Ascon. Plin. H.N. XXXVI. 3. Dion Cass. LIII. 27. Suet. Octav. 72. de ill. gramm. 17.
4 Tacit. Hist. I. 27. Plut. Galb. 24. Aul. Gell. XIII. 19.
5 Plin. H.N. XXXVI. 15.
6 Tacit. Ann. XV. 39. Suet. Ner. 31. Martial. Spect. 2.
7 Suet. Oth. 7.
8 Spartian. Sept Sev. 24. Get. 7. Ammian Marcellian. XV. 7. Comp. Suet. Tit. 1.
9 Varro I. L. V. § 164. Fest. s.v. *Romanom portam* p. 262.

erected to commemorate the capture of Jerusalem, with bas-reliefs, exhibiting the golden candlestick and various other sacred utensils, which formed part of the spoil of the temple. The inscription—SENATUS POPULUSQUE ROMANUS DIVO TITO DIVI VESPASIANI F. VESPASIANO AUGUSTO—proves that it could not have been completed until after the death of Titus.

On the side of the Velia next the forum, was the sumptuous *Templum Pacis*, erected by Vespasian after the Jewish triumph;[1] it stood in the midst of a spacious area known in latter times as the *Forum Vespasiani* or *Forum Pacis*.[2] The original temple was burned shortly before the death of Commodus,[3] and a portion of the site was probably employed by Maxentius for the vast Basilica, which, after the downfall of the usurper, was distinguished as the *Basilica Constantiniana*.

On the other side of the Velia, towards the Coliseum, stood the colossal statue of Nero, 120 feet in height,[4] which, after undergoing many transmutations in name and feature, was removed from its original position by Hadrian, to make room for the *Templum Veneris et Romae*, subsequently named *Templum Pacis*, one of the most georgeous of all the imperial structures.[5] The annexed cut, from a large brass of Hadrian, is supposed to represent the temple in question.

[1] Joseph. B. J. VII. 5. § 7. Dion Cass. LXVI. 15. Suet. Vesp. 9. Plin. H.N. XXXIV. 8. Aul. Gell. V. 21. XVI. 8.
[2] Ammian. Marcellin. XVI. 10. Procop. B. G. IV. 21. Symmach. Epp. X. 78.
[3] Dion Cass. LXXII. 24. Herod. 1. 14.
[4] Suet. Ner. 31. Vesp. 18. Plin. H.N. XXXIV 7.
[5] Dion Cass. LXIX. 4. LXXI. 31. Martial. Spect. 2. Spartian. Hadrian. 19. Lamprid. Commod. 17.

MONS AVENTINUS.

The Aventine, which rises to 150 feet above the sea, or 117 feet above the ordinary level of the Tiber, presents a more extended flat surface on its summit than any of the other hills. Immediately to the south-east of the Aventine, and separated from it by a narrow valley, is a hill of considerable magnitude, and on this we now find the modern churches of S. Saba and S. Balbina. This second hill is nowhere named in the classical writers, and it is a matter of doubt whether it was or was not regarded as a part of the Aventine. It has been ingeniously conjectured, that a difference of opinion upon this subject may have given rise to a variation in the MSS. of Dionysius, (III. 43,) some of which give twelve stadia and others eighteen stadia as the circumference of the Aventine. Twelve will correspond well with the Aventine proper, while eighteen would include both. Another curious fact connected with the Aventine embarrassed the Roman antiquaries of the empire. It was the only one of the seven hills not comprehended within the Pomoerium of Servius Tullius, and it remained excluded until the reign of Claudius.[1]

The Aventine is said to have been inhabited during the reign of Ancus Martius, who assigned it to the inhabitants of Tellene and Politorium, and other towns conquered by him;[2] but it seems, subsequently, to have been in a great measure deserted, for, towards the close of the third century, it was overgrown with wood, and formed a portion of the state lands, (*ager publicus*,) occupied by the patricians, from whom it was wrested after a hard struggle, and portioned out among the plebeians.[3] From this time forward it remained chiefly in the hands of plebeian families, and was, as it were, the stronghold of the order, even after all political distinctions between the patricians and the plebeians had been swept away.

There were several localities on the Aventine connected with the legendary history of the city. At the foot of the hill, near the *Porta Trigemina*, close to the place afterwards called *Salinae*, were the *Ara Evandri*,[4] the *Antrum Caci*,[5] and the *Ara Iovis Inventoris*,[6] reared by Hercules to commemorate the finding of his oxen; there was also pointed out on the top of the hill a spot which long bore the name of *Remoria* or *Remuria*, where Remus watched the auspices[7]— an altar to *Iupiter Elicius*,[8] which dated from Numa—the street *Lauretum*[9] where once grew a grove of laurels over the grave of king Tatius—the *Armilustrium*,[10] where a festival, bearing the same name, was celebrated, it is said, by armed men; but the nature of the solemnity is unknown. The most celebrated temple was that of Diana, and hence Martial terms the whole hill *Collis Dianae*,[11] built by Servius as the shrine where the great Latin confederacy, of which Rome must, at that period, have been regarded as the head, might offer up common sacrifice.[12] The ancient edifice appears to have been in existence in the time of Augustus, and in it was preserved, even at that epoch, the original brazen plates on which were inscribed the *Foedus Latinum* and the *Lex Icilia*. Scarcely less

---

[1] Aul. Gell. XIII. 14.
[2] Liv. I. 33. Dionys III. 43.
[3] Liv. III. 31. 32. Dionys. X. 31.
[4] Dionys. I. 32.
[5] Virg. Æn. VIII. 190. Ovid. Fast I. 551. Solin. I. 8.
[6] Dionys. I. 39.
[7] Paul. Diac. s.v. *Remurinus ager*, p. 276.
[8] Varro L. L. VI. § 94. Liv. I. 20. Plut. Num. 15.
[9] Varro L. L. V. § 152. Dionys. III. 43. Plin. H N. XV. 30.
[10] Varro L. L. V. § 153. VI. § 22. Paul. Diac. s.v. *Armilustrium*, p. 19. Plut. Rom. 23. Liv. XXVII. 37.
[11] Martial. VI. 64. VII. 73. XII. 18.
[12] Liv. I. 45. Dionys. IV. 26.

celebrated was the temple of *Iuno Regina*, built and dedicated by Camillus after the sack of Veii, and here the wooden statue of the goddess, brought from the conquered city, was deposited.[1] Near a rock, called *Saxum Rubrum*, which is probably the same with the *Remuria* noticed above, on the first downward slope of the ridge, towards the south, stood the shrine of *Bona Dea*, afterwards removed by Hadrian.[2] There was also a temple of *Minerva*, as old, at least, as the second Punic war[3]—of *Luna*[4]—and of *Libertas*.[5] With the latter, many suppose that the *Atrium Libertatis*, so frequently mentioned in the classics, was connected; but there is every reason to suppose that the latter lay somewhere between the Forum and the Campus Martius.[6]

On the narrow strip of land between the Aventine and the river, outside the Porta Trigemina, was the harbour or quay (*emporium*,) where all merchandise conveyed by the Tiber was landed. This was gradually extended, and the accommodation enlarged; and here we must look for the covered shed called *Porticus Aemilia*, set up by the aediles M. Aemilius Lepidus and L. Aemilius Paulus.[7] Here, too, as might be expected, were the corn market,[8] the public granaries, and a *Vicus Frumentarius*,[9] and this was the quarter of the wood merchants (*lignarii*.)[10]

Approaches to the Aventine.—The chief, and, in ancient times, probably the only approach to the Aventine, was by the slope called *Clivus Publicius*, so named from L. and M. Publicii Malleoli, plebeian aediles, by whom it was paved and rendered passable for wheel carriages. It ascended from the Porta Trigemina, and was the regular access from the quarter of the forum.[11]

Monte Testaccio.—To the south-west of the Aventine and included within the circuit of the Aurelian walls, rises a little hill or mound, upwards of 130 feet above the level of the Tiber, and more than a quarter of a mile in circumference, composed entirely of broken pottery; the ground all round for a considerable distance, being raised nearly twenty feet above its natural level by a mass of similar fragments. This eminence is now known as the *Monte Testaccio*, and the name *Mons Testaceus* occurs in an inscription, as old, at least, as the eighth century, while the position of the *Porta Ostiensis*, built by Honorius, proves that the surface of the ground at that point has not undergone any material change since the commencement of the fifth century. There is, however, no allusion to the Monte Testaccio in any ancient writer; and no plausible theory has yet been devised to account for such an extraordinary accumulation of potsherds in this locality.

Porta Capena.—In the valley between the Aventine and the Coelian, stood the *Porta Capena*, which gave its name to the first of the Augustan regions. This district lay altogether beyond the Servian wall, forming one of the numerous suburbs. In the immediate vicinity of the gate was the temple of *Honos*, erected

---

1 Dionys. IV. 26. X. 32. fragm. XIII. 3. Liv. V. 22.
2 Ovid. Fast. V. 148. Spartian. Hadrian. 19.
3 Fest. s v. *Quinquatrus*, p. 254. s v. *Scribas*, p. 333.
4 Liv. XL. 2. Ovid. Fast. III. 833.
5 Liv. XXIV. 16.
6 Liv. XXV. 7. XLIII. 16. XLV. 15. Cic. pro Mil. 22. ad Att. IV. 16. Another *Atrium Libertatis* was built by Asinius Pollio, who here established the first public library known in Rome. See Suet. Octav. 29. Plin. H.N. VII. 30. XXXV. 2.
7 Liv. XXXV. 10. XLI. 27.
8 Liv. XL. 51. Plin. H.N. XVIII. 3. XXXIV. 5.
9 See Becker, p. 165. 465.
10 Liv. XXXV. 41.
11 Fest. s v. *Publicius Clivus*, 238. Varro L.L. V. § 158. Liv. XXVI. 28. See also the important description of the procession in Liv. XXVII. 37.

D

by Q. Fabius Verrucosus, and repaired after the capture of Syracuse (B.C. 212,) by M. Marcellus, who attached to it a temple of *Virtus*, and decorated the twin shrines with several master-pieces of Grecian art, brought from the conquered city.[1] From this point, or from the neighbouring temple of *Mars*,[2] the Roman equites proceeded annually, on the 15th of July, in solemn procession (*transvectio*) to the capitol.[3] Beside the temple of Mars stood a sacred stone, the *Lapis Manalis*,[4] which was dragged into the city with certain ceremonies, during periods of excessive drought, in order to procure a fall of rain.

Vallis Egeriae.—Near the Porta Capena was the dell in which Numa was wont to hold nocturnal converse with the nymph Egeria, (*Hic ubi nocturnae Numa constituebat amicae*,) and the grove consecrated to the *Camoenae*, together with the sacred grotto and spring—localities minutely described by Livy and Juvenal,[5] especially by the latter, whose words are so distinct, that it is difficult to imagine how the opinion maintained by so many modern topographers, that we are to look for these spots outside the modern Porta S. Sebastiano, the *Porta Appia* of the Aurelian circuit, could ever have found supporters.

Piscina Publica.—Bordering on the region of the Porta Capena, and also outside of the Servian wall, lay the Twelfth of the Augustan regions, which took its name from the *Piscina Publica*, a large tank, in which the populace used to bathe and exercise themselves in swimming; but the pond itself had disappeared at a comparatively early epoch, although the name still adhered to the district.[6]

MONS COELIUS.

Mons Coelius.—The Coelian presents the largest level surface next to the Aventine, and rises to the height of about 158 feet above the level of the sea. It was originally, we are told, named *Mons Querquetulanus*, from the oaks with which it was clothed, and received the appellation of *Mons Coelius*, from a certain Coelius Vibennus or Coeles Vibenna, an Etruscan chief, who formed a settlement on the hill, as early as the time of Romulus, according to one account, or in the days of the elder Tarquin, according to another.[7] For a short period, under Tiberius, it was designated *Mons Augustus*, to commemorate the liberality of the emperor in supplying funds for repairing the ravages caused by a destructive conflagration.[8] It must be remarked that the surface of this hill is broken up into several divisions, by depressions and projections, and while the whole was termed *Mons Coelius*, one of the smaller heights or ridges was distinguished as *Coelius Minor* or *Coeliolus*;[9] but topographers have been unable to fix upon the portion to which this title belongs.

We hear of scarcely any public buildings of importance on the Coelian. There were chapels of *Dea Carna*[10]—of *Minerva Capta*,[11]—and of *Diana* (on the

---

[1] Ovid. Fast. VI. 191. Propert. IV. iii. 71. Serv. ad Virg. Æn. I. 292.
[2] Liv. XXV. 40. XXVII. 25. Cic. de N.D. II. 23. in Verr. IV. 54. Val. Max. 1. i. 8
[3] Dionys. VI. 13. Cic. ad Q. F. III. 7. Aurel. Vict. de viris ill. 32.
[4] Paul. Diac. s.v. *Aquaelicium*, p. 2. s.v. *Manalem Lapidem*, p. 128. Varro ap. Non. X V. s.v. *Trulleum*, p. 375. ed. Gerl. Antist. Lab. ap. Fulgent. s.v. *Manales Lapides*, p. 388. ed. Gerl.
[5] Liv. I. 21. Juv. S. III. 10. comp. Plut. Num. 13.
[6] Fest. s.v. *Piscinae publicae*, p. 213. Liv. XXIII. 32. Cic. ad Q. F. III. 7.
[7] Tacit. Ann. IV. 65. Varro L.L. V. § 46. Dionys. II. 36. Tab. Lugd. ap. Grut. XII.
[8] Suet. Tib. 48. Tacit. Ann. IV. 64.
[9] Varro L.L. V. § 46. Orat. de Harusp. resp. 15. Martial. XII. 18.
[10] Macrob. S. I. 12.
[11] Ovid. Fast. III. 857. comp. Varro L.L. V. 47.

Coeliolus)[1] —a temple to *Divus Claudius*, commenced by Agrippina, destroyed by Nero, and restored by Vespasian [2] —and a temple of *Isis*. [3]

On the Coelian was the *Aqua Mercurii*, the spring whose virtues have been celebrated by Ovid, [4] and the *Campus Martialis*, where the *Equiria* were celebrated, at times when the Campus Martius, the ordinary place of exhibition, chanced to be overflowed. [5]

We are told that Tullus Hostilius fixed on the Coelian as the site of his palace, [6] although, according to other accounts, he dwelt on the Velia. [7] In later times it was decorated by many sumptuous private dwellings, [8] of which the most celebrated were—the house of Mamurra—the *Domus Lateranorum*, belonging to the Plautii Laterani, from which the magnificent church of S. Giovanni in Laterano derives its name [9]—and the *Aedes Vectilianae*, in which Commodus perished. [10]

Almost the only memorial of ancient times now standing on the hill, is an arch, probably connected originally with some of the aqueducts in this district. It is usually known as the *Arcus Dolabellae*, having been erected, as the inscription informs us, by the consuls P. Cornelius Dollabella and C. Junius Silanus (A.D. 10.)

Ceroliensis.—The hollow between the Coelian and the Esquiline seems, as we have already stated, to have borne the name *Ceroliensis*, and here was the

[1] Orat. e Haruspic. resp. 15.
[2] Suet. Vesp. 9. Frontin. de Aquaed. 20.
[3] Trebell. Poll. trig. tyrann. 24.
[4] Ovid. Fast. V. 673.
[5] Ovid. Fast. III. 519 Paul. Diac. s.v. *Martialis Campus*, p. 131.
[6] Liv. I. 30.
[7] Cic. de R. II. 31.
[8] Val. Max. VIII. ii. 1. Plin. H.N. XXXVI. 6. Martial. XII. 18. Capitolin. M. Aurel. 1. Lamprid. Commod. 16.
[9] Juv. S. X. 18. Tacit. Ann. XV. 49. 60 Victor Epit 20.
[10] Lamprid. Commod. 16. Capitolin. Pertin. 5.

Sacellum Streniae, which marked the commencement of the Sacred Way.[1] In this valley were formed the costly fish-ponds of Nero (*stagna Neronis*,) included within the limits of the Aurea Domus; and their site was afterwards occupied by the stupendous mass of the *Coliseum*, the most impressive, perhaps, of all ancient ruins. In the same valley we can still trace the remains of the *Meta Sudans*,[2] where the water from a copious spring, rising through a conical pillar, was received into a basin of stone; and finally, at the point where this hollow is joined by that which divides the Palatine from the Coelian, stands, still entire, as represented in the cut below, the Triumphal Arch of Constantine the Great, erected to commemorate his victory over Maxentius.

ESQUILIAE S. MONS ESQUILINUS.

We have already, in our preliminary sketch, explained generally the relative position of the localities connected with the Esquiline—the *Mons Oppius*—the *Mons Cispius*—the *Carinae*—the *Vicus Cyprius*—the *Vicus Patricius*, and the *Subura*.

Mons Oppius. Carinae.—That portion of the Mons Oppius which was termed *Carinae* is now marked by the modern church of S. Pietro in Vincoli, and the extensive ruins of the baths of Titus (*Thermae Titi*.) This district seems to have formed originally a sort of independent village, for we hear in ancient times of the *Terreus Murus*[3] of the Carinae; and, according to the Servian division, the Carinae was included in the *Regio Suburana*, and not in the *Regio Esquilina*. The temple of *Tellus*, the most celebrated on the Esquiline, was situated in the Carinae. It was built by P. Sempronius Sophus, (consul B.C. 268) on the site of the mansion once occupied by Sp. Cassius, (B.C. 485.)[4] In the Carinae was the house of Cn. Pompeius,[5] and towards the close of the

[1] Varro L.L. V. § 47.
[2] Senec. Ep. 56
[3] Varro L.L. V. § 48.
[4] Dionys. VIII. 79. Liv II 41. Orat. pro dom. 38
[5] Suet. de ill. gramm 15 Tib. 15 Dion Cass. XLVIII. 38

republic it seems to have been regarded as one of the most fashionable quarters of the city. In a street leading down into the Vicus Cyprius was the *Tigillum Sororium*, a beam stretching across the pathway after the manner of a yoke. Under this, according to the legend, Horatius passed in token of humiliation, after the unhappy death of his sister; and altars were erected hard by to *Iuno Sororia* and *Ianus Curiatius*,[1] on which sacrifices were regularly offered up at stated periods by the Gens Horatia.

Mons Cispius.—The summit of the Mons Cispius is marked by the celebrated modern church of S. Maria Maggiore, in which the pavement is 187 feet above the level of the sea.

The greater portion of the Esquiline was, in ancient times, covered with wood, and although this gradually disappeared, traces of it remained in the numerous *Luci* or sacred groves scattered up and down. Among these we find especial mention made of the *Fagutal* or *Lucus Fagutalis*, with the *Sacellum Iovis Fagutalis*[2]—the *Lucus Esquilinus*[3]—the *Lucus Poetelius*[4]—the *Lucus Iunonis Lucinae*, with her temple, built in B.C. 375,[5] and the *Lucus Mefitis*.[6] The last, taken in connection with the altars to *Mala Fortuna*[7] and to *Febris*,[8] would seem to indicate that the air of this quarter was regarded as unwholesome; and it is certain that, for a long period, the greater portion of Esquiline proper was inhabited by the humbler classes only, and contained no public buildings of importance.

The amenity of the upper part of the hill must have been entirely destroyed by the vicinity of the *Campus Esquilinus*, an extensive level outside the Servian wall, which was the ordinary place of punishment for malefactors convicted of capital crimes, and served as a place of interment for all classes in the community.[9] Not only were the rich buried here, but a part of the ground was set apart for slaves and criminals, whose bodies were frequently thrown down and left to decompose or to become the prey of dogs and birds, without an attempt being made to cover them with earth.[10] But during the reign of Augustus the aspect of this region underwent an important change. Maecenas having selected the highest point for his residence, erected a lofty edifice (*turris Maecenatiana*) commanding a most extensive prospect, removed the public cemeteries to a greater distance, and laid out the ground around his mansion in spacious gardens and pleasure grounds (*horti Maecenatiani*,)[11] which descended by inheritance to Augustus, and remained for some generations in possession of his successors.

COLLIS VIMINALIS.

The Viminal was separated from the Esquiline by the *Vicus Patricius*, from the Quirinal by the *Vallis Quirini* and the *Vicus Largus*, now the Via di S. Vitale. The point where the ridges of the Viminal and Quirinal unite is 180 feet above

---

1 Liv. I. 26. Dionys. III. 21. Fest. s.v. *Sororium tigillum*, p. 297.
2 Varro L.L. V. § 49. 50. Fest s.v. *Septimontio*, p. 348. Paul. Diac. s.v. *Fagutal*, p. 87. s v *Septimontium*, p. 341.
3 Varro L.L. l.c.
4 Varro l.c.
5 Varro l.c. Dionys. IV. 15 Ovid. Fast. II. 435. Plin. H.N. XVI. 44.
6 Varro l c. Fest. s.v. *Septimontio*, p. 348.
7 Cic. de N. D. III. 25. de. legg. II. 11.
8 Val. Max. II. v. 6.
9 Plaut. Mil.Glor. II. iv. 6. Tacit. Ann. II 32 Suet. Claud. 25.
10 Cic. Philipp. IX. 7. Hor. S. I. viii. 14. and schol. Cruq. &c. Epod. V. 99. Varro L.L. V § 25.
11 Hor. S. I. viii. 14. and scholiasts. C. III xxix 10. Suet. Ner. 38.

the level of the sea; the floor of the church of S. Lorenzo is 170. No portion of the ancient city was less distinguished by public buildings or remarkable sites of any description, and hence we may conclude that it was at all times inhabited chiefly by the poorer classes. Almost the only edifice of which we find any notice was the mansion of C. Aquillius, a Roman eques, celebrated for his legal knowledge, who flourished during the last century of the commonwealth. This is said to have transcended in magnificence even the dwellings of Crassus the orator and of Q. Catulus, on the Palatine.[1] At a later period Diocletian erected, on the height where the Viminal and Quirinal join, his vast *Thermae*, the most extensive and costly of all the imperial piles of that class. A fragment of the ancient structure is included in the beautiful modern church of *S. Maria degli Angeli*.

COLLIS QUIRINALIS.

This hill, of which the highest point is at its junction with the Viminal, is said to have been originally called *Agonus*,[2] and to have received the name by which it was subsequently known, when colonized by the Sabines, (*Curetes—Quirites—Quirinus*) by whom it was inhabited during the earliest ages of Rome. The most celebrated temple was that of *Quirinus*. We hear of its existence as early as B.C. 435—it seems to have been rebuilt and dedicated in B.C. 293, by L. Papirius Cursor, in fulfilment of a vow made by his father the dictator, and it was again rebuilt by Augustus in B.C. 16.[3] Before the erection of the triple shrine to Jupiter, Juno, and Minerva upon the Capitoline, there existed a temple on the Quirinal consecrated to these deities, and although thrown into the shade by the splendour of the new edifice, it was still in existence at a very late period, and is called the *Capitolium Vetus* by Varro, while it is indicated by Martial, when he speaks of *Iovem antiquum*.[4] On the Quirinal were also temples of *Flora*;[5] of *Salus*,[6] decorated with paintings by Fabius Pictor, near which was the house of Pomponius Atticus;[7] and of *Fortuna Primigenia*.[8] Close to the *Porta Collina* was the *Campus Sceleratus*, where the Vestal virgins who had broken their vows were buried alive;[9] and beyond the gate was a temple of *Venus Erycina*.[10]

COLLIS HORTULORUM.

This hill, which, in the decline of the empire was named *Mons Pincius*,—whence the modern appellation *Monte Pincio*—rises, at its highest point, about 220 feet above the level of the sea. It was not included within the Servian wall; and, as the name imports, was laid out in gardens and pleasure grounds. Among the most celebrated of these were the *Horti Sallustiani*, in the hollow towards the Quirinal,[11] and the *Horti Luculliani*, first mentioned in connection with the downfal of Messalina.[12]

Having now completed the circuit of the high grounds, we return to the

---

1 Plin. H.N. XVII. 1.
2 Fest. s.v. *Quirinalis collis*, p. 254. Paul. Diac. s.v. *Agonium*, p. 10. comp. Dionys. II. 37.
3 Dionys. II. 63. Ovid. Fast. II. 511. VI. 795. Liv. IV. 21. X. 46. Plin. H.N. VII. 60. XV. 29. Dion Cass. LIV. 19.
4 Varro L.L. V. § 158. Martial V. 22. VII. 73.
5 Martial. V. 22. Varro L.L. l.c
6 Liv. X. 1. Plin. H.N. XXXV. 4
7 Cic. ad Att. IV. 1. XII. 45. de legg. I. 1
8 Liv. XXXIV. 53.
9 Dionys. II. 67. Plut. Num. 10. Liv. VIII. 15. Fest. s.v. *Sceleratus campus*, p. 333.
10 Liv. XXX. 38.
11 Tacit. Ann. XIII. 47. Hist. III. 82 Dion Cass. LXVI. 10. Vopisc. Aurel. 49.
12 Tacit. Ann. XI. 32. 37. Juv. S. X. 334. Plut. Lucull. 39.

vicinity of the Palatine and the Aventine, for the purpose of describing the flat between the hills and the river. But our attention is first claimed by the

CIRCUS MAXIMUS.

We have already stated that the hollow between the Palatine and the Aventine was called *Vallis Murcia*,[1] or *Ad Murciae*, or *Ad Murcim*, names derived from an altar of the goddess *Murcia*, who is represented as identical with Venus. In this hollow the *Circus Maximus* was formed, the construction and arrangement of which we shall describe more particularly hereafter. Within the Circus was the subterranean altar of *Consus*, the god of secret counsel, which was uncovered only during the celebration of the games;[2] and in the immediate vicinity of the Circus were temples—of *Sol*[3]—of *Mercurius*[4]—of *Ceres, Liber* and *Libera*, generally called simply *Aedes Cereris*[5]—of *Venus*[6]—of *Flora*[7] —of *Summanus*[8]—and of *Iuventas*.[9]

FORUM BOARIUM.

The open space extending from the Circus to the river was the *Forum Boarium* or cattle-market, in which was appropriately placed the famous bronze ox, brought from Aegina.[10] Immediately in front of the Circus was the *Ara Maxima*, sacred to Hercules, said to have been reared either by the hero himself, or by Evander, in honour of his illustrious guest,[11] and adjoining to it a shrine dedicated to the same deity.[12] In addition to this, there were other temples of Hercules in this neighbourhood, especially one of a circular form—*Aedes rotunda Herculis*,[13] adjacent to which was a chapel of *Pudicitia Patricia*.[14] In the Forum Boarium were also temples of *Fortuna Virilis*[15] and of *Mater Matuta*,[16] both of great antiquity; and near the point where the Cloaca Maxima opened upon the river was the place called *Doliola*, so named, we are told, because, at the period when Rome was taken by the Gauls, certain holy objects were buried here in earthen jars, (*condita in doliolis*,) and hence it was considered impious for any one to spit upon the spot.[17] Lastly, the Forum Boarium was the place where, down to a late period, human sacrifices were occasionally offered up.[18]

Aequimelium. Vicus Iugarius. Vicus Tuscus. Velabrum.—Adjoining the Forum Boarium, towards the Capitoline, was the open area called *Aequimelium*, the two great thoroughfares called the *Vicus Iugarius* and the *Vicus Tuscus*, and the district called the *Velabrum*.

The *Aequimelium* lay immediately under the Capitoline. The origin of the

---

1 Serv. ad Virg. Æn. VIII. 636. Varro L.L. V. § 154. Liv. I. 33. Plin. H.N. XV. 29. Claud. Cons. Stil. II. 404.
2 Varro L.L. VI. § 20. Tacit. Ann. XII. 24. Plut. Rom. 14. Serv. ad Virg. Æn VIII. 636.
3 Tacit. Ann. XV. 74.
4 Liv. II. 21. Ovid. Fast. V. 669.
5 Tacit. Ann. II. 49. Vitruv. III. 3. Plin. H.N. XXXV. 12.
6 Liv. X. 31. XXIX. 37.
7 Tacit. Ann. II. 49.
8 Liv. XXXII. 29. Ovid. Fast. VI. 731. Plin. H.N. XXIX. 4.
9 Liv. XXXVI. 36. XXI. 62. Plin. H.N. XXIX. 4.
10 Varro L.L. V. § 146. Liv. XXI. 62. Propert. IV. ix. 19. Tacit. Ann. XII. 24. Plin. H.N. XXXIV. 2.
11 Liv. I. 7. Propert. IV. ix. 67. Ovid. Fast. I. 581. Serv. ad Virg. Æn. VIII. 271.
12 Tacit. Ann. XV. 41. Plin. H.N. X. 29. XXXIV. 7. XXXV. 4
13 Liv. X. 23.
14 Liv. l.c.
15 Dionys. IV. 27.
16 Liv. V. 19. XXXIII. 27. Ovid. Fast. VI. 479.
17 Liv. V. 40. another account in Varro L.L. V. § 156.
18 Liv. XXII. 57. Plut. Marcell. 3. Q.R. 83. Plin. H.N. XXVI. 2. Dion Cass. fragm. Vales. 12.

name cannot be determined. The Romans themselves imagined that it marked the site of the house of Sp. Melius, which was razed to the ground B.C. 439.[1]

The *Vicus Iugarius*, so named from an altar of *Iuno Iuga*[2] or matrimonial Juno, ran from the *Porta Carmentalis* to the *Forum*, which it entered at the *Basilica Iulia* and *Lacus Servilius*.

The *Vicus Tuscus* was named from the Tuscans, who, under their leader, Coelius Vibenna, at first formed a settlement on the Mons Coelius, and afterwards established themselves in the plain below.[3] It ran between the Capitoline and the Palatine, connecting the Forum, which it entered between the Basilica Julia and the temple of Castor, with the Circus Maximus.[4]

The space between the *Vicus Tuscus* and the *Forum Boarium* was the *Velabrum*, which the Romans derived from *Velum*, because it was originally a swampy lake, over which boats sailed;[5] but having been drained by the Cloaca Maxima and its branches, became one of the chief marts for provisions of every

[1] Varro L.L. V. § 157. Liv. IV. 16. XXXVIII. 28. Orat. pro dom. 38. Val. Max. VI. lii. 1.
[2] Paul. Diac. s.v. *Iugarius ricus*, p. 104.
[3] Varro L.L. V. § 46. Tacit. Ann. IV. 65. Propert. IV. ii. 49.
[4] Dionys. V. 36.
[5] Varro L.L. V. § 44. Tibull. II v. 33. Ovid. Fast. VI. 401. Propert. IV. ix. 5. Plut. Rom. 5.

TOPOGRAPHY OF ROME.

kind.[1] The boundary line between the *Velabrum* and the *Forum Boarium* seems to be marked by two monuments still extant, the one termed *Arcus Argentarius*, because the inscription sets forth that it was erected in honour of Septimius Severus, his empress Julia, and his sons, by the ARGENTARII ET NEGOTIANTES BOARII HUIUS LOCI;[2] the other a massive double archway of Greek marble, commonly known as *Ianus Quadrifrons*. The former is represented on the preceding page, the latter is figured above; and it will be at once

[1] Plaut. Capt. III. i. 29. Hor. S. II. iii. 229. and schol.   [2] Orell. C. I. No. 91.

seen that the former is an arch in name only, the opening being rectangular. The whole structure is covered over with bas reliefs representing the details of an ancient sacrifice.

Between the Janus and the river are two temples in good preservation; both ancient, but neither of them, in their present state, belonging to an epoch earlier than the second or third century. One of these is circular, and hence has been named *Aedes Vestae*, the other is rectangular, and has been styled by antiquarians *Templum Fortunae Virilis;* but there is not sufficient evidence to establish the accuracy of either title. They are now employed as Christian churches, the former being dedicated to *S. Stefano delle Carozze* and *S. Maria del Sole*, the latter to *S. Maria Egiziaca*. The former is accurately represented at the bottom of the preceding page, the latter below.

We now pass beyond the limit of the Servian walls to consider the

CAMPUS MARTIUS.

Campus Martius.—We have hitherto employed this name to designate the whole of the meadow land bounded by the Tiber on one side, and on the other by the Collis Hortulorum, the Quirinal and the Capitoline; the northern and southern extremities being marked by the points where the first and the last of these hills approach within a short distance of the river. But the *Campus Martius*, strictly speaking, was that portion only of the flat ground which lies in the angle formed by the bend of the stream; the larger space contained, in addition to the Campus Martius proper, two of the Augustan regions, the seventh, called the *Via Lata*, and the ninth, called the *Circus Flaminius*. We shall consider each of these three divisions separately; but we must premise that the investigations of modern topographers have been much embarrassed by the circumstance, that the ground in question is almost entirely covered by the complicated maze of streets which form the modern city, while the seven hills and other important localities of republican Rome are to a great extent clear and open for examination.

I. **Via Lata.**—This region derived its name from a broad road which ran in a straight line from the north-east corner of the Capitoline to the point where the Collis Hortulorum approached most nearly to the river, and where the *Porta Flaminia* of the Aurelian wall was placed. After passing this point, the *Via Lata* became the *Via Flaminia*, the great highway to the north. The Via Lata is now represented by one of the principal streets of the modern city—the *Strada del Corso*. The region of the Via Lata was the level space bounded on one side by the road, and on the other by the slopes of the Collis Hortulorum, and of the Quirinal.

In this space we must look for the *Campus Agrippae*, in which was the *Porticus Polae*,[1] named after the sister of Agrippa, but known also as the *Porticus Vipsania*,[2] and as the *Porticus Europae*,[3] the latter name being derived from the subject of the pictures with which it was decorated. The Campus Agrippae was the site chosen by Aurelian for his magnificent *Templum Solis;* and in this or some other portion of the Via Lata, were the triumphal arches of Claudius and M. Aurelius, remains of which existed as late as the middle of the sixteenth century.

II. **Circus Flaminius.**—The southern portion of the meadow between the Via Lata and the river, that part, namely, which was nearest to the Capitoline, was known as the *Campus Flaminius* or *Prata Flaminia;*[4] and here, immediately under the Arx, C. Flaminius, who fell at the battle of the Thrasymene lake, formed the *Circus Flaminius*, which gave its name to the ninth Augustan region.[5] Buildings were erected in this quarter at a very early period, and before the death of Augustus, a vast number of most important edifices were here clustered together. Immediately outside of the Servian wall, at the south-west angle of the Capitoline, in front of the Porta Carmentalis, was the *Forum Olitorium*[6] or vegetable market, in and around which were several temples—that of *Apollo*, vowed in B.C. 433, on account of a pestilence, and dedicated B.C. 431, by the consul C. Julius Mento, being the only temple to that God in Rome before the time of Augustus [7]—that of *Spes*, erected by M. Atilius Calatinus, in the first Punic war, destroyed by fire in the second Punic war, rebuilt, again destroyed in B.C. 31, and again restored by Germanicus [8]—that of *Iuno Sospita*, (or perhaps *Iuno Matuta*,) vowed by C. Cornelius Cethegus, in the battle against the Insubres, B.C. 197, and dedicated B.C. 196 [9]—that of *Pietas*, vowed by M'. Acilius Glabrio at the battle of Thermopylae, B.C. 191, and dedicated ten years afterwards by his son; reared upon the spot where, according to the legend, the woman had dwelt who saved her imprisoned father from starvation by her own milk [10]—and that of *Bellona*, in which the Senate generally assembled when circumstances rendered it necessary for them to meet outside the pomoerium, as, for example, when they gave audience to the

---

[1] Dion Cass. LV. 8.
[2] Tacit. H. I. 31. Plut. Galb. 25.
[3] Martial. II. xiv. 3. III. xx. 11. VII. xxxii. 11.
[4] Liv. III. 54. 63. Varro L.L. V. § 154.
[5] Paul. Diac. s.v. *Flaminius*, p. 89. Liv. Epit. XX. Varro L.L. V. § 154. Strabo. V. 3. § 8.
[6] Varro L.L. V. § 146.
[7] Liv. IV. 25. 29. XXXIV. 43. XXXVII. 58. XLI. 17. Ascon. ad Cic. Orat. in tog. cand.
[8] Liv. XXI. 62. XXIV. 47. XXV. 7. Cic. de N. D. II. 23. de legg. II. 11. Tacit. Ann. II. 49.
[9] Liv. XXXII. 30. XXXIV. 53.
[10] Fest. s v. *Pietati*, p. 209. Val. Max. II. v. 1. Liv. XL. 34. Plin. H.N. VII. 36.

ambassadors of a state with which the Roman people were at war, or to a general who had not laid down his military command.[1] The temple of Apollo, mentioned above, was occasionally employed for the same purpose. Behind this temple was a small open space where stood the *Columna Bellica*, from whence, when war was declared against an enemy beyond the sea, the Roman Fecialis hurled a spear into the plot of ground called *Ager Hostilis*, which represented the country of the foe.[2] In addition to the above, this quarter contained the *Aedes Herculis Musarum*, built by M. Fulvius Nobilior, about B.C. 186,[3] and rebuilt by L. Marcius Philippus, the stepfather of Augustus,[4] who attached the colonnade called *Porticus Philippi*[5]—the temple of *Hercules Custos*[6]—of *Diana and Iuno Regina*, dedicated by M. Aemilius Lepidus when censor, B.C. 179[7]—of *Fortuna Equestris*, vowed by Q. Fulvius Flaccus, in a battle against the Celtiberi, B.C. 180[8]—of *Mars*[9]—of *Neptunus*, called the *Delubrum Cn. Domitii*[10]—and of *Castor* and *Pollux*.[11]

In the region of the Circus Flaminius, also, were the three great theatres of Rome—

1. *Theatrum Pompeii*, built by Pompeius Magnus upon his return from the Mithridatic war, to which were attached a spacious colonnade, the *Porticus Pompeii*,[12] where the spectators might find refuge from a sudden storm, and a hall, employed as a place of meeting for the Senate, the *Curia Pompeii*, in which Julius Caesar was murdered.[13] In the immediate vicinity of this theatre, Pompeius, who had previously lived in the Carinae, built a residence for himself and laid out gardens.[14] Adjoining the theatre was a colonnade, built by Augustus, decorated with representations of fourteen different nations, and hence called *Porticus ad Nationes*,[15] and here, too, was the triumphal arch erected by Claudius in honour of Tiberius.

2. *Theatrum Balbi*, built by L. Cornelius Balbus.[16]

3. *Theatrum Marcelli*, built by Augustus in honour of his nephew, close to the Forum Olitorium, on the site of the temple of Pietas, noticed above.[17] A great part of this theatre was destroyed by a conflagration during the reign of Titus; but considerable remains of the semicircular outer wall are still visible in the Piazza Montanara, as may be seen from the representation on the next page.

Finally, we must notice in this region the *Porticus Octavia*, otherwise called *Porticus Corinthia*, erected by Cn. Octavius, who was consul B.C. 165, in honour of his naval triumph over Perseus.[18] This structure must be carefully

---

[1] Liv. X. 19. XXVIII. 38. XXXI. 47. XXXIII. 22. XXXVI. 39. XXXIX. 29. XLI. 6. XLII. 28. 36, &c. Ovid. Fast. VI. 203. Fest. s.v *Semuncula*, p. 347. Plin. H.N. XXXV. 3.
[2] Ovid. Fast. VI. 205. Serv. ad Virg. Æn. IX. 53. Paul. Diac. s.v. *Bellona*, p. 33.
[3] Cic. pro Arch. 11. Plin. H N XXXV. 10. Plut. Q R. 59. Eumen. pro inst. schol. Aug. Macrob. S. I. 12. Serv. ad Virg. Æn. I. 8.
[4] Ovid. Fast. VI. 798. Suet. Oct. 29.
[5] Martial. V. 49.
[6] Ovid. Fast. VI. 209.
[7] Liv. XL. 52. Jul Obs. 75.
[8] Liv. XL. 40. 44, XLII. 10. Tacit. Ann. III. 71.
[9] Plin. H.N. XXXVI. 5.
[10] Plin. l.c. Liv. XXVIII. 11.
[11] Vitruv. IV. 8.
[12] Vitruv. V. 9. Ovid. A. A. I. 67.
[13] Plut. Brut. 14. Caes. 66. Appian. B.C. II. 115. Cic. de div. II. 9. Liv. Epit. CXVI. Suet. Jul. 80, 81. Octav. 31. Dion Cass. XLIV. 16. Plin. H.N. XXXV. 9.
[14] Plut. Pomp. 40. 44.
[15] Plin. H.N. XXXVI. 5. Serv. ad Virg. Æn. VIII. 721.
[16] Suet. Octav. 29. Dion Cass. LIV. 25.
[17] Plin. H.N. VII. 36.
[18] Velleius II. 1. Plin. H.N. XXXIV. 3. Fest. s.v. *Octaviae porticus*, p. 178.

TOPOGRAPHY OF ROME.   45

distinguished from the *Porticus Octaviae*, with its *Bibliotheca*, *Schola* and *Curia* attached, all comprehended under the general title *Octaviae Opera*. The latter was built close to the theatre of Marcellus by Augustus, in honour of his sister.[1] It occupied the site of the earlier *Porticus Metelli*, built by

[1] Dion Cass. XLIX. 43. Plut. Marc. 30. Plin. H.N. XXXV. 10. XXXVI. 5. Suet. de ill. gramm. 21.

Metellus Macedonicus, (consul B.C. 143,) after his triumph, and included within its circuit temples of *Iupiter Stator* and of *Iuno*.[1] The remains of the *Porticus Octaviae*, as they now exist, forming one side of the Piazza di Pescheria, the modern fish-market, are figured in the annexed cut.

III. **Campus Martius**, (in a restricted sense.)—To the north of the Prata Flaminia, and occupying the space formed by the angular bend of the stream, was the *Campus Martius* proper, frequently called simply *Campus*. According to the narrative of Livy,[2] it was the property of the Tarquins, (*ager Tarquiniorum*,) and, upon their expulsion, was confiscated, and then consecrated to Mars; but Dionysius asserts[3] that it had been previously set apart to the god, and sacrilegiously appropriated by the tyrant. This story agrees well with the statement of Livy, that it was thought impious to make use of the crop which was growing upon it at the time when the Tarquins were driven forth, and that therefore—*quia religiosum erat consumere*—the corn when reaped was cast into the river, and formed the nucleus of the *Insula Tiberina*.

During the republic the Campus Martius was employed specially for two purposes. (1.) As a place for holding the constitutional assemblies, (*comitia*,) especially the *Comitia Centuriata*, and also for ordinary public meetings, (*conciones*.) (2.) For gymnastic and warlike sports. For seven centuries it remained almost entirely open, and although subsequently built upon to a certain extent, there was still ample space left for exercise and recreation. In the Comitia, the citizens, when their votes were taken, passed into enclosures termed *Septa* or *Ovilia*,[4] which were, for a long period, temporary wooden erections; but Julius Cæsar formed a plan for constructing marble Septa, which were to be surrounded by a lofty portico, with spacious apartments, the whole extending to nearly a mile in circumference.[5] This great work, which was only commenced by the dictator, was prosecuted by Lepidus, was completed and dedicated by Agrippa, and termed *Septa Iulia* or *Septa Agrippiana*.[6] By Agrippa, also, was commenced a vast edifice, the *Diribitorium*, which was finished and dedicated by Augustus about B.C. 8. It must have been in the immediate neighbourhood of the Septa, since it was intended, as the name implies, as an office for distributing and counting the balloting tickets.[7] Close to the Septa stood the *Villa Publica*, a building employed by the censors when

numbering the people, by the consuls when holding levees, and by the Senate when receiving foreign ambassadors. We hear of its existence as early as B.C. 437, and it was rebuilt, or intended to be rebuilt, upon a magnificent scale in connection with the Septa Iulia.[8] A representation of this edifice is found on a denarius of the Gens Didia.

In the Campus Martius, also, Agrippa, in his third consulship, B.C. 27, erected a magnificent temple, with public Thermae attached, dedicated to Mars, Venus, Julius Cæsar, and all the other deities of the Julian line, and hence named the

---

[1] Velleius I. 11. Plin. H.N. XXXVI. 5.
[2] Liv. II. 5.
[3] Dionys. V. 13. Aul. Gell. VI. 7.
[4] Ovid. Fast. I. 53. Serv. ad Virg. Ecl. I. 34. Juv. S. VI. 529.
[5] Cic. ad Att. IV. 16.
[6] Dion Cass. LIII. 23. Lamprid. Alex. Sev. 26.
[7] Dion Cass. LV. 8. Suet. Claud. 18. Plin. H.N. XVI. 40.
[8] Liv. IV. 22. XXX. 21. XXXIII. 24. XXXIV. 44. Epit. LXXXVIII. Varro R. R. III. 2. Cic. ad Att. IV. 16. Val. Max. IX. ii. 1.

Pantheon.[1] Although repeatedly damaged, it was always carefully repaired, and exists almost entire at the present day, as the church of *S. Maria ad Martyres.* The belfries, however, placed at the two corners, as represented in

the annexed cut, are modern additions. Lastly, among the great works with which Agrippa embellished this district, we may notice the *Posidonium,* otherwise called the *Basilica Neptuni* or *Porticus Argonautarum,* from the pictures with which it was ornamented.[2] The first name would lead us to believe that it was a temple of Neptune; but we have no distinct information regarding it. In order to leave the Campus open, as far as possible, the greater number of the structures which we have enumerated, were grouped together at the end nearest the Prata Flaminia and the north side of the Capitoline. Hence, in the great fire which took place in this quarter during the reign of Titus, we find the following buildings named among those which were altogether destroyed or seriously injured—*Serapeum—Iseum—Septa—Templum Neptuni—Thermae* of Agrippa—*Pantheum—Diribitorium—Theatrum Balbi—Scena Pompeii— Porticus Octaviae,* ('Οκταουΐα οἰκήματα,) with the library; and the temple of Capitoline Jove, with the adjoining shrines.[3]

The only other building of great magnitude in the Campus Martius, belonging to the early empire, was the *Mausoleum Augusti,* the shell of which still remains near the Porta Flaminia, and is employed as a theatre.[4] A little to the south of this stood the great obelisk, (now on the Monte Citorio,) which was intended by Augustus to serve as the gigantic gnonom of a dial;[5] and opposite to this obelisk, on the banks of the river, we must place the *Navalia* or public dockyard.

1 Dion Cass. LIII. 27. Plin. H.N. XXXVI. 15. Ammian. Marcell. XVI. 10. Macrob. S. II. 13.
2 Dion Cass. LIII. 27. Martial. II. 14. III. 20. XI. 1. Spartian. Hadrian. 19.
3 Dion Cass. LXVI. 24.
4 Suet. Octav. 100. Strab. V. 3. § 8.
5 Plin. H.N. XXXVI. 10.

Some spots hallowed by sacred association were scattered up and down. Among these was the *Palus Capreae* (or *Caprae*,) where Romulus was believed to have vanished from the sight of men [1]—the *Petronia Aqua*, a little stream flowing from the *Cati fons*, which the magistrates crossed "auspicato" when they transacted business in the Campus [2]—*Terentum* or *Tarentum*, a place on the river bank, near the northern extremity of the plain, where was a subterranean altar to Dis and Proserpina, uncovered only on the celebration of the Ludi Saeculares [3]—an *Ara Martis*,[4] and perhaps a temple to the same deity [5]—the *Aedes Larum Permarinûm*, vowed by L. Aemilius Regillus in the naval fight against the captains of Antiochus B.C. 190, and dedicated by M. Aemilius Lepidus when censor, B.C. 179 [6]—and a temple of *Iuturna*, built by Q. Lutatius Catulus.[7]

In the fourth consulship of Cæsar, (B.C. 45,) Statilius Taurus erected in the Campus the first stone amphitheatre; but the site is altogether unknown.[8]

Among those monuments of the empire which do not properly fall within our present work, we may notice one which is still entire, the *Columna Antoniniana*, built in imitation of the *Columna Traiana*, and representing the victories of M. Aurelius over the Marcomanni. It must not be confounded with the column raised in memory of Antoninus Pius, which was a plain pillar of red granite on a white marble pedestal. The base of this alone remains, and has been removed from its original site in the Campus Martius, near the pillar of M. Aurelius, to the papal garden in the Vatican.

Finally, the modern *Piazza Navona*, which lies about half-way between the Corso and the western extremity of the angle made by the river, is supposed, from its form, to have been built upon the boundary line of an ancient circus; and modern antiquaries have imagined that the name *Navona* is a corruption of *Agonalis*. We are quite destitute of sure information with regard to it; but there was probably a stadium here in connection with the *Thermae Alexandrinae*, which stood in this neighbourhood.

Insula Tiberina.—We have already stated in what manner the Romans believed this island, sometimes called *Inter duos pontes*, to have been formed.[9] It was at all times looked upon as holy, and appropriated to sacred buildings. The first temple erected was that of *Æsculapius*, whose statue was brought to Rome from Epidaurus in B.C. 291, in consequence of a pestilence which had afflicted the city [10]—there was also a temple of *Iupiter*, dedicated B.C. 194 [11]—of *Faunus*, dedicated B.C. 196 [12]—of *Semo Sancus*, otherwise called *Deus Fidius* [13]—and of the god *Tiberinus*.[14] In the middle ages this island was named *Insula Lycaonia*, and is now known as the *Isola di S. Bartolomeo*, from a church dedicated to that saint.

---

[1] Liv. I. 16. Ovid. Fast. II. 491. Plut. Rom. 27. Aur. Vict. de viris ill. 2. Paul. Diac. s.v. *Cupralia*, p. 63.
[2] Fest. s.v. *Petronia*, p. 250. Paul. Diac. s.v. *Cati fons*, p. 45.
[3] Ovid. Fast. I. 501. Val. Max. II. iv. 5.
[4] Liv XL. 45
[5] Dion Cass. LVI. 24. Ovid. Fast. II. 860.
[6] Liv. XL. 52. Macrob. S. I. 10.
[7] Ovid. Fast. I. 463. Serv. ad Virg. Æn. XII. 139.
[8] Dion Cass. LI. 23. Suet. Octav. 29.
[9] Liv. II. 5. Dionys. V. 13. Plut. Popl. 8. Macrob. S. II. 12.
[10] Liv. Epit. XI. Ovid. Met. XV. 739. Fast. I. 291. Val. Max. I. viii. 2. Plin. H.N XXIX. 4.
[11] Liv. XXXIV. 54.
[12] Liv. XXXIII. 42. Ovid. Fast. II. 193.
[13] Justin. Mart. Apol. 2. Euseb. ii. E. H. 12
[14] Fast. Amitern. VI. Id. Dec.

Ianiculum.—Although the Janiculum was not included within the limits of the city, yet, since the ridge, which rises to the height of nearly 300 feet above the sea, and 267 above the Tiber, would, to a great extent, command the city, the expediency, and indeed the necessity, of fortifying it, must at a very early period have been forced upon the attention of the Romans. Accordingly, both Livy and Dionysius agree in asserting that, in the time of Ancus, a military fort was established on its summit, a double wall running down to the Tiber, and a communication being secured by means of a wooden bridge.

Opposite to the Forum Boarium a considerable space extends between the river and the steep slope of the hill; this must have been built upon to a considerable extent before the end of the republic, since it formed the *Regio Transtiberina*, the fourteenth of the Augustan divisions. It seems to have been inhabited by persons of the humblest grade, among whom we find particular reference to tanners, Jews, and fishermen.[1] By the latter, doubtless, the *Piscatorii Ludi* were here celebrated. We hear of no sacred localities except a temple of *Fors Fortuna*,[2] a *Lucus Furinae*,[3] and the *Arae Fontis*, near which was the grave of Numa.[4]

Beyond the Tiber, but higher up the stream than the Regio Transtiberina, were the *Mucia Prata*, bestowed on C. Mucius "virtutis causa"[5]—the *Maior Codeta*, a marshy meadow, so called from the plant with which it abounded, the *Minor Codeta* being in the Campus Martius[6]—the *Horti Caesaris*, bequeathed by the dictator to the Roman people[7]—the artificial lake (*stagnum navale*) in which Augustus exhibited his mock sea-fight (*naumachia*)[8]—and the *Nemus Caesarum*, named from Caius and Lucius.[9]

Mons Vaticanus.—The Vatican hill, which the Basilica of St. Peter and the Palace of the Pope have rendered the most remarkable quarter of the modern city, was in no way connected with ancient Rome until included within the walls of Aurelian; nor does it seem to have been built upon extensively until the decline of the empire, the insalubrity of the air being notorious,[10] and the soil not remarkable for fertility.[11] It was like the Collis Hortulorum, chiefly laid out in gardens, among which the most remarkable were the *Horti Agrippinae* and the *Horti Domitiae*, both being united to form the *Horti Neronis*.[12] Hadrian was entombed in the gardens of Domitia in the immense mausoleum constructed by himself, which is now fortified, and forms a sort of citadel, under the name of *Castello di S. Angelo*[13]—a view of which is on next page.

Before concluding our sketch of Roman topography, we must say a few words upon three topics intimately connected with the subject.

1. The bridges (*pontes*) by which a communication was established with the right bank of the Tiber.

---

1 Fest. s.v. *Piscatorii ludi*, p. 210. 238. Ovid. Fast. VI. 237. Juv. S. XIV. 202. Martial. L. 42. VI. 93
2 Varro L.L. VI. § 17. Liv. X. 46. Donat. ad Terent. Phorm. V. vi. 1.
3 Plut. C. Gracch. 17. Aur. Vict. de viris ill. 65.
4 Dionys. II. 76. Plut. Num. 22. Cic. de legg. II. 22.
5 Liv. II. 13. Dionys. V. 35.
6 Paul. Diac. s.v. *Codeta*, p. 58. Suet. Caes, 39. Dion Cass. XLIII. 23.
7 Cic. Philipp. II. 42. Suet. Caes. 83. Dion Cass. XLIV. 35. Hor. S. I. ix. 18.
8 Monum. Ancyr. Stat. Silv. IV. iv. 5. which seem to be contradicted by Tacitus (Ann XII. 56.) who says, " cis Tiberim."
9 Monum. Ancyr. Suet. Octav. 43. comp. Tacit. Ann. XIV. 15. Dion Cass. LXI. 20 LXVI. 25.
10 Tacit. Hist. II. 93.
11 Cic. de leg. agr. II. 35. Martial. VI. 92. X. 45.
12 Tacit. Ann. XV. 39.
13 Capitolin. Ant. P. 5. Spartian. Hadrian. 19. Dion Cass. LXIX. 23. Procop. B. G. I. 22.

2. The great highways (*viae publicae* s. *militares*) which branched off from Rome in different directions.

3. The aqueducts (*aquaeductus*) by which the city was supplied with water.

BRIDGES.

No subject connected with Roman topography is involved in greater obscurity than the names and positions of the different bridges. It seems certain, however, that not more than three were erected before the end of the republic.

1. **Pons Sublicius.**—By far the most ancient and the most celebrated was the Pons Sublicius, built, as we are assured, by Ancus Martius when he established a fortified post on the Janiculum.[1] It was formed, as the name implies, of timber; and both in the original structure, and in those by which it was from time to time replaced, not only the frame-work but all the bolts, bracings, and fastenings of every description, were made of wood exclusively. This system was adopted and maintained in consequence of certain superstitious feelings, for every thing connected with the work was invested with a sacred character. The repairs and renewals were always executed with a due attention to ceremonial

[1] Liv. I. 33. Dionys. III. 45. IX. 68. Plut. Num. 9.

observances, and the very term *Pontifex* was believed by the Romans to have been derived from the duties of superintendence imposed upon the highest class of priests on such occasions.[1] That the Pons Sublicius not merely retained its primitive appellation, but was actually formed of wood in the first century of the empire is proved by the words of Pliny;[2] and the name was still current in the reign of Antoninus Pius.[3] The position of the bridge has given rise to much controversy; but when we remember the purpose for which it was, in the first instance, constructed, we can scarcely doubt that it abutted upon the Forum Boarium, and that it must have crossed the river not far from the broken arches now known as the *Ponte Rotto*.

2. **Pons Aemilius s. Pons Lepidi,** commenced by the censors M. Fulvius Nobilior and M. Aemilius Lepidus, B.C. 179; but not completed until nearly forty years afterwards, in the censorship of P. Scipio Africanus and L. Mummius, B.C. 142.[4] It connected the harbour or quay under the Aventine with the opposite bank; and in this part of the river, when the water is low, the foundations of a bridge are still distinctly visible. The representation of an equestrian statue, standing upon three arches with the legend M. AEMILIO LEP., as seen on a denarius,  of which a cut is annexed, may perhaps be intended to commemorate this work.

It must not be overlooked that, before the censorship of Aemilius Lepidus, as early as B.C. 194, Livy speaks of two bridges as already existing.[5] It has hence been conjectured that, while the Pons Sublicius was kept up on religious grounds, another bridge, made of stone, had been erected in the immediate vicinity to accommodate the increasing traffic, and that the arches now called *Ponte Rotto* mark the site of the second structure. This supposition will explain the words of Ovid, who distinctly speaks, not of *a* bridge, but of bridges in the Forum Boarium;[6] and might also throw light upon an obscure expression of Servius, when he mentions the *Pons Sublicius* in connection with a *Pons Lapideus.*[7]

3. **Pons Fabricius.** 4. **Pons Cestius.**—A stone bridge connecting the Prata Flaminia with the Insula, and corresponding to the modern *Ponte Quattro Capi*, was built, B.C. 62,[8] by L. Fabricius, who was at that time, as we learn from an inscription, inspector of public highways, (*curator viarum*,) and from him it received its name.

The bridge which connected the island with the right bank, now *Ponte S. Bartolomeo*, is believed to be the *Pons Cestius*, of the Notitia and mediaeval writers. The inscription, still legible, designates it as *Pons Gratianus*, from a restoration by that emperor.

To the Notitia we are indebted for the names of four other bridges.

5. **Pons Aelius,** now *Ponte S. Angelo*, built by Hadrian[9] to connect his mausoleum with the Campus Martius.

---

[1] Varro L.L. V. § 83. Plut. l.c.
[2] Plin. H.N. XXXVI. 15. comp. Tacit. Hist. I. 86. Senec. de vit. beat. 25.
[3] Capitolin. Antonin. 8.
[4] Liv. XL. 51. Plut. Num. 9.
[5] Liv. XXXV. 21.
[6] Ovid. Fast. VI. 471.
[7] Serv. ad Virg. Æn. VIII. 646.
[8] Dion Cass. XXXVII. 45. Hor. S. II. iii. 36.
[9] Spartian. Hadrian. 19.

6. **Pons Aurelius.**—This bridge is believed to have occupied the position of the modern *Ponte Sisto*, and to have led directly to the *Porta Aurelia* on the Janiculum. In the middle ages it was called Pons Antoninus.

7. **Pons Milvius**, now *Ponte Molle*, high up the river, beyond the circuit even of Aurelian's walls. It is celebrated in history as the scene of the decisive victory gained by Constantine the Great over the usurper Maxentius.

8. **Pons Probi.**—The position of this bridge is unknown.

There was a bridge which led over to the Vatican, built before the *Pons Aurelius*, and this was designated sometimes *Pons Neronianus*, sometimes *Pons Vaticanus*.

With the exception of the *Pons Sublicius*, which is spoken of very often, and the *Pons Fabricius*, which is mentioned once by Horace and once by Dion Cassius, not one of the bridges within the walls is named in any classical author.

The cut placed below represents the *Insula*, with its two bridges in their present state.

HIGH-ROADS.

Although roads connecting Rome with the numerous cities of Latium, by which, in ancient times, it was on all sides surrounded, must have existed from the very foundation of the city, these were, in all probability, mere tracks employed by foot travellers and cattle, impassable by wheel carriages or even by beasts of burden during the rainy season. It was not until the Romans had engaged in comparatively distant wars, with the Samnites and Italiote Greeks, that the necessity of keeping up regular and secure communication with their armies became imperative; and accordingly, about the middle of the fifth century they appeared to have commenced, upon a large scale, the construction of those great military roads (*viae militares*) which have proved some of the most durable monuments of their greatness. Radiating from Rome as a centre and extending on all sides, so as to keep pace with the rapid progress of the Roman conquests, they eventually reached to the most remote extremities of the empire, throwing out innumerable subsidiary branches, which served either to connect the great trunk lines, or to open up districts which would otherwise have proved inaccessible. Milestones (*milliaria*) were erected regularly along their whole course, marking the distance from the gate at which they issued from the metropolis; and when the space between the towns and villages was great, resting places or post-houses (*mansiones*) [1] were built at moderate distances, where travellers might repose; and under the empire relays of horses were kept here for the service of the public couriers. The extraordinary durability which characterised these roads is proved by the fact, that portions of them still exist entire both in Italy and other countries, and are still available for ordinary purposes, although they have undergone no repair for many centuries. The technical phrases employed to express the making of a road are *sternere ciam* or *munire viam*, and the origin of the latter expression will be distinctly understood when we explain the nature of the operations performed.[2] Two ditches were dug, marking the limits of the road upon each side, the breadth varying from 11 to 15 feet. The whole of the loose earth was then removed from the surface, and excavation was continued until the rock or solid subsoil were reached, or, when the ground was swampy, piles were driven to secure a firm foundation. Upon the unyielding surface thus obtained (*gremium*) were laid—1. A stratum of large stones (*statumen*.) 2. A stratum, nine inches thick, of smaller stones cemented with lime (*rudus*.) 3. A stratum, six inches thick, of still smaller stones, fragments of brick, pieces of broken pottery, and such like materials, this course also being bound together by cement, and the top made flat and smooth. 4. Lastly, on the top of all were laid large flat blocks of the hardest stone which could be procured, (*silex*,) irregular in shape, but fitted and adjusted to each other with the greatest nicety, so as to present a perfectly smooth surface without gaps or interstices. This mass of building, for as such it must be regarded, being in fact a strong wall, two and a-half or three feet thick, laid flat on the ground, was slightly raised in the centre so as to allow the water to run off. The elaborate process just described was employed for the great thoroughfares, the cross-roads and those on which the traffic was light having only the under course of large stones or the *statumen*, with a coating of gravel thrown over. Hence the distinction indicated in the classical writers by the phrases *silice sternere* and *glarea sternere*.

Although a description of the Roman roads and the course which they followed, belongs properly to a work upon geography, we may here notice very briefly a few of the most important:—

1. The *Via Appia*, the Queen of roads (*Regina Viarum*) as it is termed by Statius, was commenced by Appius Claudius Caecus when censor, B.C. 312. It issued from the *Porta Capena* and ran through Aricia, Tarracina, Fundi, and Formiae to Capua, from whence it was subsequently carried across the peninsula, by Beneventum and Tarentum, to Brundusium, being the great highway from Rome to Greece and the Eastern provinces.

2. The *Via Latina*, issuing also from the Porta Capena, ran parallel to the former, but farther inland, and after passing through Ferentinum, Aquinum, Casinum, and Venafrum, joined the Via Appia at Beneventum.

---

[1] Sueton. Tit. 10. Plin. H.N. XII. 14. comp. VI. 23.
[2] For what follows see Vitruv. VII. 1. where he describes the construction of pavements and Stat. S. IV. iii. on the *Via Domitiana*

3. The *Via Praenestina s. Gabina*, issuing from the Porta Esquilina, ran straight through Gabii to Praeneste, and then joined the Via Latina.

4. 5. The *Via Collatina*, leading to Collatia, and the *Via Tiburtina*, leading to Tibur, must have both branched off from the Porta Esquilina. The latter, after reaching its destination, sent off a branch, the *Via Sublacensis*, to *Sublaqueum*, while the main line was continued northward, under the name of the *Via Valeria*, and passing through Corfinium, extended to Adria on the Upper Sea.

6. 7. The *Via Nomentana* and the *Via Salaria*, diverged from the Porta Collina; the former, after passing through Nomentum, fell into the latter, which, passing through Fidenae, ran north and east through the Sabine country, and passing Reate and Asculum, reached the Adriatic at Ancona.

8. The *Via Flaminia*, which probably issued from the Porta Carmentalis, ran north, through Narnia, and sending out numerous branches to Ancona, Ariminum, and other important towns on the east coast, formed the main line of communication with Hither Gaul, and so with the provinces beyond the Alps.

9. 10. The *Via Cassia*, branching off from the Via Flaminia, and throwing off a branch called the *Via Claudia*, traversed central Etruria.

11. The *Via Valeria* followed the line of the coast on the Lower Sea, northward, along the Etrurian shore, and passing through Genua, extended as far as Forum Julii in Gaul.

12. Lastly, the *Via Ostiensis*, issuing from the Porta Trigemina, followed the course of the Tiber, on the left bank, to the port of Ostia.

AQUEDUCTS.

Among all the wonderful undertakings of the Romans, none present more striking evidence of their enterprise, energy, and skill, and of their indifference to toil and expense when any great public benefit was to be gained, than the works commenced at an early period and extended through many successive centuries, in order to provide an abundant supply of pure water for all parts of the metropolis. Copious streams were conducted from great distances, in despite of the obstacles presented by mountains, valleys, and low-lying level plains, sometimes rushing along in vast subterranean tunnels, at other times supported upon long ranges of lofty arches, the remains of which, stretching for miles in all directions, may be still seen spanning the waste of the Campagna. The stupendous character of these monuments fully justifies the admiration expressed by the elder Pliny (H.N. XXXVI. 15.)—*Quod si quis diligentius aestimaverit aquarum abundantiam in publico, balineis, piscinis, domibus, euripis, hortis suburbanis, villis, spatioque advenientis exstructos arcus, montes perfossos, convalles aequatas, fatebitur nihil magis mirandum fuisse in toto orbe terrarum.* The Roman *Aquaeductus*, then, were artificial channels (*canales structiles*) formed of stone or brick, like sewers in our large towns, and were arched over in order to keep the water cool and free from impurity, (*eaeque structurae confornicentur ut minime sol aquam tangat;*) the circulation of a free current of air in the interior being secured by numerous small apertures or eyes (*lumina*) in the arched covering. The bottom of the channel, which was coated with a sort of cement or stucco, descended with a gradual slope or fall (*libramentum—fastigium—libramentum fastigiatum*) from the point whence the water was derived (*unde aqua concipitur*) until it reached its destination. In order to lay out the course of a channel of this nature, a knowledge of the art of levelling (*ars librandi*) was essential; and Vitruvius (VIII. 6.) gives a minute account of the instruments best adapted for this purpose. The amount of fall which he recommends is not less than six inches in every hundred feet, (*solum rivi libramenta habeat fastigiata ne minus in centenos pedes semipede;*) but the ancients do not seem to have adhered strictly to any rule upon this point, although the long circuitous sweeps by which the water was frequently conducted, proves that they were fully alive to the importance of making the fall moderate and equable. When circumstances permitted, the water, in its covered channel, was carried along the surface of the ground, resting on a base of masonry, (*substructionibus,*) when the inequalities of the surface were such as to render this impossible, it ran under ground, (*subterraneo rivo,*) when hills interposed, it flowed through them in tunnels, (*specu mersa—cuniculis per montem actis,*) which were ventilated by eyes or air holes (*lumina*) placed at intervals of 240 feet. If the tunnel (*specus*) was driven through solid rock, then the rock itself served as the channel, but if through earth or sand, it was lined with walls and arched over (*parietes cum camera in specu struantur.*) When valleys, or plains below the level, were to be crossed, the channel was supported on arches (*opere arcuato—arcuationibus—fornicibus structis.*) When the stream (*rivus*) was approaching its destination, or at some other convenient point in its course, it was, in many cases, allowed to enter large open ponds, (*contentae piscinae,*) where it reposed, as it were, (*quasi respirante rivorum cursu,*) and deposited the mud and other impurities by which it was contaminated. Hence, these receptacles (*conceptelae*) were termed *piscinae limariae*. Issuing from this piscina, the stream continued its course as before, in a covered channel, and on reaching the highest level in that part of the city to which it was conducted, it was received into a great reservoir, called *castellum* or *dividiculum*, from which it was drawn off through pipes of lead (*fistulae plumbeae*) or of earthen ware (*tubi fictiles*) into a number of smaller castella in different districts, from which it was again drawn off (*erogabatur*) to supply cisterns of private houses, (*castella privata* s. *domestica,*) the open tanks or basins in the streets, (*lacus,*) the spouting fountains, (*salientes,*) and public and private establishments of every description.

Our chief information on the aqueducts which supplied Rome is derived from the treatise *De Aquaeductibus Urbis Romae Libri II.*, composed by Frontinus, who held the office of *Curator Aquarum* under Nerva, A.D. 97; and a few additional particulars may be gleaned from Pliny[1] and Vitruvius.[2] Of modern treatises, the most complete is that of Fabretti *De Aquis et Aquaeductibus Veteris Romae*, which will be found in the fourth volume of the Thesaurus of Graevius; and many curious and accurate details have been collected in the Beschreibung der Stadt Rom, by Platner and Bunsen.

Taking Frontinus as our guide, we shall say a few words with regard to the nine aqueducts which existed when he wrote, noticing them in chronological order.

The necessity of obtaining a better supply of water for the city than could be procured from the Tiber or from wells, seems to have been first strongly felt about the middle of the fifth century, and accordingly the—

1. **Aqua Appia**, was introduced (*perducta est*) by Appius Claudius Caecus, when censor, B.C. 312. It was derived (*concepta est*) from a point about three-fourths of a mile to the left of the Via Praenestina, between the seventh and eighth milestone from Rome. The length of the artificial channel, (*ductus,*) which ended at the *Salinae* near the *Porta Trigemina*, was a little more than

[1] Plin. H.N. XXXI. 3. 6. XXXVI. 15.
[2] Vitruv. de A. VIII. 6. 7.

eleven (Roman) miles, the whole being under ground, with the exception of 100 yards at the termination, between the *Porta Capena* and the *Clivus Publicius*.

2. **Anio Vetus.**—The scheme for introducing this supply from the river Anio was formed by M'. Curius Dentatus, who was censor along with L. Papirius Cursor, B.C. 272; and it was proposed to defray the cost from the spoils taken in the war with Pyrrhus. The undertaking was not brought to a conclusion until B.C. 264; two commissioners having been appointed specially by the Senate. The works commenced beyond Tibur, and the total length of the artificial channel was about forty-four miles, entirely under ground, with the exception of three-fourths of a mile on substructions. It entered the city near the *Porta Esquilina*.

3. **Aqua Marcia**, introduced by Q. Marcius Rex, when praetor, B.C. 144, in accordance with a resolution of the Senate (Plin. H.N. XXXI. 3.) The works commenced at a point three miles to the right of the thirty-third milestone, on the *Via Valeria*; and the total length of the channel was upwards of sixty-one miles, of which about half a-mile was on substructions, nearly seven miles, (according to Pliny, nine miles) on arches, and the remainder under ground. It entered the city near the Porta Esquilina at so high a level that it gave a supply to the summit of the Capitoline. Augustus, or rather Agrippa, formed a connection with another spring nearly a mile more distant, and this branch aqueduct was named *Aqua Augusta*. The *Aqua Marcia* was held to be the purest, the coldest, and most wholesome water in Rome, and as such its praises are celebrated by Pliny (H.N. XXXVI. 15)—*Clarissima aquarum omnium in toto orbe, frigoris salubritatisque palma praeconio Urbis, Marcia est;* and so proud was the Gens Marcia of their connection with this work, that a denarius of Q. Marcius Philippus

presents upon one side a head of Ancus Martius, from whom the clan claimed descent, and on the other an equestrian statue standing on the arches of the aqueduct, with the letters AQVAM, as represented in the annexed cut. The Aqua Marcia supplied 130 castella, 700 tanks, (*lacus*,) and 105 spouting fountains (*salientes*.)

4. **Aqua Tepula**, introduced by the censors Cn. Servilius Caepio and Cassius Longinus, B.C. 125, from a point two miles to the right of the eleventh milestone on the *Via Latina*. Pliny, indeed, (H.N. XXXVI. 15.) speaks of the Aqua Tepula as considerably older than the Aqua Marcia; but the authority of Frontinus upon such a point is superior.

5. **Aqua Iulia**, introduced by Agrippa, when aedile, B.C. 33, from a point to the right of the twelfth milestone, on the *Via Latina*. The whole length of this aqueduct was about fifteen and a-half miles. One mile and a-half on substructions, six and a-half on arches, the remainder under ground. The Aqua Marcia, the Aqua Tepula, and the Aqua Iulia, after issuing from their respective *piscinae limariae*, about six and a-half miles from Rome, entered the city upon the same arches, each, however, in a separate channel, the *Aqua Iulia* being uppermost, the *Aqua Tepula* in the middle, and the *Aqua Marcia* lowest; and traces of these three channels were recently quite visible at the modern Porta Maggiore, the *Porta Praenestina* of the Aurelian circuit.

6. **Aqua Virgo**, introduced by Agrippa, B.C. 19, for the supply of his Thermae, from a swampy tract (*palustribus locis*) eight miles from Rome,

on the *Via Collatina*. The whole length of the aqueduct was about fourteen miles. It entered Rome on the side of the Pincian hill, and was conveyed upon arches into the Campus Martius. It is still available to a certain extent, and, under the name of the *Aqua Virgine*, supplies the beautiful and well known *Fontana di Trevi* and many other fountains of the modern city.

7. **Aqua Alsietina s. Augusta,** on the right bank of the Tiber, introduced by Augustus, from the *Lacus Alsietinus*, six and a-half miles to the right of the fourteenth milestone on the *Via Claudia*. The whole length was twenty-two miles, the termination being under the Janiculum; but the water was so bad that it was used for gardens only, and for filling the artifical lakes in which *naumachiae* were exhibited. The works are still partially in repair, and afford a supply to the inhabitants of the Trastevere, under the name of the *Aqua Paola*.

8. **Aqua Claudia,** introduced by Caligula and his successor, A.D. 38–52, from three very pure and abundant springs, named *Caeruleus, Curtius,* and *Albudinus,* a little to the left of the thirty-eighth milestone on the *Via Sublacensis*. The whole length was upwards of forty-six miles, of which thirty-six were under ground, and nine and a-half upon arches. This water was considered next in excellence to the *Marcia;* and many antiquarians believe that the *Aqua Felice,* which supplies numerous fountains in the modern city, is part of the *Aqua Claudia.*

9. **Anio Novus,** commenced, at the same time with the last mentioned, by Caligula, and completed by Claudius. The water was taken off from the Anio (*excipitur ex flumine*) at a point near the forty-second milestone on the Via Sublacensis; and the total length was fifty-eight and a-half miles, of which forty-nine were under ground. As it approached the city, it was carried upon arches for upwards of six miles. Frontinus calls this the largest of all the aqueducts, although he had before set down the Aqua Marcia at upwards of sixty-one miles; but it must be evident to the most cursory reader that the numbers in many parts of his treatise are in confusion.

The *Aqua Claudia* and the *Anio Novus*, after issuing from their *piscinae limariae*, entered the city upon the same arches, the latter being uppermost; and remains of the works may still be traced near the modern *Porta Maggiore*, the *Porta Praenestina* of the Aurelian circuit. There is no doubt that these two aqueducts were the grandest and most costly works of their class. Three hundred millions of sesterces (*ter millies*) were, according to Pliny, expended on the former; and some of the arches over which the latter passed were 109 feet high.

Each of the streams brought by these nine aqueducts entered the city at a different level from the rest, (*aquae omnes diversa in Urbem libra proveniunt*,) in the following order, beginning with the highest:—1. *Anio Novus*.—2. *Claudia*. 3. *Iulia*.—4. *Tepula*.—5. *Marcia*.—6. *Anio Vetus*.—7. *Virgo*.—8. *Appia*. —9. *Alsietina*. Of these, the first six had *piscinae limariae*, all about six and a-half miles from Rome, in the direction of the *Via Latina*. The last three had none. The *Anio Novus* had two, the second being near the point where the artificial channel branched off from the river; but, notwithstanding this precaution, its water was always turbid when the parent stream was in flood.

The *Anio Novus* and the *Claudia* were so elevated that they afforded a supply to the highest parts of the city. On the other hand, it will be observed that the two oldest, the *Appia* and the *Anio Vetus*, were brought in at a low level, and the works were almost entirely under ground. This, as Frontinus suggests, was probably the result of design; for at the period when they were formed the

Romans were still engaged in war with neighbouring tribes, and had these structures been exposed to view, they might have been destroyed by an invading army.

In addition to the nine aqueducts which existed when Frontinus wrote, we hear of an *Aqua Traiana*, an *Aqua Alexandrina*, the work of *Alexander Severus*, and one or two others of less importance; but we cannot ascertain with precision the names of the whole fourteen, which were still in use when Procopius flourished, (see B. G. I. 19.) i.e. A.D. 550.

It may be gathered from what has been said above, that the whole of the works by which supplies of water were brought into the city, were comprehended under the general term *Aquaeductus*, or simply, *Ductus*. The water itself was distinguished, in each case, either by the name of the person by whom it was introduced, as *Aqua Appia*, *Aqua Marcia*, &c., or by the name of the source from whence it was derived, as *Aqua Alsietina*, *Anio Vetus*, &c., or, finally, from some legend connected with its history, as *Aqua Virgo*. Again, these terms are employed to denote, not only the water conveyed, but also the aqueduct by which it was conveyed, so that *Aqua Marcia* may mean either the Marcian Aqueduct, or the water conveyed by the Marcian Aqueduct, and so for all the rest.

It may perhaps excite surprise that the Romans should have expended such a vast amount of toil and money upon the construction of aqueducts, although acquainted with the hydrostatical law, according to which, water, when conveyed in close pipes, will rise to the level of the fountain or reservoir from which the pipe proceeds. Pliny correctly enunciates this proposition when he states (H.N. XXXI. 6.)—*Subit altitudinem exortus sui*—and the distributions from the main *Castella* to the different parts of the city were actually effected upon this principle. This is clearly proved by the manner in which the authorities already quoted express themselves when describing the tubes of lead and earthenware, by the words of Frontinus, who tells us that the *Aqua Claudia* and the *Anio Novus* were introduced at so high a level as to afford a supply to the tops of the isolated hills, by the existence of numerous *Salientes* or spouting fountains—and by the line in Horace (Epp. I. x. 20.)

<blockquote>Purior in vicis aqua tendit rumpere plumbum.</blockquote>

We have no reason to believe, however, that any attempt was ever made to apply the principle upon a great scale; and it is remarkable that the experience of modern engineers goes to prove that it cannot be employed with advantage when a large body of water is to be brought from a considerable distance.

Cloaca Maxima.—But even the aqueducts of Caligula and Claudius are inferior in solid grandeur to the huge vaulted drains constructed, according to tradition, either by the elder Tarquin or by Superbus, for the purpose of drawing off the water from the swamps, which, in the earliest ages, spread over the whole of the low grounds lying around the bases of the seven hills. The main trunk, known as the *Cloaca Maxima*, may still be seen in part entire, and still conveys water into the Tiber. It consists of three concentric vaults or semicircular arches, the breadth of the innermost being about thirteen and a-half feet. All are formed of the volcanic stone called *peperino*, the blocks being five and a-half feet long and three feet thick, fitted together with the greatest accuracy, without cement. The skill as well as labour with which this colossal fabric was executed is proved by the fact, that it has undergone no change, and exhibits no trace of dilapidation or decay, although more than 2900 years have passed away since it was completed.

TOPOGRAPHY OF ROME. 59

A branch drain, running up in the direction of the *Subura*, **tributary to the Cloaca Maxima**, and formed upon the same gigantic scale, was discovered about the middle of the last century, sixty feet below the present surface. It is supposed to be the work of a somewhat later period, the stone employed being a kind of limestone, called *travertino*, which does not appear to have been used for building purposes until after the regal period.[1]

The only works of the regal epoch of which distinct traces still remain, are the Tullianum (p. 28,) the Cloaca, with the retaining wall along the bank of the river, and a few fragments of the wall of Servius. We have already given a representation of the first, and we subjoin a cut, showing the mouth of the Cloaca as it now appears, and another, taken from Sir William Gell's work on the Topography of Rome, exhibiting "one of the best and least doubtful specimens" of the Servian wall, under the church of S. Balbina, (p. 32,) in the direction of the Porta Capena.

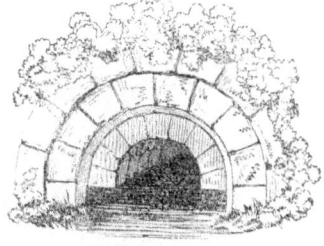

[1] On the *Cloaca Maxima* and its branches, see Niebuhr's Roman History, Vol. 1. p. 384, Engl. Trans. and his Lectures, Lecture IX.

CHAPTER II.

ON THE ORIGIN OF THE ROMAN PEOPLE, AND THEIR POLITICAL AND SOCIAL ORGANIZATION, FROM THE EARLIEST TIMES.[1]

The Romans a Mixed People.—There is no point connected with the early history of Rome more certain than that the original inhabitants were a mixed people, formed by the combination of three distinct races—*Latini, Sabini* and *Etrusci*. While tradition ascribed the actual foundation of the city to a colony of Latins from Alba Longa, under Romulus, their speedy union with a body of Sabines, under Titus Tatius, was universally acknowledged. The same unanimity does not prevail regarding the introduction of Etruscans, who, according to one account, did not form a component part of the population until the migration of the fourth king, the elder Tarquinius, while others maintained that a settlement of Etruscans, upon the Coelian hill, lent their aid to Romulus in his contest with Tatius and the Sabines. Without pretending to unravel the confused web of ancient legends, it seems perfectly clear that the triple union must have taken place before the formation of the constitution usually ascribed to Romulus, since the divisions recognised by that constitution bear a distinct reference to the three elements. The words of Florus (III. 18.) express the fact clearly and accurately—*Quippe quum populus Romanus Etruscos, Latinos, Sabinosque miscuerit et unum ex omnibus sanguinem ducat, corpus fecit ex membris et ex omnibus unus est.*

Populus Romanus. Quirites.—The appellation of the united people was *Populus Romanus Quirites*, or *Populus Romanus Quiritium*,[2] although, when no great formality was aimed at, the separate designations, *Populus Romanus* and *Quirites*, were used indifferently to comprehend the whole. The origin of the latter term must be regarded as still involved in doubt. The ancients themselves proposed two derivations, both of which pointed to the Sabines, some regarding the word as another form of *Curetes*, i.e. inhabitants of the Sabine town of *Cures*,[3] others connecting it with *Quiris*, which, in the Sabine dialect signified *a spear*. The second etymology might have been considered as satisfactory, and we might have regarded *Quirites* as equivalent to *warriors*, had it not been that *Quirites* is used emphatically to denote Romans in the full enjoyment of their

---

[1] The speculations of modern scholars upon the early history and gradual development of the Roman constitution, will be found fully expounded in the following works:—NIEBUHR, History of Rome.—NIEBUHR, Lectures upon Roman History, containing the substance of the first mentioned work in a more popular form.—ARNOLD, History of Rome.—GÖTTLING, Geschichte der Römischen Staatsverfassung.—RUBINO, Untersuchungen über Römische Verfassung und Geschichte.—HUSCHKE, Die Verfassung des Königs Servius Tullus.—HULLMAN, Römische Grundverfassung.—WACHSMUTH, Die ältere Geschichte des Römischen Staates.—WALTHER, Geschichte des Römischen Rechts.

[2] Aul. Gell. I. 12. X. 24. Macrob. S. I. 4. Liv. I. 24. 32. VIII. 6. 9. X. 28. XXII. 10. XLI 16. Varro L.L. VI. § 86. comp. Dionys. II. 46. Plut. Rom. 19.

[3] Liv. I. 13. Varro L.L. VI. § 68. Plut. Rom. 19.

civil rights as peaceful citizens; and hence Cæsar is said to have recalled his insubordinate soldiers to their duty by abruptly addressing them as *Quirites* instead of *Milites*.[1] We cannot fail to connect *Quirites* with *Quiritis*, an epithet of Juno, and with *Quirinus*, one of the titles of the god Janus, and the name under which Romulus was worshipped as a hero-god, nor to remark the verb *Quiritare*, which denotes the solemn appeal for assistance made by one citizen to another in the hour of danger—*Quiritare dicitur is qui Quiritium fidem clamans implorat*.[2]

Original Tribes.—The united people was divided into three tribes, (*tribus*,) which bore respectively the names—1. *Ramnes* s. *Ramnenses*. 2. *Tities* s. *Titienses* s. *Tatienses*. 3. *Luceres* s. *Lucerenses*. The name of the first, according to the belief of the later Romans, was taken from *Romulus*, that of the second from *Tatius*, and that of the third was connected with the Etruscan word *Lucumo*, signifying *lord* or *prince*.[3] At the head of each tribe was a captain, called *Tribunus*, and the members of the same tribe were termed, in reference to each other *Tribules*.[4]

Curiae.—Each tribe was subdivided into ten sections, called *Curiae*, each distinguished by a name,[5] so that in all there were thirty Curiae. The members of each Curia were called, in reference to each other, *Curiales*;[6] each had its own chapel—its own place of assembly, called *Curia*—its own priest, called *Curio* or *Flamen Curialis*,[7] who presided at the solemnities (*sacra*) peculiar to his Curia, and out of the thirty Curiones one was selected who presided over the whole, under the title of *Curio Maximus*.[8]

Finally, if we can trust Dionysius, each Curia was subdivided into ten decades or *Decuriae*, each Decuria having its petty officer, termed *Decurio*.[9]

Gentes Familiae.—The organization described above was entirely political; but there were also social divisions of a very important character. The Tribes and Curies were made up of clans or houses, each of which was termed a *Gens;* the individuals composing each Gens being termed, in reference to each other, *Gentiles*. Each Gens was made up of a certain number of branches or families, each of which was termed a *Familia*, and each Familia was composed of individual members. There can be no reasonable doubt, notwithstanding the assertion of Niebuhr to the contrary, that not only all the individual members of the same family, but likewise all the families of the same gens, referred their origin to a common ancestor, and hence all *Gentiles* were regarded as connected by blood more or less remotely.

Praenomen. Nomen. Cognomen. Agnomen, &c. *Gentiles* all bore a common name, which indicated the Gens to which they belonged; to this was added a second name, to designate the family, and a third name was prefixed to the two others to distinguish the individual member of the family. According to this arrangement, the name which marked the individual, answering, in some respects, to our Christian name, stood first, and was termed *Praenomen;* the name which marked the Gens stood second, and was termed *Nomen;* the name which marked the Familia stood third, and was termed *Cognomen*.

---

[1] Suet. Caes. 70. Plut. Caes. 51.
[2] Varro L.L. VI. § 68, see also Cic. ad Fam. X. 32. Liv. III. 44.
[3] Varro L.L. V. § 55. Liv. X. 6. Prop. IV. i. 31. Plut. Rom. 20.
[4] Dionys. II. 7. Plut. Rom. 20. Varro L.L. V. § 81. Digest. I. ii. 20.
[5] Plut. Rom. 20. Cic. de R. II. 8. Fest. s.v. *Novae Curiae*, p. 174.
[6] Paul. Diac. s.v. *Curiae*, p. 49.
[7] Dionys. II. 7. Varro L.L. V. § 83. Paul. Diac. s.v. *Curiales flamines*, p.
[8] Paul. Diac. s.v. *Maximus Curio*, p. 126.
[9] Dionys. II. 7.

Thus, in the full designation *Publius Cornelius Scipio*, *Publius* is the Praenomen, marking the individual; *Cornelius* is the Nomen, and marks that he belonged to the *Gens Cornelia*; *Scipio*, is the Cognomen, and marks that he belonged to that family or branch of the Gens Cornelia called *Scipio*.

Occasionally a Familia became very numerous, and sent out many branches, forming, as it were, sub-families; and in such cases it became necessary, in order to prevent confusion, to add a second cognomen. Thus, we find such appellations as, *Lucius Cornelius Lentulus Crus—Lucius Cornelius Lentulus Niger—Publius Cornelius Lentulus Spinther*—all these persons belonged to the *Gens Cornelia* and to the *Familia* of the *Lentuli*; but the Lentuli became in process of time so numerous that a number of subsidiary branches were established, whose descendants were distinguished by the additional cognomina of *Crus*, *Niger*, *Spinther*, &c. Sometimes, in the case of a family which could boast of a great number of distinguished members, it became necessary to add a third cognomen, which, however, seldom passed beyond the individual to whom it was applied. Thus, *Publius Cornelius Scipio Nasica*, (consul, B.C. 191.) had a son who was designated as *P. Cornelius Scipio Nasica Corculum*, (consul, B.C. 161 and 155.) and the son of the latter was known as *P. Cornelius Scipio Nasica Serapio*, (consul B.C. 138, killed Ti. Gracchus B.C. 131.)—*Serapio* being, in the first instance, a mere nick-name applied to him from his likeness to a certain pig merchant. The son of **Serapio** resumed the more simple appellation of his great grandfather, and was *P. Cornelius Scipio Nasica*, (consul, B.C. 111.)

Again, in addition to the ordinary name, a complimentary title was sometimes bestowed by an army, or by the common consent of the citizens, in order to commemorate some great achievement. Thus, *Publius Cornelius Scipio*, the conqueror of Hannibal, was styled *Africanus*, and the same epithet was applied to the younger Publius Cornelius Scipio, the destroyer of Carthage. In like manner *Q. Caecilius Metellus*, in consequence of his successes against Jugurtha, was styled *Numidicus*—*Publius Servilius Vatia* was styled *Isauricus*; and Roman history will furnish many other examples. Such an addition to the cognomen was called an *Agnomen*,[1] and, generally speaking, was confined to the individual who gained it, and was not transmitted to his posterity.[2]

Lastly, a peculiar modification of the name was introduced when an individual passed by adoption (of which we shall have occasion to speak more at large hereafter) out of one Gens into another. The person adopted laid aside his original names and assumed those of the person by whom he was adopted, adding, however, an epithet to mark the Gens out of which he had passed. Thus, *Publius Cornelius Scipio*, the son of the elder Africanus, having no son, adopted *L. Aemilius Paulus*, the son of L. Aemilius Paulus Macedonicus. The young Paulus, immediately upon his adoption, took the name of his adopted father, and became *P. Cornelius Scipio*; but to mark that he had once belonged to the Gens Aemilia, the epithet *Aemilianus* was annexed, so that, when at a subsequent period he received the title of Africanus, his name at full length was *Publius Cornelius Scipio Africanus Aemilianus*, to which eventually was added a second Agnomen *Numantinus!* In like manner *C. Octavius Caepias*, when adopted in terms of the last will of his maternal grand-uncle, became *C. Julius Caesar*

---

[1] See a catalogue of some of the more remarkable in Ovid. Fast. I. 587.
[2] The title of *Asiaticus* was assumed by, and not bestowed upon, L. Cornelius Scipio, the brother of the elder Africanus, and when applied to his descendants must have been regarded merely as a second cognomen. So also the title *Isernimus*, which distinguished a branch of the Claudii Marcelli.

Octavianus, and hence, at different stages in his career, he was styled *Octavius* and *Octavianus*, both being eventually superseded by the complimentary title of *Augustus*, bestowed by the Senate, B.C. 27. Very rarely we find the epithet of adoption derived from the name of the Familia, and not from that of the Gens. A son of that *M. Claudius Marcellus* who served, with distinction, under Marius in Gaul and in the social war, was adopted by a certain *P. Cornelius Lentulus*, and ought therefore to have become *P. Cornelius Lentulus Clodianus;* but there were two Gentes Claudiae, and, therefore, for the sake of distinction, and to mark the illustrious family to which he had belonged, he assumed the name *P. Cornelius Lentulus Marcellinus*, and this epithet of *Marcellinus* passed as a second cognomen to his descendants. One other anomaly deserves notice, because it occurs in the case of a famous individual, and might occasion embarrassment. *M. Junius Brutus*, the celebrated assassin of Julius Cæsar, was adopted several years before the death of the dictator, by his own maternal uncle, *Q. Servilius Caepio*, and ought therefore to have become *Q. Servilius Caepio Junianus*, but for some reason he retained his original cognomen; and we find the different appellations to which he was entitled jumbled together in great confusion. Thus by Cicero he is termed sometimes simply *Brutus*,[1] sometimes *M. Brutus*,[2] sometimes *Q. Caepio Brutus*,[3] and by Asconius,[4] *M. Caepio*.

The women of a family were, for the most part, distinguished simply by the name of the gens to which they belonged, without Praenomen or Cognomen. Thus, the daughter of Julius Cæsar was *Julia;* of Cicero, *Tullia;* of Atticus, *Pomponia*.

This system of nomenclature prevailed, without change, from the earliest epoch until the downfal of the commonwealth. It underwent considerable modification, at least in particular cases, under the earlier emperors, but these it is unnecessary to discuss here.

Patricii. Patres.—The three tribes of the *Ramnes, Tities*, and *Luceres*, divided politically into *Curiae*, and socially into *Gentes* and *Familiae*, did not, even in the earliest times, constitute the whole free population of Rome, but formed a privileged class, who enjoyed exclusively all political power and all the honours of the state. As members of this privileged class, they were comprehended under the general designation of *Patricii* or *Patres*. The latter term may have originally been confined to the chosen elders who formed the *Senatus* or great council of state; but *Patres* is employed perpetually as synonymous with *Patricii;* and even those historians who endeavour to draw a distinction between the words, and to represent the Patricii as the sons or younger branches of the Patres, do not themselves, in their narratives, maintain any such distinction.

Clientes. Patroni.—Each Patrician house had a body of retainers or dependents, who were termed the *Clientes* of the Gens, or of the Familia, or of the individuals to which or to whom they were attached, and these again were styled *Patroni*, with reference to their clients; the terms *Patroni* and *Clientes* being correlative, and the position of the parties bearing a resemblance, in some respects, to that of a feudal lord and his vassals in the middle ages. What the origin of the Clients may have been, and whence this inferiority may have proceeded, are questions which it is now impossible to answer; but the most probable hypothesis is, that they were a conquered race, and that the patricians were their conquerors. It is certain, that the relation of *Clientela*, as it was called, existed among the Sabines

---
[1] e.g. Ad Att. V. 18. 20. VI. 1.
e.g. Philipp. X. 11.
[3] e.g. Ad Fam. VII. 21. Ad Att. II. 24. Philipp. X. 11.
[4] In Milonian.

and the Etruscans, and was perhaps universal in ancient Italy.[1] The word *Cliens*, is, we can scarcely doubt, connected with the verb *clueo*, which is identical with the Greek κλύω, and although *clueo*, where it occurs in the classical writers, signifies *to be spoken of*, it may also have signified simply *to hear*, and indeed *audio* and ἀκούω are commonly used in both senses. Thus, *Clientes* or *Cluentes* would denote *hearers*, that is, persons who listened with respect and obedience to the dictates of their superiors. But although the Clientes were, in all respects, dependents and inferiors, yet the sway of the Patrons was by no means of a tyrannical or arbitrary character. On the contrary, the duties of Patrons and Clients were strictly reciprocal, and in many cases clearly defined.

The Patron was bound to expound the laws (*promere leges*) to his Client—to watch over his pecuniary and personal interests as a father over those of his son—to maintain, in a court of justice, his rights, when injured or assailed, and generally to protect him in all his relations, both public and private.

On the other hand, the Client was bound to aid and support his Patron—to furnish a dowry for the daughter, if the father were poor—to raise money for the ransom of the patron himself, or of his children, if taken prisoners in war—for the payment of fines or damages incurred in legal processes, and for the expenditure required for discharging any public office.

A Patron and his Client could not appear against each other in a court of law, either as principals or witnesses, nor assume a hostile attitude under any form. These, and similar obligations are enumerated by Dionysius, (II. 10,) who is more explicit upon this matter than any other ancient writer; and there is also a passage in Aulus Gellius, (V. 13,) in which we are told that the ties of clientship were at one time regarded as more sacred than those of blood, and that next to the name of father, that of Patronus was the most holy.

The Clientship descended from father to son on both sides; the Client bore the gentile name of his Patron, and was regarded as appertaining to the Gens, although not strictly forming a part of it.

The obligation of a Patron to protect his Client being regarded as of the most solemn character—the violation of it was a crime which rendered the perpetrator *Sacer*, i.e. devoted to the infernal gods, and, as such, an object of general abhorrence, and no longer under the guardianship of the laws. By the code of the XII. Tables it was expressly enacted—*Patronus si Clienti fraudem fecerit, sacer esto*—and among the spirits reserved for torture in the nether world, Virgil enumerates—

> "Hic quibus invisi fratres, dum vita manebat,
> Pulsatusve parens, aut fraus innexa Clienti.
> *   *   *   *
> Inclusi poenam expectant."[2]

It will still farther illustrate the position of Patron and Client if we bear in mind, that when a master granted freedom to a slave, the relation previously expressed by the words *dominus* and *servus* was now represented by *patronus* and *libertus*, and that, in legal phraseology, any advocate who pleaded for a criminal in a court of justice was termed the *patronus* of the accused.

Plebes s. Plebs.—But not only do we hear in early Roman history of the Patricians and their Clients, but from the very infancy of the state we find a body of men termed *Plebs* or *Plebes*, who at first belonged to the non-privileged class, and were entirely shut out from all participation in political power, but

[1] Liv. II. 16. Dionys. II. 46. V. 40. IX. 5. X. 14.
[2] Virgil Æn. VI. 608. see also Dionys. l.c. and Hor. C. II. xviii. 25.

who gradually increased in numbers, wealth, and influence, and at length, by slow degrees, and after many desperate struggles, succeeded in placing themselves upon a footing of complete equality with the Patricians, and in gaining admission to all the offices of state, civil, military, and sacred. Indeed, the internal history of the city, for nearly two centuries after the expulsion of the kings, is wholly occupied with details regarding the contests between the Patricians and the Plebeians; and it was not until the two orders were fully and heartily united that the career of conquest commenced, which was terminated only by the limits of the civilised world. But the question now to be considered is, Who were the Plebeians, and whence did they come?

The historians of the Augustan age believed that the term *Plebs* was another name for *Clientes*, the former being used to denote the whole non-privileged class collectively, while the latter was employed with reference to different Patrician houses to which they were individually attached. But this idea, long received without doubt or suspicion, is entirely irreconcileable with the position occupied by the Clients, as explained above, and also with the narratives of the historians themselves. The Clients, even as a body, could never have engaged in a series of fierce struggles, during which they must have constantly been brought into direct collision with their individual Patrons, nor would any Patrician have been permitted to exercise those acts of oppression and cruelty towards the Clients of another Patrician which we find often perpetrated on the Plebs in their weakness. Moreover, many passages might be quoted from Livy and Dionysius in which the Clients of the Patricians are mentioned, not merely as distinct from the Plebs, but as actively assisting their patrons to frustrate the designs of the Plebs. The most important of these are referred to below, and ought to be carefully consulted.[1]

The ingenious hypothesis of Niebuhr, although he insists with too much dogmatism on the minute details of his theory, is now generally accepted as a satisfactory solution of the difficulties which surround this subject. His views may be briefly expressed in the following propositions:—

1. *The Plebs and the Clients were originally entirely distinct.*
2. *The original population of Rome consisted solely of the Patricians and their Clients.*
3. *The Plebs was composed of the inhabitants of various Latin towns which were conquered and destroyed, their population being, at the same time, transported to Rome and the surrounding territory.* Thus, upon the taking of Alba by Tullus Hostilius, Livy records—*duplicatur civium numerus*—and again, when speaking of the conquest of Ancus—*secutusque morem regum priorum, qui rem Romanam auxerant hostibus in civitatem accipiendis, multitudinem omnem Romam traduxit.*[2]
4. *As long as the Patricians and Plebeians remained politically distinct, the former alone, with their clients, were designated as the* POPULUS.

Hence we find *Populus* and *Plebs* spoken of as different bodies, not merely in the early ages, as when we are told—*Consul Appius negare jus esse tribuno in quemquam, nisi in plebeium. Non enim* POPULI *sed* PLEBIS *eum magistratum esse*[3]—but in formal documents of a much later period, and even when the original import of the terms must have been altogether forgotten. Thus, in the prophecy published B.C. 212, during the second Punic war, enjoining the insti-

---
[1] Liv. II. 35. 56. 64. III. 14. 16. comp. VII. 18. Dionys. VI. 45-47. 63. IX. 41. X. 27.
[2] Liv. I. 30. 33.
[3] Liv. II. 56.

F

tution of games in honour of Apollo—*Is ludis faciendis praeerit praetor is, qui jus* POPULO PLEBEIQUE *dabit summum* [1]—and in the will of Augustus—*Legata non ultra civilem modum, nisi quod* POPULO ET PLEBI CCCXXXV. . . . *dedit.* [2]

When we remember the progress made by Rome during the regal period, we shall understand that the numbers of the Plebeians increased with great rapidity, and that this body must have included a vast number of families which had been noble and wealthy in the vanquished states, as well as the humble and the poor. The Plebeians had their own Gentes and Familiae, the same system of names prevailed among them as among the Patricians, and in some cases the gentile names were identical. Thus there was a Patrician *Gens Claudia* with the family names of *Pulcher, Nero,* and others; and also a Plebeian *Gens Claudia* with the family name *Marcellus.*

Amalgamation of the Clientes with the Plebs.—The old Clients were eventually mixed up with and became a portion of the Plebs; but when and by what steps this was effected, are points upon which we are entirely ignorant. It is probable, however, that the fusion was completed at the period when the Plebs succeeded in extorting from the Patricians the full concession of equal rights.

Clients of later times.—But although the clients became politically merged in the Plebs, the habits and national feelings connected with the *Clientela* remained. Many of the poorer Romans, and foreigners resident in Rome, gladly took advantage of this sentiment, and placed themselves under the protection of the rich and powerful. Even towards the close of the republic and under the early emperors, the noble Roman loved to be visited each morning by a crowd of humble dependants, and to walk abroad attended by a numerous retinue whom he was wont to assist with his advice, and occasionally to entertain at his table, or, as became the practice at a late period, to recompense by a dole (*sportula*) of food or money for their mercenary devotion.

Cities and whole provinces, in like manner, sought, as clients, to secure the good offices of particular families or individuals. The Marcelli were the patrons of Sicily—the Fabii, of the Allobroges—the Claudii, of Sparta—Cato, of Cyprus and Cappadocia; and as a proof that the connection so formed was not merely nominal, we find Octavius excusing the inhabitants of Bononia from joining in the league against his rival—*quod in Antoniorum clientela antiquitus erant* —(Suet. Octav. 17.)

Plebs of later times.—After the Plebeians had been admitted to a full participation of all social and political rights, the term *Plebs* or *Plebes* by degrees lost its original signification; it no longer indicated an order or body in the state politically distinct, but was used to denote those members of the community at large whose means were small and whose station was humble. Hence, by the writers who flourished during the last century of the republic, and under the empire, the name *Plebs* was applied to the whole mass of poor citizens, and is frequently employed disparagingly in the sense of the *mob* or *rabble*. The only trace of political or social distinction which remained was in the separation still kept up between the Patrician and Plebeian Gentes, and this was closely

---

[1] Liv. XXV. 12.
[2] Tacit. Ann. I. 8. In the Senatus Consultum, quoted by Caelius in Cic. Epp. ad Fam. VIII. 8. we read—*Si quid ea re ad populum, ad plebemve lato opus esset, uti Ser. Sulpicius, M. Marcellus Coss. praetores, tribunique plebis, quibus eorum videretur ad populum plebemve referrent*—the term *populus* may signify the people assembled in the Comitia Centuriata, as opposed to *plebs*, the people assembled in the Comitia Tributa.

observed, because, although all the great offices were open to Plebeians, there were certain magistracies (that of *Tribunus Plebis*, for example,) from which, according to an inviolable principle in the constitution, all members of the Patrician Gentes were rigidly excluded.

Nobiles. Ignobiles. Novi Homines. Ius Imaginum.—After all political distinctions between Patricians and Plebeians had been finally removed, a new aristocracy or nobility gradually sprung up. Certain high offices of state conferred upon the holder the right of using, upon public occasions, an ivory chair of peculiar form. This chair was termed *Sella Curulis;* and the offices, to be enumerated hereafter, which gave a right to the use of this seat were named *Magistratus Curules.* It was the custom for the sons or other lineal descendants of those who had held such offices to make figures with waxen faces representing their dignified ancestors, and the right bestowed by such custom or usage was called *Ius Imaginum*. These Imagines or figures were usually ranged in the public apartment (*atrium*) of the house occupied by the representative of the family—appropriate descriptive legends (*tituli*) were attached to each—they were exhibited on all great family or gentile festivals and solemnities; and the dignity of a family and of a gens was, to a certain degree, estimated by the number which it could display.[1] All persons who possessed one or more of these figures, that is to say, all who could number among their ancestors individuals who had held one or more Curule offices, were designated by the title of *Nobiles*. Those who had no figures of their ancestors, but who had raised themselves to a Curule office, were termed *Novi Homines*. All who had no figures of their ancestors, and had not, in their own persons, attained to a Curule office, were ranked together as *Ignobiles*. Even after the admission of the Plebeians to a full participation in political power, the high offices were, to a great extent, monopolised by a small number of families; these *Nobiles* became gradually more and more exclusive, and looked with very jealous eyes upon every one not belonging to their own class who sought to rise to eminence in the state.[2] Hence the fierce opposition offered to Marius, who was a *Novus Homo*, and even Cicero, who stood in the same position, was always, notwithstanding the services he rendered to the aristocracy, regarded with coldness and aversion by a large portion of the old *Nobiles*. It must be distinctly understood that this *Nobilitas* conferred no legal privileges—did not imply the possession of wealth, and was enjoyed by Plebeians and Patricians, without reference to their extraction. It has been remarked, that no Patrician is ever spoken of as an *Ignobilis* or as a *Novus Homo*. If this is really correct, it probably arises from the fact, that before these terms became of weight, every Patrician family, and the number of these was latterly very small, could number the holder of a Curule magistracy among its ancestors.

Optimates. Populares.—It will be readily understood from the last section how the state became divided into two great political parties or factions, the one composed of the Senate with the Nobiles and their adherents, who desired to keep all political power, as far as possible, in the hands of a few individuals, the other, composed chiefly of the Ignobiles, who were desirous to extend the circle, and to increase the importance of the people at large. The former, who may be termed the Aristocratic party, were styled *Optimates*, the latter, or Democratic were styled *Populares*;[3] and from the time of the Gracchi until the downfal of the

---
[1] On the subject of Roman *Imagines* our great authority is Polybius VI. 53.
[2] We find this spirit manifesting itself as early as the second Punic war.—See Law. XXII. 34.
[3] See Velleius II. 3. Cic. pro Sest. 45.

commonwealth, their contests were fierce and incessant. It must be observed, that these words, *Optimates* and *Populares*, in no way indicated rank or distinction, but solely political principles, and that although the former consisted chiefly of the *Nobiles*, yet, the most distinguished leaders of the *Populares*, the Gracchi, and Julius Cæsar, were Nobiles—the two former Plebeians, the latter a Patrician.

Local Tribes.—The Plebs, although steadily increasing in number and in strength, appear to have remained a confused mass until they received organization and political existence from the institutions of Servius Tullius. One of the most important measures of that great reformer was the division of the whole Roman territory into districts, termed *Regiones*, and of the whole free Roman population into an equal number of *Tribus*, each tribe occupying a region. The city was divided into four regions, which, as we have seen above, (p. 8,) were denominated respectively, *Suburana*, *Esquilina*, *Collina*, and *Palatina*,[1] the remainder of the Roman territory was divided into twenty-six regions,[2] so that altogether there were thirty regions and thirty tribes, twenty-six of these being *Tribus Rusticae*, and four *Tribus Urbanae*. This arrangement was strictly local; each individual possessed of landed property being enrolled in the Rustic Tribe corresponding to the region in which his property lay, and those who were not landowners being included in one or other of the City Tribes.

Some important changes took place in consequence of the convulsions and loss of lands which followed the expulsion of the kings; for in B.C. 495, fifteen years after that event, we are told by Livy—*Romae tribus una et viginti factae*.[3] From this time forward new tribes were gradually added, as the Roman territory gradually extended, until B.C. 241, when they were increased to thirty-five.[4] This number was never augmented, but remained fixed until the latest times. It is true, that upon the admission of the Italian states to the rights of citizenship, after the social war, laws were proposed and passed (*Lex Iulia*, B.C. 90—*Lex Plautia Papiria*, B.C. 89,) for the creation of eight or ten new tribes, in which the new citizens were to be enrolled;[5] but these enactments were, in this point, superseded by the *Lex Sulpicia*, (B.C. 88,) which ordained that the new citizens should be distributed among the thirty-five existing tribes;[6] and this arrangement appears to have been ratified and carried out by Sulla.[7]

The tribes instituted by Servius Tullius must be carefully distinguished from the three Patrician tribes, the Ramnes, Tities, and Luceres, which were henceforward thrown into the shade; and wherever tribes are spoken of in Roman history, we must understand that the Local tribes are meant unless the contrary is specifically stated.

The division into tribes, now described, being purely local or territorial, there can be little doubt that the Patricians and their Clients, as well as the Plebeians, were included from the very commencement; but in what relation they stood towards each other when the division into tribes was first applied to political purposes, cannot be ascertained.

The *Regiones Rusticae* were divided into a number of small districts, called

---

[1] Varro L.L. V. § 45. § 56. Dionys. IV. 14. Liv. I. 43. Epit. XX. Plin. H.N. XVIII. 3.
[2] Varro ap. Non. s.v. *viritim*, p. 30. ed. Gerl. Dionys. IV. 15.
[3] Liv. II. 21. Dionys. VII. 64.
[4] Liv. I. 43. Epit. XIX.
[5] Velleius II. 20. Appian. B.C. I. 49.
[6] Liv. Epit. LXXVII. Appian. B.C. I. 55, 64. Velleius l. c.
[7] Liv. Epit. LXXXVI.

Pagi, each of which had its *Magister Pagi* or petty magistrate; and the *Pagani*, i.e. the members of each *Pagus* had a shrine, where each year they celebrated a festival termed *Paganalia*.[1]

In like manner, the *Regiones Urbanae* were divided into *Vici*, each *Vicus* having its *Magister;* and the inhabitants of each celebrated annually, at the intersection of the streets forming their Vicus, a festival, termed *Compitalia*.[2] There were also rural festivals, termed *Compitalia*, celebrated at the point where several roads intersected each other.

Classes. Centuriae.—The division into tribes comprehended the whole body of free Romans, and was purely local; but Servius made a second distribution, not less important in every point of view, depending entirely upon the amount of fortune possessed by each citizen—this was the division into *Classes*, which were subdivided into *Centuriae*.

Classis, in the most ancient acceptation of the term, denoted *an army;* and the division into Classes and Centuries was, in one point of view, a military organization, the whole body of the people being regarded as an *Exercitus*, divided into horse and foot, with their artizans and musicians.

The Cavalry (*equites*) were divided into eighteen *Centuriae*.

The Infantry (*pedites*) were divided into five, or, according to some, into six *Classes*, the discrepancy being, however, merely nominal, as will be seen hereafter.

Each *Classis* contained a certain number of *Centuriae*, one half being Centuriae of *Iuniores*, that is, composed of men between the ages of seventeen and forty-six, and therefore liable to be called upon for active military service, the other half being Centuriae of *Seniores*, that is, composed of men above the age of forty-six.

Each class included all who possessed a certain amount of fortune, that is, whose property was valued at a certain sum; and the style of the equipments in each class was regulated by the means of those who formed the class. Thus, those in the first class had a full suit of defensive armour, helmet, large round shield, cuirass, greaves, (*galea, clypeus, lorica, ocreae,*) all of bronze, their offensive weapons being a long spear (*hasta*) and a sword (*gladius*.) Those in the second class carried a lighter oblong shield, (*scutum,*) and had no cuirass. Those in the third class had no greaves. Those in the fourth class had no defensive armour, and bore merely a long spear (*hasta*) and a light javelin (*verutum*.) Those in the fifth class were provided with slings and stones only (*fundas lapidesque missiles gerebant*.)

Our chief authorities for all the details with regard to the distribution into classes and centuries are Livy (I. 43.) and Dionysius, (IV. 16. VII. 59.) whose accounts, although agreeing in the main, present slight discrepancies. Combining the two narratives, the following scheme approaches, in all probability, nearly to the truth:—

EQUITES, ... 18 Centuries.

I^{ma}. CLASSIS.—*Fortune not less than* 100,000 *Asses or pounds of copper.*
        40 Centuriae Seniorum,⎫
        40 Centuriae Iuniorum,⎬ . . . . . 80 Centuriae.

[1] Dionys. II. 76. IV. 15. Paul. Diac. s.v. *Pagani*, p. 221. Serv. ad Virg. G. II. 382.
[2] Dionys. I. 14. IV. 14.

II$^{da.}$ CLASSIS.—*Fortune not less than* 75,000 *Asses.*
    10 Centuriae Seniorum,
    10 Centuriae Iuniorum, ... 22 Centuries.
    2 Centuriae Fabrûm,

III$^{tia.}$ CLASSIS.—*Fortune not less than* 50,000 *Asses.*
    10 Centuriae Seniorum,
    10 Centuriae Iuniorum, ... 20 Centuries.

IV$^{ta.}$ CLASSIS.—*Fortune not less than* 25,000 *Asses.*
    10 Centuriae Seniorum,
    10 Centuriae Iuniorum,   . . . 22 Centuries.
    2 Centuriae Cornicinum, &c.

V$^{ta.}$ CLASSIS.—*Fortune not less than* 12,500 *Asses.*
    15 Centuriae Seniorum,
    15 Centuriae Iuniorum, ... 30 Centuries.

    1 Centuria Proletariorum et
    Capite Censorum, ... 1 Century.

    In all 193 Centuries.

The chief points in which Dionysius and Livy differ are—

1. Livy makes the total number of Centuries to be 194, by adding to the fifth class a Centuria of *Accensi;* but it is more probable that the number should have been odd, otherwise embarrassment might have arisen from an equal division of the Centuries in voting, as will be explained in the section where we treat of the Comitia Centuriata.

2. Livy makes the fortune of the fifth class 11,000 asses, instead of 12,500; but we can see no reason why a departure should have taken place in this instance from the symmetrical reduction observed in the other cases.

3. Dionysius makes six classes, instead of five; his sixth class consisting of the one century of *Proletarii* and *Capite Censi* included by Livy in the fifth.

The *Proletarii* were those whose fortune was not above 1500 asses, and who were not called upon for military service except in extraordinary emergencies, when they were equipped at the expense of the state.

The *Capite Censi* were those who had no fortune, or whose fortune was so small that it could not be definitely fixed, and who were therefore rated "by the head," and not by the amount of their property.

It will be observed that there is a considerable gap between the fifth class, whose fortune was not less than 12,500, and the Proletarii, whose fortune was not above 1500; this space is supposed to have been filled up by the various descriptions of irregular troops, spoken of by different authors, such as, *accensi velati—adscriptitii—rorarii—ferentarii,* &c.; but whether these were included in the Centuries of the fifth class, or in the single Century of the Proletarii, we cannot tell.[1]

The citizens included in the five classes were comprehended under the general

---

[1] On the *Proletarii,* &c. see Aul. Gell. XVI. 10. Cic. de R. II. 22. Sallust. Iug. 91. Paul. Diac. s.v. *Proletarium,* p. 226.

name of *Assidui*, or (at a later period) *Locupletes*,[1] in opposition to the *Proletarii* and *Capite Censi*. Those again who, belonging to the first class, had property valued at not less than 125,000 asses, were styled emphatically *Classici*, and under this head we must suppose that the eighteen Centuries of Equites were included; those again who were included in the first, or in any of the remaining four classes, but whose fortune did not amount to the above sum, were designated as *Infra Classem*,[2] and hence the phrase *classic authors*, i.e. writers of preeminent worth, and so Aulus Gellius (XIX. 8.)—*Classicus assiduusque aliquis scriptor non proletarius.*

In conclusion, we would repeat, for the fact ought to be deeply impressed upon the young scholar, that while the division into tribes was purely local, so the distribution into classes depended upon fortune alone, and that, in so far as the local tribes and the classes were concerned, Patricians and Plebeians were, from the first, placed side by side without distinction; the great object kept in view by Servius Tullius having evidently been the establishment of political equality among the different orders of the state. This will be better understood when, in a subsequent section, we explain the relation of the tribes and centuries to the *Comitia* or constitutional assemblies.

Equites. Ordo Equester.—We must now direct our attention to that class of persons who, under the name of *Equites*, play a conspicuous part in the annals of Rome from the earliest times. The investigation of their history is highly complicated and obscure. All the materials will be found collected, discussed, and combined with great industry, acuteness and ingenuity, in the treatises quoted at the bottom of the page,[3] of which the last three deserve special attention; but many points are still involved in doubt. In pursuing our inquiries into the nature and constitution of this body as it existed at different epochs, it will be necessary to draw a broad line of distinction between the *Equites* of the primitive times and the *Equester Ordo* during the last century of the commonwealth; and it will be farther necessary to consider the ancient Equites as divided into two classes, the *Equites equo publico* and the *Equites equo privato*.

Rise and Progress of the Equites.—In the earlier ages of Rome the term *Equites* was employed exclusively in a military sense to denote the cavalry of the army, and therefore was not applied to a permanent order in the state, but to a body which was undergoing constant changes.

We are told that Romulus levied one hundred cavalry in each of the three original tribes, ten out of each Curia.

These three hundred horsemen or *tres centuriae equitum* were divided into ten squadrons (*Turmae*) of thirty men each, each Turma was subdivided into three *Decuriae* of ten men each, and at the head of each Decuria was a *Decurio*. The three *Centuriae* bore the names of the three tribes from which they were raised, and were designated respectively *Ramnes—Tities—Luceres*; and the

[1] Cic. de R. II. 22. Aul. Gell. XVI. 10. Varro ap. Non. s.v. *Proletarii*, p. 48. ed. Gerl. Charis. I. p. 58. ed. Putsch.
[2] Aul. Gell. VII. 13. comp. Paul. Diac. s.v. *Infra classem*. We have already referred to the passages of Livy (I. 43.) and Dionysius (IV. 16. VII. 59.) which afford the most distinct information concerning the constitution of Servius, and to that of Aulus Gellius (XVI. 10.) which is the most important on the *Proletarii* and *Capite Censi*; but in addition to these, there is a passage in Cicero de Republica (II. 22.) in every way remarkable, and which has given rise to animated discussion; but the text is unhappily so uncertain that it cannot be regarded as a safe guide.
[3] *Muhlert*, De equitibus Romanis, Hild. 1830.
Marquardt, Historiae equitum Romanorum, Berol. 1840.
Zumpt, Ueber die Römischen Ritter, &c.. Berol. 1840.
Madvig, De loco Ciceronis in Libro IV. de Rep., in his Opuscula Academica, Tom. 1.

squadrons were formed in such a manner that each contained ten Ramnes, ten Tities, and ten Luceres. The body collectively was termed *Equites* s. *Celeres* s. *Trossuli* s. *Flexumines*, the two latter being words of uncertain origin. The commander of the whole was styled *Tribunus Celerum*.[1]

Tullus Hostilius, after the destruction of Alba, doubled the number of the Equites, the number of Centuriae remaining the same, so that each Centuria now contained twenty Turmae and two hundred Equites.[2]

Tarquinius Priscus again doubled the number of Equites, dividing them into six Centuriae; but he was forbidden by the augur, Attus Navius, to introduce new names, and therefore the Centuriae were now distinguished as *Priores* and *Posteriores* s. *Secundi*; thus, there were the *Ramnenses priores* and the *Ramnenses posteriores*, and so for the Tities and Luceres, the whole number of Equites being now 1200. These six Centuriae were composed of Patricians exclusively, and are frequently described as the *Sex Suffragia* or *Sex Centuriae*, and were known by the latter name even when Livy wrote.[3]

Servius added to the six Centuriae twelve new Centuriae of two hundred each; these new Centuriae being selected from the leading men in the state, without reference to their position as Patricians or Plebeians. There were now altogether 3600 Equites divided into eighteen Centuriae, the number given above, when treating of the distribution of the citizens into classes. These eighteen *Centuriae Equitum* were made up of the *Sex Suffragia* of Patricians, as arranged by Tarquinius, and the twelve new Centuriae of Servius.[4]

Census Equester.—The Equites, from the commencement, were selected from the wealthiest of the citizens. The fortune necessary for admission into the first class was, as we have seen, at least 100,000 asses—the equestrian fortune was probably at least 125,000, which placed the holder among the *Classici*; but we must not suppose the 400,000 sesterces=1,600,000 asses, which was the *Census Equester* towards the close of the republic, could have been required in the infancy of the state.

Equus Publicus.—Each of the Equites, in the eighteen Centuriae, received from the public treasury a sum of 10,000 asses for the purchase of a horse, (*aes equestre*,) and hence the phrases *equo publico merere, equum publicum assignare;* he was farther allowed an annual sum of 2000 asses for its maintenance, (*aes hordearium;*) the sum necessary for the latter purpose being raised by a tax paid by unmarried women and orphans, who seem to have been exempt from ordinary imposts.[5] It seems probable that when an Eques ceased to serve, either in consequence of the regular period having expired, or from some other cause, he was required to refund the 10,000 asses advanced for the purchase of his horse, but this is not certain.[6]

Period of Service.—During the most flourishing epoch of the republic, the period of service required from an Eques was ten years, after which he was no longer obliged to take the field, but might, if he thought fit, give up his public horse and retire from the Centuriae of the Equites. It does not, however, appear that this retirement was compulsory; on the contrary, those who had obtained a place in the Senate, and were far advanced in life, sometimes retained their Equus Publicus, as in the case of the censors M. Livius Salinator and C. Claudius

---

[1] Livy. I. 13. Dionys. II. 13. Varro L.L. V. § 91. Plut. Rom. 13. 26.
[2] Paul. Diac. s v. *Celeres*, p. 55.
[3] Liv. I. 36. who, however, makes the number 1800.
[4] Liv. I. 36. 43. Cic. de R. II. 20. as interpreted by Zumpt.
[5] Liv. I. 43. Paul. Diac. s.v. *Equestre aes*, p. 81. Cic. de R. II. 20. Gaius IV. § 27.
[6] See Becker, p. 254.

Nero, B.C. 204, and indeed at one time all senators must have been included in the Centuriae Equitum. In the age of Cicero, however, these Centuriae were composed of young men exclusively.[1]

Choosing of the Equites—The Equites, we are told by Dionysius, (II. 13,) were originally selected by the Curiae. After the introduction of the Servian constitution, the duty would devolve upon the magistrate who presided over the *Census*, and hence first upon the kings, afterwards upon the consuls, and from the year B.C. 443 on the censors.[2] Once in five years the censors made a strict and solemn review of the Equites, (*equitatum recognoscere—recensere—censum equitum agere,*)[3] who passed before them on foot, in single file, each leading his horse forward as his name was called over by the public crier. Those who were approved of were desired to pass on, (*traducere equum—traduc equum,*)[4] those whose horse and equipments were in bad order, or who, from any other cause, were deemed unworthy, the censor removed from the body, (*equum equiti adimere,*) by pronouncing the words *Vende equum.*[5] After the roll was purified, the vacancies were filled up from those who possessed the necessary qualification, and no change took place until new censors entered upon office.

Equitum Transvectio.—Altogether different from the solemn review by the censors (*equitum probatio* s. *recognitio—ἱππέων ἐπίσκεψις*) was the procession called *Equitum Transvectio*, which took place annually on the Ides of July, in commemoration of the aid afforded to the Roman arms, at the battle of the lake Regillus, by the twin brethren Castor and Pollux. On the day named, the Equites, mounted on their steeds and dressed in their robes of state, (*trabeati,*) rode from the temple of Honos, outside the Porta Capena, (see above p. 34,) through the Forum to the Capitol, passing on their way the temple of the Dioscuri (see above p. 18.) This practice was first introduced by Q. Fabius Maximus Rullianus when censor, B.C. 304—*Ab eodem institutum dicitur ut equites Idibus Quintilibus transveherentur*—*Hic primus instituit uti Equites Romani Idibus Quintilibus ab aede Honoris equis insidentes in Capitolium transirent.*[6]

The *Recognitio* and the *Transvectio* of the Equites had both fallen into disuse before the downfal of the republic, but were revived, and, apparently, to a certain degree, combined by Augustus.[7]

Equites equo privato.—The eighteen Centuriae Equitum, whose constitution we have described above, were the only body of cavalry in the state until the year B.C. 403, when, in consequence of the reverses sustained by the army before Veii, and the intestine disorders which distracted the city, the Senate were thrown into great perplexity. On this emergency, a number of persons possessed of equestrian fortune, but who had not been chosen into the eighteen Centuriae, came forward and offered to serve as cavalry without receiving a horse from the state, or the usual allowance for its maintenance.[8] Their proposal was eagerly accepted. In this way a body of Equites arose, who received larger pay than the infantry, and whose period of military service was limited to ten years, but who received neither *aes equestre* nor *aes hordearium*, and who were not admitted into the eighteen Centuriae Equitum.

---

[1] Liv. XXIX. 37. Cic. de R. IV. 2. and remarks of Zumpt. Q. Cic. de pet. cons. 8.
[2] See article *Censores* in the chapter on the Roman Magistrates.
[3] Liv. XXIX. 37. XXXIX. 44 XLIII. 16.
[4] Cic. pro Cluent. 48. Val. Max. IV. i. 10.
[5] Liv. XXIX. 37. Val. Max. II. ix. 6.
[6] Dionys VI. 13. Liv. IX. 46. Val. Max. II. ii. 9. Aurel. Vict. de viris ill. 32.
[7] Suet. Octav. 38.
[8] **Liv. V. 7.** *equis se suis stipendia facturos promittunt.*

It must be remarked that towards the close of the republic, although the eighteen Centuriae were still kept up as a political body, the cavalry of the Roman armies was composed almost entirely of persons not citizens, and hence the *Equites equis privatis* must have gradually disappeared. These changes paved the way for a new body, which we now proceed to consider.

Ordo Equester.—As Rome rose and prospered, the number of those who possessed the Equestrian fortune must have greatly exceeded the demands of the armies; and when the cavalry was composed chiefly of allies and auxiliaries, a class of rich men was rapidly formed, who were not senators, and not ambitious of public distinction, but who sought to employ their time and increase their means by embarking in mercantile enterprises. We hear of such for the first time as government contractors during the course of the second Punic war;[1] and when the dominion of the republic was extended over Sicily, Greece, Asia, and Africa, they found ample occupation in farming the public revenues, and accumulated vast wealth. This body of monied men necessarily exercised great influence, and held an intermediate but ill-defined position between the nobility and the humbler portion of the community. Hence, when the struggles between the *Optimates* and the *Populares* became frequent and violent, the democratic party perceived how much they might gain by securing the hearty co-operation of the great capitalists and their retainers, and this object they effected by the bold measure of C. Gracchus, who, in B.C. 122 carried the *Lex Sempronia Iudiciaria*, in terms of which the *Iudicia*, that is, the right of acting as jurors upon criminal trials, which had hitherto been enjoyed by the senators exclusively, was transferred to those possessed of the *Census Equester*, i.e. 400,000 sesterces. In this manner a definite form was given to the body—now, for the first time, called *Ordo Equester*,[2] in contradistinction to *Ordo Senatorius*; and all necessary connection between the term *Equites* and the idea of military service ceased. The Senate, however, did not tamely resign the privilege which they had so long enjoyed, and for half a century after the passing of the Lex Sempronia, the battle of the Iudicia was fought again and again with varying success, and a constant feeling of irritation was kept up between the contending parties. To remove this, and to bring about a hearty good understanding between the Senate and the Equestrian Order, was the great object of Cicero's policy, who saw clearly that in this way only could the assaults of the democracy be repelled. This object he succeeded in accomplishing for a time, at the period of Catiline's conspiracy, which spread dismay among all who had any thing to lose. But the alliance proved short-lived, and the majority of the *Ordo Equester* threw themselves into the scale of Caesar and the *Populares*. Pliny, in the first and second chapters of the thirty-third book of his *Naturalis Historia*, communicates much information with regard to the rise and progress of the Equestrian order; but, as too common with that author, the materials are thrown together at random, and the statements, on many points, irreconcileable. The following sentences from the second chapter seem to be distinct and trust-worthy:—*Iudicum autem appellatione separari eum ordinem primi omnium instituere Gracchi discordi popularitate in contumeliam Senatus, mox ea debellata, auctoritas nominis vario seditionum eventu circa publicanos substitit: et aliquamdiu tertiae vires publicani fuere. Marcus Cicero demum stabilivit equestre nomen in consulatu*

[1] Liv. XXIII. 48, 49.
[2] It is here that the term *Ordo Equester* occurs in the earlier books of Livy, e.g. IX. 38. XXI. 59. XXIV. 18. XXVI. 36.; but the historian seems to have adopted the phraseology of his own day without reference to the period when it was first introduced. We shall have occasion shortly to notice a similar prolepsis in regard to what were called *Equites illustres*.

BADGES OF THE EQUITES. 75

suo, ei senatum concilians, ex eo se ordine profectum esse celebrans, eiusque vires peculiari popularitate quaerens. Ab illo tempore plane hoc tertium corpus in republica factum est, coepitque adiici Senatui Populoque Romano et Equester Ordo.

Insignia of the Equites.—The outward marks of distinction enjoyed by the Equites and the Ordo Equester were the following:—

1. *Annulus aureus.*—We find that golden rings were worn by senators at all events as early as B.C. 321; for we are told by Livy, that among other demonstrations of public grief, when intelligence arrived of the disaster at the Caudine forks—*lati clavi, annuli aurei positi*. During the second Punic war, we know that they were worn not only by senators, their wives and children, but also by *Equites equo publico*; since it is to these that the historian must refer when he informs us that when Mago exhibited to the Carthaginian Senate the three modii of golden rings taken from the slain at Cannae—*adiecit deinde verbis, quo maioris cladis indicium esset, neminem, nisi equitem, atque eorum ipsorum primores, id gerere insigne*. According to Pliny, who enters into many details upon the subject of rings, the greater number of the members of the equestrian order, who acted as jurors, wore, even in the time of Augustus, an iron ring only—*maior pars iudicum in ferreo annulo fuit*—from which we conclude that, after the age of Augustus, the custom or right of wearing the *annulus aureus* extended to the whole of the Ordo Equester.[1]

2. *Angustus clavus.*—While Senators and Equites equo publico had alike the privilege of wearing a golden ring, senators alone had the right of wearing a tunic with a broad vertical stripe of purple (*latus clavus*) in front, the garment being hence called *Tunica Laticlavia*, while the tunic of the Equites was distinguished by a narrow stripe, and hence called *Tunica Angusticlavia*. At what period the practice was first introduced we cannot tell, since it is seldom alluded to in the classics, and only by writers of the imperial times.[2] We learn from Dion Cassius that when the Senate, as a mark of sorrow, changed their dress, (*mutavit vestem*,) this consisted in laying aside their official garb, i.e. the *Laticlavia*, and assuming that of the Equites, i.e. the *Angusticlavia*, while the magistrates threw off their purple edged cloak, (*Toga praetexta*,) and appeared in the mantle of ordinary senators. We hear also of a change of dress under similar circumstances upon the part of the Equites and the populace; the former would, therefore, probably appear in a plain tunic, while the latter would disfigure themselves with dust and ashes, and so appear *sordidati*.[3]

3. *Quatuordecim Ordines.*—In B.C. 67, L. Roscius Otho, at that time tribune of the Plebs, passed a new law, (*Lex Roscia theatralis*,) or, perhaps, rather revived an obsolete enactment, (see Liv. I. 35,) in terms of which, fourteen rows of seats in the theatre, immediately behind those occupied by the senators, were appropriated to the Ordo Equester—a measure so unpopular that it led to a riot, which was quelled by the eloquence of Cicero.[4] From this time forward, the phrases—*sedere in quatuordecim ordinibus—in equite spectare—in equestribus sedere—sedere in pulvino equestri*—are used to indicate a member of the equestrian order; and the classics are full of allusions to Roscius and his law.[5] This ordinance, it must be observed, extended to the theatre alone, and did not

[1] Liv. IX. 7. comp. 46. XXIII. 12. XXVI. 36. Plin. H.N. XXXIII. 1. 2.
[2] Ovid. Trist. IV. x. 35. Suet. Octav. 73. Lamprid. Alex. Sev. 27. comp. Plin. H.N. XXXIII. 1.
[3] Dion Cass. XXXVIII. 14. XL. 46. LVI. 31.
[4] Liv. Epit. XCIX. Cic. pro Muren. 19. Philipp. II. 18. Plin. H.N. VII. 30. Plut. Cic. 13.
[5] Hor. Epod. IV. 16. Juv. S. III. 153. Tacit. Ann. XV. 32.

embrace the Circus, in which places were not set apart for the Senate and the equestrian order until the reign of Augustus,[1] whose regulations upon this point were modified and made more complete by subsequent emperors.[2]

Equestrian Order under the Emperors.—By the *Lex Iudiciaria* of **C.** Gracchus all persons possessing property to the value of 400,000 sesterces became, ipso facto, members of the Equestrian Order, and hence, at a very early period, the body was inundated with liberated slaves and persons, who, by disreputable means, had acquired the requisite sum. This evil was already strongly felt in the time of Augustus, who sought, in some degree, to obviate it by introducing a new division among the Equites themselves, and instituting, as it were, an upper class. With this intention, he set apart, under the name of *Equites illustres*, (sometimes called also *Equites splendidi*,) those who were of distinguished descent, and who possessed a fortune amounting to the qualification for a senator. These he regarded as forming a sort of nursery for the Senate, (*seminarium senatus:*) upon these, while still youths, he bestowed the inferior offices of state, and permitted them to wear, by anticipation, the *Tunica Laticlavia*. To this class Ovid belonged, and, as he tells us himself, when he gave up all thoughts of political distinction, and retired into private life, he was obliged to exchange the broad for the narrow stripe—*clavi mensura coacta est*.[3]

The *Equites equo publico* having long ceased to be the cavalry of the armies, would have naturally disappeared along with the *Classes* and *Centuriae* with which they were politically connected, but Augustus revived them; and while a portion of the *Equites illustres* were regarded as the stock from which the future legislators and civil magistrates were to spring, another portion, consisting of those who aimed at military distinction, were sent out as cadets under the immediate inspection of the chief generals, and appointed to subordinate commands, so as to acquire a practical knowledge of their profession. This kind of service was termed *Militia Equestris* or *Stipendia splendidae militiae;* and the individuals thus employed formed a select corps, the head of which was styled *Princeps Iuventutis*. This, however, was merely a restoration of an ancient term; for under the republic the Equites, as a body, were sometimes distinguished as *Principes Iuventutis* (Liv. XLII. 61.) Now, however, the title of *Princeps Iuventutis* was, in the first instance, restricted to two individuals, Caius and Lucius Cæsar, the grandsons of the emperor; and from this time forward it was generally bestowed upon the heir to the imperial dignity, or on one closely connected with the imperial family. Thus, it was borne by Nero from the time of his adoption by Claudius, by Titus, by Domitian, without any other title until the death of his brother, by Commodus, and by many others.

In reference to the remark in note p. 74. we have to observe that Livy makes use of the phrase *Equites illustres* when treating of the period of the second Punic war (XXX. 18.) We may readily understand, however, that the historian employed an expression with which he himself was familiar to denote what was then the higher class of Equites, viz., the *Equites equo publico*, without paying regard to the fact, that the designation did not exist as a technical term at the epoch to which his narrative refers.

Although we shall devote a separate chapter to the consideration of the consti-

---
[1] Dion Cass. LV. 22. LX. 7. LXI. 16.
[2] Tacit. Ann. XV. 32. Plin. H.N. VIII. 7. Suet. Claud. 21. Ner. 11. Dom. 8.
[3] Ovid. Trist. IV. x. 35.

tution and duties of what may be denominated the Great Council of State, we cannot conclude the present notices of the orders and divisions of the body politic from the earliest times without saying a few words upon the—

Origin of the Senate.—The *Senatus* was a deliberative body, the members of which (*Senatores*) held their office for life, established for the purpose of advising the kings and supporting their authority.[1] The name is manifestly connected with the word *Senex*, and indicates that those only were admitted into the body whose wisdom had been matured by age and long experience. The title of respect by which the members were usually designated was *Patres*, i.e. Fathers of the State; but it must not be forgotten that Livy and those writers who treat of the earlier ages of the constitution, employ the word *Patres* to denote not only the senators, but the whole body of the Patricians, the words *Patres* and *Patricii* being used, in many cases, as absolutely synonymous.

Early History of the Senate.—It is agreed by all, that Romulus chose a Senate consisting of one hundred members.[2] The prevailing tradition declared farther that one hundred additional members were added when an union was formed with Titus Tatius and the Sabines; but some writers maintained that the augmented Senate contained one hundred and fifty members while Livy takes no notice of any increase upon this occasion, but represents the Senate as consisting of one hundred only at the death of Romulus. Finally, Tarquinius Priscus increased the number to three hundred, adding one hundred if we suppose that there were two hundred previously, doubling the body if we suppose one hundred and fifty to have been the former complement.[3] We are farther told, that the senators added by Tarquinius were styled *Patres Minorum Gentium*, in contradistinction to the original senators, who were now termed *Patres Maiorum Gentium*, names which clearly point to a belief that Tarquinius increased the number of the Patricians by the incorporation of new Gentes with the old houses, and that the new senators were selected from the new Gentes.[4] If we suppose the original one hundred senators of Romulus to have been *Ramnes*, the one hundred of Tatius to have been *Tities*, then the one hundred of Tarquinius, who was from Etruria, would be *Luceres*, and thus, the three elements, of which the *Populus Romanus* was composed, would have been equally represented in the Senate; but this hypothesis, although ingenious, attractive, and, at first sight, plausible, is encumbered by many serious and almost insurmountable difficulties.

The number of three hundred, in whatever manner made up, seems long to have remained the standard. We are expressly told, that at the time of the expulsion of Tarquinius Superbus, the Senate had been so reduced in numbers by his cruelty, that it became necessary for one of the first consuls, Brutus or Valerius, to select one hundred and sixty-four new members, in order to make up the proper amount of three hundred (*ut expleret numerum senatorum* CCC.) These, according to Livy, were taken from the most distinguished of the Equites, (*primoribus equestris gradus lectis*,) and therefore must have been in part Plebeians, and these Plebeian senators were styled *Conscripti*, as being enrolled along with the other senators, to whom, as Patricians, the title *Patres* properly belonged. Hence, the united body was at first described as *Patres et Conscripti*, from which arose

---
[1] Cic. de R. II. 9.
[2] Liv. I. 8. Dionys. II. 12. Plut. Rom. 13. Fest. s.v. *Senatores*, p. 339. Dionys. II. 47. Plut. Rom. 20. but comp. Plut. Num. 2.
[3] Liv. I. 35. Dionys. III. 67. Cic. de R. II. 20. Schol. Bob. in Cic. pro Scauro.
[4] Tacitus (Ann. XI. 25.) ascribes the institution of the *Minores Gentes* to Brutus the first consul.

the title of *Patres Conscripti*, employed almost invariably, in later times, in addressing the Senate, after the distinction indicated by the terms had long since disappeared and been forgotten.[1]

From this time forward we have no definite information with regard to the number of senators. We are told by Appian that Sulla, in order to recruit the ranks of the Senate, which had been greatly diminished during the civil war, added three hundred chosen from the most distinguished of the Equestrian order, and we have direct evidence that in the time of Cicero the number must have been upwards of four hundred and fifteen.[2] Julius Cæsar, when dictator for the fourth time, (B.C. 45.) admitted a crowd of unworthy persons, by whom the number was swelled to nine hundred; and when Augustus was censor along with Agrippa (B.C. 28.) there were one thousand.[3]

[1] Liv. II. 1. Dionys. V. 13. Plut. Popl. 11. Rom. 13 Q. R. 58. Fest. s.v. *Qui Patres*, p. 254. Paul. Diac. s.v. *Allecti*, p. 7. s.v. *Conscripti*, p. 41. Unless we suppose that Plebeians gained admission at this time, we shall be at a loss to account for the fact, that Plebeians are found in the Senate (Liv. V. 12.) before they were entitled to hold any of those offices which necessarily gave admission to the body.

Livy applies the term *Conscripti* to the whole of the new senators, without any special reference to Plebeians; but the explanation given above is not only natural in itself, but is fully borne out by the words of Festus and Paulus Diaconus.

[2] Appian. B. C. I. 100. Cic. ad Att. I. 14. comp. Orat. post. red. in Sen. 10.

[3] Dion Cass. XLIII. 47. LII. 42. Suet. Oct. 35.

CHAPTER III.

ON THE GENERAL PRINCIPLES OF THE ROMAN CONSTITUTION AND THE RIGHTS OF THE DIFFERENT CLASSES OF PERSONS WHO FORMED THE POPULATION OF THE ROMAN EMPIRE.

The Roman State, regarded as a body of men politically organised and in occupation of a certain territory, was, from the earliest period to which history or tradition extend, regulated and controlled by three powers, distinct from, but not independent of, each other. These were—
1. The voice of the citizens (*Cives*) who formed the *Populus Romanus*, as expressed in their constitutional assemblies (*Comitia*).
2. The magistrates (*Magistratus*.) When we speak of the regal period, we may say, the one supreme magistrate—the King (*Rex*.)
3. The Senate (*Senatus*) or great council of state.
1. *Cives.*—The voice of the *Cives* or *Populus Romanus*, as expressed in their Comitia, was, according to the theory of the Roman constitution, absolutely supreme. To them belonged the *Summum Imperium*, and all power whatsoever emanated from them either directly or indirectly. The chief points in which the citizens exercised their power directly were—(1.) In the enacting and repealing of laws (*leges scribere*.) (2.) In the election of magistrates (*magistratus creare*.) (3.) In the declaration of war, (*bellum indicere*,) and the conclusion of peace, (*pacem facere*,) to which we may add—(4.) In deciding, as a court of last appeal, all matters affecting the life, personal freedom, or permanent political privileges of one of their own body (*de capite civis Romani iudicare*.) We may observe that (3) and (4) are in reality included in (1); for all questions concerning a declaration of war and the ratification of a peace, as well as those which involved the criminal impeachment of a citizen, were submitted to the people in the form of proposed laws (*rogationes*.)

Such were the powers of the people, as recognised in the best period of their history,[1] and exercised until the complete establishment of the imperial government under Tiberius. We cannot, however, suppose that these rights and privileges were fully developed, understood, and enforced during the ruder ages of the state, when they must have reposed much more upon traditional usage than upon written laws, and when the amount of power exerted by the kings, although controlled by public opinion, as in the case of the early Greek communities and of Arab tribes, must have depended to a considerable extent upon the temper and talents of the individual monarch.

See especially Polyb. VI. 14.

It must be observed, moreover, that the power of the people, as exercised in their Comitia, was at all times limited by two restrictions.

a. The *Comitia* could not meet unless summoned, according to prescribed forms, by one of the higher magistrates.

b. In so far as the passing of laws was concerned, no private citizen could in these assemblies originate any measure whatsoever. When called together, they were asked (*rogabantur*) to agree to some specific proposal, hence termed generally a *Rogatio*, and this they could absolutely accept or absolutely reject, but they could neither change nor modify it.

2. *Magistratus.*—The magistrates formed the executive, being individuals chosen by, and responsible to, the citizens. To them was intrusted the duty of administering the laws and carrying into effect the orders of the people. For nearly two centuries and a-half after the foundation of the city there was one supreme magistrate, raised far above all others, who retained his office for life, and bore the title of *Rex*. But in the great revolution of A.U.C. 244, the reigning king was dethroned, the office abolished, and, instead of one chief magistrate, who held his power for life, two magistrates, called *Consules*, were chosen, who were upon an equality with each other, and whose period of office was limited strictly to the space of one year. By degrees, the various functions, discharged originally by the king alone and then committed to the consuls, were distributed among a number of other magistrates, new offices being instituted from time to time.

3. *Senatus.*—The Senate was a council of state, interposed, as it were, between the people and the magistrates. Its duty was to advise, although it could not control, the former, and to watch over and guide the latter in the performance of the duties assigned to them. To the Senate was committed the management of the public money; and it discharged many most important functions connected with the administration of public affairs, which will be described at large hereafter.

We have repeatedly used the words "citizens" and "Roman people" in the above remarks, and before proceeding farther it is necessary to ascertain what constituted a *Romanus Civis*. For this purpose we must consider the classification of mankind adopted by the Romans, in so far as political and social privileges were concerned.

The first grand division was into (1.) Freemen, that is, persons possessed of personal freedom, (*liberi,*) and (2.) Slaves (*servi.*)

Again, free men might be either persons born free (*ingenui*) and who had never been in slavery to a Roman, or persons who had once been slaves but had been emancipated (*libertini.*)

Omitting, for the present, the consideration of *Servi* and *Libertini*, who will form the subject of a separate section, we shall confine ourselves to *Ingenui*, that is, persons free and free-born, and who had never been in slavery to a Roman.

Ingenui might be either (1.) *Romani Cives*, that is, members of the Roman state, or (2.) *Peregrini*, that is, persons not members of the Roman state, or (3.) *Latini*, a class who occupied a sort of intermediate place between *Romani Cives* and *Peregrini*.

ROMANI CIVES. IUS CIVITATIS.

The characteristic rights of Roman citizens were divided into—1. *Publica Iura*. 2. *Privata Iura*.

The *Publica Iura* were comprehended under the three following heads:—

1. *Ius Suffragii*, the right of voting in the popular assemblies.
2. *Ius Honorum*, the right of being eligible to all public offices, whether civil, military, or sacred.
3. *Ius Provocationis*, the right of appealing from the magistrates to the Comitia when impeached of any crime involving life, personal freedom, or a permanent loss of political and social privileges.

The *Privata Iura* were comprehended under two heads:—
1. *Ius Connubii*, the right of contracting a regular marriage.
2. *Ius Commercii*, the right of acquiring, transferring, and holding property of all kinds according to the Roman laws.

Any one who was in full enjoyment of all these rights was a *Civis Optimo Iure*; and these rights, taken collectively, constituted the *Ius Civitatis* s. *Ius Quiritium*.[1]

It is evident from what has been said in the second chapter, that, in the earliest ages of the state, the Patricians alone were *Cives Optimo Iure*. The Plebeians did not enjoy the *Ius Suffragii* at all until included in the *Classes* of Servius Tullius. The *Ius Provocationis* was first bestowed upon them by the *Lex Valeria*, passed B.C. 509, immediately after the expulsion of the kings; they were not admitted to the *Ius Connubii* until after the passing of the *Lex Canuleia* in B.C. 445; and the *Ius Honorum* was not gained without many desperate struggles, which were not brought to a close until B.C. 367, when the consulship was thrown open by the *Lex Licinia*. Within a few years from that date, in B.C. 337, the last civil barrier between the Patricians and the Plebeians was broken down by the admission of the latter to the Praetorship, and in B.C. 300, the *Lex Ogulnia* threw open the priesthood also.[2]

Mode of acquiring the Ius Civitatis.—The *Ius Civitatis*, or, as it is very frequently termed, simply *Civitas*, was acquired in one of two ways—
1. By birth. 2. By gift. To these we might add, 3. By manumission, which we shall discuss under the head of slaves. (*Ut sit civis aut natus sit oportet aut factus.*)[3]

1. **Cives (Nati.)**—The child of two persons who could contract a regular marriage, (*iustum matrimonium*,) that is, who had reciprocally the *Ius Connubii*, was by birth a Roman citizen, provided both his parents possessed the *Ius Civitatis*. The position occupied by the children of parents who could not contract a regular marriage, in consequence of the absence of the *Ius Connubii*, will be explained fully when we treat of the law of marriage, (p. 250.)

2. **Cives (Facti.)**—Foreigners (*peregrini*) might receive the *Civitas* as a gift, (*dare civitatem—donare civitate*,) either individually or as members of a community. The power of conferring this gift, at the period when the *Civitas* belonged exclusively to the Patricians, seems to have been vested in the King, acting with the consent of the *Comitia Curiata*; and the rapid increase of Rome in the earliest epoch, must be in a great measure ascribed to the liberality with which this gift was bestowed,[4] numbers having been received freely into the

[1] A distinction was drawn by the lawyers of the empire between the *Ius Civitatis* and the *Ius Quiritium*; but it is uncertain, and of no practical importance in so far as the classical writers are concerned.
[2] We must bear in mind that a considerable portion of the community, although unquestionably members of the Roman state, and entitled to the appellation of *Cives*, were not *Cives Optimo iure*. No youth, until he was of age to serve in the army, could exercise the suffrage; and Roman women, although strictly *Cives Romanae*, were under no circumstances admitted to the *Ius Suffragii* nor to the *Ius Honorum*.
[3] Quintil. I. O. V. 10. § 65.
[4] Dionys. I. 9. Liv. IV. 4. Cic. pro. Balb. 13.

ranks of the Patricians, (*per cooptationem in patres*,) when the parties brought an accession of strength to the community. One of the most notable examples upon record was the admission of the whole Gens Claudia, six years after the expulsion of the kings.[1] As the power of Rome extended, the privileges conferred by *Civitas*, became more valued, were sought with eagerness and obtained with difficulty. It was bestowed chiefly as a reward for faithful and efficient services, sometimes on individuals, and occasionally on whole communities; but during the more flourishing period of the commonwealth, an express law, passed regularly by either the Tribes or the Centuries, was indispensable.[2] Towards the close of the republic, the people occasionally delegated this power to some of their favourite leaders, such as Marius and Pompeius, while Sulla and Cæsar, when they obtained unconstitutional supremacy, exercised it freely, and apparently without challenge;[3] but this was after the privilege had become less valuable, in consequence of the admission of all the Italian states at the close of the social war. Under the empire the power was assumed by the prince, and at length Caracalla bestowed the *Civitas* on all the free inhabitants of the Roman world.

Civitas sine Suffragio. Caerites.—It sometimes happened that the *Civitas* was bestowed upon a state, with a limitation excluding the *Ius Suffragii*, and, as a necessary consequence, the *Ius Honorum*. The first example of this on record was the honour conferred upon the inhabitants of Caere, in consequence of their having received and hospitably entertained the Vestal Virgins and their *Sacra* at the time when Rome was captured by the Gauls—*Primos autem municipes sine suffragii iure Caerites esse factos accepimus, concessumque illis ut civitatis Romanae honorem quidem caperent sed negotiis tamen atque oneribus vacarent pro sacris bello Gallico receptis custoditisque*[4]—and a similar distinction was granted to the Acerrani, B.C. 332.—*Romani facti Acerrani lege ab L. Papirio praetore lata qua civitas sine suffragio data.*[5]

Aerarii.—But although the gift of the *Civitas sine Suffragio* was a high compliment and a valuable privilege to the Caerites, it was, of course, a degradation for a *civis optimo iure* to be placed upon the same footing with them, since it implied the loss of an important portion of his rights. Hence, one of the modes in which the censors marked their displeasure towards a citizen, was by omitting his name from the roll of the Tribe or Century to which he belonged and entering it in a separate register. Those who in this manner were deprived of the *Ius Suffragii* were said *referri in tabulas Caeritum;* and Horace designates men of small worth as *Caerite cera digni*. The constitutional name for this class of persons was *Aerarii;* because, although reduced to an inferior position, they were still bound to contribute, as tax-payers, to the public treasury. The censors, when they inflicted this penalty, were technically said *referre aliquem in aerarios* s. *inter aerarios* s. *in numerum aerariorum;* and on the other hand, when they reinstated an *aerarius* in his former position, *eximere ex aerariis.*[6]

---

[1] Liv. II. 16. Suet. Tib. 1.
[2] Dionys. V. 40. Liv. III. 29. IV. 4. VIII. 11. Cic. pro Balb. 8. 9. 2. 3. 24.
[3] See Cic. pro Balb. 8. 20. 21. and indeed the whole speech, pro Arch. 10. ad Fam. XIII. 36. Dion Cass. XLI. 24.
[4] Aul. Gell. XVI. 13. The Schol. Cruq. on Hor. Epp. I. vi. 62. gives a somewhat different account. Compare also Liv. V. 50. VII. 19.
[5] Liv. VIII. 17.
[6] The account of the *aerarii* given above seems to be simple and rational; but our information on this topic is sadly defective. The chief authorities are, Pseud. Ascon. in Cic. divin. in Q. C. 3. Schol. Cruq. in Hor. Epp. I. vi. 62. Aul. Gell. XVI. 13. comp. Liv. IV. 24. XXIV 18. Cic. pro Cluent. 43. de Orat. 66. Val. Max. II. ix. 6. 7.

This leads us to consider generally the various ways in which the *Civitas* might be forfeited or impaired.

Caput. Status.—The *Caput* of an individual, in the legal phraseology of the Romans, denoted his personal privileges as a free man, as a member of a family, and as the possessor of certain political rights; his *Status* was the position which he occupied in the community in virtue of his *Caput*. Hence the expressions *Crimen Capitale*—*Iudicium Capitis*—*Poena Capitalis* do not necessarily imply a charge, a trial, or a penalty, in which the life of an individual was at stake, but one which involved the forfeiture or abridgment of his political and social rights. Any loss of this nature was termed *Deminutio Capitis*, and necessarily produced *Status Permutatio*.

The jurists distinguished three degrees—

1. *Deminutio Capitis maxima.* 2. *Deminutio Capitis minor.* 3. *Deminutio Capitis minima.*[1]

1. *Deminutio Capitis maxima* consisted in the loss of personal freedom, which implied the loss of *Civitas*, for a slave had no *Caput* and no *Status*. A Roman citizen might be sold into slavery for various offences connected with military discipline—for refusing to answer to his name when the consul was holding a levy[2]—for deserting to the enemy[3]–for mutilating himself in such a manner as to become incapable of serving.[4] Several instances occur in Roman history of Roman citizens being formally handed over by the *Pater Patratus* or chief of the *Fetiales* to an enemy, (*deditio per fetiales*,) in consequence of the state refusing to ratify the engagements which these persons had formed, or because they had been guilty of some breach of public faith;[5] and thus the community at large were supposed to be relieved from the sanctity of the obligation (*exsolvi religione*— *ut religione solvatur civitas.*)[6] A citizen might also be sold into slavery for wilfully avoiding enrolment in the censor's books, in order to escape taxation;[7] and, according to the laws of the XII Tables, an insolvent debtor was liable to the same penalty,[8] but this was abrogated by the *Lex Poetelia*.[9]

When a Roman citizen was solemnly given over to an enemy by the *Pater Patratus*, it would appear that he forfeited his rights irrecoverably; but if taken prisoner in the ordinary course of war, they were only suspended. So long as he remained in the hands of the enemy he was to all intents a slave; but if he was enabled to return home, in consequence of release or escape, he recovered his *Status*, by what, in legal language, was termed *Postliminium* or *Ius Postliminii*.[10]

2. *Deminutio Capitis minor* implied loss of the *Civitas*, or at least of the full *Civitas*, without loss of personal freedom. This might happen in various ways. A Roman citizen might, in order to gain certain advantages, become a member of a *Colonia Latina*, or of another state, in which cases he ceased, ipso facto, to be a Roman citizen, and enjoyed, in reference to Rome, only those rights which belonged to all the members of the community to which he attached himself.[11] When a Roman citizen wished to escape from the penalty incurred

---

[1] Our great authority here is Gaius, I. § 159—163, see also Ulpian. Dig. IV. v. 11.
[2] Varro ap. Non. s.v. *Nebulones* et *Tenebriones*, p. 11. ed. Gerl.
[3] Liv. Epit. LV.
[4] Val. Max. VI. iii. 3. Suet. Octav. 24.
[5] e.g. Liv. Epit. XV. XXXVIII. 42. Epit. LVI. Val. Max. VI. iii. 3. VL vi. 3. VI. vi. 5.
[6] Cic. pro Caec. 34. de Orat. I. 40.
[7] Cic. pro Caec. 34. comp. Liv. I. 44.
[8] Aul. Gell. XX. i. 47.
[9] Liv. VIII. 28.
[10] Cic. Top. 8. de Orat. I. 40. Dig. XLIX. xv. 5.
[11] Cic. pro Balb. 13. pro Caec. 33.

by conviction in a criminal trial or otherwise, he betook himself to some foreign country, in which case he was said *mutare solum—vertere solum—ire exsulatum —ire in exsilium*—and his return was prevented by an order of the people, prohibiting him from the use of fire and water, (*aquae et ignis interdictio,*) so that he virtually forfeited all his political privileges as a Roman citizen, since he could have no opportunity of exercising them; he did not cease, however, to be a Roman citizen, unless he procured admission into another state; but if the interdiction was removed, (*ex exsilio revocare,*) he might return and resume his former position. Thus, *Exsilium* is said by Cicero to be unknown in Roman law as the name of a punishment—*exsilium enim non supplicium est sed perfugium portusque supplicii, nam qui volunt poenam aliquam subterfugere aut calamitatem, eo solum vertunt, hoc est, sedem ac locum mutant*—and so far it is true that sentence of *Exsilium* was never passed; but the going into banishment was a voluntary act, although followed up by measures which rendered absence compulsory.[1] Under the empire, however, two forms of banishment, in the ordinary acceptation of the term, were introduced, and became common. These were *Relegatio* and *Deportatio*. *Relegatio* consisted in simply sending away an offender from Rome to some place more or less distant, where he was compelled to remain, enjoying, however, personal freedom, and retaining his *Civitas*. There was in this case no *aquae et ignis interdictio*, and hence, probably, the position of a *relegatus* was nominally better than that of an *exsul*; for Ovid, when speaking of his own banishment to Tomi, and praising the clemency of the emperor, declares (Trist. V. xi. 21.)

> Ipse relegati non exsulis utitur in me
> Nomine . . . .

Deportatio, on the other hand, although it did not reduce the criminal to the condition of a slave, was accompanied with personal restraint, for he was usually conveyed to one of the small rocky islets off the coast of Italy, or in the Aegean, which were in reality state prisons.

3. *Deminutio Capitis minima* was in no way connected with *Libertas* or *Civitas*, but resulted in certain cases from a change of family (*mutatio familiae*.) Thus, a citizen who was his own master, (*sui iuris,*) if adopted into another family, became subject to parental authority (*patria potestas*.) There were other procedures which involved the lowest *Deminutio Capitis*, some of them depending upon mere legal fictions, but these do not require notice here.

Infamia.—Closely connected in its results, but not identical with *Capitis Deminutio minor*, was the state called *Infamia*. If a Roman citizen was found guilty of a crime which involved personal turpitude, (*turpi iudicio damnatus,*) although the legal penalty might be only a pecuniary fine, such as theft, (*furtum,*) wilful fraud, (*dolus malus,*) assault or libel, (*iniuria,*) of an aggravated description, or if he followed any disgraceful occupation, such as the profession of an actor or of a gladiator, he became, in the eye of the law, *Infamis*, and incapable of holding any honourable office—*turpi iudicio damnati omni honore ac dignitate privantur*[2]—although it cannot be proved, as some celebrated scholars maintain, that he forfeited the *Ius Suffragii*.

Ignominia, again, was the result of the expressed disapprobation of the Censors, and persons who incurred their censure were said to be *ignominia notati*. This, in certain cases involved the loss of the *Ius Suffragii;* but, as we shall explain

[1] Cic. pro Caec. 34. Orat. pro dom. 30.
[2] Cic. pro Cluent. 42. comp. pro Sull. 31. 32.

fully when treating of the office of Censor, the effects produced were only temporary, while in the case of *Infamia* they were permanent.

PEREGRINI.

The term *Peregrinus*, with which in early times *Hostis* (i.e. stranger) was synonymous, embraced, in its widest acceptation, every one possessed of personal freedom who was not a *Civis Romanus*.

Generally, however, *Peregrinus* was not applied to all foreigners indiscriminately, but to those persons only, who, although not *Cives*, were connected with Rome. Thus, during that period of the republic which preceded the organic changes introduced by the social war, the term comprehended—

1. All the free inhabitants of Italy who did not enjoy *Commercium* and *Connubium* with Rome.
2. All the free subjects of Rome in the provinces, including persons belonging by birth to foreign states, but who had settled in the dominions of Rome.
3. All the free subjects of states in alliance with Rome.
4. All Romans who had either temporarily or permanently forfeited the *Civitas*.

Persons who belonged to states at war with Rome, or to states which had no league or connection with Rome, were not properly styled *Peregrini*, but either *Hostes*, or *Barbari*, as the case might be.

After the termination of the social war, all the inhabitants of Italy became *Cives Romani*, and the term *Peregrini* was confined to those included in the last three of the above classes.

Peregrini resident at Rome were incapable of exercising any political functions, and, in the eye of the law, had no civil rights. Hence—

1. They had no *locus standi* in a court of law, and could be heard only when represented by a *patronus*, under whose protection they had placed themselves, (*cui sese applicuissent*,)[1] like the Clients of the early ages, who appear to have occupied, with regard to the Patricians, a position in many respects analogous to that in which, at a later period, the Peregrini stood in reference to the citizens at large. But although formally excluded from the courts in their own person, Peregrini had no difficulty, during the last two centuries of the republic at least, in obtaining redress for their wrongs; for, as we shall see hereafter, a judge (*Praetor peregrinus*) and a court of commissioners (*Recuperatores*) were appointed for the special purpose of taking cognizance of those suits in which their interests were involved.

2. They were prohibited from wearing the *Toga*, the national Roman dress.[2] The object of this restriction was probably to prevent foreigners from fraudulently intruding themselves into the assemblies of the people and exercising the franchise.[3]

3. They could be expelled from Rome as often as seemed good to the Senate or people.[4] The object of this rule may have been to prevent them from taking part in any popular commotions.

Peregrini dediticii, a term to which we must recur, denoted properly the inhabitants of a foreign state, who, having been conquered in war, surrendered at discretion.

Hospitium. Hospes.—We may take this opportunity of adverting to a bond

---
[1] Cic. de Orat. I. 39.
[2] Plin. Epp. IV. 11.
[3] Dionys. VIII. 72. Plut. C. Gracch. 12. Appian. B.C. I. 23.
[4] Cic. de Off. III. 11. Appian. l.c.

of union which frequently subsisted in ancient times between individuals belonging to different states, and which is so often alluded to in the classical writers that it calls for explanation. In the earlier stages of society, especially in Greece and Italy, where the population consisted of numerous independent tribes constantly at variance with each other, every stranger was looked upon with suspicion, as likely to prove an enemy or a spy, and even in those cases where the personal safety of a traveller was not endangered, he must have found it difficult to supply his wants or procure shelter, in consequence of the absence of all places of public entertainment. Hence, it became common for a person who was engaged in commerce, or any other occupation which might compel him to visit a foreign country, to form previously a connection with a citizen of that country, who might be ready to receive him as a friend and act as his protector. Such a connection was always strictly reciprocal. If A agreed to entertain and protect B when B visited A's country, then B became bound to entertain A when A visited B's country. An alliance of this description was termed *Hospitium*, the parties who concluded it were termed *Hospites* in relation to each other, and thus the word *Hospes* bore a double signification, denoting, according to circumstances, either *an entertainer* or *a guest*. The obligations imposed by the covenant were regarded as of the most sacred character, and any treachery practised by one of the parties towards the other (*sacra hospitii temerare*) was deemed sacrilege of the worst kind, entailing upon the perpetrator the direct wrath of *Jupiter Hospitalis*, the special guardian of these mutual duties, and their avenger when violated. One of the parties might, however, break off and terminate the *Hospitium* by a solemn and public renunciation, (*hospitium renunciare,*) of which we have a curious example in Liv. XXV. 18.

The league of *Hospitium*, when once formed, was hereditary, descending from father to son, (*paternum hospitium,*) so that persons might be *hospites* who had not only never seen each other, but whose ancestors, for generations, might have had no direct intercourse. In order to prevent confusion, suspicion, and fraud, when the alliance was in the first instance concluded, the parties interchanged tokens, by which they or their descendants might recognise each other. This token, called *tessera hospitalis*, was carefully preserved; and after any lapse of time an individual claiming the rights of *Hospitium* in a foreign land, sought out his *Hospes* and exhibited his *tessera*, which, if found correct, entitled him at once to the good offices which he required. We have an excellent illustration of the manner in which the system worked presented to us in the Poenulus of Plautus, where a Carthaginian merchant, Hanno by name, arriving at Calydon in Ætolia, inquires for his *Hospes*, whom he had never seen—

> Verum ego hospitium hic habeo: Anthidamae filium
> Quaero: commostra si novisti Agorastoclem.

It happens that Agorastocles, the person sought, is actually present, and upon his making himself known, the following dialogue ensues:—

> HANNO.—Si ita est, tesseram
> Conferre si vis hospitalem, eccam, attuli.
> AGOR.—Agedum huc ostende: est par probe: nam habeo domi.
> HAN.—O mi hospes, salve multum! nam mihi tuus pater,
> Pater tuus ergo, hospes Anthidamas fuit:
> Haec mihi hospitalis tessera cum illo fuit.
> AGOR.—Ergo hic apud me hospitium tibi praebebitur
> Nam haud repudio hospitium.[1]

[1] Plaut. Poen. V. ii. 82.

Hospitium appears to have been originally confined to individuals, and to have been purely a private compact for mutual convenience; but in process of time, among both the Greeks and Romans, it became common for a state, when it desired to pay a marked compliment to any individual, to pass a resolution declaring him the *Hospes* of the whole community. Such a person was termed *Hospes Publicus*. Thus, Cicero tells us (In Verr. IV. 65.) that the Senate of Syracuse conferred this honour on his cousin Lucius—*Decernunt statim ut cum L. fratre hospitium publice fieret*, and again (Pro Balb. 18.) *Gaditani cum L. Cornelio hospitium publice fecerunt*. So also the Rhodian ambassadors, in their speech to the Roman Senate, (B.C. 189. Liv. XXXVII. 54.) explain the position in which they stood towards Eumenes by stating, *cum quo uno maxime regum et privatum singulis, et, quod magis nos movet, publicum civitati nostrae hospitium est*.

It is almost unnecessary to point out that *Hospes* and *Hospitium* are perpetually employed in a general sense by the best writers, the former denoting *a stranger*, or *a guest*, or *an entertainer*, the latter *the reception or entertainment of strangers or guests*, or *a place of entertainment or shelter*, without reference to the technical meaning. So also the adjective *Hospitalis*.

LATINI.

It is well known that towards the close of the kingly era, Rome stood at the head of the Latin confederation; and although even then *Connubium* did not exist between Rome and the Latin states, they must have had certain reciprocal rights and privileges, amounting probably to *Commercium*. After Rome had ceased to be recognised as the head of the Latin confederation, and an unbroken series of wars had removed all traces of ancient friendship, the various Latin towns and states, as they one by one fell under the sway of Rome, were admitted into alliance (*recepti in societatem*) on terms which differed for almost every individual community. Hence, during the more flourishing epoch of the republic, the term *Latini* is employed merely to describe those inhabitants of Latium who were not Roman citizens, and does not denote any uniform standard of rights nor any definite political position. But after the whole of Italy had received the *Civitas*, at the close of the social war, the term *Latini* was introduced by jurists to denote the inhabitants of states who were not Roman citizens, but who enjoyed certain privileges, short of the full *Civitas*, in virtue of which they occupied a position intermediate between *Cives* and *Peregrini*. What these privileges were is a question which has given rise to much discussion; but it seems probable that they comprehended the *Iura Privata*, that is the *Ius Connubii* and the *Ius Commercii*, to the exclusion of the *Iura Publica*.

The term employed to designate these rights was *Ius Latii* or *Latinitas*, (Cic. ad Att. xiv. 12.) or simply *Latium*, for Pliny (H.N. III. 20.) mentions certain Alpine tribes as *Latio donati*.

The *Ius Latii* was bestowed, soon after the social war, upon all the Trans padani, and by Vespasian upon all Spain (Plin. H.N. III. 4.)

Closely connected with the subjects which we have been discussing in the preceding paragraphs, is the political position of those towns which were designated respectively by the terms *Coloniae—Municipia—Praefecturae*, and these we shall consider in succession.

COLONIAE.[1]

As the Romans gradually extended their conquests over Italy, each state which had offered a determined resistance to their arms, was, when subjugated, generally deprived of a portion of its territory. A part of the territory thus acquired was usually retained, under the administration of the Senate, as a source of revenue, and another portion was frequently divided among the poorer Roman citizens, who quitted Rome, established themselves in the chief town of the conquered country, and took possession, as cultivators, (whence the name *coloni*,) of the land assigned to them. A settlement of this kind was called a *Colonia*, and these being spread every where over the conquered districts, answered many important purposes. They served to keep the vanquished races in check, and were in reality so many permanent posts of occupation, or, as Livy and Cicero term them, garrisons, fortifications, and watch towers (*praesidia—propugnacula—speculae*.) They, at the same time, tended to diffuse widely the language, laws and institutions of Rome, and to pave the way for a general amalgamation. They were excellent nurseries for hardy and well trained soldiers, and, finally, they provided an outlet for the more needy portion of a rapidly increasing population. Indeed, in later times, after Italy and Cisalpine Gaul had been completely subdued, colonies were very frequently formed with no other object than to make a provision for a poor and discontented populace; and on many occasions, when there was no newly acquired territory available, a portion of the *Ager Publicus*, or land which was the property of the state, was given up. To this part of the subject we shall return when treating of the Agrarian Laws.

When it had been resolved to plant a colony, (*coloniam deducere*,) a law was passed in accordance with a resolution of the Senate, (*ex senatus consulto*,) fixing the quantity of land to be set apart, and the manner in which it was to be divided. This law served as the foundation charter, (*formula*,) and specified, among other matters, the burdens to be borne by the colonists, and especially the contingent of troops which they were to become bound to furnish. At the same time, commissioners, (*curatores*,) two or more in number (*duumviri, triumviri agro dando—coloniae deducendae agroque dividundo*,) were nominated to lead forth the settlers, and to make all the arangements necessary for carrying into effect the provisions of the law. These were generally persons of high standing; they were elected by the people in the Comitia, and their office lasted for three and sometimes for five years,[2] during which period they exercised supreme jurisdiction.

Those who were desirous to join the settlement were invited to give in their names, (*dare nomina*,) and when the list was filled up and all the preliminaries arranged, the whole body marched forth in military array, with colours flying, (*sub vexillo*,)[3] to take possession of their new homes. When no city or fortified place already existed which they could occupy, a new town was founded with all the solemnities already described; (p. 4;) and one of the most common devices upon colonial coins is a representation of the founder tracing out the walls or the boundaries of the city with the plough.

---

[1] Consult Sigonius, De Antiquo iure Italiae, in the Thesaurus of Graevius; Heyne, Opuscula, Tom. I. p. 290. Tom. III. p. 79; Madvig, De coloniarum P.R. iure et conditione, in his Opuscula Academica; and Rein, s.v. *Colonia*, in the Encyclopaedie der Alterthumswissenschaft.
[2] Liv. XXXII. 29. XXXIV. 53. Cic. de leg. agr. II. 11. 13.
[3] Cic. Phil. II. 40. de leg. agr. II. 32.

Colonies, in so far as their political privileges were concerned, were divided into two classes—
1. *Coloniae civium Romanorum.* 2. *Coloniae Latinae.*

1. *Coloniae civium Romanorum* consisted exclusively of Roman citizens (*coloni ab urbe missi*) who retained all their rights and privileges. The colonies first planted were of this description, such as Velitrae and Lavici—*Volscis devictis Veliternus ager ademtus: Velitras coloni ab urbe missi et colonia deducta.* (Liv. II. 31.) *Senatus censuit frequens coloniam Lavicos deducendam: coloni ab urbe mille et quingenti missi bina iugera acceperunt.* (Liv. IV. 47.)

The *Coloniae Maritimae* belonged to this class, being colonies of Roman citizens, and were distinguished only by their position on the sea coast, and by some peculiar exemptions which the inhabitants (*coloni maritimi*) enjoyed or claimed. (Liv. XXVII. 38. XXXVI. 3.) Ostia, Antium, Anxur, Minturnae, Sinuessa, and several others were maritime colonies.

2. *Coloniae Latinae* consisted of a mixed body of Romans and members of some of the Latin states. In this case, the Roman citizens who joined such a community suffered a *deminutio capitis*, and lost the full *civitas*; for these colonies had only *Commercium* and *Connubium* with Rome, but not *Suffragium*.[1] Bononia was a colony of this description—*Eodem anno* [B.C. 189.] *a. d. III. Kal. Ian. Bononiam Latinam coloniam ex senatus consulto L. Valerius Flaccus, M. Atilius Serranus, L. Valerius Tappus triumviri deduxerunt: tria millia hominum sunt deducta: equitibus septuagena iugera, ceteris colonis quinquagena sunt data. Ager captus de Gallis Boiis fuerat: Galli Tuscos expulerant.* (Liv. XXXVII. 57.)

Both alike had a regular government for the administration of justice, and the regulation of their internal affairs, which was an imitation, on a small scale, of the government at Rome—(*effigies parvae simulacraque populi Romani*—Aul. Gell. XVI. 13.) They had a senate, the members of which were termed *Decuriones* or *Senatores.* Their chief magistrates, usually two in number, but sometimes four, and hence styled *Duumviri* or *Quatuorviri*, were elected annually by the colonists, and might be regarded as representing the consuls of the republic, and, in fact, were in some colonies designated *Consules*, and in others *Praetores.* There were also various subordinate magistrates, such as *Quinquennales*, corresponding to Censors; *Aediles, Quaestores*, and others. Not only their laws but their sacred rites were those of Rome, and therefore the ministers of religion were *Pontifices, Flamines* and *Augures*, as in the mother city—*Iura institutaque omnia populi Romani non sui arbitrii habent.* (Aul. Gell. XVI. 13.)

When a colony was established in a town already existing, the population must have consisted of two distinct classes. 1. The new *coloni.* 2. The old inhabitants. How far the latter shared the privileges of the former it is impossible to determine; but we cannot doubt that they occupied an inferior position, and were compelled to exchange their own laws and institutions for those of their rulers. In process of time, however, a certain degree of fusion would take place, and in some cases we find that the union became so close that the combined population revolted and attempted to throw off the Roman yoke. (Liv. VIII. 14.)

After the termination of the social war and the passing of the *Lex Iulia* and the *Lex Plautia Papiria*, the distinctions between the *Coloniae civium Romanorum* and the *Coloniae Latinae*, as well as any inequality in the social and

---

[1] Cic. pro Caec. 33. Orat. pro dom. 30. Liv. XXXIV. 42. 53. XXXV. 9. XXXIX. 55.

political position of the different races in the same colony, were completely removed, in so far as Italy was concerned, and all alike were admitted to a full participation in the rights and privileges of Roman citizens, and the same advantages were gradually extended to the colonies in the provinces, until, by the edict of Caracalla, the full *Civitas* was bestowed on all the free inhabitants of the Roman empire.

Coloniae Militares.—Although the colonies described above were highly serviceable in a military point of view, they differed in their origin from the *Coloniae Militares*, which were composed entirely of veterans, who received allotments of land as a reward for their services. The first example of a colony of this description was the grant to the soldiers who, under the command of Scipio, brought the second Punic war to a happy conclusion; but the practice did not become common until towards the close of the republic, from which time forward it was the ordinary mode of providing for the legionaries whose period of service had expired (Tacit. Ann. I. 17. XIV. 27.) The oppression and misery to which these distributions gave rise during the civil wars of Marius, Sulla, Cæsar, and the Triumvirs, are familiar to every reader of history; and the downfal of the republic was certainly hastened by the estrangement of Pompeius from the Senate, caused by the opposition which they offered to his scheme of dividing the public land in Campania among the soldiers who had served under his command in the East.

After the accession of Augustus, the military colonies were planted in the provinces as a matter of necessity, and not unfrequently on the disturbed frontiers as a matter of policy.

Finally, it is to be remarked, that under the empire, various provincial towns were permitted, as a mark of favour, to style themselves *Coloniae*, the word, when thus employed, being merely a complimentary title.

MUNICIPIA.[1]

Many towns in Italy, especially in the immediate vicinity of Rome, formed, at a very early period, an alliance with Rome, upon terms of perfect equality; (*foedus aequum;*) many others submitted to the Roman arms without a struggle, or yielded after a slight resistance, or succeeded after a protracted contest, in securing an honourable treaty. The whole of these were comprehended under the general name of *Municipia*, and their inhabitants were designated as *Municipes*, words compounded of *Munia* and *Capere*. Two characteristics were common to all Municipia—

1. The inhabitants of a *Municipium*, if they came to reside at Rome, were liable to the same obligations and burdens (*munia*) as ordinary Roman citizens, and hence the name.

2. The *Municipes* themselves administered the internal affairs of their own town.

Eventually, all the states of Italy which were not absolutely annihilated in war, or held in check by colonies, or actually incorporated with and swallowed up by Rome, so as to lose all independent existence, (such as Aricia—Caere— Anagnia,) entered into an alliance (*foedus*) of some sort with Rome. The terms of this league would necessarily vary according to the circumstances of each

---

[1] Consult Dirksen, Observ. ad Tab. Heracl. Berol. 1817. Zumpt, Ueber die Römische Ritter, &c. Berol. 1840. Walther, Geschichte des Römischen Rechts, Kap. VII—X. XX. XXIV. Grauer, De re Municipal. Rom. 1840. Fest. s.v. *Municeps*, p. 131. 142. Paul. Diac. s.v. *Municipium*, p. 127.

individual case; and a multitude of minute distinctions and gradations would and did prevail in their position relatively to the ruling power. The same state might, moreover, occupy a very different position at different periods in consequence of receiving additional privileges as a reward of fidelity, or in consequence of being deprived of former advantages as a punishment for disaffection or revolt. Of the latter we have a conspicuous example in Capua.

Although it is now impossible to ascertain what these distinctions may have been in each particular case, we can, at all events, divide *Municipia* into three well defined classes.

1. *Municipia* enjoying Isopolity. In these there was simply an alliance on equal terms between Rome and one of the neighbouring towns, in virtue of which *Connubium* and *Commercium* were established, so that intermarriage was freely allowed; and if a citizen of one of the two states forming the league took up his residence in the other, he enjoyed all the privileges of a native, in so far as private rights were concerned, but was excluded from the popular assemblies and from all share in the government. This relation is very similar to what the Greeks termed ἰσοπολιτεία, and hence the name given above, which has been adopted by many modern scholars as convenient and appropriate. To this class belonged the *Municipia* of the earliest period, and in it were included the Latin and Hernican towns, with which Rome formed a very close connection in the treaties concluded by Sp. Cassius, B.C. 485, and B.C. 479. But after the great Latin war, (B.C. 340,) quickly followed by the complete subjugation of Latium, this class of Municipia may be said to have disappeared altogether, and the Isopolite treaties to have been cancelled; for although some towns may have nominally retained their former position, their most important privilege, namely, independence in their foreign relations, was now lost; and from this time forward all *Municipia*, however favourable the terms of their alliance, were in reality the subjects of Rome, and necessarily belonged to one or other of the two following divisions:—

2. *Municipia sine Suffragio.* [1]—These enjoyed *Connubium* and *Commercium* with Rome, but could not vote in the popular assemblies, nor be elected to any political office in the city. They retained the internal regulation of their own affairs, which were administered by a senate, (*decuriones*,) elected their own magistrates, administered justice according to their own local laws and usages, (*leges municipales*,) and worshipped what divinities they pleased according to their own rites (*municipalia sacra*.)

3. *Municipia cum Suffragio* enjoyed the same privileges as the foregoing, with this addition, that all the *Municipes* were enrolled in a Roman tribe, and accordingly, when resident at Rome, were *Cives Romani optimo iure*. To this class belonged Tusculum and Arpinum; the inhabitants of the former were enrolled in the *Tribus Papiria*, of the latter in the *Tribus Cornelia*. (Liv. VIII. 37. XXXVIII. 36.)

It is a matter of some doubt whether the Municipia belonging to this class were not compelled to adopt the Roman laws, to the exclusion of their own provincial codes. It is certain that some did, although this may have been a voluntary act, and it is clear that all Municipia must have been bound by all laws enacted at Rome which did not refer to mere local interests.

The inhabitants of *Municipia cum Suffragio* being all enrolled in Roman tribes, would be liable to pay taxes and to serve as soldiers in the legion on

See Liv. IX. 43. 45.

the same footing as citizens actually residing in Rome, while the obligations imposed upon the other Municipia were determined by the stipulations contained in their treaties of alliance, (*ex foedere*,) and those of the colonies by their foundation charter (*ex formula*.) Hence, the *Municipia sine Suffragio* seem to have been comprehended under the general title of *Civitates Foederatae* or *Populi Foederati.*[1]

Municipia after the Social War.—With the *Lex Iulia* and the *Lex Plautia Papiria*, both passed immediately after the social war, a new era commenced in the history of the *Municipia*. All the cities in Italy now became *Municipia cum Suffragio*; and the distinctions between *Municipia* and *Coloniae* were, in a great measure, removed. Thus, we find Placentia, Cremona, Suessa, Thurii,[2] and many other colonies styled *Municipia* after this epoch; and although the term *Colonia* was still applied to towns in Italy even subsequent to the reign of Augustus, it was more usually employed with reference to the provincial colonies. In process of time, many cities in foreign countries, especially in Spain, were raised to the rank of *Municipia*,[3] until, by the edict of Caracalla, bestowing the *Civitas* upon the whole of the free inhabitants of the Roman world, the privileges implied by the name were extended to all.

Populi Fundi.—It would appear that the *Lex Iulia* merely offered the full *Civitas* to those towns in Italy which chose to accept of it; and when the offer was accepted the inhabitants were said to become *fundi*, (i.e. *auctores*,) to become parties to the law in question, and hence the term *Populi Fundi*. To this Cicero alludes when he says—*accusator . . . negat, ex foederato populo, quemquam potuisse,* NISI IS POPULUS FUNDUS FACTUS ESSET, *in hanc civitatem venire*. And again—*Ipsa denique Iulia, qua lege civitas est Sociis et Latinis data,* QUI FUNDI POPULI FACTI NON ESSENT, *civitatem non haberent. In quo magna contentio Heracliensium et Neapolitanorum fuit, cum magna pars in iis civitatibus foederis sui libertatem civitati anteferret.*[4]

PRAEFECTURAE.[5]

The characteristic of a *Praefectura*, from which it received its name, and by which it was distinguished from an ordinary *Colonia* or *Municipium*, was, that the chief magistrate was not chosen by the citizens of the town, but that a PRAEFECTUS *iuri dicundo* was sent annually from Rome to administer justice—a circumstance which seems to indicate that in such towns Roman law was employed exclusively, since a Roman officer, appointed annually, could scarcely have been qualified to decide controversies according to the principles and practice of a provincial code. The definition given by Festus is clear and satisfactory—*Praefecturae eae appellabantur in Italia in quibus et ius dicebatur et nundinae agebantur et erat quaedam earum res publica, neque tamen magistratus suos habebant: in quas his legibus praefecti mittebantur quotannis qui ius dicerent.*[6] Consequently, all towns in Italy which did not enjoy the privilege of electing their own magistrates and administering their own affairs, would fall under the head of *Praefecturae*. But although this seems unquestionable, there appears to

---

[1] See particularly Liv. IX. 43. 45.
[2] Cic. in Pison. 23. Philipp. XIII. 8. Tacit. Hist. III. 34. Caes. B.C. III. 22.
[3] These provincial Municipia were unknown in Greece and Asia, where all the principal towns had ancient constitutions.
[4] Cic. pro Balb. 8.
[5] Savigny, in his *Geschichte des Roemischen Rechts*, &c. first pointed out the true nature of a *Praefectura*. See also Sigonius, *De antiquo iure Italiae*; Madvig, in his *Opuscula Academica*; and Zumpt l.c.
[6] Festus s.v. *Praefecturae*, p. 233.

be no good grounds for the conclusion at which all the earlier writers on Roman antiquities have arrived, that a *Prefectura* was necessarily in a position far inferior to a *Colonia* or a *Municipium*. It is true that Capua, the example upon which they chiefly rely, was made a *Praefectura*, when recovered after its revolt to Hannibal; and it is evident, that when a *Colonia* or a *Municipium* was, as a punishment, deprived of the right of administering its internal affairs, it must have become a Praefectura. Thus, when after the revolt and capture of Privernum, (Liv. VIII. 19-21,) the inhabitants became Roman citizens, we cannot doubt that they lost all right of internal government, and that their town became a *Praefectura*; and something of the same kind took place with regard to Arpagnia (Liv. IX. 43.) But, on the other hand, it is equally certain that many towns were Praefecturae which never incurred the displeasure of the Romans, and which could not be regarded as holding a degraded or inferior position. Volturnum, Liternum, and Puteoli in Campania were all *Coloniae civium Romanorum*, and, at the same time, *Praefecturae*. In like manner, Fundi, Formiae, and Arpinum are included in the list of Praefecturae; but these were at first *Municipia sine Suffragio*—they then became *Municipia cum Suffragio*, and may very possibly have passed into *Praefecturae* when they adopted fully the Roman code. In like manner, we shall find in Festus several towns specified as Praefecturae which are elsewhere mentioned as Municipia, some with and some without the Suffragium. Moreover, although all towns which possessed no independent jurisdiction were Praefecturae, it by no means follows that all Praefecturae had entirely forfeited internal jurisdiction: the only fact indicated by the name being, that the chief magistrate was a Praefectus, sent from Rome instead of the Duumviri, Quatuorviri, Consules or Praetores of ordinary Municipia and Coloniae. We may conclude, therefore, as in the case of Municipia, that the term Praefectura includes a wide range, and that the actual condition of the towns where justice was administered by Praefecti would depend entirely upon their history.

We gather from the passage in Festus already referred to, that there were ten Praefecturae in Campania, and that, for the administration of justice in these, four Praefecti were appointed annually by the Roman people; while the Praefecti for the other Praefecturae scattered over Italy, were nominated annually by the *Praetor Urbanus*.

After the passing of the *Lex Iulia* and the *Lex Plautia Papiria*, all Praefecturae in Italy, as well as the Municipia and Coloniae, received the full Civitas. Great changes were necessarily introduced, at this period, into the internal administration of the provincial towns; and although many retained their ancient title of Praefecturae, they were no longer under the jurisdiction of Praefecti. The magistrates of Arpinum, in the time of Cicero, were *Triumviri aediliciae potestatis*;[1] those of Cumae, *Quatuorviri*;[2] while Horace speaks of a *Praetor* at Fundi;[3] yet all of these at an earlier period were Praefecturae.

Oppida. Fora. Conciliabula. Vici. Castella.—Each of the *Coloniae Municipia* and *Praefecturae*, was, for the most part, the metropolis of a considerable district, which contained numerous small market towns and hamlets, distinguished by one or other of the above names; and these occupied the same dependent position, with regard to their own Municipium or Colonia, which the villages round Rome occupied in regard to the great city.

[1] Cic. ad Fam. XIII. 11. Val. Max. VI. ix. 14.
[2] Cic. ad Att. X. 13. the words, however, are not quite distinct.
[3] Hor. S. I. v. 34.

Socii. Nomen Latinum.—During the period which intervened between the complete subjugation of Italy and the social war, the citizens of all those Italian states whose members did not enjoy the full Roman *Civitas*, were comprehended under the general appellation of *Socii*, a term subsequently applied to the subjects of Rome in the provinces also. In consequence, however, of the close connection which had subsisted from the earliest times between Rome and the Latin confederacy, the citizens of the towns who formed that league, and of the *Coloniae Latinae*, are sometimes distinguished from the rest of the *Socii* as *Latini*—*Socii Latini*—*Nomen Latinum*—*Socii Latini nominis*, and must be carefully distinguished from the members of those states who, *after* the social war, enjoyed the legal rights designated as **Ius Latii**—*Latinitas*—*Latium*. See above p. 87.

Having now taken a rapid view of the position occupied by the different classes of persons subject to the dominion of Rome, in so far as *Ingenui* are concerned, we proceed to consider the condition of those who were either actually in slavery, (*servi*,) or who, having been once slaves, had obtained their freedom, (*libertini*,) reserving all farther observations with regard to the free inhabitants of the Roman provinces, until we shall have given an account of the Roman magistrates.

SERVI.[1]

A slave, when regarded as a person bound to obey the commands of a master, was called *Servus*; when regarded as a piece of property, *Mancipium*; when regarded as a saleable commodity, *Venalis*; when regarded as a domestic, *Famulus* or *Puer*; but these words, in ordinary language, were considered interchangeable, and were employed without distinction. The whole body of slaves in one mansion was comprehended under the designation *Familia*. One slave, however, did not constitute a *familia*, nor even two, but fifteen certainly did—*Quindecim liberi homines, populus est: totidem servi, familia; totidem vincti, ergastulum*; but the term may be applied to a smaller number, as by Seneca, to a body of eleven.[2]

Persons might become slaves in different ways—they might be born in the servile state, or, having been born free, might be made slaves—(*servi aut nascuntur aut fiunt*)—

1. *By Birth.*—The child of a female slave (*ancilla*) was a slave, whatever might be the condition of the father, and belonged to the master of the mother. It was held, however, by the lawyers of the empire, that if the mother of a child, although in slavery at the period of its birth, had been free for any time, however short, during the ten months which preceded its birth, then the child was to be regarded as free born (*ingenuus*.) A slave born in the house of his master was called *Verna*.[3]

2. *By Captivity.*—Prisoners of war (*captivi*—*bello capti*) were, by the ancient law of nations, the absolute property of the captors, and, as such, were

---

[1] Full information with regard to slavery among the Romans at all periods of their history, will be found in the following works:—PIGNORIUS, De Servis et eorum apud veteres ministeriis. POPMA, De operis Servorum. GORI, Columbarium Libertorum et Servorum Liviae Augustae. BLAIR, An inquiry into the state of slavery among the Romans, Edinb. 1833. BECKER, Gallus, dritter Excurs. zur I. Scene. GESSNER, De Servis Romanorum publicis, Berol. 1814. The three first mentioned tracts will be found in the Supplement of Polenus to the Thesaurus of Graevius.

[2] Cic. pro Caecin. 19. Digest. L. xvi. 40. Apulei. Apolog. 482. Senec. Epp. 27.

[3] Cic. de N. D. III. 18. Digest. I. v. 5. XL. ii. 19. Instit. I. 3. 4. For some modifications, see Tacit. Ann. XII. 53. Suet. Vesp. 11. Gaius I. § 82—86. Ulpian. fragm. V. 9.

either retained for the service of the state, and employed in public works, or were sold by auction. The practice, in early times, was to expose captives for sale with chaplets round their heads, and hence the phrase, *sub corona vendere s. venire*, i.e. to sell, or to be sold, for a slave. The chaplet indicated that the seller gave no warranty (*id autem signum est nihil praestari a populo.*) [1]

3. **By Judicial Sentence.**—In certain cases freeborn Roman citizens were condemned to be sold as slaves, as a punishment for heinous offences. See above, under *Capitis deminutio maxima*, p. 83.

Condition of a Slave.—A slave had no personal nor political rights. He was under the absolute power (*dominium—potestas dominica*) of his master, (*dominus,*) who could scourge, brand, torture, or put him to death at pleasure. Under the republic there was no restriction whatsoever placed on the caprice or cruelty of masters, except the force of public opinion. An attempt was made by the emperor Claudius to put a stop to some revolting barbarities in relation to the exposure of sick slaves; but it was not until the reign of Hadrian that a master was forbidden to put his slave to death, unless condemned by a court of justice— an ordinance confirmed and enforced by Antoninus Pius. [2] The *Lex Petronia*, of uncertain date, but probably belonging to the reign of Augustus, in terms of which, a master was prohibited from compelling his slave to fight with wild beasts, seems to have been the first legislative enactment of a protective character. [3]

Contubernium.—A slave could not contract a regular marriage; but any connection which he might form with one of his own class, was termed *Contubernium*. [4] The offspring of these alliances were the *Vernae*.

Names given to Slaves.—A slave was named according to the fancy of his master, not in the Roman fashion, however, with Praenomen and Nomen, but from his country, or some other characteristic, or in many cases the name was altogether fanciful. Hence such appellations as *Syrus*, *Phryx*, *Geta*, *Afer*, *Tiro*, *Davus*, *Dama*, *Castor*, *Croesus*, &c. In the earlier ages, they seem to have received a designation from the name of their masters, thus, *Marcipor*, (i.e. *Marci puer,*) *Quintipor*, (i.e. *Quinti puer,*) *Lucipor*, (i.e. *Lucî puer.*) See Quintil. I. O. 1. 4. § 7. Plin. H.N. XXXIII. 1.

Injuries to Slaves.—A slave being regarded as a thing rather than a person, if he were insulted, or assaulted, or killed, the law did not regard this as a wrong done to the slave, but to his master, who might bring an action, under the *Lex Aquillia*, for the injury suffered by his property. [5] Again, if a slave was guilty of any offence against the property of another person, such as theft or assault, the master of the offender had it in his option either to make compensation to the injured party, or to give up his slave to be dealt with by the public authorities—*domino damnati permittitur aut litis aestimationem sufferre aut hominem noxae dedere.* [6]

Peculium.—It follows as a necessary consequence, from what has been said above, that no slave could acquire property independent of his master, and that if a slave obtained possession of money or objects of any description, his master might at any time seize and appropriate the whole. [7] But although this was

---

[1] Aul. Gell. VII. 4. Fest. s.v. *Sub corona*, p. 306. Liv. V. 22. Caes. B. G. III. 1.
[2] Gaius I. § 52. 53. Suet. Claud. 25. Dion Cass. LX. 29. Spartian. Hadrian. 18.
[3] Aul. Gell. V. 14. Digest. XVIII. i. 42. XLVIII. viii. 11.
[4] Plaut. Cas. prol. 67.
[5] Gaius III. § 211. Digest. IX. ii.
[6] Gaius III. § 222. IV. § 75. Instit. IV. 8.
[7] Gaius I. § 52. II. § 87. Ulpian. frag. XIX.

the letter of the law, it was almost universally the practice to allow a slave to retain any property which he might have acquired honestly. The hoard formed in this manner was termed the *Peculium* of the slave, and sometimes amounted to a sum which enabled him to purchase his freedom.[1] Occasionally a slave purchased a slave for himself, who was termed his *Vicarius*;[2] and the Vicarius might have a Peculium. But according to the strict principles of the law, the Peculium of the Vicarius belonged to the slave who was his master, while both slaves and their Peculia were at the disposal of the free master.

Slave Dealing.—In addition to the public sales of prisoners, which generally took place at the seat of war, slave-dealing became, towards the close of the republic, and under the empire, a very common and lucrative trade, prosecuted by a class of persons called *Mangones* s. *Venalitii*, who collected slaves from all quarters, and disposed of the least valuable portion of their stock (*mancipia viliora*) in open market, and of the more precious in private shops (*tabernae*.) Those sold in the market were stripped and exhibited in a sort of wooden cage, called *Catasta*, where intending purchasers might examine and handle them, in order to ascertain whether they were sound and in good condition. A label (*titulus*) was attached to the neck of each, describing the age, country, qualities and defects of the individual, and whether he was new (*novitius*) or had previously been in servitude; (*veterator*;) those belonging to the latter class being less valuable, from a belief that they were more likely to be idle and cunning. If the representations contained in this statement were afterwards discovered to be false, the purchaser might raise an action of damages against the seller. If the seller declined to give any warranty, (*praestare*,) the slave was exposed for sale with a cap upon his head (*pileatus*.) Slaves newly imported from abroad had their feet whitened (*gypsatos s. cretatos pedes*.) When put up to auction, the *praeco* placed them on an elevated stone, so as to be visible to all, and hence Cicero calls two of his opponents, who had been openly and notoriously bribed, *duos de lapide emtos tribunos*.[3]

Price of Slaves.—The price of slaves must, as a matter of course, have varied at different epochs, according to the abundance of money, the demand, and the supply. But it would be as impossible, even in reference to any given time, to name a definite sum as the value of an article varying so much in quality, as it would be in our own day to fix, in general terms, the cost of horses. In the Augustan age, it would appear that a common domestic slave, possessed of no particular merits, would fetch from sixteen to twenty pounds sterling, while one of a higher order, such as a skilful workman, was worth three times as much.[4] But when individuals endowed with rare and valuable accomplishments came into the market, they brought fancy prices, regulated by accident only and the caprice of the purchaser. Under the early emperors, beautiful youths, Asiatics especially, were in great request as pages (*salutigeruli pueri*) and cupbearers. Such, if we can believe Martial, were worth between eight and nine hundred pounds, or even double that amount (*centenis quod emis pueros et saepe ducenis;*) and Pliny tells us that M. Antonius gave the latter sum (200,000 sesterces) for a pair of boys, uncommonly well matched, and represented (though falsely) to be twins.[5]

---

[1] Tacit. Ann. XIV. 42. Gaius IV. § 78. Digest. XV. i. 53.
[2] Digest. XV. i. 17. Plaut. Asin. II. iv. 28. Cic. in Verr. III. 28. Martial. II. xviii. 7.
[3] Cic. in Pison. 15. de Off. III. 17. Aul. Gell. IV. 2. VII. 4. Plaut. Bacch. IV. vii. 17. Tibull. II. ii. 59. Propert. IV. v. 5. Hor. S. II. iii. 285. Epp. II. ii. 14. Pers. S. VI. 77. Juv. S. I. 111. Martial. VI. 6. IX. 60. Digest. XVIII. i. 19. 43. XIX. i. 13. XXI. i. 1. 19. 31. 37. 65.
[4] Hor. S. II. vii. 43. Epp. II. ii. 5. Columell. R. R. III. 3.
[5] Juv. S. V. 56. XI. 145. Martial. III. 62. XI. 70. Plin. H. N. VII. 12.

Number of Slaves.—In the days of primitive simplicity, the number of slaves possessed even by the wealthy was exceedingly small, and individuals of distinction had frequently not more than two or three to provide for their wants.[1] At this period also, the great majority of agricultural labourers were freemen, and all ordinary trades were plied by Roman citizens. Before the passing of the Licinian Rogations, however, (B.C. 367,) slave labour began to preponderate in the country, an evil which went on increasing, notwithstanding the efforts made to remedy it, until, in the seventh century of the city, the estates of extensive landowners were tilled almost exclusively by slaves; and before the close of the republic, few citizens would submit to the degradation of practising any handicraft.[2] By degrees it was reckoned discreditable and mean for any one in easy circumstances to be scantily provided with personal attendants; the division of labour in the houses of men of moderate means was as great as in India at the present day, while the throngs maintained by the rich (*familiarum numerum et nationes*) were multiplied to an extent which almost transcends belief; those occupied in the same departments being so numerous that it was, in many cases, necessary to divide them into *Decuriae*.[3]

The obstinate and bloody wars in Sicily, (B.C. 135-132, B.C. 103-99,) in the latter of which a million of slaves is said to have perished; and the struggle with Spartacus in Italy, (B.C. 73-71,) in which 60,000 fell along with their leader when he was finally defeated by Crassus, bear evidence to the multitudes which must have been employed in rural affairs. As to the numbers employed in one Familia for domestic purposes, it is impossible to speak generally—they must have varied within such very wide limits. When Horace wrote, ten and two hundred were regarded as the opposite extremes of a small and a large establishment; for a Praetor to travel to his country house with a retinue of five only, was a mark of sordid parsimony. The household of Pedanius Secundus, prefect of the city, under Nero, contained 400; Scaurus is said to have had 4000; and C. Caecilius Claudius Isidorus, a freedman, whose fortune had suffered much during the civil wars, left behind him at his death, during the reign of Augustus, 4116. A large portion of the enormous wealth of Crassus consisted of slaves; but of these, many were artizans, whose labour yielded a highly profitable return, his architects and masons alone amounting to 500.[4]

Classification of Slaves.—The whole body of slaves belonging to one master was usually classed under two heads:—

1. *Familia Rustica*, the slaves who lived upon the country estates of their master, and were employed in the cultivation of the soil, or in tending flocks and herds.

2. *Familia Urbana*, the slaves employed for domestic purposes.

The *Familia Rustica* was again separated into two divisions—*Servi Vincti* and *Servi Soluti*. The former consisted of those who, as a punishment for refractory conduct, or in consequence of their barbarous habits and savage temper, were compelled to work in chains (*compede vincti*) while abroad, and were kept confined, when at home, in a sort of underground prison, termed *Ergastulum*. The *Servi Soluti*, on the other hand, were not placed under any personal restraint. The whole of the Familia Rustica, *Servi Soluti* and *Servi Vincti* alike, were under the superintendence of a steward or manager, termed

---

[1] Plin. H.N. XXXIII. 1. Apulei. Apolog. 430.
[2] Appian. B.C. I. 7—10. Suet. Jul. 42. Cic. de Off. I. 42.
[3] Petron. 47.
[4] Hor. S. I. iii. 11. vi. 107. Tacit. Ann. III. 53. XIV. 43. Plin. H.N. XXXIII. 10. Plut. Crass. 2.

Villicus or *Actor*, with whom, in large establishments, a book-keeper, called *Procurator*, was frequently associated; the Villicus and the Procurator being themselves, for the most part, slaves or freedmen.

The *Familia Urbana* also was separated into two divisions—*Ordinarii* and *Vulgares*, or upper and under slaves.[1]

The *Ordinarii* comprehended all slaves who held offices of trust and responsibility in the establishment. Most of these had sub-slaves, (*vicarii*,) who formed part of their *peculium*, or assistants placed under their orders by the master of the house. The general term for those who took charge of particular departments in the household was *Procuratores*, among whom we reckon the cashier (*Dispensator*,)[2]—the house-steward and butler (*Cellarius* s. *Promus*, called by Plautus, *Condus Promus* and *Procurator Peni*)[3]—the groom of the chambers, (*Atriensis*,) and the *Decuriones* of the different *Decuriae*, into which the under slaves who performed particular duties were distributed; as, for example, the *Decurio Cubiculariorum* and the *Decurio Ostiariorum*.[4] To the *Ordinarii* belonged also the highly educated slaves, (*Literati*,) among whom were the reader, (*Anagnostes* s. *Lector*,)[5]—the copying-clerk, (*Librarius* s. *Scriba*,) and many others, who were named *Servi ab epistolis*—*a manu*—*a bibliothecis*—*a studiis*, &c. according to the duties which they executed.

The *Vulgares* were the menials of the household, such as the Hall-porter (*Janitor*) and other Doorkeepers, (*Ostiarii*,)—Chamber-men, (*Cubicularii*,) who cleaned out and attended upon the different apartments,—Footmen, (*Pedisequi*,)—Palanquin-bearers, (*Lecticarii*,)—Running-footmen to clear the way, (*Anteambulones*,)—Couriers, (*Tabellarii*,) while, in the culinary department, there were Cooks, (*Coqui*,)—Bakers, (*Pistores*,)—Confectioners, (*Dulciarii*,)—Carvers, (*Carptores* s. *Structores* s. *Scissores*,) and a host of others.

Mediastini,[6] who were to be found in the *Familia Rustica* as well as in the *Familia Urbana*, seem to have been common drudges, scullions and servants-of-all-work, who had no special duties, but performed the lowest offices; and the *Quales-quales*, mentioned by Ulpian in the Digest, must have been something of the same sort.[7]

There were very many slaves who cannot be conveniently included in the above classes, such as *Familia Gladiatoria*, the prize-fighters, of whom vast numbers were trained for the amphitheatre, both by the rich, for the sake of ostentation, and by speculators, as a source of profit—*Medici* and their assistants, (*iatraliptae*,) who sometimes were merely house physicians, and sometimes gained large sums by general practice—*Opifices*, skilled artizans of all descriptions, whose earnings, when they worked for the public, belonged to their master—*Ludiones*, stage-players, who were let out on hire to those who exhibited theatrical shows; and many others, generally kept for the private amusement of the owner, such as Choristers (*Cantores*,)—Musicians, (*Symphoniaci*,)[8]—Dancing-girls, (*Saltatrices*,)—Merry-Andrews, (*Moriones*,)[9]—male and female dwarfs, (*Nani, Nanae; Pumiliones*,) and, strangest of all, idiots of both sexes (*Fatui, Fatuae*.)[10]

[1] Digest. XLVII. x. 15.
[2] Cic. de R. V. 3. ad. Att. XI. 1. Suet. Galb. 12. Vesp. 22. Juv. S. I. 91.
[3] Plaut. Pseud. II. ii. 13.
[4] Suet. Dom. 17. see Orelli. C. I. No. 2874.
[5] Corn. Nep. Att. 16. Plin. Epp. III. 5.
[6] Cic. in Cat. II. 3. Columell. R. R. I. 9. II. 13. Hor. Epp. I. xiv. 14.
[7] Digest. XLVII. x. 15.
[8] Cic pro Mil. 21. Senec. Epp. 54. Petron. 33. 47.
[9] Martial. VIII. 13.
[10] Senec. Epp. 50.

Vernae, as we have noticed above, were the slaves born in the house of their master—the children of his female slaves. Being trained from infancy, they naturally were particularly expert in the discharge of their functions, were generally treated with greater kindness and familiarity than others, and hence their sauciness became proverbial.[1]

Dress and Food of Slaves.—*Peregrini* being forbidden to appear in the *Toga*, the prohibition, a fortiori, extended to slaves also; and *Ancillae* were not allowed to assume the *Stola*, which was characteristic of the Roman matrons. Slaves, however, had no distinctive dress until the age of Alexander Severus; and a proposal made in the Senate, at an earlier period, to establish some badge of servitude, was rejected as dangerous, since it would have enabled the persons who bore it to form an estimate of their own numbers and strength.[2] The absence of the Toga would excite no attention, for this garment could not be worn by any class of persons engaged in manual labour; and, consequently, slaves, in this respect, did not differ from the humbler citizens, the *tunicatus popellus* of Horace (Epp. I. vii. 65.)

Each slave received a certain allowance, consisting of corn or bread, (*cibaria,*) wine, (*vinum,*) and something to give a relish to the farinaceous food, (*pulmentarium,*) usually olives or salt fish (*halec.*) This allowance, in consequence of being measured out, was termed *Demensum;* and according as the distribution took place daily or monthly, it was called *Diarium* or *Menstruum*. The precise quantity and quality of each article of food and raiment to be supplied to slaves in the country are minutely detailed by the writers on agriculture.[3] With regard to the condition of town slaves, in this respect, our information is not so precise. Donatus says, that the ordinary allowance of corn per month was four modii; and Seneca mentions, that a slave stage-player received five modii of grain and five denarii in money. By saving a portion of these allowances, slaves were sometimes enabled to accumulate a *peculium,* sufficient to purchase their freedom— *Peculium suum quod comparaverunt ventre fraudato, pro capite numerant.*[4]

Punishments inflicted upon Slaves.—These depended entirely upon the caprice of the master—were of many different kinds, and were often diversified with savage ingenuity. One of the mildest was the transference of a slave from the *Familia Urbana* to the *Familia Rustica*, in which he was allowed less freedom, enjoyed fewer luxuries, and performed more severe labour. When the offence was of a serious character, the culprit was not only sent to the country, but was placed among the *Servi vincti*, and compelled to work in chains in the fields, or to grind corn in the bakehouse, (*ferratus in pistrino—praeferratus apud molas—irrigatum plagis pistori dabo,*) or to toil in stone quarries (*ibis porro in latomias lapidarias.*)[5] The most common infliction for trifling transgressions, was the lash, which was unsparingly applied, and to increase the effect, the sufferer was sometimes hung up by the hands and weights attached to his feet.[6] The flogging of slaves, which, in large establishments, was performed by a regular body of scourgers, (*lorarii,*) affords an inexhaustible theme for jests in the comic writers; and the vocabulary of Plautus and Terence is peculiarly rich in terms connected with this species of domestic discipline. One of the ordinary epithets of reproach applied to one who had been repeatedly

---

[1] Hor. S. II. vi. 66. Epp. II. ii. 6. Martial. I. 42. X. 3. Senec. de Prov. 1.
[2] Senec. de clem, I 24.
[3] See especially Cato de R. R. 56—59.
[4] Senec. Epp. I. 24. 80. Terent. Phorm. I. i. 9. and Donat. ad. loc.
[5] Plaut. Bacch. IV. vi. 11. Pers. II. iii. 17. Epid. I. ii. 17. Capt. III. v. 63.
[6] Plaut. Asin. II. ii. 21. Most. V. ii. 45. Trin. II. i. 19. Terent. Phorm. I. iv. 42.

admonished by the lash is *Verbero* (or *Verbereum Caput* or *Verberea Statua;*) but in addition to this, we meet with *Mastigia—Ulmitriba—Flagitriba—Plagitriba—Plagipatida—Plagigerulus—Ulmorum Acheruns—Gymnasium flagri—Virgarum lascivia*, and a multitude of others.

A heavy collar of wood, shaped like the letter V, and hence termed *Furca*, was frequently attached to the necks of offenders, who were compelled to bear it about from place to place, and were sometimes scourged as they moved painfully along (*caesus virgis sub furca.*) One to whom this kind of torture had been applied, was jeeringly addressed as *Furcifer.*

Runaways (*fugitivi*) and thieves were usually branded (*notati*) with a red hot iron, and were styled *Inscripti—Inscripta Ergastula,* or, jestingly, *Literati,* because the letters F V R were often imprinted indelibly upon their persons, and hence the taunting address—*Tune* TRIUM LITERARUM HOMO *me rituperas?* i.e. *thief that thou art.*

When slaves were capitally punished, crucifixion was the death specially reserved for them. In Rome, the execution took place outside of the *Porta Esquilina*, and the offender carried his cross through the streets, with his arms attached to the transverse beam, (*patibulum,*) while the executioners goaded him on, thus, Plautus (Mil. II. iv. 6.)

> Credo ego istoc exemplo tibi esse eundum actutum extra portam
> Dispessis manibus patibulum cum habebis. . . . . [2]

When the master of a family was murdered in his own house, either by one of his own slaves, or by a person unconnected with the establishment, or by an unknown assassin, the whole of the slaves who were in the mansion at the time the murder was perpetrated were put to death. A remarkable example of the rigorous enforcement of this ancient law took place during the reign of Nero, when four hundred slaves were executed, in consequence of the murder of their master, Pedanius Secundus, prefect of the city.[3]

Finally, we may remark, that when slaves were examined judicially, in a criminal trial, they were always interrogated under torture.

Liberation of Slaves.—The release of a slave from slavery (*manumissio*) might be effected by his master, regularly, in three ways.[4]

1. *Vindicta.*—This was the most ancient and the most formal mode, and was essentially a public acknowledgment in court on the part of the master, that the slave was free. The master appeared with his slave before one of the higher magistrates, usually the Praetor, and a third person came forward, laid a rod called *Virga* s. *Festuca* s. *Vindicta* upon the head of the slave, and claimed him as a free man, in the set form, *Hunc ego hominem liberum esse aio.* The master laid hold of the slave, and turning him round, replied, *Hunc hominem liberum esse volo,* gave him a slight blow upon the cheek (*alapa*) and let him go (*emittebat eum e manu.*) The magistrate then pronounced him free, by giving judgment in favour of the claimant, (*addicebat.*) and the ceremony was complete. The Lictor of the magistrate usually, in later times at least,

---

[1] Martial. VIII. 75. Juv. XIV. 24. Plaut. Cas. II. vi. 49. Aul. II. iv. 46.
[2] Plaut. Mil. II. iv. 19. Most. I. i. 52. Tacit. Ann. II. 32. Senec. Epp. 101. Some commentators suppose that in the above and similar passages where the *patibulum* is mentioned, the punishment of the *furca* only is indicated; but this certainly does not hold good generally. A curious enumeration of a vast variety of slave punishments will be found in Plaut. Asin. III. ii. 1. seqq.
[3] Tacit. Ann. XIV. 42. XIII. 32. comp. Cic. ad. Fam. IV. 12.
[4] Cic. Top. 2. pro Caec. 34. Schol. Cruq. ad. Hor S. II. vii. 76. Galus. I. § 17. Ulpian. frag. I. 9.

acted as the claimant (*assertor*) who asserted the freedom of the slave (*vindicatio liberali causa*.)¹

2. *Censu.*—If the master applied to the Censor to enrol his slave as a *Civis*, the slave became free as soon as the entry was made.

3. *Testamento.*—A master might, by his will, either bestow freedom at once (*directo*) on a slave, or he might instruct his heir to manumit the slave. In the latter case, the freedom was said to be granted *per fideicommissum*. Sometimes freedom was bequeathed, subject to the performance of certain conditions, (*certa conditione proposita*,) and on these conditions being fulfilled, the slave became free, and was termed *statu liber*.

Libertinus. Libertus. Patronus.—Manumission, completed according to any of these three methods, was *Justa et legitima Manumissio*, and the freedom thus acquired, *Justa Libertas*. The liberated slave was now termed *Libertinus* when described in reference to his social position, but *Libertus* when spoken of in connection with his former master, who was now no longer his *Dominus*, but his *Patronus*. Thus, a liberated slave was called *Homo Libertinus;* but *Libertus Caesaris, Pompeii, Ciceronis*, &c.—never *Libertinus Caesaris*, &c. nor *Libertus Homo*.

The relation which existed between the Patronus and his Libertus resembled very closely the ancient tie of Patron and Client. The freedman was required to pay a certain degree of respect, and to perform certain duties to his patron, (*obsequium praestare*,) and this respect and these duties appear, under the republic, to have been seldom withheld or neglected.² But examples of ingratitude and insolence on the part of freedmen towards their patrons became, under the empire, so frequent and flagrant, that laws were passed rendering such conduct penal, and the punishment extended, in some cases, to the cancelling of the manumission.³

A slave freed *directo* by will, having no living Patronus, was called *Libertus Orcinus;* but when freed *per fideicommissum* he became the freedman of the person by whom he was actually manumitted. One whose freedom depended upon the performance of certain conditions was, until these conditions were fulfilled, called *Libertus futurus*.⁴

Names of Libertini.—A Libertinus usually received the *Praenomen* and *Nomen* of his former master, the appellation by which he had been previously distinguished being added as a *Cognomen*. Of this practice we have examples in such names as *M. Terentius Afer, M. Tullius Tiro, L. Cornelius Chrysogonus*. When a public slave was liberated, it would seem that he adopted the name of the magistrate before whom his manumission took place.

The *Praenomen* marked the *Status* of the individual at once as a Roman citizen possessed of *Caput*, (see above p. 83,) and hence, newly made Libertini were especially flattered when addressed by their Praenomen (*gaudent Praenomine molles auriculae*.)⁵ With regard to the *Nomen*, it must not be supposed that a Libertinus, although nominally belonging to the Gens of his Patron, was admitted, in ancient times at least, to all the privileges of a *Gentilis*.

Cap of Liberty.—As soon as a slave received his freedom he shaved his head and put on a conical cap, called *Pileus;* the right of wearing such a covering

---
1 Liv. II. 5. XLI. 9. Plaut. Mil. IV. i. 15. Phaedr. II. 5. Hor. S. II. vii. 76. Pers. S. V. 88. 175. Gaius. IV. § 16.
2 Cic. ad Q. F. I. i. 4. Digest. II. iv. 4. XXXVIII. i. 7. § 2. § 3. li. 1.
3 Suet. Claud. 25. Tacit. Ann. XIII. 26. Lactant. *De Ver. Sap.* IV. 3. Digest. I. xvi. 9. XXV. iii. 6. XXXVII. xiv. 1.
4 Gaius II. § 226. Ulpian. frag. II. 8. Orelli. C. I. No. 2980. 5006.
5 Hor. S. II. v. 32. comp. Pers. V. 79.

being a distinctive mark of a free citizen. Hence the phrases, *servos ad pileum vocare—pileum capere—hesterni capite induto Quirites*, and hence the idea of a cap as an emblem of freedom both in ancient and modern times. Sometimes a wreath of white wool was substituted for the *Pileus*.[1]

Political Condition of Libertini.—From the time of Servius Tullius[2] until the close of the republic, Libertini, whose manumission had been completed according to any one of the three regular forms, became invested with the rights and privileges appertaining to members of the Plebeian order, and, as such, were enrolled in a tribe. They were originally confined to the four city Tribes; but in the censorship of Appius Claudius, B.C. 312, in common with the humbler portion of the community, were dispersed among all the Tribes indifferently; and although the arrangements of Appius were overthrown in B.C. 304, by Q. Fabius Rullianus, we find it stated, that about eighty years afterwards, (B.C. 220,)—*Libertini in quatuor tribus redacti sunt, quum antea dispersi per omnes fuissent: Esquilinam, Palatinam, Suburanam, Collinam*. Finally, in B.C. 169, it was determined that all Libertini should be enrolled in one only of the city Tribes, to be determined by lot, and the lot fell upon the *Tribus Esquilina*. This state of things remained unaltered until the close of the republic, at least we have no account of any farther change.[3] The right of granting manumission remained unlimited until the age of Augustus, when the disorders arising from the multitude of disreputable and worthless characters turned loose upon the community, in the full enjoyment of the *Civitas*, rendered some legislative enactment imperative. Accordingly, by the *Lex Aelia Sentia*, passed A.D. 4, the following restrictions were introduced upon *Manumissio per Vindictam*,[4]

1. Any slave who had been convicted of a serious crime and punished as a malefactor, or who had been trained as a gladiator, was not, if manumitted, admitted to the rights of a Roman citizen, but was placed in the same class with *Peregrini dediticii*—(see above, p. 85.)

2. A slave, if under the age of thirty when manumitted, or any slave manumitted by a master who was under the age of twenty, was not admitted to the full rights of citizenship, unless the reasons assigned for the manumission were considered satisfactory (*iusta causa approbata*) by a board (*consilium*) appointed for the purpose of considering such cases.

Again, by the *Lex Furia Caninia*, passed A.D. 8, a master was prohibited from manumitting *Per Testamentum* more than a certain proportion of the whole number of his slaves—one half, if he possessed not more than ten—one third, if not more than thirty—one fourth, if not more than a hundred—one fifth if not more than five hundred; but in no case was the total number manumitted to exceed one hundred.

No restriction was placed upon manumission *Per Censum*, because that could not be effected without the direct concurrence of the government.

Social Condition of Libertini.—Although Libertini, under the republic, were nominally invested with all the rights and privileges of Roman citizens, they were virtually, by the force of public opinion and feeling, excluded from all high and honourable offices in the state. Not only the Libertinus himself, but his descendants, for several generations, were looked down upon as inferiors by

[1] Plaut. Amphit. I. i. 306. Liv. XXiV. 16. XLV. 44. Pers. S. III. 106. Non. s.v. *Qui liberi*, p. 361. ed. Gerl.
[2] Dionys. IV. 22—24.
[3] Dionys. IV. 22. Liv. IX. 46. Epit. XX. XLV. 15. Val. Max. II. ii. 2. The evidence afforded by these passages overpowers the assertion of Plut. Popl. 7.
[4] Gaius I. § 13. § 18—20. § 38. § 44. Ulpian. fragm. I. 11—13. Suet. Octav. 40. Dion Cass. LV. 13. LVI. 33.

those who had no taint of servile blood. We shall have occasion to point out hereafter, that *Ingenuitas*, for two generations at least, was considered an indispensable qualification in a candidate for the office of Tribune of the Plebs, and we cannot doubt that this rule applied to all the higher magistracies. Appius Claudius, when Censor, (B.C. 312,) was the first who "polluted" the Senate by admitting the sons of Libertini; (*senatum primus libertinorum filiis lectis inquinaverat;*)¹ but although public indignation was so strong that the consuls were borne out when they refused to acknowledge the persons so nominated, yet it is nowhere hinted that Appius violated any law in making such a choice. During the disorders produced by the civil wars, the Senate became crowded with Libertini; and the satirists always speak with special bitterness of the wealth and influence enjoyed by the favourite Liberti of the early emperors. Under the empire, also, the Status of *Ingenuitas* was sometimes bestowed upon Libertini by a special grant.² It would appear that the marriage of an *Ingenuus* with a *Libertina* entailed *Ignominia* (see above, p. 84,) on the former; for among the various rewards bestowed upon Hispala Fecenia, the Libertina who, in B.C. 186, gave information with regard to the excesses practised in the Bacchanalian orgies, it was decreed—*Uti ei ingenuo nubere liceret: neu quid ei, qui eam duxisset, ob id fraudi ignominiaeve esset* (Liv. XXXIX. 19.)

Informal Manumission.—In addition to the regular and legally recognised forms of manumission, a slave might be liberated in various ways, by the mere expression of a wish to that effect on the part of his master; but in this case his position was less secure. Thus we hear of *Manumissio inter amicos* s. *Libertas inter amicos data*, when a master, in the presence of his friends, pronounced his slave free—*Manumissio per epistolam*, when, being at a distance, he wrote a letter to that effect—*Manumissio per mensam*, when he permitted his slave to sit at table with him. A slave who was able to prove any one of these acts on the part of his master, could, by an appeal to the Praetor, resist any attempt to bring him back to slavery. His position, however, was dubious. He was said *in libertate morari* or *in libertatis forma servari;* and any property which he might accumulate belonged of right to his Patron. The political privileges of such persons was first defined by the *Lex Iunia Norbana*, passed about A.D. 19, which bestowed upon all slaves irregularly manumitted the *Ius Latii*, (see above, p. 87,) and hence the name *Latini Iuniani*, by which they are sometimes designated. A slave liberated in an irregular manner, might be again manumitted according to one of the three regular methods; and this process, termed *iteratio*, conferred full citizenship upon a *Latinus Iunianus*.

Manumission of Slaves by the State.—The state itself occasionally bestowed freedom upon slaves, as a recompense for long service, or for some signal benefit conferred on the community, such as giving information against conspirators or the perpetrators of heinous crimes; and if such slaves were not public property, (*servi publici*,) they were purchased with the public money from their masters.³ One of the most remarkable examples of manumission by the state, on a large scale, is to be found in the case of the *Volones*, that is, the slaves who, to the number of 8000, volunteered to serve as soldiers during the second Punic war, and who received their freedom after the battle of Beneventum, (B.C. 214,) as a reward for their efficient bravery.⁴

1 Liv. IX. 46. comp. Cic. pro Cluent. 47. Suet. Claud. 24. Dion Cass. XL. 63. XLIII. 47.
2 Dion Cass. XLVIII. 45. Appian. B.C. V. 80.
3 Liv. IV. 45. XXII. 33. XXVI. 27. XXVII. 3. XXXII. 26. Cic. pro Balb. 9. pro Rabir. perd. reo. 11.
4 Liv. XXII. 57. XXIV. 14—16. XXV. 20. 22. XXVII. 38.

CHAPTER IV.

THE COMITIA.[1]

We stated, at the commencement of the preceding chapter, that, according to the theory of the Roman constitution, all power proceeded from the voice of the citizens, as expressed in their constitutional assemblies, called *Comitia*—that no magistrate could be elected, no law enacted, no Roman citizen tried for a criminal offence, except by these assemblies. The citizens, however, could not lawfully assemble for the discharge of these duties, nor for any political purpose, except when formally summoned by a civil magistrate. They might be called together by a magistrate for one of two purposes.[2]

1. For the purpose of being addressed upon some matter of public interest, without any proposition being submitted to them upon which they were required to vote. In this case the assembly was called *Concio*.

2. For the purpose of having some proposition submitted to them, which they were required to accept or to reject by their votes. In this case the assembly was called, *Comitia*, or anciently *Comitiatus*.[3] *Comitium* never denotes the assembly, but the part of the Forum where the popular assemblies met in the earliest times. See p. 12.

Conciones.—A *Concio*, in so far as its objects were concerned, corresponded in many respects to what we now term a "Public Meeting." The magistrate by whom it was summoned employed a public crier, (*praeco*,) and was said *advocare* s. *convocare concionem;* the multitude merely listened to the oration of the person by whom they had been called together, and of those persons whom he introduced to their notice, (*produxit in concionem*,) for no private person could come forward and address them without obtaining permission from the presiding magistrate.[4]

The word *Concio* in the best writers is used for a public meeting in the restricted sense above described, and is sharply distinguished from *Comitia;*[5] but it would appear that originally *Concio* was employed in a more comprehensive signification to denote all public assemblies regularly summoned, including, of

---

[1] Full information with regard to the Roman Comitia will be found in SCHULZE, Von den Volksversammlungen der Römer, Gotha, 1815; in BECKER, Handbuch der Römischen Alterthümer, IIter. Theil. 1te. Abtheil. p. 353—394, Leipz. 1844; and in the continuation of the work by MARQUARDT, Leipz. 1849.

[2] We throw out of view here those occasions when the people were called together for the purposes of a military levy, (*delectus*,) of the *Census*, of solemn sacrifices, and the like, as not pertaining to the present subject.

[3] Cic. de legg. III. 12. 18. Aul. Gell. XIII. 15.

[4] Dionys. V. 11. Liv. III. 71. XLII. 34. Cic. ad Att. II. 24. IV. 2. pro Sest. 63. in Vatin. 10.

[5] Aul. Gell. XIII. 15. Liv. XXXIX. 15. Cic. pro Sest. 50.

course, Comitia, and that the phrases—*Inlicium vocare*—*In concionem vocare*—*Ad Comitia vocare*—*Ad Conventionem vocare*—were regarded as synonymous.[1]

Concio, however, in the purest authors, is constantly employed to denote, not only a public meeting, but also a speech delivered to such a meeting, and thus, *Concionem habere* is equivalent to *Verba facere*, that is, to deliver a harangue;[2] and hence such phrases as *Conciones scriptae*—*Legi tuam concionem*—*Concio funebris*—*Dare concionem alicui*, (to grant any one permission to speak,) and the verb *Concionari*.[3]

The right of calling a *Concio* belonged, during the regal period, in all probability, to the king alone, or to his immediate representatives, the *Tribunus Celerum* or the *Praefectus Urbis*. Under the republic it was exercised by all the higher magistrates, including the Tribunes of the Plebs. The ordinary places of meeting were the Comitium, the lower Forum, the Capitol, and the Campus Martius. The presiding magistrate usually occupied a *Templum*, that is, a place consecrated by the Augurs, and opened the proceedings on this, as on other occasions when the people were addressed, by a solemn prayer (see Liv. XXXIX. 15.)

Concilium.—While *Comitia* denoted an assembly of the whole people, called together for the purpose of voting upon some measure, *Concilium* is sometimes used to denote a similar assembly, consisting of a portion only of the community—*Is, qui non universum populum, sed partem aliquam adesse iubet, non* COMITIA, *sed* CONCILIUM, *edicere debet.*[4] Hence *Concilium Plebis*, or simply *Concilium*, is employed to denote the *Comitia Tributa*, because that assembly consisted originally of Plebeians only, and the term having been once recognized, remained in use after the Comitia Tributa included all classes.[5] On the other hand, *Concilium Populi* denotes the *Comitia Centuriata*, which, from the first, embraced the whole *Populus*.[6]

Concilium is also frequently employed to denote a promiscuous assemblage, without any reference either to *Conciones* or *Comitia*.

Comitia.—When a magistrate summoned *Comitia* it was invariably for the purpose of *asking* the people to do something, (*ut rogaret quid populum*,) and in submitting the matter to their consideration, he was said *agere cum populo*, which became the technical phrase for dealing with the people in their Comitia —*Cum populo agere est rogare quid populum quod suffragiis suis aut iubeat aut vetet.*[7]

There were three kinds of Comitia, which were named from the three modes in which the people were organized politically. These were—
1. *Comitia Curiata*, in which the people voted in *Curiae*.
2. ———— *Centuriata*, ... *Centuriae*.
3. ———— *Tributa*, ... *Tribus*.

To these some add a fourth, *Comitia Calata*, the nature of which we shall explain at the close of this chapter.

In none of the three first named did the people vote promiscuously, but,

---

[1] Varro L.L. VI. § 88. Paul. Diac. s.v. *Contio*, p. 38. s.v. *Inlicium*, p. 113.
[2] *Concionem habere est verba facere ad populum sine ulla rogatione.* Aul. Gell. XIII. 15.
[3] Cic. in Vatin. 1. ad Fam. IX. 14. ad Att. IV. 2. pro Flacc. 7.
[4] Lael. Fel. ap. Aul. Gell. XV. 27.
[5] Liv. VII. 5. XXXVIII. 53. XXXIX. 15. XLIII. 16.
[6] Liv. III. 71. VI. 20.
[7] Aul. Gell. XIII. 15. comp. Cic. de. legg. III. 4. in Vatin. 7. Sallust. Cat. 51. Macrob. S, I. 16. We find in Liv. XLII. 34. the phrase *agere* AD *populum* used with reference to a speech delivered to a *Concio*.

according to the nature of the Comitia, each voted in the *Curia*, in the *Centuria*, or in the *Tribus* to which he belonged, and in no case was the result decided simply by the majority of the gross number who gave their votes.

Thus, in the *Comitia Centuriata*, each *Centuria* had one vote, and the vote of each Centuria was determined by the majority of the individual voters which it contained. The vote of each Centuria being determined in this manner, the question under consideration was decided by the majority of the Centuries. But since the different Centuries did not all contain the same gross number of voters, some containing a much larger number than others, it did not by any means follow, that a majority of the Centuries expressed the opinion of a majority of the gross number of individual voters in the community at large.

Exactly the same principle was followed in the *Comitia Curiata* and in the *Comitia Tributa*, the majority of *Curiae* in the one, and of the *Tribus* in the other, decided the question, while the vote of each Curia and of each Tribus was determined by the majority of the individuals which it contained.

Since Comitia were summoned regularly every year during the period of the republic, for the election of magistrates, the word *Comitia* is not unfrequently used as equivalent to *elections*, sometimes by itself and sometimes with the addition of an adjective, indicating the magistrates for whose election the assembly was summoned. Thus, the sentence *Jam Comitiorum appetebat tempus* means, *the period for the annual elections was now approaching;* and in like manner, *Clodius quum videret ita tracta esse Comitia anno superiore* means, that the *elections* had been deferred for so long a period, &c.; while *Comitia Consularia — Praetoria — Aedilicia — Censoria* s. *Censorum — Pontificia* s. *Pontificum —* are phrases denoting the assemblies held for *the election* of Consuls —Praetors—Aediles, &c.

Functions of the Presiding Magistrate.—The magistrate who summoned a meeting of Comitia also presided, (*comitiis praeerat,*) and was said *habere Comitia:* in submitting any measure for the approval of the people, which he did commencing with the form *Velitis Jubeatis, Quirites,* he was said *agere cum populo — consulere populum — ferre ad populum — rogare,* and the latter verb, which implies the *asking,* the essential characteristic of all Comitia, is also applied to the object upon which the people were required to vote, as, for example *rogare legem — rogare magistratus — rogare consules — rogare praetores,* i.e. *to propose* a law—magistrates, consuls, &c. the phrases being elliptical abbreviations for *rogare populum legem — rogare populum consules,* &c.; so in like manner, *irrogare multam* s. *poenam* is to ask the people to inflict a fine or penalty, and *arrogatio* is asking leave to take to yourself or adopt the child of another. When the president called upon the people to give their vote, he was said *mittere populum* s. *centurias* s. *tribus in suffragium*—or, *in suffragium vocare;* the voters, on the other hand, were said *ire in suffragium — suffragium inire — ferre suffragium — ferre sententiam.* When he dismissed the assembly after the business was concluded, he was said *dimittere populum —comitatus dimittere;* when the assembly was broken up suddenly without coming to a decision, it was said *dirimi* s. *rescindi.*

Rogatio. Lex.—Since the essence of the procedure consisted in asking the people to vote upon something, the word *Rogatio* is frequently used to denote a *Bill* proposed to the people; hence *promulgare Rogationem* means *to publish a bill* previous to its being submitted to the Comitia; and according as the people accepted or rejected it, they were said *jubere* or *antiquare rogationem.* After a *Rogatio* was passed (*lata est*) it became a *Lex;* but in practice *Rogatio*

COMITIA IN GENERAL. 107

and *Lex* were frequently used as convertible terms, just as *Bill* and *Law* are by ourselves. The verb *Rogo* and its compounds enter into many technicalities connected with the passing of laws. To repeal a law, was *legem abrogare;* to repeal a portion but not the whole, *aliquid legi derogare;* to add new clauses to an existing law, *aliquid legi subrogare;* and when the provisions of an old law were altered or in any way affected by a new law, the former was said *obrogari*.[1]

The presiding magistrate being the person who submitted the measure to the people and announced the result, was said, individually, as it were, *ferre* s. *perferre legem* when the law was passed, and so, in the case of elections, he was said *creare consules—creare praetores*, &c. as if it were his own act and deed. Thus, *Dictator primo comitiali die creavit consules—Duo consules comitiis centuriatis a praefecto urbis creati sunt—Brutus collegam sibi creavit comitiis centuriatis—Per interregem consules creati*.[2]

Power of the Presiding Magistrate.—In addition to the mere ministerial functions performed by the presiding magistrate, and to the influence which he naturally exercised as president of the meeting, he wielded considerable constitutional powers—

1. No one could address the meeting without his permission, except a magistrate of equal or superior rank to himself, or a Tribune of the Plebs, although in some cases perhaps a senator might insist upon being heard.[3] We find examples, however, of private individuals, when refused liberty of speech by the consuls, obtaining it by an appeal to the Tribunes;[4] and since the Tribunes, in virtue of their office, could prevent a person from speaking, it was customary to ask permission of them as well as of the president.[5]

2. He had the power, if he thought fit, of fixing a limit to the space during which an orator was to speak, in order to prevent persons from wasting time needlessly, or from wilfully delaying the proceedings, with a view to frustrate the measure under discussion.[6]

3. At an election he could refuse to admit the name of any candidate whom he regarded as legally disqualified, and in doing this he was said *aliquem non accipere—nomen alicuius non accipere—rationem alicuius non habere*—and if, notwithstanding a declaration to this effect, votes were tendered for such a candidate, he might refuse to receive them, (*suffragia non observare*,) or refuse to return him as elected (*renuntiare*.) Of course, the presiding magistrate incurred responsibility in adopting such a course, and was liable to be called to account at a subsequent period, if it should appear that he had been actuated by personal enmity or factious motives.[7]

But although the president could refuse to return another candidate, he was not permitted, under any circumstances, to return himself, and hence the indignation and disgust excited by the conduct of Appius when he presided at his own re-election as Decemvir.[8]

Manner of Voting.—For a long period the votes in the Comitia were given vivâ voce, and hence the phrase *dicere aliquem consulem*,[9] i.e. to vote for a person to be consul; but voting by ballot (*per tabellas*) was introduced at the

---

[1] Ulpian. frag. I. 3. Liv. XXV. 2. I. 60. II. 2. III. 55.
[3] Liv. III. 63. 72. VI. 38. 40. XXXIV. 1. XLII. 34. XLV. 21.
[4] Liv. III. 71.
[5] Liv. XLII. 34.
[6] Plut. Cat. min. 43. Dion Cass. XXXIX. 34.
[7] Liv. III. 21. IX. 46. X. 15. XXXIX. 39. Cic. Brut. 14. Val. Max. III. viii. 3.
[8] Liv. III. 35. see also X. 15. XXVII. 6.
[9] Liv. X. 13. 22. XXIX. 22.

beginning of the seventh century by a succession of laws which, from their *subject*, were named *Leges Tabellariae*.[1] Cicero tells us that there were in all four, namely:—

1. *Lex Gabinia*, passed B.C. 139, by Gabinius, a Tribune of the Plebs, enacting that, in the election of magistrates, the votes should be given by ballot.[2]

2. *Lex Cassia*, carried in B.C. 137, by L. Cassius, Tribune of the Plebs, after strong opposition. We gather that this law provided for the ballot *in judicio populi*, except in cases of *Perduellio*. Considerable controversy has arisen as to the interpretation of the expression *judicio populi*, but there can be little doubt that it here includes *all criminal trials*, whether held before the people, in their *Comitia*, or before commissioners to whom the people delegated their jurisdiction.[3]

3. *Lex Papiria*, passed B.C. 131, by C. Papirius Carbo, Tribune of the Plebs, which provided that the ballot should be introduced *in legibus jubendis ac vetandis*.

4. *Lex Caelia*, passed B.C. 107, by C. Caelius, in terms of which the ballot was extended to trials for *Perduellio*, which had been specially excepted by the *Lex Cassia*.

Arrangements for Collecting the Votes.—On the day of the Comitia, a number of small enclosures, called *Septa* or *Ovilia* were erected in the Forum, in the Campus Martius, or wherever the assembly was to be held. These, when set up in the Forum, were of course removed as soon as the proceedings were over; but in the Campus Martius, towards the end of the republic at least, there were permanent structures devoted to this purpose (see above, p. 46.) Each *Septum* was entered by a narrow passage or plank termed *Pons* s. *Ponticulus*, and egress was afforded by a similar *Pons* upon the opposite side. On the *Pontes* at each end of the *Septum* stood vases called *Cistae* s. *Cistellae* s. *Sitellae* s. *Urnae*. When the Tribes or Centuries were called up to vote, each individual, as he passed along the Pons, received a certain number of tickets (*tabellae*) from persons who took them out of the vases, and who, from their office of distribution, were called *Divisores* s. *Diribitores*, and in performing this duty were said *Tabellas diribere*, the operation itself being termed *Suffragiorum diribitio*.[4]

When the subject under discussion was a law, each voter, it would appear, received two tickets; on one of these were marked the letters V.R. the initials of the words *Uti Rogas*,[5] i.e. let it be *as you ask*, and this he used if he was favourable to the measure; on the other was marked the letter A. the initial of the word *Antiquo*, i.e. *antiqua probo*, I prefer *the old state of matters*, and this he used if he voted against the Bill, whence the phrase *antiquare legem* signifies *to reject a law*.[6]

In the case of a criminal trial, the voter received three tickets, one marked A. for *Absolvo*, another C. for *Condemno*, and a third N.L. for *Non Liquet*, i.e.

---

1 The *locus classicus* is in Cic. de. legg. III. 16. and is well worthy of being read.
2 Cic. Lael. 16.
3 Cic. Brut. 25. 27. pro Sest. 48 fragm. Cornel. 24. Ascon. in Cornel. p. 78. Pseud. Ascon. in Verr. p. 141. Schol. Bob. p. 303. ed. Oreil. Consult also Cic. pro Planc. 6. and Plin. Epp. III. 20.
4 Cic. in Pison. 15. 40. pro Planc. 6. Orat. pro. Harusp. resp. 20. It is believed by some, however, that the operation implied by *diribere* was the arrangement and classification of the votes after the tickets had been dropped into the urn. On the *Diribitorium* see above, p. 46.
5 *Tabellae ministrabantur ita ut nulla daretur* UTI ROGAS, Cic. ad Att. I. 14. comp. de legg. III. 17.
6 Liv. V. 30. VI. 38. VIII. 37. Cic. de. legg. II. 10. Paul. Diac. s.v. *Antiquare*

I cannot make up my mind; and to employ this was virtually to decline giving a vote.

In the case of elections it would seem probable—but we have no distinct information upon this point—that each voter received a blank tablet, on which he wrote the initial letters of the names of his favourite candidates.

The voters having received their tickets, passed into the *Septum*, where they probably remained for a short time in consultation, and then each as he passed out was asked for his ticket by persons called *Rogatores*, stationed for the purpose, by whom they were dropped into the urn.[1] As soon as the Septum was emptied, the tablets were shaken out, arranged and counted under the inspection of tellers, called *Custodes*, who, in performing this operation, were said—*Suffragia dirimere—Suffragia describere—Tribus describere.*[2]

In illustration of what has been said above, we may refer to the denarius of the Gens Cassia, engraved in p. 15, where we see on one side of the temple a representation of the *Sitella* or Balloting Urn, and on the other a *Tabella* with the letters A C, (*Absolvo Condemno;*) on another denarius of the same Gens, of which a cut is annexed, we see a voter in the act of dropping his ticket into the box. The figures on a denarius of the Gens Hostilia, of which also we annex a cut, are generally supposed to be voters passing along the the Pons into the Septum, but on this we cannot speak with certainty.

The vote of each Tribe or Century having been thus ascertained was reported to the presiding magistrate, who proclaimed (*renuntiavit*) the result to those around, and made it known to those at a distance by means of the public criers, (*praecones*,)[3] and in like manner, when all the Tribes and Centuries had voted, the general result was declared.

If the votes for and against any measure were equal, which might happen from an equality of voices in individual Tribes or Centuries, the measure was lost; in the case of a criminal trial, such a result was regarded as equivalent to an acquittal.

As to the manner in which the votes were collected when given vivâ voce, we are almost totally destitute of information. It seems probable that the voters, in passing along the *Pontes*, were questioned by the *Rogatores*, and that their reply was noted down by a dot pricked upon a tablet. Hence the word *punctum* is constantly used in the sense of *a vote*, and *ferre puncta* means *to gain votes*, thus *Nonnullas tribus punctis paene totidem tulerunt Plancius et Plotius— Recordor quantum hae quaestiones . . . punctorum nobis detraxerint;*[4] and the well known Horatian line—

        Omne tulit punctum qui miscuit utile dulci.

---

[1] Cic. in Pison. 15. 40. de. Divin. II. 36. de. N. D. II. 4.
[2] Cic. in Pison. 5. 15. 40. de leg. agr. II. 10. pro Planc. 6. 20. ad Q. F. III. 4. Orat. post red. 7. Varro R. R. III. 2. comp. Plin. H.N. XXXIII. 2.
[3] *Coepti sunt a praecone renuntiari quem quaeque Tribus fecerint aedilem*, Varr. R. R. III. 17. See also Cic. in Verr. V. 15. de leg. agr. II. 2. 9. pro Muren. 1.
Cic. pro Planc. 22. pro Muren. 34.

After the votes had been taken and the result announced, the presiding magistrate invited the assembly to disperse by the form—*Si vobis videtur, discedite, Quirites*—and the same words were employed when he called upon them to separate for the purpose of voting.[1]

Quorum.—Although the presence of a certain fixed number of individuals was not held necessary to constitute a lawful assembly, it would appear that, occasionally, when the number in attendance was very small, the business was deferred and the Comitia dismissed.

In the case of an election, however, it was necessary for a candidate to obtain the votes of a certain number of Centuries or Tribes, and if, in consequence of the votes being divided among several competitors, the individual who had a majority over his rivals, failed to obtain the full number necessary, he was said —*non explere tribus—non conficere legitima suffragia*.[2]

In a consular election, if one consul was duly elected, while the candidate who stood second failed to procure the necessary number of votes, the consul duly elected had the right of nominating his colleague, without the matter being again referred to the Comitia, and a similar practice prevailed in the election of Tribunes of the Plebs.[3] This did not hold for Praetors, Aediles and Quaestors; but if the election of these magistrates was interrupted from this or from any other cause, the Comitia were summoned again and again, until they arrived at a legal decision. It may be inferred, however, from a passage in Cicero, that if two competitors for the Aedileship received an equal number of votes, then their pretensions were decided by lot.[4] On the other hand, in the election of Censors, if both did not obtain the full number of votes, then neither was elected.[5]

Auspicia.—The Romans, in the earlier ages of their history, never entered upon any important business whatsoever, whether public or private, without endeavouring, by means of divination, to ascertain the will of the gods in reference to the undertaking (*nisi auspicato—nisi auspicio prius sumto.*) This operation was termed *sumere auspicia*; and if the omens proved unfavourable, the business was abandoned or deferred—*Apud antiquos non solum publice sed etiam privatim nihil gerebatur nisi auspicio prius sumto—Auspiciis hanc urbem conditam esse, auspiciis bello ac pace domi militiaeque omnia geri, quis est qui ignoret?—Auspicia, quibus haec urbs condita est, quibus omnis respublica atque imperium continetur*.[6]

No meeting of the Comitia Curiata nor of the Comitia Centuriata could be held unless the auspices had been previously taken; and although this rule did not apply originally to the Comitia Tributa, that assembly also was, in later times, to a certain degree, dependent upon the auspices.[7]

In the earlier ages of the state, the Patricians claimed the exclusive right of taking auspices, asserting that this power was vested in them alone, (*nobis propria sunt auspicia—sunt auspicia more maiorum penes Patres*,) and hence the Patricians were said *habere auspicia*, i.e. to be in possession of the auspices.[8]

---

[1] Liv. II. 56. III. 11.
[2] Liv. III. 64. IX. 34. XXXVII. 47.
[3] Liv. ll. cc.
[4] Liv. XL. 59. Aul. Gell. XIII. 15. Cic. pro Planc. 20. 22. ad Att. IX. 9.
[5] Liv. IX. 34.
[6] Val. Max. II. i. 1. Liv. VI. 41. Cic. in Vatin 6. de. Divin. I. 16.
[7] Liv. I. 36. Dionys. II. 6. These passages would seem to imply, that even in the infancy of the state the meetings of the Plebs were dependent upon auspices.
[8] Liv. V. 14. X. 8. Aul. Gell. XIII. 15.

But as far as public proceedings were concerned, no private individual, even among the Patricians, had the right of taking auspices. This duty devolved upon the supreme magistrate alone, so that during the regal period, the kings only could take the auspices, and during the republic the consuls only, as long as they remained in the city. In an army this power belonged exclusively to the commander-in-chief; and hence all achievements were said to be performed under his auspices, even although he were not present; and a victory gained by one of his subordinate officers, a *legatus*, for example, was said to have been won *auspiciis Consulis, ductu Legati*. This principle was still observed after the downfal of the free constitution; and the emperor being, in virtue of his office, general-in-chief of all the armies of the state, every military exploit, in whatever part of the world it might be performed, was regarded as falling under his *Auspicia*.

The fact, that the chief magistrate alone could take the auspices, and the assumption that no one but a Patrician possessed the privilege, formed one of the arguments most strenuously urged against the admission of the Plebeians to the consulship, (*quod nemo Plebeius auspicia haberet*,) it being maintained that no Plebeian consul could, without sacrilege, attempt to make the requisite observations—*Quid igitur aliud, quam tollit ex civitate auspicia, qui plebeios consules creando, a Patribus, qui soli ea habere possunt, aufert*.[1] Upon like grounds the Patricians opposed the intermarriage of Plebeians with their order, because the taking of auspices formed part of the nuptial ceremonies, and they alleged that the whole discipline would be thrown into confusion by these ill-assorted unions and a hybrid progeny—*Perturbationem auspiciorum publicorum privatorumque afferre—ideo decemviros connubium diremisse ne incerta prole auspicia turbarentur*.[2]

When, however, a king died, then the Patricians, as a body, were required to take the auspices before they could elect his successor or choose an Inter-rex; and in this case the auspices were said *Redire ad Patres*, to return, as it were, to the source from whence they had been derived; and the same took place under the commonwealth, when both consuls died or resigned before they had held the Comitia for the election of a successor, or had named a Dictator for that purpose. Whenever it became necessary from this, or from any other cause, to seek the auspices at the fountain whence they were supposed to flow, the process was termed—*auspicia de integro repetere—auspicia renovare—per interregnum renovare auspicia*.[3]

Auspicia in Connection with the Comitia.—Neither the Comitia Curiata nor the Comitia Centuriata could be held unless the auspices had been taken and pronounced favourable. The objects observed in taking these auspices were birds, the class of animals from which the word is derived (AUSPICIUM *ab ave spicienda*.) Of these, some were believed to give indications by their flight, and were technically termed *Alites* s. *Praepetes*, others by their notes or cries, and hence were termed *Oscines*, while a third class consisted of chickens (*Pulli*) kept in cages. When it was desired to obtain an omen from these last, food was placed before them, and the manner in which they comported themselves was closely watched. If they refused to feed, or fed slowly, the auspices were regarded as unfavourable; on the other hand, if they fed voraciously, and especially if a portion of their food, falling from their bills, struck the ground,

---
[1] Liv. IV. 6. VI. 41.
[2] Liv. IV. 2.
[3] Liv. V. 17. 31. 52. VI. 1. 5. VIII. 3. 17.

which was termed *Tripudium Solistimum*,[1] the omen was regarded as in the highest degree propitious. The three forms of divination from birds are alluded to in Cicero when he says—*Non ex alitis involatu, nec e cantu sinistro oscinis, ut in nostra disciplina est, nec ex tripudio solistimo, tibi auguror.*[2]

The manner of taking the auspices previous to the Comitia was as follows:— The magistrate who was to preside at the assembly arose immediately after midnight on the day for which it had been summoned, and called upon an augur to assist him (*augurem in auspicium adhibebant.*) With his aid a region of the sky and a space of ground, within which the auspices were observed, were marked out by the divining staff (*lituus*) of the augur, an operation which was termed *Templum capere*, the whole space thus designated being called *Templum*, and the spot on which they stood *Tabernaculum*, in consequence, very probably, of a tent or hut being erected for the occasion.

This operation was performed with the greatest care; for if it was discovered at any future time that any irregularity had been committed in this, or in any other point connected with the auspices, (*tabernaculum non recte captum—tabernaculum vitio captum—auspicia parum recte capta—auspicia vitio contacta*,) the whole of the subsequent proceedings became null and void, and if magistrates had been elected under such circumstances, they were said to be *vitio creati*, and compelled at once to resign their office. In making the necessary observations, the president was guided entirely by the augur, who reported to him the result. This formal report, if favourable, was termed *Nuntiatio*, if unfavourable, *Obnuntiatio*; in the former case he declared *Silentium esse videtur*, i.e. there is no evil sight or sound; in the latter case he postponed the proposed assembly by pronouncing the words *Alio die*. The auspices observed in the manner above described, formed an indispensable preliminary to all meetings of the Comitia Centuriata, and, we have every reason to believe, of the Comitia Curiata also; and these observations could be taken by the presiding magistrate only, with the aid of the augur whom he invited to attend him.[3]

Servare de Coelo.—There was, however, another class of omens or auspices connected with the Comitia, which exercised an important influence, especially towards the close of the republic. The nature of these has been frequently misunderstood, and must therefore be distinctly explained.

According to the discipline of the augurs, no popular assembly could continue its proceedings if thunder or lightning were observed, or if a storm of any kind arose—*Jove tonante, cum populo agi non esse fas—Jove fulgente nefas esse cum populo agi, augures omnes usque a Romulo decrevere—In nostris commentariis scriptum habemus, Jove tonante fulgurante Comitia populi haberi nefas—Fulmen sinistrum auspicium optimum habemus ad omnes res praeterquam ad Comitia*[4]—and accordingly, if such appearances manifested themselves, the meeting at once broke up; (e.g. *Praetorum Comitia tempestas diremit;*)[5] but no distinct rules, as far as we know, were laid down in the earlier ages of the commonwealth with regard to observing and reporting such phenomena.

About the year B.C. 156, a law, or perhaps two laws, one being supplementary

---

[1] *Cum igitur offa cecidit ex ore pulli, tum auspicanti* TRIPUDIUM SOLISTIMUM *nuntiant.* Cic. de Divin. II. 34. comp. I. 15.
[2] Cic. ad Fam. VI. 6.
[3] Cic. de Divin. I. 17. II. 35. de N. D. II. 4. de Legg. II. 12. III. 4. Liv. IV. 7. VIII. 17. 30. Fest. s v. *Silentio.* p. 348.
[4] Cic. Philipp. V. 3. in Vatin. 8. de Div. II. 18. 38.
[5] Liv. XL. 59. comp. Tacit. H. I. 18.

to the other, were passed by Q. Aelius Paetus and M. Fufius, Tribunes of the Plebs, which are frequently referred to by Cicero, as *Lex Aelia Fufia* or *Lex Aelia et Lex Fufia.*

One of the chief provisions of these enactments was, that it should be lawful for any of the superior magistrates to watch the heavens (*servare de coelo*) on the day on which assemblies of the people were held, whether Comitia Centuriata or Comitia Tributa, and if they saw lightning, to report this (*obnuntiare*) to the presiding magistrate. The right of observing the heavens, termed *Spectio*, belonged to the magistrates alone, and hence Cicero says, (Philipp. II. 32,) *Nos* (sc. augures) NUNTIATIONEM *solam habemus, at consules et reliqui magistratus* SPECTIONEM.

But, by another principle in the discipline of the augurs, it was unlawful to hold Comitia while any one was known to be engaged in taking the auspices or watching the heavens, while the will of the gods might therefore be regarded as not yet fully ascertained (Orat. pro. dom. 15.)

Hence, if, on the day when a meeting of Comitia was about to be held, one of the higher magistrates thought fit to announce to the presiding magistrate that he was engaged in observing the heavens, (*se servare de coelo*,) or if he gave notice previously that he intended to be so engaged on the day fixed for an assembly, this was held to be an *Obnuntiatio*, and the proceedings were stopped.

The great object and effect of these laws was to impede hasty and rash legislation, by putting it in the power of every magistrate to stay proceedings; and hence they are described as *propugnacula et muros tranquillitatis et otii* by Cicero, (In Pison. 4,) who declares in another place, (In Vatin. 7,) *ea saepenumero debilitavisse et repressisse tribunicios furores.* These laws, after having been strictly observed for nearly a century, were disregarded by Cæsar and by Vatinius, during the consulship of the former, B.C. 59; for they persisted in forcing through several measures in defiance of a formal *Obnuntiatio* on the part of Bibulus and others. This violation of the constitution forms a theme of bitter invective in the speech of Cicero against Vatinius; and the opponents of Cæsar maintained that all his own proceedings, (*acta*,) as well as those of his satellite, were in reality null and void. The *Lex Aelia et Fufia* was repealed by Clodius, or perhaps rather suspended, for it seems to have been in force at a period subsequent to his tribuneship (see Cic. pro Sest. 61. ad Q. F. III. 3. Philipp. II. 32.)

Notice of Comitia.—The Comitia Centuriata and the Comitia Tributa were summoned by a written proclamation, (*edictum*,) issued by the consul or other magistrate who was to preside.[1] It appears to have been customary, from a very early period,[2] to issue this proclamation seventeen days beforehand, and this space of time was termed *Trinundinum*, because, in this way, the subject to be discussed became known to the people for three successive market-days (*nundinae*) before they were called upon to give their votes. But although this may have been the practice sanctioned by custom, there can be no doubt that it was often departed from in cases of emergency, and laws were passed, and magistrates were elected, sometimes even upon a single day's notice.[3] But by the *Lex Caecilia Didia*, passed B.C. 98, it was positively enacted that no law could be proposed to the people for their acceptance until its provisions had been

[1] Liv. XXXV. 24. Aul. Gell. XIII. 15.
[2] Liv. III. 35. Macrob. S. I. 16.
[3] Liv. IV. 24. XXIV. 7. XXV. 2.

published for the space of *Trinundinum* at least, (*ut leges Trinundino die promulgarentur*,) this publication being termed *Promulgatio*, whence *Promulgare legem* means *to propose a law*. The provisions of the Lex Caecilia Didia were subsequently made more stringent by the *Lex Licinia Junia*, passed, probably, in B.C. 62. Cicero makes repeated allusion to these laws, and laments their violation during the troublous period when he lived.

Dies Comitiales.[1]—Comitia could be held upon particular days only, which were, from this circumstance, marked in the Kalendars as *Dies Comitiales*; and these could not have been very numerous if we observe those which we know to have been excluded. These were—

1. All *Dies Festi*, i.e. all days consecrated to the worship of the gods, and celebrated by sacrifices, banquets or games. Among these were included the Calends and Ides of every month, the former being sacred to Juno, the latter to Jupiter.

2. The *Nundinae* or market days on which the country people came into the city to buy or sell, and which fell every eighth day. This restriction, however, may have been in part removed by the *Lex Hortensia* of B.C. 286, which declared that it should be lawful to transact legal business on the Nundinae.

3. It appears that by a *Lex Pupia*, regarding which we know little but the name, that it was forbidden to hold a meeting of the Senate on a *Dies Comitialis*, so that many days open for ordinary business could not have been *Dies Comitiales*.

Hour of Meeting.—We know nothing as to the period of the day at which the Comitia usually assembled; but it was a general constitutional rule, that no public business of any kind could be transacted before sunrise or after sunset.[2]

Events which might abruptly put an end to a Meeting of Comitia.—We have already seen that if the auspices were unfavourable the assembly was put off; but even after the Comitia had met, the meeting might be broken up without coming to a vote by various circumstances.

1. If any magistrate of equal or superior rank to the presiding magistrate gave formal notice (*obnuntiavit*) that he was watching the heavens (*se servare de coelo*.) See above, p. 113.

2. If lightning was seen or if a sudden storm arose.[3] See above, p. 112.

3. If any individual present was seized with Epilepsy, a disease which was hence named *Morbus Comitialis*.[4]

4. By the intercession of one of the Tribunes of the Plebs. This right, which will be fully explained when we treat of the magistracy itself, could only be exerted, in the case of a law, after the law had been read over, but before the people had begun to vote.[5]

5. By night-fall coming on before the business was concluded.

6. If the standard hoisted on the Janiculum was lowered; but this applied to the Comitia Centuriata alone, and will be noticed in treating specially of that assembly.

But although the assembly was broken up abruptly by a storm, by intercession, by night-fall, or the like, the meeting might be held to be merely adjourned,

---

[1] See Macrob. S. I. 15. 16. Varro L.L. VI. § 29. Fest. s.v. *Nundinas*, p. 173. Paul. Diac. s.v. *Comitiales*, p. 38. Aul. Gell. V. 17. Cic. ad. Q. F. II. 13. ad Fam. I. 4. de prov. cons. 19. Plin. H.N. XVIII. 3.
[2] Dionys. IX. 41. Cic. in Cat. III. 12. Dion Cass. XXXIX. 65. Plut. Aem. Paul. 20.
[3] Liv. XL. 59.
[4] Fest. s.v. *Prohibere Comitia*, p. 234. Aul. Gell. XIX. 2.
[5] Cic. frag. pro Corn. Liv. XLI. 21.

and the same question might be again submitted to the people even on the day following.[1]

The above remarks apply, in a great measure to all Comitia. We now proceed to consider these assemblies separately.

COMITIA CURIATA.

There can be no doubt that the *Comitia Curiata*, instituted, we are told,[2] by Romulus, formed the original, and, for a considerable time, the only popular assembly among the Romans; but the period during which this assembly exercised any considerable influence or control over public affairs belongs exclusively to that epoch of history which is involved in the deepest obscurity, and hence our information upon all matters of detail is extremely limited and uncertain. The following points seem to be fully established:—

1. The constituent body of the *Comitia Curiata*, as the name implies, was composed of the thirty *Curiae*. The Curiae being made up of Patrician Gentes, it follows that the Plebeians must have been altogether excluded from these assemblies. Whether, in ancient times, the Clients of the Patricians took a part in the proceedings, is a question which has been much agitated; but it is very difficult to understand how a class of persons so completely under the influence of their Patrons as the Clients were, could have exercised any independent political power, and hence we are led to adopt the opinion of those who maintain that the Patricians alone had the right of voting.

2. The Comitia Curiata being the only popular assembly up to the time of Servius Tullius, wielded all those constitutional powers, civil and religious, which were held to belong to the citizens as a body, although those powers, in the earlier ages of the state, could not have been very clearly defined. It elected the kings, all priests,[3] and perhaps the quaestors also,[4] enacted laws,[5] declared war, or concluded peace,[6] and was the court of last appeal in all matters affecting the life or privileges of Patricians.[7]

It would be vain if we were to attempt to enter into details with regard to the forms and ceremonies observed in holding the Comitia Curiata, indeed we ought always to bear in mind that the few particulars recorded rest, for the most part, upon the evidence of writers who flourished many centuries after the customs which they describe had entirely passed away, and who were ever prone to represent the usages of their own times as having existed unchanged from the most remote ages. On one or two topics we can speak with tolerable certainty.

Each Curia had one vote, and the vote of each Curia was determined by the majority of voices in that Curia, every citizen voting individually (*viritim*) in the Curia to which he belonged. The question under discussion was decided by the majority of the Curiae. The Curia called up to vote first was termed *Principium;* but since we know that the same Curia did not always vote first, it is probable that the precedence was, on each occasion, determined by lot. The number of the Curiae being thirty, it might happen that they would be equally divided upon a question; but what provision was made to meet such a contingency is nowhere indicated. The debate regarding the disposal of the property

[1] Liv. VII. 17. X. 9. XL. 59. comp. XXXI. 6. 7.
[2] Dionys. II. 14.
[3] Dionys. II. 22. Aul. Gell. XV. 27.
[4] See the conflicting testimonies of Junius Gracchanus ap. Ulpian. Dig. I. 13. and Tacit. Ann. XI. 22.
[5] Pompon. Dig. I. ii. 2.
[6] Liv. I. 24. 32. 38. 40. Aul. Gell. XVI. 4. Dionys. VIII. 91. IX. 69.
[7] See Liv. I. 26. VIII. 33. Dionys. III. 22.

of the Tarquins turned, according to Dionysius, upon a single vote, so that the Curiae must have stood sixteen against fourteen.[1]

During the regal period, the Comitia Curiata could not meet unless summoned by the king, or by his representative, the Tribunus Celerum, or, in the absence of the king, by the Praefectus Urbis, or, when the throne was vacant, by an Inter-rex. These magistrates could not summon the Comitia unless authorized by a decree of the Senate; and no measure passed by the Comitia was held valid until ratified by a decree of the Senate. Notice of the assembly was given by Lictors, one being attached to each Curia, (*Lictor Curiatus,*) who went round and summoned the members individually (*nominatim.*) Public criers (*praecones*) were sometimes employed for the same purpose. The place of meeting was the *Comitium*, where the tribunal of the king was placed (COMITIUM *ab eo quod coibant eo Comitiis Curiatis et litium causa.*)[2]

Under the republic, when a *Lex Curiata* was required, one of the Consuls, a Praetor or a Dictator might preside. In cases of adoption and when matters of a purely religious character were debated, a Pontifex could hold the assembly, and we can scarcely doubt that the *Curio Maximus* (see p. 61.) must have, in some instances, enjoyed a similar privilege.[3]

It would seem that the same solemnities, with regard to auspices, sacrifices, and prayers, were observed in meetings of the Comitia Curiata which afterwards characterised the Comitia Centuriata, and to these we shall advert more particularly in the next section.

Gradual Decline of the Comitia Curiata.—The first blow to the influence of the Comitia Curiata was the establishment, by Servius Tullius, of the Comitia Centuriata, which included all classes of the community, and was doubtless intended to supersede, in a great measure, the most important functions of the existing assembly. The powers of both alike were, probably, almost entirely suspended during the despotic sway of the second Tarquin; but upon his expulsion, the Patricians recovered their power to such an extent that although the consuls were elected by the Comitia Centuriata, no measure passed by that body was binding until it had received the sanction of the Comitia Curiata, in which many of the most important measures with regard to the infant republic were originated and decided; and when the question arose with regard to the compilation of a new code of laws, the Patricians boldly declared—*datarum leges neminem nisi e Patribus.*[4] But this controlling power was altogether lost when, by the *Lex Publilia*, passed by Q. Publilius Philo, dictator, B.C. 339, the *Patres*, i.e., Patricians, were compelled to ratify beforehand whatever laws the Comitia Centuriata might determine—*ut legum quæ Comitiis Centuriatis ferrentur ante initum suffragium Patres auctores fierent* (Liv. VIII. 12.)[5]

Moreover, the foundations upon which the dominion of the Patricians and the Comitia Curiata rested were gradually undermined after the expulsion of the kings, by the steadily increasing influence of the Plebeians, who first of all extorted the right of electing, from their own body, magistrates invested with great powers for the protection of their interests: then organised their own constitutional assemblies, the *Comitia Tributa*; then by the *Lex Licinia* (B.C. 367) obtained a share in the consulship; and finally, by the *Lex Publilia*, passed at the same time and

---

[1] Dionys. II. 14. IV. 20. 84. V. 6. Liv. I. 42. IX. 38.
[2] Dionys. II. 7. 14. 50. IV. 71. IX. 41. Liv. I. 17. 59. VI. 41. Varro L L. V. § 155. Lael. Felix ap. Aul. Gell. XV. 27.
[3] Cic. de leg. agr. II. 11. 12. Liv. IX. 38. Aul. Gell. V. 19.
[4] Dionys IX. 75. 84. V. 6, 57. VI. 89. VII. 38. 59. Liv. II. 56. III. 11. 31.
[5] Confirmed by the *Lex Maenia*, B.C. 286. See Cic. Brut. 14. pro Planc. 3. comp. Liv. I. 17.

by the same person with that mentioned in the last paragraph, established the important principle that all laws passed in the Comitia Tributa should be binding on the whole community—*ut Plebiscita omnes Quirites tenerent* (Liv. l.c.) Upon this topic we shall say more in treating of the *Comitia Tributa*.

From this time forward we hear little of the Comitia Curiata, whose influence may be regarded as having completely ceased when the Plebeians were admitted to a full participation in all political rights; and this assembly would probably have altogether disappeared had it not been closely connected with certain religious observances, which, according to the ideas of the people, could not, without sacrilege, have been committed to any other body. Of these, the most important were—

1. The granting of *Imperium* or supreme military command. Although the kings were elected by the Comitia Curiata, it was essential that a second meeting of the same Comitia should be held for the purpose of conveying to the new sovereign *Imperium*, with which was always combined the right of taking the *Auspicia* in the field, a duty and privilege appertaining to the commander-in-chief alone. Now, although the doctrine long and strenuously maintained by the Patricians, that they, and they alone, possessed the right of taking auspices, was set aside upon the election of Plebeians to the consulate, it was still admitted that the power of taking auspices must emanate from and be conferred by the Patricians; and hence, after the election of consuls by the Comitia Centuriata, a law passed by the Comitia Curiata (*Lex Curiata de Imperio*) conferring *Imperium* and the *Auspicia* was, in practice, held to be essential down to the very close of the republic.[1] Thus, *Comitia Curiata quae rem militarem continent—Consuli, si Legem Curiatam non habet, attingere rem militarem non licet—Demus igitur Imperium Caesari sine quo res militaris administrari, teneri exercitus, bellum geri non potest.*[2]

This meeting of the Comitia Curiata, although never dispensed with, became in process of time a mere form, and in the age of Cicero, the ceremonies were performed by an assemblage of the thirty *Lictores Curiati*, each representing his own Curia—*Comitiis . . . illis ad speciem atque ad usurpationem vetustatis per XXX. lictores* AUSPICIORUM CAUSA *adumbratis—Nunc quia prima illa Comitia tenetis, Centuriata et Tributa, Curiata tantum* AUSPICIORUM CAUSA *remanserunt.*[3]

It would appear from an expression dropped by Cicero—*Maiores de omnibus magistratibus bis vos sententiam ferre voluerunt*[4]—that a meeting of the Comitia Curiata was anciently required to ratify the election of all magistrates; but that when the procedure became a mere form, it was held to be essential in the case of the consuls only who thus received the auspices.

2. *Arrogatio.*—When an individual passed by adoption into a Gens to which he did not previously belong, the sanction of the Comitia Curiata was held requisite, because, since each Gens and Familia had its own peculiar rites, (*gentilitia sacra—sacra privata*,) the act of passing from one Gens into another, implied that the individual adopted must be relieved from the obligation to perform one set of rites, and must bind himself to maintain new observances. In this case, the question being regarded as one of a purely religious character, the assembly

---

[1] That there were some disputes upon this matter in theory appears from Cic. ad Fam. L ix. 13.
[2] Liv. V. 52. Cic. de leg. agr. II. 12. Philipp. V. 16. comp. ad Fam. L ix. 13, ad Att. IV. 18, ad Q. F. III. 2.
[3] Cic. de leg. agr. II. 10. 12.
[4] Cic. de leg. agr. II. 10.

was held by a Pontifex, and to this we find an allusion in the words addressed by Galba to Piso—*Si te privatus Lege Curiata apud Pontifices, ut moris est, adoptarem*.[1]

When a foreigner was admitted into a Patrician Gens, the process was termed *Cooptatio*; when a Plebeian entered a Patrician Gens, *Adlectio*; when a Patrician passed from one Patrician Gens to another. *Adoptio*; when a Patrician passed into a Plebeian Gens, *Transductio ad Plebem*, and he was said *Transire ad Plebem*, the term *Arrogatio* comprehending all the varieties.[2]

3. Since it appears that the *Curio Maximus* was elected by Comitia, we can scarcely doubt that the Comitia in question must have been the Comitia Curiata, although the words of Livy might lead to a different conclusion.[3]

COMITIA CENTURIATA.

We have already (p. 69.) described the distribution of the whole body of Roman citizens by Servius Tullius into *Classes* and *Centuriae*. One of the chief results of this division was the establishment of the *Comitia Centuriata*, which, during the whole period of the republic, was regarded as the most important of the constitutional assemblies, and was styled *Comitiatus Maximus*.[4] The great characteristic of the Comitia Centuriata was, that from the period of its institution it was, in the strictest sense, a *national* assembly, and not an assembly of one class or order. While the Comitia Curiata was, at all times, composed exclusively of the Patrician Gentes, and while the Comitia Tributa was, for a considerable period, confined to the Plebeians, the Comitia Centuriata, from the very beginning, comprehended all citizens whatsoever, (*universus Populus Romanus*,)[5] the leading principle of classification being property, although both age and station exercised influence to a certain extent in the subordinate details. *Cum ex aetate et censu suffragium feratur Centuriata Comitia esse*.[6]

Original Constitution of the Comitia Centuriata.—We have seen (p. 70.) that the whole body of citizens was divided into 193 Centuries. When any question was submitted to the Comitia Centuriata it was decided by a majority of these Centuries. Each Century had one vote, and the vote of each Century was decided by the majority of the individuals who were included in that Century. Consequently, ninety-seven Centuries would form a majority in the Comitia Centuriata. But it will be observed that the first class, together with the eighteen Centuries of Equites made up ninety-eight Centuries, so that, if the Centuries of Equites and of the first class were unanimous, they would alone decide any question, whatever might be the views and wishes of the remaining Classes. Moreover, since the Equites and the first class were composed entirely of the most wealthy citizens, the aggregate of individuals contained in these ninety-eight Centuries must have been much smaller than in any other class; in fact, the number of individuals in each class would increase as the qualification became lower, and the lowest class, the sixth, would doubtless contain a larger number of individuals than all the other Classes taken together. Hence, the obvious effect of this system was to throw the whole power of the state into the hands of the wealthy, while those possessed of moderate means, and those who had little

---

[1] Tacit. Hist. I. 15. See also Suet. Octav. 65. Dion Cass. XXXVII 51. Appian. B.C. III. 94.
[2] Liv. IV. 4. 16. Suet. Tib. I. 1. Ner. 1. Octav. 2. There is an important passage on Adoptions in Aul. Gell. V. 19.
[3] Liv. XXVII. 8.
[4] Cic. de legg. III. 19. comp. Orat. post. red. in Sen. 11.
[5] Cic. de leg. agr. II. 2.
[6] Lael. ap. Aul. Gell. XV. 27.

or no realized capital would have a mere nominal voice without real influence, except when dissension prevailed among the rich. This must have been the object of Servius, who intended the Comitia Centuriata to be the supreme constitutional assembly, and this design was probably carried into execution while he lived;[1] but during the sway of the second Tarquin, all the principles and forms of the constitution were, in a great measure, set at naught, and his reign approached to a pure despotism.

Comitia Centuriata at the Commencement of the Republic.—After the overthrow of the monarchy, the whole power of the state was for a time wielded by the Patricians; and although the Comitia Centuriata was not abolished, it occupied a dependent position, since no measure could be submitted to the Centuries without the sanction of the Senate, and no vote of the Centuries was held valid until ratified by the Comitia Curiata.

But in the year B.C. 339, one hundred and seventy years after the expulsion of the Tarquins, the *Leges Publiliae* were passed, (see above p. 116,) which virtually abrogated the power possessed by the Comitia Curiata by declaring that the Patricians should be required to sanction by anticipation whatever laws might be passed in the Comitia Centuriata, and, at the same time, checked and limited the influence of the latter, by raising up a rival co-ordinate power in the Comitia Tributa, which was now elevated to the rank of a national assembly, and its ordinances, originally applicable to the Plebeians alone, were now made binding upon the whole community.

Centuria Praerogativa.—According to the constitution of Servius Tullius, when the Centuries were called up to vote they were summoned in regular order, beginning with the Equestrian Centuries, then the Centuries of the first class, and so on in succession.[2] Hence, as pointed out above, if the Equestrian Centuries and those of the first class were unanimous, the question was decided, and it was unnecessary to proceed further with the vote. But at an early period of the commonwealth,[3] a very important modification of these arrangements was introduced, the Centuries were no longer called up in regular order, beginning with the most wealthy and gradually descending, but the Century first called upon to vote was fixed by lot. The Century upon which the lot fell was termed *Centuria Praerogativa*, those which immediately followed were called *Primo vocatae*,[4] the rest *Iure vocatae*. This precedence in voting, which we might, at first sight, regard as of no moment, was rendered of great importance by the superstition of the Romans. The decision by lot was believed to be regulated by the Gods; and thus, the vote given by the *Centuria Praerogativa* was looked upon as an indication of the will of heaven, (*Praerogativam, omen comitiorum*, Cic. de Div. II. 40,) and as such, was followed, in elections at least, by a majority of the Centuries. This is known to have happened not merely in particular instances, as when Livy (XXVI. 22.) tells us—*auctoritatem Praerogativae omnes Centuriae secutae sunt*—but Cicero expressly declares that there was no example upon record of a candidate for a public office having failed to carry his election if he obtained the suffrage of the *Praerogativa—An tandem una Centuria*

---

[1] Dionys. IV. 20.
[2] Liv. I. 43. comp. XLIII. 16. Dionys. IV. 20. VII. 59.
[3] The first allusion to the practice seems to be in Liv. V. 18. where the historian is recording the events of B.C. 396.
[4] The *primo vocatae* may have been the Equestrian Centuries, but the matter is very doubtful. Livy (X. 22.) uses the expression—*eumque et praerogativa et primo vocatae omnes centuriae consulem dicebant*; elsewhere (XXVII. 6.) he speaks of the Centuries which followed the *praerogativa* as *iure vocatae*, while the Pseudo Asconius (Act. I. in Verr. 9.) says, *Praerogativae sunt tribus quae primae suffragium ferunt ante iure vocatas.*

Praerogativa tantum habet auctoritatis ut nemo unquam prior eam tulerit quin renuntiatus sit. Cic. pro Planc. 20.

In this way the influence of the wealthy Centuries, although the chances were in their favour, might sometimes be neutralized, and a Century of the fifth class, or even the *Capite Censi*, might decide the fate of a candidate.

Incorporation of the Centuries with the Tribes.—A change, apparently of a vital character, was introduced into the constitution of the Comitia Centuriata at some time or other during the commonwealth, but, unfortunately, every thing connected with the history of this change, important as it must have been, is enveloped in such impenetrable obscurity that we can determine neither the period when it took place nor form a distinct conception of its nature and extent. All that we know with certainty amounts to this, that the Centuries were somehow arranged so as to form component parts of the local Tribes, and hence the Tribes are repeatedly mentioned in connection with the Comitia Centuriata, with which originally they had certainly nothing in common.[1]

Various schemes have been drawn up with much ingenuity by different scholars, pointing out how this might have been effected without totally destroying the fundamental principles upon which the Comitia Centuriata were based. But it must be borne in mind that these attempts to solve the problem are little better than pure hypotheses, the notices contained in ancient writers being so scanty and imperfect that they can, without violence, be accommodated to plans the most opposite.

Business transacted in the Comitia Centuriata.—This was threefold.—1. Election of magistrates.—2. Enacting or repealing laws.—3. Criminal trials affecting the personal and political privileges of Roman citizens, to which we may add—The declaration of war and the conclusion of peace, although this is included under (2.)

Magistrates.—The magistrates always elected in the Comitia Centuriata, were the Consuls, the Praetors and the Censors, to which we may add the *Decemviri* during the brief period of their existence, and the *Tribuni Militares consulari potestate*.[2] It would appear that the Curule Aediles and the Quaestors might be chosen either in the Comitia Centuriata or in the Comitia Tributa, at least such seems to have been the case in the time of Cicero.[3] We find also that in special cases the Comitia Centuriata nominated Proconsuls, and once it appointed a Prodictator.[4] There is some reason to believe that during the first years of the commonwealth the Comitia Centuriata could not vote for any candidates for the consulship unless such as had previously received the sanction of the Senate; but this restriction, if it ever existed, seems to have been removed about B.C. 482. See Zonaras, as quoted by Niebuhr, vol. II. p. 205.

Laws.—Any proposal for enacting a new law or repealing one already in force, might be submitted to the Comitia Centuriata by the presiding magistrate, provided it had previously received the sanction of the Senate (*ex senatusconsulto.*)

Criminal Trials.—According to the laws of the XII Tables, no charge which involved the *Caput* (see p. 83.) of a Roman citizen, could be tried before any tribunal except the Comitia Centuriata—*Tum leges praeclarissimae de*

---
[1] e.g. Liv. XXIV. 7. XXVII. 6. XXIX. 37. Cic. de leg. agr. II. 2.
[2] Liv. III. 33. 35. V. 52.
[3] Cic. pro Planc. 20. ad Att. IV. 3. ad Fam. VII. 30.
[4] Liv. XXVI. 18. XXII. 8.

XII Tabulis tralatae duae: quarum altera privilegia tollit: altera de Capite civis rogari, nisi maximo comitiatu, vetat.—Cic de legg. III. 19. pro Sest. 34. From an early period, however, the Comitia Centuriata was in the habit of delegating its authority to commissioners, as we shall explain more fully in the chapter on criminal trials.

Magistrates who could Summon and Preside at the Comitia Centuriata.—Of the ordinary magistrates, the *Consul*, the *Praetor Urbanus*, and the *Censor* possessed this privilege,[1] and also the *Decemviri* and the *Tribuni Militares consulari potestate*, at the period when these offices were in existence; of the extraordinary magistrates, the *Dictator*, the *Magister Equitum*, and the *Inter-rex;* but all had not the same powers.

When one only of the Consuls was in the city, it belonged to him to summon and preside at these assemblies, whatever the business might be—if both consuls were present, they usually decided by lot which of them should perform this duty—and when both were obliged to quit the city, they arranged beforehand which should return and preside at the elections.[2] The *Decemviri*, the *Tribuni Militares consulari potestate*, the *Dictator* and the *Magister Equitum*, stood exactly in the same position as the Consuls.

The *Praetor Urbanus* could hold the Comitia Centuriata for trials only,[3] except in some rare cases in which he received special authority, and which must therefore be regarded as exceptions to the rule.[4] The Censors could preside only when the assembly was convoked for matters connected with their peculiar duty of taking the Census, and the Inter-rex, probably, at elections only. The first Consuls, according to Livy, (I. 60,) were elected in the Comitia Centuriata by the *Praefectus Urbi;* but on this point he is contradicted by Dionysius (IV. 84.)

Preliminary Forms.—To some of these we have already adverted—

1. The Senate fixed the day on which the assembly was to be held, having, in the case of laws, given their sanction to the measure which was to be proposed.

2. Public notice of the day of meeting and of the business was given by a written proclamation, (*edictum*,) usually seventeen days (*trinundinum*) beforehand. See above p. 113.

3. Immediately after midnight, on the morning fixed for the assembly, the auspices were taken as described, p. 112.

4. On the day of assembly a formal verbal proclamation was made by a public servant, a *praeco, accensus*, or *cornicen*, and in later times, according to Varro, by an *Augur*, calling upon the people to meet before the Consul.[5]

Place of Meeting.—The organization of the Classes and Centuriae being originally essentially military, the people were wont, in ancient times, to assemble in martial order, and probably fully armed. Hence the Comitia Centuriata is frequently termed, especially in legal or sacred formularies, *Exercitus urbanus*—*Exercitus centuriatus*, or simply *Exercitus*—the presiding magistrate was said *Imperare exercitum*, and when he dismissed the assembly, *Exercitum remittere*.[6] But since it was contrary to the principles of the constitution that any body of armed men should congregate within the walls of the city, it was

---

[1] To these, some would add the *Quaestores*, at least in so far as trials in the earliest ages were concerned. See Varro. L.L. VI. § 90. comp. Liv. III. 24.
[2] Liv. XXXV. 6. 20. XXIV. 10.
[3] Liv. XXVI. 3. XLIII. 16. Dion Cass. XXXVII. 27.
[4] Liv. XXV. 7. XXVII. 5.
[5] Aul. Gell. XV. 27. and a somewhat obscure passage in Varro L.L. VI. § 95.
[6] Varro L.L. VI. § 88. § 94. Fest. s.v. *Remisso*, p. 289. Liv. I. 43. XXXIX. 15. Aul. Gell. XIII. 15. XV. 27

necessary that the Comitia Centuriata should be held outside the *Pomoerium*. From the earliest times the Campus Martius was the regular place of meeting, and on one occasion only do we find the Centuries assembling in a different locality, (the *Lucus Poetelinus*, outside of the *Porta Nomentana*, beyond the Viminal,) but this was for the special object of avoiding the sight of the Capitoline.[1] Even after the practice of assembling in arms had long been discontinued, the Campus Martius continued to be the place of meeting; and as a memorial of the precautions observed in ancient times, when Rome was surrounded by hostile tribes up to her very walls, to prevent a surprise, a detachment of men was posted upon the Janiculum with a red banner (*vexillum rufi coloris*) displayed. In the early ages, when this banner was lowered it was a signal that danger was at hand, and the Comitia immediately broke up. The rule was never formally set aside; and accordingly, in the time of Cicero, we find that the consul Metellus gave orders for the flag on the Janiculum to be struck while the trial of Rabirius was proceeding, and thus succeeded in breaking up the assembly before it came to a vote.[2]

Form of Procedure.—The citizens being assembled, and no interruption being announced from the auspices, the proceedings were opened by a solemn prayer, (*solemne carmen precationis—solemnis ista comitiorum precatio—longum illud comitiorum carmen*,) offered up by the presiding magistrate, and the prayer was generally, if not always, preceded by a sacrifice.[3] The religious rites being completed, the president submitted to the meeting the matter upon which they were required to decide, and introduced his statement (*praefabatur*) by the solemn formula—*Quod bonum, faustum, felix, fortunatumque sit.*[4] In the case of an election, he read over the names of the different candidates, and might, if he thought fit, make observations upon their comparative merits.[5] After he had concluded, any magistrate of equal or superior rank, or any of the Tribunes of the Plebs, might address the multitude, and then private individuals,[6] if they could obtain permission from the president and the tribunes, might come forward to argue in favour of, or against, the measure—*Ad suadendum dissuadendumque prohibant—Romanis pro concione suadere et dissuadere* (sc. rogationem) *moris fuit.*[7] This portion of the proceedings being brought to a conclusion, if no tribune interposed his Veto, and no declaration of an unfavourable omen (*obnuntiatio*) was announced by a qualified person, the president called upon the people to separate for the purpose of voting—*Si vobis videtur, discedite Quirites—Ite in suffragium bene iuvantibus Dis.* The crowd, which had hitherto been standing promiscuously, then separated, each Century having, probably, a position assigned to it. Then followed the casting of lots to decide which Century should vote first (*sortitio praerogativae.*) The names of the different Centuries, written upon tickets (*sortes*) were thrown (*coniiciebantur*) into a vase, (*urna* s. *sitella*,) were shaken together, (*aequabantur*,) and one of them was thrown or drawn out, that which came first (*quae prima exierat*) being the *praerogativa.* When the *Centuria praerogativa* had given its vote,

---

[1] Liv. VI. 20.
[2] Liv. XXXIX. 15. Macrob. S. I. 16.
[3] Dionys. VII. 59. IX. 41. X. 4. 32. Liv. XXXVIII. 48. XXXIX. 15. Cic. pro Muren. 1. Plin. Paneg. I. 63.
[4] Cic. de Divin. I. 45.
[5] Liv. X. 22. XXII. 34.
[6] It would appear from Dion Cass. XXXIX. 35. that private persons, occasionally at least spoke before the magistrates.
[7] Liv. XXXIV. 1. XLII. 34. Quintil. I. O. II. 4.

the other Centuries were called up in regular succession, beginning with the Equestrian Centuries and the first class, an arrangement which seems to have remained unaltered in the days of Cicero, although a bill was brought in by C. Gracchus to determine the precedence of the whole by lot—*lex quam C. Gracchus in tribunatu promulgaverat, ut ex confusis quinque classibus sorte centuriae vocarentur.* But although it does not appear that this proposal ever became law, it would seem that the Centuries sometimes voted without paying attention to any regular order of succession, and were in that case said *inire confusum suffragium.*[1] The manner of taking and counting the votes, of announcing the result, and dismissing the assembly, being common to all Comitia alike, have been already detailed in p. 108.

COMITIA TRIBUTA.

As the *Comitia Curiata* were at all times composed of Patricians alone, so there is every reason to believe that the *Comitia Tributa* were originally confined to the Plebeians; the *Comitia Centuriata* being the only one of the three popular assemblies which, from the first, comprehended the members of both orders. Hence the *Comitia Tributa* are frequently termed *Concilia Plebis*, a name which they retained even after they had ceased to be meetings of the Plebs exclusively,[2] and the decrees passed in them were called *Plebiscita* in opposition to the *Leges* of the Comitia Centuriata; the resolutions of the Plebs being technically expressed by the verb *sciscere*, while the people at large were said *iubere*—*Nullam illi nostri,* [maiores,] *sapientissimi et sanctissimi viri vim concionis esse voluerunt. Quae sciscerct Plebes, aut quae Populus iuberet; summota concione, distributis partibus, tributim et centuriatim descriptis ordinibus, classibus, aetatibus, auditis auctoribus, re multos dies promulgata et cognita, iuberi vetarique voluerunt.*[3]

Origin and Progress of the Comitia Tributa.—There can be little doubt that the Tribes, from the time of their organization by Servius Tullius, would occasionally assemble individually or collectively, for the discussion of matters connected with their local or general interests; but these meetings did not assume the form or dignity of regular Comitia until the year B.C. 491, when the Tribes were convoked to give their verdict on the charges against Coriolanus, and this is regarded by Dionysius as the first example of a meeting of the *Comitia Tributa* properly so called.[4] But even this might be regarded as an extraordinary procedure, not to be recognised as a precedent, and we can scarcely consider the Comitia Tributa to have been placed upon a regular footing until twenty years later, (B.C. 471,) when Publilius Volero, Tribune of the Plebs, passed a law which ordained that the Plebeian magistrates, who had hitherto been chosen by the Comitia Curiata, should for the future be elected in the Comitia Tributa.[5] This secured regular meetings at stated periods; but the legislative powers of the Comitia Tributa, in so far as the community at large was concerned, were not fully established until a much later period. We find three distinct enactments on this subject—

---

[1] Cic. Philipp. II. 33. pro. Muren. 23. pro Cornel. fragm. Liv. XXIV. 7. XLIII. 16. Val. Max. VI. iii. 4. Sallust. de ordin. rep. Epp. II. 8.
[2] Liv. III. 54. XXV. 3. 4. XXVII. 5. XXXIX. 15.
[3] Cic. pro Flacc. 7. Aul. Gell. X. 20. XV. 27. Fest. s.v. *Populi*, p. 233.
[4] Dionys. VII. 59.
[5] Liv. II. 56. Dionys. IX. 41. Zonar. VII. 17.

1. *Lex Valeria Horatia*, passed by L. Valerius and M. Horatius when Consuls, B.C. 449, who *legem Centuriatis Comitiis tulere, ut quod tributim Plebes iussisset, Populum teneret.*[1]

2. *Lex Publilia*, passed by Q. Publilius Philo when Dictator, B.C. 339— *Ut Plebiscita omnes Quirites tenerent.*[2]

3. *Lex Hortensia* passed by Q. Hortensius when Dictator, B.C. 286—*Ut Plebiscita universum Populum tenerent.*[3]

It would, at first sight, appear that these laws, although spread over a space of a hundred and sixty years, were absolutely identical, each providing that the *Plebiscita*, or ordinances passed by the Plebs in the Comitia Tributa, should be binding not on the Plebs alone, but on the whole body of the Roman people (*Quirites—universus Populus Romanus.*) The difficulty may be explained by supposing that the *Lex Valeria Horatia* gave to *Plebiscita* the force of *Leges*, provided they were sanctioned by the Senate before being submitted to the Tribes, and subsequently ratified by the Comitia Curiata, that the *Lex Publilia* deprived the Comitia Curiata of all right to interfere, and that the *Lex Hortensia* declared the consent of the Senate to be unnecessary. This, it must be understood, is merely a hypothesis; but it is not improbable in itself, and is in accordance with what we know positively with regard to the progress of the constitution.

From the passing of the *Lex Valeria Horatia*, the Comitia Tributa assumed the right of discharging functions of the same nature as those committed to the Comitia Centuriata, that is, the election of magistrates, the enactment of laws, and the trial of criminals. And we can have little doubt, that from this time forward the Patricians and their Clients voted in these assemblies, while we have no evidence to prove that this took place before the enactment of the laws of the XII Tables, B.C. 450. It is true that, theoretically, those matters alone ought to have been submitted to the Comitia Tributa which were conceived to affect peculiarly the interests of the Plebs; but it is easy, at the same time, to perceive that this principle, even if fully recognised, would admit of great latitude of interpretation in times of popular excitement. After the Plebeians were admitted to a full participation in the honours of the state, there appears to have been little collision between the *Comitia Centuriata* and the *Comitia Tributa*, each assembly had its own duties defined with sufficient distinctness, to which they, for the most part, confined themselves.

Those which fell to the Comitia Tributa in the three departments noticed above, may be briefly enumerated.

Magistrates.—1. The purely Plebeian magistrates, in terms of the law of Publilius Volero, namely, the *Tribuni Plebis* and *Aediles Plebeii*.

2. The *Aediles Curules* and the *Quaestores*, during a considerable period; but upon this point we shall speak more at large when treating of these offices.

3. The members of the great colleges of priests, after the passing of the *Lex Domitia*, B.C. 104.

4. Most of the inferior magistrates such as *Triumviri Monetales*; *Triumviri Capitales*, and others to be specified hereafter (Aul. Gell. XIII. 15.)

5. Such of the *Tribuni Militum* as were not nominated by the general (Sall. Jug. 60. Liv. VII. 5.)

6. The commissioners, (*Curatores*,) appointed from time to time for portioning

---

[1] Liv. III. 55. Dionys. XI. 45.
[2] Liv. VIII. 12.
[3] Aul. Gell. XV. 27. Liv. Epit. XI. Plin. H.N. XVI. 10. Gaius I § 3.

out grants of the public land among the poorer classes (*Duumviri, Triumviri, &c. agris dividundis.* Cic. de leg. agr. II. 7.)

Trials.—These were originally limited to cases which involved a charge of having invaded or infringed the rights and privileges of the Plebeians as an order. Such were the trials of Coriolanus, of Kaeso Quinctius, of Appius the Decemvir, and of Caius Sempronius.[1] Subsequently this jurisdiction was extended,[2] in so far as the nature of the offences was concerned; but by the laws of the XII. Tables, the Comitia Tributa were prohibited from inflicting any punishment more severe than the imposition of a fine—(*multae irrogatio*)—an offence involving the *Caput* of a Roman citizen, could be tried before the Comitia Centuriata only.

Laws.—It is a matter of great difficulty to fix, in general terms, what class of laws could be legitimately submitted to the Comitia of the Tribes, and indeed it would seem that this point was never very clearly defined. According to the theory of the constitution, it would be those only which bore upon the interests of the Plebs as a separate order; but this limitation would manifestly prove almost worthless in practice, for no measure whatsoever could be brought forward which might not be proved to bear either directly or indirectly on the interests of the Plebeians. The difficulty was increased by the circumstance that the Senate, when extraordinary dispatch was required, or when it seemed unnecessary to observe all the tedious forms required for the Comitia Centuriata, frequently requested the Tribunes of the Plebs to submit matters to the Comitia Tributa which, under ordinary circumstances, would have been placed before the Comitia Centuriata.

That the powers of the Comitia Tributa were held to be limited is clear from a passage in Livy, (XXXVIII. 36. B.C. 188,) where C. Valerius Tappus, a Tribune of the Plebs, is represented as having brought in a law for bestowing the full *Civitas* on the the inhabitants of Fundi, Formiae and Arpinum, on which four of his colleagues were about to place their Veto, on the ground that it had been introduced without the sanction of the Senate, (*quia non ex auctoritate Senatus ferretur,*) but withdrew their opposition—*edocti populi esse non Senatus ius, suffragium quibus velit, impartiri.* But although the powers of the Comitia Tributa were, to a certain extent, ill defined, there were some matters, such as the election of consuls and other superior magistrates, in which they never attempted to interfere.

Magistrates who Summoned and Presided in the Comitia Tributa. —The *Tribuni Plebis* were naturally the persons by whom the Comitia Tributa were, in most cases, summoned, and who presided. When a measure was proposed by one Tribune specially, with the consent, however, of all his colleagues, which was essential, he would obviously preside at the meeting called to consider it. When matters were brought forward in which the whole college of Tribunes might be supposed to feel an equal interest, then, in all probability, the presidency was decided by lot (Liv. III. 64.)

The *Aediles Plebeii* also had the right of holding the Comitia Tributa, but only, it would seem, for impeachments and matters of police immediately connected with their own peculiar jurisdiction.[3]

The Consuls and Praetors frequently presided at the election of such magistrates as the *Aediles Curules* and the *Quaestores*, and also at trials, but very rarely when laws were proposed; and it seems certain that no measure whatsoever

---

[1] Dionys. VII. 59. Liv. II. 35. III. 11. 56. IV. 44.
[2] e.g. Liv. XXV. 3. Val. Max. VI. i. 7.
[3] Liv. III. 31. Dionys. X. 48. Val Max. VI. i. 7.

could be proposed to the Tribes, nor any business be transacted without the permission of the Tribunes.[1]

Mode of Summoning.—The Comitia Tributa might be summoned at the discretion of the Tribunes of the Plebs. Notice was given of the proposed meeting, sometimes verbally from the *Rostra*, more frequently by means of a proclamation (*edictum*) hung up in the Forum, and the Viatores of the Tribunes were sent round to warn the country voters within reach. When the public notice was given the nature of the business was explained, and when a law was to be proposed, a copy of the law, with the names of its most strenuous supporters, (*auctores*) was publicly exposed, such publication (*promulgatio*,) after the passing of the *Lex Caecilia Didia* (see above, p. 113,) taking place at least a *Trinundinum* before the day fixed for the assembly.

Place of Meeting.—The Comitia Tributa not being like the Comitia Centuriata, essentially a military assemblage, might be held any where either within or without the walls, provided the distance from the Pomoerium was not more than a mile, beyond which limit the Tribunes had no jurisdiction. The ordinary place of meeting within the city was the lower Forum, and more rarely the Capitol; without the city, the Campus Martius, or the Prata Flaminia.[2]

Preliminary Forms.—All the formalities with regard to auspices[3] and sacrifices were dispensed with in the Comitia Tributa. The only obstacle seems to have been the formal announcement, (*obnuntiatio*,) by a qualified person, that he was observing the heavens (*se servare de coelo*.) See above, p. 113. Comp. Cic. in Vatin. 2.

Mode of Procedure.—The people having assembled, the president explained to the meeting the matter for which it had been called together; if a law was proposed, it was read over by a clerk (*scriba*) or public crier; (*praeco;*) if an election was to take place, the names of the candidates were proclaimed by the president, who then introduced those who were desirous of speaking. No one could address the assembly without his permission except a Tribune, any one of whom could at once put an end to the proceedings by his Veto.

Voting.—When the matter had been sufficiently discussed, the multitude, who had been standing promiscuously, now separated and divided into their respective Tribes. Lots were then cast, deciding the order in which each tribe should vote, that which was called upon to vote first being styled *Tribus Principium* or *Tribus Praerogativa* and the Tribes which followed *Iure Vocatae*. The votes were originally given vivâ voce, afterwards by ballot, as explained above, p. 108. Each Tribe had one vote, the vote of the Tribe being decided by the majority of individuals who composed the Tribe, and the majority of Tribes deciding the question at issue.

Although the Comitia Tributa was the most democratic in its constitution of all the popular assemblies, the classification of the voters, depending entirely upon their place of residence, without reference to descent, fortune, or age, it must not be supposed that the suffrage of each citizen had equal weight in deciding a question, since this could only have been the case had each Tribe contained exactly the same number of voters. When Servius Tullius first distributed the people into local tribes, the sum total of those who lived constantly in the city

---

[1] Liv. II. 56. III. 31. 55. 64. IV. 57. V. 17. XXV. 3. 4. XXVII. 20. XXX. 41. Dionys. VI. 89. IX. 41. seqq. X. 48. Cic. pro Sest. 33. de leg. agr. II. 9. pro Planc. 20. in Vatin. 6. Aul. Gell. IV. 14. Val. Max. VI § 7.
[2] Liv. III. 54. XXV. 3. XXVII. 21. XXXIII. 25. XLIII. 16. Cic. ad Fam. VII. 30. ad Att. I. 1. IV. 3. Plut. C. Gracch. 3.
[3] On this a doubt may exist, see p. 110. and the references in note.

was not very great, and the Roman territory was divided among a very large body of small proprietors, so that the number of individuals in each of the four regions of the city did not, probably, greatly exceed the number of those who were enrolled in the twenty-six country districts. But, as the population of Rome increased, the estates around became more extensive, and the number of proprietors and of free labourers diminished, so that the disparity of numbers in the City and the Rustic Tribes must have been striking, although this was, to a certain extent, counterbalanced by the enrolment in one or other of the Rustic Tribes of the inhabitants of those Municipia who, from time to time, were admitted to the full *Civitas*. The Tribe to which each citizen belonged was, strictly speaking, determined by the place of his abode ; but a wide discretion seems to have been left to the censors, under whose inspection the lists were made up. Accordingly, we find that Appius Claudius, (censor B.C. 312,) who seized every opportunity of mortifying the aristocracy, in order to render the Comitia Tributa more democratic, and to neutralize the influence of the country voters, dispersed the lowest class of citizens among all the Tribes (*humilibus per omnes tribus divisis Forum et Campum corrupit* . . . *Ex eo tempore in duas partes discessit civitas. Aliud integer populus, fautor et cultor bonorum, aliud forensis factio tenebat.*)[1] This arrangement was, however, overthrown by Q. Fabius Rullianus, who, when censor, (B.C. 304,) enrolled the whole of the "forensis turba" in the four city tribes, and thus gained for himself and his descendants the title of *Maximus*—*Fabius, simul concordiae causa, simul ne humillimorum in manu Comitia essent, omnem forensem turbam excretam in quatuor tribus coniecit, urbanasque eas appellavit.*[2]

The changes which took place from time to time regarding the Tribes in which *Libertini* were enrolled have been already noticed. See p. 102.

COMITIA CALATA.

In addition to the *Comitia Curiata*, *C. Centuriata* and *C. Tributa*, we find a fourth species of Comitia mentioned, although rarely, by ancient writers, under the name of *Comitia Calata*, and much discussion has taken place among scholars with regard to the nature and object of these assemblies. Our chief information is derived from the following passage, in Aulus Gellius (XV. 27.)—

In libro Laelii Felicis ad Q. Mucium primo scriptum est, Labeonem scribere, CALATA COMITIA *esse, quae pro collegio pontificum habentur aut Regis aut Flaminum inaugurandorum causa. Eorum autem alia esse* CURIATA, *alia* CENTURIATA. *Curiata per lictorem Curiatum calari id est, convocari: Centuriata per cornicinem. Iisdem Comitiis quae* CALATA *appellari diximus, et Sacrorum Detestatio et Testamenta fieri solebant. Tria enim genera testamentorum fuisse accepimus; unum, quod in Calatis Comitiis, in concione populi fieret,* &c.

It appears from this—

1. That the *Comitia Calata* was an assembly held by the Pontifices, and here we may remark that the verb *Calare*, meaning *to summon*, was in ordinary use among the Roman priests, whose attendants were termed *Calatores*.

2. That the people assembled sometimes in *Curiae* and sometimes in *Centuriae*.

---
[1] Liv. IX. 46.
[2] Liv. l.c.
[3] Varro L. L. V. § 13. VI. § 16. 27. Paul. Diac. s.v. *Calatores*, p. 38. Macrob. S. L 15, Serv. ad Virg. G. I. 268. Æn. VIII. 654.

3. That the objects for which these meetings were held were threefold—(*a*) For the consecration of certain priests, the *Rex Sacrificulus* and the *Flamines*—(*b*) For the making of wills—(*c*) For the *Detestatio Sacrorum*.

From a full consideration of the above, and all other passages bearing upon this subject, it appears probable that these assemblies were of the same nature as those held in the Capitol, in front of the *Curia Calabra*, (see p. 26,) to which the people were convoked (*calabantur*) on the appearance of each new moon, when one of the Pontifices or the Rex Sacrificulus made proclamation (*calando prodebat*) of the distribution of the Nones and Ides for the month, and also of the days consecrated to the worship of the gods. It seems certain, moreover, that in the Comitia Calata, for whatever purpose summoned, the people at large were altogether passive, being merely listeners receiving information, or witnesses beholding some formal procedure.[1]

With regard to the making of wills, we find a distinct assertion in Gaius (II. § 101.)—*Testamentorum autem genera initio duo fuerunt: nam aut Calatis Comitiis faciebant, quae Comitia bis in anno testamentis faciendis destinata erant*, &c.—and then proceeds to say, that the practice of making wills in this manner had fallen altogether into disuse. A will made in the Comitia Calata was, in all probability, a formal public declaration by the testator, of the manner in which he wished his property to be disposed of after death, and this method was resorted to at a period when written documents were little employed, in order that his real wishes might be proved by a multitude of witnesses, and all dispute and litigation thus obviated.

With regard to the *Detestatio Sacrorum* it is impossible to speak with confidence, since the expression is found nowhere except in the passage quoted above. It is generally believed to have been a formal declaration upon the part of an heir, that he renounced certain sacred rites which were occasionally attached to property,[2] such renunciation requiring the sanction of the Pontifex Maximus, given in presence of the assembled people.

If the views explained above are correct, it follows that Comitia Calata approached more nearly in their character to *Conciones* than to *Comitia* properly so called, since the essence of *Comitia* was wanting, the people not being *asked* to vote upon any proposal, but summoned merely to see and to hear; and this is confirmed by the expression of Aulus Gellius—*Tria enim genera testamentorum fuisse accepimus unum quod Calatis Comitiis* IN CONCIONE POPULI *fieret*, &c.

Comitia under the Empire.—This subject may be dismissed in a very few words.

Comitia Curiata.—The Comitia Curiata continued to meet under the Empire, for the purpose of confirming adoptions. *Leges Curiatae* were passed, ratifying the adoption of Tiberius by Augustus and of Nero by Claudius. The ceremony is alluded to as common in the speech of Galba, reported by Tacitus, and although at a later period the consent of the Senate was held to be sufficient, the ancient practice was not formally abrogated until a law was enacted (A.D. 286) by Diocletian declaring—*Arrogatio ex indulgentia principali facta, perinde valet apud Praetorem vel Praesidem intimata, ac si per Populum iure antiquo facta esset*.[3]

---

[1] Varro L.L. V. § 13. VI. § 16. 27. Paul. Diac. s.v. *Calatores*, p. 38. Macrob. S. I. 15. Serv. ad Virg. G. I. 263. Æn. VIII. 654.
[2] Cic. de legg. II. 21.
[3] Suet. Octav. 65. Tacit. Ann. XII. 26. 41. Hist. I. 15. Dion Cass. LXIX. 20. LXXIX. 17. Cod. Iust. VIII. xlviii. 2.

Comitia Centuriata and *Comitia Tributa*.—We have seen that the prerogative of the people, as exercised under the republic, in these Comitia, was fourfold—1. To declare war and to conclude peace. 2. To act as a supreme court of criminal judicature in all cases affecting the life and privileges of a Roman citizen. 3. To enact laws. 4. To elect magistrates.

1. With regard to the first of these matters, the people seem never to have been consulted after the battle of Pharsalia.[1]

2. Their direct interference with the second had been, in a great measure, rendered unnecessary, by the institution of the *Quaestiones Perpetuae*, which we shall discuss at large hereafter. They still, however, even in the age of Cicero, acted as judges in causes, such as that of Rabirius, for which no separate court had been established, and their control over criminal prosecutions was fully acknowledged in theory until they were finally deprived of all jurisdiction by Augustus.[2]

3. They retained the power of enacting laws, ostensibly at least, for a longer period.

Augustus submitted several measures to the people in their Comitia according to ancient forms, and in some instances met with such strenuous opposition that he was compelled to modify his proposals. His example was followed to a certain extent by Tiberius and Claudius; and the assemblies appear to have been occasionally summoned for legislative purposes as late as the reign of Nerva. Gradually, however, the epistles and decrees of the Prince and the resolutions of the Senate, passed with his approbation, superseded all other legislation; and we have no reason to believe that any bill was ever submitted to the Comitia after the close of the first century.[3]

4. The Comitia were still summoned for the election of magistrates in the second century, but they did not possess even a shadow of power. Julius Caesar and Augustus *recommended*, as the phrase was—*Commendo vobis*—the persons whom they desired to raise to the Consulship, and also one half of the number of candidates requisite to fill the other offices of state, professing to leave the remaining places open to free competition, and Augustus even went through the farce of canvassing the electors in person on behalf of those whom he had named.[4] But under Tiberius, the little which had been left by his predecessor was taken away; and while the Emperor still continued to nominate the Consuls and a certain number of the magistrates of inferior grade, the rest were selected by the Senate. However, when Tacitus says (Ann. I. 16)—*Tum primum e Campo Comitia ad Patres translata sunt*—he does not mean to assert that popular assemblies for the election of magistrates were no longer held, but merely that they thenceforward ceased to exercise any real influence.[5] The Comitia Centuriata were regularly summoned, and met, as in the olden time, in the Campus Martius; and down to the period indicated above, the proceedings seem to have been conducted with due regard to all ancient forms and ceremonies. A Consul presided, auspices were observed, prayers and sacrifices were offered up, and even the red flag was hoisted on the Janiculum;[6] but the people, instead of

---

[1] See Dion Cass. XLII. 20.
[2] Dion Cass. LVI. 40.
[3] Suet. Octav. 34. Vesp. 11. comp. Senec. de benef. VI. 32. Gaius I. § 4. 5. Digest. I. ii. 2. § 12. iii. 9. iv. 1. The words of the Institutions I. ii. 5. are very distinct.
[4] Suet. Caes. 41. Octav. 40. 56. Vitell. 11. Tacit. Hist. I. 77. comp. Dion Cass. XLII. 20. XLIII. 45. 47. 51. LIII. 21. LV. 34. Appian. B.C. I. 103.
[5] Tacit. Ann. I. 16 81. Velleius II. 124. 126. Dion Cass. LVIII. 20.
[6] Suet. Vesp. 5. Dom. 10. Plin. Panegyr. 63. seqq. Dion Cass. XXXVII. 28. LVIII. 20. comp. Vopisc. Tacit. 7.

being called upon to choose freely from a numerous body of aspirants, were required merely to give their sanction to a list, previously drawn up by the Prince and the Senate, containing the exact number of individuals requisite to fill the vacant offices, and no more. An attempt was made by Caligula to make over once more the elections to the people, but the arrangements of Tiberius were soon restored.[1] Although the people were thus altogether excluded, the power of selection intrusted to the Senate was, under some emperors at least, exercised freely. This appears from the accounts transmitted to us by the younger Pliny of the zeal with which the Senators were canvassed and bribed, just as the larger constituencies had been in former days; of the violent party spirit exhibited, and of the scenes of tumult and confusion which arose, and which rendered the introduction of the ballot expedient, forcibly contrasting these disorders with the grave and dignified composure which had characterized the proceedings under the first Emperors.[2]

It would appear that at the beginning of the fourth century the people had ceased to be called together even as a matter of form, and by writers who flourished at the close of that century the Comitia are spoken of as political institutions understood by antiquarians only.[3] The words of Symmachus (fl. A.D. 380) are very distinct as to the practice in his time—*Intelligamus nostri seculi bona: abest cera turpis, diribitio corrupta clientelarum cuneis, sitella venalis. Inter Senatum et Principes Comitia transiguntur: eligunt Patres, confirmant Superiores.* (Orat. ined. p. 40. ed. Mai.)

---

[1] Suet. Cal. 16. Dion Cass. LIX. 9. 20. comp. Juv. S. X. 77. Modest. Digest. XLVIII. xiv 1. Dion Cass. LII. 30.
[2] Plin. Epp. III. 20. comp. IV. 25. VI. 19. Tacit. Ann. IV 2. XIII. 29. Dion Cass. LXXVIII. 22.
[3] Arnob. adv. gent. II. 67. Ammian. Marcell. XIV.

CHAPTER V.

MAGISTRATES OF THE REGAL AND REPUBLICAN PERIODS AND UNDER THE EARLY EMPERORS.[1]

REGES.

For two hundred and forty-four years after the foundation of the city, the administration of public affairs was in the hands of one supreme magistrate, who held his office for life, with the title of *Rex*.

Duties discharged by the King.—The functions of the King were threefold—

1. He was the supreme civil magistrate, the upholder of order and the laws; he alone had the right to summon meetings of the Senate and of the Comitia and to guide their deliberations, and he presided in all courts of justice.
2. He was commander-in-chief of the armies of the state.
3. He was chief priest, and as such, exercised a guiding influence over all matters connected with public religion.

Mode of Election.—Although the office of King was held for life, it was not a hereditary but an elective monarchy. When a King died, the supreme power (*summa potestas*) having proceeded from the Patricians, who constituted the *Populus*, was supposed to return to them (*res ad patres rediit.*) They were forthwith summoned (*convocabantur*) by the Senate; they assembled in the Comitia Curiata, and proceeded at once to choose, out of their own body, a temporary King (*prodere interregem*) to discharge the duties of the regal office until matters were ripe for a new election. This *Interrex* remained in office for five days, and then himself nominated (*prodidit*) his successor, who continued in office for a like period. It was understood that the Comitia for the choice of a new King was not to be held by the first Interrex, but the second might proceed to the election; if a longer period was required for deliberation, a number of Interreges might follow in succession. At length the Interrex and the Senate having, in all probability, made arrangements as to the person to be proposed, and the Comitia Curiata, consisting entirely of Patricians, having been regularly summoned by the Interrex, the individual nominated by a majority of the Curiae was chosen (*creatus est*) King; but the Curiae were restricted to those candidates who had received the sanction of the Senate, and were proposed by the Interrex—*Tullum Hostilium populus Regem, interrege rogante, Comitiis Curiatis creavit.* When the result had been announced by the Interrex who presided, the monarch elect was conducted by an Augur to the Arx, and there seated on a stone called the Auguraculum, with his face to the south. The omens

---

[1] The best summary of all that is known with regard to the Roman magistrates will be found in BECKER, Handbuch der Römischen Alterthümer, Iter. Theil. Ite. Abtheil. p. 291 —339; 2te. Abtheil. p. 1—456. and the continuation by MARQUARDT.

were then observed, and if favourable, the fact was announced by the augur to the multitude assembled in the Forum below; and the choice of the Curiae, in so far as the priestly character of the monarch was concerned, was declared to be ratified by the approval of the gods.[1] Finally, the new King summoned the Comitia Curiata, and submitted to them a law conferring *Imperium* upon himself,[2] and this having been passed,[3] the ceremonies were held to be complete.

Such, as far as we can gather, from the indistinct and inconsistent statements of those writers who have touched upon this obscure period, were the forms anciently observed. The accounts with regard to the Interrex are especially contradictory, and the authors who speak with the greatest precision, evidently took it for granted that all the rules and usages connected with the Interrex of the republican times were identical with those in force in regard to the functionary who bore the same appellation in the days of the Kings.[4]

Servius Tullius was, we are told, the first King who seated himself upon the throne without having been duly elected by the Comitia Curiata, (*iniussu populi*,) but he obtained their sanction to a *Lex Curiata de imperio* (Cic. de R. 21.)

Insignia of the Kings.[5] —These were—

1. Twelve attendants, called *Lictores*, each bearing a bundle of rods, with an axe in the midst, (*fasces cum securibus*,) emblematic of the power of scourging and of life and death.

2. *Sella Curulis*, a chair of state ornamented with ivory.

3. *Toga Praetexta*, a white cloak or mantle with a scarlet border, or sometimes a *Toga Picta*, a cloak embroidered with figures.

4. *Trabea*, a tunic striped with scarlet or purple.

TRIBUNUS CELERUM.

The *Tribunus Celerum* or commander of the cavalry, occupied the second place in the state, being a sort of aid-de-camp to the King, and his representative in military affairs;[6] on the other hand, the

CUSTOS URBIS S. PRAEFECTUS URBI

was an officer appointed by the King to act as his deputy when compelled to quit the city.[7] There were also

QUAESTORES;

but we shall reserve our remarks upon these until we discuss the Quaestors of the commonwealth.

We now proceed to treat of the magistrates under the republic, commencing with the—

CONSULES.

Origin of the Office.—Upon the expulsion of the Kings, it was resolved, in accordance, we are told, with a suggestion contained in the commentaries of

---

1 Liv. I. 18. Plut. Num. 7. Paul. Diac. s.v. *Auguraculum*, p. 18.
2 Cic. de R. II. 13. 17. 18. 21.
3 This last sanction was expressed by the phrase *Patres auctores fiunt—Patres auctores fuerunt*. See Liv. I. 17.
4 The chief authorities are, Cic. de R. II. 12. Liv. I. 17. 32. III. 40. IV. 7. V. 31. VI. 41. VII. 17. 21. VIII. 23. Dionys. II. 57. 60. III. 36. IV. 34. 40. 80. VIII. 90. Plut. Num. 2. Applan. B.C. I. 98. Dion Cass. XL. 45. Ascon. et Schol. Bob. in Cic. pro Milon. 5.
5 The whole of these seem to have been of Etruscan origin. Liv. I. 8. Cic. de R. II. 17. Plin. H.N. VIII. 48. IX. 39. Macrob. S. I. 6. Ovid. Fast. I. 37. II. 501. Juven S. VIII. 259.
6 Dionys. IV. 71. Lyd. de magist. I. 14. Pompon. de orig. iuris, Digest. I. ii. 15.
7 Tacit. Ann. VI. 11.

Servius Tullius, who, it was believed, contemplated the establishment of a republican constitution, to place the executive in the hands of two supreme magistrates, who might act as presidents of the infant commonwealth.[1]

These two magistrates were originally designated PRAETORES,[2] that is, leaders, (*quod populo praeirent,*) and sometimes *Iudices*;[3] but both of these appellations were superseded at an early period[4] by the title of CONSULES, bestowed, it would seem, because it was their duty to deliberate for the welfare of the state, (*consulere reipublicae,*) while the names of *Praetor* and *Iudex* were eventually transferred to other functionaries.

Original Jurisdiction of the Consuls.—The Consuls at first exercised precisely the same powers, both civil and military, as the Kings—*Uti consules potestatem haberent tempore dumtaxat annuam, genere ipso et iure regiam—Regio imperio duo sunto;*[5] but from the immutability believed to attach to things sacred, it was held that certain holy rites, which in times past had been performed by the Kings, could not be duly solemnised by persons bearing a different title and holding office according to a different tenure. Accordingly, a priest was chosen for the special purpose of discharging these duties, and was designated *Rex Sacrorum* or *Rex Sacrificulus.*

But although the civil and military functions of the Kings were transferred to the Consuls, the power wielded by the latter was very different in consequence of numerous important limitations and restrictions—

1. The Consuls were always two in number (*imperium duplex.*) When both were in the city or in the camp together their power was equal, and neither could take any step without the consent of the other. Moreover, an appeal lay from the judicial sentence pronounced by the one to the other (*appellatio collegae*) who had the right of cancelling the decision (*intercessio collegae.*)[6] If a Consul died or resigned while in office, the remaining Consul was obliged to summon the Comitia for the election of a colleague (*subrogare* s. *sufficere collegam*) to fill the vacant place for the remainder of the year; and a Consul so chosen was termed *Consul suffectus*, in contradistinction to *Consules ordinarii*, elected in usual manner.

There are only four, or rather two, instances upon record of this rule having been violated during the period of the republic—one in B.C. 501, soon after the institution of the office, when the death happened so near the close of the official year that a new appointment was considered unnecessary—the other in B.C. 68, when L. Caecilius Metellus having died, and the *Consul suffectus* chosen to fill his place having also died before entering upon office, a second election was regarded as ominous, and Q. Marcius Rex remained sole Consul. Cn. Papirius Carbo, after the death of his colleague Cinna, (B.C. 84,) remained sole Consul for nearly a year; but this was during a period of civil war, when the forms of the constitution were altogether disregarded; and again, in B.C. 52, Cn. Pompeius was deliberately elected *Consul sine collega;* but this was at a juncture when the extraordinary disorders in the state called for extraordinary remedies, and

---

[1] Liv. I. 48. 60. Dionys. IV. 40.
[2] Liv. VII. 3. where the Consul is styled *Praetor Maximus*. Plin. H.N. XVIII. 3. Varro L.L. V. §. 80. Fest. s.v. *Maximum Praetorem*, p. 161. Aul. Gell. XX. 1.
[3] Varro L.L. VI. § 88. Liv. III. 55. Cic. de legg. III. 3. It may be doubted, however, whether the term *Iudices*, which manifestly refers to their judicial functions, was ever applied as a general title.
[4] According to Zonaras (VII. 19.) the title *Consul* was introduced in B.C. 449, upon the expulsion of the Decemvirs.
[5] Cic. de R. II. 32 de legg. III. 3.
[6] Dionys. X. 17. Liv. II. 18. 27. III. 34. 36.

Pompeius, after holding office alone for five months, assumed his father-in-law, Q. Caecilius Metellus Pius Scipio, as his colleague.[1]

2. The Kings held office for life, and were irresponsible; the Consuls remained in office for the fixed period of one year only, (*annuum imperium*,) and when they laid down their magistracy, might be brought to trial before the people if accused of malversation. It very rarely happened that the same individual was Consul for two years consecutively, and when this did happen, it could only take place after a fresh election, and no one, when presiding at an election for this or any other office, could receive votes for himself. The only exception to the above rule is to be found in the case of Cinna and Marius, who, in B.C. 84, continued in the Consulship without re-election; but this was an open and avowed violation of the constitution (Liv. Epit. LXXX.)

3. The *Lex Valeria*, passed in the year of the first Consulate (B.C. 509,) by P. Valerius Poplicola, ordained—*Ne quis magistratus civem Romanum adversus provocationem necaret neve verberaret* (Cic. de R. II. 31.) Of this and of the other laws *De Provocatione*, which were the great charters of the personal freedom of Roman citizens, we shall speak more fully when we treat of the administration of the laws.

4. The control exercised by the Tribunes of the Plebs, (B.C. 494,) of which we shall treat in the next section.

5. In process of time their influence was still further diminished by the institution of several new magistracies, to the holders of which, the Praetors, Aediles, Censors, &c. were committed many duties originally intrusted to the Consuls.

But notwithstanding these limitations, the power of the Consuls was at all times very great, and the office was always regarded as the highest in the state, the great object of ambition to all who aimed at political distinction.

We must consider their power under two heads—
1. As civil magistrates (*potestas*.)
2. As military commanders (*imperium*.)

Potestas of the Consuls.—While the Consuls remained in the city they were at the head of the government, and all other magistrates, with the exception of the Tribunes of the Plebs, were subject to their control. They alone could summon meetings of the Senate and of the Comitia Centuriata; they alone could preside at such meetings and propose subjects for deliberation to the former, and laws for the approbation of the latter;[2] and they formed the medium of communication between the Senate and foreign powers. Until the establishment of the Praetorship and the Censorship, they acted as supreme judges in the civil and criminal courts, and superintended the enrolment and classification of the citizens. In virtue of their office, they possessed the right of summoning any one to appear before them, (*vocatio*,) and if he delayed or refused, they could order him to be brought by force, (*prehensio*,) whether present or absent. In order to execute their commands, each was attended by twelve officers, called *Lictores*, who marched in single file before the Consul, the individual nearest to the magistrate being termed *proximus Lictor*, and being regarded as occupying a more honourable post than the rest. When the office of Consul was first instituted, each Lictor carried a bundle of rods (*fasces*) with an axe (*securis*) stuck in the midst, to indicate that the Consul possessed the power of scourging and putting

[1] Liv. XLI. 18. Epit. LXXXIII. CVII. Velleius II. 24. Dionys. V. 57. Dion Cass. XXXV. 4 XL. 50, 51.
[2] To what extent the Tribunes of the Plebs arrogated to themselves several of these functions will be seen in the next section.

to death those who disobeyed his commands. But by the *Lex Valeria*, (see above, p. 134,) it was ordained that the axe should be removed from the *Fasces* of the Consul while in the city, *secures de fascibus demi jussit*, (Cic. de R. II. 31,) and when the Consuls appeared in the Comitia, their Lictors were compelled to lower their Fasces (*fasces submittere*) as an acknowledgment of the sovereignty of the people.

Imperium of the Consuls.—The vote of the Comitia Centuriata, by which the Consuls were elected, conferred upon them civil authority only, (*potestas*,) but as soon as they entered upon office, military power also, (*imperium*,) and the right of taking the auspices (*auspicia*) were bestowed by the Comitia Curiata. This, under the republic, was, as we have seen, a mere form, but a form never dispensed with. (Read what has been said upon this subject when treating of the Comitia Curiata, p. 117, see also p. 110.)

The Consuls were, for several centuries, occupied almost exclusively with military operations, and in this capacity they had the supreme command of the armies committed to their charge, and of all matters connected with the prosecution of war in the field; but they could not make peace or conclude a binding treaty without the consent of the Senate and the Comitia, and by the former the number of troops to be employed, their pay, clothing, and all other necessary supplies were voted (e.g. Liv. XLIV. 16.) In their capacity of generals-in-chief, the Consuls were invested with absolute power over their soldiers, and could inflict, if they saw fit, even the punishment of death, and hence, when in the field, their Lictors bore axes in the Fasces.

Relation in which the Consuls stood to each other.—We have already remarked that the two Consuls were upon a footing of perfect equality, and that one might at any time stop the proceedings of the other, or, when appealed to, cancel his decisions. But when both Consuls were in the city, it was the invariable practice, in order to prevent confusion and collision, that each Consul should in turn, usually for the space of a month at a time, assume the principal place in the direction of public affairs. That Consul whose turn it was to take the lead, was attended in public by his twelve Lictors, who marched before him as above described, while his colleague appeared either altogether without Lictors, or his Lictors walked behind him, and he was preceded by an ordinary messenger, termed *Accensus*. Hence, the acting Consul is described as the one *penes quem fasces erant*, or *cuius fasces erant*.[1] The individual who had the *Fasces* during the first month seems to have been termed *Maior Consul*, and the precedence was probably determined by seniority in years.[2]

When both Consuls were with the same army the troops were divided between them, each taking special charge of one half, and they assumed the supreme command upon alternate days, unless one voluntarily yielded to the other.[3]

When any doubt or competition arose with regard to the performance of particular duties, the matter was usually settled by lot.[4] More will be said upon this point in treating of the provinces.

Mode of Election.—The Consuls, from the period when the office was instituted until the downfall of the republic, were always chosen by the Comitia Centuriata, and the assembly convoked for that purpose could be held by no magistrate except one of the Consuls, or a Dictator, or an Interrex. The election,

---
1 Cic. de R. II. 31. Liv. II. 1. VIII. 12. IX. 8. Dionys. V. 2. IX. 43. Suet. Caes. 20.
2 See on this controverted point Cic. de. R. II. 31. Val. Max. IV. i. 1. Plut. Popl. 12. Dionys. VI 57. Aul. Gell. II. 15. Fest. s.v. *Maximum Praetorem*, p. 161.
3 Liv. III. 70. XXII. 27. 41. XXVIII. 9. Polyb. III. 110. VI. 26.
4 Liv. II. 8. IV. 26. XXIV. 10.

towards the close of the republic, if not interrupted by civil commotion, generally took place in July, some months before the Consuls entered upon office, in order to give full time for ascertaining that no corrupt practices had been resorted to. This, however, was not the case in the earlier ages, and at no period was a specific time fixed for holding the election, nor was there any law requiring that a certain space should intervene between the election and the induction into office.

Order from which the Consuls were chosen.—The Consuls were originally chosen from the Patricians exclusively; but after a fierce and protracted struggle, continued for nearly eighty years, (B.C. 445—367,) towards the close of which, if we can trust the narrative of Livy, the republic was left for five years in succession (B.C. 375-371,) without Consuls or any other magistrates who might supply their place, (*solitudo magistratuum*, Liv. VI. 35;) at length the *Lex Licinia* was passed, (B.C. 367,) which ordained that in all time coming one of the Consuls should be a Plebeian. This arrangement remained undisturbed for eleven years; but in B.C. 355, the Patricians succeeded in evading the law, for in that year both Consuls were Patricians; and the constitution was violated in a similar manner six times during the thirteen following years, until in B.C. 342, after the meeting at Capua, a law was passed re-enacting more stringently the *Lex Licinia*, with the addition, that it should be lawful for the people, if they thought fit, to choose both Consuls from the Plebs—*Uti liceret Consules ambos Plebeios creari*. From this time forward, after some ineffectual resistance on the part of the Patricians, the principle, that one Consul must be a Plebeian was fully recognised and acted upon. No example, however, occurs of both Consuls being Plebeians until the year B.C. 215, when a successful attempt was made to set aside the election on religious grounds, but the practice after this time soon became common. [1]

Day of Induction into Office.—The Consuls appear to have, originally, entered upon office on the Ides of September, and on this day, in ancient times, the Consul drove a nail into the temple of Jupiter Capitolinus, thus marking the lapse of a year—*Eum clavum, quia rarae per ea tempora litterae erant, notam numeri annorum fuisse ferunt* (Liv. VII. 3. Dionys. V. 1.) Since the Consuls, according to a fundamental rule of the constitution, held office for one year only, this would have continued to be the day of induction in all time coming had matters proceeded with unvarying regularity. But it occasionally happened that, in consequence of the resignation of the Consuls, or from some other cause, the office became vacant before the year was completed, in which case two new Consuls were chosen, who held office for a year from the period of their election; and more frequently, in consequence of civil commotions, it came to pass that the year of office had expired before a new election could take place. In the latter case, since the Consuls whose term was finished, could no longer exercise any of their functions, the Senate nominated (*prodebat*) a temporary magistrate, who, like his prototype in the regal period, bore the title of *Interrex*. The *Interrex* held office for five days only, when a successor was chosen; and a succession of Interreges were appointed in this manner until tranquillity was restored, when the Interrex for the time being held the Comitia for the election of Consuls, who immediately entered upon their duties, and remained in office for a year. In this way the day was repeatedly changed. At first, as we have seen, it was the Ides of September—in B.C. 493, the Kalends of September—in B.C. 479, the Kalends of August—in B.C. 451, the Ides of May—in B.C. 443, the Ides of December—in B.C. 401, the Kalends of October—in B.C 391,

[1] Liv. VI. 35. 42. VII. 1. 17—28. 42. X. 8. 15. XXIII. 31. XXVII. 34. XXXIX. 32. XXXV. 10. 24. Aul. Gell. XVII. 21. Cic. Brut. 14.

the Kalends of July—at the commencement of the second Punic war, B.C. 218, it was the Ides of March, and this continued to be the day until B.C. 154, when it was enacted that, in all time coming, the whole of the ordinary magistrates, with the exception of the Tribunes of the Plebs, should enter upon office upon the Kalends of January, and that if an Interregnum or any other circumstance should prevent them from entering upon office until later in the year, they should, notwithstanding, lay down their office on the last day of December, and their successors commence their duties on the first of January, just as if there had been no interruption. This system commenced with the consulship of Q. Fulvius Nobilior and T. Annius Luscus, who entered upon office on the first of January, B.C. 153, and henceforward the civil and the political year commenced on the same day. [1]

Ceremonies of Induction.—The day on which the Consuls and other ordinary magistrates assumed office was marked by peculiar solemnities. The new Consuls usually arose at day-break, took the auspices, and then arrayed themselves in the *Toga Praetexta* before the domestic altar. A solemn procession (*processus consularis*) was marshalled, headed by the new magistrates in their robes of state, attended by the Senate and the dignified priests, and accompanied by a numerous throng composed of all classes of citizens. The whole assemblage marched in order to the Capitol, where white steers were sacrificed before the great national shrine, and prayers and vows offered up for the prosperity of the Roman people. A meeting of the Senate was then held, and the new Consuls proceeded to make arrangements in the first place for the due performance of public religious rites, and then to consider the internal condition of the state and its foreign relations. [2]

Insignia of the Consuls.—The twelve Lictors, and the *Toga Praetexta*, a cloak with a scarlet border, have already been adverted to; and in addition to these outward badges of distinction, the Consuls, upon public occasion, used a seat ornamented with ivory, termed *Sella Curulis* (see above, p. 67.) This was somewhat in the form of a modern camp stool, and we can form a correct idea of of its form, as well as of the appearance of the *Fasces*, from the numerous representations which occur upon ancient coins and monuments of every description.

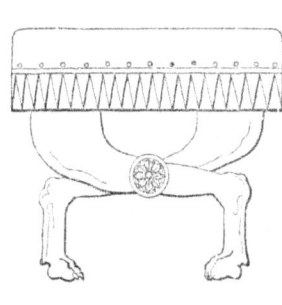 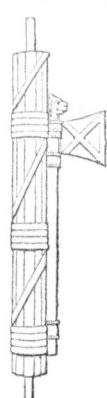

---

[1] Dionys. VI. 49. XI. 63. Liv III. 6. 36. IV 37 V 4. 52. VIII. 20. XXII. 1. XXX. 39. XLIV. 19.
[2] Dionys. II. 6. Liv. XXI. 63. Dion Cass. LVIII 5. Ovid. Fast. I. 79. Epp. ex. P. IV. ix.

Naming of the Year after the Consuls.—In all annals, sacred and civil, as well as in public and private documents of every description, the dates were usually determined by naming the Consuls for the year. Thus, any event belonging to A. U. C. 684, B.C. 70, would be fixed by saying that it took place *Pompeio et Crasso Consulibus*. Hence the phrase *numerare multos consules* is equivalent to *numerare multos annos*; and Martial, (I. xv. 3,) when reminding his friend that he was nearly sixty years old, employs the expression,

His iam pene tibi Consul trigesimus instat.

The practice continued under the Empire down to a very late period. Historians occasionally defined the period of a remarkable event by calculating the number of years which had elapsed from the foundation of the city; but in all ordinary cases followed the computation by Consuls.

The Consulship under the Empire.[1]—A *Plebiscitum* was passed as early as B.C. 342, prohibiting any individual from holding the same office twice within ten years—*ne quis eumdem magistratum intra decem annos caperet* (Liv. VII. 42.) This law was suspended during a period of great alarm, in favour of Marius, who was Consul six times in the space of eight years, (B.C. 107—B.C. 100,) was openly violated by Cinna, Carbo, and Sulla, during the disorders of the civil war, and may be regarded as having been finally set aside when Julius Cæsar was invested with the Consulship and the Dictatorship in perpetuity (*continuum Consulatum, perpetuam Dictaturam*.)[2] After the death of Cæsar and the battle of Philippi, the Triumvirs arrogated to themselves the right of disposing of the Consulship; and from the time when Augustus succeeded in establishing an undivided sway, the office was entirely in the hands of the Emperors, who conferred it upon whom they pleased, and assumed it in person as often as they thought fit, being guided in this matter by no fixed rule, but solely by their own discretion. Augustus was Consul in all thirteen times, sometimes for several years in succession,(B.C. 31—B.C. 23;) but during the last thirty-six years of his life (B.C. 22—A.D. 14) twice only; (B.C. 5 and B.C. 2;) Vitellius proclaimed himself perpetual Consul;[3] Vespasian was Consul eight times during his reign of ten years; Domitian seventeen times, for the first time A.D. 71, ten years before his accession, for the last time A.D. 95, the year before his death; Hadrian, on the other hand, assumed the Consulship during the first three years of his sway, (A.D. 117—119,) but never afterwards (A.D. 120—138.)

Consules Ordinarii. Consules Suffecti.—Under the republic two individuals, and no more, held the Consulship in the course of one year, except when a vacancy occurred from death or any other unexpected circumstance, in which case a successor was substituted (*suffectus est*.) Julius Cæsar, however, in A.D. 45, having entered upon the office along with M. Aemilius Lepidus, they both resigned before the end of the year, in order to make room for Q. Fabius Maximus and C. Trebonius, and the former having died on the last day of his office, C. Caninius Rebilus was elected for the few remaining hours, an appointment which afforded Cicero a theme for many a bitter jest. The example thus set was caught up and adopted by the successors of Cæsar, and it soon became the established practice to have several pairs of Consuls during one year, the

---

[1] An excellent account of the Consulship during the Imperial period will be found in the Doctrina Numorum Veterum of ECKHEL, Tom VIII. p. 325 seqq. who is closely followed by MARQUARDT. Consult also the article CONSUL by REIN, in the Encyclopaedie der classischen Altherthumswissenschaft.
[2] Suet. Caes. 76. Dion Cass. XLII. 20. XLIII. 45.
[3] Suet. Vitell. 11.

number varying according to the number of persons whom the Emperor felt desirous of gratifying. Under ordinary circumstances, two months was the period of office, so as to allow of twelve Consuls in each year; in B.C. 69 there were fifteen, and under the corrupt administration of Cleander, the chamberlain of Commodus, there were no less than twenty-five nominated for A.D. 189.[1]

Those Consuls who entered upon office on the first of January, were termed *Consules Ordinarii*, gave their name to the year, and were held in higher honour than those who followed, and who were termed *Consules Suffecti* or *Consules Minores* (σμικροτέρους σφᾶς ὑπάτους ἐπεκάλουν.)

It is true that after this system was fully recognised, we find examples of persons retaining the consulship for a whole year, as in the case of Germanicus A.D. 12, and Cn. Domitius A.D. 32; but these were rare exceptions, since even the Emperors, who, when they assumed the Consulship, generally took office as *Consules Ordinarii*, appear to have been in the habit of resigning within a short period, in order to make way for others (Tacit. H. I. 77. Dion Cass. LIII. 32.)

Under the later empire the *Consules Suffecti* disappear almost entirely;[2] but we find mention made of *Consules Honorarii*,[3] as distinguished from *Consules Ordinarii*. These honorary Consuls had probably no duties imposed upon them, and enjoyed little more than the *Ornamenta Consularia*, to be described below.

Consules Designati.—Under the republic a Consul was never elected except for the year immediately following the election, and during the months or days which elapsed between his election and his induction, was styled *Consul Designatus*. But in B.C. 39, Consuls were nominated by the Triumvirs for eight years prospectively.[4] Of these, the year B.C. 34, together with B.C. 31, were assigned to Antonius. Hence, from the year B.C. 44, in which he was for the first time Consul, until B.C. 39, he is styled on medals simply Cos., from B.C. 39 to B.C. 34, Cos Desig. Iter. et Tert., from B.C. 34, Cos. II. Des. III. until B.C. 31, when he appears as Cos. III. Octavianus, who, in B.C. 39, was in like manner nominated Consul for B.C. 33 and B.C. 31, passed through the same variety of titles.

Augustus, in B.C. 6, named his grandson, Caius, at that time fourteen years old, *Consul Designatus;* but with the proviso, that he was not to enter upon office until five years had elapsed, and accordingly, he actually held the Consulship in A.D. 1. His brother Lucius was, in B.C. 2, named *Consul Designatus* upon the same terms; but he died before the five years were completed. In like manner, Nero, when fourteen years old, became *Consul Designatus*, although it was arranged that he was not to enter upon office until he had attained the age of twenty; and Vitellius, when he assumed the Imperial dignity—*Comitia in decem annos ordinavit, seque perpetuum Consulem* (Suet. Vitell. 11.)

Ornamenta Consularia.—We are told by Suetonius (Caes. 76) that Julius Cæsar—*decem praetoriis viris Consularia Ornamenta tribuit*—by which we must understand that he bestowed the title and outward badges of the Consulship upon ten persons who did not hold, and who never had held, the office of Consul. This statement is fully corroborated by Dion Cassius, (XLIII. 47,) who mentions in another place (XLVI. 41) that the Senate, at the death of Hirtius and Pansa, being unwilling to elevate Octavius to the Consulship, in consequence of his extreme youth, endeavoured to get rid of his claims by bestowing upon him

---

[1] Cic. ad Fam. VII. 30. Macrob. S. II. 3. Dion Cass. XLIII. 46. XLVIII. 35. LXXII. 12.
[2] Symmachus, however, (fl. A.D. 370,) speaks of a *Consul suffectus*, Epp. VI. 40.
[3] Justinian. Cod. X. xxxi. 66. Nov. LXXXI. 1.
[4] Appian (B.C. V. 73.) says for *four* years, Dion Cassius, (XLVIII. 35,) who is borne out by ancient monuments, says for *eight*.

Consular Honours (ταῖς δὲ δὴ τιμαῖς ταῖς ὑπατικαῖς ἐκόσμησαν.)[1] From this time forward numerous examples occur of persons being invested with what may be termed a *Titular Consulship*, the expression usually employed to designate this mark of favour being *Ornamenta Consularia* s. *Insignia Consularia*.[2] The practice was extended to other offices of state, since we read, not only of *Ornamenta Consularia*, but also of *Ornamenta Praetoria*, of *Ornamenta Aedilitia*, and of *Ornamenta Quaestoria*. The phrase *Ornamenta Tribunitia* does not occur, perhaps because the Tribunes of the Plebs had no external symbols of rank; but we find the emperors bestowing *Dignitates Tribunitias*, which comes to the same thing (Capitolin. M. Aur. 10.)

Power and Dignity of the Consuls under the Empire.—The Consuls, except in so far as they were the organs of the Imperial will, were mere cyphers in the state; and, in fact, the short period during which they held office must in itself have prevented them from possessing any weight. They were, however, allowed to preside in the Comitia and at meetings of the Senate, retaining all the ancient forms; they occasionally administered justice in civil suits, and from the reign of Claudius to that of M. Aurelius, they exercised special jurisdiction in cases relating to minors.[3] But although shorn of all real power, the Consulship down to the very extinction of the western empire, was nominally the most exalted and most honourable of all dignities—*Consulatus praeponendus est omnibus fastigiis dignitatum*—*Divinum praemium consulatus*—*Summum bonum primumque in mundo decus*—are the phrases employed by writers of the fourth, fifth, and sixth centuries;[4] and there can be no doubt that the office was invested, especially during the period just mentioned, with a greater amount of external pomp and splendour than in the days of freedom. The Consuls, when inducted into office, (*solennitas consularis—processus consularis.*) appeared in a dress, which was a gorgeous imitation of that worn by generals of old when celebrating a triumph. They were arrayed in the ample folds of a richly embroidered cloak, (*Toga picta*,) beneath which was a tunic striped with purple (*Trabea*) or figured with palm leaves (*Tunica palmata*.) On their feet were shoes of cloth of gold (*Calcei aurati*.) In their hand they bore a sceptre (*Scipio*) surmounted by an eagle. Before them marched their Lictors with Fasces and Secures wreathed in laurel (*Fasces laureatae*.) Their *Sella Curulis* was placed in a lofty chariot, and from this seat they scattered handfuls of money upon the crowd below, while they presented their friends with ivory diptychs, (*Pugillaria eburnea*,) silver boxes, (*Canistelli argentei*,) and other trinkets, bearing inscriptions commemorative of the auspicious day, which was closed by the exhibition of sumptuous games. If we can believe Procopius, an individual called upon to fill the office of Consul, at the time when he wrote, (A.D. 560,) was compelled to expend a sum little short of one hundred thousand pounds upon this vain display.[5]

---

[1] We find a trace of something similar even under the republic, (B.C. 67,) but Dion Cassius, who is our authority, (XXXVI. 23,) although he uses the words τιμαῖς ὑπατικαῖς enters into no details.

[2] This distinction was sometimes bestowed even on foreigners, as by Claudius on Agrippa, the grandson of Herod the Great, the same individual having previously received *Praetoria Ornamenta* from Caligula.

[3] Tacit. Ann. IV. 19. Plin. Epp. IX. 13. Suet. Claud. 23. Capitolin. M. Aurel. 10. comp. Tacit. Ann. XIII. 4. Aul. Gell. XIII. 24. Dion Cass. LXIX. 7.

[4] Cassiodor. Var. VI. 1. Lyd. de Mag. II. 8. Cod. Theod. VI. vi. 1. IX. xl. 17. Iornandes de R. G. 57.

[5] Vopisc. Aurelian. 13. Cassiodor. Var. II. 2. VI. 1. Claud. Eutrop. II. prol. 7. Prob. et Olybr. 230. Symmach. Epp. I. 1. II. 81. VI. 40. Procop. Hist. arc. 26. Comp. Iustinian. Nov. CV. Auth. Const. XXXIV. On the liberality occasionally manifested by the emperors to a poor Consul, see a curious passage in Vopisc. Aurelian. 12.

TRIBUNI PLEBIS.

Origin of the Office.—We have already had occasion to point out that the constitution of Servius Tullius bestowed political existence upon the Plebs, and the object of that great legislator was, we can scarcely doubt, to abolish ultimately all exclusive privileges. His untimely death, however, prevented him from carrying out his design; and under the cruel sway of his successor, all orders in the state were alike oppressed. After the expulsion of the second Tarquin, the Patricians strained every nerve, and for a time with success, to regain the position which they had occupied under the earlier kings, arrogating to themselves the control of public affairs and the possession of all the great offices of the state, which, at this time, although nominally a republic, was in reality an oligarchy in its worst form. At length, however, the tyranny, insolence, and cruelty of the dominant class became so intolerable, that the Plebs were roused to vigorous resistance, and in B.C. 494, sixteen years after the expulsion of the Tarquins, they quitted the city in a body and retired (*secessit*) to an eminence beyond the Anio, which from that time forward bore the name of MONS SACER. The Patricians, now thoroughly alarmed, immediately opened negotiations with the leaders of the movement, concord was restored, and the Plebs agreed to return upon the following conditions:—

1. That magistrates should be elected annually, under the name of *Tribuni Plebis*, whose sole duty should be to watch over and protect the interests of the Plebeian order and the persons of its members, and that they should be armed with powers sufficient to secure these objects.

2. That these magistrates should be chosen exclusively from the Plebs.

3. That the persons of these magistrates should be hallowed, (*sacrosancti*,) so that if any one offered personal violence to a Tribune, or impeded him in the performance of his duty, he should, ipso facto, become *sacer*, i.e. devoted to the infernal gods, and that, as such, he might be put to death with impunity and his property confiscated to Ceres. Hence, the magistracy was termed *Sacrosancta Potestas*, (ἱερὰ καὶ ἄσυλος ἀρχή,) and the laws which conferred these privileges *Leges Sacratae*.[1]

4. That the Tribuni Plebis should have the right to interfere, (*intercedere*,) so as to stop any procedure which might appear to be detrimental to the Plebs as a body, or to any member of the order.

Number of Tribunes.—Every thing connected with the history of the early years of the Tribunate is involved in deep obscurity, and the statements of the historians present irreconcilable discrepancies. It would appear that at first two only were chosen, then five, and finally, in the year B.C. 457, ten, which continued to be the number ever afterwards.[2] The ten Tribunes were regarded as forming a corporation, and as such, were styled collectively *Collegium Tribunorum Plebis*.

Mode of Election.—We are told expressly by Cicero and Dionysius that the Tribunes were originally chosen by the Comitia Curiata; but that in B.C. 473, Publilius Volero, one of the Tribunes, proposed a law—*Ut Plebeii magistratus Tributis Comitiis fierent*—which, although violently resisted, was carried in the following year, (B.C. 472,) and that, from that time forward, the Tribunes were always chosen by the Comitia Tributa, one of the Tribunes already in office being

---

[1] On the *Sacrosancta Potestas* see Dionys. VI. 89. Liv. III. 55. Cic. pro Balb. 14. Dion Cass. LIII. 17. Fest. s.vv. *Sacrosanctum, Sacratae, Sacer*, p. 318.
[2] The chief authorities are, Liv. II. 33. 44. 58. III. 30. IV. 16. VI. 35. 38. Cic. de R. II. 34. pro Cornel. and note of Ascon. Dionys. VI. 89. IX. 2. 41.

selected by lot to preside.[1] During the sway of the Decemvirs, the functions of all the ordinary magistrates were suspended; but on the downfal of Appius with his colleagues, the Pontifex Maximus presided at the election of new Tribunes.[2]

In the earlier years of the Tribunate it was considered lawful for the presiding magistrate to call upon the electors to choose a certain number of Tribunes less than the full complement, at his own discretion, and then to permit those who were thus chosen to select their own colleagues, until the entire number was made up. When vacant places in any corporation were supplied in this manner by the votes of the members of the corporation, the process was called *Cooptatio*. The practice of *Cooptatio*, in so far as the *Collegium* of the Tribunes was concerned, was forbidden by the *Lex Trebonia*, passed in B.C. 448.[3]

Qualifications.—The office was open to all Roman citizens, under the following restrictions:—

1. No one could be elected who was not himself *Ingenuus* and the son of an *Ingenuus*. We find no violation of this rule until the time of Augustus.[4]

2. No one could be elected except he belonged to the Plebs. We find one exception to this rule in the earlier ages, but the procedure was unquestionably illegal.[5] It was not necessary for a candidate to be by birth a member of a Plebeian family; it was held sufficient if he had been adopted into a Plebeian family, as in the case of Cicero's enemy, Clodius Pulcher, who was by birth a Patrician.

3. In the earlier ages the same individual was frequently elected Tribune for two or more years in succession.[6] But this practice was stopped by the *Plebiscitum* of B.C. 342, which enacted—*Ne quis eumdem magistratum intra decem annos caperet*—and hence the attempt of Tiberius Gracchus to procure his own re-election was unconstitutional.

Day of Induction.—The first Tribunes entered upon office on the 10th of December. (IV. Id. Dec.) and the day remained unchanged during the whole of the republic and under the earlier emperors.[7] There is no instance of the office having been suspended or interrupted, (except under the Decemvirs,) and although the Tribunes in office could, under no pretext, lengthen out their period, they were forbidden, under pain of death, to leave the Plebs without its legal protectors.[8] Towards the close of the republic, the election of new Tribunes always took place a considerable time before they entered upon their duties.

Power of the Tribunes.—The powers of the Tribunes, according to the views of those by whom the office was first established, were very moderate and entirely of a defensive character. They were required to afford assistance (*auxilium*) to a member of the Plebs, when oppressed by a Patrician; the person feeling himself aggrieved was entitled to call upon the Tribunes for aid, (*appellare tribunos*,) and when they granted the aid sought they were said *esse auxilio*. In order to render this aid effectual, they possessed the *Ius Intercessionis*, that is, the right of *interfering*, and at once putting a stop to any measure which they deemed injurious to their order; in exerting this right they were said *intercedere*, and the mode of exerting it was by pronouncing the

---
[1] Cic. pro Cornel. as above. Dionys. ll. c. Liv. III. 64.
[2] Liv. III. 54. Cic. l. c.
[3] Liv. II. 33. III. 64. 65. V. 10.
[4] Dion Cass. LIII. 27.
[5] Liv. III. 65. comp. V. 10. Suet. Octav. 10
[6] Liv. II. 56. III. 14. 21. 24. 29. VI. 35. 38.
[7] Liv. XXXIX. 52. Dionys. VI. 89.
[8] Liv. III. 55. Cic. de legg. III. 3.

solemn word *Veto*.[1] In order that they might always be at hand in case of need, a Tribune was, under no pretext, allowed to be absent from the city for twenty-four hours, except during the celebration of the *Feriae Latinae*, and he was bound to allow the doors of his house to remain open day and night, that he might be at all times accessible. Finally, in order to protect their persons from violence, they were declared *Sacrosancti* (see above, p. 141.)

Within a very brief period it was discovered that these protective powers might be made efficient as weapons of offence in a manner not originally contemplated. The Tribunes were themselves the sole judges of what was to be regarded as injurious to the Plebs, and consequently, when they desired to carry any measure on behalf of their order, or to extort any extension of power for themselves, in opposition to the Patricians, they had the means of producing the greatest embarrassment and danger until their demands were complied with. Thus, they frequently prevented the election of the ordinary magistrates—they refused to allow troops to be levied or supplies voted in pressing emergencies—they suspended all business in the Senate, and, in fact, brought the whole machine of the state to a dead stop. By pursuing these tactics they succeeded, after many hard fought battles, in destroying, one after another, all the bulwarks of Patrician exclusiveness, in procuring the complete emancipation of the Plebs from all political disabilities, and their full and free admission to all the honours of the state. So far their efforts, although not always moderate and judicious, were, in so far as the end in view was concerned, in the highest degree praiseworthy; and after complete concord was established between the orders, the Tribunes appear, for a series of years, to have generally exerted their influence with most patriotic singleness of purpose. But towards the close of the republic, they became the tools of the violent leaders of conflicting parties; they factiously abused their power for the promotion of the most unprincipled and ruinous schemes, and were the foremost instigators of those scenes of riot and bloodshed which cast such a gloom over the last struggles of the constitution, and which terminated in the utter extinction of freedom. Hence, it is not wonderful that those who viewed the Tribunician power under the aspect which it presented in those evils days, should have characterised it as—*Postestas pestifera, in seditione, et ad seditionem nata*.[2]

A Tribune had no right to summon a citizen to appear before him; that is, he did not possess the *Ius Vocationis:* but he had the *Ius Prehensionis;* that is, he could order any one, who, in his presence, was violating the rights of the Plebs, to be taken into custody, and for this purpose each tribune was attended by an officer, termed *Viator*. This *Ius Prehensionis* was sometimes stretched so far that there are examples of a Tribune giving orders for the arrest even of Consuls and Censors, and commanding them to be led off to prison.[3]

Relation of the Tribunes to the Senate.—The Tribunes originally had no right to enter the Senate-house; but they were wont to sit upon benches (*subsellia*) at the doors, in order that they might be able to watch the proceedings, and, if they thought fit, put a negative on any proposed decree. By the *Plebiscitum Atinium*, however, they became, *ex officio*, members of the Senate. The date of this ordinance is unknown; but as early as B.C. 456 they assumed

---

[1] Liv. VI. 35.
[2] Cic. de legg. III. 8. where he makes his brother Quintus the organ of the sentiments entertained by those who were hostile to the Tribunician power.
[3] Liv. II. 56. IV. 26. Epit. XLVIII. LV. Cic. in Vatin. 9. ad Att. II. 1. de leg. agr. II. 37. de legg. III. 9. Val. Max IX. v. 2.

the right of summoning meetings of the Senate, and we find one of their body speaking in the Senate eleven years later (B.C. 445.)[1]

Relation of the Tribunes to Public Meetings and Comitia.—From the commencement the Tribunes had the right of calling public meetings (*conciones*) of the Plebs; and in the year after the institution of the office, (B.C. 493,) the *Lex Icilia* was passed ordaining that no *Concio*, summoned by a Tribune, could be disturbed or called away (*avocari*) by any Patrician magistrate. This law remained in force at all periods, for although we are told by Messala, as quoted by Aulus Gellius—*Consul ab omnibus magistratibus et comitiatum et concionem avocare potest*—it is clear, from various examples, that this rule did not extend to meetings at which Tribunes of the Plebs presided.[2]

After the *Comitia Tributa* were established, it was one of the peculiar duties of the Tribunes to summon these assemblies, to preside, and to propose laws, (*agere cum populo*,) and such laws were hence frequently termed *Leges Tribuniciae*. During the struggles which agitated the state after the secession to the Mons Sacer, we find Tribunes on several occasions impeaching Patricians and bringing them to trial before the Comitia Tributa, even when the charge involved a *Poena Capitalis*;[3] the pretext alleged being always, apparently, some violation of the *Leges Sacratae*. But after the legislation of the Decemvirs, it would appear that all trials which involved the life or privileges of a Roman citizen could be held before the Comitia Centuriata only, and the Tribunes could propose no higher punishment in the Comitia Tributa than the imposition of a fine (*irrogatio multae*.)

Limitations of the Tribunitian Power.—1. It was exclusively civil. They had *Potestas*, but were never invested with *Imperium*.

2. It was confined to the city and to a circuit of one mile outside the walls. Beyond this the Tribunes were subject to the consular power as if *Privati*.[4] It would seem, from two passages in Livy, that the Senate could invest them with extraordinary powers, extending even to foreign countries; but such cases must be regarded as exceptions, depending entirely upon a special decree.[5]

3. The most important limitation to their power resulted from the relation in which they stood towards each other. When a Tribune was appealed to and requested to interfere on behalf of any individual who sought his aid, his *auxilium* could not be granted until the whole *collegium* had been consulted and had passed an unanimous resolution, (*decretum*,) granting the assistance sought, which resolution was publicly announced on the part of the college, (*pro collegio*, s. *ex collegii sententia pronuntiare*,) by one of its members. If the Tribunes were not unanimous the appeal was not allowed. On the same principle, a single Tribune might put his Veto upon any law proposed in the Comitia, or any resolution submitted to the Senate, although supported or originated by all his colleagues.

Hence the Patricians were enabled on many occasions to baffle the efforts of a majority of the Tribunes, and altogether to neutralize their influence by gaining over one or more members of the College and persuading them to put a negative upon the measures promoted by the rest.

---

[1] Zonar. VII. 15. Dionys. X. 31. Aul. Gell. XIV. 8. Liv. IV. 1. Val. Max. II. ii. 7. who tells us that in ancient times when a decree of the Senate passed without opposition on the part of the Tribunes, the letter T was written at the bottom to indicate their consent.
[2] Aul. Gell. XIII. 15 Liv. XLIII. 16. Val. Max. IX. v. 2. Aurel. Vict. III. 73.
[3] e.g. Coriolanus—Appius Claudius, Liv. II. 61—Kaeso Quinctius, Liv. III. 12.
[4] Dionys. VIII. 87. Liv. III. 20. Appian. B.C. II. 31. Dion Cass. LI. 19.
[5] Liv. IX. 36. XXIX. 20.

4. The temporary check placed upon the Tribunes by the nomination of a Dictator will be explained in the next section.

5. The power of the Tribunes was, for a time, greatly reduced by a *Lex Cornelia* of Sulla, which deprived them of all that they had acquired or usurped during four centuries, leaving them nothing but the *Ius Intercessionis*, with which they had been originally invested.[1] But this, like most of the changes introduced by Sulla, was disregarded after his death; and the Tribunes were formally reinstated in all their former rights and privileges by Cn. Pompeius when Consul for the first time, B.C. 70.

Insignia of the Tribunes.—Although the Tribunes wielded so much real power, they had scarcely any external symbols of dignity. They wore no *Toga Praetexta* nor other official dress, they had not the right of the *Sella Curulis*, but sat on benches or stools, called *Subsellia*, and they had no Lictors; but, as remarked above, each was attended by a single *Viator*.

Tribunes of the Plebs under the Empire.—At no period of Roman history were the Tribunes more active or more corrupt than during the last struggles of the free constitution. It was an alleged infringement of their prerogative by the Senate which furnished Cæsar with a plausible pretext for crossing the Rubicon and marching upon the city. But from that moment the office became little better than an empty name. The unfettered exercise of power such as they had wielded for four centuries and a-half, was altogether incompatible with the dominion held by Julius, by the Triumvirs, and eventually by Augustus and his successors. During the first century, however, they still retained some outward show of their ancient authority. They still summoned and presided at meetings of the Senate; they were still appealed to for their *auxilium*, and still exerted, or threatened to exert, their right of intercession; but they prudently ascertained beforehand whether such a course would be pleasing to the Emperor, or, if they for a moment forgot their position, and showed an inclination to act independently, they were quickly checked and humbled.[2] The office was introduced at Constantinople by Constantine, and was in existence in the west during the fifth century.

The Tribunes, under the empire, were generally selected by the Senate, with the concurrence of the prince, from persons who had held the office of Quaestor.[3] Augustus intrusted to them, along with the Praetors and Aediles, the general superintendence of the fourteen regions into which he portioned out the city, and this charge they seem to have retained as late as the reign of Alexander Severus, by whom new arrangements were introduced. They appear also to have exercised, for a brief period, extensive jurisdiction in civil suits; but this was much curtailed by Nero.[4]

The office presented so few attractions, that even under Augustus it was difficult to find candidates, and a law was found necessary, ordaining that the Tribunes of the Plebs should be chosen by lot out of those who had served as Quaestors, and had not yet attained to the age of forty.[5] Pliny endeavours to represent the Tribuneship as still worthy of being regarded as a high and sacred dignity; but it is evident that by his contemporaries in general it was looked upon as a mere title, implying no honour—*inanem umbram et sine honore nomen* (Epp. I. 23.)

[1] Caes. B.C. I. 5. 7.
[2] Dion Cass. LL 47. LVII. 15. LIX. 24. LX. 16. 28. LXXVIII. 37. Suet. Caes. 79. Tib. 23. Tacit. Ann. I. 13. VI. 12. 47. XIII. 28. XVI. 26. Hist. II. 91. IV. 9.
[3] Suet. Octav. 10. 40. Dion Cass. LIV. 26. 30.
[4] Dion Cass. LV. 8. Lamprid. Alex. Sev. 33. Tacit. Ann. XIII. 28.
[5] Suet. Octav. 10 40. Dion Cass. LIV. 26. 30.

DICTATOR.

Origin of the Office.—Soon after the establishment of the republic it became evident that emergencies might arise in which a divided authority, such as that exercised by the Consuls, restricted, moreover, by the right of appeal to the people, would prove insufficient to protect the state. Accordingly, when a powerful and united effort was about to be made, by a large number of the Latin states, for the restoration of the Tarquins, a suspicion having arisen that the Consuls for the year were friendly to the cause of the exiles, it was proposed that it should be lawful, as a last resort in times of great difficulty and danger, (*ultimum auxilium—in rebus trepidis ultimum consilium,*) to appoint a single magistrate, who should possess, for a limited period, absolute power, without appeal, over all members of the community, and a law to that effect (*Lex de Dictatore creando*) received the sanction of the Comitia. The name given to this new magistrate was originally *Magister Populi;* but subsequently he was styled *Dictator*, a title already familiar to the Latin states. Considerable doubt existed when Livy wrote as to the precise year in which the office was instituted, and as to the individual first nominated; but the accounts which he deemed most trustworthy declared that Titus Larcius was the first Dictator, and that he was named in B.C. 501, nine years after the expulsion of the Tarquins, and eight years before the establishment of *Tribuni Plebis.* [1]

Mode of Election.—A Dictator was named by one of the Consuls, in pursuance of a decree of the Senate. Hence DICERE *Dictatorem* is the strict technical phrase, although *creare, nominare* and *legere* are also occasionally employed. The Consul could not name a Dictator unless armed with the authority of the Senate, nor could he, if required to name a Dictator, refuse to comply with the order; but, on the other hand, although the Senate frequently recommended a particular individual, and although this recommendation was generally adopted, they could not limit the choice of the Consul, who by no means uniformly attended to their wishes. [2] In one remarkable case we find the *Comitia Tributa*, at the request of the Senate, fixing upon the individual who was to be named Dictator by the Consul (Liv. XXVII. 5.) No magistrate, except a Consul, or one who occupied the position of a Consul, such as a *Tribunus Militaris consulari potestate*, (see p. 152.) could name a Dictator; and hence the nomination of Sulla by an Interrex, and of Julius Cæsar by a Practor, must be regarded as direct violations of the constitution. [3] The nomination, under ordinary circumstances, took place at Rome, and we find examples where Consuls were summoned from a distance for the purpose; but in cases of necessity a Dictator might be named in the camp, provided it was not beyond the limits of the *Ager Romanus*, which, in the time of the second Punic war, was understood to comprehend all Italy. It having been settled by mutual agreement, by a special resolution of the Senate, by lot, or otherwise, which of the two Consuls should perform the task, the Consul so selected rising (*surgens s. oriens*) in the dead of night, (*nocte silentio,*) if no unfavourable omen presented itself, named whom he thought fit *Dictator.* [4]

---

[1] Liv. II. 18. IV. 56. VI. 38. Cic. de. R. I. 40. II. 32. de legg. III. 3. Dionys. V. 70. 72. Varro L.L. V. § 82. VI. § 61. ap. Macrob. S. 1. 8. Fest. s.v. *Optima lex*, p. 198.
[2] Liv. IV. 17. 21. 23. 26. 46. 57. V L 2. VII. 12. VIII. 12. 15, 17. IX. 7. 29. 38. X. 11. Epit. XIX. XXII. 57. XXVII. 5. Cic. de. legg. III. 3.
[3] Liv. IV. 31. Cic. de leg. agr. III. 2. ad Att. IX. 15. Caes. B.C. II. 21. Dion Cass. XLI 36.
[4] Liv. IV. 21. 26. VII. 19. 21. VIII. 12. 23. IX. 38. X. 40. XXIII. 22. XXVII. 5. Dionys X. 11.

DICTATOR.

Qualifications.—The original law, *de Dictatore creando*, enjoined that no one should be named Dictator unless he had held the office of Consul, (*consularis*,) but this rule seems to have been dispensed with at an early period, since A. Postumius Tubertus was Dictator in B.C. 434, although he had not previously been Consul; but the exceptions were certainly rare.[1] The Dictator was chosen originally from the Patricians exclusively; but after the Plebs succeeded in gaining admission to the Consulate, the Dictatorship (*Dictatura*) also was thrown open. The first Plebeian Dictator was C. Marcius Rutilus, named B.C. 356, ten years after the Consulship of L. Sextius.

Objects for which a Dictator was Named.—We have stated above that the object originally contemplated in naming a Dictator was to avert some danger of a character so threatening that the ordinary resources of the constitution were deemed insufficient—*Imperio, quo priores ad vindicandam maximis periculis rempublicam usi fuerant—Quando duellum gravius discordiaeve civium escunt . . . Populi Magister esto.*[2] Dangers of this description might arise either from external enemies or from intestine discord, and hence a Dictator was generally named either for the prosecution of a war (*rei gerundae causa*) or for the suppression of a popular tumult (*seditionis sedandae causa.*) But in process of time it was found convenient to appoint a Dictator for the performance of less important, but indispensable duties, when the functionaries on whom they properly devolved were prevented by some unforeseen event from discharging them. Thus, a Dictator was frequently appointed to preside at the annual elections, (*comitiorum habendorum causa,*) when, in consequence of death, sickness, or the demands of military service, it was impossible for either of the Consuls to be present in the city. In like manner, a Dictator was sometimes appointed for the purpose of making arrangements with regard to the *Feriae Latinae* (*Feriarum constituendarum causa*) and the celebration of solemn games; (*ludorum faciendorum causa;*) for presiding at trials of an unusual character; (*quaestionibus exercendis;*) for fixing the nail in the temple of Jupiter Capitolinus, which marked the succession of years; (*clavi figendi causa;*) on one occasion for supplying vacancies in the Senate; (*senatui legendo;*) on another for recalling a Consul, who had overstepped his duty by quitting his province.[3] It must be observed also, that in the earlier ages, the Senate and the Patricians had often recourse to the nomination of a Dictator when no real danger threatened the state, in order that they might frustrate the schemes of the Tribunes, or accomplish some other party purpose. Hence some historians, reasoning apparently from these abuses, ascribe the origin of the office to a desire on the part of the Patricians to coerce the Plebs, who, overwhelmed with debt and crushed by oppression, had become indifferent to the dangers which were threatening the community at large, and were refusing to serve as soldiers.[4]

Extent of a Dictator's Power.—As soon as a Dictator was named he was invested with *Imperium* by the Comitia Curiata,[5] (see above, p. 117,) and forthwith all the independent powers of the ordinary magistrates were suspended; they did not resign their offices nor cease to perform their duties, but so long as the Dictator remained in office they were in all respects subject to his control, resuming their former position when he retired. The Dictator was, for the time

---

[1] Liv. IV. 24. so also in B.C. 352, C. Iulius Iulus.
[2] Velleius II. 28. Cic. de legg. III. 3.
[3] Examples of the above will be found in Liv. VII. 28. XXVII. 33. IX. 26. VII. 3. VIII. 18. IX. 28. XXIII. 22. XXX. 24.
[4] Dionys. V. 63—72. Zonaras, VII. 13.
[5] Liv. IX. 38, 39.

being, supreme; he was a temporary despot, armed with full power to adopt what measures he thought expedient, without consulting the Senate, and to dispose of the lives and fortunes of the citizens without appeal (*sine provocatione*.)[1] Even the *auxilium* of the Tribunes was powerless against the might of the Dictator;[2] and the few cases upon record in which the former were called upon to interfere were those in which a Dictator, when appointed for a special purpose, was endeavouring to pass beyond the limits of his commission.[3] Finally, a Dictator was irresponsible, and he could not be called to account for his acts after he had laid down his office.

We might infer from a passage in Festus[4] that there was an appeal from the Dictator to the people, and we know that the *Lex Valeria Horatia* (Liv. III. 55) enacted—*Nequis ullum magistratum sine provocatione crearet;* but no reliance can be reposed in this place on the text of Festus, and the *Lex Valeria* must be understood to have applied to ordinary magistrates only. We find no example in history of an appeal from the commands of a Dictator having been prosecuted with success, and only one instance of such an appeal having been threatened (Liv. VIII. 33.)

The very nature of the office rendered it impossible that there should be more than one Dictator at the same time. The only apparent exception is to be found in the case of M. Fabius Buteo, who was named Dictator in B.C. 216, for the special purpose of filling up vacancies in the Senate, M. Junius Pera having been previously named *rei gerundae causa*. The procedure was, however, at this time regarded as altogether irregular and anomalous, and to be justified only on the plea of necessity (Liv. XXIII. 22. 23.)

Limitations to the Power of a Dictator.—1. A Dictator was named for six months only, (*semestre imperium*,) and there is no example of any one having ever attempted to retain the office beyond that period.[5] On the contrary, a Dictator seldom retained the office even for six months, except when named *rei gerundae causa*, and even in that case, if he succeeded in bringing the struggle to a speedy termination, he resigned in a few weeks or days. But when chosen for any of the special purposes enumerated above, he was expected, as a matter of course, to resign (*abdicare se dictatura*) as soon as the duty was discharged. Indeed, as indicated above, if a Dictator, when appointed for a special purpose, endeavoured to exert his power in reference to other matters, he might be successfully resisted.[6]

The perpetual Dictatorships of Sulla and of Caesar were open violations of the constitution, resulting from the disorders of civil war.

2. It must be understood that, although a Dictator could enforce absolute obedience to his orders, and although these orders could not be disputed, in any matter connected with military operations, when he was named *rei gerundae causa*, yet, when called upon to perform an ordinary constitutional act, he was bound to perform that act according to the established principles and laws of the constitution. Thus, a Dictator, when presiding at the annual elections, was obliged to observe all the ordinary forms connected with the *Comitia*, and to take the votes in the manner prescribed by law; and hence, when T. Manlius

---

[1] Liv. II. 18. 29. 30. III. 20. IV. 13. XXII. 11. XXIII. 30. Cic. de legg. III. 3. Dionys. V. 70. Polyb. III. 87.
[2] Polybius l c. makes an exception with regard to the Tribunes, but they also appear to have been unable to resist. See Liv. VI. 16.
[3] Liv. VII. 3. 21. IX. 26.
[4] s.v. *Optima Lex*, p. 198.
[5] Liv. III. 29. IX. 34. XXIII. 23. Cic. de legg. III. 3.
[6] Liv. III. 29. IV. 46. VI. 29. VII. 3. IX. 26. 34. XXIII. 23.

(Liv. VII. 21) attempted to neglect the *Lex Licinia*, in holding the Consular Comitia, he was resisted, and failed to effect his purpose.

3. We are told by a late writer, whose statement is, however, to a certain extent corroborated by Livy, that a Dictator could not expend the public money without permission from the Senate.[1]

4. It seems to have been a recognised principle that no one should be allowed to exercise, beyond the limits of Italy, the extraordinary powers bestowed upon a Dictator. This rule was violated upon one occasion only, when, during the first Punic war, Atilius Calatinus commanded an army in Sicily (B.C. 249.)[2]

Abolition of the Office.—From the year B.C. 249 until B.C. 217, no Dictator was named *rei gerundae causa*; the office, in a great measure, fell into desuetude and was almost forgotten.[3] But, in consequence of the terror caused by the successes of Hannibal, Q. Fabius Maximus, in B.C. 217, and M. Junius Pera, in B.C. 216, were named *rei gerundae causa*, while others were named, up to B.C. 202, *comitiorum causa*; the last of these being C. Servilius Geminus. With the termination of the second Punic war the office of Dictator may be said to have become extinct; for we cannot regard the perpetual Dictatorships of Sulla and of Cæsar as revivals of the constitutional magistracy. Upon the death of the latter, the name and office of Dictator were formally abolished by law.[4]

Decretum Ultimum—After the office of Dictator had fallen into disuse, the Senate, in seasons of great peril, recurred to an ancient usage,[5] and armed the Consuls with extraordinary powers by passing a resolution, which is termed by Cæsar *Decretum extremum atque ultimum*, couched in these terms—VIDEANT (s. DENT OPERAM) CONSULES NE QUID DETRIMENTI RESPUBLICA CAPIAT, the nature, object and effects of which are briefly, but distinctly, described by Sallust (Cat. 29)—*Itaque, quod plerumque in atroci negotio solet, Senatus decrevit, darent operam Consules, ne quid respublica detrimenti caperet. Ea potestas per Senatum, more Romano, magistratui maxima permittitur, exercitum parare, bellum gerere, coercere omnibus modis socios atque cives, domi militiaeque imperium atque iudicium summum habere; aliter sine populi iussu nulli earum rerum consuli ius est.*

Insignia of the Dictator.—Since the Dictator represented, in his single person, both Consuls, he appeared in public with twenty-four Lictors, who marched before him with *Fasces*, to which the *Secures*, emblematic of his absolute power, were attached even within the city.[6] We cannot doubt that he wore the *Toga Praetexta* and used the *Sella Curulis*, although we do not find these specially mentioned as badges of his office.

PRODICTATOR.

On one single occasion of great embarrassment and alarm, immediately after the battle of the *Lacus Thrasymenus*, when one of the Consuls was dead, and it was difficult, if not impossible, to reach the other, by whom alone a Dictator could be named, the people elected (*creavit*) Q. Fabius Maximus *Prodictator*, in which capacity he exercised all the powers of an ordinary Dictator (Liv. XXII. 8.)

[1] Zonaras VII. 13. Liv. XXII. 23.
[2] Liv. Epit. XIX. Dion Cass. XXXVI. 17.
[3] Liv. XXII. 8. 11.
[4] Cic. Philipp. I. 1. Liv. Epit. CXVI. Dion Cass. XLIV. 51. LIV. 1.
[5] See also Cic. Cat. I. 2. pro Milon. 26. pro Rabir. perd. reo. 7. Sallust. fragm. H. Lib. L. Caes. B. C. I. 5. Dion Cass. XXXVII. 31.
[6] Polyb. III. 87. Dionys. V. 75. X. 24. Plut. Fab. 24. Liv. II. 18. There must be some mistake in the statement found in Liv. Epit. LXXXIX. that Sulla was the first who ever appeared in public with twenty-four Lictors.

MAGISTER EQUITUM.

As soon as a Dictator had been named, he himself named (*dixit*) a lieutenant or deputy, who was styled *Magister Equitum*, probably because he headed the cavalry in the field, while the Dictator led the legion. The *Magister Equitum* executed the orders of the Dictator when the latter was present, and acted as his representative when he was absent, being in all respects subordinate to him, and bound to yield implicit obedience. The only case in which we find the services of a *Magister Equitum* dispensed with, was when M. Fabius Buteo was named Dictator (B.C. 216) for the purpose of filling up vacancies in the Senate; but, as we have noticed above, the position of Buteo was altogether anomalous, for there was another Dictator in office, M. Junius Pera, who had been named *rei gerundae causa*.

The earliest *Magistri Equitum* were all persons who had held the office of Consul, (*consulares*,) and although when the rule was departed from in the case of the principal, it could not have been enforced in the case of the deputy, the exceptions were not numerous. The first Magister Equitum, not a *Consularis*, upon record, was L. Tarquitius, B.C. 458. We infer, moreover, from scattered notices, that the *Magister Equitum* was required to have held the office of Praetor at least, and that his rank and insignia were the same as those of a Praetor.[1]

DECEMVIRI LEGIBUS SCRIBENDIS.

Origin and duration of the Office.—The Plebs having gained a secure position in the state by the institution of the Tribuneship, their next efforts were directed towards a reform in the administration of justice. This, after the expulsion of the Tarquins, was in the hands of the Consuls exclusively, who decided all causes according to their own discretion, and acting under the influence of excited party feelings, showed little disposition to discharge the judicial functions with impartiality. Written laws, if they existed at all, were few in number, and a knowledge of these, as well as of the law of custom, (*Ius Consuetudinis*,) by which chiefly all legal proceedings were regulated, was confined to the Patricians, who jealously refrained from communicating information on such subjects to persons not belonging to their own order. Accordingly, in B.C. 462, forty-seven years after the institution of the Consulship, and thirty-two years after the institution of the Tribuneship, C. Terentillus Arsa, a Tribune of the Plebs, brought forward a bill to the effect, that five commissioners should be elected for the purpose of drawing up laws to define and regulate the power of the Consuls—*Ut quinqueviri creentur legibus de imperio consulari scribendis*.[2] This proposal was violently resisted by the Patricians, and the contest was prolonged for ten years. In B.C. 454, however, the Patricians yielded so far as to consent that three ambassadors should be sent to Athens for the purpose of obtaining a copy of the famous laws of Solon, and of making themselves acquainted with the laws and usages of the other states of Greece. After their return, a bill was carried in B.C. 452, that ten commissioners should be elected for a year, not merely with the limited object first proposed, but for drawing up a complete body of statutes, which should be made known to all, and be binding on all members of the community; and that, during the period of their office, they should be the sole magistrates of the republic. The whole of the commissioners thus chosen were Patricians, it having been previously stipulated that they should

---
[1] Polyb. III. 87. Cic. de legg. III. 3. Dion Cass. XLII. 21. 27. Plut. Anton
[2] Liv. III. 9. Dionys. X. 1.

not be permitted to annul or alter those laws which secured by a solemn sanction (*leges sacratae*) the privileges of the Plebeian order.

The first *Decemviri legibus scribendis*, as they were styled, entered upon office on the Ides of May, B.C. 451, and exercised their power in such a manner as to give general satisfaction. They drew up a Code consisting of ten divisons, or *Tables*, as they were termed, which was accepted and ratified by the Comitia Centuriata. It having been represented, however, that the work was still imperfect, and that two additional Tables were required to render the system complete, the people consented to appoint Decemviri, upon the same terms, for another year. The members of the second board were, according to Livy, all different, with the exception of one individual, Appius Claudius, who, although he presided at the election of the new commissioners, returned himself as one of the number, in violation of the usage established in such cases (see above, p. 107.) The new Decemvirs, headed by Appius, were as remarkable for their insolence and tyranny as their predecessors had been for mildness and moderation. Having finished the task assigned to them, by the addition of two Tables to the existing ten, there was no longer any pretext for them to remain in office; but they allowed the year to elapse without summoning the Comitia for the election of Consuls or other magistrates, and without showing any intention of resigning their power. This usurpation was, however, soon brought to a close, by the outrage perpetrated by Appius in regard to the daughter of Virginius, when the Decemvirs, in order to escape from the storm of popular indignation, formally abdicated. Tribunes of the Plebs were forthwith elected at a meeting of the Comitia Tributa, held by the Pontifex Maximus—Consuls at a meeting of the Comitia Centuriata, held by an Interrex; and the previous form of government was at once restored.[1]

Powers and Duties of the Decemviri.—The *Decemviri* were, for the time being, the sole magistrates of the republic, performing all the duties of state, both civil and military—the office even of the Tribunes of the Plebs having been suspended; their power was absolute, and without appeal to the people— *Placet creari Decemviros sine provocatione, et ne quis eo anno alius magistratus esset.*[2] The first Decemvirs exercised supreme jurisdiction by turns, one only appearing in public with twelve lictors and the other insignia of Consular power, while his colleagues were accompanied each by a single *accensus*, and each permitted an appeal from his legal decisions to another member of the body (*quum priores Decemviri appellatione collegae corrigi reddita ab se iura tulissent.*)[3] But the second board not only declared the decision of each individual member absolute and final, but each appeared in public attended by twelve lictors, with *fasces* and *secures*, thus thronging the forum with a troop of one hundred and twenty armed attendants, and striking terror into high and low alike by this display of despotic force.

Laws of the Decemviri.—But although the office of Decemvirs quickly passed away, and the individuals who had held it were forgotten, or remembered with detestation, the work which they had performed remained a durable monument of their toils, and the code of the XII Tables, engraved on plates of bronze and hung up to public view, (*in aes incisas in publico proposuerunt,*) served in all time coming as the foundation of the whole fabric of Roman Law (*fons omnis publici privatique iuris.*) It seems to have embodied the laws and usages

---

[1] Liv. III. 31—55. Dionys. X. 1. seqq. Cic. de R. II. 36. 37. de legg. III. 8.
[2] Liv. III. 32. Cic. de R. l.c.
[3] Liv. III. 33. 36. comp. Dionys. X. 57.

in force among the Romans at the time it was compiled, together with numerous selections from foreign sources, (*accitis quae usquam egregia,*) the whole having been collected, digested, and combined under the superintendence of an Ephesian exile, Hermodorus by name, to whom, in testimony of his services, a statue was erected at the public expense, in the Comitium.[1]

TRIBUNI MILITARES CONSULARI POTESTATE S. CONSULARI IMPERIO.

Origin and Duration of the Office.—In B.C. 445, four years after the abdication of the Decemvirs, C. Canuleius, a Tribune of the Plebs, proposed two laws, the one for establishing the right of intermarriage (*connubium*) between Patricians and Plebeians, which had been formally prohibited by the Code of the XII Tables, the other for declaring Plebeians eligible to the Consulship. The former was carried in the same year after considerable opposition, the latter was more fiercely resisted by the Patricians; who perceiving, however, that if matters were pushed to an extremity, they would, in all probability, be vanquished, agreed to a compromise, in terms of which it was resolved that, instead of two Consuls, a larger number of magistrates, to be called *Tribuni Militares Consulari potestate*, invested with the same powers as Consuls, should be elected annually, and that it should be lawful to choose these from the Patricians and Plebeians, without distinction (*promiscue ex patribus ac plebe.*)[2] This arrangement continued partially in force for nearly eighty years, (B.C. 444—B.C. 367,) until the passing of the Lex Licinia, (B.C. 367,) by which the Consulship was thrown open to the Plebeians. During the above period the Senate seems to have had the power of fixing, each year, whether the magistrates for the following year should be Consuls or *Tribuni Militares C. P.* and their decision appears to have been generally regulated by the state of parties. When the Tribunes of the Plebs were supine or had little prospect of being able to carry a law similar to that of Canuleius, then two Patrician Consuls were chosen; but when the agitation was pushed with greater vigour, then a decree was passed for the election of *Tribuni Militares C. P.* During the space indicated above these Tribunes were elected fifty times, Consuls twenty-three times; and during five consecutive years, (B.C. 375—B.C. 371,) the struggle connected with the Licinian Rogations deprived the state altogether of supreme magistrates (see above, p. 134.)

Number of Tribuni Militares C. P.—In the four elections which took place from B.C. 444—B.C. 427, three were chosen for each year; in the thirteen elections, from B.C. 426—B.C. 406, the number was four, except in B.C. 418 and B.C. 408, when there were three only; during the remaining period, commencing with B.C. 405, the number was uniformly six.

Mode of Election, Powers, and Duties.—These magistrates were elected by the Comitia Centuriata, and the duties which they performed were precisely the same with those which devolved upon the Consuls. One of their number usually remained in the city for the purpose of administering justice, presiding at meetings of the Senate, holding Comitia, and performing other civil functions, the rest went forth either singly or in pairs to command the armies and prosecute the wars in which the state might be engaged. When acting together, they assumed the supreme command upon alternate days, as already described in the case of the Consuls.[4]

---

[1] Dionys X. 57. Tacit. Ann. III. 26. Liv. III. 34. Plin. H.N. XXXIV. 5. Pompon. de orig. iur. Digest. I. ii. 4.
[2] Liv. IV. 6. comp. Dionys. XI. 60.
[3] Liv. IV. 12. Dionys. l c.
[4] Liv. V. 13. 52. IV. 31. 36. 45. 46. 59. VI. 1. 30.

Insignia.—It has been doubted whether the *Tribuni Militaris C. P.* were regarded as Curule Magistrates; but it is clear, from the words of Livy, (IV. 7,) that their *imperium* and the emblems of their authority were the same with those of the Consuls. There is no record, however, of any one of them having ever celebrated a triumph, although they gained victories which might have entitled them to that distinction.

It may be asked what the Patricians gained by consenting to the institution of this new magistracy, which was thrown open to the Plebeians, while they still strenuously resisted their admission to the Consulship. On this point historians supply no clear explanation; but it will be seen (in the section on CENSORES) that, at the period when the change was introduced, the duty of taking the *Census*, to which the Patricians doubtless attached great importance, and which had hitherto been performed by the Consuls, was committed to two magistrates, then first appointed for that special purpose, and who, for a considerable period, were chosen from the Patricians exclusively. It has, moreover, been conjectured, with much plausibility, that the Patricians made some stipulation or arrangement, by which the *Tribunus* who remained in the city for the purpose of administering justice should be a member of their own body; for even after the admission of Plebeians to the Consulship, the Patricians clung to the privilege of appointing one of their own order to act as supreme judge in the civil courts, as we shall explain in the article on PRAETORES. We shall find, moreover, that although in several instances the *Tribuni Militares C. P.* were all Patricians, there is no example of their having been all Plebeians.

PRAETORES.

Origin of the Office.—When the Patricians were at length compelled to acquiesce in the passing of the *Lex Licinia*, (B.C. 367,) by which the Consulship was thrown open to the Plebeians, (see above, p. 134,) they stipulated that the judicial functions hitherto discharged by the Consuls, should be separated from their other duties, and that a new Curule Magistrate should be appointed, from the Patricians exclusively, to act as supreme judge in the civil courts (*qui ius in urbe diceret.*) On this magistrate the title of PRAETOR was bestowed, (*Praetorem iura reddentem,*) which, it will be remembered, (see above, p. 133,) was originally the designation of the Consuls. The Praetorship was retained by the Patricians longer than any of the other great offices of state, no Plebeian having been admitted until B.C. 337.[1]

Number of Praetors at Different Times.—At first there was one Praetor only; but towards the close of the first Punic war (about B.C. 244) the number of *Peregrini* (see above, p. 85) residing in Rome had increased to such an extent that it was found necessary to elect an additional Praetor, who should confine his attention to suits between *Peregrini*, or between citizens and *Peregrini*.[2] From this time forward the Praetor who decided causes between citizens alone was termed *Praetor Urbanus* or *Praetor Urbis*, and to him belonged, in technical phraseology, the *Provincia s. Sors Urbana—Urbana Iurisdictio—Iurisdictio inter cives;* while his colleague was said to hold the *Provincia s. Sors Peregrina—Peregrina Iurisdictio—Iurisdictio inter peregrinos—Iurisdictio inter cives et peregrinos*, and was, in later times at least, styled *Praetor Peregrinus.*[3]

[1] Liv. VI. 42. VII. 1. VIII. 15.
[2] Liv. Epit. XIX. Pompon. de orig. iur. Digest. I. ii. 28.
[3] According to Becker the title *Praetor Peregrinus* occurs first in inscriptions belonging to the age of Trajan. See Orelli C. I. L. No. 2369. 2760.

About B.C. 227 the number of Praetors was increased to four, in order that one might proceed annually to Sicily to act as governor of that province, while another might, in like manner, take the command in Sardinia. In B.C. 197 the number was further increased to six, in order to provide rulers for the two Spains. A *Lex Baebia* was passed, probably in B.C. 180, ordaining that the number of Praetors should be six and four, in alternate years; but this statute seems to have been put in force once only, namely, in B.C. 179. By Sulla the number of Praetors was augmented to eight, by Julius Caesar to ten, twelve, and eventually to sixteen.[1]

Duties of the Praetors.—The charge intrusted to each Praetor was, under ordinary circumstances, determined by lot,[2] and the nature of their duties has been indicated above. The *Praetor Urbanus* and the *Praetor Peregrinus* remained in the city to exercise their respective jurisdictions, (*duae urbanae provinciae*,) while the remainder proceeded with *Imperium* to Sicily, Sardinia, and the Spains. But not only might these last be employed elsewhere at the discretion of the Senate, but occasionally the Praetor Peregrinus was called upon for military service, in which case his duties were thrown upon the Praetor Urbanus, who was himself, in times of great emergency, sometimes required to take the command of an army.[3]

After the institution of the *Quaestiones Perpetuae*, (see Chapter on Roman Law and administration of justice, p. 290,) that is, about B.C. 144, a great change took place in the arrangements described above. From that time forward the whole of the Praetors remained in the city during their year of office, two of their number presiding, as formerly, in the civil courts, while the remaining four, or, after the time of Sulla, the remaining six, took cognizance of criminal causes, as we shall explain more fully hereafter. This, however, is the proper place to say a few words upon the position occupied by—

The Praetor Urbanus specially.—The original, and, at all times, the chief duty of the Praetor Urbanus was to act as supreme judge in the civil court; and he took his seat on his curule chair, on his *Tribunal*, for this purpose on every *Dies Fastus*, that is, on every day on which it was lawful to transact legal business. He also, ex officio, presided at the *Ludi Apollinares* and the *Ludi Piscatorii*. These duties he performed even when both Consuls were in the city; but in their absence his powers and occupations were greatly extended. He then discharged most of the functions which had formerly devolved on a *Praefectus Urbi*, and, in fact, acted in every respect as the representative of the Consuls, except in so far that it was not competent for him to name a Dictator nor to preside either at the Consular or the Praetorian elections.

Mode of Election, Dignity and Insignia of the Praetors.—They were elected by the Comitia Centuriata, under the same auspices with the Consuls, at first on the same day with the Consuls, subsequently, one or several days later. A *Praetor* was styled *Collega Consulis*, although inferior to him in rank, and was regarded as occupying the second place among the higher magistrates.[4] He wore the *Toga Praetexta*, used the *Sella Curulis*, and was attended by two Lictors within the city, and by six when on foreign service, and hence he is termed by Polybius ἑξαπέλεκυς ἡγεμών or ἑξαπέλεκυς στρατηγός and the office

---

[1] Liv. Epit. XX. XXXII. 27. XL. 44. Sueton. Caes. 41. Dion Cass. XLII. 51. XLIII. 47. 51.
[2] The Senate however, occasionally assumed the right of fixing, *extra ordinem*, the duties to be performed by one or more of the Praetors, e. g. *Comitiis praetorum perfectis, Senatus consultum factum est, ut Q. Fulcio extra ordinem urbana provincia esset*. Liv. XXIV. 9.
[3] Liv. XLII. 28. XLIV. 17. XXIV. 44. XXV. 3. 41. XXX. 40. XXIII. 32.
[4] Liv. VII. 1. VIII. 32. X. 22. XXVII. 35. XL. 59. XLIII. 11. XLV. 44.

ἐξαπέλεκυς ἀρχή.¹ The Praetor Urbanus was regarded as superior in dignity to the rest, and hence was designated *Praetor Maior*.²

The Praetorship under the Empire.—The number of Praetors, which had been increased by Cæsar to sixteen, was, in the first instance, reduced by Augustus to ten, then again raised to sixteen, and finally fixed by him at twelve. From A.D. 14 until A.D. 96, it varied from twelve to eighteen—eighteen held office under Nerva, and no change seems to have taken place under Trajan, Hadrian, and the Antonines.³

The functions of the Praetors, under the empire, were, to a considerable extent, altogether different from those which they discharged under the commonwealth. The supreme jurisdiction, both in the criminal and civil courts, was transferred, in a great measure, to the Senate and the *Praefectus Urbi*, although particular departments were, from time to time, committed to the Praetors. Augustus made over to the *Praetor Urbanus* and the *Praetor Peregrinus* much of the jurisdiction which had formerly belonged to the Aediles; Claudius committed to two Praetors, and Titus to one, the decision of questions concerning trust estates; (*Praetor de Fideicommissis;*) Nerva appointed another to preside in all causes which arose between private individuals and the Imperial exchequer; (*Fiscus;*) Antoninus consigned to another all matters connected with the affairs of minors, and hence this judge was entitled *Praetor s. Iudex Tutelaris*.⁴

But although the Praetors, as a body, were now little called upon to exercise purely judicial functions, new duties were imposed upon them. A certain number, in conjunction with the Aediles and the Tribunes of the Plebs, were charged with the general superintendence of the XIV Regions into which Augustus divided the city, and this arrangement appears to have remained unchanged until the reign of Alexander Severus. Augustus and Vespasian placed the public exchequer (*Aerarium*) under the management of two Praetors, and the former made over to the Praetors exclusively the whole charge of the public games, which had previously belonged to the Aediles. But these occupations were not found to afford at all times sufficient employment for the whole of these magistrates, and some of them occasionally enjoyed the honour and title without being called upon for any active exertion.⁵

The name, at least, of *Praetor Urbanus* endured as long as the Roman empire in the west, that of *Praetor Peregrinus* fell out of use after the time of Caracalla, who bestowed the full *Civitas* on all the inhabitants of the Roman world; and both the *Praetor Urbanus* and the *Praetor Tutelaris* found a place among the officers of state at Constantinople.

AEDILES.⁶

Two sets of magistrates bore the name of *Aediles*, being distinguished from each other as *Aediles Plebeii* and *Aediles Curules*. We must, in the first place, consider them separately.

---

¹ On the much contested point of the number of Lictors assigned to a Praetor, the chief authorities are, Plaut. Epid. I. i. 26. Censorin. de die nat. 24. Cic. de leg. agr. II. 34. in Verr. V. 54. Polyb. II. 24. III. 40. 106, frag. lib. XXXIII. I. The most embarrassing passage is Val. Max. I. i. 9. unless we suppose that the ceremonial there described was regarded as a sort of military spectacle.

² Fest. s.v. *Maiorem Consulem*, p. 161.

³ Velleius II. 89. Tacit. Ann. I. 14. II. 32. Dion Cass. LIII. 32. LVI. 25. LVIII. 20. LIX. 20. LX. 10. Pompon. Digest. I. ii. 2. § 32.

⁴ Pompon. Digest. l.c. Ulpian. XXV. 12. Digest. XXVI. v. 8. XXVII. i. 35. 6. §. 13. Tacit. Ann. VI. 17. Dion Cass. LIII. 2.

⁵ Dion Cass. LIII. 32. LV. 8. Tacit. Hist. IV. 9. Agric. 6. Suet. Octav. 30. 36. Lamprid. Alex. Sev. 33.

⁶ In addition to the chapter in Becker, the student may consult, with advantage, the elaborate monograph of Schubart, De Romanorum Aedilibus. Regimont. 1828.

Origin of the Aediles Plebeii.—At the time when the arrangement was concluded between the Patricians and the Plebeians with regard to the institution of *Tribuni Plebis*, (B.C. 494, see p. 146,) it was agreed that, in addition to the Tribunes, two Plebeian magistrates should be elected annually under the name of *Aediles*. These appear to have been, originally, regarded merely as assistants to the Tribunes: and the only special duty which they were required to perform was to act as custodiers of the Tablets on which the laws passed by the people in their Comitia and the decrees of the Senate were inscribed. These were, at that period, deposited in the temple of Ceres; and the Plebs had probably stipulated that they should be given in charge to officers selected out of their own body, from an apprehension that the great charters of their freedom might have been tampered with if left in the hands of the Patricians.

Origin of the Aediles Curules.—In B.C. 367, one hundred and twenty-seven years after the institution of the *Aediles Plebeii*, the long protracted strife between the Patricians and the Plebeians was brought to a close by the admission of the latter to the Consulship; but it was determined, at the same time, that three new magistrates should be introduced, to be chosen from the Patricians exclusively, viz. the *Praetor*, of whom we have spoken in the preceding article, and two *Aediles Curules*, whose chief duty, ostensibly at least, was to be the celebration, with extraordinary magnificence, of the *Ludi Romani*, in honour of the harmony now established between the two orders in the state.[1]

The Tribunes, however, having remonstrated against the unfairness of instituting three magistrates exclusively Patrician, while one place only in the Consulship had been conceded to the Plebeians, the Senate gave way and consented (B.C. 366) that the Curule Aediles should be chosen in alternate years from the Plebeians, and, soon after, that they should at all times be chosen from the Patricians and Plebeians indifferently. Henceforward there were four annual magistrates called *Aediles*, two termed *Aediles Plebeii*, chosen from the Plebeians exclusively, two termed *Aediles Curules*, chosen from Patricians and Plebeians without distinction.

Relative Position of the Aediles Plebeii and Aediles Curules.—In so far as external marks of dignity were concerned, the superiority of the *Aediles Curules* was unquestionable; for they had the privilege of wearing the *Toga Praetexta* and using the *Sella Curulis*, symbols of honour not enjoyed by their Plebeian colleagues. On the other hand, there can be no doubt that the persons of the *Aediles Plebeii* were, on the first institution of the office, declared inviolable, (*sacrosancti*, see above, p. 146,) and they probably retained the privileges bestowed by the *Leges Sacratae* to their full extent, as long as they were regarded in the light of mere assistants to the *Tribuni Plebis*. But after they became, in a great measure, independent of the Tribunes, and were called upon to discharge numerous and complicated duties—duties, moreover, which did not bring them into collision with violent political partizans—it would seem that their inviolability dropped out of view, and that the higher magistrates claimed and exercised the right of controlling, and even, in extreme cases, of imprisoning them; so that, towards the close of the republic, it became a topic of speculative discussion whether the *Aediles Plebeii* had any right to the title of *Sacrosancti*.[2] In regard to a separation of duties between the Plebeian and Curule Aediles, if any such existed, it is impossible now to discover the line of demarcation, except in so far that the charge of certain of the more important public games, the *Ludi*

---
[1] Liv. VII. 42.
[2] Liv. III. 55. 57. Festus. s.v. *Sacrosanctum*, p. 318.

Romani and the *Megalesia* especially, devolved upon the Curule Aediles, while, as a matter of course, the *Ludi Plebeii* were the province of the Plebeian Aediles.

Mode of Election.—The *Aediles Plebeii*, from the year B.C. 472, were elected by the *Comitia Tributa*, in terms of the *Lex Publilia* of Volero, (see above, p. 123,) before that time probably by the *Comitia Curiata*.[1] The *Aediles Curules* were probably elected originally by the *Comitia Centuriata*, but subsequently by the *Comitia Tributa*:[2] the *Curules* and the *Plebeii* were not, however, elected on the same day, at least in the time of Cicero; but the *Comitia Aedilium Plebis* took place before the Comitia for the *Curules*.[3] The presiding magistrate at the election of the *Aediles Plebeii* seems, as far as our single authority can be depended upon, to have been himself a Plebeian Aedile; the first Curule Aedile was chosen by Camillus when Dictator, afterwards a Consul presided, or, in his absence, the *Praetor Urbanus*.[4]

Day of Induction into Office.—There is no doubt that the Curule Aediles, from the period of their institution, entered upon office on the same day with the Consuls and Praetors, and consequently, from the year B.C. 154, (see above, p. 135,) on the first of January.[5] From the close connection which originally subsisted between the Plebeian Aediles and the Tribunes, one might have concluded that the former would have entered upon office on the same day with the latter, that is, on the tenth of December. But all the evidence we possess goes to prove that the Plebeian Aediles, as well as their Curule colleagues, entered upon office on the same day with the Consuls and Praetors.[6]

Duties of the Aediles.—These were of a most multifarious character; but, following the example of Cicero, they may be conveniently classed under three heads—*Suntoque Aediles curatores urbis, annonae, ludorumque solennium*.

1. It was their duty to act as burgh magistrates and commissioners of police (*Curatores Urbis*.)
2. To superintend the supply of provisions to the public (*Curatores Annonae*.)
3. To take charge of the exhibition of the public games (*Curatores ludorum solennium*.)

I. *Curatores Urbis*.—As burgh magistrates and commissioners of police, the Aediles were called upon to preserve peace and good order within the city, and within the circuit of a mile from the walls, which was the limit of their jurisdiction; to frame and enforce such regulations as might be necessary for the preservation of property and for the safety and comfort of the community. Within five days after their election, or, at all events, after they entered upon office, they divided by lot the districts into which the city was portioned out for police purposes. Each was specially required to keep the streets within his own district in good order, to see that the necessary repairs were executed from time to time, to have them swept regularly, to remove all nuisances, to prohibit encroachments, on the part of private individuals, which might obstruct the thoroughfare, to quell all brawls and disturbances, and generally to enforce order and regularity among the passers to and fro.[7] To them was intrusted the superintendence of

---

[1] Dionys. IX. 41.
[2] Aul. Gell. XIII. 15. Dionys. IX. 49. comp. Liv. IX. 46. XXV. 2.
[3] The testimony of Coelius ap. Cic. ad Fam. VIII. 4. is perfectly distinct, although at variance with Plut. Mar. 5.
[4] Piso ap. Aul. Gell. VI. 9. Liv. VI. 42. Cic. ad. Att. IV. 3. pro Planc. 20. Varro R.R. III. 2. Dion Cass. XXXIX. 7. 32.
[5] Cic. in Verr. Act. I. 12.
[6] Liv. XXVIII. 10. 38. XXIX. 38. XXX. 26. XXXI. 50.
[7] See Tabul. Heracl. Plaut. Stich. II. ii. 23. Capt. IV. ii. 26. Suet. Vesp. 5. comp. Cic. Philipp. IX. 7. Ovid. Fast. VI. 663. Digest. XLIII. x.

the temples (*procuratio aedium sacrarum*) and of public buildings in general; and they had a right to insist that private mansions should not be allowed to fall into such a state of disrepair as to endanger the safety of the people.[1] The duty of making contracts for the execution of great public works belonged to the Censors, as we shall point out in the article devoted to those magistrates: but since Censors were in office for eighteen months only during each space of five years,(*lustrum*,) the task of seeing their projects carried out must, in many cases, have fallen upon the Aediles. The Aediles also exercised a certain surveillance over public health and public morality, by placing the baths, taverns, and eating-houses under proper restrictions,[2] by preventing the introduction of disorderly foreign rites,[3] and by coming forward as the public accusers of females charged with disgraceful conduct (*probrum*.)[4] They had the right of issuing proclamations (*edicta*) containing rules connected with their department, and of punishing the infringement of these or of the ordinary police laws by the infliction of a fine upon offenders.[5]

But, in addition to these matters, all of which naturally formed part of their duties as police magistrates, we find them, especially the Plebeian Aediles, instituting prosecutions against three classes of persons.

1. Those who were in occupation of more than the legal quantity of the *Ager Publicus*, that is, the land belonging to the state (Liv. X. 13.)

2. Those tenants of the public pastures (*Pecuarii*) who had increased their flocks beyond the legal limits (Liv. X. 23. 47. XXXIII. 42. XXXIV. 53. XXXV. 10.)

3. Money lenders (*feneratores*) who exacted more than the legal rate of interest (Liv. VII. 28. X. 23. XXXV. 41.)

These were affairs which might be regarded as peculiarly affecting the interests of the Plebs, and hence such prosecutions were probably originally instituted by the Plebeian Aediles in their character of assistants to the Tribunes. On this subject we shall say more in the chapter on the *Ager Publicus*.

II. *Curatores Annonae*.—From the earliest times the Aediles acted as inspectors of the markets, and hence they are termed ἀγορανόμοι by the Greek writers on Roman history. In this capacity they were called upon to see that the provisions exposed for sale were sound and wholesome, that the weights and measures were in accordance with the legal standard, and that the prices charged were not exorbitant.[6] But in addition to this, they were required to perform the more important and difficult task of securing an adequate supply of corn (*cura annonae*) at all times, and of making arrangements for importation from abroad when any apprehension prevailed of a scarcity from ordinary sources, and of superintending the warehousing and distribution of the large cargoes, which, towards the close of the republic, were regularly despatched to Rome from the provinces. Hence, they assumed the right of inflicting fines upon those dealers (*frumentarii*) who hoarded up large stocks (*ob annonam compressam*) in seasons of scarcity, in the hope of realizing an extravagant profit.

In times of great emergency, however, a commissioner was chosen for the special purpose of procuring supplies, under the name *Praefectus Annonae;* and

---

[1] Tabul. Heracl. Cic. in Verr. V. 14.
[2] Senec. Epp. 86. Suet. Tib. 34. Claud. 38. Martial. V. 84. XIV. 1.
[3] Liv. IV. 30. XXV. 1.
[4] Liv. VIII. 18. 22. X. 31. XXV. 2. Aul. Gell. X. 6. comp. Val. Max. VI. i. 7. Laber. ap. Aul. Gell. XVI. 7. Tacit Ann. II. 85.
[5] Liv. X. 23. 31. 47. XXX. 39. XXXIII. 42. XXXIV. 53. XXXV. 10. 41. XXXVIII. 35.
[6] Plaut. Rud. II. iii. 42. Juv. X. 100. Digest. XIX. ii. 13. § 8.

Julius Cæsar instituted two additional Plebeian Aediles, under the designation of
Aediles Cereales.[1] A denarius, certainly struck before the end of the republic, presents on one side a head of Saturn with a sickle behind, and the legend PISO. CAEPIO. Q.; on the other, two men clothed in the toga seated with an ear of corn before and behind, the  legend being AD. FRU. EMU. EX. S.C. from which we infer that the duty of purchasing corn for the public was sometimes laid upon the Quaestors.

III. *Curatores ludorum solennium.*—The *Aediles Curules*, as we have seen, from the first took charge of the *Ludi Romani*; but the general superintendence exercised by these magistrates over the public games was closely connected with the obligation imposed upon them as heads of the police, to maintain order and regularity at the great festivals which, in the earlier ages of the state, were exhibited at the public cost exclusively. The decoration of the *Argentariae*, (see above, p. 18,) with the gilded shields of the Samnites, at the triumph of Papirius, in B.C. 309, is said to have first suggested to the Aediles the idea of ornamenting the Forum and its vicinity with statues, pictures, embroidery, and other works of art, during solemn processions and the celebration of the public games. This species of display was, towards the close of the republic, conducted upon such an extensive scale that works of art were borrowed for the purpose, not only from private individuals in Rome, but from public bodies in all the provinces, by the Aediles, who spared neither trouble nor expense in this nor in any other matter connected with the splendour of the great festivals, each being eager to surpass his predecessor, and hoping that, by gratifying the curiosity and feasting the eyes of the multitude, he would be able to secure their suffrages when candidate for the higher offices of state.[2] It is to be observed that, although the arrangement and regulations of these national shows devolved upon the Aediles, one of the higher magistrates, a Consul or a Praetor usually acted as President.[3]

We may conclude this article by quoting from Cicero (In Verr. V. 14) the catalogue of the duties which devolved on him in his capacity of *Aedilis Curulis*, and of the honours which formed the recompense of his labours—*Nunc sum designatus Aedilis: habeo rationem, quid a Populo Romano acceperim: mihi ludos sanctissimos maxima cum caeremonia Cereri, Libero, Liberaeque faciundos; mihi Floram matrem populo plebique Romanae ludorum celebritate placandam; mihi ludos antiquissimos, qui primi Romani sunt nominati, maxima cum dignitate ac religione Iovi, Iunoni, Minervae esse faciundos; mihi sacrarum aedium procurationem, mihi totam Urbem tuendam esse commissam: ob earum rerum laborem et sollicitudinem fructus illos datos, antiquiorem in Senatu sententiae dicendae locum, Togam Praetextam, Sellam Curulem, Ius Imaginis ad memoriam posteritatemque tradendae.*

Aedileship under the Empire.—The *Aediles Plebeii* and the *Aediles Curules*, together with the *Aediles Cereales*, instituted by Julius Cæsar, continued to exist as distinct magistrates until the reign of Alexander Severus, when they

---

[1] Liv. X. 11. XXX. 26. XXXI. 4. 50. XXXIII. 42. XXXVIII. 1. Sueton. Caes. 41. Dion Cass. XLIII 51. Pompon. de orig. iur. Digest. I. ii. 2. § 32.
[2] Liv. IX. 40. XL. 44. Cic. in. Verr. I. 19. 22. IV. 3. and notes of Pseud. Ascon. de N. D. I. 9.
[3] Val. Max. I. i. 16. Liv. XXXIV. 44. Macrob. S. II. 6. Tabul. Heracl.

disappeared altogether. But although the office was thus retained for more than two centuries and a-half after the downfal of the commonwealth, the duties were reduced within very narrow limits, all the most important tasks performed by them under the republic having been by degrees committed to other hands. The general superintendence of the XIV Regions into which the city was divided by Augustus, was indeed intrusted to the Praetors, Aediles, and Tribunes of the Plebs; but the most important and onerous portion of this charge fell upon the *Magistri Vicorum*, the *Praefectus Vigilum* and various *Curatores*, nominated for particular departments. The Aediles seem to have retained little except the inspection of the streets, of baths and of taverns, the exercise of a literary censorship, and the enforcement of the sanitary laws. The *Cura ludorum solennium* was left with them for a time; but the expenses entailed by this charge being ruinous to men of moderate means, and popular favour being no longer an object of ambition, persons could not be found, even under Augustus, willing to accept the office, so that he was obliged upon several occasions to compel those who had held the Quaestorship and the Tribuneship of the Plebs to decide by lot which of them should assume the Aedileship. Eventually, as stated above, he made over the whole superintendence of the public games to the Praetors, whom he assisted, for a time, by a grant of public money.[1]

QUAESTORES.

Origin of the Office.—No subject connected with Roman antiquities is involved in more doubt and confusion than the origin and early history of the Quaestorship; (*Quaestura*;) but without entering into a tedious critical examination of the various opinions which have been advanced and maintained, we may state at once that much of the embarrassment has arisen from the circumstance, that two sets of magistrates, both bearing the name of *Quaestores*, but whose functions were entirely different, existed from a very early period.

1. *Quaestores Aerarii* or keepers of the treasury, ordinary magistrates, who took charge of the public money, receiving and disbursing it under the orders of the Senate.

2. *Quaestores Parricidii*, extraordinary magistrates, appointed in the primitive ages to preside at criminal trials, originally, as the name imports, at trials for homicide. When we proceed to inquire into the administration of justice among the Romans, we shall find that, at all periods of the republic, commissioners specially appointed to preside at criminal trials were termed *Quaesitores*, which is merely another form of *Quaestores*, and that *Quaestio* is the technical word for a criminal trial. The *Decemviri Perduellionis* nominated by Tullus Hostilius (Liv. I. 26) to try Horatius must be regarded as affording the first example of *Quaestores Parricidii*; and again, at a much later period, (B.C. 384.) Livy (VI. 20) found in some of his authorities that Manlius was tried and convicted by *Duumviri* appointed for the purpose of investigating the charge of treason. It is quite true that in the earlier books of Livy mention is made of *Quaestores* in connection with criminal trials, where apparently the ordinary *Quaestores* are the persons indicated; but in these instances they are spoken of as accusers, not as judges;[2] and that the ordinary *Quaestores* were the

---

[1] Tacit. Ann II. 85. III. 52. 55. IV. 35. XIII. 28. Plin. H.N. XXXVI. 15. Senec. de vit. beat. 7. Epist. LXXXVI. Suet Tib. 34. 35. Vesp. 5. Dion. Cass. XLIX. 43. LIII. 2. LIV. 2. 10. LV. 24. 31. LVI. 27. LVII. 24. LIX. 12.

[2] Liv. II. 41. the first passage in which he mentions *Quaestores*, III. 24. 25. VI. 20. 25. See also Cic. de R. II. 35.

magistrates to whom the prosecution of criminals was frequently intrusted, especially in the absence of the Consuls, is proved by the assertion of Varro, that for this purpose, and for this only, they had the right of summoning the *Comitia Centuriata*—*Alia de causa hic magistratus non potest exercitum urbanum convocare.* [1]

In what follows, therefore, we shall confine our attention exclusively to those Quaestors who, for the sake of distinction, were called *Quaestores Aerarii*, reserving all remarks upon the criminal judges called *Quaesitores* or *Quaestores*, whom we believe to have been perfectly distinct from the others, until we treat of criminal trials. [2]

But even after we have drawn this line of separation, we do not yet find our authorities agree as to the period when the ordinary magistrates called *Quaestores* were first introduced. According to Junius Gracchanus, as quoted by Ulpian, they were as old as the time of Romulus and Remus, and Tacitus says that they unquestionably existed under the Kings—*quod Lex Curiata ostendit ab Lucio Bruto repetita.* Livy, on the other hand, and Plutarch state as positively that the office was not instituted until after the establishment of the commonwealth. [3] That there must be officers in every regularly organized state to take charge of the public treasury appears so obvious that, even if the statements of Gracchanus and Tacitus had been less positive than they are, we should at once have preferred their authority, and we may therefore conclude that the office passed over from the regal to the republican period without material change.

Number of Quaestores.—The number of Quaestores was originally two, and they discharged the duties of their office within the city. But in B.C. 421 the number was increased to four; two remained in the city, and were styled *Quaestores Urbani*, while two accompanied the Consuls with the armies to the field, taking charge of the military chest and disposing of the plunder. [4] The number was again increased to eight about the beginning of the first Punic war, when the whole of Italy had been subjugated; but we hear of no further increase until the time of Sulla, who raised the number to twenty, while by Julius Cæsar it was augmented to forty. [5] We read in Joannes Lydus (De magistr. I. 27) of twelve *Classici Quaestores* chosen about B.C. 267; but whether they were so named from being appointed to the fleet, or how far we can at all trust the information afforded by such a writer, it is not easy to determine.

Mode of Election.—Here again we find nothing but positive contradictions. Tacitus asserts that the right of nomination lay with the Kings, and after their expulsion, was exercised for sixty-three years by the Consuls. Gracchanus, on the other hand, assures us that, even during the regal period, they were chosen by the votes of the people. We can scarcely doubt that, from the commencement

---

[1] Varro L L. VI. § 90—93. Dionys. VIII. 77.
[2] We have distinct statements with regard the *Quaestores Parricidii* in Paulus Diaconus s v. *Parrici Quaestores*, p. 221, and in Pomponius de orig. iur. Digest. I. ii. 2. § 23. who tells us that they were named in the laws of the XII Tables. The words of Festus s.v. *Quaestores*, p. 258. are unfortunately so mutilated as to yield no information. Varro, again, (L.L. V. § 81.) although sufficiently clear upon one point, seems to have supposed that the *Quaestores Aerarii* and the *Quaestores Parricidii* were originally identical, while Zonaras, (VII. 13,) if we consider his testimony of any weight in a matter of this sort, believed that the *Quaestores* were originally criminal judges, to whom, on the establishment of the commonwealth, the charge of the public money was consigned.
[3] Digest. I. xiii. Tacit. Ann. XI. 22. Liv. IV. 4. Plut. Popl. 12.
[4] Here we follow Livy, (IV. 43,) whose narrative is clear and consistent while the account given by Tacitus, (Ann. XI. 22,) which is, upon some points, directly opposed to that of Livy, is confused and improbable.
[5] Liv. Epit. XV. Tacit. l.c. Suet. Caes. 41. Dion Cass. XLIII. 47.

of the republic at least, the election was in the hands of the Comitia—first of the *Comitia Curiata*, and subsequently of the *Comitia Tributa*.[1]

From what Order Chosen.—The Quaestors, like all the other great officers of state, were at first taken from the Patricians exclusively; but when, in B.C. 421, the number was increased to four, it was settled, after a sharp contest, that, for the future, the magistracy should be open to Patricians and Plebeians without distinction. For eleven years, however, the Patricians contrived to exclude the Plebeians; but, in B.C. 409, a reaction took place, and the Plebeians succeeded in securing three places out of four.[2]

Day of Induction into office.—There can be no doubt that the *Comitia Quaestoria* took place after the *Comitia Consularia*, and we should naturally conclude that the Quaestors entered upon office on the same day with the Consuls, Praetors, and Aediles; but it has been inferred, from a passage in one of the Verrine Orations, and the Scholium by which it is accompanied, that, in the age of Cicero, the Quaestors entered upon office upon the 5th of December (*Nonis Decembribus*.) Perhaps, however, it would be unsafe to pronounce upon this confidently, in the absence of more conclusive evidence.[3]

Duties of the Quaestors.—The Quaestors, after their election, usually decided by lot where each should serve, although occasionally the Senate assigned a particular duty specially (*extra sortem*) to a particular individual, and sometimes a General was permitted to select his own Quaestor.[4] When the number was four, two, as we have seen, remained in the city, and one was assigned to each Consul; at a later period, perhaps not until the number was increased to twenty, one was always sent to Ostia, to take charge of the dues paid upon exports and imports, and this seems to have been what was termed the *Provincia Aquaria*, which was regarded as the most disagreeable and troublesome of all; another was stationed at Cales in Campania, another in Cisalpine Gaul, while the rest were distributed in the provinces in attendance upon the provincial governors.[5] It is to be observed, that the connection between a provincial governor and his Quaestor was held to be a tie of the closest description, and the same feelings of affection and confidence were supposed to exist between them as between a father and his son; so that any act of hostility on the part of Quaestor towards one under whom he had served, was regarded as odious and unnatural. Cicero insists strongly upon this plea when pointing out the unfitness of Q. Caecilius to conduct the impeachment of Veres—*Sic enim a maioribus nostris accepimus, Praetorem Quaestori suo parentis loco esse oportere: nullam neque iustiorem neque graviorem causam necessitudinis posse reperiri, quam coniunctionem sortis, quam provinciae, quam officii, quam publicam muneris societatem. Quamobrem si iure posses eum accusare, tamen quum is tibi parentis numero fuisset, id pie facere non posses.*[6]

The *Quaestores Urbani* took charge of the *Aerarium*. The proceeds of all

---

[1] That they were chosen in the *Comitia Tributa* in the age of Cicero seems certain from Epp. ad fam. VII. 30.
[2] Liv. IV. 43. 54.
[3] Liv. IV. 44. 54. Cic. in Verr. Act. I. 10.
[4] Cic. ad Q. F. I. 1. ad Att. VII. 6. Div. in Q. C. 14. in Verr. I. 13. in Catil. IV. 7. Liv. XXX. 33.
[5] Cic. pro Muren. 8. pro Sest. 17. in Vatin. 5. Dion Cass. LV. 4. Tacit. Ann. IV. 27 Suet. Claud. 24. Plut. Sert. 4.
[6] Cic. div. in Q. C. 19. and again in Cap. 14, when anticipating the arguments that would be employed against Caecilius by the advocate of Verres—*Quid? quum commiserari, conqueri, et ex illius invidia deonerare aliquid, et in te tracere coeperit? commemorare Quaestoris cum Praetore necessitudinem constitutam? Morem maiorum? Sortis religionem? Poterisne eius orationis subire invidiam?*

QUAESTORES.   163

taxes, whether direct or indirect, were paid into their hands, and all monies belonging to the state, from whatever source derived, were received by them.[1] By them, also, all disbursements on account of the public service, whether for public works, for the pay of troops, or for any other object, were made. In this they acted only ministerially, since they could make no payment whatsoever without the direct and express authority of the Senate, who held the entire control over the finances of the state.[2]

The military standards also were deposited in the *Aerarium*, and when an army marched forth from the city, they were taken out by the Quaestors and delivered to the general—*Signa a Quaestoribus ex aerario prompta delataque in Campum*.[3]

In like manner, in the provinces, all pecuniary transactions of every description, connected with the public money, were conducted through the Quaestors, who accounted to the Senate directly, or through the medium of the *Quaestores Urbani*.

The *Aerarium*, as we have already stated, (p. 28,) was in the temple of Saturn, on the *Clivus Capitolinus*, and immediately connected with it was the *Tabularium*, or Record-office, where state papers of every description were deposited; and these, towards the close of the republic, were in the custody of the Quaestors, having at an earlier period been kept in the temple of Ceres, under the care of the Aediles.[4] Officials, both civil and military, on resigning their charge, deposited in the *Aerarium* the documents connected with their offices, and took an oath as to their accuracy before the Quaestors.[5]

Dignity of the Quaestors.—The Quaestorship was the lowest of the great offices of state, and was regarded as the first step (*primus gradus honoris*) in the upward progress towards the Consulship. Such, at least, was the light in which it was viewed in later times, but in the earlier ages we hear of individuals who had held the office of Consul serving afterwards as Quaestors.[6]

While in office, the Quaestors had the right of taking part in the deliberations of the Senate, and had a claim to be chosen permanent members of that body, after those who had held higher offices had obtained seats.[7]

They do not appear to have enjoyed any outward mark of distinction, neither the *Sella Curulis* nor the *Toga Praetexta*, and not being invested with any summary jurisdiction, were not attended by either *Lictores* or *Viatores*.[8]

Quaestorship under the Empire.—The number of Quaestors was increased by Julius Caesar to forty. We have no specific statement with regard to any diminution in this number; but it has been inferred from the words of Tacitus, who notices the augmentation of Sulla only, that they must have been speedily reduced to twenty.[9] A vital change took place in the duties of the office soon after the downfal of the commonwealth; for the charge of the public exchequer (*Aerarium*) was committed by Augustus, in the first instance, to commissioners selected from persons who had held the office of Praetor the previous year, and

---

[1] Liv. IV. 15. V. 26. XXVI. 47. XXXIII. 42. XXXVIII. 60. XLII. 6. Dionys. V. 34. VII. 63. VIII. 82. X. 26.
[2] Liv. XXIV. 18. XLIV. 16. XLV. 44. Cic. Philipp. IX. 7. XIV. 14. Val. Max. V. 1. 1. Polyb. VI. 13.
[3] Liv. III. 69. IV. 22. VII. 23.
[4] Polyb. III. 26. Liv. XXXIX. 4. Tacit. Ann. III. 51. Suet. Octav. 94.
[5] Liv. XXIX. 37. Val. Max. II. viii. 1. Appian. B. C. I. 31.
[6] Liv. III. 25. Dionys. X. 23.
[7] Auct. ad Herenn. I. 12. Plut. Cat. min. 18. Liv. XXIII. 23. Val. Max. II. ii. 1.
[8] Varr. ap Aul. Gell. XIII. 12.
[9] Dion Cass. XLIII. 47. Tacit. Ann. XI. 22.

subsequently to two of the annual Praetors. This arrangement was overthrown by Claudius, who again made over the *Aerarium* to two Quaestors, with this alteration, that these individuals were to retain office for three years instead of one. By Nero *Praetorii* were again employed; *Praetores* by Vespasian, and no further change took place until the reign of Trajan. When the commissioners employed were Praetors, they were termed *Praetores Aerarii*, when chosen from *Praetorii* they were called *Praefecti Aerarii*. From the time of Trajan we hear of *Praefecti Aerarii* only, but we are not told from what class they were taken.[1]

Another change commenced under the Triumvirs, by whom two Quaestors were assigned to each Consul. Hence, so long as two of the Quaestors continued to preside over the treasury, six Quaestors remained each year in the city; and the titles *Quaestores Urbani* and *Quaestores Consulis* are used as synonymous. The *Quaestores Consulis*, as well as the other Quaestors, remained in office for a whole year, and consequently served under a succession of Consuls. The governors of those provinces which were under the administration of the Senate were, as in ancient times, each attended by a Quaestor.[2] But in addition to the ordinary *Quaestores Consulis* and the *Quaestores Provinciarum*, a Quaestor was always assigned specially to the Emperor, and styled *Quaestor Principis* or *Quaestor Candidatus Principis* or simply *Candidatus Principis*. This individual was nominated by the Emperor, and it was his duty to communicate to the Senate the imperial Rescripts, which were, for the most part, drawn up by himself. It is almost unnecessary to observe that he was regarded as much superior in dignity and influence to his colleagues, occupying, in many respects, the position of a principal Secretary of State, but holding office for one year only. When the Emperor was Consul he had two Quaestors in virtue of his office, who were called *Quaestores Caesaris*; but we know not whether in this case there was a *Quaestor Principis* in addition.[3] By an ordinance of Alexander Severus the *Quaestores Principis*, were immediately promoted to the Praetorship, and upon them was imposed the exhibition of certain public games, hence termed *Quaestorii Ludi*— *Quaestores Candidatos ex sua pecunia iussit munera populi dare, sed ut post Quaesturam Praeturas acciperent et inde Provincias regerent* (Lamprid. Alex. Sev. 43.)

CENSORES.

Origin of the office.—As soon as the constitution of Servius Tullius was established, it became necessary that the whole body of the Roman citizens should be registered at regular periods, and that the age of the individual members of the state, together with the value of their property, should be correctly ascertained, in order that the amount of tax (*tributum*) for which each was liable, might be determined, and that each might be assigned to his proper Class and Century, so as to secure order and accuracy in the arrangements of the *Comitia Centuriata*. The business connected with this Registration, and the solemn rites by which it was accompanied, were originally performed by the Kings, and after the revolution by the Consuls, until the increase of public business, and a desire upon the part of the Patricians to prevent duties, which they regarded as peculiarly sacred, from being discharged by Plebeians, led to the institution of a new magistracy termed *Censura*, the magistrates who held the office being called CENSORES, i.e. *Registrars*. This took place in B.C. 443, the law for

---

[1] Tacit. Ann. I. 75. XIII. 28. 29. Hist. IV. 9. Suet. Octav. 36. Claud. 24. Plin. Panegyr. 91. Epp. X. 20. Dion Cass. LIII. 2. 32. LX. 4. 10. 24.
[2] Dion Cass. XLVIII. 43. Plin. Epp. VIII. 23.
[3] Ulpian. Digest. I. xiii. Plin. Epp. VII. 16. Tacit. Ann. XVI. 27. Suet. Tit. 6.

the election of *Tribuni Militares consulari potestate* having been passed in B.C. 445.[1]

Number. Mode of Election. Qualification, &c.—The Censors were always two in number, and were originally chosen from the Patricians exclusively. In B.C. 351, we find for the first time a Plebeian Censor, C. Marcius Rutilus. In B.C. 339, a *Lex Publilia* was passed by Q. Publilius Philo when Dictator, enacting that at least one of the Censors must be a Plebeian. In B.C. 280, the solemn sacrifice of the *Lustrum*, with which each Registration was closed, was performed for the first time by a Plebeian Censor, Cn. Domitius, and in B.C. 131, we have the first example of two Plebeian Censors.[2]

The Censors were chosen by the Comitia Centuriata. The assembly for their election (*Comitia Censoria—Comitia Censoribus creandis,*) was held by the Consuls soon after they entered upon office, and the Censors appear to have commenced their duties immediately after their election, and, therefore, upon no fixed day.[3]

As a general rule, no one seems to have been considered eligible who had not previously held the office of Consul; but we have no reason to suppose that there was any law enforcing such a restriction, although when an exception occurs, it is mentioned as something extraordinary.[4]

Peculiarities connected with the office.—The Censorship was characterized by several peculiarities which distinguished it from all the other great offices of state.

1. While all the other magistrates of the republic remained in office for one year only, (*annui,*) the Censors originally retained their office for five, that being the stated period (*lustrum*) which elapsed between each Registration. But in B.C. 434, nine years after the institution of the Censorship, a feeling having arisen that freedom might be endangered if the same individuals were suffered to exercise power for such a lengthened period, the *Lex Aemilia* was passed by Mam. Aemilius, at that time Dictator, enacting that the Censors should hold office for one year and-a-half only; (*ne plus quam annua semestris Censura esset;*) and, accordingly, from that time forward, all Censors, with one exception, resigned at the close of the above-named period. It would seem, however, that they could not be forcibly ejected, for Appius Claudius Caecus, (B.C. 312,) on the pretext that the *Lex Aemilia* applied to those Censors only during whose magistracy it had been passed, persisted in retaining office after the eighteen months had expired, although his colleague had retired, and although all classes united in reprobating his conduct—*Summa invidia omnium ordinum solus Censuram gessit.*[5]

2. In B.C. 393, it happened, for the first time, that one of the Censors, C. Iulius, died while in office, and his place, according to the system followed with regard to the Consulship, was filled up by the appointment of P. Cornelius Maluginensis. Three years afterwards, (B.C. 390,) before the period for the election of new Censors had arrived, Rome was captured by the Gauls. Hence a superstitious feeling arose, and it became an established rule that, if a Censor died while in office, his place was not to be filled up, but that his colleague must resign, and two new Censors be elected. It happened upon one occasion that this second set of Censors were found to be disqualified, which was regarded as an

---

[1] Liv. III. 3. IV. 8. 28. Dionys. VI. 96.
[2] Cic. de legg. III. 3. Liv. VII. 22. X. 8. VIII. 12 Epit. XIII. Epit. LIX.
[3] Liv. XXIV. 10. XXVII. 11. XXXIV. 44. XXXIX. 41. XLI. 27. XLIII. 14.
[4] Liv. XXVII. 6. 11. comp. Fast. Capitolin. s.a. 500.
[5] Liv. IV. 24. IX. 34.

indication that the Gods desired the office to be suspended for that *Lustrum*, and no third election took place.[1]

3. C. Marcius Rutilus having been elected Censor for a second time in B.C. 265, an honour, apparently, never before conferred upon any individual, he publicly declared his disapprobation of the procedure, and passed a law by which it was forbidden that any one should hold the office twice. From this transaction, the epithet of *Censorinus* was borne, as a second cognomen, by one of the branches of the *Gens Marcia*.[2]

4. It was necessary that both Censors should be elected on the same day. If one only of the candidates obtained the necessary number of votes he was not returned, but the proceedings were renewed upon a subsequent day—*Comitiis Censoriis, nisi duo confecerint legitima suffragia, non renuntiato altero, comitia differantur.*[3] See above, p. 110.

Insignia of the Censors.—The Censors had the *Sella Curulis*, and we gather from Polybius that their state dress was not the *Toga Praetexta* but a *Toga Purpurea*, that is, a cloak not merely bordered or fringed with purple, but all purple. They had no lictors.[4]

Dignity of the Censors.—The nature and extreme importance of the duties performed by the Censors, as described below, taken in connection with the circumstance that the office was almost invariably filled by Consulars, placed these magistrates in a pre-eminent position. Although far inferior in actual power to a Dictator, to a Consul, or even to a Praetor, the Censor was invested with a certain sacred character which always inspired the deepest respect and reverence. To be chosen to fill this post was regarded as the crowning honour of a long life of political distinction—Κορυφὴ δέ τίς ἐστι τιμῆς ἁπάσης ἡ ἀρχὴ καὶ τρόπον τινὰ τῆς πολιτείας ἐπιτελείωσις.[5]

Duties of the Censors.—The duties of the Censors, which at first were easy and simple, became, in process of time, highly complicated and multifarious; but they were all closely connected with each other, being, in fact, merely developments and extensions of their original functions. They may be conveniently classed under three heads:—[6]

1. The Registration (*Census.*)
2. The superintendence of public morals (*Regimen morum.*)
3. Arrangements for the collection of the public Revenue and the execution of public works.

These we shall consider separately.

I. The *Census* or *Registration*.—The fundamental and, originally, the sole duty of the Censors was to draw up a complete catalogue of the citizens of Rome, stating in detail the age of each, the amount of his property, including slaves, and the number of his children—*Censores populi aevitates soboles familias pecuniasque censento*. This registration was technically termed *Census*,[7] and the Censors, in performing the duty, were said *censum censere* s. *agere* s. *habere* s. *facere*. When they made an entry in their books (*Tabulae Censoriae*)

---

[1] Liv. V. 31. VI. 27. IX. 34. XXIV. 43. XXVII. 6. comp. Plut. Q. R. 50. Fast. Capitolin. passim.
[2] Val. Max IV. i. 3. Plut. Cor. 1.
[3] Liv. IX. 34.
[4] Liv. XL. 45. Polyb. VI. 53. but comp. Athenaeus XIV. 79. Zonar. VII. 19.
[5] Plut. Cat Mai. 16. Flaminin. 18. Zonar. VII. 19. Suid. p. 3569, ed. Gaisf.
[6] Liv. IV. 8. Cic. de legg. III. 3. Zonar. VII. 19. Ulpian. Digest. L. xv. 3. 4.
[7] Hence the word *Census* frequently signifies *fortune* or *property*, as in the phrases *In pretio pretium nunc est, dat* Census *honores*—Census *amicitias; Privatus illis* Census *erat brevis; Homo tenui* Censu; Census *Senatorius*, i.e. the money qualification for a Senator; Census *Equester*, &c.

under the proper head, they were said *Censere*¹ s. *Censeri*² s. *Censum accipere.*³ The different objects to be taken into account in estimating a man's fortune, were defined by a law entitled *Lex censui censendo;* and hence lands which belonged in full property to Roman citizens, and which it was necessary to enter in the Censors' books, were termed by lawyers *Agri censui censendo.*⁴ When the citizens assembled for the purpose of being registered they were said to meet *ut censerentur* s. *censendi causa.*⁵ The schedule filled up in reference to each individual was the *Formula censendi,* and this was regulated according to the discretion (*Censio*) of the Censor.⁶ A person when regularly registered was said *censeri,*⁷ and called *census,* while a person not registered was styled *incensus,* and heavy penalties were inflicted upon those who wilfully evaded registration (see p. 83, under *Deminutio Capitis maxima.*) No one had a right to be registered (*ius censendi*) except he was his own master, (*sui iuris,*) and thus sons, while under the control of their father, (*in patria potestate,*) were not registered independently, but were included in the same entry with the person to whose authority they were subject (*cuius in potestate fuere.*)⁸ Unmarried women (*viduae*) not under the control of parents, together with orphans, (*orbi orbaeque—pupilli,*) were ranked together and arranged in a compartment by themselves, their rights being guarded by *Tutores.*

When the Registration was completed the Censors proceeded to revise the lists of the Tribes, Classes and Centuries, and to make such alterations as the change of circumstances, since the former Registration, demanded. They next drew up a catalogue of the Equites who were entitled to serve *equo publico,* (see p. 72,) and finally proceeded to make up the roll of Senators, (*Album Senatorium,*) supplying the vacancies which had been occasioned by death or other causes. In performing this task they were said *legere Senatum,* and the principles by which they were guided will be explained in the chapter where we treat of the Senate itself.

*Place and Manner of Registration.*⁹—The Census was taken in the Campus Martius, in a spot consecrated by the Augurs, (*Templum Censurae,*) much of the business being transacted in the *Villa Publica* (see above, p. 46.) The night before the day fixed for taking the Census, the Auspices having been observed and pronounced favourable, a public crier (*praeco*) was ordered to summon all the citizens (*omnes Quirites*) to appear before the Censors, and he made proclamation to that effect, first upon the spot, (*in templo,*) and then from the city walls (*de moeris.*) At daybreak the Censors and their clerks (*scribae*)

---

1 e.g. *In qua tribu denique ista praedia* CENSUISTI, i.e. Did you make entry of. Cic. pro Flacc. 32.
2 *Censeri* is used as a deponent verb in such phrases as, CENSUS ES *praeterea numeratae pecuniae sestertiorum triginta millia*—CENSUS ES *mancipiis Amyntae,* i.e. You registered or made an entry of. Cic. l.c.
3 e.g. *In* CENSIBUS *quoque* ACCIPIENDIS *tristis et aspera in omnes ordines censura fuit.* Liv. XXXIX. 44.
4 See Liv. XLIII. 14. Thus Cicero asks (Pro Flacc. 32) *Illud quaero, sintne ista praedia* CENSUI CENSENDO? Comp. Paul. Diac. s.v. *Censui censendo,* p. 58.
5 CENSOR, *ad quoius* CENSIONEM, *id est, arbitrium, censeretur populus.* Varro L.L. V. § 81.
6 e.g. *Haec frequentia totius Italiae . . . . quae convenit ludorum* CENSENDIQUE *causa.* Cic. in Verr. Act. I. 18.
7 Here *Censeri* is a passive verb, with *Census* for its participle, e.g. *Ne absens* CENSEARE, *curabo edicendum,* &c. Cic. ad Att. I. 18.—*Convenerat autem ex municipiis cuiuscunque modi multitudo . . . . ut* CENSERETUR *apud Censores Gellium et Lentulum.* Pseud. Ascon. in Cic. Verr. Act. I. 18—*Lustro a Censoribus condito,* CENSA SUNT *capita civium ducenta septuaginta unum millia ducenta viginti quatuor.* Liv. Epit. XIV.
8 Liv. XLIII. 14. Paul. Diac. s.v. *Duicensus,* p. 66.
9 On the matter contained in this section consult the curious extracts from the *Tabulae Censoriae,* (a general name for all written documents connected with the office,) preserved in Varro L.L. VI. § 86. also the *Tabula Heracleensis;* Dionys. IV. 15. and Aul. Gell. IV.

were anointed with perfumed oil (*murrha unguentisque unguentur*.) Upon the arrival of the Praetors, the Tribunes of the Plebs, and others invited to act as assessors, (*in consilium vocati*,) the Censors cast lots which of them should offer the great purificatory sacrifice, with which the whole proceedings closed (*Censores inter se sortiuntur uter Lustrum faciat*.) The meeting was then constituted by the Censor on whom the lot had fallen, and he must have been looked upon as the president. These preliminaries concluded, the Tribes were called in succession, the order in which they were to be summoned having been probably decided by lot. Each Paterfamilias, who was *sui iuris*, was called up individually, and required to declare his name, the name of his father, or, if a freedman, of his patron, his age, and the place of his abode. He was then asked whether he was married or single, and if married, the number of his children and their ages (*Equitum peditumque prolem Censores describunto*.) Finally he was obliged to state what property he possessed, and an estimate was formed of its total amount, the Censor being assisted in this matter by sworn valuators, who seem to have been called *Iuratores*.[1] The whole of these particulars were taken down by the *Scribae* and entered in the registers, (*Tabulae Censoriae*,) which were deposited in the *Atrium Libertatis*[2] (see above, p. 33.) It is evident that, as the population increased, the operations described above must have become very tedious, and have occupied a long space of time.

II. *Morum Regimen*.—But the Censors were required to perform, not only the mere mechanical duties of the *Census*, but, in process of time, were fully recognised as the inspectors of public morals (*mores populi regunto*) and the organs of public opinion. In this capacity they were empowered to brand with disgrace (*ignominia*) those who had been guilty of acts which, although not forbidden by any penal statute, were pronounced by the voice of society to be disgraceful in a Roman, or of such as were calculated to prove injurious to the wellbeing of the state and the interests of the community at large. Hence, not only gross breaches of morality in public and private life, cowardice, sordid occupations, or notorious irregularities, fell under their corrective discipline, but they were in the habit of denouncing those who indulged in extravagant or luxurious habits, or who, by the careless cultivation of their estates, or by wilfully persisting in celibacy, omitted to discharge obligations held to be binding on every citizen. It was the exercise of this discretionary power which invested the Censor with so much dignity; for the people, when they elected any individual to fill this office, by so doing, pronounced him qualified to sit in judgment on the character and conduct of the whole body of his fellow citizens.

An expression of disapprobation on the part of a Censor was termed *Notio s. Notatio s. Animadversio Censoria*, and the disgrace inflicted by it *Nota Censoria*; for when attached to the name in the register, it was regarded as a brand of dishonour stamped upon the fame of the culprit—*Qui pretio adductus eripuerit patriam, fortunas, liberos civi innocenti, is* CENSORIAE SEVERITATIS NOTA NON INURETUR?[3] No previous judicial investigation nor examination of witnesses was held necessary; but in affixing the mark they assigned the reason, (*Subscriptio Censoria*,) and occasionally, when any doubt existed in their minds, they allowed those whose character was impeached an opportunity of

---

[1] Plaut. Poen. Prol. 55. Trin. IV. ii. 30. Liv. XXXIX. 44. These passages, however, can scarcely be regarded as decisive.
[2] Liv. XLIII. 16.
[3] Cic. pro Cluent. 46.

CENSORES. 169

defending themselves. The only effect of the *Animadversio Censoria*, in itself, was to affix a stigma (*ignominia*) on the individual—CENSORIS *iudicium nil fere damnato nisi ruborem affert. Itaque ut omnis ea iudicatio versatur tantummodo in nomine, animadversio illa* IGNOMINIA *dicta est;*[2] but, in addition to the mere disgrace thus inflicted, the Censors could, to a certain extent, deprive the object of their displeasure of substantial honours and political privileges. If he were a Senator they could omit his name from the *Album Senatorium*, whence such persons were termed *Praeteriti Senatores*, and thus expel him the body; (*movere senatorem senatu;*) if he were an *Eques equo publico*, they might deprive him of his horse; (*equum equiti adimere;*) and any ordinary citizen might be transferred from a *Tribus Rustica* to one of the *Tribus Urbanae*, or his name might be left out of the list of registered voters altogether and placed among the *Aerarii* (see above, p. 82.) It must be remarked, however, that neither the dishonour nor the degradation were necessarily permanent. The Censors next elected could reverse the sentence of their predecessors, and reinstate those whom they had disgraced (*notaverant*) in all their former dignities, so that we find examples of persons, who had been *marked* by Censors, rising afterwards to the highest offices of the state and even becoming Censors themselves.[3] It is to be observed further, that the *Nota* of one Censor had no force unless his colleague concurred, and accordingly persons were sometimes removed from the Senate by one Censor and then replaced by the other; and upon one occasion Rome witnessed the unseemly spectacle of two Censors who mutually marked and degraded each other.[4] But when the duties of the office were discharged harmoniously (*concors Censura*) there was no appeal from their decision to any other court. On one occasion, indeed, when Appius Claudius (Censor B.C. 312) had displayed notorious partiality in choosing the Senate, the Consuls of the following year refused to recognise the new list, and summoned the Senate according to the previous roll—*Consules . . . questi apud populum deformatum ordinem prava lectione Senatus, qua potiores aliquot lectis praeteriti essent: negaverunt, eam lectionem se, quae sine recti pravique discrimine ad gratiam ac libidinem facta esset, observaturos: et Senatum extemplo citaverunt eo ordine, qui ante Censores Appium Claudium et C. Plautium fuerat.*

Notwithstanding the assertion of Zonaras, (VII. 19,) it seems certain that the Censors had not the right of proposing laws in the *Comitia Centuriata*. No doubt we find mention made of *Leges Censoriae*, but although this expression has a twofold meaning, in no case does it denote laws in the ordinary sense.

1. *Leges Censoriae* were the ordinances and rules laid down by successive Censors with regard to the forms to be observed in performing their duties, and these at length formed a sort of code, which Censors were held bound to respect.[5]

2. *Leges Censoriae* is a phrase used also to denote the conditions and stipulations contained in the contracts entered into by the Censors on behalf of the public.[6]

III. *Arrangements for the Collection of the Revenue.*—One of the earliest taxes imposed upon the Romans was the *Tributum*, which, being a property-tax, the amount paid by each individual depended upon the value assigned to his

---
1 Liv. XXIV. 18.
2 Cic. de R. ap. Non. Marcell. s.v. *Ignominia* p. 15. ed. Gerl.
3 Liv. IV. 31. Cic. pro Cluent. 42. Pseud Ascon. ad Cic. Div. in Q. C. 3. Val. Max. II. ix. 9.
4 Cic. pro Cluent. 43. Liv. XL. 51. XLII. 10. XLV. 15. comp. XXIX. 37.
5 Plin. H.N. VIII. 51. 57. XXXVI. 1.
6 Cic. in Verr. I. 55. de N. D. III. 19.

property. This value being fixed by the Censors, the task of making arrangements for the collection of the tax naturally devolved upon them; and as the income of the state gradually increased, although by far the largest portion of it was derived from sources in no way connected with their jurisdiction, they were still intrusted with the extended charge. We shall reserve all details upon this subject for the chapter in which we treat of the Roman Revenue; but we may here state generally, that few of the imposts were collected directly, but were farmed out upon lease to contractors, who paid a fixed sum annually. The business of the Censors was to frame these leases or contracts, which were for a period of five years, and to let them out to the highest bidder. It must be understood, however, that the Censors had no concern whatsoever with the actual payments into the treasury, which were made by the contractors to the Quaestors, nor with the expenditure of the public money, which was regulated by the Senate, and, therefore, in no sense could they be said to administer the finances of the state.

IV. *Superintendence of Public Works.*—When the Senate had resolved to execute any public works, such as highways, bridges, aqueducts, harbours, court-houses, temples, and the like, the Censors were employed to make the necessary contracts and superintend the progress of the undertakings, and hence the most important of these were frequently distinguished by the name of the Censor to whom the task had been assigned. Thus we have the *Via Appia*, the *Via Flaminia*, the *Aqua Appia*, the *Basilica Aemilia*, and a multitude of other examples.

Not only did the Censors take measures for the execution of new works, but they also made the necessary arrangements for keeping those already in existence in good repair, and in doing this they were said, in so far as buildings were concerned, *sarta tecta exigere*, i.e. to insist upon their being wind and watertight.

Finally, they provided various objects required for the state religion, such as the victims offered up at public sacrifices, horses for the games of the Circus, food for the Capitoline geese, and red paint for the statue of Capitoline Jove.

Every thing was done by contract; and we may take this opportunity of explaining the technical terms employed with reference to such transactions.

The person for whom any work was to be performed by contract was said LOCARE *opus faciendum;* the person who undertook to perform the work for a stipulated payment was said CONDUCERE s. REDIMERE *opus faciendum*, and was called REDEMTOR. If, after the work was finished and inspected, the person for whom it had been executed was satisfied, he was said *opus probare*, and formally took it off the contractor's hands—*in acceptum retulit;* but, on the other hand, if the work had not been executed in terms of the agreement, then— *negavit opus in acceptum referre posse.*

The sums expended upon the objects indicated above were comprehended under the general term *Ultrotributa*, and hence the Censors, in letting contracts for the performance of such works, or furnishing such supplies, were said *Locare Ultrotributa.*

Lustrum. Condere Lustrum.—After the Censors had concluded the various duties committed to their charge, they proceeded in the last place to offer up, on behalf of the whole Roman people, the great expiatory sacrifice called *Lustrum*, and this being offered up once only in the space of five years, the term *Lustrum* is frequently employed to denote that space of time. The Censor to whose lot it fell to perform this rite was said *Lustrum facere* s. *Condere Lustrum*. On the day fixed, the whole body of the people were summoned to assemble in the

Campus Martius in martial order, (*exercitus*,) ranked according to their Classes and Centuries, horse and foot. The victims, consisting of a sow, a sheep, and a bull, whence the sacrifice was termed *Suovetaurilia*, before being led to the altar, were carried thrice round the multitude, who were then held to be purified and absolved from sin, and while the immolation took place the Censor recited a set form of prayer for the preservation and aggrandizement of the Roman state.

Downfal and Gradual Extinction of the Censorship.—The Censorship was instituted, as we have seen above, in B.C. 443, and continued in force, with a few occasional interruptions, for about four hundred years. It was first directly attacked by the *Lex Clodia*, B.C. 58, which ordained that no one should be expelled from the Senate unless he had been formally impeached, found guilty, and the sentence confirmed by both Censors. This law was, indeed, repealed six years afterwards, but the circumstances of the times were such as to render the office powerless, and during the civil wars it was altogether dropped. An attempt to revive it was made by Augustus, who having held the office in B.C. 28 along with Agrippa, caused L. Munatius Plancus and Paullus Aemilius Lepidus to be nominated Censors in B.C. 22, but with them the office may be regarded as having expired.

The Emperors, under the title of *Praefecti Morum*, undertook the regulation of public morals and the selection of Senators, while the other duties of the magistracy were assigned to various functionaries. Claudius, in A.D. 48, took the title of Censor, assuming as his colleague L. Vitellius, the father of the Emperor Vitellius, and the same course was followed by Vespasian, who, in A.D. 74, assumed his son Titus as his colleague, while Domitian styled himself *Censor Perpetuus*. We find *Censor* among the titles of Nerva, but it does not appear again until the reign of Decius, when Valerian was named Censor without a colleague.

PRAEFECTUS URBI.[1]

We have already had occasion to mention (p. 130,) that when the king was compelled to quit the city he committed his power to a deputy styled *Praefectus Urbi*, or, originally, perhaps, *Custos Urbis*, whose office was probably permanent, although no duties were attached to it except in the absence of the monarch. During the earlier ages of the republic, when both Consuls were required for military service, a *Praefectus Urbi* was named by the Senate to act during their absence. He was, it would seem, invariably a person who had held the office of Consul, (*consularis*,) and he enjoyed during the period of his office the same powers and privileges within the walls as the Consuls themselves. During the sway of the *Tribuni Militares*, C. P., that individual of the body who remained in the city seems to have been designated as *Praefectus Urbi*. After the establishment of the Praetorship the duties which, in the absence of the Consuls, would have devolved on a *Praefectus Urbi* were discharged by the *Praetor Urbanus*, and the office fell, for all practical purposes, into disuse, until revived in a permanent form under the Empire.[2] But although the magistracy fell into disuse for all practical purposes, it was nominally retained during the whole of the republic, for a *Praefectus Urbi* was nominated annually to hold office during the celebration of the *Feriae Latinae*. This festival was solemnized on the *Mons Albanus*, and from the period of its institution was attended by all the higher magistrates and the whole body of the Senate. Hence, in the

[1] The forms *Praefectus* URBIS and *Praefectus* URBI are both found in the best writers.
[2] Liv. I. 59. 60. III. 3. 5. 9. 24. 29. IV. 36. comp. IV. 31. 45. 59. VI. 30. Dionys. V. 75. VI. 13. VIII. 64. X. 23. 24. Tacit. Ann. VI. 11.

earlier ages, the appointment of a *Praefectus Urbi*, who might take measures for protecting the city from any sudden attack on the part of the numerous enemies by which it was surrounded, was absolutely necessary; but after all danger from without had passed away, the practice was retained in consequence of its connection with religious observances; and under the Empire, when the *Praefectus Urbi* had become one of the ordinary magistrates, another *Praefectus* appears to have been nominated for the period of the festival, who was usually some youth of distinction.[1]

GENERAL REMARKS ON THE HIGHER MAGISTRATES.

We shall now proceed to consider some matters connected with all, or with the greater number of, the higher magistrates of the republic, but to which we could not advert fully until we had discussed each office separately.

The Kings and the Magistrates of the Republic.—The essential distinction between the regal and the republican governments, as they existed among the Romans, was, that under the former the whole executive power, civil, military, and religious, was vested and concentrated in the person of one individual, who held office for life and was irresponsible, while under the latter, the performance of the most important public duties was committed, in the first instance, to two, and gradually to a much larger number of persons, included under the general designation *Magistratus*, who, with the single and not important exception of the Censors, retained their authority for one year only, (*annui magistratus*,) received their appointments directly from the people, (*per suffragia populi*,) and were responsible to them for the manner in which they executed the tasks intrusted to them. (Polyb. VI. 15.) The term *Magistratus*, let it be observed, denotes alike an office and an official, a *magistracy* or a *magistrate*.

The Kings disposed of a certain amount of revenue from lands belonging to the state; the Magistrates of the republic received no salary for their services, but the different appointments being regarded as marks of confidence bestowed by the sovereign people were always eagerly sought after, and held to be the most honourable of all distinctions. Hence *Honorem gerere* and *Magistratum gerere* are convertible terms, and all the offices of state were comprehended in the single word *Honores*. It is true that, towards the close of the republic, the government of the Provinces, which fell to those who had held the chief magistracies, was conducted in such a manner as, in many cases, to procure vast wealth for the governors, but the means resorted to in order to gain this end were, for the most part, altogether illegal, and forbidden by a series of the most stringent enactments. This abuse, which affords one of the most glaring proofs of the degeneracy of moral feeling among men in exalted station during the decline of the commonwealth, was in many cases produced by the pecuniary embarrassments of provincial governors, who were tempted to reimburse themselves for the enormous sums which they had expended, when Aediles, on public shows and games, (see above, p. 159,) and in direct bribery previous to their elections.

Election of Magistrates.—All the ordinary magistrates, without exception, were elected by the votes of the people in their Comitia. The *Consules*, *Praetores* and *Censores* were elected in the *Comitia Centuriata*, as were also the

---

[1] Tacit. Ann. IV. 36. Suet. Ner. 7. Claud. 4. Capitolin. M. Aur. 4. Aul. Gell. XIV. 8. See also Dion Cass. XLI. 14. XLIII. 29. XLIX. 16. 42. LIII. 33. LIV. 17. Some particulars with regard to the *Praefectus Urbis* will be found in Lydus, (De Mens. 19. De Magistr. I. 34. 38. II. 6,) but no confidence can be reposed in his statements unless corroborated by **other authorities**.

GENERAL REMARKS ON THE HIGHER MAGISTRATES.

Decemviri legibus scribendis and the *Tribuni militum consulari potestate*, all others, during the last two centuries at least, by the *Comitia Tributa*.

Qualification as to Birth.—We have already stated that no one could be chosen Tribune of the Plebs or Plebeian Aedile except he was actually a member of a Plebeian family, either by birth or by adoption. We have also pointed out that all the other great offices were originally filled by Patricians exclusively, but that the Plebeians succeeded gradually in breaking down every barrier until they were admitted to a full participation in all political privileges, with this positive advantage, that while only one place in the consulship and the censorship could be filled by a Patrician, both might be filled by Plebeians. After this state of matters was established, any Roman citizen was eligible to any public office, provided he was free-born (*ingenuus*) and the son of free-born parents, so that *Libertini* and the sons of *Libertini* were excluded; but this seems to have been the result of popular feeling rather than of any legislative provision, and we have an exception in the case of Cn. Flavius, who although the son of a *Libertinus*, was Curule Aedile in B.C. 304; (Liv. IX. 46;) but the feeling, under ordinary circumstances, was so strong that in the early ages of the commonwealth it was deemed necessary that the paternal ancestors of a candidate should have been free for two generations at least (*patre avoque paterno ingenuus*.)[1]

Qualification as to Age.—For more than three centuries after the expulsion of the kings, there was no law defining the age at which a citizen might become a candidate for one of the higher magistracies.[2] Men of mature years and extensive experience would, as a matter of course, generally be preferred; but although we find the Tribunes of the Plebs objecting to Scipio, on account of his youth, when he stood for the Aedileship—*negantes rationem eius habendam esse, quod nondum ad petendum legitima aetas esset*[3]—their opposition proved unavailing, and it is clear that there was no positive enactment on the subject. The words of Tacitus (Ann. XI. 22) are perfectly explicit—*Ac ne aetas quidem distinguebatur, quin prima iuventa Consulatum ac Dictaturam inirent;* and accordingly we find that M. Valerius Corvus was consul at the age of twenty-three; that the elder Scipio received an important command when twenty-four years old, and was consul at thirty.[4] But in B.C. 180, L. Villius, a Tribune of the Plebs, passed a law, known as *Lex Villia Annalis*, which determined, in reference to each of the higher magistracies, the age at which a citizen was to be held eligible—*quot annos nati quemque magistratum peterent caperentque.* We are nowhere told expressly what the several ages were, but the case of Cicero is usually regarded as supplying the requisite information; for he declares that he had been chosen to each office *suo anno*, which is understood to mean, as soon as he was legally eligible.[5] Now Cicero, when Quaestor, was thirty-one years old, when Curule Aedile thirty-seven, when Praetor forty, when Consul forty-three. It is to be understood that the demands of the law were held to be satisfied if the individual was in his thirty-first, thirty-seventh, fortieth and forty-third years, although he had not completed them,[6] and this was, in fact, the case with Cicero, for his birth-day was the third of January, and he entered on the above offices two days before he had completed his thirty-first, thirty-seventh,

---
[1] Such is the inference we draw from Plin. XXXIII. 2. Liv. VI. 40. Suet. Claud. 24.
[2] Cic. Philipp. V. 17. Tacit. Ann. XI. 22.
[3] Liv. XXV. 2. comp. Polyb. X. 4.
Liv. VII. 26. XXVI. 18. XXVIII. 43. Val. Max. VIII. xv. 5.
[5] Cic. de Off. II. 17. de. leg agr. II. 2. Philipp. V. 17. Brut. 94.
[6] This principle seems to have held good generally in Roman law See Ulpian. Digest. L. iv. 8.

fortieth and forty-third years respectively. It is manifest also from the passages referred to, at the bottom of the page,[1] that, in the time of Cicero, at whatever age a citizen was chosen Aedile, it was necessary that two clear years should intervene between the Aedileship and the Praetorship, and the same space between the Praetorship and the Consulship. A difficulty arises, however, with regard to the Quaestorship. Polybius, who flourished half a century after the passing of the Lex Villia, tells us (VI. 19) that no one could hold any political office until he had completed ten years at least of military service. But since the regular age for entering the army was seventeen, we should conclude that the Quaestorship might be held at the age of twenty-seven, and this is confirmed by the fact, that both Tiberius and Caius Gracchus were exactly that age when they held the office.[2] On the other hand, we have seen that Cicero completed his thirty-first year two days after he entered on the Quaestorship. But it does not necessarily follow that his assertion, that he held each of the *honores* as soon as he was eligible—*suo anno*—is erroneous. For,—

1. In the first place, he probably refers to the Curule magistracies alone, the Aedileship, the Praetorship and the Consulship; indeed, we know that the Quaestorship was not, strictly speaking, accounted a *Magistratus* at all. This is evident from a well known passage in the speech of Cicero on behalf of the Manilian Rogation, (cap. 21,) where he says that Pompeius, in virtue of a special dispensation from the Senate—*ex Senatus consulto legibus solutus*—was elected Consul—*antequam ullum alium magistratum per leges capere potuisset*. But Pompeius was in his thirty-sixth year when he entered on his first Consulship, (B.C. 70,) and therefore, under any supposition, must have been eligible for the Quaestorship, but not for the Aedileship, which is here evidently regarded as the lowest office to which the term *Magistratus* applied.

2. Secondly, it is highly probable that some change may have taken place after the time of Polybius, by which the *Aetas Quaestoria* was advanced to thirty-one. At all events, circumstances were now completely changed with regard to the term of military service, which seems to have been almost entirely dispensed with. Cicero, for example, served only one campaign altogether.

We cannot tell whether any particular age was required by law in a candidate for the Tribunate of the Plebs, this office standing apart, and, as it were, independent of all others.

Succession of Magistracies.—(*Certus ordo magistratuum*.)—In the earlier ages of the republic it was not held essential that the different magistracies should be held according to any fixed rule of succession, although naturally the usual course would be to ascend gradually from the Quaestorship, through the Aedileship and Praetorship, until the highest point, the Consulship, was attained (Liv. XXII. 25.) Accordingly, we find striking violations of this arrangement noticed as remarkable, but not as illegal; and, in like manner, it was not necessary that any stated period should elapse between two offices. Thus, nothing could be more irregular than the career of Appius Claudius Caecus—he was Censor (B.C. 312) before he had been Consul or Praetor; he was Consul in B.C. 307, and again in B.C. 296, and then Praetor in B.C. 295. Tiberius Gracchus was Curule Aedile B.C. 216 and Consul the year following. Q. Fulvius Flaccus, after having been Consul and Censor, was City Praetor in B.C. 215. P. Sulpicius Galba was Consul in B.C. 211, although he had not previously held any

---

[1] Cic. de leg. agr. II. 2. 18 ad fam. X. 25.
[2] Plut. Tib. Gracch. 3. C. Gracch. 1. 2.

Curule office; and numerous examples occur of persons holding the Praetorship the year immediately following their Aedileship.¹

In all probability, however, the Lex Villia, when it defined the age at which the different offices might be held, contained provisions also with regard to a regular succession—*certus ordo magistratuum*. It is certain, as we have seen, that, in the days of Cicero, it was required that two clear years (*biennium*) should elapse between the Aedileship and the Praetorship, and the same space between the Praetorship and the Consulship;² but it does not appear that the Aedileship was necessarily included in the Curriculum. The *Lex Cornelia de Magistratibus* of Sulla prohibited any one from being chosen Praetor who had not previously been Quaestor, and from being Consul who had not been Praetor,³ without making any mention of the Aedileship; and it would appear that the Tribunate of the Plebs was at all times held to be an equivalent.

Restrictions on Re-election.—The duration of all the great offices, with the exception of the Censorship, was limited to the period of one year; but, in the early ages, the same individual might be re-elected to the same office for a succession of years, and this practice was, at one time, very common in the case of Tribunes of the Plebs, who, when strongly opposed in their efforts to carry out any important measure, were re-elected (*reficiebantur*) again and again, in order to give them greater facilities in the prosecution of their object. As early as B.C. 460 the Senate passed a resolution to the effect, that the re-election of the same individuals to a magistracy, making special mention of the Tribunes, was injurious to the interests of the state—*In reliquum magistratus continuari et eosdem Tribunos refici iudicare Senatum contra Rempublicam esse*;⁴ but this expression of opinion appears to have been disregarded until B.C. 342, when Plebiscita were carried, enacting that it should not be lawful for any one to be re-elected to the same office until ten years had elapsed from his first appointment, and that no one should be permitted to hold two magistracies in the same year—*Aliis Plebiscitis cautum, ne quis eumdem magistratum intra decem annos caperet, neu duos magistratus uno anno gereret.*⁵ The latter rule did not apply to an extraordinary magistracy, for Tiberius Gracchus was *Aedilis Curulis* and also *Magister Equitum* in B.C. 216;⁶ but it must be remembered, that during the sway of a Dictator the independent functions of all the ordinary magistrates were virtually suspended.

Not only was it forbidden to re-elect to the same office until after a lapse of ten years, but, at some period before B.C. 134, a law had been passed, enacting that no one should hold the office of Consul twice.⁷ In looking over the *Fasti* it will be seen that no example occurs from B.C. 151 to B.C. 104 of the same individual being twice Consul, except in B.C. 134, when a special exception was made in favour of the younger Scipio. These laws, however, were altogether neglected after the time of Marius until Sulla revived the original regulation with regard to the interval of ten years, a part of which Carbo had proposed to repeal by a bill brought forward in B.C. 131—*Ut eumdem Tribunum Plebis quoties vellet, creare liceret.*⁸ But the laws were unquestionably in force in

---

¹ Liv. IX. 29. 42. X. 15. 22. XXIII. 24. 30. XXV. 41. XXIV. 9. 43. XXXV. 10. 24. XXXIX. 39.
² Cic. de leg. agr. II. 9.
³ Appian. B.C. 100. 101. Cic. Philipp. XI. 5. pro Planc. 21.
⁴ Liv. III. 21.
⁵ Liv. VII. 42. comp. X. 13. XXXIX. 39. Cic. de legg. III. 3.
⁶ Liv. XXIII. 24. 30.
⁷ Liv. Epit. LVI.
⁸ Liv. Epit. LIX. Appian. B.C. I. 100. 101.

B.C. 133; and hence the murder of Tiberius Gracchus was justified upon the plea that he was openly violating the constitution by insisting upon his own re-election to the Tribuneship the year after he had held it.

Relaxation of the above mentioned Laws regarding Qualification.—Although the laws enumerated above with regard to age, the regular succession of offices, and re-election, were enforced under all ordinary circumstances, the people, and even the Senate reserved to themselves the right of granting dispensations, in great emergencies, in favour of particular individuals. Persons exempted in this manner from the regular operation of the laws were said to be *Soluti legibus*, and to hold office *Praemio legis*.[1] Thus the younger Scipio was elected Consul at the age of thirty-eight, before he had held either the Praetorship or the Aedileship, and was elected Consul for a second time at a period when such a practice was altogether forbidden.[2] So also Pompeius was elected Consul at the age of thirty-six, and C. Marius, during the terror of the Cimbric war, was Consul for the second time, B.C. 104, only three years after his first Consulship, (B.C. 107,) and held the office for five years in succession (B.C. 104—100.) So also, at an earlier epoch, in the second year of the second Punic war, the Senate and the *Comitia Tributa* agreed that the law regarding re-election should be suspended in regard to Consulars as long as the enemy remained in Italy.[3]

Formalities Observed in Standing Candidate for an Office.—We hear of no restrictions being placed upon candidates as to the time, place, and manner of declaring their wishes, until the last days of the commonwealth. The practice of the earlier ages, as we find it described in Livy and elsewhere, fully proves that no preliminary forms whatsoever were required. Persons were frequently elected to high offices who had not only refrained from offering themselves, but who were with difficulty persuaded to accept the honour thrust upon them; and if the people were dissatisfied with the actual competitors, they were not prohibited by law or usage from passing them over and selecting individuals who appeared more worthy. The attendance of a candidate on the day of election was certainly not required; for we find many examples of persons being elected when serving with the armies at a distance, and on more than one occasion all the chief magistrates were chosen in their absence (*omnes absentes creati sunt*.) The first proof we meet with of a change in this respect occurs in the case of Catiline, who, at the time when he was seeking the Consulship, was impeached of malversation in the province which he had governed after his Praetorship. The Consul who was to preside at the election, L. Volcatius Tullus, announced that, under these circumstances, he would not allow the name of Catiline to be placed on the list of candidates, and although he was acquitted when brought to trial, it was then too late; for Sallust, in narrating the circumstances, uses the expression—*Catilina pecuniarum repetundarum reus, prohibitus est consulatum petere quod intra legitimos dies profiteri nequiverit*—thus clearly pointing out that at the period in question (B.C. 66) a candidate was required by law to make a formal announcement of his intentions a certain time before the day of election.[4]

A second example is presented by the position of Caesar when he was for the first time candidate for the Consulship, B.C. 60. When the day of election was approaching he was with his army outside the walls, negotiating for a triumph, and this honour he must have abandoned had he entered the city. His enemies

---

[1] Cic. pro leg. Manil. 21. Philipp. XI. 5. Acad. IV. 1. Liv. Epit. LVI.
[2] Cic. de amicit. 3. Liv. Epit. L. LVI. Appian. Pun. 112.
[3] Liv. XXVII 6
[4] Cic. Orat. in tog. cand. frag 11. and note of Ascon. Sallust. Cat. 18.

therefore threw every obstacle in the way of a decision on his claims, in order that he might thus be prevented from declaring himself a candidate in due form, and they positively refused to grant him an exemption from the law. Having in vain endeavoured to bring about an arrangement, he at length determined to sacrifice his prospect of a triumph to what he regarded as the more important object, and accordingly, entering the city, made the requisite announcement. From the words of Cicero in reference to this matter, we learn that the shortest space allowed by law was a *Trinundinum* or seventeen days, so that no candidate could come forward after public notice had been given of the day fixed for the election.[1]

That no such law existed in B.C. 180 is certain, for in that year a case is recorded exactly parallel. Q. Fulvius Flaccus having returned from Spain, was waiting outside the walls in hope of a triumph, was chosen Consul, and triumphed a few days afterwards (Liv. XL. 43.)

The *Lex Pompeia de iure magistratuum*, passed by Pompeius in his third Consulship, (B.C. 52,) expressly declared that no one could stand candidate for an office when absent, (*a petitione honorum absentes submovebat*,) and on this law the Consul Marcellus founded his opposition to the request of Cæsar, who was desirous to be elected Consul for the second time without quitting his troops in Gaul.[2]

Thus we perceive, that before the downfal of the republic, three restrictions had been placed upon candidates. They were obliged—

1. To declare themselves not less than seventeen days before the election, (*intra legitimos dies*,) in order probably, that the proclamation which summoned the assembly might contain a list of the competitors.

2. To declare themselves in person, (*praesens profiteri*,) which could be done within the city only, apparently in the Forum.

3. To appear in person at the election.

The date of the first enactment is altogether unknown; but it may have been included in the provisions of the *Lex Caecilia Didia*. See above, p. 113. The third seems to have been introduced by Pompeius. The second must belong to some period between B.C. 63 and B.C. 60; for in the latter year it was, as we have seen, enforced against Cæsar, while Cicero, in one of his speeches on the Agrarian law of Rullus, (II. 9,) delivered in the early part of his consulship, positively asserts that there was no law which required a candidate for one of the regular magistracies to announce himself in person.

But although there may have been no law to enforce the presence of candidates until the very close of the republic, in the great majority of cases, the aspirants to public offices were not only on the spot, but were most actively engaged in canvassing for months before each election.

Toga Candida. Candidati.—The first intimation was made, in accordance with a very ancient practice, by the candidate appearing in public dressed in a *Toga Candida*, that is to say a *Toga* which had been artificially whitened by the application of chalk or some similar substance, the natural colour of the wool, as commonly worn, being described by the epithet *Alba*. Persons so arrayed were styled *Candidati*, and hence our English word *Candidate*. This conspicuous dress was forbidden by a *Plebiscitum* as early as B.C. 432—*Ne cui album in vestimentum addere petitionis liceret causa*—but this ordinance must

---
[1] Cic. ad fam. XVI. 12. Suet. Caes. 18. Plut. Caes. 13. Appian. B.C. II. 8. comp. Macrob. S. L. 16.
[2] Suet. Caes. 28. Dion Cass. XL. 56. comp. 59.

have been repealed, or, in process of time, neglected; for the *Toga Candida* is frequently alluded to during the two last centuries of the republic, as the characteristic dress; and we are assured by Plutarch that, on these occasions, it was customary to wear the *Toga* without any *Tunica* under it, in imitation, probably, of the primitive simplicity of the olden time.[1] Marked out by this attire from the crowd of citizens, they were wont to repair day after day to all places of public resort, to go round among the people, (*ambire—ambitio—concursare toto foro*,) to shake hands with them, (*prensare*,) and to recommend themselves as best they might.[2] They were usually attended by a numerous retinue of clients and supporters, (*assidua sectatorum copia*,) who repaired to their dwellings at an early hour, escorted them down to the Forum, (*deducebant—deductores*,) followed them about (*sectatores*) from place to place, and exerted all the influence they possessed on their behalf. When the population had increased to such an extent that it was impossible for a candidate to know all the voters even by sight, he was accompanied by a slave termed a *Nomenclator*, whose sole business it was to become acquainted with the persons and circumstances of the whole constituency, and to whisper such information into his master's ear, when he passed from one to another in the crowd, as might enable him to salute each individual correctly by name, (*appellare*,) and to greet him as an acquaintance.[3] After the social war, when the *Ius Suffragii* was extended to nearly all the free inhabitants of Italy, the provincial towns exercised no small influence in the elections, and hence it was found expedient to canvass the Coloniae and Municipia as well as Rome.[4] When party spirit ran high, and the competition was likely to prove keen, the principal supporters (*suffragatores*) of the rival candidates were in the habit, not only of soliciting individually, but of organizing clubs and committees (*sodalitates—sodalitia*) for securing the return of their friends, and of portioning out the constituency into sections, (*conscribere s. describere s. decuriare populum*,) so as to ensure a thorough canvass; and when they succeeded in obtaining pledges from a majority in any Century or Tribe they were said *Conficere Centuriam s. Tribum*.[5] It was not unusual for two candidates to form a coalition (*coitio*) and unite their interests, in order to throw out (*deiicere honore*) a third who was likely to prove formidable to either singly. In this way Catiline and Antonius caballed to exclude Cicero, (*coierant ut Ciceronem Consulatu deiicerent*,) Lucceius and Balbus to exclude Caesar; but the plan failed in both instances.[6] These and various other devices were accompanied, towards the close of the republic, by so many disorders and so much violence, that it became necessary to check them by legislative prohibition; but they must be regarded as pure and innocent when compared with the wholesale bribery (*ambitus*) practised during the last half century. How crying this evil had become is sufficiently indicated by the number of laws (*Leges de ambitu*) passed within a few years for the repression of the offence, each rising above its predecessor in the severity of the penalties denounced, and all alike ineffectual. We shall enumerate the most important of these when treating of the adminis-

---

[1] Liv. VI. 25. XXXIX. 39. Polyb X. 4. Val. Max. IV. v. 3. Plut. Q. R. 49. Coriol. 14. and we have fragments of a speech of Cicero delivered *In Toga Candida*, when he stood for the Consulship.
[2] Varro L.L. V. § 28. Liv. III. 35. IV. 6. Cic. de Orat. I. 24. Val. Max. IV. v. 4. VII. v. 2.
[3] Cic. pro Muren. 36. ad Att. IV. 1.
[4] Cic. ad Att. I. 1. Philipp. II 30. Caes. B. G. VIII. 50.
[5] Cic. pro Planc. 18. ad fam. XI. 16. Q. Cic. de pet. cons. 5.
[6] Liv III. 35. XXXIX. 41. Cic. ad Q. F. III. 1. Ascon. ad Cic. Orat. in Tog. cand. p. 82 ed. Orell. Suet Caes. 19.

tration of the criminal law; but at present we have only to remark that, during the period above-mentioned, bribery was reduced to a system—regular agents (*interpretes*) were employed, who bargained with large bodies of the voters for their suffrages, the money promised was, in order to secure good faith upon both sides, deposited until the elections were over, in the hands of trustees (*sequestres*) appointed by the parties mutually, and was eventually distributed by paymasters (*divisores*) employed for the special purpose. A most extraordinary, complicated, and villanous example of corruption and of meditated perjury, is to be found in the scheme of Memmius and Domitius, as detailed by Cicero in a letter to Atticus (IV. 18.)

The technical term denoting a suitor for any office is *Petitor*, and the act, *Petere* and *Petitio;* hence the phrases *Petere Consulatum, Praeturam*, &c. In making a formal announcement of his intentions, the candidate was said *Profiteri* (sc. *se petere* s. *se petiturum esse*.) Those who were canvassing for the same office were termed *Competitores*, and when a candidate was defeated he was said *ferre repulsam*.

Candidates under the Empire.—We have already pointed out, that, under the Empire, the Consuls and a certain number of the magistrates of inferior grade were nominated, or, as the phrase was, *recommended*, by the Prince, while the selection of the remainder was left to the Senate. The nominees of the Emperor were styled *Candidati Principis* s. *Imperatoris* s. *Augusti* s. *Caesaris*, and in process of time simply *Candidati*, while the term *Petitores* was applied to those only who solicited the votes of the Senate.[1] Since those who held office in consequence of their influence at court were proud of this distinction, we find it frequently recorded in inscriptions that an individual had been PRAETOR CANDIDATUS—TRIBUNUS PLEBIS CANDIDATUS—QUAESTOR CANDIDATUS—and among these is a tablet dedicated to one who had been DIVI HADRIANI AUG. IN OMNIBUS HONORIBUS CANDIDATO IMPERAT.[2]

The peculiar duties performed by the *Quaestor Candidatus* or *Quaestor Principis* have been detailed above, see p. 164.

Magistratus Designati. Abdicatio.—After a magistrate had been regularly chosen by the Comitia and returned (*renuntiatus*) by the president, he was distinguished by the title of *designatus* (*Consul designatus; Praetor designatus*, &c.) The election could not be cancelled unless he formally resigned, (*abdicavit se magistratu*,) and this resignation was always voluntary, except under the following cirumstances:—

1. If it was discovered at any subsequent period that there had been any irregularity in observing the auspices before the Comitia, or that an unfavourable omen had been overlooked or wilfully neglected, then the magistrates elected at such an assembly were said to be *Vitio creati*, and immediate resignation was compulsory.

2. If a *Magistratus designatus* was impeached and found guilty of having secured his election by bribery or other illegal means, he was compelled to resign. In this manner Sulla and Autronius, when *Consules designati* in B.C. 66, were forced to retire, while, on the other hand, the attempt made in B.C. 63 to oust Murena, upon a similar charge, failed.

No magistrate under any other circumstances, whether merely *designatus* or after he had entered upon his duties, could be forcibly deprived of office. A

[1] Thus, Spartian. Sept. Sev. 3.—*Praetor designatus a Marco est* NON IN CANDIDA SED IN COMPETITORUM GREGE *anno aetatis XXXII.*
[2] Grut. C. 1. L. p. CCCCI.VII. comp. Velleius II. 124. Quintil. I. O. VI. iii. 62.

Dictator, indeed, might suspend his own *Magister Equitum*, or even a *Consul;* but, in point of fact, during the sway of a Dictator no magistrate could exercise jurisdiction except by his permission (Liv. III. 29. VIII. 36.)

Certain honours and privileges belonged to the *Magistratus designati.* They were asked their opinion in the Senate before ordinary Senators ; if called upon to plead in a court of justice, they spoke from the bench (*de sella ac Tribunali—de loco superiore*) and not from the bar, (*ex subselliis—ex loco inferiore,*) and they had the right of publishing proclamations (*edicta*) with regard to the manner in which they intended to discharge the duties of their respective offices.

Oath of Office.—Every magistrate was compelled, within five days after he entered upon office, to swear obedience to the laws, (*iurare in leges,*) and, in like manner, when the period of his office had expired and he tendered his formal resignation, (*abdicare se magistratu—magistratum deponere,*) he was required to swear that he had not wilfully violated the laws, and hence the phrase *eiurare magistratum.* This ceremony took place in the Forum, on the day before the new magistrates entered upon office. The retiring magistrates, at least the Consuls, usually ascended the *Rostra* and delivered an oration, (*concio,*) in which they took a review of their proceedings while in office. It is well known that Cicero, when about to deliver an address, according to custom, on the last day of December B.C. 63, was stopped by Metellus Nepos, a Tribune of the Plebs, and ordered to restrict himself to the simple oath, upon which, to use his own words—*Sine ulla dubitatione iuravi, rempublicam atque hanc urbem mea unius opera esse salvam . . . . Populus Romanus universus illa in concione, . . . meum iusiurandum tale atque tantum, iuratus ipse, una voce et consensu approbavit* (In Pison. 3. Ad fam. V. 2.)

Marks of Respect paid to Magistrates.—When one of the higher magistrates, especially the Consul, appeared in any place of public assemblage, such as the Senate-house, the Circus, or the Theatre, where the persons present were seated, all were wont to rise up to do him honour, (*assurgere,*) and the same took place if he paid a visit to a private dwelling ; when he was walking abroad in the streets, all who met him made way for him (*decedere de via*) and uncovered their heads, (*aperire caput.*) and if on horseback, dismounted until he had passed by ; and these marks of consideration were paid, not only by the community at large to the magistrates, but by the inferior magistrates to their superiors. Thus, the Praetor ordered his Lictors to lower their Fasces (*fasces submittere*) when he chanced to meet the Consul, and, if seated, rose from his *Sella Curulis* as the latter passed.[1]

Titles bestowed upon those who had held the great offices of State.—The six great offices of state being the *Consulatus, Praetura, Aedilitas, Tribunatus, Quaestura, Censura,* those who had held these offices were styled respectively *Consulares, Praetorii, Aedilitii, Tribunitii, Quaestorii, Censorii.* These titles originally merely stated a fact, for under the republic no one was ever designated as *Vir Consularis, Vir Praetorius,* &c. unless he had been regularly elected to, and had actually discharged the duties of the office indicated by the epithet. But an important change in this respect took place under the empire. After the practice of bestowing *Ornamenta Consularia, Ornamenta Praetoria,* &c. the nature of which we have explained above, (p. 139,) was

---

[1] See Cic. in Verr. IV. 62. in Pison. 12. Liv. IX. 46. XXIV. 44. Sallust. ap. Non. Marcell. s.v. *Apertum*, p. 161. ed. Gerl. Val. Max. II. ii. 4. V. ii 9. VIII. v. 6. Suet. Caes. 80. Claud. 12. Nero. 4. Aul. Gell. II. ii. 13. VII. vi. 9. Plut. C. Gracch. 3. Q. R. 10.

introduced, not only those who had really held the office of Consul, of Praetor, &c. were styled *Consulares, Praetorii,* &c. but those also who had merely received the *Ornamenta*. These persons formed a numerous body ; and although they wielded no real power in virtue of their titles, they formed distinct classes, each enjoying for life a certain amount of rank, consideration, and precedence, (*Dignitas praetoria—D. Aedilitia—D. Tribunitia,*) similar to that possessed in modern times by those belonging to the different orders of knighthood. When an individual was admitted to such privileges he was said to be *allectus inter Consulares, allectus inter Praetorios,* &c. and thus a number of grades were introduced into the Senate, since a member might be *Senator Consularis,* or *Senator Praetoriae Dignitatis,* or *Senator Aedilitiae Dignitatis,* &c. In choosing new members of the Senate it appears to have been not uncommon to bestow upon them at the same time a specific rank ; thus we are told that M. Aurelius—*Multos ex amicis in Senatum allegit cum Aedilitiis aut Praetoriis Dignitatibus—Multis Senatoribus vel pauperibus sine crimine Dignitates Tribunitias Aedilitiasque concessit.* (Capitolin. 10.)

Hence the historians of the empire sometimes distinguish an individual who had actually held one of the great offices from a mere Titular, by designating the former as *Consulatu functus, Praetura functus,* &c. ; but this is by no means uniformly observed.

Insignia.—These having been specified when treating of the different offices separately, it is unnecessary to repeat what has been stated under each head.

Potestas.—Every Roman magistrate was, in virtue of his election by the Comitia, invested with a certain amount of civil power, technically termed *Potestas,* by which he was entitled to discharge the duties of his office, and, if impeded, to enforce obedience to his lawful orders by fine, by imprisonment, or otherwise.[1] The amount of *Potestas* varied according to the office. Those magistrates who had the right of being attended by *Lictors,* namely, the Consuls and Praetors,[2] had not only the right of arresting any one who was present, (*Prensio,*) but they had also the right of summoning any one not present to appear before them and to enforce his attendance (*Vocatio.*) Those, again, who were attended by *Viatores,* the *Tribuni Plebis,* for example, had only *Prensio* and not *Vocatio.* Those who had neither *Lictores* nor *Viatores,* the Quaestors for example, had neither *Vocatio* nor *Prensio* and therefore no summary jurisdiction.[3]

Imperium.—It was a fundamental principle of the constitution, that election by the *Comitia Centuriata* or the *Comitia Tributa* conferred *Potestas* only, and that no magistrate could take the command of an army, or hold a meeting of the Comitia Centuriata, which was always regarded as an assembly of a military character, (*Exercitus Urbanus,*) until *Imperium* was bestowed upon him by a *Lex Curiata,* concerning which we have already spoken at length.[4]

Whatever step a magistrate took in virtue of his official authority he was said *Pro magistratu agere,*[5] and this step would be taken *Pro Potestate* or *Pro Imperio* as the case might be. When a magistrate was deforced in the exercise of his *Potestas* he was said *In ordinem cogi.*[6]

[1] The right of inflicting a fine belonged to Consuls only, until the passing of the *Lex Aternia Tarpeia,* (B.C. 454,) by which it was extended to all ordinary magistrates. Dionys. X. 50. Cic. de R. II. 35. Aul. Gell. XI. 1.
[2] It is unnecessary here, and elsewhere, when speaking of the ordinary working of the constitution, to refer to the Dictators who were, for the time being, above the laws.
[3] This is very clearly explained by Varro in a passage quoted by Aulus Gellius XIII. 12.
[4] See p. 117.
[5] Liv. VIII. 36. IX. 7.
[6] Liv. III. 51. VI. 38. XXV. 4. XLIII. 16.

Prorogatio Imperii.—A magistrate was never, under any pretext, allowed to retain his office, without re-election, after the expiration of a year; but when, by the gradual extension of the Roman conquests, the seat of war was gradually removed farther and farther from the city, it was felt that it might at times prove both inconvenient and hazardous to recall or supersede a general actively engaged in important and critical military operations. These considerations forced themselves so strongly upon the public mind during the war against the Greeks in Campania, (B.C. 327,) when danger was apprehended on the side of Samnium, that the Tribunes, at the request of the Senate, proposed to the people, that when the Consul Q. Publilius Philo had ceased to hold office, he should be armed with the same powers for the prosecution of the war as if he were still Consul, and that these should continue until the war was brought to a conclusion—*Actum cum Tribunis est ad populum ferrent, ut, quum Publilius Philo consulatu abisset* PRO CONSULE *rem gereret, quoad debellatum cum Graecis esset.* This was accordingly done, and Publilius was not only the first upon whom such a command was conferred, but the first Roman general who ever celebrated a triumph after the period of his office had expired.[1] From this time forward it became common for the people in the *Comitia Tributa* to prolong the military command of a general, sometimes for six months, sometimes for a year, and sometimes, as in the case of Publilius, for an indefinite space, until the undertaking in which he was engaged should be brought to a close. During the second Punic war, especially, we find examples of the same individuals being continued in their command for several years in succession.[2] This prolongation was termed *Prorogatio* s. *Propagatio Imperii*, and the phrase *Prorogare Imperium* must be carefully distinguished from *Continuare Consulatum*, which was employed when the people elected the same individual to the Consulship for two years consecutively.

When the people conferred extended *Imperium* in this manner, they were understood to reserve to themselves, in all cases, the right of annulling their own act even when a definite period had been fixed, and in doing this they were said *Abrogare Imperium*, (Liv. XXVII. 20. XXIX. 19,) but a regular *Plebiscitum* was always required for the *Prorogatio* or *Abrogatio* of *Imperium*.

When the *Imperium* of a Consul was prolonged, he was said *rem gerere* PRO CONSULE, i.e. to exercise in so far as the particular service was concerned the power of a Consul, although not holding the office; and in like manner, when the *Imperium* of a Praetor or of Quaestor was prolonged, they were said *rem gerere* PRO PRAETORE, PRO QUAESTORE, &c. Hence, in process of time, the words *Proconsul, Propraetor, Proquaestor* were formed and applied to designate those who were intrusted for special service, with powers and rank belonging to the magistrates indicated by these terms. Generally speaking, the title *Proconsul*, and the phrases *Proconsulare Imperium* and *Pro consule* were applied to those only who had actually held the office of Consul; and the same holds good for *Propraetor* and *Proquaestor*. The rule was not, however, universally observed; for the elder Scipio, when twenty-four years old, was sent as *Proconsul* into Spain,

---

[1] Liv. VIII. 23. At a much earlier date (B.C. 464) we read (Liv. III. 4.) that T. Quinctius, who had been Consul the previous year, was despatched from Rome with a reinforcement *pro consule*; but these words may be understood to mean merely *instead of the Consul*, the Consul having been detained in the city, comp. Dionys. IX. 16. 63. who uses the terms with which he was familiar when he wrote. But see the section below, p. 194, on the *Different Applications of the term Proconsul*.

[2] Liv. IX. 42. X. 16. 20. 22. XXIII. 25. XXIV. 10. 11. XXV. 6. XXX. 1.

although he had held no office previously; and Pompeius, at the age of thirty-one, was sent *Pro consule* against Sertorius.[1] See below, p. 194.

The *Imperium* of Proconsuls and Propraetors differed, however, in some important particulars from the *Imperium* enjoyed by Consuls and Praetors while in office. The Proconsul or Propraetor exercised *Imperium* in that particular district or province only to which he was specially appointed, and if at any time he entered the city, he, ipso facto, lost his *Imperium*. Hence, when a Proconsul or a Propraetor solicited a triumph, he was obliged to remain with his army outside the city until his claims were considered; but if, from any cause, he entered the city before the matter was decided, he at once lost his *Imperium* and became incapable of celebrating a triumph. If a triumph was voted by the Senate, then a special Plebiscitum was required, granting him the privilege of retaining his *Imperium* within the city upon the day of the pageant. On the other hand, a Consul who had received *Imperium* could exercise it anywhere without the city, and although it was suspended, as it were, each time he entered the city, he could enter and leave the city repeatedly without being obliged to apply for a renewal of his *Imperium*. This is well illustrated by the following passage in Livy, (XXVI. 9)—*Inter hunc tumultum Q. Fulvium Proconsulem profectum cum exercitu a Capua affertur: cui ne minueretur Imperium, si in urbem venisset, decernit Senatus, ut Q. Fulvio par cum Consulibus Imperium esset*.

Classification of Magistrates.—Various classifications of the Roman Magistrates have been proposed by writers upon antiquities, some of which were recognized by the ancients themselves. We shall notice the most important.

1. *Magistratus Ordinarii. Magistratus Extraordinarii.*—The former were regularly elected at stated intervals, the latter were not. The principal *Magistratus Ordinarii* were the Consuls, Praetors, Aediles, Quaestors, Tribunes of the Plebs, and Censors; the principal *Magistratus Extraordinarii* were the Dictator, the Magister Equitum, and the Interrex. The *Decemviri legibus scribendis* and the *Tribuni Militares consulari potestate* existed under circumstances which prevent us from ranking them with propriety under either head, although, according to our definition, they would, strictly speaking, fall under the *Extraordinarii*. The *Praefectus Urbi* was a *Magistratus Ordinarius* under the kings, *Extraordinarius* during the period of the republic, and again became *Ordinarius* under the empire.

2. *Magistratus Curules. M. non Curules.*—The former, as we have had occasion to observe repeatedly, were the Consuls, Praetors, Curule Aediles, Censors, and in all probability the Dictator, the Magister Equitum, and the Warden of the city. To these we may doubtless add the *Decemviri legibus scribendis* and the *Tribuni Militares C. P.* This distinction is so far important that the descendants of those who had borne curule offices were *Nobiles*, and enjoyed the *Ius Imaginum*. See p. 67.

3. *Magistratus Patricii. M. Plebeii.*—Originally all the great offices of state were filled by the Patricians exclusively, except the Plebeian Tribunate and the Plebeian Aedileship, to which, from the period of their institution down to the close of the republic, and even later, Plebeians alone were eligible. We have seen, however, in treating of the different offices separately, that the Plebeians fought their way gradually until they obtained admission to all without distinction, so that after B.C. 337, when the first Plebeian Praetor, Q. Publilius Philo,

[1] Liv. XXVI. 18. XXVIII. 43. Epit. XCI. Cic. pro leg. Man. 21. Philipp. XL 8.

was elected, the term *Magistratus Patricii* ceased to be applicable to any class of public officials with the exception of certain priests.

4. *Magistratus Maiores. M. Minores.*—We sometimes find the inferior functionaries, such as the *Triumviri Capitales* and the *Triumviri Monetales*, of whom we shall speak more particularly below, termed by some of the classical writers *Minores Magistratus* in opposition to the great dignitaries, the Consuls, Praetors, Aediles, Tribunes, Quaestors, and Censors.[1] But the division of magistrates into *Maiores* and *Minores* was contemplated by other authors from a very different point of view. A work by Messala, quoted in Aulus Gellius, (XIII. 15,) teaches us that the *Auspicia* were believed to possess greater efficacy when observed by one particular class of magistrates—*Patriciorum auspicia in duas sunt potestates divisa*—and hence were distinguished as *Maxima s. Maiora Auspicia* and *Minora Auspicia*. The *Maiora Auspicia* belonged to the Consuls, Praetors, and Censors, to whom we ought to add the Dictator, who is not specified by Messala, because the office no longer existed when he wrote, and these therefore were the *Maiores Magistratus*, while, according to this principle, the Curule Aediles and the Quaestors were *Minores Magistratus*. (Compare with Messala the words of Cic. de legg. III. 3.)

Secondly, although the Consuls, Praetors, and Censors had the *Maiora Auspicia*, the *Auspicia* of the Censors were different in quality, though not in degree, from those of the Consuls and the Praetors; and these two sets of *Auspicia* were independent of each other, so that the *Auspicia* taken by a Censor could not interfere with or disturb those taken by a Consul or a Praetor, nor those taken by a Consul or a Praetor disturb those taken by a Censor.

Thirdly, since the Praetor had the same *Auspicia* as the Consul, he was styled *Collega Consulis*; but although he had the same *Auspicia* he had not the same *Imperium*. The Consuls had *Maius Imperium*, relative to the Praetors, who had reciprocally *Minus Imperium*, relative to the Consuls. Now, it was a principle of the constitution, that no magistrate could preside at the election of another magistrate who enjoyed *Maius Imperium*. Hence a Praetor could not preside at the *Comitia* for the election of Consuls, because the latter had *Maius Imperium*; nor could a Praetor preside at the *Comitia* for the election of Praetors, for in that case he would have been presiding at the election of a magistrate who was the *Collega* of the Consul, and therefore the *Collega* of a magistrate who had *Maius Imperium*.[2]

Lastly, while the Consuls had *Maius Imperium* relatively to the Praetors, the Dictator had *Maius Imperium* relatively to the Consuls, and to his own master of the horse, being supreme over all. This is distinctly laid down by Livy (VIII. 38. XXX. 24. XXXII. 7.)

PROVINCES OF THE MAGISTRATES.

General signification of the term Provincia.—Whatever may be the origin of the word *Provincia*, and no scholar has as yet succeeded in discovering a satisfactory etymology, it denotes, when used with reference to a Roman magistrate, *the sphere of action* within which he was called upon to discharge the duties of his office. For several centuries the Consuls were occupied, almost exclusively, in leading the armies of the state; and accordingly the war which a Consul was appointed to conduct, or the region in which it was prosecuted, or the people

---

[1] Liv. XXXII. 26. Suet. Caes. 41.
[2] This curious doctrine is very clearly stated by Messala in the passage above referred to, and by Cicero ad Att. IX. 9. See also Val. Max. II. viii. 2.

against whom it was waged, were alike termed his *Provincia*. So also the Praetor who acted as supreme judge in the civil courts at Rome was said to have the *Urbana Provincia*; the Quaestor who superintended the exportation and importation of merchandise at Ostia and elsewhere was said to have the *Aquaria Provincia*; and, in the ordinary language of familiar conversation, *Provincia* means *a duty, a task*, or *an occupation* of any description.[1]

Arrangement and Distribution of the Provinces.—It was the prerogative of the Senate, under ordinary circumstances, to fix the *Provinciae Consulares*, that is, to determine where and how the Consuls should be employed in the service of the state (*decernere s. nominare Provincias*.) When the *Provinciae* were marked out, the Consuls were generally allowed to settle with each other regarding their distribution, (*comparare inter se Provincias*,) or, if they could not come to an agreement, they decided the question by lot (*sortiri Provincias*) —*Quum Senatus, aut sortiri aut comparare inter se Provincias, Consules iussisset*;[2] but occasionally the Senate itself assigned a particular Province to a particular individual, in which case that body was said *dare Provinciam extra sortem s. extra ordinem*;[3] and it sometimes assigned the same province to both Consuls.[4]

In the earlier ages of the republic one Consul was usually sent forth to carry on military operations, while the other remained to protect the city and administer the ordinary business of the state; when the war was of a very formidable character, both Consuls proceeded to the army and assumed the supreme command on alternate days; (see p. 135;) and when danger threatened from different quarters the Consuls commanded separate armies, acting independently of each other. In every case the limits of the Province, that is, the limits within which the operations of the Consul were to be carried on, were strictly defined; and it was considered a most serious offence for a Consul to overstep the bounds of his own Province without express permission.[5]

We have said that it was the prerogative of the Senate to arrange and distribute the Provinces, and in point of fact it will be found that this was regarded as one of the ordinary and regular duties of that body. But since, according to the theory of the constitution, all power proceeded from the people, acting in their constitutional assemblies, it happened in times of strong political excitement, when party spirit ran high, that the Tribes exercised the right of assigning particular Provinces to their favourites, without regard to the opinion or decision of the Senate. Thus, although the Senate had passed a resolution that Metellus should continue to prosecute the war against Jugurtha during the year B.C. 107, the people having been asked (*rogatus*) by Manilius Mancinus, one of the Tribunes of the Plebs—*Quem vellet cum Iugurtha bellum gerere*—decided by a great majority

[1] One or two examples will suffice to illustrate what has been said above—*Consules T. Sicinius et C. Aquillius, Sicinio Volsci, Aquillio Hernici* PROVINCIA *evenit.* Liv. II. 40.
T. Manlio Consuli Etruria PROVINCIA *evenit.* Liv. X. 11.
Praetores PROVINCIAS *sortiti sunt: P. Cornelius Sulla Urbanam et Peregrinam, quae duorum ante sors fuerat; Cn. Fulvius Flaccus Apuliam; C. Claudius Nero Suessulam; M. Iunius Silanus Tuscos.* Liv. XXV. 3.
PAL. *Lepide facitis. Nunc hanc tibi ego impero* PROVINCIAM.
ACR. *Impetrabis, imperator, quod ego potero, quod voles.*
PAL. *Militem lepide et facete et laute ludificarier.* Plaut. Mil. Gl. IV. iv. 23.
Tunc tuus pater, Corneli, ... illam sibi officiosam PROVINCIAM *depoposcit, ut . . . . . me in meo lectulo trucidaret.* Cic. pro Sulla 18.
[2] Liv. XXXVII. 1.
[3] e.g. Liv. III. 2. VIII. 16.
[4] *Consulibus ambobus Italia Provincia . . . . . decreta*, i.e. they were both ordered to stay at home. Liv. XXXIII 25. and again XXXV. 20.
[5] Liv. X. 37. XXIX. 19. XXXI. 48 XLI 7. XLIII. 1. comp. XXVII. 43. XXVIII. 17. 42. XXIX. 17. 19.

that it should be committed to Marius. In this instance it might be argued that Marius, being actually Consul, had a better right to the command than Metellus, whose Imperium had been already prolonged; but exactly the reverse took place in B.C. 88, for the war against Mithridates having been assigned by the Senate to Sulla, one of the Consuls for the year, as his Province, the Tribes were persuaded by Marius to cancel the appointment and bestow it upon himself, a procedure which led to the first great civil war. So also in B.C. 59, the people bestowed the command of Gallia Cisalpina and Illyricum upon Cæsar, at the instigation of the Tribune Vatinius, who brought in a bill (*Rogatio Vatinia*) for that purpose, and carried it in direct opposition to the wishes and arrangements of the Senate.

Exactly the same system was followed with regard to the Provinces of the Praetors. It was decided usually by lot, which should act as Praetor Urbanus, which as Praetor Peregrinus, (hence these Provinces are frequently termed *Sors Urbana* and *Sors Peregrina*,) and then the foreign Provinces were divided among the remainder, or, as took place during the last century of the republic, when all usually remained in the city during their year of office, the lot decided in which court each should preside.

Provincia in a restricted sense.—A country or district beyond the confines of Italy, completely subjugated, deprived of its independence, and ruled by a Roman governor, was termed a *Provincia*, and when reduced to this condition was said technically *redigi in formam Provinciae*. It must be remarked that a conquered country was not always at once converted into a *Province*. Thus, Macedonia, although fully subdued in B.C. 168, did not become a Province until B.C. 146, and in like manner, neither Asia nor Achaia became Provinces for many years after they had been entirely under the control of Rome. It is to *Provinciae* in this restricted sense that we shall confine the observations made in the following paragraphs.

Constitution of the Provinces.—When the Senate had resolved that a country should be reduced to the form of a Province, they commonly sent ten *Legati*[1] or commissioners from their own body, who, in conjunction with the victorious general, arranged the terms of peace with the vanquished people, determined the exact limits of the Province to be formed, and drew up a constitution, by which the future condition and government of the state was defined. These matters having been arranged upon the spot, were, upon the return of the Legati to Rome, submitted to the people in the form of one or more Rogations, which if sanctioned, formed the Charter which regulated the powers and jurisdiction of the provincial governors. Of this description were the *Lex Rupilia* for Sicily, the *Lex Aquillia* for Asia, and the *Leges Aemiliae* for Macedonia; but these and similar laws, although serving as the groundwork of the constitution, might in each case be altered, modified, and explained by new Laws, Decrees of the Senate, and the Edicts of the provincial governors themselves.

Provincial Governors.—These at first were Praetors, two Praetors having been added, about B.C. 227, to the previous number, for the special purpose of acting as governors of Sicily and of Sardinia; and two more in B.C. 197, for the two Spains (see above p. 154.) But towards the close of the republic, the number of Provinces having greatly increased, they were divided into two classes, *Provinciae Consulares* and *Provinciae Praetoriae*; and since both Consuls and Praetors, at this period, usually passed the whole of their year of

---

[1] Liv. XXXIII. 43. XLV. 16. 17. 18. Cic. Philipp XII. 12.

THE PROVINCES.

office in the city, they were again invested with *Imperium* after they had laid down their offices and proceeded to the different Provinces allotted to them, which they ruled with the titles of *Proconsules* and *Propraetores* respectively.

The Senate determined, each year, which should be *Provinciae Consulares* and which *Provinciae Praetoriae*, the Consuls then cast lots, or came to an understanding with regard to the *Provinciae Consulares*, and, in like manner, the Praetors with regard to the *Provinciae Praetoriae*, unless the Senate saw fit to make a special (*extra ordinem*) appointment, or the *Comitia Tributa* took the matter into their own hands. Generally speaking, the Consular Provinces were those in which there was war or the apprehension of war, either external or internal, while the Praetorian Provinces were those in which tranquillity prevailed and was not likely to be disturbed. In this manner a Province at one time Consular might become Praetorian, and vice versa; but changes of this kind seem to have been effected frequently without reference to warlike considerations.[1]

Departure of a Proconsul or Propraetor for his Province.—When the time had arrived for a Proconsul or Propraetor to leave Rome for his Province, he received his equipments from the Senate, who decided by what number of *Legati* he was to be assisted, the amount of troops which were to be placed under his command, the allowance for outfit (*Vasarium*) to be paid from the public treasury, and all other things requisite, in voting which they were said *Provinciam Ornare* s. *Instruere*.[2] Having then received *Imperium* by a *Lex Curiata*, and his vows having been offered up in the Capitol, (*votis in Capitolio nuncupatis*,)[3] he took his departure in great state from some point beyond the walls, arrayed in the robe of a military commander, (*paludatus*,) his Lictors, twelve or six as the case might be, marching before him with *Fasces* and *Secures*, escorted on his way by a numerous train of friends and clients, and attended by his personal staff, (*Cohors Praetoria*,) consisting of his *Quaestor*, his *Legati*, various subordinate officers, (*Praefecti*,) clerks and secretaries, (*Scribae*,) servants of all kinds, (*apparitores*,) public slaves, (*publici servi*,) and a throng, who, under the general appellations of *Comites*, *Amici*, *Familiares*, hoped to share his power and benefit by his patronage.[4] He was bound to travel direct to his Province, the inhabitants of the towns through which he passed being obliged to find lodging, forage, means of transport, and to satisfy various other demands, which, until regulated by the *Lex Iulia*, frequently afforded a pretext for great extortion and oppression.[5] When a sea voyage was necessary, ships were provided by the state.[6]

Commencement and Duration of a Provincial Command.—The command of a governor commenced on the day when he entered his Province, or, at all events, on the day when he reached one of the chief towns, (Cic. ad Att. V. 15,) and, under ordinary circumstances, was understood to continue for one year only. It was, however, very frequently prolonged by a decree of the Senate; and even when no formal *Prorogatio* took place, a governor could remain and exercise his power until the arrival of his successor. We gather

---

[1] Cic. ad Att. I. 13. 16. de Prov. Cons. 7. 15. Plut. Pomp. 61. Dion. Cass. XXXVII. 33.
[2] Cic. ad Att. III. 24. de leg. agr. II. 13. in Pison. 35. ad Q. F. II. 3. Suet. Caes. 18.
[3] Liv. XLII. 49. Cic. ad fam. I. 9.
[4] Liv. XXXI. 14. XLII. 49. Cic. in Verr. V. 13 ad fam. XV. 17. ad Att. VII. 2. ad. Q. F. I. 1. Caes. B. C. I. 6.—*Quos vero aut ex domesticis convictionibus, aut ex necessariis apparitionibus tecum esse voluisti, qui quasi ex* COHORTE PRAETORIA *appellari solent, horum non modo facta, sed etiam dicta omnia nobis praestanda sunt.* Cic. ad Q. F. I. 1. § 4. *Cohors Praetoria*, in a more limited sense, signified the military body guard of the governor. Cic. ad. fam. XV. 4.
[5] Cic. ad Att. V. 10. 16.
[6] Cic. in Verr. V. 18. ad Att. V. 13. VI. 8.

from what took place in the case of Cicero, that if no formal vote of *Prorogatio* had been passed, a governor might, at the end of his official year, commit his Province to his Quaestor or to one of his Legati and return home. But this was a contingency so little to be looked for that it would appear that no provision was made to meet it.

Although the power of the provincial governor ceased at once on the arrival of his successor, he retained his *Imperium* and his Lictors until he entered Rome (Cic. ad Att. XI. 6. Appian. B.C. 1. 80.)

Power and Duties of a Provincial Governor.—These were partly military and partly civil.

1. In virtue of his *Imperium* the Proconsul or Propraetor was commander-in-chief of all the troops, whether Roman or auxiliary, stationed in the Province, and could, in emergencies, order a local levy (*delectus provincialis*.) These forces he could employ as he thought fit, either for the purpose of repelling invasion from without, or suppressing rebellion within; but on no account, as already observed, could he quit the limits of his Province without express orders from the Senate.

2. In virtue of his *Imperium* and *Potestas*, he had supreme jurisdiction in all causes, criminal as well as civil, and could imprison, scourge, or even inflict the punishment of death upon the provincials; but Roman citizens, although resident abroad, had, in all criminal causes, the right of appeal (*provocatio*) to Rome. The law or laws by which the constitution of each Province was established usually settled the mode in which justice was to be administered;[1] and a large number of suits were tried before local and domestic tribunals, although there seems to have been, in every instance, a right of appeal to the governor, who was assisted in his decisions by a board of assessors, termed his *Consilium*. For the sake of convenience in administering justice, a Province was usually divided into districts, called *Conventus*, and the governor made the circuit of these at least once in the year, holding his court in the principal town. In performing this duty he was said *Agere Conventus*.[2]

3. Besides the above duties, the Proconsul or Propraetor regulated all matters connected with the internal government and interests of the various towns and communities contained in the Province, in so far as his interference was demanded or warranted (Cic. ad. Q. F. I. 1.)

Honours bestowed on Provincial Governors.—When the inhabitants of a Province entertained feelings of attachment and gratitude towards their ruler, or deemed it expedient to feign such sentiments, they were wont to erect temples, statues and other memorials (*monumenta*) in the *fora* of the chief towns, they instituted solemn festivals to keep alive the recollection of his virtues,[3] they despatched embassies to Rome to pronounce his panegyric before the Senate; and when he had achieved any military exploit, they subscribed money, termed *aurum coronarium*, to assist in defraying the expenses of a triumph. Such

---

[1] Cicero (in Verr. II. 13. 15. 27.) gives many details with regard to Sicily which are very instructive.

[2] *Conventus* denotes properly an assemblage of persons who have met, not by chance, but for a fixed purpose. Hence, specially—
    1. An assemblage of persons in the Provinces meeting together to attend a court of justice.
    2. The day or days on which these assemblages took place.
    3. The place in which they were held.
    4. The district of which the inhabitants assembled.
Conventus is used also to denote an union or association of Roman citizens dwelling in a Province. See REIN s v. in the Encyclopaedie der Alther thumswissenschaft.

[3] Such were the *Marcellia* in Sicily, the *Mucia* and *Lucullia* in Asia.

demonstrations may, in some rare instance, have been called forth by a gentle and paternal exercise of power; but in later times at least, when they were most common, they were in general to be regarded as expressions of terror and servile flattery. They were frequently demanded and enforced as a matter of right by the most unworthy, and large sums were extorted by the corrupt and unscrupulous as contributions towards honorary testimonials.[1]

Landed Property in the Provinces.—In a newly subjugated Province the whole of the landed property fell under one of two heads, it was either, 1. *Ager Privatus*, belonging to private individuals, or, 2. *Ager Publicus*, belonging to the governing body, or to different communities and corporations, the proceeds of which were applied to public purposes. The whole of the soil, whether *Ager Privatus* or *Ager Publicus*, was regarded, theoretically, as belonging, by right of conquest, to the victors, and entirely at their disposal. In practice, however, the lands of private proprietors in the Provinces were seldom confiscated by the Romans; but the owners were allowed to retain possession and full right of property on payment of a moderate land tax. The *Ager Publicus*, on the other hand, was usually regarded as part of the spoils of war, and was disposed of in various ways—1. A portion was frequently sold and the proceeds paid into the Aerarium—2. A portion was farmed out to tenants who possessed no right of property in the soil which they cultivated, but paid a fixed rent—3. A portion was frequently left in the hands of the corporation or community by whom it had been formerly held, but became subject to certain payments to Rome.

Taxation and Burdens in the Provinces.—In like manner as the *Ager Publicus* in the Provinces was in most cases seized by the Romans, so they appropriated the revenues which had been raised from other sources in the different countries when independent. Such were the duties levied on exports and imports, the profits realised from salt works, mines, and many other objects which would vary in different localities.

In addition to the land-tax paid by the provincials, they were often subjected to a property-tax, (*Tributum*,) which was levied from each individual in proportion to the amount of his means. For the purpose of ascertaining the necessary data, a provincial Census became necessary. To this we find many allusions in the classical writers,[2] and every one is familiar with the narrative of St. Luke, which informs us that Joseph undertook the journey from Nazareth, which immediately preceded the Nativity, in order that he might be registered at Bethlehem.

But not only were the provincials required to pay a fixed sum in the form of land-tax, property-tax, and other well defined imposts, but they were liable to various demands of an arbitrary character, which varied for different times and different places. Thus they might be required to provide winter quarters for troops, to equip and maintain fleets for war or transport, to afford supplies for the table of the governor and his retinue, (*frumentum in cellam*,) and to submit to many other burdens which were peculiarly galling, since they were, to a great extent, regulated by the discretion of their rulers, and therefore could be, and often were employed by them as engines of intimidation, oppression, and extortion.[3]

[1] Cic. in Verr. II. 21. 57. 63. IV. 10. 67. pro Flacc. 15. 23. 25. 26. 40. in Pison. 37. ad Q. F. I. § 9. ad fam. III. 7. 9. Plut. Q. Flaminin. 16.
[2] e.g. Cic. in Verr. II. 49. 53. seqq. Liv. Epit. CXXXIV. CXXXVII. Plin. Epp. X. 83. 112. Dion Cass. LIII. 22.
[3] Cic. pro leg. Man. 14. Div. in Q. C. 10. in Verr. I. 34. 38. II. 60. III. 5. 81. 86. 87. V. 17. 23. 81. 38. 52. pro Flacc. 12. 14. Philipp. XI. 12.

Privileges enjoyed by Particular Communities in the Provinces.—Although a Province as a whole was subject to the control of the law or laws by which it was constituted, and to the sway of the governor by whom these laws were administered, yet almost every Province contained within its limits communities, which enjoyed special privileges. These communities, for the most part, belonged to one or other of the following classes:—

1. *Municipia.*—On *Municipia* in general see p. 90. With regard to the provincial Municipia we can say little. In all probability, no two of these towns had exactly the same constitution; but their common characteristic was the right of internal self-government.

2. *Coloniae.*—These, as in Italy, might be either *Coloniae Civium Romanorum* or *Coloniae Latinae*, or, in the frontier provinces especially, *Coloniae Militares.* See p. 88—90.

3. *Civitates Liberae.*—These were cities or communities which, by a special law, were, in return for some benefit conferred upon Rome, or from motives of policy, permitted to administer their own affairs without any interference upon the part of the provincial governor; and although subjects of Rome were no more under his Imperium than if they had actually been living in Rome. Thus, Byzantium and Cyzicus both received *Libertas*, as a reward for their good service in the war against Mithridates; but Cyzicus forfeited this privilege during the reign of Tiberius, in consequence of alleged misconduct (Cic. de Prov. Cons. 3. 4. Tacit. Ann. IV. 36.)

4. *Civitates Immunes.*—These were cities or communities which were exempted from the taxes and other imposts for which the ordinary inhabitants of the Provinces were liable. *Immunitas* was by no means necessarily a consequence of *Libertas*, for a state might be a *Civitas Libera* and yet heavily taxed. Thus, Byzantium, which enjoyed *Libertas*, was so overwhelmed by the public burdens imposed upon it that Claudius saw fit, upon petition, to grant it an exemption from tribute for five years. (Tacit. Ann. XII. 62. 63.) In like manner, a *Civitas* might be *Immunis* without being *Libera*.

5. *Civitates Foederatae.*—All cities and communities were comprehended under this title whose position with regard to Rome was defined by a treaty separate and distinct from those laws which provided for the general regulation of the province. The fact that a *Civitas* was *Foederata* did not necessarily imply the enjoyment of high privileges. It might be *Libera* or *Immunis*, or both, in virtue of its *Foedus;* but it did not follow as a matter of course that it was either. *Civitates Liberae, Civitates Immunes,* and *Municipia* were sometimes all included in the general designation of *Civitates Foederatae;* but, generally speaking, the right implied by *Libertas* and *Immunitas* were perfectly simple in themselves, and were the result of a free gift, which might be cancelled at the pleasure of the giver, while the condition of the *Civitates Foederatae* was secured by a formal treaty, and the relations established were frequently of a complicated nature.

Number of Provinces under the Republic.—1. The earliest Province was that portion of *Sicilia* which had belonged to Carthage, and which was ceded to Rome at the close of the first Punic war, B.C. 241; but after the capture of Syracuse in B.C. 212, and of Agrigentum in B.C. 210, it embraced the whole island. 2. *Sardinia* and *Corsica*, subdued in B.C. 238. 3. *Hispania Citerior;* and 4. *Hispania Ulterior.* The exact period when these were constituted Provinces is uncertain; but it was probably in B.C. 206, when the Carthaginians were finally subdued. Livy, when treating of the events of that year says—*Itaque* *ergo prima Romanis inita Provinciarum quae quidem Continentis sint, postrema omnium, nostra demum aetate, ductu auspicioque Augusti Caesaris perdomita est.* 5. *Macedonia*, although fully subjugated as early as B.C. 168, was not reduced to the form of a Province until B.C. 146. 6. *Illyricum*, called also *Dalmatia*, about the same time as Macedonia. 7. *Africa*, after the destruction of Carthage by Scipio in B.C. 146. 8. *Asia*, in B.C. 129. 9. *Gallia Transalpina*, comprehending originally (B.C. 121) the country of the Allobroges only and the south-east corner of Gaul. In order to distinguish it from the other divisions of that country, this was sometimes termed *Gallia Narbonensis* or, emphatically *Provincia*. Caesar conquered the whole of Gaul and divided it into three Provinces. 10. *Gallia Cisalpina* was subdued as early as B.C. 190; but we are unable to fix the period when it became a Province. It ceased to be a Province in B.C. 43, when it was included within the limits of Italy. 11. *Achaia*, although fully under the sway of the Romans after the capture of Corinth, B.C. 146, did not become a Province for some years subsequent to that date. 12. *Cilicia* was certainly a Province as early as B.C. 80. 13. *Bithynia*, in B.C. 74. 14. *Syria*, in B.C. 64, after the conquests of Pompeius. 15. *Creta* and *Cyrenaica*, in B.C. 63.

Of these fifteen provinces, seven were in the year B.C. 51, *Provinciae Consulares*, viz. the two Gauls and Illyricum, the two Spains, Cilicia and Bithynia, which now included Pontus. The remainder were *Provinciae Praetoriae*.

Laws with regard to the Provinces.—In addition to the laws which defined the constitution of each Province separately, general statutes were passed from time to time, which applied to all alike. Of these the most important were—

Lex Sempronia de Provinciis Consularibus, passed by C. Gracchus in B.C. 123, which enacted that, in each year, before the election of Consuls took place, the Senate should determine what two Provinces were to be assigned to the Consuls about to be chosen, and that the Consuls after their election should, by mutual agreement, or by lot, decide which of these two Provinces was to be assigned to each. Thus, we read in Sallust (Jug. 27)—*Lege Sempro ia Provinciae futuris Consulibus Numidia atque Italia decretae.* The obje of this law was to put a stop to the intrigues and corrupt practices by which Consuls elect were in the habit of endeavouring to influence the Senate to grant them those Provinces which were likely to be most agreeable or most profitable, without regard to the interests of the public service. [1]

Lex Cornelia de Provinciis ordinandis, passed by Sulla. The provisions of this law known to us were—

1. It limited the amount to be expended by provincial communities in sending embassies to Rome for the purpose of praising their governors.

2. It declared that those to whom Provinces had been assigned in terms of the *Lex Sempronia* should be allowed to retain their *Imperium* until they had entered the city. Thus we find Cicero retaining his Imperium for many months after he had quitted his Province and returned to Italy, in the hope of eing at length permitted to celebrate a triumph.

3. It ordered a provincial governor to quit the Province (*decedere*) within thirty days after the arrival of his successor. [2]

---

[1] Cic de Prov. Cons. 2. 3. pro Balb. 27. ad Fam. I. 7. Orat. pro dom. 9.
[2] Cic. ad fam. I. 9. III. 6. 8. 10.

Lex Iulia de Provinciis, passed by Julius Cæsar. In this, or in the *Lex Iulia de Repetundis*, it was enacted—

1. That a provincial governor, on quitting his Province, must make up three copies of his accounts, and deposit two copies in the Province, (*rationes confectas collatasque deponere*,) one in each of the two chief towns, the third to be deposited in the *Aerarium* at Rome (*rationes ad Aerarium referre*.) Thus, Cicero tells us that, in obedience to this law, he left copies of his accounts at Laodicea and Apamea—*lex iubebat, ut apud duas civitates, Laodicensem et Apameensem, quae nobis maximae videbantur, quoniam ita necesse erat, rationes confectas collatasque deponeremus.*

2. That, in the Praetorian Provinces, the governor should not remain beyond the space of one year, and in the Consular Provinces not beyond two years.

3. That no governor should be permitted to receive *Aurum Coronarium* from his Province, until after a triumph had been actually voted him by the Senate.

4. That it should not be lawful for a Proconsular governor to administer justice in a *Civitas Libera*.

By this, or some other *Lex Iulia*, the amount of accommodation and supplies to be afforded to Roman governors when journeying to their Provinces, by the towns and states through which they passed, was strictly specified.[1]

In B.C. 52 the Senate, in order to repress the corrupt practices which, notwithstanding the operation of the *Lex Sempronia*, still prevailed with regard to the distribution of the Provinces, passed a resolution, that no Consul or Praetor should be allowed to enter upon the government of a Province until five years had elapsed from the period when he had held office in the city; and that, in order to meet the demands of the public service in the meantime, all persons who had held the office of Consul or Praetor previous to the year B.C. 56, and had not yet acted as provincial governors, should be required to supply the vacancies. In this manner Cicero, much against his wishes, was compelled to leave Rome in B.C. 51, in order to act as Proconsul of Cilicia.[2]

The Provinces under the Empire.—Arrangements entirely new were introduced by Augustus. The whole of the Provinces were now divided into two classes—

1. *Provinciae Imperatoriae*, which were under the direct and sole control of the Emperor.

2. *Provinciae Senatoriae*, which were administered by the Senate.

The *Provinciae Imperatoriae* comprehended all the frontier Provinces which required the constant presence of large bodies of troops. These armies, and the Provinces in which they were quartered, were commanded by military officers, styled *Legati Caesaris* or *Legati Augusti*, who were named by the Emperor, he himself being commander-in-chief of all the armies of the state. The revenues of these Provinces were received by imperial agents, termed *Procuratores Caesaris*, and the proceeds were paid into the private exchequer (*Fiscus*) of the Prince. Some of the smaller imperial Provinces, or portions of the larger Provinces, such as Judaea, in which the presence of a *Legatus* was not held to be necessary, were ruled by a *Procurator* alone.

The *Provinciae Senatoriae* were those which, being in the enjoyment of long established peace, and removed to a distance from foreign foes, did not require

---

[1] Cic. de Prov. Cons. 4. in Pison. 16. 25. 37. ad fam. II. 17. V. 20. ad Att. V. 10, 16, 21. VI. 7. Philipp. I. 8. III. 15 V. 3. VIII. 9.
[2] Dion Cass. XL. 30, 46, 56.

THE PROVINCES. 193

any troops, except such as were employed for purposes of show or of police. These, as formerly, were governed by persons who had held the office of Consul or of Praetor; but all such governors were now, without distinction, styled *Proconsules*.[1] They were attended by Quaestors, who received the revenues and paid them into the public *Aerarium*, which was managed by the Senate. With the exception of military duties, the functions of the provincial Proconsuls under the empire were much the same as under the republic; they had the same external marks of honour, were attended by a numerous retinue of personal followers, and received equipments and allowances from the Senate. Their appointment was for one year, and was nominally regulated by the Senate; but if the Emperor thought fit to interfere, his wishes were never disputed.[2]

In addition to the ordinary imperial *Legati*, and the Senatorial *Proconsules*, the Emperor and the Senate conjointly sometimes granted, for a time, supreme power over a number of provinces to one individual. Thus, under Tiberius, the whole of the East was committed to Germanicus, and under Nero to Corbulo. With regard to the former Tacitus thus expresses himself—*Tum decreto Patrum permissae Germanico Provinciae quae mari dividuntur, maiusque imperium, quoquo adisset, quam iis qui sorte aut missu Principis obtinerent*[3]—where the word *sorte* indicates the Proconsuls.

All provincial governors under the empire are frequently included under the general title *Praesides Provinciarum;* but *Praeses* is more frequently employed with reference to the imperial governors, and eventually denoted an inferior class of officers. Many other terms, such as *Iuridici, Rectores, Correctores* were introduced at different times; but upon these we cannot enter here.

Changes occasionally took place in the distribution of the Provinces; but, according to the original division, the *Senatoriae* were twelve in number—

1. *Africa*.—2. *Asia*.—3. *Hispania Baetica*.—4. *Gallia Narbonensis.*—5. *Sicilia*.—6. *Sardinia*.—7. *Illyricum* and *Dalmatia*.—8. *Macedonia.*—9. *Achaia*.—10. *Creta et Cyrenaica*.—11. *Cyprus*.—12. *Bithynia et Pontus*.

The *Imperatoriae* were also twelve—

1. *Hispania Lusitanica*.—2. *Hispania Tarraconensis*.—3. *Gallia Luglunensis.*—4. *Gallia Belgica*.—5. *Noricum*.—6. *Pannonia*.—7. *Vindelicia et Rhaetia*.—8. *Moesia*.—9. *Alpes Maritimae*.—10. *Cilicia*.—11. *Galatia*. —12. *Syria*.

Illyricum and *Dalmatia* were soon transferred to the Emperor. Tiberius took *Achaia* and *Macedonia* from the Senate; but they were restored by Claudius.[4]

The following Provinces were subsequently added to the *Imperatoriae:*—*Germania Superior et Inferior*, on the left bank of the Rhine—*Cappadocia*—*Mauritania*—*Lycia*—*Cottiae Alpes*—*Britannia*—*Commagene*—*Thracia*—*Dacia*—*Armenia*—*Arabia*—*Mesopotamia*.

Italia was reckoned as a province from the time of Hadrian. The position of *Aegyptus* was altogether peculiar. From the period of its final subjugation it was regarded as a private estate of the Emperors, rather than as a part of the dominions of the Roman people. It was placed under the sway of a *Praefectus*, called frequently *Praefectus Augustalis*, who was nominated by the Emperor,

---
[1] Dion Cass. LII. 23. LIII. 13. Suet. Octav. 47. Tacit. Ann. XVI. 18.
[2] Dion Cass. LIII. 13. Suet. Octav. 47. Tacit. Ann. III. 32. 35.
[3] Tacit. Ann. II. 43. XV. 25. Velleius II. 93. So Augustus had upon two occasions, B.C. 23. and B.C. 16, invested Agrippa with supreme command over all the Eastern Provinces.
[4] Tacit. Ann. I. 76. Suet. Claud. 25. Dion Cass. LIII. 12. LX. 24.

and chosen from the Equestrian order. No Senator or Eques of the higher class was permitted to enter Egypt without receiving express permission from the Prince; and Tiberius sharply rebuked Germanicus for having ventured to visit Alexandria without leave. The cause of these jealous regulations is briefly explained by Tacitus—*Augustus inter alia dominationis arcana, vetitis nisi permissu ingredi Senatoribus aut Equitibus Romanis Illustribus, seposuit Ægyptum, ne fame urgeret Italiam quisquis eam Provinciam claustraque terrae ac maris, quamvis levi praesidio adversum ingentes exercitus, insedisset*—and in another passage—*Ægyptum copiasque, quibus coerceretur, iam inde a Divo Augusto, Equites Romani obtinent loco regum: ita visum expedire, Provinciam aditu difficilem, annonae fecundam, superstitione et lascivia discordem et mobilem, insciam legum, ignaram magistratuum, domi retinere.*[1]

Different applications of the term Proconsul under the Republic.— It may prevent confusion to bear in mind that the term *Proconsul* is uniformly employed to denote an individual who, although not actually holding the office of Consul, exercised in some particular locality all the powers of a Consul. We may distinguish four varieties of Proconsuls.

1. Occasionally a distinguished leader who was *Privatus*, i.e. out of office, but who, at some former period, had held the office of Consul, was specially appointed to perform some particular duty, and was *for that purpose* armed with the same powers which he would have wielded had he been actually Consul. Thus, T. Quinctius, who was Consul in B.C. 465, was hastily despatched from Rome in the course of the following year to relieve Sp. Furius, who was besieged in his camp by the Aequi, and, in so far as necessary for the accomplishment of that object, was armed with the powers of a Consul—*Optimum visum est* PRO CONSULE *T. Quinctium subsidia castris cum sociali exercitu mitti*—(Liv. III. 4,) and when the object was accomplished the power ceased. So also Pompeius, in B.C. 67, three years after his consulship, was invested by the *Lex Gabinia* with the title of *Proconsul*, and with very ample powers, in order that he might prosecute the war against the pirates (Velleius II. 31.)

2. It happened, in some very rare instances, that a private individual, who had never held the office of Consul, was sent forth upon a mission as a Proconsul. This came to pass in the case of the elder Scipio Africanus, who, in B.C. 211, was sent into Spain as Proconsul at the age of twenty-four; and again in the case of Pompeius, who, in B.C. 76, at the age of thirty-one, before he had held any of the great offices of state, was appointed Proconsul to conduct the war against Sertorius. See above, p. 182.

3. When a Consul, at the close of his year of office, had his Imperium prolonged, in order that he might be enabled to carry out some undertaking, (see above, p. 182,) he continued to command with the title Proconsul. The first example upon record is that of Q. Publilius Philo, B.C. 326, (Liv. VIII. 23— 26.) and the procedure subsequently became common.

4. Towards the close of the republic the Consuls usually remained in the city during their year of office, and after this had expired proceeded, as Proconsuls, to assume the government of a province.

It will be seen that the Proconsuls who belong to the three first heads were officers who received extraordinary appointments in consequence of a special decree of the Senate, or of a Rogation submitted to the people, while the

---

[1] Tacit. Ann. II. 59. XII. 60. Hist. I. 11. Comp. Liv. Epit. CXXXIII. Velleius. II. 39. Dion Cass. LI. 17. LIII. 12.

Proconsuls who belong to the fourth class were, for a considerable period, appointed as a matter of ordinary routine.[1]

A controversy has been maintained by grammarians, both ancient and modern, whether it is more correct to employ the form *Pro Consule* in two distinct words, or *Proconsul* declined as an ordinary noun, or whether each is in itself correct, but the signification different. It is sufficient here to remark, without entering into details, that if we consult inscriptions and the oldest MSS. we shall find both forms used indifferently by the best authors to convey the same idea, it being observed that *Pro Consule* can be employed only when the sentence is thrown into a particular shape.

Interchange of the terms Consul, Praetor, Proconsul, Propraetor.—A *Proconsul* is sometimes styled *Consul*, as in Liv. XXVI. 33. XXVIII. 39; but this may be merely an oversight or an inaccurate expression.

A *Proconsul* is sometimes styled *Praetor*, as in Cic. ad Att. V. 21. ad. Fam. II. 17. XIII. 15. In this case *Praetor* is probably employed in its general and ancient signification of *General* or *Commander* (see above, p. 133.)

On the other hand, a provincial governor is sometimes styled *Proconsul*, although he had never held any office higher than the Praetorship. Thus, C. Sempronius Tuditanus who was elected Praetor for B.C. 197, (Liv. XXXII. 27,) is soon afterwards spoken of (XXXIII. 25) as *C. Sempronium Tuditanum Proconsulem in Citeriore Hispania;* and in like manner, M. Fulvius, who was elected Praetor for B.C. 193, and received Hispania Ulterior as his province by lot, (Liv. XXXIV. 54. 55,) is called, the following year, *M. Fulvius Proconsul* (Liv. XXXV. 22.)[2] This apparent inconsistency is generally, if not always, to be explained by the fact that the Senate, when the condition of a Praetorian Province was such as to demand the influence and might of the highest power, were wont to invest the Praetor, who was about to take the command, with *Proconsulare Imperium*, thus entitling him, during the period of his government, to bear all the insignia and exercise all the authority of a Consul. Hence, Q Cicero (the brother of the orator) who, after having been Praetor, acted as governor of Asia, is styled indifferently *Propraetor* and *Proconsul*, the former denoting the office which he had actually held in Rome, the latter the dignity which he enjoyed, and the power which he possessed, in his province.[3]

INFERIOR MAGISTRATES UNDER THE REPUBLIC.

In addition to the great functionaries, whose duties we have described above, there were a considerable number of officials who performed tasks of an important, but less dignified character. These were comprehended under the general designation of *Minores Magistratus*;[4] but we must carefully distinguish this use of these words from the more extended application of the same phrase, as

---

[1] It will be gathered from what has been said above, that a Proconsul assumed the insignia of his office as soon as he quitted the city; but he could exercise no power, civil or military, except within the limits of his Province. He retained, however, both his *Imperium* and the outward symbols of his dignity until he re-entered the city. These rules applied to the Proconsuls of the empire as well as of the republic. The statements of Ulpian are distinct and precise—*Proconsul ubique quidem proconsularia insignia habet statim atque urbem egressus est: Potestatem autem non exercet, nisi in ea Provincia sola quae ei decreta est*—and again—*Proconsul portam Romae ingressus deponit Imperium*—Ulpian. Digest. I. xvi. 1. 16. comp. Cic. ad Att. VII. 1. 7. Liv. XLV. 35. Tacit. Ann. III. 19.

[2] For other examples see Cic. in Vatin. 5. (C. Cosconius,) pro Ligar. 1. (C. Considius,) ad fam. XII. 11. 12. XIII. 78. 79. (Cassius and Allienus.)

[3] Cic. ad Q. F. I. 1. de Divin. I. 28. Suet. Octav. 3. comp. Velleius II. 42. 69. Cic. Philipp. XI. 12.

[4] Cic. de legg. III. 3. Liv. XXXII. 26. XXXVI. 3. XXXIX. 14. Suet. Caes. 41.

explained above, p. 184. Of the *Minores Magistratus*, in the restricted sense, the most conspicuous were—

I. **Triumviri Capitales**, instituted, according to Livy, about B.C. 289. These may be regarded as police commissioners, subordinate to the Aediles. Among the tasks specially imposed upon them were, the charge of the gaols, and the execution of those criminals who were put to death in prison. They exercised jurisdiction, sometimes of a summary character, over slaves and peregrini; their tribunal being placed beside the Columna Maenia in the Forum (see above, p. 17.) They appear to have presided at preliminary investigations in cases of murder and other heinous offences against the person; they committed to prison those accused, and occasionally acted as public impeachers. They existed under the earlier emperors; and we hear of them in inscriptions as late as the third century. [1]

II. **Triumviri Nocturni** are generally believed to have been distinct from the TRIUMVIRI CAPITALES, and to have been specially charged with preserving the peace of the city by night, patrolling the streets, arresting those whom they found prowling about under suspicious circumstances, enforcing precautions against fire, and taking prompt measures for quenching conflagrations which might arise. There can be no doubt that this magistracy is distinctly mentioned by Livy at a period prior to that which he fixes for the institution of the *Triumviri Capitales;* but, on the other hand, the same historian, when giving an account of the panic which arose in consequence of the disclosures regarding the Bacchanalia, details certain duties imposed upon the *Triumviri Capitales*, which must have devolved upon the *Triumviri Nocturni* had they been separate officers—*Triumviris Capitalibus mandatum est, ut vigilias disponerent per urbem, servarentque ne qui nocturni coetus fierent: utque ab incendiis caveretur; adiutoresque Triumviris Quinqueviri uti cis Tiberim suae quisque regionis aedificiis praeessent.* Moreover, *Triumviri Nocturni* are not included in the list of *Minores Magistratus*, as they existed before Augustus, given by Dion Cassius, although he distinctly describes the *Triumviri Capitales*—οἵ τε τοῖς οἱ τὰς τοῦ θανάτου δίκας προστεταγμένοι. In very many cases where allusions are made to the subordinate police magistrates, they are spoken of simply as *Triumviri* or *Treviri*, without the addition of any epithet. [2]

III. **Quatuorviri Viis in Urbe Purgandis.**

IV. **Duumviri Viis extra Urbem Purgandis.**

These must have acted directly under the orders of the Aediles (see above, p. 157.) The former, as the name implies, being charged with cleansing the streets within the city, the latter those in the suburbs. [3]

V. **Decemviri Stlitibus Iudicandis.**—Pomponius asserts that this court was established after the institution of the office of *Praetor Peregrinus*, and at the same time with the *Triumviri Capitales*. Many antiquarians, however, believe that the board existed from a much earlier period, and that it is alluded to in the *Lex Valeria Horatia* passed immediately after the abdication of the *Decemviri Legibus Scribendis*, in B.C. 449—*Ut qui Tribunis Plebis Aedilibus*

---

[1] Liv. Epit. XI. XXV. 1. XXXII. 26. XXXIX. 14. 17. Cic. de legg. III. 3. in Q. C. Divin. 16. and note of Pseud. Ascon. pro Cluent. 13. Ascon. argument. in Milon. Varro. L.L. V. § 81. IX. § 85. Fest. s.v. *Sacramentum*, p. 344. Sallust Cat. 55. Tacit. Ann. V. 9. Agric. 2. Senec. Controv. III. 16 Val. Max. V. iv. 7. VI. i. 10. VIII. iv. 2. Spartian. Hadrian. 4. 15. 23. Aul. Gell. III. 3. Pompon. Digest. I. ii. 2. § 30. Plaut. Aul. III. ii. 2. Asin. I. ii. 5. Hor. Epod. IV. 11.

[2] Liv. IX. 46. Epit. XI. XXXIX. 14. comp. 17. Plaut. Amphit. I. i. 3. Val. Max. VIII. i. 6 6. Paul. Digest. I. xv. 1. Dion. Cass. LIV. 26.

[3] Tabul. Heracl. Pompon. Digest. I. ii. 2. § 30. Dion. Cass. LIV. 26.

Iudicibus Decemviris nocuisset eius caput Iovi sacrum esset: familia ad aedem Cereris Liberi Liberaeque venum iret—in which case they must have been Plebeian magistrates. They are noticed by Cicero, but not in such a manner as to define the nature or extent of their jurisdiction, and the words of Pomponius yield no satisfactory information—*Deinde quum esset necessarius magistratus qui Hastae praeesset Decemviri in litibus iudicandis sunt constituti*. By Augustus they were placed at the head of the *Centumviri*, who will be mentioned more particularly when we treat of the administration of justice; but they still existed as a separate and independent body down to the end of the fifth century.[1]

VI. **Triumviri Monetales**—Commissioners of the mint, to whom the charge of coining money was committed. The names of individuals holding this office appear frequently upon coins struck very near the close of the commonwealth, with the addition of the letters A. A. A. F. F. denoting *Auro Argento Aeri Flando Feriundo*. Pomponius states that they were instituted at the same period with the *Triumviri Capitales;* (B.C. 289;) but if this be the case they could not have been, as he says they were, *aeris argenti auri flatores*, for silver was not coined, according to Pliny, until B.C. 269, and gold not until a much later epoch. They are alluded to by Cicero (Ad. Fam. VII. 13) in a complicated joke, when warning his friend Trebatius against encountering the warlike nation of the Treviri in Gaul—*Treviros vites censeo, audio Capitales esse, mallem auro, aere, argento essent*. The number of these officers was increased by Julius Cæsar to four, as appears from coins struck while he held sway; but it was again reduced to three by Augustus (Suet. Caes. 41. Dion Cass. LV. 26. Pompon. Digest. I. ii. 2. § 30. Plin. H.N. XXXIII. 39.)[2]

In addition to the above, who seem to have been elected regularly every year in the Comitia Tributa, commissioners were, from time to time, nominated for the performance of special temporary duties, and all of these would, for the time being, be ranked as *Minores Magistratus*. Such were the commissioners appointed for distributing public lands, (*agris dividundis,*) for planting colonies, (*coloniis deducendis,*) for erecting, dedicating or repairing temples, (*aedibus faciundis—dedicandis—reficiendis,*) for relieving some extraordinary pressure in the money market, (*Triumviri s. Quinqueviri Mensarii,*) and many others, the nature of whose offices are sufficiently explained by the epithets employed, and by the narratives of the historians by whom they are mentioned.

Augustus formed a sort of corps or board of the Minor Magistrates, which he termed the *Vigintiviratus*, comprehending the *III Viri Capitales*, the *III Viri Monetales*, the *IV Viri Viis in Urbe purgandis*, and the *X Viri Stlitibus iudicandis*. The members were selected exclusively from those possessed of the *Census Equester*, and admission to the body was regarded as the first step towards public distinction. Hence Ovid tells us—

> Cepimus et tenerae primos aetatis honores
> Eque *viris* quondam pars *tribus* una fui.[3]

PUBLIC SERVANTS OF THE MAGISTRATES.

I. **Scribae.**—The most important were the *Scribae* s. *Scribae librarii*,[4] the

---

[1] Pompon. Digest. I. ii. 2. § 29. Cic. Orat. 46. de legg. III. 3. pro Caecin. 33. Orat. pro dom. 29. Varro L.L. IX. § 85. Suet. Octav. 36. Dion Cass. LIV. 26. Sidon. Apollin. Epp. I. 7. II. 7.
[2] For full information on the *Triumviri Monetales* see Eckhel, *Doctrina Numorum Veterum*, Tom. V. Cap. iv. p. 61.
[3] Dion Cass. LIV. 26. Ovid. Trist. IV. x. 33.
[4] Varro R. R. III. 2. Tabul. Heracl. But Frontinus de Aquaed. 100. seems to draw a distinction between *Scribae* and *Scribae Librarii*. comp. Cic. de leg. agr. II. 13.

government clerks, a certain number of whom were attached to the Senate, and to all the different departments of the public service. Their duty was to take down and record the proceedings of the public bodies, to transcribe state papers of every description, to keep the books and accounts (*rationes perscribere—conficere*) connected with the different offices, to supply the magistrates with the written forms required in transacting public business, to read over public documents in the Senate, in the courts of justice, and in the assemblies of the people, and to perform a great variety of services of a similar description. When we recollect that the principal magistrates remained in power for one year only, and that many of them entered upon office without any experience or previous knowledge of business, it is manifest that they must have depended entirely upon their subordinate assistants, who, being engaged permanently in the performance of the same tasks, would be able to inform and guide their superiors. Aid of this description would especially be necessary in the case of the Quaestorship, which was the first step in the ascent to political power, but which must, at the same time, have demanded an extensive and accurate knowledge of a multitude of minute details connected with the finances of the republic. This knowledge must have been supplied by the *Scribae ab aerario*, the chief of whom were designated *Sexprimi*.

The *Scribae* were so numerous that they are spoken of as forming a separate class in the state—*Ordo Scribarum*—and were regarded as occupying a humble but highly respectable position in the community.

II. **Lictores.**—We have already had occasion to describe the Lictors, as the attendants of the Kings, Consuls, Praetors, and Dictators. They executed the orders of the magistrate especially where force was required, cleared the way before him, and dispersed a crowd when it impeded public business (*summovere turbam*.) When any one failed to pay proper respect to a dignified functionary, he ordered his Lictor *to mark* the offender, (*animadvertere*,) and hence *animadvertere* frequently denotes to *censure* or *punish*.

III. **Accensi** were messengers or orderlies, one of whom always attended upon the higher magistrates to convey messages or commands. We hear of them in connection with Consuls, Proconsuls, Praetors, and the Decemvirs.

IV. **Viatores** were also attendants upon the magistrates, and executed their orders. They are most frequently mentioned in connection with the Tribunes of the Plebs; but we find them employed also by the Senate, by Dictators, and by Consuls. When the territory of Rome extended but a short distance beyond the walls, *Viatores* were sent round the rural districts to give notice to those residing in the country of meetings of the Senate and of the Comitia. [1]

V. **Praecones**—criers, were employed on all occasions when it was necessary to make public proclamation verbally of any matter. They also acted as auctioneers, both for public and private property.

All the above were included under the general appellation of *Apparitores*, (that is, persons *qui apparent s. parent magistratibus*,) a term which may be applied to the public servants belonging to any one class or to the whole collectively. [2] It must be understood that the *Apparitores* were all free men; many of them *Ingenui*, a larger number, especially under the empire, *Libertini*, [3] and as such were completely distinct from the numerous body of *Servi Publici*, who were

---

[1] Liv. VI. 15. VIII. 18. XXII. 11. Plin. H. N. XVIII. 3. Aul. Gell. IV. 10. XIII. 12.
[2] Cic. in Verr. III. 66. de leg. agr. II. 13. Frontin. de Aquaed. 79.
[3] Liv. II. 55. Cic. pro Quinct. 3. Val. Max. IX. i. 8. Tacit. Ann. XIII. 27.

employed in inferior capacities. The *Apparitores* were ranked together in *Decuriae*, each *Decuria* apparently comprehending those who were connected with one particular department and class of duties, so that the body from whom the Lictors of the Consuls were taken formed the *Decuria Consularis*, the Scribes attached to the Quaestors formed the *Decuria Quaestoria*, and so, in like manner, we hear of *Scribae Aedilitii, Tribunicii Viatores*, &c.

They received payment for their services,[1] and kept their places for an indefinite period, two circumstances which at once distinguished them from Magistrates, properly so called, even of the humblest grade. In whom the appointment of these persons was vested, and according to what tenure they held their situations, are points on which we do not possess satisfactory information. Occasionally, at least, the Scribae certainly purchased their posts, and hence the expressions—*emere decuriam*—*scriptum quaestorium comparare*—*decuriam quaestoriam comparare*; and the choice in some cases lay with the Quaestors (hence *Scribam legere*.)[2]

An *Accensus* seems to have been nominated for the time being by the magistrate to whom he was attached, and to have been usually one of his own freedmen.[3]

NEW MAGISTRATES UNDER THE EMPIRE.

We have seen that all the ordinary magistrates of the republic continued to exist in name at least for nearly three centuries after the overthrow of the free constitution, many of them much longer; that they were ostensibly chosen by the Comitia, and that, as in ancient times, they retained office for one year only. They were, however, gradually deprived of all their most important functions, at least of all which conferred any real influence. Most of these were concentrated in the person of the Emperor; but it became necessary for him to possess organs of the high and varied powers with which he was invested, and consequently several new offices were instituted. The most important of these we shall notice very briefly, premising that the new magistrates differed in at least three essential points from the magistrates of the commonwealth—

1. They were nominated directly by the Emperor, without reference to the wishes of the Senate or the people.

2. No limit was fixed to the period during which they held office. This depended entirely upon the Emperor, who could dismiss them at pleasure.

3. They possessed no independent authority. All their acts were subject to the revision and sanction of the Emperor, who could confirm, reverse, or modify their decisions as he thought fit. They were, in fact, merely the ministers of his will.

PRAEFECTUS URBI.

Origin of the Office.—The Imperial *Praefectus Urbi* had little in common, except the name, with the republican magistrate who bore the same title. When Augustus was compelled to quit Rome in B.C. 36, in order to prosecute the war against Sextus Pompeius in Sicily, he placed the City and all Italy under the control of Maecenas, and again, in B.C. 31, he again imposed the same charge upon Maecenas in conjunction with Agrippa. In B.C. 25 he established the

---

[1] Cic. in Verr. III. 78. Frontin. de Aquaed. 79.
[2] Cic. in Verr. III. 79. Sueton. Vit. Horat. Schol. Juv. S. V. 3. Liv. XL. 29. Cic. pro Cluent. 45.
[3] Cic. in Verr. III. 67. ad Att. IV 16. ad Q. F. I. 1.

Praefectura Urbana as a permanent office, to be held by *Consulares* only, and bestowed it upon Messala Corvinus, who resigned in a few days, pleading that he felt unfit for the task; he was succeeded by Agrippa, Agrippa by Statilius Taurus, and Taurus by L. Piso, who discharged his duties for twenty years with great reputation, and died in A.D. 32. From that time forward there was a regular succession; and after the removal of the chief seat of government to Constantinople, there was a Praefectus Urbi for each of the capitals.[1] The original duty of the *Praefectus Urbi* was to maintain peace and good order, and remedy the social disorders produced by long protracted civil wars—Augustus . . . . . . *rerum potitus, ob magnitudinem populi ac tarda legum auxilia sumsit e consularibus qui coerceret servitia et quod civium audacia turbidum nisi vim metuat* (Tacit. l.c.) For this purpose he was armed with ample powers for the suppression and punishment of all offences which threatened public tranquillity, his jurisdiction extending not only over the city, but to the distance of a hundred miles beyond the walls. By degrees he became the supreme judge in all causes criminal as well as civil, except such as were reserved by the Prince for the special consideration of the Senate, and, with the assistance of a board of assessors, (*consilium*,) decided all appeals sent up from the inferior courts in Rome, Italy, and the Provinces. He also engrossed much of the power formerly committed to the Praetors and Aediles, and, as a matter of course, all the police magistrates of every grade were bound to obey his commands. Ulpian and Paulus, who flourished in the early part of the third century, each wrote a treatise *De Officio Praefecti Urbi*. These are quoted in the Digest, (I. xii. 1. 2,) from which, and from other compilations of Roman law, much information concerning the varied and constantly increasing duties of the office may be derived.

The *Praefectus Urbi*, moreover, wielded not only civil, but also military power; for he was, in virtue of his office, the commander of the *Urbanae Cohortes*, a sort of militia or national guard, divided into five battalions, of which we shall speak more at large in the section on military affairs.

PRAEFECTUS PRAETORIO.

The *Praefectus Praetorio*, the general of the imperial life guards, although discharging duties of a more simple character, was, in real power and influence, superior even to the *Praefectus Urbi*, since the succession to the throne was, in many cases, decided by the troops under his immediate command. Of this officer, and of the corps of which he was the head, we shall say more in the section on military affairs.

PRAEFECTUS VIGILUM.

Augustus organized seven battalions, consisting chiefly of *Libertini*, under the name of *Cohortes Vigilum*, who watched the city by night, one cohort being assigned to every two of the *XIV Regiones*. The whole were under the command of a *Praefectus Vigilum*, chosen from the Equites, who was himself subordinate to the *Praefectus Urbi*.[2]

PRAEFECTUS ANNONAE S. REI FRUMENTARIAE.

As early as B.C. 440 we find a commissioner appointed under the title of

---

[1] Dion Cass. XLIX. 16. LI. 3. LII. 21. LIV. 6. 19. Tacit. Ann. VI. 11. XIV. 41 Velleius II. 88. 127. Suet. Oct. 33. 37. Hieron. Chron. Euseb.
[2] Suet. Octav. 25. 30. Dion Cass. LIV. 4.

Praefectus Annonae to procure provisions for the city during a period of scarcity. Towards the close of the republic, when Rome was almost entirely dependent upon foreign countries for corn, the importance of securing a steady supply and regulating the price must have forced itself upon the attention of all connected with the government. In B.C. 57 a law was passed by which Pompeius was intrusted with the charge for five years—*Legem Consules conscripserunt qua Pompeio per quinquennium omnis potestas rei frumentariae toto orbe daretur;* but no permanent magistracy was established for this purpose until Augustus, having himself undertaken the task—*curam . . . frumenti populo dividundi*—ordained that for the future two *Praetorii* should be appointed annually to distribute corn to the people, and this number he subsequently increased to four. Eventually he confided the trust to two Consulars, and, in addition to these, nominated an Inspector-general of the corn market, who, under the ancient appellation of *Praefectus Annonae*, held office without limitation as to time, was chosen from the Equestrian order, and was regarded as occupying a very dignified position. The office continued to exist until the downfal of the empire, but latterly was held in little esteem.[1]

NEW INFERIOR MAGISTRATES UNDER THE EMPIRE.

Curatores Viarum.—To these Augustus committed the charge of inspecting and keeping in repair the military roads, (see above, p. 52,) each great line being intrusted to a separate individual, so that we read of *Curator Viae Appiae, Curator Viae Flaminiae, Curator Viae Valeriae,* and so on. Although the office did not confer any direct political power, it was regarded as very honourable, and was bestowed on those only who had been Consuls or Praetors. Besides the *Curatores Viarum,* there was one or more *Curatores Operum publicorum,* a *Curator Aquarum,* who took charge of the aqueducts, *Curatores Alvei et Riparum Tiberis et Cloacarum Urbis,* i.e. sewer commissioners, and many others.[2]

Magistri Vicorum.—These existed under the republic, and are spoken of by Livy as holding the lowest place (*infimum genus*) among magistrates. When Augustus divided the city into *XIV Regiones* and *CCLXV Vici,* he placed the former under the general superintendence of the Praetors, Aediles, and Tribunes of the Plebs, the latter were committed to local *Magistri,* chosen from the humbler portion of the population; (*Magistri e Plebe cuiusque viciniae lecti;*) but they occupied a higher position than formerly, for they now took charge of the fire police, of the celebration of district rites, and on certain state occasions were permitted to wear the *Toga Praetexta,* and to be attended by two Lictors.[3]

Curatores Urbis. s. Curatores Regionum.—The fourteen Augustan regions were placed by Alexander Severus under the charge of *XIV Curatores,* chosen *ex consularibus viris,* who were conjoined with the *Praefectus Urbi,* to whom before this time, the general superintendence, formerly intrusted to the Praetors, Aediles, and Tribunes of the Plebs, had been transferred.[4]

---

[1] Liv. IV. 12. Epit. CIV. Cic. ad Att. IV. 1. Tacit. Ann. I. 7. XL 31. Hist. IV. 68. Plin. Panegyr. 29. Suet. Octav. 37. Dion Cass. XXXIX. 9. LII. 24. LIV. 1. 17. LV. 26. 31. Boeth. Consol. 3.
[2] Suet. Octav. 37. Lips. ad. Ann. III. 31. Tacit. Ann. I. 77. 79. Dion Cass. LVII. 14. Frontin. de Aquaed. Urb. Rom. 95. seqq.
[3] Liv. XXXIV. 7. Suet. Octav. 30. Dion Cass. LV. 8.
[4] Lamprid. Al. Sev. 33. comp. Capitolin. M. Aur. 11.

THE EMPERORS.

It does not fall within the limits or province of this work to investigate the causes which led to the downfal of the republic, nor to enumerate the various processes by which the free constitution was converted into a military despotism, nor to enlarge upon the skill displayed by Augustus in organizing the new order of things and in providing for the stability of the monarchy. It is enough for our present purpose to point out that under his sway the whole might of the government was concentrated in his own person, while the Comitia, the Senate, and the Magistrates, although retaining their ancient names and apparently discharging their ancient functions according to ancient forms, were, in reality, mere machines, whose every movement was regulated and guided by his will. The successors of Augustus did not deem it necessary to adhere so closely to all the details of the commonwealth; but it may be gathered from what has been said in the preceding pages, that although the vital workings of the free constitution were completely paralysed, few of the institutions themselves were formally abrogated until the whole system was remodelled by Constantine.

The powers wielded by the Emperors were all such as had been exercised by the legitimate authorities under the republic, although never before combined and concentrated in one individual, and these powers, which were understood to be received from the Senate, were expressed by a series of titles, which we shall proceed to examine in succession. It is true that Augustus might have effected his purpose completely had he, following the example of Sulla and of Caesar, accepted the name and office of *Dictator Perpetuus;* but the name and office of Dictator had been formally abolished by law upon the death of Julius, (see above, p. 149,) and even had this been disregarded, the very idea of a *perpetual* Dictator was a monstrous violation of the fundamental principles of the magistracy. True, therefore, to his determination of avoiding every thing which might give a rude shock to public feeling by being glaringly irregular and offensive, he steadily refused to assume any name or exercise any power for which a precedent could not be found in the ordinary usages of the commonwealth. We begin with the most important of the titles indicated above, that which has ever since been employed by many nations of Europe to denote the highest grade of sovereignty.

Imperator.—There can be no doubt that the title *Imperator* properly signifies one invested with *Imperium*, and it may very probably have been assumed in ancient times by every general on whom *Imperium* had been bestowed by a *Lex Curiata*. It is, however, equally certain, that in those periods of the republic with the history and usages of which we are most familiar, the title *Imperator* was *not* assumed as a matter of course by those who had received *Imperium*, but was, on the contrary, a much valued and eagerly coveted distinction. Properly speaking, it seems to have been in the gift of the soldiers, who hailed their victorious leader by this appellation on the field of battle; but occasionally, especially towards the end of the commonwealth, it was conferred by a vote of the Senate. One of the earliest allusions to the former practice is to be found in the words ascribed by Livy (XXVII. 19) to Africanus when the Spaniards were desirous of styling him king—*Sibi maximum nomen* IMPERATORIS *esse dixit, quo se milites sui appellassent;* but the best and most explicit testimony upon this point is to be found in Tacitus (Annal. III. 74)—*Id quoque Blaeso tribuit, ut* IMPERATOR *a legionibus salutaretur, prisco erga duces honore, qui, bene gesta republica, gaudio et impetu victoris exercitus conclamabantur, erantque plures simul Imperatores, nec super ceterorum aequalitatem.* The latter practice is stated with equal clearness by Cicero in many passages, e.g. (Philipp

XIV. 4)—*At si quis Hispanorum aut Gallorum aut Thracum mille aut duo millia occidisset; non eum, hac consuetudine quae increbuit,* IMPERATOREM *appellaret Senatus.*

It is manifest that an honour of this kind might be bestowed more than once upon the same individual, and thus, on some of the coins of Sulla we read IMPER. ITERUM, on those of Pompeius M. simply IMP., on those of Cæsar and of Sext. Pompeius IMP. ITER., on those of Antonius IIIVIR. IMP. IIII. After the power of Augustus was fully established, the title was very sparingly bestowed on personages not imperial. We find that it was granted to Tiberius before his adoption, and to his brother Drusus, but apparently not to Agrippa. The last private individual who enjoyed it was Blaesus, on whom it was conferred by Tiberius after the defeat of Tacfarinas.

Augustus and his successors constantly assumed this title, and inscribed it upon their coins, with the figures I. II. . . . V. VI. . . . added according to circumstances, it being understood, it would appear, although the rule was not strictly adhered to, that it could be bestowed once only in the same war. The last Emperor who inscribed it on his medals was Caracalla, if we except IMP. V. and IMP. X. on coins of Postumus. It occurs occasionally, but rarely, in inscriptions, after the age of Caracalla. We must observe that *Imperator*, when used in this sense, was always placed *after* the name of the individual who bore it.

But the designation *Imperator* was employed under the empire in a manner and with a force altogether distinct from that which we have been considering. On this point we have the distinct testimony of Dion Cassius, (XLIII. 44. comp. LIII. 17,) who tells us that, in B.C. 46, the Senate bestowed upon Julius Cæsar the title of *Imperator*, not in the sense in which it had hitherto been applied, as a term of military distinction, but as *the peculiar and befitting appellation of supreme power*, and in this signification it was transmitted to his successors, without, however, suppressing the original import of the word. Again, the same Dion (LII. 41) informs us that Octavius, in B.C. 29, received the name of *Imperator*, not in the ancient sense in which it was bestowed after a victory, but *to point out that he was invested with the supreme power*. See also (LIII. 17.) Suetonius, in like manner, among the excessive honours heaped upon Julius Cæsar, reckons the *Praenomen Imperatoris*.

This last expression is valuable, because it points out the fact which we learn from medals, that *Imperator*, when used to denote supreme power, comprehending in fact the force of the titles *Dictator* and *Rex*, is usually, although not invariably, placed before the name of the individual to whom it is applied. Thus we constantly read such legends IMP. CAES. VESPASIAN.—IMP. NERVA CAES.; and upon a denarius of the *Gens Pinaria* we find IMP. CAESARI. SCARPUS IMP. where the first IMP. is applied to Augustus in his capacity of supreme ruler, the second to Scarpus as a victorious general.

Not unfrequently, however, *Imperator* in this sense is used as a cognomen; thus, we find generally on the coins of Nero, NERO CÆSAR AUG. IMP., more rarely IMP. NERO CÆSAR, and on the coins of Vitellius we find invariably A. VITELLIUS GERMANICUS IMP.; but it may be fairly questioned, when IMP. occurs in this position, whether it is not intended as the military title, the more ambitious appellation being suppressed. Whenever a number is added this is unquestionably the case, as when we read on the obverse of a medal CÆSAR VESPASIANUS AUG. and on the reverse IMP. XIII.

Not unfrequently both titles occur on the same coin, one on the obverse, the other on the reverse, as IMP. TITUS. CAES. VESPASIAN. AUG. and on the reverse

IMP. XV., so in like manner IMP. NERVA CAES. AUG. and on the reverse IMP. II.

Tribunicia Potestas.—Among the many honours conferred upon Julius Cæsar after the battle of Pharsalia, the Senate voted that he should possess for life the powers of a Tribune of the Plebs; and on the 27th of June B.C. 23, a similar vote was passed in favour of Augustus, and renewed regularly on the accession of each succeeding Emperor.[1] In virtue of this the person of the Prince was at all times sacred and inviolable; he could summon meetings of the Senate, and could at once put a stop, by intercession, to any procedure on the part of a magistrate or public assembly which might be contrary to his wishes. The *Tribunitia Potestas* of the Emperor, however, differed materially in many respects from the power wielded by the Tribunes of the Plebs under the republic, and was in every respect superior.

1. Neither Augustus nor any of his successors ever assumed the name of *Tribunus Plebis*, but the attribute *Tribunitia Potestas*. Indeed, all the Emperors were either by birth Patricians, or were, immediately upon their elevation, adopted into a Patrician Gens, so that they could not have become *Tribuni Plebis* without violating one of the fundamental principles of the office.[2]

2. The *Tribuni Plebis*, from the institution of the magistracy, entered upon office on the 10th of December, and remained in office for one year only. The *Tribunitia Potestas* of the Emperors commenced on no fixed day and continued for life.

3. The *Tribuni Plebis* were not allowed to absent themselves from the city even for a single night, except during the *Feriae Latinae*, and their jurisdiction extended to a mile only from the walls. Those invested with *Tribunitia Potestas* might absent themselves from the city or from Italy for any length of time without forfeiting their privileges, and their jurisdiction extended over the whole circuit of the Roman dominions (e.g. Suet. Tib. 11.)

It must be borne in mind also that while the Emperors were invested with *Tribunitia Potestas*, the ordinary *Tribuni Plebis* continued to be chosen for centuries, (see above, p. 145,) although their influence was merely nominal.

It was not unusual for the Emperors to permit those with whom they were closely connected, especially their children or the individual selected to be their successor, to participate in the *Tribunitia Potestas*. Thus, Augustus bestowed it for five years on Agrippa, and prolonged it for an additional five years; for five years on Tiberius, but when the period had expired it was not immediately renewed; after the death of his grandson, however, it was again given to Tiberius for ten years, and subsequently continued. Tiberius bestowed it on his son Drusus, Vespasian on Titus, Nerva on Trajan, Hadrian on Aelius, and subsequently on Antoninus. It is unnecessary to multiply examples.[3]

The *Tribunitia Potestas* was considered to be in the gift of the Senate, by whom it was regularly conferred on each new occupant of the throne, and when the Emperor desired that it should be bestowed on another, he always made a special request to that effect. So completely was this form established, that Dion Cassius keenly censures Eagabalus as guilty of indecent haste, because he assumed the title without waiting for the resolution of the Senate.[4]

Consul.—We have already spoken of the Consulship under the empire, (see above, p. 138,) and of the manner in which the Emperors assumed it at pleasure.

---

[1] Dion Cass. XLII. 20. LIII 32. comp. LI. 19. and Oros. VI. 18. Tacit. Ann. I. 2. 7. III. 56.
[2] Dion Cass. LIII. 17. 32 Spartian. Did. Julian. 3.
[3] See Dion Cass. LIV. 12. 28. Tacit. Ann. III. 56.
[4] Tacit. l.c. Dion Cass. LXXIX. 2.

The name implied no powers which they could not exercise as *Imperatores* or in virtue of the *Tribunitia Potestas*, and therefore it was not thought necessary to include it among the permanent titles of the supreme ruler. Dion Cassius indeed, asserts (LIV. 10) that Augustus received the *Consularis Potestas* for life, (τὴν ἐξουσίαν τὴν τῶν ὑπάτων διὰ βίου ἔλαβεν,) but this seems to refer rather to the dignity which he enjoyed, and the right of being attended by twelve Lictors than to any actual title.

Censor.—We have stated above (p. 171) that after B.C. 22 the office became virtually extinct. Claudius, however, Vespasian with Titus for his colleague, Domitian, and Nerva, each received the title; but other Emperors were content with exercising the *Censoria Potestas* under the designation of *Praefecti Morum*, (although Trajan refused even this appellation,) or styled themselves *Censores* merely while actually engaged in performing the duties of the Registration.[1] Thus, we are told of Augustus—*Recepit et morum legumque regimen aeque perpetuum: quo iure quamquam sine Censurae honore Censum tamen populi ter egit, primum ac tertium cum collega, medium solus* (Suet. Oct. 27)—and on the Monumentum Ancyranum we read—*Senatum ter legi.*

Proconsul. Proconsulare Imperium.—Although the title of *Proconsul* does not (with one or two very dubious exceptions) appear upon the medals of the Emperors until the time of Diocletian, it is certain, from historical records and other monuments, that they were regularly invested with *Proconsulare Imperium.*

Dion Cassius relates (LIII. 32) that among other honours conferred upon Augustus, in B.C. 23, it was decreed that he should possess the *Proconsulare Imperium* for ever, (ἡ γερουσία ἔδωκεν αὐτῷ τὴν ἀρχὴν τὴν ἀνθύπατον ἐσαεὶ καθάπαξ ἔχειν,) that it should not cease when he entered the Pomoerium, that it should not be necessary to renew it, and that, in each Province, this *Imperium* should be considered superior to that of the actual governors of the Provinces. Moreover, we are told by Capitolinus (Vit. Anton. Pii.) that Antoninus Pius, after his adoption by Hadrian—*factus est in Imperio Proconsulari et in Tribunitia Potestate conlega;* and there can be no doubt, although the fact is not specified in every particular case, that each Emperor, on his accession, was invested with the *Proconsulare Imperium* on the same terms as when it was originally bestowed on Augustus.

With regard to the object gained by this appellation it may be observed, that although the title *Imperator*, when used as a Praenomen, gave to the possessor supreme command over all the armies of the state, and hence absolute power both at home and abroad, both within and without the city, yet since there were certain Provinces nominally under the control of the Senate, whose governors, termed Proconsuls, were appointed by the Senate, and whose revenues were paid into the public Exchequer administered by the Senate, it was considered expedient to bestow upon the Prince a title implying powers which should place beyond all doubt or question his authority over the ordinary magistrates of the Senatorial Provinces, as well as over the officers of the Imperial Provinces. This *Proconsulare Imperium* of the Emperors differed from the powers granted to ordinary and extraordinary Proconsuls under the republic (see above, p. 194) in several important points—

1. It was universal, extending, without restriction, over every part of the empire.

[1] Dion Cass. LIII. 17. 18. LIV. 10. 16. 30. Suet. Oct. 27. 38. 39. Cal. 16. Claud. 16. Vesp. 8. 6. Tit. 6. Dom. 18 Tacit. Ann. II. 33. 48. IV. 42. XI. 13. 25. XII. 4. 52. Hist. L 9.

2. It was not for a limited period, but perpetual, requiring no renewal.

3. It was in force as well within as without the *Pomoerium*. This last condition is, in fact, comprehended in the first, but it deserves to be particularly noticed, because we find that the Emperors occasionally permitted others to exercise the *Proconsulare Imperium* without the walls; thus, at the request of Claudius—*Senatus libens cessit, ut vicesimo aetatis anno consulatum Nero iniret, atque interim designatus Proconsulare Imperium extra urbem haberet;* (Tacit. Ann. XII. 41:) and, in like manner, Marcus Aurelius, by the desire of Antoninus—*Tribunitia Potestate donatus est, Imperio extra urbem Proconsulari addito* (Capitolin. Vit. M. Aur. 6.)

Pontifex Maximus.—Since we shall be called upon, when treating of the religion of the Romans, to describe in detail the position occupied and the duties performed by this priest, it will be sufficient at present to state, in general terms, that he was regarded as the chief personage in the whole ecclesiastical establishment, and as such, exercised a general superintendence over all things sacred. The office was for life; and Lepidus having been chosen after the death of Caesar, continued to retain it after he had been stripped, in B.C. 36, of all political power and banished to Circeii. Upon his death, however, in B.C. 13, Augustus in the following year agreed to accept this dignity, which ever after was regularly conferred upon each new Emperor by a vote of the Senate. Although many of the Emperors, during the first two centuries, granted the *Tribunitia Potestas*, and the titles of *Imperator, Augustus* and *Caesar*, to those whom they associated with themselves in the administration of public affairs, it was held that under no circumstances could there be more than one *Pontifex Maximus*, and this principle was never violated until Balbinus and Pupienus were named joint Emperors by the Senate, (A.D. 237.) when both assumed the title. From this time forward no attention was paid to the ancient rule, but whenever the Prince assumed a colleague he permitted him to be styled *Pontifex Maximus* as well as Augustus. Of this we have examples in the younger Philip, in Volusian, in Carinus, and in many others, as may be seen from their medals, and in a proclamation of Galerius Maximianus, preserved by Eusebius (H. E. VIII. 8.) Maximianus himself, Constantinus and Licinius are all designated *Pontifices Maximi*.

In order to secure a complete control over all matters connected with religion, the Emperors, not content with the office of *Pontifex Maximus*, became members of all the four great corporations of priests, which will be enumerated in chapter X. Of this fact we are positively assured by Dion Cassius, (LIII. 17.) and his assertion is confirmed by an inscription, in which Tiberius is styled PONTIF. MAX. AUGURI. XVVIRO. S. F. VIIVIRO. EPULON.; and Nero, after his adoption

by Claudius, was, by a decree of the Senate, admitted a supernumerary member of all the four colleges, as appears from the coin of which we annex a cut, which represents upon the obverse a youthful head of Nero, with the legend NERO CLAUD. CAES. DRUSUS. GERM. PRIN. IUV. and on the reverse various sacerdotal instruments with the legend SACERD. COOPT. IN. OMN. CONL. SUPRA. NUM. EX. S. C.

Augustus.—When Octavianus had firmly established his power, and was now left without a rival, the Senate, being desirous of distinguishing him by some peculiar and emphatic title, decreed, in B.C. 27, that he should be styled

THE EMPERORS AND THEIR TITLES.

Augustus, an epithet properly applicable to some object demanding respect and veneration beyond what is bestowed upon human things—

> *Sancta* vocant AUGUSTA *patres*, AUGUSTA *vocantur*
> *Templa, sacerdotum rite dicata manu.*

This being an honorary appellation, analogous to the epithets *Torquatus*, *Felix*, *Magnus*, *Pius*, &c. bestowed upon Valerius, Sulla, Pompeius, and Metellus, it would, as a matter of course, have been transmitted by inheritance to his immediate descendants. Hence it was at once assumed after his decease by Tiberius, his adopted son; and Livia, having been adopted by the will of her husband, took the names of *Iulia* and *Augusta*.

In like manner, it was rightfully assumed by Caligula, he being the adopted grandson of Tiberius; nor did he altogether depart from the idea that it was a title appertaining exclusively to the Julian line when he bestowed it upon his grandmother Antonia, for she was the daughter of Octavia, who was the grand-niece of Julius Caesar. Claudius, who was the son of the same Antonia, and Nero, who was her great-grandson, both assumed the title of *Augustus* on their accession; but although the Julian dynasty became extinct upon the death of the latter, their example was followed by all succeeding rulers, (Vitellius alone having for a while hesitated,) who communicated the title of *Augusta* to their consorts, and this was carried so far that Domitilla, the wife of Vespasian, is styled *Augusta* on medals, although she died while her husband was still a subject.

The title of *Augustus* was sometimes bestowed by the Emperor upon a second person, who was thenceforward regarded as a colleague in the empire, although still inferior to the individual who bestowed it. Thus, M. Aurelius shared the distinction first with his adopted brother, L. Verus, and then with his son, Commodus. So also Septimius Severus associated with himself, first his eldest son Caracalla and subsequently his younger son Geta also, so that towards the close of his reign there were three *Augusti*. In these and similar cases the *Augusti* did not really possess the same authority; but the peculiar circumstances under which Balbinus and Pupienus were elevated to the throne, placed them upon an absolute equality. The system introduced by Diocletian was a complete departure, both in theory and practice, from the former constitution; for he established several *Augusti* and several *Caesares*, who were entirely unconnected with each other by ties of relationship.

Caesar.—Caesar was originally a cognomen belonging to the *Gens Iulia*, it was assumed by Octavianus after his adoption by Julius Caesar, was transmitted, in like manner, by Octavianus to his three grandsons, Caius, Lucius and Agrippa, and to his step-son and son-in-law Tiberius. By the latter it was communicated to his son Drusus, and to his adopted son Germanicus, and by Germanicus to his own sons, among whom was Caligula. Thus far the succession was perfectly regular, all the individuals by whom it was assumed being, according to Roman law and usage, regarded as members of the *Gens Iulia*. But it did not of right appertain to Claudius, and, in fact, he never bore the name until after his accession; but still he and his adopted son Nero were regarded as belonging to the Julian line in consequence of their connection with Augustus—the paternal grandmother of Claudius being Livia, the wife of Augustus, and his maternal grandmother being Octavia, the sister of Augustus.

With Nero all traces of the Julian stock disappeared, and yet Galba, immediately upon his accession, assumed the name of *Caesar*, his example was followed by Otho, and subsequent Emperors, as a matter of course, assumed the appellations of *Augustus* and *Caesar*, with the exception of Vitellius, who assumed the former after considerable hesitation, but steadily refused the latter.

After the elevation of Vespasian it became customary for Emperors to bestow the title of *Caesar* on the individual whom they destined for their successor, either adding or withholding as seemed fit to them, the additional honour of the title *Augustus*, the *Tribunitia Potestas*, and other designations, and conferring upon them a greater or smaller amount of real power according to their pleasure. Thus, L. Aelius Verus, when adopted by Hadrian, became *Aelius Caesar*, and received the *Trib. Pot.* Commodus received the title of *Caesar* from his father when five years old, A.D. 166, in A.D. 177 he was invested with the *Trib. Pot.* and the Consulship, and with the titles of *Augustus* and *Pater Patriae*.

The system introduced by Diocletian need not be detailed here.

Princeps.—Under the republic the senator whose name was placed first upon the roll of the Censors was styled *Princeps Senatus*, a title which was regarded as in the highest degree honourable, but which conferred no power nor privilege. In B.C. 28, Octavianus, when Censor along with Agrippa, became *Princeps Senatus*, and with the feigned moderation which so strongly stamped his character, selected this ancient constitutional expression as the appellation by which he was to be distinguished—*Lepidi atque Antonii arma in Augustum cessere, qui cuncta discordiis civilibus fessa nomine* PRINCIPIS *sub imperium accepit.*[1] From this time forward the term *Princeps*, the addition *Senatus* being usually omitted, is perpetually employed by historians and in inscriptions to designate the Emperor.

Princeps Iuventutis.—In the earlier ages of the republic, when the *Equites* were composed of the flower of the nobility, it was customary to designate them as a body under the complimentary appellation of *Principes Iuventutis* (Liv. XLII. 61.) This term would appear to have gradually fallen into desuetude as the *Ordo Equester* assumed a distinct form and lost its military character. We certainly have no evidence that it was ever applied as a mark of honorary distinction to one or two individuals, until we read in Tacitus (Ann. I. 3) that Augustus was most eager that his grandsons Caius and Lucius should be styled *Principes Iuventutis*, and learn from medals that they actually received this distinction. From this time forward the title of *Princeps Iuventutis* was frequently bestowed upon the person marked out as the heir of the imperial dignity, or on some one otherwise closely connected with the imperial family. Thus, it was borne by Nero from the time of his adoption by Claudius; by Titus; by Domitian, without any other title until the death of his brother; by Commodus, and by many others.

It was not, however, assumed by any Emperor until the days of Gordian III. who united it with *Augustus* on his coins; but from this time forward it occurs very frequently upon the medals of reigning sovereigns. There are, it is true, a very few examples before Gordian III., but these are ascribed by the best numismatologists to mistakes on the part of the moneyers.

Pater Patriae s. Parens Patriae.—Romulus, when snatched from earth to heaven is said to have been hailed as *Parens Urbis Romae*, words which might be applied to him in a literal sense as founder of the city. Camillus, after he had recovered Rome from the Gauls, was, according to Livy, (V. 49,) styled *Romulus ac Parens Patriae conditorque alter Urbis;* but the first individual, belonging to an epoch strictly historical, who received this title was Cicero, to whom

[1] Tacit. Ann. I. 1. comp. Dion Cass. LIII. 1.

it was voted by the Senate after the suppression of the Catilinarian conspiracy. It was bestowed upon Julius Cæsar after his victory in Spain, B.C. 45, and it appears for the first time on a medal of Augustus struck about B.C. 2. From this time forward it seems to have been offered to every Emperor immediately upon his accession, and was either at once accepted, or deferred, or altogether rejected, according to the temper and feelings of the individual. It was steadily refused by Tiberius; it is not found upon the coins of Galba, of Otho, and of Vitellius, which may be perhaps ascribed to the shortness of their sway; by M. Aurelius it was not adopted until the fifteenth year of his sovereignty, and consequently never appears upon the money of his colleague L. Verus. The general practice seems to have been to accept the distinction forthwith, and hence it ranks among the ordinary titles of constant recurrence from the commencement, or nearly the commencement of each reign.

Pius. Felix.—The epithet *Pius* was bestowed, under the republic, upon the son of Metellus Numidicus, somewhat later upon Sextus Pompeius, and perhaps upon others also. Caligula, as we are informed by Suetonius, (Calig. 22,) desired to be distinguished by this appellation; but the first Emperor on whom it was regularly conferred was Antoninus. It was assumed by Commodus; Septimius Severus decreed that it should belong to himself and to his sons; and thus it gradually became one of the ordinary titles of the Augusti.

Felix was first connected with the name of Sulla, and among the Emperors, first adopted by Commodus. After Commodus, the first who combined the epithets *Pius* and *Felix* was Caracalla, who used them sparingly; they occur frequently on the monuments of Elagabalus, and after his time were introduced conjointly among the ordinary and regular designations of the sovereign.

Pius and *Felix* were never combined with the simple *Caesar*, except in the case of Carinus, who is styled on a medal M. AUR. CARINUS. P. F. NOB. CAES.; but we know that Carinus had sometimes IMPERATOR prefixed as a praenomen to his CAESAR.

Dominus.—The appellation *Dominus*, which properly implies, *the master of a slave*, was rejected with real or feigned disgust by both Augustus and Tiberius.[1] Caligula was the first who permitted himself to be addressed by this invidious designation; but as early as the reign of Claudius the term was applied in society as an expression of courteous civility even to persons not imperial, and hence it is not surprising that it is constantly employed by Pliny in his correspondence with Trajan. As early as the age of Antoninus Pius we find Κύριος on Greek coins; and on a medal of the colony of Antioch in Pisidia, bearing the heads of Caracalla and Geta, we read VICT. DD. NN. (*Victoria Dominorum Nostrorum.*) But no example of this title appears upon money of a Roman stamp until the time of Aurelian, who first suffered the legend DEO ET DOMINO NOSTRO AURELIANO to appear upon his coinage, and his example was followed by Carus. D. N. (*Dominus Noster*) is used as a sort of praenomen on the pieces of Diocletian and Maximianus, after they had resigned the empire; thenceforward the term became common as a praenomen, applied, however, in the first instance more commonly to the Cæsars; but from the time of the sons of Constantine, was introduced on the imperial coins as a substitute for *Imperator*, which fell into disuse.

Deus. Divus.—Even under the republic, altars and temples were erected and sacrifices were offered by the provincials, especially the Greeks, in honour

[1] Dion Cass. LVII. 8. Suet. Tib. 27. 24. Tertull. Apolog. 34.

of their governors. As a matter of course this species of adulation was addressed, with increased eagerness and servility, to each Emperor in succession. But although the Senate had voted to Julius Cæsar, while alive, honours scarcely inferior to those paid to the deities, neither he, nor Augustus, nor Tiberius suffered themselves to be actually worshipped in the city or even within the limits of Italy, while they graciously permitted themselves to be adored as gods in foreign countries.[1] Caligula, however, set up his own effigy in Rome, between those of the Dioscuri; it was the pleasure of Domitian that he should be addressed as *Dominus et Deus*, and victims were offered to both of these Princes;[2] but with the exception of *Hercules Romanus* on the coins of Commodus, and the inscription noticed in the last paragraph on those of Aurelian and Carus, the Emperors seem to have avoided any permanent memorial of their assumption of divine attributes.

Soon after the death of Julius Cæsar, the Senate formally decreed that homage should be rendered to him as to one translated to heaven; a similar resolution was passed upon the decease of Augustus, a College of priests being, at the same time, formed, who, under the designation of *Sodales Augustales*, were to conduct and preside over the holy rites now instituted; and the example was followed in the case of all succeeding Princes, except when the new ruler thought fit to mark his disrespect for the memory of his predecessor, as happened to Tiberius, Caius, Nero, Galba, Otho, Vitellius, and Domitian. This deification, termed *Consecratio* by the Romans, and ἀποθέωσις by the Greeks, was solemnised by gorgeous ceremonies, of which a full description will be found in Dion Cassius (LVI. 34. 42. LXXIV. 5.) and Herodian (IV. 1.) The individual thus hallowed was thenceforward distinguished by the epithet *Divus*, which, it must be understood, was never, until a late period, applied to a living personage.

This epithet, and the divine honours which it indicated, were bestowed, not only on those who had enjoyed the supreme power, but occasionally also on those nearly connected with them; on their consorts, as on Livia, Poppaea, Domitilla, Plotina, Sabina, the two Faustinas, and Julia Domna; on their children, as on Claudia, the daughter of Nero, and Julia, the daughter of Titus; on their parents, as on Trajan, the father of Trajan, and even on other relatives, as on Marciana the sister, and Matidia the niece of Trajan.

The medals struck in honour of the imperial personages thus deified, bear appropriate devices, such as an eagle, a blazing altar, a funeral pyre, a sacred car drawn by elephants; in the case of females, a *Carpentum* drawn by mules, the spirit of the departed ascending to the skies on a peacock, and several others. Of these we have given a few examples at the end of the chapter, taken from coins of Augustus, Agrippina, Antoninus Pius and Julia Domna.

Rex.—Βασιλεύς was commonly employed by Greek writers with reference to the Emperors, and it occasionally appears upon Greek medals of Commodus and Caracalla; but the obnoxious *Rex* never found a place upon any coin of Roman mintage.

Titles derived from Conquered Countries.—These require little comment. Numerous examples occur under the republic, such as *Africanus*, *Asiaticus*, *Numidicus*, *Isauricus*. Under Augustus, Drusus, the younger brother of Tiberius, gained for himself, by his exploits, the cognomen of *Germanicus*; from him it passed, as it were by inheritance, to his sons Germanicus and Claudius, of whom the latter transmitted it to Nero. It was subsequently borne by

---

[1] Suet. Jul. 76. Octav. 52. Tacit. Ann. I. 10. 78. IV. 37. 55.
[2] Suet. Cal. 22. Dom. 13. Plin. Panegyr. 52.

Vitellius, Domitian, Nerva, Trajan, Hadrian, and many others. *Britannicus* was probably first assumed by Claudius, whose son was distinguished by this epithet as his proper name, and it was at a later period adopted by Commodus, Sept. Severus, Caracalla and Geta. In addition to these, we find *Parthicus, Dacicus, Sarmaticus, Medicus, Adiabenicus, Arabicus, Armeniacus, Carpicus, Gothicus*, all intended to commemorate conquests real or imaginary.

Such were the titles assumed by the Emperors, and in virtue of the powers which these implied, they performed the various acts of absolute sovereignty. The most important were bestowed upon Augustus by a succession of separate votes, and were regularly renewed at intervals of ten years;[1] but upon later Emperors they were conferred all at once and for life. Thus—*Decernitur Othoni Tribunitia Potestas et nomen Augusti et omnes Principum honores;* and again —*Romae Senatus cuncta Principibus solita Vespasiano decernit.*[2] It will be observed that several of them, especially those not adopted until a late period, were merely complimentary, the essence of the imperial dominion being concentrated in the epithets *Imperator—Tribunitia Potestas—Pontifex Maximus*— which were stretched so as to embrace all power, military, civil, and sacred. Indeed, the first alone would have been sufficient had there not been a desire in all but the worst rulers to keep up a decent show of constitutional usages; for since it was understood to convey the right of supreme command over all the armies of the state, of levying troops to any extent, of imposing taxes for their support, and of deciding upon all questions of war and peace, it placed the personage invested with it in a position to enforce immediate obedience to his wishes. Hence, when an Emperor adopted the usual formality of consulting the Senate and requesting their consent to a proposal, he occasionally reminded them that this was purely an act of grace and courtesy, and accordingly we find such communications as the following—*Antonino autem divinos honores et miles decrevit et nos decrevimus et vos, Patres Conscripti, ut decernatis* CUM POSSIMUS IMPERATORIO IURE PRAECIPERE, *tamen rogamus* (Capitolin. Macrin. 6.)

Succession to the Throne.—The imperial power not having been formally established by a new constitution recognised by all orders in the state; but being essentially an usurpation, and being exercised under false colours, no legislative provision, regulating the succession to the throne, was attempted during the first three centuries. Augustus, and those who followed him, tacitly assumed the right of nominating their successors, by, in each case, admitting the individual selected as *Collega*[3] in some of their most important duties, such as the *Tribunitia Potestas* and the *Proconsulare Imperium*, or associating him still more closely with themselves under the designation of *Caesar* or *Augustus*. This system proved generally successful when time was given for preparation, and when the demise of the reigning Prince was not attended by any scenes of violence, although it was at all times felt, especially after the Julian line had became altogether extinct, that every thing depended upon the disposition of the soldiers, and hence the eagerness displayed by each Emperor on his accession to propitiate them by the most extravagant largesses. But when a social convulsion took place, in consequence of the unexpected death of the sovereign by assassination or otherwise, the nomination of a new monarch depended, in the first instance, upon the will of the Praetorians, who could always

---
[1] Dion Cass. LIII. 13. 16. LIV. 12. LV. 6. 12. LVI. 28. LVII. 24.
[2] Tacit. Hist. I. 47. IV. 3. comp. Dion Cass. LIII. 18.
[3] e.g. Tacit. Ann. III. 56. XII. 41. Capitolin. Antonin. P. 4.

212 THE EMPERORS AND THEIR TITLES.

overawe the capital; but it seldom happened that the powerful armies on the frontiers were ready to acquiesce in the decision of the household troops or to agree with each other, and hence the bloody and complicated struggles which ensued upon the death of Nero, of Commodus, and of many others. It is true that, in every instance, the Senate was the body with whom, in theory, the nomination lay, since the powers of the Emperor were all conferred by their vote; but the Senate were mere puppets in the hands of the armies, except in one or two rare examples, where the latter exhibited singular moderation.[1]

[1] Vopisc. Aurel. 40. 41. Tacit. 2—9. 12. Florian 56. Prob. 10. Especially after the death of Aurelian. See the narrative of Vopiscus with regard to the election of Tacitus. Vit. Tacit. 2—9. comp. Aurelian 40 41. Florian. 56. Prob. 10.
Every thing connected with the various titles bestowed upon the Emperors will be found explained and illustrated in the best manner at the end of the eighth volume of Eckhel's *Doctrina Numorum Veterum*.

CHAPTER VI.

THE SENATE.

We have already, at the end of chapter II. (p. 77. comp. p. 80.) given some account of the origin, early history, and numbers of the Senate. We now proceed to describe more minutely the constitution and duties of that body.

Manner of Choosing the Senate.—(*Lectio Senatus.*) Under the regal government the Senate was chosen in the first instance and vacancies were filled up by the king, (*legit sublegitque,*) of his own free will, without reference to hereditary claims or to the voice of the Curiae.[1] After the expulsion of the Tarquins, the power of choosing Senators was at first committed to the Consuls, but after B.C. 443, to the Censors, whose task it was, each *Lustrum*, to revise the list, (*Album Senatorium,*) to omit the names of those who had rendered themselves unworthy of remaining members of the supreme council, and to supply the vacancies caused in this manner or by death. Although the power of the Censors in discharging this duty does not seem to have been defined or restricted by any legislative enactment, until the passing of the *Lex Ovinia*,[2] (the date is uncertain,) in terms of which they were bound to elect upon oath the most deserving, (*optimum quemque,*) we have no reason to suppose that their proceedings were altogether arbitrary. The powers intrusted to them may, at times, have been abused from the influence of personal or party feelings; but it must, from the commencement, have been regulated by certain principles which gradually became fixed, and which, except in extraordinary cases, they could not have ventured to disregard. What these principles were at the period of the second Punic war is clearly demonstrated by the statement of Livy, (XXIII. 23,) with regard to the proceedings of the Dictator, who was named for the special purpose of filling up the blanks caused by the slaughter at Cannae, for the proceedings described evidently indicate the ordinary rule—*Recitato vetere senatu, inde primos in demortuorum locum legit, qui post L. Aemilium et C. Flaminium Censores curulem magistratum cepissent, necdum in Senatum lecti essent; ut quisque eorum primus creatus erat: tum legit, qui aediles, tribuni plebei, quaestoresve fuerant: tum ex iis, qui magistratum non cepissent, qui spolia ex hoste fixa domi haberent, aut civicam coronam accepissent*—thus carrying out the rule which he had previously declared that he would follow—*ut ordo ordini, non homo homini praelatus videretur.*

It is to be observed that all the higher magistrates, from the Quaestor upwards, had, during the period of their office, the right of sitting and speaking in the Senate; but they were not necessarily Senators, unless they had been enrolled

---

[1] Fest. s.v. *Praeteriti Senatores*, p. 246. Dion Cass. fgmt. Mai. Nov. Coll. II. p. 138. fgmt. Peir. XXII. 1. XXIII. 2. Cic. de R. II. 8. Liv. I. 49.
[2] Fest. l.c.—*Lex Ovinia Tribunicia intervenit, qua sanctum est ut Censores ex omni ordine optimum quemque curiati in Senatu legerent.* Where the word *Curiati* is corrupt.

as such before the close of the preceding *Lustrum*. Hence the distinction observed between *Senatores* and those *quibus in Senatu sententiam dicere licet*.[1] Therefore, when the Censors supplied the vacancies, they began by selecting in order of rank and seniority those who had filled offices in virtue of which they had been admitted to sit and to speak. Such persons were regarded as possessing the first claim; and Livy, (XXII. 49,) when enumerating the victims at Cannae, makes use of the expression—*octoginta praeterea, aut Senatores aut qui eos magistratus gessissent unde in Senatum legi deberent*. When the Censors, in making up the new roll, omitted the name of any Senator, they were said *movere s. eiicere Senatu* the individual in question; if, on the other hand, they did not include in the list of new Senators any one who had a claim to be selected according to the principle explained above, while they gave a place to one or more who were his juniors or inferiors in rank, then they were said *praeterire* the individual in question, and such persons were termed *Praeteriti*. This distinction is not, however, always observed, and *Praeterire* is used generally with reference to those passed over by the Censors, whether previously Senators or not.[2]

We are told by Appian (B.C. I. 100) that Sulla, when he made a large addition to the numbers of the Senate from the Equestrian order, left the choice of the individuals to the Tribes; but this statement is not confirmed by other writers.

Princeps Senatus.—The Censors, as we have seen, drew up a list of the Senate. The Senator whose name was placed by them at the head of the roll was styled *Princeps Senatus*, and this position was highly valued, although it conferred no substantial power or privilege. Under ordinary circumstances, the senior of the *Censorii*, that is, of those who had held the office of Censor, was the person selected as the *Princeps*; but this was by no means an imperative rule (Liv. XXVII. 11. XXXIV. 44.)

Qualifications as to Birth, Occupation, Age, Fortune, &c.—Although the choice of the Censors, during the best ages of the republic, was regulated, to a certain extent, by established usage, any one possessing the full *Civitas* was regarded as eligible without any limitation as to birth except *ingenuitas* for two generations. Hence, the son of a *Libertinus* would be shut out; but this exclusion seems to have rested upon public opinion rather than upon any specific law, for we find that persons belonging to this class were actually admitted in the Censorship of Appius Claudius, (B.C. 312)—*qui Senatum primus libertinorum filiis lectis inquinaverat*—but that popular indignation was so strongly expressed that the Consuls of the following year refused to acknowledge them.[3] The same feeling, although neglected during the troubles of Marius and Sulla, was revived in the age of Cicero, but altogether disregarded by Julius Caesar.[4]

No Senator, in the earlier ages at least, was allowed to follow any lucrative trade, or to engage in traffic except in so far as selling the produce of his lands; and hence, by an ancient *Lex Claudia*, no Senator nor son of a Senator, was permitted to possess a sea-going ship of more than 300 amphorae burden. A vessel of that size was deemed sufficient for the transport of his crops and—

---

[1] Fest. s.v. *Senatores*, p. 339. Liv. XXIII. 32. XXXVI. 3. Val. Max. II. ii. 1. Aul. Gell. III. 18.
[2] Liv. XXXIX. 42. XLI. 27. Epit. XCVIII. Fest. s.v. *Praeteriti Senatores*, p. 246.
[3] Liv. IX. 30. 46. Cn. Fulvius in virtue of his office of Curule Aedile must have held a seat in the Senate.
[4] Cic. pro Cluent. 47. Dion Cass. XL. 63. XLIII. 47. XLVIII. 34.

Quaestus omnis Patribus indecorus visus. But this law had fallen into desuetude in the days of Cicero.[1]

There can be little doubt, that towards the close of the republic there was a fixed age, before which no one was eligible; and hence Cicero, when dwelling on the early career of Pompeius exclaims—*Quid tam praeter consuetudinem, quam homini peradolescenti, cuius Senatorio gradu aetas longe abesset, imperium atque exercitum dari?*[2] and this age probably depended on the *Lex Villia Annalis;* (see above, p. 173;) but when there was no restriction as to the age at which a citizen could be chosen to fill the highest magistracies it is not probable that there could have been any fixed *Aetas Senatoria*. Under the Empire the *Aetas Senatoria* seems to have been twenty-five, since, under ordinary circumstances, no one could hold the Quaestorship until he had attained to that age.[3]

That the Senators, as a body, formed the wealthiest class in the state seems unquestionable, and examples occur in which they were called upon to contribute more largely than any other portion of the community to the necessities of the commonwealth. But we nowhere find any hint given that, under the free constitution, the want of a certain amount of fortune was held as a disqualification. As far as our authorities go, Augustus was the first who required a definite sum (*Census Senatorius*) as indispensable for those who desired to become candidates for the higher offices of state and to gain admission to the Senate. This sum he, in the first instance, fixed at 400,000 sesterces, the same with the *Census Equester* introduced by the Gracchi, (see above, p. 74,) but afterwards raised it to a million of sesterces, (*decies,*) after which we hear of no further change.[4]

Powers and Duties of the Senate.—Although the Senate, from the very foundation of the city, was recognised as an integral and indispensable member of the body politic, it seems to have occupied a very subordinate position under the kings, except during an *Interregnum*. The monarch held his office for life, and was irresponsible; consequently, although compelled, to a certain extent, by public opinion and custom to ask the advice of the Senate, he might accept or reject their counsel as he thought fit.[5] The Senators could not assemble unless summoned by him, nor deliberate upon any matter not submitted to them by him, and they had no means of enforcing their opinions and wishes. The King might, and probably did, for the sake of convenience, place many of the details of government in their hands; but the nature and extent of the authority thus committed to them depended entirely upon his will and pleasure. As soon, however, as the republic was established, the powers of the Senate were at once greatly enlarged. The chief magistrates now retained office for one year only, while the Senate, being a permanent body, a vast mass of public business necessarily devolved upon them alone. By degrees the independent powers of the Consuls and other magistrates became narrower, while the influence of the Senate was, in like proportion, extended, until, ere long, the magistrates were

---

[1] Cic. in Verr. V. 18.
[2] Cic. pro leg. Manil. 21.
[3] Dion Cass. LII. 20. 32. LIII. 15. 28. comp. Velleius II. 94. Digest. I. xiii. 3. L. iv. 8. Tacit. Ann. XV. 28. Hist. IV. 42.
[4] Dion Cass. LIV. 17. comp. LIV. 26. 30. Tacit. Ann. I. 75. II. 37. 86. Juv. VI. 137. X. 335. Martial. II. 65. If we can believe Suetonius, (Octav. 41,) the *Census Senatorius* was at one time fixed by Augustus at 800,000 sesterces, and finally raised by him to 1,200,000; but this statement is not corroborated.
[5] Liv. I. 32. 49. Cic. de R. II. 9. Dionys. II. 14. 56. III. 22. 26. 37. Plut. Rom. 27. Dion Cass. fgmt. Mai. Nov. Coll. II. p. 138.

little more than the servants who executed the orders of the Senate, by whose decision the whole administration of public affairs was regulated and controlled.

The people in their Comitia alone had the right of enacting or repealing laws, of electing magistrates, of declaring war or concluding peace, and of deciding upon charges which involved the life or privileges of a citizen; but with these exceptions, the powers of the Senate were almost unlimited. Hence, we might content ourselves with this negative description of their duties; but there are certain important matters which we may briefly notice as falling more especially under their control—

1. To the Senate exclusively belonged the administration of foreign affairs. They conducted all negotiations, appointed ambassadors selected from their own body, gave audience to the envoys of independent states, and concluded treaties. They received the deputations sent from the provinces, granted or refused their requests, inquired into their complaints and redressed their grievances.[1] The people, as we have repeatedly observed, had alone the power of declaring war or concluding peace; but no proposition with regard to these points could be submitted to them except through the medium of the Senate, and when an attempt to pass over the Senate was made, it was regarded as little better than a direct violation of the constitution—*novum malumque exemplum*.[2] All matters connected with the general conduct of the war were left to their wisdom. They named the different Provinces and their limits, they distributed them among the different magistrates, they fixed the amount of troops to be placed under the orders of each, they provided the necessary supplies of provisions, clothing, warlike stores and money, and after a victory they voted thanksgivings, (*Supplicationes*,) and greater or lesser triumphs (*Triumphi—Ovationes*.)[3]

2. With the assistance of the great Colleges of priests, they exercised a general superintendence over the religion of the state, arranged the periods for the celebration of the moveable feasts and for the exhibition of extraordinary games.

3. To them belonged the whole management of the public Exchequer. They were the auditors of the public accounts, and all disbursements were made by their orders.

4. Up to the passing of the *Lex Sempronia Iudiciaria* of C. Gracchus, (B.C. 122,) the jurors in criminal trials (*iudices*) were taken exclusively from the Senate.

5. The Senate assumed to itself, on several occasions, under pressing circumstances, the right of suspending for a time, in favour of some particular individual, the provisions of a positive law. This was, however, regarded as a stretch of their prerogative, to be justified only by extraordinary emergencies; and C. Cornelius, Tribune of the Plebs, B.C. 67, brought in a bill to stop this practice —*promulgavit legem qua auctoritatem Senatus minuebat, ne quis nisi per populum legibus solveretur*. See Ascon. in Cic. Orat. pro Cornel. arg. p. 57. ed. Orelli.

6. In seasons of great danger or alarm they assumed the right of investing the Consuls with Dictatorial power, by what was termed a *Decretum Ultimum* s. *Extremum*. See above, p. 149.

7. Although the Senate never claimed the power of making or repealing laws, it is certain that, in the earlier ages of the republic, no law was submitted to the

---

[1] Polyb. VI. 13. Liv. XXX. 17. XXXI. 11. XL. 58.
[2] As to war. Liv. IV. 30. XXXVI. 1. XLV. 21. As to peace. Liv. XXX. 37. 43. XXXIII. 13. 30. XXXIV. 35. XXXVII. 45. 55.
[3] Polyb. VI. 13. Liv. XXX. 17. XXXI. 11. XL. 58.

Comitia Centuriata until it had been revised and sanctioned by the Senate. But as the power of the Tribunes of the Plebs increased, and especially after the *Lex Publilia*, (see above, pp. 117. 124,) by which *Plebiscita* were rendered binding upon all orders in the state, the right of previous sanction, προβούλευμα, as it was termed among the Greeks, even if it was fully admitted, became of comparatively little importance, (Dionys. VII. 38. IX. 41. Appian. B.C. I. 59.)

But while the Senate discharged these and many other functions of the highest importance, for the most part without question or opposition, still the people being, according to the principles of the constitution, (see above, p. 79,) supreme, occasionally interfered and reversed the arrangements of the Senate. Thus, no prerogative of the Senate was more completely recognized and was, for ages, less disputed, than their title to distribute the Provinces according to their discretion;[1] yet, as we have seen above, (p. 185,) the Tribes, upon three important occasions, took the matter into their own hands; and other examples of a similar nature will be found recorded, from time to time, by the historians.

Relation in which the Senate stood towards the Magistrates.—The Senate, although nominally, in a considerable degree, under the control of the higher magistrates, were in reality their masters. It is true that the Senate could not meet unless summoned by one of the great functionaries, and could neither decide nor even deliberate upon any question unless regularly brought under their notice by the president. But, on the other hand, the magistrates were unable to discharge their ordinary duties without the sanction and assistance of the Senate, and would have been utterly powerless without their support. Difference of opinion occasionally arose, when, if the Senate were resolute, and the Consuls refused to yield, (*in potestate* s. *in auctoritate Senatus esse*,) the Senate, as a last resource, might insist upon the nomination of a Dictator, or might appeal for assistance to the Tribunes of the Plebs, who were ever ready to interfere upon such occasions, and could, in an extremity, order the Consuls to prison.[2]

Even when in actual command of an army, the generals were dependent upon the Senate, for they were strictly confined within the limits of their Province, and to the Senate they looked for all supplies, and for the ratification of all their proceedings.[3]

Meetings of the Senate.—The Senate could not meet unless summoned by a magistrate, and certain magistrates only possessed the power (*Vocare* s. *Cogere Senatum.*) Among the ordinary magistrates, the privilege belonged to the Consuls; in their absence, to the Praetor Urbanus, or to those magistrates who, for a limited period, were substituted for the Consuls—the *Decemviri legibus scribendis* and the *Tribuni militares consulari potestate*. The Tribunes of the Plebs also, after a time, assumed and maintained the right of summoning the Senate. Of the extraordinary magistrates, to the Dictator, the Interrex and the Praefectus Urbi.[4]

Mode of Summoning. Attendance.—When it was necessary to summon the Senate in great haste, it was done by means of a *Praeco* and *Viatores*; but, under ordinary circumstances, a public notice (*edictum*) was posted up a few days beforehand. There were no fixed days for meetings of the Senate until the

---

[1] See especially Cic. in Vatin. 15.
[2] Liv. III. 21. 52. IV. 26. 56. V. 9.
[3] Liv. V. 27. VI. 26. VIII. 1. 36. X. 5. 36.
[4] Aul. Gell. XIV. 7. who quotes Varro. Cic. de Orat. III. 1. de legg. III. 4. who, if his text be correct, adds the Magister Equitum to the above list.

time of Augustus,[1] who ordained that the Senate should meet regularly twice every month, on the Kalends and the Ides, and hence arose the distinction between *Senatus legitimus*, an ordinary, and *Senatus indictus*, an extraordinary meeting.

The attendance of Senators was not optional, but might be enforced by the summoning magistrate, and they were liable to a fine if absent without good reason; but this appears to have been seldom exacted. Under the empire, members of the Senate were exempted from attendance after their sixtieth (or, perhaps, sixty-fifth) year.[2] A full meeting of the Senate was called *Senatus frequens*, a thin meeting, *Senatus infrequens*. When the subjects to be proposed for deliberation were of importance, it was not unusual, in the *Edictum*, to request a large attendance.

Place of Meeting.—The Senate could hold their meetings in a *Templum* only, that is, in a place consecrated by the Augurs. The ordinary council hall for many centuries was the *Curia Hostilia*, which stood upon the north side of the *Comitium*; (see above, p. 14;) but occasionally we find other *Templa* employed for the same purpose. Towards the close of the republic and under the empire several magnificent edifices were erected, with the express object of serving as Senate-houses, and of these we have noticed the *Curia Julia* and others.

When the Senate gave audience to the ambassadors of a hostile state, or to the generals who wished to retain their *Imperium*, which they would have forfeited by passing the *Pomoerium*, then the ordinary places of meeting were the Temple of Bellona or the Temple of Apollo, both in the *Prata Flaminia*. See above, p. 43.

Manner of Conducting Business.—Before proceeding to business the auspices were taken and a sacrifice offered by the magistrate who had called the meeting.[3]

The magistrate or magistrates, for both Consuls appear to have frequently acted jointly, who had called the meeting and who presided, had alone the right, in the first instance, to submit any matter for deliberation, and in doing this he usually commenced with things sacred, and then passed on to secular affairs (*de rebus divinis priusquam humanis*.)[4] When the president simply made a statement for the purpose of communicating intelligence, he was said *rem ad Senatum deferre*, when he brought before them any question for discussion, *rem ad Senatum referre*.[5]

When the presiding magistrate had finished the business for which the meeting had been summoned, it was competent for a Tribune of the Plebs, or any other magistrate who possessed the right of holding the Senate, to propose a subject for debate;[6] but under no circumstances could this be done by a private Senator. It was not unusual, however, for the house, as a body, to call upon the president to bring some matter under their consideration—*postulare uti referrent*—*conclamatum est ex omni parte curiae uti referret Praetor*, &c.[7]

In submitting any matter he was said, as noticed above, REFERRE *rem ad*

---

[1] Liv. III. 38. XXVIII. 9. Cic. ad fam. XI. 6. Appian B.C. I. 25. Dion Cass. LV. 3. LVIII. 21. Capitolin Gordian. 11.
[2] Liv. III. 38. XXXVI. 3. XLIII. 11. Cic. de legg. III. 4. Philipp. I. 5. Aul. Gell. XIV. 7. Senec. de brevit. vit. 20. Senec. Controv. 7.
[3] Aul. Gell. XIV. 7. Cic. ad fam. X. 12. Sueton. Caes. 81. Appian. B.C. II. 116.
[4] Aul. Gell. l.c. comp. Liv. XXII. 9. 11. XXIV. 11.
[5] e.g. Liv. II. 28. XXXIX. 14.
[6] e.g. Cic. Philipp. VII. 1. pro. leg. Man. 19. ad fam. X. 16.
[7] Liv. XXX. 21. XLII. 3. Cic. ad fam. X. 16. Tacit. Ann. XIII. 49.

THE SENATE.

Senatum or REFERRE *ad Senatum de aliqua re*, and the question or subject submitted was called *Relatio*. After the *Relatio* had been briefly explained, he proceeded to ask the opinion of the house, (*consulere Senatum*,) which he did in the words *Quid de ea re fieri placet*, and this opinion was elicited by calling upon each Senator by name (*nominatim*) to declare his sentiments, (*sententiam rogare* s. *interrogare*,) employing the form *Dic* . . . (here the name of the individual addressed) . . . *quid censes*. A certain rule of precedence was followed (*gradatim consulere*.) If the elections for the following year were over, the Consuls elect were first called upon to speak, (*censere—decernere—sententiam dicere*,) then the Princeps Senatus, then those who had held the office of Consul, (*Consulares*,) those who had held the office of Praetor, (*Praetorii*,) and so on through the inferior offices. Again, in adjusting the order of precedence between those belonging to the same class, the rule of seniority was generally followed; but a certain degree of latitude was allowed to the presiding magistrate, who might mark his respect for particular individuals by calling upon them out of their turn at an early stage of the debate.[1] Considerable importance was attached to the privilege of speaking early, for we find Cicero enumerating among the various honours and rewards which he would enjoy in consequence of being elected Curule Aedile—*antiquiorem in Senatu sententiae dicendae locum* (In Verr. V. 14.)

A Senator, when named, usually rose up (*surrexit*) and expressed his views briefly or at length as he thought fit. It does not appear that any limit was fixed to the length of an oration, and hence factious attempts were sometimes made to stave off a question by wasting the whole day in speaking (*diem consumere—diem dicendo eximere*.)[2] We have stated that no private Senator was permitted to originate any motion; but any one was at liberty, when called upon for his opinion, to digress from the subject in hand, and to state his opinion upon topics foreign to the actual business. In doing this he was said *egredi relationem*.[3] Occasionally, in matters of great importance, when a Senator was desirous to express himself with deliberate solemnity, he read his speech (*de scripto sententiam dicere*.)[4]

Many contented themselves with simply assenting to a proposition, without rising and delivering a formal harangue, (*verbo adsentiri—sedens adsentiri*,) while others gave a silent vote, (*pedibus in sententiam ire*.)[5]

When every Senator had had an opportunity of explaining his sentiments, (*perrogatis sententiis*,) if a difference of opinion had arisen, the president proceeded to state the various propositions in succession, (*pronuntiare sententias*,) and a division (*discessio*) took place, those who supported the first proposition being desired to pass to one side of the house, while those who did not approve of it were to pass to the other—*Qui hoc censetis, illuc transite, qui alia omnia in hanc partem*—ALIA OMNIA, being the technical form used to denote every opinion except the one upon which the vote was in the act of being taken.[6] From

---

[1] Aul. Gell. IV. 10. XIV. 7. Liv. XXVIII. 45. Cic. in Verr. V. 14. Philipp. V. 13. ad Att. I. 13. XII. 21. The words of Sallust (Cat. 50.) with regard to the *Consul designatus* are perfectly explicit—*Tum D. Junius Silanus, primus sententiam rogatus, quod eo tempore Consul designatus erat*. The privilege, however, does not seem to have extended to the other magistrates elect; for, as we learn from the narrative of Appian, in the debate above referred to, Caesar, although Praetor elect, did not speak until after many Senators had supported the views of Silanus.
[2] Cic. in Verr. II. 39. ad fam. I. 2. ad Att. IV. 2. ad Q. F. II. 1.
[3] Tacit. Ann. II. 38.
[4] Cic. ad fam. X. 13. Att. IV. 3.
[5] Liv. XXVII. 34.
[6] Cic. ad fam. I. 2, VII. 13. X. 12. Caes. B.C. I. 2. Liv. VII. 35.

the circumstance of the Senators walking to opposite sides of the house arose the common formulae which expressed the act of voting in favour of a measure—*discedere in sententiam—ire in sententiam—pedibus ire in sententiam.* We have already observed that the last of these was applied to those who gave a vote without speaking, and hence the members who did this habitually were termed *Pedarii Senatores*, at least this is the most reasonable explanation of the phrase.

Sometimes a proposition might consist of different heads, and while some persons might agree to a portion of it, they might be unwilling to assent to the whole. In this case they insisted that the president should separate the proposition into clauses, and take the sense of the house upon each separately—*postulatum est ut sententia divideretur.* [1]

On the other hand, when a magistrate hurried through a proposition consisting of several heads, without time being allowed for the discussion of the clauses in detail, he was said *per saturam sententias exquirere.* [2]

When a speedy decision was indispensable, or when it was known that men's minds were made up, the president did not ask the opinion of the Senators in succession, but proceeded at once to the vote, and hence the distinction drawn between *Senatus-consultum per relationem* and *Senatus-consultum per discessionem;* but it must be observed that the latter phrase may be applied to every decree of the Senate upon which a vote was taken, whether preceded by a debate or not. [3]

When the Senate had separated and were standing upon opposite sides of the house, the president, who appears to have had no vote, proceeded to count, and announced the result by the formula—*Haec pars maior videtur.* Occasionally, although a difference of opinion had been expressed, the vote was unanimous, and in this case was termed—*Sine ulla varietate discessio.* [4]

Senatus Consultum. Senatus Auctoritas.—A proposition sanctioned by a majority of the Senate, and not vetoed by one of the Tribunes of the Plebs, who might interrupt the proceedings at any stage, was called *Senatus-Consultum* or *Senatus-Decretum,* the only distinction between the terms being that the former was the more comprehensive, since a *Senatus-Consultum* might include several orders or *Decreta.*

But if a Tribune of the Plebs put his veto on a proposition which a majority of the Senate had sanctioned, then the resolution of the Senate was called *Senatus Auctoritas*, and became a mere formal expression of opinion without legal efficacy.

When a *Senatus-Consultum* had been passed, it was reduced to writing (*perscriptum est.*) Those who had taken the greatest interest in the measure superintended this process, (*scribendo adfuerunt,*) and their names, styled *auctoritates perscriptae,* were included in the body of the document.

In like manner a *Senatus Auctoritas* was frequently written out, serving as a sort of protest, and recording the names of those who had supported the motion as well as of the Tribune or Tribunes who had interceded. [5]

When one or more Tribunes had put their veto upon a measure approved of by a large majority, the Consuls were sometimes requested to remonstrate with

---

[1] Cic. ad fam. I. 2. (*postulatum est ut Bibuli sententia divideretur*) comp. Ascon. ad Cic. pro Milon. 6. and Schol. Bob. in loc.
[2] See Sallust. Iug. 29. comp. Fest. s.v. *Satura*, p. 314.
[3] Aul. Gell. XIV. 7.
[4] Cic. in Cat. III. 6. pro Sest. 34. Senec. de vit. beat. 2
[5] Cic. ad fam. I. 2. VIII. 8.

THE SENATE.

the Tribunes, (*agere cum Tribunis,*) and to endeavour to induce them to withdraw their opposition. Sometimes, under similar circumstances, the Consuls proceeded immediately to consult the Senate upon the propriety of having recourse to strong measures, whether, for example, it might not be expedient to make an appeal to the people or to arm the Consuls with Dictatorial power.[1]

Not only a Tribune but one of the Consuls might interfere to prevent the passing of a *Senatus-Consultum,* such interference being termed *intercessio collegae,* or, generally, any magistrate possessed of authority equal to or greater than that of the magistrate who brought forward the proposition.[2]

Ordinary Senators, although they could not positively forbid the passing of a resolution, might in various ways impede, delay, and thus eventually frustrate it,—1. By speaking against time.—2. By demanding that each individual Senator should be called upon to speak (*ut singuli consulantur.*)—3. By requiring that each clause should be discussed separately (*ut sententiae dividerentur.*)—4. By calling upon the president, again and again, to count the house, (*Numerare Senatum,*) in order to ascertain that there was a proper number present.[3] This leads us, finally, to consider the question of a

Quorum.—That the presence of a certain number of Senators was necessary, in order that the proceedings might be valid, seems beyond a doubt; but it is equally clear that this quorum must have varied at different periods under the republic, and perhaps according to the nature of the business, for we find in different places a hundred, a hundred and fifty, and two hundred spoken of as a Quorum.[4] Under Augustus the presence of four hundred was, at one period, required; but it would appear that this rule was subsequently relaxed, at least when the questions discussed were not of special importance. At a later epoch the quorum was reduced to seventy and even to fifty.[5]

Insignia of Senators.—Senators, from an early period, were distinguished from ordinary citizens by certain peculiarities in their dress, to which other privileges were subsequently added. They wore—

1. *Tunica Laticlavia,* an under garment, ornamented with a broad vertical purple stripe (Hor. S. I. vi. 27.)

2. *Annulus Aureus,* a golden ring. See above, p. 75.

3. *Calceus Senatorius,* a shoe of a particular form fastened by four straps, (*corrigiae,*) the *Lora patricia* of Seneca, which were fastened round the calf of the leg. To some part of this shoe a piece of ivory in the form of a crescent (*lunula*) was attached. From the words of Juvenal (S. VII. 192)—

Appositam nigrae lunam subtexit alutae,

compared with Horace, (S. I. vi. 27,) it has been concluded that the *Calceus Senatorius* was black, while others have inferred from Martial (II. 29) that it was scarlet. If the latter opinion be correct it was probably the same with what is elsewhere termed the *Mulleus.*[6]

Seats were reserved for the Senators in that part of the theatre called the *Orchestra,* and at a subsequent period they enjoyed a similar privilege

---

1 Cic. ad Att. IV. 2. ad fam VIII. 8.
2 Aul. Gell. XIV. 7. Liv. XXX. 43.
3 See an obscure passage in Festus s.v. *Numera Senatum,* comp. Cic. ad fam. VIII. 11. ad Att. V. 4.
4 Senat. C. de Bacchanal. Liv. XLII. 28. Ascon. in Cic. pro Corn. p. 58. ed. Orell.
5 Dion Cass. LIV. 35. LV. 3. Lamprid. Al. Sev. 16. Cod. Theod. VI. iv. 9.
6 Cic. Philipp. XIII. 13. Senec. de Tranq. An. 11. Plut. Q. R. 76. Martial. I. 50. II. 29. Philostrat. vit. Herod. Att. II. 8.

in the circus, as we shall mention more particularly when discussing the Public Games.

Legatio Libera.—One of the most substantial advantages enjoyed by a Senator was, that when he quitted Italy for his own private business he usually received, by a vote of his colleagues, a *Legatio Libera*, in virtue of which he was invested with the character of an ambassador, and was entitled, in all foreign countries, to the same respect and consideration as if he had actually been despatched upon some special mission by the state.[1]

Senate under the Empire.—The influence of the Senate under the Empire was, ostensibly, prodigiously increased; for it not only retained all its former rights, but was, to a great extent, invested with those powers which, under the commonwealth had formed the exclusive prerogative of the people.

1. We have seen above (p. 129) that the election of magistrates was arranged between the Emperor and the Senate, the Comitia being merely called upon to approve of a list, previously prepared, which they could neither reject nor alter.

2. In like manner, the legislative functions of the Comitia were entirely suspended by the Decrees of the Senate and the Constitutions of the Prince, which were submitted to the Senate for ratification.

3. All criminal trials of importance, all which could be classed under the head of state trials, including charges in any way affecting the government, the person of the Emperor, the proceedings of Senators or their families, or the character of the Proconsular governors, were referred to the decision of the Senate.

4. Even questions with regard to war and peace, although naturally appertaining to the Emperor in his capacity of supreme military commander, were occasionally left in the hands of the Senate (e.g. Dion Cass. LX. 23. LXVIII. 9.)

5. Lastly, the Senate elected and deposed the Emperors themselves, and all the powers in virtue of which the Emperors exercised dominion were nominally conferred by vote of the Senate.

But these privileges, vast in name, were, in reality, a mere empty show. It formed part of the policy of Augustus and of the most judicious among his successors to govern through the Senate, which became the mere organ of the imperial will, executing with ready submission all orders communicated directly, and watching with servile eagerness and anxiety for the slightest indications which might enable it to divine the secret thoughts and anticipate the wishes of the Prince, while, in addition to the sanction readily accorded by the body in its corporate capacity, each individual Senator was required, at regular periods, generally at the commencement of each year, to approve and ratify upon oath the proceedings of the Emperor (*iurare in acta Principis*.)[2] The actual position of the Senate in the state was very different at different times, depending almost entirely upon the temper of the sovereign. By some it was altogether disregarded or treated with open contempt, insult, and cruelty; by others it was allowed to discharge the most weighty functions of the government, and to exercise extensive patronage without question or interference; but, in every case, all distinctly understood and felt that they acted by permission only, and that they were, in fact, agents who were allowed a greater or smaller amount of discretionary power according to the convenience or caprice of their employer.

In cases when an attempt was made to dethrone the reigning Emperor, or

---

[1] Cic. ad fam. XI. 1. XII. 21. ad Att. II. 18. XV. 11. pro Flacc. 34. Val. Max. V. iii. 2. Sueton. Tib. 31. On the abuses to which this practice gave rise, see Cic. de leg. agr. I. 3. II. 17.

[2] See Dion Cass. LI. 20. LIII. 28. LVII. 8. 17. LX. 25. Tacit. Ann. XVI. 22.

THE SENATE UNDER THE EMPIRE. 223

when the succession was disputed, the position of the Senate was peculiarly painful and hazardous. Compelled to submit to the dictates of the chief, who, for the time being, was in military possession of the capital, the members were liable, upon each change of fortune, to be treated as rebels and traitors by the conqueror.

Number of Senators under the Empire.—We have stated above (p. 78) that at the period of the first Census, held after the battle of Actium, there were one thousand Senators. Augustus reduced the number to six hundred;[1] but we have no distinct information of what took place in this respect under subsequent Emperors, each of whom, in virtue of his *Censoria Potestas*, drew up, at pleasure, lists of the Senate, admitting new members and excluding the unworthy.[2]

Persons entitled to Summon and Consult the Senate.—As under the republic, the Senate might be summoned by the Consuls, Praetors, or Tribunes of the Plebs. When the Emperor was Consul he presided in that capacity; at other times, when present, he occupied a Curule chair, placed between those of the two Consuls.[3] The Emperor, in virtue of his *Tribunitia Potestas*, could at any time call a meeting, and even when not presiding, was allowed to originate a motion and submit it for deliberation. This privilege was eventually extended, so as to empower him to bring several distinct matters under consideration, and was termed *Jus tertiae—quartae—quintae relationis*.[4]

Ordo Senatorius.—This expression was used under the republic to denote the members of the Senate collectively; but under the empire it seems to have included all the children of Senators and their direct descendants, who then formed a distinct and privileged class. The sons of Senators especially inherited a sort of nobility. As soon as they assumed the *Toga Virilis* they were permitted to wear the *Tunica Laticlavia*, to be present as auditors at meetings of the Senate, and enjoyed various rights and exemptions, both military and civil,[5] many of which were shared by the *Equites illustres*, of whom we have spoken above (p. 76.)

Consilium Principis.—Augustus employed the services of a committee composed of the Consuls, of one individual from each of the classes of higher magistrates, and of fifteen ordinary Senators chosen by lot, who acted for six months as his advisers, assisting him in preparing and maturing the measures which were afterwards to be submitted to the whole body of the Senate, and in the prosecution of judicial investigations.[6]

The *Consilium Principis*, as it was termed, gradually underwent very momentous changes, both in its constitution and in the extent of the powers which it exercised. The number of members was increased, individuals were admitted who were friends or personal attendants of the Emperor, but who had no connection with the Senate,[7] the most weighty questions of policy were discussed and finally decided by this privy council; and as early as the time of

---

[1] Dion Cass LIV. 13. 14.
[2] e.g. Dion Cass. LIV. 13. 14. LV. 3. Tacit. Ann. IV. 42. Suet. Vesp. 9.
[3] Plin. Epp. II. 11. Dion Cass. LV. 16.
[4] Tacit. Ann. III. 17. Dion Cass. LIII. 32. LV. 16. Capitolin. M. Aurel. 6. Pertin. 5. Lamprid. Alex. Sev. 1. Vopisc. Prob. 12.
[5] Dion Cass. LII. 31. LIII. 15. LIV. 26. Suet. Octav. 38. Digest. I. ix. 5—10. XXIII. ii. 44. L. i. 22. § 5. comp. Tacit. Hist. II. 86.
[6] Dion Cass. LIII. 21. Suet. Octav. 35.
[7] The *Amici et Comites Augusti*, as they were styled, formed the personal staff of the Emperor, and were divided by Tiberius into three classes, according to their dignity (*tribus classibus factis pro dignitate cuiusque*, Suet. Tib. 46.) In the jurists we find them frequently referred to as *amici* s. *comites primi—secundi—tertii ordinis* s. *loci*.

Hadrian, it had usurped the most important functions of the legislature and the courts of justice. It did not, however, assume a regular and definite form until the reign of Diocletian, when it was established under the name of *Consistorium Principis*, and henceforward was fully recognized as an independent and powerful department of the government.[1]

[1] Dion Cass. LVI. 28. 41. LVII. 7. LX. 4. Suet. Tib. 35. Ner. 15. Tit. 7. Plin. Panegyr. 68. Epp. VI. 21. Spartian Hadr. 22.

A Lictor, from an ancient bas relief.

CHAPTER VII.

ON THE PUBLIC LANDS AND THE AGRARIAN LAWS.[1]

Ager Publicus was the general term for all lands which belonged in property to the state and not to private individuals. A domain of this description, the proceeds of which were applied to the public service, formed part of the Roman territory from the earliest times.[2] Originally it must have been very limited in extent; but as the Romans gradually subjugated Italy, they were in the habit of mulcting those tribes which resisted their arms of a considerable portion of their lands, and, in process of time acquired immense tracts. In this way, for example, the Hernici and the Privernates were deprived of two-thirds of their territory, (*agri partes duae ademtae,*)[3] the Boii forfeited one half,[4] and, upon the recovery of Capua, after its revolt to Hannibal, the whole *Ager Campanus*, the most fertile district in the peninsula, was confiscated.[5]

A portion of the lands thus acquired was frequently sold by public auction, in order to provide funds for the immediate wants of the state. The remainder was disposed of in different ways, according to its nature and condition; for it might be, (1.) Arable, or meadow-land, or vineyards, or olive gardens, in a high state of cultivation. (2.) Land of good quality, capable of producing the best crops, but which was lying waste and depopulated in consequence of the ravages of war. (3.) Wild hill and forest pasture, of which there are vast districts in the mountainous regions of central and southern Italy, and also on some parts of the coast.

(1.) The rich land in good condition was usually disposed of in three ways—

If at no great distance from the city, or if not in an exposed situation, it was frequently made over (*assignatum*) in small allotments, usually of seven jugers, to the poorer citizens, those chiefly who had acquired a claim upon the state by long military service.

If, on the other hand, it lay upon an exposed frontier, or in the midst of hostile tribes, a *Colonia* was established according to the policy already explained (see above, p. 88.)

---

[1] Extended information on the subjects treated of in this chapter will be found in the Prolusion of Heyne, entitled "Leges Agrariae pestiferae et execrabiles." contained in the fourth volume of his "Academica;" in the chapters of Niebuhr's Roman History, "On the Public Land and its Occupation "—"The Assignments of Land before the time of Sp. Cassius"—"The Agrarian Law of Sp. Cassius," and "The Licinian Rogations." Our most valuable ancient authority is Appian. B.C. I. 7. seqq. whom Niebuhr supposes to have here followed Posidonius.

[2] Consisting, probably, chiefly of pasture land, and hence *Pascua* was the ancient term for the revenue of the state, from whatever source derived. See Plin. H.N. XVIII. 3.

[3] Liv. II. 41. VIII. 1.

[4] Liv. XXXVI. 39.

[5] Liv. XXVI. 16.

In both of these cases the lands so assigned ceased to be *Ager Publicus*, and were made over in full property to the recipients, subject, in so far as colonies were concerned, to the conditions of the foundation charter (*formula*.)

Lastly, land of this description was sometimes left in the hands of the subjugated proprietors, who were, however, transformed from owners into mere tenants, who held the land on lease for a fixed period, and paid a fair rent to the Roman Exchequer for the farms which they occupied.[1] In this case the land remained the property of the state, and formed part of the *Ager Publicus*.

(2.) (3.) It is manifest that the arrangements with regard to the lands which had been laid waste by the operations of war must have been of a very different description. Here the farm houses and buildings of every description would be in ruins, the population killed or dispersed, the vines and fruit trees cut down or destroyed, and not only much labour, but large capital would be required to render them again productive. In like manner, the wide ranges of wild pasture land would be available to those only who were able to stock them with flocks and herds and to provide troops of slaves to attend and guard their property. Hence the state was in the habit, in the earlier ages at least, of inviting persons to enter upon the occupation of such districts upon very favourable terms, the payment, viz. of one-tenth of the produce of corn lands, and one-fifth of the produce of vines and fruit trees, when the land should have been again brought under cultivation, and of a moderate sum per head for sheep and cattle grazing on the public pastures. These lands fell, as a matter of course, in the earlier ages, into the hands of the Patricians exclusively, the only class possessed of capital, and afterwards the wealthy Plebeians also obtained a share. The persons who so occupied the lands were of course tenants of the state; but they did not hold leases for a fixed period, but were tenants at will, (*precario*,) who kept possession so long as the state did not desire to apply the land to any other purpose, but who might be lawfully ejected whenever the state thought fit. On the one hand no length of occupancy could bestow a right of property upon the occupier, for it was a fundamental principle of Roman law, that prescription could not be pleaded against the state; but, on the other hand, it does not appear that the state ever attempted to displace one occupier in order to make room for another occupier, but when it resumed possession it was for the purpose of applying the land to a different purpose. Hence, occupiers of the public lands, although liable to be dispossessed at any time by the state, might, and frequently did, retain possession of these lands for many generations; and the right of occupancy might not only be transferred to an heir, but might be sold for a price, the purchaser taking into account, of course, the precarious nature of the title.

A piece of land occupied in this manner was called *Possessio*, the occupier was called the *Possessor*, and he was said *Possidere*; the act of occupancy was *Usus*, the benefit derived by the state *Fructus*. Much of the obscurity connected with the Agrarian Laws has arisen from a misapprehension of the words *possidere*, *possessor*, *possessio*, which when used as technical legal terms, never denote an absolute right of property but merely occupancy by a tenant.[2]

It will be seen, from what we have said above, that the tenants of the *Ager Publicus* were divided into two classes, which stood in a very different position.

---

[1] See Appian B.C. I. 7. seqq. Some of the lands in Sicily were held according to this tenure, (Cic. in Verr. V. 6,) and it was very common in the provinces beyond the seas.
[2] Fest. s.v. *Possessio*, p. 233. Cic. de Off. II. 22. adv. Rull. III. 23. Liv. II. 61. IV. 36. 51. 53. VI. 5. 14. 37. Epit. LVIII. Flor. III 13. Oros. V. 18. *Mancipium* is the old word for property, and is opposed to *Usus*, the mere right of occupancy, as in the Lucretian line—
Vitaque *mancipio* nulli datur omnibus *usu*.

1. Those who had entered upon farms in full cultivation, who held leases for a limited period, and who paid a fair rent for the land. Such individuals might be either the original owners, or Roman citizens, or any persons whatsoever. They stood in the same relation to the state as an ordinary tenant to his landlord in modern times; and if, at the termination of the lease, either party was dissatisfied, the connection would terminate without the other having a right to complain.

2. Those who had entered upon the occupation of land lying waste and desolate in consequence of the ravages of war or from any other cause, who were bound, as the land was reclaimed, to pay to the state a certain moderate proportion of the produce, and who were tenants at will, upon an understanding, however, that they were not liable to be displaced in order to make room for another rent-paying tenant. The state reserved to itself the power of resuming possession when it thought fit, and unquestionably had a legal right at any time to eject the tenant; but it does not follow that this right could at all times be exercised with equity, especially after long occupation. Those who, in the first instance, had become the tenants of the state, had probably in most cases expended large sums in the erection of buildings, in the purchase of slaves and agricultural stocking, and in improvements of various descriptions. As the productiveness of the land was increased, the tax of one-tenth or one-fifth, as the case might be, would become less and less burdensome, and a very large reversion would accrue to the occupier, the result, in a great measure, of his own industry, skill, and capital. Here it is evident, that if the state, after allowing such occupants to remain in occupation for a lengthened period, and encouraging them to invest larger and larger sums in improvements, had suddenly required them to remove, without, at the same time, offering adequate compensation, it would have been guilty of gross injustice and bad faith. But this was not all. Land held in this manner being a source of great profit, the right of occupancy was, as we have mentioned above, frequently sold and transferred from one occupier to another for a large sum, and the validity of such sales and conveyances was fully recognized by law. Hence, if the state, by allowing occupation to remain undisturbed for generations, had, as it were, permitted the precarious nature of the tenure to fall out of view, the purchaser who had paid a large sum for the right of occupancy would have naturally regarded the sudden resumption by the state as little better than an arbitrary confiscation of his fortune.

The original occupiers of the public pastures were in a more favourable position, because here the capital was not sunk in buildings or in the improvement of the soil, but was laid out upon cattle and slaves, which were at all times sure of finding purchasers, although loss might be sustained by forced sales. Those, however, who had purchased the right of pasturing their stock upon a particular district would, as a matter of course, have lost the purchase money if called upon by the state to surrender their right soon after they had acquired it.

Having thus explained the origin of the Ager Publicus and its occupation, we now proceed to consider the

Leges Agrariae.—It is impossible to form a distinct idea of the Roman constitution unless we fully comprehend the nature and object of the laws so frequently mentioned by historians under this appellation—laws which were upon many occasions the source of furious and fatal discord. Their character was totally mistaken by scholars for many centuries after the revival of letters. It was universally believed that they were intended to prohibit Roman citizens from holding property in land above a certain amount, and for confiscating and dividing among the poorer members of the community the estates of private persons in so far as they exceeded the prescribed limits. Although the expediency of such a doctrine was never recognized in any well regulated state, ancient or modern, although it is at variance both with the principles and practice of the Roman constitution, and although the expressions of ancient writers, when correctly interpreted, give no support to the supposition that such ideas were ever mooted, yet the opinions first broached with regard to the Agrarian Laws were received and transmitted by successive generations of learned men almost without suspicion, and the innumerable embarrassments and contradictions which they involved were overlooked or passed by in silence. It was not until the latter end of the last century, (1795,) amid the excitement caused by the wild schemes of the French revolutionary leaders, that Heyne first distinctly pointed out the real nature of these enactments. His views were almost immediately embraced by Heeren, while the penetrating and vigorous Niebuhr quickly perceiving and appreciating their vast importance, brought all his vast learning and acuteness to bear upon the discussion, and succeeded so completely in developing and demonstrating the truth, that all are now astonished that the subject could have been so long and so grossly misunderstood.[1]

The discovery, for such it must be regarded, thus happily made, may be enunciated in the following proposition—

The LEGES AGRARIAE *of the Romans were in no case intended to interfere with or affect private property in land, but related exclusively to the* AGER PUBLICUS.

The *Ager Publicus* having been acquired and occupied as explained above, numerous abuses arose in process of time, especially among the tenants belonging to the second class. These being, as we have seen, in the earlier ages, exclusively Patricians, who, at the same time, monopolized the administration of public affairs, they were in the habit of defrauding the state, either by neglecting altogether to pay the stipulated proportion of the produce, or by paying less than was due, or, finally, by claiming what was in reality Ager Publicus as their own private property, it being easy, of course, in the absence of all strict superintendence and of scientific surveys, to shift the land-marks which separated public from private property. Meanwhile, the deficiencies in the public treasury were made up by heavier taxes; and the Plebeians complained that they were impoverished by new imposts, while the lands belonging to the community, which they had acquired by their blood, if fairly managed, would yield a sufficient return to meet all demands upon the Exchequer, or, if portioned out in allotments among themselves, afford them the means of supporting the increased burdens. These complaints, unquestionably founded in justice, were soon vehemently expressed, and were revived from time to time more or less loudly and enforced more or less earnestly, according to the state of public feeling and the energy of the popular champions. It is true, that the wealthier Plebeians soon became tenants of the *Ager Publicus* as well as the Patricians; but although this circumstance materially strengthened the hands of the occupiers, it did not improve the condition of the poor or make them less keenly alive to the injustice of the system against which they protested. Hence, from an early period in the commonwealth, *Leges Agrariae* were employed as most formidable and efficient weapons of offence by the Tribunes of the Plebs, and by the leaders of the democratic party.

[1] Even Arnold, in his excellent articles which appeared in the Encyclopædia Metropolitana about the year 1827, proceeded upon the supposition that the laws of the Gracchi were intended to limit private property. Before publishing his history of Rome, however, which was printed about eleven years later, he had fully adopted the views of Heyne and Niebuhr

THE PUBLIC LANDS AND THE AGRARIAN LAWS. 229

According to our definition, the term *Lex Agraria* will include any enactment with regard to the disposal of the *Ager Publicus;* but it was usually employed to denote, (1.) Those measures which had for their object a reform in management of the public lands, by enforcing the regular payment of rent on the part of the occupiers, prohibiting them from occupying more than a certain extent, demanding the surrender of portions and dividing these in small allotments among the poorer citizens; and, (2.) Those which were intended to prevent the occupation of newly acquired territory, by insisting upon its immediate application to the establishment of colonies or its distribution to individuals (*viritim.*) It is manifest that Agrarian Laws, belonging to the first class, were those which would give rise to the most bitter contests, because they would more nearly affect existing interests.

The first Agrarian Law upon record was the *Lex Cassia*, proposed and passed by Sp. Cassius Viscellinus when Consul, B.C. 486, (*tum primum Lex Agraria promulgata est, nunquam deinde usque ad hanc memoriam sine maximis motibus rerum agitata.*) Cassius was a Patrician, and the measure must, in all probability, have originated in some intestine feud among the dominant class. His opponents proved too strong for him; for as soon as he laid down his office he was impeached of treason and put to death, while his law, regarding the provisions of which we have no precise information, seems not to have been enforced.[1] We hear no more of Agrarian Laws, until the years B.C. 424,[2] 417, 416,[3] when much agitation prevailed on the subject, but without any marked result. By far the most important measure of this class was the *Lex Licinia*, carried, after a protracted struggle, by C. Licinius Stolo, in B.C. 367,[4] which served as the foundation of almost all later Agrarian Laws. The chief provisions were—

1. That no one should occupy more than five hundred jugers of the *Ager Publicus* (*ne quis plus D. iugera agri possideret.*)[5]
2. That no one should have more than a hundred large and five hundred small cattle grazing upon the public pastures.[6]
3. That each occupant of the *Ager Publicus* should employ a certain proportion of free labourers in cultivating it.[7]

The enforcement of these regulations seems to have been intrusted to the Plebeian Aediles, whom we find, on several occasions, prosecuting and fining those who had transgressed;[8] one of the first convictions under the new law being that of C. Licinius Stolo himself who had, by a legal fraud, obtained possession of one thousand jugers, and was, in consequence, sentenced to pay ten thousand asses.[9]

In addition to these fundamental provisions, the law would doubtless contain regulations for ascertaining correctly the boundaries of the *Ager Publicus* and private property, for the regular payment of rent to the state on the part of the occupants, and for ascertaining the amount to be paid in each case. Niebuhr has endeavoured to reproduce the law in full; but in descending to details, we

---

[1] Liv. II. 41. Dionys. VIII. 76.
[2] Liv. IV. 36. *Agri publici dicidendi coloniarumque deducendarum spes ostentatae.*
[3] Liv. IV. 47. 48. *Discordia domi ex agrariis legibus fuit . . . . et quum* (Tribuni) *legem promulgassent ut ager ex hostibus captus viritim divideretur,* &c.
[4] Liv. VI. 42.
[5] Liv. VI. 35.
[6] Appian. B.C. I. 7. 8.
[7] Appian. l c.
[8] e.g. Liv. X. 13. 23. 47. XXXIII. 42. XXXV. 10. Ovid. Fast. V. 283.
[9] Liv. VII. 16.

have little to guide us beyond conjecture. (See Niebuhr's Roman History, Vol. III. p. 11. Engl. trans.)

For upwards of two centuries after the passing of the Lex Licinia no attempt was made to interfere with the actual occupants of the *Ager Publicus*. Meanwhile immense additions had been made to the domains of the commonwealth during the contests which terminated in the subjugation of all Italy, and, during the second Punic war, by the confiscations of lands belonging to those states which had revolted to Hannibal. Large portions of the territory thus acquired had, it is true, been assigned to the faithful allies of Rome, had been disposed of in the foundation of colonies, and made over to the veterans of Scipio, but, at the same time, vast tracts had been retained as *Ager Publicus;* and no division among the poorer citizens individually (*viritim*) had taken place since the Lex Agraria passed, greatly to the disgust of the Senate, by C. Flaminius when Tribune of the Plebs, (B.C. 233,) in terms of which the lands conquered from the Senones, south of Ariminum, had been portioned out in small lots; and hence the district received the name of *Ager Gallicus Romanus*.[1] Moreover, although the *Lex Licinia* had never been repealed, the most important provisions had been violated. A large number of the wealthier families had gradually become occupiers, many of them, doubtless, by purchase and inheritance, of an extent far beyond five hundred jugers, their flocks and herds grazing on the public pastures greatly exceeded the lawful number, and the free agricultural labourers had been almost entirely superseded by slaves,[2] who, especially after the conquest of Macedonia, could be obtained at a very low price. On the other hand, the estates of small proprietors had been almost all swallowed up by the rich landholders, and the number of the poor was everywhere increasing. It was to arrest the downward progress of the humbler classes, and to remedy the abuses by which it had been caused that Tiberius Gracchus introduced his celebrated *Lex Sempronia Agraria*, the declared object of which was to revive, under a modified form, the ancient Lex Licinia. It proposed that no single individual should occupy more than five hundred jugers of the *Ager Publicus*, but that a father should be allowed a further amount of two hundred and fifty jugers for each of his sons, not exceeding two, so that no one should hold for himself and family more than one thousand jugers; that the surplus remaining over after this new adjustment had taken place should be divided among the poorer citizens, and that funds should be advanced to them out of the treasures bequeathed by Attalus sufficient to enable them to stock their allotments. It is evident, from what has been said above, (see p. 226,) that a sweeping change of this nature suddenly introduced, although containing clauses providing for compensation in certain cases, would entail heavy loss on a large class of persons, and would, in many instances, amount to a confiscation of property. Hence, the bill was met by the most violent opposition; but it was passed notwithstanding, and a standing commission appointed to carry it into effect. The difficulties and obstinate opposition encountered at every step rendered the progress of this body very slow; and the reader of history is well aware, that this and all the other enactments of Tiberius Gracchus and his brother were set aside or eluded after the death of the latter.[3]

In the civil strife which preceded the final dissolution of the commonwealth,

---

[1] Cic. Brut. 14. Acad. II. 5. De Inv II. 17. Val. Max. V. iv. 5. Varro R. R. I. 2. Polyb. II. 21.
[2] See on this point Plut. Tib. Gracch. 8.
[3] Plut. Tib. Gracch. 3 seqq. Liv. Epit. LVIII. Velleius II. 2. Appian. B.C. I 9. Cic. pro. Sext. 48. Victor de vir. ill. 64.

a very large portion of the public lands in Italy were alienated from the state and made over, by the establishment of military colonies, to the soldiers of the great commanders—Sulla, Pompeius, Julius Cæsar, and the Triumvirs. A considerable quantity, however, still remained up to the time of Vespasian, by whom assignments in Samnium were made to his veterans, and the little that was left was disposed of by Domitian, after whose reign the state possessed scarcely any property in land in Italy.

In addition to the *Lex Cassia—Lex Licinia—Lex Flaminia*, and *Lex Sempronia*, which have been adverted to in the above sketch, the following *Leges Agrariae* deserve notice.—

Lex Thoria, passed by Sp. Thorius, Tribune of the Plebs, B.C. 107. The object of this law, as far as we can gather from Appian, was to prohibit any farther distribution of land under the *Lex Sempronia*, and to ordain that the rents paid by the occupiers, who were to be left in undisturbed possession, should, in all time coming, be divided among the poorer citizens instead of being made over to the public Exchequer.[1]

Lex Appuleia, passed by L. Appuleius Saturninus when Tribune of the Plebs, B.C. 100. This was the law to which Q. Metellus Numidicus refused to swear obedience, and was, in consequence, forced to go into exile.[2]

Lex Servilia, proposed by P. Servilius Rullus, Tribune of the Plebs, B.C. 63, for the division of the *Ager Campanus*, and strenuously opposed by Cicero, in consequence of whose exertions it was thrown out. The speeches delivered against this law throw much light upon various topics connected with the *Ager Publicus*.[3]

Lex Julia, passed by Julius Cæsar during his Consulship, B.C. 59, in terms of which the *Ager Campanus* was distributed among twenty thousand citizens. It would appear that this territory was not occupied by large holders, but was portioned out in a number of small farms, and the holders of these were probably tenants belonging to the class described above (see p. 226.) Hence, there was no tumultuous opposition to this measure. The chief objection was the impolicy of depriving the state of the large revenue derived from this region which is described by Cicero as—*Caput vestrae pecuniae, pacis ornamentum, subsidium belli, fundamentum vectigalium, horreum legionum, solatium annonae* (De Leg. agr. II. 29.)[4]

[1] Appian. B.C. I. 27. We have taken it for granted that the true reading in this passage is Θόριος and not Βόριος. See also Cic. Brut. 36. De Orat. II. 70.
[2] Liv. Epit. LXIX. Cic. pro Sest. 16. 47. Victor de vir. ill. 62. Appian. B.C. I. 29.
[3] See the speeches of Cicero against Rullus passim; also in Pison 2.
[4] Cic. ad Att. II. 16. 18. ad Fam. XIII. 4. Liv. Epit. CIII. Velleius II. 44. Suet. Caes. 20. Appian. B.C. II. 10. Plut. Cat. min. 31.

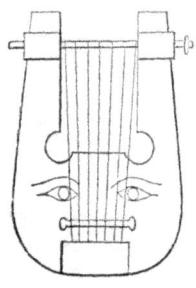
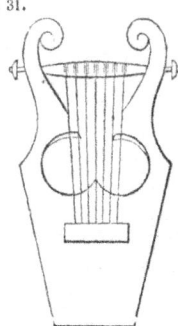
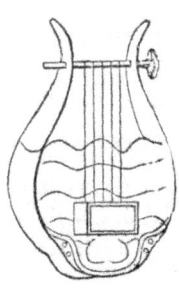

CHAPTER VIII.

THE ROMAN REVENUES.[1]

Different Words signifying Revenue.—*Pascua*—*Vectigalia*—*Publicum* —are the terms employed to denote generally the Revenues of Rome, from whatever source derived.

Pascua, i.e. Pasture lands, signified *Revenue*; because, in the earliest ages, the public income was derived solely from the rent of pastures belonging to the state. Thus Pliny declares—*Etiam nunc in Tabulis Censoriis* PASCUA *dicuntur omnia ex quibus Populus reditus habet, quia diu hoc solum Vectigal fuerat.*[2]

Vectigal is the word used more frequently than any other to denote the Revenue of the state generally. It is probably connected etymologically with *Veho*, and may be regarded as equivalent to the Greek φόρος, which bears the same meaning.

Publicum, in its widest acceptation, comprehended every thing which belonged to the community at large, and hence included not only the domain lands, their produce, and the Exchequer, but also roads, bridges, and public buildings of all descriptions. In a more limited sense, it signified *Revenue*, the word *Vectigal* being, in this case, understood. Indeed, the ellipse is sometimes supplied, as when Cicero says—*Diognotus, qui ex publicis vectigalibus tanta lucra facit.*[3]

Sources of the Roman Revenue.—The Roman Revenues were derived partly from lands, mines, and other property held by the state, partly from taxes paid by Roman citizens and by the subjects of Rome. Those subject states who paid a fixed sum in money were styled *Stipendiarii*,[4] those who paid a proportion of the produce of their soil, *Vectigales*; and the latter were regarded as occupying a more favourable position than the former. The terms, however, are frequently used indifferently, and, in point of fact, the provincials, in many cases, paid a portion of their taxes according to one system, and a portion according to the other.

Revenue derived from Land.—The Revenue derived from land was of two kinds, according as the land was the property of the state, (*Ager Publicus*, see last chapter,) and the occupiers merely tenants at will or upon leases of limited duration, or was the absolute property of the occupiers, subject to certain burdens

---

[1] The chief ancient authorities on the Roman Revenues will be found collected and arranged in the treatise by Peter Burman, entitled, *Vectigalia Populi Romani*, 4to. Leid. .734.
[2] Plin. H.N. XVIII. 3.
[3] Cic. in Verr. III. 38.
[4] *Impositum Vectigal est certum quod Stipendiarium dicitur, ut Hispanis et plerisque Poenorum, quasi victoriae praemium ac poena belli.* Cic. in Verr. III. 6. comp. IV. 60. Div. in Q.C. 3. de Prov. Cons. 5. de legg. III. 18. pro Balb. 18. Liv. XXIV. 47. XXXVII. 55. Caes. B. G. I. 44. VII. 10.

in favour of the state. In the former case, the Revenue received was, in the strictest sense, *a rent* paid by a tenant to his landlord, in the latter case, it was what we now term a *land-tax*. By far the larger portion of the public Revenue derived from land in Italy during the commonwealth proceeded from *Ager Publicus*, and was therefore *rent*. In the Provinces beyond the seas, on the other hand, Sicily, Sardinia, Africa, Macedonia, Asia, and others, the inhabitants were, for the most part, left in possession of their lands, but were required to pay a fixed sum in money or a certain proportion of the produce of the soil. The amount so paid would of course vary according to the circumstances of each particular Province and of each district; and we are acquainted with the details in a very few cases only. Rome, however, unquestionably possessed *Ager Publicus* in the Provinces as well as in Italy. Thus, we are told by Cicero that Sicily was the most favoured of all the Provinces; for when it had passed into the hands of the Romans, the inhabitants paid them no more than they had previously paid to their own kings and rulers. But although this applied to Sicily generally, a few states were in a worse position—*Perpaucae Siciliae civitates sunt bello subactae quorum ager cum esset publicus P. R. factus tamen illis est redditus. Is ager a censoribus locari solet.*[1] In this case, although the ancient proprietors were allowed to remain on their estates, they were no longer proprietors, but tenants, who held upon short leases, and paid a full rent for the land which they occupied, and which the state might take from them at any time and dispose of at pleasure (p. 226.) So also many of the larger cities in the Provinces possessed, previous to their subjugation by the Romans, *Ager Publicus* of their own, which in certain cases they would be permitted to retain, while in others it would be transferred to their conquerors.

This being premised, the Revenue derived from land, under whatever tenure it might be held, was divided into two heads, according as it was received from cultivated or uncultivated land. In the former case it was termed *Decumae*, in the latter, *Scriptura*.

Decumae.—We have already pointed out (p. 226) that the occupiers of the *Ager Publicus* in Italy, who were tenants at will, paid to the state one-tenth of the produce of the arable lands. This was the proportion paid by the proprietors of estates in Sicily in the shape of land-tax,[2] and this was the amount of land-tax in Sardinia also; for we are expressly told that Cæsar punished the Sulcitani in that island by ordering them to pay an eighth instead of a tithe (*et pro decumis octavas pendere iussi.*)[3] The tithe being therefore the ordinary amount levied in Italy and in the Provinces first subdued, was used as the general term to denote the proportion of the produce of arable land paid to the state in the shape of rent or of land-tax, whatever that proportion might be in reality. Thus, although vineyards and oliveyards usually paid a fifth, this was included under the designation of *Decumae;* and Cicero, when enumerating the various extortions connived at by Verres, uses such phrases as the following —*Quid? Amestratini miseri, impositis* ITA MAGNIS DECUMIS, *ut ipsis reliqui nihil fieret, nonne*, &c.[4] A great mass of curious information with regard to the working of the tithe system in Sicily, in all its details, will be found embodied in the third oration of the second action against Verres, the whole of that division of the speech being devoted to this subject. The occupiers of the public lands

[1] Cic. in Verr. III. 6.
[2] Cic. in Verr. III. 6. 8. et passim.
[3] Hist. de bello Afr. cap. ult.
[4] Cic. in Verr. III. 39.

who paid *Decumae* are usually termed *Aratores*, and as such are opposed to the *Pecuarii* or *Pastores*, to be mentioned in the next paragraph.

Scriptura.—In addition to the arable lands from which *Decumae* were exacted, the state possessed vast tracts of wild woody and mountain pasture (*silvae—saltus—pascua—pastiones*) in various parts of Italy, especially in Samnium and Lucania, to which sheep and cattle were driven in summer from the hot plains on the sea coast, (*greges ovium longe abiguntur ex Apulia in Samnium aestivatum,*)[1] a system still followed, and indeed rendered necessary by the climate and natural features of the country. Those who turned out their flocks and herds on the public pastures were termed *Pecuarii*[2] or *Pastores*, and were obliged to make a declaration to the Collector of Revenue for the district (*ad Publicanum profiteri*) of the number, which was written down in a register kept for the purpose, and hence the money levied was called *Scriptura*, and the land itself *Ager Scripturarius*[3] (*Scripturarius ager publicus appellatur, in quo ut pecora pascantur, certum aes est: quia Publicanus scribendo conficit rationem cum pastore.*) If any one was detected in turning out cattle not registered (*si inscriptum pecus paverint*)[4] he was liable to be prosecuted by the Collector of the Revenue; but a fraud of this description must be distinguished from a violation of the *Lex Licinia*, committed when an individual turned out a greater number of sheep and oxen upon the public pastures than the provisions of that law allowed to any one individual (p. 229.) The Plebeian Aediles are generally mentioned as the persons who instituted proceedings against transgressors of the statute (p. 158.)

There were public pastures in Sicily also, in Asia, in Africa, and doubtless in nearly all the provinces.[5]

Metalla, &c.—In addition to the income derived from *Decumae* and *Scriptura*, large sums were obtained from mines, (*metalla,*) including minerals of every description, which, together with the timber and other productions of the public forests, may be classed under the head of *Ager Publicus*. An ancient decree of the Senate forbade the working of mines in Italy; but mines of gold, silver, copper, iron, lead, and cinnabar, the property of the state, were worked with great profit in the Provinces, especially in Spain, which was above all other countries rich in mineral wealth, (*Metalla auri—argenti—aeris—ferri—plumbi—minii; fodinae aurariae—argentariae—ferrariae—miniariae; aurifodinae—argentifodinae.*)[6] In like manner, Revenue was obtained from stone quarries, (*lapicidinae,*) especially the grindstone quarries of Crete, (*Cotoriae,*)[7] from chalk-pits, (*cretifodinae,*)[8] and, above all, from salt-works, (*salinae,*) which were turned to advantage from a very early period.[9] The Revenue derived from the value of the salt itself must be distinguished from the tax upon salt, (*vectigal ex salaria annona,*) instituted by the Censors C. Claudius and M. Livius,[10] (B.C. 204,) and we may perhaps infer, from a passage in Livy,[11] that the sale of salt under the republic was a government monopoly.

1 Varro R. R. II. 1. Hor. Epod. I. 27.
2 Liv. X. 23. 47. XXXIII. 42. XXXV. 10.
3 Fest. s.v. *Saltum*, p. 302. s.v. *Scripturarius*, p. 333. Lucil. fragm. lib. XXVI. Plaut. Truc. I. ii. 41. seqq.
4 Varro l.c.
5 Cic. in Verr. II. 2. pro leg. Manil. 6. ad Fam. XIII. 65. Plin. H.N. XIX. 3. 15.
6 Plin. H.N. XXXIII. 4. 7. XXXIV. 10. 17. XXXVII. 13. Liv. XXXIV. 21. XXXIX. 24. XLV. 18. 29. Strab. III. p. 146.
7 Digest XXXIX. iv. 15.
8 Digest. VII. i. 13. XXIV. iii. 7.
9 Plin. H.N. XXXI. 7. Liv. I. 33. Cic. pro leg. Man. 7.
10 Liv. XXIX. 37.
11 Liv. II. 9.

Finally, under this head we may class the money raised from the sale of timber and from the tar works (*picariae*) in the public forests.[1]

Portoria.—The export and import dues levied at the various seaports in Italy and the Provinces formed another very important branch of Revenue. We hear of the existence of *Portoria* during the regal period, and of their temporary abolition by Publicola.[2] The amount of the *Portoria* was augmented as the empire itself extended, both by the vast increase of the foreign trade of Italy, and also by the duties levied in other countries, which were appropriated by the Roman treasury when the countries themselves were subjugated.[3] Q. Caecilius Metellus Nepos, when Praetor, (B.C. 60,) passed a law abolishing *Portoria* in Italy;[4] but they were revived by Caesar,[5] and continued by succeeding emperors.[6]

Burman has pointed out that the term *Portorium*, although properly denoting what we call *Customs*, was sometimes applied to a toll paid on crossing a bridge, and also to transit dues for goods merely passing through a country.[7]

It cannot be doubted that both the articles subject to duty and the amount of the duty must have varied for different places and for different periods; but upon these points we are almost totally destitute of information. It would appear that at Syracuse, in the time of Cicero, the *Portoria* were an ad valorem duty of five per cent.[8] Under the empire, the ordinary tax upon articles imported into Italy seems to have been two and a-half per cent. ad valorem;[9] and this is probably what Suetonius terms *Publicum Quadragesimae*.[10]

The *Portoria*, *Decumae*, and *Scriptura* formed the three chief sources of Revenue during the most flourishing period of the republic, and as such, are classed together by Cicero—*Ita neque ex portu, neque ex decumis, neque ex scriptura vectigal conservari potest . . . . . . saepe totius anni fructus uno rumore periculi, atque uno belli terrore, amittitur* (Pro. leg. Man. 6.)

Tributum was a property tax, being a per centage levied upon the fortune of each Roman citizen, as rated in the books of the Censors. The sum raised in this manner does not appear to have been considerable until the practice of granting pay to the troops was introduced. From this time forward the proceeds of the *Tributum* were chiefly, if not altogether, applied to make provision for the *aes militare* and other expenses of war.[11] It was paid by all citizens who were *censi*, Patricians and Plebeians alike.[12] We find, indeed, on one occasion, a claim for exemption preferred by the pontiffs and augurs, but it was not allowed.[13] The amount raised annually varied according to the demands of the public service, and was fixed by the Senate, who were said *indicere tributum*, while the people correlatively were said *conferre tributum*. Since the amount required varied from year to year, the rate per cent. must, in like manner, have varied; and we cannot feel certain that property of every description was rated equally. It is stated that Cato, whose Censorship (B.C. 184) was marked

---

[1] Cic. Brut. 22. Digest. L. xvi. 17. *Vectigal salinarum, metallorum et picariarum.*
[2] Liv. II. 9. Dionys. V. 22.
[3] Liv. XXXII. 7. XL. 51. Velleius II 6. Cic. in Verr. 72—75. de leg. agr. II. 29.
[4] Cic. ad Att. II. 16. comp. ad Q. F. I. 1. Dion Cass. XXXVII. 51.
[5] Suet. Caes. 43.
[6] Dion Cass. XLVIII. 34. Tacit. Ann. XIII. 51.
[7] Senec. de const. sap. 14. Plin. H N. XII. 14. Sueton. Vitell. 14.
[8] Cic. in Verr. II 75.
[9] Quintil. declam 359.
[10] Sueton. Vesp. 1. comp Symmach. Epp. N 62. 63.
[11] Liv. IV. 60 V 10. VI. 32.
[12] Liv. IV. 60. The relaxation mentioned in Liv. II. 9. does not appear to have been permanent.
[13] Liv. XXXIII. 42.

by singular severity, taxed certain articles of luxury at 1-30th per cent. on a greatly exaggerated valuation.[1]

Tributum seems to have been regularly levied from the institution of the Census by Servius Tullius[2] until the triumph of Aemilius Paulus, in B.C. 167, after the complete subjugation of Macedonia, when such vast sums were poured into the Roman treasury that this tax was abolished as no longer necessary (*Omni Macedonum gaza, quae fuit maxima, potitus est Paulus: tantum in aerarium pecuniae invexit, ut unius imperatoris praeda finem attulerit tributorum.*)[3] This immunity continued for one hundred and twenty-four years; but in the Consulship of Hirtius and Pansa, (B.C. 43,) a few months only after Cicero wrote the paragraph quoted above, the impoverished state of the exchequer rendered it necessary to reimpose the *Tributum*, which was regularly levied under the empire.[4]

Although *Tributum*, in the restricted sense of the word, was paid by Roman citizens alone, a tax of the same nature, and sometimes designated by the same name, was levied in the Provinces also. Thus, we are told by Cicero, that in Sicily—*Omnes Siculi ex censu quotannis tributa conferunt;*[5] we hear from the same authority of a poll tax in the Province of Cilicia, which included part of Phrygia, (*audivimus nihil aliud nisi imperata ἐπικεφάλια solvi non posse*,)[6] and Appian,[7] who flourished under Hadrian, informs us that in his time the Syrians and Cilicians paid a poll tax annually, amounting to one per cent. on the property of each individual; but that the impost on the Jews was heavier in consequence of their frequent rebellions.

Another tax, dating from an early period of the commonwealth, was the—

Vigesima Manumissionum—a duty of five per cent. on the value of manumitted slaves. This tax was instituted B.C. 357, under very extraordinary circumstances, the law by which it was imposed having been passed, not in the Comitia at Rome, but in the camp at Sutrium.[8] This is the tax spoken of by Cicero when he says—*Portoriis Italiae sublatis, agro Campano diviso, quod vectigal superest domesticum, praeter vicesimam?*[9] and it appears to have continued without change until the reign of Caracalla, (A.D. 211—217,) by whom it was raised to ten per cent.; (*decima manumissionum;*) but his immediate successor Macrinus reduced it to the original rate.[10] The money realised from this source was termed *Aurum Vicesimarium*, and in the earlier ages of the republic was hoarded, "*in sanctiore aerario*," to meet extraordinary emergencies.[11]

The charges entailed by the large standing armies maintained under the empire, and the bounties paid to soldiers on their discharge, taken in connection with the rapid diminution of the Revenue derived from the *Ager Publicus* in Italy, rendered the imposition of new taxes inevitable. The most remarkable of these were—

Vectigal Rerum Venalium.—This was introduced after the civil wars, and consisted of a per centage levied upon all commodities sold by auction or in

---

[1] Liv. XXXIX. 44.
[2] Dionys. IV. 15. 19.
[3] Cic. de Off. II. 22. and so also Plin. H.N. XXXIII. 3.
[4] Plut. Aem. Paul. 38. Cic. ad Fam. XII. 30. Philipp. II. 37.
[5] Cic. in Verr. II. 53 and following chapters.
[6] Cic. ad Att. V. 16. comp. ad Fam. III. 8.
[7] Appian. de rebus Syr. 50.
[8] Liv. VII. 16. *Ab altero consule nihil memorabile gestum: nisi quod legem, novo exemplo ad Sutrium in castris tributim de vicesima eorum, qui manumitterentur, tulit.*
[9] Cic. ad Att. II. 16.
[10] Dion Cass. LXXVII. 9. LXXVIII. 12.
[11] Liv. **XXVII.** 10.

open market. It was originally one per cent. upon the price (*centesima rerum venalium.*) Tiberius, soon after his accession to the throne, was earnestly solicited to abolish this tax; but he refused upon the plea—*militare aerarium eo subsidio niti.* Two years afterwards, however, (A.D. 17,) when Cappadocia was reduced to a Province, he lowered the duty to one half per cent. (*ducentesimam in posterum statuit;*) but in A.D. 31 he found it necessary to return to 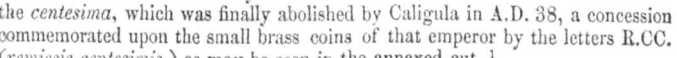 the *centesima*, which was finally abolished by Caligula in A.D. 38, a concession commemorated upon the small brass coins of that emperor by the letters R.CC. (*remissis centesimis,*) as may be seen in the annexed cut.[1]

Vectigal Mancipiorum Venalium.—The last mentioned tax did not apply to the sale of slaves, upon the price of whom Augustus levied a duty of two per cent. (*quinquagesima,*) which he applied to military purposes and to the payment of night watchmen. This two per cent. had been augmented to four per cent. before the second Consulship of Nero, (A.D. 56,) by whom it was at that time modified in so far that he made it payable by the seller and not by the buyer (*Vectigal quoque quintae et vicesimae venalium mancipiorum remissum, specie magis quam vi, &c.*)[2]

Vigesima Hereditatium.—Instituted by Augustus A.D. 6. It was, as the name implies, a tax of five per cent. on successions and legacies, none being exempt except very near relations, (πλὴν τῶν πάνυ συγγινῶν,) that is, probably, those who were technically termed *sui heredes* and poor persons who inherited to a small amount.[3] The discontent occasioned by this impost was deep, and was loudly expressed, and the people submitted only from a dread of something still more obnoxious.[4] Modifications were introduced by Nerva and Trajan; but no important change took place until the reign of Caracalla, by whom, in this case as well as in the *vigesima manumissionum*, the five per cent. was raised to ten per cent.; but his successor Macrinus restored matters to their former footing.[5]

Quadragesima Litium.—Among the various new taxes (*vectigalia nova et inaudita*) imposed by Caligula, was a duty of two and a-half per cent. on the amount in dispute in all suits at law (*pro litibus atque iudiciis, ubicumque conceptis, quadragesima summae de qua litigaretur.*)[6] This was probably the tax whose abolition is commemorated, on large brasses of Galba, by the legend R. XL. or REMISSAE XXXX. or QUADRAGENS. REMISSAE.

What the *Quadragesima* and *Quinquagesima*, repealed by Nero may have been we have no means of deciding; but the words of the historian, who records their abolition, seem to imply that they were illegal exactions.[7]

[1] The chief authorities regarding the *Centesima* are, Tacit. Ann. I. 78. II. 42. Dion C· 38. LVIII. 16. LIX. 9. Suet. Cal. 16.
[2] Dion Cass. LV. 31. Tacit. Ann. XIII. 31.
[3] Dion Cass. LV. 25. Suet. Octav. 49.
[4] Dion Cass. LVI. 28.
[5] Plin. Paneg. 36. Dion Cass. LXXVII. 9. LXXVIII. 12. comp. Ulpian. in collat. leg. Mos. tit. XVI. § ult.
[6] Suet. Cal. 40.
[7] Tacit. Ann. XIII. 51.

Mode of Collecting the Revenue.—The Roman Revenue was, for the most part, not collected directly, but the different taxes in Italy and in the Provinces were farmed out, that is, were let upon lease to contractors, who undertook, at their own risk and cost, to levy the dues, and to pay a fixed sum annually into the treasury.

The persons who entered into these contracts with the state were regarded as forming a distinct class, (*ordo*,) and were all comprehended under the general name of PUBLICANI; (*quia publico fruuntur;*) but those who farmed particular taxes were frequently distinguished by a title derived from the impost in which they were specially interested, and thus the terms *Decumani, Scripturarii*, and *Portitores*[1] are applied to the lessees of the *Decumae, Scriptura*, and *Portoria;* the persons from whom these taxes were collected being respectively the *Aratores, Pecuarii*, and *Mercatores*. Occasionally also, the contractors who farmed the taxes of a particular district or Province were named from the country in question, and hence *Asiani* is used by Cicero to denote the *Publicani* who farmed the Revenues of the Roman Province of Asia.[2]

The state, in granting the lease, was said *locare vectigalia*, and the process was called *locatio;* those who took the lease were said *conducere* or *redimere*, and hence *redemtores*, which is a general term for contractors of any kind, is sometimes employed as synonymous with *Publicani*.

To farm the Revenues, or even a portion of the Revenues, of a large Province, required an immense establishment of slaves and subordinates of every kind, as well as vast warehouses for storing, and fleets of merchantmen for transporting from place to place, the produce collected. An enterprise of this magnitude was obviously beyond the means of any private individual, however wealthy, and was always undertaken by joint stock companies, which were called *societates*, the partners being termed *socii*. The *Publicani* had become a body of importance as early as the second Punic war,[3] and their numbers, wealth, and influence increased with the extension of the Roman empire and the increase of its Revenue. The *societates*, during the last century of the republic and under the early emperors,[4] were composed chiefly of members of the Equestrian order, who, as we have already explained, (p. 74,) were in reality the class of monied men. In fact, the *Equites*, as a body, may be said to have had a monopoly of this department of mercantile speculation; and in all matters relating to the collection of the public revenue *Equites* and *Publicani* became convertible terms. Although the Romans looked with little respect upon traffic conducted upon a small scale, the *Publicani* were always treated with great respect; and by Cicero, who, however, had a special object in view, they are complimented in the most high flown language—*Flos enim equitum Romanorum, ornamentum civitatis, firmamentum reipublicae, Publicanorum ordine continetur*; (Pro. Planc. 9;) and it would appear that among the different classes of *Publicani* the farmers of the *Decumae* held the most honourable place—*Decumani, hoc est, principes et quasi Senatores publicanorum* (In. Verr. II. 71.)

The duty of letting the different branches of the Revenue to the *Publicani* devolved, as we have seen, (p. 169,) on the Censors, and hence these leases

---

[1] It is doubtful, however, whether the word *Portitor* is not confined to the persons in the employment of those *Publicani* who farmed the *Portoria*, to the tide-waiters, namely, who watched the vessels as they loaded and discharged, and exacted the duties, see Non. s.v. *Portitores*, p. 15. ed Gerl.
[2] Cic. ad Att. I. 17.
[3] Liv. XXIII. 48. 49.
[4] Tacit. Ann. IV. 6.

were generally for a period of five years. The *locatio* of the taxes for all the Provinces, except Sicily,[1] took place in the forum, by public auction; the upset price was augmented by the bidding (*licitatione*) of the competitors, the person who offered the advance holding up his finger, hence the phrases *tollere digitum—digito liceri*.[2] Sometimes, led away by the ardour of competition, a sum was offered beyond the real value of the tax; and we find examples of the *Publicani* petitioning the Senate to cancel, or at least modify, the terms of the bargain (*Asiani, qui de Censoribus conduxerant, questi sunt in Senatu, se cupiditate prolapsos, nimium magno conduxisse: ut induceretur locatio postulaverunt.*[3]

Each *Societas* had a chairman or president called *Manceps*,[4] who conducted the bidding at these auctions, (hence termed *auctor emptionis*,) and who gave security to the state for the due performance of the conditions of the sale and the terms of the contract,[5] which, from being drawn up by the Censors, were called *Leges Censoriae*. In addition to the *Manceps*, each *Societas* had a Manager styled *Magister Societatis*,[6] a business man, who generally remained at Rome, kept the accounts, conducted the correspondence, and exercised a general superintendence over the affairs of the company. Under his immediate control were a number of officials, who took charge of different departments, and these inspectors were said *dare operas pro magistro* or *esse in operis societatis*; hence we find in Cicero such expressions as the following—*P. Terentius, meus necessarius, operas in portu et scriptura Asiae pro magistro dedit:—In maiorem modum a te peto, Cn. Papium, qui est in operis eius societatis, tueare, curesque ut eius operae quam gratissimae sint sociis—Canuleius vero, qui in portu Syracusis operas dabat*,[7] &c.

Although nearly the whole of the Roman Revenue was collected according to the system described above, the *Tributum*, paid by Roman citizens, formed an exception. This tax was originally applied to the payment of the army, (*aes militare*,) and was, it would seem, levied by persons entitled *Tribuni aerarii*, by whom it was disbursed to the soldiers, without passing through the public treasury. Every thing, however, connected with these *Tribuni aerarii* is involved in the greatest obscurity and doubt.[8]

Total Revenue.—It has been stated, on the authority of Plutarch, (Pomp. 45,) that the total amount of the income of the state, from every source, was, before the conquests of Pompeius in the east, 200 millions of Sesterces, and that it was increased by him to 340 millions, the former sum being equivalent, in round numbers, to £1,600,000 sterling, the latter to £2,800,000. But it is scarcely possible to believe that either of these sums would have been sufficient to cover the expenditure of the commonwealth at that epoch; and it will be seen, upon referring to the original, that the words of the biographer do not necessarily imply that he comprehended the whole revenue derived by Rome from all her

---

[1] The taxes of Sicily were let in the island itself. Cic. in Verr. II. 3. 64.
[2] See Cic. in Verr. I. 54. III. 11.
[3] Cic. ad Att. I. 17.
[4] Paul Diac. s.v. *Manceps*, p. 151. Pseud. Ascon. in Cic. div. in Q. C. 10. says—*Mancipes, publicanorum principes*, and hence *Mancipes* is sometimes used as equivalent to *Publicani*.
[5] Varro L. L. V. § 40. Ascon. ad Cic. in Verr. I. 54. Polyb. VI. 15.
[6] e.g. *Cn. Plancius, eques Romanus, princeps inter suos, maximarum societatum auctor, plurimarum magister*. Cic. pro Planc. 13.
[7] Cic. ad Att. XI. 10. ad Fam. XIII. 9. in Verr. II. 70. comp. in Verr. III. 41. ad Fam. XIII. 6⁵.
[8] See Plaut. Aul. III. 8. 52. Cato ap. Aul Gell. IX. 10. Varro. L.L. V. y 181. Paul. Diac. s.v. *aerarii tribuni*, p. 2. Pseud. Ascon. ad Cic. in Verr. I. 13. Every thing known upon this subject will be found in the essay of Madvig, *De Tribunis Aerariis*, contained in the second volume of his *Opuscula Academica*.

possessions, and very probably his observation applied to the Eastern Provinces alone.[1] Gibbon has calculated (Decline and Fall, Chapter VI.) that the general income of the Roman Provinces could seldom have amounted, after the accession of Augustus, to less than fifteen or twenty millions of our money, while both Wenck and Guizot consider this estimate too low.

[1] Πρὸς δὲ τούτοις ἔφραξε διὰ τῶν γραμμάτων, ὅτι πεντακισχίλιαι μὲν μυριάδες ἐκ τῶν τελῶν ὑπῆρχον, ἐκ δ'ὧν αὐτὸς προσεκτήσατο τῇ πόλει, μυριάδας ὀκτακισχιλίας πεντακοσίας λαμβάνουσιν. Moreover, these expressions, if strictly interpreted, must mean that the sum of 340 millions of Sesterces (85 millions of drachmae) was added by Pompeius to the former revenue, not that the revenue was made up to that sum by his conquests.

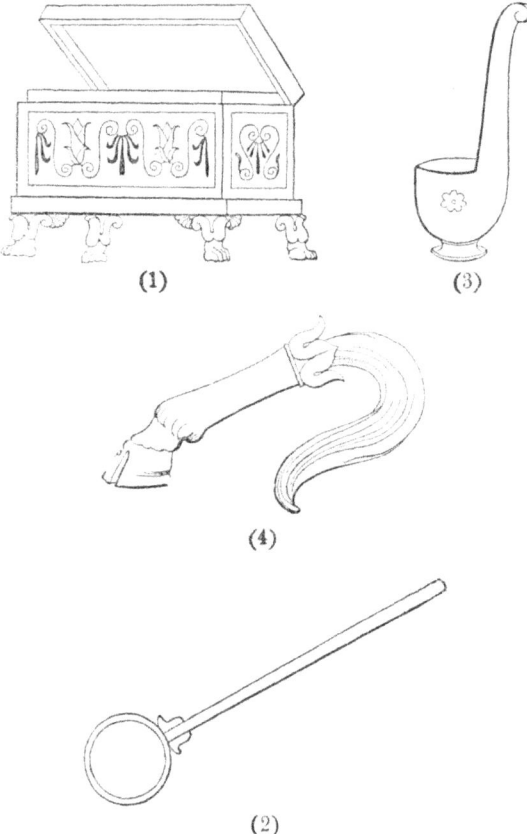

Sacred Utensils, (see page 343.) from the frieze of the temple of Jupiter Tonans at Rome.

CHAPTER IX.

ROMAN LAW AND THE ADMINISTRATION OF JUSTICE.

It must not be supposed that we are now about to sketch even a faint outline of Roman Law considered as a science. To execute such an undertaking in a satisfactory manner would require the space of a large volume instead of a short chapter. Our object is very limited. We propose—In the first place, to name the different sources from which Roman Law was derived. In the second place, to advert very briefly to those portions of the national code, a certain acquaintance with which is absolutely indispensable before we can form a distinct idea of the political and social state of the people; and here we must confine ourselves to an exposition of the broad and simple principles recognised and understood by the community at large, without attempting to explain the complicated modifications and subtle refinements which were introduced by jurisconsults, especially under the empire. Lastly, to convey a general idea of the mode of procedure, both in civil suits and in criminal impeachments.[1]

It will be remembered that in chapter III. p. 80, we made a statement of the characteristic rights of Roman citizens and of the subdivisions of those rights. The *Ius Suffragii* and the *Ius Honorum* we have now discussed and illustrated as fully as our limits will permit; and in addition to what has been already said regarding the *Ius Provocationis*, some farther remarks will be made in the concluding portion of this chapter, when treating of criminal trials. As yet we have said nothing upon the *Ius Connubii* and the *Ius Commercii*, the former comprehending the relations existing between parents and children as well as between husbands and wives, the latter embracing the different modes in which property might be legally acquired, held, transferred and defended. These topics will now occupy our attention; but before entering upon any portion of the Civil Law, we must examine into the foundations on which it rested.

Signification of the word Ius.—IUS, when used in a general sense, answers to our word *Law* in its widest acceptation. It denotes, not one particular law nor collection of laws, but the entire body of principles, rules and statutes, whether written or unwritten, by which the public and the private rights, the duties and

---

[1] The following works will be found highly useful to the student who may desire to examine closely into the topics touched upon in this chapter.—Corpus Iuris Civilis Anteiustiniani, edd. *Boecking, Bethmann-Hollweg*, &c. Bonn. 1835, &c.—*Hugo*, Lehrbuch d. Geschichte d. Roemischen Rechts bis auf Iustinian, Berlin, 1832 (eleventh edition.)—*Savigny*, Geschichte d. Roemischen Rechts im Mittelalter; the Das Recht des Besitzes, and, indeed all the writings of the same author.—*Bethmann-Hollweg*, Handbuch d. Civilprocesses, Bonn. 1834.—*Zimmern*, Geschichte d. Roemischen Privatrechts, Heidelb. 1826.—*Rein*, Das Roemische Privatrecht und der Civilprocess, Leips. 1836.—*Rein*, Das Criminalrecht d. Roemer Leips. 1844.—*Geib* Geschichte d. Roemischen Criminalprocesses, Leips. 1842.

the obligations of men, as members of a community, are defined, inculcated, protected and enforced. Roman writers usually recognise a threefold division—
1. *Ius Naturale*—2. *Ius Gentium*—3. *Ius Civile*.

1. *Ius Naturale*, comprehending those duties which are acknowledged and performed by the great mass of mankind, whether civilized or barbarous. Such are, the union of the sexes in marriage or otherwise, the rearing of children, and the submission of the latter to their parents.

2. *Ius Gentium*, comprehending the principles of right and wrong, which are generally acknowledged and acted upon by all bodies of men who have attained to political organization—*quod semper aequum et bonum est*. Such are, the plain rules of honesty and equity, the importance of truth, the expediency and necessity of adhering to treaties and compacts deliberately concluded.

For most practical purposes the *Ius Naturae* and the *Ius Gentium* may be included under one head, the latter being, in reality, included in the former, and thus Cicero (Tusc. I. 13) declares—*Consensio omnium gentium* LEX NATURAE *putanda est*. This will not, however, hold good universally; for, by the *Ius Naturale* all men enjoyed personal freedom, although the condition of slavery was recognised by all, or nearly all, the civilized nations of antiquity, and hence the remark of Florentinus (Dig. I. v. 4)—*Servitus est* CONSTITUTIO IURIS GENTIUM *qua quis dominio alieno* CONTRA NATURAM *subiicitur*.

3. *Ius Civile*, comprehending all the usages and laws which serve to regulate the internal administration of any particular community. Hence, when speaking of the Romans, *Ius Civile* denotes the whole body of Roman Law, from whatever source derived.[1] The most important of these sources we shall now proceed briefly to enumerate.

I. **Leges XII Tabularum.**—Formal laws were enacted under the kings, first in the Comitia Curiata, and subsequently in the Comitia Centuriata also, after the establishment of that assembly by Servius Tullius. A few fragments of these *Leges Regiae*, as they were termed, have been preserved by Livy and Dionysius.[2] We have no reason, however, to suppose that any attempt was made to draw up and introduce a system which should establish general principles and rules of practice, binding upon all classes of the community, until the appointment of the ten commissioners—the *Decemviri*—for that special purpose, in B.C. 451, fifty-nine years after the expulsion of the kings. We have already had occasion to mention (p. 151) that the result of their labours was the far-famed Code of the XII Tables, which although necessarily brief and imperfect, was ever after regarded as the spring in which the ample and constantly increasing stream of Roman Law took its rise (*fons omnis publici privatique iuris*.) During the period of the republic it was committed to memory by every well educated youth, (Cic. de legg. I. 5. II. 4,) and was regarded with so much veneration that, after the lapse of two centuries and a-half, the most learned were unable to speak of the compilation without using the language of hyperbole—*Bibliothecas mehercule omnium philosophorum unus mihi videtur XII Tabu-*

---

[1] See Gaius I. § 1. *Ius Civile*, as we shall point out below, is sometimes used by late writers in a restricted sense, to denote that particular source of Roman Law which was contained in the writings and opinions of celebrated jurists.

[2] The *Leges Regiae*, published by Marbanus, are modern forgeries. With regard to the nature of the *Ius Papirianum*, said to have been a collection of the *Leges Regiae*, and to have been compiled during the reign of Tarquinius Superbus, (Dionys. III. 36. Pompon. Digest. I. ii. 2. § 2. 35,) we know nothing certain. We gather from the words of Paulus in the Digest (L. xvi. 144.) that it was commented on by Granius Flaccus, who was contemporary with Julius Caesar. See *Dirksen*, Versuchen zur Kritik, &c. der Quellen des Roemischen Rechts. Leips. 1823.

SOURCES OF ROMAN LAW.

larum libellus, si quis legum fontes et capita viderit, et auctoritatis pondere et utilitatis ubertate superare, (Cic. de Orat. I. 44,) and again (De R. IV. 8) —*admiror nec rerum solum sed verborum etiam elegantiam.*

The *Leges XII Tabularum* were doubtless derived in part from the earlier *Leges Regiae*, and in part from the laws of other states, (p. 152,) but must, in all probability, have been founded chiefly upon long established use and wont, the *Ius Consuetudinis* of Cicero, (De Inv. II. 22,) the *Ius non scriptum* of later writers, which, taking its rise in the tastes, habits and prejudices, as well as in the wants of a people, long precedes statutory enactments, and long serves as a guiding rule in young communities which work out their own civilization.

II. **Leges Curiatae.**—Laws passed in the Comitia Curiata. These can scarcely be accounted as a source of Roman Law after the establishment of the republic, or, at all events, after the introduction of the Decemviral Code.

III. **Leges Centuriatae.**—Laws passed in the Comitia Centuriata. These, from the first, were binding upon all orders in the state, and formed, during the republic one of the chief sources of Law.

IV. **Leges Tributae s. Plebiscita.**—Laws passed in the Comitia Tributa. These were, originally, binding upon the Plebeians alone; but after the passing of the *Lex Valeria Horatia*, in B.C. 449, confirmed and extended by the *Lex Publilia*, in B.C. 339, and by the *Lex Hortensia*, in B.C. 286, they possessed the same efficacy as the *Leges Centuriatae*. See the details given in p. 124.

V. **Senatus-Consulta.**—It was a subject of controversy among the jurists of the empire whether, even at that period, a decree of the Senate could be regarded as a law, (Gaius I. § 4. See above, pp. 229. 222.) and according to the theory of the constitution, it certainly could not. But in practice, even under the republic, although a decree of the Senate could not overturn any existing law, it was regarded as possessing the force of a law (*legis vicem obtinet*) in matters not provided for by an existing law.

VI. **Edicta Magistratuum.**—The higher magistrates, such as the Consuls, Praetors, Aediles, Quaestors, Censors, as well as the Provincial Governors and the Pontifices, were in the habit of publishing *Edicta* or public notices, with reference to the jurisdiction conferred by their respective offices; and these notices or proclamations constituted what was termed *Ius Honorarium*. The magistrates could in no sense be regarded as lawgivers; but those portions of their edicts which were adopted in the practice of the courts acquired, in process of time, the force of laws. By far the most important were the *Edicta Praetorum*, especially of the Praetor Urbanus, to whom was committed the control over civil suits. From an early period it became customary for the Praetor Urbanus, when he entered upon office, to put forth an *Edictum*, in which he stated the forms to which he would adhere in the administration of justice, and, at the same time, took occasion to explain or supply any details connected with the ordinary course of procedure, with the application of the laws, and with previous decisions which appeared obscure or imperfect.

The Edict of the Praetor Urbanus, from being published regularly every year, was styled *Edictum Perpetuum* or *Lex Annua*, in contradistinction to an Edict referring to some special occurrence, termed *Edictum Repentinum*. These *Edicta Perpetua* being carefully preserved, began, in process of time, to be regarded as a source of law, in so far as its interpretation was concerned; and in the days of Cicero the *Ius Praetorium* was studied by youths along with the XII Tables. It was not uncommon for a Praetor to include in his Edict passages borrowed from those of his predecessors; and a section transferred in this manner was distinguished as *Caput Tralaticium*.[1]

The *Edicta* of the Praetors, from the earliest times, were collected, arranged, and digested by Salvius Iulianus during the reign of Hadrian, and thus rendered more easily available.

VII. **Res Iudicatae. Praeiudicia.**—Decisions passed by a competent court in cases of doubt or difficulty, although not absolutely binding upon other judges, were naturally held to be of great weight when any similar combination of events happened to occur.

VIII. **Responsa Prudentium. Iuris-Peritorum Auctoritas.**—The brevity with which the Laws of the XII Tables were expressed rendered explanations and commentaries absolutely necessary for the application and development of the code. Moreover, particular technical forms, called *Legis Actiones*, were introduced into the practice of the courts, and without the use of these no suit could be prosecuted. Lastly, a certain number of days in the year were set apart for hearing civil suits, these days being termed *Dies Fasti*. All knowledge regarding these matters was, for a long period, confined to the Patricians, and especially to the Pontifices, who devoted themselves to legal studies, and who, as part of their official duty, regulated the Calendar. This knowledge was studiously concealed by a privileged few until, in B.C. 304, a certain Cn. Flavius, secretary (*scriba*) to Appius Claudius, divulged the carefully guarded secrets—*Civile Ius, repositum in penetralibus Pontificum, evulgavit, Fastosque circa forum in albo proposuit, ut, quando lege agi posset, sciretur*—and published, for general use, a collection of forms and technicalities, which was named *Ius Flavianum*.[2] Those who had previously enjoyed a monopoly of legal practice made an effort to retain their influence by drawing up a new set of forms; but these also were made public, about B.C. 200, by L. Aelius Paetus Catus, in a work quoted under the title of *Ius Aelianum*, which appears to have contained the text of the XII Tables, with a commentary and appropriate *Legis Actiones*.[3] The difficulties which had hitherto surrounded the study of Civil Law being now in a great measure removed, it attracted general attention, and towards the close of the republic was cultivated with so much diligence and zeal that it gradually assumed the dignity of a science, whose professors were styled *Iuris-periti, Iuris-consulti, Iuris-auctores*. Persons who were known to have devoted themselves to this pursuit were constantly appealed to for assistance and advice; treatises were drawn up and published by them on various branches; and it became common for young men who were desirous to acquire distinction as pleaders to attach themselves for a time to some celebrated doctor, as Cicero did when he placed himself as a disciple, first under Q. Mucius Augur, and, after his death, under Q. Mucius Scaevola.

The taste for Law as a science increased under the empire, rising to its highest point during the reign of Hadrian and his immediate successors; (A.D. 130—230;) a vast number of works were compiled, both upon general principles and on particular departments; and to this period belong the great names of Gaius, Papinianus, Ulpianus, Paulus and Modestinus. In proportion as statutes became more complicated, and the number of new and embarrassing questions, which

---

[1] Cic. de Inv. II. 2. in Verr. I. 42, III. 14, 44. de legg. I. 5. ad Fam. III. 8. ad Attic. V. 21. Aul. Gell. III 18.
[2] Liv. IX. 46. Cic. pro Muraen. 10. ad Att. VI. 1. Plin. H.N. XXXIII. 1. Aul. Gell. VI. 9.
[3] Cic. Brut. 20. de Orat. I. 56. III. 33. Cod. Iustin. VII. vii. 1. Digest. I. ii. 2. § 38.

arose out of a highly artificial state of society, increased, the value attached to the written treatises and oral responses of jurists of reputation was enhanced, and their importance was still farther augmented by an ordinance of Augustus, followed up by a decree of Hadrian, the effect of which was to confer upon the opinions of the most learned doctors, when in harmony with each other,[1] the force of laws (Gaius I. § 7.)

The term *Ius Civile* is sometimes applied, in a restricted sense, by late writers to denote the *Responsa Prudentium* alone.

IX. **Constitutiones Principum.**—We have seen that the popular assemblies were virtually suppressed soon after the downfal of the republic, (pp. 128. 129.) and thus the principal source of new laws was cut off. On the other hand, the legislative functions of the Senate were, ostensibly at least, greatly extended, (p. 222.) and the Emperor being viewed as the fountain of all civil as well as military power, decrees emanating from the imperial will had all the force of laws. These *Constitutiones*, as they were termed, assumed four forms.

1. *Edicta*.—Ordinances with regard to matters in which new laws, or modifications of existing laws, were deemed requisite.
2. *Mandata*.—Instructions to magistrates and other officials.
3. *Rescripta*.—Answers to magistrates and other officials, when they applied to the Emperor for information and advice.
4. *Decreta*.—Decisions upon doubtful points of law, referred to the Emperor as the highest court of appeal.

Systems of Roman Law.—From the publication of the Laws of the XII Tables until the accession of Justinian, (B.C. 450—A.D. 527,) a space of nearly a thousand years, during which, republican laws, imperial constitutions, senatorial decrees, praetorian edicts, and the writings of the jurists, had accumulated to an immense extent, no attempt had been made to reduce this vast mass to a well ordered system. Collections had indeed been formed from time to time of the Imperial Constitutions, such as the *Codex Gregorianus* and the *Codex Hermogenianus*, (the latter probably a supplement to the former,) known to us from fragments only, which embrace Constitutions from the age of Septimius Severus to that of Diocletian and Maximinian (A.D. 196—A.D. 305.)

Much more important than either is the *Codex Theodosianus*, still extant, the first work of the kind published under authority. It was drawn up by the command of Theodosius the younger, and with its supplement entitled *Novellae Constitutiones*, comprehended the Imperial Constitutions from the time of Constantine the Great down to A.D. 447, being, in fact, a continuation and completion of the two previous *Codices*. These compilations, however, were both limited in design and imperfect in execution. To Justinian belongs the honour of having formed the grand scheme of collecting, arranging, and digesting the enormous heterogeneous mass of Roman Law; and to the learned men whom he employed belongs the still higher glory of having achieved their task in such a manner as to command the admiration of all succeeding ages. The results of

---

[1] It could not be expected that those who devoted themselves with the greatest ardour to legal studies could always agree in opinion, and hence sects arose among jurists, as well as among philosophers. As early as the reign of Augustus we hear of two schools, the founders of which were Antistius Labeo and Ateius Capito; the disciples of the former were named, from the most distinguished of his successors, *Proculeiani* or *Pegasiani*, those of the latter, in like manner, *Sabiniani* or *Cassiani*. It is difficult to discover the points on which these two sects principally differed; but it is believed that the *Sabiniani* were inclined in all cases to adhere to the *strict letter* of the law, while the *Proculeiani* endeavoured to discover the circumstances out of which each enactment had arisen, and then to decide according to its *spirit*.

their labours have fortunately descended to us entire, consisting of the following parts:—[1]

1. *Codex Iustinianus*, in twelve books, containing the Imperial Constitutions of the Gregorian, Hermogenian, and Theodosian Codes, collected, revised, compressed and reduced to one consistent and harmonious whole. This undertaking was executed by a commission of ten jurists at the head of whom was Tribonianus; it was commenced in February, A.D. 528, and finished in April, A.D. 529.

2. *Pandectae* s. *Digesta*, in fifty books, containing an abstract of the decisions, conjectures, controversies, and questions of the most celebrated Roman jurists. The substance of two thousand treatises was comprised in this abridgment, and it was calculated that three millions of sentences had been reduced within the compass of one hundred and fifty thousand. This stupendous task was executed in the short space of three years, (A.D. 530—A.D. 533,) by a commission of seventeen jurists, head by Tribonian.

3. *Institutiones*, in four books, containing an elementary treatise on Roman Law, serving as an introduction to the Digest, and published one month before it.

"The Code, the Pandects, and the Institutes, were declared to be the legitimate system of civil jurisprudence; they alone were admitted in the tribunals, and they alone were taught in the academies of Rome, Constantinople, and Berytus." Taken together, with the addition of the *Authenticae*, that is, one hundred and sixty-eight *Novellae Constitutiones* of Justinian; of thirteen *Edicta*, issued by the same Justinian; of one hundred and thirteen *Novellae* of the Emperor Leo, and some smaller tracts, they form what has been termed *Corpus Iuris Civilis*, which has been adopted as the basis of the legal code in many states of modern Europe.

Much light has been thrown upon Roman Law within the last few years, by the discovery of the *Institutiones* of Gaius, a celebrated jurist contemporary, it is believed, with Hadrian, a work which served as a model for the *Institutiones* of Justinian, considerable portions of the latter having been transferred verbatim from the earlier treatise.

Our direct knowledge of Roman Law is derived principally from the following sources:—

1. Fragments of the Laws of the XII Tables, preserved in the classical writers and in the compilations of the jurists. These will be found under their best form, accompanied by a great mass of curious and important illustrations, in the work of Dirksen, entitled *Uebersicht der bisherigen Versuche zur Kritik und Herstellung des Textes der XII Tafelfragmente*, Leips. 1824.

2. Fragments of Laws and Senatus-Consulta passed during the republic, which have been discovered in modern times inscribed on tablets of stone or metal. These will be found collected in the *Monumenta Legalia* of Haubold, published after his death by Spangenberg, Berlin, 1830.

3. *Institutiones Iuris Romani* of Gaius. The best edition is that by Klenze and Böcking, Berlin, 1829.

4. *Domitii Ulpiani Fragmenta*. The best edition is that of Böcking, Bon 1836.

5. The fragments of the *Codex Gregorianus* and the *Codex Hermogenianus*, which will be found under their best form in the *Jus Civile Anteiustinianum*, Berlin, 1815.

---

[1] For what follows see the XLIVth Chapter of Gibbon's Decline and Fall, which exhibits a masterly outline of the leading features of Roman Jurisprudence.

6. *Codex Theodosianus.* An excellent edition is that of Gothofredus, Lyons, 1665, reprinted under the inspection of Ritter, at Leipsic, 1736—1745. But the latest, and most complete, is that of *Hänel*, Bonn. 1837.

7. *Corpus Iuris Civilis.* The best editions are those of Gothofredus, Lyons, 1583, often reprinted, and of Spangenberg, Götting. 1776. 1791.

Objects to which Ius refers.—These were threefold—
I. PERSONAE. II. RES. III. ACTIONES. *Omne ius quo utimur vel ad Personas pertinet, vel ad Res, vel ad Actiones,* Gaius I. § 8. These we shall briefly discuss in succession.

I. PERSONAE.

All *Personae*, in the eye of the law, belonged to one of two great classes. They were either *Liberi*, i.e. in the enjoyment of personal freedom, or *Servi*, i.e. slaves.

Again, *Liberi* might be either *Ingenui*, i.e. born in a state of freedom, or *Libertini*, i.e. emancipated slaves.

Lastly, *Ingenui* might be—1. *Cives Romani optimo iure.* 2. Persons enjoying an imperfect *Civitas*, such as *Latini* and *Aerarii*. 3. *Peregrini.*

We have already, in Chapter III. spoken of the rights of *Personae*, regarded from the above points of view; but there was another classification of *Personae* recognized by law, involving considerations of much importance. According to this division *Personae* were ranked as—

1. *Personae sui iuris.* Persons subject to no external control.
2. *Personae alieni iuris.* Persons subject to the control of others.

The first division, being merely negative, will include all not comprehended in the second. The *Personae alieni iuris* were—

1. *Servi in potestate dominorum.*
2. *Liberi in potestate parentum.*
3. *Uxores in manu maritorum.*
4. *Personae in Tutela.*
5. *Personae in Mancipio.*

The position occupied by *Servi* we have already examined, (see above, pp. 94—103,) and we therefore pass on to

PERSONAE IN POTESTATE PARENTUM.

Nature and Extent of the Patria Potestas. [1]—From the most remote ages the power of a Roman father over his children, including those by adoption as well as by blood, was unlimited. A father might, without violating any law, scourge or imprison his son, or sell him for a slave, or put him to death, even after that son had risen to the highest honours in the state. This jurisdiction was not merely nominal, but, in early times, was not unfrequently exercised to its full extent, and was confirmed by the laws of the XII Tables.

In extreme cases it seems to have been always the custom to summon a domestic court, (*consilium*,) composed of the nearest relatives of the family, before whom the guilt or innocence of the child was investigated; but it does not appear that such a *Consilium* could directly set aside the decision of the parent. It had the effect, however, of acting as a check; and taken in connection with the force of

---

[1] See Cic. de R. II. 35. de Fin. 1. 7. Orat. pro dom. 29. Liv. Epit. LIV. Val. Max. III. v. 1. V. viii. 2. 3. 5. ix. 1. VI. i. 5. 6. Plin. H. N. XXXIV. 4. Tacit. Ann. XVI. 33. Aul. Gell. II. 2. V. 19. Sallust. Cat. 39. Dionys. II. 26. 27. VIII. 91. 11. Plut. Num. 17. Dion Cass. XXXVII. 36.

public opinion, as expressed by the Censors, must have tended to repress any savage abuse of the power in question.

By degrees the right of putting a child to death (*ius vitae et necis*) fell into desuetude; and long before the close of the republic, the execution of a son by order of his father, although not forbidden by any positive statute, was regarded as something strange, and, unless under extraordinary circumstances, monstrous.[1] But the right continued to exist in theory, if not in practice, for three centuries after the establishment of the empire, and was not formally abrogated until A.D. 318.

Such being the nature and extent of the *Patria Potestas*, it is almost unnecessary to state that a child *In Potestate Patris* could neither hold nor dispose of property independent of the father, to whom every thing acquired by the child belonged of right. A son *In Potestate* could not lawfully contract debts, nor even keep an account book (*Tabulas, qui in potestate patris est, nullas conficit*, Cic. pro Coel. 7.) He indeed might, like a slave, possess a *peculium;* but this could be acquired by special permission only, which was granted as an act of grace and favour, and might, at any time, be recalled.[2] An exception seems to have been made, under the empire at least, in favour of property acquired by a soldier on military service, which was termed *Peculium Castrense*.[3] It must be understood that the children of a son who was *In Potestate* were themselves *In Potestate* of their grandfather; so also were great-grandchildren, provided their father and grandfather were both *In Potestate:* and the same principle applied to descendants even more remote.

Extinction of the Patria Potestas.—The *Patria Potestas* might be extinguished in various ways—

1. By the death of the father—*Morte patris filius et filia sui iuris fiunt*, (Ulpian X. 2,) and the grandson now came under the *Patria Potestas* of his father.

2. If the father or the son ceased to be a Roman citizen by undergoing *Capitis Deminutio maxima*, (p. 83,) or otherwise, for *Patria Potestas* could exist only in the case of parties both of whom were Roman citizens. If the father was taken prisoner, his *Patria Potestas* was suspended while he remained in captivity, but resumed when he recovered his other political rights by *Postliminium* (p. 83.)

3. If a son became *Flamen Dialis* or a daughter a *Virgo Vestalis*.[4]

4. If either father or son was adopted by a third person.

5. If a daughter, by a formal marriage, (see below, p. 250,) passed into the hands of a husband, she exchanged paternal for marital slavery.

6. By the triple sale of a son by his father. If a father sold his son as a slave, and the person to whom he had been made over emancipated him, the son did not become *sui iuris*, but returned again under the *Patria Potestas*. If, however, the process of formal conveyance, (*mancipatio*,) and release, (*emancipatio*,) was repeated three times, then the son was finally relieved from the *Patria Potestas*, and had the *Status* (p. 83) of a freeborn (*ingenuus*) Roman citizen, and not of a *Libertinus*. This was expressly enacted by the Laws of the XII Tables—*Si pater filium ter venum duit, filius a patre liber esto.* Accordingly, when circumstances rendered it desirable that a son should

---

[1] Senec. de clem. I. 14. 15.
[2] Dionys. VIII. 79. Suet. Tib. 15. Senec. de Benef. VII. 14. Gaius II. § 86.
[3] Juv. S. XVI. 52. Pompon. Digest. XLIX. xvii. 11.
[4] Tacit. Ann. IV. 16. Aul. Gell. I. 12. Ulpian. X. 5

be released from the *Patria Potestas* in the lifetime of his father, this end was attained by a series of fictitious sales. A person was provided who bound himself to liberate the son when transferred to him as a slave, this person being termed *Pater fiduciarius*. To him the son was formally sold and conveyed (*mancipatus*) according to the legal ceremonies of *Mancipatio*, which will be detailed hereafter; he was immediately liberated (*manumissus—emancipatus*) in the manner already described when treating of the manumission of slaves, (p. 100,) and this process having been twice performed, he was sold a third time and immediately reconveyed by the *Pater fiduciarius* to the father, by whom he was forthwith finally manumitted and became his own master—*filius ter mancipatus, ter manumissus sui iuris fit* (Ulpian. X. 1.) It will be observed that matters were so arranged that the final manumission was made by the father, and not by the *Pater fiduciarius*, otherwise the latter would have become the *Patronus* (p. 101) of the liberated son. A daughter or granddaughter was released from the *Patria Potestas* by a single *Mancipatio* and *Emancipatio* (Gaius I. § 132. Ulpian. X. 1.)

7. If a son was actually the holder of a public magistracy the *Patria Potestas* was suspended for the time being, and the son might, in virtue of his office, exercise control over his father; but as soon as the son resumed the position of a private individual the paternal authority was re-established in full force.

8. If a son concluded a marriage with the consent of his father, the latter lost the right of selling him for a slave.

A father was entitled to expose or put to death a new born infant, provided he previously exhibited it to five neighbours and obtained their consent. This rule was evidently intended to apply to deformed children only; (*partus deformis;*) for a father was expressly forbidden to kill a male child or a first-born daughter, if under the age of three years.[1]

PERSONAE IN MANU. MARRIAGE.

In order that any valid marriage might be contracted according to the Civil Law, it was required—

1. That the consent of both parties should be obtained, if they were *sui iuris*, or of the father or fathers, if one or both happened to be *In Patria Potestate*. Under the empire, by the *Lex Iulia et Papia Poppaea*, (about A.D. 9,) a father might be compelled to give his consent, if he had no reasonable ground for refusing it.

2. That the parties should both be *puberes*, i.e. should have respectively attained to manhood and womanhood. No marriage could take place between children.

3. That the parties should both be unmarried. Polygamy was entirely prohibited.

4. That the parties should not be nearly related to each other. The determination of the prohibited degrees was a matter rather of public opinion and feeling than of positive enactment, until the passing of the *Lex Iulia et Papia Poppaea;* but it may be regarded as having included the unions of all direct ascendants and descendants, whether by blood, adoption, or marriage—parents with children, grandparents with grandchildren, fathers-in-law and mothers-in-

---

[1] Dionys. II. 15. 27.   Cic. de legg. III. 8.   Liv. XXVII. 37.   Senec. de ira I. 15.   Macrob. S. VII. 16.

law with sons-in-law and daughters-in-law, stepfathers and stepmothers with stepchildren, of brothers with sisters, whether by blood, adoption, or marriage—of uncles and aunts with nephews and nieces, until the time of Claudius ;[1]—and, at one period, of cousins even of the fourth degree, although the practice in this respect seems to have varied at different epochs.[2]

5. That both parties should be free.

These indispensable preliminary conditions being satisfied, all marriages were divided into two classes—1. *Nuptiae Iustae* s. *Matrimonium Iustum*. 2. *Nuptiae Iniustae* s. *Matrimonium Iniustum*, which we may term *Regular* and *Irregular Marriages*.

1. *Nuptiae Iustae.*—No regular marriage could be concluded except *Connubium* (i.e. *Ius Connubii*) existed between the parties. Hence, in ancient times, there could be no *Nuptiae Iustae* between a Patrician and a Plebeian, because there was no *Connubium* between the orders ; and this state of things continued until the passing of the *Lex Canuleia* (B.C. 445, see above, p. 81.) Hence, also, a marriage between a Roman citizen and a *Latinus* (a) or a *Peregrinus* (a) not enjoying *Connubium* with Rome was a *Matrimonium Iniustum*.

The children born in *Nuptiae Iustae* were termed *Iusti Liberi*, and enjoyed all the rights and privileges of their fathers.

2. *Nuptiae Iniustae.*—When a marriage took place between parties who did not mutually possess the *Ius Connubii*, as, for example, between a Roman citizen and a *Latinus* (a) or a *Peregrinus* (a) not enjoying *Connubium* with Rome, the children belonged to the *Status* (see above, p. 83) of the inferior party. Thus, the son of a *Latinus* or a *Peregrinus* and a Roman woman was himself a *Latinus* or a *Peregrinus*; the son of a *Civis Romanus* and a *Latina* or a *Peregrina* was, in like manner, a *Latinus* or a *Peregrinus*. The rule of law is expressed by Gaius (I. § 67) as follows—*Non aliter quisquam ad patris conditionem accedit quam si inter patrem et matrem eius connubium sit*.

In the case where the mother was a *Civis Romana* and the father a member of a state which enjoyed *Connubium* with Rome, but not the full *Civitas*, then the son stood precisely in the same position as his father ; but when the father was a *Civis Romanus* and the mother a member of a state which enjoyed *Connubium* with Rome, but not the full *Civitas*, then the son was a Roman citizen *optimo iure* (pp. 81. 85. 87.)

Although a *Matrimonium Iniustum* affected the civil rights of the children, it was no stain upon the moral character of the persons who contracted it ; but was probably regarded in the same light as we ourselves view an alliance where a wide difference exists between the social position of the parties.

But when a man and woman cohabited without contracting a marriage at all, they were said to live in a state of *Concubinatus*—the woman was called the *Concubina*, or, poetically, the *Amica*, of the man, while the term *Pellex*, although originally used with reference to the woman, was applied, at least in later times, to either party. The children born from such connections were bastards, (*spurii*,) did not become subject to the *Patria Potestas*, and, indeed, in the eye of the law, had no father at all (Gaius I. § 59. 64.)

No legal marriage could take place between slaves, but their union was termed *Contubernium* s. *Serviles Nuptiae*; the children were slaves, and were generally styled *Vernae*. See p. 95.

[1] Tacit. Ann. XII. 5—7. Suet. Claud. 26. Gaius I. § 62.
[2] Tacit. l. c. Liv. I. 42. XLII. 34. Dionys. IV. 28. Ulpian. V. 6.

In so far as the marriage of *Libertini* with *Libertinae* was concerned, it would appear that, in the earlier ages at least, those only could marry whose Patrons belonged to the same *Gens*; and hence, among the rewards bestowed upon Hispala Fecenia (Liv. XXXIX. 19) we find *Gentis enuptio* enumerated. With regard to the marriage of an *Ingenuus* with a *Libertina* see p. 103.[1]

Different kinds of Nuptiae Iustae.—*Nuptiae Iustae* were of two kinds—
1. *Cum Conventione in Manum.*
2. *Sine Conventione in Manum.*

1. When a marriage took place with *Conventio in Manum* the woman passed entirely from under the control of her father or guardian, (*exibat e iure patrio*, Tacit. Ann. IV. 16,) and from the *Familia* to which she belonged into the *Familia* of her husband, to whom she became subject, and to whom, in so far as her legal rights were concerned, she stood in the relation of child to parent so long as the marriage subsisted. Hence she could hold no property, but every thing which she possessed at the time of her marriage, or inherited afterwards, was transferred to her husband; and if he died intestate she inherited as a daughter. If she committed any crime, her husband was the judge in a court (*consilium*) composed of the nearest relations upon both sides.

2. When a marriage took place without *Conventio in Manum*, the woman remained under the legal control of her father, or of her guardian, or was *sui iuris*, as the case might be, and when *sui iuris*, all the property which she possessed or inherited was at her own disposal, with the exceptions to be noted hereafter when treating of the *Dos*.

Marriages *Cum Conventione in Manum*, although common in the earlier ages, gradually fell into disuse, and, towards the close of the republic, had become very rare.

It would appear, from the statements of the grammarians, that *Uxor* was the general term applied to a wife, without reference to the nature of the marriage; *Mater familias* to the wife who was *in Manu mariti*; *Matrona* to the wife when not *In Manu*; but these distinctions are by no means strictly observed.

Different Forms of Marriage Cum Conventione.—A marriage *Cum Conventione* might be legally contracted in three different modes,[2] viz. by 1. *Confarreatio.* 2. *Coemptio.* 3. *Usus.*

1. *Confarreatio* was a religious ceremony performed in the house of the bridegroom, to which the bride had been conveyed in state, in the presence of at least ten witnesses and the *Pontifex Maximus*, or one of the higher Flamens. A set form of words (*carmen—verba concepta*) was repeated, and a sacred cake made of *Far* (*farreus panis*)—whence the term *Confarreatio*—was either tasted by or broken over the parties who sat during the performance of the various rites, side by side, on a wooden seat made of an ox-yoke covered with the skin of the sheep which had previously been offered in sacrifice. The children born of such an union were named *Pa'rimi et Matrimi*, and such were alone eligible to the priestly offices of *Flamen Dialis*, of *Flamen Quirinalis*, and of *Flamen Martialis*.[3]

2. *Coemptio* was purely a legal ceremony, and consisted in the formal conveyance of the wife to the husband, according to the technical procedure in the sale of *Res Mancipi* (see below, p. 258.) An imaginary sale took place on the part of the parent or guardian in the presence of five Roman citizens of mature

---
[1] Comp. Cic. Philipp. II. 2. 36. III. 6, ad Att. XVI. 2. 11. Senec. Controv. III. 21.
[2] See Gaius I. § 108.
[3] Gaius I. § 108—115.

age, and a balance-holder, (*libripens,*) the husband or fictitious purchaser being termed *Coemptionator*.[1]

3. *Usus.* A woman who remained with her husband during one whole year without absenting herself for three nights consecutively, passed *in Manum mariti* by prescription (*usu*) as effectually for all legal purposes as if the ceremonies of *Confarreatio* or *Coemptio* had been performed. Gaius lays down the condition distinctly (I. § 111)—*Usu in manum conveniebat, quae anno continuo nupta perseverabat, nam velut annua possessione usucapiebatur, in familiam viri transibat, filiaeque locum obtinebat. Itaque lege XII Tabularum cautum erat, si qua nollet eo modo in manum mariti convenire, ut quotannis trinoctio abesset atque ita usum cuiusque anni interrumperet.*[2] Gaius adds, that at the time when he wrote, (i.e. probably in the early part of the second century,) the whole of the ancient law with regard to marriage *Cum Conventione in Manum* by *Usus* had ceased to be in force, having been in part repealed by positive enactments, and in part suffered to fall into desuetude.

When a marriage took place *Sine Conventione in Manum*, the ceremonies were entirely of a domestic character; and these we shall briefly describe when treating of the private life of the Romans.

Dissolution of a Marriage.—A marriage might be dissolved in various ways:
1. By the death of one of the parties.
2. By one of the parties losing the *Connubium* in consequence of *Capitis Deminutio* (p. 83) or otherwise. In this case a *Matrimonium Iustum* either became a *Matrimonium Iniustum*, or was entirely annulled, at the discretion of the party whose *Status* remained unchanged.
3. By divorce. The technical terms for *a divorce* are *Repudium—Divortium —Discidium—Renuntiatio—Matrimonii dissolutio.* Of these *Repudium* applies properly to the act of divorce when originating with the man, *Divortium* to the act when originating with the woman; but these distinctions are frequently neglected.

We can say little with regard to the law or practice of divorce in the earlier ages of Rome, for we are positively assured that no example of a divorce occurred for more than five centuries after the foundation of the city; and this statement is borne out by the fact that, with one single exception, there is no record of any such event until B.C. 231, when Sp. Carvilius Ruga put away a wife, to whom he was tenderly attached, because she was unfruitful. We know, however, that there were provisions with regard to divorce in the Laws of the XII Tables, and we cannot doubt that contracts solemnly concluded might be solemnly rescinded.[3] Accordingly, we hear in the grammarians of a rite termed *Diffarreatio* for dissolving marriages by *Confarreatio*, although Dionysius asserts that such unions were indissoluble; and we are told that a marriage by *Coemptio* could be cancelled if the woman was conveyed back again (*remancipata*) by the husband *cui in Manum Convenerat.* It is asserted, moreover, that in the days of Romulus no woman could divorce her husband, but that a husband might lawfully divorce his wife if she was convicted of infidelity, of sorcery, or of drinking wine (εἴ τις οἶνον εὑρεθείη πιοῦσα γυνή.) Under these circumstances it is probable that a regular domestic trial took place before the husband and the nearest relatives of both parties.[4]

---

[1] Gaius l.c.
[2] Comp. Aul. Gell. III. 2.
[3] Aul. Gell. IV. 3. XVII. 21. Val. Max. II. ix. 2. Cic. Philipp. II. 28.
[4] Paul. Diac. s.v. *Diffarreatio*, p. 74.—Fest. s.v. *Remancipatum*, p. 277. Dionys. II. 25. Plut. Rom. 22. Orelli. C. I. L. n. 2648.

It would seem that marriages *sine Conventione in Manum* could at any time be dissolved by either party. When this was done directly the husband used the form of words *Tuas res tibi habeto;* but it was more usual to announce the divorce formally through a third party, and hence the phrase *Nuntium mittere uxori* (s. *marito*) signifies *to divorce.* This facility of divorce was eagerly taken advantage of towards the end of the republic, and under the empire, when free marriages had almost entirely superseded the stricter union *Cum Conventione.* Divorces took place upon the most frivolous pretexts, and frequently without any pretext at all, and such was the laxity of public morals, that little or no disgrace was attached to the most flagrant abuse of this license.[1] Augustus endeavoured, by the provisions of the *Lex Julia et Papia Poppæa,* to place some restrictions upon divorce, but apparently without any practical result; and certainly the example set by himself was not calculated to give weight to such an enactment.[2]

Dos.—When a marriage was contracted either with or without *Conventio in Manum,* the woman was in every instance expected to bring with her some fortune as a contribution towards the expenses of the establishment. The sum would, of course, depend upon the station and means of the parties, but something was considered indispensable; and in the case of death or absolute inability on the side of the father, the nearest relatives were held bound to supply what was requisite.[3] The fortune thus brought by the woman to her husband was technically termed *Dos,* if furnished by her father, *Dos Profectitia,* if by some other party, *Dos Adventitia* (see Ulpian, VI. 3.)

In the case of a marriage with *Conventio in Manum,* whatever property the woman was possessed of passed at once into the hands of the husband—*quum mulier viro in manum convenit omnia quae mulieris fuerunt viri fiunt* DOTIS *nomine.* Cic. Top. 4.

But in a marriage without *Conventio in Manum,* whatever property a woman possessed remained under the control of herself or her guardians, with the exception of the *Dos,* which was made over to the husband, and hence the influence and sometimes tyranny exercised by rich wives.[4] The property retained by a wife in her own power was termed *Bona Receptitia,* (*quae ex suis bonis retinebat neque ad virum tramittebat ea recipere dicebatur*—Aul. Gell. XVII. 6,) a phrase which seems to have been equivalent to the word *Parapherna,* introduced at a later period.

Disposal of the Dos when the Marriage was Dissolved.—For many years, during which the dissolution of a marriage, except by the death of one of the parties, was scarcely contemplated, the rule seems to have been that the *Dos* fell to the survivor. But when divorces became transactions of ordinary occurrence, stringent rules became necessary in addition to established usage; and these were introduced partly by legislative enactments, which laid down general principles, and partly by special agreements or marriage contracts, (*dotalia pacta,*) by which the *Dos* was secured, (*cautio rei uxoriae,*) and for the fulfilment of which suits, called *Actiones rei uxoriae,* could be instituted. During the last century and a-half of the republic and the early part of the empire, the law and practice with regard to the *Dos,* when a marriage was dissolved, seems to have been as follows:—

---

[1] Val. Max. VI. iii. 10—15. Plut. Cic. 41. Cic. de Orat. I. 40. 56 ad Att. XI. 23. ad Fam. VIII. 7. Martial. VI. 7, X. 41. Senec. de Provid. 3. de Benef. III. 16.
[2] Suet. Octav. 74.
[3] Although the passages which state this most explicitly are found in the Comic Dramatists, they seem, without doubt, to refer to Roman manners. See Plaut. Aul. II. ii. 13. 61. 80. Terent. Phorm. II. i. 66. iii. 64.
[4] Plaut. Asin. I. i. 73. Aul. III. v. 58. Senec. Controv. I. 6

1. The *Dos* was sometimes paid down at once, but generally when an alliance was in contemplation the amount was first settled and then a regular obligation was granted for the payment, (*Dos aut datur, aut dicitur aut promittitur*—Ulpian. VI. 1,) which was effected by three instalments (*tribus pensionibus*) at intervals of a year.[1]

2. If the marriage was dissolved by the death of the husband the *Dos* returned to the wife.

3. If the marriage was dissolved by the death of the wife the disposal of the *Dos* varied according to circumstances.

a. If the wife died after her father, or if the *Dos* was *Adventitia*, in either case the whole remained with the husband, unless the person who had given the *Dos* had specially stipulated that it should be returned to him, in which case it was termed *Dos Receptitia* (Ulpian. VI. 4.)

b. If the wife died childless, before her father, a *Profectitia Dos* returned to her father; but if there were children, one fifth was retained by the husband for each child.

4. If a marriage was dissolved by divorce, the disposal of the *Dos* depended upon the circumstances under which the divorce took place.

a. When the divorce was the result of mere caprice upon the part of the husband, or, although promoted by the wife, was provoked by the gross misconduct of the husband, he was obliged to refund the whole *Dos* and to maintain the children—*Si viri culpa factum est divortium, etsi mulier nuntium remisit, tamen pro liberis manere nihil oportet*—Cic. Top. 4.

b. When the divorce was the result of caprice on the part of the wife, or of persuasion on the part of her father, without any reasonable ground of complaint, the husband was entitled, if there were children, to retain one-sixth of the *Dos* for each child, provided the whole amount so retained did not exceed one-half of the *Dos*. This was termed *Retentio propter liberos* (Ulpian. VI. 10.)

c. But when the divorce was caused by the bad conduct of the wife, the husband was entitled, even when there were no children, to withhold a portion of the *Dos* as *Solatium* or damages, this being termed *Retentio propter mores*. We have reason to believe that, in ancient times, a wife, if guilty of one of the highest offences, such as infidelity or wine-drinking, forfeited the whole *Dos*. When Ulpian wrote, she forfeited one-sixth for offences of the highest class, one-eighth for those of a less serious nature; but if there were children, the husband could withhold one portion on account of the children and another as punishment for misconduct.[2]

Disputes with regard to the facts of matrimonial misconduct and the amount of pecuniary compensation, seem to have formed the subject of legal processes even under the republic; and a regular *iudicium de moribus* was instituted by Augustus for the purpose of determining to which party blame attached.[3]

When a divorce took place by mutual consent, the disposal of the *Dos*, if not settled previous to the marriage by the *Pactum Dotale*, must have been arranged privately by the persons interested.

PERSONAE IN TUTELA.[4]

When children of unripe years, (*impuberes*,) and those who, in the eye of the

---

[1] Polyb. XXXII. 13. Cic. ad Att. XI. 2. 4.
[2] Plin. H.N. XIV. 13. Ulpian. VI. 11. 12.
[3] Plin. l.c. Aul. Gell. X. 23. Quintil. I. O. VII. 4.
[4] Gaius I. § 142—200.

law, were incapable of regulating their own affairs, were deprived by death or otherwise of a father's protection, they were placed in wardship, (*in Tutela*,) under the control of guardians, termed *Tutores*, and were themselves designated *Pupilli* s. *Pupillae*. In certain cases guardians were styled *Curatores*.

Appointment of Tutores.—A father had the right of nominating guardians by will (*testamento Tutores dare*) for those of his male children who might be of tender years or born after his death, for all his daughters who were *In Potestate*, for his wife if *In Manu*, for his daughter-in-law if *In Manu mariti*, and for the grandchildren under his *Potestas*, provided their father was dead. Such guardians were termed *Tutores dativi*.

A husband might grant permission by will to his wife, if *In Manu*, to nominate her own guardians, (*Tutores optare*,) and this either without restriction or under certain limitations—*aut plena optio datur aut angusta*. Such guardians were termed *Tutores optivi*.

If a man died without appointing guardians by will, then, by the Laws of the XII Tables, the charge devolved upon the nearest *Agnati*, (see below, p. 265,) a regulation which continued in force under the empire in regard to males, but was superseded in the case of females by a *Lex Claudia*. Such guardians were termed *Tutores legitimi*.

If no guardians had been appointed by will, or if the guardians appointed died or were unable to act, and if there were no *Agnati* qualified to undertake the charge, then, in virtue of a *Lex Atilia*, the date of which is unknown, the Praetor Urbanus, with the sanction of a majority of the Tribuni Plebis, appointed a guardian. Such guardians were termed *Tutores Atiliani*.

Duration of Tutela.—*Tutela* was intended for the protection and control of *impuberes* only. According to the imperial laws, boys ceased to be *impuberes* at the age of fourteen, and consequently at that age the authority of the *Tutor* ceased. With women the case was different, for although they ceased to be *impuberes* at the age of twelve, they were held to be unfit to take charge of their own affairs at any period of life; and hence a female was held to be at all times either *In Potestate patris*, or *In Manu mariti*, or *In Tutela*. The only exceptions were in favour of Vestal Virgins, and, after the passing of the *Lex Julia et Papia Poppaea*, (about A.D. 9,) of women who had borne three children, four being required for *Libertinae*. But although this was the strict legal view, it was, in later times at least, altogether disregarded in practice; and women of mature years who were not *In Potestate patris* nor *In Manu mariti* were regarded as *sui iuris*, and were allowed to administer their own affairs, but were obliged, when called upon to perform certain legal acts, such as the conveyance of *Res Mancipi* (see below, p. 257) and making a will, to obtain, as a matter of form, (*dicis causa*,) the sanction of their legal guardian.

Curatores.—Although the control of a *Tutor* ceased when the *Pupillus* had attained to manhood and become invested with his political rights, it must have frequently happened that the youth would be involved in business which he would be incapable of regulating with advantage at that early age, and would, at all events, if wealthy, be open to fraud and imposition. Hence arose the practice of nominating a *Curator*, whose authority extended to the twenty-fifth year of the ward, but who did not necessarily, like a *Tutor*, exercise a general superintendence, being frequently nominated for one special purpose. The appointment of a *Curator* lay with the Praetor Urbanus, as in the case of a *Tutor Atilianus*—he could not be fixed by will, but might be recommended, and the recommendation confirmed by the Praetor.

Curatores were appointed also to manage the affairs of persons beyond the age of **twenty-five**, who, in consequence of being insane, deaf and dumb, or affected with some severe incurable disease, were incapable of attending to their own concerns.

Since *Tutores* and *Curatores* were chiefly occupied in administering the pecuniary affairs of those under their charge, they were often required to give security (*satisdare*) for their intromissions; and a *Tutor*, when his *Pupillus* attained to mature age, was called upon to render a formal account of his transactions—*Cum igitur Pupillorum Pupillarumque negotia Tutores gerunt post pubertatem tutelae iudicio rationem reddunt* (Gaius I. § 191.)

PERSONAE IN MANCIPIO.[1]

A free person when made over to another according to the legal form of *Mancipatio*, (see below, p. 258,) was said to be *In Mancipio*, and suffered *Deminutio Capitis*, (p. 83,)—*Deminutus Capite appellabatur qui . . . liber alteri mancipio datus est* (Paul. Diac. s.v. *Deminutus Capite*.) An example of this *Status* is afforded by the condition of a son who had been conveyed by his father to a third person by *Mancipatio*, and who, except when this was done in order to compensate the person in question for some wrong which he had sustained, (*ex noxali causa*,) was *In Mancipio* for a moment only, (*plerumque hoc fit dicis gratia uno momento*, Gaius I. § 141.)

A person *In Mancipio* was not, in the eye of the law, absolutely a *Servus*, but *tanquam Servus s. Servi loco*. He was bound to obey the commands of his master, and could hold no property save by his permission. On the other hand he could not, like a slave, be subjected to injurious treatment, much less put to death, by his master, and if he recovered his freedom, received, at the same time, the *Status* of *Ingenuitas*.

A wife who had been married by *Coemptio* was also *In Mancipio*; but since she was also *In Manu*, the relation in which she stood towards her husband was of a complicated nature.

II. RES.

On the Classification of Res.—*Res* were variously classed by Roman lawyers according to the point of view from which they were regarded. The most important divisions were—

A. *Res Divini Iuris*.—Things appertaining to the gods.
B. *Res Humani Iuris*.—Things appertaining to men.

A. *Res Divini Iuris* were divided into—

1. *Res Sacrae*, places or objects openly set apart and solemnly consecrated to the gods by a deliberate act of the state, such as groves, altars, chapels and temples.

2. *Res Religiosae* s. *Sanctae*, places or objects which acquired a sacred character from the purposes to which they were applied, such as sepulchres and the walls of a fortified city.

B. *Res Humani Iuris* were divided into—

a. *Res in nullius Patrimonio*.
b. *Res in privatorum Patrimonio*.

Again, a. *Res in nullius Patrimonio* might be—

a. 1. *Res Communes* s. *Publicae*, objects which belonged to all mankind alike, such as the air we breathe, the sea and its shores.

a. 2. *Res Universitatis*, objects belonging to a society, but not to a single

---
[1] See Gaius I. § 116—123. § 138—141.

individual, such as streets, theatres, halls of justice, which belonged to the whole body of the citizens in a state, and under this head was ranked the property of mercantile companies (*societates*) and of corporations (*collegia*.)

a. 3. *Res nullius*, in a restricted and technical sense, was applied to an inheritance before the heir entered upon possession.

b. Res Privatae s. *in privatorum Patrimonio*, objects belonging to individuals, were divided into—

b. 1. *Res Mancipi*, and,
b. 2. *Res nec Mancipi*.

Res Mancipi was a term applied, according to the usage of Roman Law, to a certain class of objects which could not be conveyed, in the earlier ages at least, except by a formal process, termed *Mancipatio*, which will be explained immediately. The *Res Mancipi* were probably very numerous; but the most important were—1. Lands and houses (*praedia*) in Italy.[1] 2. Slaves. 3. Domestic beasts of burden, such as horses, asses, mules, and oxen; but not animals naturally wild, although tamed and broken in, such as camels and elephants.

Res nec Mancipi comprehended all objects which were not *Res Mancipi*.

Right of Property and Modifications of this Right.—An individual might possess a right of property in various ways. Of these the most important were—

1. *Dominium.* 2. *Iura in re.* 3. *Ususfructus.*

1. *Dominium. Dominium Quiritarium.* The right by which any one exercised control over property, and by which he was entitled to retain or alienate it at pleasure, was termed *Dominium.* When this right was exercised by Roman citizens in the most complete manner (*pleno iure*) over property acquired according to all the forms of law, and not situated in a foreign country, it was termed *Dominium legitimum* s. *Dominium Quiritarium* s. *Dominium ex iure Quiritium.*

2. *Iura in Re* s. *Servitutes.* An individual although he had not *Dominium* over an object, might yet possess a certain legal control over that object. Such rights were denominated *Iura in Re*, or *Servitutes*, and when applicable to houses or lands, *Servitutes Praediales.* These again might be either *Servitutes Praediorum Urbanorum*, or *Servitutes Praediorum Rusticorum.*

Of the *Servitutes Praediorum Urbanorum* we may take as examples—
1. When one of the two proprietors of adjoining houses could prevent the other from removing a wall or a pillar which, although forming part of the building belonging to the latter, was necessary to insure the stability of the building belonging to the former. This was *Servitus Oneris.* 2. When one proprietor had the right of introducing a beam for the support of his own house into the wall of his neighbour's house. This was *Servitus Tigni immittendi.*
3. When one proprietor had the right of conveying the rain-drop from his own house into the court or garden of his neighbour. This was *Servitus Stillicidii.*
4. Of carrying a drain through his neighbour's property, *Servitus Cloacae.*
5. Of preventing his neighbour from building a wall above a certain height, *Servitus non altius tollendi*, or from disturbing his lights, *Servitus Luminum.*

Among the *Servitutes Praediorum Rusticorum* we may enumerate—1. A

---

[1] When the Roman territory extended over but a small portion of Italy, the *praedia*, which ranked under *Res Mancipi*, were confined within the same limits. At a subsequent period the *praedia*, in certain districts in the provinces, were regarded as *Res Mancipi*, provided those districts enjoyed what was termed the *Ius Italicum.*

right of way through the lands of another, which, according to circumstances, might be—*a*. Merely a foot-path or a bridle-road (*Iter.*) *b*. A drift-road, along which a beast of burden or a carriage might be driven, but not if loaded (*Actus.*) *c*. A highway (*Via.*) 2. The right of conveying water through the property of another (*Aquaeductus.*)

The *Servitutes Praediorum Rusticorum* were classed by all lawyers under the head of *Res Mancipi;* with regard to the *Servitutes Praediorum Urbanorum* a difference of opinion existed.

3. *Ususfructus.* An individual might be in the lawful occupation and enjoyment of property either for life or for a limited period, without having the power of alienating the property in question. This was termed *Ususfructus.* Similar to this, as we have seen above, was the tenure under which the *Ager Publicus* was frequently held by those in possession.

Different modes of acquiring Property.—The most important of these were—

1. *Mancipatio.* 2. *In Iure Cessio.* 3. *Usus.* 4. *Traditio.* 5. *Adiudicatio.* 6. *Lex.*

1. *Mancipatio.*[1] This ancient and purely Roman mode of transferring property was under the form of an imaginary sale and delivery. It was necessary that the buyer and seller should be present in person, together with six male witnesses, all arrived at the age of manhood, (*puberes,*) and all Roman citizens, of whom one, called *Libripens*, carried a balance of bronze. The buyer (*is qui mancipio accipit*) laying hold of the property, if moveable, or a representation of it, if immoveable, employed the technical words, *Hunc ego hominem* (supposing the object to be a slave) *ex iure Quiritium meum esse aio isque mihi emptus est hoc aere aeneaque libra*, upon which he struck the balance with a piece of brass, which he then handed over to the seller (*is qui mancipio dat*) as a symbol of the price.

This form was applicable to *Res Mancipi* alone, and a conveyance of this nature could take place between Roman citizens only, or between a citizen and one having the *Ius Commercii* with Rome.

2. *In Iure Cessio.*[2] This was a formal transference of property in the presence of a Roman magistrate. The parties, buyer and seller, appeared before the Praetor, if at Rome, or the provincial governor, if abroad, and the person to whom the property was to be conveyed (*is cui res in iure ceditur*) laying hold of the object, claimed (*vindicavit*) it as his own, in the technical words, *Hunc ego hominem, ex iure Quiritium meum esse aio*, upon which the magistrate turned to the other party (*is qui cedit*) and inquired whether he set up any opposing claim, (*an contra vindicet*,) and on his admitting that he did not, or remaining silent, the magistrate made over (*addixit*) the object to the claimant. There were in this process three principal actors, the former proprietor, the claimant or new proprietor, and the magistrate, whose relations to each other are expressed by the three verbs, *cedere, vindicare*, and *addicere. In iure cedit dominus, vindicat is cui ceditur, addicit Praetor.*

In order that this form of conveyance might be valid, it was necessary that three conditions should be satisfied.

(1.) That the parties should appear in person before the magistrate.

(2.) That they should both be Roman citizens, or if one was not, that he should have the *Ius Commercii* with Rome.

[1] Gaius I. § 119.
[2] Gaius II. § 24.

(3.) That the property should be of such a kind as to admit of *Dominium Quiritarium*, and hence lands in the Provinces were excluded.

3. *Usus s. Usucapio.* Prescription. When an individual remained in undisputed possession of any object, whether a *Res Mancipi* or a *Res nec Mancipi*, for a certain length of time, he acquired a full right to it although it might not have been formally conveyed to him. The period fixed for prescription by the laws of the XII Tables was one year for moveable property, and two years for houses or lands. In order that *Usus* might apply, it was essential that the person holding the object should be a *bonae fidei possessor*, that is, that he should honestly believe that he had a just title to the property—*si modo bonâ fidê acceperimus*. But prescription did not apply to objects stolen or taken by force from their lawful owner, even although the person in actual possession might not be cognizant of the theft or robbery.[1]

4. *Traditio.* The simple handing over of a piece of property by one person to another is the earliest and most simple form of conveyance, and by Roman Law conferred full possession (*Dominium Quiritarium*) in the case of *Res nec Mancipi*, to which alone it properly applied.

But if the owner of a *Res Mancipi* made over the object to another, without going through the form of *Mancipatio* or *In iure cessio*, the new owner did not acquire the *Dominium Quiritarium* until the full period of *Usus* had expired. During the intermediate period, lawyers distinguished the actual possession from the full right of property by the term *Dominium in bonis*.

5. *Adiudicatio.* When several persons had claims upon a piece of property, a *iudex*, or umpire, was appointed by the Praetor to make a legal division, and his award, called *adiudicatio*, conveyed to each individual full right of property in the share allotted. A process of this nature for portioning out an inheritance among co-heirs (*coheredes*) was termed *Formula familiae erciscundae;* for dividing waste land among several proprietors, *Formula communi dividundo;* for defining the boundaries of conterminous landholders, *Formula finium regundorum*, &c.[2]

6. *Lex* is the general term for all modes of acquiring property, when made over by a magistrate to the claimant, in terms of some specific law.

Disposal of Property by Will.[3] — Property might be lawfully conveyed and acquired by Will also.

The right of conveying property by Will (*Factio Testamenti*) belonged to all Roman citizens who were *puberes* and *sui iuris*. Under the empire, soldiers, although not *sui iuris*, were permitted to dispose by Will of any property they might have acquired during military service (*peculium castrense*.) Women above the age of twelve, not *In Potestate* nor *In Manu*, might make a Will with the sanction of their guardians (*Tutoribus auctoribus*.)

Different modes of making a Will.—In the earliest times the law recognised two modes only of making a will.

1. In *Comitia*, summoned twice a-year for the purpose, and called *Comitia Calata*. Of this assembly we have already spoken at length, see p. 127.

2. *In Procinctu*, by a soldier, publicly in the presence of his comrades, when about to go into action; *Procincta Classis* being an ancient term for an army equipped and drawn up in battle order.

These two modes were originally thought sufficient to provide for a deliberate

---

[1] Cic. pro Caecin. 19. 26. Top. 4. Gaius II. § 42.
[2] Cic. de Orat. I. 56. Ulpian. XIX. 16. Aul. Gell. I. 9. Serv. ad Virg. Aen. VIII.
[3] Gaius I. § 101—104.

or a hasty settlement, but in process of time, as early at least as the legislation of the Decemvirs, a third was added.

3. *Per aes et libram.* When a citizen found death approaching, and had not time to submit his Will to the *Comitia Calata*, he made over his whole property according to the forms of *Mancipatio*, (p. 258,) to a friend, who thus became the nominal heir, and at the same time gave instructions for the disposal of his effects, trusting to the good faith of the individual to whom they had been conveyed.

Eventually, the first two modes of Will-making fell into disuse, and were superseded by the third, which, however, underwent a material change. The maker of the Will (*Testator*) conveyed his property, as before, in a fictitious sale, by *Mancipatio*, to an individual who was introduced for form's sake, (*dicis causa*,) and termed *familiae emptor;* but, instead of giving verbal instructions to the imaginary purchaser, he had previously drawn up a regular written deed, (*Tabulae Testamenti.*) which he exhibited to the witnesses present, repeating the technical words, *Haec ita, ut in his tabulis cerisque scripta sunt, ita do, ita lego, ita testor, itaque vos, Quirites, testimonium mihi perhibitote.* This act was termed *Testamenti Nuncupatio*, the word *nuncupare* signifying properly *to make a public declaration.*

Before the age of Justinian these forms of the Civil Law with regard to Wills, had been essentially modified by Praetorian edicts and imperial constitutions. The act of *Mancipatio* was now altogether dispensed with, and it was held sufficient that the written Will should be signed by the *Testator*, and attested by the signatures and seals of seven competent witnesses, who represented the *Emptor*, the *Libripens*, and the five witnesses of the ancient *Mancipatio*.[1]

Conditions necessary to render a Will valid.—In order that a Will might be valid, it was requisite not only that the *Testator* should possess the right of making a Will, (*Factio Testamenti*,) and should have duly performed the ceremonies above described, but also that the nomination of the Heir (*institutio heredis*) should be regularly expressed (*solenni more*) in certain set words. Thus the regular form (*solennis institutio*) was *Titius heres esto*, for which might be substituted, *Titium heredem esse iubeo*, but if the words employed were *Titium heredem esse volo*, the deed was worth nothing.[2]

Many other legal niceties were insisted upon. Thus, if a father wished to disinherit (*exheredare, exheredem facere*) a son who was *In Potestate* it was necessary to state this expressly in established phraseology, such as, *Titius filius meus exheres esto*, but if he merely bequeathed his property to another without specially excluding the son *In Potestate*, the Will was invalid.[3]

A Will was also rendered null and void by any material change having taken place in the position of the *Testator*, with regard to his own family or to society at large, after the Will had been made. Thus, if an individual, after he had made a Will, adopted a son or married a wife *Cum Conventione in Manum*, or if a wife *In Manu*, at the time of executing the Will, subsequently passed *In Manum* of another husband, or if a son who had been sold returned under his *Potestas*, or if he himself suffered *capitis deminutio*, any one of these circumstances was sufficient to cancel the Will. Moreover, any Will was cancelled by another of later date—*Posteriore testamento superius rumpitur.*[4]

Strictly speaking, a Will which, in consequence of some informality, was,

[1] Iustin. Instit. II. X. 1—3.
[2] Gaius II. § 116.
[3] Gaius II. § 123, 127.
[4] Gaius II. § 138—143.

from the first, null and void, was said *non iure fieri;* when it was originally valid, but was rendered null by some event which happened after it had been executed, it was said *rumpi* s. *irritum fieri*.

The Persons to whom Property was bequeathed. [1]—The general term for a person who succeeded to property on the death of another was *Heres*. When a person nominated as an Heir (*institutus heres*) accepted the bequest, he was said *cernere hereditatem;* when he entered upon the inheritance, *adire hereditatem*. A person might bequeath his property to whom he pleased, as well as to slaves as to free men. If he bequeathed property to his own slave, he was compelled to grant him freedom at the same time, in the form *Stichus servus meus liber heresque esto*. If he bequeathed property to the slave of another, the bequest was invalid unless the master of the slave gave him permission to accept and enter upon the inheritance.

Classification of Heirs. [2]—Heirs were divided into three classes, according to the relation in which they stood to the deceased.

1. *Heredes Sui et Necessarii*, more frequently termed simply *Heredes Sui*.—2. *Heredes Necessarii*.—3. *Heredes Extranei*.

1. *Sui Heredes*. A man's *Sui Heredes* were such of his children, whether by blood or adoption, as were *In Potestate* and those persons who were *in liberorum loco*. We have thus as *Sui Heredes*, [3]

a. Sons and daughters *In Potestate*, but those who from any cause had ceased to be *In Potestate*, ceased at the same time to be *Sui Heredes*. A son born after the death of his father (*postumus*) who, if his father had lived until his birth, would have been *In Potestate*, ranked as a *Suus Heres*.

b. A wife *In Manu* was a *Sua Heres*, because in the eye of the law she was *in loco filiae*.

c. Grandchildren through a son—*nepos neptisque ex filio*—provided they were *In Potestate* of their grandfather, and provided their father had, from death or some other cause, ceased to be *In Potestate*.

d. Great-grandchildren in the direct male line—*pronepos proneptisque ex nepote ex filio nato*—and so on for more remote descendants, provided the male person nearer in the direct male line had ceased by death or otherwise to be *In Potestate*—*si praecedens persona desierit in potestate parentis esse*—it being essential to the character of a *Suus Heres* that he should be *In Potestate* of the person to whom he bore that relation, and that he should not, upon the death of that person, fall under the *Patria Potestas* of any other person.

e. A son's wife (*nurus*) provided she had passed *In Manum mariti*, and provided her husband had ceased to be *In Potestate*, for in that case she became in the eye of the law *neptis loco*. In like manner a grandson's wife might become *proneptis loco*, and so on for the wives of more remote descendants.

Heredes Sui were also *Heredes Necessarii*, because they were held in law to be the heirs of the person to whom they succeeded, even if he died intestate, as we shall explain more fully in a subsequent paragraph. But although this was the strict letter of the Civil Law, they might, if the person to whom they succeeded died insolvent, by making application to the Praetor, receive permission to refrain (*abstinere*) from accepting the inheritance, in order to save their own property, if they possessed any, from the creditors.

2. *Heredes Necessarii*. Slaves when nominated heirs by their masters

---
[1] Gaius II. § 185—190.
[2] Gaius II. § 152—173.
[3] Gaius II. § 156. III. § 1.

became *Heredes Necessarii*, being compelled to accept the inheritance; and on this account a person who had doubts regarding his own solvency, sometimes nominated one of his slaves as his heir, in order that the disgrace resulting from the sale of his effects, (*ignominia quae accedit ex venditione bonorum*,) for behoof of his creditors, might fall upon the slave rather than upon the members of his own family.

3. *Heredes Extranei.* All heirs not included in the two divisions described above were classed together as *Heredes Extranei.* Thus, sons not *In Potestate* to whom their father bequeathed property ranked as *Heredes Extranei*, and in like manner, all sons to whom property was bequeathed by their mother, for no woman could have her children *In Potestate.* A *Heres Extraneus* had full power either to accept or to refuse an inheritance, the act of deciding being termed *Cretio.* If he determined to accept he announced his resolution by the formula—*Quod me Publius Titius testamento suo heredem instituit, eam hereditatem adeo cernoque*—but if he failed to do this within a certain period he lost all interest in the bequest, or if he entered upon the administration of the inheritance without going through this form, various penalties were imposed by law varying with the circumstances of the case.

It was customary in drawing up a will to define the period within which the heir must make his election, and, should he fail to do so, to provide for the succession, by naming one or more persons under like conditions, thus—*Lucius Titius heres esto, cernitoque in diebus centum proximis quibus scies poterisque, quodni ita creveris, exheres esto. Tum Maevius heres esto, cernitoque in diebus centum*, &c. The heir first named was called *Primo gradu scriptus heres*, the person who, failing him, was to succeed, *Heres substitutus*, and of these there might be any number, *Heres substitutus secundo—tertio—quarto*, &c. *gradu.* [1]

Division of an Inheritance.—A person might bequeath his whole property to one individual, or he might divide it among several in fixed proportions. The unit of all objects which could be weighed, measured, or counted, was called *As*, and the divisions of an inheritance were expressed according to the subdivisions of the *As*, as will be explained in the chapter upon Weights and Measures.

Legata. Legatarii. [2]—When a person bequeathed his property to a single individual, or to several individuals in fixed proportions, the individual or individuals was or were termed *Heres* or *Heredes.* But a *Testator* might not nominate an heir or heirs in this sense, but he might think fit to leave special bequests or gifts to one or more individuals, such bequests or gifts not forming a definite proportion of the whole property, but falling to be subtracted from it before it was made over to the *Heres* or divided among the *Heredes*, or these bequests might be left as a burden upon the succession of one or more of the *Heredes* as the case might be. Such a gift or bequest was termed *Legatum*, and the person to whom it was made *Legatarius*, the verb *Legare* denoting the act of making such a bequest. The civil law recognised four modes in which *Legata* could be bequeathed.

1. *Per Vindicationem*, in which the form was—*Lucio Titio* (. . . here the object was named . . .) *do lego.* This form was applicable to those objects only which were actually in the full possession of the *Testator* at the period of his death.

2. *Sinendi Modo*, in which the form was—*Heres meus damnas esto sinere*

[1] Gaius II. § 174—178.
[2] Gaius II. § 191—223.

Lucium Titium (. . . here the object . . .) *sumere sibique habere.* This form was applicable not only to objects actually in the possession of the *Testator* at the period of his death, but also to those actually in the possession of his heir.

3. *Per Damnationem*, in which the form was—*Heres meus* (. . . here the object . . .) *Lucio Titio dare damnas esto.* This form was applicable to objects in the possession of any person whatsoever, the *Heres* being bound either to procure the object for the *Legatarius* or to pay him its estimated value.

4. *Per Praeceptionem*, in which the form was—*Lucius Titius* (. . . here the object . . .) *praecipito.* This form was applicable only when the *Legatarius* was also one of the *Heredes*, and it authorised him to take the object specially named beforehand, (*praecipere,*) and in addition to the fixed proportion to which he was entitled over and above.

The Law of the XII Tables—*Uti legassit suae rei ita ius esto*—was held to justify a *Testator* in bequeathing his whole property in *Legata*, so that nothing would be left for the persons named as heirs general. Hence the *Scripti Heredes* if not *Sui* nor *Necessarii*, frequently refused to intromit with the estate, (*ab hereditate se abstinebant*,) and in that case the will fell to the ground, for no *Legatum* could be bequeathed except *through* a *Heres*, or as it was technically expressed, AB *Herede*,[1] who was bound to pay it. To provide a remedy for this grievance various legislative enactments were framed. First a *Lex Furia*, (of uncertain date,) which limited the amount of a *Legatum*, but not the number of the *Legatarii;* next the *Lex Voconia*, (B.C. 169,) which provided that no *Legatarius* should receive more than the *Heredes;* but both of these statutes having been found defective, they were superseded by the *Lex Falcidia*, (B.C. 40,) in terms of which no *Testator* could will away in *Legata* more than three-fourths of his property, so that one-fourth at least was, in every case, left for the heir or heirs, and this law was still in force when Gaius wrote.

Law of succession to the Property of an Intestate.[2]—According to the Laws of the XII Tables, if a person died without making a will, or if his will was found to be, from any cause, invalid, the succession to his property was arranged as follows:—

1. The *Sui Heredes* (p. 261,) inherited first. The property was divided among all *Sui Heredes* without distinction as to proximity—*pariter ad hereditatem vocantur nec qui gradu proximior est ulteriorem excludit*—but the division took place, as lawyers expressed it, *non* IN CAPITA *sed* IN STIRPES. That is, if the intestate had been the father of two sons, one of whom was alive and *In Potestate* at the time of his father's death, while the other was dead or had ceased to be *In Potestate*, but had left three sons who were *In Potestate* of their grandfather, the intestate, then the son *In Potestate* and the three grandsons all inherited; but the inheritance was not divided into four equal parts, but into two equal parts, the son received one-half, and the remaining half was divided equally among the three grandchildren, who thus received what would have been their father's portion had he been alive and *In Potestate* at the time of the intestate's death. So, in like manner, if an intestate left behind him—1. A wife *In Manu*. 2. A daughter unmarried, or who, if married, had not passed *In Manum mariti*. 3. A daughter-in-law who had been married to his son *Cum Conventione in Manum*, but whose husband had ceased to be *In Potestate* at

[1] Hence the phrase in Cicero pro Cluent.12. *Ei testamento legat grandem pecuniam* A *filio.*
[2] Gaius III. § 1—38. Ulpian. XXVI. 1.

the time of the intestate's death. 4. A son (A) still *In Potestate*. 5. Three grandchildren (*b b b*) *In Potestate* by a son (B) who had ceased to be *In Potestate*. 6. Two great-grandchildren (*c c*) through a son (C.) and a grandson (D,) both of whom had ceased to be *In Potestate*. 7. And, finally, if the wife of the intestate gave birth after his death to a child (*p*). Then the widow, the son A, the daughter, the posthumous child *p*, and the daughter-in-law, would each have received one-seventh of the whole property, one-seventh would have been divided equally among the three grandchildren *b b b*, each receiving a one-and-twentieth of the whole, and the remaining seventh would have been divided equally among the two great-grandchildren *c c*, each receiving one-fourteenth of the whole.

2. Failing *Sui Heredes*, the inheritance was divided equally among the *Consanguinei* of the intestate, that is, his brothers and sisters by the same father, but it was not necessary that they should be by the same mother.[1] A mother or a step-mother who by *Conventio in Manum* had acquired the rights of a daughter relatively to her husband, ranked in this case as a sister—*sororis loco*.

3. Failing *Sui Heredes* and *Consanguinei*, the inheritance passed to the nearest *Agnati*—*his qui proximo gradu sunt*—that is, the nearest male kindred in the male line, and if there were several *Agnati* who stood in the same degree, then the inheritance was divided *in capita* and not *in stirpes*.

Thus, supposing that of three brothers A, B, C.—B died first leaving sons, and then A died intestate leaving no *Sui Heredes*, C inherited A's property, to the exclusion of the sons of B, but if the intestate left no brother, but two nephews by B, and three nephews by C, then the succession was divided equally among the five nephews.

4. Failing *Agnati*, the laws of the XII Tables ordained that the inheritance should go to the *Gentiles* (p. 61) of the intestate—*si nullus Agnatus sit, eadem lex XII Tabularum Gentiles ad hereditatem vocat*—but when Gaius wrote, the whole *Ius Gentilicium* had fallen into desuetude.

It will be observed that by the above ancient arrangement, the following persons were altogether excluded :—

1. All sons who, by emancipation or otherwise, had ceased to be *In Potestate* at the time of the intestate's death, and the children born after their father had ceased to be *In Potestate*.[2]

2. All daughters who had passed *In Manum mariti*.

3. All females, except those in the direct line of descent through males, sisters, and those who were *sororis loco*. No aunt, no niece, no female cousin, could succeed.

The rigour of this scheme was modified in favour of blood relations, by various Praetorian Edicts, and the law of succession became very confused and uncertain, until the legislation of Justinian placed it upon a firm and satisfactory basis.

Before quitting this subject it may be proper to say a few words on the Degrees of kindred, and to explain the signification of the terms *Cognati*, *Agnati*, and *Adfines*.

---

[1] Strictly speaking *Germani* was applied to those children born of the same father and the same mother. *Consanguinei*, to those born of the same father but of different mothers. *Uterini*, to those born of the same mother but of different fathers.

[2] This would not apply to a posthumous child if his father had been *In Potestate* when he died.

Cognati. Agnati.—The tie of *Cognatio* existed among all who could trace their descent from one pair who had been legally united in marriage, and hence included all blood relations, male and female, however remote the root of the genealogical stem might be. Those only were *Agnati* who could trace their relationship by blood through an unbroken succession of males. *Cognatio*, although the more general term, did not necessarily include all *Agnati*, for adopted sons, in so far as legal rights were concerned, occupied in every respect the position of natural sons, and ranked as *Agnati*, but not as *Cognati*. On the other hand, *Agnatio*, in the eye of the law, was broken and dissolved by any one of the following circumstances.

1. By Adoption. When adoption took place, the son adopted passed out of the *familia* to which he belonged by birth, and entered the *familia* of his adopted father.

2. By the dissolution of the *Patria Potestas* in any way except by death.

3. By *Capitis Deminutio Maxima* (p. 83,) for *Agnatio* could exist between Roman citizens only.

The following Table exhibits the different degrees of *Cognatio* as recognised in the Institutes of Justinian :—

GRADUS COGNATIONIS.

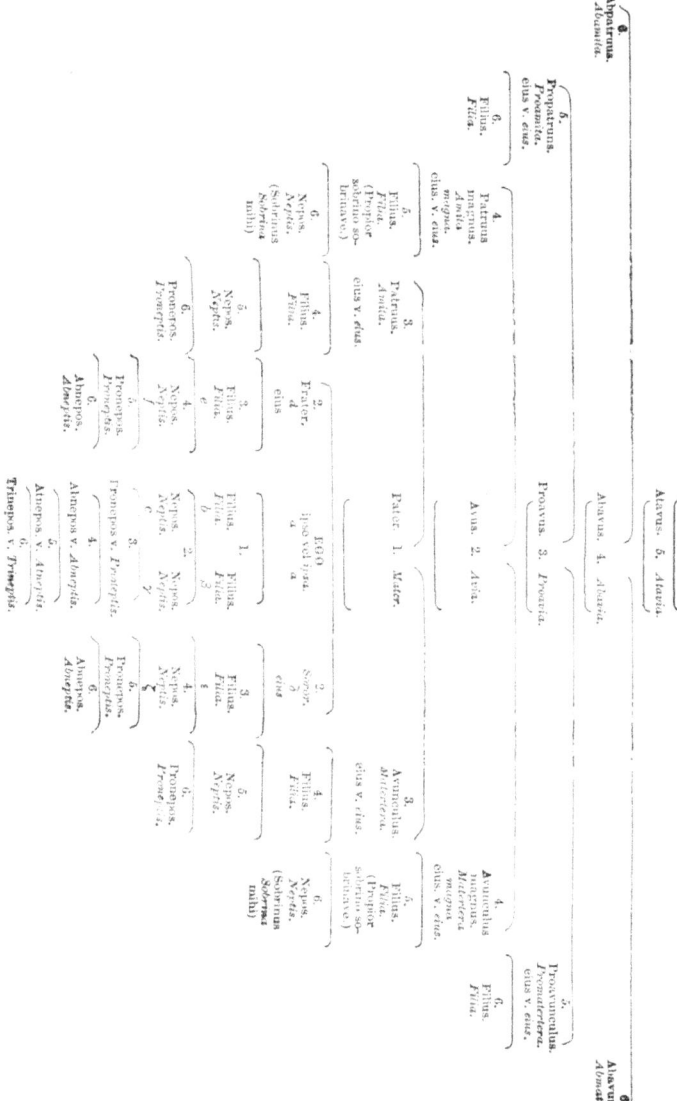

b and e are *Fratres* or *Sorores Patrueles*
β and ε are *Consobrini* or *Consobrinae*
$\left.\begin{array}{l}b \text{ and } \varepsilon \\ \beta \text{ and } e\end{array}\right\}$ are *Amitini* or *Amitinae*
$\left.\begin{array}{l}f \text{ and } c\,\gamma\,\zeta \\ c \text{ and } f\,\zeta \\ \gamma \text{ and } f\,\zeta \\ \zeta \text{ and } f\,c\,\gamma\end{array}\right\}$ are *Sobrini* or *Sobrinae*

To each other.

The father or mother of a *Sobrinus* or *Sobrina* is *Propior Sobrino* v. *Sobrinâ* to the other *Sobrinus* or *Sobrina*.

The term *Consobrini* was applied, in popular language, to the children of two brothers as well as to the children of two sisters (Gaius III. § 10.)

Adfines.—*Adfinitas* is the connection which subsisted after a legal marriage had been contracted between two parties, between the husband and the *Cognati* of his wife, and between the wife and the *Cognati* of her husband, the persons between whom the connection subsisted being termed, relatively to each other, *Adfines*. There were no degrees of *Adfinitas* recognised by law, for no legal relation existed between *Adfines*. The *Adfines* of whom we hear most frequently and for whom distinctive terms existed, were *Gener*, (son-in-law,) *Socer*, (father-in-law,) *Nurus*, (daughter-in-law,) *Socrus*, (mother-in-law,) *Privignus*, *Privigna*, (stepson, stepdaughter,) *Vitricus*, (stepfather,) *Noverca*, (stepmother.) *Levir* is a husband's brother, and *Glos* a husband's sister, relatively to his wife.

Adoptio. Arrogatio.—We have already had occasion to speak of adoption in connection with the *Comitia Curiata*; but one consideration with regard to the persons adopted was necessarily deferred. The person selected for adoption, if a Roman citizen, might be either—

1. *Sui Iuris*, or, 2. *In Potestate Patris*.

1. In the first case, it was necessary that the adoption should take place with the consent of the people assembled in the *Comitia Curiata*, (p. 117,) and when the adoption was completed, the individual adopted ceased to be *Sui iuris*, and passed under the *Potestas* of his adopted father.

2. In the second case, it was necessary that his natural father should convey him, according to the forms of *Mancipatio*, in the presence of the Praetor, to the father by whom he was adopted.

Here, strictly speaking, the former process only was an *Arrogatio*, because it alone included a *Rogatio ad populum* (p. 106.) Compare what has been said above (p. 117) on the different terms employed to denote an adoption.

It must not be forgotten that a son, legally adopted, stood, in the eye of the law, in the same relation in every respect to the father by whom he was adopted as a son begotten in lawful marriage.

III. Actiones.

Definition of the term Actio.—*Actio*, in its strict legal sense, denotes the right of instituting proceedings in a court of justice for the purpose of obtaining something to which the person possessing this right conceived himself to be entitled—*Ius persequendi sibi iudicio quod sibi debetur;*[1] but the word is more generally used to signify, not the right of instituting a suit, but *the suit* itself. The person who instituted the suit was termed *Actor* or *Petitor*, the defendant *Reus*.

[1] Justin. Instit. IV. vi. 1.

Classification of Actiones.—*Actiones*, when considered with reference to the nature and object of the claim, were divided into—[1]
 1. *Actiones in Personam.* 2. *Actiones in Rem.*
 1. *Actiones in Personam* were brought by the *Actor*, in order to compel the *Reus* to perform a contract into which he had entered, or to make compensation for some wrong which he had inflicted—*Cum intendimus Dare Facere Praestare oportere.*
 2. *Actiones in Rem* were brought to establish the claim of the *Actor* to some corporeal object (*res*) in opposition to the claim of the *Reus*, or to compel the *Reus* to concede some right, such as a *Servitus*, which was claimed by the pursuer and denied by the defendant.
 Actiones, again, when considered with reference to the manner in which the claim was made, were divided into—
 1. *Actiones stricti iuris.* 2. *Actiones arbitrariae* s. *Ex fide bona.*[2]
 1. In *Actiones stricti iuris* a specific claim was made either for a definite sum of money (*pecunia certa*) or for a particular object; and if the pursuer failed to substantiate his claim to the letter he was nonsuited.
 2. In *Actiones arbitrariae*, on the other hand, the claim was of an indefinite character, as, for example, in an ordinary action of damages; and it was left to the judge to decide the kind and amount of compensation which ought in equity to be awarded.
 Definition of the term Obligatio.—*Obligatio*, in Civil Law, denotes a relation subsisting between two parties, in virtue of which one of the parties is legally bound to do something for, or permit something to be done by the other party—*Dare Facere Praestare.* In every *Obligatio* there must be two persons at least, the person who is bound and the person to whom he is bound. These were termed respectively *Debitor* and *Creditor.*
 By comparing the definition of an *Actio* with that of an *Obligatio* it will be seen that they are correlative terms; every *Actio* presupposes the existence of an *Obligatio*, and every *Obligatio* implies an *Actio.*
 Classification of Obligationes.[3]—All *Obligationes*, considered with reference to their origin, were divided into—
 A. *Obligationes ex Contractu*, arising from a compact or agreement between the parties.
 B. *Obligationes ex Delicto*, arising from an injury inflicted by one party on the other.

A. *Obligationes ex Contractu.*

These were fourfold—*a. Re.—b. Verbis.—c. Litteris.—d. Consensu.*
 a. Obligationes Re.[4] Of Real-Contracts the most important were—1. *Mutui Datio.*—2. *Commodatum.*—3. *Depositum.*—4. *Pignus.*
 1. *Mutui Datio.* This term was applied to the giving on loan objects which could be weighed, measured, or counted—*Res quae pondere, numero, mensura constant*—such as bullion, corn, wine, oil, and coined money, all of which were lent on the understanding that the borrower, on making repayment, was bound to restore an equal amount of the object borrowed, but not the identical metal, corn, wine, oil, or pieces of money which he had received. The contract in this

---
[1] Gaius IV. § 2. 3.
[2] Gaius IV. § 55—68. Quintil. I. O. IV. 1. VII. 3. Cic. de Invent. II. 19. 6. Off. III. 70. pro Rosc. Comoed. 4.
[3] Gaius III. § 88.
[4] Gaius III. § 90. Iustin. Instit. III. xiv. 1. § 1—4.

case implied that exactly the same amount was to be restored as had been received; but from a very early period the practice of paying interest upon money borrowed prevailed at Rome. On this subject we shall speak hereafter.

2. *Commodatum.* This term also denoted a loan; but in this case the temporary use of some object was granted—*Res utenda datur*—and the borrower was required to restore (*reportare*) the self-same object which had been lent, such as a horse, a slave, or the like. The *Obligatio* contracted *Ex Commodato* was very different, in the eye of the law, from that imposed by *Mutui Datio*; for in the latter case the borrower was required to restore a like quantity of the object received, even although what he had received might have been stolen or destroyed while in his possession. But if an object had been *Commodatum*, and had been properly watched and used while in the possession of the borrower, he was not liable, if it was stolen, lost, or destroyed, to be called upon to replace it, unless *Culpa* could be proved. Thus, if a horse or a slave died of disease, or was struck by lightning, or perished by any unavoidable accident, the loss fell upon the lender.

3. *Depositum.* When a sum of money or any piece of property was lodged for safety in the hands of another it was termed *Depositum*, and the person to whom it had been consigned was bound to restore it (*reddere depositum*) to the lawful owner, provided he did not deny having received it—*Si depositum non infitietur*. If he refused, then the depositor might sue him by an *Actio Depositi*, and endeavour to prove his case.

4. *Pignus.* In like manner, if any one deposited a pledge (*pignus*) with another as a security for a loan or any other engagement, the holder of the pledge was bound to restore it as soon as the loan was repaid or the engagement fulfilled, otherwise a suit (*Actio pignoratitia*) might be raised to compel restitution.

b. Obligationes Verbis.[1] Of Verbal-Contracts the most important were—
1. *Nexum.* 2. *Stipulatio.*

1. *Nexum.*[2] This term originally denoted any transaction whatever entered into *per aes et libram* according to the forms of *Mancipatio* (p. 258.) It subsequently became restricted in its signification, and was applied to the obligation imposed by the formal acknowledgment of a pecuniary loan, ratified by a symbolical transfer in the presence of witnesses. The process by which this *Obligatio* was incurred was called *Nexi datio*, the *Obligatio* itself being *Nexum;* the state or condition of the debtor was called *Nexus*,[3] when he incurred the *Obligatio* he was said *Nexum ire*, and became *Nexus*[4] or *nexu vinctus*. An obligation so contracted took precedence of all others in ancient times; and the law of debtor and creditor was characterised by extreme harshness and cruelty. If a person who was *Nexus* failed to pay his debt at the period fixed, and if the debt was acknowledged or had been proved in court—*aeris confessi, rebusque iure iudicatis*—he was allowed thirty days' grace. After these had expired, if he could not find any one to become responsible for him, (*vindex*) the creditor might bring him by force (*manus iniectio*) before the magistrate, by whom he was made over bodily (*addictus*) to the creditor. The creditor then kept him in bonds for sixty days, and during this period made public proclamation

---
[1] Gaius III § 92—96.
[2] Varro L.L. VII. § 105. Fest. s.v. *Nexum*, p. 165. Cic. de Orat. III. 40. Aul. Gell. XX. 1. Liv. II. 23. VI. 27. 34. VIII. 28. xxiii. Val. Max. VI. i. 9.
[3] *Nexus* is here a noun of the fourth declension.
[4] *Nexus* is here a passive participle.

upon three market days, demanding payment of his debt. If, at the end of this term, no one appeared to release the debtor, he became the slave of his creditor, who might employ him in work, or sell him, or even put him to death. Nay, if there were several creditors, the Laws of the XII Tables, if literally interpreted, gave them permission to divide the body of the debtor into pieces proportionate to the claims of each. Although there is no record of such barbarity having been actually perpetrated even in the worst times, it would appear, from the narrative of Livy, that in the early ages the treatment of debtors by their creditors was very cruel; and this state of things continued until the passing of the *Lex Poetilia*, (B.C. 326,) by which the condition of debtors was greatly ameliorated. It would seem that the personal slavery of a debtor to his creditor was not abolished by this enactment, but provision was made that he should be humanely treated; the right of selling him was probably taken away, and if released from bondage—*Nexu solutus*—he was at once reinstated in all his privileges as a Roman citizen.

2. *Stipulatio*.[1] In process of time the *Nexum* seems to have fallen altogether into desuetude, and verbal contracts were usually concluded by *Stipulatio* and *Restipulatio*, which consisted in a formal demand for a promise on the one side and a suitable reply on the other, the giver (*Stipulator*) employing the words *Dari Spondes*, the receiver (*Restipulator*) replying *Spondeo*. A third person, named *Adstipulator*, frequently took part in the proceedings, who, in case of the death or absence of the *Stipulator*, was entitled to enforce the claim.

c. *Obligationes Litteris*.[2] Of written contracts the most important were—
1. *Expensi Latio.* 2. *Syngraphae.*

1. *Expensi Latio* was an entry to the debit of one party in the account book of another party. In order to understand the nature and origin of this obligation it is necessary to bear in mind, that among the Romans, not only mercantile men, but every master of a house, kept regular accounts with the greatest accuracy. In doing this he was said *domesticas rationes scribere—tabulas s. rationes conjicere;* and to fail or be negligent in keeping such accounts was regarded as disreputable. The entries were first made roughly in day-books, called *Adversaria* or *Calendaria*, and were posted at stated periods in ledgers, called *Codices Expensi et Accepti*, which were divided into two columns, in one of which all sums received were entered and in the other all sums paid out.

Nomen was the general name for any entry, whether on the debtor or the creditor side of the account; and hence, *facere—scribere—perscribere nomen* may, according to circumstances, signify to record a sum as paid out, or a sum as received, and thus *facere nomen* may mean either to *give a loan* or *to contract a debt*.

When any one keeping books entered a sum of money as received from any one, from *Titius*, for example, he was said *ferre s. referre acceptum Titio*, that is to place it to the credit of Titius: when, on the other hand, he entered a sum as paid to Titius he was said *ferre s. referre expensum Titio*, that is, to place it to the debit of Titius; and hence, figuratively, *ferre aliquid acceptum alicui* is to acknowledge a debt or a favour, *ferre aliquid expensum alicui* is to set up a claim.

Entries of a particular class were termed *Nomina transcriptitia*, and these were of two kinds.

---
[1] Gaius III. § 92. 110—14. 117. 215. IV. § 113. Fest. s.v. *Reus*, p. 273.
[2] Gaius III. § 128—134.

(1.) *Nomen transcriptitium* s. *Transcriptio a Persona in Personam.* This was made when, A owing a sum to B, and B owing a sum to C, C, with the consent of B, entered the sum as actually paid by C to A.

(2.) *Nomen transcriptitium a Re in Personam,* when B owed a balance to C on any transaction, and C entered that sum in his books as having been actually paid to B.

Towards the close of the republic the Romans frequently kept their ready money in the hands of bankers or money changers. These persons were called *Argentarii*, or, in consequence of sitting in the forum with tables or counters before them, *Mensarii* s. *Trapezitae.* Debts were frequently paid, as in modern times, by orders on these bankers, a transaction expressed by the phrase *Scribere* s. *Perscribere* s. *Solvere* AB *Argentario,* i.e. to write an order for payment *through* a banker, i.e. *to give a cheque upon a banker.* This will illustrate the expression in Livy, (XXIV. 18,) in reference to the trust money belonging to wards and unmarried women which had been lent to government—*Inde, si quid emptum paratumque pupillis ac viduis foret, a Quaestore perscribebatur,* i.e. the money so expended was paid by a bill or *cheque on* the Quaestor. See also Cic. ad Att. IV. 8. XII. 51. XVI. 2. ad Fam. VII. 23. pro Planc. 42. Hor. Epp. II. i. 45.

This being premised, the entry of a sum in a regularly kept account book constituted, in law, an *Obligatio Litteris.* Of course, if a sum was claimed in consequence of such an entry on the *Expensum* side of one man's ledger, and no corresponding entry was found on the *Acceptum* side of the ledger of that person from whom it was claimed, some further proof than the mere entry would be demanded, and this collateral evidence would, in some cases, be derived from an examination of the books themselves.

2. *Syngraphae* s. *Syngrapha,* i.e. bonds, formed another species of *Obligationes Litteris;* but these were resorted to for the most part, if not exclusively, in transactions with foreigners.

d. Obligationes Consensu.[1] A consensual contract, as it is sometimes called, that is, a contract by mutual consent, was concluded by a simple verbal agreement between the parties, although no tangible object had been actually transferred from one to the other, no legal form of words had been interchanged, and no writing or entry been made. Of consensual contracts the most important were—

1. *Emtio et Venditio.*—2. *Locatio et Conductio.*—3. *Societas.*—4. *Mandatum.*

1. *Emtio et Venditio,* buying and selling. A sale was held binding when the parties had come to an agreement as to the price, although there had been no delivery, no money actually paid, and no earnest-penny (*arra*) received. The giving of the *Arra* might be adduced as a proof that the contract had been entered into; but it did not in itself form a necessary part of the contract. A suit brought to compel fulfilment of a contract of this kind was termed *Actio Empti* or *Actio Venditi,* according as it was instituted by the buyer or the seller.

2. *Locatio et Conductio,* letting and hiring. The relation between these terms will best be understood by considering their true original signification. *Locare* is properly applied to a party who sets down or supplies (*locat*) some object which another party takes away (*conducit*) and applies to some purpose. This being premised, it is necessary to draw a distinction between the use of

[1] Gaius. III. § 135–162.

Locare in the phrase *Locare aliquid faciendum* and in the phrase *Locare aliquid utendum.*

Locare aliquid faciendum. If a party were desirous of having some article manufactured by a skilful workman, he might be required *to place down* or supply (i. e. *Locare*) the raw material, while the artizan would be called upon to take up and carry away with him (i. e. *Conducere*) the material so supplied. Hence, if we use the word *Contract* in its limited colloquial sense, both *Locare* and *Conducere* may be correctly translated by the verb *To Contract*. *Locare aliquid faciendum* is to bind oneself to pay for the execution of a work, or in common language, *To contract for the execution of a work*, while *Conducere aliquid faciendum*, is to bind oneself to perform a work in consideration of receiving a certain remuneration, or in common language, *To contract for the execution of a work*. Hence, if we say in English, that a party has *made a Contract for building a house*, the expression is ambiguous, but in Latin, *Locare aedes faciendas* would be employed with reference to the party *for* whom the house was to be built, *Conducere aedes faciendas* to the party *by* whom the house was to be built, and who was to receive payment for so doing. The party *for* whom the work was to be performed was *Locator*, the party *by* whom the work was to be performed, *Conductor* s. *Manceps* s. *Redemtor*. The *Locator* was entitled to demand a strict performance of the terms prescribed (*exigere*) from the *Conductor*, and hence it was the duty of the Aediles and Censors, who were the *Locatores* in making contracts for keeping the public buildings in repair, *exigere sarta tecta*, i. e. to insist that the buildings should be kept wind and water tight, and we read in Cicero of *Censoriae leges in sartis tectis exigendis* (see p. 170.)

Locare aliquid utendum. Again, *Locare* may be used somewhat differently in the sense of setting down or supplying some object which, for a consideration, we permit another party to make use of and enjoy for a time. Thus, in the expressions, *Locare aliquid utendum* and *Conducere aliquid utendum*, *Conducere* applies to the paying party, and *Locare* is equivalent to the English *To let on Hire*, while *Conducere* means *To Hire*, or pay a consideration for the use of an object. In this sense we have the common phrases, *Locare aedes* and *Conducere aedes*, applied respectively to the landlord, who lets the house and receives the rent, and to the tenant, who hires the house and pays the rent.

3. *Societas* in its widest acceptation denotes two or more persons who unite or combine for the prosecution of a common object; in its more restricted sense it denotes a mercantile partnership or company, the individual members being termed *Socii*. Such were the companies of *Publicani*, described above, formed for leasing the revenues.

4. *Mandatum* properly denotes *a commission*. In many cases a person might find it convenient to intrust (*mandare*) legal or pecuniary business to an agent or attorney, who was termed *Mandatarius* or *Procurator*, and if any one who undertook such a task was found guilty of fraud, or even of carelessness, his principal might seek redress by an *Actio Mandati*. See specially, Cic. pro Rosc. Amer. 38, 39.

In all *Obligationes ex Contractu* it is necessary to draw a very sharp line between the legal essence of the *Obligatio* and the proof. Thus, in real contracts, the delivering on the one hand, and the receiving on the other, constituted the legal obligation, but in order that an *Actio*, founded on this *Obligatio*, might be successfully maintained, it would be necessary for the Plaintiff *to prove that the object had been actually delivered to the Defendant*. In verbal contracts the symbolical transfer constituted the obligation, and this was always susceptible of proof, because the presence of a certain number of witnesses was a necessary part of the form. In literal contracts the *Latio Expensi* in the ledger of one party constituted the obligation, and if corroborated by a corresponding *Latio Accepti* in the ledger of the other party, the proof was complete, but if no such entry appeared in the ledger of the Defendant, then the mere fact of the *Latio Expensi* standing in the ledger of the Plaintiff could not be accepted as proof, because it might be a false entry, and hence it would be necessary to seek collateral evidence. This, as hinted above, might in some cases be afforded by the books themselves, for if those of the one party were found to have been kept in a clear, regular, and methodical manner, while those of the other were confused, imperfect, and disfigured by erasures (*liturae*,) then a strong presumption would arise in favour of the former.

We now proceed to consider the s cond great division of *Obligationes*.

B. *Obligationes ex Delicto*.[1]

These also were fourfold—
a. *Furtum*. b. *Iniuria*. c. *Damnum iniuria datum*. d. *Rapina* s. *Bona vi rapta*.

a. *Furtum*, theft.[2] According to the definition of Sabinus,—*Qui alienam rem attrectavit quum id se invito domino facere iudicare deberet*, FURTI TENETUR. A distinction was drawn from the earliest times between—
1. *Furtum manifestum*, and 2. *Furtum nec manifestum*.

1. *Furtum Manifestum*. According to the Laws of the XII Tables, a *Fur manifestus*, that is, a thief caught in the fact, if detected in plundering by night, might be lawfully put to death on the spot; and so also a *Fur manifestus* by day, if he defended himself with a lethal weapon, (*cum telo*,) but if he did not resist, then the owner of the property might seize, scourge, and detain him in bonds.

2. *Furtum nec Manifestum*. By the same Code a *Fur nec manifestus* was compelled to restore double the amount of the property stolen; but both in this case and also in the case of *Furtum manifestum*, the person plundered was allowed to make a private arrangement with the thief.

According to a very ancient usage, if a person suspected that property which had been stolen from him was concealed in the house of another, he was allowed to search for it, provided he entered the house naked save a girdle (*licio* s. *linteo vinctus*) and holding a large dish (*lanx*) with both hands. A search so conducted was called *Furti per Lancem et Licium Conceptio*. The thief, if detected in this manner, was punished as a *Fur manifestus*, and the person in whose house the property was discovered, although not himself the thief, was bound, by the Laws of the XII Tables, to restore three times the amount of what had been stolen, the suit for enforcing this penalty being termed *Actio Furti concepti*, while an *Actio Furti oblati* lay against any one who had conveyed stolen property and lodged it in the hands of another.

In process of time the law against theft was in so far relaxed that in the case of a *Furtum Manifestum*, when not aggravated by darkness or violence, the thief was not placed under personal restraint, but was compelled in an *Actio Furti* to restore the stolen property fourfold.

[1] Gaius III. § 182—225.
[2] Gaius III. § 186. § 189. § 195. IV. § 111. Aul. Gell. XI. 18. Plaut. Pers. I. ii. 10.

b. Iniuria.[1] An *Actio Iniuriarum* lay against any one who had assaulted or offered violence, not merely in deeds but words, to any Roman citizen, whether *Sui Iuris,* or *In Potestate,* or *In Manu,* or *In Tutela.*

1. By the Laws of the XII Tables, the *Lex Talionis,* "an eye for an eye and a tooth for a tooth," might be enforced in the case of personal injuries. This, however, was not applied universally; for the compensation fixed for a broken bone was three hundred Asses if the sufferer was a free man, and one hundred and fifty if he was a slave, the master of the slave, in the latter case, being, in the eye of the law, the aggrieved party. For assaults of a more trifling character the fine was twenty-five Asses.

2. *Mala Carmina. Famosi Libelli.* The Laws of the XII Tables were particularly severe in the matter of libellous verses—*Nostrae* (says Cicero) *duodecim tabulae, quum perpaucas res capite sanxissent, in his hanc quoque sanciendam putaverunt, si quis occentavisset, sive carmen condidisset, quod infamiam faceret flagitiumve alteri*—the punishment, if we can believe Porphyrio and other scholiasts, being flogging the offender to death.

In process of time the *Lex Talionis* and other penalties for *Iniuria,* fixed by the ancient laws, fell altogether into disuse, and *Actiones* for pecuniary compensation, founded upon Praetorian Edicts, were substituted. By the *Lex Cornelia de Iniuriis,* any one who had inflicted bodily injury upon another was liable to be criminally indicted, and, if convicted, might be banished or condemned to work in the mines.

c. Damnum Iniuria datum,[2] damage done to the property of another. It would seem that, by the Laws of the XII Tables, any one who in any way had damaged the property of another could be compelled to make compensation. By the *Lex Aquillia,* (B.C. 286,) any one who, through malice, or culpable neglect (*dolo aut culpa*) caused the death of a slave or any fourfooted domestic animal belonging to his neighbour, could be compelled to pay the highest price at which a similar object had been sold during the space of a year antecedent to the offence; any other damage to the property of another was to be compensated for by paying the highest price which the object had borne during the space of a month antecedent.

d. Rapina. Bona vi rapta. Robbery by open violence seems, in ancient times, to have been included in the *Actio damni iniuria dati;* but when the crime became common during the civil wars, M. Lucullus, when Praetor, endeavoured to repress these disorders by introducing a new *Actio bonorum vi raptorum,* by which the robber was compelled to restore the property plundered threefold, and, in some cases, fourfold.

In addition to the two great classes of *Obligationes,* which we have enumerated, the Roman lawyers reckoned two sub-classes, viz.:—

1. *Obligationes quasi ex Contractu,* and, 2. *Obligationes quasi ex delicto.*

Examples of the *Obligationes quasi ex Contractu* are offered by three *Actiones,* founded upon them, to which we have adverted above (p. 259.) 1. *Actio Familiae erciscundae.* 2. *Actio Communi dividundo.* 3. *Actio Finium regundorum.*

Obligationes quasi ex delicto,[3] upon which an *Actio Damni infecti* might be founded, arose when any procedure, on the part of one individual threatened

---

[1] Cic. de R. IV. 10. Porphyr. ad Hor. Epp. II. 152. Fest. s.v. *Talionis,* p. 363. Aul. Gell. XVI. 10. XX. 1.
[2] Gaius III. § 210—219. Cic. pro Rosc. Com. 11. Fest. s.v. *Rupitias,* p. 265.
[3] Cic. Verr. I. 56. Top. 4. 9. 10. Iustin. Instit. IV. v. 1.

to prove injurious to the person or property of another individual, in which case, the latter might call upon the former to take measures to prevent such an injury as was anticipated, or to give security that, if the injury was inflicted, adequate compensation would be made.

THE ADMINISTRATION OF THE LAWS.

All judicial proceedings were comprehended under the general term *Iudicia*, and these were naturally divided into *Iudicia Publica* and *Iudicia Privata*, which correspond closely with what we designate as *Criminal Trials* and *Civil Suits;* the subject of the former being those offences which may be regarded as affecting the interests of the community as a body, such as murder, treason, embezzlement of public money, forgery, malversation in a provincial governor, and many others; the subject of the latter being those disputes, chiefly regarding property, which arise between individuals, and in which the state has no interest beyond that of providing the means for a legal and equitable decision. Cicero (Pro Caecin. 2) points out the distinction very clearly [1]—*Omnia iudicia, aut distrahendarum controversiarum, aut puniendorum maleficiorum caussa reperta sunt;* but, at the same time, it must be observed that certain wrongs which among ourselves are made the grounds of criminal prosecutions, were regarded by the Romans as subjects for a civil suit only, and *vice versa.* Thus, during the later centuries of the republic prosecutions for theft were *Iudicia Privata*, while adultery exposed the offender to a criminal impeachment.

I. IUDICIA PRIVATA.

In explaining the details of a civil suit we may consider—1. *The Persons concerned.* 2. *The actual Process.* The persons concerned belonged to two classes.

1. The persons who decided the suit.
2. The persons who carried on the suit, i.e. the *Actor* and the *Reus*, with their counsel, agents, witnesses, &c.

The Judges in Civil Suits.—In the earliest ages the Kings acted as supreme judges in civil as well as in criminal trials; and after the expulsion of the Tarquins these functions were, for a time, discharged by the Consuls. The Consuls were relieved from judicial duties after the institution of the Praetorship, (B.C. 367,) and from that time until the downfal of the republic, the Praetor Urbanus and the Praetor Peregrinus presided in the civil courts. Some of the other magistrates, such as the Aediles and the Quaestors, had the right of acting as judges (*iurisdictio*) in matters pertaining to their own departments; but all ordinary controversies between man and man were submitted to the Praetor. In the Provinces, the Provincial Governor, and in the cities of Italy which adopted Roman forms, the chief magistrate had *Iurisdictio*, and exercised the same powers as the Praetor at Rome.

Mode in which the Praetor exercised Jurisdiction.—In very simple causes the Praetor at once decided the matter in dispute, and the process was termed *Actio Extraordinaria;* but in the great majority of causes, hence termed

---

[1] Cicero employs the phrases *Iudicia Privata* (Top. 17) and *Causa Publica;* (pro Rosc. Amerin. 21;) but it seems doubtful whether the technical division into *Iudicia Publica* and *Iudicia Privata* was recognised until employed in the writings of the jurists of the empire, and even by them the former term is used in a restricted sense (Macer. Digest. XL. i. 1.) The words of Ulpian (Digest. L. i. 1,) clearly points to the division adopted above—PUBLICUM IUS *est quod ad statum rei Romanae spectat*, PRIVATUM, *quod ad singulorum utilitatem.*

Actiones Ordinariae, he appointed one or more umpires, for whom the general term is *Iudex*, to inquire into the facts of the case, and to pronounce judgment; but he previously instructed the *Iudex* as to the points of law involved, and laid down the principles upon which the decision was to be based. After the *Iudex* had pronounced judgment, it became the duty of the Praetor to give effect to that judgment.

Hence the jurisdiction of the Praetor was said to be expressed by three words Do, Dico, Addico.

Dabat Actionem et Iudices, he gave permission to bring the suit into court, and appointed one or more umpires.

Dicebat Ius, he laid down the law for the guidance of the *Iudices*.

Addicebat Bona vel Damna, he gave effect to the decision of the *Iudices* by formally making over the property in dispute to the lawful owner, or by awarding compensation for an injury sustained. To these words Ovid refers in his definition of *Dies Fasti* and *Dies Nefasti*, when he says—

> Ille *Nefastus* erit per quem Tria Verba silentur.
> *Fastus* erit per quem lege licebit agi.[1]

The Praetor had full powers, in virtue of his office, to take all the steps described without consultation with others; but, for his own satisfaction, he frequently sought the advice of those who were learned in the law, and who, when called in to assist him, were termed his *Consiliarii* or *Assessores*.[2]

The Iudices in Civil Suits were distinguished by different names, according to the manner of their election, and the nature of the duties which they were called upon to discharge.

1. *Iudices* in a restricted sense. When the question turned upon a simple matter of fact, the parties themselves, or, if they could not agree, the Praetor, nominated a single umpire, who, under these circumstances, was named specially *Iudex*.

2. *Arbitri*. When, in addition to simple matters of fact, it was necessary for the umpire to pronounce upon questions of equity, he was termed *Arbiter*. Hence, a *Iudex* would be appointed in an *Actio stricti iuris*, an *Arbiter* in an *Actio ex fide bona*, (see p. 268,) and a lawsuit, when founded on *Actio stricti iuris*, was termed *Iudicium*, when founded on *Actio ex fide bona*, was termed *Arbitrium*.[3]

3. *Centumviri*. Matters of an important and complicated nature were usually referred by the Praetor to the judicial college of the *Centumviri*. This consisted of individuals elected annually, probably in the Comitia Tributa, three from each of the thirty-five Tribes, making in all one hundred and five, or, in round numbers, *Centumviri*. The period when this body was instituted is unknown. The name cannot be older than B.C. 241, for then first the Tribes were increased to thirty-five; (p. 68;) but a similar board may have existed at a much earlier epoch, (see Liv. III. 55,) in the *Decemviri Stlitibus iudicandis*, of whom we have spoken above, (p. 196,) and may have been gradually augmented. We are unable to determine the precise limits of their jurisdiction, which appears, in certain cases, to have extended even to criminal trials; but it would appear that causes connected with wills and successions were very frequently submitted

---

[1] Ovid. Fast. I. 47. Macrob. S. I. 16. Varro L.L. VI. § 30.
[2] Cic. pro Planc. 38. de Orat. I. 37. in Verr. II. 29.
[3] See Cic. pro Roscio Comoed. 4. where these distinctions are fully explained, and comp. Top. 7.

to them, and, in addition to these, Cicero (De Orat. I. 38) gives a long, but, as he himself indicates, by no means a complete catalogue of *Causae Centumvirales.*

In later times, under the empire, the Praetor himself sat as president in the court of the Centumviri; their numbers were increased to one hundred and eighty, and they were divided into two, and sometimes into four, sections, (*quadruplex iudicium,*) which, in certain cases, judged separately. [1]

When the *Centumviri* sat in judgment (*Centumvirale Iudicium*) a spear was set upright before them, and hence the phrases *Iudicium hastae—Centumviralem hastam cogere—Centum gravis hasta virorum—Cessat centeni moderatrix iudicis hasta,* &c.[2] According to the explanation of Gaius, (IV. § 16,) the *Hasta,* being a symbol of legal right of ownership, (*iusti dominii,*) was held to be a suitable emblem for a court which settled conflicting claims—*maxime enim sua esse credebant quae ex hostibus cepissent: unde in Centumviralibus iudiciis hasta praeponitur.*

4. *Recuperatores.* This name was originally given to a mixed body of commissioners, appointed by a convention between two states for the purpose of adjusting any claims and disputes which might have arisen between the members of those states. Subsequently a judicial corporation, consisting of three or five individuals, who bore the name of *Recuperatores,* was established at Rome, under the immediate control of the Praetor Peregrinus, for the purpose of acting as umpires in suits in which Peregrini were concerned. In trials before the *Recuperatores* all those tedious and complicated formalities which characterised ordinary processes between citizens, were dispensed with; and hence, it would appear that when a speedy decision was desired, the parties, although both Roman citizens, sometimes, by mutual consent, submitted their cause to the *Recuperatores.* [2]

The Parties in Civil Suits.—The parties in a civil suit were, as already mentioned, the plaintiff, termed *Actor* s. *Petitor,* and the defendant, termed *Reus* s. *Adversarius,* the name *Adversarius* being, however, applicable to either party. It was not essential that the parties should appear in person, either or both might conduct their case by means of an agent, who, according to circumstances, was styled *Cognitor* or *Procurator.* A *Cognitor* appears to have been named in court, with certain formalities, in the presence of both parties, and hence the party for whom he appeared became at once responsible for his acts. A *Procurator,* on the other hand, was not necessarily named in court, and might be appointed without the knowledge of the opposite party, and therefore was obliged himself to give security that his acts would be adopted by his principal. We shall reserve our remarks upon the counsel (*patroni*) employed to plead, until we treat of criminal trials.

Before considering the regular steps of a suit, it is necessary to explain the signification of two terms closely connected with the history of civil processes. These are *Legis Actiones* s. *Actiones Legitimae* and *Formulae.*

Legis Actiones.—In the earlier ages of the republic, when a party instituted a suit against another, he was obliged to make his claim according to a certain prescribed form of words, derived directly from the law upon which the claim was founded, and to this form it was necessary to adhere strictly. The form

---

[1] Cic. de leg. agr. II. 17. Ovid. Trist. II. 91. Phaedr. III. x. 35. Plin. Epp. I. 5. 18. II. 14. IV. 24. V. 1. VI. 4. 33. IX. 23. Quintil. I. O. IV. i. 57. V. ii. 1. VII. 2. XI. 1. XII. 5. Dialog. de causis C. E. 38. Val. Max. VII. viii. 1. Suet. Oct. 36. Aul. Gell. XVI. 10. Paul. Diac. s.v. *Centumviralia iudicia,* pp. 54. 64.
[2] Fest. s.v. *Reciperatio,* p. 274. Liv. XLIII. 2. Cic. in Verr. III. 11. Gaius I. § 104.

employed was termed *Legis Actio*, and the person who employed it was said *Lege Agere*. The *Legis Actio* varied according to the nature of the case; and if any plaintiff selected a wrong *Legis Actio*, or departed a hair's breadth from the precise words of the proper form, he was at once nonsuited—*eo res perducta est, ut, vel qui minimum errasset, perderet* (Gaius IV. § 30.) The knowledge of these forms was, for a long period, confined to the Patricians and especially to the Pontifices, and hence the whole administration of the Civil Law was, for a lengthened period, virtually in their hands. Gaius (IV. § 12) enumerates five classes of these *Legis Actiones*—*Lege autem agebatur modis quinque: Sacramento: Per Iudicis Postulationem: Per Condictionem: Per Manus Iniectionem: Per Pignoris Captionem.*

1. *Sacramento.* So called, because at the commencement of the process, each of the contending parties deposited or gave security for a certain sum, called *Sacramentum*, which was forfeited to the public by the loser. According to the Laws of the XII Tables, the amount of the Sacramentum was 500 Asses in suits where the value of the property in dispute amounted to 1000 Asses or upwards, and 50 Asses when the value was below 1000 Asses. The parties resorting to this kind of *Legis Actio*, which appears to have been applicable to a great variety of cases, were said *Contendere Sacramento*. The term *Sacramentum* may have been adopted in consequence of the parties having been originally required to take an oath upon depositing the sum, or from the circumstance of the forfeited deposit having been originally applied to holy purposes. See Varro L.L. V. § 180.

2. *Per Iudicis Postulationem.* When both parties, by mutual consent, appeared before the Praetor and requested him to name a *Iudex*.

3. *Per Condictionem.* When the plaintiff formally summoned the defendant to appear before the magistrate on the thirtieth day after the summons, for the purpose of choosing an umpire—*Actor adversario denuntiabat, ut ad iudicem capiendum die tricesimo adesset.*

4. *Per Manus Iniectionem.* When a party had been judicially sentenced to pay a sum of money to another, and had failed to discharge the debt within thirty days, then the creditor was entitled—*lege iudicati*—to lay hands upon the defaulter and bring him by force before the magistrate, with the view of compelling payment. The *Legis Actio per Manus Iniectionem* was, by subsequent laws, extended to various cases in which there had been no previous judicial sentence. These are enumerated by Gaius IV. § 21—26.

5. *Per Pignoris Captionem.* In certain cases a creditor was entitled to distrain the goods of his debtor without a judicial sentence, provided he made use of certain prescribed forms. This *Legis Actio* was permitted to a soldier or an *Eques*, when the parties bound to furnish *Stipendium* or *Aes Hordearium* had failed to perform the obligation, to the seller of a victim for sacrifice, and to *Publicani*, when tax payers failed to pay a legal impost. See Gaius IV. § 26 —29. comp. Cic. in Verr. III. 11.

Formulae.—The difficulties, and inconveniences, and uncertainties attendant upon the employment of the *Legis Actiones* were so numerous and became so insupportable, that as lawsuits became more frequent and more complicated, they gradually fell into desuetude, and at length, by a *Lex Aebutia* and two *Leges Iuliae*, (the precise date of these enactments is unknown,) they were formally abolished, except in a few special cases, and the procedure by *Formulae* s. *Verba Concepta* substituted.

The grand distinction between the use of *Legis Actiones* and *Formulae* consisted, originally, in this, that while the former were selected and employed by plaintiffs at their own risk, the latter proceeded from the supreme judge, and were, in fact, carefully worded instructions to the *iudex*, adapted to the circumstances of the case, after these had been ascertained from the statements of the parties. Indeed, the *Formulae*, in many instances, corresponded closely with what we term the *Issues* submitted to a jury, when trials by jury are resorted to in civil suits.

Eventually, indeed, the *Formulae* adapted to cases of a particular class became fixed, and the number of these established *Formulae* was constantly increased by the annual Edicts of the Praetors, by whom new *Formulae* were, from time to time, introduced to meet new circumstances. In the days of Cicero these established *Formulae* had accumulated to such an extent that the orator declares that provision had been made for every possible contingency; and it appears that at this period, the plaintiff was in the habit of selecting the *Formula* according to which he wished his case to be tried, although the technical precision of the *Legis Actiones* was no longer essential—*Sunt iura, sunt* FORMULAE *de omnibus rebus constitutae, ne quis aut in genere iniuriae, aut ratione actionis errare possit. Expressae sunt enim ex unius cuiusque damno, dolore, incommodo, calamitate, iniuria, publicae a Praetore* FORMULAE, *ad quas privata lis accommodatur.* Cic. pro Rosc. Comoed. 8.

Formulae were divided into two classes—
1. *Formulae in Ius conceptae.*
2. *Formulae in Factum Conceptae.*

The former were employed when the facts of a case were admitted, and it was necessary merely to determine the legal consequences or results of those facts, and whether, in the eye of the law, any damage had been sustained by the plaintiff, and if damage had been sustained, to decide the amount. The latter were employed when the *Iudex* was called upon to decide with regard to the truth of conflicting statements as well as on the legal validity of the claim. An example of each, taken from Gaius (IV. § 47) will make the nature of the *Formulae* belonging to each class sufficiently distinct. In what follows it is to be observed that *Aulus Agerius* and *Numerius Negidius* are fictitious names representing an imaginary *Actor* and *Reus.*

1. *Iudex esto. Quod Aulus Agerius apud Numerium Negidium mensam argenteam deposuit, qua de re agitur, quidquid ob eam rem Numerium Negidium Aulo Agerio dare facere oportet ex fide bona eius, id iudex Numerium Negidium Aulo Agerio condemnato . . . . . . Si non paret; absolvito.*

2. *Iudex esto. Si paret, Aulum Agerium apud Numerium Negidium mensam argenteam deposuisse, eamque dolo malo Numerii Negidii Aulo Agerio redditam non esse, quanti ea res erit, tantam pecuniam iudex Numerium Negidium Aulo Agerio condemnato: si non paret, absolvito.*

Form of Process in a Civil Suit.—Although it is manifest that the form of process must have undergone many changes in details during the long period which elapsed from the foundation of the city to the downfal of the constitution, and must have been much influenced by the gradual transition from the *Legis Actiones* to the *Formulae;* yet, in so far as our authorities enable us to judge, it appears to have varied little in its general outline. It always consisted, as may be inferred from what has been said above, of two parts—
1. Proceedings before the Praetor, said to be *In Iure.*
2. Proceedings before the *Iudex*, said to be *In Iudicio.*

Proceedings in Iure.—It must be borne in mind, that no suit could be brought into court except upon a *Dies Fastus*, and the knowledge of these was jealously guarded by the Pontifices until betrayed, along with other secrets, by Cn. Flavius (p. 244.) The Praetor, during the earlier ages, administered justice in the *Comitium*, (p. 12,) seated on his *Sella Curulis*, which was placed upon an elevated platform, termed *Tribunal*, around which, but on a lower level, a number of seats, called *Subsellia*, were arranged for the convenience of the parties who had business to transact. Towards the close of the republic and under the empire the Tribunal of the Praetor was usually placed in one of the stately *Basilicae* (p. 19,) which surrounded the Forum.

Vocatio in Ius. The first procedure on the part of the plaintiff was to summon the defendant to appear before the Praetor, (*vocare in ius*,) and in case of a refusal or an attempt to escape, the plaintiff was authorized, by the Laws of the XII Tables, to drag him to the judgment-seat by force; but he was required, in the first place, to call upon a bystander to bear witness (*antestari*) to the facts. This ancient practice seems to have been in force even when Horace wrote, as we gather from the well known scene at the conclusion of Sat. I. ix. A defendant could not, however, be dragged from his own house; but if it could be proved that he was wilfully concealing himself, in order to avoid an appearance in court, the Praetor might confiscate his property for the benefit of the plaintiff—*Actor in bona mittebatur.*

A defendant was not obliged to appear personally if he could find another to undertake his cause, and such a representative was originally termed *Vindex*. The *Vindex*, who, in ancient times, gave surety that the defendant would be forthcoming when necessary, seems gradually to have passed into the *Cognitor* or *Procurator*.

Intentio. Actionis Postulatio. Exceptio, &c. The parties having appeared before the Praetor, the plaintiff made a statement of his claim, (*Intentio*,) and asked leave to bring the suit into court (*Actionem postulabat*.) The defendant then simply denied his liability, or gave in a plea in law (*exceptio*.) The Praetor, if he required further information, might order the plaintiff to answer the *Exceptio*, which was done by a *Replicatio*, and to this, again, the defendant might make a rejoinder, called, at this stage, *Duplicatio*, and the *Duplicatio* might be followed by *Triplicatio*, a *Quadruplicatio*, &c.

If the Praetor considered that a prima facie case had been made out, he gave the plaintiff leave to bring his suit into court, (*dabat Actionem*.) and the plaintiff then declared what *Actio* he intended to employ (*edebat Actionem*.) After the *Formulae* were substituted for the *Legis Actiones*, the appropriate *Formula* was selected sometimes, as we have seen, by the Praetor, more frequently in later times by the plaintiff.

Iudicis Datio. Comperendinatio. These preliminaries having been concluded, the parties were required to present themselves again before the Praetor, and the *Lex Pinaria* (Gaius IV. § 15) fixed that this second appearance should take place within a limited period after the first. If the parties, during this interval, had been unable to come to any arrangement, then the Praetor referred the matter to a *Iudex*, an *Arbiter*, or the *Centumviri*, as the cause might require; and the parties were obliged to prosecute their suit on the next day but one—*Dies Perendini—Dies Comperendini*—and hence the term *Comperendinatio*.

Litis Contestatio. This finished the proceedings before the Praetor, that is, the proceedings *in iure*, and the whole of these proceedings were comprehended under the general term *Litis Contestatio*, a phrase which seems originally to have been confined to the notice given by both parties to their witnesses to appear before the *Iudex*. At this stage the cause was termed by jurists *Iudicium acceptum* s. *ordinatum*.

Vadimonium. At different stages of the proceedings *in iure* the plaintiff might call upon the defendant to give bail—*Dare Vades*—*Dare* s. *Facere Vadimonium*—for his appearance, and in so doing was said *Vadari Reum*, that is, to hold the defender to bail, or to let him go on his sureties. When the defendant appeared at the appointed time and place he was said *Sistere* s. *Obire Vadimonium;* but if he failed to appear, he was said *Deserere Vadimonium;* the cause was called *Iudicium desertum*, and the Praetor at once gave judgment for the plaintiff. Generally, at any stage in the suit, either *in iure* or in *iudicio*, if one of the parties failed to appear personally or by his agents without being able to allege a valid apology, (*iusta excusatio*,) then the judgment was given by default in favour of the opposing party.

Vades. Praedes. Sponsores. These words may all be rendered by the English *Sureties*. According to Ausonius and Paulus Diaconus, *Vas* denotes a surety in a *Res Capitalis;* *Praes*, a surety in a Civil Suit.

> Quis subit in poenam Capitali Iudicio? Vas—
> Quid si Lis fuerit Nummaria, Quis dabitur? Praes.

But it cannot be proved from classical writers that this distinction was observed either in legal phraseology, or in the language of ordinary life.[1] *Praedium* originally signified any property which a *Praes* assigned in security to the state, but in process of time was used in a general sense for Landed Property. *Praediator*, as we learn from Gaius,[2] was one who bought from the people a *Praedium* which had been pledged to them.

Sponsor was a person who became surety to a *Creditor* for the performance of an *Obligatio* on the part of a *Debitor* (p. 268.) When there were several *Sponsores* jointly bound, they were called relatively to each other, *Consponsores*. A surety, according to the nature of the *Obligatio*, was sometimes termed *Sponsor*, sometimes *Fidepromissor*, sometimes *Fideiussor*.[3]

Proceedings in Iudicio.—The parties appeared on the appointed day before the *Iudex*, who took an oath to decide impartially, and was usually assisted by persons of high reputation learned in the law—*His, quos tibi advocasti, viris electissimis civitatis*—are the words ·of Cicero when addressing a *Iudex* (Pro Quinct. 2.)

A statement of the case was then made by both parties, (*Causae Collectio* s. *Coniectio*,) evidence was adduced, both oral (*Testes*) and documentary, (*Tabulae*—*Epistolae*—*Codices*—*Rationes*,) depositions were read, (*Testimonium recitare*,) the advocates (*Patroni*) commented at length upon the details; and after a full hearing, the *Iudex* or *Iudices* pronounced sentence at once, or, if doubts still remained, put off the cause (*proferre iudicium*) for further debate, and this was sometimes repeated again and again (*saepius prolato iudicio*, Cic. pro. Caec. 4.)

The final sentence, when in favour of the plaintiff, was termed *Condemnatio*, when in favour of the defendant, *Absolutio*.

---

[1] Varro L. L. VI. § 74. Auson. Eidyll. XII. Paul. Diac. s. v. *Vadem* p. 377. s. v. *Manceps* p. 151. Pseud. Ascon. in Cic. in Verr. Act. II. i. 45. 54.
[2] Gaius II. § 61. comp. Cic. ad Att. XII. 14. 17. pro Balb. 20. Val. Max. VIII. xii. 1. Suet. Claud. 9.
[3] Gaius III. § 115.

Vindiciae. Vindicatio.—The proceedings detailed above were common to *Actiones in Rem* and *Actiones in Personam* alike. But in *Actiones in Rem*, the Plaintiff, upon receiving leave to bring his suit into court, usually made a claim (*Vindiciae*) for temporary possession of the object in dispute until the suit should be finally settled; (*pendente lite ;*) this was commonly met by a counter claim on the part of the Defendant, and the Praetor was called upon, in the first instance, to decide upon this preliminary claim. The technical term for a claim of this nature was *Vindiciae*, the act of making the claim *Vindicatio* s. *Postulatio Vindiciarum*, the discussion which followed *Lis Vindiciarum*, the Praetor, in pronouncing his decision, was said *Dare* s. *Dicere Vindicias secundum alterum*, and the party to whom he awarded temporary possession was said *Ferre Vindicias*. Thus, if it were asserted that an individual, who was living as a slave in the possession of a master, was in reality a freeman and ought to be set at liberty, or, vice versa, if it were asserted that an individual, nominally free, was in reality a slave, then the Plaintiff in the former case would be said *Vindicare* s. *asserere in libertatem* s. *liberali causa*, in the latter case *Vindicare in servitutem*, and according as the Praetor decided that the individual whose freedom was in dispute, should, during the prosecution of the suit, be treated as one free or one in slavery, he was said *Dare Vindicias secundum libertatem* or *Dare Vindicias secundum servitutem* s. *Dicere Vindicias ab libertate*. See Liv. III. 44. 47. 57.

The party in whose favour the *Vindiciae* had been pronounced, was required to give security that the object should suffer no loss or damage until the proceedings were closed. This act was expressed by the phrase *Dare Praedes Litis et Vindiciarum*.

Forms observed in a Vindicatio.—When the object claimed was moveable, it was produced in court before the Praetor; the claimant, (*qui vindicabat,*) holding a rod, called *Festuca* s. *Vindicta*, in his hand, laid hold of the object, a slave, for example, saying—*Hunc ego hominem ex iure Quiritium meum esse aio secundum suam causam ut dixi*—and then touching him with the rod, added—*Ecce tibi Vindictam imposui*. The Defendant (*adversarius*) did the like.

When the object was not moveable, a piece of land, for example, it was the practice at an early period, in accordance with the rule prescribed in the Laws of the XII Tables, for the parties to proceed along with the Praetor to the land which was claimed by both, and there to commence a mock struggle, (*manum conserere,*) each endeavouring to drag (*deducere*) his opponent off the ground; this species of ejectment being termed *Vis Civilis* s. *Quotidiana*. At a later epoch, when the extent of the Roman territory and the press of business rendered it impossible for the magistrate to visit the spot, the parties having appeared before him, summoned each other to repair to the ground for the purpose of struggling to gain or keep possession of it—*Institutum est contra XII Tabulas ut litigantes non in iure apud Praetorem manum consererent sed ex iure manum consertum vocarent, id est, alter alterum ex iure ad manum conserendam vocaret*—(Aul. Gell. XX. 10.)—and having gone forth, they brought a clod (*gleba*) of earth from the disputed land, and placing it in the court, before the Praetor, went through the forms of *Vindicatio* in reference to this as a representative of the whole estate. Eventually a fiction was substituted for the act of proceeding to the ground. The claimant summoned his opponent in these words—*Fundus, qui est in agro, qui Sabinus vocatur, eum ego ex iure Quiritium meum esse aio, inde ego te ex iure manum consertum voco*—the *Adver-*

sarius replied—*Unde tu me ex iure manum consertum vocasti, inde ego te revoco* [1]—the Praetor then ordered them to go forth, each attended by his witnesses—*Suis utrisque superstitibus* [2] *praesentibus, istam viam dico: inite viam*—the parties then made a few steps as if to depart, when the Praetor called upon them to return in the words—*Redite viam*—and then the ceremonies of the *Vindicatio* proceeded. Observe that *Conserere Manum* originally indicated the actual contest, and hence *Conserere Manum in iure* became the technical phrase for laying claim formally, in court, to property, while *Conserere Manum ex iure* is to be explained from the practice of quitting, or pretending to quit, the court (on this see Aul. Gell. XX. 10.)

Sacramentum. After the Plaintiff had made his claim and the Defendant his counter claim, in *Actiones stricti iuris*, the Plaintiff deposited a sum of money, termed *Sacramentum*, and challenged his opponent to do the like, using the words—*Quando tu iniuria vindicavisti D aeris sacramento te provoco*, to which the *Adversarius* replied—*Similiter ego te*, &c. The amount of the *Sacramentum* was fixed by the Laws of the XII Tables.

Formula Petitoria. Sponsio.—After the *Legis Actiones* fell into disuse, the *Vindicatio* and *Sacramentum* were, in a great measure, superseded by the *Formula Petitoria*, or by the *Sponsio*.

In the *Formula Petitoria* the Plaintiff laid claim to the property—*Petitoria Formula haec est qua actor intendit rem suam esse*—and the parties mutually called upon each other by *Stipulatio* and *Restipulatio* (p. 270) to give security that they would be prepared to fulfil the decision of the court (*judicatum solvi.*)

The *Sponsio*, again, was a sort of judicial wager, of which one of the forms has been preserved by Gaius—(IV. § 93)—*Si homo, quo de agitur, ex iure Quiritium meus est, sestertios viginti quinque nummos dare spondes*—to which the *Adversarius* replied—*Spondeo*. When the *Sponsio* was made by one party only, as in the above example, it was termed *Sponsio Praeiudicialis*, and was adopted merely as a convenient form of bringing the matter to an issue, the sum not being exacted if the Plaintiff was successful. In other cases, however, mentioned by Gaius, the *Sponsio* was mutual, and took the form of *Stipulatio* and *Restipulatio*; the amount named was forfeited by the losing party, as in the case of the *Sacramentum*, and the term employed was *Sponsio Poenalis* (Gaius IV. § 13. 141. 171. Cic. pro Rosc. Comoed. 4.)

Interdictum. [3]—In some particular cases, those especially which referred to the possession of an object, a Plaintiff, instead of bringing an action in the regular form, applied to the Praetor to issue, in the first instance, an *Interdictum* or summary order to secure the rights of the applicant, by preventing any thing from being done to deteriorate or injure the object in question. Strictly speaking, a judicial order by the Praetor, commanding something to be done, was termed *Decretum*; an order forbidding something to be done, *Interdictum*; but *Interdictum* is constantly employed by jurists to comprehend both. *Interdicta* were applied for when some wrong had been done, or was likely to be done, which it was necessary to redress or prevent at once, without waiting for the ordinary technicalities *in iure* and *in iudicio*. *Interdicta*, according to their character, were divided into three classes—

1. *Restitutoria.* 2. *Exhibitoria.* 3. *Prohibitoria.*

[1] Cic. pro Muren. 12.
[2] Fest. s.v. *Superstites*, p. 305.
[3] Gaius IV. § 13.

1. If the actual possessor of a property had been forcibly ejected (*vi, hominibus armatis*) by a claimant, the person so dispossessed might apply for an *Interdictum Restitutorium*, ordering him to be reinstated until the rights of the parties had been decided by a competent court. The speech of Cicero pro Caecina is chiefly occupied with an argument concerning an *Interdictum Restitutorium*.

2. If any one had gained possession of a person or of a thing which was the subject of conflicting claims, and if there was reason to apprehend that the person or thing in question might suffer irreparable injury if allowed to remain in the custody of the Defendant until the suit was decided, the Plaintiff might apply for an order to have the object produced in court, and such an order was an *Interdictum Exhibitorium*.

3. In like manner, if the value of an estate was likely to be materially lessened by some meditated act of the person in possession, such as cutting down timber, uprooting vineyards, or the like, an *Interdictum Prohibitorium* might be applied for, forbidding any such act.

The object of an *Interdictum* was manifestly to prevent any wrong from being suffered by either of the parties in a suit until their respective claims were decided, and did not in itself prejudge those claims which were to form the subject of a deliberate independent discussion. But an application for an *Interdictum* often led to a preliminary lawsuit, for the Praetor might refuse to grant it until he had heard the opposite party, and might eventually refer the propriety of granting or refusing it to the decision of a *Iudex*. Even after an *Interdictum* had been granted, questions frequently arose as to whether the order of the Praetor had been duly obeyed, and on this question a separate litigation might arise, with protracted proceedings both *in iure* and *in iudicio*. The subject of *Interdicta* is somewhat difficult and complicated, and those who desire full information will do well to study the Chapter of Gaius (IV. § 139—170) devoted to this topic, and the remarks of Savigny in his *Das Recht des Besitzes*.

II. IUDICIA PUBLICA.

Criminal Jurisdiction of the Kings.—In so far as our authorities permit us to investigate this obscure period of Roman history, it seems clear that the Kings were the supreme judges in all criminal trials, and that their sentence was final. It would appear that they exercised this power in cases of importance only, those of trivial character being committed to the decision of the Senate.[1] The King, moreover, might, if he thought fit, delegate his authority to commissioners, as took place when Horatius was tried for the murder of his sister; and when this was the case the accused had the right of appealing from the commissioners to the Comitia Curiata.[2] When the King judged in person it was usual, but not imperative, for him to have the assistance and advice of a *Consilium*, composed of the whole or of a portion of the Senate;[3] at least we find it made the subject of complaint against the elder Tarquin, that he dispensed with the aid of a *Consilium* in criminal trials of importance—*Cognitiones capitalium rerum sine Consiliis per se solus exercebat* (Liv. I. 49.)[4] What the power of the *Consilium* may have been it is impossible to determine; but, probably, although it might advise and guide, it could not control nor gainsay the resolution of the monarch.

---

[1] Dionys. II. 14. 29. 53. 56. III. 73. IV. 5. 25. 36. 42. 62. Liv. I. 26. 40. 41.
[2] Liv. I. 26.
[3] Dionys. III. 26. Zonaras VII 9.
[4] So with regard to Romulus, Dionys. II. 56.

Criminal Jurisdiction of the Consuls and other Magistrates.—Upon the expulsion of the Kings the whole of the authority which they had enjoyed was transferred, in the first instance, to the Consuls, and consequently the latter, at the commencement of the republic, succeeded to the judicial functions of the former, and jointly exercised the power of life and death, as in the proceedings against the sons of Brutus.[1] This excessive power was, however, speedily limited, and in process of time altogether neutralized, chiefly by the *Ius Provocationis*, which we have already defined, in general terms, (p. 81,) to have been the right possessed by every Roman citizen of appealing to the people in their Comitia from the sentence of a magistrate in any matter which involved life, corporal punishment, or a permanent loss of political and social privileges.

Origin and Development of the Ius Provocationis.—It was positively asserted in certain priestly books, extant in the time of Cicero, that there was right of appeal even under the Kings—*Provocationem autem etiam a Regibus fuisse declarant pontificii libri, significant etiam nostri augurales* (Cic. de R. II. 31)—but, if it existed at all,[2] it must originally have been enjoyed by the Patricians alone, who would appeal to the Comitia Curiata. That a similar provision in favour of the Plebeians also may have been made upon the institution of the Comitia Centuriata is highly probable, but the rights of all classes alike would be altogether disregarded during the tyrannous dominion of the second Tarquin.

The right of *Provocatio* was revived and extended so as to include all classes of citizens, Plebeians and Patricians alike, by the *Lex Valeria*, of Poplicola, passed B.C. 509, immediately after the expulsion of the Kings—*Poplicola . . . legem ad populum tulit eam quae Centuriatis Comitiis prima lata est*, NE QUIS MAGISTRATUS CIVEM ROMANUM ADVERSUS PROVOCATIONEM NECARET NEVE VERBERARET, (Cic. de R. II. 31,)[3] and this law was always regarded by the Romans as the Magna Charta of their freedom. It was subsequently renewed, and its provisions made more stringent by the following statutes:—

Lex Valeria et Horatia, passed by L. Valerius Potitus, and M. Horatius Barbatus, when chosen Consuls B.C. 449, upon the abdication of the Decemvirs, which enacted—*Ne quis ullum magistratum sine Provocatione crearet: qui creasset, eum ius fasque esset occidi: neve ea caedes capitalis noxae haberetur* (Liv. III. 55. comp. Cic. de R. II. 31.)

Lex Duilia, passed in the same year with the above, by M. Duilius, Tribune of the Plebs, which enacted—*Qui Plebem sine Tribunis reliquisset, quique magistratum sine Provocatione creasset, tergo ac capite puniretur* (Liv. III. 55.)

Lex Valeria, passed by M. Valerius Corvus, when Consul, B.C. 300, which is noticed by Livy (X. 9) in the following terms—*Eodem anno M. Valerius consul de Provocatione legem tulit, diligentius sanctam. Tertio ea tum post reges exactos lata est, semper a familia eadem. Causam renovandae saepius haud aliam fuisse reor, quam quod plus paucorum opes, quam libertas plebis, poterant. Porcia tamen Lex sola pro tergo civium lata videtur: quod gravi*

---
[1] Dionys. IV. 73. V. 8. X. 1. Liv. II. 1. 4. Cic. de R. II. 32. Val. Max. V. viii. 1. Cassiodor. Var. VI. 1.

[2] In the case of Horatius, as detailed by Livy, (I. 26,) the King nominated, in accordance with an existing law—*secundum legem*—two commissioners (*duumviri*) to try the accused; but the same law which provided for the nomination of *Duumviri* by the King to act as judges in cases of *Perduellio* expressly allowed an appeal from these *Duumviri*—DUUMVIRI PERDUELLIONEM IUDICENT. SI A DUUMVIRIS PROVOCARIT, PROVOCATIONE CERTATO.

[3] See also Liv II. 8. III. 55. X. 9. Val. Max. IV. i. 1. Dionys. V. 19. Pompon. Digest. I. ii. 2. § 16.

poena, si quis verberasset necassetve civem Romanum, sanxit. Valeria Lex, quum eum, qui provocasset, virgis caedi securique necari vetuisset, si quis adversus ea fecisset, nihil ultra quam improbe factum, adiecit. Id (qui tum pudor hominum erat) visum, credo, vinculum satis validum legis.

A *Lex Porcia*, whose tenor was similar to that of those mentioned above, is mentioned by Livy in the passage just quoted, and is alluded to both by Cicero and Sallust.[1] It is generally believed to have been passed by P. Porcius Laeca, who

was Tribune of the Plebs B.C. 197. The chief evidence for assigning it to him is derived from a denarius, of which we annex a cut, representing on one side the usual helmeted head of Rome, with the legend P. LAECA, and on the other an accused person standing in a suppliant attitude before a magistrate, behind whom is a Lictor carrying a sword in one hand and two rods in the other, the legend at the bottom of the coin being PROVOCO.

Again, by an express Law of the XII Tables, it was ordained that no measure affecting the *Caput* (p. 83) was valid unless ratified by the Comitia Centuriata —*De Capite civis nisi per Comitiatum Maximum ne ferunto.*

Even the power of imposing a pecuniary fine was confined within narrow limits as early as B.C. 454 by the *Lex Aternia Tarpeia*.[2]

These restrictions reduced the criminal judicial powers of the Consuls and other magistrates to nothing in times of peace and tranquillity; but when civil commotions arose, and the liberties of the people were endangered by sedition or rebellion, either a Dictator was named or the Consuls were invested, by a decree of the Senate, with extraordinary powers, in virtue of which they executed summary justice upon all offenders without regard to the ordinary course of legal procedure (p. 149.)

Criminal Jurisdiction of the Senate.—We have already stated that our scanty sources of information lead us to believe that during the regal period the Kings sat as judges in all criminal causes of moment, assisted by a *Consilium* composed of the whole Senate, or of a committee of that body, while all trials of small importance were referred at once to the Senate.

During the republic the Senate appear to have possessed no regular independent jurisdiction whatsoever in criminal causes in so far as Roman citizens were concerned, the right of judging in all such matters being vested exclusively in the popular assemblies. In times of great alarm, indeed, when the state was threatened with destruction from internal treachery, the Senate, in conjunction with the Consuls, assumed the right of adopting whatever measures they thought necessary for the security of the public, and of inflicting summary punishment upon those by whom it was endangered. Of this we have conspicuous examples in the proceedings against the Gracchi, and against the conspirators associated with Catiline; but such measures were viewed with great jealousy, as involving a dangerous and unconstitutional stretch of power, to be justified only by the last necessity; while all parties concerned incurred a heavy responsibility, and were liable to be called to account before the people at a subsequent period, as

---

[1] Sallust. Cat. 51. Cic. pro Rabir. 3. 4. in Verr. V. 63. In these three passages Cicero speaks of the *Lex Porcia* in the singular number; but in de R. II. 31. after speaking of the earlier laws *De Provocatione*, adds, *Neque vero* LEGES PORCIAE, QUAE TRES SUNT TRIUM PORCIORUM, *ut scitis, quicquam praeter sanctionem attulerunt novi.*

[2] Aul. Gell. XI. 1. Dionys. X. 50. Cic. de R. II. 35. Festus. s.v. *Peculatus*, p. 237.

happened to Cicero, although at the moment of peril all parties acknowledged that Rome had been preserved from imminent hazard by his prompt decision.

Occasionally, also, crimes were committed which appeared to be stamped with a character so strange and awful, that a departure from ordinary forms was deemed requisite, and the Senate, with the consent of all classes, undertook to investigate or to order the investigation of the offences and to punish the guilty. Of this description were the poisonings recorded by Livy as having taken place in B.C. 331, when one hundred and seventy matrons were found guilty, and an occurrence of a similar nature in B.C. 180.[1]

But although the Senate, under ordinary circumstances, possessed no criminal jurisdiction over Roman citizens, it formed the regular court for the trial and punishment of state crimes, such as treachery or insurrection, committed by the allies,[2] and sometimes took cognizance of crimes of a private nature, such as murders and poisonings,[3] although these and lesser offences were usually disposed of by local tribunals.

It has been stated by some authors that the Senate inquired into charges of oppression preferred against Provincial Governors or military commanders, and punished the guilty. But although the Senate was the body to which such complaints were probably addressed by foreign ambassadors, it does not appear that the members ever arrogated to themselves the functions of judges. The example chiefly relied on—that of Pleminius (Liv. XXIX. 16)—does not bear out such an assertion, and the circumstances were altogether special.

Criminal Jurisdiction of the Comitia.—At the commencement of the republic the popular assemblies appear to have performed the functions of a court of justice in those cases only where an appeal was made from the sentence of a magistrate. But while the power of the magistrates, when acting as criminal judges, was always viewed with great and constantly increasing jealousy, and became more and more restricted by the enactment of successive laws, so, in like degree, the direct jurisdiction of the Comitia was more distinctly recognised, till at length they became the regular and ordinary courts for the investigation and punishment of all the more serious crimes. Throwing out of consideration the Comitia Curiata, to which an appeal was made in the case of Horatius, but which, even before the expulsion of the Kings, had ceased to take cognizance of matters affecting the community at large, we find that both the Comitia Centuriata and the Comitia Tributa acted as supreme courts of criminal judicature. The Comitia Tributa originally claimed the right of sitting in judgment upon those offences only which were regarded as infringements of the rights and privileges of the Plebs as an order; but as the power of the Plebs increased, and their Tribunes grew more bold and grasping, disputes and collisions must have constantly taken place between the two assemblies, had not the Laws of the XII Tables expressly ordained that no citizen could be tried for any offence involving his *Caput* (p. 83) except by the *Comitiatus Maximus*, that is the *Comitia Centuriata*. At the same time the jurisdiction of the Comitia Tributa was extended to embrace all causes for which the penalty was a pecuniary fine only, even although not bearing directly upon the interests of the Plebs (p. 125.)

Notwithstanding the positive injunction contained in the Code of the XII Tables, it seems probable, that, after harmony was completely established

---

1 Liv. VIII. 18. XL. 37. Val. Max. II. V. 3.
2 Liv. IV. 23. VI. 13. 17. VIII. 19. 20. IX. 26. X. 1. XXVIII. 10. XXIX. 36. XXXII. 26. XXXIII. 36. Polyb. VI. 13.
3 Liv. XXXIX. 41. XL. 37. 43. Cic. Brut. 22. Polyb. l.c.

between the two orders in the state, the jurisdiction of the Comitia Tributa was occasionally resorted to, with the consent of the Senate and the parties interested, even in cases which did not properly fall under its control, in consequence of the greater facilities afforded for summoning and holding that assembly; but the expressions of the classical writers are not so precise as to enable us to speak with confidence upon this point.

Form of Procedure in Criminal Trials before the Comitia.—No one could act as an accuser except a magistrate who had the right of holding the Comitia before which the charge was to be tried; and no one could be brought to trial while holding any of the higher offices of state. The magistrate who had resolved to impeach a citizen, gave public notice of his intention in a *Concio*, and named the day on which he would summon the Comitia for the purpose of instituting proceedings—hence the phrase *Diem dicere alicui* signifies *to give formal notice of an impeachment.*

Meanwhile the accused was thrown into prison, unless he could find sureties (*vades*) for his appearance on the day fixed. This point is said to have been first settled when Quinctius Kaeso was impeached of murder, by A. Virginius, a Tribune of the Plebs (B.C. 461.) Virginius insisted that he should be kept in bonds until the day of trial; but the College of Tribunes, when appealed to, decided that the accused must be forthcoming at the appointed time, (*sisti reum,*) and that bail must be given for his appearance; (*pecuniamque, nisi sistatur, populo promitti;*) and it was fixed that ten sureties must be found, (*vades dare placuit: decem finierunt: tot vadibus accusator vadatus est reum,*) each of whom became bound for three thousand pounds of copper. Livy concludes his narrative (III. 13) by stating—*Hic primus vades publicos dedit.*

When the day fixed arrived, the accuser stated the charge, examined witnesses, and adduced other evidence in proof. This portion of the procedure was termed *Anquisitio*, (Varro L.L. VI. § 90,) and according as the charge which the accuser sought to establish was one which involved the *Caput* of the accused, or merely a pecuniary fine, he was said, in the one case, *capite s. capitis anquirere*, in the other, *pecunia anquirere*.[1] Sometimes, when the investigation had been commenced with reference to a capital charge, the accuser departed from this, and was content to prosecute for a fine—*In multa temperarunt tribuni, quum capitis anquisissent: duo millia aeris damnato multam dixerunt,* (Liv. II. 52.) and, vice versa, we find—*Quum Tribunus bis pecunia anquisisset, tertio capitis se anquirere diceret*.... (Liv. XXVI. 3. comp. VIII. 33.)

When the *Anquisitio* was concluded, the magistrate then brought in a bill (*Rogatio*) ordaining the infliction of certain penalties on the accused, and this *Rogatio* was published, discussed, and accepted or rejected, as the case might be, with all the formalities required in submitting any ordinary legislative measure to the Comitia. Hence the phrases *Irrogare multam—poenam—supplicium alicui.*

Criminal Jurisdiction of Quaesitores.—Although the Comitia possessed the unquestionable right of acting as a supreme court in all criminal causes affecting Roman citizens, it must soon have become evident that it was highly inconvenient, and frequently impossible, for a popular assembly to examine into

---

[1] Occasionally *anquirere* is used in a more general sense—*Sunt qui per duumviros, qui* DE PERDUELLIONE ANQUIRERENT, *creatos, auctores sint damnatum,* (Liv. VI. 20)—*Id solum Germanico super leges praestiterimus, quod in curia potius quam in foro, apud senatum quam apud iudices* DE MORTE EIUS ANQUIRITUR (Tacit. Ann. III. 12.)

the details of a complicated charge, and to sift and weigh a mass of confused and contradictory evidence. Hence, from an early period it became common for the Comitia to delegate their power to one or more persons, who acted as judges, and were entitled *Quaesitores* or *Quaestores*, the investigation or trial being termed *Quaestio;* and hence the phrases—*Quaestioni praeficere*—*Quaestionem exercere*—*Quaestionem habere*—employed in relation to those who conferred and to those who exercised this authority. Such an appointment is specially mentioned for the first time in B.C. 413, (Liv. IV. 51,) when the Comitia Tributa, at the request of the Senate, and with the consent of the Comitia Centuriata, nominated a commission to inquire into the murder of Postumius by his own soldiers, and in this instance the Consuls were the Commissioners.

By degrees, as the population increased, and criminal trials became more numerous, the Comitia very rarely exercised their judicial functions directly, and the great majority of criminal trials were conducted under the presidency of *Quaestores*.

There are several points connected with these officials to which we must pay particular attention—

1. The judicial *Quaesitor* or *Quaestor* must be carefully distinguished from the *Quaestores*, who acted as Commissioners of the Treasury. The latter denominated, by way of distinction, *Quaestores Aerarii*, were regular ordinary magistrates, called upon to discharge a routine of duties, and elected every year. The former, the judicial *Quaestores*, were appointed specially for the purpose of presiding at a particular trial, they possessed no powers beyond, and as soon as this duty was discharged, their authority ceased. The *Quaestiones* were *Special Commissions*, the *Quaestores* were the *Special Commissioners*.

2. The judicial *Quaestor* acted as a Judge, and was uniformly assisted by a *Consilium* or body of assessors resembling, in many respects, a modern Jury. This *Consilium*, up to the passing of the *Lex Sempronia*, in B.C. 122, consisted of Senators exclusively. How far the power of the *Consilium* may have extended in early times is unknown; but there is no doubt that at the period when the above law was passed a majority of their number could condemn or acquit the accused person without reference to the opinion of the *Quaestor*.

3. The *Quaestor* being the delegated representative of the people, the sentence passed in his court was final.

4. Although the Commission nominated in B.C. 413 is the first example which can be fairly regarded as historical, we find traces of a similar usage from the most remote ages. Thus, the *Duumviri* appointed by Tullus Hostilius for the trial of Horatius, were a species of judicial *Quaestores*, and the *Quaestores Parricidii*, mentioned in Paulus Diaconus, were probably instituted at a very early epoch—*Parrici Quaestores appellabantur, qui solebant creari causa rerum capitalium quaerendarum*.[1]

5. Since the *Quaestores* were the representatives of the people, we cannot doubt that they must have been uniformly elected by the Comitia, as in the case already cited; but the manner in which the *Consilium* was chosen in the earlier ages is quite unknown.

6. Where the Senate had jurisdiction, they also usually appointed a *Quaesitor* out of their own body; and at times we find a resolution passed in the Comitia enjoining the Senate to appoint Commissioners for the investigation of certain acts alleged to be criminal.[2]

[1] Paul. Diac. s.v. *Parrici Quaestores*, p. 221. comp. Varro L.L. V. § 81. Lyd. de Mag. I. 26.
[2] See Liv. XXXVIII. 54. XLII. 21.

Institution of the Quaestiones Perpetuae.—As the population of Rome increased, and offences of every description became more and more numerous, the plan of appointing a Special Commission to try each cause became more and more inconvenient and embarrassing. Hence the idea naturally suggested itself of appointing *Standing Commissions* for trying those accused of the crimes which were of the most frequent occurrence. The first step towards this new arrangement was made by L. Calpurnius Piso, a Tribune of the Plebs, who, in B.C. 149, passed a law (*De Repetundis*) to check the oppression of Provincial Governors, one of the provisions being that a Commission should be established to sit permanently throughout the year for the hearing of all charges preferred under that law.[1] The experiment was found to work so well that from time to time new laws were passed, by which new Courts or Commissions of a similar description were instituted for the investigation of different offences, until at length the system was brought into general operation by a *Lex Cornelia* of Sulla. From that time forward until the final establishment of the imperial government, the jurisdiction of all other courts in criminal prosecutions was, in a great measure, superseded, and the whole of the ordinary criminal business was conducted by Standing Commissions, and these *Commissions* or *Courts* were distinguished as the QUAESTIONES PERPETUAE.

With regard to these, it must be remarked—

1. That each court or *Quaestio* took cognizance of one class of offences only. Thus, there was a *Quaestio Perpetua*, which was occupied exclusively with cases connected with the misgovernment or oppression of the Provincials, (*De Repetundis*,) another with embezzlement of the public money, (*De Peculatu*,) another with bribery on the part of the candidates for public offices, (*De Ambitu*,) another with violations of the dignity of the imperial people, (*De Maiestate*,) and so forth.

2. Although these Courts were permanent, they were viewed exactly in the same light as the former Special Commissions, and were regarded as exercising power directly delegated to them by the people. The supreme jurisdiction of the Comitia Centuriata was still fully recognised in principle, and the assemblies of the people were still called together for the purpose of holding trials or for the appointment of Special Commissions in all extraordinary cases, for which no provision had been made in the laws establishing the *Quaestiones Perpetuae*.

3. It was no longer necessary that a magistrate should act as the accuser; any citizen might now come forward and prefer a charge.

4. Each *Quaestio* was established by a separate law, and all the proceedings in each Court were regulated by the terms of the law under which its sittings were held, and these proceedings were, from time to time, modified or altogether changed by new laws.

5. Hence, there was no general form of procedure applicable to all the Courts alike; and although we may be able to ascertain the details of a process in one Court, in that for trying causes *De Ambitu*, for example, at one particular period, we cannot infer that the same formalities were observed at the same period in trying cases *De Maiestate* or *De Repetundis*, or at a different period in trying cases *De Ambitu*.

6. There was, however, one general principle applicable to all without exception—every case submitted to a *Quaestio Perpetua* was tried by a Judge and a Jury. The duty of the Judge was to preside and to regulate the proceedings in

---

[1] Cic. Brut. 27. de Off. II. 21. in Verr. III. 84. IV. 25.

terms of the law under which he acted. The duty of the Jury was, after hearing the pleadings and the evidence, to pronounce upon the guilt or innocence of the accused.

7. In addition to this general principle, we have every reason to believe that the ordinary course of procedure was similar in the different Courts, and that many forms were common to all, although each had its peculiarities; and we know that, from time to time, *Leges Iudiciariae* were passed for the regulation of the Courts, and that these were applicable to all.

8. The general name for the Judge was *Quaesitor* or *Quaestor:* the Jury as a body was termed *Consilium:* the individuals who composed the Jury were the *Iudices.* It must be carefully remarked by the young scholar that wherever the word *Iudices* occurs in the plural in any phrase relating to a criminal trial, it must always be rendered into English by the word *Jury* or *Jurors,* never by *Judges.* In Civil Suits, as we have seen above, *Iudex* denotes an umpire or arbiter, that is, in reality, a Jury composed of one individual: in criminal trials the presiding Judge or *Quaesitor* was, in certain cases, named *Iudex Quaestionis;* but this is a special technicality, which will be illustrated below.

These things being premised, we shall proceed to state what our authorities enable us to ascertain with regard—1. To the Judge and Jury, and, 2. To the ordinary course of procedure; and we shall conclude with a short account of the most important of those crimes which formed the subjects of investigation in the criminal courts.

Presiding Judges in the Quaestiones Perpetuae.—In the earlier *Quaestiones* or Special Commissions, the Judge or *Quaesitor* was nominated by the people, in their Comitia, and any one, without restriction, might be appointed at their pleasure. After the institution of the *Quaestiones Perpetuae,* the case was altered. The presiding Judge was now either—

1. One of the *Praetores,* or, 2. An officer denominated *Iudex Quaestionis.*

1. At the period when the first *Quaestio Perpetua* was instituted by the passing of the *Lex Calpurnia de Repetundis,* there were six Praetors. The *Praetor Urbanus* and the *Praetor Peregrinus* remained in the city during their year of office and presided in the Civil Courts, the remaining four acted as the Provincial Governors of Sicily, Sardinia, and the two Spains. Upon the passing of the *Lex Calpurnia,* the duty of presiding in the Court for trying cases *De Repetundis* was assigned to the *Praetor Peregrinus;*[1] but as legal business, both civil and criminal, rapidly increased, and new *Quaestiones Perpetuae* were established, the *Praetor Urbanus* and the *Praetor Peregrinus* were obliged to give the whole of their attention to Civil Suits, while the four remaining Praetors were retained in the city during their year of office, in order that they might act as Judges in the new Criminal Courts, and did not proceed to their Provinces until their year of service in the city had expired. When the Criminal Code was remodelled by Sulla, and the number of *Quaestiones Perpetuae* increased, it was found necessary to increase the number of Praetors also, which was now augmented to eight, so that six were left free to act as Criminal Judges, and these divided the duties of the different Courts among each other by lot, and, when spoken of in their judicial capacity, were usually named *Quaesitores.*[2]

2. But towards the close of the republic, the increase in criminal business was so great, that even this additional number of Praetors proved insufficient for the

[1] See Klenze, Fragmt. leg. Servil. p. 27.
[2] Cic. in Verr. Act. I. 8. pro Sest. 40. in Pison. 15. pro Milon. 15. Orat. post. red. 9. Dion Cass. XLII. 51. Varro L.L. V. § 81.

work, and it became necessary to appoint supplementary Judges, each of whom was called a *Iudex Quaestionis*.

All detailed information with regard to these personages is extremely deficient; but our authorities enable us to assert that a *Iudex Quaestionis* was the supreme Judge in the court in which he sat, and, for the time being, enjoyed the full authority of an ordinary Praetor. This is proved by the accounts preserved of the trial of Oppianicus, and of the trial of Cluentius, in the former of which a certain C. Junius, and in the latter a Q. Voconius Naso, acted as *Iudex Quaestionis*. We know, moreover, that a *Iudex Quaestionis* was not held to be an ordinary magistrate, for he could himself be brought to trial before the close of the year in the course of which he served; and when about to preside at a trial, he was obliged to take an oath like an ordinary Juryman, a form from which a Praetor was exempted.[1] But whether each Praetor had a *Iudex Quaestionis* attached to him during his year of office, to whom, as his deputy, he might make over the business which he himself was unable to overtake; or whether a *Iudex Quaestionis* had a particular department set aside for him in the criminal courts altogether independent of any particular Praetor; or whether a *Iudex Quaestionis* was nominated specially for a particular trial; whether the appointment, according to any of the above suppositions, was made by the people or by the Praetors themselves, and what the qualifications may have been for holding the office, are questions to which no satisfactory reply can be offered. In reference to the last point, two individuals are mentioned as having held this office, both of whom are stated to have been previously Aediles, and a third subsequently became a Praetor; but no induction from such a limited number of facts can be conclusive.[2]

The Iudices or Iurors in the Quaestiones Perpetuae.—The duty of the presiding Judge in one of the *Quaestiones Perpetuae* was merely that of a superintendent, who was bound to see that the provisions of the law under which the trial took place were strictly complied with, but who exercised no direct influence upon the final result of the trial. He might unquestionably take advantage of technical formalities to aid or embarrass one or other of the parties; and this will account for the exhortations to impartiality so often addressed to the Judge in the orations of Cicero; or if recklessly corrupt, he might, at his own peril, make a false declaration of the state of the votes given by ballot; but he was not able, in the fair exercise of his functions, to influence the decision, which rested entirely with the *Iudices*. Hence the power possessed by those who acted as *Iudices* was necessarily very great, and was often abused for party purposes. Some of the most serious internal dissensions during the last century of the republic were closely connected with the contests between different orders in the state for the privilege of acting as *Iudices*; and the different *Leges Iudiciariae* relating to this point were a source of great and frequently renewed excitement.

Class of persons from which the Iudices were chosen.—From the earliest period until the time of the Gracchi, the *Consilium* in all Criminal Trials, whether held before Special Commissions, or *Quaestiones Perpetuae*, had been composed exclusively of Senators. But in B.C. 122, the *Lex Sempronia Iudiciaria* of C. Gracchus was passed, in terms of which the *Iudicia*, that is *the right of acting as jurors on criminal trials*, were transferred from the Senate

---

[1] Cic. pro Cluent. 33—35. 53. 54. in Verr. Act. I. 10, and note of Pseud. Ascon. Digest. XLVII. viii. 1.
[2] Cic. Brut. 76. pro Cluent. 29. pro Rosc. Amer. 4.

to the Equestrian Order, which, in fact, first received a definite form in consequence of this ordinance.¹

After the death of C. Gracchus, the Senate made strenuous efforts to recover the privilege of which they had been deprived; and various laws were brought forward by the representatives of different parties, whose object was to reverse, confirm, or modify the provisions of the *Lex Sempronia.* Such were the *Lex Servilia* (B.C. 106) of Q. Servilius Caepio, by which the *Iudicia* were to be restored to the Senate; the *Lex Servilia* of C. Servilius Glaucia, by which the provisions of the Lex Sempronia against Senators were rendered more stringent; the *Lex Livia* (B.C. 91) of M. Livius Drusus, which endeavoured to bring about a compromise between the Senate and the Equestrian Order; and the *Lex Plautia* (B.C. 89) of M. Plautius Silvanus, which proposed that the people should, each year, nominate fifteen *Iudices* out of each tribe, without reference to the fact of their being Senators, members of the Equestrian Order, or simple citizens.²

But these laws, if they ever actually came into operation, remained in force for a very brief period, and the *Iudicia* remained in the hands of the Equestrian Order for forty-two years, until Sulla, following out his deliberate scheme of increasing by all means the influence of the *Optimates,* restored, in B.C. 81, the state of things which existed before the passing of the *Lex Sempronia,* giving back the *Iudicia* to the Senate.³

The reaction which immediately followed the death of the Dictator, rendered a continuance of this exclusive privilege impossible; and accordingly in B.C. 70, the *Lex Aurelia* of L. Aurelius Cotta, one of the Praetors of that year, was passed, ordaining that the *Iudices* were to be selected from three bodies or orders in the state—the *Senatus,* the *Ordo Equester,* and the *Tribuni Aerarii,* (p. 239,) each order forming a *Decuria.*⁴

By the *Lex Pompeia,* passed by Pompeius Magnus in his second consulship, B.C. 55, the *Iudices* continued to be chosen from the three orders named in the *Lex Aurelia,* but the most wealthy only were eligible; and by the *Lex Iulia* of Caesar, passed B.C. 46, the *Tribuni Aerarii* were excluded. Antonius, after the death of Caesar, endeavoured to render the constitution of the body more democratic than ever, by the admission of legionary soldiers; but his enactments remained in force for a very limited space. Finally, Augustus restored the three *Decuriae* of the Aurelian law, and added a fourth from the humbler classes of the community, while a fifth *Decuria* was introduced by Caligula; but before that period, the importance of the office had passed away.⁵

Qualification as to Age.—So long as the *Iudicia* remained in the hands of the Senate, no regulations were necessary upon this head; but when other orders were admitted, certain restrictions were introduced. By the *Lex Servilia,* no one could act as a *Iudex* under the age of thirty, or above the age of sixty; and this regulation seems to have continued in force until Augustus reduced the legal age to twenty-five.⁶

Disqualifications for the Office.—No one could act as a *Iudex* who was invested with any of the higher offices of the State, or who did not live in Rome

---

¹ Velleius II. 6. 13. 32. Tacit. Ann. XII. 60. See above. D 74.
² Tacit. Ann. XII. 60. Liv. Epit. LXX. LXXI. Velleius II. 13. Cic. pro Scauro I. 2. Fragmt. leg. Servil. 6. 7.
³ Cic. in Verr. Act. I. 13. Velleius II. 32. Tacit. Ann. XI. 22.
⁴ Cic. pro Corn. in Pison. 39, and note of Ascon. ad Att. I. 16. ad Q. F. II. 6.
⁵ Ascon. in Cic. in Pison. 39. Cic. Philipp. I.S. V. 5, XIII 2. 3. ad Fam. XII. 14. Dion Cass. XLVI. 36. Sueton. Octav. 32. Calig. 16. Plin. H. N. XXXIII. 1, 2.
⁶ Fragmt. leg. Servil. 6. Suet. Octav. 32; but the text is doubtful.

or the immediate vicinity; nor any one who had ever been found guilty of any charge affecting his *Status* as a *Civis Romanus optimo iure*.¹

Number of Iudices.—On the first institution of the *Quaestiones Perpetuae*, it would appear that a certain number of *Iudices* were appointed each year for each *Quaestio*, out of which the proper number for each trial—and this number appears always to have been fixed by the law under which the trial was held—was selected. Thus, from the fragments which have been preserved of the *Lex Servilia de Repetundis*, we know that 450 *Iudices* were nominated yearly to serve on the *Quaestio de Repetundis*. But when the *Quaestiones Perpetuae* gradually embraced almost all criminal causes, it would appear that a certain number of *Iudices* were selected for the whole, and subsequently distributed among the different *Quaestiones*. Thus the number fixed by the *Lex Livia* was 600; by the *Lex Plautia* 525 (being 15 out of each tribe,) unless we suppose, with some writers, that this number was chosen for each *Quaestio*. We have no farther information until the time of Augustus, when the number was about 4000. On the occasion of Milo's trial, 360 *Iudices* were set apart; and it appears to have been the intention of Pompeius to appropriate this number for each *Quaestio*; but it is well known that the changes in the criminal law introduced by him remained in force for a very short time only.²

Manner of choosing the Iudices.—In what manner the *Iudices* were chosen annually out of the qualified classes, is a matter involved in much obscurity. So long as a fixed number was set apart for each *Quaestio*, it would appear that the Praetor, or *Iudex Quaestionis*, who presided over that *Quaestio*, chose whom he thought fit; at least this was the case under the *Lex Servilia de Repetundis*, in which the *Praetor Peregrinus* is enjoined to select 450. After the *Iudices* for the whole of the *Quaestiones Perpetuae* were chosen in a mass, we infer, from a passage in Cicero, that the duty devolved upon the *Praetor Urbanus*, who selected, upon oath (*iuratus*,) the persons whom he deemed best qualified, although it would seem from the words of Dion Cassius, that the *Quaesitor*, in some instances, chose them by lot. The list of *Iudices* for the year, however chosen, was termed *Album Iudicum*, and the individuals included in this list, *Iudices Selecti*.³

Decuriae Iudicum. We have stated above that by the *Lex Aurelia*, the whole number of *Iudices* was divided into three sections or *Decuriae*, each order forming a *Decuria*. Thus there was a *Decuria* of Senators, a *Decuria* composed of members of the Equestrian Order, and a *Decuria* of *Tribuni Aerarii*. By the law of Augustus, also noticed above, the number of *Decuriae* was increased to four, and by that of Caligula to five. In the period also between the *Lex Cornelia* of B.C. 81, and the *Lex Aurelia* of B.C. 70, during which Senators only could act as *Iudices*, we hear of *Decuriae Iudicum*, but we are altogether ignorant of the principle upon which this arrangement or distribution was founded.⁴

ORDINARY FORM OF PROCESS IN CRIMINAL TRIALS DURING THE EPOCH OF THE QUAESTIONES PERPETUAE.

The various steps in a criminal prosecution, without reference to the particular *Quaestio*, or the special law by which they were regulated, seem to have been as follows:—

---
1 Fragmt. leg. Servil. 6. 7. Cic. in Verr. Act. I. 10.
2 Fragmt. leg. Servil. 6. 7. Appian. B. C. 1. 35. Plin. H. N. XXXIII. 1. Velleius II. 76. Plut. Pomp. 55.
3 Fragmt. leg. Servil. 6. 7. Cic. pro Cluent. 43. Dion Cass. XXXIX. 7.
4 Cic. in Verr. I. 61. II. 32. pro Cluent. 37.

Postulatio.[1]—An application on the part of the impeacher to the Praetor, or *Iudex Quaestionis*, who presided over the court to which the charge belonged, for leave to prefer an accusation. This, although in most cases a mere formality, was a necessary preliminary, because it might happen that the applicant was disqualified by law from acting as an impeacher of any one, or from acting as the impeacher of the particular individual whom he desired to prosecute; or he might have been forestalled, which leads us to consider,

Divinatio.[2]—Two or more persons might make application at the same time for leave to prefer the same charge against the same individual. It thus became necessary to decide which of the applicants had the best claim to conduct the prosecution, and this question was decided formally by a *consilium* of *iudices*, (who were, however, not upon oath—*iniurati*,) after the different applicants had been fully heard in support of their pretensions. This preliminary process was termed *Divinatio;* and Cicero affords an example, who contended with a certain Q. Caecilius for permission to bring a criminal charge against C. Verres, and delivered a speech, still extant, entitled *Divinatio in Q. Caecilium*.

Nominis s. Criminis Delatio.[3]—These preliminaries having been adjusted, the accuser made a formal declaration of the name of the person whom he intended to impeach, and of the crime which he laid to his charge, and in so doing was said—*Deferre Nomen—Deferre Crimen*—and hence, under the empire, *Delatores* was the term used to denote that class of persons who made a trade of impeaching.

Citatio.[4]—At this stage, it would appear that the accused was formally summoned (*citatus*) to appear befor the Praetor or *Iudex Quaestionis*, and hear in person the charge preferred.

Interrogatio.[5]—The accuser then put certain questions to the accused, which he was, of course, at liberty to answer or not as he thought fit. The object of these questions was to ascertain how much the accused was willing to admit, in order that the question submitted to the Jury might assume a definite form and be compressed within narrow limits.

Inscriptio. Subscriptio.[6]—A formal document was next drawn up stating precisely the nature of the charge and the name of the accused. This was signed by the accuser and also by those who intended to give him their support and countenance in conducting the prosecution, and who were hence termed *Subscriptores*. The accused then became technically *Reus*, and as such was legally disqualified from becoming candidate for any public office.

Nominis Receptio.[7]—The presiding Judge then formally registered the name of the accused, and in so doing was said *Nomen Recipere*.

Finally, a day was fixed for proceeding with the trial. This, under ordinary circumstances, was the tenth after the *Nominis Receptio;* but the interval was sometimes regulated by the special law under which the *Quaestio* was held, and sometimes a lengthened space was granted in those instances where it was necessary to procure evidence from a distance, as in the accusation of Verres,

---

1 Cic. Div. in. Q. C. 20. Epp. ad Fam. VIII. 6.
2 Cic. ad Q. F. III. 2. Pseud. Ascon. Argumt. in Cic. Div. in Q. C. Quintil. I. O. III. x. 3. VII. iv. 33. Aul. Gell. II. 4.
3 Cic. Div. in Q. C. 3. 15. 19. 20. pro Cluent. 4. 8. 17. Epp. ad Fam. VIII. 6.
4 Cic. in Verr. II. 28.
5 Pseud. Ascon. in Cic. in Verr. Act. I. 2. Schol. Bob. p. 342. ed. Orell. Sallust. Cat. 18. 31. Velleius II. 13.
6 Cic. pro Cluent. 31. 47. Ascon. in Milonian. 35. Orat. pro dom. 20.
7 Cic. in Verr. II. 38. IV. 19. Epp. ad Fam. VIII. 8. Val. Max. III. vii. 9.

when Cicero was allowed one hundred and ten days, although he did not avail himself of the permission to the full extent.[1]

On the day appointed, the Judge having taken his seat upon the tribunal, the names of all those *Iudices* who were liable to serve upon this particular *Quaestio* were called over, and at the same time the accuser and defendant were summoned to appear by the Crier of the Court (*ciebantur a Praecone praetorio*.)[2]

There can be no doubt that the Judge possessed the power of enforcing the attendance of such *Iudices* as did not answer when called upon, and of inflicting punishment on such as could not afford a satisfactory excuse for their absence (Cic. Philipp. V. 5.) If the accuser did not appear, the defendant was at once dismissed from the bar, it being left open, however, to any one to institute a new process. If the accused did not appear, and if no one appeared to account for his absence, then, towards evening, he was pronounced guilty, and sentence was passed upon him in terms of the law under which the Court sat.[3] If all the parties were in attendance, the first business was balloting for the Jury.

Iudicum Sortitio.[4]—The names of all those *Iudices* who were liable to serve were thrown into the balloting urn, those only being excluded who were closely connected by blood, marriage, or any other strong tie, with either of the parties.

The presiding Judge then drew out of the urn the number of names proper to constitute the Jury. This number depended entirely upon the provisions of the particular law under which the trial took place, and we accordingly find examples of 32, 50, 70, 75, and other numbers.[5]

Iudicum Reiectio.—It was a principle in Roman Law, that in all causes, both civil and criminal, the person or persons who decided a controversy should be appointed with the full consent of the contending parties (Cic. pro Cluent. 43.) To have carried out this principle to its full extent in criminal causes would have, manifestly, been impracticable; but after the requisite number of Jurors had been chosen by ballot, both parties were allowed to challenge (*reiicere*) a certain number, if they thought fit. It was not necessary that the party challenging should state his reasons, the right was absolute, and he alone was the judge of the expediency of exercising it. The number of Jurors which each party was allowed to challenge appears, like the number of the Jury, to have been fixed by the laws regulating each *Quaestio*, and on this point we have but little general information.[6]

Iudicum Subsortitio.—The vacancies in the *Consilium*, caused by the challenges, were filled up by the Judge, who drew fresh names from the urn. This operation was termed *Subsortitio*.[7]

Iudicum Editio.—The appointment of a Jury by ballot was the rule followed in a great majority of criminal causes; but it was not universal, for some laws, prohibiting particular offences, directed that the Jury should be appointed in a different manner. Thus, by the *Lex Servilia de Repetundis*, each party nominated (*edebat*) one hundred Jurors, and each challenged fifty of those nominated

---

1 Cic. ad Q. F. II. 13. in Vat 14. Ascon. Arg. in Cic. Cornelian. Pseud. Ascon. Argumt. in Cic. in Verr. Act. I. Plut. Cic. 9.
2 Pseud. Ascon. in Cic. in Verr. I. 1. Ascon. Argumt. in Cic. Cornelian. Cic. in Verr. II. 17. 40. Pro Cluent. 17. 18. 21. Plut. Brut. 27.
3 Cic. in Verr. II. 17. 38. 40. Ascon. in Cic. Milonian. 35. Velleius II. 24. Caes. B. G. VI. 44. Plut. Brut. 27. Dion Cass. XLVI. 48. LIV. 3.
4 Pseud. Ascon. in Verr. Act. I. 6. Schol. Gronov. ibid.
5 Cic. pro Cluent. 27. pro Flacc. 2. ad Q. F. III. 4. in Pison. 40.
6 Cic. de Orat. II. 70. in Verr. II. 31. III. 60. in Vatin. Philipp. XII. 7.
7 Cic. in Verr. I. 19. 61. pro Cluent. 33. 35. Pseud. Ascon. in Verr. Act. 1. 6

by his opponent, so that the *Consilium*, when thus reduced, consisted of one hundred; but this procedure was abrogated by subsequent laws *De Repetundis*, and the ordinary methods of *Sortitio* and *Subsortitio* substituted.[1] Again, by the *Lex Licinia de Sodalitiis*, the accuser named four Tribes, the accused had the right of challenging or rejecting one of these Tribes; and then the accuser selected the Jury out of the remaining three Tribes, without, it would seem, any farther right of challenge being granted to the accused.[2] Jurors appointed in this, or in a similar manner, were called *Iudices Editicii*, as distinguished from those named by *Sortitio*.

The Jury, being finally adjusted, were then sworn, and hence they are frequently designated simply by the epithet *Iurati*. A *Iudex Quaestionis* was, in like manner, sworn; but a Praetor was not, his general oath of office being considered sufficient; and this circumstance alone seems to prove that the *Iudex Quaestionis* was not regarded in the light of an ordinary magistrate.

The pleadings then commenced. The prosecutor or his counsel (of whom more hereafter) opened the case, the defender replied in person or by his counsel, and then the evidence was led.

Testimonia.—The evidence might be of different kinds, Oral, (*Testes*,) Documentary, (*Tabulae*,) and mixed, that is, consisting of declarations by corporate bodies, (*Testimonia publica*,) supported by the verbal testimony of deputies (*Legati*) sent for the purpose.

Testes.—Witnesses might be either free men or slaves; and, if free men, they might be either Roman citizens or Peregrini.

All free men alike were examined upon oath—*iurati*—but much less importance attached to the evidence of foreigners than of citizens, and Greek witnesses especially were regarded with peculiar suspicion. Witnesses might give evidence of their own free will (*voluntarii*) or upon compulsion; but the right of compelling a person to appear as a witness (*Denuntiare—Testibus denuntiare —Testimonium denuntiare*) was possessed by the accuser alone. It was customary for the accused to call witnesses to speak, not only to facts, but to character, and such were termed *Laudatores*, the number usually brought forward for this purpose being ten.[3]

With regard to the position of slaves as witnesses, several points deserve particular notice—

1. It was a principle in Roman Law that no declaration on the part of a slave could be received in evidence unless emitted under torture. Hence the word *Quaestio*, when employed in reference to the examination of slaves, always implies the application of torture.[4]

2. In the great majority of cases in which we read of the judicial examination of slaves, in the earlier period of Roman history, the persons charged with the crimes were the masters of the slaves, the slaves themselves being implicated as accomplices, and the chief object was to force from the slave a confession of his own guilt; and no slaves were examined except those belonging to the accused party.

3. In no case could a slave, when not charged with participation in the crimes, be admitted as an ordinary witness *against* his own master. It was only when

---

[1] Klenze, Fragmt. leg. Servil. 8. 12.
[2] Cic. pro Planc. 15—17. and the Prolegomena of Wunder to that speech.
[3] Cic. in Verr. I. 19. II. 4. 5. 26. 27. V. 22. pro Rosc. Amerin. 38. pro Flacc. 6. 17. pro Fontei. 16. Ascon. in Cic. pro Scaur. Quintil. I. O. V. vii. 9. Plin. Epp. VI. 5.
[4] Liv. XXVI. 27. XXVII. 3. Cic. Partit. Orat. 34. pro Sull. 28. Rhet. ad Herenn. II. 7.

ready to bear testimony in his favour that he could be heard in court, and torture was applied in this case upon the principle that an extraordinary sanction was necessary to give value to evidence which, it was presumed, must have been delivered under a strong bias.[1]

4. The two last rules were modified in later times, in so far as crimes which involved the safety of the state were concerned, or those which related to some daring act of sacrilege. In both these cases the evidence of a slave against his master was admitted. Moreover, towards the close of the republic, the slaves not only of the accused, but also of third parties were sometimes examined under torture, the permission of their masters having been previously obtained.[2]

5. In the earlier ages the torture was applied in public—*medio foro*—but during the period of the *Quaestiones Perpetuae*, it seems, as far as our authorities extend, to have been customary to apply the torture out of court, and consequently the depositions must have been taken down in writing.[3]

Tabulae.—Written evidence consisted of private account books, (*Tabulae accepti et expensi* p. 270,) of letters, (*Epistolae,*) and of memoranda (*Libelli*) of every description. The accuser had a right to call for all documents of this nature, and to compel their production. When received, they were regularly sealed up (*obsignatae*) in the presence of witnesses, (*obsignatores,*) delivered over to the Judge, and opened by him in the presence of the Court. Besides these private papers, the accounts of the Collectors of the Revenue (*Tabulae Publicanorum*) were sometimes brought forward, but in this case it was not necessary to present the originals, an authenticated copy being admitted.[4]

A second species of written evidence consisted in the depositions of those witnesses who, from bad health, age, distance, or any satisfactory cause, were unable to appear in person, and were therefore allowed to have their depositions taken down in writing, (*Testimonia per tabellam dare,*) these depositions being authenticated by the signature of commissioners (*signatores*) in whose presence they were made.[5]

Lastly, under this head we must reckon the *Testimonia Publica*, which, when in favour of the accused, were termed *Laudationes*, that is, public declarations, regarding particular facts, or upon the general merits of the case, emanating from public meetings held in the provincial towns, or from the magistrates, or from some recognised corporation. These, which were employed very extensively in cases *De Repetundis*, were always conveyed to Rome by an embassy appointed for the purpose, and the members of the deputation attended in court, during the trial, for the purpose of authenticating the documents which they presented, and of giving such oral explanations as might be required by either party.

The evidence being concluded, the Jury were called upon by the Judge to give their verdict, who, in doing this, was said *mittere iudices in consilium*, while the Jurors were said *ire in consilium*. Originally, they voted openly; but after the passing of the *Lex Cassia*, (B.C. 137, p. 108,) by ballot, (*per tabellas,*) excepting during a short period, when, in accordance with one of Sulla's laws, the defendant had the right of choosing whether the Jury should vote openly or

---

[1] Tacit. Ann. II. 30. Cic. pro Rosc. Amer. 41. pro Deiot. 1. pro Milon. 22.
[2] Cic. Partit. Orat. 34. pro Milon. 22. pro Rosc. Amer. 28. 41. 42. Val. Max. VI. viii. 1.
[3] Cic. pro. Sull. 28. pro Milon. 22. Ascon Argum. in Cic. Milonian.
[4] Cic. in Verr. I. 19. 23. 38. II. 74. 76. 77. III. 66. IV. 63, 66. pro Flacc. 9.
[5] Dialog. de C. C. E. 36. Quintil. I. O. V. vii, 1. 2. 25. 32.

secretly; but it is uncertain whether this regulation was general, or applicable to a particular class of trials only.¹ Each Juror received a small tablet covered with wax; upon this he wrote his verdict, and threw it into the ballot-box (*sitella*.) The verdict might be expressed in three ways, (except in cases *De Repetundis*, to be noticed below,)
1. By the letter A, which denoted *Absolvo*—Not Guilty.
2. ———————— C, ——————— *Condemno*—Guilty.
3. ———letters N. L, ——————— *Non Liquet*—No Verdict.
the last indicating, that, from the uncertain or contradictory nature of the evidence, the Juror could not make up his mind either to acquit or to condemn. The result was decided by the majority of votes, and announced by the Judge. If the majority gave the verdict *Guilty*, it was proclaimed by the words *Fecisse Videtur*; if *Not Guilty*, by *Non Fecisse Videtur*; but if the majority voted N. L., then the Judge said *Amplius*.² In the case of an equality of votes, the result most favourable to the defendant was held to be the verdict.

Ampliatio.—The announcement *Amplius* denoted that a more full investigation into the merits of the case was requisite, and accordingly the Judge fixed a day for a second hearing. When this arrived, the same formalities were observed as on the first hearing; the pleadings were renewed, the evidence already tendered was probably read over, and new evidence brought forward; but notwithstanding, the result might be the same as before, and a majority might still vote N. L. In this case, a fresh *Ampliatio* took place; a day was fixed for a third time, and the same process was repeated again and again,—in one cause upon record, seven times,³—until the Jury could give a positive verdict. It would appear that—we know not from what cause—the verdict N. L. fell gradually into desuetude,⁴ at least we can find no example of an *Ampliatio* in the time of Cicero.

Comperendinatio.—We remarked above that the verdict might appear in three forms, except in cases *De Repetundis*. After the passing of the *Lex Servilia*, (about B.C. 104,) the process in trials of this nature was altogether peculiar, for at that period *Comperendinatio* was introduced. By the arrangement so designated, all trials *De Repetundis* were divided into two distinct parts, termed respectively *Actio Prima* and *Actio Secunda*. In the *Actio Prima*, the accuser gave an outline of the case, more or less complete, according to circumstances and the judgment of the pleader; the defender then replied; and the witnesses upon both sides were examined. The Jury did not now, however, proceed at once to give their verdict, but the proceedings were suspended until the next day but one, (*tertio die*—*perendie*, and hence the word *Comperendinatio*,) when a second hearing, the *Actio Secunda*, took place. The accuser and the accused had now an opportunity of commenting upon the evidence already tendered, and of bringing forward additional testimony. When this second hearing was concluded, the Jury was called upon to give a verdict of condemnation or acquittal, no option being left to them of saying *Non Liquet*.

We have an excellent example of a trial of this description in the prosecution against Verres, which presents us with the preliminary *Divinatio*, the *Actio Prima*, and the *Actio Secunda*, on the part of the impeacher, although the *Actio Prima* was unusually short, in consequence of the peculiar policy which

---

1 Cic. pro Cluent. 20. 27.
2 Cic. pro Caecin. 10. Pseud. Ascon. in Verr. I. 9. 29.
3 Cic. Brut. 22. Val. Max. VIII. 1. 11.
4 Cic. pro Cluent. 28.

Cicero felt himself obliged to adopt, and the speeches which form the *Actio Secunda* were never actually delivered, the defendant having given up his case in despair. The speeches *Pro Fonteio*, *Pro Flacco*, and the fragment *Pro Scauro*, were all delivered in an *Actio Secunda*, as we learn from internal evidence. It is generally stated in works on Roman Antiquities, on the authority of the Pseudo-Asconius, that the *Actio Secunda* was distinguished by a remarkable peculiarity; that while in the *Actio Prima* the pleadings were commenced by the accuser, who was followed by the defendant, this order was reversed in the *Actio Secunda*, the defender being called upon to speak first, and the pleadings concluded by the accuser. But this statement is not only repugnant to reason, but is directly at variance with several expressions in Cicero, which all clearly point out that the order of the pleadings in the *Actio Secunda* was the same as in the *Actio Prima*.[1]

Litis Aestimatio.—In Criminal Trials of a certain class, such as those *De Repetundis* and *De Peculatu*, when a *Reus* was found guilty, he was compelled, as a part of his punishment, to make restitution of what he had unlawfully appropriated, and sometimes, according to the provisions of the law under which he was tried, of double, treble, or quadruple the amount. It was part of the duty of the *Iudices*, after they had brought in their verdict, to determine the sum to be paid. This part of the process was the *Litis Aestimatio*. There is an obscure passage in Cicero (Pro Cluent. 41) from which we may infer that considerable latitude was allowed to the *Iudices* in this matter, and that they might not only remit a portion of the pecuniary damages, but might even substitute a milder punishment for the *Poena Capitalis*.[2]

The term *Litis Aestimatio* was employed in Civil Suits also when the umpire or umpires were required to fix the amount of pecuniary compensation due to one who had sustained damage.[3]

We now proceed to give some details with regard to those offences which most frequently afforded subjects of investigation in the criminal courts, and especially in the *Quaestiones Perpetuae*.

Perduellio.—*Perduellis*, derived from *duellum* i.q. *bellum*, properly speaking signifies *a public enemy*, and hence *Perduellio* was employed in legal phraseology to denote the crime of *hostility to one's native country*, and is usually represented as corresponding, in a general sense, to our term *High Treason*.

Many scholars maintain that, originally, *Perduellio* was applied to any crime of great atrocity involving the life of a citizen, for the murder committed by Horatius is called *Perduellio* by Livy, (I. 26,) while Festus (s. v. *sororium*, p. 297,) designates it as *Parricidium*.

During the sway of the Kings, any attempt against the life or privileges of the monarch would constitute *Perduellio*. Under the republic, any attempt to restore the exiled Tarquins, or to assume regal power, (*regni affectatio*,) was regarded in the same light; also any attempt to subvert, by violence, the established form of government, and, in general, any act of hostility on the part of a citizen towards the welfare of Rome, whether indicated by exciting internal rebellion against the constitution, (*seditio*,) or by favouring and aiding the designs

---
[1] Cic. in Verr. I. 28. II. 72. III. 88. V. 1. 13 pro Fontei. 13.
[2] See also Cic. in Verr. Act. I. 13. and note of Pseud. Ascon. Act. II. i. 38. ii. 18. iv. 10. v 49. pro Rabir. Post. 4. ad Fam. VIII. 8. Tacit. Ann. I. 74. Lex Servil. de repet. 18–20.
[3] Aul. Gell. IV. 4. Cic. pro Tull. 7.

of external foes (*proditio.*) In like manner, any open invasion of the more sacred rights of the Plebs, such as assaulting one of their Tribunes, was construed as Treason; or if a magistrate, taking advantage of his official station, put to death a Roman citizen not legally convicted; (*caedes civis indemnati;*) and from this point of view, some explain why the deed of Horatius was termed indifferently *Perduellio* and *Parricidium.* Hence, too, it is a prosecution for *Perduellio* with which Cicero threatens Verres, (In Verr. Act. II. i. 5,) should he be acquitted upon other charges, for Verres was said to have put Roman citizens to death illegally while governor of Sicily.

No *Quaestio Perpetua* was ever instituted for the trial of charges of *Perduellio*, which were, comparatively speaking, of rare occurrence; and towards the close of the republic, many offences which might have been considered, at an earlier period, as involving *Perduellio*, were classed under the head of *Maiestas* or of *Vis*, for which separate Courts were established.

Hence all trials for *Perduellio* took place either before the Comitia, or before Special Commissioners.

Of trials for *Perduellio* before the Comitia, we have an example in the case of Spurius Cassius Viscellinus, who was charged, in B.C. 485, with having aimed at kingly power—*propter consilia inita de regno*—*propter suspicionem regni appetendi*. He was put to death, and his house was razed to the ground.[1] In like manner, M. Manlius Capitolinus, who had saved his country during the Gaulish invasion, was impeached before the Comitia—*propter suspicionem regni appetendi*—and found guilty. He was hurled from the Tarpeian rock, his house was razed, and his property was confiscated.[2] In B.C. 249, P. Clodius Pulcher was tried for having engaged Adherbal off Drepanum in despite of unfavourable auspices, whereby a large portion of the Roman fleet was destroyed. The assembly of the people was broken off by a storm, and Clodius thus escaped. In later times, he would have been tried for *Maiestas*, not for *Perduellio*.[3] Lastly, in B.C. 107, C. Popilius Laenas was impeached of *Perduellio*, for having displayed carelessness and cowardice while acting as *Legatus* to the consul C. Cassius, and for having concluded a very unfavourable treaty with the Tigurini. He was convicted and banished.[4] This was the first instance in which the people had voted by ballot in a trial for *Perduellio*. See p. 108.

The first trial upon record for *Perduellio*, that of Horatius for the murder of his sister, is said to have taken place before two Special Commissioners, nominated by the king, an appeal from their sentence being permitted. The last trial on record for *Perduellio* under the republic, that of C. Rabirius, in B.C. 63, for the murder, 37 years previously, of L. Appuleius Saturninus, Tribune of the Plebs, took place, in like manner, before two Special Commissioners, C. Julius Caesar and L. Caesar, who were nominated by the Praetor, and not by the people. Rabirius, having been found guilty by the Commissioners, appealed to the Comitia Centuriata, whose deliberations were abruptly broken off by a bold expedient on the part of the Praetor, Q. Metellus Celer, who pulled down the banner hoisted on the Ianiculum, and thus, in accordance with ancient usage, broke up the assembly. See p. 122. The speech delivered by Cicero on behalf of Rabirius is still extant.

---

[1] Liv. II. 41. IV. 15. Dionys. VIII. 77. Cic. Philipp. II. 44. Val. Max. VI. iii 1.
[2] Liv. VI. 20. Plut. Camill. 36. Dion Cass. XLV. 32. fragmt. Peiresc. 31. Cic. Philipp. I. 13. II. 44. de R. II. 37.
[3] Liv. Epit. XIX. Polyb. I. 51. Val. Max. VIII. i. 4.
[4] Cic. de legg. III. 16. de R. I. 3. Rhet. ad Herenn. I. 15. IV. 24.

IUDICIA PUBLICA.

Maiestas.—*Maiestas*, as a legal term, was employed to express, briefly, *Crimen Maiestatis minutae*, and signified, in its widest acceptation, any procedure on the part of a Roman citizen, by which the power or dignity of the Roman people was impaired or degraded. MAIESTATEM MINUERE *est, de dignitate aut amplitudine aut potestate populi aut eorum quibus populus potestatem dedit aliquid derogare* (Cic. de Inv. II. 17.) Offences of this description during the sway of the Kings, and during the greater portion of the republican period, were included under *Perduellio*, and made the subject of special investigation. No law designating a crime by the term *Maiestas* was passed until about B.C. 100, and consequently no *Quaestio Perpetua* for the trial of such a crime could have been instituted before that date. The principal enactments, taken in chronological order, were,

1. *Lex Appuleia*,[1] passed in B.C. 102 or B.C. 100, by L. Appuleius Saturninus, Tribune of the Plebs.

Under this law, Q. Servilius Caepio was impeached (B.C. 100) for having violently interfered to prevent the people from giving their votes on the *Lex Frumentaria* of Saturninus—*Impetum fecit, pontes disturbat, cistas deiicit, impedimento est quo secius feratur lex;* ARCESSITUR MAIESTATIS (Rhet. ad Herenn. 12.)

Under this law also another Q. Servilius Caepio was condemned, B.C. 95, on the charge of having, by his misconduct, while Proconsul, caused the defeat, by the Cimbri, of the Roman army under his command (*de amissione exercitus.*) Caepio went into exile to Smyrna, and his property was confiscated. The following year, his accuser, C. Norbanus, was himself impeached *De Maiestate*, for having forcibly prevented two of his colleagues from interposing their Veto in favour of Caepio; but by the exertions of his counsel, M. Antonius, he was acquitted.

2. *Lex Varia*,[2] passed B.C. 92 by Q. Varius Hybrida, Tribune of the Plebs. Its object was to declare those guilty of *Maiestas* who instigated or aided the designs of the Italian allies, or other enemies against Rome—*Quorum dolo malo Socii ad arma ire coacti essent.*

M. Aemilius Scaurus was impeached, B.C. 92, under this law, on the charge of having excited the allies to revolt, (*socios ad arma coegisse,*) and of having received a bribe from Mithridates to betray his country (*ob rempublicam prodendam.*) His bold, dignified, and triumphant defence is well known from the narrative of Valerius Maximus.

3. *Lex Cornelia*, passed B.C. 81, by Sulla when Dictator, was more important and comprehensive than either of the preceding, defining and explaining much that had been left vague and obscure. This, indeed, together with the

4. *Lex Julia* of Julius Caesar, which comprehended those cases which might still have been ranked under *Perduellio*, served as the foundation of all the imperial enactments.

Under the *Lex Cornelia*, C. Cornelius, who had been Tribune of the Plebs in B.C. 67, was impeached in B.C. 66, for having prevented his colleagues from exercising their right of Intercession. He was defended by Cicero, fragments of whose speech still remain, and was acquitted. (See Ascon. in Cornelian.)

Under this law also, A. Gabinius was impeached in B.C. 54, because, while Proconsul of Syria, he had, without orders from the Senate and people, quitted

---

[1] Cic. de Orat. II. 25. 27. 39. 47. de Off. II. 14. Brut. 35. Rhet. ad Herenn. I. 14. Val. Max. IV. vii. 3. VIII. v. 2.
[2] Val. Max. III. vii. 8. VIII. vi. 4. Ascon. in Cic. pro Scauro.

his Province, and marched an army into Egypt to reinstate Ptolemy Auletes. Out of 70 Jurors, 32 brought in a verdict of Guilty, and 38 Acquitted him.

After the establishment of the empire, the law of *Maiestas* served, in the hands of evil Princes, as one of the grand instruments of tyranny, and offered irresistible temptations to bands of needy informers, (*delatores*,) for not only acts tending to subvert the imperial constitution were regarded as penal, but any thing written or spoken which could in any way be construed as reflecting on the character of the supreme ruler, was now held to involve *Minuta Maiestas*. How fearfully this engine of oppression was worked from the time of Tiberius downwards, is familiar to every reader of Tacitus, by whom the change of principle introduced after the downfal of the republic, is distinctly explained,—LEGEM MAIESTATIS *reduxerat;* (Tiberius;) *cui nomen apud veteres idem, sed alia in iudicium veniebant: si quis proditione exercitum, aut plebem seditionibus, denique male gesta re publica* MAIESTATEM POPULI ROMANI MINUISSET : *facta arguebantur, dicta impune erant. Primus Augustus cognitionem de famosis libellis, specie legis eius, tractavit, commotus Cassii Severi libidine, qua viros feminasque illustres procacibus scriptis diffamaverat. Mox Tiberius, consultante Pompeio Macro, Praetore, an iudicia Maiestatis redderentur, exercendas leges esse, respondit.* (Tacit. Ann. I. 72.)

Vis.—*Vis*, as a legal term, was understood to denote the organizing and arming of tumultuous bodies of men for the purpose of obstructing the constituted authorities in the performance of their duty, and thus interrupting the ordinary administration of the laws. No such offence was recognised by the Criminal Code until the last century of the republic, when violent riots by hired mobs became so frequent, that M. Plautius Silvanus, Tribune of the Plebs, B.C. 89, passed the *Lex Plautia de Vi*, in terms of which, those convicted of such practices were banished. The law is described by Cicero as—*Legem quae de seditiosis consceleratisque civibus, qui armati Senatum obsederint, magistratibus vim attulerint, rempublicam oppugnarint, quotidie quaeri iubeat* (Pro Coel. 1.) The concluding words in the above sentence indicate a peculiarity by which the statute was characterized, namely, that trials under it might be held on any day whatsoever—*quotidie quaeri iubeat . . . diebus festis ludisque publicis omnibus, negotiis forensibus intermissis, unum hoc iudicium exerceatur*. It does not appear, however, that a *Questio Perpetua de Vi* was established until the Dictatorship of Sulla.

The *Lex Lutatia*, passed in B.C. 78, seems to have been merely supplemental to the *Lex Plautia*.

The *Lex Pompeia de Vi*, passed by Pompeius Magnus in his third consulship, B.C. 52, was intended specially for the punishment of those who had taken part in the murder of Clodius, and in the subsequent disturbances, when the Senate house was burned, and the mansion of M. Lepidus, the Interrex, attacked. After these cases had been disposed of, the *Lex Plautia* and the *Lex Lutatia* were again resorted to until superseded by the

Lex Iulia de Vi, passed by Julius Caesar while Dictator, by which, or by some of the *Leges Iuliae* of Augustus, the distinction between *Vis Publica* and *Vis Privata*, unknown before, was introduced, and a wide field opened up for lawyers, both speculative and practical.

Of the extant speeches of Cicero, those *Pro Sulla*, (B.C. 62,) *Pro Sestio*, (B.C. 56,) and *Pro Coelio*, (B.C. 56,) were delivered on behalf of individuals impeached under the *Lex Plautia*, and of these, that *Pro Sestio* especially presents a most vivid picture of the disorders which prevailed at that epoch. After the execution of the ringleaders in the Catilinarian conspiracy, five or six persons deeply implicated were impeached *De Vi* under the *Lex Plautia*, found guilty and banished (Cic. pro Sull. 2.)

The trial of Milo (B.C. 52) was of course conducted under the *Lex Pompeia*, by which the proceedings were made shorter, and the penalty more severe. The chief provisions were [1]—

1. That the trial should commence with the examination of witnesses upon both sides, and that three days should be allowed for that purpose.

2. That one day should intervene, and then that the speeches of the accuser and the defendant should be delivered on one and the same day, that is the fifth, two hours being allowed to the former and three to the latter.

2. That 81 *Iudices* should be chosen by lot, who should hear the whole proceedings, but that, before they retired to vote, the accuser and the defendant should each have the right of challenging five out of each *Ordo* or *Decuria*, so that the number who actually voted would be reduced to 51.

4. That the president of the court (*Quaesitor*) should be elected by the Comitia (*suffragio populi*) out of those who had held the office of Consul.

Milo was found guilty by a majority of 38 to 13 : one of his chief supporters and abettors, M. Saufeius, was acquitted, a few days afterwards, by a majority of 26 to 25, and having been again brought to trial, soon afterwards, under the *Lex Plautia*, was acquitted by a majority of 32 to 19 ; which seems to prove that the ordinary number of Jurors under the *Lex Plautia*, as well as under the *Lex Pompeia*, was 51.

Incendium.—*Arson.* It has been inferred from a passage in the Digest, (XLVII. ix. 9.) that by the Code of the XII Tables, any one convicted of wilful (*sciens prudens*) fire-raising, was himself to be burned alive. How long this statute, if ever acted upon, remained in force, we cannot tell ; but towards the close of the republic, the crime of Arson was included in the *Lex Cornelia de Sicariis*, and punished with *Aquae et Ignis Interdictio*. The crime, when connected with a riot, was included also in the *Lex Pompeia de Vi*, and the *Lex Iulia de Vi*.

Parricidium.—Until the period of the Empire, when the term *Homicidium* was introduced, the word *Parricidium* was employed not only to denote the murder of a parent, but in an extended sense to signify the wilful malicious (*dolo sciens*) murder of any free citizen, and even a person guilty of sacrilege was called, figuratively perhaps, *Parricida*. [2]

By the Laws of the XII Tables ordinary wilful murder was punished by decapitation. In the earlier ages the crime was of very rare occurrence, (Cic. pro Tull. 9.) and when it was committed, the people either judged the case directly in the Comitia Centuriata, or appointed Commissioners, who seems to have been called *Parricidi Quaestores*,[3] or the matter was investigated, with the consent of the people, and under the direction of the Senate, by the chief magistrates. [4]

No new law against murder was enacted from the promulgation of the XII Tables until the last half century of the republic, when the insecurity of property and life, which resulted from the disorganization of society in the civil wars, became so fearful that Sulla endeavoured to check the evil by his *Lex Cornelia*

---

[1] See Asconius in Milonian.
[2] Paul. Diac. s. v. *Parrici Quaestores*, p. 221. Plut. Rom. 22. Cic. de Legg. II. 9.
[3] Paul. Diac. l. c.
[4] See particularly the details regarding the proceedings upon the murder of Postumius, Liv. IV. 50. 51. Also Cic. Brut. 22. de Fin. II. 16. de N.D. III. 33.

de Sicariis et Veneficis, and by the establishment of a *Quaestio Perpetua* to carry out its provisions. This enactment was of a character much more comprehensive than its title would import, and formed the kernel of the Imperial ordinances, as we find from the Digest which contains large extracts. Not only assassins, (*sicarii*,) and all persons who had actually committed murder, but every one who could be proved to have carried weapons with the intent of committing murder or robbery—*qui cum telo ambulaverit hominis necandi furtive faciendi causa, hominemve occiderit*—or who had compounded, sold, bought, been in possession of, or administered poison with felonious intent—*quicunque fecerit, vendiderit, emerit, habuerit, dederit venenum necandi hominis causa*— or who had procured the condemnation of an innocent man for murder by corrupting witnesses or jurymen, became liable to the penalty imposed, which, for a free citizen, was *Aquae et Ignis Interdictio*, to which Julius Cæsar added confiscation of property.[1]

We are acquainted with the details of two most interesting trials held under this law, that of Statius Albius Oppianicus in B.C. 76, for the murder at Rome of a certain young man of Larinum, named Asuvius; and that of Aulus Cluentius Habitus in B.C. 66, for having suborned the Jury upon the trial of Oppianicus and subsequently poisoned Oppianicus himself. The particulars are given at great length in the speech of Cicero *Pro Cluentio*.

With regard to *Parricidium* proper, or the murder of a parent, it was ordained by a very ancient law that the individual convicted of such atrocious guilt (*crimen asperrimum—nefas ultimum*) should, after being scourged to the effusion of blood (*virgis sanguineis verberatus*,) be sewed up in a leather bag (*insui in culeum*) and thrown into the deep sea or a running stream, (*obvolutus et obligatus corio devehebatur in profluentem*,) and this punishment seems to have been retained in the *Lex Cornelia*.[2] It is said that no example of this crime occurred for upwards of five centuries from the foundation of the city. The first individual convicted of murdering his father, was a certain L. Hostius, after the close of the second Punic war, and the first murderer of a mother was Publicius Malleolus before the Cimbric war.[3] As an example of the prosecution of an alleged parricide under the *Lex Cornelia*, we have the trial of Sextus Roscius of Ameria, impeached, B.C. 80, of the murder of his father, and successfully defended by Cicero in a speech still extant.

Pompeius in his second consulship, B.C. 55, passed the *Lex Pompeia de Parricidio*, in which *Parricidium*, even in a restricted sense, comprehended the murder of all near relations, whether by blood or marriage, and also of a *Patronus* by his *Libertus*, but the punishment of the sack was retained in the case of those only who had murdered a father, a mother, a grandfather, or a grandmother, an unsuccessful attempt being visited with the same severity as the completed crime.

It must be borne in mind, that under the republic and the early empire, the

---

[1] See Cic. pro Rabir. perduell. reo 6. Pro Cluent. 52—57. 71.
[2] Modestinus in the Digest (XLVIII. ix. 9,) when commenting on the *Lex Pompeia de Parricidis*, states *Poena Parricidii, more maiorum, haec instituta est: ut Parricida virgis sanguineis verberatus, deinde culleo insuatur cum cane, gallo gallinaceo, et vipera, et simia: deinde in mare profundum culleus iactatur. Hoc ita, si mare proximum sit: alioquin bestiis obiicitur secundum Diri Hadriani Constitutionem.* But although Modestinus uses the phrase *more maiorum*, the addition of the animals must have been after the establishment of the empire. Seneca refers to the serpents, and Juvenal to the apes, but Cicero in a highly ornamented and rhetorical passage on this very topic takes no notice of any thing but the sack.— *Maiores nostri . . . . insui voluerunt in culeum vivos, atque ita in flumen deiici.* (Pro Rosc. Amer. 25.) Moreover, there were no monkeys in Italy.
[3] Plut. Rom. 22. Rhetor. ad Herenn. I. 13. Liv. Epit. LXVIII. Oros. V. 16.

murder of a slave by his master involved no penalty, while the murder of a slave belonging to another subjected the perpetrator merely to an action of damages on the part of the owner.

Although ordinary murders may, for a long period, have been rare, we find mention made on several occasions of poisoning, which, if we can put any faith in the details, was sometimes practised upon a most extensive scale. Thus in B.C. 331, two Patrician matrons fell under the suspicion of having caused a pestilence, which was ravaging the city. They were found guilty and—*comprehensae extemplo earum comites magnum numerum matronarum indicaverunt: ex quibus ad centum septuaginta damnatae. Neque de Veneficiis ante eam diem Romae quaesitum est.* (Liv. VIII. 18.) In B.C. 184, we find Q. Naevius Matho, one of the Praetors, appointed to the government of Sardinia —*et ut idem de Veneficiis quaereret*—and we are told that he was detained for four months by—*Quaestiones Veneficii quarum magnam partem extra urbem per Municipia Conciliabulaque habuit, quia ita aptius visum erat. Si Antiati Valerio credere libet, ad duo millia hominum damnavit.* (Liv. XXXIX. 38. 41.) In B.C. 180, on occasion of a pestilence, a suspicion of poisoning arose— *et Veneficii Quaestio ex S. C. quod in urbe, propiusve urbem decem millibus passuum esset commissum, C. Claudio, Praetori . . . ultra decimum lapidem per Fora Conciliabulaque C. Maenio, priusquam in Sardiniam provinciam transiret, decreta*—and soon after C. Maenius wrote a letter to the Senate acquainting them—*Se iam tria millia hominum damnasse et crescere sibi Quaestionem indiciis.* (Liv. XL. 37. 43.) Comp. Liv. Epit. XLVIII. Val. Max. II. v. 3. VI. iii. 8.

Repetundae.—The *Crimen Repetundarum* (sc. *pecuniarum*) in its original etymological signification denoted a charge of extortion preferred against a Roman provincial governor. The provincials who brought the charge were said according to ancient phraseology—*res repetere*—and part of the punishment inflicted, when an offence of this nature was proved, was a restitution of the sum or objects illegally appropriated, and hence such sum or such objects were *Res Repetundae*. In process of time, however, the *Crimen Repetundarum* was held to apply to any act of misgovernment or oppression on the part of a provincial governor—*male administratae Provinciae crimen*.

During the earlier ages of the republic we find Roman magistrates accused, from time to time, either of extortion, properly so called, or of misgovernment generally. Such cases were sometimes tried by the people directly in the Comitia Centuriata, or by special Commissioners appointed by the Comitia, or the matter was referred to the Senate, who appointed Commissioners or submitted the whole matter to the Tribunes of the Plebs.[1]

Soon after the termination of the second Punic war the *Lex Porcia*, of M. Porcius Cato, was passed with a view to check the malversation of provincial governors, but no regular court was instituted until the passing of the *Lex Calpurnia* (see p. 290,) in B.C. 149, by which the first *Quaestio Perpetua* was introduced. From that time forward the rapid degradation in the morals of public men, demanded a series of enactments each more comprehensive and more severe than its predecessor, and all equally inefficacious.

These, taken in chronological order, were—

1. *Lex Calpurnia*, B.C. 149.

[1] For examples and illustrations, see Liv. VI. 1. X. 46. XXIV. 43. XXVI. 26. 30. 33. 34. XXIX. 8. 16. XXXVIII. 24. XXXIX. 3. 5. XLII. 1. XLIII. 2. 7. Epit. XLIX. Val. Max. VIII. i. 2. Plut. Cat. 15. Aul. Gell. IV. 17.

IUDICIA PUBLICA. 307

2. *Lex Iunia*, passed by M. Iunius, a Tribune of the Plebs. Date unknown.
3. *Lex Servilia*, passed by C. Servilius Glaucia, Tribune of the Plebs. B.C. 105.
4. *Lex Acilia*, passed by M'. Acilius Glabrio, Tribune of the Plebs. B.C. 101.
5. *Lex Cornelia*, passed by Sulla. B.C. 81.
6. *Lex Iulia*, passed by Iulius Cæsar in his first Consulship. B.C. 59.

Consequently all the trials *De Repetundis* in which Cicero took a part, e.g. that of C. Verres, B.C. 70—M. Fonteius, B.C. 69—P. Oppius, B.C. 69—C. Manilius, B.C. 65—L. Valerius Flaccus, B.C. 59—C. Antonius, B.C. 59—M. Aemilius Scaurus, B.C. 54—A. Gabinius, B.C. 54—were under either the *Lex Cornelia* or the *Lex Iulia*. The proceedings against Verres afford an example of a trial *De Repetundis* under the *Lex Cornelia* in its most complete form, except that the opening speech, the *Actio Prima*, is less full than it would have been under different circumstances.

Falsum.—*Forgery.* No special law against this crime existed until the time of Sulla, by whom the *Lex Cornelia de Falsis* was passed, and a *Quaestio Perpetua* instituted.[1] The chief offences of which this court took cognisance were—

1. Forging, destroying, concealing, altering, or in any way tampering with a will—*Testamentum—falsum scribere—surripere—supprimere—celare—delere—interlinere: Signum adulterinum sculpere—facere—exprimere*, &c.

2. Coining base money, &c.—*Nummos aureos, argenteos—adulterare—lavare—conflare—radere—corrumpere—vitiare . . . Aes inaurare—argentare*, &c.

3. Bearing false testimony and corrupting witnesses—*Ob falsum testimonium perhibendum vel verum non perhibendum pecuniam accipere—dare*. This crime was provided for in the Code of the XII Tables, and punished by hurling the offender from the Tarpeian rock.

The penalty attached to the *Lex Cornelia de Falsis*, as indeed to all the laws of the Cornelian criminal code, was *Aquae et Ignis Interdictio*.

Peculatus denotes *the embezzlement of public property*, while *Furtum* is the abstraction of the property of an individual.

This crime was of rare occurrence in the earlier ages, and many of the trials upon record were the result of party feeling rather than of any corruption on the part of the person accused. Among the most remarkable were those of—M. Furius Camillus (B.C. 391)[2]—of M. Livius Salinator, afterwards Consul and Censor[3] (B.C. 219)—of the brothers P. Cornelius Scipio Africanus and L. Cornelius Scipio Asiaticus[4] (B.C. 187)—and of M'. Acilius Glabrio[5] (B.C. 139.)

We learn from the speech of Cicero for Murena (c. 20) that a *Quaestio Perpetua* had been established for the trial of cases of *Peculatus* as early as B.C. 90, but when it was first instituted, and under what law it was administered we cannot determine. Whatever the law may have been, it would seem that it remained in force until the enactment of a *Lex Iulia* by Julius Cæsar or Augustus. In the *Lex Iulia de Peculatu* was comprehended the crime of *Sacrilegium*, in so far as it extended to abstracting or injuring the property belonging to a temple or to the services of religion.

[1] Act. in Verr. I. 42. de N. D. III. 30.
[2] Liv. V. 32. Plut. Cam. 12.
[3] Aurel. Vict. de vir. ill. 50.
[4] Liv. XXXVIII. 50. XXXIX. 22. 52. Val. Max. III. vii. 1. V. iii. 2. VI. i. 8. VIII. l. 1 Aul. Gell. IV. 18. VII. 19.
[5] Liv. XXXVII. 57.

The *Crimen de Pecuniis Residuis* was closely connected with the *Crimen de Peculatu*. Looking to the etymology we should be led to believe that it originally signified a prosecution for the recovery of a balance of public money, remaining in the hands of some official who had not accounted fully to the government. Faustus Sulla, son of the Dictator, was frequently threatened with an impeachment of this nature, in reference to sums received by his father, but no trial actually took place.[1] The *Crimen de Residuis* formed one of the chapters in the *Lex Iulia de Peculatu*.

Ambitus.—*Bribery* employed by a candidate for some public office in order to secure his election. This offence was almost unknown in the earlier ages of the republic. Laws were indeed enacted from time to time whose object was to check the eagerness of rival competitors, such as that passed in B.C. 432, prohibiting candidates from wearing a conspicuous dress; (p. 177;) and the *Lex Poetelia* of C. Poetelius, Tribune of the Plebs, B.C. 358, intended to repress the excessive zeal displayed in canvassing (Liv. VII. 16.) Towards the close of the commonwealth, however, bribery prevailed to an extraordinary extent, and was reduced to a regular system. There were Brokers (*Interpretes*) who undertook to arrange the terms upon which the votes of electors were to be purchased; Trustees (*Sequestres*) in whose hands the money agreed upon was deposited until the service was performed; and Distributors (*Divisores*) who portioned out the sum among the venal citizens. These proceedings became notorious, and a series of enactments were passed in rapid succession for the repression of such practices, each more severe than its predecessor; but as happened *De Repetundis*, the temptation proved too strong, and the crime went on increasing in enormity until the final overthrow of the constitution. The laws *De Ambitu*, taken in chronological order, were the following:—

1. *Lex Cornelia Baebia*, passed by the Consuls of B.C. 181, P. Cornelius Cethegus and M. Baebius Tamphilus. Of its provisions we know nothing.

2. *Lex Cornelia Fulvia*, passed by the Consuls of B.C. 159, Cn. Cornelius Dolabella and M. Fulvius Nobilior. Those convicted under this law were disqualified from standing for any public office for ten years. (Liv. Epit. XLVII. Schol. Bob. in Orat. pro. Sull. 5.)

3. *Lex Maria*, passed by C. Marius when Tribune of the Plebs, B.C. 119. Some scholars believe that this was the law under which the *Quaestio Perpetua de Ambitu* was established. (Cic. de Legg. III. 17. Plut. Mar. 4.)

4. *Lex Fabia*, prohibiting the candidates from being escorted by a long train of clients and followers—*De numero Sectatorum*. (Cic. pro Muren. 34.)

5. *Lex Acilia Calpurnia*, passed by the Consuls of B.C. 67, C. Calpurnius Piso and M'. Acilius Glabrio, of a more stringent character than its predecessors —*severissime scripta* (Cic. pro Muren. 23.) It imposed a pecuniary fine on those convicted, and disqualified them from ever becoming candidates for any public office. The necessity for a new law had been made manifest by the notorious bribery resorted to by the agents of Verres in B.C. 70, in order to prevent Cicero from being elected Aedile.

6. *Lex Tullia*, passed by Cicero when Consul, B.C. 63. He proposed this law, which was much more severe than the *Lex Calpurnia*, (*multo severior quam Calpurnia*, Schol. Bob. in Vat.) in consequence of the corrupt practices of his competitors of the preceding year, Catiline and Antonius. In addition to the penalties fixed by the *Lex Calpurnia*, it was enacted that those convicted should

---

[1] See Cic. pro Cluent. 34. 53. de Leg. Agr. I. 4. Ascon. ad Cornelian.

be banished for ten years. Many practices were prohibited which tended to influence the electors improperly, even when money was not offered, such as the presence of crowds of hired attendants, public banquets, and the exhibition of gladiatorial shows, except under peculiar circumstances. (Cic. pro Muren. 32. in Vatin. 15.)

7. *Lex Licinia*, passed by M. Licinius Crassus when Consul, B.C. 55. This referred chiefly to the suppression of electioneering clubs, (*sodalitates—sodalitia*,) the members of which (*sodales*) acted as bribing agents. A *Senatus-Consultum* to the same effect had been passed the year before. The punishment inflicted was *Aquae et Ignis Interdictio;* but the chief peculiarity and harshness of the law lay in the constitution of the Jury, which was composed of *Iudices Editicii*, (see p. 297,) a majority of whom were virtually nominated by the accuser.

Under this law, Cn. Plancius was tried in B.C. 54, and the speech of Cicero in his defence is still extant.

8. *Lex Pompeia*, passed by Pompeius Magnus in his third Consulship, B.C. 52. The changes introduced by this law related chiefly to the form of process, which was shortened and simplified, and thus the escape of the guilty was rendered less easy. Finally, we have

9. *Lex Iulia*, passed by Augustus, B.C. 18, in consequence of the disturbances which took place at the Consular Comitia of B.C. 22, during his absence.

Punishments recognised in Roman Criminal Law.—Of these we may specially notice—

1. *Mors.* The punishment of death appears to have been inflicted, not unfrequently in the earlier ages, by hanging, (*infelici arbore reste suspendere,*) scourging, and beheading, (*virgis caedere securique ferire* s. *percutere,*) and hurling from the Tarpeian rock (*de saxo Tarpeio deiicere.*)[1] By degrees, however, the sacred character with which the person of a Roman citizen was invested, rendered capital punishments much less frequent, and for a long period before the close of the republic, judicial executions may be said to have, in a great measure, been abolished. Indeed, the right which every one accused possessed of remaining at large upon bail, until his trial was concluded, always placed it in the power of a criminal, when he perceived that condemnation was inevitable, to escape. The arrest, imprisonment, and death by strangling, (*laqueo gulam frangere,*) of Lentulus and Cethegus, took place under circumstances altogether unprecedented, and it must be remembered that they were never brought to trial.

2. *Sacratio Capitis.* In the earlier ages also, the penalty attached to the violation of certain laws, hence termed *Leges Sacratae*, was *Sacratio Capitis;* that is, the offender was declared to be *Sacer*, i.e. devoted, life, family, and property, to a deity, and might be slain by any one with impunity, the act of putting him to death being regarded, not as murder, but, as it were, a sacrifice, a presentation to the deity of an object which belonged to him. Thus, according to the definition of Festus, (s. v. *Sacratae*, p. 318)—*Sacratae leges sunt quibus sanctum est, qui quid adversus eas fecerit, sacer alicui deorum sicut familia pecuniaque;* and again—*neque fas est eum immolari, sed qui occidit, parricidi non damnatur.* Such was the law of Poplicola—*de sacrando cum bonis capite eius qui regni occupandi consilia inisset;* (Liv. II. 8;) and such was the law in virtue of which persons of the Plebeian magistrates became *sacrosancti*—*nam*

---

[1] Liv. I. 26. II. 5. VI. 20. VII. 19. XXVI. 15.

lege Tribunicia prima cavetur, si quis eum qui eo plebei-scito sacer sit occiderit, parricida ne esto (Fest. s. v. *Sacer*, p. 318, comp. what has been said in Chap. V. p. 141.)

3. *Aquae et Ignis Interdictio.* On the nature of this punishment, as well as on the meaning of the words *Exsilium*, *Relegatio*, and *Deportatio* we have spoken in p. 84.

4. *Servitus.* We have already adverted to those offences which rendered a citizen liable to be sold as a slave, (p. 83,) most of which were in reality breaches of military discipline. We have also pointed out the severity with which the ancient law visited insolvent debtors; and by the XII Tables, a similar fate awaited the *Fur Manifestus.* Thus Gaius (III. § 189)—*Poena Manifesti Furti ex lege XII Tabularum capitalis erat nam liber verberatus addicebatur ei cui furtum fecerat*; and Aulus Gellius, after Cato (XI. 18)—*Fures privatorum furtorum in nervo atque in compedibus aetatem agunt;* but lawyers did not agree as to whether such persons could be strictly regarded as slaves. The rigour of the ancient code upon both these points was relaxed as the state advanced in civilization: after the passing of the *Lex Poetelia Papiria*, (B.C. 326, Liv. VIII. 28,) a creditor could no longer attach the person of his debtor—*pecuniae creditae bona debitoris non corpus obnoxium esset;* and by degrees, in virtue of various Praetorian edicts, theft of every description was regarded as falling under the head of *Obligationes ex delicto*, and as such, formed the ground of a purely Civil Action (pp. 268, 273.) In point of fact, even when the punishment was most severe, and most rigorously exacted, it does not appear that prosecutions of insolvent debtors, and of *Fures Manifesti*, were ever regarded as *Iudicia Publica*, but were always conducted before the civil magistrate.

In like manner *Noxae Deditio* was altogether a civil procedure. This took place under the following circumstance. If a son *In Potestate*, or a slave, had been guilty of *Furtum* or *Iniuria* on the property of another, it constituted an *Obligatio ex delicto* against the father or master, and the person wronged might bring an *Actio Noxalis*. In this case the father or master might either abide the result of the suit, or he might at once settle the claim by making over the offender by *Mancipatio* to the plaintiff, and this surrender of the person of the offender, as a compensation to the sufferer, was legally termed *Noxae Deditio*, and the offender was said *ex noxali causa mancipio dari*.

5. *Carcer. Vincula.* Simple imprisonment, that is, imprisonment not combined with slavery, does not seem to have been resorted to, under the republic, as a punishment.

A person accused of any heinous crime might be detained in prison until his guilt or innocence was decided by a trial, but after the proceedings which took place at the impeachment of Kaeso Quinctius, in B.C. 461, it seems to have been established that an accuser, although he might require the accused to give bail for his appearance, had no right to throw him into prison if sureties could be found, indeed such imprisonment would have been altogether inconsistent with the fully recognised right possessed by every Roman citizen when publicly impeached, of withdrawing into voluntary exile at any period before his guilt had been formally pronounced.

In cases of extraordinary emergency only, when the safety of the whole state was in peril, and when the worst consequences might have been apprehended from permitting a suspected traitor to remain at large, the Senate assumed the responsibility of committing him to prison. Of this we find an example in the proceedings adopted towards some of those who were accused of participating in the conspiracy of Catiline. But except in an extreme case, even when it was deemed necessary to refuse ordinary bail, a more gentle restraint was imposed, and the individual was placed in what was termed *Custodia Libera*, that is, he was not sent to gaol, but was intrusted to the charge of one of the higher Magistrates, or of a Senator of distinction, who became responsible for his safe keeping.[1]

5. *Mulcta.* The infliction of pecuniary fines as a penalty for certain offences was common from the earliest times, and at the commencement of the republic the Consuls seem to have assumed a discretionary power. This was, however, regulated and limited by the *Lex Aternia Tarpeia*, passed by Aulus Aternius and Sp. Tarpeius, when Consuls, B.C. 454, after which no magistrate in exercise of summary jurisdiction could impose a fine beyond a certain fixed limit, and when the penalty proposed exceeded this it became the subject of a *Iudicium Publicum.*[2]

*Poena Capitalis—Crimen Capitale—Iudicium Capitis—Causa Capitalis —Aliquem rerum capitalium reum facere—Accusare rei capitalis—Facinora capitalia facere—Fraudem capitalem admittere—*on the true signification of these and similar phrases, see p. 83.

Under the empire, new and cruel punishments were introduced, such as compelling criminals to fight with each other as Gladiators, or with wild beasts, (*dare ad bestias—bestiis obiicere—condemnare ad bestias—tradere ad bestias depugnandas;*) burning to death, which was not unfrequently carried into execution by clothing the victim in a shirt steeped in pitch, (*Tunica molesta,*) and then setting it on fire; and various other tortures. These, however, were generally inflicted upon culprits of the lowest class only, criminals of distinction, especially those convicted of offences against the state, being generally permitted to choose whatever form of death, by their own hands, appeared to them least painful.

Pleaders in Civil and Criminal Trials.—As long as Criminal Trials were held in the Comitia, or before Commissioners specially appointed by the Comitia, the accuser was the magistrate by whom the Assembly had been summoned, and the accused conducted his own defence in person, aided only by his nearest relations.[3] We find no trace of the accuser having received assistance until B.C. 149, when Cato is represented as having acted as a *Subscriptor* (p. 295) to the Tribune, Scribonius Libo; and on this occasion also, Sergius Galba, the accused, was defended by Fulvius Nobilior, who had no immediate concern with the cause. It may be doubted, however, whether the procedure in question was in the form of a regular judicial impeachment.[4] It is certain that up to this period, the existence of a class of persons who made it their chief occupation to undertake the impeachment or defence of accused persons, in whom they felt no direct personal interest, was entirely unknown. But in the very year above mentioned, the first *Quaestio Perpetua* was introduced by the *Lex Calpurnia*, (p. 290,) and a new order of things rapidly arose. The law *De Repetundis* was intended expressly for the protection of the provincials against the oppression of their Roman governors; but it was impossible for the injured parties to appear personally as accusers in the Roman courts, and the services of a magistrate were no longer necessary. Hence the accusers would naturally seek to obtain the assistance of that individual who was likely to conduct their cause with the greatest amount

---
[1] Sallust. Cat. 47. 48. &c. Cic. in Cat. IV. 5. Tacit. Ann. VI. 3. Dion Cass. LVIII. 3.
[2] Aul. Gell. XI. 1. Dionys. X. 50. Cic. de R. II. 35. Festus s. v. *Peculatus*, p. 237.
[3] Liv. III. 5. 8. VIII. 33. XXXVIII. 58. Dionys. X. 5.
[4] Liv. Epit. XLIX. Cic. Brut. 23. de Orat. I. 53. Val. Max. VIII. i. 2.

of ability and zeal ; while the defendant, if not gifted with native powers, would soon feel the necessity of adopting the same course. On the other hand, it was soon found that the new Courts afforded an excellent stage for the display of oratory and wit, and that in no way could a young ambitious man more speedily or more effectually make known his talents for public business, and secure the support of admirers and partizans. Thus the value of eloquence and dialectic skill became every day more and more evident, and the art of forensic speaking was more and more cultivated, until it reached its culminating point in the age of Cicero, when success at the Bar opened up one of the most direct avenues to political power.

Those who thus undertook to represent another in a Court of Justice, discharged one of the duties most imperative, in ancient times, on Patrons in relation to their Clients ; and hence the general name for a pleader in a Court of Justice, whether Civil or Criminal, who acted as counsel for another, was *Patronus*. Any one learned in the law, (*iuris-consultus*,) who was called in to give his advice on legal technicalities and on the best mode of conducting the case, was termed *Advocatus;* but this word was never employed to denote a *Pleader* until the imperial times.[1] In the earlier period of forensic pleading, it was the practice for a *Patronus* to conduct the whole cause intrusted to him single-handed ; but it gradually became customary in impeachments, for the accuser to be aided by *Subscriptores*, who spoke occasionally, but played a part altogether subordinate to that sustained by the leading counsel. The number of these assistants varied, one, two, and three being mentioned in different processes.[2] But while there was only one leading counsel, assisted by subordinate *Subscriptores*, for the impeachment, the arrangements for the defence were different. Here there were several counsel-in-chief, all alike distinguished by the name of *Patroni*, the ordinary number being four, which was sometimes increased to six, as in the case of Scaurus, and occasionally rose as high as even twelve.[3]

Time allowed for Speaking. It is uncertain whether any restrictions were placed, at an early period, on the length of time during which a pleader might speak. The author of the Dialogue on the Decline of Eloquence ascribes (38) the introduction of a regulation of this nature to Pompeius, by one of whose laws for the regulation of the Criminal Courts, the speech of the accuser was limited to two hours, and that of the defender to three ;[4] but it is clear from the words of Cicero upon several occasions—*Si utar ad dicendum meo legitimo tempore* (In Verr. Act. I. 11)—*Nisi omni tempore* QUOD MIHI LEGE CONCESSUM EST *abusus ero* (In Verr. I. 9. comp. pro Flacc. 33.)—that some limitation must have been imposed at an earlier date, although we know not the precise nature, nor the extent of it, nor whether it was rigidly enforced.

Remuneration of Pleaders. Although a great number of persons, during the last century of the republic, devoted themselves to the business of the Law Courts, in cases both Civil and Criminal, the *Profession* of a Pleader, as a means of gaining money, was absolutely unknown, the only reward sought being fame or political influence. The position occupied by the Pleader being,

---

[1] Cic. de Off. I. 10. II. 14. de Orat. II. 74. in Verr. II. 30. pro. Cluent 40. pro Sull. 29. Sueton. Claud. 15. 33. Dialog. de caus. C. E. 1. Quintil. I. O. IV. i. 7. VI. iv. 22. Plin. Epp. I. 23. III. 4. Pseud. Ascon. in Cic. Div. in Q. C. 4.
[2] Cic. pro Cluent 70. pro Fontei. 12. pro Flacc. 33. pro Muren. 27. pro Coel. Div. in Q. C. 15. and note of Pseud. Ascon. Epp. ad Fam. VIII 8. Val. Max. IV. ii. 5. Ascon. in Milonian.
[3] Ascon. Argum. in Cic. pro Scaur. Dialog. de caus. C. E. 38.
[4] Ascon. Argum. in Milonian. Cic. Brut. 94. de Finn. IV. 1. Dion Cass. XL. 52.

in principle, that of a Patron to a Client, it was considered disreputable to receive pecuniary remuneration, or even gifts, for executing a task, the due performance of which was a sacred duty. However, as early as B.C. 204, the *Lex Cincia Muneralis* was passed—*qua cavetur ne quis ob causam orandam pecuniam donumve accipiat*[1]—which proves that the practice of accepting fees, in Civil Suits at least, had at that early epoch, begun to excite attention, and to call for legislative interference.

After the overthrow of the republic, the position of Pleaders, with regard to the people at large, was entirely changed. The latter were no longer, as formerly, the dispensers of all political distinctions, and therefore the former had no longer the same inducements to court their favour. Moreover, the most important Criminal Trials now took place in the Senate, from whose deliberations the public were excluded. Hence persons could not be easily found willing to devote their time and talents to the service of those from whom they could obtain no acknowledgment, and the practice of taking fees seems to have rapidly become general. Augustus endeavoured to restore the ancient discipline in this matter, by passing an enactment, that Pleaders, convicted of having accepted remuneration, should be compelled to refund the amount fourfold; but from the change of circumstances, it is manifest that such a regulation could not have been enforced with advantage to those parties whom it was intended to protect. Accordingly, we read that Claudius, when a proposal was made during his reign to revive the *Lex Cincia*, found it expedient to fix the maximum which it should be lawful for a Pleader to receive, (10,000 sesterces,) instead of making a vain attempt to forbid the practice altogether.[2] From this time forward, pleading at the bar became fully recognised as a *Profession*, in the modern acceptation of the word. Those who followed this calling were now usually termed *Causidici*; and Juvenal, when complaining of the want of encouragement for men of letters, reckons the *Causidici* among those whose exertions were inadequately rewarded.

It may be seen, from the examples given by Valerius Maximus (VIII. iii.) that women were not prohibited from pleading in a Court of Justice.

Offences committed by Pleaders. We have seen above, that after the institution of the *Quaestiones Perpetuae*, it was competent for any Roman citizen to prefer a charge in these Courts.

This privilege might be abused in various ways, and in process of time it was found necessary to restrain certain offences connected with public prosecutions by penal enactments. The offences against which these statutes were directed were chiefly—

1. *Tergiversatio.* 2. *Praevaricatio.* 3. *Calumnia.*—*Accusatorum temeritas tribus modis detegitur et tribus poenis subiicitur, aut enim* CALUMNIANTUR, *aut* PRAEVARICANTUR, *aut* TERGIVERSANTUR.

The nature of these we shall briefly explain.

1. *Tergiversatio.* When an accuser, after having brought a charge against any individual, was induced, by corrupt motives, to abandon the accusation, either by not appearing on the day fixed for the trial, or by formally abandoning the case before the trial had been brought to a regular conclusion, he was said *Tergiversari*. The result of such a step was the erasure of the name of the defendant from the roll of accused persons; and during the period of the republic

---

[1] Tacit. Ann. XI. 5. comp. XIII. 42. Cic. Cat. Mai. 4. ad Att. I. 20. Liv. XXXIV. 4. Paul. Diac. s. v. *Muneralis*, p. 123.
[2] Tacit. Ann. XI. 5—8.

no proceedings seem to have been taken against the accuser, who would merely suffer generally in character. But the practice of extorting money by threatened prosecutions became so frequent under the empire, that in the reign of Nero, a measure was passed by C. Petronius Turpilianus, Consul, A.D. 61, cited sometimes as the *Lex Petronia*, and sometimes as the *Senatus-Consultum Turpilianum*, in terms of which *Infamia* (p. 84,) and a fine of five pounds weight of gold were inflicted upon any one convicted of *Tergiversatio*.

2. *Praevaricatio.* When an accuser was induced, by corrupt motives, to conduct his case in such a manner as to secure the acquittal of the accused, which might be done in many ways—as, for example, by passing over lightly the most important charges, or by refraining from calling the most important witnesses, or by challenging upright jurors, and allowing those to remain who were known to be friendly to the defendant,—he was said *Praevaricari*. We find no traces of any separate enactment directed specially against this offence before the imperial times, although the practice became common towards the close of the republic, at the period when so many of the Criminal Trials were of a political and party character; but various laws seem to have contained clauses providing for the punishment of such treachery. Any one whose acquittal had notoriously been procured in this manner, could again be brought to trial for the same offence. The new accuser was bound, in the first instance, to impeach the former accuser before the same Court which had pronounced the acquittal; and if the first accuser was found guilty of *Praevaricatio*, the condemnation of the original defendant followed almost as a matter of course.[1] The punishment for *Praevaricatio* was first placed upon a formal footing by the *Lex Petronia*, spoken of in the last section.

We have examples of trials for *Praevaricatio* in the case of Livius Drusus, who was charged with this crime[2] in B.C. 54, but acquitted; and of M. Servilius Geminus, whose case is detailed by Coelius; (Epp. ad Fam. VIII. 8;) and if we can believe Cicero, the motive which induced Q. Caecilius to seek the privilege of impeaching Verres, was a desire to procure his acquittal. (See Divin. in Q. C. passim.)

The term *Praevaricatio* is sometimes employed in a general sense to denote the conduct of a *Patron* who wilfully betrays the interests of his Client, and, thus might be employed to denote the treachery of a Pleader who endeavoured to procure the condemnation of the party whom he was ostensibly defending; but this is not the technical and legal import of the word.

3. *Calumnia.* This word, in its most general acceptation, is used to denote any fraud or treachery on the part of one engaged in conducting a Criminal Trial, and hence comprehends the two offences already specified. It is, however, for the most part employed in a more restricted sense to signify the crime of wilfully, and with malice aforethought, preferring a false accusation—in the language of the jurists—*Calumniosus est qui sciens prudensque per fraudem negotium alicui comparat*. From a very early period, an accused person had the right to administer to his accuser an oath called *Iusiurandum Calumniae*, in terms of which the latter made a solemn declaration that he sincerely believed in the guilt of the accused. An oath of this description seems to have been demanded as a necessary preliminary in the various laws providing for the administration of Criminal Justice—*Si deiuraverit Calumniae causa non pos-*

---

[1] See Lex Servil. de Repet. p. 7. 64. ed. Klenze. Plin. Epp. III. 9.
[2] Cic. ad Q. F. II. 16.

IUDICIA PUBLICA. 315

tulare—and hence any one suspected of having taken this oath falsely, was liable to impeachment.[1]

A *Lex Remmia* was passed under the republic for the repression of *Calumnia*; but when, or by whom, is not known. Nor are we acquainted with its provisions, except in so far that it has been inferred, from a passage in Cicero, (Pro Rosc. Amer. 19. 20.) that branding upon the forehead (with the letter K) was one of the penalties.

The Parties in Criminal Trials.—In addition to what has been said above, we may remark, that the terms *Actor* and *Reus* (p. 267) were employed alike in Civil Suits and in Criminal Trials; but *Petitor* was applied to the plaintiff in the former only, and *Accusator* to the impeacher in the latter only.

[1] Frag. Leg. Servil. 8. Liv. XXXIII, 47. Cic. ad Fam, VIII. 8. pro Rosc. Comoed. 1. pro Sull. 31. Ascon. in Cic. Cornelian.

Sacrificial Axe and Knives, (see p. 343,) from the frieze of the temple of Jupiter Tonans at Rome.

CHAPTER X.

RELIGION OF ROME.

The subject naturally divides itself into three heads.
1. The Gods worshipped, their names, attributes, history, and mutual relations.
2. The Ministers by whom their worship was conducted.
3. The Mode of worship.

I. THE GODS WORSHIPPED.

General Characteristics of Roman Mythology.—In order that we may be able to form any distinct conception of Roman Mythology, it is essentially necessary to bear in mind the fact that the Romans were originally a mixed people, formed by the coalition of at least three distinct races—Latins—Sabines—Etruscans—and that at all events the first of these races was itself compound, being made up of Pelasgians, grafted upon some early Italian stock. Hence, when united, their religion could not fail to present confused and heterogeneous combinations. The simple belief of the primitive mountain tribes, stamped by a pure and somewhat stern morality, was mingled with the more soft and imaginative system of the pastoral Pelasgians, and with the dark and gloomy superstition of the Etruscans, from whom, avowedly, all that was gorgeous and imposing in the national ritual was derived. The fusion and amalgamation of these materials seems, however, to have been fully completed at a very early epoch, since we find no traces of jealousy or collision between inconsistent and contending creeds. But there was another and still more important source of complication. As the Romans gradually became acquainted with the colonists of Southern Italy, and extended their conquests beyond the Ionian Sea, they found several Greek divinities bearing a marked resemblance, both in name and attributes, to their own, just as might be expected from the Pelasgian element common to both nations. This circumstance having attracted notice, it would appear that all classes in the community speedily arrived at the conclusion, that the Religion of Greece and that of Rome were in all respects radically the same. Hence every Greek God was identified with some member of the Roman Pantheon, even where the resemblance was very slight, or where there was no resemblance at all, and the genealogy, history, and adventures of the one, were unhesitatingly transferred to the other. In so far as the early Italian religion was concerned, the tales connected with their deities appear to have been meagre, and not peculiarly interesting. A considerable number of these native legends has been preserved by Ovid in his Fasti, and others will be found scattered in Propertius, Tibullus, and Virgil; but the great mass of the mythology in these writers, as well as in Catullus, Horace, and the later poets, is almost purely Greek.

It is evident, therefore, that a full account of all the Gods celebrated in the

Latin Classics would involve a complete treatise upon Greek Mythology, a subject which does not fall within the compass of a work like the present. We must be content, in this place, simply to name the most important divinities, adopting, as far as it goes, the classification recognised by the Roman authors themselves.

Dii Consentes.—The Romans and the Etruscans recognised Twelve Great Gods, six male and six female, who met together in council and regulated all things in heaven and on earth. There were the *XII. Dii Consentes* s. *Complices* whose gilded statues were ranged along the Forum, (Varro R. R. I. 1,) the same, doubtless, with those enumerated by Ennius—

    Iuno, Vesta, Minerva, Ceres, Diana, Venus, Mars,
    Mercurius, Iovis, Neptunus, Vulcanus, Apollo.

1. IOVIS, IOVIS PATER, IUPITER, DIESPITER, the $Ζεύς$ of the Greeks, the TINA or TINIA of the Etruscans, was Lord Supreme. He was worshipped on the Capitoline under the titles of *Optimus Maximus*, *Capitolinus*, and *Tarpeius*; on the Alban Mount he received the homage of the Latin Confederacy, as *Iupiter Latiaris*. Of his numerous titles, many were derived from the sway which he exercised over the elements. Hence he was termed *Lucetius*, *Diespiter*, *Tonans*, *Fulguritor*, *Imbricitor*, and, from a legend that he had been drawn down from heaven, in the age of Numa, to teach how his wrath, when indicated by storms, might be appeased, *Elicius*. The Ides of each month were sacred to Jove, and a great festival, the *Feriae Latinae*, was celebrated in honour of him annually on the Alban Mount. It is said to have been instituted by Tarquinius Superbus in order to cement the union between Rome and the Latin States; but it probably originated at a much earlier epoch. The sacred banquet, called *Epulum Iovis*, was held on the 13th November (*Non. Novembr.*)

2. IUNO, a modified form of IOVINO, the wife of IOVIS, and Queen of Heaven, (*Iuno Regina*,) was identified with the $Ἥρα$ of the Greeks, and the CUPRA of the Etruscans. One of her chief duties was to preside over married life, and hence she was addressed as *Matrona*, *Iugalis*, *Pronuba*. When lending aid at childbirth, she was styled *Lucina*, and in this capacity was identified with the Greek $Εἰλείθυια$. In her temple on the Arx, she was worshipped as *Iuno Moneta*, which seems to mean, the *Warning Goddess*, and adjacent to this shrine was the public mint. Her rites were celebrated from a very early epoch with peculiar sanctity at Lanuvium, where she was named *Iuno Sospita* s. *Sispita*, i.e. the *Saviour*. The Kalends of each month were sacred to Juno, and she received special homage on the *Matronalia*, celebrated by the Matrons on the first of March.

3. MINERVA, the MENRVA of the Etruscans, was identified with the $Παλλάς$ $Ἀθήνη$ of the Greeks. She was the patroness of all learning, science, and art, and exercised a special superintendence over spinning and weaving, the two chief departments of female industry. Her great festival was the *Quinquatrus* s. *Quinquatria*, which commenced on the 19th of March, and eventually was prolonged for five days. A second festival was celebrated on the Ides of June, and termed *Quinquatrus Minusculae*. Since *Minerva* was goddess of learning, schools were under her protection. School-boys had holidays during the greater *Quinquatria*, and at this season each brought a gift to his master, which was termed *Minerval*.

It would appear that *Iovis*, *Iuno*, and *Minerva*, were worshipped jointly in the citadel of every great Etruscan city; and we have seen that they were regarded as the special protectors of Rome, and occupied the great national temple on the Capitoline (p. 25.)

On the 4th September, (*Prid. Non. Septembr.*) and for several days following, the great games, styled by way of distinction, *Ludi Magni*, or *Ludi Romani*, were celebrated in honour of these three deities.

4. VESTA, who must be regarded as the same with the ʹΕστία of the Greeks, seems to have been a Pelasgic goddess. She was worshipped in every mansion as the protectress of the domestic hearth; and the ever-blazing altar of her circular temple beside the Forum was looked upon as the hearth of the whole Roman people considered as one family. In the most sacred recesses of this sanctuary were preserved certain holy objects, upon which the safety of the City was supposed to depend; and when Greek superstition became rife, it was believed that chief among these was the *Palladium*, the image of Pallas, which fell from heaven when Ilus was founding Ilium, and which was brought to Italy by Æneas, along with the Phrygian Penates. The festival of Vesta, the *Vestalia*, was celebrated on the 9th of June (*V. Id. Iun.*)

5. APOLLO, whose name appears on Etruscan monuments under the form APLU, is the Φοῖβος ʹΑπόλλων of the Greeks, who was eventually identified with ʺΗλιος, the Sun-God. The worship of Apollo was not introduced at Rome until a comparatively late period. No temple was erected to him until B.C. 428, and the *Ludi Apollinares*, celebrated each year on the 5th of July (*III. Non. Quintil.*) were not instituted until B.C. 212.

6. DIANA, or LUNA, the Moon-Goddess, must be regarded as the same with the LOSNA, or LALA, of the Etruscans, and was identified with the Greek Hunting-Goddess, ʺΑρτεμις, the sister of Phœbus Apollo, who was herself identified, by post-Homeric poets, with Σελήνη. There can be no doubt that DIANA is a contracted form of DIVA s. DIA IANA, *Iana* being the wife of *Ianus*, who was anciently regarded by the Italians as the Sun-God. But how *Diana* came to be separated from her husband in the enumeration of the Twelve Consentian Deities, and how the Greeks and Romans should have established a connection between Artemis or Diana, and Hecate or Proserpina, goddesses of the nether world, so as to make up the *Diva Triformis*, (*Tria virginis ora Dianae*,) worshipped as *Luna* in heaven, as *Diana* upon earth, and as *Proserpina* in the realms below, are questions which would lead to very complicated and perplexing investigations. Her statues were frequently erected at a point from which three roads or streets diverged, and hence she is styled *Trivia*. There was a sacrifice to *Diana* on the Aventine, on 31st March, (*Prid. Kal. Apr.*) but her chief festival was on the 13th August (*Id. Sextil.*) There was a celebrated shrine of *Diana* on the *Lacus Nemorensis* near Aricia, where a festival called the *Nemoralia* was celebrated on the 13th August (*Id. Sextil.*) The priest in this temple was always a fugitive slave, who had gained his office by murdering his predecessor, and hence went armed that he might be prepared to encounter a new aspirant.

7. VENUS, identified with the TURAN of the Etruscans, and the ʹΑφροδίτη of the Greeks, was the Goddess of Love and Beauty. She was worshipped in the Forum under the title of *Cloacina*, or *Cluacina*, i.e. *The Purifier*, and in the Circus Maximus as *Venus Murtea*, an epithet derived probably from the myrtle, her favourite plant. The two festivals named *Vinalia*, the first celebrated on 23d April, (*IX. Kal. Mai.*) and the second, the *Vinalia Rustica*, on 19th August, (*XIV. Kal. Septr.*) were sacred to *Iovis* and *Venus*.

8. CERES, identified with the Greek Δημήτηρ, i.e. *Mother-Earth*, was the Goddess of Corn and Agriculture. Her worship, as we are assured by Cicero, (Pro Balb. 24.) was derived from Greece, and conducted by Grecian priestesses,

The festival of *Ceres*, the *Cerealia*, commenced on the 12th of April (*Prid. Id. Apr.*) and lasted for several days. There were also rustic festivals in honour of this goddess, the *Paganalia* and the *Feriae Sementivae* in seed-time, and the *Ambarvalia* before harvest. The latter was so called because the victim was led thrice round the fields before it was sacrificed. (See Virg. G. I. 338. Tibull. II. i. 1.)

9. MARS s. MAVORS s. MAMERS s. MARSPITER, the God of War, was the Αρης of the Greeks, and with him was associated a female goddess, BELLONA, but the name of his wife was NERIA or NERIENE. As the god who strode with warlike step to the battle-field, he was worshipped under the epithet *Gradivus*; and as the protector of the country, he was styled *Mars Silvanus*. *Quirinus*, i.e. *Spear-Bearer* or *Warrior*, was also an epithet of Mars, but was employed more frequently as the appropriate appellation of deified Romulus. Horse races in honour of *Mars*, called *Equiria*, took place on the 27th February (*III. Kal. Mart.*) and on the 14th March, (*Prid. Id. Mart.*) and chariot races on 15th October, (*Id. Octobr.*) on which occasion a horse, called *Equus October*, was sacrificed to the god in the *Campus Martius*. The festival of *Bellona* was on the 4th of June (*Prid. Non. Iun.*)

10. NEPTUNUS, the Lord of the Sea, whose name appears as NETHUNS on Etruscan monuments, was identified with the Greek Ποσειδῶν. There was also a PORTUNUS, the God of Harbours. The festival of *Neptunus*, the *Neptunalia*, was celebrated on the 23d July (*X. Kal. Sextil.*).

11. VULCANUS s. MULCIBER, the God of Fire, the SETHLANS of the Etruscans, was identified with the "Ηφαιστος of the Greeks, the artificer in metals, the smith who forged the armour of the gods and the thunderbolts of Zeus. The festival of *Vulcanus*, the *Vulcanalia*, was celebrated on the 23d August (*X. Kal. Septembr.*)

12. MECURIUS, the God of Traffic and of Gain, the TURMS of the Etruscans, whose name is manifestly derived from *Merx*, was identified with the Ἑρμῆς of the Greeks. The festival of *Mercurius* was celebrated on the 15th May, (*Id. Mai.*) that being the day on which this temple was dedicated in B.C. 498 (Liv. II. 21.)

Varro, at the commencement of his treatise on Agriculture, invokes to his assistance Twelve Consentian Deities, (some of whom are different from the twelve named above,) those powers, namely—*Qui maxime agricolarum duces sunt*. These he arranges in pairs: 1. *Iovis* et *Tellus*. 2. *Sol* et *Luna*. 3. *Ceres* et *Liber*. 4. *Robigus* et *Flora*. 5. *Minerva* et *Venus*. 6. *Lympha* et *Bonus Eventus*.

1. IOVIS et TELLUS, or *Heaven* and *Earth*. *Tellus*, or *Terra Mater*, was a personification of the productive powers of the earth, and as such, identical with *Ceres*. As the source of wealth, she was styled *Ops*, and as the giver of all good things, *Bona Dea*. *Fatua* is said to have been another appellation of the same goddess, the name clearly indicating a prophetic or oracular divinity. *Maius* and *Maia*, from whom the month of May derived its name, seem to have been a pair of equivalent deities, worshipped at Tusculum, and probably in the other states of ancient Latium. The festival of *Ops*, the *Opalia*, was celebrated on 19th December; (*XIV. Kal. Ian.;*) the rites of the *Bona Dea* were performed on the 1st May (*Kal. Mai.*) by women only, every male creature being scrupulously excluded.

2. SOL et LUNA. These, according to the popular belief, were regarded as identical with *Apollo* and *Diana*.

3. CERES et LIBER. *Liber*, or, as he is more frequently termed, *Liber Pater*, together with his wife, *Libera*, seem to have been the ancient Italian patrons of agriculture. When Greek deities became mixed up with those already worshipped in Rome, *Ceres*, or Δημήτηρ, was regarded as the protectress of the husbandman, *Libera* was identified with her daughter Περσεφόνη, or *Proserpina*, while *Liber* was identified with the Wine-God, Διόνυσος, otherwise called Βάκχος, the PHUPHLUNS of the Etruscans. The festival of *Liber*, the *Liberalia*, was celebrated on the 17th March (*XVI. Kal. Apr.*) But although the Romans recognised their own *Liber* in the Greek Διόνυσος, they long repudiated the disgusting and frantic rites by which the worship of the latter was characterised in the East; and the attempt made to introduce the nocturnal *Bacchanalia* in B.C. 186 called forth most stringent prohibitions.

4. ROBIGUS et FLORA must be regarded as two antagonistic powers, the latter a beneficent goddess, who watched over the early blossom, the former a worker of evil, who destroyed the tender herbs by mildew, and whose wrath was to be averted by prayer and sacrifice. *Robigus* is elsewhere associated with a female *Robigo*. The festival of *Flora*, the *Floralia*, commenced on the 28th of April, (*IV. Kal. Mai.*) and continued until the 1st of May (*Kal. Mai.*) inclusive. The festival of *Robigus*, the *Robigalia*, was celebrated on the 25th April (*VII. Kal. Mai.*) We find classed along with *Robigus*, a God AVERRUNCUS; (Aul. Gell. V. 12. comp. Varro L. L. VII. § 102;) but this word must be regarded as an epithet, equivalent to the Greek ἀποτρόπαιος, applicable to any God when invoked to avert calamity.

5. MINERVA et VENUS, the former as the patroness of all the useful arts, the latter as the goddess of reproduction, were appropriately ranked among the great rural deities. There can be no doubt that *Venus* was occasionally viewed as a male power; the termination might lead us to suspect this, and the symmetry of the Twelve Rural *Dii Consentes*, six male and six female, can be maintained only upon this supposition. (See Macrob. S. III. 8.)

6. LYMPHA et BONUS EVENTUS, *Moisture* and *Good-Luck*, close the catalogue.

Dii Selecti.—In a fragment of Varro we find twenty deities ranked together as Great Gods, and designated, by an epithet borrowed from the *Iudices* of Law Courts (p. 294,) *Dii Selecti*.[1] These are *Ianus, Iovis, Saturnus, Genius, Mercurius, Apollo, Mars, Vulcanus, Neptunus, Orcus, Liber Pater, Tellus, Ceres, Iuno, Luna, Diana, Minerva, Venus, Vesta*. Of these, four are not included in either of the lists of *Dii Consentes* detailed above, viz.:—

1. IANUS, the deity represented with two faces (*Biceps--bifrons*) looking in opposite directions, seems to have been one of the chief objects of worship among the Italian tribes from the most remote epoch, but was totally unknown to Greek Mythology. There can be no doubt that he was the Sun-God, and that his wife *Iana* was the Moon-Goddess. He presided over all beginnings and entrances; as opener of the day he was hailed as *Matutinus Pater*, his name was first invoked in every prayer, and his festival was appropriately celebrated on the 1st January, (*Kal. Ian.*) that is, on the first day of the first month, that month being named after him. The festival of the *Agonalia*, celebrated on the 9th January, (*V. Id. Ian.*) was also in honour of *Ianus*.

2. SATURNUS. We can scarcely doubt that this name is connected etymologically with *Sat, Satur, Satio*, and that *Saturnus* was originally purely a rural

---

[1] In like manner Cicero (Tusculan. I. 13.) speaks of *Di Maiorum Gentium*.

RELIGION OF ROME.   321

deity. In later times, however, by some process which it is very hard to explain, he was identified with the Titan Κρόνος, the father of Zeus, while the female Titan 'Ρέα, the wife of Κρόνος, was identified with *Ops*. We find mention made of another female deity, called *Lua Mater*, in connection with *Saturnus*. The *Nundinae* were sacred to *Saturnus*, but his great festival, the *Saturnalia*, which was characterised by extravagant mirth, serving as the prototype of the modern Carnival, was celebrated on the 17th December (*XVI. Kal. Ian.*) The two following days were added by Augustus, and two more by Caligula.

3. ORCUS, otherwise named DITIS, DIS, or DIS PATER, was the monarch of the nether world, and as such was identified with the MANTUS of the Etruscans, and with the ῎Αδης or Πλούτων of the Greeks. His wife, the MANIA of the Etruscans, the Περσεφόνη of the Greeks, was, we have noticed above, called *Proserpina* by the Romans, and identified with the Italian *Libera*.

4. GENIUS. This was a spiritual being who presided over the birth of man, and attended and watched over him during life. Each individual had a separate *Genius*, who regulated his lot, and was represented as black or white according to his fortunes. Women were attended by similar spirits, who were termed *Iunones*, and not only persons, but places also, were guarded by their *Genii*. Closely allied to the *Genii* were the

Domestic Gods. Lares. Penates.—LARES were the departed spirits of ancestors who watched over their descendants, and were worshipped as tutelary gods in every mansion, and as such termed *Lares Familiares*. The whole city being the dwelling of the Roman people, who might be regarded as forming one great family, had its *Lares Praestites*, whose appearance and festival, celebrated on the 1st of May, (*Kal. Mai.*) are described in the Fasti of Ovid (V. 129 seqq.) In like manner there were groupes of *Lares Publici*, worshipped as *Lares Rurales*, *Lares Compitales*, *Lares Viales*, *Lares Permarini*, &c.

PENATES were deities selected by each family as its special protectors, and were worshipped along with the LARES in the *Penetralia* of each mansion, that is, at the *Focus* or hearth, which was the centre of the dwelling, and therefore the spot most remote from the outer world. The term *Penates* is frequently used to denote all the Gods worshipped at the domestic hearth, and in this sense comprehends the *Lares*, who must not, however, be considered as identical with the *Penates*, when the latter term is used in its restricted sense.

As there were Public *Lares* so there were Public *Penates*. Amidst the obscurity and contradictions which surround the statements of ancient writers on this subject, we are led to the conclusion that the *Penates Populi Romani*, were worshipped under the form of two youthful warriors who, in later times at least, were regarded as identical with Κάστωρ and Πολυδεύκης (CASTOR and POLLUX,) the Διόσκουροι of the Greeks, and were believed to have some connection with the mysterious *Dii Cabiri* of Samothrace. They are generally represented on horseback bearing long spears, with conical caps on their heads, whence they are called by Catullus, *Fratres Pileati*.

Dii Novensiles.—This is the Roman term for the Nine Gods, who were believed by the Etruscans to possess the power of wielding thunderbolts. The names of seven only of these can be ascertained. 1. TINIA or IOVIS. 2. CUPRA or IUNO. 3. MENRVA or MINERVA. 4. SUMMANUS, who was probably identical with ORCUS, hurling his bolts by night, while those of IOVIS were launched by day. 5. MARS. 6. SETHLANS or VULCANUS. 7. VEDIUS or VEIOVIS, a

Y

deity with regard to whose nature and attributes great diversity of opinion prevailed among the Romans themselves in the Augustan age. See Ovid Fast. III. 429. Dionys. I. 15. Aul. Gell. V. 12. Macrob. S. III. 9.

Dii Indigetes, i. e. *Gods natives of the Soil,* were mortals, who by their bravery and virtues had won for themselves a place among the celestials. Such were HERCULES, whose rites were established in Italy at a very remote epoch, his altar, called *Ara Maxima,* in the *Forum Boarium,* having been erected, according to tradition, by Evander; ÆNEAS, to whom sacrifice was offered yearly on the banks of the Numicius, under the name IUPITER INDIGES; and ROMULUS, worshipped under the name of QUIRINUS, whose festival, the *Quirinalia,* was celebrated on the 17th February (*XIII. Kal. Mart.*) The festival of FORNAX, the goddess of bake-houses, the *Fornacalia,* was held on the same day, which was also, for some reason not known, styled *Festa Stultorum.*

Semones.—All of the personages mentioned in the last paragraph were, it will be observed, divine by one parent, and hence might be appropriately termed *Semones,* i. e. *Semihomines.* The deity most frequently mentioned under this title was the Sabine SEMO SANCUS, the God of Good Faith, who was held to be the same with the Latin DIUS FIDIUS, both being identified with the Greek or Pelasgian HERCULES. See Ovid Fast. VI. 213. His festival was celebrated on the 5th June (*Non. Iun.*)

Rural Deities.—As might have been expected among tribes devoted to agriculture and a pastoral life, the Italian Pantheon was very rich in Rural Gods. Among the most notable of these, in addition to the *XII. Dii Consentes* of the Country, enumerated above, were FAUNUS, whose festivals, the *Faunalia,* were celebrated on the 13th February, (*Id. Febr.*) on 13th October, (*III. Id. Octobr.*) and on 5th December (*Non. Decembr.*) and in addition to *Faunus* regarded as an individual God, there was a class of rural deities called FAUNI, who, in many respects, corresponded to the Σάτυροι of the Greeks: there was also a female power, FAUNA, who is sometimes identified with *Tellus, Ops, Bona Dea,* and *Fatua:* LUPERCUS, whose festival, the *Lupercalia,* was celebrated at a spot on the Aventine, called *Lupercal,* on the 15th February (*XV. Kal. Mart.:*) *Faunus* and *Lupercus,* together with a third, named INUUS, were, in later times, identified with each other, and with the Arcadian PAN: PICUS and SILVANUS, Gods of the Woods: PALES, the deity of shepherds, represented by some writers as a male, and by others as a female power, whose festival, the *Palilia,* celebrated on the 21st April, (*XI. Kal. Mai.*) was believed to mark the day on which the city was founded (*Dies Natalis urbis Romae:*) POMONA, the Goddess of fruits: VERTUMNUS, the God of the changing seasons: ANNA PERENNA, the Goddess of the circling year, whose festival was celebrated on the 15th March (*Id. Mart.:*) TERMINUS, the God of Boundaries, whose festival, the *Terminalia,* was celebrated on 23d February (*VII. Kal. Mart.*)

Personifications of Moral Qualities, &c.—A striking characteristic of Roman mythology was the homage paid to the Moral Qualities, the various Affections of the mind, and many other Abstractions. Thus temples were erected and sacrifices were offered to VIRTUS, HONOS, FIDES, SPES, PUDOR, PAVOR, CONCORDIA, PAX, VICTORIA, LIBERTAS, SALUS, IUVENTAS, MENS, FAMA, and a multitude of others, among whom FORTUNA or FORS FORTUNA, the NORTIA of the Etruscans, must not be forgotten.

Some other deities, who do not fall under any of the above classes, may be mentioned here. Such were MATER MATUTA or AURORA, goddess of the early dawn, the THESAN of the Etruscans, the 'Ηώς of the Greeks, whose festival, the *Matralia*, was celebrated on 11th June (*III. Id. Iun.*) CONSUS, God of Secret Counsel, whose altar was buried in the earth in the Circus Maximus, and uncovered once a year only at his festival, the *Consualia*, which was celebrated on the 18th August, (*XV. Kal. Sept.*) the anniversary of the abduction of the Sabine maidens. LIBITINA, Goddess of Funerals, identified with VENUS. LAVERNA, Goddess of Thieves. FERONIA, originally a Sabine goddess, whose attributes are very doubtful, but who was probably in some way connected with SORANUS, the Sabine God of the Lower World. VACUNA, also a Sabine goddess, who was variously identified with *Ceres, Diana, Venus, Minerva*, and *Victoria*. CARMENTA, identified with the prophetic mother of Evander, whose festival, the *Carmentalia*, was celebrated on 11th January (*III. Id. Ian.*) CAMENAE or CASMENAE, nymphs analogous to the Greek Muses, one of whom was *Egeria*, the mistress of Numa. FATA s. PARCAE, the Goddesses of Destiny. FURIAE s. DIRAE, identified with the Greek 'Ερινύες, the Goddesses who inspired raging madness. MANES, the spirits of the departed, called LEMURES when they exhibited themselves in frightful forms, whose festivals, the *Feralia* and *Lemuria*, were celebrated, the former on 18th February (*XII. Kal. Mart.*) the latter on 9th May (*VII. Id. Mai.*) MANIA, whom we have named above as the wife of ORCUS, is sometimes termed mother of the *Manes*, while the mother of the *Lares* was LARA or LARUNDA or LARENTIA, whose festival, the *Larentalia*, was celebrated on the 23d December (*X. Kal. Ian.*) In later times, LARA or LARENTIA was held to be *Acca Larentia*, the wife of *Faustulus*. Varro (L.L. V. § 74.) states, on the authority of the *Annales*, that King Tatius dedicated altars to *Ops, Flora, Vedius, Iovis, Saturnus, Sol, Luna, Volcanus, Summanus, Larunda, Terminus, Quirinus, Vortumnus*, the *Lares, Diana*, and *Lucina*. In another place (L.L. VII. § 45.) he names *Volturnus, Diva Palatua, Furrina*, and *Falacer Pater*, among the deities to whom separate priests were assigned by Numa. According to Servius, the ancient Romans gave the title of *Pater* to all Gods (Serv. ad Virg. Æn. I. 55.)

Foreign Deities.—Although the Romans were readily induced, by very slight resemblances, to identify their national gods with those of Greece, they, for a long period, looked with jealousy upon the introduction of deities avowedly foreign, and few were admitted, except in obedience to the dictates of an oracle or prophecy. Among those imported in this manner were—

AESCULAPIUS, God of the Healing Art, whose worship was introduced from Epidaurus in B.C. 291, in consequence of instructions contained in the Sibylline Books, which had been consulted two years previously as to the steps to be taken for averting a pestilence.

CYBELE, the great Phrygian Goddess of Nature, whose worship was introduced from Pessinuns in B.C. 205, in obedience to an injunction contained in the Sibylline Books. By the Greeks, she was identified with 'Ρέα, and styled μεγάλη μήτηρ θεῶν, and hence her festival, which was celebrated with great pomp at Rome on the 4th of April (*Prid. Non. Apr*) and following days, was named *Megalesia*.

PRIAPUS, the God of Gardens, belongs to this class, since he was imported from Lampsacus on the Hellespont into Greece, and thence passed into Italy, superseding, to a great extent, the native *Horta*.

Towards the close of the republic, the worship of the Egyptian ISIS became fashionable, and, under the empire, OSIRIS, ANUBIS, SERAPIS, and a multitude of outlandish deities were eagerly cultivated.

Holy Things and Holy Places.

There are several terms which express the religious feelings entertained by the Romans, which it may be proper to explain before entering upon the second division of our subject.

Fas. Nefas. Fatum. Fanum. Profanus. Fanaticus.—All of these words are connected etymologically with the verb FARI. *Fas* denotes the Law or Will of the Gods, including every thing which has received the express sanction of the divine Word. *Nefas* is every thing opposed to that Law or Will. *Fatum* is that which has been spoken or decreed by the deity, and which must therefore inevitably come to pass. *Fanum* is a place consecrated by holy words. *Profanus* is applied to any object not within the limits of a *Fanum*, and is merely a negative epithet, signifying *not consecrated*. *Fanaticus* is properly one who dwells in a *Fanum*, and is inspired by a God; and since, according to the views of the ancients, inspiration was frequently accompanied by frantic enthusiasm, *fanaticus* often denotes *mad* or *fatuous*; nor is the epithet confined to animate objects, for *fanaticum carmen* is a prophecy, and *fanatica arbor* means *a tree struck by lightning* (Paul. Diac. p. 92.) With regard to the adjectives, *Fastus*, *Nefastus*, *Festus*, *Profestus*, which are generally used with reference to time, we shall speak at large in the next chapter.

Sacer. Sacrum. Sacrarium. Sacerdos. Sacramentum. Sacrare. Obsecrare. Resecrare.—Any object whatever, set apart and hallowed by man to the Gods, was termed *Sacer*, and in setting it apart he was said *Sacrare* s. *Consecrare*. *Sacrum*, used as a substantive, is any holy offering, any holy place, any holy observance. *Sacerdos* is one who ministers in things holy. *Sacrarium* or *Sacellum*, a holy place. *Sacramentum* an asseveration confirmed by an appeal to the Gods, i.e. a holy oath. To offer a solemn prayer to the Gods is *Obsecrare*, and the act of praying *Obsecratio*: if any one repented of a petition he had offered, and wished to cancel it, he was said *Resecrare* (Plaut. Aul. IV. vii. 4.)

An individual might become *Sacer* in two ways:—

1. He might present himself as a voluntary offering to the Gods—in doing which he was said *Devovere se*—as in the case of the Decii, who made themselves over to death (*Diis Manibus Tellurique*) for the preservation of their country.

2. Any one who had been guilty of heinous sacrilege might be declared by the state to be *Sacer* to the deity whom he had outraged; and hence an individual who took the life of such an one was not held guilty of murder, but was rather regarded as having performed a religious act in making over to the God what of right belonged to him.

Sanctus, from *Sancire*, is applied to any object believed to be under the direct protection of the Gods. Any person or object which had been formally placed by man under the protection of the Gods, and which the Gods had received under their protection, was *Sacrosanctus*, and any injury done to such an object would involve sacrilege.

Religio, from *Religare*, is the consciousness of the tie which unites man to the Gods, and binds him to obey their behests. Hence *Religio* not unfrequently signifies that feeling which causes a man to shrink from the performance of any

---

[1] On the subject of this section, and indeed on all matters connected with Roman Mythology, the student will find much instruction in the work of HARTUNG entitled *Die Religion der Roemer*, Erlang. 1836.

act, or to dread the neglect of any observance, lest in so doing he should call down the wrath of Heaven.

Templum, Fanum, Delubrum, are the words most commonly employed to denote *a sacred place.*

The original meaning of *Templum* was, in all probability, a spot marked out with certain solemnities by an *Augur* when about to take auspices; and on this was the *Tabernaculum* (p. 112) from which he made his observations. The term was applied also to the quarter or district of the heavens which the Augur defined with his staff of office, (*Lituus,*) and to which his observations were limited. Hence the verb *Contemplari* signifies *To survey.* In process of time, *Templum* became the technical term for any piece of ground separated and set apart (*liberatus et effatus*) for some sacred purpose by an Augur.

Fanum, in its widest acceptation, is a place consecrated by holy words. In its restricted sense, it was a piece of ground consecrated for the erection of a temple (*locus templo effatus*) by the *Pontifices*.

Delubrum is more comprehensive than either of the two others, being a place hallowed by sacred associations, by the presence of a deity, or by the erection of an altar or sanctuary; but it does not necessarily follow that the place had been formally dedicated by any of the higher priests.

No one of these words necessarily implies the existence of a building, (*aedes,*) although they are all commonly used as equivalent to our word *Temple.* In order that an edifice destined for the service of the Gods might be erected in due form, the ground was usually, in the first place, *liberatus et effatus* by an *Augur,* and thus it became a *Templum;* it was then consecrated by a *Pontifex,* and thus it became a *Fanum;* finally, after the building was erected, a third ceremony, termed *Dedicatio,* took place, by which it was made over to a particular God. It was by no means essential, however, that all edifices erected for public worship should be *Templa.* Thus the *Aedes Vestae,* perhaps the most holy shrine in Rome, was not a *Templum.* On the other hand, many structures were *Templa,* although not employed directly in the worship of the Gods; such were the *Rostra* and the *Curia Hostilia* (pp. 13, 14.)

Lucus is a holy grove; *Sacrum, Sacrarium,* and *Sacellum* frequently designate a holy place where there was an altar but no covered building.

A TEMPLUM, in the restricted sense of an edifice set apart for the worship of the Gods, consisted essentially of two parts only, a small apartment or sanctuary, the *Cella,* sometimes merely a niche (*Aedicula*) for receiving the image of the God, and an altar (*Ara—Altare*) standing in front of it, upon which were placed the offerings of the suppliant. The general form, whether circular, square, or oblong; whether covered with a roof, or open to the sky; whether plain and destitute of ornament, or graced by stately colonnades with elaborately sculptured friezes and pediments,—depended entirely upon the taste of the architect and the liberality of the founders, but in no way increased or diminished the sanctity of the building. In so far as position was concerned, we learn from Vitruvius that a Temple, whenever circumstances permitted, was placed East and West, the opening immediately opposite to the *Cella* being on the West side, so that those who stood before the altar with their eyes fixed upon the God, looked towards the East. [2]

---

[1] In the case of Vesta, it was held that her Temples must be circular.
[2] On *Templa, Fana,* &c. see Liv. I. 21. X. 37. XL. 51. Varro L. L. VI. § 54. VII. § 13. Vitruv. IV. 5. Aul. Gell. XIV. 7. VI. 12. Macrob. S. III. 4. 11. Serv. ad Virg. Æn. I. 450. II. 225. IV. 200.

II. MINISTERS OF RELIGION.

These may be conveniently divided into two classes.

A. Those who exercised a general superintendence over things sacred, or over particular departments, but who were not specially attached to one particular God.

B. Priests of particular Gods.

We commence with the former, of whom the most important were—1. *Pontifices.* 2. *Augures.* 3. *XV-viri Sacrorum.* 4. *Epulones.* These Corporations formed the four great *Collegia* of Priests, who are emphatically described by Dion Cassius as Τὰς τέσσαρας ἱερωσύνας, and by Suetonius as *Sacerdotes Summorum Collegiorum.*[1]

1. *Pontifices.*

Institution. Number.—The institution of *Pontifices* was ascribed to Numa, the number being originally five—*Sacris e Principum numero* PONTIFICES *quinque praefecit*—four ordinary *Pontifices* and a president styled *Pontifex Maximus*, the whole being Patricians exclusively.[2] This state of things continued until B.C. 300, when the *Lex Ogulnia* was passed by Q. and Cn. Ogulnius, Tribunes of the Plebs, which enacted that four additional *Pontifices* should be chosen, and that these four should be selected from the Plebeians. The number remained fixed at nine until the time of Sulla, by whom it was augmented to fifteen.[3] Under the empire, the number was not strictly defined, but depended upon the will of the Prince, who, in his capacity of *Pontifex Maximus*, used his own discretion.[4] *Pontifices* continued to exist as late as the end of the fourth century at least.[5] Among the numerous etymologies proposed by the Romans themselves, the most rational was that which regarded *Pontifex* as a compound of *Pons* and *Facio*, resting upon the explanation that one of their most sacred duties in ancient times was the repair of the *Pons Sublicius*, to which a holy character was always attached.[6]

Mode of Election.—For a long period, whenever a vacancy occurred, it was filled up by the process technically termed, in this and similar cases, *Cooptatio*, that is, the existing members of the Corporation themselves selected their new colleague, who, after the consent of the Gods had been ascertained by observing the auspices, was formally admitted by the solemn ceremony of *Inauguratio.* But by the *Lex Domitia*, passed by Cn. Domitius Ahenobarbus, Tribune of the Plebs, in B.C. 104, the right of election was transferred to the *Comitia Tributa*, which nominated an individual, who was then admitted into the College of Pontifices by *Cooptatio* and *Inauguratio*, the former being now reduced to a mere name. It must be observed that the *Comitia Tributa* proceeded, according to the above named law, in a manner altogether peculiar. The whole of the thirty-five Tribes did not vote, but a minority of them, seventeen namely, were taken by lot, and by these the new *Pontifex* was elected. The *Lex Domitia* was repealed, B.C. 81, by the *Lex Cornelia de Sacerdotiis* of Sulla, who restored to the College their ancient rights in full; but it was re-enacted by the

---

[1] Dion Cass. LIII. 1. LVIII. 12. Suet. Octav. 100. comp. Tacit. Ann. III. 64.
[2] Cic. de R. II. 14. Dionys. II. 73. Flor. I. 2. Livy, however, expresses himself (I. 20.) as if there had been originally one *Pontifex* only.
[3] Liv. X. 6—9. Epit. LXXXIX. Aurel. Vict. de vir. ill. 75.
[4] Dion Cass. XLII. 51 XLIII. 51. LI. 20. LIII. 17. Suet. Claud. 22.
[5] Symmach. Epp. IX. 123.
[6] Varro L. L. V. § 83. Dionys. II. 73. III. 45. Plut. Num. 9 Serv. ad Virg. Æn. II. 166.

Lex Atia of Labienus, Tribune of the Plebs, B.C. 63, with this modification, that the choice of the Tribes was now restricted to one of two persons previously nominated by the College. The *Lex Atia* was confirmed by Julius Cæsar; b the original practice was revived for a brief space by M. Antonius in B.C. 43. Upon the abrogation of his laws, the right of choice fell into the hands of Augustus and his successors.[1]

With regard to the *Pontifex Maximus*, the arrangements were somewhat different, since the people had a voice in his election from a much earlier epoch. When a *Pontifex Maximus* died, an ordinary member of the College was admitted in the usual manner, and then the people, in a meeting of the *Comitia Tributa*, at which the newly chosen *Pontifex* presided, determined which of the number, now complete, should be *Pontifex Maximus*. After the time of Tiberius, the disposal of the office seems to have rested ostensibly with the Senate, by whom it was bestowed as a matter of course, upon each Emperor on his accession.

Pontifices Minores.—That some of the *Pontifices* were styled *Minores* is certain; but we have no means of ascertaining upon what basis the distinction was founded, and it would be fruitless to detail the numerous conjectures which have been proposed from time to time. The most obvious and probable solution is, that the epithet was applied to the three junior members, of whom the youngest in standing was termed *Minorum Pontificum minimus*, and the eldest *Minorum Pontificum maximus*.[2] The words of Livy (XXII. 57)—*L. Cantilius, scriba pontificis, quos nunc Minores Pontifices appellant . . . . a Pontifice Maximo eo usque virgis in Comitio caesus erat, ut inter verbera exspiraret*—are particularly embarrassing, and have led some to imagine that the *Minores Pontifices* were mere secretaries, not members of the College at all. See also Capitolin. vit. Macrin. 7.

Duties and Powers of the Pontifices.—The *Pontifices* were not attached to the service of any particular deity, but exercised a general superintendence and regulating power over all matters whatsoever connected with the Religion of the State and Public Observances. To enumerate all their functions would be at once tedious and unprofitable; but the words of Livy, (I. 20. comp. Dionys. II. 73,) when describing the establishment of this priesthood by Numa, will show that their sphere of action embraced a very wide range—*Pontificem deinde Numa Marcium Marci filium, ex Patribus legit, eique sacra omnia exscripta exsignataque adtribuit: quibus hostiis, quibus diebus, ad quae templa sacra fierent, atque unde in eos sumtus pecunia erogaretur. Cetera quoque omnia publica privataque sacra Pontificiis scitis subiecit: ut esset, quo consultum plebes veniret: ne quid divini iuris, negligendo patrios ritus, peregrinosque adsciscendo, turbaretur. Nec coelestes modo ceremonias, sed iusta quoque funebria placandosque Manes, ut idem Pontifex edoceret; quaeque prodigia, fulminibus aliove quo visu missa, susciperentur atque curarentur: ad ea elicienda ex mentibus divinis, Iovi Elicio aram in Aventino dicavit, Deumque consuluit auguriis, quae suscipienda essent.*

To the *Pontifices* also was intrusted, in the earlier ages, the entire regulation of the year and of the Kalendar. They alone could determine the *Dies Fasti*, on which legal business might be lawfully transacted; and they alone were

---

[1] Cic. de leg. agr. II. 7. ad Brut. I. 5. Philipp. II. 2. Ascon. in Cornelian. Pseud. Ascon. in Div. in Q. C. Velleius II. 12. Suet. Octav. 3. Claud. 22. Nero 2. Tacit. Ann. III. 19. Hist. I. 2. Dion Cass. XXXVII. 37. XLIV. 53. LI. 20. LIII. 17.
[2] Fest. s.v *Minorum Pontificum* p. 161. Orat. de Harusp. resp. 6. Macrob. S. I. 15.

acquainted with the technical forms which litigants were obliged to employ in conducting their suits. Hence Pomponius, (Digest. I. ii. 2. § 6.) after explaining the origin of the *Legis Actiones*, (p. 277,) in the Laws of the XII Tables, adds—*Omnium tamen harum* (sc. legum) *et interpretandi scientia et actiones apud Collegium Pontificum erant,*—and Valerius Maximus (II. v. 21.) in like manner—*Ius Civile per multa secula inter sacra ceremoniasque Deorum immortalium abditum solisque Pontificibus notum, Cn. Flavius . . . vulgavit.* Compare the quotation from Livy, to the same effect, in p. 244.

Powers of the Pontifex Maximus.—It belonged to the *Pontifex Maximus* to announce publicly the decisions (*decreta—responsa*) at which the College had arrived in regard to any matter which had been submitted to their consideration —*Pro Collegio* s. *Ex auctoritate Collegii Respondere,*—and he would naturally possess considerable influence in their deliberations. But although he is designated by Festus (p. 185) as—*Iudex atque Arbiter rerum divinarum humanarumque*—it is certain that he was obliged to submit to the decision of a majority of the College, although opposed to his own views (e g. Liv. XXXI. 9.) Indeed there were only two matters in which we have any reason to believe that he exercised independent authority, namely, in choosing and, when necessary, inflicting punishment on the *Virgines Vestales*, of whom we shall speak below, and in compiling the annual record of remarkable events, civil as well sacred, which was known as *Annales Maximi*, and which must not be confounded with the *Libri Pontificales* s. *Pontificii* s. *Pontificum*, which were the volumes containing instructions and liturgies for the celebration of all manner of holy rites, and the decisions of all manner of questions connected with sacred observances (*Ius sacrum.*) A portion of their contents was divulged by Cn. Flavius, as noticed above, (comp. p. 244,) and eventually the study of the *Ius Pontificium*, in general, occupied the attention of many of the most distinguished lawyers towards the close of the republic and under the earlier Emperors.

Although the power of the *Pontifex Maximus* and his colleagues was, in things sacred, unquestionably very great, Dionysius goes much too far when he asserts (II. 73.) that they were subject to no control on the part either of the Senate or of the People. Not only did the People, as we have seen above, increase the number, admit Plebeians, and change the mode of election, but we can find many examples where they exercised the right of passing under review the decisions of the College, partially confirming and partially annulling them. e.g. Liv. XXXVII. 51. Cic. Philipp. XI. 8.

2. *Augures.*

The Romans, like many Eastern nations in modern times, never entered upon any important undertaking either in public or private life, without endeavouring beforehand to ascertain the feelings of the Gods upon the subject, and hence to infer the probable issue of the enterprise. The science by which this information was obtained was termed *Divinatio*, and the various signs which were believed to indicate the disposition of the Supreme Powers were comprehended under the general name of *Omina*. There was scarcely any sight or sound connected with animate or inanimate nature which might not, under certain circumstances, be regarded as yielding an *Omen;* but the greatest reliance was placed upon the manifestation of the divine will afforded by thunder and lightning, by the appearances exhibited in the entrails of victims offered in sacrifice, and, above all, by the cries, the flight, and the feeding of birds, regarding which we have already had occasion to speak when treating of the preliminary ceremonies of the *Comitia Centuriata* (p. 111.) This feeling was not peculiar to the Romans, but was shared in its full extent by the Greeks, so that the words Ὄρνις and Οἰωνός in the one language, and *Avis* in the other, although properly denoting simply *a bird*, are commonly used to signify *an omen*. The lines of Aristophanes apply as forcibly to the Romans as to the Athenians,—

"Ὄρνιν τε νομίζετε πάνθ', ὅσαπερ περὶ μαντείας διακρίνει
Φήμη γ' ὑμῖν ὄρνις ἐστίν, πταρμόν τ' ὄρνιθα καλεῖτε,
Ξύμβολον ὄρνιν, φωνὴν ὄρνιν, θεράποντ' ὄρνιν, ὄνον ὄρνιν·

Nor aught there is by augury, but for a BIRD may pass;
A word, a sign, a sound, a sneeze, a servant or an ass.[1]

Institution, Number, Mode of Election, &c.—The whole system of Divination, in so far as the public service was concerned, was placed under the control of the Corporation or *Collegium* of *Augures*. The institution of this priesthood is lost in the darkness of remote antiquity, the statements of ancient writers being full of doubt and contradiction. Romulus is said to have employed the aid of *Augures* in founding the City, and to have nominated three, one from each of the original Tribes, the *Ramnes*, the *Tities*, and the *Luceres*. At the period when the *Lex Ogulnia* was passed, (see above p. 326,) i.e. B.C. 300, there were four, and five being added from the Plebeians by that enactment, the total number became nine, which was subsequently increased by Sulla to fifteen, and by Julius Cæsar to sixteen.[2] The president was styled *Magister Collegii*, but he did not occupy such a conspicuous position in relation to his colleagues as the *Pontifex Maximus* with regard to the ordinary *Pontifices*.

The mode of electing *Augurs* underwent exactly the same vicissitudes as that of electing *Pontifices*, described above. They were originally chosen by *Cooptatio*, which was followed by *Inauguratio*. In terms of the *Lex Domitia*, the right of filling up vacancies was transferred from the College to seventeen out of the thirty-five Tribes, was restored to the College by the *Lex Cornelia*, was modified by the *Lex Atia*, and again restored by the *Lex Antonia*, which was, however, speedily annulled. Eventually the appointment lay with Augustus and his successors, who increased or diminished the number at pleasure.

Ius Augurum s. **Ius Augurium**.—The rules constituting the science (*disciplina*) of Augury were derived in a great measure, if not exclusively, from the Etruscans, and formed the *Ius Augurum*, by which the proceedings of the College were regulated. When doubt or uncertainty arose in any matter connected with this department, it was customary to submit it to the College, (*referre ad Augures*,) and their decisions were termed *Decreta* s. *Responsa Augurum*.[3]

Insignia, Privileges, &c.—In common with all the higher priests, they wore the *Toga Praetexta*, in addition to which they had the purple striped tunic called *Trabea*, their characteristic badge of office being the *Lituus*, a staff bent round at the extremity into a spiral curve. This they employed to mark out the regions of the heaven when taking observations, and it is constantly represented on coins and other ancient monuments in connection with those who had borne the office.[4] See cut annexed.

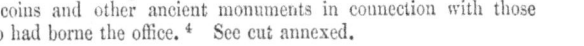

[1] Cary's Translation of the Birds of Aristophanes, Act. I. Sc. VI.
[2] Liv. l. 20. IV 4. X. 6. Epit. LXXXIX. Dionys. II. 22. 64. Cic. de R. II. 9. 14. de Div. L 40. Plut. Num. 15. Dion Cass.
[3] Cic. de Div. I. 17. II. 28. 33. 35. 36. de N. D. II. 4. de Legg. II. 12, 13. de R. II. 31.
[4] Serv. ad Virg. Æn. VII. 612. Cic. de Div. I. 17.

330   MINISTERS OF RELIGION.

The *Inauguratio*, or solemn admission into office, was celebrated by a sumptuous repast, the *Coena Auguralis* s. *Aditialis*, at which all the members of the College were expected to be present.

Two individuals belonging to the same *Gens* could not be *Augures* at the same time, and no one could be chosen who was openly upon bad terms with any member of the Corporation. [1]

The office of Augur (*Auguratus*) was for life. A person once formally admitted could not, under any circumstances, be expelled—*Honore illo nunquam privari poterant, licet maximorum criminum convicti essent* (Plin. Epp. IV. 8. Plut. Q. R. 99.)

3. *Quindecemviri Sacrorum.*

The prophetic books purchased by King Tarquin from the Sibyl, and hence termed *Libri Sibyllini*, were consigned to the custody of a College of Priests, whose duty it was to consult them (*libros inspicere* s. *adire*) when authorized by a decree of the Senate, and to act as the expounders (*interpretes*) of the mysterious words. The number of these Oracle-keepers was originally two, but in B.C. 369, was increased to ten, of whom, after B.C. 367, one half were chosen from the Plebeians, and by Sulla was increased to fifteen. [2] Their title was of a general character, being *Duumviri* s. *Xviri* s. *XVviri Sacrorum* s. *Sacris faciundis*, and in early times their duties were not confined to the custody and exposition of the sacred volumes, but they were, in certain cases, intrusted with the task of carrying out the injunctions found therein, and in the celebration of various rites. Thus we find them taking charge of *Lectisternia*, of the festival of Apollo, and of other solemnities—*Decemviros Sacris faciundis, Carminum Sibyllae ac Fatorum populi huius interpretes, antistites eosdem Apollinaris sacri caeremoniarumque aliarum Plebeios videmus.* [3]

4. *Epulones.*

The superintendence of banquets, in honour of the Gods, according to the arrangements of Numa, formed part of the duty of the *Pontifices*—*Quum essent ipsi a Numa ut etiam illud ludorum epulare sacrificium facerent instituti*—and we have stated above, that the *Lectisternia* were frequently conducted by the *Duumviri* or *Decemviri Sacrorum*. But in B.C. 196, in consequence of the pressure caused by the multitude of ceremonial observances—*propter multitudinem sacrificiorum*—a new Corporation of three priests was instituted, to whom was committed the regulation of sacred *Epulae*, and who were hence called *Triumviri Epulones*. The number was subsequently increased, probably by Sulla, to seven, by Caesar to ten, while under Augustus and his successors it would vary, but they are usually designated by the style and title of *Septemviri Epulones*. In common with the *Pontifices* and other higher priests, they had the right of wearing the *Toga Praetexta*. [4]

There were several other inferior *Collegia Sacerdotum*, not attached to any one particular deity. The names and functions of these we shall notice very briefly.

---

[1] Liv. XXX. 20. Cic. ad Fam. III. 10. VII. 26. ad Att. XII. 13. 14. 15. Brut. 1. Varro R. R. III. 6. Plin. H. N. X. 23. Suet. Cal. 12. Claud. 22.
[2] Liv. V. 13. VI. 37. 42. Cic. de Div. I. 2. ad Fam. VIII. 4. Tacit. Ann. XI. 11. Suet. Caes. 79. Dion Cass. XLIV. 15. LIII. 1.
[3] Liv. X. 8. comp. V. 13. XXII. 10.
[4] Cic. de Orat. III. 19. Orat. de Harusp. resp. 10. Liv. XXXIII. 42. Tacit Ann. III. 64. Lucan I. 602. Aul. Gell. I. 12. Paul. Diac. s.v. *Epulones* p. 78.

Fratres Arvales. A college of twelve priests, whose institution is connected with the earliest legends relating to the boundaries of the city. It is generally believed that their duty was, each year on the 15th of May (*Id. Mai.*) to propitiate those Gods upon whose favour the fertility of the soil depended, by a sacrifice termed *Ambarvale Sacrum*, the victims offered (*Hostiae Ambarvales*) being driven round the ancient limits of the Roman territory. In this manner the fields were purified (*lustrare agros.*) A portion of one of the Litanies employed by this priesthood is still extant, and is regarded as the most ancient monument of the Latin language. Private *Ambarvalia* were celebrated by the rustic population in various localities, for the purification of their own districts, and some scholars maintain that the *Ambarvale Sacrum*, was in all cases a private rite. There is certainly no conclusive evidence that it was ever offered by the *Fratres Arvales.* [1]

Rex Sacrorum s. *Sacrificus* s. *Sacrificulus.* This, as we have already had occasion to point out, (p. 133,) was a priest appointed upon the expulsion of the Tarquins, to perform those sacred duties which had devolved specially upon the Kings. The title of *Rex* having been retained in the person of this individual from the feeling that holy things were immutable, a certain amount of dignity was unavoidably associated with the office; but the greatest care was taken that no real power, religious or secular, should be in any way connected with the detested name. The *Rex Sacrificulus* was necessarily a Patrician, was nominated, it would seem, by the *Pontifex Maximus*, or by the College of *Pontifices*, and was consecrated in the presence of the *Comitia Calata*. He held his office for life, and took formal precedence of all other priests, but was placed under the control of the *Pontifex Maximus*: the tasks assigned to him were for the most part of a very trivial character, and he was not permitted to hold any other office, civil, military, or sacred. His wife, by whom he was assisted in certain rites, was styled *Regina*, and his residence on the *Via Sacra* was known as the *Regia*.

Although this priesthood was of small importance, and was so little coveted that towards the close of the republic it fell into abeyance, it was revived under the empire, and existed down to a very late period. [2]

Haruspices or *Extispices*, whose chief was termed *Summus Haruspex*, presided over that very important department of Divination in which omens were derived from inspecting the entrails of victims offered in sacrifice. Their science, termed *Haruspicina* s. *Haruspicum Disciplina*, was derived directly from Etruria, and those who practised it were said *Haruspicinam facere*. The inferiority of the *Haruspices* to the *Augures* is clearly indicated by the fact, that while the most distinguished men in the State sought eagerly to become members of the latter college, Cicero speaks of the admission of an *Haruspex* into the Senate as something unseemly. [3]

Fetiales, [4] a college of Priests said to have been instituted by Numa, consisting, it would appear, of twenty members, who presided over all the ceremonies connected with the ratification of peace, or the formal declaration of war,

---

[1] A most elaborate investigation with regard to the origin and duties of the *Fratres Arvales* is to be found in the work of Marini, published in 1795,under the title *Atti e monumenti d. fratelli Arvali*, &c. Aul. Gell. VI. 7. Plin. H.N. XVIII. 2. Tibullus. II. i. 1. Virg. Georg. I. 345. Macrob. S. III. 5. Paul. Diac. s. v. *Ambarvales Hostiae*, p. 5, and the note of Mueller.
[2] Liv. II. 2. III. 39. VI. 41. XL. 42. Dionys. IV. 74. V. 1. Plut. Q. R. 60. Fest. s. v. *Sacrificulus*, p. 318. Varro L.L. VI § 13. 28. 31. Macrob. S. I. 15. Aul. Gell. XV. 27. Serv. ad Virg. Æn. VIII. 654. Orat. pre dom. 14. Ovid. Fast. I. 21. 323. V. 727.
[3] Cic. de Div. I. 2. II. 12. 18. 24. ad Fam. VI. 18.
[4] Frequently written *Feciales*. The orthography and etymology are alike uncertain.

including the preliminary demand for satisfaction, (*res repetere*,) as well as the actual denunciation of hostilities (*Clarigatio*.) Their chief was termed *Pater Patratus*, and was regarded as the representative of the whole Roman people in taking the oaths and performing the sacrifices which accompanied the conclusion of a treaty. When despatched to a distance for this purpose they carried with them certain sacred herbs called *Verbenae* or *Sagmina*, which were gathered on the Capitoline Hill, and which were considered as indispensable in their rites, and they took also their own flints for smiting the victim; thus at the close of the second Punic War—*Fetiales quum in Africam ad foedus feriendum ire iuberentur, ipsis postulantibus, Senatus-consultum in haec verba factum est: Ut privos lapides silices, privasque verbenas secum ferrent: uti Praetor Romanus his imperaret, ut foedus ferirent, illi Praetorem Sagmina poscerent. Herbae id genus ex arce sumtum dari fetialibus solet* (Liv. XXX. 43.)[1] The inferiority of the *Fetiales* to the four great Colleges is distinctly laid down in Tacitus, Ann. III. 64.

Curiones. Of these, thirty in number, as well as of the *Curio Maximus*, who was chief over all, we have already had occasion to speak (p. 61.) The ordinary *Curiones* were elected each by the *Curia* over the rites of which he presided, the *Curio Maximus* seems originally to have been elected by the *Comitia Curiata*, but in later times by the *Comitia Centuriata* or *Tributa*. The *Curiones* and the *Curio Maximus* must, in the earlier ages, have been all Patricians, but in B.C. 210, when the political significance of the *Curiae* had passed away, a Plebeian was, for the first time, chosen to fill the office of *Curio Maximus*.[2]

We now proceed to consider those Priests whose ministrations were confined to particular Gods. The most important were—1. *Flamines*. 2. *Salii*. 3. *Vestales*.

1. *Flamines*.

Flamines was a general name for certain Priests whose services were appropriated to one deity. There were in all fifteen *Flamines*, three *Maiores Flamines* instituted by Numa, who were at all times chosen from the Patricians, and twelve *Minores Flamines*, who might be taken from the Plebeians. The *Flamines* were, it would appear, originally nominated by the *Comitia Curiata*, but after the passing of the *Lex Domitia* (p. 326) by the Comitia Tributa in the manner described above. They were then presented to and received by (*capti*) the *Pontifex Maximus*, by whom, with the assistance of the *Augures*, their consecration (*Inauguratio*) was completed, and under ordinary circumstances they held office for life. The three *Maiores Flamines* were—1. *Flamen Dialis*, the priest of *Iovis*. 2. *Flamen Martialis*, the priest of *Mars*. 3. *Flamen Quirinalis*, the priest of *Quirinus*. First in honour was the—

Flamen Dialis. No one was eligible except the son of parents who had been united by *Confarreatio*, (p. 251,) a condition which applied probably to all the *Maiores Flamines*. When a vacancy occurred, three qualified candidates were named (*nominati—creati—destinati*) by the Comitia, and from these the new *Flamen Dialis* was selected (*captus*) by the *Pontifex Maximus*. He was assisted in his duties by a wife to whom he had been united by *Confarreatio*,

---

[1] Liv. I. 24 32. X. 45. XXXVI. 3. Dionys. II. 72. Cic. de Legg. II 9. Varro L.L. V, § 86. Non. Marcell. s. v. *Fetiales* p. 362. ed. Gerl. Aul. Gell. XVI. 4. Plin. H. N. XXII. 2.
[2] Dionys. II. 23. Liv. XXVII. 8.

MINISTERS OF RELIGION.

and who was termed *Flaminica*. Her aid was indispensable, and he was prohibited from marrying twice, so that if the *Flaminica* died her husband was obliged to resign. The privileges of the *Flamen Dialis* were numerous and important. As soon as he was formally admitted he was emancipated from parental control, (*Patria Potestas*, p. 247,) and became *Sui iuris*. He was entitled to a seat in the Senate, used the *Sella Curulis*, and wore the *Toga Praetexta*, but when sacrificing assumed, in common with other *Flamines*, a robe called *Laena*. His characteristic dress was a cap of a peculiar shape, termed *Albogalerus*, of which we annex a representation, and which it will be perceived, like the cap of all the higher priests terminated in a sharp point, formed of a spike of olive wood wreathed round with white wool. This peak was the *Apex*, a word applied frequently to denote the head-dress of any priest.

To counterbalance the advantages which he enjoyed, the *Flamen Dialis* was fettered by a multitude of restrictions and ceremonial observances enumerated by Aulus Gellius (X. 15.) Of these the most important was, that he was not permitted to quit the city even for a single night, and hence could never undertake any foreign command.

The office of *Flamen Dialis* was interrupted for seventy-six years, from the death of Merula in B.C. 87 until the consecration of Servius Maluginensis in B.C. 11. The duties during this interval were discharged by the *Pontifex Maximus*.

With regard to the *Flamines Minores* we are acquainted with the names of a few and nothing more, the attributes of the deities to whom some of them were attached being in several instances quite unknown. Thus we hear of the *Flamen Pomonalis—Carmentalis—Floralis—Volcanalis—Volturnalis—Furinalis—Palatualis—Falacer*, &c.;[1] but in what relation they stood to each other we cannot distinctly ascertain.

2. *Salii*.

In addition to the *Flamen Martialis*, a college of twelve priests of *Mars Gradivus*, was instituted by Numa. They were all chosen from the Patricians, and to their custody the twelve holy shields, called *Ancilia*, one of which was believed to have fallen from heaven, were committed. Every year, on the Kalends of March, and for several days following, they made a solemn progress through the city, chanting hymns (*Saliaria Carmina*) called *Axamenta*, and dancing sacred war dances—whence the name of *Salii*. On these occasions they were arrayed in an embroidered tunic, on their heads was the conical priest's cap, on their breasts a brazen cuirass, swords by their sides, spears or long wands in their right hands, while in their left they bore the *Ancilia*, which were sometimes suspended from their necks—*Salios duodecim Marti Gradivo legit*

---

[1] With regard to the *Flamen Dialis* and other *Flamines*, see Liv. I. 20. V. 52. Epit. XIX. XXVII. 8. XXIX. 38. XXX. 26. XXXI. 50. XXXVII. 51. Tacit. Ann. III. 58. 71. IV. 16. Dionys. II. 64. Plut. Num. 7. Q. R. 39. 43. 107. 108. Cic. de Legg. II. 8. Brut. I. 14. Philipp. II. 43. Orat. pro dom. 14. Velleius II. 20. 22. 43. Suet. Iul. 1. Octav. 31. Val. Max. I. i. 2. 4. VI. ix. 3. IX. xii. 5. Dion Cass. LIV. 36. Gaius I. § 112. 130. Aul. Gell. X. 15. XV. 27. Varro L.L. V. § 84. VII. § 44. Fest. s v. *Maximae dignationis* p. 154. Paul. Diac. s.v. *Maiores Flamines* p. 151. Serv. ad Virg. Æn. IV. 262. VIII. 664.

(sc. Numa) *tunicaeque pictae insigne dedit, et super tunicam aeneum pectori tegumen: coelestiaque arma, quae Ancilia adpellantur, ferre, ac per urbem ire canentes carmina cum tripudiis iussit.* Annexed is a denarius of Augustus, on the reverse of which are represented two of the *Ancilia*, with an *Apex* between them. The splendour of the banquet by which the solemnities terminated is commemorated both by Cicero and Horace, and indeed the phrases *Saliares dapes* and *Epulari Saliarem in modum* seem to have passed into a proverb. Different members of the college bore the titles of *Praesul*, *Vates*, and *Magister*.

In addition to the twelve *Salii* instituted by Numa, to whom the Ancilia were consigned, and whose sanctuary was on the Palatine, twelve other *Salii* were instituted by Tullus Hostilius, and these had their sanctuary on the Quirinal. Hence, for the sake of distinction, the former were sometimes designated *Salii Palatini*, the latter *Salii Agonales* s. *Agonenses* s. *Collini*.[1]

3. *Vestales.*

Institution. Numbers.—The *Vestales* were the Virgin Priestesses of Vesta, instituted we are told by Numa, although the legends with regard to the foundation of the city imply the existence of a similar sisterhood at Alba Longa. Two were originally chosen from the *Ramnes*, two from the *Tities*, and, subsequently, two from the *Luceres*, making up the number of six, which ever afterwards remained unchanged.

Qualifications. Mode of Election.—No one was eligible except a spotless Patrician maiden, perfect in all the members of her body, between the ages of six and ten, the child of parents free and free-born, who had been united in marriage by *Confarreatio* (p. 251.) The *Vestales* were originally nominated by the kings, but under the republic and the empire by the *Pontifex Maximus*, the technical phrase being CAPERE *Virginem Vestalem*. Towards the end of the commonwealth, in consequence of the unwillingness of parents to resign all control over their children, it became difficult to find individuals willing to accept the office, and a *Lex Papia* (Aul. Gell. I. 12) was enacted, in terms of which, when a vacancy occurred, the *Pontifex Maximus* was authorised to draw up a list of twenty damsels possessing the requisite qualifications, and one of these was publicly fixed upon by lot. The difficulty, however, seems to have increased, in consequence perhaps of the rite of *Confarreatio* having fallen into disuse, for we find that under Augustus even *libertinae* were admitted.

Period of Service. Duties.—The office was not necessarily for life, the length of service being fixed at thirty years. During the first ten, a *Vestalis* was supposed to be occupied in learning her duties, during the second ten in performing them, and during the last ten in giving instructions to the novices (*discipulae*.) During the whole of this time they were bound to remain pure and unwedded. When the full period had elapsed, the Vestal might, if she thought fit, return to the world, and even marry; but this rarely happened, and

---

[1] Liv. I. 20, 27. Dionys. II. 70, III. 32. Cic. de Div. I. 26, II. 66, de R. II. 14, ad Att. V. 9. Tacit. Ann. II. 83. Suet. Claud. 33. Capitolin vit. M. Anton. 4, 21. Paul Diac. s. v. *Aramenta*, p. 3. Quintil. I. O. I. vi. 40. Varro L. L. VI. § 14, VII. § 2, 26. Virg. Æn. 286, 663. Hor. C. I. xxxvii. 2, Epp. II. i. 86. Lucan. I. 603, IX. 478. Ovid. Fast. III. 387. Juv. S. II. 125.

MINISTERS OF RELIGION. 335

such unions were looked upon as of evil omen. The Senior was termed *Vestalis Maxima;* the three Seniors, *Tres Maximae*. Their chief duty was to watch and feed the ever burning flame which blazed upon the altar of Vesta, the extinction of which, although accidental, was regarded with great horror. They also cleansed and purified, each day, the temple of the Goddess, within the precincts of which they lived, guarding the sacred relics deposited in the penetralia; and in consequence of the inviolable character of the sanctuary, wills and other documents of importance were frequently lodged in their hands for safe custody. They also occupied a conspicuous place in all great public sacrifices, processions, games, and solemnities of every description.

Honours and Privileges.—The confinement and restrictions imposed upon the Vestals, were fully compensated by the distinctions they enjoyed. From the moment of their election they were emancipated from the *Patria Potestas* and became *Sui iuris*. In public they were treated with the most marked respect; they might go from place to place in a chariot; in later times a Lictor cleared the way before them; a seat of honour was reserved for them at the public shows; the Fasces of a Praetor or Consul were lowered to do them reverence; and if they met a criminal on his way to execution, he was reprieved.

Punishments for violation of Duty.—The Vestals were under the control and subject to the jurisdiction of the Pontifex Maximus. The two great offences which exposed them to condign punishment were—1. Permitting the sacred fire of Vesta to be extinguished through neglect. 2. Breaking their vow of chastity. In the first case the culprit was punished with stripes inflicted by the *Pontifex Maximus;* in the second, a terrible fate was reserved for the guilty one. She was buried alive in a spot called the *Campus Sceleratus*, close to the *Porta Collina* (p. 38.)[1]

Of less importance than the preceding were the—

Luperci, a very ancient Corporation, instituted, it is said, by Numa, who, on the 15th of February in each year, celebrated the festival of the *Lupercalia* in a sacred enclosure on the Palatine called *Lupercal*, the animals sacrificed being goats and dogs. The *Luperci* then stripped themselves naked, threw the skins of the slaughtered goats over their shoulders, and with thongs in their hands cut from the hides, ran through the most frequented parts of the city, smiting all whom they encountered, the blow being believed to possess a purifying influence. Marcus Antonius is taunted by Cicero with having exhibited himself in this guise when Consul, and this was the occasion when he offered a diadem to Caesar. The *Lupercal* was popularly supposed to mark the den of the wolf which suckled Romulus and Remus; and the later Romans considered that the ceremonies belonged to the worship of the Arcadian Pan. The *Luperci* were divided into two Colleges, termed respectively the *Fabii* s. *Fabiani* and the *Quinctilii* s. *Quinctiliani*. The legend invented to account for these names will be found, together with many other details concerning the *Luperci* and the *Lupercalia*, in Ovid. Fast. II. 267—426, comp. V. 101.[2]

[1] On the *Vestales*, see Liv. I. 3. 20. IV. 44. VIII. 15. XXII. 57. XXVI. 1. XXVIII. 11. Plut. Num. 10. Tib. Gracch. 15. Q. R. 93. Dion Cass. XXXVII. 45. XLVII. 19. XLVIII. 37. 46. LIV. 24. LV. 22. LVI. 10. LXV. 18. LXVII. 3. LXXVII. 16. fragm. Peiresc. XCI. XCII. Val. Max. I. i. 6. 7. V. iv. 6. Cic. de Legg. II. 8. 12. pro Muren. 35. Ovid. Fast. III. 11. IV. 639. Tacit. Ann. I. 8. III. 64. 69. IV. 16. XI. 32. Hist. III. 81. IV. 53. Suet. Iul. 83. Octav. 31. 44. 101. Tib. 2. 76. Vitell. 16. Domit. 8. Senec. Controv. VI. de Vit. beat. 29. de Provid. 5. Gaius I. § 145. Plin. Epp. IV. 11. Aul. Gell. I. 12. VI. 7. X. 15. Festus s.v. *Probrum virginis Vestalis*, p. 241. *Sceleratus Campus*, p. 333.
[2] See also Virg. Æn. VIII. 343. and note of Servius. Liv. I. 5. Cic. Philipp. II. 34. Plut. Caes. 61. Suet. Iul. 79. Octav. 31. Paul. Diac. s.v. *Faviani et Quintiliani* p. 87. Fest. p. 257. whose text is much mutilated in this place.

Potitii et Pinarii.—These, according to the legend, were two illustrious families dwelling nigh the Palatine at the time when the *Ara Maxima* was raised to Hercules by Evander, and were by him appointed to minister at that shrine. Of these, the *Pinarii*, who became extinct at an early epoch, were, from the first, through their own neglect, inferior to, and merely assistants of, the *Potitii*, who for many ages continued to act as priests of the Hero-God—*Potitii ab Evandro edocti, antistites sacri eius per multas aetates fuerunt* (Liv. I. 7.) But in B.C. 312, having, by the advice of Appius, the Censor, given instructions to public slaves, in order that they might delegate to them the performance of the sacred rites, the whole race (*genus omne*) was cut off in one year, and Appius himself, not long afterwards, was stricken with blindness.[1]

Sodales Titii.—There was in ancient times a College of Priests bearing this appellation. Tacitus in one place (Ann. I. 54.) says that they were instituted by Titus Tatius for the purpose of keeping up the Sabine ritual, (*retinendis Sabinorum sacris,*) and in another, (Hist. II. 95.) that they were instituted by Romulus in memory of Tatius. The account of Varro is totally different (L.L. V. § 85. comp. Lucan. I. 602.) The *Titii Sodales* are said to have suggested the idea of the

Sodales Augustales, first instituted A.D. 14, in honour of the deified Augustus, the number being twenty-five, of whom twenty-one were taken by lot from the leading men of the state, and Tiberius, Drusus, Claudius, and Germanicus were added to make up the number (Tacit. Ann. I. 54.) Similar Colleges were instituted in honour of other emperors, so that we read in inscriptions of *Sodales Claudiales, Sodales Flaviales, Sodales Titiales Flaviales, Sodales Hadrianales,* &c. In addition to these Corporations, we find that a single individual priest also was sometimes nominated, who, under the title of *Flamen Augustalis,* devoted himself to similar duties.[2]

General Remarks on the Roman Priests.

Several points connected with the Roman Priests deserve particular attention. Some of these can be inferred from the statements made above, but it may be useful to exhibit them in one view.

1. They did not form an exclusive class or caste, nor was any preliminary education or training requisite. Persons were elected at once to the highest offices in the priesthood who had never before performed any sacred duties.

2. Sacred and Civil offices were not incompatible, but might be held together. Thus P. Licinius Crassus being *Pontifex Maximus,* was also *Censor* in B.C. 210 (Liv. XXVII. 6.) Q. Fabius Pictor was *Praetor* and *Flamen Quirinalis* in B.C. 189, (Liv. XXXVII. 50;) and of the two Consuls in B.C. 131, P. Licinius Crassus was also *Pontifex Maximus,* and L. Valerius Flaccus was *Flamen Martialis.*

3. Two of the higher priesthoods might be held together. Thus Ti. Sempronius Longus was in the same year (B.C. 210) chosen *Augur* and also *Xvir Sacris faciundis,* (Liv. XXVII. 6;) Q. Fabius Maximus, who died in B.C. 203, was at once an *Augur* and a *Pontifex,* (Liv. XXX. 26;) C. Servilius Geminus, who died in B.C. 180, was both *Pontifex Maximus* and *Xvir Sacrorum* (Liv. XL. 42.)

4. No qualification as to age was insisted upon. Mature years were, indeed,

[1] Liv. I. 7. IX. 29. Dionys. I. 40. Virg. Æn. VIII. 269. and note of Servius.
[2] Tacit. Ann. I. 54. III. 64. Suet. Claud. 6. Galb. 8. Dion Cass. LVI. 45. LVIII. 12. LIX. 7—11. Orelli. C. I. L. 3944. 364. 2432. 918. 3186. 2761.

at first required (Dionys. II. 21.) and for a long period, very young men were seldom chosen. Thus in B.C. 204, we are told that Ti. Sempronius Gracchus was elected *Augur—Admodum adolescens, quod tunc perrarum in mandandis sacerdotiis erat* (Liv. XXXIX. 38. comp. XXV. 5.) Again, in B.C. 196—*Q. Fabius Maximus Augur mortuus est admodum adolescens, priusquam ullum magistratum caperet* (Liv. XXXIII. 42.) In B.C. 180, Q. Fulvius was chosen *IIIvir Epulo* while still *Praetextatus*, that is before he had assumed the manly gown; and Julius Cæsar was elected *Flamen Dialis* at the age of seventeen (Velleius II. 43. Suet. Iul. 1.)

5. All the higher priests were originally chosen from the Patricians exclusively, but after the Plebeians had been by law admitted to the Pontificate and the Augurate, it is probable that all class distinctions were abolished, except in the case of the *Rex Sacrificus*, the three *Maiores Flamines*, the *Salii*, and the *Virgines Vestales*, who were at all times necessarily Patricians, probably because none were eligible except *Patrimi et Matrimi*, that is, the children of parents who had been united by *Confarreatio*, (p. 251.) a rite which appears to have been confined to Patricians.

6. It appears certain, that, originally, all priests were appointed by the Kings. In the earlier ages of the republic, the members of the four great Colleges, and probably of all priestly Colleges, were nominated by *Cooptatio;* but this system was, in all the more important Corporations, set aside by the *Lex Domitia*. The *Vestales*, and perhaps some of the *Flamens*, were selected (*capiebantur*) by the *Pontifex Maximus;* some other priests were chosen (*creati*) by the *Comitia Curiata;* but in every case, formal admission or consecration was a ceremony never dispensed with, and since this could not be performed without taking the auspices, it was termed *Inauguratio*. Generally speaking, the *Inauguratio* followed the election as a matter of course, for if the auspices were unfavourable at first, fresh observations were made, and fresh sacrifices offered, until the Gods were propitiated. When Julius Cæsar, however, was elected *Flamen Dialis*, his *Inauguratio* was stopped by Sulla.

7. As a general rule, after a priest **was** consecrated, his office was held for life. In the *Augurs*, as stated above, the character was absolutely indelible; and we are assured by Pliny (H.N. XVIII. 2.) that the same was the case with the *Fratres Arvales*. Augustus, when he stripped Lepidus of all power, did not venture to deprive him of the office of *Pontifex Maximus*, which was retained by him, though in exile, until his death. One of the higher *Flamens*, however, might be forced to resign, (Val. Max. I. 1. 4.) and the *Flamen Dialis* was at once disqualified by the death of the *Flaminica*. A Vestal also, when the thirty years of her service had expired, might unconsecrate herself, (*exaugurare se*,) and return to the world.

8. In so far as formal precedence was concerned, the *Rex Sacrificus* ranked first; next came the *Flamen Dialis;* the *Flamen Martialis* was third; the *Flamen Quirinalis* fourth; and the *Pontifex Maximus* occupied the fifth place only. There is no doubt, however, that the *Pontifex Maximus* stood first in real power, and exercised authority over all the others. [1]

III. Worship of the Gods.

The worship of the Gods consisted of two parts:—
A. *Prayers*. B. *Offerings*.

[1] Festus s v. *Ordo Sacerdotum*, p 185. Liv II. 2. Epit. XIX. XXXV II. 51. Cic. Philipp. XI. 8. Tacit. Ann. III. 59.

A. Prayers.

Prayers, for which the general term is *Preces* s. *Precationes*, might be either private or public, that is, they might either be offered up by individuals on behalf of themselves and of their friends, or on behalf of the community at large. Private prayers might be of a general character, simple requests for the favour and protection of Heaven, (*preces*,) or they might be thanksgiving for special benefits received, (*gratiarum actiones—gratulationes*,) or they might be appeals to the deity, entreating him to avert or stop some calamity impending or in progress (*obsecrationes*.) When prayers had reference to the future, they were generally accompanied by a promise on the part of the suppliant, that, if his request were complied with, he would perform some act in return. A prayer of this description was called *Votum*, the worshipper was said *Vota facere—suscipere—nuncupare—concipere—votis caput obligare*, and to be—*Voti religione obstrictus*. When the prayer was accomplished, he became *Voti compos*, and at the same time *Voti reus* s. *Voti damnatus*, i.e. a debtor for his part of the obligation; and in discharging this debt he was said—*Vota solvere—exsolvere—persolvere—reddere—exsequi—Voto jungi*, and was then *Voto liberatus*. It was not uncommon to commit a *Votum* to writing, such a document being a *Votiva Tabella*,[1] and to attach it with wax to the knee of the deity addressed; and hence Juvenal, (S. x. 55.) when speaking of the things which men chiefly desire, characterizes them as those

> Propter quae fas est genua incerare deorum.

Public prayers, termed *Supplicationes* s. *Supplicia*, were offered in the temples thrown open for the purpose, or, occasionally, in the streets, and were addressed sometimes to one, sometimes to several divinities, according to the *edictum* of the Senate, of the magistrate, or of the priest by whom they were ordained. They might be either *obsecrationes* or *gratulationes*, and were not unfrequently combined with the feast called a *Lectisternium*.[2]

Supplicatio is often employed in a restricted sense to denote a public thanksgiving, voted by the Senate in honour of a victory achieved by a General at the head of his army, and such a *Supplicatio*, especially towards the close of the republic, was very frequently the forerunner of a Triumph (Cic. ad Fam. XV. 5.) The period during which the festivities were to continue was fixed by the *Senatus-Consultum*, and was understood to bear a relation to the importance of the exploit and the character of the commander. In the earlier ages, one, two, or three days were common; upon the taking of Veii the *Supplicatio* lasted for four—*Senatus in quatriduum, quot dierum nullo ante bello, supplicationes decernit* (Liv. V. 23.) Subsequently five days became not unusual, but towards the close of the commonwealth we hear of *Supplicationes* extending to ten, fifteen, twenty, forty, and even fifty days.[3] On one occasion only was a thanksgiving of this nature decreed in honour of a citizen holding no military command,

---

[1] *Tabella*, or *Tabula Votiva*, may also denote a picture hung up in a temple in discharge of a *Votum*: such were often vowed by the mariner in the hour of danger, and afterwards presented to commemorate his escape. So *Votivus sanguis—Votiva iuvenca—Votiva tura—Votiva carmina—Votivi ludi*—denote offerings of various kinds promised by a vow.

[2] Numerous Examples of *Supplicationes* will be found in Livy, e.g. III. 7. V. 21. VII. 28. X. 23. XXI. 62. XXII. 10. XXIV. 11. XXVII. 7. 23. XXX. 17. 42. XXXI. 8. 22. XXXVIII. 36. XL. 28. XLI. 28. XLV. 2.

[3] Liv. XXX. 21. XXXIII. 24. XXXV. 40. Cic. de prov. cons. 10. 11. Philipp. XIV. 11. 14. Caes. B. G. II. 35. IV. 38. VII. 90. Suet. Caes. 24.

(*togatus,*) of Cicero, namely, after the suppression of the Catilinarian conspiracy.¹

Forms observed in Praying.—When an individual was about to give utterance to a prayer, he covered his head with his garment, raised his right hand to his lips, (hence the verb *adoro,*) made a complete turn with his body, moving towards the right—*in adorando dextram ad osculum referimus totumque corpus circumagimus* ²—and sank upon his knees, or prostrated himself to the earth, his face towards the East, or if in a temple, towards the sanctuary, and at the same time laid hold of the horns of the altar, or embraced the knees of the God. In the act of prayer the hands were turned up or down according as the deity addressed was one of the celestials, or belonged to the nether world.

Words of the Prayer.—The utmost importance was attached to the phraseology employed, because it was universally believed that the words themselves possessed a certain efficacy altogether independent of the feelings entertained by the suppliant. Hence, when a magistrate was offering up a public prayer for the whole community, he was usually attended by one of the *Pontifices* who dictated (*praeire verba*) the proper expressions, for any mistake in this respect might have entailed the wrath of heaven upon the whole State. It was the practice to call in the first place upon Janus, as the power who presided over the beginning of all things; then upon Jupiter, as lord supreme; then upon the God or Gods specially addressed; and, finally, to wind up by an invocation of the whole heavenly host, or of all who presided over some particular department of nature, as when Virgil, at the opening of his Georgics, after naming the chief patrons of the labours of the husbandman, concludes by an appeal to—*Dique Deaeque omnes studium quibus arva tueri*. Moreover, when a God had several titles, these were carefully enumerated, lest that one might have been passed over in which he principally delighted—*Matutine pater, seu Iane libentius audis*—and the person who prayed usually guarded himself against the consequence of omission by adding—*aut quocunque alio nomine rite vocaris*—or some such phrase.

B. *Offerings.*

Offerings to the Gods may be classed under four heads,—

1. Those which were of a permanent character, the *Donaria* of the Romans, the ἀναθήματα of the Greeks. 2. Those which passed away and were destroyed at the very moment when they were offered to the deity, such were properly termed *Sacrificia.* 3. Banquets (*Epulae.*) 4. Games (*Ludi.*)

Donaria.—These were gifts presented to the Gods and deposited in their shrines, by individuals or by public bodies, or by whole nations, who thus hoped to give efficacy to their prayers, to display their gratitude for benefits received, or to fulfil a vow. The things dedicated were of a very multifarious character; any object remarkable for its beauty, its rarity, or its magnificence, being regarded as an acceptable present. In this way the Temples of Greece and Rome, especially of the former, were crowded with gorgeous statues, pictures, tapestry, richly chased plate, and other costly works of art, while a considerable portion of the plunder gained in war was almost invariably disposed of in this manner. Frequently, however, *Donaria* possessed no intrinsic value, and served

---

¹ Cic. in Cat. III. 15. IV. 10. pro Sull. 30. in Pison 3. Philipp. II. 6. Quintil. II. 16.
² Plin. H. N. XXVIII. 5. comp. Plaut. Curc. L i. 70. Suet. Vitell. 2. Macrob. S. III. 2.

merely to commemorate some remarkable epoch in the life of the worshipper, when he felt peculiarly called upon to acknowledge the power and sue for the protection of the God. Thus boys when they assumed the manly gown (*Toga virilis*) hung up to the *Lares*, the *Bulla*, which had served as an amulet to save their childhood from the terrors of the Evil Eye; maidens when entering upon womanhood dedicated their dolls (*Pupae*) to Venus; the shipwrecked sailor suspended his dripping garments in the shrine of Neptune, and fixed to the walls a picture representing his disaster;[1] while the convalescent who had been relieved from a grievous malady, placed in the temple of Aesculapius a *Tabula Votiva*, detailing the symptoms by which he had been afflicted, and the process of cure, or, if the affection had been external, a model of the diseased member executed in the precious metals.

Donaria does not occur in the singular number. Judging from the analogy of *Sacrarium, Lararium,* and similar words, it must signify properly *a receptacle for gifts*, that portion of temples set apart for gifts, the θησαυροί of the Greeks, and in fact, in the purest authors it is employed in the general sense of *a temple* or *an altar*, e.g.—*uris = Imparibus ductos alta ad donaria currus* (Virg. G. III. 533.)—*Si tua contigimus manibus donaria puris* (Ovid. Fast. III. 335.)

Sacrificia.—Sacrifices, properly so called, may be divided into two classes, according as the objects offered were inanimate or animate, that is, bloodless or bloody sacrifices.

Bloodless offerings consisted for the most part of the first-fruits of the earth, (*frugum primitiae*,) of flowers, cakes, (*liba*,) honey, milk, wine, salt, and above all, frankincense, (*tus*,) for without the perfumed smoke arising from fragrant gums no sacred rite was regarded as complete and acceptable.

Bloody offerings consisted of animals of all kinds, which were put to death with certain solemnities, and were comprehended under the general designations of *Victimae* or *Hostiae*. These were usually the ordinary domestic animals, oxen, sheep, goats, and swine, but various other living creatures were offered, and even human victims, in the earlier ages at least of Greece and Rome, were by no means uncommon.[2] Full grown victims, such as bulls, cows, rams, ewes, boars, and sows, were termed *Hostiae Maiores;* those which had not come to maturity, such as calves, lambs, kids, or young pigs, *Hostiae lactentes* (Cic. de Legg. II. 12. Liv. XXII. 1.) Particular animals were believed to be particularly grateful to particular Gods; the bull, for example, to Jupiter, the goat to Bacchus, the sow to Ceres, the ass to Priapus, and a knowledge of all matters connected with the sex, age, colour, and other circumstances which rendered each victim an appropriate offering to the power which it was wished to propitiate, formed an important department of priestly lore—*Iam illud ex institutis Pontificum et Haruspicum non mutandum est, quibus hostiis immolandum cuique Deo, cui maioribus, cui lactentibus, cui maribus, cui feminis* (Cic. de Legg. II. 12. compare the quotation from Livy, in p. 327.) Upon ordinary occasions only one animal was sacrificed at once, but sometimes large numbers of the same

---

[1] Thus Horace, when congratulating himself on escape from danger of another kind, exclaims figuratively—*Me Tabula sacer = Votiva paries indicat uvida = Suspendisse potenti = Vestimenta maris Deo.* C. I v. 13.

[2] There seems to be little doubt that as late as B.C. 216, four human beings—*Gallus et Galla, Graecus et Graeca*—were, in order to propitiate the Gods, buried alive in the *Forum Boarium* where similar rites had been performed at an earlier epoch (Liv. XXII 57.) The immolation of two of the soldiers of Julius Caesar to Mars, narrated by Dion Cassius, (XLII. 24,) ought perhaps to be regarded as an exercise of military discipline, invested with awful solemnities, rather than as a sacrifice in the proper acceptation of the term.

RELIGION OF THE ROMANS—SACRIFICES. 341

kind, as in the ἑκατόμβη of the Greeks, sometimes several of different kinds, as in the sacrifice offered by the Romans whenever purifications took place upon a large scale, and called *Suovetaurilia* s. *Solitaurilia*, because it consisted of a sow, a sheep, and a bull. The animals selected for sacrifice were always such as were perfect in form and free from all blemish. Bulls and heifers destined for this purpose were usually set apart from the time of their birth (*aris servare sacros*) and exempted from all agricultural labours (*Hostiae iniuges—intacta cervice iuvencae*.) The victims commonly employed in the public solemnities in honour of Capitoline Jove were milk white steers from Umbria, and we find numerous allusions in the classics to the herds which fed on the banks of the Clitumnus, a region rendered famous by producing this valued breed of cattle (e.g. Iuv. S. XII. 13.)

Forms observed in offering Sacrifice. — No important undertaking, whether affecting the whole community, public bodies, or individuals, was ever commenced without offering sacrifice, and hence the division into *Sacrificia Publica* and *Sacrificia Privata*. We shall describe the various ceremonies of a Public Sacrifice when offered on behalf of the State, many of these being, of course, omitted or modified in domestic and private worship.

The persons actively engaged were—

1. The individual by whom the sacrifice was offered, who would in this case be one of the Consuls, a Praetor, a General about to set out on foreign service, or some other high official personage, acting as representative of the people.

2. One of the *Pontifices*, and, in the case of sacrifices to Iupiter, Mars, or Quirinus, one of the higher *Flamines*, by whom the performance of all the rites would be directed and superintended.

3. Various assistants of the *Pontifex*, termed VICTIMARII, POPAE, CULTRARII, &c., whose duty it was to bring the victim up to the altar, to slaughter and dismember it, and to perform all the menial offices.

4. An *Haruspex* to inspect the entrails.

5. A *Tibicen* to play upon the flute during the progress of the rites.[1]

6. A *Praeco*.

7. In certain cases the officiating priest was assisted by a CAMILLUS, i.e. a free-born youth, the son of parents who had been united by *Confarreatio*, (*puer patrimus et matrimus*,) p. 251.

On great occasions, in addition to the ordinary crowd, there would be a throng of Senators, magistrates, and other dignitaries.

All who took a part in the performance of the rites were required previously to purify themselves by bathing in a running stream, to appear in fair white garments, wearing on their brows chaplets (*coronae*) formed from the leaves of the tree or plant believed to be most acceptable to the deity at whose shrine the act of homage was performed. All the priests present wore on their heads the sacred band of white wool, (*infula*,) wreathed round with white ribbons, (*vittae*,) and a similar decoration was attached to the victim and to the altar. When all things were ready, the public crier (*praeco*) commanded the assembled multitude to preserve a solemn silence, (*ut linguis faveret*,) the persons offering the sacrifice washed their hands in pure water, veiled their heads with their robes, in order that no ill-omened sight might meet their eyes, while the flute-player (*tibicen*) played a solemn strain, in order that no ill-omened sound might fall upon their ears. The victim, adorned with *serta* and *vittae*, and with gilded

---
[1] How indispensable the presence of *Tibicines* for the due performance of sacred rites appears from the whimsical story in Liv. IX. 30.

horns, was now led up by the *Popae* gently to the altar, if possible with a slack rope, all violence being carefully avoided, for an unwilling sacrifice was believed to be distasteful to the Gods, and hence any reluctance on the part of the animal was regarded as of evil augury. The sacrificer then repeated a form of prayer dictated by the *Pontifex;* wine, incense, and the flour of *Far*, mixed with salt, (*mola—mola salsa—fruges salsae,*) were sprinkled upon its head, with the words *Macte hoc vino et ture esto,*[1] and a few hairs were cut off from between the horns, and thrown upon the altar. The sacrificer repeated a form of prayer dictated by the *Pontifex*, and the *Popa* then asked the officiating priest whether he should proceed, using the established form—*Agone?* if he received the expected and appropriate reply—*Hoc Age*—he struck down the victim with a mallet, (*malleus,*) and then stabbed it with a knife (*culter.*) The blood was received in a basin, and poured upon the altar, together with wine, incense, and sacred cake (*libum—feretum.*) The victim was now cut up, and the entrails examined by the Haruspex; (*exta consulebat;*) if the appearances presented were favourable, (*exta bona,*) then the sacrificer was pronounced to have presented an acceptable offering, (*litâsse,*) but if any thing unusual or unnatural presented itself, (*exta tristia,*) then it was held necessary that another victim should be slaughtered, (*sacrificium instaurabatur,*) and this was, if necessary, repeated until the desired result was obtained. The priest then sprinkled the choicest portions of the entrails with meal, wine, and incense, and threw the whole upon the flames.[2] The portions of the victims so presented were called—*praesecta* s. *prosiciae* s. *ablegmina*,—the priest in presenting them was said—*exta pollucere* s. *porricere* s. *obmovere*—*aris exta imponere*, and all the ceremonies between the slaughtering of the victims and the solemn presentation of the entrails, were said to take place *inter caesa et porrecta*. Another prayer or invocation was then made by the *Pontifex*, who finally dismissed the multitude by pronouncing the word *Ilicet*. It would appear that from time to time during the progress of the rites, fresh libations of wine were poured upon the altar, and additional incense thrown upon the flames.

The flesh of the victim was never, under ordinary circumstances, consumed on the altar, but was reserved for a family feast in private sacrifices, and for a priestly banquet (*epulae sacrificales—polluctum*) on public occasions.

There were certain distinctions observed in the forms of sacrificing to the Celestial Gods (*Di Superi*) and to the Gods of the Nether World (*Di Inferi*.)

In sacrificing to the Celestial Gods, the ceremonies were performed by day. The altar was placed upon the surface of the ground; the sacrificer was arrayed in white robes, and when he prayed, raised his hands to heaven; the victims were, if possible, white; when slaughtered, the neck was turned upwards, and the knife thrust in from above, (*imponebatur,*) the blood was poured upon the altar, and the entrails alone were consumed.

In sacrifices to the Gods of the Nether World, (*Inferiae,*) all these circumstances were, as far as possible, reversed. The ceremonies were performed by night; the altar was placed in a trench; the sacrificer wore black garments, and prayed with his hands turned down; the victims were always of a dark colour; when slaughtered, the head was turned down, and the knife thrust in from below, (*supponebatur,*) the blood was poured into the trench, and the

---

[1] See Cato R. R. 132, 134, 139. Serv. ad Virg. Æn. ix. 641. Paul Diac. s v. *Mactus*, p. 125. Hence the verbs MACTARE and IMMOLARE are used in the general sense of *To offer in sacrifice*.
[2] When sacrifice was offered to sea or river Gods, the entrails were cast into the waves or a stream.

RELIGION OF THE ROMANS—SACRED UTENSILS.

whole animal was consumed, because it was held unlawful to turn to the service of man any object which had been devoted to the infernal powers. Even the libations were made in a different manner. In one case, the ladle (*patera*) was held with the palm of the hand turned upwards, (*manu supina*,) and the wine was poured out by a forward inclination; in the other, the hand was inverted, and the *patera* turned upside down,—the former act was termed *Libare*, the latter *Delibare*.

Sacred Utensils.—We shall give a list of these, accompanied by illustrations of the different objects, some of which have been placed at the end of Chapters VIII. and IX.

Acerra s. *Turibulum* s. *Arcula Turaria*.—The box in which incense was contained and brought to the altar. It must not be confounded with the Censer employed in Jewish rites, a vessel in which incense was consumed. Hor. C. III. viii. 2. Virg. Æn. V. 744. Ovid. Epp. ex P. IV. viii. 39. Pers. S. II. 5. comp. Paul. Diac. s.v. p. 18. Cic. de Legg. II.24. See (1) p. 240.

Patera s. *Patella* signifies generally *a flat plate* or *shallow saucer*; but in connection with sacrifices denotes a ladle with or without a handle, used for pouring libations of wine upon the altar. Many *paterae*, formed of earthenware and bronze, have been preserved, and may be seen in all considerable collections. See (2) p. 240.

Simpuvium s. *Simpulum* is defined by Paulus Diacon. s.v. p. 337, to be— *Vas parvulum non dissimile cyatho, quo vinum in sacrificiis libabatur*. It is very frequently represented on coins and other ancient monuments, and being always of small size, gave rise to the proverb, *excitare fluctus in simpulo*, i.e. to make much ado about nothing. Varro L.L. V. § 124. et ap. Non. s.v. *Simpuvium* p. 375. ed. Gerl. Cic. de Orat. II. 51. de Legg. III. 16. See (3) p. 240.

Guttus.—A bottle with a long narrow neck, used for the same purpose as the *patera* and the *simpulum*. Varro L.L. V. § 124. Plin. H.N. XVI. 38. An excellent representation is given on the first of the two large coins engraved in the next page.

Praefericulum is defined to be—*Vas aeneum sine ansa patens summum, velut pelvis quo ad sacrificia utebantur*. Festus and Paul. Diac. s.v. p. 248. 249.

Adspergillum is a word not found in any classical author, but is used by writers on antiquities to denote an object very frequently represented in connection with Roman sacrifices, and which was evidently a sort of brush used for sprinkling. See (4) p. 240.

Secespita, *Culter*, *Securis*, all denote knives and axes employed in slaughtering and disembowelling the victims. Several instruments of this kind, varying in shape, are frequently represented on coins and bas reliefs; but it is extremely difficult to decide which of them was the *Secespita*, notwithstanding the definition, unfortunately mutilated, of it given by Festus (s.v. p. 348.) after Antestius Labeo, and by Paulus Diaconus (s.v. p. 336.) Comp. Serv. Virg. Æn. IV. 262. and Sueton. Tib. 25. See p. 315.

On the denarius of Nero, figured in page 206, are represented a *Simpulum*, a *Tripus*, a *Patera*, and a *Lituus*, the first being generally regarded as the symbol of the *Pontificatus*, the second of *XVviratus*, the third of *VIIviratus*, and the fourth of the *Auguratus*. On the Denarius of Cæsar, of which a cut is annexed, are represented a *Simpulum*, a *Securis* or *Dolabra*, an *Aspergillum*, and the *Apex*, the symbol of the *Flaminium*. On the Aureus of Augustus, of which also we annex a cut, we see the *Simpulum* and the *Lituus*,

while on the reverse, the founder of a new colony is represented marking out the holy circuit of the walls with a plough. (See pp. 4, 88.)

On the first of the coins figured below, which is the reverse of a large brass of M. Aurelius, are represented a *Simpulum*, a *Lituus*, a *Guttus*, an *Aspergillum*, and a *Culter* or *Secespita*.

On the second, which is the reverse of a large brass of Caligula, the Emperor is represented sacrificing at an altar placed before the portico of a temple, with a *patera* in his hand, and with his head covered; (*capite velato*;) in front of him is a *Popa*, naked to the waist, holding the victim, and at his side a *Camillus*, bearing, perhaps, a *Praefericulum*, or some such vessel.

Lances were large plates or dishes employed at banquets and at sacrifices, upon which the viands or portions of the victims were laid, as when Virgil, in describing rich soil, declares

> hic fertilis uvae,
> Hic laticis, qualem pateris libamus et auro,
> Inflavit quum pinguis ebur Tyrrhenus ad aras
> Lancibus et pandis fumantia reddimus exta,—G. II. 191.

Banquets.—*Epulum. Epulae.*—Every year, during the *Ludi Romani*, and at other periods also, a feast termed *Epulum Jovis* was spread in the Capitol. The statue of Jupiter was placed at table in a reclining posture, while those of Juno and Minerva sat upright on each side of him, Senators being admitted to share in the banquet.[1] Moreover, the temples of many Gods, probably of all belonging to the highest class, contained couches or sofas termed *Pulvinaria*, and it was not uncommon for the Senate in seasons of great exultation or depression, to order the statues of some or of all these deities to be laid upon the couches in pairs, and banquets to be served up to them, either in the temples themselves or in some place of public resort, and such a solemnity was termed *Lectisternium*. The first display of this kind is said to have taken place B.C. 399, during the ravages of a pestilence, in obedience to an injunction contained

[1] Aul. Gell. III. 8. XII. 8. Val. Max. II. i. 1. 2. Liv. XXXI. 4. XXXIII. 42. XXXVIII. 57. Cic. de Orat. III. 19. Orat. de Haruspic. resp. 10. Arnob. VII. 32. Dion Cass. XLVIII. 52.

in the Sibylline books—*Duumviri sacris faciundis*, LECTISTERNIO *tunc primum in urbe Romana facto, per dies octo Apollinem Latonamque, Dianam et Herculem, Mercurium atque Neptunum tribus, quam amplissime tum apparari poterat, stratis lectis placavere* (Liv. V. 13.)—*Tum Lectisternium per triduum habitum, Decemviris Sacrorum curantibus. Sex pulvinaria in conspectu fuere: Iovi ac Iunoni unum: alterum Neptuno ac Minervae: tertium Marti ac Veneri: quartum Apollini ac Dianae: quintum Vulcano ac Vestae: sextum Mercurio ac Cereri* (Liv. XXII. 10. B.C. 217.)—*In foris publicis ubi Lectisternium erat, Deorum capita, quae in lectis erant, averterunt se* (Liv. XL. 59. B.C. 179.)

The above passages, it will be observed, all refer to extraordinary solemnities of rare occurrence; for although the first *Lectisternium* was celebrated in B.C. 399, there were only three others during the next seventy years; (Liv. VIII. 25;) but it would appear that as early as B.C. 191, *Lectisternia* formed part of the ordinary worship of certain Gods, and were going on during the greater part of the year—*P. Cornelium Cn. filium Scipionem et M'. Acilium Glabrionem Consules, inito magistratu, Patres, priusquam de provinciis agerent, res divinas facere maioribus hostiis iusserunt in omnibus fanis,* IN QUIBUS LECTISTERNIUM MAIOREM PARTEM ANNI FIERI SOLET . . . *ea omnia sacrificia laeta fuerunt, primisque hostiis perlitatum est* (Liv. XXXVI. 1; the words printed in capitals occur again in XLII. 30.)

A *Supplicatio* was frequently combined with a *Lectisternium;* and it is probable that the latter is always implied when we meet with such expressions as— *Decretum, ut quinque dies circa omnia pulvinaria supplicaretur* (Liv. XXX. 21.)—*Quoniam ad omnia pulvinaria supplicatio decreta est* (Cic. in Cat. III. 10.)—*Miro certamine procerum decernuntur supplicationes ad omnia pulvinaria* (Tacit. Ann. XIV. 12.)

Sellisternium.—Since it was the practice for women among the Romans to sit and not to recline at meals, when a banquet was presented to female deities alone, it was denominated not *Lectisternium*, but *Sellisternium*.[1]

Convivium Publicum, a public banquet, was also a religious rite, connected sometimes with a *Lectisternium,* sometimes with other solemnities; but the expression is not always employed in the same sense. It occasionally signifies an exercise of hospitality on the part of all householders who prepared repasts, threw open their doors, and invited all who passed by to partake. Thus Livy, after recording the first *Lectisternium* in the words quoted above from V. 13, proceeds—*Privatim quoque id sacrum celebratum est. Tota urbe patentibus ianuis, promiscuoque usu rerum omnium in propatulo posito notos ignotosque passim advenas in hospitium ductos ferunt.* Again, when we read (Liv. XXII. 1. B.C. 217)—*Postremo Decembri iam mense ad aedem Saturni Romae immolatum est, lectisterniumque imperatum (et eum lectum Senatores straverunt) et convivium publicum*—it may be a matter of doubt whether the Senate enjoined the citizens in general to keep open house, or voted a sum of money from the public funds for a repast, of which all who thought fit might partake at that festive season. Again, the *Epulum Iovis,* to which Senators were admitted, might be regarded, in a restricted sense, as a *Convivium Publicum;* and lastly, the magnificent entertainments given in the forum or some temple by persons of wealth, especially towards the close of the republic, in which large bodies of

---

[1] Val. Max. II. i. 2. Tacit. Ann. XV. 44. Festus s.v. *Solla*, p. 298. Serv. ad Virg. Æn. III. 176.

their friends, and sometimes the community at large, were the guests, fell under the head of *Convivia Publica*. These frequently formed part of funeral solemnities, (*epulum funebre*,) as, for example, that given by Q. Maximus on the death of Africanus, to which he invited the whole Roman people—*Quum epulum Q. Maximus Africani patrui sui nomine populo Romano daret* (Cic. pro Muren. 36;) and that in honour of P. Licinius Crassus, who had been *Pontifex Maximus*, of which Livy says (XXXIX. 46. B.C. 183)—*P. Licinii funeris causa visceratio data, et gladiatores CXX pugnaverunt, et ludi funebres per triduum facti, post ludos Epulum. In quo, quum toto foro strata triclinia essent*, &c. So Julius Cæsar—*Adiecit epulum, et viscerationem ac, post Hispaniensem victoriam, duo prandia;* (Sueton. Caes. 38;) and in Africa, upon the accession of Otho—*Crescens Neronis libertus Epulum plebi ob laetitiam recentis imperii obtulerat* (Tacit. Hist. I. 76.)

Games, and their Classification.—Public Games (*Ludi*) formed an important feature in the worship of the Gods, and in the earlier ages were always regarded as religious rites; so that the words *Ludi*, *Feriae*, and *Dies Festi*, are frequently employed as synonymous. Games celebrated every year upon a fixed day were denominated *Ludi Stati*. Such were the *Ludi Romani* s. *Magni*, held invariably on the 4th of September; the *Megalesia* on 4th April; the *Floralia* on 28th April; and many others. Games celebrated regularly every year, but on a day fixed annually by the public authorities, were called *Ludi Conceptivi*. Such were the *Feriae Latinae*. The *Ludi Apollinares* were *Conceptivi* from the period of their institution in B.C. 212, until B.C. 208, when they became *Stati*, being fixed to the 5th of July (Liv. XXV. 12. XXVII. 23.) Games celebrated by order of the Senate, of the magistrates, or of the higher priests, to commemorate some extraordinary event, such as a victory, or to avert a pestilence, were called *Ludi Imperativi*; those celebrated in fulfilment of a vow, *Ludi Votivi*. Entertainments of a similar nature were sometimes celebrated by private persons, especially at the obsequies of a near kinsman. Such were *Ludi Funebres*. Another classification of *Ludi* was derived from the place where they were exhibited and the nature of the exhibition; and this we shall adopt in the following sections. Viewed from this point, they may be divided into—1. *Ludi Circenses*, chariot races and other games exhibited in a Circus. 2. *Ludi Scenici*, dramatic entertainments exhibited in a theatre. 3. *Munera Gladiatoria*, prize-fights, which were usually exhibited in an Amphitheatre.

1. *Ludi Circenses*.

These consisted chiefly of Chariot Races, a species of contest in which the Romans took special delight from the earliest epochs. Tradition declared that Romulus celebrated in this manner the *Consualia*, (p. 328,) and he is said to have instituted also, in honour of Mars, the horse races called *Equiria*, which continued down to a late period, and were held twice a-year, on the 27th February (*III. Kal. Mart.*) and 14th March (*Prid. Id. Mart.*) in the Campus Martius, or, when this plain was overflowed by the river, on a flat space on the Coelian Hill, hence termed *Minor Campus*.[1]

Circus Maximus.—In order that such shows might be exhibited with greater

---

[1] Liv. I. 9. Dionys. I. 33. II. 31. Ovid. Fast. II. 857 III. 199. 519. Auson. Eclog. de feriis 19. Tertullian. de Spectac. Varro L.L. VI. 20. Paul. Diac. s.v. *Consualia*, p. 41. s.v. *Equiria*, p. 81. s.v. *Martialis Campus*, p. 131. Serv. ad Virg. Æn. VIII. 635.

magnificence, Tarquinius Priscus formed the Race Course, ever after distinguished as the CIRCUS MAXIMUS, in the hollow between the Palatine and Aventine called the *Vallis Murcia*, and surrounded the space with scaffolding for the convenience of the spectators. The Circus of Tarquinius, which must have been repeatedly altered and repaired under the republic, was reconstructed upon a grander scale by Julius Cæsar; and almost every succeeding emperor seems to have done something either to increase the splendour of the edifice, or to add to the comfort of the public.[1]

Tarquinius, we are assured, not only constructed the Circus, but first arranged the shows in a systematic form, and introduced gymnastic contests, the performers having been brought from Etruria. He also instituted a new festival in honour of Jupiter, Juno, and Minerva, which was observed with great pomp every year, the games represented being styled emphatically *Ludi Romani*, or *Ludi Magni* (Liv. I. 35.)

Since the first Circus was constructed by Tarquinius, the name of *Ludi Circenses* first arose at this period; and thus the *Ludi Romani* instituted by him are frequently termed κατ' ἐξοχήν, *Ludi Circenses*. But there were a great many other festivals during which games were exhibited in the Circus, and which, although altogether distinct from the *Ludi Romani*, were with equal propriety termed *Ludi Circenses*. Thus *Ludi Circenses* were exhibited during the festivals of Ceres, (*Cerealia*,) of Apollo (*Ludi Apollinares*,) of Cybele, (*Megalesia* s. *Ludi Megalenses*,) of Flora, (*Floralia*,) and many others.

General Form of the Circus.—The most complete account of the *Circus Maximus* is to be found in Dionysius (III. 68.) It is to be observed, that although he refers the first construction of the Circus to Tarquinius, his description relates to the appearance which it presented in his own times. The substance of the passage in question is to the following effect : " Tarquinius formed the greatest of all the Circi, that which is situated between the Aventine and the Palatine. . . . This work was destined in the course of time to become one of the most beautiful and wonderful structures of the city. The length of the Circus is three stadia and a half, (about 700 yards,) and the breadth four plethra ; (about 135 yards;) around it, along the two greater sides and one of the lesser, a trench (*Euripus*) has been dug for the reception of water, ten feet in breadth and in depth, and behind this trench a triple row of covered porticoes, one above the other, has been built. The lowest of these has stone seats, like those in the theatres, of small elevations, but the seats in the upper porticoes are of wood. The two larger sides of the Circus are brought together and unite, being connected by one of the shorter sides, which is semicircular in shape, so that the three form one continuous portico like an amphitheatre, eight stadia (about 1620 yards) in circumference, sufficient to contain 150,000 persons. But the remaining smaller side being left uncovered, contains starting places arched over, which are all opened at once by means of a single barrier. There is also another covered portico of one story, which runs round the Circus on the outside, containing workshops and dwelling houses above them. Through this portico, beside each workshop, are entrances and staircases for those who come to see the shows, so that no crowding takes place among so many tens of thousands passing in and coming out."

Reserved Seats.—According to the description given in Dionysius of the

---

[1] Liv. I. 35. Dionys. III. 68. Plin. H.N. XVI. 24. Suet. Iul. 39. Dom. 5. Dion Cass. LXVIII. 7.

Circus Maximus as constructed by Tarquinius, each of the thirty *Curiae* had a space assigned to it, and from these the Plebeians must have been excluded. After all political distinctions between the different orders in the state had disappeared, the people seem to have sat promiscuously, until Augustus ordained that the front seats at all public exhibitions of every description should be reserved for Senators; and places were set apart for the Equites also at the *Ludi Circenses* by order of Nero.[1]

Area of the Circus.—The flat space encompassed by the porticoes was carefully levelled, and being strewed with sand, was called the *Arena*. The straight wall by which the Circus was terminated at one end had one large entrance in the centre, by which the solemn processions filed into the interior. On each side of the central entrance were smaller openings, (*Ostia*,) which led from the outside into small arched chambers called *Carceres*, where the chariots stood before the commencement of the race. The *Carceres* were closed towards the *Arena* by doors termed *Claustra* or *Repagula*, fastened by a cross bar, and so contrived that they could be flung open all at once, and thus allow the chariots to dart forward with a fair start. The wall which contained the *Carceres* was ornamented at the top with battlements, and from this circumstance is sometimes termed *Oppidum*.[2] Down the Arena, parallel to the two larger sides, but not reaching to either extremity, and nearer to the left hand side than to the right, ran a low wall, the *Spina*. At each end of the *Spina* rose a group of three small conical pillars clustered together; these were the *Metae*. Between the *Carceres* and the nearest *Meta*, a straight line was drawn with chalk across the Circus; this was variously termed *Alba Linea, Creta, Calx*.[3] On the top of the Spina stood small frames or tables supported on pillars, and also small pieces of marble in the shape of eggs or dolphins. The frames were the *Phalae;* the pieces of marble, according to their form, *Ova* or *Delphini*. Finally, Augustus erected in the *Circus Maximus* an obelisk which he transported from Egypt, the same which now stands in the Piazza del Popolo; and a second obelisk of much larger dimensions was brought to Italy by Constantius, and placed also in the Circus. It now stands in front of the great church of St. Giovanni in Laterano.

The description of Dionysius, and what has been said in the last paragraph, will be more easily understood by referring to the ground plan in the next page, which is taken chiefly from a Circus of which considerable remains are still visible in the immediate vicinity of Rome, and which is commonly known as the Circus of Caracalla. Annexed to the plan are cuts from two large brass coins, one of Trajan, in which we clearly distinguish the obelisk of Augustus, the external portico, the *Spina*, the *Metae*, the *Phala* with its *Ova*, and the Temple of the Sun; the other of Balbinus, representing one of the groups of *Metae*.

In addition to the *Circus Maximus*, we hear of the *Circus Flaminius*, constructed in the *Prata Flaminia* by C. Flaminius when Censor, B.C. 220; of the Circus of Flora, which lay between the *Collis Quirinalis* and the *Collis Hortulorum;* of the Circus of Nero which occupied the ground on which St. Peter's now stands; and of some others of less note; but although these differed from the *Circus Maximus*, and from each other in magnitude, we have no reason to suppose that there was any variation in the general disposition of the

---

[1] Suet. Octav. 44. Claud. 21. Ner. 11. Dom. 8.
[2] Varro L. L. V, § 153. Liv. VIII. 20. Suet. Claud. 21. Cassiodor. Var. III. 51.
[3] Cassiodor. l. c. Ovid. Met. X. 106. Liv. XXXVII. 27. Plin. H. N. VIII. 65. XXXV 17. Senec. Epp. CVIII. Hor. Epp. I. xvii. 79.

GAMES OF THE CIRCUS.

different parts. Having therefore described the general form of a Roman Circus, we may now proceed to give some account of the shows exhibited.

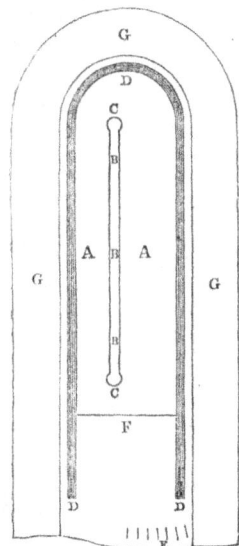

A. The *Arena*.

B. The *Spina*.

C. The *Metae*.

D. The *Euripus*.

E. The *Carceres*.

F. The *Alba Linea*.

G. The Seats.

Chariot and Horse Races.—The most important and the most ancient portion of the shows consisted of Chariot Races. The chariots were drawn sometimes by four horses, (*Quadrigae,*) sometimes by two, (*Bigae,*) and sometimes, though rarely, by three (*Trigae*.) There were races between mounted horses also, (*Equi singulares,*) and occasionally each rider had two horses, vaulting from one to the other (*Desultores—Equi desultorii.*) When Chariot Races were about to begin, *Desultores* rode round the course to announce the commencement of the sports; and we learn from ancient monuments on which Chariot Races are depicted, that the chariots were frequently attended by riders, whose business was, in all probability, to give them assistance in case of any accident, and to cheer them on.[1]

Missus. Curricula.—The number of chariots which contended together in one race was always four, until the time of Domitian, by whom it was increased to six. Each of these matches was termed a *Missus,* and the number of *Missus* in one day was regularly twenty-four, although in ancient times a twenty-fifth was added, and the cost defrayed by voluntary contributions. The four chariots being placed each in a separate *Carcer,* the signal for starting was given by the President of the Games, (*Editor Spectaculi,*) who was usually one of the higher magistrates, by throwing down a napkin, (*Mappa,*) upon which the *Repagula* were flung back simultaneously, and the chariots dashed out. They

[1] Dionys. VII. 73. Liv. XLIV. 9. comp. XXIII. 20. Suet. Iul. 39. Tiber. 26. Claud. 21. Domit. 4. Propert. IV. ii. 35. Cassiodor. Var. III. 51.

ran seven times round the *Spina*, keeping it always on the left hand; and the chariot which first crossed the *Alba Linea* as it completed the seventh round was the conqueror. Each circuit was termed a *Curriculum*; and that no confusion might arise with regard to the number of circuits which had been performed, at the termination of each round one of the *Ova* or of the *Delphini* was placed on one of the *Phalae*, and then the spectators could at a glance perceive the progress of the race. It was of course a great object to keep close to the *Spina* and to turn round the extremities as sharply as possible. Hence the accidents which frequently happened by the wheels striking against the *Meta*, (as in the famous description of a Chariot Race in the Electra of Sophocles,) and hence the phrase in Horace—*Metaque fervidis evitata rotis.* It is almost unnecessary to add, after what has been said in the preceding paragraphs, that although we may fairly render *Carceres* by *the starting post*, we can never with propriety translate *Meta* as the *goal* or *winning post*. In modern racing there is nothing corresponding to the *Meta*; and in the Circus the *Alba Linea* was the goal. [1]

Factiones Circi.—The drivers (*Aurigae—Agitatores—Bigarii— Quadrigarii —Factionarii*) of the chariots were distinguished from each other by the colour of their garments, one being always dressed in white, another in green, the third in red, and the fourth in blue. Hence, from the keenness with which different persons espoused the cause of the different colours, arose four parties or *Factiones Circi*, which were named respectively the *Factio Albata*, the *Factio Prasina*, the *Factio Russata*, and the *Factio Veneta*. The eagerness of those who favoured the contending colours frequently rose, as might be anticipated, to furious excitement and tumult, and on one celebrated occasion, at Constantinople in A.D. 532, produced the terrible riot and massacre known in history as the *Nika* sedition, in which upwards of 30,000 persons are said to have perished. The progress of this appalling calamity has been depicted with terrible force by Gibbon (Chap. XL.)

When Domitian introduced the practice of making six chariots start in each *Missus*, two new *Factiones* were necessarily added, the gold and the purple—*Factio Aurata—Factio Purpurea*; but these were soon dropped, or, at least, not steadily maintained.

It would appear that the *Factio Prasina*, the *Viridis Pannus* of Juvenal, was the favourite of the greater number of the Emperors, and hence most generally popular. [2]

Athletae.—Gymnastic contests also formed a part of the *Ludi Circenses*, and as the Greeks had their πένταθλον, so the Romans combined the five chief exercises into a *Quinquertium*,[3] consisting of foot races, (*Cursus*,) leaping, (*Saltus*,) wrestling, (*Lucta*,) throwing the quoit, (*Disci jactus*,) and hurling the javelin (*Iaculatio*.) Sometimes the group was varied, and boxing (*Pugilatus*) substituted for one of the above. Youths, from the earliest times, were in the habit of passing a portion of each day in the *Campus Martius*, practising these manly sports, as well as riding (*Equitatio*) and swimming,

---

[1] Cassiodor. Var. III. 51. Suet. Dom. 4. Ovid. Halieut. 68. Varro ap. Aul. Gell. III. 10. Propert. II. xxv. 25. Serv. ad Virg. Georg. III. 18. who is, however, contradicted by Dion Cass. LIX. 7. Liv. XLI. 27. Dion Cass. XLIX. 43. Varro R.R. I. 2. Iuv. S. VI. 588. Paul. Diac. s.v. *Falae*, p. 88. Quintil. I. O. I. 5. Martial. XII. 29. Suet. Ner. 22.

[2] Suet. Dom. 7. Dion Cass. LXI. 6. LXVII. 4. On the *Prasina*, see Sueton. Cal. 55. Ner. 22. Capitolin. vit. Ver. 4. 6. Iuv. S. XI. 196. Martial. XI. 33. Dion Cass. LIX. 14. LXIII. 6. LXXII. 17. LXXIX. 14. On the *Veneta*, Sueton. Vitell. 14. Martial. X. 48. Dion Cass. LXXVII. 10. On the *Albata*, Plin. H.N. VIII. 65. On the *Russata*, Plin. H.N. VII. 54. comp. Martial. XIV. 131.

[3] Fest. s.v. p. 257. The performers were termed *Quinquertiones*.

(*Natatio,*) while under the empire large courts called *Gymnasia* or *Palaestrae* were generally attached for this purpose to the great *Thermae* or public bathing establishments.

Ludus Troiae.—A sort of mock fight performed by Patrician youths on horseback, well understood from the spirited description of Virgil (Æn. V. 545 —603.) This show was said to have been instituted at a very remote period, was revived by Julius Cæsar, and cultivated under succeeding Emperors.[1]

Pugna.—Sham battles were also exhibited, in which infantry, cavalry, and elephants contended, the camps of the opposing hosts being pitched in the *Area* of the Circus.[2]

Naumachia.—Sea fights (*Navalia Proelia*) were occasionally represented in the Circus, the Arena being filled with water. Julius Cæsar, Augustus, and Domitian dug ponds for this special purpose near the Tiber; Claudius organized a magnificent *Naumachia* on the *Lacus Fucinus;* Nero usually employed an amphitheatre. Observe that *Naumachia* is used to signify not only the sea-fight, but also the lake or tank in which it took place.[3]

Venatio.—As the Roman arms extended to a greater and greater distance from Rome, the productions of foreign countries, especially strange animals, were from time to time shown off in public. Thus three elephants taken from Pyrrhus formed a most attractive spectacle in the triumph of Curius Dentatus; and 142 were brought over from Sicily in B.C. 251 by Lucius Metellus, and displayed in the Circus. The populace, however, soon demanded that the wild beasts should not merely be exhibited, but that they should be matched against each other or against armed men; and to such contests the term *Venationes* was applied. The first *Venatio*, properly so called, took place at the games of M. Fulvius Nobilior, B.C. 186, after which they gradually became more and more frequent, until towards the close of the republic, no *Ludi Circenses* would have been considered complete without its Wild Beast Hunt; and Julius Cæsar found it necessary to cause the *Euripus* to be dug as a protection to the spectators. Under the empire, the great Amphitheatres were usually employed for these shows.

The number of animals destroyed on many occasions almost transcends belief. In the second consulship of Pompeius, B.C. 55, 500 lions, 410 panthers and leopards, and 18 elephants, were killed in five days; Julius Cæsar turned 400 lions loose all once; Caligula, at a festival in honour of Drusilla, caused 500 bears to be put to death in one day ; and in the games celebrated on the return of Trajan from Dacia, 11,000 wild animals were butchered.[4]

Venatio Direptionis.—The elder Gordian, when Quaestor, planted the area of the Circus with trees, so as to resemble a forest, and turned loose a multitude of deer, wild sheep, elks, boars, and other kinds of game. The populace were then invited to enter the enclosure, and carry away whatever they could kill. His example was followed by Philip, by Probus, and by others; amusements of this description being styled *Venationes Direptionis.*[5]

---

[1] Dion Cass. XLIII. 23. XLVIII. 20. LI. 22. Suet. Iul. 39. Octav. 43. Tib. 6. Cal. 18. Claud. 21. Nero. 7.
[2] Suet. Iul. 39. Claud. 21. Dom. 4.
[3] Dion Cass. XLIII. 23. XLVIII. 19. LX. 33. LXI. 9. LXVI. 25. Suet. Iul. 39. Octav. 43. Tib. 72. Claud. 21. Dom. 4. Nero 12. Tacit. Ann. XII. 56. XIV. 15.
[4] Liv. XXXIX. 22. XLIV. 18. Plin. H.N. VIII. 6, 7. 20. 40. Cic. ad Fam. VII. 1. VIII. 9. Sueton. Iul. 39. Octav. 23. Claud. 21. Tit. 7. Dion Cass. XLIII. 23. LI. 22. LV. 10. LVI. 25. LXI. 9. LXVIII. 15.
[5] Capitolin. Gord. 3. 33. Vopisc. Prob. 19.

Rewards of Victory.—Branches of the palm tree were presented to the conquerors in the different contests, and also more substantial rewards, such as wreaths made of gold and silver wrought in imitation of leaves, sums of money, horses, silken tunics, linen vestments embroidered with gold, and the like. All these are frequently included under the general title of *Palmae*.[1]

Pompa Circi.—We have already adverted to the fact, that *Ludi* in general were regarded as religious rites; and accordingly we find that the *Ludi Circenses* commenced with a solemn procession, which defiled from the Capitol, and passing through the Forum, entered the *Circus Maximus*. The principal magistrates headed this *Pompa Circi*, as it was called; youths on the verge of manhood, organised in bands as cavalry and infantry, followed; next came the performers who were about to take a part in the sports; then numerous bodies of dancers and musicians; and lastly the images of all the most important deities, carried on frames called *Fercula*, or in sacred vehicles called *Thensae*, preceded by men who bore incense boxes of gold and silver. After the various personages and objects composing this train had occupied the places assigned to them, the chief magistrate present, assisted by the higher priests, proceeded to offer sacrifice. When this was concluded, the shows commenced.[2]

2. *Ludi Scenici*.

Origin and Progress of the Roman Drama.—Dramatic exhibitions were entirely unknown at Rome for nearly four centuries after the foundation of the city. But in B.C. 361, among other expedients for appeasing the wrath of heaven during the ravages of a pestilence, scenic sports—*Ludi Scenici*—were introduced from Etruria, the performers in which were termed *Ludiones* or *Histriones*, the latter word being formed from *Hister*, which, according to Livy, signified a *Stage-Player* in the Tuscan tongue. These entertainments were at first of a very simple nature, consisting solely of dances accompanied by the music of the flute. By degrees a sort of unpremeditated farce was added to the dance, but the art continued in a very rude state until about B.C. 240, when Livius Andronicus, a Greek freedman, introduced Comedies and Tragedies, translated from his native language, and his example was followed by Naevius, Ennius, Plautus, Pacuvius, Accius, Terentius, and many others, whose pieces, as far as our knowledge extends, were all close imitations or adaptations of Greek originals, and this character was stamped upon the Roman Drama until the extinction of their literature. In addition to plays with regular plots, (*Fabulae*,) farces or interludes, called *Mimi*, abounding in practical jokes and coarse humour, found great favour with the public, and also *Atellanae*, (sc. *fabulae*,) so called from *Atella* in Campania—entertainments indigenous in Southern Italy, in which the characters made use of the Oscan dialect, the dialogue being in a great measure extemporaneous. These *Atellanae* were the only class of stage-plays in which a Roman citizen could appear as an actor without incurring *Infamia*. (p. 84.) Different from either of the above were the *Pantomimi*, imported from Alexandria during the reign of Augustus. In these there was neither dialogue nor soliloquy, but a single performer undertook to

---

[1] Liv. X. 47. Plin. H.N. XXI. 3. Suet. Octav. 45. Claud. 21. Vopisc. Aurelian. 12.
[2] Dionysius has transmitted a detailed and very curious account of the *Pompa Circi*, in which he professes to follow the description given by Fabius, the earliest Roman historian, of the games decreed by the Senate, in fulfilment of the vow made by Aulus Postumius, (B.C. 487,) when about to enter upon the war against the Latin States, who were endeavouring to restore Tarquinius.

represent in dumb show, by means of gesticulations alone, all the events of a complicated tale.

Roman Theatre.—Although formal dramas were exhibited in B.C. 240, and although such exhibitions necessarily imply the existence of a stage, of scenery, and of decorations, no attempt was made for nearly a century to provide comfortable accommodation for the spectators, who, unless they chose to recline upon the ground, must have been content with rough scaffolding. The construction of a regular theatre was first commenced in B.C. 155, but the work was stopped at the instance of Scipio Nasica, at that time Consul, and the Senate passed a decree sternly forbidding such effeminate indulgences.[1] A few years afterwards, however, Lucius Mummius, the destroyer of Corinth, vanquished the prejudices of his countrymen, for among the various shows which enlivened his Triumph, a drama was performed for the first time, in a theatre erected after the Greek fashion. (Tacit. Ann. XIV. 21.) This, it must be observed, and all which followed it for nearly a hundred years, were merely temporary structures formed of wood, which, although frequently of enormous size and splendidly ornamented, were erected for a particular occasion and demolished as soon as the holiday was over.

The first permanent theatre was the work of Pompeius Magnus after his return from the Mithridatic War. (B.C. 61.) It was built of hewn stone, upon the model of one which he had seen at Mitylene, and calculated to hold 40,000 persons.[2] A second, the work of Cornelius Balbus, was opened a few years after the battle of Actium; and a third, the most splendid of all, still a noble ruin, (see page 45,) bore the name of the amiable Marcellus, the nephew of Augustus. These are constantly alluded to as the three theatres of Rome, are mentioned repeatedly both singly and collectively, and the number was still the same in the reign of Nero; but we must take into account also the temporary structures, of which several, as we are informed by Vitruvius, were built up and pulled down every year.[3]

Arrangement of the different parts of a Roman Theatre.—With regard to the internal economy of the more ancient temporary structures we can know but little, but a description of two of the most remarkable, one the work of Scaurus, the step-son of Sulla, when Aedile; the other, erected by Curio, who perished in the civil wars of Cæsar and Pompeius, has been transmitted to us by Pliny, and is well worthy of attention. (H.N. XXXVI. 15.) In so far as the permanent theatres of stone are concerned, notwithstanding the information contained in the works of ancient writers upon architecture, and frequent allusions to the different parts in the ordinary classics, antiquarians found, for a long period, much difficulty in adjusting the details, none of the existing ruins being sufficiently perfect to resolve some important doubts. By the discoveries at Pompeii, where two theatres and an amphitheatre, all entire, have been excavated, every difficulty has been removed as to the disposition of the different parts.

A theatre, ancient or modern, may be conveniently separated into two divisions,—1. The part devoted to the spectators. 2. The part devoted to the actors. The former was comprehended under the general name of *Cavea*, the latter under that of *Scena*.

The *Cavea* was semicircular, and consisted of steps—*Gradus*—of stone or

---

[1] Liv. Epit. XLVIII. Val. Max. II. iv. 2. Velleius, I. 15. Applan. B.C. I. 28. Tertullian. de Spectac. 10. Augustin. C. D. I. 31.
[2] Tacit. Ann. XIV. 20. 21. Plut. Pomp. 52. Plin. H.N. VII. 3.
[3] Ovid. A. A. III. 394. Trist. III. xii. 23. Tacit. Ann. III. 64. 72.

marble, rising in succession one above the other, each row being of course farther removed from the stage than the one in front of it. In order that the spectators might gain easy access to the different parts of the house, and might enter or retire without confusion—no easy matter when thirty or forty thousand persons were present at one time—the rows of steps or seats were divided at intervals by broad passages, called *Praecinctiones*, running round the whole semicircle. These compartments were again divided into smaller spaces by staircases—*Scalae*—converging towards the centre, these *Scalae* cutting across the *Gradus*, which formed the seats, and dividing them into wedge-shaped compartments, which were termed *Cunei*. The various *Praecinctiones* and *Scalae* communicated with apertures called *Vomitoria*, which led to the porticoes, which, rising story above story, ran round and encompassed the whole building.

The *Scena* consisted of the *Scena* in a restricted sense, answering to the modern *Scene*, and the *Pulpitum* or stage. The scene itself, in accordance with a critical canon observed with much solicitude by the Grecian dramatists, was very rarely changed during the course of the same play, although the *Scena Versatilis*, the turning scene, and the *Scena Ductilis*, the shifting scene, were not altogether unknown. The *Pulpitum* again was divided into the *Proscenium* or space in front of the scene, where the actors stood while actually engaged in the business of the play, and the *Postscenium*, or space behind the scene, to which they retired when they made their exits.

Orchestra.—We have as yet said nothing with regard to the semicircular area, included by the straight line which bounded the stage in front and the first row of the ascending steps. This was the *Orchestra*, and the purposes to which it was applied constitute the principal distinction between the arrangements of the Grecian theatres and those of Italy. *Orchestra* is derived directly from ὀρχεῖσθαι, (to dance,) and in the Greek theatre this space was always occupied by the *Chorus*, which formed such a conspicuous feature in Greek Tragedy and in the old Comedy of Athens. Here the individuals composing the *Chorus* performed their sacred dances; here they chanted their songs; and whilst the different characters were conversing, the leader of the *Chorus*, the *Coryphaeus*, stood upon the altar, (θυμέλη,) which rose to a level with the stage, observing the progress of the action, and ready, as their representative, to take a part in the dialogue. On the other hand, in Roman Comedy, which was derived from the New Comedy of Athens, there was no *Chorus;* and in Roman Tragedies, both the *Chorus* and the musicians were placed upon the stage itself, so that the whole of the *Orchestra* was left vacant for the spectators.

On the next page we have given a ground plan of two theatres; the first has been delineated from the descriptions handed down by Vitruvius and other ancient writers; the other represents one of the theatres actually excavated at Pompeii.

Reserved Seats.—All ranks sat promiscuously until B.C. 193, when the elder Scipio Africanus passed a law by which places separate from the rest of the spectators were assigned to the Senators, and when regular theatres were constructed, the *Orchestra* was set apart for their use. In the year B.C. 68, a certain L. Roscius Otho carried a bill (*Lex Roscia*) in terms of which fourteen rows of benches, immediately behind those of the Senators, were made over to the Equites; and although the first attempt to enforce this measure occasioned a riot, which was with difficulty quelled by the eloquence of Cicero, the distinction thus introduced was maintained; and to say that a person sat upon the fourteen benches, (*in quatuordecim ordinibus sedere,*) was equivalent to an assertion of his equestrian rank.[1]

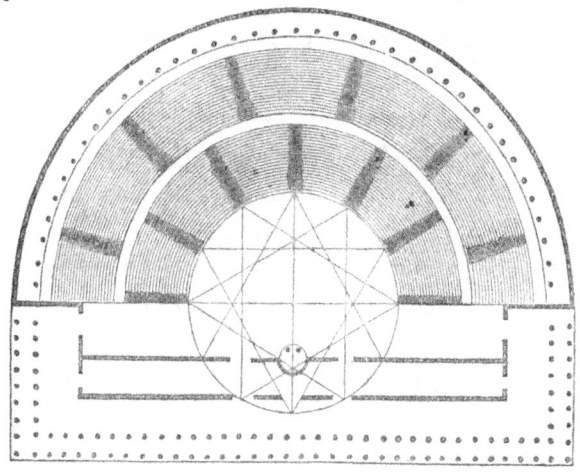

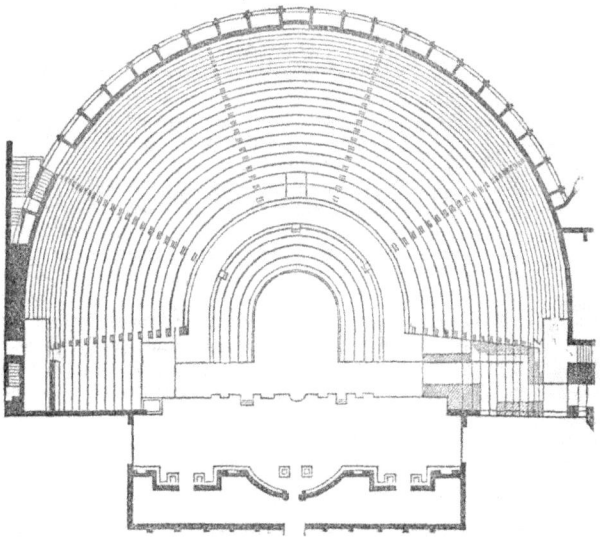

[1] Cic. pro Muren. 19. Ascon. in Cornelian. p. 79. ed. Orelli. Plin. H.N. VII. 30. Macrob. S. II. 10. Plut. Cic. 13. Hor. Epod. IV. 15. Iuv. S. III. 154—159.

Aulaeum, Siparium.—Before a play commenced, or in the interval between two pieces, the stage was concealed by a curtain called *Aulaeum* or *Siparium*, which was not pulled up, as those in modern theatres are, when the performance commenced, but was drawn down under the stage, so that when Horace wishes to express that certain spectacles were sometimes prolonged for four hours or more, he says—

Quatuor aut plures AULAEA PREMUNTUR in horas.

i.e. *the curtain is kept down*, and therefore the exhibition continues for that space.

Dress of Actors.—The actors (*Histriones—Ludiones*) in Tragedy always wore a boot called *Cothurnus*, (κόθορνος,) which reached half-way up the leg, and sometimes almost to the knees, with a very thick sole to increase the apparent stature of the performer. The actors in Comedy always wore a thin slipper called *Soccus*, and hence *Cothurnus* and *Soccus* are employed figuratively to denote respectively Tragedy and Comedy. Thus Horace, when speaking of Iambic measure (Ep. ad Pis. 80.)—*Hunc Socci cepere pedem grandesque Cothurni*; and again—*Grande munus Cecropio repetes Cothurno* (C. II. i. 11.) *Indignatur item privatis ac prope Socco = Dignis carminibus narrari coena Thyestae* (Ep. ad Pis. 90.) On the other hand, the actors in Mimes (*Mimi*,)[1] appeared with bare feet, and hence were termed *Planipedes*, and the farces themselves *Planipediae*.[2] Actors, generally speaking, concealed their features with masks, (*Personae*,) which were fabricated with great care and skill, so as to convey, by their features, a general idea of the character represented by the wearer.

Amphitheatres.—It will be convenient to explain here the distinction between a Theatre and an Amphitheatre. The very name *Amphitheatrum* or ἀμφιθέατρον, i. e. *a double theatre*, or a theatre *all round*, is almost enough. If we suppose the whole of the *Cavea*, including the *Orchestra*, of one theatre to be applied to the *Cavea* of another theatre of the same dimensions, or, which comes to the same thing, if we suppose the semicircular rows of *Gradus*, instead of being terminated by the straight line which bounded the *Pulpitum*, to be continued round along with their *Praecinctiones*, *Scalae*, *Cunei*, and Exterior Porticoes, so as to complete the circle, we shall form an accurate idea of a Roman Amphitheatre, with this difference, that instead of being perfectly circular, it was usually of an elliptical or oval shape. The space in the centre formed by the *Orchestras* of the two theatres, which we have supposed to be applied to each other, was called the *Arena*, being strewed with sand, and this was the spot upon which the various exhibitions to which the building was devoted were represented. It was sunk several feet under the level of the lowest row of seats, in order that the spectators might not be exposed to danger from the wild beasts which were frequently admitted; and for still greater security, a sort of balustrade called *Podium*, covered with trellis or net-work, was raised on the summit of the bounding walls, and through the interstices those who occupied the front seats gazed on the scenes below. Several doors opened from the *Arena*, communicating with various apartments, by which the combatants were intro-

---
[1] Observe that the words *Mimi* and *Pantomimi* denote alike the actors and the entertainments.
[2] Iuv. S. VIII. 189. Aul. Gell. I. 11. Macrob. S. II. 1. Diomed. III. p. 487. ed. Putsch. Donat. de Comoed. et Tragoed.

luced and withdrew. With regard to these combatants and the contests in which they engaged, we shall speak at length in the section on Gladiators.

Amphitheatres, like theatres, were originally temporary buildings of wood. Such was the curious structure of Curio, to which we have already alluded; such were the amphitheatres of Julius Cæsar, (Dion Cass. XLIII. 22.) and of Nero, (Tacit. Ann. XIII. 31. Suet. Ner. 12.) although a stone edifice of this description was erected in the Campus Martius by Statilius Taurus during the reign of Augustus (Dion Cass. XLI. 23.) But these and all similar works sunk into insignificance when compared with the Colosseum, that stupendous fabric commenced by Vespasian and completed by his son, a memorial of the triumphant conclusion of the Jewish war. It was upwards of 180 feet in height, one-third of a mile in circumference, and capable of containing easily 100,000 persons.[1] A sketch of the ruin as it now exists will be found in p. 35; and we annex a cut taken from a large brass of Titus, struck probably to commemorate the completion of the pile.

Below is a view of the Amphitheatre excavated at Pompeii, which will explain at a glance the general appearance and internal arrangements of such buildings.

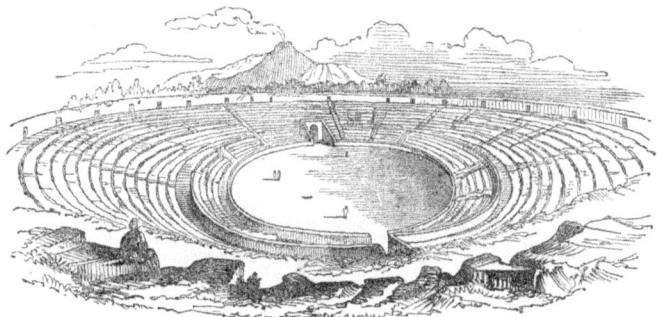

Vela.—The ancient theatres and amphitheatres, at least all of large size, were open to the sky, and hence they were generally surrounded by porticoes to which the spectators might retire in the event of a sudden shower. In order to afford shelter from the scorching rays of the sun, it was customary to spread an awning (*Vela*) of white or coloured canvas over the whole of the interior; and on the outside wall of the Colosseum, rings hewn out of the blocks of stone which form part of the edifice, are still visible, which were destined to receive the tall poles by means of which these coverings were supported. It was, of course, impossible, during

---

[1] A detailed account of the present state and original plan of the Colosseum will be found in the Beschreibung der Stadt Rome, referred to in page 1, and in almost every work descriptive of the modern city and its ancient remains. An elaborate treatise on ancient amphitheatres in general, and on that of Verona in particular, forms the first volume of the *Verona Illustrata* of Maffei.

a high wind, to hoist or manage such an unwieldy expanse of cloth; and in this case the people were obliged to shade themselves with a sort of broad brimmed hat called a *Causia*, or to hold up parasols (*Umbracula*.)[1] The hues thrown upon the stage, the performers, and the audience, by the coloured canvas, afforded Lucretius an illustration of one of his doctrines regarding colour; and in another place he endeavours to explain the origin of thunder, by comparing the action of the clouds to the flapping of the awning when agitated by a sudden gust.[2]

Sparsiones. Missilia, &c.—No cost was spared, during the last century of the republic and under the empire, which could tend to increase the splendour of the exhibitions, or gratify the craving of the crowd for novelty. The Scene was overlaid sometimes with silver, sometimes with ivory, sometimes with gold; all the instruments used on the stage were formed of the precious metals; while in the amphitheatre the sand of the *Arena* was strewed with vermillion, the seats of the *Podium* intertwined with golden cords, and the knots covered with amber; streams of water were introduced, which coursed between the seats, and diffused a grateful coolness as they murmured along; statues were placed on the stage and in different parts of the house, which were constructed in such a manner as to rain down perfumes on the *Pulpitum* and the spectators, these showers being termed *Sparsiones*. To increase the good humour of the multitude, at the conclusion of the sports, little balls of wood were thrown down (and hence the name *Missilia*) from the upper story, and scrambled for by those below, each of these *Missilia* containing a ticket (*Tessera*) upon which was written the name of some object of greater or less value. Sometimes it was merely a basket of fruit, sometimes a horse, or a robe, or a slave, or a piece of plate, or a sum of money; and the holder of a ticket in this lottery without blanks was entitled to receive the article inscribed upon it, by making application to an officer appointed for the purpose.[3] Many of these refinements became common even in the small country towns as early as the latter half of the first century; for we find in one of the play-bills scrawled upon the walls of Pompeii, the exhibitor endeavouring to attract a large audience by promising—SPARSIONES VELA ERUNT.

3. *Munera Gladiatoria.*

We now proceed, in the last place, to notice that species of exhibition which, towards the close of the republic and under the empire, was more popular than any other, and which has been justly regarded as the foulest blot upon the national character of the Romans.

Origin and progress of Gladiatorial Shows.—GLADIATORES were persons armed with deadly weapons who fought with each other in cold blood, usually in pairs, for the amusement of the spectators, until one (or both) of the combatants was killed or disabled. The origin of this practice must be traced to the belief existing among the Greeks and Romans, from the earliest periods, that the spirits of the dead took delight in human blood. Hence Achilles is represented by Homer as slaying twelve Trojan captives, and casting their bodies on the funeral pyre of Patroclus, while Æneas, in like manner, offers up eight of his prisoners to appease the *Manes* of Pallas the son of Evander. (Æn. X. 517.) Passing on to historical times, the custom is said to have been imported into

[1] Martial. XIV. 28. 29.
[2] Lucret. IV. 73. VI. 105.
[3] Plin. H.N. XXXIII. 27. XXXVII. 11. Suet. Ner. 11. Martial VIII. 78.

Rome from Etruria, and the first example is afforded by Marcus and Decimus Brutus, who, in B.C. 264, matched together gladiators in the *Forum Boarium*, when celebrating the obsequies of their father—*D. Junius Brutus munus gladiatorium in honorem defuncti patris edidit primus.* (Liv. Epit. XVI. Val. Max. II. iv. 7.) The practice from this time forward gradually gained ground. There were *Ludi funebres* in B.C. 216, at which twenty-five pairs fought, (*gladiatorum paria duo et viginti,*) the same number in B.C. 200, and sixty pairs in B.C. 183.[1] As the taste for these spectacles increased they were no longer confined to funereal rites, but formed a part of every important public solemnity, and were introduced occasionally even at private banquets. Julius Cæsar at one festival presented three hundred and twenty pairs to the people, and Trajan, during the great rejoicings on his return from Dacia, which extended over one hundred and twenty days, matched together ten thousand gladiators. Attempts were made by various persons at different times to restrain the extravagance of private individuals, who were tempted by vanity or ambition to lavish enormous sums on these displays. Laws were proposed and passed by Cicero, by Augustus, by Tiberius, and by other Emperors, to limit the number of fighters, and to check excessive expenditure, but these were neglected or repealed during the sway of worthless princes, and no attempt was made to interdict such exhibitions entirely until the reign of Constantine the Great. They were partially revived under Constantius, Theodosius, and Valentinianus, and finally suppressed by Honorius.

Training of Gladiators.—It was natural that much care should be bestowed on the preparations for shows to which thousands looked forward with intense eagerness. Regular academies, called *Ludi gladiatorii*, or simply *Ludi*, were devoted to the instruction of these prize-fighters, in which the most important practical duties were committed to a trainer, called *Lanista*, by whom the *Tirones*, or undrilled novices, were instructed in the principles of their art, fighting with heavy wooden swords, called *Rudes*, while their bodies were brought into condition by regular exercise and nourishing food (*sagina gladiatoria.*) Many of these *Ludi* were kept upon speculation by *Lan tae*, who trained large bodies of men, whom they sold or let out for hire to those who were desirous of procuring recruits for public games.

Class of persons who fought as Gladiators.—The most copious supply was at all times derived from prisoners of war, or refractory slaves sold by their masters to the *Lanista*. Malefactors also were occasionally condemned to fight as gladiators, and occasionally Roman citizens offered themselves voluntarily for hire, and to such the specific term *Auctorati* was applied, their pay being called *Auctoramentum*. Under the more worthless and dissolute emperors, Equites, priests, and senators did not scruple to contend in the arena, in the hope of attracting the attention and gaining the favour of the prince; and even highborn women were found who consented to pander to the appetite for novelty, by fighting with each other or with dwarfs.

Classification of Gladiators.—Gladiators were divided into classes according to the manner in which they were equipped, and were in many cases named from the nation whose characteristic arms they bore. The representatives of different nations were frequently matched against each other, and the comparative efficiency of their weapons offensive and defensive, was thus put to the test. The classes most frequently mentioned are—

[1] Liv. XXIII. 30. XXXI. 50. XXXIX. 46. comp. XXVIII. 21.

Threces, armed as Thracians, with a light circular buckler (*parma*) and short crooked cutlas; (*sica;*) *Samnites*, who, we cannot doubt, were furnished like the Samnites of old (Liv. IX. 40.) with a convex shield, (*scutum*,) broad and even at top, (*summum latius fastigio aequali*,) the two sides gradually converging to a point, (*ad imum cuneatius*,) a wadded breast-plate, (*spongia pectori tegumentum*,) crested helmet, (*galea cristata*,) and with a greave on the left leg: (*sinistrum crus ocrea tectum;*) *Mirmillones*, a word of doubtful origin, equipped as Gaulish warriors; *Hoplomachi*, in a complete suit of mail like those who fought in the front ranks of the Grecian phalanx.

Retiarii were provided with a net (*Iaculum—Rete*) and a three-pointed spear (*Fuscina*) with a long handle, but were destitute of defensive armour; they were usually paired with a heavy armed opponent, a *Mirmillo* for example, who was in this case designated *Secutor;* the *Retiarius* being no match for his antagonist in a hand-to-hand fight, endeavoured, as the latter approached, to throw his net so as to entangle him in its meshes, and, if successful, stabbed him with the *fuscina* before he could extricate himself. If the cast failed he was compelled to take to flight, was chased by the *Secutor*, (and hence the name,) and if overtaken easily despatched. If, however, the *Retiarius* contrived to evade his pursuer until he was prepared for a second throw, then the contest was renewed as at first, and continued until one or the other was baffled or exhausted. A most vivid description of a combat of this nature will be found in the eighth Satire of Juvenal (199—210.)

Less frequently named than the preceding were *Dimachaeri*, who fought with two swords; *Laquearii*, analogous to the *Retiarii*, but who had lassos or nooses instead of nets; *Andabatae*, who wore helmets with close visors, so that they fought blindfold; *Essedarii*, who fought from Celtic war chariots; (*Esseda;*) *Meridiani*, who fought in the middle of the day, inferior performers, it has been conjectured, who were brought forward at an hour when the majority of the spectators had retired to repose during the noontide heat; *Provocatores*, of whom we know nothing, except that they were occasionally matched with *Samnites*. Gladiators, as remarked above, generally fought in pairs, and all such were termed *Ordinarii;* at times, however, by way of variety, a number rushed together in a meleé, and such were named *Catervarii*. *Bestiarii* were those who, in the *Venationes*, already described, fought with wild beasts.

Munus. Editor.—The term *Munus* is applied specially to denote a Gladiatorial show, either in consequence of the connection which originally subsisted between these displays and funeral obsequies, which were specially termed *Munera*, or from the circumstance that they were regarded in the light of a gift, bestowed by the magistrate or the private individual at whose cost they were exhibited, and who presided under the title of *Editor* (*Spectaculi*) or *Munerarius*, the latter term having been, as we are told, first employed by Augustus.[1]

Place of Exhibition.—The first show of Gladiators took place, as stated above, in the *Forum Boarium*, and when they were brought forward in connection with funeral rites, they would always be exhibited near the funeral pyre or in some place of general resort. When they formed a part of great public solemnities, they at first fought in the *Circus Maximus*, but subsequently Amphitheatres were erected as the kind of edifice best adapted for these contests.

Mode of Procedure.—When the day of the show had arrived, of which public

---

[1] *Munus* is applied also, though less frequently, to games or shows in general.

notice was given some time beforehand, accompanied by a description of the number, names, and previous exploits of the combatants, (*Libellus munerarius,*) the Gladiators marched in procession into the Arena of the Amphitheatre, and were there arranged in pairs, much pains having been previously bestowed upon matching individuals nearly equal in strength and skill. Their arms and equipments were then produced and carefully examined; a prelude (*Prolusio*) followed, in which the parties fenced with wooden swords and pointless spears, exhibiting the graceful attitudes and dexterous evolutions which they had been taught by the *Lanista*. The strife then commenced in earnest upon a signal given by the *Editor*. As soon as a Gladiator succeeded in inflicting a decided wound on his adversary, he exclaimed in a loud voice, *Hoc Habet*—It is a hit. If the injury appeared to be of such a nature as to disable the sufferer, and prevent him from continuing the fight, the *Editor* replied, *Habet*, and the life or death of the wounded man, who now held up his finger in token of submission, depended upon the pleasure of the president, who usually, as a matter of courtesy, referred it to the audience. If the man was a favourite, had fought well, and betrayed no symptoms of terror, the crowd testified their approbation by shouts and clapping of hands, and he was allowed to retire; but if he had, from any cause, incurred their displeasure, they depressed their thumbs in silence, and the conqueror, in obedience to a look from the *Editor*, plunged his weapon into the body of the unresisting victim. The attendants then rushed in, dragged off the corpse by a hook to an apartment called the *Spoliarium*, sprinkled fresh sand on the Arena, and new actors entered to perform like tragedies. [1]

[1] Much information with regard to various matters connected with Gladiatorial contests may be gathered from a very curious series of bas reliefs discovered at Pompeii, which are accurately delineated in the great work of Mazois, and in the *Museo Borbonico*.

Jupiter, Juno, and Minerva, in an ancient style of art, from a bas relief in the Capitol.

CHAPTER XI.

THE ROMAN CALENDAR.

In giving an account of the Roman Calendar, it will be convenient to discuss, in the first place, that portion of the subject concerning which our information is full and complete; and then to pass on to the consideration of those points, which are comparatively doubtful and obscure. According to this plan, we shall commence with an account of the constitution of the *Julian Year*.[1]

Julian Year.—At the time when Julius Cæsar attained to supreme power, the Calendar had, from causes which will be afterwards explained, fallen into great confusion. The Dictator, therefore, resolved to reform the whole system, and being himself versed in astronomy,[2] with the aid of Sosigenes, a peripatetic philosopher of Alexandria, the great school of the sciences, introduced B.C. 45, that division of time which, with a few modifications, is still employed by all Christian nations, and received from its author the name of the *Julian Year*.

The solar year, or the period between two vernal equinoxes, was supposed to contain $365\frac{1}{4}$ days; but to prevent the inconvenience which would have arisen from the use of fractional parts, three years out of four were regarded as consisting of 365 days, while every fourth year had 366.

Months of the Julian Year.—The Roman year had from a very early period been divided into twelve months. This number and the ancient names were retained, but the distribution of the days was changed. By the new arrangement, *Ianuarius*, the first month, had 31 days; *Februarius*, 28 in ordinary years, and every fourth year, 29; *Martius*, 31; *Aprilis*, 30; *Maius*, 31; *Iunius*, 30; *Quintilis*, 31; *Sextilis*, 31; *September*, 30; *October*, 31; *November*, 30; *December*, 31.

In the year B.C. 44, Marcus Antonius, at that time Consul, proposed and carried a law by which the name of *Quintilis* was changed to *Iulius*, in honour of *Iulius Cæsar*, whose birth-day was on the 12th of that month;[3] and at a subsequent period, B.C. 8, by a similar piece of flattery, the name *Sextilis* was changed to *Augustus*, because the emperor had in that month entered upon his first Consulship, had achieved some remarkable victories, and had celebrated three triumphs.[4] Other princes rejected,[5] or courted like distinctions. *September*

---

[1] The principal authorities are Plutarch. Vit. Cæs. 59. Dion Cassius XLIII. 26. Appian. B.C. II. 154. Ov. Fast. III. 155. Sueton. Jul. 40. Plin. H.N. XVIII. 25. Censorinus 20. Macrob. S. I. 14. Ammian. Marcell. XXVI. 1.
[2] See Macrob. S. I. 16.
[3] Macrob. S. I. 12. Dion Cass XLIV. 5. Appian. B.C. II. 154.
[4] Sueton. Octav. 31. Dion Cass. LV. 6. Macrobius has preserved the decree of the Senate, the date is given by Censorinus 22.
[5] Sueton. Tib. 26.

was for a while known as *Germanicus*,[1] and *October* as *Domitianus*;[2] but while the names of *July* and *August* still endure, the others soon reverted to their primitive designations.

Divisions of the Month.—Julius Cæsar retained also the ancient divisions of the month by *Calendae, Nonae*, and *Idus*. The *Calendae* fell uniformly on the first day of each month; the *Idus* on the 13th, except in March, May, July, and October, when they fell on the 15th; the *Nonae* were always eight (according to the Roman computation *nine*) days before the *Idus*, and therefore on the 5th, except in March, May, July, and October, when they fell on the 7th.

Method of Dating.—When an event did not happen exactly on the Calends, Nones, or Ides of any month, they calculated the day by reckoning backwards from the next division of the month. Thus, if it happened between the Calends and the Nones, it was said to take place so many days before the Nones; if it happened between the Nones and Ides, it was said to take place so many days before the Ides; if it happened after the Ides, it was said to take place so many days before the Calends of the ensuing month.

In the second place, in making these computations, the day *from* which they reckoned was always included, as well as the day *to* which they reckoned. Thus, the 3d of January was called the third day before the Nones of January; the 10th of March the 6th day before the Ides of March; the 14th of June the 18th day before the Calends of July. We observe an analogy to this practice in the Scotch phrase, " this day eight days ;" the German " acht Tage," which alike denote a space of *seven days*; and the French " quinze jours," which stands for *a fortnight*.

The form of expression was likewise remarkable. When an event took place on the Calends, Nones, or Ides, it was said to happen, *Calendis—Nonis—Idibus Ianuariis—Februariis*, &c. or *Ianuarii—Februarii*, &c.; (sc. mensis;) when it took place on the day before one of these divisions, then it was said to happen, *Pridie Calendas—Nonas—Idus Ianuarias—Februarias*, &c.; but in other cases the formula generally employed was, *Ante diem tertium—quartum—quintum—sextum*, &c. *Calendas—Nonas—Idus Ianuarias—Februarias*, &c. Thus the 31st of January was, *Pridie Calendas Februarias;* the 6th of March, *Pridie Nonas Martias;* the 12th of April, *Pridie Idus Apriles;* the 27th of April, *Ante diem quintum Calendas Maias;* the 2d of May, *Ante diem sextum Nonas Maias;* the 6th of June, *Ante diem octavum Idus Iunias;* the 15th of August, *Ante diem decimum octavum Calendas Septembres*. Sometimes, but less frequently, the preposition is omitted, and the numeral put in the ablative. Thus we find, *Quarto Calendas Septembres*, for the 29th of August; *Decimo sexto Calendas Novembres*, the 17th of October; *Quinto Idus Decembres*, the 9th of December, and so on. In ancient monuments and old MSS., the words *Ante diem* are very frequently indicated by initial letters only, A.D., and the number by the Roman numeral—thus, A.D. IV. IDUS OCTOBRES; A.D. VI. CALENDAS DECEMBRES; A.D. III. NONAS NOVEMBRES; or farther abbreviated, A.D. IV. ID. OCTOB.; A.D. VI. KAL. DEC.; A.D. III. NON. NOV. The *Ante diem*, or its abbreviation, are often omitted altogether, and the numeral stands alone—IV. ID. OCTOB.; VI. KAL. DEC.; III. NON. NOV.

Scaliger and others have attempted, with no great success, to account for the origin of the expression *Ante diem tertium*, &c. instead of what would appear to be the more natural form, *Diem tertium* (or, *die tertio*) *ante*.[3] However the

---
[1] Sueton. Cal. 15.
[2] Sueton. Dom. 13. Macrob. S. 1. 12.
[3] We have in Tacit. Ann. XII. 69, *tertio ante Idus Octobres*, but such a combination is rare

phrase may have arisen, the combination *ante diem* appears practically to have been a formula, which was regarded as a single word, and hence we occasionally find another preposition prefixed to the *ante*. Thus Cic. Phil. III. 8.—IN ANTE DIEM *quartum Calendas Decembres distulit*, i.e. He put off (the meeting of the Senate) to the 28th of November; and again, Ep. ad. Att. III. 17.—*De Quinto fratre nuntii nobis tristes nec varii venerant* EX ANTE DIEM *Non. Iun. usque ad Prid. Kal. Sept.* i.e. From the Nones of June until the day before the Calends of September. Nay, we even meet with *ante diem* introduced adverbially where no date is given, as in Caes. B. C. I. 11.—ANTE QUEM DIEM *iturus sit*, for *quo die*, and the Greek writers translate the phrase literally, when computing time according to the Roman fashion. Thus Plutarch[1] tells us that Rome was founded ἡμέρα τῇ πρὸ ἕνδεκα Καλανδῶν Μαίων, i.e. 21st April.[2]

Intercalation of the Julian Year.—The day added every fourth year, as explained above, was inserted in February, immediately after the festival of the Terminalia, which fell *VII. Kal. Mart.* (23d February.) In such years, the 6th day before the Calends of March (*VI. Kal. Mart.*) was repeated twice, from which circumstance the day inserted was termed *Bissextum*,[3] or *Dies Bissextus*,[4] and the year itself *Annus Bissextus*.[5] The adjective *Bissextilis*, from whence comes the modern word *Bissextile*, is a barbarism. We find that the Roman lawyers decided that of the two days which were called *VI. Kal. Mart.* the latter, or that nearest to March, was, strictly speaking, to be considered in all contracts as the inserted day; but that since these two days were one in the eye of the law, any person born on the inserted day was, in ordinary years, to consider the *VI. Kal. Mart.* as his birth-day, while any person born on the *VI. Kal. Mart.* in an ordinary year, was, in the *Annus Bissextus*, to consider the former of the two days called *VI. Kal. Mart.* as his birth-day.[6]

The edict published by Julius Cæsar which explained the changes introduced, and pointed out the steps to be followed, in order to secure regularity for the future, seems to have been expressed ambiguously. The *Julian Era* commenced on the 1st of January, B.C. 45; Cæsar was assassinated on the Ides of March, the year following, and almost immediately after the *Pontifices* fell into an error, and inserted a day every third year, instead of every fourth. This was continued for thirty-six years, in the course of which twelve days were added, instead of nine, when the mistake was rectified by Augustus, who gave orders that the insertion of the *bissextum* should be omitted for twelve years, by which a compensation would be made for the three supernumerary days, after which the insertion was to proceed regularly every fourth year, according to the original intention of the author of the Calendar.[7] A slight correction must on this account be applied to the dates of events which took place within the above period of thirty-six years, when they descend to days. Thus the battle of Actium, which we are told was fought on the 2d of September, B.C. 31, really happened on the 3d.

Nundinae.—From the earliest times the Romans made use of a week of eight days. During seven days the husbandman devoted himself to his rural toils,

---

[1] Vit. Rom. 12.
[2] Observe also Caes. B.C. I. 6. *Is dies erat ante diem V. Cal. Aprilis*, and Liv. VI. I. *Tum de diebus religiosis agitari coeptum, diemque ante diem XV. Calendas Sextiles . . . insignem . . . fecerunt.*
[3] Censorin. 20. Amm. Mar. XXVI. 1.
[4] Ulpian. Digest. IV. iv 3.
[5] Augustin Ep. CXIX. ad Januar. c. 7. See also Macrob. S. I. 14.
[6] Digest. IV. iv. 3.
[7] Macrob. S. I. 14. Plin. H.N. XVIII. 57. Sueton. Octav. 26. Solin. Polyh. I

and on the eighth he repaired to the city to transact business, and exercise his political privileges. These market days were called *Nundinae*, a word evidently formed from *Nonus*, because, according to the Roman method of computation, they recurred every ninth day, *nono quoque die*. We have seen above (p. 113,) that in the year B.C. 98, a law was passed by the Consuls Q. Cæcilius Metellus and T. Didius, thence called *Lex Caecilia Didia*, which, among other provisions, enacted that every bill should be exhibited for the inspection of the people for three market days before it was submitted to the Comitia. This space of time, which could not be less than seventeen days, was from that time forward called *Trinundinum* or *Trinum Nundinum*.[1] The *Nundinae* ran on with perfect regularity; but it was considered unlucky for them to fall upon the first day of the year, or upon the Nones of any month.[2] Such coincidences were carefully guarded against in the infancy of the republic by the priests, who controlled the Calendar, and even so late as B.C. 40, five years after the adoption of the Julian reform, an extraordinary day was inserted to prevent the first of January in the following year from coinciding with one of the *Nundinae*,[3] the superstition having been revived, it would seem, by the circumstance that the war of Lepidus (B.C. 78) broke out in a year which commenced in this inauspicious manner.

The Jewish week of seven days (*Hebdomas*) was known to the Romans from the time of Pompeius, but was not generally adopted until after Christianity became the established religion of the State.

Classification of Days.—We may now proceed to explain the epithets by which the days of the Roman year were distinguished individually, when considered with reference to religion and the ordinary business of life.

Dies Fasti were the days upon which the Courts of justice were open, and legal business could be transacted before the Praetor, the *Dies Nefasti* were those upon which the Courts were closed. Certain days were *Fasti* during one portion, *Nefasti* during another,[4] and such were named *Intercisi*, (halved,) or, according to the more ancient form of the word, *Endotercisi*.

All days consecrated to the worship of the Gods by sacrifices, feasts, or games, were named *Festi;* those hallowed by no such solemnities, *Profesti*.

The holy days (*Feriae, Festa,*) included under the general denomination of *Festi dies*, were divided into two classes, *Feriae Publicae*, and *Feriae Privatae*, the former celebrated by the community at large, the latter peculiar to particular clans, families, or individuals. The *Feriae Publicae* again were either,

Feriae Stativae, observed regularly every year on a fixed day, such as the *Terminalia* on the 23d of February, the *Festum Annae Perennae* on the Ides of March, and many others; or,

Feriae Conceptivae, observed regularly every year, but on days fixed by the priests or magistrates for the time being. Such were the *Feriae Latinae*, the *Sementiva, Compitalia*, &c. There were also

Feriae Imperativae, extraordinary holidays, being for the most part days of supplication or thanksgiving, appointed by the magistrates on occasions of

---

[1] See Cic. Phil. V. 3. Ep. ad Att. II. 3. Ep. ad Fam. XVI. 12.   Liv. III. 33.   Quintil. I, O. II. iv. 35.
[2] Macrob. S. I. 13.   Dion Cass. XLVIII. 33.   See also XL. 47.
[3] We cannot doubt, however, that a day would be subsequently dropped to compensate for this irregularity.
[4] *Fastus* is derived from *fas*, or from *fari*, as being the days on which it was *lawful* for the Praetor *to speak* the words which expressed his jurisdiction. Thus Macrobius S. I. 16.— INTERCISI—*illorum enim dierum quibusdam horis fas est, quibusdam fas non est ius dicere. nam, cum hostia caeditur, fari nefas est: inter caesa et porrecta fari licet: rursus, cum adoletur, non licet.*

national distress or triumph. We ought also to notice *Dies Comitiales*, days on which it was lawful to hold assemblies of the people, being for the most part such as were neither *Fasti* nor *Festi* nor *Intercisi*.

Nor ought we to forget the *Dies Atri*, on which it was thought unlucky to undertake any business of importance. To this class belonged the day after the Calends, Nones, and Ides of each month, as we are told by Ovid. Fast. I. 57. Macrobius gives a full account of the origin of this superstition (I. 16.)

Fasti.—For nearly four centuries and a-half after the foundation of the city, the knowledge of the Calendar was confined to the Pontifices alone, whose duty it was regularly to proclaim the appearance of the New Moon, to announce to the people the days of the month on which the Nones and Ides would fall, and to give notice of the *Dies Festi*, *Fasti*, *Nefasti*, and *Comitiales*. These secrets which might be, and doubtless often were, employed for political ends, were at length divulged in the year B.C. 314, by Cn. Flavius, (see p. 224. 328,) who drew up tables embracing all this carefully-treasured information, and hung them up in the Forum for the inspection of the public.[1] From this time forward documents of this description were known by the name of *Fasti*, and were exhibited for general use in various parts of the city. They contained, for the most part, an enumeration of the days of the year in regular order; to each was attached a mark pointing out whether it was *Fastus*, *Nefastus*, *Intercisus*, *Comitialis*, *Ater*, &c.; the position of the Nones and Ides, and different Festivals, was also laid down, and sometimes a brief notice of some great victory, the dedication of a temple, or similar event, was added, especially in later times, when in this manner a compliment could be paid to the reigning prince.

These *Fasti*, in fact, corresponded very closely to a modern Almanac, and the poem of Ovid which he entitled *Fasti* may be considered as a poetical *Year-Book*, or *Companion to the Roman Almanac*, according to the order of the Julian Calendar. All the more remarkable epochs are examined in succession, the origin of the different festivals is explained, the various ceremonies described and such illustrations added as were likely to prove useful or interesting to the reader.

Several specimens of *Fasti*, or ancient Almanacs, engraved on stone, have been discovered at different times more or less perfect, and copies are to be found in the larger collections of Roman antiquities and inscriptions.[2]

Upon a careful examination and comparison of the marks by which the days of the year are distinguished in these monuments, we obtain the following classification:—

```
38 days are marked,.................. F.
63      —           .................. N.
54      —           .................. N. P.
 1      —           .................. F. P.
 2      —           .................. Q. Rex C. F.
 1      —           .................. Q. St. D. F.
 8      —           .................. EN.
181     —           .................. C.
17      —           .................. Sine Nota.
———
365
```

[1] Liv. IX. 46. Val. Max. II. 5. Macrob. S. I. 15. Cic. pro Mur. 11.
[2] See *Graevius*, Thesaurus Antiqq. Romm. Vol. VIII.: *Gruter*. Corpus Inscrip. Latt.: *Foggini*, Fastorum Verrianorum reliquiae, &c.; *Van Vaassen*, Animadverss. ad Fastos Rom. sacros, &c.

proved by the names of those which follow June, namely *Quintilis* or the fifth month, *Sextilis* the sixth, *September* the seventh, and so on to *December* the tenth. In addition, many sacred rites and ancient customs long retained point to the same conclusion. On the first of March, the holy fire was renewed on the altar of Vesta; at the commencement of the month the old laurels were taken down from the *Regia*, from the houses of the *Flamines*, and from the different *Curiae*, and replaced by fresh branches; sacrifices were offered to *Anna Perenna*, the goddess of the circling year; the salaries of instructors were paid; the taxes farmed out; and matrons gave an entertainment to the slaves, as the masters of families did on the *Saturnalia*, the object of the latter being to reward the domestics for their industry during the year that was past, of the former to stimulate their exertions for the future.[1]

The year of 304 days corresponds with the course neither of the sun nor of the moon, and many hypotheses have been formed with regard to its origin and import. By far the most ingenious and profound of these, so ingenious indeed that it almost carries conviction, is the theory propounded by Niebuhr. He supposes it to have been employed along with a lunar year for the purpose of making the solar and lunar years coincide at certain fixed epochs. He moreover finds traces of it in history at a period long after it is generally believed to have fallen into disuse, and by its aid explains several of the chronological anomalies and contradictions so frequent in the early annals. His calculations are too intricate to be developed here, but well deserve the attention of all interested in such researches.[2]

Year of Numa.—The year of Romulus was succeeded by a pure lunar year, introduced, according to the prevailing tradition, by Numa,[3] who retained the names of the ten months already in use, and added two more, *Ianuarius*, from the god *Ianus*, and *Februarius*, from *Februus*, the deity who presided over expiatory rites.

The true length of a lunar month, that is, the interval between two successive New or Full Moons, is 29 days, 12 hours, 44 minutes, 2.87 seconds, and hence twelve lunar months contain 354 days, 8 hours, 48 minutes, 34.386 seconds. The Athenians made their lunar year consist of 354 days; but Numa, influenced, it is said, by the virtue attributed to odd numbers,[4] added another to make up 355.

Calendae. Nonae. Idus.—Each month was divided into three periods by the *Calendae*, *Nonae*, and *Idus*. The *Calendae* marked the first of the month, the day following the evening upon which the slender crescent of the *New Moon* was first visible in the sky; the *Nonae* the *First Quarter*; the *Idus* the *Full Moon*. The origin of these terms must be explained. Macrobius has preserved the record of the ancient practice (S. I. 15.)

Priscis ergo temporibus, antequam Fasti a Cn. Flavio scriba invitis patribus in omnium notitiam proderentur, Pontifici Minori haec provincia delegabatur, ut novae lunae primum observaret adspectum, visamque Regi Sacrificulo nuntiaret, itaque sacrificio a Rege et Minore Pontifice celebrato idem Pontifex, KALATA, *id est,* VOCATA *in Capitolium plebe iuxta Curiam Kalabram, quae*

---
[1] See Macrob. S. I. 12. Ov. Fast. III. 135. seqq. Plutarch. Q. R. 19.
[2] Niebuhr's Roman History, Vol. I. Chapter "On the secular cycle."
[3] Censorin. 20. Solin. 1. Macrob. S. I. 13. On the other hand Junius Gracchanus maintained (Censorin. 1. c.) that this change was introduced by Tarquinius (Priscus.)
[4] Thus Virgil. E. VIII. 75—*Numero deus impare gaudet.* Plin. H.N. XXVIII. 5—*Impares numeros ad omnia vehementiores credimus;* and Paulus Diaconus s. v. *Imparem,* p. 109—*Imparem numerum antiqui prosperiorem hominibus esse crediderunt.*

F. denotes *Fastus;* N. *Nefastus;* N. P. *Nefastus priore,* (parte,) that is *Nefastus* in the early part of the day, and therefore we conclude, *Fastus* in the after part; F. P. *Fastus priore,* the converse of the preceding; Q. *Rex* C. F. *Quando Rex Comitiavit Fastus;* that is, *Fastus* after the *Rex Sacrificulus* has performed sacrifice in the *Comitium,* this mark is attached to the 24th of March and the 14th of May; Q. *St.* D. F. *Quando Stercus Defertur Fastus;* that is, *Fastus* after the sweepings and other filth have been carried out of the temple of Vesta and conveyed to the Tiber, a ceremony performed once a-year on the 15th of June, as we learn from Ovid and Varro; EN. *Endotercisus;* C. *Comitialis.*

There is some difficulty in explaining the difference between the days which were N. P. and those which were EN. The Ides of each month were N. P. and most of the other days bearing this mark were sacred to different deities, while those marked EN. do not appear to been hallowed by any solemnity whatever.

The *Fasti* just described have, to prevent confusion, been called *Calendaria* or *Fasti Calendares,*[1] and must be carefully distinguished from certain compositions also named *Fasti* by the ancients.

These were regular chronicles in which were recorded each year the names of the Consuls and other magistrates, together with the remarkable events, and the days on which they occurred. The most important were the *Annales Maximi,* kept by the *Pontifex Maximus;* but similar records appear to have been compiled by other magistrates, and by private individuals, and we find many allusions to works of this description, which must have afforded valuable materials to the historian.[2]

In the year 1547, several fragments of marble tablets were dug up at Rome, which were found to contain a list of Consuls, Dictators, Censors, &c. from the foundation of the city, until the age of Augustus. These were collected and adjusted as far as possible, and deposited by Cardinal Alexander Farnese in the Capitol, from which circumstance they have been styled the *Fasti Capitolini,* and similar collections derived from different sources have received the names of *Fasti Consulares, Fasti triumphales,* and the like.

We may now turn our attention to the Roman Calendar as it existed in ages more remote, and to the different forms which it assumed before the Julian Era. Every part of this subject is involved in darkness and uncertainty, and the statements of the ancient writers, who appear to have been themselves very ignorant in such matters, are most perplexing and irreconcileable.

Year of Romulus.—There can be little doubt that a year was in use among the Romans in the earliest times, and therefore denominated the *Year of Romulus,* which consisted of 304 days, divided into 10 months—*Martius, Aprilis, Maius, Junius, Quintilis, Sextilis, September, October, November, December.* Of these, March, May, Quintilis, and October, contained 31 days, the rest 30.[3]

That the month of March was originally the first in the year is sufficiently

---

[1] These expressions are not classical.
[2] See Hor. C. III. xvii. 1. IV. xiii. 13. S. I. iii. 112.
[3] Among the older historians, Licinius Macer and Fenestella maintained that the Romans from the first employed a solar year of 12 months, (see Censorin. 20. and Plutarch also Vit. Num. 18.) that the number of the months was originally 12, and that the number of days in each varied from 20 to 35, the sum total being 360. But on the other side we have Junius Gracchanus, Fulvius, Varro, and others, (see Censorin. as above,) to whom we may add Ov. Fast. I. 27. 43. III. 99. 119. 151. Aul. Gell. III. 16. Macrob. S. I. 12. Solin. Polyh. I.; all of whom speak without any doubt of the 10 months year. The number of days in each month is given by Censorinus, Solinus, and Macrobius.

*Casae Romuli proxima est, quot numero dies a Kalendis ad Nonas superessent
pronuntiabat: et* QUINTANAS *quidem dicto quinquies verbo* καλῶ, SEPTIMANAS
repetito septies praedicabat, verbum autem καλῶ *Graecum est, id est,* VOCO, *et
hunc diem qui ex his diebus qui Kalarentur primus esset, placuit* KALENDAS
vocari. hinc et ipsi Curiae, ad quam vocabantur, KALABRAE *nomen datum est.
Ideo autem Minor Pontifex numerum dierum qui ad Nonas superessent
Kalando prodebat, quod post novam lunam oportebat Nonarum die populares
qui in agris essent confluere in urbem accepturos causas feriarum a Rege
Sacrorum, scripturosque quid esset eo mense faciendum.*

It appears from this that the *Kalendae* were derived from *Kalo*, the same with
the Greek καλῶ, because immediately after the appearance of the New Moon, the
people were called together that they might be told on what day the Nones would
fall. It must be observed that the *New Moon* in question was not the astronomical New Moon or period of conjunction, but the first appearance of the crescent in
the evening twilight. Now, according to circumstances, the New Moon is sometimes visible on the evening after conjunction, sometimes not for two or three
days. Hence the *Nones* or First Quarter would fall sometimes as early as the fifth
of the month, sometimes as late as the seventh; and thus the *Ides* or Full Moon
would fall sometimes as early as the thirteenth, sometimes as late as the fifteenth.
The pontiffs appear by ancient custom to have been confined to the extremes,
and hence according to the appearance of the New Moon they proclaimed that
the Nones would be on the fifth, in which case they were called *Quintanae*, or
on the seventh, and then they were called *Septimanae*. *Idus* is derived from an
Etruscan verb *iduare*, signifying *to divide*, because the Full Moon divides the
lunar months; *Nonae* is the plural of *Nonus* "the ninth," because the Nones
were always just nine days before the Ides, according to the Roman system of
computation explained above.

January and February having been added to the ten months of the old year,
a question arises as to the order of succession then or subsequently established.

That February was in the first instance the last month of the year, seems
scarcely to admit of doubt; thus Cicero de Legg. II. 21.—*Venio nunc ad
Manium iura, quae maiores nostri et sapientissime instituerunt et religiosissime coluerunt. Februario antem mense, qui tunc extremus anni mensis erat,
mortuis parentari voluerunt,*—and Varro (L.L. VI. § 13.)—TERMINALIA, *quod
is dies anni extremus constitutus. Duodecimus enim mensis fuit Februarius.* [1]

We have no satisfactory evidence to determine the epoch at which January
and February became the first and second months. Plutarch supposes them to
have been from the first the eleventh and twelfth. According to Ovid, who
supposes them to have been added by Numa, January was placed at the beginning of the year, February at the end, and the new arrangement, by which
February was placed second, was introduced by the Decemvirs. [2] It is perfectly
clear, however, from the various ceremonies described above, that March must
have been looked upon as the commencement of the year at the time when those
rites were established. *Ianuarius*, therefore, may have been called after *Ianus*,
the deity presiding over the beginning of all things, not because it was the first
month of the sacred or of the civil year, but because it was the month which

---

[1] See also Paul. Diac. s.v. *Februarius*, p. 85, and Servius on Virg. G. I. 43. Macrobius S. I.
11. 13. asserts that January and February were placed by Numa as the first and second
months of the year, and in the last quoted chapter contradicts himself downright—*Omni
intercalationi mensis Februarius deputatus est, quoniam is ultimus anni erat.*
[2] Fast. II. 49.

immediately followed the winter solstice, when the sun may be said to resume his career.[1] We know that from B.C. 153, the consuls always entered upon their office on the 1st January, but we cannot positively assert that this day was considered the first of the civil year before that time, although it undoubtedly was looked upon as such ever after.

Intercalation of the Lunar Year.—The lunar year of the Greeks consisted of 354 days, that of the Romans of 355, while the length of the solar year, upon which depends the return of the seasons, is $365\frac{1}{4}$ days nearly. Hence almost all nations who have adopted a lunar year have had recourse to *intercalations*, that is, to the insertion of additional days or months from time to time, which, if managed skilfully, will insure a correspondence between the civil and natural year at fixed periods, and prevent the dislocation of the seasons. The insertion of a day every fourth year in the Julian Calendar, which has no reference to the moon, is also an *intercalation*, the object being to compensate for the error arising from making the solar year consist of an exact number (365) of days, instead of $365\frac{1}{4}$, and we shall see how it became afterwards necessary to modify this intercalation in order to compensate for the error arising from supposing the solar year to be exactly 365.25 days in length, instead of 365.242264, &c., as it really is.

Octaeteris of the Athenians.—If we reckon the lunar month at $29\frac{1}{2}$ days, and the solar year at $365\frac{1}{4}$ days, and the earliest astronomers did not arrive at greater accuracy, then twelve lunar months, or 354 days, will fall short of a solar year by $11\frac{1}{4}$ days, which in eight lunar years will amount to 90 days. If, therefore, in the space of eight lunar years we add three lunar months, or, in other words, make three lunar years out of every eight consist of thirteen lunar months instead of twelve, then at the end of eight years there will be a difference of only one day and a-half between the solar and lunar years. This correction was at one time employed by the Athenians; the intercalary months were added at the end of the third, fifth, and eighth years, and the period, or to use the technical phrase, the *Cycle* of eight years was termed ὀκταετηρίς.

Cycle of Meton.—With the progress of science a more convenient correction was introduced. According to the most accurate calculations,

19 Solar years contain..........................6939.603016 days.
235 Lunar months.....................⎫
or, 19 Lunar years and 7 months........⎬ contain 6939.68718 days.

so that if seven lunar months are intercalated during nineteen lunar years, or if, in other words, seven out of every nineteen lunar years are made to consist of thirteen lunar months instead of twelve, then the difference between the solar and lunar years at the end of that period will amount to only .084164 of a day, and the error will be less than one day in two hundred years. This ἐννεαδεκατηρίς, or cycle of nineteen years, is usually named, from its inventor, the *Cycle of Meton*, and came into use at Athens on the 16th of July, B.C. 432. It was afterwards corrected by Calippus of Cyzicus, who invented a cycle of seventy-six years, which in its turn was corrected by Hipparchus, who invented a cycle of three hundred and four years.

It seems to be certain that the Romans for a considerable period made use of a pure lunar year, the introduction of which, as we have seen above, was usually

---

[1] *Bruma novi prima est, veterisque novissima solis:*
Principium capiunt Phoebus et annus idem.—Fast. I. 163.

ascribed to Numa, and it can scarcely be doubted that intercalations were employed resembling some of those described above, in order to bring about a correspondence with the solar or natural year. On this subject, however, the ancient writers are silent, with the exception of Livy, (I. 19.) but unfortunately his language is extremely obscure, and the text of the passage disputed.

The intercalations which we do find described by Macrobius, Censorinus, and Plutarch, and which were certainly in use at the time of the Julian reform, belong to a system essentially different. The scheme which they describe is the following. The year of Numa consisted of 355 days. The Romans having become acquainted with the Grecian Octaeteris, according to which 90 days were to be intercalated in a cycle of eight years, applied it thus. They intercalated at the end of every two years a month, which consisted alternately of twenty-two and twenty-three days, thus making up the sum of 90 days at the end of eight years.[1] It was soon discovered, however, that the year of the Greeks contained 354 days only, while their own had 355, and hence it followed that in the cycle of eight years there was an excess of eight days. To remedy this, a new cycle was invented of twenty-four years, and in the last eight years of this twenty-four days were omitted, sixty only being intercalated instead of 90, thus compensating for the excess which would have taken place in the whole period had the full number been employed.

At what time this (or any other) system of intercalation was brought into use, we cannot tell. The Roman antiquaries themselves were at variance. Some referred the introduction of intercalations to Romulus, some to Numa, some to Servius, some to the Decemvirs, while some brought it down as low as the consulship of Manius Acilius Glabrio in the Ætolian war, B.C. 191.[2] Whatever opinion we may adopt on this matter, it is important to attend to the following consideration.

So long as we make use of a year, the months of which are regulated by the phases of the moon, it is evident that all intercalations employed to produce a correspondence with the solar year, must be in the form of entire lunar months. As soon as a period is inserted either longer or shorter than one lunar month, or an exact number of entire lunar months, from that time forward all regular connection between the phases of the moon and the commencement of the months and years is destroyed. Hence as soon as the Romans began to employ the intercalary months of twenty-two and twenty-three days, from that moment they virtually abandoned the lunar year, and adopted a solar cycle, the same in substance as that afterwards perfected by Julius Cæsar, but less accurate and less convenient. The old names of Calends, Nones, and Ides were retained, but these would no longer answer to the first appearance of the New Moon, to the First Quarter, and to Full Moon, more than the first, fifth, and thirteenth of any month at the present time. Ideler believes the change from the pure lunar year to have taken place during the sway of the Decemvirs, an opinion of which we find some trace in Macrobius.[3] Hence he supposes that the Roman Calendar assumed three different shapes before the Julian reform. These he distinguishes as—

I. *The Year of Romulus* of 10 months and 304 days.

[1] So Censorinus 20. and Macrob. S. I. 13. Plutarch, on the other hand, says that Numa doubled the difference between the solar and lunar year, and thus made a month of 22 days, which was intercalated every alternate year, but makes no allusion to the month of 23 days.
[2] Macrob. S. I. 13. See also Cic. de Legg. II. 12.
[3] Macrob. S. I. 13. It is clear from Ov. Fast. II. 54, that there was a tradition that the Decemvirs had made *some* changes in the Calendar.

II. *The Year of Numa*, a pure lunar of 12 lunar months and 355 days, with suitable intercalations.

III. *The Year of the Decemviri*, nominally a lunar year like the former, but which, from the intercalations employed, ceased to correspond with the phases of the moon.

We have not yet mentioned the distribution of the days among the twelve months of the year of 355 days. It was as follows:[1]—

Januarius,...29	Aprilis,......29	Quintilis,....31	October,.....31
Februarius,..28	Maius,.......31	Sextilis,.....29	November,..29
Martius,......31	Junius,......29	September,...29	December,...29

This arrangement, which remained in force until the Julian reform, is usually referred to the time of Numa; but as the number of days in the different months is inconsistent with a lunar calendar, it can scarcely have been introduced until the intercalary months of twenty-two and twenty-three days were employed. The position of the Calends, Nones, and Ides was the same as in the year of Cæsar, the Calends always marked the 1st of every month, the Nones and Ides the 5th and 13th, except in March, May, July, and October, when they fell upon the 7th and 15th. All dates of works written before B.C. 45, must of course be calculated by the above table. Thus when Cicero, in a letter written B.C. 51, says that he arrived at the camp in Lycaonia, *VII. Kal. Sept.* we must not translate this "the 26th of August," as we should do had it been written after the beginning of B.C. 45, but "the 24th of August," because Sextilis at that time had 29 days only.

Plutarch names the intercalary month twice; in the life of Numa he calls it Μερκιδίνος; in the life of Cæsar, Μερκηδόνιος. It is remarkable that this term is not to be found in any Roman writer; the expressions *mensis intercalaris* and *mensis intercalarius* being alone employed by them.

The intercalations took place in the month of February, between the *Terminalia* and the *Regifugium*; that is, between the 23d and the 24th, at least such was the rule, although it may have been violated at times. The remaining five days belonging to February were added after the intercalary month, probably from some superstition; but all the calculations of time in intercalary years were founded upon the supposition that in such years February contained 23 days only. Thus in ordinary years, the day after the Ides of February was *A.D. XVI. Kal. Mart.*, but in the intercalary years, *A.D. XI. Calendas Intercalares*. The *Terminalia* in ordinary years fell *A.D. VII. Kal. Mart.*, in intercalary years, *Pridie Calendas Intercalares*.

The intercalary month had its own Calends, Nones, and Ides, with the addition of the epithet *intercalares*, the day after the Ides would be *A.D. XV.* or *A.D. XVI. Kal. Mart.*, according as the month contained 22 or 23 days, the five remaining days of February being added, and in either case the *Regifugium* would always stand as *A.D. VI. Kal. Mart.*[2]

Irregularities in the Roman Year previous to the Julian reform.—We have seen that the whole management of the Calendar was originally in the hands of the *Pontifices*, and even after Cn. Flavius had divulged the secrets of the Fasti, they retained the privilege of adjusting the intercalation.[3] This trust they shamefully betrayed, and to gratify their private animosities, or show

---

[1] Macrob. I. 14. Censorin. 20.
[2] For examples, see Fast. Capit. Liv. XXXVII. 59. Cic. pro Quinct. 25.
[3] Pontificum Arbitrio intercalandi ratio permissa. Censorin. 20.

favour to their friends, in order that a magistrate might remain in office for a period shorter or longer than the law permitted, that a farmer of the taxes might be defrauded of his just right, or obtain an unfair advantage, they curtailed or drew out the year at pleasure, until the whole Calendar was involved in a degree of uncertainty and confusion, to which we can find no parallel in the history of a civilized people.[1] The ignorance which prevailed with regard to the years in which the intercalations ought to take place, and the mystery observed by the priests, is well illustrated by the expressions of Cicero. Thus in Ep. ad Att. V. 21, we find—*Cum scies Romae intercalatum sit, necne, velim ad me scribas;* again in Ep. ad Fam. VII. 2—*Quotidie vota facimus ne intercaletur, ut quam primum te videre possimus;* and in Ep. ad Att. VI. 1. we find—*Accepi tuas literas. A.D. quintum Terminalia;* that is, on the 19th of February, this singular method of fixing the date being employed to prevent ambiguity, since the day would be *A.D. XI. Kal. Mart.* in a common year, and *A.D. VI. Kal. Intercal.* in an intercalary year, and Cicero knew not when he wrote, whether an intercalation had or had not taken place.

Annus Confusionis.—Accordingly, when Cæsar became Dictator, the year was about two months in advance of the seasons; the spring festivals happened in what were nominally the summer months, and those of summer in autumn.

To take a single example.—Cicero, in one of his Epistles to Atticus, (X. 17.) says that at the time when he was writing his journey was delayed by the equinox. The date affixed to this letter is *XVII. Kal. Jun.* i.e. 16th May.

In order to remedy these defects, it was found necessary to add 67 days to the year B.C. 46; these days were divided into two intercalary months, and inserted between November and December. In this year the ordinary intercalations of 23 days took place in February, so that it contained, in all—

Ordinary length of year,........................355 days.
Intercalary month, ...23 —
Two additional intercalary months,................ 67 —

Total, ...445 days.

Such was the year B.C. 46, which among modern chronologers has received the name of *Annus Confusionis*, although, as Ideler observes, Macrobius has more correctly termed it *Annus Confusionis ultimus.*

Censorinus says that 90 days were added to that year, Dion Cassius 67; but there is no contradiction here, for the former includes the ordinary intercalation of 23 days in February, which is not taken into account by the latter.[2] The two additional months seem to have been called *Mensis intercalaris prior*, and *Mensis intercalaris posterior*, for we find in Cic. Ep. ad Fam. VI. 14—*Ego idem tamen cum A.D. V. KALENDAS INTERCALARES PRIORES, rogatu fratrum tuorum venissem mane ad Caesarem*, &c.

Gregorian Calendar.—The Julian Calendar was founded upon the supposition, that the length of the solar or tropical year was exactly 365 days, 6 hours, or 365.25 days. Therefore

---
[1] See Censorin. 20. Macrob. I. 14. Plutarch. Vit. Caes. 59. Ammianus Marcellinus XXVI. 1. Solinus I.
[2] See Censorin. 15. Dion Cass. XLIII. 26. Macrob S. I. 16. Plin. H.N. XVIII. 17. Ammian. l. c. Macrob. XXVI. 1. Suet. Cæsar 40. Ov. Fast. III. 155. Appian. B.C. II. 154.

THE ROMAN CALENDAR.

The length of the Julian Year being ....365d. 6h.
But the true length of the Solar Year being ...365d. 5h. 48m. 51½s.

It follows that the Julian Year is too long by   11m. 8½s.
This excess in   10 years will amount to......   1h. 51m. 25s.
    —   in 100   —   ......   18h. 34m. 10s.
    —   in 1000   —   ...... 7d. 17h. 41m. 40s.

To correct this accumulating error, Pope Gregory XIII. published a Bull in 1582, by which it was ordained that common years should consist of 365 days, and that a day should be added every fourth year as formerly, with this difference, that the intercalation was to be omitted in the last year of those centuries not divisible by 4; and thus that 97 days instead of 100 should be inserted in 400 years.[1] The Gregorian Calendar was almost immediately adopted in all Roman Catholic countries, and to compensate for the error already incurred, 10 days were dropped. The change was not admitted into England until 1752, when 11 days were dropped between the 2d and 14th September, from which arose the distinction between *Old* and *New Style*. Russia and other countries which follow the Greek church, still retain the original Julian Calendar, and hence their dates are now 12 days behind those of the rest of Europe.

According to the Gregorian scheme by which three leap years are omitted in 400 years—

Length of the Gregorian Year being .... 365d. 5h. 49m. 12s.
True length of the Solar Year being .. .. 365d. 5h. 48m. 51½s.

Therefore the Gregorian Year is too long by........................ 20½s.
An excess which will not amount to 1 day in 4500 years.

If the insertion of a day be omitted each 4000th year—
Length of year according to cycle of 4000 years, 365d. 5h. 48m. 50½s.

which is too short by 1 second—a deficiency which will not amount to a day in 70,000 years.

Lustrum. Seculum.—We may now say a few words with regard to the longer divisions of time, the *Lustrum* and the *Seculum*.

The word *Lustrum*, (see p. 170,) derived from *Luo*, signified properly the expiatory sacrifice offered up for the sins of the whole people by the Censors at the end of every five years, the period during which these magistrates originally held office. Hence *Lustrum* was used to denote *a space of five years*, and the Censors in performing the sacrifice, were said *Condere lustrum*, to bring the *Lustrum* to a close. Varro, in explaining the term, derives it from *Luere*, in the sense of *to pay*—LUSTRUM *nominatum tempus quinquennale a luendo, id est solvendo, quod quinto quoque anno rectigalia et ultrotributa per censores persolvebantur.* (L.L. VI. § 2.)

It is to be observed here that *quinto quoque anno*, according to the Roman method of computation, might mean *every fourth year*, and *quinquennale tempus*, a term of *four years*, just as Cicero (De Orat. III. 32.) calls the Olympic games—*Maxima illa quinquennalis celebritas ludorum*;[2] but since we know

---

[1] Thus no intercalation takes place in the years 1900, 2100, 2200, 2300, 2500, because the numbers 19, 21, 22, 23, 25, are not divisible by 4, but all of these, according to the old system, would have been leap years.
[2] This is evidently in reference to the Greek expression πεντατηρίς.

from other sources that the Censors originally held office for five years, and that the taxes were farmed out upon five years' leases, the interpretation of the above passage is not open to doubt. We may add, that wherever the word *Lustrum* occurs in the older writers, it is always in connection with the duties of the Censors.

When we come down to the age of Ovid, a confusion seems to have arisen, and the meaning of *Lustrum* was no longer definite; in Amor. III. vi. 27.—*Nondum Troia fuit lustris obsessa duobus*—it unquestionably stands for five years; and also in Fast. III. 119, where the 10 month year of Romulus is described—*Ergo animi indociles et adhuc ratione carentes = Mensibus egerunt lustra minora decem*, i.e. the *Lustra* were too short by 10 months. But with singular inconsistency, a few lines farther on, (165,) where he is explaining the Julian Year, and the intercalation of the *Dies Bissextus*—*Hic anni modus est; in lustrum accedere debet = Quae consummatur partibus una dies*—*Lustrum* must certainly denote *four years.*

Again, in Trist. IV. x. 96. compared with the E. ex P. IV. vi. 5. we see the Roman *Lustrum* identified with the Grecian Olympiad, each being supposed equal to five years. As we come down lower, Pliny twice in one chapter (H.N. II. 47.) calls the four-year cycle of the Julian year a *Lustrum;* we find in inscriptions the intervals between the successive exhibitions of the Capitoline games instituted by Domitian, and celebrated every four years, designated as *Lustra;*[1] and in the third century, the original force of the term seems to have been quite forgotten, for Censorinus, in defining the *Lustrum* or *Annus Magnus*, seems to be ignorant that it ever did differ from the Olympiad, or denote any period but four years.

This uncertainty may probably be traced to the irregularity with which the sacrifice of the *Lustrum* was performed. It was omitted sometimes from superstitious motives, as when we read in Livy III. 22.—*Census actus eo anno.* (B.C. 460,) *Lustrum propter Capitolium captum, consulem occisum, condi religiosum fuit*—and often from other causes, for upon looking over the Fasti Capitolini, in which the Censors are registered, and the letters L. F. attached to the names of those who completed this rite, we shall find that although the usual interval is five years, yet not unfrequently six and seven were allowed to elapse, while occasionally it was repeated after four only. These facts seem to account for the inconsistencies of the later Roman writers, without going so far as Ideler, who maintains that *Lustrum* never was used for a fixed space of time.

The duration of the *Seculum* was a theme of controversy among the Romans themselves in the days of Augustus. The historians and antiquaries seem all to have agreed that the *Seculum* was a period of 100 years, while the Quindecemviri, the priests to whom was intrusted the custody of the Sibylline books, reposing, it would seem, upon the testimony of their sacred registers, asserted that 110 years was the interval at which the solemn *Ludi Seculares*, which marked the close of each *Seculum*, had ever been and ought to be celebrated. The *Locus classicus* on this subject is in Censorinus (17.)[2]

Censorinus has preserved also the conflicting statements with regard to the actual celebration of these games from the time of their institution, and his dates are all fixed by the consuls in office at the time. They are as follows:—

---

[1] Gruter C. I. CCCXXXII. 3. Censorin. 18.
[2] See also Varro L.L. VI. § 11. Paul. Diac. s.v. *Seculares Ludi*, p. 328. The corresponding passage in Festus is too much mutilated to afford any information.

The first Secular games were celebrated according to…	{ Valerius Antias,............ A.U.C. **245** The Commentaries of XV-viri, ... ——— 298 }
The second, ...	{ Antias,....................... ——— 305 XV-viri, ——— 408 }
The third, ...	{ Antias and Livy, ... ——— 505 XV-viri, ——— 518 }
The fourth, ...	{ Antias, Varro, and Livy, ——— 605 Piso Censorinus, Cn. Gellius, and Cassius Hemina, who lived at the time, ... ——— 608 XV-viri, ——— 628 }

The fifth by Augustus,............................ A.U.C. 737 or B.C. 17
The sixth by Claudius,............................ A.U.C. 800 or A.D. 47
The seventh by Domitian,........................ A.U.C. 841 or A.D. 88
The eighth by Septimius Severus, ... A.U.C. 957 or A.D. 204

To attempt to discover the causes which led to this strange disagreement would be absolute waste of time. We can scarcely hesitate to believe that the computations of the XV-viri were trimmed to serve an end; but it is remarkable that the period chosen by Augustus does not absolutely agree with their views, since the 5th games ought to have been held A.U.C. 738, and not 737, as they really were.

A Standard-bearer and two Legionaries, from Trajan's column.

CHAPTER XII.

THE MILITARY AND NAVAL AFFAIRS OF THE ROMANS.

I. MILITARY AFFAIRS.

In all discussions with regard to the Military affairs of the Romans, the extent of the subject should never be forgotten. For nine hundred years they pursued an almost uninterrupted career of conquest, and thirteen centuries more passed away before the empire thus formed was completely dismembered. If we confine ourselves to the former period alone, and bear in mind that the whole energies of a large portion of the nation were devoted to the cultivation of war both as a science and an art, it becomes evident that the changes and modifications in general principles and in practical details introduced during that lengthened space, must have been almost countless, and that we shall be guilty of a grievous error if we suppose that statements which are true with regard to any one epoch will hold good for all. We must therefore endeavour, as far as our materials will permit, to exhibit a view of a Roman Army at epochs far removed from each other, and thus, if possible, to form some idea of what took place during the intervals. With regard to one epoch only is our information full and satisfactory. Polybius, himself an experienced commander, who, as the friend and companion of the younger Scipio, had the best opportunities of studying the military system of Rome, when the discipline of her armies was most perfect, and when the physical and moral character of her soldiers stood highest, has transmitted to us an account of the Roman Army, as it existed when he composed his history, so complete in every particular that our curiosity is fully satisfied. With regard to other epochs, however, we depend entirely upon scattered notices contained in the classical writers; but although these are very numerous, and are dispersed over the works of authors in every department of literature, they but too often convey little instruction, for the writers and those for whom they wrote were so familiar with such topics, that there is very rarely more than a passing allusion, unaccompanied by comment or illustration. In what follows we shall, in accordance with the plan hitherto pursued, restrict ourselves in a great measure to the period of the republic, adding a few explanations of the more important alterations introduced under the earlier Emperors.[1]

Constitution of a Roman Army.—A regular Roman Army, consisting of

---

[1] I would venture to refer for fuller information on some of the matters treated of in this Chapter to the articles, ACIES, AGMEN, ALA, CASTRA, EXERCITUS, FECIALES, OVATIO, SPOLIA, TRIUMPHUS, written by me for the Dictionary of Greek and Roman Antiquities, edited by Dr. W. Smith. We may also refer here, once for all, to our great authority, Polybius, VI. 19--42.

Infantry (*Peditatus*) and cavalry, (*Equitatus*.) was, in the earlier ages, composed of Roman citizens exclusively, who were enrolled in Brigades termed *Legiones*.

As Latium and the rest of Italy were gradually subjugated, the different states received into alliance became bound by the terms of their respective treaties to furnish, when called upon, a contingent of soldiers, horse and foot. These were enrolled in battalions distinct from those composed of Roman citizens, were designated *Socii nomenque Latinum*, or simply *Socii*, and were clothed, equipped, and paid by the communities to which they belonged.

When Rome had extended her dominion beyond Italy, foreign Kings or Chiefs in alliance with the republic frequently supplied bodies of troops, who, under the name of *Auxiliares* or *Auxilia*, served along with the *Romani* and *Socii*. Thus as early as B.C. 218, we find *Galli Equites* under Scipio at the battle of the Ticinus, and soon afterwards we are told that no less than 2200 (*duo millia peditum et ducenti equites*) of the *Auxiliares Galli* deserted to Hannibal (Liv. XXI. 46. 48.)

Foreigners receiving pay, that is, Mercenaries in the limited sense of the word, were not employed until B.C. 213, when the Celtiberi in Spain offered to serve under the Roman Generals for the same hire which they had received from the Carthaginians, and their proposal was accepted (Liv. XXIV. 49.) For a considerable period, however, the mercenaries in a Roman Army were few in number, and consisted chiefly of Corps raised in particular localities, where the natives were celebrated for their skill in the use of some particular weapon. Such were the Slingers (*Funditores*) from the Balearic Isles, the Archers (*Sagittarii*) of Crete, and the Javelin-men (*Iaculatores*) of Mauretania.

After the Social War, (B.C. 88,) when all the subject states of Italy were admitted to the full *Civitas*, the distinction between *Romani* and *Socii* altogether disappeared, and the armies from that time forward were made up of *Romani milites* and *Auxilia*, the latter being in part furnished by foreign princes who were allowed to retain a nominal independence under the title of allies, but principally mercenaries recruited among the most warlike tribes of Gaul, Germany, Illyria, Pannonia, Thrace, and other frontier provinces. The number of these went on constantly increasing, and in the first century of the empire they already formed a large proportion of the really efficient troops.

The Roman Soldier.—It was a fundamental principle in the Roman polity that the state had at all times a right to demand military service from its members, and hence every male citizen between the ages of seventeen and forty-six was bound, when required, to enrol himself in the ranks. But service in the Army was regarded not merely as a duty and an obligation, but as a privilege. For many ages, the only avenue to favour and power was by the path of military distinction; and as late as the time of Polybius, no one could stand candidate for the lowest of the great offices of state until he had served for twenty years in the Infantry or ten years in the Cavalry. Moreover, by the constitution of Servius Tullius, none were permitted to serve as regular troops, except *Ingenui* belonging to the five classes; *Libertini*, *Proletarii*, and *Capite Censi* being alike excluded, except in seasons of great emergency, when all, without distinction, were called out, and even youths under seventeen and men above forty-six were enrolled. On one occasion during the second Punic War, when Rome was reduced to the last extremity, a large corps of volunteer slaves was raised, who eventually received their freedom as a reward for their faithful and efficient aid.[1] One of the most momentous of the democratic changes introduced by

[1] Liv. X. 21. XXII. 11. 57. XXIII. 32. XXIV. 11. 14. Aul. Gell. XVI. 10.

Marius was the free admission of the poorest citizens to the Legions,[1] a measure which, especially after the enfranchisement of the subject states in Italy, had the effect of introducing a new class of persons, who, from this time forward, formed the great bulk of the ordinary levies. But even before this period, the social position of the Roman soldiers had by degrees assumed an aspect totally different from that which it exhibited for five centuries after the foundation of the city. At first, they were mere militia, called out to repel or retaliate the hostile incursions of neighbouring tribes, and as soon as the brief campaign was over, each man returned to his home and resumed his peaceful occupations. But in proportion as the power of the commonwealth increased, the wars in which it was involved became more complicated and tedious, and the same army was compelled to keep the field for years in succession, especially when the scene of operations was removed to Greece and Asia. Hence the characters of citizen and soldier, which were long inseparably connected, gradually became distinct, the line of demarcation became more and more broadly marked, and after the time of Marius, the ranks were filled with men who were possessed of no property whatever, who were dependent for subsistence upon their pay, and who were consequently soldiers *by profession*. It was not, however, until the imperial government was established that the principle of maintaining at all times a large standing army was fully recognized; but from that time forward military men formed a large and powerful order in the state altogether distinct from civilians.

Levying Soldiers.—The Senate, at their first meeting after new Consuls entered upon office, voted the number of troops to be raised for the current year, and the Consuls then made proclamation (*edixerunt*) of the day on which they proposed to hold a levy, (*Delectum habere*,) giving notice that all liable for service must attend. The proceedings usually took place in the Capitol. The Consuls, seated on their Curule Chairs, assisted by the *Tribuni Militares*, caused the tribes to be summoned in succession, the order being determined by lot. The list of all who were of the legal age (*Aetas Militaris*) was read over, those individuals were selected who appeared most suitable, and their names were entered on the muster roll (hence *scribere* s. *conscribere milites*.) Under ordinary circumstances, the youth came forward eagerly to volunteer their services; (*dare nomina*;) but if any one absented himself, or, being present, refused to answer when cited, (*militiam detrectabat*,) he might be punished summarily with the utmost severity, and even sold as a slave,[2] unless a Tribune of the Plebs interfered on his behalf.

After the number was complete, the military oath (*Sacramentum*) was administered to all the recruits, (*Sacramento adigere* s. *Rogare*—*Sacramentum* s. *Sacramento dicere*,) in terms of which they swore to obey their leaders, and never to desert their standards. It would appear from a passage in Paulus Diaconus compared with Polybius, that one individual was chosen to repeat the formal words (*verba concepta*) of the oath, while all the rest took upon themselves the same obligation (*iurabant in verba*) by making the response IDEM IN ME.[3] After these preliminaries were concluded, the new levies were dismissed, notice having been given to them to meet at a given place on a given day.

---

[1] Aul. Gell. l. c. Sallust. Iug. 86.
[2] Liv. IV. 53. VII. 4. Cic. pro Caecin. 34.
[3] Liv. II. 24. III. 20. IV. 53. VII. 11. XXII. 38. Cic. de Off. I. 11. Caes. B.C. I. 76. Aul. Gell. XVI. 4. Paul. Diac. s.v. *Praeiurationes*, p. 224. There is a very obscure passage in Livy XXII. 38. about a second military oath which no commentator has ever explained in a satisfactory manner. Comp. Polyb. VI. 10. seqq.

When any panic arose, (*Tumultus,*) such as in ancient times was caused by the report of an inroad of the Gauls, (*Gallicus Tumultus—Tumultus Gallici fama atrox*, &c.) the formalities described above were dispensed with, and all who could bear arms, young and old, rich and poor alike, were called upon to rise in a mass for the protection of their country, such soldiers being termed *Tumultuarii* or *Subitarii*. When, under similar circumstances, there was time to hold a levy, it was conducted with the utmost rigour, (*delectus omnis generis hominum,*) all the ordinary pleas of exemption, (*vacationes,*) such as length of service or special indulgence, (*beneficium,*) being suspended, and hence the phrases—*Scribere exercitus sine ulla vacationis venia—Delectus sine vacationibus.* [1]

When a levy was about to be held at Rome, formal intimation was made to the allied states of the number of troops which they would be required to furnish —*Item ad Socios Latinumque nomen ad milites ex formula accipiendos mittunt;* (Liv. XXII. 57;) and the same course was probably adopted with regard to the distant *Coloniae Civium Romanorum.*

It is manifest that after the termination of the Social War, when all the inhabitants of Italy were admitted to the rights of Roman citizens, the system described above could not have been pursued, at least exclusively. When, therefore, volunteers did not come forward in sufficient numbers, persons termed *Conquisitores* were despatched to different districts, who superintended all the details of the Conscription, which in this case was properly called *Conquisitio*, as opposed to the ancient *Delectus* held in the city; but eventually *Conquisitio* and *Delectus* were used indifferently. Hence in Cicero and Caesar we meet with the phrases—*Exercitus ille noster, superbissimo Delectu et durissima Conquisitione collectus* (Cic. Prov. Cons. 2.)—*In omnes partes legatos Conquisitoresque Delectus habendi causa miscrant;* (Hirt. de bell. Alex. 2.) and under the empire, we find Tiberius assigning as one of the reasons which rendered it necessary for him to make a progress through the provinces—*Delectibus supplendos exercitus: nam voluntarium militem deesse, ac si suppeditet, non eadem virtute ac modestia agere, quia plerumque inopes ac vagi sponte militiam sumant* (Tacit. Ann. IV. 4.) A similar plan was adopted occasionally at an earlier period when great difficulty was experienced in procuring men, as in B.C. 212, when we find two commissions consisting each of three individuals appointed—*alteros, qui citra, alteros qui ultra quinquagesimum lapidem in pagis forisque et conciliabulis omnem copiam ingenuorum inspicerent: et, si qui roboris satis ad ferenda arma habere viderentur, etiamsi nondum militari aetate essent, milites facerent* (Liv. XXII. 6.)

Legio.—A Roman Army, from the foundation of the city, until the downfal of the Western Empire, always contained one or more Brigades, called LEGIONES, a term which comprehended Infantry, Cavalry, and, after the use of military engines became common, Artillery (*Machinae—Tormenta*) also. The *Legio*, under the republic, was composed of Roman citizens exclusively; and, therefore, in the earlier ages, an army consisted entirely of one or more *Legiones*, but after the subjugation of Latium and other states, the words, *Legiones* and *Legionarii Milites*, indicated those who were Roman citizens, in contradistinction to the *Socii* and *Auxilia*. The number of *Legiones* raised annually, necessarily varied according to the demands of the public service. Originally, four was the ordinary number, two for each consul, and down to the close of the republic, **two**

---

[1] Liv. I. 37. II. 26. III. 4. 30. VI. 6. VII. 11. 28. VIII. 20. X. 21. XXXV. 2. XL. 26.

Legions, with their complement of *Socii* and *Auxilia*, formed a *Consularis Exercitus*. During the Second Punic War, the forces under arms rose as high as eighteen, twenty, twenty-one, and even twenty-three Legions; under Tiberius, the standing army amounted to twenty-five *Legiones*, besides *Auxilia* about equal in strength to the Legions, and the Imperial Life Guards.[1] The Legions were at first numbered according to the order in which they were raised, *Prima, Secunda . . . Decima*, &c., and when they became permanent bodies, they retained the same numbers, like regiments in our own service, with the addition of epithets derived from various circumstances; these epithets being, in many cases, rendered necessary by the fact, that different Legions frequently bore the same number. Then under the empire we read of the *Prima Italica*, the *Prima Adjutrix*, the *Prima Minervia*, and the *Prima Parthica;* of the *Sexta Victrix* and the *Sexta Ferrata*. So also there were five numbered *Secunda*, and five numbered *Tertia*, &c. The men belonging to the *Prima, Secunda, Tertia . . . Duodevicesima . . . Vicesima*, &c., were designated respectively, as *Primani, Secundani, Tertiani . . . Duodevicesimani . . . Vicesimani*, &c.

Number of Pedites in a Legion. 1. The Legion, as established by Romulus, contained 3000 foot-soldiers, and we have no evidence of any increase or diminution of this number during the regal period.[2] 2. From the expulsion of the Tarquins, until the beginning of the second Punic War, the number varied from 4000 to 4200, although, on emergencies, the strength was raised to 5000, and even 5200.[3] 3. From the beginning of the second Punic War, until the age of Marius, (B.C. 100,) the number varied from 4200 to 5200, seldom falling below 5000, and, in some cases, rising as high as 6000.[4] 4. From B.C. 100, until the downfal of the empire, the number varied from 5000 to 6200. From the accession of Augustus, until the time of Hadrian, 6000 seems to have been regarded as the regular complement.[5]

Number of Equites in the Legion. From the first establishment of the Legion, until the time of Marius, the number of Cavalry seems to have been invariably 300, except in some rare special cases, when it was augmented to 330 and to 400.[6] After the time of Marius, the Cavalry in the Roman armies consisted chiefly of foreign troops, and, consequently, were not considered as forming part of the Legion. Down to the latest period, however, we find Cavalry, occasionally at least, incorporated with the Legion, but not in regular fixed numbers, as during the first six centuries of the City.

Organization of the Infantry in the Legion. This, as we have indicated above, must have passed through many changes, which it is impossible to follow step by step, in their gradual course, but we are able to trace the general outlines of the system at certain epochs widely distant from each other.

[1] Liv VIII. 8. II. 30. VII. 25. XXIV. 11. XXVI. 28. XXVII. 22. XXVI. 1. XXVII. 36. Tacit. Ann. IV. 4.
[2] Varro L.L. V. § 89. Plut. Rom. 13.
[3] Liv. VL 22. VII. 25. XXVIII. 28. XXI. 17. Dionys. VI. 42. IX. 13. Polyb. I. 16. II. 24. III. 72.
[4] Liv. XXII. 36. XXVI. 28. XXXVII. 39. XXXIX. 38. XL. 1. 18. 36. XLI. 9. 21. XLII.31. XLIV. 21. Polyb. III. 107. VI. 20.
[5] Paul. Diac. s.v. *Sex millium et ducentorum*, p. 336. Plut. Mar. 35. Sull. 9. Appian. Mithrid. 72. Lamprid. Alex. Sev. 50. Veget. II. 6. Serv. ad Virg. Æn. VII. 274. Isidor. Orig. IX. iii. 46. Suidas, Hesychius, s.v.
[6] The Roman authorities, and Dionysius, all agree upon this point; but Polybius, in one passage, (III. 107. comp. II. 24.) states that the Cavalry of the Legion amounted to 200 under ordinary circumstances, and was increased to 300 in great emergencies only. Elsewhere, however, (VI. 20.) he gives 300 as the number, without comment. For numbers beyond 300, see Liv. XXIII. 34. XL. 36. XLIII. 12.

(*First Epoch.*) We can say nothing of the state of matters until the time of Servius Tullius, whose division of the whole body of the citizens into Classes and Centuries, was inseparably connected with military considerations. Those possessing the largest amount of fortune, were bound to serve as Cavalry, while the arms, offensive and defensive, of the five Classes, were distinctly specified, and depended upon the means possessed by the members of each Class. When we take these statements in connection with the positive assertion of Livy, (VIII. 8,) we cannot for a moment doubt, that the Legion, in the earliest times, was marshalled in one compact solid body, according to the principles of the Grecian Phalanx. The foremost ranks were occupied by the citizens belonging to the first Class, whose fortune enabled them to provide themselves with a complete suit of defensive armour; the different portions of which we have enumerated in p. 69, and which will be seen represented in the annexed cut of a Greek heavy-armed warrior. Behind these, those of second and third Classes, less exposed, and therefore requiring less complete equipments, took their places, while those belonging to the fourth and fifth Classes skirmished with missiles; and when the conflicting hosts came to close quarters, fell into the rear of the phalanx, adding weight and consistency to the mass in the charge.

(*Second Epoch.*) How long this system lasted, we cannot with certainty determine; but Livy says (l.c.) that the change took place *postquam* (Romani) *stipendiarii facti sunt*—that is, after the commencement of the siege of Veii,—and conjecture has fixed upon Camillus the great Captain of the fourth century, as the individual by whom a new order was introduced. It is certain that in B.C. 340 we find that the unwieldy mass of the Phalanx had been broken up into three distinct lines, each line composed of small companies called *Manipuli*, the whole being arranged in such a manner that while each line and each company could act separately, they mutually supported each other, and executed combined movements with great facility, rapidity, and precision. The details are given in the chapter of Livy, already twice referred to above, which is unfortunately obscure if not corrupt; but although doubt may exist with regard to the force of some expressions, we can form a distinct conception of the leading features of the new system. The whole Legion when in battle order was arrayed in three lines.

The foremost line (*prima acies*) was composed of youths in the first bloom of manhood, (*florem iuvenum pubescentium ad militiam habebat,*) who were classed together under the general name of *Hastati*, and were divided into fifteen companies called *Manipuli*, which were drawn up separately at a short distance from each other (*distantes inter se modicum spatium.*) Each *Manipulus* contained sixty rank and file, two officers called *Centuriones*, and one standard bearer called *Vexillarius*. Of the sixty soldiers in the *Manipulus*, twenty carried only a spear (*hasta*) and javelins, (*gaesa*,) the remaining forty had oblong shields, (*scuta*,) and probably body armour also.

The second line was composed of men in the full vigour of life, (*robustior aetas,*) who were classed together under the general name of *Principes*, and, like the *Hastati*, were divided into fifteen *Manipuli*. The whole of the *Principes* were heavily armed, and their equipments were of the best kind (*scutati omnes insignibus maxime armis.*)

The thirty *Manipuli* of *Hastati* and *Principes* were comprehended under the general name of *Antepilani*.

The third line was composed, like each of the two former, of fifteen *Manipuli*, but each of the *Manipuli* in the third line was divided into three sections, which were called *Vexilla*, because each section had its separate standard. Under the first *Vexillum* in each of these triple *Manipuli*, were ranged the *Triarii*, veteran soldiers of tried bravery; under the second *Vexillum* the *Rorarii*, men younger and less distinguished; under the third *Vexillum* the *Accensi*, less to be depended upon than either of the foregoing, (*minimae fiduciae manum,*) and therefore placed in the rear.

The tactics of the period cannot be described more briefly or more clearly than in the words of the historian:—

Ubi his ordinibus exercitus instructus esset, Hastati omnium primi pugnam inibant. Si Hastati profligare hostem non possent, pede presso eos retrocedentes in intervalla ordinum Principes recipiebant: tunc Principum pugna erat; Hastati sequebantur: Triarii sub vexillis considebant, sinistro crure porrecto, scuta innisa humeris, hastas subrecta cuspide in terra fixas, haud secus quam vallo septa inhorreret acies, tenentes. Si apud Principes quoque haud satis prospere esset pugnatum, a prima acie ad Triarios sensim referebantur, inde rem AD TRIARIOS REDISSE, *quum laboratur, proverbio increbruit. Triarii consurgentes, ubi in intervalla ordinum suorum Principes et Hastatos recepissent, extemplo compressis ordinibus velut claudebant vias: unoque continenti agmine, jam nulla spe post relicta, in hostem incedebant; id erat formidolosissimum hosti, quum, velut victos insecuti, novam repente aciem exsurgentem auctam numero cernebant.*

(*Third Epoch.*) The principles adopted in the Second Epoch probably received their full development during the wars against the Samnites, the Greeks in Southern Italy, and the Carthaginians. The Third Epoch may be regarded as extending from B.C. 300 to B.C. 100 or 107. Here our great authority is Polybius, whose remarks apply to a Legion of 4000 men, although the number was usually greater in his day.

The Legion, as during the Second Epoch, was marshalled in three lines, which still bore the names of *Hastati*, *Principes*, and *Triarii*. The *Hastati*, 1200 in number, were, as formerly, young men, and formed the first line; the *Principes*, men in the prime of life, also 1200 in number, formed the second line; while the *Triarii*, experienced veterans, 600 in number, formed the third line In addition to these, there was a corps of light armed skirmishers, first organised B.C. 211, at the siege of Capua, (Liv. XXVL 4,) under the name of *Velites* or *Procubitores*, 1000 in number, who represented the irregular bodies termed *Accensi* and *Rorarii* in the earlier ages. When the number in the Legion was above 4000, the additional men were distributed equally among the *Hastati*, *Principes*, and *Velites*, the number of the *Triarii* being fixed at 600.

The defensive arms of the *Hastati*, *Principes*, and *Triarii*, were the same, all alike being equipped in a full suit of mail, consisting of a helmet (*galea*) of bronze, a breastplate of chain or scale armour, (*lorica*,) or a small cuirass, (*thorax* s. *pectorale*,) a greave for one leg, (*ocrea*,) and a large shield, (*scutum*,) made of thick rectangular planks, four feet long and two and a-half broad, bent round with the convexity outwards, covered with hide and bound with iron. As to their offensive weapons, all were furnished with the short, straight, pointed, two-edged Spanish sword; (*gladius*;) in addition to which the *Triarii* bore long pikes, (*hastae*,) while each man in the *Hastati* and *Principes* carried two of the formidable heavy javelins, upwards of six feet in length, called *Pila*. The *Velites* had merely a light casque covered with skin, a round buckler, (*parma*,) a sword, and a bundle of darts (*hastae velitares*.)

The *Hastati*, *Principes*, and *Triarii* were each divided into 10 *Manipuli*, and each *Manipulus* into two *Centuriae*, so that every Legion contained 30 *Manipuli* and 60 *Centuriae*. The *Velites* were not divided into Maniples and Centuries, but were dispersed equally among the three heavy armed lines. The word *Ordo* is very frequently employed as equivalent to *Centuria*, and rarely as equivalent to *Manipulus*. (See Liv. VIII. 8, and compare XLII. 34.)

As early as the second Punic War, perhaps earlier, (Aul. Gell. XVI. 4.) the *Manipuli* of the Legion were combined together in battalions called *Cohortes*. Each Legion contained ten *Cohortes*; each *Cohors* contained three *Manipuli* or six *Centuriae*, viz. one *Manipulus* of *Hastati*, one of *Principes*, and one of *Triarii*, with their complement of *Velites*. Observe that the word *Cohors* is also frequently employed as a general term to denote any body of soldiers unconnected with the Legion, (Liv. IV. 39. VII. 7. X. 40. XXV. 14. XXX. 36,) but when used with reference to the Legion, always bears the definite signification explained above.

It would appear that during the Second Epoch, the *Triarii* alone carried the *Pilum*, and were styled *Pilani*, and hence the two front lines, the *Hastati* and *Principes* were collectively termed *Antepilani*, (Comp. Varro L.L. V. § 39,) and these terms were still employed to designate the same divisions after the *Pilum* of the *Triarii* had been transferred to the *Hastati* and *Principes*. The standards, or at least the principal standard, must have originally been borne between the *Principes* and the *Hastati*, and hence the latter, or, in general, those who fought in the foremost ranks, are occasionally designated as *Antesignani*,[1] the front ranks themselves being called *Principia*.[2]

Cavalry of the Legion.—This branch of the service seems to have undergone little change in organization during the three Epochs which we have discussed. The regular complement (*iustus equitatus*) attached to each Legion was, as we have seen, 300. These were divided into ten squadrons called *Turmae*, of thirty men each, and each *Turma* into three *Decuriae* of ten men each. At the head of each *Decuria* was a *Decurio*, who had an *Optio* under him. The senior *Decurio* in each *Turma* commanded the squadron, and the whole body of Cavalry was under the command of an officer who, in later times, at least, was named *Praefectus Alae*, the term *Ala* being used to denote the Cavalry of the Legion, in consequence of their having been originally employed in the field to cover the flanks of the Infantry, which in the Phalanx were always vulnerable. The equipment of the Cavalry was originally made as light as possible, in order to secure rapidity in their evolutions, and their chief weapon was a long, thin,

---

[1] Liv. II. 20. VII. 33. VIII. 11. IX. 39. XXII. 5. XXX. 33.
[2] Liv. II. 65. III. 22. VIII. 10. Sallust Iug. 54. Tacit. Hist. II. 43.

flexible lance. But, before the time of Polybius, it had been found advisable to furnish them with a cuirass, a substantial buckler, and a strong heavy spear. Under the empire foreign Cavalry were to be found in the Roman ranks who were clad both man and horse in a complete suit of chain or scale armour, like those who formed part of the host of Antiochus, and were called *Cataphracti* or *Loricati* (Liv. XXXV. 48. XXXVII. 40.) Such is the Dacian represented in the annexed cut, taken from Trajan's column.

Socii of the Third Epoch.—When the Senate had resolved to levy a certain number of Legions, the *Socii* were called upon to furnish an equal number of Infantry, and twice the number of Cavalry. These troops were, we have every reason to believe, armed, equipped, organized, and disciplined exactly in the same manner as the Roman Legions, the whole of the expense being defrayed by the states to which they belonged. Both in the camp and when drawn up in order of battle, the Infantry of the allies was placed on the wings of the Legions, and hence the words *Ala, Alarii,* and *Cohortes Alariae* are employed to designate the whole force of the allies, both horse and foot, and the two divisions were distinguished as *Dextera Ala* and *Sinistra Ala. Ala,* when used in this sense, must be carefully distinguished from *Ala* when it signifies the 300 Roman horse which formed the Cavalry of the Legion, and which received their name in like manner from having been in ancient times employed to cover the flanks. After the social war the terms *Alarii* and *Alariae Cohortes* were applied to the *Auxiliares.*[1]

One third of the Cavalry and one fifth of the Infantry were always selected from the whole body *Socii* in each army, and attended upon the Consul, under the name of *Extraordinarii.*[2]

(*Fourth Epoch.*) This may be regarded as including the century which immediately preceded and that which immediately followed the Christian Era. We have already had occasion to notice important innovations which belong to the earlier portion of this Epoch—the free admission of *Proletarii, Capite Censi,* and probably of *Libertini* also, which took place under the influence of Marius —the removal of all distinctions between *Romani Milites* and *Socii,* which was a result of the Social War—and, finally, the employment of foreign Cavalry to the almost total exclusion of *Romani Equites.* But in addition to these general changes in the constitution of the army, there are some matters connected with the organization of the Legion itself which force themselves upon our attention.

1. From the commencement of this Epoch, the names *Hastati, Principes,* and *Triarii,* as applied to classes of Legionary soldiers, altogether disappear, and we must conclude that the ancient order of battle had fallen into disuse. The distribution of the men into *Centuriae, Manipuli,* and *Cohortes* still prevailed, the mutual relations of these divisions being the same as during the third Epoch,

---
[1] Aul. Gell. XVI. 4. Liv. X. 40. 43. XXVII. 2. XXX. 21. XXXI. 21. Caes. B.G. I. 51. B.C. I. 73. Cic. ad Fam. II. 17.
[2] Liv. XXVII. 13. XXXV. 5. Polyb. VI. 28.

that is to say, each *Legio* contained ten *Cohortes*, each *Cohors* three *Manipuli*, and each *Manipulus* two *Centuriae*.

2. The *Velites* are no longer mentioned, their place being supplied by *Iaculatores*, *Funditores*, *Sagittarii*, and other light-armed auxiliaries, comprehended under the general expression, *Levis Armatura*. The ancient word *Ferentarii* is used both by Sallust and Tacitus to designate the skirmishers of an army. (Sallust.Cat. 60. Tacit. Ann. XII. 35. Varro L.L. VII. § 57. Non. Marcell. s.v. *Decuriones*, p. 356, and s.v. *Ferentarii*, p. 357. ed Gerl. Paul. Diac. s.v. *Ferentarii*, p. 85. 93.)

3. The whole of the Legionaries were now equipped exactly alike. All wore the same defensive armour, and all were armed with the *Pilum* to the exclusion of the *Hasta*.

4. When it became necessary to execute any rapid movement, a certain number of the most active Legionaries were selected, and, having been relieved of the heavier portion of their equipments, were, for the time being, called *Expediti Milites*, *Expeditae Cohortes*, or the like, but these terms do not designate a separate class of soldiers.

5. The foreign Troops were distributed into *Cohortes* of Infantry and *Alae* of Cavalry, but of the internal organization of these bodies we know little or nothing.

Officers of the Legion.—Tribuni. Centuriones. Optiones. The officers of highest rank in the Legion were the *Tribuni*, of whom there were originally three; but when Polybius wrote, the number had been increased to six. For a long period the nomination of the *Tribuni* was vested in the Consuls, who commanded the Legions to which they were attached, but in B.C. 361, the people assumed the right of electing as many as they thought fit, and from that time forward, or at least from B.C. 311, a portion of them were always chosen in the Comitia Tributa, and the choice of the remainder left, as before, to the commanders-in-chief.[1] Polybius asserts, that no one could be nominated *Tribunus* until he had served for ten years in the Infantry, or five in the Cavalry, and this rule, although occasionally violated, as in the case of the elder Scipio, (Liv. XXII. 53,) was probably observed with considerable strictness during the republic. But among the privileges granted by Augustus to Senators, he permitted their sons to assume the *Latus Clavus*, (p. 223,) and, if they entered the army, they at once received commissions as *Tribuni*, and hence such persons were denominated *Tribuni Laticlavii*.[2]

Each battalion of *Socii*, corresponding in numbers to the Roman Legion, was commanded by six *Praefecti Sociorum*, who were nominated by the Consul, and corresponded to the *Tribuni* in the Legion.

Next in rank to the *Tribuni*, were the *Centuriones*, sixty in number, each having the command of a *Centuria*. They were nominated by the *Tribuni*, who were bound to select the most meritorious; and it would appear that the appointments were subject to the approbation of the commander-in-chief. (Liv. XLII. 33.) Although each Centurion had the command of one *Centuria*, and no more, they were not all upon an equality in rank, but a regular system of precedence was established, extending to the whole number. We are led to the conclusion that not only was service in the ranks of the *Triarii* regarded as more honourable than in those of the *Principes*, and in the *Principes*

---

[1] Liv. VII. 5. 34. IX. 30. XXVII. 36. XLII. 31. XLIII. 12. Polyb. VI. 19.
[2] Suet. Octav. 38. Dom. 10. comp. Otho. 10, where we find mention made of a *Tribunus Angusticlavius*.

than in the *Hastati*, but that the Maniples in each line were numbered from one to ten, and took precedence according to these numbers. Hence there would be a regular gradation from the Centurion who commanded the right wing or Century of the first Maniple of the *Triarii*, down to the Centurion who commanded the left wing or Century of the tenth Maniple of the *Hastati*. The Centurion who commanded the right wing of the first Maniple of the Triarii, was entitled *Primipilus*, or *Centurio primipili*, and was said *Ducere primum pilum*. To his charge was committed the *Aquila* or great standard of the Legion. He ranked next to the Tribunes, and had a seat in the *Consilium*, or Council of War. The first Centurion of the Principes was styled *Primus Princeps;* the first Centurion of the *Hastati*, in like manner, *Primus Hastatus;* and these and similar designations were retained after the classes of *Hastati, Principes* and *Triarii* were no longer to be found in the Legion. We have remarked above, that *Ordo* is by most writers used as synonymous with *Centuria*, and hence, with reference to the comparative rank of the different Centuries, we meet with such phrases as *primi ordines, superiores ordines, inferiores ordines, infimi ordines;* and a Centurion who commanded one of the higher companies was said *Ducere honestum ordinem*.

Each Centurion had under him a subaltern or lieutenant, named by himself, who was termed *Optio*, and there was also, in each century, an ensign or standard-bearer, (*signifer*,) who was probably regarded as a petty officer.

Legati. In addition to the regular officers of the Legion, a general or provincial governor usually nominated, with the consent of the Senate, *Legati*, that is lieutenant-generals who were not attached to any one corps, but who exercised a general superintendence under his orders, when he was present, and acted as his representatives when he was absent. We hear of *Legati* under Consuls and Dictators from a very early period; the number seems to have been originally two, one for each of two Legions which constituted a *Consularis Exercitus*, but in after times the number varied according to the magnitude of the army, and the nature of the service.[1]

Agmen.—The arrangement of a Consular Army on the March (*Agmen*) as described by Polybius, will be understood from the annexed representation. A, *Extraordinarii Pedites*. B, *Dextera Ala Sociorum* (*Pedites*.) C, *Impedimenta* belonging to A and B. D, *Legio Romana*. E, *Impedimenta* of D. F, *Legio Romana*. G, *Impedimenta* of F. H. *Impedimenta* of K. K, *Sinistra Ala Sociorum*.

[1] Liv. II. 59. IV. 17. XLIII. 1. Sallust. Iug. 28. Cic. pro Sext. 14. Nepos Att. 6.

The Cavalry did not maintain a fixed position, sometimes riding in advance, or upon the flanks, as circumstances might demand, and sometimes falling into the rear of the division to which they belonged. When any apprehension was entertained of an attack, the different corps followed each other closely, so as to exhibit a compact body, and this was termed—*Quadrato agmine incedere.* When danger was anticipated from behind, the *Extraordinarii* brought up the rear instead of leading the van.

Acies.—The disposition of an army in battle order (*Acies*) must, to a great extent, have depended upon the nature of the ground, and upon tactics adopted by the force opposed to them. Certain general principles were, however, observed during the different epochs, to which we have referred above, in drawing up the constituent parts of each Legion, so as to insure the greatest amount of mutual support, whether acting on the offensive or defensive.

During the First Epoch, the whole body of the Infantry being marshalled in the solid mass of a phalanx, the great object would be to keep the front of the phalanx, which presented an impenetrable wall of warriors clad in full suits of armour, turned towards the enemy, an attack upon the rear or flanks being fatal, if executed with boldness and resolution.

The system pursued during the Second Epoch is sufficiently intelligible from the narrative of Livy as given above, (p. 382,) according to which A will repre-

```
 ─── ─── ─── ─── ─── ─── ─── ─── A
     ─── ─── ─── ─── ─── ─── ─── ── B

(1) ──  ───  ───  ───  ───  ───  ───  ─── ⎫
(2) ──  ───  ───  ───  ───  ───  ───  ─── ⎬ C
(3) ──  ───  ───  ───  ───  ───  ───  ─── ⎭
```

sent the 15 Maniples of *Hastati,* B the 15 Maniples of *Principes,* and C the 15 triple Maniples, consisting of (1) *Triarii,* (2) *Rorarii,* and (3) *Accensi.*

During the Third Epoch we have still the three lines, A being the 10 Maniples of *Hastati* in front, B the 10 Maniples of *Principes* in the centre, and C the 10

```
 ───  ───  ───  ───  ───  ───  ───    A
    ───  ───  ───  ───  ───  ───  ─── B
 ───  ───  ───  ───  ───  ───  ───    C
```

Maniples of *Triarii* in the rear as a reserve, while the *Velites,* or skirmishers, acted in front or on the flanks as circumstances might demand, and when driven in, retired through the openings between the Maniples, and rallied in the rear.

When we reach the Fourth Epoch, the *Hastati, Principes,* and *Triarii* have disappeared, and the Roman generals found by experience that it was necessary to vary their tactics according to the varying modes of warfare practised by their barbarian foes. It would appear that Cæsar did not adhere to any fixed system, but each cohort was kept distinct, and spaces, as of old, were left between the Maniples; the young soldiers were no longer placed in front, but the van was led by the Veterans.

We may now proceed to notice some classes of soldiers which sprung up immediately after the establishment of the Empire. Under this head we shall describe, 1. *Praetoriae Cohortes.* 2. *Cohortes Urbanae.* 3. *Cohortes Vigilum.* 4. *Vexillarii.*

1. **Praetoriani.**—The commander-in-chief of a Roman army was attended by a select detachment, which, under the name of *Cohors Praetoria*, remained closely attached to his person in the field, ready to execute his orders, and to guard him from any sudden attack. Unless Livy (II. 20) has carelessly transferred the usages with which he himself was familiar, to the earliest ages of the commonwealth, something analogous to a *Cohors Praetoria*, was to be found in the Roman armies soon after the expulsion of the Kings; but Festus seems to have ascribed the institution to Scipio Africanus.[1] At all events, bodies of this description are frequently mentioned towards the close of the republic, but they consisted of individuals selected from the ordinary troops, for a special purpose, and never constituted a distinct branch of the service.[2]

Augustus, following his usual line of policy, retained the ancient name of *Praetoriae Cohortes*, while he entirely changed their character. He levied in Etruria, Umbria, ancient Latium, and the old Colonies, nine or ten Cohorts,[3] consisting of a thousand men each, on whom he bestowed double pay and superior privileges. These formed a permanent corps, who acted as the Imperial Life Guards, ready to overawe the Senate, and to suppress any sudden popular commotion. To avoid the alarm and irritation which would have been excited by presence of such a force in the capital, three Cohorts only were stationed in Rome itself, whilst the remainder were dispersed in the adjacent towns of Italy. But after fifty years of peace and servitude, Tiberius ventured on a decisive measure which riveted the fetters of his country. Under the pretence of relieving Italy from the burden of military quarters, and of introducing stricter discipline among the guards, he assembled them at Rome in a permanent camp, (*Castra Praetoria*,) strongly fortified, and placed on a commanding situation at the northern extremity of the Viminal.[4] Their number was subsequently increased by Vitellius, to sixteen thousand.[5]

The power wielded by the Praetorians was necessarily so great, and was so fully appreciated by themselves, that each Prince, upon his accession, found it expedient to propitiate their vanity by flattering compliments, and to purchase their allegiance by extravagant donations. Their insolence was increased by every fresh concession, until at length it reached a climax when, after the murder of Pertinax, they put up the empire to sale, and made it over to Didius Julianus, as the highest bidder. After the downfal of this pretender, they were disgraced and disbanded by Septimius Severus, who, however, revived the institution upon a new model, and increased the number to about 40,000. The Praetorians had, originally, been recruited in Italy exclusively, and, in process of time, in Macedonia, Noricum, and Spain also. But under Severus they were composed of picked men and tried warriors, draughted from all the frontier legions, who, as a reward for good service, were promoted into the Cohorts of the Household Troops.

After the lapse of another century, they were gradually reduced, and their

---

[1] Paul. Diac. s.v. *Praetoria Cohors*, p 223.
[2] Sallust. Cat. 60. Iug. 98. Cic. in Cat. II. 11. Caes. B. G. I. 40. Appian B.C. III. 67. V. 3.
[3] Tacitus says *nine*, (Ann. IV. 5,) Dion Cassius *ten* (LV. 24.)
[4] I have used here, and in the sentences which follow, almost the very words of Gibbon, Cap. 5.
[5] On the rise and progress of the Praetorians, see Tacit. Ann. IV. 1—5. Hist. I. 84. II. 93. III. 84. Suet. Octav. 49. Tib. 37. Dion Cass. LII. 24. LV. 24. LVII. 19. LXXIV. 2. Herodian. III. 13. Aurel. Vict. de Caes. 39. 40.

privileges abolished by Diocletian, who supplied their place in a great measure by the Illyrian legions, called Jovians and Herculians; they were again increased to their former strength by Maxentius, and finally suppressed by Constantine the Great.

The office of General of the Guards—*Praefectus Praetorio*—which was vested originally in two, under Tiberius in one, and, at a later period, occasionally in three or four individuals, increased in importance as the power of the Praetorians themselves increased, and at times was but little inferior to that of the Emperor himself. Their duties, in the reign of Commodus, were extended so as to comprehend almost all departments of the government, and hence the post was sometimes filled by Civilians, as in the case of the celebrated Ulpian.

2. **Cohortes Urbanae.**—These were a sort of city militia or national guards, whose duties seem to have been confined to the preservation of order in the metropolis. They were instituted by Augustus, and divided, according to Tacitus, into three, or, according to Dion Cassius, into four Cohorts, amounting in all to six thousand men. They were under the immediate command of the *Praefectus Urbi*, and hence Tacitus tells us, that when Flavius Sabinus was incited to take up arms against Vitellius, he was reminded—*esse illi proprium militem Cohortium Urbanarum*. (Hist. III. 64.)[1]

3. **Cohortes Vigilum.**—Augustus established also a body of armed night-police who patrolled the streets, and whose special task was to take all precautions against fire. They were divided into seven Cohorts, were composed of *Libertini*, and were commanded by a member of the Equestrian Order, who was denominated *Praefectus Vigilum*. (See p. 200.)[2]

4. **Vexillarii. Vexilla.**—By comparing the different passages in Tacitus where these terms occur, we shall arrive at the conclusion that they bear a double meaning, one general, the other special. 1. *Vexillarii* and *Vexilla*, in their widest acceptation, are applied to any body of soldiers, horse or foot, serving under a *Vexillum* apart from the Legion, whether connected or not connected with the Legion, and hence may be used to denote a body of legionaries detached upon particular duty, or a body of recruits not yet distributed among the ranks of the Legion, or a body of foreign troops altogether independent of the Legion. Thus we read of *Vexilla Tironum—Germanica Vexilla—Manipuli . . . Nauportum missi . . . Vexilla convellunt*, &c. 2. *Vexillarii* and *Vexilla*, in a special sense, are applied to the Veterans who, in accordance with a regulation introduced by Tiberius, (see below p. 392,) had at the end of sixteen years' service, been discharged from the ranks of the Legion, but who, enjoying various exemptions and privileges, were retained for four years longer under a *Vexillum*, which accompanied the Legion in which they had been previously enrolled. When *Vexillarii* or *Vexilla* is employed to denote this class of soldiers, some expression is usually introduced to mark their connection with the corps to which they had previously belonged. Thus—*Vexillarii discordium Legionum—Vexillarii vicesimani—Vexilla nonae secundaeque et vicesimae Legionum*, &c.[3]

We must carefully distinguish these *Vexilla* which belong to the imperial times exclusively, from the *Vexilla* of the Second Epoch, (see above p. 383,) which denoted the different sections of the Triple Maniples of the third line.

[1] See Tacit. Ann. IV. 5. Dion Cass. LV. 24, who terms them οἱ τῆς πόλεως φρουροί, and sometimes (e.g. LIX. 2) simply οἱ ἀστικοί.
[2] Sueton. Octav. 25. 30. Tacit. Hist. III. 64. Dion Cass. LV. 26, who calls them νυκτοφύλακες. Digest. I. xv.
[3] Tacit. Ann. I. 20. 38. II. 78. XIV. 34. Hist. I. 31. 53. 70. II. 11. III. 22.

Military Pay.—Each of the *Equites equo publico*, from the earliest times, received a sum of money for the purchase of his horse, and was allowed 2000 Asses annually for its support (p. 72.) The Infantry, however, for three centuries and a-half received no pay. During the whole of that period, the Legions usually remained on service for a very limited period each year, being called out merely for the purpose of repelling a sudden inroad, or of making a foray into the territory of a neighbouring state. As soon as the brief campaign was over, the soldiers dispersed to their abodes, and resumed the tillage of their farms and the other occupations in which they had been engaged. But when it became necessary for the troops to keep the field for a lengthened period, it became necessary also to provide for their support, and to afford them such compensation for their loss of time as might enable them to contribute towards the maintenance of the families they had left at home. Accordingly, in B.C. 406, exactly three years before the period when the Roman army for the first time passed a winter in the field, encamped before Veii, the Senate passed a resolution that soldiers should receive pay out of the public treasury—*Ut stipendium miles de publico adciperet, quum ante id tempus de suo quisque functus eo munere esset* (Liv. IV. 59.) [1] Three years afterwards, when the blockade had been actually commenced, (B.C. 403,) those who were possessed of the *Census Equester*, but to whom no *Equus Publicus* had been assigned, volunteered to serve as Cavalry, and to them also the Senate voted pay (Liv. V. 7.) The practice thus introduced was never dropped—*facere stipendia—merere stipendia* —became the ordinary phrases denoting military service, and when a numeral was attached to *stipendium*, it indicated the number of campaigns.

Livy does not state the amount of the pay when it was first instituted; and with the exception of a casual expression in Plautus, (Mostell. II. i. 10,) we have no distinct information until we come down to Polybius, in whose time a private foot-soldier received $3\frac{1}{3}$ asses per day, a centurion double, a dragoon three times as much, that is, a *Denarius*.[2] By Julius Cæsar, the amount was doubled—*Legionibus stipendium in perpetuum duplicavit;* (Suet. Iul. 26;) by Augustus it was farther increased to 10 asses per day, the denarius being now in this as in ordinary computations held to be equivalent to 16 asses, (Tacit. Ann. I. 17. comp. Suet. Octav. 49,) and thus each man would receive (in round numbers) 9 aurei per annum, to which Domitian added three more—*Addidit et quartum stipendium militi, aureos ternos,* (Suet. Dom. 7,) thus making the sum an aureus, or 25 denarii, per month. The Praetorians had double pay. (Dion Cass. LIII. 11. LIV. 25. Tacit. l. c.)

The state provided the soldier with clothes and a fixed allowance of corn; but for these a deduction was made from his pay, and also for any arms which he might require. (Polyb. Tacit. ll. cc. comp. Plut. C. Gracch. 5.)

The allied troops (*Socii*) were clothed and paid by their own states, and received gratuitously from the Romans the same quantity of corn as the legionaries. (Polyb. l. c.)

Praemia. Commoda.—Towards the close of the republic and under the empire, it became customary, when soldiers received their discharge upon com-

---

[1] This is one of the many instances in which Niebuhr refuses to admit the accuracy of Livy's statements; but I am unable to perceive the force of his arguments, or, rather, assertions.

[2] Polybius (VI. 37.) says that the legionary received 2 obols a-day; but he, in common with other Greek and Roman writers considered the Greek drachma and the Roman denarius as equivalent, and we know from Pliny (H.N. XXX. 3) that for a long period the *Denarius*, in computing military pay, was held to be equal to ten asses only. (See Tacit. Ann. I. 1*t*)

pleting their regular period of service, to assign to each a portion of land or a gratuity in money. Sometimes large bodies of veterans, in accordance with the policy followed during the subjugation of Italy, (p. 88,) were transported to the remote frontier provinces, and there established as military colonies. All such rewards for service were comprehended under the general term *Praemia* or *Commoda Missionum*—*Commoda emeritae militiae*, &c.—and corresponded with the system of military pensions common in modern times.[1]

Period of Service.—In the earlier ages, when the campaigns were of short duration, every Roman citizen possessed of a certain fortune, and between the ages of seventeen and forty-six, was bound to enrol himself as a soldier, if called upon, without reference to his previous service. In process of time, however, when large armies were constantly kept on foot, and the legions often remained long in foreign countries, it was found expedient to limit the period, and before the time of Polybius it had been fixed to twenty years for the Infantry and ten years for the Cavalry. Each individual who had completed this term was exempted for the future, was styled *Emeritus*, and was entitled to a regular discharge (*Missio.*) A discharge granted in this manner was termed *Missio honesta*, but if obtained in consequence of bad health or any special plea, *Missio causaria*. Those who thought fit to remain in the Legions after they had a right to demand their *Missio* were called *Veterani*, and those who had received their *Missio* but were induced again to join in compliance with some special request, were named *Evocati*. Augustus, in B.C. 13, restricted the regular period of service for the Legionaries to sixteen years, and for the Praetorians to twelve, (Dion Cass. LIV. 25.) but subsequently (A.D. 5) it would appear that the old system was renewed, the Praetorians being required to serve for sixteen and the Legionaries for twenty years, at the end of which they were to receive a bounty (*praemium*) of 20,000 sesterces and 12,000 sesterces respectively (Dion Cass. LV. 23.) This arrangement was again modified under Tiberius, in consequence of the mutiny in Pannonia, to this extent, that the Legionaries were not to be entitled to the full *Missio* until after twenty years, but that after sixteen years they were to receive a partial discharge, termed *Exauctoratio*, in virtue of which they were to be separated from the Legion, to be exempted from all ordinary laborious tasks, and to be marshalled by themselves under a distinct banner—*Missionem dari vicena stipendia meritis; exauctorari qui sena dena fecissent, ac retineri sub vexillo ceterorum immunes nisi propulsandi hostis* (Tacit. Ann. I. 36.) It is by no means clear, however, that this was not the system which had been introduced by Augustus when he revived the ancient period of service, and that the mutiny was not partly caused by a want of good faith in carrying out these rules.

Military Standards.—(*Signa. Vexilla.*) The military standard of the primitive ages is said by Ovid (Fast. III. 117) to have been a wisp or handful of hay or straw attached to the end of a long pole. Pliny (H.N. X. 4) tells us that up to the second consulship of Marius, (B.C. 104,) the eagle and four other animals formed the standards of the Legion, the eagle holding the first place, but that after that date the eagle alone was retained—*Romanis eam* (sc. *aquilam*) *legionibus C. Marius in secundo consulatu suo proprie dicavit. Erat et antea prima cum quatuor aliis: Lupi, Minotauri, Equi, Aprique singulos ordines anteibant. Paucis ante annis sola in aciem portari coepta erat: reliqua in castris relinquebantur.* But although the eagle (*Aquila*) continued

---

[1] Tacit. Ann. I. 17. Suet. Octav. 49. Calig. 44.

to be at all times the great standard of the Legion, and as such was committed to the custody of the *Primipilus*, we must not suppose that it was the only standard; on the contrary, it is certain that each *Cohors* and each *Centuria* had its own standard, and judging from the numerous representations of such objects on coins, on the column of Trajan and other ancient monuments, they must have assumed a great variety of different forms. The Denarius of M. Antonius, of which we annex a cut, represents the form of the legionary eagle, and two other standards, at the close of the republic. (See also the figure in page 376.) It has been con- 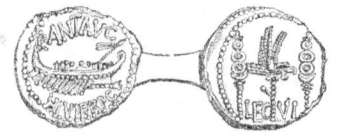 jectured that while *Aquila* denotes the great standard of the whole Legion, *Signum* denotes that of a *Cohors*, and *Vexillum* that of a *Centuria*, but these distinctions are certainly not uniformly observed.

The standards *marked* out the various divisions and subdivisions of the Legion, so as to enable each soldier readily to fall into his place, and the movements of the standards in the field indicated at once to a spectator the evolutions performed by the different corps to which they belonged. Hence the phrases *Signa inferre*, to advance; *S. referre*, to retreat; *S. Convertere*, to wheel; *Signa conferre—Signis collatis confligere*, to engage; *urbem intrare sub signis—sub signis legiones ducere*, in regular marching order; *ad signa convenire*, to muster; *a signis discedere*, to desert; and many others which can occasion no embarrassment. The expression *Milites Signi unius* (e.g. Liv. XXV. 23. XXXIII. 1.) is, however, of doubtful import, and we cannot with certainty decide whether it signifies the soldiers of *one Maniple* or of *one Century*.

Military Rewards.—These may be classed under two heads, according as they were bestowed upon the commander-in-chief, or upon the subordinate officers and soldiers. The great object of ambition to every general was a *Triumphus*, or, failing that, an *Ovatio*; the distinctions granted to those inferior in rank to the general consisted, for the most part, of personal decorations, *Coronae, Phalerae*, &c.

Triumphus.—A Triumph was a grand procession, in which a victorious general entered the city by the *Porta Triumphalis*, in a chariot drawn by four horses, (*Quadriga*,) wearing a dress of extraordinary splendour, namely, an embroidered robe, (*Toga picta*,) an under garment flowered with palm leaves, (*Tunica palmata*,) and a wreath of laurel round his brows. He was preceded by the prisoners taken in the war, the spoils of the cities captured, and pictures of the regions subdued. He was followed by his troops; and after passing along the *Sacra Via* and through the *Forum*, ascended to the Capitol, where he offered a bull in sacrifice to Jove. A regular Triumph (*iustus Triumphus*) could not be demanded unless the following conditions had been satisfied. 1. The claimant must have held the office of Dictator, of Consul, or of Praetor. It is true that Pompeius triumphed twice (B.C. 81 and B.C. 71,) before he had held any magistracy, but the whole of his career was exceptional. 2. The success upon which the claim was founded must have been achieved by the claimant while commander-in-chief of the victorious army; or in other words, the operations must have been performed under his *Auspicia*. (p. 111.) 3. The campaign must have been brought to a termination, and the country reduced to such a state of tranquillity as to admit of the withdrawal of the troops, whose presence at the ceremony was indispensable. 4. Not less than 5000 of the enemy must have fallen in one engagement. 5. Some positive advantage and extension of dominion must have been gained, not merely a disaster retrieved, or an attack repulsed. 6. The contest must have been against a foreign foe; hence the expression of Lucan, when speaking of Civil Wars [1]—

> Bella geri placuit nullos habitura triumphos.—I. 12.

When any important exploit had been performed by an army, the general forwarded a despatch wreathed with laurel (*Literae laureatae*) to the Senate, who generally ordered a public thanksgiving, (*Supplicatio*,) and upon his return gave him audience in some temple outside the walls. The Senate at all times maintained that it was their prerogative to decide whether the honours of a Triumph should be conceded or withheld; but in this, as in all other matters connected with public business, the people occasionally asserted their right to exercise supreme control, and consequently we find examples of generals celebrating a Triumph by permission of the people in opposition to the opinion of the Senate. [2] When it was settled that a Triumph was to take place, one of the Tribunes of the Plebs applied to the *Comitia Tributa* for a *Plebiscitum* to suspend the principles of the constitution during the day of the ceremony, in order that the general might retain his *Imperium* within the city. [3]

Roman generals who had petitioned for a Triumph, and had been refused, frequently indulged in a similar display on the *Mons Albanus*, concluding with a sacrifice to *Jupiter Latiaris*. [4]

Triumphus Navalis.—A Triumph might be celebrated for a victory gained by sea. These were comparatively rare; but we have examples in the case of C. Duillius, (B.C. 260,) of Lutatius Catulus, (B.C. 241,) and a few others. [5]

Triumphs under the Empire.—The Prince being sole commander-in-chief of the armies of the state, all other military commanders were regarded merely as his *Legati*, and it was held that all victories were gained under his *Auspicia*, however distant he might be from the scene of action; consequently he alone was entitled to a Triumph. Hence, although Augustus in the early part of his

career, before his position became secure and well defined, permitted his subordinates to celebrate Triumphs, this honour was not granted to any one not belonging to the imperial family after B.C. 14; but instead of Triumphs, certain titles and decorations, termed *Triumphalia Ornamenta*, were instituted and freely bestowed. [6]

Decorated arches were frequently built across the streets through which the triumphal procession defiled. These were originally, in all probability, mere temporary structures; but under the empire they frequently assumed a permanent form, were designed with great architectural skill, and ornamented with elaborate sculptures. Of this description

---

[1] See various details with regard to Triumphs in Liv. VIII. 26. XXVI. 21. XXVIII. 29. 38. XXX. 48. XXXI. 5. 20. 48. 49. XXXIII. 22. XXXIV. 10. XXXIX. 29. XL. 38. Val. Max. II. viii. 1. 2. 5. 7.
[2] Liv. XXVI. 21. XXXVI. 39. XXXIX. 4. and on the other hand Liv. III. 63. VII. 17. X. 37. Polyb. VI. 13. Dionys. XI. 50.
[3] Liv. XXVI. 21. XLV. 35.
[4] Liv. XXVI. 21 XXXIII. 23. XLII. 21. XLV. 38. Plin. H.N. XV. 38. Plut. Marcell. 22.
[5] Liv. Epit. XVII. XXXVII. 60 XLV. 42. Val. Max. II. viii. 2.
[6] Tacit. Ann I. 72. II. 52. III. 72. Hist. I. 79. II. 78. Suet. Octav. 9. 38. Dion Cass XLIX. 42. LIV. 11. 24.

are the arches of Titus, of Severus, and of Constantine, still extant, of which we have given representations in Chapter I., and such objects are often delineated upon coins, as in the cut at the bottom of the last page, from a large brass of Nero.

Ovatio.—This was a procession of the same nature as a Triumph, but much less gorgeous, and was conceded to those who had distinguished themselves against the enemy, without having performed any achievement of sufficient importance to entitle them to a Triumph, or who were unable to fulfil all the conditions enumerated above. In this case, the general entered the city on foot, or, in later times, on horseback, attired in a simple *Toga Praetexta*, frequently unattended by troops, and the display terminated by the sacrifice not of a bull, as in the case of a Triumph, but of a sheep—and hence the name *Ovatio*. [1]

Coronae, Phalerae, &c.—*Coronae* were wreaths or chaplets worn on the head, or carried in the hand, on public occasions, and were distinguished by various names, according to their form and the circumstances under which they were won. The most honourable of all was the *Corona Civica*, bestowed upon those who had saved the life of a citizen ; (*ob Cives Servatos ;*) it was made of oak leaves, and hence termed *Quercus Civilis*—the *Corona Vallaris* s. *Castrensis* was given to the individual who first scaled the rampart in assaulting the camp of an enemy—the *Corona Muralis* to him who first mounted the breach in storming a town—the *Corona Navalis* to him who first boarded a hostile ship—a *Corona Rostrata* was presented by Augustus to Agrippa after the defeat of Sex Pompeius—a *Corona Obsidionalis* was the offering of soldiers who had been beleaguered to the commander by whom they had been relieved, and was made of the grass which grew upon the spot where they had been blockaded. [2]

Phalerae were ornaments attached to horse furniture, or to the accoutrements of the rider ; besides which, various decorations for the person, such as collars of gold, (*Torques,*) Armlets, (*Armillae,*) Clasps, (*Fibulae,*) and similar objects, were among the marks of honour given and received.

Spolia, that is, armour or weapons taken from the person of a vanquished foe, were always exhibited in the most conspicuous part of the house of the victor, and the proudest of all military trophies were *Spolia Opima*, which could be gained only when the commander-in-chief of a Roman army engaged and overthrew in single combat the commander-in-chief of the enemy, (*quae dux Populi Romani duci hostium detraxit.*) Roman history afforded but three examples of legitimate *Spolia Opima*. The first were won by Romulus from Acro, King of the Ceninenses, the second by Aulus Cornelius Cossus from Lar Tolumnius, King of the Veientes, the third by M. Claudius Marcellus from Virodomarus, a Gaulish chief, (B.C 222.) In all cases they were dedicated to Jupiter Feretrius, and preserved in his temple. [3]

Military Punishments.—Slight offences were punished with stripes or with blows with a stick, and these were generally inflicted summarily by the centurions, who, for this purpose, carried a vine sapling, which was regarded as

---

[1] Liv. III. 10. XXVI. 21. Paul. Diac s.v. *Ovantes.* p. 195. Aul. Gell. V. 6. Plin. H.N. XV. 29. Flor. III. 19. Plut. Marcell. 22. Dion Cass. XLVIII. 31. XLIX. 15. LIV. 8. 33. LV. 2. Serv. ad Virg. Æn. IV. 543.

[2] See Aul. Gell. V. 6. Liv. VI. 20. VII. 10. 26. 37. 47. 44. IX. 46. X. 44. 47. XXII. 51. 52. XXIV. 16. XXVI. 21. 48. XXX. 15. XXXIX. 31. Epit. CXXIX. Tacit. Ann. II. 9 83. III. 21. XV. 12. Plin. H.N. VII. 30. XXI. 4. XXII. 4. 5. Suet. Claud. 17. Paul. Diac. s. v. *Navali corona*, p. 163. Vopisc. Aurelian. 13.

[3] Liv. I. 10. IV. 20. Epit. XX. Fest. s.v. *Opima spolia*, p. 186. Plut. Marcell. 8. Corn. Nep. vit. Att. 20. comp. Val. Max. III. ii. 6. Dion Cass. XLIV. 4. Ll. 24.

their badge of office.[1] More serious violations of discipline, such as disobedience, desertion, mutiny, or theft, were visited with death. The sentence was carried into effect in various ways, by beheading, by crucifixion, and sometimes by the *Fustuarium*, which was analogous to running the gauntlet. When a soldier was condemned to undergo this, one of the tribunes touched him with a stick, upon which all the soldiers of the legion fell upon him with stones and clubs, and generally despatched him. He was, however, allowed to run for his life, but if he escaped, could never return home.[2] When some crime had been committed which involved great numbers, every tenth man was chosen by lot for punishment, and this was called *Decimatio*.[3] Under the empire we hear also of *Vicesimatio* and *Centesimatio*. (Capitolin. Macrin. 12.)

Encampments.—When a Roman army was in the field, it never halted, even for a single night, without throwing up an entrenchment capable of containing the whole of the troops and their baggage. This field-work was termed *Castra*, and such an essential feature in their system did it form, that the word is frequently used as synonymous with *a day's march*, and also with *warfare* in general, as in the expressions—*Consul tertiis Castris Ancyram pervenit* (Liv. XXXVIII. 24.)—*Septuagesimis Castris Tarraconem rediit* (Liv. XXVIII. 16.) —*Vir, nescias utilior in Castris, an melior in Toga* (Velleius II. 125.)

Polybius has bequeathed to us such a minute description of a Roman Camp, accompanied by accurate measurements, that we can have no difficulty in describing the form and arrangements which it exhibited at the epoch when the discipline of the Romans was in its most perfect state.

Officers possessed of the necessary skill and experience, were always sent forward in advance of an army on the march, to choose suitable ground for the encampment, (*capere locum castris*,) attended by practical engineers, called *Metatores*, who, after the spot had been selected upon which the tent of the general (*Praetorium*) was to be erected, taking this as their base, made all the measurements, and drew all the lines necessary to enable the soldiers to begin working as soon as they came up, and laid off the spaces appropriated to each of the various divisions of which the army was composed, so that each individual knew at once where his quarters were to be found.

The form of the camp was a square, each side of which was 2017 Roman feet in length. The defences consisted of a ditch, (*fossa*,) the earth dug out, being thrown inwards so as to form a rampart, (*agger*.) upon the summit of which a palisade (*vallum*) was erected of wooden stakes, (*valli—sudes*,) a certain number of which were carried by each soldier, along with his entrenching tools. A clear space of 200 feet (*intervallum*) was left all round between the *vallum* and the tents. The relative position of the different parts will be readily understood by studying the annexed plan, and the explanation by which it is accompanied, it being premised, that the camp represented is one calculated to accommodate a consular army, consisting of two legions, each containing 4,200 infantry and 300 cavalry, together with the usual complement of *socii*, that is, an equal number of infantry and double the number of cavalry, in all 16,800 infantry and 1,800 cavalry.

---

[1] Tacit. Ann. I. 17. 18. 23. Liv. Epit. LVII. Plin. H N. XIV. 1.
[2] Liv. II. 59. V. 6. Epit. XV. XXVIII. 29. XXX. 4. Polyb. VI. 37. Cic. Philipp. III. 6. Tacit. Ann. III. 21.
[3] Liv. II. 59. Cic. pro Cluent. 46. Polyb. VI. 38. Plut. Crass. 10. Suet. Octav. 24. Galb. 12. Tacit. Hist. I. 37. Dion Cass XLI. 35. XLIX. 27. 38. For various minor punishments, see Liv. X. 4. XXIV. 16. XXV. 6. XXVI. 1. XXVII. 13. XL. 41. Val. Max. II. vii. 9. 15. Suet. Octav. 24.

ROMAN ARMY—THE CAMP.

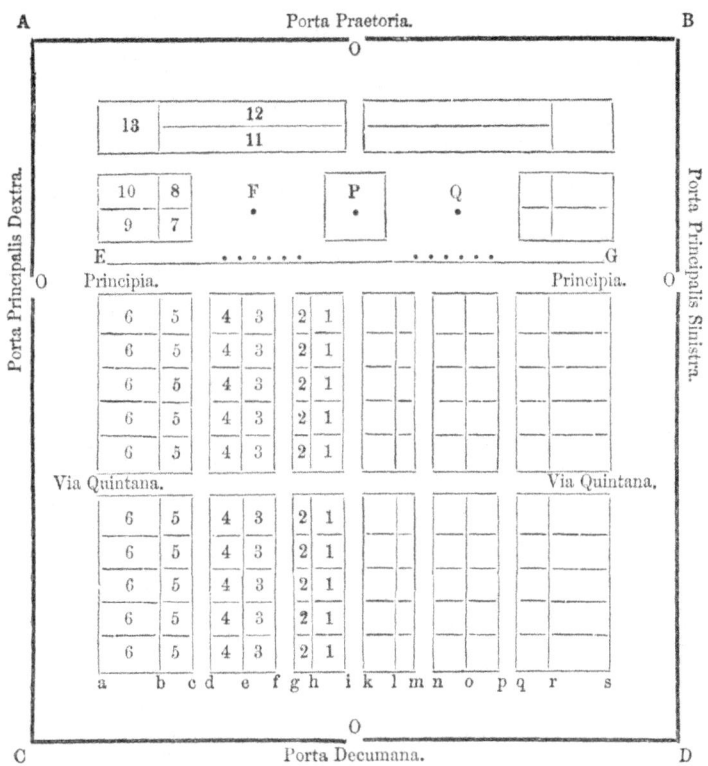

AB, AC, CD, DB, are the four sides or ramparts enclosing the Camp; P is the *Praetorium*, the quarters of the general-in-chief, which, as remarked above, served as the base in making the measurements and laying off the different areas. We have supposed the *Praetorium* to face towards CD; but this is a disputed point.

In the middle of the side AB, which was always the side nearest to the enemy, was a gate, O—the *Porta Praetoria*.

In the middle of CD, the side farthest from the enemy, was a second gate, O —the *Porta Decumana*.

The whole Camp was divided into two unequal parts, which we may distinguish as the Upper and the Lower portions, by a road, 100 feet broad, which ran right across parallel to the sides AB, CD. This road was called *Principia;* and at each extremity of the *Principia* a gate, O, was formed in the sides AC, BD; these were respectively the *Porta Principalis Dextra*, and the *Porta Principalis Sinistra*.

The Upper portion of the Camp, that, namely, which lay between the *Prin-*

cipia and the side AB, contained about one-third of the space embraced by the lower portion. The principal object in this division was the *Praetorium*, (P) which stood in the centre of an open square, extending 100 feet on each side of it. Right and left of the *Praetorium*, at Q and F, were the *Quaestorium*, the quarters of the Quaestor and of those immediately connected with his departments, and the *Forum*, the public market of the Camp; but it is uncertain on which side of the *Praetorium* they were respectively situated.

Along the straight line, EG, which forms the upper boundary of the *Principia*, were ranged at the points marked by dots, the tents of the twelve *Tribuni* belonging to the two legions; and, in all probability, along the same line, nearer to its extremities, were the tents of the *Praefecti Sociorum*.

The *Principia* may be regarded as the great thoroughfare of the Camp. Here the altar for sacrifice was raised, and beside the altar, as befitted their sacred character, stood the standards, or at all events, the *Aquilae* of each legion.

In the spaces marked 7, 8, 9, 10, and the corresponding spaces on the opposite side of the *Praetorium*, were the staff of the general, including probably the *Legati*, together with the *Praetoria Cohors*, the body guard of the general, consisting chiefly of picked men selected from the *Extraordinarii*; 7 and 8 were cavalry, facing towards the *Praetorium*; 9 and 10 infantry, facing towards the *Agger*. In 11 were the remainder of the *Extraordinarii Equites*, facing towards the *Principia*; in 12, the remainder of the *Extraordinarii Pedites*, facing towards the rampart. The space 13 was devoted to troops not included in a regular Consular Army, who might chance to be serving along with it.

The Lower portion of the Camp, that, namely, which lay between the *Principia* and the side CD, was devoted to the quarters of the ordinary troops, Infantry and Cavalry, Legionaries and Allies. It was divided into two equal parts by a road, 50 feet wide, which ran parallel to the *Principia*, and was called *Via Quintana*. The tents were all pitched in the twelve oblong compartments represented on the plan, six above and six below the *Via Quintana*. Each of these compartments was divided from the one next to it by a road or passage (*Via*) 50 feet broad; each compartment was 500 feet long, and each was divided transversely into five equal compartments, each 100 feet long, by lines drawn parallel to the *Principia*, and again longitudinally into two compartments by lines drawn parallel to the sides AC, BD, ab being in length 200 feet, bc 133$\frac{1}{3}$, de 100, ef 100, gh 50, hi 100, the remainder of the same dimensions in a reverse order, kl 100, lm 50, no 100, op 100, qr 133$\frac{1}{3}$, rs 200. We have thus the twelve large compartments each divided into ten rectangular spaces, and from the data given above, we can at once calculate the area of each.

It will be seen that a line drawn from the *Porta Praetoria* to the *Porta Decumana* would pass through the centre of the *Praetorium*, dividing the Camp into two equal parts; and it will be seen by referring to the plan, that these two parts are in every respect perfectly symmetrical. In explaining how the troops were arranged, it will be necessary to describe their distribution on one side of this line only, for one Legion, with its complement of *Socii*, lay on the right hand, and the other on the left hand, while every compartment, both in the upper and lower portion of the Camp, belonging to the Legion upon one side, had a compartment exactly similar corresponding to it, and belonging to the Legion on the other side.

In the spaces marked 1, each containing 10,000 square feet, were the *Equites* of the Legion, each of the ten spaces being occupied by one *Turma* of 30 men and horses.

In the spaces marked 2, each containing 5000 square feet, were the *Triarii* of the Legion, each of the ten spaces being occupied by a *Manipulus* of 60 men.

In the spaces marked 3, each containing 10,000 square feet, were the *Principes* of the Legion, each of the ten spaces being occupied by two *Manipuli* of 60 men each.

In the spaces marked 4, each containing 10,000 square feet, were the *Hastati* of the Legion, each of the ten spaces being occupied by two *Manipuli* of 60 men each.

In the spaces marked 5, each containing about 13,300 square feet, were the *Equites Sociorum*, each of the ten spaces being occupied by 40 men and horses, making in all 400, the remaining 200 being quartered apart in the upper Camp among the *Extraordinarii*.

Finally, in the spaces marked 6, each containing 20,000 square feet, were the *Pedites Sociorum*, each of the ten spaces being occupied by 240 men, making in all 2400, the remaining 600 being quartered apart in the upper Camp among the *Extraordinarii*.

The tents all faced towards the *Viae* which formed their boundaries; those in the spaces 1, 3, 5 facing towards BD, those in 2, 4, 6, towards AC.

It will be observed that nothing has been said regarding the quarters of the *Velites*. Polybius leaves us altogether in the dark upon this point.

Watching the Camp.—Pickets of Cavalry and Infantry, called *Stationes*, were thrown forward in advance of the different gates, to give timely notice of the approach of a foe; and in addition to these, a strong body of *Velites* was posted at each gate to prevent the possibility of a surprise. These were called *Custodes* s. *Custodiae*. Finally, a number of sentinels, (*Excubiae*,) taken also from the *Velites*, kept guard (*agere excubias*) along the ramparts, while others taken from the Legions were stationed at the quarters of the general-in-chief and other principal officers, and were dispersed among the tents and *Viae*. All these precautions were observed during the day, and were of course redoubled during the night, which, reckoning from sunset to sunrise, was divided into four equal spaces called *Vigiliae*, the night guards being termed specially *Vigiles*, (*agere Vigilias*,) while *Excubiae* and *agere Excubias* applied both to night and to day. The ordinary duty of going the rounds (*Vigilias circuire*) was committed to eight *Equites*, four from each Legion, who were changed daily, and the most effectual precautions were taken to ascertain that they performed their task fully and faithfully.

The watchword (*Signum*) for each night was not passed verbally, but was inscribed upon small tablets of wood, (*Tesserae*,) which were delivered, in the first instance, by the commander-in-chief to those legionary Tribunes who were upon duty, and by these to four men in each Legion called *Tesserarii*, by whom the *Tesserae* were conveyed to the tents most remote from the *Principia*, and thence passed along the line from *Turma* to *Turma*, and from *Manipulus* to *Manipulus*, until they again reached the hands of the *Tribuni*.

Attack and Defence of Fortified Places.—In laying siege to a fortified town or other place of strength, one of two methods was adopted: either, 1. An attempt was made to force an entrance, in which case the process was termed, *Oppugnatio*, and, if successful, *Expugnatio:* or, 2. A blockade was formed, and the assailants calculated upon starving out the defenders. This was called *Obsidio*.

Oppugnatio. Urbem Oppugnare. If the town was of small size, and accessible on every side, while the force at the disposal of the besiegers was large, a ring of soldiers was drawn round the walls, (*oppidum corona cingere,*) a portion of whom kept up a constant discharge of missiles upon those who manned the battlements, (*propugnatores,*) while the rest, advancing on every side simultaneously, with their shields joined above their heads so as to form a continuous covering, like the shell of a tortoise, (*testudine facta,*) planted scaling ladders (*scalae*) against a number of different points, and, at the same time, endeavoured to burst open the gates.

When the town, from its size, the strength of its defences, and the numbers of the garrison, could not be attacked in this manner with any reasonable prospect of success, a regular siege was formed; one or two points were selected, against which the operations were to be principally directed, and elaborate works were constructed. The great object was to demolish the walls, so as to make a practicable breach, and this might be effected in two ways. 1. By undermining them (*muros subruere* s. *suffodere.*) 2. By battering them with repeated blows from an enormous beam of wood shod with a mass of iron forged into the shape of a ram's head, which gave the name of *Aries* to the whole machine. But in order to enable the soldiers who were to be engaged in filling up the ditch, in undermining the walls, and in working the Ram, to approach with safety, it was necessary to protect them from the missiles hurled down from the battlements. The means resorted to in order to gain this end, were twofold.

1. A number of large wooden sheds, called, according to their various forms, *Vineae—Testudines—Plutei—Musculi*, open at the two ends, but with strong roofs overlaid with raw hides, and wattled at the sides, were placed upon rollers, and pushed forwards up to the very walls (*rotis subiectis agebantur.*) Under some of these there were Rams which the men could work with comparative security, being sheltered from arrows and darts, while others afforded cover to those who were digging under the foundations of the walls.

2. In order to annoy and distract the defenders, a huge mound of earth—*Agger*—was thrown up opposite to the points selected for attack, and as it was gradually advanced nearer and nearer to the walls, it was at the same time raised so as to equal them in elevation. Upon the summit of this, one or more towers—*Turres*—were built of such altitude as completely to overtop the battlements, and thus to enable the archers and javelin-throwers, with which the successive stories (*Tabulata*) were crowded, to look down upon the ramparts, and to take deliberate aim at the townsmen. When the nature of the ground, or other circumstances, rendered it difficult or impossible to construct an *Agger*, *Turres* were fabricated at a distance, and rolled up on wheels like the *Vineae*, but their unwieldy weight and height rendered such an operation very difficult and hazardous.

Occasionally also, mines (*cuniculi*) were driven with a view of passing under the walls, and opening out within the town, as in the problematical tale regarding the capture of Veii. (See Liv. V. 19. 21. XXIII. 18. XXXVIII. 7.)

The mode of attacking a fortified place would necessarily depend in its details upon a variety of circumstances, which would vary for each particular case; and the skill of the engineers would be taxed in devising schemes for the removal of new and unlooked-for obstacles. But the general principles remained the same; and we find the *Agger*, the *Turres*, the *Aries*, and the *Vineae*, constantly recurring in the descriptions of sieges recorded by historians. When the use of *Balistae, Catapultae, Scorpiones*, and similar machines, (*Tormenta,*) which discharged arrows, darts, and stones, in showers, became common, they were employed with great effect by both parties, but they appear to have been directed entirely to the destruction of life, and not, although some of them shot stones of immense size, to battering in breach.

Obsidio. Urbem Obsidere s. Obsidione Cingere. It is obvious that the system described above could not have been pursued against a town or castle built upon a lofty eminence, or strongly fortified by nature. Hence, when it was desired to reduce a place of this description, recourse was had to *Obsidio.* In order to render this effectual, the place besieged was, if practicable, surrounded by a double wall, (*Circumvallare—Circumvallatio,*) strengthened at intervals with towers, the inner wall being intended to resist any sally upon the part of the townsmen, the outer to repel any attempt at relief from without.

The defence, on the other hand, was in each case varied to meet the particular form of attack. Every effort was made to delay the progress of the works, and destroy the machines, by frequent sallies, (*eruptiones,*) and since the materials employed in constructing the *Vineae* and *Turres* were all of a combustible nature, it often happened that they were repeatedly consumed by fire. Ingenious contrivances were devised for deadening the shock of the *Aries*, and for seizing and lifting it up, so as to prevent it from being propelled with effect; huge masses of stone were cast down upon the *Vineae,* crushing every thing before them by their weight; mines were met by counter mines—*tranversis cuniculis hostium cuniculos excipere;* Turres were erected opposite to, and more lofty than those upon the *Agger;* the Agger itself was undermined, and the earth withdrawn; when a portion of the wall was shattered, a deep trench was dug behind the breach, a new wall raised behind the trench, and a multitude of schemes contrived and executed, which may be best learned by reading the accounts which have been transmitted to us of some of the more remarkable sieges of antiquity, such as those of Syracuse, (Liv. XXIV. 33, &c.,) of Ambracia, (Liv. XXXVIII. 4,) of Alesia, (Caes. B. G. VII. 68.) of Marseilles, (Caes. B. C. II. 1.) and of Jerusalem, as recorded by Josephus.

Military Dress.—The cloak, or upper garment, worn by the soldiers on service, was termed *Sagum,* in contradistinction to *Toga,* the garb of the peaceful citizen. In the case of any sudden panic, it was assumed by the whole body of the people, who in such a case were said—*Saga sumere—Ad Saga ire—In Sagis esse.* It seems to have been worn by officers as well as common soldiers, for we find the garment of the latter sometimes distinguished as *Gregale Sagum.* The characteristic dress, however, of the general-in-chief and his staff, was the *Paludamentum,* which, although less cumbrous than the *Toga,* was more ample and graceful than the *Sagum.* When a Roman magistrate quitted the city to take the command of an army or of a Province, he threw off the *Toga* as soon as he had passed the gates, and assumed the *Paludamentum.* Hence he was said—*Exire paludatus,* and on such occasions he was usually preceded by *Lictores paludati.*

The *Caliga* was a shoe, or rather a sandal, worn by the common soldiers, who are hence termed *caligati,* and is used figuratively to denote service in the ranks. Thus Seneca—*Marium Caliga dimisit? Consulatus exercet.* (De brev. vit. 17.) Again—*Ingratus C. Marius, ad Consulatum a Caliga perductus.* (De Benef. V. 16.) And Pliny—*Iuventam inopem in Caliga militari tolerasse.* (H.N. VII. 43.) It was very heavy, and studded with nails. Hence

[1] Cic. Philipp. V. 12. VIII. 11. XIV. 1.
[2] Liv. VIII. 34. comp. XXVII. 19. XXX. 17. Sil. IV. 518. XVII. 527
[3] Cic. ad Fam. VIII. 10. Liv. XLI. 10. XLV. 39.

Juvenal enumerates, among the inconveniences of jostling in a crowd—*Planta mox undique magna = Calcor et in digito clavus mihi militis haeret* (S. III. 248.)—and again, when descanting on the folly of exciting the hostility of a throng of soldiers—*Cum duo crura habeas, offendere tot caligas, tot = Millia clavorum* (S. XVI. 24.) Caius, the son of Germanicus, who was reared in the camp, wore the *Caliga* when a child, out of compliment to the soldiers, and hence acquired the nickname of *Caligula*, by which he was familiarly distinguished.[1]

It must be observed, that the most striking illustrations of military costume and equipments contained in Montfaucon, and other great works upon Antiquities, are derived to a great extent from the sculptures upon Trajan's column, and therefore depict the soldier of the empire. We have given, in p. 376, representations of two legionaries and a standard-bearer, and we now subjoin a figure of the Emperor himself in his dress as a general, and also of a stone caster and of a slinger, all taken from the monument in question. These show clearly the general aspect of the common legionary soldiers and also of the irregular troops. The cloak worn by the *Signifer* is probably the ordinary *Sagum*, while that of the Emperor is unquestionably the *Paludamentum*.

II.—SHIPS AND NAVAL WARFARE.[2]

In no one of the arts which have been practised by mankind from the earliest times, was the inferiority of the ancients to the moderns more conspicuous than in Navigation. Even those nations which became most celebrated for their skill in this department, scarcely ever attempted to keep the sea during winter, but were wont to haul up (*subducere*) their vessels upon dry land towards the close of autumn, and not to haul them down (*deducere*) to sea until the stormy equinoctial gales of spring were past, operations which they performed by machines (*Trahuntque siccas machinae carinas*) called *Phalangae*,[3] consisting of

---

[1] Tacit. Ann. I. 41. Suet. Octav. 25. Calig. 9. Vitell. 7.
[2] The most important passages in ancient writers connected with Ships and Naval Warfare, are collected in SCHEFFERUS *De militia navali veterum*, Upsal, 1654. Much valuable information will be found in a recently published work by Mr. Smith of Jordanhill, entitled, *The Voyage and Shipwreck of St. Paul*, Lon. 1848.
[3] Hor. C. I. iv. 2. Varro ap. Non. s.v. *palangae*, p. 111. ed Gerl.

a system of rollers, acting probably somewhat in the same manner as what is now called a patent slip. The Romans especially, notwithstanding the great extent of sea coast presented by Italy, never became addicted, as a people, to maritime pursuits; and in all matters connected with nautical affairs, were far surpassed by the Phœnicians and Tyrrhenians of the early ages, and by the Athenians, Carthaginians, Cretans, and Rhodians of a later epoch. Hence we shall not be surprised to find their language very defective in the technical terms connected with ships; and although ancient vessels, especially in so far as the rigging was concerned, were infinitely more simple in their structure than those now in use, there are many essential parts which we never find named in any Latin classical author, and several others, preserved in the grammarians, which have been borrowed without change from the Greek.

All sea-going vessels, throwing out of view for the present mere boats, skiffs, and small craft, may be divided into two classes, with reference to the purposes to which they were applied.

1. Merchantmen. (*Naves mercatoriae—onerariae.*)
2. Ships of War. (*Naves bellicae—longae—rostratae—aeratae.*)

The former were propelled chiefly by sails, the latter, although often fully rigged, depended, in all rapid evolutions, upon rowers, of whom they carried great numbers.

We shall first describe an ancient ship generally, including those parts which were common to both classes, and then point out the peculiarities which distinguished the war galleys.

Every ship (*Navis*) may be regarded as consisting of two parts: 1. the Hull, (*Alveus,*) and 2. the Tackling (*Armamenta.*)[1]

Alveus.—The *Alveus* was made up of, 1. The Keel (*Carina.*) 2. The Prow or fore part of the ship (*Prora.*) 3. The Stern or after-part of the ship (*Puppis.*) 4. The Hold, (*Alveus* in its restricted sense,) which contained the cargo, crew, and ballast (*Saburra.*) The Well, or bottom of the Hold, was called *Sentina;* into this the bilge-water (*Nautea*) drained, and was drawn off by a pump (*Antlia.*) The Ribs or frame-work were termed *Costae* or *Statumina;*[2] the Planking *Tabulae*, the seams of which were payed with wax, pitch, or similar substances (hence *Ceratae puppes.*) Undecked vessels were *Naves apertae*, as opposed to *Naves tectae* s. *constratae*, the decks themselves being *Tabulata* s. *Pontes*.[3] Very frequently vessels were only partially decked, and the sailors passed from one end to the other by means of gangways, (*Fori,*) or from side to side by cross planks (*Transtra* s. *Iuga.*) The *Fori* and *Transtra* served also as benches for the rowers.[4]

Armamenta.—Of these, the most important were—

1. *Anchorae*, the anchors, of which there were usually several,[5] resembling closely in form those now employed, fitted with cables (*Ancoralia.*) The anchor was thrown from the prow (*Ancora de prora iacitur*) when the ship was required to ride, (*Consistere ad ancoram—stare* s. *expectare in ancoris—tenere navem in ancoris,*) and on going to sea was weighed (*Ancoram tollere* s. *Vellere*, or in the case of great haste, *Praecidere.*) A ship in harbour was

---

1 *Alveus* and *Armamenta* stand opposed to each other in Liv. XXXIII. 34.
2 Pers. S. VI. 31. Caes. B.C. I. 54.
3 Val. Flacc. VIII. 305. Tacit. Ann. II. 6.
4 Cic. de S. 6. Isidor. XIX. ii. 2. 5. Virg. Æn. VI. 411. Charis. p. 19. ed. Putsch. Diomed. p. 314. ed Putsch.
5 *e.g.* The ship in which St. Paul sailed had four. (Act. Apost. xxvii. 29.)

moored by hawsers, (*Retinacula—Orae,*) [1] which were unloosed when the ship went out, and hence the phrases—*Oram resolvere*—*Navem solvere*—or simply *Solvere*—signify *to set sail.*

2. *Gubernaculum,* the rudder, with the *Clavus,* its handle or tiller. [2] The

ancient rudders were not hinged to the stern posts as ours are, but were what are technically termed *paddle-helms,* and of these there were usually two in the ship, placed one on each side of the stern. A rudder of this kind is seen in the annexed cut, taken from a tomb at Pompeii, and ships were commonly steered in this manner as late as the fourteenth century.

3. *Mali,* the masts, with their yards, (*Antennae* s. *brachia,*) whose extremities, the yard arms, were termed *Antennarum cornua.* The mast rested in a socket, or *step* called *Modius,*[3] and high up above the main-yard the mast was embraced by a sort of cup-shaped cage called *Carchesium,*[4] corresponding to what is now termed *a top.* It served as a look-out place; and in ships of war, men and military engines were sometimes stationed in the *Carchesium* to command the decks of an opponent. The ships of the ancients, even when of large size, had seldom, if ever, more than two masts, and the second mast was usually very small, and placed very far forward. The masts were, especially in smaller vessels, often made moveable, and might be stepped or unstepped at pleasure, whence the phrases—*Malum attollere* s. *erigere,* and *M. ponere* s. *inclinare.*

4. *Vela,* the sails, called also, from the materials of which they were fabricated, *Lintea* or *Carbasa.* There was usually one very large square sail (*Acatium*) on the mainmast, and above it was hoisted, in calm weather, a small topsail (*Supparum* s. *Suppara velorum.*) [5] The sail attached to the foremast (*Velo prora suo*) was also very small, and seems to have been termed *Dolon* or *Artemon.* [6] Pliny alludes to a mizen sail also, called *Epidromos* by Isidorus, but how it was rigged we know not—*Iam vero nec vela satis esse maiora navigiis, sed quamvis amplitudini antennarum singulae arbores sufficiant, super eas tamen addi velorum alia vela, praeterque alia in proris, et alia in puppibus pandi ac tot modis provocari mortem.* [7]

5. *Funes* s. *Rudentes* are words which comprehend the whole rigging, whether standing or running. The ropes specially named being the *Pedes,* that is, the ropes attached to the two lower corners of the square sail, what are now termed the *sheets* and *tacks,* the tack being sometimes called *Propes,* [8] to distinguish it from the *Pes,* or sheet proper—the *Opisphorae,* [9] or braces attached to the

---

[1] The authorities for *Ora* in the sense of a *cable* or *hawser,* are Liv. XXII. 29. XXVIII. 36. Quintil. IV. 2.
[2] Virg. Æn. V. 176, and note of Servius.
[3] Isidor. XIX. ii. 9.
[4] Lucil. ap. Non. s.v. *Carchesia,* p. 274. ad Gerl. Serv. ad Virg Æn. V. 77. Apulei. Florid. IV. 22.
[5] Isidor. XIX. iii. 2. Lucan. V. 428. Stat. S. III. ii. 27. Senec. Epp. LXXVII. Fest. s. v. *Supparus. Supparum* pp. 310. 340.
[6] Juv. S. XII. 69. Isidor. l.c.
[7] Plin. H.N. XIX. prooem. Isidor. l.c.
[8] Isidor. XIX. iv. 3.
[9] Isidor. XIX. 4. 6.

extremity of the yard, by which it was trimmed—the *Ceruchi*,[1] which attached the two extremities of the yard to the top of the mast, and the *Anquina*,[2] which attached the centre of the yard to the top of the mast. The large ropes, now called stays, which support the mast, were called πρότονοι by the Greeks, but the Latin name does not occur. *Remulcum* was a hawser used by one vessel when towing another.

6. *Remi*, the oars, the flat blades of which were the *palmulae* or *tonsae*, were attached each to its thole or pin, (*scalmus*[3] s. *paxillus*,) by a leather strap called *stropha* or *struppus*,[4] the τροπωτήρ of the Greeks.

Insigne s. *Figura* (παράσημον) was the figure-head attached to the prow, which gave its name to the ship, in addition to which, the bows were frequently decorated with an eye, represented in painting or carving, and both the stem and stern generally terminated in a tapering extension which was shaped so as to resemble the head and neck of a goose, and was hence termed *Cheniscus* (χηνίσκος.) See cut in p. 404.

Aplustre (pl. *Aplustra* s. *Aplustria*.) This was a decoration made of wood, attached to the stern, and bearing a resemblance to a plume of feathers. We have nothing corresponding to it in ordinary modern ships, but it is an object constantly represented upon ancient sculptures and medals, may be seen in the annexed cut, taken from a large brass of Commodus.

Sacellum. In the after part of the vessel also was a niche or small chapel containing images of the god or gods to whose protection the vessel was consigned, (*ingentes de puppe deos*,) and hence this part of the ship was named *Tutela*.

Vexillum—*Taenia*—*Fascia*, were used to designate a small streamer attached to a pole placed sometimes on the prow, and sometimes on the stern, which served as a vane to indicate the direction of the wind. See the cut given above, and the coin of M. Antonius, in p. 393.

Naves Longae.—Ships of war differed from merchant ships in their general form, being long and narrow, in order to ensure speed, while the latter were broad and round so as to afford capacious stowage.

The leading characteristic of the war ships of the ancients was, that they were galleys, depending upon rowers chiefly as the propelling power, (*Remus*, an oar—*Remex*, a rower—*Remigium*, the whole rowing apparatus,) and they were rated according to the number of ranks of oars (*ordines remorum*.) Thus those vessels which carried one rank of oars, (*quae simplice ordine agebantur*,) were called *Monocrota* (μονήρεις)—two ranks, *biremes*—*dicrota* s. *dicrotae* (διήρεις)—three ranks, *triremes*, (τριήρεις)—four ranks, *quadriremes* (τετρήρεις) —five ranks, *quinqueremes*, (πεντήρεις,) and so on for higher numbers.

No question connected with the mechanical contrivances of ancient times, has given rise to greater discussion, than the manner in which the ranks of oars were arranged. The ordinary supposition that they were placed in horizontal tiers, one row directly above another, occasions little difficulty, if we do not go beyond

---

[1] Val. Flacc. I. 469. Lucan. VIII. 176. X. 495.
[2] *Anquinae*, and not *anchorae*, is the true reading in Non. p. 367. See also Isidor. XIX. iv. 7.
[3] Vitruv. X. 8.
[4] Isidor. XIV. iv. 9.

two or even three rows, but the length and weight of the oars belonging to the upper tier of a quinquereme must have been such as to render them most unwieldy, if not altogether unmanageable, and when we come to deal with ships of six, seven, ten, sixteen, and even forty rows of oars, which are mentioned by ancient writers, the difficulty becomes absolutely insuperable. Nor do ancient monuments afford much aid, for, although they abound in representations of ships, the figures are not sufficiently distinct to render effectual assistance, but it cannot be concealed that, as far as they go, they lend no support to any opinion which supposes the oars to have been placed otherwise than in parallel tiers.

Rostrum (ἔμβολος.) Another characteristic of a ship of war was the *Rostrum*, a huge spike, or bundle of spikes, made of bronze or iron, projecting from the bow of the vessel, on a level with or below the water line. The purpose to which this instrument was applied, will be explained below.

Propugnacula. Turres.—Towers, or elevated platforms, were occasionally erected on the decks of war galleys, which were manned with soldiers, who poured down darts and other missiles upon their opponents, such vessels being termed *Naves Turritae*.

Crew of a Ship.—The crew of a merchant vessel are usually designated simply as *Nautae*, the pilot was called *Gubernator*, and might or might not be at the same time the commander of the vessel, the *Magister navis*, who is sometimes designated by the Greek word *Nauclerus*. The captain of a ship of war was called *Praefectus* or *Navarchus*, the admiral of a fleet, *Praefectus Classis*, and his ship *Navis Praetoria*. The rowers (*Remiges*) as well as those who navigated and fought the galleys, were comprehended under the expression *Navales Socii* or *Classici*. These, especially the rowers, were frequently slaves or freedmen, and, as in the case of the land forces, a certain number were furnished by the allied states and by the *Coloniae Maritimae*. In addition to the *Socii Navales*, there were always a considerable number of regular soldiers on board, who, when the Romans first engaged in naval warfare, were ordinary troops of the line, but were afterwards raised as a separate corps (*in classem scripti*) from those classes of the citizens whose fortune did not entitle them to serve in the legions. These marines are generally styled *Classiarii*, or, by adoption of the Greek equivalent, *Epibatae*; and under the empire, when two fleets were constantly kept ready for action, one at Ariminum, and the other at Misenum, they were organized in legions (*Legio Classica*.)[1]

Naval Warfare.—When two ships engaged individually, if tolerably well matched, the great object aimed at by each, was, either by running up suddenly alongside of the enemy, to sweep away (*detergere*) or disable a large number of his oars, or, by bearing down at speed, to drive the Rostrum full into his side or quarter, in which case the planks were generally stove in, and the vessel went down. But if one of the parties was so decidedly inferior in seamanship, as to be unable to cope with his antagonist in such manœuvres, he endeavoured, as he approached, to grapple with him, and then the result was decided, as upon land, by the numbers and bravery of the combatants. It was in this way that the Romans, under Duillius, achieved their first great naval victory (B.C. 260)

---

[1] Liv. XXI. 49. 50. XXII. 11. 57. XXIV. 11. XXVI. 17. 35. 48. XXVII. 42. XXVIII. 45. XXIX. 25. XXXII. 23. XXXVI. 43. XXXVII. 16. XLII. 48. Cic. in Verr. I. 20. II. 55. III. 80. V. 17. 24. Hirt. de bell. Alex. 11. de bell. Afric. 20. 62. Tacit. Ann. IV. 5. 27. XIV. 8. XV. 51. Hist. I. 6. 31. 36. 87. II. 8. 11. 14. 17. 22. 67. III. 55. Suet. Octav 16. Nero 34. Galb. 12. Dion Cass. LXIV. 3.

over the Carthaginians, to whom they were at that time far inferior in nautical experience and skill. The machines employed on this occasion, called *Corvi*, have been minutely described by Polybius; (I. 22;) and grappling-hooks and gear of various forms, (*Manus ferreae atque Harpagones*,) are incidentally mentioned in the descriptions of sea-fights recorded by ancient writers.[1]

We subjoin an imaginary representation of an ancient ship, taken from the work of Scheffer, which will serve to explain the relative position of the different parts described above.

aa, Alveus; *bb*, Prora; *cc*, Puppis; *d*, Gubernaculum; *e*, Malus; *ff*, Antennae; *gg*, Cornua; *h*, Carchesium; *kk*, Acatium; *ll*, Supparum; *m*, Dolon (?); *nn*, Pedes; *oo*, Opisphorae; *pp*, Ceruchi; *qq*, πρότονοι.

[1] Caes. B. C. I. 57. Q. Curt. IV. 2. 4. 9. Liv. XXVI. 39. XXX. 10. Flor. Plin. H. 2 H.N. VII. 57. Dion Cass. XLIX. 3. L. 32. 34.

CHAPTER XIII.

ROMAN WEIGHTS AND MEASURES—COINS—COMPUTATION MONEY—INTEREST OF MONEY.

A vast number of elaborate treatises have been composed on the subjects enumerated in the title to this Chapter. We must content ourselves with stating the general results at which the most patient and acute inquirers have arrived, without attempting to enter into the lengthened and, in many cases, very complicated investigations upon which these conclusions are founded.[1]

I. WEIGHTS.

As.—The unit of weight was the As or LIBRA, which occupied the same position in the Roman system as the POUND does in our own. According to the most accurate researches, the *As* was equal to about $11\frac{1}{2}$ oz. Avoirdupois, or .7375 of an Avoirdupois Pound.

Divisions and Multiples of the As.—The *As* was divided into 12 equal parts called *Unciae*, and the *Uncia* was divided into 24 equal parts called *Scrupula*, the *Scrupulum* being thus the $\frac{1}{288}$ part of the *As*. The following nomenclature was adopted to distinguish various multiples of the *As*, *Uncia*, and *Scrupulum*:—

Divisions of the As.			Divisions of the Uncia.			
As,	$= 12$ UNCIAE.		*Semuncia*,...	$= \frac{1}{2}$ UNCIA	$= \frac{1}{24}$ As.	
Deunx,	$= 11$	—	*Duella*,.....	$= \frac{1}{3}$	—	$= \frac{1}{36}$ —
Dextans,	$= 10$	—	*Sicilicus*,....	$= \frac{1}{4}$	—	$= \frac{1}{48}$ —
Dodrans,	$= 9$	—	*Sextula*,......	$= \frac{1}{6}$	—	$= \frac{1}{72}$ —
Bes s. *Bessis*,	$= 8$	—	*Semisextula*,	$= \frac{1}{12}$	—	$= \frac{1}{144}$ —
Septunx,	$= 7$	—	*Scrupulum*,..	$= \frac{1}{24}$	—	$= \frac{1}{288}$ —
Semis s. *Semissis*,	$= 6$	—	*Siliqua*,......	$= \frac{1}{144}$	—	$= \frac{1}{1728}$ —
Quincunx,	$= 5$	—	Multiples of the As.			
Triens,	$= 4$	—	*Dupondius*,............	$= 2$ ASSES.		
Quadrans s. *Teruncius*,	$= 3$	—	*Tripondius* s. *Tressis*,...	$= 3$	—	
Sextans,	$= 2$	—	*Octussis*,............	$= 8$	—	
Sescunx s. *Sesuncia*,...	$= 1\frac{1}{2}$	—	*Decussis*,............	$= 10$	—	
Uncia,	$= 1$	—	*Vicessis*,............	$= 20$	—	
			Centussis,............	$= 100$	—	

[1] Of the numerous works which have from time to time appeared in connection with these topics, the following are the most celebrated—BUDAEUS, *De Asse*, 1516; GRONOVIUS, *De Pecunia vetere*, 1643; GREAVES, *Discourse of the Roman Foot and Denarius*, 1647; EISENSCHMIDT, *De Ponderibus et Mensuris, veterum*, 1708; ECKHEL, *Doctrina Numorum veterum*, 1792; HUSSEY, *Essay on Ancient Weights and Money*, 1836; BOECK, *Metrologische Untersuchungen*.

The *Drachma* and the *Obolus*, which were properly Greek weights, are occasionally employed by Roman writers—

The *Drachma* was reckoned as $=\frac{1}{8}$ of the *Uncia* $=\frac{1}{96}$ of the *As*.
The *Obolus*   — $=\frac{1}{48}$ — $=\frac{1}{576}$ —

The term As, and the words which denote its divisions, were not confined to weight alone, but were applied to measures of length and capacity also, and in general to any object which could be regarded as consisting of 12 equal parts. Thus they were commonly used to denote the shares into which an inheritance was divided. When an individual inherited the whole property of another, he was designated as *Heres ex asse;* if one-half, *Heres ex semisse;* if one-third, *Heres ex triente*, &c.; Cicero will supply (Pro Caecin. 6.) an excellent example —*Testamento facto mulier moritur. Facit heredem ex deunce et semuncia Caecinam, ex duabus sextulis M. Fulcinium libertum superioris viri, Aebutio sextulam adspergit*. The account stands thus—

Caecina inherited 11 *Unciae* and a *Semuncia*, $= 11\frac{1}{2}$ *Unciae*.
Fulcinius   —   2 *Sextulae*, ... $= \frac{2}{6}$ —
Æbutius   —   1 *Sextula*,..................... $= \frac{1}{6}$ —

Making up in all 12 *Unciae*,..................... $=$ 1 *As*, or the whole inheritance.

II. MEASURES OF LENGTH.

Pes.—The unit of Lineal Measure was the PES, which occupied the same place in the Roman system as the FOOT does in our own. According to the most accurate researches, the *Pes* was equal to about 11.64 inches imperial measure, or, .97 of an English foot.

The *Pes* being supposed to represent the length of the foot in a well proportioned man, various divisions and multiples of the *Pes* were named after standards derived from the human frame. Thus—

Pes,......... $=$ 16 *Digiti*,.... i.e. Finger-breadths.
  — .... $=$ 4 *Palmi*,.... i.e. Hand-breadths.
Sesquipes,.. $=$ 1 *Cubitus*, { i.e. Length from elbow to extremity of middle finger.

The *Pes* was also divided into 12 *Pollices*, i.e. thumb-joint-lengths, otherwise called *Unciae* (whence our word *inch*.) When the division of the *Pes* into *Unciae* was adopted, then the different divisions of the *Pes* from one *Uncia* up to twelve were designated by the names given in the preceding section for the divisions of the *As*, viz. the *Deunx*, *Dextans*, &c.

The measures longer than the *Pes*, in common use, were—

Palmipes, ... $=$ 1 *Pes* $+$ 1 *Palmus* $=$ 20 *Digiti* $=$ 15 *Unciae*.
Cubitus, ... $=$ 1 *Sequispes*, ... $=$ 24 *Digiti* $=$ 18   —
Gradus, ... $=$ 2½ *Pedes*, ... $=$ 40 *Digiti*.
Passus, ... $=$ 5 *Pedes*, ... $=$ 2 *Gradus*.
Decempeda s. *Pertica*, $=$ 10 *Pedes*, ... $=$ 2 *Passus*.
Actus,.................. $=$ 120 *Pedes*, ... $=$ 12 *Decempedae*.
Mille Passuum, ... $=$5000 *Pedes*, ... $=$ 1000 *Passus*.

There was also a *Palmus maior* = 3 *Palmi* = 12 *Digiti* = 9 *Pollices* or *Unciae*.
It appears from this, that since

The English statute mile = 1760 yards ...... = 5280 English feet.
The Roman mile .... = 5000 Roman feet = 4850 English feet.

Therefore the Roman mile is shorter than the English mile by 430 English feet, or 144 yards nearly.

Ulna, the Greek ὠλένη, from which the English word *Ell* is derived, varied in signification when used to indicate a measure. Sometimes it represents the distance from the shoulder to the wrist, sometimes from the shoulder to the extremity of the middle finger, sometimes it is regarded as synonymous with *Cubitus*, and sometimes it denotes the distance between the tips of the middle fingers, when the arms are stretched out in the same plane with the body, i.e. the full extent which can be embraced by the outstretched arms, in which case it would be held as equivalent to 6 *Pedes*.

In applying the divisions of the *As* to measures of length, the *Pes* was regarded as the *As* and the *Pollex* as the *Uncia*. Hence we read in Columella (III. 13.)—DUPONDIO ET DODRANTE *altus sulcus*, i.e. a ditch 2 feet 9 inches deep; and again (VI. 19.)—*Habet in latitudinem pars prior* DUPONDIUM SEMISSEM, i.e. is two feet and a-half broad.

III. MEASURES OF SURFACE.

We have seen above that the lineal *Actus*, which was the normal length of a furrow, was 120 Roman feet; the *Actus Quadratus* was a square, whose side was a lineal *Actus*; a *Iugerum* consisted of two *Actus* put together, and was therefore a rectangular plot of ground 240 Roman feet long and 120 Roman feet broad. Reducing Roman feet to English feet, it will be found that the *Iugerum* contains 27097.92 square feet English, while the English Acre contains 43560 square feet; hence the Roman *Iugerum* was less than ⅔ of an English Acre.

Less frequently mentioned than the *Iugerum* are—the *Heredium* = 2 *Iugera*; the *Centuria* = 100 *Heredia* = 200 *Iugera*; and the *Saltus* = 4 *Centuriae* = 800 *Iugera*.

We hear also of the *Versus*, which contained 10,000 square feet, and the *Actus minimus*, which contained 480 square feet.

In applying the divisions of the *As* to measures of surface, the *Iugerum* was regarded as the *As*, and fractions of the *Iugerum* were represented by the sub-divisions of the *As*. Hence we meet with such expression as the following (Liv. V. 24.)—*Triumviri ad id creati* TERNA IUGERA ET SEPTUNCES *viritim diviserunt*, i.e. assigned to each individual seven Jugers and $\frac{7}{12}$ of a Juger.

IV. MEASURES OF CAPACITY.

The unit of Capacity was the AMPHORA or QUADRANTAL, which contained a cubic foot, and therefore, according to the computation of the Roman foot given above, must have been equal to 5.687 imperial gallons, or 5 gallons 2 quarts 1 pint 2 gills nearly.

The *Amphora* was the unit for both Liquid and Dry Measures, but the latter were generally referred to the *Modius*, which contained one-third of an *Amphora*, that is, 1.896 imperial gallons, or .948 of an imperial peck.

This being premised, we may enumerate the divisions of the *Amphora* and the *Modius*.

Liquid Measure.			Dry Measure.		
AMPHORA	=	2 *Urnae*.	MODIUS	=	2 *Semimodi*.
—	=	8 *Congii*.	—	=	16 *Sextarii*.
—	=	48 *Sextarii*.	—	=	{32 *Heminae* s.
—	=	{96 *Heminae* s.	—	=	{ *Cotylae*.
—	=	{ *Cotylae*.	—	=	64 *Quartarii*.
—	=	192 *Quartarii*.	—	=	128 *Acetabula*.
—	=	384 *Acetabula*.	—	=	192 *Cyathi*.
—	=	576 *Cyathi*.	—	=	768 *Ligulae*.
—	=2304 *Ligulae*.				

The *Culeus* was equal to 20 *Amphorae*.

In applying the divisions of the *As* to the above Liquid Measures, the *Sextarius* was regarded as the *As* and the *Cyathus* as the *Uncia*; hence we read in Martial (XI. 37.)—

> Quincunces et sex cyathos bessemque bibamus
> Caius ut flat, Iulius et Proculus :

i.e. let us drink five, and six, and eight *Cyathi*, i.e. 19 *Cyathi*, 19 being the number of letters in the name *Caius Iulius Proculus*.

From *Congius* is derived the word *Congiarium*, which properly signifies a vessel holding a *Congius*, but was frequently employed, especially in later times, to denote a gratuity of wine or oil bestowed upon the people at large; e.g. *Lucullus millia cadûm* IN CONGIARIUM *divisit amplius centum;* (Plin. H.N. I. 14;) also a gratuity of edibles whether wet or dry—*Ancus Marcius rex salis modios sex mille* IN CONGIARIO *dedit populo;* (Plin. H.N. XXXI. 7.) and finally, a gratuity in money—CONGIARIA *populo frequenter dedit, sed diversae fere summae, modo quadringenos, modo tricenos, nonnumquam ducenos quinquagenos numos* (Suet. Octav. 41.) Under the empire, a gratuity of this nature, when bestowed on the soldiers, was usually termed *Donativum*—*Populo* CONGIARIUM, *militi* DONATIVUM *proposuit* (Suet. Ner. 7.)

V. COINS.[1]

There can be little doubt that the Romans, in the earlier ages of their history, were unacquainted with coined money. Their circulating medium consisted of lumps or ingots of copper, (*Aes,*) which were weighed, and not counted, the name of an ingot of this description being *Stipes* or *Stips*, from which was formed *Stipendium*. According to Pliny, copper money was first coined by Servius Tullius, and stamped with the figure of a sheep, (*nota pecudum,*) but it is very doubtful whether any such pieces were ever minted at Rome, and it is not unlikely that the story was invented in order to supply a plausible derivation for the word *Pecunia*. Of the coinage as it actually existed from a remote period, we can, however, speak with confidence. The practice of hoarding was carried to such an extent in the ancient world, that scarcely a year elapses in which large numbers of Greek and Roman coins are not discovered in various

---

[1] The *Locus Classicus*, on the rise and progress of the Roman mint, is in Pin. H. N XXXIII. 13.; a passage full of curious information, but containing many evident errors and absurdities. The best modern account of the subject will be found in the *Prolegomena* to the *Doctrina Numorum veterum* of ECKHEL.

parts of Europe, Asia, and Northern Africa, while the extensive collections which have been formed afford most valuable information on a multitude of topics connected with classical antiquity.

The metals employed by the Romans in their coinage were copper, (*Aes*,) silver, (*Argentum*,) and gold, (*Aurum*,) but these were not introduced all at once, but in succession.

Copper Coinage of the Republic.—For nearly 500 years after the foundation of the city, the Romans coined no metal except copper. If any gold or silver pieces were in circulation, they must have been of foreign stamp.

The ordinary copper coins of the republic were six in number, each being distinguished by a particular device, which is preserved with almost perfect uniformity. The names of these coins were—

1. *As*,.................. presenting on its obverse a head of *Ianus*.
2. *Semis*, the half *As*, — *Ioris*.
3. *Triens*, one-third of the *As*, — *Minerva*.
4. *Quadrans*, the quarter *As*, — *Hercules*.
5. *Sextans*, the half *Triens*, — *Mercurius*.
6. *Uncia*, one-twelfth of the *As*, — *Minerva*.

The device on the reverse is the same in all, being a rude representation of the prow of a ship. On the *As* we find the numeral I, on the *Semis* the letter S, while on the rest round dots indicate the number of *Unciae*; thus the *Triens* is marked o o o o, the *Quadrans* o o o, the *Sextans* o o, the *Uncia* o. Many of them have the word *ROMA*, and it gradually became common for the magistrate under whose inspection they were struck, to add his name.

Weight of the As at different periods.—The *As*, regarded as a coin, originally weighed, as the name implies, one Pound, and the smaller copper coins those fractions of the Pound denoted by their names. By degrees, however, the weight of the *As*, regarded as a coin, was greatly diminished. We are told, that about the commencement of the first Punic War, it had fallen from Twelve Ounces to Two Ounces; in the early part of the second Punic War, (B.C. 217,) it was reduced to One Ounce; and not long afterwards, by a *Lex Papiria*, it was fixed at Half-an-Ounce, which remained the standard ever after.[1] We subjoin a series of cuts taken from existing specimens of the *As* and the smaller denominations, in which will be seen the different devices and marks enumerated above.

It will be observed that in this series, the *Semis* is smaller than the *Triens*, proving that the particular specimen of the *Triens* from which the cut was made belongs to a period when the *As* was heavier than it was at the period when the specimen of the *Semis* was struck.

Copper Coinage of the Empire.—Upon the establishment of the imperial

---

[1] According to the statement of Pliny, the weight of the *As* was reduced at once from 12 ounces to 2 ounces, by order of the Senate, in order to relieve the financial embarrassments under which the state was labouring; or, in other words, the Senate resolved to defraud the public creditors by a sudden and enormous depreciation of the currency. This representation, which is in itself incredible, since it is totally at variance with the scrupulous good faith which the government is known to have observed on other occasions in its pecuniary transactions, is completely disproved by the fact, that *Asses* are still in existence exhibiting a series of weights descending gradually from nearly 12 ounces, through 11, 10, 9, 8, &c. ounces, till we reach the final ½ ounce. The diminution in the weight of the *As* arose in all probability from the value of copper, in relation to silver, increasing gradually as the latter metal became more common and the former in greater demand.

COPPER COINAGE.

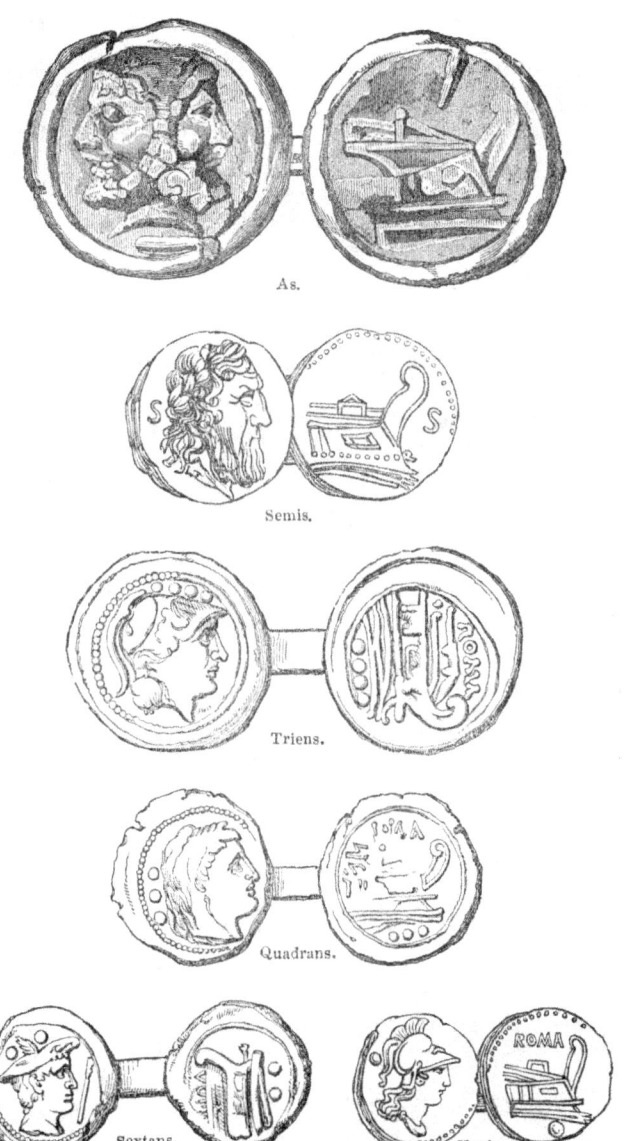

As.

Semis.

Triens.

Quadrans.

Sextans. Uncia.

government under Augustus, the old *As* and its divisions ceased to be struck, and a new copper coinage was introduced, consisting—

1. Of those pieces which are commonly called *Imperial Large Brass*, and which form a series extending from Augustus down to Postumus. They are generally about the size of an English Penny; they exhibit, for the most part, on the obverse, the head of the reigning Prince, or of some member of the imperial family, accompanied by a legend expressive of the name and titles of the individual represented, while on the reverse we find a great variety of most interesting and instructive devices. These pieces are usually of very good workmanship, are in many cases composed, not of ordinary copper, but of fine yellow brass (*aurichalcum*,) and are supposed to have passed for 4 *Asses*. Several illustrations, taken from the reverse of coins belonging to this class, have been given in the course of the work, and we annex a cut of a Large Brass

of Antoninus Pius, bearing upon one side the head of the Emperor, with the legend ANTONINUS AUGUSTUS PIUS, and on the reverse the figure of Æneas bearing off his father from Troy and leading his boy by the hand, with the legend PP. TR. POT. COS. III. S.C. (*Pater Patriae, Tribunicia Potestas, Consul Tertium, Senatus Consulto.*)

2. Of those pieces commonly called *Imperial Middle Brass*, which resemble the Large Brass, except in so far that they are only half the size. We annex a

cut taken from one of the earliest of the series, exhibiting on the obverse the head of Augustus, with the legend CAESAR AUGUSTUS TRIBUNIC. POTEST., and on the reverse the name of one of the *Triumviri Monetales* (p.197) C. GALLIUS LUPERCUS IIIVIR A. A. A. F. F. (p. 197) and S. C. in the field.

3. Of those pieces commonly called *Imperial Small Brass*. These do not, like the two former classes, form a regular series; they vary much in size; they

seem seldom to have been struck in large numbers, and not to have been struck at all by many Emperors. We have given a specimen in p. 237 of one belonging to the reign of Caligula.

Silver Coinage.—According to Pliny, silver was first coined at Rome in B.C. 269, five years before the commencement of the first Punic War, in pieces of three denominations.

1. The *Denarius* equivalent to 10 *Asses*.
2. The *Quinarius* — 5 —
3. The *Sestertius* — 2½ —

But when the weight of the *As* was reduced in B.C. 217 to One Ounce, it was ordained at the same time that

The *Denarius* should be held equivalent to 16 *Asses*.
The *Quinarius* — — 8 —
The *Sestertius* — — 4 —

and this relation subsisted ever after between the silver coins bearing the above names and the *As*.

The *Denarius* and the *Quinarius* continued to be the ordinary silver currency down to the age of Septimius Severus and his sons, by whom pieces composed of a base alloy were introduced, and for several reigns entirely superseded the pure metal. The silver *Sestertius* does not appear to have been coined under the empire, its place being occupied by the Large Brass which was of the same value.

The devices originally stamped upon all three denominations were, on the obverse a female head helmeted and winged, with the legend ROMA; on the reverse the *Dioscuri* on horseback, with spears couched and with conical caps, a star being placed above the head of each. The *Denarius*, *Quinarius*, and *Sestertius* were severally distinguished by the numerals X, V, and IIS, placed behind the helmeted head, and even after they passed respectively for 16, for 8, and for 4 *Asses*, the same numerals were retained as corresponding to their names.

In *Denarii* of a somewhat later date, instead of the *Dioscuri*, we generally find a figure of Jupiter, or some other deity, in a chariot drawn by four or by two horses, and hence such pieces were known as *Quadrigati* and *Bigati*. We annex a cut of a *Bigatus*, in which Victory is the charioteer. At an early period

also it was not uncommon to notch the edges of the coin, in order, probably, to render forgery more difficult, and hence such pieces were known as *Serrati*.

Quinarii bore originally, as we have seen, the same device as *Denarii*; but it soon became the practice to stamp upon the reverse of all *Quinarii*, a figure

of the goddess *Victoria*, who appears in various attitudes, sometimes standing, sometimes flying, sometimes in a chariot, sometimes crowning a trophy, and hence the term *Victoriatus* is frequently employed as synonymous with *Quinarius*. On the obverse of both *Denarii* and *Quinarii*, the helmeted head gradually disappeared, and was replaced by various heads, sometimes of gods, sometimes of mortals, but never, under the republic, of living personages.

On the earliest silver coins there is no legend except the word ROMA, but it soon became common for the magistrate intrusted with the task of coining, to mark upon the pieces his own name or that of an illustrious member of the family to which he belonged, and the devices, of which there are a great variety, frequently bear reference to some legend, or exploit, or honour, connected with the house. Of this, several examples will be found in *Denarii* introduced as illustrations in the preceding pages; and on the *Serratus*, figured above, we see a representation of Ulysses recognised by his dog, the name on the coin being C. MAMILIUS LIMETANUS, but the *Mamilii* came from *Tusculum*,

and *Tusculum* was said to have been founded by Telegonus, son of Ulysses, (*Telegoni iuga parricidae*.) The *Denarius*, of which we annex a cut, bears the name T. CARISIUS, on the obverse is a head of the goddess *Moneta*, on the reverse are represented the tools of the coiner. The number of silver coins belonging to the republican period, which have come down to modern times, is enormous, and from this source alone we can make up a catalogue of nearly two hundred *Familiae*, whence coins of this class are frequently designated as *Nummi Familiarum*.

The silver coinage of the empire consisted of *Denarii* and *Quinarii*, and differed little from that of the republic, except that the obverse represented almost uniformly the head of the reigning Prince, or of some member of the imperial family, while the pieces themselves gradually decreased in weight. The first of the two specimens annexed exhibits on the obverse a veiled head of Julius Cæsar,

 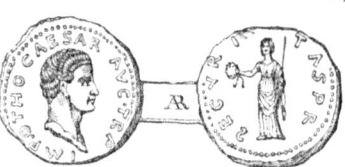

with the *Lituus* and the *Apex*, the legend being PARENS PATRIAE CAESAR, and on the reverse the name of one of the commissioners of the mint under Augustus, C. COSSUTIUS MARIDIANUS, with the letters A. A. A. F. F. The second has on the obverse, the head of Otho, with the legend IMP. OTHO CAESAR

Aug. Tr. P., and on the reverse a figure of *Securitas*, with the legend SECURITAS P. R.

Gold Coinage.—Pliny asserts that gold was first coined in B.C. 207, and a few pieces are still extant which correspond with his description, but they are now generally regarded as having been struck in Magna Graecia. The number of gold coins, undoubtedly Roman, belonging to the republican period, is so small, that the best numismatologists are of opinion that this metal did not form part of the ordinary and regular currency until the age of Julius Caesar, the want having been supplied by Greek *Philippi*. The principal gold coin of the empire was the *Denarius Aureus*, which is generally termed simply *Aureus*, but by Pliny uniformly *Denarius*. The *Denarius Aureus* always passed for 25 silver *Denarii*. Half *Aurei* were also minted, but these are comparatively rare. A specimen of an *Aureus*, with the head of Augustus, will be found in p. 344, and we annex a representation of another, belonging to the same period, exhibiting on the obverse, the head of *Ammon*, and on the reverse a man arrayed in the vestments of an *Augur*, and crowned by *Iuno Sospita*, who follows behind, the legend being Q. CORNUFICI AUGUR. IMP.

VI. COMPUTATION OF MONEY.

Sums of money were computed either
1. By *Asses*; or, 2. By *Sestertii*,

the latter denomination having been generally employed after the introduction of a silver currency. Before considering these separately, it is necessary to explain the system pursued with regard to the numerals.

1. In expressing all sums, from one *As* or one *Sestertius* up to a thousand *Asses* or *Sestertii*, the cardinal or distributive numerals employed agree in case with *As* or *Sestertius*. Thus we say, *Decem Asses—Viginti Sestertii—Ducenti Asses—Tricenos Asses—Quinquagenis Sestertiis—Mille Sestertii*, &c.

2. All sums from one thousand up to one hundred thousand inclusive, are expressed by the cardinal or distributive numerals, followed by *As* or *Sestertius* in the genitive plural. Thus we say, *Duo millia . . . Decem millia . . . Bina millia . . . Tricena millia . . . Centum s. Centena millia Assium vel Sestertiorum*. As to the numeral *Mille*, we may say with equal propriety, *Mille Asses* v. *Sestertii*, or *Mille Assium* v. *Sestertiorum*. [1]

3. All sums above one hundred thousand are expressed by prefixing a numeral adverb to *Centena millia*, the word *Assium* or *Sestertiorum* following in the genitive. Thus we say, *Bis centena millia . . . Quater centena millia . . . Decies centena millia Assium* v. *Sestertiorum*, to denote 200,000; 400,000; 1,000,000, &c.

But in the great majority of cases the words *Centena millia* are omitted, and the numeral adverb is placed alone, it being the rule that a numeral adverb is never employed in expressing sums of money, except when the words *Centena millia* are either expressed or understood. Thus we say, *Decies . . . Centies . . . Millies . . . Bis millies . . . Tricies quinquies . . . Centies millies . . . Quadringenties millies . . . Quater decies millies Sestertiorum*, &c., to

---

[1] Instead of *Sestertiorum*, the contracted genitive *Sestertium* is common, as we shall notice below.

denote 1,000,000; 10,000,000; 100,000,000; 200,000,000; 3,500,000; 10,000,000,000; 40,000,000,000; 4,000,000,000, &c.

This being premised, we proceed to explain some details with respect to the computation by *Asses* and by *Sestertii*, considered separately.

1. *Computation by Asses.*—The *As* being a copper coin, the word *Aes* is used in computing sums of money as equivalent to *As*. e.g. *Ex eis, qui centum millium aeris, aut maiorem censum haberent* (Liv. I. 43.)—*Qui millibus aeris quinquaginta census fuisset* (XXIV. 11.)—*Qui supra trecenta millia usque ad decies aeris*[1] (ibid.) As long as the *As* retained its original weight of a pound, no confusion could arise between *As* signifying a coin, and *As* denoting a pound weight of metal. But after the *As*, regarded as a coin, underwent successive diminutions in weight, it became necessary to distinguish between the original weight of the coin and the coin actually current, and hence the expression *aes grave* was introduced when a sum was computed according to the ancient standard, that is, when a certain number of *Asses* or full pounds of metal were to be designated, and not the coin called *As* of inferior weight. Hence we read—*M. Postumius . . . decem millibus aeris gravis damnatur* (Liv. IV. 41.)—*Quia nondum argentum signatum erat aes grave plaustris ad aerarium convehentes* (IV. 60.) —*Indici data libertas et aeris gravis viginti millia* (XXII. 33.)—*Ei centum millia gravis aeris dari Patres iusserunt: servis vicena quina millia aeris et libertatem* (XXXII. 26.)

2. *Computation by Sestertii.*—The word *Sestertius*, contracted for *Semistertius*, is properly an adjective signifying *two and a-half*,[2] the substantive understood being *Nummus*, and *Nummus* is frequently used by itself as equivalent to *Sestertius*, the *Nummus Sestertius* having beeen emphatically *the Nummus* or coin of account from the time when a silver currency was introduced. Thus the statement—*Populo trecenos* NUMMOS *viritim divisit*—denotes that each individual received 300 *Sestertii*. When *Nummus* is employed to denote any other coin, then an adjective is invariably added, fixing the coin in question; e.g. *In capita Romana trecenis* NUMMIS QUADRIGATIS, *in socios ducenis* (Liv. XXII. 52.) where the epithet *Quadrigatis* indicates that *Denarii* are meant (p. 415.)

We have seen that in expressing sums from one up to a thousand *Sestertii*, the numerals agree in case with *Sestertius*, and that in expressing all sums above a thousand, the numeral is joined with *Sestertiorum* in the genitive, for which the contracted form *Sestertiûm* is very frequently substituted.

But the word *Sestertiorum* or *Sestertiûm* is often omitted, and the numeral is placed alone; thus Cicero (Pro Coel. 7.)—*Cuius hic in aediculis habitat* DECEM, *ut opinor* MILLIBUS—i.e. *decem millibus Sestertiorum;* and in like manner Velleius (II. 10.)—*Lepidum Aemilium augurem quod* SEX MILLIBUS *aedes conduxisset adesse iusserunt augures*, i.e. *sex millibus sestertiorum*. In like manner the numeral adverbs *decies, . . . centies, . . . millies*, &c. are placed alone without the addition of *Sestertiorum* to denote one million, ten millions, one hundred millions of *Sestertii*.

It must be carefully observed, that wherever *Sestertium* is found in the pure text of any classical writer, it is invariably to be regarded as the contracted genitive plural for *Sestertiorum*. It cannot be proved that the form *Sestertium* as a neuter nominative singular anywhere exists.

---

[1] In these and similar phrases, some grammarians suppose that there is always an ellipsis of the word *Assium* before *Aeris*.

[2] Literally, *The third a half one*. By a similar idiom in Greek, τίταρτον ἡμιτάλαντον signifies *Three Talents and a-half*.

In writers of the Empire, however, we find the word *Sestertia* used as a neuter plural to denote *a sum of one thousand Sestertii*. Thus in Suetonius (Octav. 101.)—*Reliqua legata varie dedit, produxitque quaedam ad* VICENA SESTERTIA,[1] i.e. 20,000 *Sestertii;* and in Juvenal (S. IV. 15.)—*Mullum sex millibus emit = Aequantem sane paribus* SESTERTIA *libris*, i.e. he paid six thousand sesterces for a mullet, at the rate of a thousand sesterces for each pound. (See also Hor. Epp. I. vii. 80. Martial VI. 20.)

The *Sestertius* having been originally equivalent to two *Asses* and a-half, although it subsequently became equivalent to four *Asses*, (p. 415,) was represented in writing by the symbol IIS, that is, two units and a-half, (S denoting *Semis*,) a line being drawn through the figures (thus HS) to mark that they were to be taken together. It appears probable that the symbol and not the word was always employed in ancient documents, and that much confusion and many blunders have been introduced by the ignorance of transcribers when changing the symbol into a word. To this cause we must ascribe the corrupt forms which disfigure the texts of many editions of the classical authors. Thus in Nepos (Att. 14.)—*Atticus tanta usus est moderatione ut neque in* SESTERTIO VICIES, *quod a patre acceperat, parum splendide se gesserit, neque in* SESTERTIO CENTIES *affluentius vixerit quam instituerat;* in Suetonius (Caes. 50.)—*Serviliae* SESTERTIO SEXAGIES *margaritam mercatus est;* in Livy (XLV. 4.)—*Argenti ad summam* SESTERTII DECIES *in aerarium rettulit;* and in Cicero (Philipp. II. 37.)—*Syngrapha* SESTERTII CENTIES : in which, and in all similar passages, *Sestertio* and *Sestertii* are corrupt forms for *Sestertiorum* or *Sestertiûm*, and in the older MSS. these words were probably represented by the symbol HS.

Comparison of Roman with English Money.—According to accurate calculations, based upon the weight and assay of the most perfect specimens of *Denarii*, the value of the silver *Sestertius* at the close of the republic may be fixed at twopence sterling. After the reign of Augustus, the coinage underwent a sensible deterioration, both in weight and in purity, and we cannot reckon the *Sestertius* higher than 1¾d. from the age of Tiberius down to Septimius Severus. Taking the higher value, the following table may be useful in converting sums from Roman into English currency:—

		£	s.	d.			£	s.	d.
1 *Sestertius*	=	0	0	2	10,000 *Sestertii* =		83	6	8
10 *Sestertii*	=	0	1	8	100,000 —	=	833	6	8
100 —	=	0	16	8	1,000,000 —	=	8333	6	8
1000 —	=	8	6	8	10,000,000 —	=	83333	6	8

VII. Interest of Money.

A Capital Sum lent out at Interest was termed *Caput* or *Sors;* the Interest paid upon it was termed *Fenus* or *Usura*, the latter word being generally used in the plural *Usurae*. The rates of Interest most frequently mentioned in the classics are the *Fenus Unciarium* and the *Usurae Centesimae;* but the real import of these expressions has proved a fruitful source of controversy. Niebuhr, in the third volume of his History, has a masterly dissertation on this subject,

---

[1] It may be doubted whether here, and in similar passages in prose writers, the true reading is not *IIS vicena*, i.e. *vicena millia Sestertiorum*, but we cannot apply the same remedy to the passages found in the poets.

and his conclusions appear to be impregnable. We shall briefly consider each rate separately.

Fenus Unciarium.—The Capital being regarded as the *As* or Unit, and the Interest being calculated by the year, then *Fenus Unciarium*, or Uncial Interest, would be one-twelfth part of the Capital, that is, $8\frac{1}{3}$ per cent. per annum. But if we suppose, with Niebuhr, that this rate was introduced while the year of ten months was still observed, then $8\frac{1}{3}$ per cent. for a year of ten months, will be exactly 10 per cent. for a year of twelve months.

According to Tacitus (Ann. VI. 16.) the first legislative enactment on the subject of Interest was contained in the Laws of the XII Tables, which provided, (B.C. 451—449,) that the *Fenus Unciarium* should be maximum rate of Interest—*Nam primo Duodecim Tabulis sanctum ne quis* UNCIARIO FENORE *amplius exerceret;* but Livy seems (VII. 16.) to refer the introduction of this restriction to the *Lex Duillia Maenia* of B.C. 357, nearly a century later. The same historian records (VII. 27. comp. Tacit. l.c.) that in B.C. 347, the legal rate of interest was reduced one-half—*semunciarium tantum ex unciario fenus factum;* and again we find (VII. 42. B.C. 342.)—*Invenio apud quosdam L. Genucium, Tribunum plebis, tulisse ad populum ne fenerare liceret;* and Tacitus (l.c.) declares that a law to that effect was actually passed,[1] but if this was really the case, it must, from its very nature, have been absolutely powerless.

Usurae Centesimae.—Towards the close of the republic, we hear for the first time of *Usurae Centesimae*, which must signify Interest amounting to 100th part of the Capital, or 1 per cent. But this was probably introduced along with the Greek fashion of paying Interest monthly, so that *Usurae Centesimae* was 1 per cent. per month, or 12 per cent. per annum.

Usurae Centesimae being 12 per cent., when a lower rate was charged the proportions were expressed by the divisions of the *As*. Thus *Usurae Besses, U. Semisses, U. Trientes, U. Quadrantes,* signify respectively, 8, 6, 4, and 3 per cent.

On the other hand, when the security was bad, a higher rate was exacted, and we hear of *Binae Centesimae*, i.e. 24 per cent.; *Quaternae Centesimae*, i.e 48 per cent.; and when Horace uses the phrase *Quinas hic Capiti mercedes exsecat*, he must mean *Quinae Centesimae*, i.e. 60 per cent. (Cic. in Verr. III. 70. ad Att. VI. 2. Hor. S. I. ii. 14.)

[1] His words are—*Postremo vetita versura*—where it must be observed that this is not the usual import of *Versura*, which is generally employed to express the *conversion* of the original Capital into a new Capital by the addition of Interest due upon it, according to the principle of Compound Interest, otherwise termed *Centesimae renovatae* or *Anatocismus*, Simple Interest being expressed by the phrase *Centesimae perpetuae* (Cic. ad Att. V. 21. VI. 2.)

CHAPTER XIV.

PRIVATE LIFE OF THE ROMANS.

I. Customs connected with particular Epochs of Life.

Infancy.—As soon as a child was born it was laid down at the feet of the father, who, if the babe was free from any serious deformity, and if he was prepared to acknowledge it (*agnoscere*) as his legitimate offspring, lifted it from the ground, (*a terrâ levabat*,) and thus declared that he was willing to rear it (*alere*) as his own. Hence the expressions *Tollere* s. *Suscipere liberos* signify *to bring up or educate children*. Infanticide, as we have seen above, was not prohibited by law, and, in the earlier ages of the state, was, probably, not uncommon.[1]

Boys on the ninth, and girls on the eighth day after birth underwent a religious purification termed *lustratio*, and on this day, which was called *Dies lustricus*, the former received their *Praenomen* (*nomen accipiebant*.) Boys, until they attained to manhood, and girls, until they were married, wore a *Toga Praetexta*, i.e. a cloak with a narrow scarlet border, and from the necks of boys was suspended a hollow disk called *Bulla*, made of gold, silver, or, in the case of the poor, of leather, containing a charm or amulet against the fascination of the Evil Eye. The *Toga Praetexta* and the *Bulla* were both of Etruscan origin, (hence the latter is called *Etruscum aurum* by Juvenal,) and were at first confined to the offspring of Patricians, but before the close of the republic were assumed by all *Ingenui*.[2]

Education.—Elementary schools (*Ludus literarius—Ludi literarum*) for both girls and boys, seem to have existed from a very early epoch, as may be seen from the story of Virginia, and these were originally situated in the immediate vicinity of the Forum. For several centuries the instruction communicated was confined to reading, writing, and arithmetic, but after a taste for Greek literature had been formed, the Greek language was eagerly cultivated. Before the close of the republic, a familiar knowledge of that tongue was considered indispensable to every one in the upper ranks, and Quintilian recommends (I. O. I i. 12) that a boy should study Greek before his mother tongue. In the age of Cicero, and for some centuries afterwards, a complete course of education for youths consisted of, at least, three parts, which followed each other in regular progression under different masters. 1. Reading, Writing, and

---

[1] Plaut. Amph. I. iii. 3. Trucul. II. 1:. 45. Terent. Andr. I. iii. 14. Heaut. IV. i. 15. Hor. S. II. v. 45. Suet. Octav. 65. Ner. 5. Cic. Philipp. XIII. 10. de legg. III. 8. Senec. de Ira I. 15. de Benef. III. 13.
[2] Macrob. S. I. 6. 16. Liv. XXVI. 36. Cic. in Verr. I. 44. Philipp. II. 18. Propert. IV. i. 131. Sueton. de clar. Rhet. 1. Plut. Q. R. 101. Vit. Rom. 25. Isidor. XIX. xxxi. 11

Arithmetic, taught by the *Ludi Magister* s. *Literator*. 2. A critical knowledge of the Greek and Latin languages, taught by the *Grammaticus* s. *Grammatistes*. 3. Composition and Oratory, taught by the *Rhetor Latinus*, to which some added, 4. A course of Moral and Metaphysical Philosophy; [1] to obtain the last in perfection it was not unusual to resort to Athens, or to some other famous foreign seat of learning, although numerous Greek Professors of these sciences were to be found at Rome. Persons of easy fortune had frequently domestic tutors called *Paedagogi*, answering in many respects to what we now term Nursery Governesses, who taught children the first rudiments of literature, and afterwards attended them to school, while men of great wealth sometimes hired distinguished *Grammatistae*, *Rhetores*, and *Philosophi*, to superintend the training of their sons at home, and, as among ourselves, the comparative advantages of a public and a private education seem to have been a common subject of discussion.[2]

Holidays were given regularly on the *Quinquatria* and *Saturnalia*. The former festival was regarded as the commencement of the scholastic year, and at this time a gratuity termed *Minerval*, was presented by the pupil to his preceptor, but this was, apparently, distinct from the ordinary school fees.[3]

Mode of Teaching.—Children were tempted to learn their alphabet (*elementa velint ut discere prima*) by encouraging them to play with pieces of ivory on which the different letters were marked, (*eburneae literarum formae;*) they were taught to write upon waxen tablets, (*tabulae ceratae—cerae,*) on which a copy had been previously traced, (*puerile praescriptum—praeformatae literae;*) a knowledge of arithmetic was communicated through the medium of a calculating board (*abacus*) and counters, (*calculi.*) while the memory was strengthened, and practice given in Writing and Orthography, by the master repeating aloud passages from some popular author, which were taken down and committed to memory. Such lessons were termed *Dictata*.[4] The children of the rich were escorted to school not only by *Paedagogi*, but also by slaves called *Capsarii*, who carried in boxes (*Capsae*) the books, writing tables, bags with counters, (*Loculi*,) and other school utensils of their young masters.

Entrance upon Manhood.—When the education of a youth was completed, and he was regarded as fit to enter upon the business of life, he threw off the *Toga Praetexta* and assumed a plain gown termed *Toga Virilis* s. *Toga Pura* s. *Toga Liberior*. This act, which was regarded as an important domestic ceremony, was usually performed on the *Liberalia*, in the presence of the relations and friends of the family, who afterwards attended the young man down to the Forum, (*in Forum deducebant,*) the formal introduction into public life being termed *Tirocinium Fori*. The event was always solemnised by holy rites, and, in the case of great personages, a public sacrifice was offered up in the Capitol.[5]

The age at which the *Toga Virilis* was assumed is a matter of doubt. Some scholars have named the completion of the fourteenth year, others of the fifteenth, others of the sixteenth as the stated period, and all have been able to support

---

[1] Dial. de C. E. 35 Suet. de cl. Rhet. 1. Aul. Gell. XV. 11. Appulei. Florid. 20. Plut. Q. R. 59.
[2] Plin. H.N. XXXV. 14. Plut. Cat. Maj. 20. Quintil. I. O. I. ii. 1.
[3] Varro R.R. III. 2. Hor. Epp. II. ii. 197. Ovid. Fast. III. 829. Juvenal S. VII. 228. X. 114. Martial. V. 84.
[4] Quintil. l. i. 26. 27. viii. 5. V. xiv. 31. Senec. Epp. 94. Hor. S. I. i. 25. vi. 72. Epp. II. l. 16. ii. 42. Cic. de legg. II. 23. ad Q. F. III. 1. Suet. de Ill. Gramm. 16. de clar. Rhet. 1. 2.
[5] Cic. ad. Fam. V. 8. XIII. 10. XV. 6. Brut. 88. Suet. Octav. 26. Tib. 15. 54. Calig. 10. Claud. 2. Ner. 7 Val. Max. V. iv. 4.

their opinions by examples and plausible arguments. In reality, it would appear that the time was never fixed by any invariable custom. In the earlier ages the completion of the seventeenth year was undoubtedly the ordinary age, for the young man then became liable for military service, but in later times this period was generally anticipated, the decision depending entirely upon the wishes of the father (*iudicium patris.*) We may, however, lay it down as a general rule, that the completion of the fourteenth and of the seventeenth years were the two extremes, and that *Praetextati* rarely threw off the badges of boyhood until upon the verge of their fifteenth birth-day, and rarely retained them after their sixteenth was passed.[1]

Marriage Ceremonies.—We have already (p. 249) fully discussed marriage from a legal point of view: it only remains for us to notice those customs and ceremonies, which may be regarded as of a strictly domestic character, and which were commonly practised at all marriages, whether *Cum Conventione in Manum*, or *Sine Conventione*.

Betrothment.—When a man had resolved to demand a woman in marriage, he communicated his wishes to her father or legal guardian, whose consent was indispensable, and if he found that this consent would not be refused, he then put the formal question *Spondesne?* to which the appropriate reply was *Spondeo*. After this the parties were considered as fully engaged to each other, and were called respectively *Sponsus* and *Sponsa*. The ceremonial of the betrothment was termed *Sponsalia*, and was usually celebrated by a festival, and on this occasion the *Sponsus* frequently presented a ring, the *Annulus pronubus*, to his *Sponsa*, who offered him some gift in return.[2] The proposal of marriage and the negotiations connected with it, were named *Conditio*, and hence this word is used in the general sense of *a matrimonial alliance*, as in the phrase *Conditionem filiae quaerendam esse* (Liv. III. 45.[3]) Hence, also, when one of the parties wished to break off the engagement, (*sponsalia dissolvere*,) this might be done verbally by making use of the formal words *Conditione tua non utor*, but when the announcement was made through a third person, the same expressions were employed as in the case of a divorce, viz., *Repudium renuntiare* s. *remittere*, or simply *Nuntium mittere*.[4]

Marriage Day.—Popular prejudice forbade any marriage to be solemnized in May—*Mense malas Maio nubere vulgus ait* (Ovid. Fast. V. 490.)—but we are quite ignorant of the origin of this superstition. The Kalends, Nones, and Ides of each month, and the day after the Kalends, Nones, and Ides, were also avoided, as well as those days on which sacrifices were offered to the spirits of the dead, and all *Dies Atri*. The period most propitious for the ceremony was probably decided by an *Auspex*, who was in attendance to avert the consequences of any evil omen. (See Cic. de Div. I. 16. pro Cluent. 5. 16. Inv. S. X. 336.)

Dress of the Bride.—The Bride (*Nova Nupta*) was attired in an under garment named *Regilla* or *Tunica Recta*, woven after a peculiar fashion, and was fastened round the waist by a woollen girdle (*cingulum factum ex lana ovis.*) Her hair was divided into six locks, (*senis crinibus nubentes ornantur,*)

---

[1] When Nero assumed the *Toga Virilis* at the age of fourteen, Tacitus remarks, *Virilis Toga Neroni Maturata*, (Tacit. Ann. XII. 41. comp. Suet. Claud. 43.) On the other hand, Caius was not permitted by Tiberius to throw off his *Toga Praetexta* until he was twenty, (Suet. Cal. 10.) but this was the result of jealous despotism.
[2] Plaut. Aul. II. ii. Trin. II. iv. 98. Poen. V. iii. 36. Plin. H. N. XXXIII. 1. Juvenal. 8. VI. 25. Dion Cass. XLVIII 44. LIX. 12. LXIII. 13.
[3] See also Plaut. Aul. III. v. 2. Stich. I. ii. 81. Nep. Att. 12. Suet. Galb. 5.
[4] Digest. I. xvi. 101. XXIII. i. 110. Plaut. Aul. IV. x. 53. Terent. Phorm. IV. iii. 72. Suet. Caes. 21. Octav. 62. Tacit. Ann. XII. 3. Dion Cass. XLVI. 56. Plut. Cat. Min. 7.

PRIVATE LIFE—MARRIAGE.

which were parted with the point of an instrument called *hasta coelibaris*, either really a spear or some article of the toilet in the form of a spear, which was held on this occasion in a particular position, with the point turned back (*comat virgineas* HASTA RECURVA *comas*.) On her head was placed a yellow net, (*Reticulum luteum*,) and a veil of the same colour, (*Flammeum*,) while her feet were covered with yellow shoes (*Socci lutei*.)[1]

Nuptial Procession, &c.—The bride was invariably conducted (*ducere s. deducere nubentem*,) on the evening of the marriage day, from the home of her parents, to her new home, in a regular procession (*Pompa nuptialis*) formed by the friends and relations of both parties, attended by minstrels, who played upon the flute, (*Tibicines*,) and chanted the nuptial song called *Hymenaeus* by the Greeks, and *Thalassio* by the Romans, which must not be confounded with the *Epithalamium*, which was sung at the door of the nuptial chamber after the bride had retired to rest. The lady was escorted by three boys, (who, when the rite was solemnised by *Confarreatio*, were necessarily *Pueri patrimi et matrimi*,) of whom two supported her, one on each side, while the third marched before bearing a blazing torch made of the white thorn; (*Spina alba*;) other torch-bearers were likewise included in the procession, and hence the words *Faces, Taedae*, &c. either with or without the epithets, *Nuptiales, Iugales*, &c. are perpetually employed in reference to marriage. A fourth youth, called *Camillus*, was also in attendance, who carried an open basket (*cumerus*) containing a distaff, a spindle, and other implements of housewife toil (*nubentis utensilia*.) When they reached the mansion of the bridegroom, the bride wreathed sacred fillets of white wool (*vittae*) round the door posts, and anointed the latter with oil or lard, (*axungia*,)—whence some derive the word *Uxor*—after which she was carefully lifted over the threshold, to avoid the possibility of an ill omened stumble.[2]

On entering the house, she was received by the husband, whom she addressed in the solemn words *Ubi tu Caius ego Caia*, and was presented by him with fire and water, to indicate, probably, that all things essential to life were thenceforward to be shared by them in common.[1] These ceremonies concluded, the company partook of the *Coena Nuptialis*, at the close of which nuts were scattered among the guests, and the bride was then escorted to her nuptial chamber (*thalamus nuptialis*) by her *Pronubae*, who corresponded to our bride's-maids, but among the Romans were matrons who had not been married more than once. In the annexed cut, taken from the celebrated

---

[1] Fest. s. vv. *Regillis*, p. 286. *Rectae*, p. 277. *Senis crinibus*, p. 339. Paul. Diac. s. vv. *Cingulo*, p. 63. *Coelibari hasta*, p. 62. *Flammeo*, p. 89. Plin. H. N. VIII. 48. XXI. 8. Catull. LXI. 10. 167. Ovid. Fast. II. 559. Juv. S. VI. 224. Plut. Q. R. 86.
[2] Plaut. Aul. II. i. 88. Trin. V. ii. 64. Cas. IV. iii. 1. iv. 1. Catull. LXI. LXII. Propert. IV. iii. 13. Fest. s v. *Patrimi*, p. 245. Paul. Diac. s.vv. *Cumerus*, p. 50. *Cumeram*, p. 63. Varro L. L. VII. § 34. Plut. Q. R. 29. 31. 81. Plin. H.N. VIII. 48 XVI. 18. XXVIII. 9. Juv. S. VI. 79. 227. Plut. Rom. 15. Liv. I. 4. Dionys. II 30. The number of torches carried in a nuptial procession was always five, neither more nor less. Plut. Q R. 2.

painting known as the *Aldobrandini Marriage*, we see the bride with the *flammeum* on her head, seated on a couch, probably the *Lectus genialis*, with a *Pronuba* by her side. [1]

On the day after the marriage, the new mistress of the house entered upon her duties by offering sacrifice on the domestic altar, and in the afternoon an entertainment was given by the bridegroom, which was called *Repotia*. [2]

The verb *Nubere* signifies properly *to veil*, and is therefore used exclusively with reference to the act of the woman in contracting a marriage, while on the other hand, *Ducere*, which denotes the ceremony of *leading* home the bride, is confined to the man; thus we say *Nubere viro* and *Ducere uxorem*, never *Nubere uxori* or *Ducere virum;* e.g. *Nubere Paulla cupit nobis, ego ducere Paullam* = *Nolo: anus est: vellem si magis esset anus:* and again, *Nubere vis Prisco, non miror, Paulla, sapisti,* = *Ducere te non vult Priscus, et ille sapit* (Martial IX. 6. X. 8.)

Funeral Rites.—We shall describe the ceremonies observed in celebrating the obsequies (*Exsequiae*) of a man of rank and fortune; but it must be understood that several of these would be omitted in the case of individuals belonging to the middle and humbler classes of society.

As soon as life was extinct, those who surrounded the couch of the deceased raised a loud shout of woe, (*clamor supremus,*) and hence *conclamata corpora* signify bodies in which no trace of life remains, as in the expressions—*Conclamata et desperata corpora—ecce iam ultimum defletus atque conclamatus processerat mortuus—tum corpora nondum* = *Conclamata iacent—At vero domui tuae iam defletus et conclamatus es.* [3] Notice of the death was immediately sent to the temple of *Venus Libitina*, where a register was kept and a fee paid, (*Auctumnusque gravis Libitinae quaestus acerbae*, Hor. S. II. vi. 19.) and where undertakers, hence called *Libitinarii*, were constantly in attendance to provide all things necessary for interment. By one of these, a slave, called *Pollinctor*, was forthwith despatched, by whom the corpse was washed with hot water, anointed, dressed in the garb which it had worn on ceremonial occasions when alive, and laid out upon a couch (*Lectus funebris*) in the Atrium, with its feet towards the door. In performing these offices, the *Pollinctor* was said *curare corpus ad sepulturam*. A cypress tree or a pine was then placed before the house, partly as an emblem of death, partly to give warning to priests or others, who might have incurred pollution by entering incautiously. [4]

Many funerals, especially those of a private or humble description, took place by night, and hence torches are frequently mentioned in connection with the rites of sepulture, as well as with those of marriage. Thus in one of the elegies of Propertius (IV. xi. 46.) the spirit of a wife boasts—*Viximus insignes inter utramque facem*, i.e. *from the day of marriage until the hour of interment;* and one of Ovid's heroines (Heroid. XXI. 173.) exclaims in her misery—*Et face pro thalami fax mihi mortis adest*. The procession was marshalled by a sort of master of ceremonies called *Designator*, who was aided by assistants

---

[1] Plut. Q.R. 1. 30. Cic. pro Muren. 12. Quintil. I.O. I. vii. 28. Paul. Diac. s.vv. *Aqua*, p. 2. *Facem*, p. 87. Ovid. Fast. IV. 792. Digest. XXIV. i. 66. Stat. Silv. I. ii. 1. seqq.
[2] Macrob. S. I. 15. Festus s.v. *Repotia*, p. 281. Porphyr. on Hor. S. II. ii. 60.
[3] Quintil. Declam. VIII. 10. Ammian. Marcellin. XXX. 10. Ovid. Trist. III. iii. 43. Lucan. Phar. II. 22. Apulei. Met. I. 5. II. 38.
[4] Plut. Q.R. 23. Dionys. IV. 15. Hor. S. II. vi. 19. Suet. Ner. 39. Plaut. Asin. V. ii. 60. Digest. XIV. iii. 5. Liv. XXXIV. 7. XL. 19. Iuv. S. III. 171. Plin. H.N. VII. 8. XVI. 10. Serv. ad Virg. Æn. III. 64.

called *Lictores*, attired in mourning—*dum ficus prima calorque = Designatorem decorat lictoribus atris* (Hor. Epp. I. vii. 61.) First came the musicians, *Tibicines*, *Cornicines*, and *Tubicines;* then the *Praeficae*, hired female mourners, some of whom chanted dirges, (*Naeniae*,) while others shrieked aloud, beat their breasts, and tore their hair; then dancers, dressed up like satyrs; then actors, (*Mimi*,) among whom was one termed the *Archimimus*, who mimicked the appearance, movements, and language of the dead man; then the *Imagines* of illustrious ancestors in long array.[1] The body itself followed, extended upon the *Lectus funebris*, which was spread upon a frame or bier called *Feretrum* or *Capulus*, and this was supported sometimes by the children or near kinsmen of the deceased, sometimes by those among his *Liberti* to whom freedom had been bequeathed by his will, and in the case of slaves, or of those among the poor who had no relatives, by bearers called *Vespillones*, furnished by the *Libitinarius*. The bier was followed by all the family, connections, and friends, attired in black, (*atrati*,) the newly liberated freedmen wearing the *pileus* on their heads.[2] The lines of Persius (S. III. 103.) contain allusions to several of the points noticed above. Speaking of one who had died of gluttony—

> Hinc Tuba, Candelae, tandemque beatulus alto
> Compositus Lecto, crassisque lutatus amomis
> In portam rigidos calces extendit, at illum
> Hesterni capite induto subiere Quirites.

The *Pompa* defiled into the forum, and, in the case of persons of distinction, halted beneath the *Rostra*, when some one of the relatives or admirers of the departed ascended the platform, and delivered a panegyrical harangue (*Laudatio funebris—Solemnis laudatio*.)[3] This being concluded, the procession resumed its course, and proceeded to the place where the body was to be interred or burned; and it was ordained by the Laws of the XII Tables that this place must, in either case, be outside of the city walls—*Hominem in urbe ne sepelito neve urito*. Inhumation was generally practised in the earlier ages; but towards the close of the republic, and during the first four centuries of the empire, the body was, in the great majority of cases, consumed by fire, and the ashes consigned to the tomb in an urn. The pile of wood raised for this purpose was termed *Rogus* or *Pyra;* the place where it was erected, *Ustrina;* and what remained after the flames were extinguished, *Bustum*, the latter word being frequently employed in a general sense, to denote a place of interment. The corpse having been placed on the *Rogus*, perfumes and various tokens of affection were thrown upon it, and then the son or nearest relation, with averted face, applied a torch to the structure. When the whole was consumed, the glowing embers (*favilla*) were extinguished with wine, the charred bones were collected, sprinkled first with wine, then with milk, dried with a linen cloth, mixed with the most costly perfumes, and enclosed in an urn of earthenware, marble, glass, or metal, which was deposited in one of the niches, (*loculi*,) arranged

---

[1] Hor. Epod. VIII. 2. S. I. vi. 43. A.P. 431. Ovid. Amorr. II. vi. 6. Pers. S. III. 106. Non s.v. *Praeficae*, p. 47. ed. Gerl. s.v. *Nenia*, p. 99. Varro L.L. VII. § 70. Paul. Diac. s.v. *Praeficae*. p. 223. Dionys. VIII. 72. Suet. Vesp. 19. Polyb. VI. 53. Plin. H N. XXXV. 2. Propert. II. xiii. 19. Dion Cass. LVI. 34.

[2] Velleius I. 11. Plut. Q.R. 14. Serv. ad Virg. Æn. VI. 222. The *Lectica* or *Lectus funebris* must not be confounded with the *Sandapila*, a covered coffin in which the humblest portion of the community were conveyed to the tomb, the *Vilis Arca* of Horace, the *Orciniana Sponda* of Martial. Mart. II. 81. VIII. 75. X. 5. Hor. S. I. viii. 9. Iuv. S. VIII. 175. Suet. Dom. 17.

[3] Polyb. VI. 53. Dionys IV. 40. V. 17. IX. 54. XI. 39. Plut. Poplic. 9. Camill. 8. Liv. V. 50. VIII. 40. Cic. Brut. 16. de Orat. II. 11.

in regular rows in the interior of a family tomb, (*Sepulcrum*,) which, from the appearance thus presented, was sometimes termed *Columbarium*.[1] Annexed is a representation of a place of sepulture of this description, as it now exists at Pompeii.

Nine days after the interment, a repast, called *Coena Feralis*, consisting of a few simple articles of food, was placed beside the tomb, and of this the *Manes* were supposed to partake. The solemnities performed when this sacrifice or offering was presented, were comprehended under the terms *Novemdiale Sacrum*, or *Feriae Novemdiales*. The *Coena Feralis* must not be confounded with the *Coena Funeris*, a banquet given in honour of the deceased, by his representative, at the family mansion; and the *Coena Funeris* must be distinguished from the *Silicernium*, a repast taken beside the tomb.[2]

When any great public character died, the whole community were requested to attend, and such a funeral was styled *Funus Publicum*, or, in consequence of the invitation being given by a public crier, *Funus Indictivum*. These were frequently accompanied by shows of gladiators and games (*Ludi funebres*) of all descriptions, and concluded by a magnificent banquet, (*Epulum funebre*,) to which the most distinguished members of the community were asked, while a distribution of food (*Visceratio*) was made to those of inferior grade. The most gorgeous ceremonies were usually lavished on the last rites of one who had held the office of Censor, and hence any funeral conducted in the same manner was called a *Funus Censorium*.[3]

We need not feel surprised at the extreme importance attached to these observances by the ancients, when we remember that a belief prevailed among almost all nations, that unless the body was decently committed to the earth, the spirit was unable to gain admission to its appointed abode, but wandered about in restless misery. The dead were regarded as lawfully entitled to a decent burial from the living, and hence the ordinary phrases which express the fulfilment of this obligation are *Iusta* (s. *debita*) *facere* s. *reddere* s. *solvere*. Any one who chanced to find an unburied corpse, although it were that of a stranger, was held to be guilty of impiety if he did not perform the rites of sepulture in their most simple shape, by thrice casting a handful of earth upon the remains; (Hor. C. I. xxviii. 22. &c.;) and if the body of any member of a family was known to be unburied in consequence of death by shipwreck or from any other cause, then an empty tomb (*Cenotaphium*) was raised to his memory, and his heir

---

[1] Cic. de legg. II. 22. 23. Plin. H.N. VII. 54. Virg. Æn. VI. 216. seqq. Tibull. III. ii. 9—30. Stat. Silv. V. i. 208—241.
[2] Hor. Epod. XVII. 48. and Schol. Iuv. V. 84. Serv. ad Virg. Æn. V. 64. Paul. Diac. s.v. *Resparsum vinum*, p. 263, and the corresponding passage in Festus, which is sadly mutilated. Pers. V. 33. Liv. VIII. 22. XXXIX. 46. Cic. pro Muren. 36. Non. s. v. *Silicernium*, p. 33. ed. Gerl.
[3] Varro L L. V. § 160. Cic. de legg. II. 24. Tacit. Ann. IV. 15. XIII. 2.

was obliged to sacrifice each year a victim termed *Porca Praecidanea*, to Tellus and Ceres, in order to free himself and kinsmen from pollution.[1]

But even after the ordinary funeral rites had been performed with all due honour, oblations, in this case called *Inferiae*, were, by many persons, regularly made at the tombs of parents and near relations by their surviving children and kindred, from feelings of affection, because such tributes were believed to be grateful to the *Manes*. Those who made offerings of this description were said *Parentare*; and the period of the year chiefly set apart for this purpose was the festival of the *Feralia* in February, (the month of purifications,) and hence the days during which these solemnities were continued were called *Parentales Dies*, and the gifts presented *Parentalia*. *Parentare* is used also in the general sense of propitiating the dead, without particular reference to relations.[2]

The most important passages in the Latin Classics relating to the interment of the dead will be found collected in KIRCHMANN, *De funeribus Romanorum*, first published at Hamburgh in 1605, and frequently reprinted.

II. CUSTOMS CONNECTED WITH EVERY-DAY LIFE.

Martial has an epigram in which he describes the ordinary mode of spending the day at Rome:—

> Prima salutantes atque altera continet horas,
> Exercet raucos tertia causidicos.
> In quintam varios extendit Roma labores,
> Sexta quies lassis, septima finis erit.
> Sufficit in nonam nitidis octava palaestris,
> Imperat exstructos frangere nona toros.—IV. viii.

The occupations here indicated are—1. *Paying and receiving visits.* 2. *Professional business.* 3. *The noontide Siesta.* 4. *Exercise.* 5. *The Repast.* We shall say a few words upon each of these in succession, commencing with an explanation of the system according to which the day was divided into hours, and inserting some account of the Bath, which is not specifically noticed by Martial, probably because he regarded it as inseparably connected with exercise.

Divisions of the Day and the Night.—In their computations of time, the Romans made use of the Natural Day and Natural Night, the former extending from Sunrise to Sunset, the latter from Sunset to Sunrise.

Divisions of the Day.—The space from Sunrise to Sunset was supposed to be divided into twelve equal spaces, each of which was called *Hora*, but since this interval varies from day to day, it is manifest that the length of a Roman hour was never the same for two days consecutively, that it went on constantly increasing from the winter solstice, (*Bruma*,) when it was shortest, until the summer solstice, (*Solstitium*,) when it was longest, and coincided in length with our own hours at two points only in the year, namely, at the Equinoxes. Sunrise was *Solis Ortus*; Noon, *Meridies*; Sunset, *Solis Occasus*; *Mane* was an indefinite word, denoting the early part of the day; *Tempus Antemeridianum* comprehended the whole space from Sunrise to Noon, *Tempus Pomeridianum* from Noon to Sunset, *Meridiei Inclinatio* the turn of the day after Noon.

Divisions of the Night.—The space from Sunset to Sunrise was divided into

---

[1] Varro ap Non. s.v. *Praecidaneum*, p. 111. ed Gerl. Paul. Diac. s.v. *Praecidanea*, p. 223. Marius Victor, p 2470. ed. Putsch. comp. Cic. de legg. II. 22.
[2] Ovid. Fast. II. 547. Cic. de legg. II. 21. pro Flacc. 38. Philipp. I. 6.

MEASUREMENT OF TIME.

four equal spaces called *Vigiliae*, severally distinguished as *Prima . . . Secunda . . . Tertia . . . Quarta Vigilia*, each *Vigilia* containing three *Horae Noctis*. As in the case of the hours of the day, the length of the *Vigiliae* constantly varied, they were longest in winter and shortest in summer, containing three of our hours at the Equinoxes only. In every-day life eight divisions of the night were adopted, which were, however, altogether indefinite. These, taken in order, were, 1. *Vespera* s. *Crepusculum;* 2. *Prima Fax* s. *Prima Lumina* s. *Primae Tenebrae;* 3. *Concubia Nox;* 4. *Intempesta Nox*, corresponding to Midnight; 5. *Mediae Noctis inclinatio;* 6. *Gallicinium;* 7. *Conticinium;* 8. *Diluculum.*[1]

Modes of Measuring Time.—The progress of the day and the night must, for a long period, have been guessed from observing the position of the sun and of the stars, for no contrivance for the measurement of time was known at Rome until the latter end of the fifth century. According to one account, the first sun-dial was brought from southern Italy, and placed in front of the temple of Quirinus, by L. Papirius Cursor, about B.C. 293; according to another account, the first sun-dial was brought by M. Valerius Messala, from Catania in Sicily, in B.C. 263, and fixed near the *Rostra*. Neither of these having been constructed for the latitude of Rome, the indications they afforded were necessarily incorrect and inconsistent with each other, but they were followed as guides for nearly a hundred years, until Q. Marcius Philippus (Consul, B.C. 169) set up a more accurate instrument In B.C. 159, P. Scipio Nasica, at that time Censor, introduced *Clepsydrae*, which were contrivances resembling in principle our hour-glasses, but in which water was employed instead of sand. These appear to have been extensively used, and it is manifest that whatever space of time they were constructed to measure, it must have been fixed like our own hours, and could not have varied like the Roman hours with the season of the year. Ingenious and complicated contrivances, which gave results similar to those afforded by modern clocks, were invented by Greek mechanicians, and were doubtless known to the Romans, but they were regarded merely as curiosities, and certainly never superseded the *Solarium* and the *Clepsydra*, which, in courts of justice, were watched by an Accensus, who reported to the magistrates the hours as they passed, while in large private establishments a slave was kept for the purpose.

The words which strictly denote sun-dials are *Solaria* and *Sciaterica*, while *Horaria* and *Horologia* may indicate any instruments for measuring time; *Solarium*, however, was used as equivalent to *Clepsydra*—*Solarium vel descriptum vel ex aqua*, (Cic. de N. D. II. 34. comp. Censorin. 23,) but *Clepsydra* was confined to water-clocks.[2]

Salutatio. Sportula.—In the early ages of the state, it was part of the duty of Clients to be assiduous in their attendance on their Patron, to escort him down to the Forum, and to swell his train upon all occasions of ceremony; while on the other hand, the house of the Patron was always open to his Clients, who sought

---

[1] Varro L. L. VI. § 4—8. § 89. Plin. H. N. VII. 60. XXXVI. 10. Macrob. S. I. 3. Censorin. 23. 24. Isidor. V. xxxi. 5—14.
[2] Varr. Plin. Censorin. ll. cc. Vitruv. IX 8. 9. Athenae. IV. 75. Pliny (Epp II. 11) speaks of the Clepsydra being used in courts of justice for measuring the time during which each pleader was allowed to speak—*Dixi horis pene quinque, nam duodecim Clepsydris quas spatiosissimas acceperam sunt additae quatuor*, so that, if the reading be correct, these *Clepsydrae* must have measured about one-third of an hour. Observe, that the words *quas spatiosissimas* do not indicate, as Becker supposes, that there were different *Clepsydrae*, but simply, that he was allowed large measure, i.e. that some little time was allowed after the water had run out of the vessel, before it was filled again.

his advice and assistance in all cases of perplexity or danger (pp. 63, 64.) After political distinctions between Patrons and Clients were entirely at an end, the old names and the old feelings were still retained, the high-born noble still loved to be surrounded by a throng of obsequious followers, and multitudes were still to be found among the poorer citizens, especially *libertini* and their descendants, who were eager to attach themselves to the persons of the rich and powerful, and to repay, with coarse flattery, the protection and aid which they received. Towards the close of the republic, and under the empire, it became customary for those who, from their wealth, connections, or high stations, possessed extensive influence, to hold daily regular levees, which were attended by many who simply desired to testify their respect and regard for the individual,[1] but by many more who hoped to benefit by his power and patronage, (*salutatio meritoria*,) and in the case of Clients and dependents, such visits were regarded as an imperative duty (*officium*.) The regular hour of reception, as indicated by Martial, was sunrise, and hence the expressions *Salutatio matutina—Officia antelucana—ingentem foribus domus alta superbis = Mane Salutantum totis vomit aedibus undam* (Virg. G. II. 461)—nor have the Satirists failed to present us with lively pictures of the crowds who rose in haste and hurried through the streets in the cold dark rainy mornings of winter, all in full dress, (*togati*,) each alarmed lest his rival should be beforehand with him in rendering homage— *sollicitus ne = Tota salutatrix iam turba peregerit orbem*. (Iuv. S. V. 21.)

During the republic, when even the most humble possessed a certain amount of political influence, it was usual for the great man to invite his retainers occasionally to his table. Under the empire, the luxurious habits universal among the rich, and the absence of any strong inducement to cultivate the favour of the poorer classes, caused this practice to fall in a great measure into disuse,[2] but as a sort of compensation, all who were recognised as Clients of the house were entitled to receive occasionally, or daily, as the case might be, an allowance of cooked provisions. This gratuity being carried off in a basket provided for the purpose, was termed *Sportula*, and these baskets or trays were sometimes fitted up with small stoves or braziers to keep the viands hot while transported to a distance.

> Nonne vides quanto celebretur Sportula fumo?
> Centum convivae; sequitur sua quemque culina.—Iuv. S. III. 249.

In process of time, many found it convenient to substitute a small sum in money for the allowance of provisions, and the amount thus bestowed seems to have been fixed at a hundred *Quadrantes*, that is, about a shilling sterling.

It is clear from the words of Juvenal and Martial, that, when they wrote, the persons who applied for and received the *Sportula* were by no means exclusively the lowest and poorest of the community; for while the latter, in many cases, depended entirely upon the *Sportula* for the necessaries of life, many who had risen to high offices did not disdain to calculate the profits arising from this source as a regular item in their income.

> Sed quum summus honor finito computat anno,
> Sportula quid referat, quantum rationibus addat;
> Quid facient comites, quibus hinc toga, calceus hinc est,
> Et panis fumusque domi?—Iuv. S. I. 117.

[1] See Cic. ad Fam. IX. 20. ad. Att. I. 18. Senec. Ep. XXIX. comp. de Benef. VI. 33.
[2] If a poor client by any chance was honoured with an invitation to his patron's board, he was subjected to all manner of slights and insults. See the whole of the 5th Satire of Juvenal and comp. Plin. Epp. II. 6.

We learn also, that in each great house a regular list was kept of persons entitled to the *Sportula*, who might be either males or females, and that, to prevent imposture, all were required to make their claim in person. An amusing description will be found in Juvenal of the tricks resorted to in order to evade this regulation.

As to the time of doling out the *Sportula*, our two great authorities in this matter, Juvenal and Martial, are at variance, the former (S. I. 128) represents it as the first act of the day, the latter leads us to believe that the distribution took place immediately before the evening meal (X. 70.)

We may conclude from Seneca, compared with Juvenal and Martial, that, even during the first century, the *turba mane salutantum* was divided into three classes—1. Those who were the friends and equals of him who held the levee, and who visited him from courtesy only—such had the first entrée (*Primae Admissiones.*) 2. Those who, although desirous to solicit interest and favours, occupied a respectable position—such had the *Secundae Admissiones*. 3. The throng of needy retainers, who were not admitted to the presence at all, but received their *Sportula* at the door (*primo limine.*)[1]

Professional Business.—The first and second hours of the day having been consumed by visits of ceremony, the third, fourth, and fifth, according to the arrangements described above, were devoted to various toils, the third especially calling forth the energies of the judicial pleader. The space set apart for the active occupations of life appears, at first sight, altogether inadequate, but it must be remembered that the ideas entertained by the countrymen of Martial with reference to what we call Professional Business, were altogether different from our own. During the earlier ages of the republic, the time of a citizen was divided between war and agriculture, the latter was regarded as the only pursuit by which gain could be honourably acquired, and the Romans, at all periods of their history, were enthusiastic lovers, in theory at least, of the country and the labours of the farmer. In process of time, as the intercourse with distant countries became more frequent, the merchants (*Negotiatores*) engaged in foreign trade commanded a certain degree of respect in consequence of their wealth, but a great number of these resided abroad, while the rest were constantly moving from place to place, so that they never exercised much political influence, and, therefore, never occupied a high position in the community. The members of *Ordo Equester* indeed, which, from the time of the Gracchi, was composed of the class of monied men, (p. 74,) invested their funds in the joint-stock companies (*societates*) which farmed the public revenues, (p. 238,) but they merely furnished the capital required to conduct these enterprises, the whole burden of the practical details being in the hands of subordinate agents and managers. We have seen in former chapters (pp. 312,379,) how the Army and the Bar eventually became *Professions*, in the modern acceptation of the term, but the number of professions open to persons in the upper ranks of life was not increased for centuries, the practice of all the other liberal arts and sciences, by which fortunes could be realised, being for the most part in the hands of Greeks.

If the merchant on a large scale was treated with a certain degree of consideration, the retail dealer (*Institor*) and the artizan (*Opifex*) were at all times regarded with contempt, and this feeling became so strong, as the dignity of

---

[1] On the *Salutatio* in general, see Iuv. III. 126. V. 19. 76. Senec. Ep. LXVIII. de Benef. VI. 34. de Brev. vit. 14. Plin. Epp. III. 12. Martial. IV. 8. IX. 100. X. 10. XII. 26. On the *Sportula*, see Iuv. S. I. 95 seqq. 117. seqq. III. 249. Martial. I. 60. III. 7. 14. 46. IV. 25. 68. VII. 39. VIII. 42. 50. IX. 86. 101. X. 27. 28. 70 74. 75. comp. Suet. Ner. 16. Dom. 7.

Rome rose high, that we have reason to believe that, towards the close of the commonwealth, the great majority of those who followed such callings were slaves or *libertini*, and the absence of all means of earning an honest livelihood with credit, may, in some degree, account for the excessive venality which prevailed among the lower class of citizens. The same dislike to industry prevailed under the empire, and a large number of the freeborn citizens passed their lives in absolute idleness, depending upon the pittance yielded by the *Sportula*, (p. 430,) and on the gratuitous distributions of grain and other largesses proceeding from the liberality or the policy of successive princes. If, however, their poverty was abject, their desires were moderate, they demanded nothing but bread, and the public shows

> Qui dabat olim
> Imperium, Fasces, Legiones, omnia, nunc se
> Continet, atque duas tantum res anxius optat
> PANEM ET CIRCENSES.

The Siesta.—This requires no illustration. The practice of retiring to rest during the hottest portion of the day still prevails in Southern Italy, as well as in Spain and in tropical countries.

Exercises.—*Exercitationes.*—The martial character of the Romans led them to cultivate with enthusiasm all kinds of manly and athletic sports. From the very commencement of the republic, the Campus Martius was specially set apart as the public exercising ground, and here the youth were accustomed to assemble each day, in order to acquire, by practice, skill in the use of warlike weapons, and to gain power and agility of limb by severe and assiduous training. Here they found ample scope for horsemanship, for launching the javelin, for hurling the quoit, for pugilistic encounters, for running, leaping, wrestling, swimming, and similar gymnastic feats, among which trundling a hoop (*Trochus*) was included.[1] In order to increase the violence of the exertion, some ran or leaped, swinging in their hands heavy weights called *Halteres*, answering the purpose of modern dumb-bells;[2] while others, instead of fencing with their comrades, armed themselves with large wicker shields, twice as heavy as the legionary *Scutum*, and with clubs twice as heavy as the legionary sword, and thus equipped, levelled a series of blows against a tall post (*palus s. stipes*) set up as an antagonist.[3]

But in addition to the *Exercitationes campestres equorum et armorum*, in which none but the young and vigorous could engage, other amusements were pursued with great eagerness, which demanded dexterity rather than physical strength, and from which, therefore, persons advanced in years were not excluded. Chief among these were various games at ball, (*ludere pila*,) to which we find very many allusions in the writers of the empire. It appears that there were three kinds of balls, differing from each other in size and materials—

1. *Pila*, which is the general name for any ball, but which, when used in a restricted sense, denotes the ordinary small hand-ball.
2. *Pila Paganica*, larger than the common *Pila*, and stuffed with feathers.

---

[1] *Ibi cursu, luctando, hasta, disco, pugillatu, pila, = Saliendo, sese exercebant* (Plaut. Bacch. III. iii. 24.) *Sunt illis celeresque pilae, inculumque, trochique = Armaque, et in gyros ire coactus equus* (Ovid. A. A. III. 383.)—*Usus equi nunc est, levibus nunc luditur armis = Nunc pila, nunc celeri volvitur orbe trochus* (Trist. III. xii. 19.)
[2] Martial. VII. 67. XIV. 19. Senec. Epp. XV. LVI. The athletes who used these were termed *Halteristae*.
[3] Veget. I. 11. Iuv. S. VI. 247. Martial. VII. 32.

3. *Follis* s. *Folliculus*, larger than either of the two others, inflated with air like our foot-ball, but struck with the hand.[1]

To these some would add the *Trigon* or *Pila Trigonalis* and the *Harpastum*, but these were not the names of balls, but of particular games played with the common *Pila*. Thus Horace, when speaking of the former (S. I. vi. 126.)—

<blockquote>Ast ubi me fessum sol acrior ire lavatum
Admonuit, fugio Campum LUSUMQUE TRIGONEM.</blockquote>

Various expressions occur with regard to the manner of playing, which we can explain by conjecture only. Thus *Ludere datatim* seems to indicate the throwing and catching of the ball by the players in turn, and to this mode belong the phrases *Dare* s. *Mittere Pilam*, and *Accipere* s. *Excipere Pilam*,[2] and then *Reddere* s. *Remittere Pilam*.

Again, *Ludere expulsim* must imply striking the ball away by a sharp blow, while the player opposite struck it back in like fashion; to the former operation we apply the phrase *Expulsare Pilam*; to the latter *Repercutere* s. *Geminare Pilam*, while *Revocare Pilam* means to catch it up just as it was on the point of falling to the ground.[3]

In the *Trigon* or *Pila Trigonalis*, the players stood, as the name denotes, so as to form a triangle. The ball was either thrown or struck from one to another, and when the performers were skilful, the left hand only was employed.[4]

In the *Harpastum*, to which the phrase *Ludere raptim* belongs, there was a struggle for the ball among the players, who endeavoured to snatch it from each other, but we are quite ignorant of the details.[5]

Since exercise of some sort was considered as a necessary preliminary to the daily bath, just as the bath was considered a necessary preliminary to the evening meal, spacious courts for athletic sports, designated by the Greek words *Gymnasia* and *Palaestrae*, were always attached to the *Thermae* or great bathing establishments, and a *Sphaeristerium* or Ball-room was not unfrequently to be found even in private mansions. (Plin. Epp. V. 6.)

Baths.—In a climate so hot as that of Italy, the comfort and salubrity of frequent ablutions must have been felt and acknowledged by even the rudest tribes, but we are assured that in the earlier ages of the republic the Romans were not wont to purify themselves thoroughly more frequently than once a-week —*nundinis toti lavabantur* (Senec. Ep. 86.) Towards the close of the republic, however, and under the empire, the daily bath became a necessary of life, and an indispensable preliminary to the evening meal, and the magnificent piles erected for the convenience of the public by the liberality or ostentation of princes and private individuals, placed the luxurious indulgence of this habit within the reach of the humblest classes in the community, the ordinary charge being a *Quadrans* only—about half-a-farthing of our money.

No subject connected with antiquarian research ought to admit of more complete illustration than that of which we now treat. We have the scientific descriptions of professed architects, extensive ruins in Rome and in various provinces minutely described by local antiquaries, a complete establishment

---

[1] Martial. VII. 32. XIV. 45. 47. The exercise of the *Follis* was particularly gentle. *Ite procul iuvenes, mitis mihi convenit aetas.*=FOLLE *decet pueros ludere,* FOLLE *senes.*
[2] Plaut. Curcul. II. iii. 17. Non. s. v. *Datatim* p. 67. ed. Gerl. Senec. de Benef. II. 17. Manil. V. 165.
[3] Martial. XIV. 46. Senec. l. c. Saleius Paneg. in Pison. 173.
[4] Hor. S. I. vi. 125. Martial. VII. 72. XII. 83. XIV. 46.
[5] Martial. IV. 19. VII. 67. XIV. 48. Non. s.v. *Datatim*, p. 67. ed. Gerl.

disclosed by the excavations at Pompeii, and numerous allusions in writers upon all subjects. But, perhaps, nothing has contributed more effectually to dispel doubt and correct misapprehension, than a pictorial representation found upon a wall in one of the rooms of the Thermae of Titus, in which the interior of a public bath is opened up to view, and the names of the different apartments painted in legible characters upon each.[1] See the sketch in the next page.

In what follows, we do not propose to give a detailed account of the gorgeous structures of the empire—the *lavacra in modum provinciarum exstructa*, as they are termed by Ammianus (XVI. 10.)—such as those reared by Caracalla and Diocletian, which contained within their vast compass gardens, colonnades, halls, saloons, libraries, courts for all varieties of athletic sports, every thing which could minister to the comfort or amusement of visitors of all ranks and tastes,—but to confine ourselves to a description of those parts which were essential in a complete Bathing establishment, in which a bath might be taken in three ways: 1. Cold Water. 2. Hot Water. 3. Hot Air. This being premised, we shall consider the different rooms in succession.

1. *Frigidarium* s. *Cella Frigidaria*, an apartment not warmed artificially. Visitors entered this first, and here probably those undressed who intended to take the cold bath. Accordingly, at Pompeii we find opening out of it on one side a—

2. *Natatio* s. *Natatorium* s. *Piscina* s. *Baptisterium*. The cold plunge bath, which was generally large enough to allow those who entered it to swim about; the *Natatorium* in the *Thermae* of Diocletian was 200 feet long and 100 feet broad.

Beyond the *Frigidarium*, that is farther removed from the outer door, was

3. *Tepidarium*, a room heated artificially, but not to a very high temperature. Here the great body of the bathers left their clothes under the charge of slaves called *Capsarii*, by whom they were deposited in boxes or cupboards kept for the purpose. The apartment, from this circumstance, was sometimes called *Apodyterium*. Beyond the *Tepidarium* was the

4. *Caldarium* s. *Sudatorium* s. *Concamerata Sudatio*, under the pavement of which were formed a number of flues, (*Suspensurae Caldariorum*,) through which circulated the hot air and flames of the furnace (*Hypocaustum*.) In one corner was placed a cylindrical hollow pillar called *Laconicum*, communicating directly with the flues, closed at top by a disk of metal (*Clypeus aeneus*.) When this was raised, the heated air and even the flames could be admitted directly into the chamber, and thus the temperature elevated to any height. Around the walls were benches rising one above another, on which the bathers sat until they burst out into a profuse perspiration, after which they were scraped with a bronze instrument called a *Strigil*, thin and flexible like a hoop, by which all impurities were removed from the skin, they were then *shampooed*, rubbed down with towels, (*Lintea*,) and their bodies anointed with oil by an attendant called *Aliptes*, after which they returned to the *Tepidarium*, where they attired themselves, and cooled gradually before returning to the open air. Some persons, however, in addition to, or as a substitute for, the vapour bath, took the hot water bath, in which case they proceeded into the room which was called

5. *Balneum*, (in a restricted sense,) and here they might bathe in hot water

---

[1] See especially Vitruv. V. 10. Pallad. I. 40. Senec. Epp. LI. LVI. LXXXVI. Plin. Epp. II. 17. V. 6. Stat. S. I. 5. Martial. VI. 42. For speculations on the *Thermae* of Titus, Caracalla, and Diocletian, see the works of BUNSEN and CANINA; for an account of the baths at Pompeii, the works of GELL and of MAZOIS, and the *Museo Borbonico*.

in two ways, either standing in a large tub called *Labrum*, in which case, probably, the hot water was thrown over them, or immersing themselves in a tank of hot water called *Alveus*, sunk below the level of the floor. The *Balneum* represented below is heated with flues like the *Caldarium*, so that those who entered it would enjoy at once a hot water bath and a hot vapour bath, the vapour here being moist, while in the *Caldarium* it would be dry.

The *Labrum* and *Alveus* were supplied from a connected series of three vessels, the water entered cold from the cistern into the first, passed from thence into the second, which stood lower and received a certain degree of warmth from the furnace, and attained to the required heat in the third, which stood lowest. These three vessels bore respectively the same names as the chambers to which they corresponded in temperature, being styled *Frigidarium*, *Tepidarium*, and *Caldarium*.

We have described the arrangements exactly as they are represented in the subjoined sketch, and we shall perceive that in this there is still another apartment, the *Elaiothesium*, in which the various perfumed oils employed in anointing are seen ranged on shelves, like the bottles in an apothecary's shop.

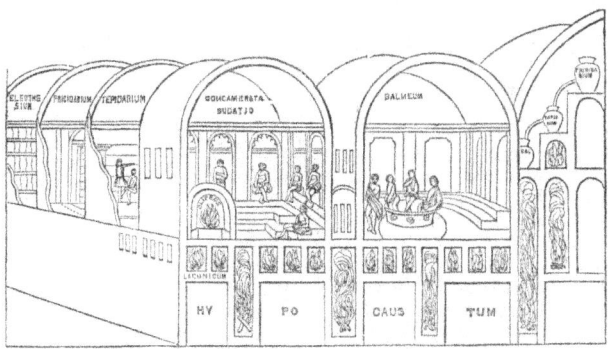

According to the extent of the structure, the number of distinct apartments was increased or diminished. In some, the visitors undressed and were anointed in the *Tepidarium;* in others, there were an *Apodyterium* and an *Unctorium* distinct from the *Tepidarium*. In the Baths at Pompeii, the *Alveus* and the *Labrum* were placed in the *Caldarium*. Again, the mode of bathing differed according to individual taste. Some persons took the cold bath alone; some, after taking the hot air bath, or the hot water bath, or both, cooled themselves in the *Tepidarium;* some, on leaving the hot chambers, plunged at once into the cold *Piscina*, just as the Russians, after enduring for a time the intense heat of their vapour baths, roll themselves in the snow.

We have seen *Balneum* applied in a restricted sense, to signify the hot water bath; but *Balinea*, *Balnea*, *Balineae*, *Balneae*, are used in a general sense to denote baths of any description, either those in a private mansion, or those open for the accommodation of the public. These words, however, are usually confined to establishments upon a moderate scale appropriated to bathing exclusively, while the foreign term *Thermae* was applied to the immense edifices alluded to above, the first of which was raised by Agrippa, whose example was followed by Nero, Titus, Caracalla, and Diocletian. We are expressly told by Dion Cassius (LIV. 29,) that Agrippa bequeathed his baths to the people, in order that they might bathe free of cost; and we cannot doubt that the founders of the other great *Thermae* were equally liberal; but from the constant mention of the *Quadrans*[1] in connection with public baths, we are led to believe that this trifling sum must have been contributed by all, perhaps to cover the expense of oil and attendance, even when the admission was nominally gratuitous. There were besides, in every quarter of Rome, baths kept by private speculators, and at these the charges would be higher, and the visitors, probably, more select.

The period at which the bath was usually taken must have been between the eighth and ninth hours, according to the distribution of the day detailed in the epigram of Martial quoted above. But the same author, in two other passages, (III. 36. X. 70,) speaks of the tenth hour or even later; Pliny (Epp. III. 1,) of the ninth hour in winter and the eighth in summer; while Juvenal (S. XI. 205,) tells his friend that, on a holiday at least, he might, *salva fronte*, repair to the *Balnea* before noon. It is manifest that in matters like this, every thing must have depended upon individual tastes and habits.

Meals. The Romans, during that period of their history with which we are best acquainted, took only two regular meals in the day; the *Prandium* in the morning, and the *Coena*, which was always the principal repast, in the afternoon. It has been conjectured that in the earliest times they took three, the *Prandium* at an early hour, the *Coena* about mid-day, and the *Vesperna* in the evening, corresponding to the ἄριστον, the δεῖπνον, and the δόρπον of the Homeric Greeks, but the evidence for this is altogether defective.[2]

To fix the hours of the *Prandium* and *Coena* is clearly impossible, since these must have varied not only with the fashions and social habits of different ages, but with the stations and employments of different individuals in the same age. All we can decide with certainty is, that during the first century of the empire, the ordinary time for the *Coena*, in the fashionable world, was the commencement of the ninth hour, which at midsummer would be about half-past two, and in midwinter about half-past one, according to our mode of computation. Persons who desired to devote a longer period than was customary to the pleasures of the table, anticipated the usual hour, and hence such entertainments were called *Tempestiva Convivia*, and those who partook of them were said *Epulari de die*.

We are told of Vitellius, who was proverbial for his gluttony—*Epulas trifariam semper, interdum quadrifariam dispertiebat, in* IENTACULA, *et* PRANDIA, *et* COENAS, COMMISSATIONESQUE. (Suet. Vitell. 13.) The *ientaculum*, which is not often mentioned elsewhere,[3] was in the strictest sense a *break-fast*, being food taken immediately upon getting up in the morning, and thus would correspond to the Greek ἀκράτισμα, which was a morsel of bread dipped in wine.

---

[1] e.g. Hor. S. I. iii. 137. Martial III. 30. Iuvenal. S. VI. 447. Senec. Ep. LXXXVI.

[2] See Paul. Diac. s. vv. *Coena*, p. 54. *Prandium*, p. 223 *Vesperna*, p. 368. Fest. s. v. *Scensas*, p. 339, and the notes of Mueller. Paulus says, COENA *apud antiquos dicebatur, quod nunc est* PRANDIUM: VESPERNA, *quod nunc* COENAM *appellamus*.

[3] Isidor. XX. ii. 10. In Apuleius Met. I. 14, two travellers are represented as making their *ientaculum* upon bread and cheese, and, in I. 2, a horse cropping the grass as he moves along, is said *affectare ientaculum ambulatorium*, see also IX. 187. XI. 257. When Martial (XIV. 223) says—*Surgite, iam vendit pueris ientacula pistor*, it is clear that *ientaculum* must mean a roll or cake, which boys eat as their breakfast, and *ulere puerum ad ientaculum* in Plautus (Truc. II. vii. 37.) seems to denote rearing a child until it is able to feed itself. See also Plaut. Curcul. I. i. 72. where *ientaculum* is an offering to the gods, and comp. Apulei. Met. IX. 187. For the verb *ientare*, see Non. s. v. p. 86. Suet. Vitell. 7. Martial. VIII. 67.

Commissatio properly signifies a drinking party after the *Coena*, and implies noisy revelry.[1] Besides these, we hear of the *Merenda*,[2] which is sometimes used as synonymous with *Prandium*, but appears to have been, strictly speaking, a luncheon interposed between the *Prandium* and the *Coena*.

Food.—The national dish of the ancient Romans was a sort of porridge or hasty-pudding made of *Farina*, that is, the flour of *Far*, a coarse species of wheat, the *Triticum Spelta* of Botanists, which is said to have been cultivated in Italy before any other kind of grain, and was, therefore, invested with a sort of sacred character, and used exclusively in religious ceremonies. This porridge was called *Puls*, and, along with vegetables, (*olera*,) fruits, fresh and dried, and dairy produce, constituted, in the primitive ages, the principal article of diet for all classes in the community; any thing savoury eaten along with *Puls*, in order to give it a relish, being termed *Pulmentum* or *Pulmentarium*.[3] Animal food was little used except on holidays, when the smoked flitch of bacon afforded a treat, or, after a sacrifice, when those who had assisted at the rite partook of the flesh of the victim—*Accedente nova si quam dabat hostia carne* (Juv. S. XI. 82.) The trade of a Baker was unknown at Rome until the time of the war against Perseus, (B.C. 172,) but the bread for each family was made by the female slaves. The word *Pistores*, which eventually signified *bakers*, originally denoted *Millers*, properly those *qui far pinsebant*, i.e. who separated from the *far* the husk which adheres to it with great tenacity, an operation which necessarily preceded the grinding of the corn into flour. For a long period, also, Cooks did not form part of an ordinary establishment, but were hired in upon great occasions, the statement of Pliny upon this point—*Nec Cocos vero habebant in servitiis, eosque ex macello conducebant*—being fully confirmed by Plautus, and since it would be part of the duty of such an artist to prepare the bread and cakes necessary for the entertainment, we can understand how it should be said that in ancient times the baker and the cook were the same—*Cocum et Pistorem apud antiquos eundem fuisse accepimus*.[4] In later times, in so far as the wealthy were concerned, earth, air, and water were ransacked to furnish forth their banquets, on which enormous sums were lavished [5]—*Interea gustus elementa per omnia quaerunt = Nunquam animo pretiis obstantibus*, (Iuv. S. XI. 14,) and which were frequently characterised by the coarsest and most revolting gluttony—*Vomunt ut edant, edunt ut vomant* (Senec. ad Helv. 9.) It would be out of place were we to enumerate here all the beasts, birds, fishes, and other dainties under which their tables groaned, since we could do little more than give a mere catalogue of names, but we shall say a few words upon the subject of wines, and explain the arrangements of a formal *Coena*, that being the meal to which guests were usually invited.

Wines.—We do not profess in the present work to treat of the industrial arts practised by the Romans, and therefore cannot enter into details with regard to agriculture and the topics allied to it; but the allusions in the classics to the

---

[1] Liv. I. 57. XL. 7. 9. 13. Cic. pro Coel. 15. Suet. Tit. 7. Domit. 21. Senec. ad Helv. 10. de Benef. VI. 32.
[2] Plaut. Mostell. IV. ii. 50. Non. s. v. *Merenda*, p. 19, ed Gerl. Paul. Diac. s. v. *Merendam*, p. 123. Isidor. XX. ii. 12. iii. 3. Calpurn. Ecl. V. 60.
[3] Varro L.L. V. § 105. 108. Plin. H. N. XVIII. 8. Val. Max. II. v. 5. Pers. S. VI. 140. Iuv. S. XI. 58. XIV. 170. Charis. p. 56. ed. Putsch. Cato R. R. 58. Plaut. Mil. Glor. II. iii. 78. Pseud. I. ii. 84. Hence Plautus makes a foreigner call an Italian workman, *Pultiphagus opifex barbarus*, (Mostell. III. ii. 141,) and Persius, when depicting the death of a glutton—*Uncta cadunt laxis tunc Pulmentaria labris* (S. III. 102.)
[4] Plin. H. N. XVIII. 11. Plaut. Aul. II. iv. 1. Pseud. III. ii. 1. Paul. Diac. s. v. *Cocum*, p. 58.
[5] See Senec. Consol. ad. Helv. 9. *C. Caesar . . . HS. centies coenavit uno die.*

various processes connected with making and preserving wine are so numerous, that we must briefly illustrate them.[1] When the season of the vintage (*Vindemia*) had arrived, the grapes were gathered in baskets (*Corbes—Fiscinae*) and conveyed to an apartment or shed called *Calcatorium* or *Torcularium*, where they were thrown into a large receptacle which formed part of the winepress, (*Prelum—Torcular,*) and beneath this was a cistern (*Lacus Torcularius.*) The juice which drained from the clusters in consequence of their bearing upon each other, called *Protropum*, (Plin. H.N. XIV. 9,) was collected and set apart, the grapes were then gently trodden by the naked feet, (*Calcare*, and hence *Calcatamque tenet bellis Socialibus uvam*, Iuv. S. V. 31,) and the juice thus obtained, called *Mustum lixivium*, (Columell. XII. 41,) was also set apart; the grapes were now fully trodden, and the force of the press being moderately applied, they yielded nearly the whole of their juice, which was called *Mustum pressum*, or more frequently simply *Mustum*. Lastly, water was thrown among the stalks and husks, and the full power of the press called into action, the liquid thus obtained being called *Mustum tortivum* (Columell. XII. 36.) These four products were kept separate from each other. The first two were usually preserved in their sweet state; the third was fermented for wine; (*Vinum*;) the fourth was also fermented, and the result was a thin acid beverage known as *Lora* (Plin. XIV. 10.)

The process of fermentation was allowed to commence in the *Lacus*, the liquor was then conveyed to the *Cella Vinaria*, a cool apartment, the floor of which was usually sunk below the surface of the ground, and here it was poured into large earthenware vats (*Dolia—Cupae—Seriae*) carefully coated in their interior with pitch, (*Dolia picata*,) and in these the fermentation was completed. The inferior qualities intended for immediate consumption underwent no farther preparation, but the contents were drawn off as required, and hence the expressions *Vinum Doliare* s. *Vinum de Cupa*, i.e. *Draught-Wine* (Digest. XVIII. vi. 1. Cic. in Pison. 27.) The more choice and full bodied kinds were mixed with a number of substances, which were believed to heighten their flavour and to make them keep better. Such were, sweet grape juice (*Mustum*) boiled down to a sort of jelly, decoctions of various spices, drugs, and aromatic herbs, to which were frequently added pitch, rosin, turpentine, and sea water. The mixture was then racked off (*Diffundere*, hence *Ipse capillato diffusum consule potat*, Iuv. S. V. 30. comp. Hor. Epp. I. v. 4. and Ovid. Fast. V. 517.) from the *Dolium* into jars called *Amphorae*, *Cadi*, or *Lagenae*, on which were stamped or painted the names of the Consuls for the current year (*Titulus* Iuv. S. V. 33.)—thus marking the date of the vintage. The mouths of these vessels were then closed with plugs of wood or cork (*Cortex*) carefully plastered over with pitch, clay, or gypsum, so as to exclude the air. They were then conveyed to a repository (*Apotheca—Horreum*) in the upper part of the dwelling house, frequently constructed so as to communicate directly with the chimneys, the heat and smoke being supposed to accelerate the ripening of the wine, and in this case the apartment was called *Fumarium*. A single stanza in one of the Odes of Horace (III. viii. 19,) comprises references to many of the particulars now enumerated:

---

[1] The technicalities concerning the making and compounding of wines will be found scattered over the works of the *Scriptores de Re Rustica*, Cato, Varro, and Columella; in the collection entitled *Geoponica*; and in the *Historia Naturalis* of Pliny, especially XIV. 6. seqq. Much curious and interesting information is contained in HENDERSON's *History of Ancient and Modern Wines*.

Hic dies anno redeunte festus,
Corticem adstrictum pice demovebit
Amphorae fumum bibere institutae
Consule Tullo.

Comp. III. xxi. 1. 7. xxviii. 7. The annexed cut, taken from the sign of a wine shop in Pompeii, represents the ordinary shape of the Amphorae, the mode of transporting them from place to place, and the position in which they were stored in the cellars, either imbedded in the ground or leaning against the walls.

Observe that *Mustum* is strictly the sweet juice of the grape before it had undergone any chemical change, although this word is sometimes used loosely for wine, as when Martial (I. 19,) speaks of—*In Vaticanis condita musta cadis;* after fermentation it became *Vinum;* if the fermentation was pushed too far, or if the wine was kept too long, it was changed into *Acetum;* the vinegar itself in process of time underwent decomposition and was transformed into an insipid useless liquor to which the name *Vappa* was given. Hence the latter term is sometimes employed to denote wine of the most miserable quality, (Hor. S. II. iii. 144,) and sometimes, figuratively, a fool or a good-for-nothing reprobate (Hor. S. I. 1. 103. Pers. S. V. 77.)

Mustum was preserved from fermentation by boiling, and was distinguished by different names according to the degree of inspissation. When boiled down to two-thirds of its original bulk, it became *Carenum*, to one-half *Defrutum*, to one-third *Sapa*, and these jellies were used for a great number of domestic purposes.

The ripe grapes, instead of being conveyed at once to the press, were in some cases exposed to the rays of the sun until partially dried, and from these, sweet wines, called *Vinum Diachytum* and *Vinum Passum*, were manufactured.

In consequence of the numerous heterogeneous substances mixed with the newly made wine when transferred to the *Amphora*, it was always necessary to filter it (*Defaecare—Liquare—Colare—Saccare*) before it was used, and this was effected by passing it either through a woollen bag (*Saccus vinarius*) or a metal strainer perforated with small holes, (*Colum vinarium,*) and in order to cool it by the same operation, it became common to fill the *Saccus* or *Colum* with snow. Hence we find two epigrams of Martial (XIV. 103. 104,) with the Lemmata, *Colum Nivarium* and *Saccus Nivarius*. On the other hand, wine mixed with hot water was a favourite beverage, (Martial. I. 12. VIII. 68,) and a very ingenious vessel, constructed upon the principle of a modern tea-urn, has been found at Pompeii, intended, it is believed, to keep the water or the mixture hot at table. The *Thermopolia* mentioned by Plautus [1] were unquestionably taverns where hot mulled wine was sold; but it may be doubted whether the words of the dramatist apply to Roman usages.

[1] Curcul. II. iii. 13. Rud. II. vi. 45. Trin. IV. iii. 6.

Mulsum was a term applied to two different combinations; 1. To a mixture of honey with the finest *Mustum* taken fresh from the *Lacus* (Columell. XIII. 41.) 2. To a mixture of honey and wine—*Mulsum ex vetere vino utilissimum* (Plin. H.N. XXII. 4.)

The finest Italian wines were all the growth of Campania, and of these the *Caecubum* from the poplar swamps of Amyclae, anciently held the first place, but before the time of Pliny it had been superseded by the *Setinum*. The *Falernum* and the *Massicum*, from the southern slopes of the hills which divide Campania from Latium, held the next rank; the vineyards of Vesuvius were also very celebrated, and the *Calenum*, the *Surrentinum*, and the *Fundanum*, all enjoyed high reputation. Of those not Campanian, the *Albanum* stood first, (*Albani veteris pretiosa senectus*,) and among the poorest were the *Sabinum*, the *Vaticanum*, and the *Veientanum*.

Greek wines also were imported to a considerable extent, the most esteemed being the *Thasium*, the *Chium*, the *Lesbium*, the *Cyprium*, and the *Clazomenium*.

Triclinium.—In early times, the whole family eat together in the *Atrium*, or public room; but when mansions were built upon a large scale, one or more spacious banqueting halls commonly formed part of the plan, such apartments being classed under the general title of *Triclinia*. The word *Triclinium*, however, in its strict signification, denotes not the apartment, but a set of low divans or couches grouped round a table; these couches, according to the usual arrangement, being three in number, and arranged as represented in the annexed figure. A, B, C, are the three couches (*Lecti—Lecti Tricliniares*,) the space, M, was occupied by the table, (*Mensa*,) and the side, Z, left open for the attendants to put down and remove the dishes. Each couch was calculated to hold three persons, although four might be squeezed in, and since it was expected that each couch would have at least one occupant, the saying arose, that the company at a *Coena* should not exceed the number of the Muses, nor fall short of the number of the Graces.

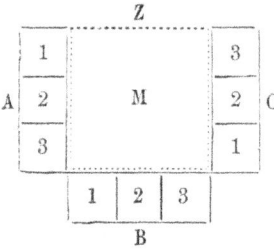

Men always reclined at table (and thus *Accumbere* s. *Discumbere Mensae* was the established phrase) resting on the left elbow, their bodies slightly elevated by cushions, (*pulvini*,) and their limbs stretched out at full length. Thus the individual who lay at 1 on the couch A had his limbs extended behind the body of the individual who lay at 2, the head of the latter being opposite to the breast of the former. In like manner the limbs of A 2, extended behind the body of A 3, whose head was opposite to the breast of A 2, and so for the two other couches.

The couch A was termed *Summus* (*Lectus*)—B, *Medius* (*Lectus*)—C, *Imus*, (*Lectus*,) and the three places, 1, 2, 3, on each couch and the individuals who occupied them were in like manner termed respectively *Summus*, *Medius*, *Imus*. Hence the person who occupied A 1 was said *Discumbere Summus in Summo*, or simply *Discumbere Summus*—A 2, *D. Medius in Summo*—A 3, *D. Imus in Summo*—B 1, *Summus in Medio*—C 2, *Medius in Imo*, and so for the rest. The couch A was considered the most honourable, B the second, C the lowest; and the numbers 1, 2, 3, indicate the precedence of the different places on each couch. To the order thus described there was one exception, the most honourable place at the whole table was B 3, the *Imus in Medio*, and as this was always assigned to the Consul when he was among the guests, it was named *Locus Consularis*. The master of the house, in order that he might be as near as possible to the great man, usually occupied C 1, that is, he was *Summus in Imo*. When the relative position of two individuals upon the same couch was described, the one who occupied the more honourable position was said *Discumbere superior*, or *D. supra alterum*, the other *Discumbere inferior*, or *D. infra alterum*. If we apply what has been said above to the well-known description of the *Coena Nasidieni*, given by Horace, (S. II. viii.) we shall see that the different personages mentioned were arranged as follows:—A 1, Horace; A 2, Viscus Thurinus; A 3, Varius; B 1 and 2, Vibidius and Servilius Balatro, the two *Umbrae*, i.e. uninvited guests whom Maecenas had brought along with him; B 3, Maecenas, in the *Locus Consularis*; C 1, Nomentanus, who acted as a sort of master of ceremonies, and therefore took the place of Nasidienus, who was C 2; C 3, Porcius. A still more interesting example is afforded by the account given in a fragment of Sallust, preserved by Servius, (Ad Virg. Æn. I. 702,) of the arrangement of the guests in the banquet, given by Perperna, at which Sertorius was murdered —*Igitur discubere: Sertorius inferior in medio; super eum L. Fabius Hispaniensis senator ex proscriptis; in summo Antonius et infra scriba Sertorii Versius; et alter scriba Maecenas in imo medius inter Tarquinium et dominum Perpernam.* In this case there were two persons only on the *Summus Lectus*, and two on the *Medius Lectus*, of whom Sertorius, the great man, was *inferior*. Curiously enough, Servius adduces this passage to prove that in ancient times the middle place upon the couch belonged to the master of the house, while it distinctly shows that Perperna was *Summus in Imo*.[1]

It is to be observed that, down to the imperial times at least, women sat at table, and the grammarians assure us that such was the practice among men also at a remote period.[2] We have already had occasion to point out that at the *Epulum Iovis*, Iuno and Minerva were placed upright, while Iove was extended on a couch, and that a solemn feast in honour of goddesses was termed *Sellisternium*. (p. 345.)

Arrangement of the Coena.—A complete banquet (*Coena recta*) was composed of three parts.

1. *Gustus* s. *Gustatio* s. *Promulsis*, consisting of objects intended to provoke rather than to satisfy the appetite, such as lettuces, shell-fish, and especially eggs, (Plin. Ep. I. 15,) to which was frequently added a cup of wine sweetened with honey, (*mulsum*,) and flavoured with aromatic herbs, this last being strictly the *Promulsis*.

2. The *Coena* proper, consisting of several courses. Each course was brought up upon a tray called *Ferculum*, and hence the number of *Fercula* decided the number of courses, which varied according to circumstances; thus we are told of Augustus—*Coenam ternis Ferculis, aut, cum abundantissime, senis praebebat*, (Suet. Octav. 74,) and Juvenal exclaims (S. I. 95) . . . *Quis Fercula Septem = Secreto coenavit avus?*—The word *Missus* is used in the same sense as when it is recorded of Pertinax—*quotquot essent amici, novem libras carnis per*

---

[1] We have followed Becker in describing the position of the different couches, and the arrangement of the guests upon the *Triclinium*, although his views differ from those of most of the earlier writers on convivial antiquities. The position of the *Locus Consularis* is determined by a passage in Plutarch, Sympos. I. 3.
[2] Val. Max. II. i. 2. Serv. ad Virg. Æn. I. 218. 712.

tres Missus ponebat (Capitolin. Pertin. 12)—and of Elagabalus—*Celebravit item tale convivium ut apud amicos singulos singuli Missus appararentur* (Lamprid. Elagab. 30.) *Repositoria*, mentioned occasionally in Pliny, appear to have been stands upon which dishes or drinking vessels were placed, but to have been different from the *Fercula* (Plin. H.N. XVIII. 35. XXIII. 11. XXVIII. 2.)

3. *Mensae Secundae*, consisting of cakes, sweetmeats, (*Bellaria*,) and fruit of all kinds.

The fact that the repast commenced with eggs and ended with fruit gave rise to the proverb—*Ab* Ovo *usque ad* Mala, (Hor. S. I. iii. 6. comp. Cic. ad Fam. IX. 20.) i.e. *from beginning to end.*

The various dishes were set in order on the *Ferculum*, and the whole arrangements of the banquet conducted by a superintendent named *Structor*, while the carving was performed with graceful gestures by a person called *Carptor* or *Scissor*, who had been regularly educated by a professor of the art. We infer from a passage in Juvenal, (S. V. 120,) who is our great authority upon this subject, that the offices of *Structor* and *Carptor* were commonly united in the same individual.

Spoons (*Cochlearia—Ligulae*) are occasionally mentioned, but knives and forks for the use of the guests were altogether unknown. Each one must, therefore, have helped himself, and torn his food into morsels with his fingers, (Ovid. A. A. III. 736,) as is the practice in the East at this day. Hence, before the meal commenced, and probably at its termination also, slaves went round with vessels of water for washing the hands, and towels (*Mantelia*) for drying them, (Virg. G. IV. 376. Æn. 701,) but the guests brought with them their own napkins (*Mappae*.) Horace, (S. II. viii. 11,) when describing the banquet of Nasidienus, notices, that when one of the courses was removed, a slave—*Gausape purpureo mensam pertersit*—which seems to prove that tablecloths were not known at that period, and, when Lampridius wrote, it was believed that they were first introduced under Hadrian (Lamprid. Elagab. 27. Alex. Sev. 37.)

Drinking Customs.—Drinking Vessels, &c.—The Romans seldom drank their wine pure, (*Merum*,) but usually mixed it with water, hot or cold, which, when called for, was handed to them (*Frigida non desit, non deerit calda petenti*, Martial. XIV. 105) in jugs called *Urceoli Ministratorii* (Martial. Ibid.) by the slaves in attendance, those who were employed in such services by the wealthy being often beautiful boys brought from the East (*Flos Asiae*, Iuv. S. V. 56,) and purchased for immense sums. The relative proportions of the wine and the water were regulated by the addition of a certain number of *Cyathi*[1] of wine to a fixed quantity of water in the *Poculum* or drinking cup, the precise number of *Cyathi* being determined by various considerations. Thus Horace, in one of his Bacchanalian Odes, (C. III. xix. 11,) proposes to take the number either of the Graces or of the Muses as the standard—*tribus aut novem*=*Miscentor Cyathis pocula commodis*—indicating, at the same time, that the former combination was the more prudent; and in another passage when calling upon Maecenas to drink deep in honour of his friend's escape, he hyperbolically exclaims —*Sume, Maecenas, Cyathos amici*=*Sospitis centum.* When it was proposed to drink the health of any one, it was not uncommon to take a *Cyathus* of wine for every letter in the name, as in the epigram upon Caius Iulius Proculus, quoted from Martial in page 411, and again we find (I. 72)—*Naevia sex Cya-*

---
[1] The *Cyathus*, as we have seen above, p. 411, was one-twelfth of the *Sextarius*.

DRINKING CUSTOMS—GAMES OF CHANCE. 443

this, septem Iustina bibatur=Quinque Lycas, Lyde quatuor, Ida tribus.[1] When any one was toasted in this manner, *Bene* was prefixed to his name, as we learn from Tibullus (II. i. 3)—*Sed,* BENE MESSALAM, *sua quisque ad pocula dicat* —and from the lively scene in the Persa of Plautus (V. i. 18).

A summo septenis Cyathis committe hos ludos: move manus: propera, Paegnium! tarde Cyathos mihi das: cedo sane: BENE MIHI, BENE VOBIS, BENE AMICAE MEAE.

When a person drank wine *with* another, he first tasted of the cup himself, and then handed it to his friend with the words *Propino tibi,* (Cic. Tusc. I. 40, Iuv. S. V. 127,) receiving his in return. It must be understood that *Cyathus* always indicates a measure for adjusting the proportions of the wine and the water, and never a drinking cup. The general word for the latter is *Poculum,* but *Pocula* were distinguished by a vast variety of names, according to the forms which they assumed, such as *Calices—Canthari—Carchesia—Ciboria—Cululli—Paterae—Phialae—Scyphi—Trientalia—Trullae,* and many others. The materials of which they were composed were also greatly diversified. *Pocula* of wood, (*fagina*, &c.,) of pottery, (*fictilia*,) and of glass, (*vitrea*,) were in everyday use. More precious were those of rock crystal, (*crystallina,*) of amber, (*capaces Heliadum crustas,* Iuv. S. V. 37,) and of the precious metals, (*argentea—aurea,*) the latter being frequently decorated with chasings, (*Toreumata,*) or with figures in high relief, (*Crustae—Emblemata,*) or with precious stones, (*Calices gemmati—Aurum gemmatum.*)[2] What the *Vasa Murrhina,* the most highly valued of all, may have been, no one has yet been able to decide, but they were certainly brought from the East, and, judging from the expressions of Propertius (IV. v. 26)—*Murrheaque in Parthis pocula cocta focis*— may very probably have been porcelain.

Under ordinary circumstances, each guest would mix the wine and water in his own cup (*temperare poculum*) so as to suit his individual taste, but when the *Coena* was succeeded by a regular *Commissatio,* then the wine and water were mixed for the whole company in a large bowl called *Crater,* from which the *Pocula* were filled. In this case the strength of the beverage, the toasts to be drunk, and all other matters connected with the festivities, were regulated by one of the party, who was formally elected to the office of *Arbiter Bibendi,* (the Συμποσίαρχος of the Greeks,) i.e. *Master of the Revels.* The choice was usually determined by throwing the dice—*Quem Venus arbitrum=Dicet bibendi* (Hor. C. II. vii. 25,) and again—*Nec regna vini sortiere talis* (I. v. 18)—which leads us to speak of the

Games of Chance and other amusements which were frequently introduced after the *Coena.* The dice used by the Romans were of two kinds:—

1. *Tesserae,* (κύβοι,) which were regular cubes corresponding in every respect with modern dice.

2. *Tali,* (ἀστράγαλοι,) which were of an oblong shape, and rounded at the two ends, so that they could not rest upon either of these. They were, therefore, marked upon four sides only, and bore the numbers I. III. IV. VI.—I. and VI. being on opposite sides.

Tesserae and *Tali* alike were thrown from a cylindrical box, called *Fritillus* s. *Phimus* s. *Pyrgus* s. *Turricula,* upon a board called *Abacus* s. *Alveus,* or simply *Tabula* (sc. *lusoria.*) The best throw was termed *Venus* s. *Casus*

[1] Comp. Ovid. Fast. III. 532. Plaut. Stich. V. iv. 24. 30.
[2] See Cic. in Verr. IV. 18 seqq. Iuv. S. I. 76. Martial. XIV. 109. 111. 115.

Venereus s. *Iactus Venereus*, the worst *Canis*. The mode of playing, however, was different according as *Tesserae* or *Tali* were used.

In playing with *Tesserae*, it appears that, generally, although perhaps not invariably, the person who threw the highest number won, which was termed by the Greeks, πλειστοβολίνδα παίζειν. Hence, it was the *Iactus Venereus* when all the dice came up sixes, (*Seniones*,) and the *Canis* when they all came up aces, (*Uniones*,) and thus *Canis* is used in a general sense for *an ace* whether in *Tesserae* or *Tali* (Suet. Oct. 71.) Any number of *Tesserae* might be employed, but three was the usual number, as we see from the Greek proverb, ἢ τρὶς ἓξ ἢ τρεῖς κύβοι, which Becker has rightly explained to mean, *three sixes or three aces*, i.e. *all or nothing*.

On the other hand, they always played with four *Tali*, neither more nor less, for here it was reckoned the *Iactus Venereus* when they all came up different, (Martial. XIV. 14.) and the *Canis* when they all came up the same. In a game of *Tali*, described by Suetonius, (Octav. 71,) whoever threw a six or an ace put a *Denarius* into the pool for each six and each ace so thrown, and this went on until some one threw the *Venus*, which swept the board.

Alea may signify *a die*, as in the exclamation of Julius Cæsar, when passing the Rubicon—*Iacta Alea esto*, (Suet. Iul. 32,) but is more commonly used to mean *gambling* in general, and especially those games of chance in which money was staked and dice were used. Such amusements were forbidden by law as early at least as the time of Cicero, except during the festive license of the *Saturnalia*, and professed gamblers (*Aleatores*) were always looked upon as disreputable, but the enactments for the suppression of this vice do not appear to have been at any time rigidly enforced, and, under many emperors, were altogether neglected.[1]

Other games of a less objectionable character are occasionally mentioned. Such are the *Ludus Latrunculorum* and the *Ludus duodecim Scriptorum*. The former, which by some scholars has been compared to chess, and by others to draughts, is described at considerable length in the Panegyric on Calpurnius Piso, attributed to Saleius Bassus, and is alluded to more than once by Ovid. The men were called *Calculi, Milites, Latrones, Latrunculi*, were made of glass, and were of different colours.[2] The latter has been supposed to resemble backgammon, because the movements of the pieces were to a certain extent regulated by throwing dice.[3]

We may also mention the games of *Odd and Even*, (*Ludere par Impar*,) which was by no means confined to children, as we might suppose from the words of Horace, (S. II. iii. 48,) being sometimes introduced along with *Tali* at the banquet, (Suet. Oct. 71;) of *Pitch and Toss*, in which the cry was *Capita aut Navia*, in allusion to the devices on the *As*, (Macrob. S. I. 7;) and of *Micare*, (*Digitis*,) which is identical with the modern *Morra*, so popular among the lower classes in Southern Italy (Cic. de N. D. 41. de Off. 19. Suet. Octav. 13. Calpurn. Ecl. II. 25.)

Chaplets.—Towards the close of the *Coena*, before the drinking (*Compotatio*) fairly commenced, chaplets or garlands (*Serta—Coronae—Corollae*) were distributed among the guests. At what period the custom of wearing these was first introduced it is impossible to determine, but an anecdote told by

---

[1] Cic. Philipp. II. 23. Hor. C. III. xxiv. 58. Digest. XI. v. 1. seqq. Martial. IV. 14. V. 84. XI. 6. Iuv. S. I. 89. XIV. 4.
[2] Ovid. A. A. II. 207. III. 35. Trist. II. 477. Senec. de Tranq. 14. Martial. XIV. 17. 20.
[3] Cic. ap. Non. s.v. *Scripta*, p. 110. ed. Gerl. Ovid. A. A. II. 203. III. 363. Quintil. I. O. XI. 2.

Pliny (XXI. 3.) proves that it prevailed as early as the second Punic War.[1] They were originally assumed not merely for ornament, or to gratify the senses, but from a belief that the odour of certain plants neutralized the intoxicating properties of wine, and hence we find that they were formed not of fragrant flowers alone, such as roses or violets, but of parsley, ivy, myrtle, and various other plants, simple or combined . . . . *est in horto = Phylli, nectendis Apium coronis = Est Hederae vis* (Hor. C. IV. xi. 3.) . . . *Quis udo = Deproperare Apio coronas = Curatve Myrto* (II. vii. 23.) But after the habit was once established such considerations were altogether thrown aside, so that in winter artificial chaplets, called *Coronae Ægyptiae* s. *hibernae*, made of coloured horn, (*ramento e cornibus tincto,*) or of dyed silks, (*e veste serica versicolores,*) or of copper foil, plated, or gilded, (*e lamina aerea tenui inaurata aut argentata,*) were substituted. To the last mentioned, those of copper foil, the double diminutive *Corollarium* was, according to Pliny, properly applied, on account of the great tenuity of the metallic leaves.

Sometimes the materials employed were plaited together, (*Coronae plectiles,*) sometimes pinned or pasted together, (*Coronae pactiles,*) sometimes sewed together, (*Coronae sutiles,*) sometimes tied together with coloured ribbons termed *Lemnisci*, or with strips of lime-tree bark (*Philyrae coronarum Lemniscis celebres.* Plin. H.N. xvi. 4.), and sometimes a simple tendril of ivy or a sprig of myrtle sufficed, without any previous preparation—*Displicent nexae Philyra coronae* . . . . *Simplici Myrto nihil adlabores* (Hor. C. I. xxxviii. 2. 5.)

The artificial chaplets of copper foil worn at banquets must be distinguished from *Corollaria*, made of the precious metals, with *Lemnisci* to match, which are said to have been first introduced by Crassus, and bestowed by him on the successful competitors at his games. Soon after this it seems to have become a common practice to bestow such tokens of approbation upon actors and other public performers who had distinguished themselves, and hence the word *Corollarium* is used in a general sense to denote something given beyond what is strictly due, *a gratuity* or *donation*—COROLLARIUM *si additum praeter quam quod debitum eius: vocabulum fictum a Corollis. quod eae, cum placerent actores, in scena dari solitae.* Varro L.L. V. § 178. Phaedr. V. vii. 34. For examples see Cic. in Verr. II. 50. IV. 22. Senec. de Ben. VI. 17. Suet. Octav. 45.[2]

Perfumes.—Not less essential than *Coronae* to the full enjoyment of a banquet, was a supply of perfumes. The taste prevailed from a very early period among the Greeks, was first developed among the Romans after their Asiatic conquests, so that about a century later, B.C. 89, the Censors, P. Licinius Crassus, and L. Iulius Cæsar, found it necessary to issue an ordinance—*Ne quis venderet unguenta exotica* (Plin. H. N. XXI. 3. comp. Aul. Gell. VII. 12.) and towards the close of the republic amounted to a passion. The ancients being unacquainted with the art of distillation, their only vehicle for odorous essences was oil, and hence perfumes of every description were comprehended under the general term

---

[1] The ornamental *Corona* seems to have originated in a simple band called *Strophium* or *Strophiolum*, worn round the head to confine the hair. Thus Plin. H. N. XXI. 2. *Tenuioribus* (sc. *coronis*) *utebantur antiqui.* STROPHIA *appellantes; unde nata* STROPHIOLA.

[2] Most of the particulars given above with regard to *Coronae* are taken from Pliny H. N. XXI. 2. seqq. A great mass of curious matter will be found in Athenaeus XV. 8–34. See also Plut. Sympos. III. 1. Plaut. Bacchid. I. i. 37. Pseud. V. ii. 8. Ovid. Fast. I. 403. II. 739. V. 335. Martial. V. 65. IX. 91. X. 19 Petron. Arb. 60. Paul. Diac. s. v. *Corolla* p. 63. With respect to *Lemnisci* see Paul. Diac. s.v. p. 115. Serv. ad Virg. Æn. V. 209. Capitolin. Ver. 5. The *Lemniscus* was generally regarded as an ornamental addition not essential to the *Corona*. Plin. H.N. XXI. 3. comp. Cic. pro Rosc. Amerin. 35.

Unguenta. Of these there was an immense variety obtained from all manner of sweet smelling herbs and flowers, and large quantities were consumed for anointing the body, an operation which many performed regularly three times a-day (Senec. Ep. LXXXVI.)—before taking exercise, after taking exercise, and after the bath. The coarser kinds were kept in large shells (. . . . *funde capacibus = Unguenta conchis* . . . . Hor. C. II. vii. 22.) or bottles of swelling globular form called *Ampullae;*[1] the finer sorts, which were very costly, being extracted from rare plants imported from the most distant regions of the East,[2] were kept in small flasks, made of a species of gypsum called *Lapis Alabastrites* s. *Onychites* s. *Onyx*, which was believed to possess the property of preserving their fragrance from being dissipated—*Lapidem Alabastriten* . . . . *cavant ad vasa unguentaria quoniam optime servare incorrupta dicitur* (Plin. H. N. XXXV. 12.) Such a flask was termed *Alabastron* or *Onyx*, and was shaped with a long narrow neck, which allowed the contents to escape drop by drop only, so that when it was desired to obtain the whole at once, it was necessary to break off the neck, a circumstance which fully explains the passage in the New Testament, where the woman who came to visit our Saviour is represented as having broken the "Alabaster box of very precious ointment." (St. Matt. xxvi. 7. St. Mark xiv. 3).

The finer *Unguenta* were introduced at a banquet along with the *Coronae*, and these two luxuries are constantly mentioned in connection with each other, and with the wine, thus, Horace, C. III. xiv. 17.

> I, pete unguentum, puer, et coronas
> Et cadum Marsi memorem duelli,

and again II. iii. 13,

> Huc vina, et unguenta et nimium brevis
> Flores amoenae ferre iube rosae.[3]

The perfumes, when handed round, were applied to anoint the hair and face— *cum interea Apronius caput atque os suum unguento perfricaret* (Cic. in Verr. III. 25.)—*Saepe coronatis stillant unguenta capillis* (Ovid. Heroid. XXI. 161.) . . . . *coronatus nitentes = Syrio Malabathro capillos* (Hor. C. II. vii. 7.) and they sometimes formed *Coronae* out of the leaves of the *Nardus*, and steeped these in the liquid odour—*Lautissimum quippe habetur e Nardi foliis eas* (sc. *Coronas*) *dari* . . . . *unguentis madidas* (Plin. H.N. XXI. 3. comp. Lucan. Phars. X. 164.) They were not content, however, with applying them externally, but actually mixed them with the wine—*At hercle iam quidam in potu addunt* (Plin. H.N. XXIII. 3,) or poured the wine into the shells or bottles containing perfumed oil, and drank off the compound. To this strange practice we find allusions both in Juvenal and Martial, the former when describing a debauch, mentions among other characteristics (S. VI. 303,)

> Cum perfusa mero spumant unguenta Falerno,
> Cum bibitur Concha . . . . .

---

[1] Cic. de Finn. IV. 12. Hor. A. P. 97. Apulei. Florid. II. 9. § 2.
[2] Among these the far-famed *Nardus*, or emphatically *Folium*, held the first place, the oil impregnated with it being termed *Nardinum* or *Foliatum*.
[3] In another Ode, IV. xii. 11, when inviting a friend to join him in making the necessary preparations for a jovial party, he offers to supply the wine, provided Virgilius will contribute the perfume—*Nardo vina merebere = Nardi parvus Onyx eliciet cadum = Qui nunc Sulpiciis accubat horreis.*

and the latter has the following epigram on an *Ampulla* which bore the name of the celebrated perfumer Cosmus:—

> Hac licet in gemma quae servat nomina Cosmi,
> Luxuriose, bibas, si FOLIATA sitis.—XIV. 110.

Sometimes the wine was flavoured with the perfume before it was transferred to the Amphora, and of such Plautus speaks (Mil. Gl. III. ii. 11)—*Deprompsit Nardini amphoram cellarius*—where *Nardinum* is wine that had been mixed with Nard.[1]

The great seat of the manufacture in Italy was Capua, where a whole street or quarter called *Seplasia* was occupied by the *Unguentarii*.[2]

Music, &c.—The presence of musicians at a formal banquet seems to have been considered indispensable from a very early period, for in the Aulularia of Plautus, Megadorus, when making preparations for the marriage feasts to be held in his own house and in that of his intended father-in-law, hires and sends home from the market not only two cooks, but also two female minstrels (*Tibicinae*.) Singing women (*Psaltriae—Sambucistriae*) who accompanied their voices with the Lyre, were introduced at a somewhat later epoch, and towards the close of the republic regular concerts (*Symphoniae*) were performed by bands of youthful choristers (*Pueri symphoniaci*) trained for the purpose.[3] That such an addition to the pleasures of the table, although not essential, was by no means uncommon, is evident from the words of Horace (A. P. 274 comp. Cic. in Verr. III. 44.)

> Ut gratas inter mensas Symphonia discors
> Et crassum unguentum, et Sardo cum melle papaver,
> Offendunt, *poterat duci quia coena sine istis*.

Under the empire, dancing girls (*Saltatrices*) from Spain and Syria, were frequently introduced, whose performances seem to have resembled those of the *Almeh*, still common in the East, while in addition to these, dwarfs, tumblers, with mountebanks of every description, (*Nani—Moriones*, &c.) and even gladiators, displayed their feats.[4] Sometimes, however, in graver society, more intellectual amusements were provided. The productions of celebrated poets were recited or sung, just as in ancient times, ballads, recounting the glories of high-born warriors had been chanted by boys to the note of the flute, or repeated without music, (*assa voce*,) and sometimes the talents of an *Improvisatore* were exercised to the admiration of his hearers.[5]

All entertainments, such as those noticed above, whether addressed to the eye or to the ear, were comprehended under the Greek term *Acroamata*, (e.g. Suet. Vesp. 19,) but this word is more frequently employed to signify, not the performances themselves, but the *persons* who performed. Thus Suetonius (Octav. 74) says of Augustus—*Et aut acroamata et histriones aut etiam triviales ex Circo ludios interponebat ac frequentius aretalogos*—and Nepos of Atticus (14) *Nemo in convivio eius aliud acroama audivit quam anagnosten*. Taking this in connection with what has been said above on the word *Corollarium*, we are enabled to understand the expressions used by Cicero (In Verr. IV. 221,) when recounting the thefts of Verres in abstracting figures from drinking cups—*Hic,*

---

[1] As in the case of *Coronae*, our most copious sources of information regarding *Unguenta* are Pliny (XIII. 1. seqq.) and Athenaeus (XV. 34—47.)
[2] Cic. de leg. agr. II. 34. pro Sest. 8. Plin. H. N. XVI. 10. XXXIV. 11. Val. Max. IX. 1.
[3] Plaut. Aul. I. iv. 1. Liv. XXXIX. 6. Cic. Div. in Q. C. 17. pro Milon. 21.
[4] Iuv. 8. XL 162. seqq. Martial. V. 78. Macrob. S. II. 1. Aul. Gell. XIX.
[5] Cic. Tuscul. IV. 2. Brut. 19. Val. Max. II. i. 10. Non. s.v. *assa*, p. 54. ed. Gerl. Hor. O. IV. xv. 29. Iuv. S. XL 77. Cic. pro Arch. 8.

quasi festivum Acroama, (i.e. a hired performer at a banquet,) *ne sine Corollario,* (i.e. a gratuity,) *de convivio discederet, ibidem, convivis inspectantibus, emblemata avellenda curavit.*[1]

Musical Instruments.—We may take this opportunity of naming the musical instruments in general use among the Romans, whether introduced at banquets or otherwise. These may be divided into two classes.

1. *Wind Instruments.* 2. *Stringed Instruments.*

1. *Wind Instruments.* By far the most important of these was the *Tibia,* which, in ancient times at least, was a necessary accompaniment to every solemn sacrifice, to every dramatic exhibition, and to all processions, whether of a grave or jovial character.

> Temporibus veterum Tibicinis usus avorum
> Magnus, et in magno semper honore fuit.
> Cantabat fanis, cantabat Tibia ludis,
> Cantabat moestis Tibia funeribus.—*Ovid. Fast.* VI. 657.

The English term *Flute* is generally given as an equivalent for *Tibia,* but *Clarionet,* or *Flageolet,* would be more appropriate, for, while the *Tibia* in so far resembled the flute that it was a cylindrical tube, perforated with holes, and frequently made of box-wood,

> Prima terebrato per rara foramina buxo
> Ut daret effeci Tibia longa sonos—*Ovid. Fast.* VI. 697.

it was not held horizontally, nor were the notes produced by blowing into one of the holes, but it was held vertically, and the notes were produced through the medium of a mouth-piece (*Ligula*—γλῶσσις.) Moreover, although a single *Tibia* was frequently employed, the Romans, judging from the representations on ancient monuments, generally employed a combination of two . . . . *biforem dat Tibia cantum* (Virg. Æn. IX. 618.)—*Saepe duas pariter, saepe Monaulon habet* (sc. *Tibicina,* Martial. XIV. 64.) The two *Tibiae* were not, however,

joined together and united to a common mouth-piece, as in our double flageolet, but each was kept distinct, and two separate mouth-pieces were applied to the lips of the player, which were bound round with a strap, called Φορβεία by the Greeks, which enabled him to confine and regulate his breath. This is seen distinctly in the annexed figure taken from a painting at Pompeii. *Tibiae* were formed of different materials according to the purposes to which they were to be applied—*Nunc Sacrificae Tuscorum (tibiae) e Buxo, ludicrae vero Loto, Ossibusque asininis et Argento fiunt* (Plin. H.N. XVI. 36,) and those intended for the theatre were sometimes of such large dimensions, that it became necessary to hoop them with brass rings, and then the instrument must have been analogous to the modern Hautboy—in ancient times, says Horace,

> Tibia non ut nunc, aurichalco vincta, tubaeque
> Aemula, sed tenuis, simplexque foramine pauco.—A. P. 202.

---

[1] The *Tibia Phrygia* was curved round at its extremity. Tibull. II. i. 86. Virg. Æn. XI. 737. Ovid. Fast. IV. 190, who calls it *Lotus adunca.*

When two *Tibiae* were united in this manner, that which was held in the right hand was called *Tibia Dextra*, or, because it played the Air on the Treble notes, *Tibia Incentiva*, while that held in the left hand was called *Tibia Sinistra* s. *Laeva*, or, because it played the Bass accompaniment, *Tibia Succentiva* (Varr. R. R. I. 2.) Sometimes instead of uniting a Treble and a Bass, two Trebles or two Basses were connected, and hence we read of *Tibiae Dextrae* and *Tibiae Sinistrae*. Again, *Tibiae*, as we have seen above, were divided into *Sacrificae* and *Ludicrae*, and they were also classified according to the character of the Music for which they were constructed, and since the three principal *Modi* ($\tau\acute{o}\nu o\iota$) were the Lydian, the Dorian, and the Phrygian, there were *Tibiae Lydiae*, *Tibiae Phrygiae*, &c. adapted to the *Lydius Modus*, the *Phrygius Modus*, and the *Dorius Modus*. When two *Tibiae* adapted to the same *Modus* were united, they were termed *Tibiae Pares;* when adapted to different *Modi*, they were called *Tibiae Impares*. Hence we find in the Didascalia attached to the plays of Terence, such expression as—*Tibiae pares Dextrae et Sinistrae* —*Tibiae duae Dextrae*, &c.—at least this is the most plausible explanation of these phrases, although the matter is involved in much obscurity, in consequence of our ignorance of the technical details of ancient music.

The *Fistula* was the $\Sigma \acute{v} \rho \iota \gamma \xi$ of the Greeks, the Pandean pipe, which properly consisted of seven hollow reeds (*calami*) of different lengths and diameters—*Est mihi disparibus septem compacta cicutis = Fistula*. (Virg. Ecl. II. 36.)

Bag-pipes also were not unknown, for we are told by Suetonius that Nero made a vow that he would appear in public as a *Hydraula* and as a *Choraula* and as an UTRICULARIUS. Ner. 54.

The other wind instruments in common use were of a martial character. The *Tuba* was a straight metal trumpet, the *Cornu*, made of the same material, was curved round like a French Horn—*Non Tuba directi non aeris Cornua flexi*, (Ovid. Met. I. 98,) while the *Lituus*, as the name implies, resembled in form the staff of the Augur, and was, therefore, a straight or slightly bent tube with a short spiral curl at the extremity. See representations, pp. 206. 329. 344.

2. *Stringed Instruments.* Chief among these was the Lyre, (*Fides—Lyra* —$\lambda \acute{v} \rho \alpha$,) called also, poetically, *Testudo* or *Chelys*, ($\chi \acute{\epsilon} \lambda \upsilon \varsigma$—$\chi \epsilon \lambda \acute{\omega} \nu \eta$,) because, according to the legend recounted at full length in the Homeric hymn, the frame of the first Lyre was formed by Hermes out of the shell of a tortoise. The number of strings (*Nervi—Chordae—Fides—Fila*) was different at different periods, and we meet with many variations in this respect, as well as in the general shape of the instrument, in the numerous representations which appear on ancient monuments, of which we have given a few examples in p. 231, and one in p. 450. When it assumed its most perfect form, however, they did not exceed seven, and they were struck either with the fingers, especially the thumb, or with a pointed instrument resembling a pencil in shape, (see cut in p. 450,) called by the Romans *Pecten*, or, when they adopted the Greek term, *Plectrum*, ($\pi \lambda \tilde{\eta} \varkappa \tau \rho o \nu$.) Thus Orpheus in Virgil (Æn. VI. 646,)

> Obloquitur numeris septem discrimina vocum,
> Iamque eadem digitis, iam pectine pulsat eburno.

Many other stringed instruments are occasionally mentioned, such as the *Cithara* and the *Barbitos*, differing, probably, from the Lyre, but we cannot

2 G

speak with any certainty respecting their characteristics. The *Sambuca* was triangular, and the strings, therefore, of unequal lengths, as in the harp.

Tambourines, (*Tympana*,) Cymbals, (*Cymbala*,) and Castanets, (*Crotala*,) were employed chiefly in the orgiastic rites of Dionysus, Cybele, and the Syrian Goddess. Nor ought we to pass over the *Sistrum*, so often alluded to by the Roman writers of the first century in connection with the worship of Isis, who, in the annexed cut, is represented bearing it in her hand.

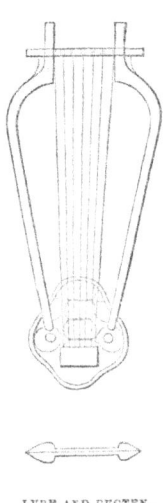

LYRE AND PECTEN.

III. DRESS.

Dress of Men.[1]—The dress of men among the Romans was, during the whole of the best period of their history, extremely simple, consisting of a loose upper garment or plaid of ample dimensions, called *Toga*, and of an under garment or shirt which fitted more closely to the person, called *Tunica*. The feet were protected either by sandals, called *Soleae*, or by shoes, called *Calcei*. The head was not usually covered, but those who were much exposed to the weather sometimes used a felt cap called *Pileus*, or had a hood or cowl called *Cucullus* attached to their cloaks. The *Causia* and the *Petasus* were broad brimmed hats worn by those who had weak eyes, and by travellers. Both are Greek words, and hence we may infer that the objects which they represented were foreign importations.

Toga.—The *Toga* was in all ages regarded as the characteristic garb of the Romans, who were hence designated as emphatically the *Gens Togata*—

---

[1] The most important Treatises on this subject are, OCTAVIUS FERRARIUS, *De Re Vestiaria*, and his *Analecta De Re Vestiaria*; ALBERTUS RUBENIUS, *De Re Vestiaria praecipue de Lato Clavo*; J. B. DONIUS, *De utraque Paenula*; ALDUS MANUTIUS, *De Toga Romanorum*, and *De Tunica Romanorum*; all of which are contained in the sixth volume of the *Thesaurus of* GRAEVIUS.

DRESS OF MEN.

Romanos rerum dominos GENTEMQUE TOGATAM. Although too cumbrous to be worn by those engaged in manual labour, and probably often thrown aside in the domestic circle, it was always assumed by persons in the upper classes when they appeared in public, and, at a late epoch, under the empire, when it had been in a great measure superseded in ordinary life by other forms of apparel, it was still regarded as the dress in which a Roman was expected to appear in the presence of the Prince.[1] The *Toga* was not only the characteristic dress of a Roman citizen, while the Greek *Pallium* distinguished foreigners, but the right of wearing it was the exclusive privilege of citizens, its use being forbidden to *Peregrini* and slaves (p. 85.)[2] It was, moreover, the garb of peace in contradistinction to the *Sagum* (p. 401) of the soldier, and hence the word *Toga* is employed to denote *Peace*, as in the well-known line of Cicero—*Cedant arma* TOGAE, *concedat laurea linguae.*

The shape of the *Toga* and the manner in which it was worn, have given rise to many controversies, and although much information is afforded by the statements of ancient writers, and especially by ancient statues and other works of art, these do not in all instances harmonize with each other. Indeed, it is reasonable to believe, that, while the general character of the garment remained the same, fashion would introduce changes and modifications both in the shape, the dimensions, and the mode of adjustment, and something would at all times depend upon individual fancy. We may rather feel surprised when we consider the long space of time over which the accounts and representations extend, that the variations from something like a fixed standard should not be more numerous and more complicated. There can be no reasonable doubt that, while the Greek *Pallium* was a square, or, at least, a rectangular piece of cloth, the outline of the *Toga* was partly curved. Dionysius expressly terms it (III. 61) περιβόλαιον ἡμικύκλιον, while Quintilian, who gives minute directions regarding the most graceful mode of arranging it, declares (I. O. XI. 3.)—*Ipsam togam* ROTUNDAM ESSE *et apte caesam velim.* We must not, however, press these expressions so closely as to conclude that the *Toga* must have been exactly semicircular, a figure which cannot be reconciled with the appearance which it bears in works of art; but if we assume, with Becker, that, while the upper edge or chord of the curve was straight, extending, as we learn from Horace, (Epod. IV. 8.) in the case of fops, to six *Ulnae*, it was deeper in its greatest breadth than if the lower edge had been exactly semicircular, we shall find many difficulties removed. But, even if we suppose the shape and the dimensions to have been fixed, it is manifest that great room must have been left for the exercise of individual taste in arranging the voluminous folds (*Sinus*) so as to produce the most graceful effect, and, it must be confessed, that the manner in which this huge mass of cloth was thrown round the figure and kept in its place, is very obscure. The two illustrations, A and B, given below, both taken from ancient statues, represent two different adjustments, one evidently much more simple than the other, but it will be found extremely difficult to reproduce either of them. It would appear that the ordinary mode was to throw the whole *Toga* over the left shoulder, leaving one extremity to cover the left arm, and to bring it round the back and under the right arm, which remained at liberty, the second end being carried again over the left shoulder. In this way, the broadest part of the cloth hung down in front, a large bunch or mass of plaits, termed *Umbo*, lay across the breast, and the second extremity, which was carried across, served

---
[1] Suet. Octav. 40. Spartian. vit. Sever. 1. comp. Lamprid. Commod. 16.
[2] Plin. Epp. IV. 11. Suet. Claud. 15. Comp. Cic. pro Rabir. 9. in Verr. IV. 24. V. 13. 33

as a sort of belt (*Balteus*) to secure the whole. Compare A and B with Quintilian I. O. XI. iii. 137. On certain occasions of extraordinary solemnity,

as when a Consul was about to declare war in the name of the Roman people, or to devote himself to death for his country, the *Toga* was brought over the head and girded round the body, according to what was termed the *Cinctus Gabinus*. The details have been described by Servius in his Commentary on the Æneid, (VII. 612,) and the illustration marked C, taken from the celebrated Vatican MS. of Virgil, is intended to represent this adjustment. See also Liv. V. 46. VIII. 9.

Tunica. Subucula.—The *Tunica*, as indicated above, was a sort of shirt worn under the *Toga*, and buckled round the waist by a girdle (*Cinctus—Cingula—Cingulum.*) It reached an inch or two below the knees, and the sleeves were so short that they merely covered the shoulders, for although Tunics hanging down to the ancles, (*Tunicae talares,*) and with sleeves extending to the wrists and terminating in fringes (*Tunicae Manicatae et Fimbriatae*) were not unknown towards the close of the republic, they were always regarded as indications of effeminate foppery.[1] An under shirt, termed *Subucula*, appears to have been an ordinary piece of dress in the days of Horace—*rides si forte Subucula pexae = Trita subest Tunicae*, (Epp. I. i. 95,) and Augustus was so intolerant of cold, that he enveloped himself in a thick *Toga*, four *Tunicae*, a *Subucula*, and a bosom-friend, besides swathes for the legs and thighs—*Hyeme quaternis, cum pingui* TOGA, TUNICIS *et* SUBUCULA, *et* THORACE *laneo, et* FEMINALIBUS *et* TIBIALIBUS (Suet. Oct. 82.)

Indusium or *Intusium* is explained by Nonius and Varro to mean a *Tunica*, but while the former expressly states that it was an under Tunic—*vestimentum*

---

[1] Quintil. I.O. X. iii. 137. Aul. Gell. VII 12. Cic. in Cat. II. 10. Suet. Iul. 5. Ner. 51. Plin. H.N. XXVIII. 9.

DRESS OF MEN.

quod corpori intra plurimas vestes adhaeret—the words of the latter, although obscure, imply that it was an upper Tunic—that while *Capitium* was the general term for an under garment, (*ab eo quod capit pectus,*) the *Subucula* was the under Tunic, and the *Supparus* the upper Tunic, and, farther, that there were two varieties of the *Supparus*, one called *Indusium* and the other *Palla*.

Varro, in the same passages, classes all garments under two heads, those which were of the close shirt-like form, and those which were thrown loosely round the person—*Prius dein* INDUTUI, *tum* AMICTUI *quae sunt tangam.*[1]

It is stated by Aulus Gellius, (VII. 12,) that the Romans originally wore the *Toga* alone, but this must be understood to mean that they did not wear both the *Toga* and the *Tunica* at the same time, for the former could never have been the sole garment of men employed in any pursuit requiring active bodily exertion. Hence, in later times, we find those who affected primitive simplicity were wont to appear in public without a Tunic, and especially candidates for public offices, in order, perhaps, that they might the more readily display the scars of any wounds they had received in front.[2] What a graceful effect might be produced by the simple *Toga*, may be seen from the figure (1) below, which is taken from a statue of Jupiter in the gallery at Florence.

(1) (3) (2)

Fasciae, &c.—Coverings for the legs did not form a regular part of ordinary dress, but the limbs were generally left bare, except in so far as they were covered by the *Tunica* and *Toga*. Occasionally, however, strips of cloth, called *Fasciae* or *Fasciolae*, were swathed round the legs like bandages, a fashion still common among the peasants of southern Italy, and, according as they were applied above or below the knees, were termed *Feminalia*, *Cruralia*, *Tibialia*, and sometimes *Fasciae crurales*, and *Fasciae pedules*, besides which

---

[1] Varro L.L. V. § 131. ap. Non. s.v. *Capitia*, p. 371. ed. Gerl. Non. s.v. *Indusium*, p. 369. ed. Gerl. The word was written *Indusium* or *Intusium*, according as it was derived from *Induo* or from *Intus*.
[2] Plut. Cor. 14. Cat. Min. 6. Q. R. 49. Liv. III. 26. Dionys. X. 17.

we hear of *Ventralia*, to protect the abdomen. Cravats, also, or something corresponding to them, were not entirely unknown, for Horace enumerates, among the equipments of a coxcomb, *Fasciolas, Cubital, Focalia*, (S. II. iii. 255,) where *Focalia* must signify a *throat-muffler*.[1]

Calcei, &c.—The *Calceus*, as indicated above, was a shoe covering the whole foot, the *Solea*, a sandal consisting of a sole only, without upper leathers, fastened round the instep and ancle by straps (*ligulae*.) Both of these were strictly Roman, and are opposed to the *Crepida* of the Greeks,[2] just as the *Toga* is opposed to the *Pallium*. The various shapes which *Calcei* and *Soleae* assumed,

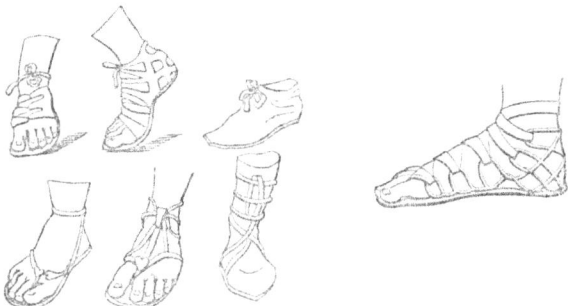

and the different methods of fastening them, will be better understood by studying the annexed representations selected by Becker from ancient monuments, than from the most elaborate description in words.

During inclement weather, additional clothing was required, and we are acquainted with the names of various upper cloaks, but are almost entirely in the dark as to their characteristic shape. Those most frequently mentioned are the *Lacerna*, the *Laena*, and the *Paenula*, to which we may add the *Synthesis*, the *Abolla*, and the *Endromis*. The *Lacerna* and the *Laena* were properly thrown over the *Toga* for warmth, but under the empire seem to have been often adopted as a substitute for it, and were then made of the finest materials, and dyed of the most showy colours;[3] the *Paenula* is generally believed to have resembled what is now called a *poncho*, that is, to have been a thick blanket with a hole cut in the centre, through which the head was inserted. The statue represented above, and marked (2) is supposed to be dressed in a *Paenula*, but this is a mere conjecture. The *Synthesis* was a loose easy robe worn at table instead of the more unwieldy *Toga*, and seems to have been the prototype of the modern *domino*, since every one appeared with it in public during the Saturnalia, but at no other season; of the *Abolla* we can say almost nothing, except that Juvenal speaks of it as the dress of the Stoics; (S. III. 115. comp. IV. 76;) the *Endromis* was a cloth wrapped round the body by athletes after violent exertion, in order to guard against a chill.

Official Dresses.—These have been for the most part already noticed in

---

[1] Non. s.v. *Calantica*, p. 367, ed. Gerl. Quintil. I.O. XI. iii. Cic. ad Att. II. 3. Val. Max. VI. ii. 7. Suet. Octav. 82. Plin. H.N. VIII. 48. 57. Digest. XXXIV. ii. 25.
[2] *Non hic qui in* CREPIDAS GRAIORUM *ludere gestit*. Pers. S. 1. 127. See also Liv. XXIX. 19, and Suet. Tiber. 13.
[3] The *Laena*, or, at all events, a robe called *Laena*, was worn by the *Flamines*, when offering sacrifice (Cic. Brut. 14. Serv. ad Virg. Æn. IV. 262.

connection with the different offices to which they belonged. The most common of these was the *Toga Praetexta*, a *Toga* with a purple border, worn by Dictators, Consuls, Praetors, Curule Aediles, the higher orders of Priests, by all freeborn youths until they assumed the *Toga Virilis*, and by girls until they were married, or had, at least, attained to mature years. The *Trabea* was an upper garment with broad purple stripes, which is said to have been the dress of the kings, and was subsequently assumed by the *Equites* in their solemn processions, and perhaps by the Augurs. The *Toga Picta*, an embroidered robe, was the garb in which the statue of Jupiter Capitolinus was arrayed, and was worn by generals when they triumphed, along with the *Tunica Palmata*. The Emperors, on state occasions, appeared in a *Toga*, all purple, and some have supposed that this belonged to the Censors under the republic. Of the *Tunica Laticlavia*, and the *Tunica Angusticlavia* we have already said enough when describing the Insignia of Senators, and of the *Ordo Equester* (pp. 75, 221.) The meaning of the phrase *Mutare Vestem* has been already explained, p. 75.

Hair, Beard, &c.—In the earlier ages the Romans wore long flowing hair and beards. Hence when Juvenal wishes to indicate that the master of a feast was drinking wine of great age, he says—*Ipse* CAPILLATO *diffusum* CONSULE *potat*—while Tibullus and Ovid speak of their countrymen in the olden time as *Intonsi avi*. Varro and Pliny inform us that hair-dressers (*Tonsores*) came from Sicily in B.C. 300, (*antea intonsi fuere*,) and that the younger Scipio Africanus was the first person of note who shaved every day (*radi quotidie instituit.*) This operation was performed in two different modes. They either shaved off the beard smooth (*tondere strictim*) with a razor, (*novacula—Culter,*) or merely clipped it short through a comb (*tondere per pectinem*) with scissors (*Axicia.*) The custom of wearing beards was revived under the empire, by Hadrian, who is frequently represented on coins and other monuments *Barbatus*. The barber's-shop (*Tonstrina*) seems, from a very early period, to have been a favourite lounging-place, as we gather from Plautus, who enumerates all the apparatus employed, knife or razor (*Culter*) for the beard and nails, scissors, (*Axicia,*) comb, (*Pecten,*) Tweezers (*Volsellae*) for plucking out stray hairs, curling tongs, (*Calamistrum,*) mirror, (*Speculum,*) towel, (*Linteum,*) and dressing-gown (*Involucre iniicere vestem ne inquinet.*)[1]

Ornaments.—The only personal ornaments worn by men were rings, (*Annuli,*) and these were originally made of iron and carried for use, in sealing letters and other documents, (*Obsignare,*) rather than for decoration. On the right of wearing a golden ring during the republic we have already spoken fully (p. 75.) Under the empire all restrictions seem to have been removed, and it was not uncommon to wear a ring on every finger, or several on the same finger, while some persons, like Crispinus in Iuvenal, varied them according to the season of the year,

> Ventilet aestivum digitis sudantibus aurum
> Nec sufferre queat maioris pondera gemmae,

and kept those not in use, in cases called *Dactyliothecae.*[2]

Dress of Women.—Although we must conclude from two well-known passages in Plautus, (Aul. III. v. 34—47. Epid. II. ii. 39—50.) that even at the

---

[1] Iuv. S. V. 30. Tibull. II. i. 34. Ovid. Fast. II. 30. Liv. V. 41. Plin. H. N. VII. 59. Varro R. R. II. 11. Aul. Gell. III. 4. Plaut. Capt. II. ii. 16. Epid. II. ii. 13. Asin. II. ii. 86. Curcul. IV. iv. 21. Martial. III. 74. VIII. 47. IX. 28.

[2] Pliny gives numerous details with regard to the history of Rings XXXVII. 1. Comp. Iuv. S. I. 28. XI. 43. Martial. XI. 37. 59. XIV. 123. Quintil. I. O. XI. 3.

early epoch to which that dramatist belongs, Roman ladies employed a great variety of stuffs in adorning their persons, and that their wardrobes exhibited many different fashions, yet the garments themselves were few in number, and their general character always the same. The dress of a matron consisted of three parts—

1. The *Tunica interior* s. *intima*, or, as it was termed at a later period, *Interula*, a short shift fitting close to the body, over which was placed a belt, called *Mamillare* or *Strophium*, to give support to the bosom.[1]

2. The *Stola*, a loose tunic, to the bottom of which a border or flounce, called *Instita*, was sewed, the whole reaching down so low as to conceal the ancles and part of the feet—*Quaeque tegis medios Instita longa pedes* (Ovid. A.A. I. 32.) The *Stola*, with the *Instita* attached, was the characteristic dress of the Roman matron. Hence when Horace wishes to indicate matrons as a class, he styles them—*illas* = *Quarum subsuta talos tegit Instita veste;* (S. I. ii. 29;) and Martial (I. 36.) employs the phrase *Stolatum pudorem*. The *Stola* was gathered and confined at the waist by a girdle, (*Zona*—*Cingulum*—*Cinctus*,) and frequently ornamented at the throat by a coloured border called *Patagium*.

3. The *Palla*, a shawl so large as to envelope the whole figure, thrown over the *Stola* when a lady went abroad—*Ad talos Stola demissa et circumdata Palla* (Hor. S. I. ii. 99.)[2]

In the cut marked (3) in p. 453, taken from a statue of the Empress Livia, found at Pompeii, we see distinctly the *Tunica Interior*, the *Stola*, and the *Palla*. Here it will be observed that the inner Tunic has sleeves, while the *Stola* is fastened over the shoulders by simple straps; but this was not the case universally, for several ancient monuments show the inner Tunic without, and the *Stola* with, sleeves.

Just as men occasionally wore a *Lacerna* or a *Laena* over the *Toga*, so women occasionally threw a second cloak over the *Palla*. This, in the most ancient times, was called *Ricinium*. Livy and Ovid, when describing something of the same kind, use the general terms, *Amiculum* and *Amictus*.[3]

Peregrinae, *Libertinae*, and all women of doubtful reputation, instead of wearing the *Stola* and *Palla*, were attired in a shorter Tunic, without the *Instita*, and in a *Toga*, the latter usually of a dark colour.[4] The word *Palla* is applied to the robe of tragic actors and of musicians; but we know not whether this was identical in form with the *Palla* of women.[5]

Head Dress.—Great pains were bestowed upon plaiting and arranging the hair, as may be seen from the numerous representations upon ancient coins and statues; the aid of hair dressers (*Ciniflones*—*Cinerarii*) and curling tongs (*Calamistra*) was called in, various unguents and dyes were applied, and the great object of ambition under the empire being yellow hair, wigs of this colour (*Galerus flavus*) were substituted for the natural locks.[6] Coverings of different kinds for the head were also common, such as nets, (*Reticula*,) veils, (*Ricae* s. *Riculae*,) as well as caps and turbans of various shapes (*Mitrae*, *Calanticae*, &c.)

Ornaments, &c.—These consisted of necklaces, (*Monilia*,) bracelets or arm-

[1] Aul. Gell. VI. 10. X. 15. Apulei Florid. II. 9. § 1. Met. VIII. 159. Catull. LXIV. 65. Martial. XIV. 66. Non. s.v. *Strophium*, p. 368 ed. Gerl.
[2] Comp. Senec. Troad. I. 91. On the manner in which the *Palla* was adjusted, see Apulei. Met. XI.
[3] Varro L L. V. § 131. Liv. XXVII. 4. Ovid. Met. XIV. 262.
[4] Hor. S. I. ii. and Schol. Cruq. on the passage. Tibull. IV. x. 3.
[5] Hor. A.P. 278. Auct. ad Herenn. IV. 47.
[6] Ovid. A.A. III. 163. Iuv. S. VI. 120. Martial. V. 68. XII. 23.

lets, (*Armillae,*) earrings, (*Inaures,*) chains, (*Catellae,*) made of gold and decorated with pearls (*Margaritae—Uniones*) and precious stones of every description, which were kept in jewel boxes (*Arculae.*) The toilet furniture (*Mundus muliebris*) consisted of mirrors made of polished metal, (*Specula,*) perfume bottles, (*Vasa unguentaria,*) combs, (*Pectines,*) and a countless variety of cosmetics, (*Medicamina faciei,*) among which rouge (*Purpurissum*) and white paint (*Cerussa*) were not forgotten.[1]

Materials of Dress.—All the garments of both sexes, although differing widely in texture and quality, according to the seasons of the year and the circumstances of the wearer, were for many centuries made of wool exclusively, and although various new fabrics, composed of silk, cotton, and flax, were introduced towards the close of the republic and under the empire, they were never adopted by any large portion of the community. The wool was not dyed but was allowed to retain its natural colour, white, (*alba,*) under ordinary circumstances, and black (*pulla*) for those who were in mourning, and who, when dressed in their dark apparel, were said to be *Pullati* or *Atrati*. The various articles of dress, when cleansed, were not simply washed, but were elaborately scoured with sulphur and other purifying substances, by a class of persons called *Fullones*. Those who were impeached of any offence against the State, frequently endeavoured to excite public sympathy, by appearing abroad *Sordidati*, i.e. with *Vestes Sordidae*, typifying by the neglect of their personal appearance the mental depression under which they were labouring. The term opposed to *Sordidati* is *Candidati*, which has been already explained, p. 177.

The Roman conquests in the East led to the importation of silk, (*Sericum,*) but the cost of the raw material was so great, that thin gauzes (*Coae vestes*) were chiefly employed, or cloths in which the woof was of silk (*Trama ex Serico*) and the warp of flax, (*Stamine lineo,*) these stuffs being termed *Vestes subsericae*, in contradistinction to the *Vestes holosericae*, composed entirely of silk. Dresses of such materials were at first almost confined to women, and so unbecoming was it considered for a man to appear in them, that during the reign of Tiberius, the Senate passed a decree—*Ne Vestis Serica viros foedaret* (Tacit. Ann. II. 33.) Although this regulation may have soon been disregarded or evaded, it is evident that while silk was worth its weight in gold, its use must have been very limited.[2] Cotton also, although not unknown, was rare; but it appears very strange and unaccountable that flax, although cultivated in Italy, and used for many domestic purposes, was never employed generally, until a late epoch, for articles of dress, insomuch that the priests of Isis were at once marked out to the eye as a distinct class by the circumstance of their being robed in linen (*linigera turba.*)

It is generally assumed that the words *Byssus, Carbasus, Linum, Sindon, Supparus* s. *Supparum,* signify different kinds of flax and of linen cloth; that *Bombyx, Vestes Bombycinae, Coae Vestes, Sericum, Sericae Vestes,* all indicate silk; and that *Gossipium* and *Xylinum* (sc. *linum*) mean cotton. But on examining carefully the passages in ancient authors where these words occur, it will be found that much obscurity and confusion prevail; that the terms usually

---

[1] Plaut. Mostell. I. iii. 91, seqq. Ovid. Medic. fac. passim. A.A. III. 197. Cic. Orat. 23. Iuv. S. VI. 481. It is doubtful whether the *Periscelis* mentioned in Horace was an article of dress or an ornament worn round the ancle (Hor. Epp. I. xvii. 56.) The most complete account of all matters connected with the toilet of a Roman lady under the empire is to be found in the work of BOETTIGER entitled *Sabina.*
[2] Plin. H.N. VI. 17. Senec. de Ben. VII. 9. Dion Cass. XLIII. 24. LII. 15. Suet. Calig. 52. Lamprid. Alex. Sev. 40. Elagab. 26. Vopisc. Aurelian. 45. Tacit. 10. Isidor. XIX. xxii.

translated *Silk* and *Silken* must in many cases refer to muslins or other delicate manufactures of cotton, which, like silk, were brought from the far East, and that although nothing is more certain than that, in ordinary language, *Linum*, with its derivatives, *Lineus*, *Linteus*, *Linteo*, and *Lintearius*, all refer to flax, yet we shall find *Linum* and *Byssus* both used to denote cotton, while *Sindon* is sometimes linen, sometimes muslin or calico.[1]

Spinning and Weaving.—Not only were woollen stuffs employed exclusively for many centuries, but in the earlier ages the cloth was all home-made. Spinning and Weaving were considered honourable in themselves, and formed the chief occupation of females in every rank. The family loom long stood in the *Atrium*, the public apartment of the mansion, and here the mistress of the house sat and toiled, surrounded by her female slaves.

A quantity of wool was weighed out to each handmaid, (hence *Pensum* signifies a task,) which she was required first to card, (*carpere—carpere herile pensum*,) and then to spin into yarn. The latter operation was performed by means of a distaff (*Colus*) and spindle, (*Fusus*,) the method practised in this country at no very remote epoch, and still almost universal in southern Italy. A most graphic and charming description of the process will be found in Catullus, where he represents the Fates plying their task at the nuptials of Peleus and Thetis (LXIV. 312-320.) The different parts of the Loom and of the Web are in like manner enumerated by Ovid when describing the struggle of Arachne with Minerva, and are frequently alluded to in the classics.[2] The frame of the Loom, which was generally placed vertically, and not horizontally, was called *Jugum*, the web was *Tela*, the loops, which are now called *Heddles*, were the *Licia*, the warp or longitudinal threads of the web *Stamen*, the woof or cross threads *Trama* or *Subtemen*, the reed by which the threads of the warp were kept separate, so as to afford a passage for the shuttle, was *Arundo*, the shuttle itself was *Radius*, the lay by which the threads of the woof are driven home was *Pecten* (*Illa etiam radio* STANTES *percurrere* TELAS = *Erudit et rarum* PECTINE DENSET OPUS. Ovid. Fast. III. 819.)

IV. WRITING MATERIALS, BOOKS, LIBRARIES, &c.

We may pass over very briefly those substances which were resorted to from the most remote epochs for recording and preserving public acts and national documents of every description, and on which the characters were cut and not inscribed. Such were slabs of stone. (*incisa notis marmora publicis*, Hor. C. IV. viii. 13.)—plates of copper or bronze, (*leges Decemvirales . . . in aes incisas publice proposuerunt*, Liv. III. 57.) which were employed almost exclusively, down to a very late period, for registering the ordinances of the People and the decrees of the Senate—sheets of lead, the *plumbea volumina* of Pliny (H.N. XIII. 11.)—and slabs of wood (*oppida moliri, leges incidere ligno*, Hor. A.P. 399.)[3] Nor can we enter into any examination of the use of palm leaves, (*in palmarum foliis primo scriptitatum*, Plin. l. c.) nor of the bark of trees, (*liber*,) still manufactured for such purposes in the East; nor of the prepared linen of which the ancient *Lintei libri*, referred to by Livy (IV. 7. 13. 20.)

---

[1] On these and all topics connected with the textile fabrics of the ancients, see the masterly treatise of YATES, entitled *Textrinum Antiquorum*, a work which, to the regret of every scholar, has not yet been completed.

[2] Ovid. Met. VI. 54. comp. Fast. III. 816—820.

[3] In Aulus Gellius (II. 12.) we read—*In legibus Solonis illis antiquissimis, quae Athenis* AXIBUS LIGNEIS (alii leg. *asseribus*) *incisae sunt*, &c.

must, as their name implies, have been composed. We confine ourselves to the consideration of the materials which were in ordinary use after the Romans had become a literary people, and when writings of all descriptions were multiplied to an extent altogether unknown in the earlier ages.

These materials may be divided into two classes, according as the writing was intended for permanent preservation, or consisted of notes made for a temporary purpose only. In the former case, the materials employed were either Paper (*Charta*) or Parchment, (*Membrana*,) in the latter, thin pieces of board coated with wax (*Tabulae ceratae*.)

1. Paper, termed *Charta*, was made from the reedy plant called *Papyrus*, the *Cyperus Papyrus* of modern botanists, which grew in great abundance amid the stagnant waters left by the inundations of the Nile. Paper from the *Papyrus* was used in Egypt at a period far beyond the records of authentic history, for fragments of it covered with writing are found attached to the oldest mummies. It was imported into Rome from Alexandria in large quantities towards the close of the republic and under the empire, and manufactories (*Officinae*) existed in the metropolis for the purpose of making it up into different forms. Eight varieties were known during the early part of the first century; the best quality was *Charta Augusta*, the second *Liviana*, the third *Hieratica*, this in ancient times having been the epithet applied to the best; the lowest was called *Emporetica*, and was used for tying up parcels only. In consequence of certain improvements introduced by the emperor Claudius, the *Charta Claudia* eventually took precedence even of the *Augusta*. The mode in which the *Papyrus* was manufactured into paper has been minutely described by Pliny, who is our great authority upon this topic, (H.N. XIII. 11, 12.) but he is more than usually obscure and confused in his phraseology when describing the process. We gather, however, from his words, that the stem of the *Papyrus* was cut into lengths, and that the inner substance was separated into very thin strips or slices (*philyrae*) by a sharp pointed instrument (*acus*.) Two of these *philyrae* were placed one above the other, the direction of the fibres in the one being at right angles to the fibres of the other, and glued together to form the thickness of the paper; several of these strips were then placed side by side and glued together to form a strip of the proper breadth, which was now termed *Scheda*, or *Pagina*, or *Plagula*, the breadth varying in the different qualities, that of the *Augusta* being 13 *Digiti*, (p. 409,) that of the *Hieratica* 11. Again, several *Schedae* or *Plagulae* were glued together to form a full sized sheet called *Scapus*, the number of *Plagulae* so united never exceeding twenty. The *Claudia* was thicker than any of the other kinds, being composed of three *philyrae* placed above each other; in breadth, too, it exceeded even the *Augusta*, being a foot wide, (*pedalis*,) and the particular variety called *Macrocolum* or *Macrocollum* [1] was a foot and a-half wide (*cubitalis*.)

2. Parchment or Vellum, termed *Pergamena* (sc. *membrana*) because the invention of it was ascribed to one of the early kings of Pergamus, was also extensively used, but being much more costly than *Charta* made of the *Papyrus*, was employed for those documents only which were regarded as of great importance and value.

Pens and Ink.—The pen for writing upon paper or parchment was made of a reed, and hence is termed *Arundo* s. *Calamus* s. *Fistula*, and was formed into the proper shape by a penknife—the *Scalprum librarium*. Ink, termed *Atramen-*

---

[1] The term *Macrocollum*, applied to paper of large size, was known to Cicero, see Epp. ad. Att. XIII. 25. XVI. 3.

tum, was generally composed of lamp-black (obtained by burning pitch or rosin) mixed with gum water or some other glutinous liquid. *Sepia* also, the dark fluid contained in the bag of the cuttle fish, was used as a substitute for *Atramentum*.[1]

Since the common *Atramentum* contained no mordant, it did not necessarily make an indelible mark upon parchment, but might be easily obliterated by the application of a wet sponge; if, however, in consequence of the skin not being properly dressed, or from some other cause, the black marks could not be removed in this manner, the surface of the *membrana* might be rendered available for the reception of fresh writing by scraping it with pumice-stone or any similar substance, and hence second-hand parchment renovated in this manner was called *Palimpsestus*.[2]

Writing was confined to one side of the *Charta* or *Membrana*, except when an author was hard pressed for room, or when old MSS. were given to boys in order that they might copy out their exercises on the back. Such writing was distinguished by the epithet *Opisthographus*.[3]

3. *Tabula* properly signifies *a board*, and the commonest of all writing materials were small thin boards (*Tabellae*) covered with a coating of wax, (*Cera rasis infusa tabellis*,) the characters being formed by an iron pencil termed *Stilus* or *Graphium*, which was ground to a sharp point at one end for scratching the wax, and flattened at the other for smoothing the surface when it was desired to obliterate what had been inscribed—hence the phrase *Vertere Stilum* signifies *To make an erasure*. When several of these *Tabellae* were united together, they formed books, which were termed *Codices* s. *Codicilli*; (*Plurium Tabularum contextus*;) when these were of small dimensions, they were called *Pugillares*, and according as they consisted of two, three, or more leaves, were distinguished as *Diptychi, Triptychi, Triplices, Quincuplices*, &c. Instead of common deal, the precious *Citrus* wood was sometimes employed for *Pugillares*, and they were frequently decorated with costly ornaments.[4]

Although the words *Tabulae, Tabellae, Codices, Codicilli*, properly refer to tablets covered with wax, they are constantly employed in a general sense to denote written documents of any description, whatever might be the material employed. Thus *Tabulae Testamenti* is the received phrase for a *Will*, although such a deed would doubtless be generally engrossed on paper or parchment, and Horace designates the first page of a Will as *Prima cera* (S. II. V. 53.) But *Pugillares* might be made of parchment or of ivory; and thus one of the Epigrams of Martial (XIV. 7.) bears as its Lemma *Pugillares Membranei*, and another (XIV. 5.) *Pugillares Eborei*, while in an inscription (Orelli No. 3838) we read of *Pugillares membranaceos cum operculis eboreis*.

Liber.—Observe that *Liber* signifies properly the inner bark of a tree, especially of the *Tilia* or Linden-tree, and that *Philyrae* are the thin layers or membranes of which the *Liber* is composed. This substance having been prepared in early ages for writing, just as the *Philyrae* of the *Papyrus* were in Egypt, the word *Liber*, in process of time, was employed like *Tabulae*, to denote a book or document of any description without reference to the material—LIB-RORUM *appellatione continentur omnia volumina, sive in charta, sine in mem-*

---

[1] Pers. S. III. 11. seqq.   Cic. ad Att. VI. 8.   Suet. Vitell. 2.   Tacit. Ann. V. 8.   Vitruv. VII. 10   Plin. H.N XXXV. 6. XXXVII. 7.
[2] Cic. ad Fam. VII. 18. Catull. XXII. 14.
[3] Iuv. S. I. 5. Martial. IV. 86 Plin. Epp. III. 5. Digest XXXVII. xi. 4.
[4] Ovid. A.A. I. 437.   Hor. S. I. x. 72.   Cic. in Verr. IV. 41.   Senec. de brev. vit. 13. Martial. XIV. 3. Senec. Ep. CVIII. Auson. Epigr. 146. Very small *Pugillares* were called *Vitelliani*, Martial. XIV. 8. 9.

brana sint, sive in quavis alia materia. Sed et si in Philyra, aut Tilia, ut nonnulli conficiunt, aut in aliquo corio, idem erit dicendum. Ulpian. Digest. XXXII. 52.

Letters.—Letters were generally written upon waxed tablets, but also upon paper and parchment.[1] When Chrysalus in the Bacchides of Plautus tells Pistoclerus to fetch her all things necessary for writing a letter, she names

Stilum, Ceram, et Tabellas, et Linum.—IV. iv. 64.

The *Cera* mentioned here is for sealing the string (*Linum*) with which the tablets were tied together; and when the wax was thus applied, it was stamped with the impression of a signet-ring, this operation being termed *Obsignare*. Thus, in the scene above quoted, after the letter is finished, the writer exclaims,

Cedo tu Ceram ac Linum actutum, age OBLIGA, OBSIGNA, cito.

Hence, when a letter was opened, the first operation was to destroy the seal—*Resignare*—the next to cut the string—*Linum incidere* (Cic. in Cat. III. 5.) Instead of wax, a sort of clay, or perhaps gypsum, called *Cretula*, was in common use (Cic. in Verr. IV. 9.)

Transmission of Letters.—Since the Roman government had no post-office establishment, persons of small means were obliged to take advantage of any opportunity which might occur for transmitting their letters, while the rich and the *Societates* of *Publicani* kept regular couriers, called *Tabellarii*, for the purpose.[2]

Book-Binding, Libraries, &c.—When a work was completed, the different strips of paper or parchment on which it was written were glued to each other in regular order, so as to form one long sheet. To the lower extremity a cylindrical piece of wood was attached, round which the whole was rolled, and thus a *Volumen* was formed. The two circular ends of the wooden cylinder, the only portions of it visible when the MS. was rolled up, were termed *Umbilici*, and hence the word *Umbilicus* was used to denote the cylinder itself, which gave rise to the phrase *Ad umbilicum adducere*, signifying *to bring to a conclusion*. The two *Umbilici* were sometims decorated with colours, (hence, *picti umbilici*,) and sometimes two knobs, called *Cornua*, were attached to them. The rough outside edges of the roll, named *Frontes*, were cut even and smoothed with pumice stone, (*geminae poliantur pumice Frontes*,) the back of the roll was rubbed over with oil of cedar, (*oleum ex Cedro*, Vitruv. II. 9,) which was believed to possess the property of preserving it from the attacks of moths and other insects (*Tineae—Blattae*.) An outside wrapper (the σιττύβη of the Greeks) dyed of some bright colour, yellow or purple, (*Lutea sed niveum involvat membrana libellum—Nec te purpureo velent vaccinia fuco*,) was then fitted on, and secured by red strings (*lora rubra*.) Finally, the title (*Index—Titulus*—Σιλλύβος) was written in scarlet letters (*Titulus notetur minio—Index rubeat cocco*) on thin parchment, (*membranula*,) and attached to one of the *Umbilici* or of the *Cornua*. Reference will be found at the bottom of the page to the different passages in ancient writers from which the above account has been pieced together.[3]

[1] Cic. ad Fam. VII. 18. ad Q.F. II. 15. Martial. XIV. 11. Digest. XXXIII ix. 3.
[2] Cic. in Verr. III. 79. ad Fam. XII. 12. XIV. 22. Philipp. II. 31.
[3] Catull. I. 1. XXII. Tibull. III. i. 10. Ovid. Trist. I. 1. 5. III. i. 13. E.P. IV. xiii. 7. Hor A.P. 331. Epp. I. xx. 2. Martial. I. 67. 118. III. 2. IV. 91. V. 6. VI. 13. VIII. 61. 72. X. 93. XI. 1. 107. Cic. ad Att. IV. 4. 5. 8. Lucian. advers. indoct. 16.

When books were collected in Libraries, they were deposited in presses or shelves termed *Armaria* s. *Foruli* s. *Loculamenta*, or figuratively, *Nidi*, and when carried about from place to place were packed in boxes called *Scrinia* or *Capsae*.[1] The material most esteemed for the construction of such repositories was the wood of the cypress tree, which was believed to be more durable than any other, and to possess antiseptic properties—hence the exclamation of Horace, (A. P. 331.)

>——————— Speramus carmina fingi
>Posse linenda cedro, et levi servanda cupresso.

Librarii is the general term for that class of slaves who were in any way connected with the book or writing department in an establishment. Hence this name is given to the Transcribers who made copies of works for their master's use or for sale, to Secretaries of every description, (*Librarii ab epistolis—ad manum—a manu—a studiis*,) as well as to those domestics who took charge of the apartment in which the books were kept (*Servi a bibliotheca*.[2])

Librarius is used also to denote *a bookseller*, for these persons, when in a small way of business, would copy out with their own hands the works which they retailed. The names of the books which they had in stock were affixed to posts or pillars (*Pilae—Columnae*) in front of their shops, (*Tabernae Librariae*,) and hence Horace when he declares that he had no wish that his writings should be hawked about, uses the expression (S. I. iv. 71)—*Nulla Taberna meos habeat neque Pila libellos*—and again, in allusion to the same practice (A.P. 372)—*mediocribus esse poetis* = *Non homines, non di, non concessere Columnae*. The *Argiletum* and the *Vicus Sandalius* seem to have been the chief quarters of booksellers under the empire, and the fame of the *Sosii* under Augustus, of *Dorus* under Nero, and of *Tryphon* under Domitian, has been preserved by Horace, Seneca, Martial, and Quintilian.[3]

V. Houses.

The arrangement of a Roman dwelling-house (*Domus—Aedes privatae*) has proved a source of much embarrassment to scholars, and although strong light has been thrown upon the various subjects of discussion by the extensive excavations at Herculaneum and Pompeii, many points are still doubtful, and ample room is still left for controversy. We shall mention in succession the constituent parts which usually made up the town mansion of a man of fortune, during the first century of the empire, and endeavour to determine their relative position in the plan (A) placed at the end of the volume, which represents the ground plan of one of the largest houses at Pompeii, that which is usually distinguished as the *House of Pansa*. It must be borne in mind that many of the rooms there represented were altogether dispensed with in dwellings occupied by persons of small means, while, on the other hand, the most sumptuous edifice in a small provincial town such as Pompeii was, could not vie either in the number

---

[1] Vitruv. VII. Praef. Plin. Epp. II. 17. Senec. de Tranquill. 9. Iuv. S. III. 219. Martial. I. 118. VII. 17. Vopisc. Tacit. 8.

[2] On booksellers, who were frequently designated by the Greek term *Bibliopolae*, and their shops, see Aul. Gell. II. 3. V. 4. XIII. 30. XVIII. 4. See also Cic. de Legg. III. 20. Philipp. II, 9. Hor. Epp. I. xx. 2. A.P. 345. Senec. de Ben. VII. 6. Martial. I. 118. II. 8 IV. 71, 72. XIII. 3. Quintil. I.O. Praef. On the price of popular new publications, see Martial. I. 67. 118. XIII. 3.

[3] On the subject of this section consult Mazois, *Le Palais de Scaurus ou Description d'une Maison Romaine.* Paris. 1822; and the great work of the same author on Pompeii. These, together with the first Excursus to the second scene of Becker's *Gallus*, contain all the materials requisite for the student who may wish to investigate this difficult subject.

or the scale of its apartments with the palaces of the metropolis. The two sources from which we derive the greatest amount of direct information, are the sixth book of Vitruvius, and two letters of the younger Pliny (II. 17. V. 6.) The former, however, contains chiefly architectural precepts for the construction of a house, the different portions of which, in so far as their uses and juxta position were concerned, were familiar to his readers, while in the latter, two Villas are described which, it would appear, differed materially from ordinary town houses.[1]

Insula.—We must begin by explaining this term, which bears two distinct significations. It originally denoted a mass of building, consisting of one or of several houses, surrounded on all sides by streets or lanes, and thus completely detached from other buildings. Even when an *Insula* contained only one regular mansion, there were frequently shops in different parts of the ground story, as is common in Roman and Neapolitan palaces in modern times. Such a mass of building was frequently raised to the height of several stories, and laid out in lodging-houses for the accommodation of single individuals, or of small families belonging to the middle or lower classes, these individuals and families living completely apart, but still under the same roof, as takes place in the *Flats* of a Scotch *Land*, or the *Etages* of a French *Hotel*. Hence *Insula* is employed to denote a single lodging-house, or set of apartments, and the person employed by the proprietor to exercise a general superintendence over the whole of the separate *Insulae*, which were included in the large *Insula*, was named *Insularius*, his duties being probably analogous to those of a *Concierge* in French establishments of a similar nature. The mass of building represented in the plan (A) at the end of the volume is an *Insula* in the first sense, containing not only the mansion, called the *House of Pansa*, but also a number of shops marked (x), and four small lodgings marked (z), none of which had any communication with the House of Pansa, and would thus be termed *Insulae* in the second sense.[1]

Vestibulum. Area.—The door of the house was frequently thrown back to a considerable distance from the street, and an open space was left in front, which was sometimes planted with trees, and was large enough to admit of a portico on each side, ornamented with triumphal chariots, statues, and other works of art. The open space was termed *Area*, and this, together with the colonnades, seats, &c., constituted the *Vestibulum*, which, it must be understood, was altogether on the exterior of the mansion. The houses in Pompeii have no *Vestibulum*, but open upon the street, as in the case of that represented in (A.)

Ostium, Ianua, were the names given to the principal entrance, the door by which it was closed being usually folding, as indicated by the plural words *Valvae* and *Fores*, the latter, however, is used also in the singular *Foris*. The door was generally left open during the day, but a Porter—*Ianitor*—*Ostiarius*—kept watch in a small lodge or box, (*Cella ostiarii*,) observing all who passed in and out.

Prothyrum.—A passage or small entrance hall leading from the outer door to the interior of the house.

Atrium.—This, for a long period, was the most important apartment in a Roman house. It was generally more spacious than any other, and existed in some shape in every mansion, great or small, from the earliest down to the

[1] Vitruv. I. 6. II. 8. Paul. Diac. s.v. *Insulae* p. 111. Cic. pro Coel. 7. ad Att. XIV. 9. XV. 1.. Tacit. Ann. XV. 53. Suet. Ner. 38. Senec. de ira. III. 35.

latest times. It was always placed opposite to the principal entrance, and was, in the great majority of cases, lighted by an aperture in the centre of the ceiling, open to the sky, which was called *Impluvium*, because the surrounding roof sloped towards it so as to conduct the rain down into a reservoir called *Compluvium*, formed in the pavement below for its reception. The *Atrium* was originally the public room, open to all members of the family, to friends, and to visitors. In the middle was placed the fire-place of the house, (*Focus*,) where all culinary operations were conducted, the smoke escaping through the *Impluvium* above; beside the *Focus* a small altar was erected, upon which were placed the offerings to the domestic Gods, the Lares and Penates, who occupied niches hard by, and the *Focus* being the spot farthest removed from the exterior of the mansion, the space which it occupied was sometimes termed *Penetralia* or *Foci Penetrales*. In the *Atrium* stood the marriage couch (*Lectus genialis*) immediately opposite to the door, and hence it was sometimes distinguished as *Lectus adversus;* here, too, all the members of the household shared the common repast; here stood the looms; here the mistress plied her labours surrounded by her maidens; here the master received his visitors; here, when a death occurred, the corpse was laid out previous to the funeral, with feet towards the outer door; and here were arranged the waxen images of illustrious ancestors in which the *Nobiles* (p. 67) took such pride. This description must be understood to apply, in so far as persons belonging to the higher ranks were concerned, to the primitive ages only, when the *Atrium* was the sole public apartment. In process of time, separate rooms for cooking, for banqueting, and for carrying on ordinary domestic toils were constructed, a private chapel was provided for the Gods, and in the houses of the great the *Atrium* was set apart for the reception of clients, and of those who sought assistance from, or desired to testify their respect for, the lord of the mansion.

Cavaedium.—As houses became more spacious and the dimensions of the *Atrium* were increased, it became necessary to support the roof with pillars, one being placed at each corner of the *Impluvium*. In process of time a room was found to possess many advantages in point of coolness and ventilation in which the aperture was made larger than was absolutely required for the admission of light, more pillars were in this case required for the support of the beams, and a small open court was then formed below the *Impluvium*, surrounded by a colonnade. An apartment formed upon this plan was termed a *Cavaedium*.

Peristylium.—When the size of this court was considerably enlarged, so as to leave merely covered cloisters between the pillars of the colonnade and the walls, the court and cloisters were termed *Peristylium*.

Houses on a great scale had an *Atrium*, a *Cavaedium*, and a *Peristylium*, all spacious, but occasionally the *Atrium* was contracted to a mere ante-chamber, and the *Cavaedium* became the great reception hall. When this was the case, the *Atrium* was sometimes roofed over completely (*Atrium testudinatum*) receiving light from the *Cavaedium* on one side, and from the outer door on the other.

It is clear that it must have been difficult to determine the exact point at which an *Atrium* passed into a *Cavaedium*, and a *Cavaedium* into a *Peristylium*, and it is not surprising that the expressions employed by ancient writers in reference to these matters should be occasionally ambiguous. It is quite unnecessary to enter upon the details of the controversy maintained by those upon the one hand, who maintain that *Atrium* and *Cavaedium* are absolutely synonymous, or at all events, that the *Cavaedium* was merely the small court in the centre of the *Atrium*, and by those who insist that these words always represent apartments entirely distinct. It is enough to bear in mind that the *Atrium* was never dispensed with, that neither the *Cavaedium* nor the *Peristylium* were essential, and that when we find one only it may be difficult to determine to which of the classes it properly belongs. Then in the house A we have the *Atrium* distinctly marked, but we may hesitate, whether the court behind marked 9, ought to be regarded as a *Cavaedium* or a *Peristylium*.[1]

Tablinum. Alae.—The *Atrium* at its lower end was divided into three apartments open in front; the largest, that in the centre, was the *Tablinum*, and the two smaller, on each side, were the *Alae*. Here were deposited the genealogical records and archives, and all documents commemorating the exploits which had been performed or connected with the high offices which had been filled by members of the family.

Fauces was the general name for narrow passages leading from one portion of the house to another, and of these there was generally one on each side of the *Tablinum*.

The *Tablinum* with its *Alae* served to separate the public from the private apartments; and hence when there was both an *Atrium* and a *Cavaedium*, the *Tablinum* would be placed at the bottom of the *Cavaedium*.

Triclinia, dining rooms. When there were several of these, they varied in size according to the number of guests which they were designed to contain, and were built so as to offer different exposures suited to the different seasons of the year.

Cubicula s. Dormitoria, bed-rooms. These also were arranged so as to suit the seasons. Some had an antechamber or dressing-room attached, called *Procoeton*, ($\pi\varrho o \varkappa o \iota \tau \acute{\omega} \nu$,) in others, the bed was placed in a recess or alcove termed *Zotheca*.

Oeci.—This is a general term for *Saloons*, which might be used as diningrooms, as private sitting rooms for females, or for any other purpose. They received different appellations according to their form and architectural decorations. Thus an *Oecus* which was square and ornamented with four pillars, was named *Tetrastylos*, others were called *Corinthii*, *Cyziceni*, *Aegyptii*, &c., according to the style in which they were constructed and fitted up.

Exedrae were conversation rooms, (*parlours*,) furnished with seats, which were frequently placed in semicircular recesses (*Hemicyclia*.)

In many cases the name alone sufficiently indicates the purpose for which the apartment was designed. To this class belong the *Bibliotheca*, (library,) the *Pinacotheca*, (picture-gallery,) the *Lararium*, (chapel,) the *Culina*, (kitchen,) with its *Latrina* (scullery) attached, the *Pistrinum*, (bake-house,) *Cella Penuaria*, (store-room,) *Cella Vinaria*, (wine-cellar,) and many others.

The cut marked B represents one of the numerous attempts to lay down the plan of a Roman house according to the description of Vitruvius. Many of the arrangements, as here represented, are, however, very doubtful, and the space which is marked as a *Vestibulum* ought to be designated as a *Prothyrum*.

[1] The passages chiefly relied upon by those who entertain conflicting opinions with regard to the relation between an *Atrium* and a *Cavaedium* (or *Cavum aedium*, as it is sometimes termed,) are—Varro L.L. V. § 161. Vitruv. VI. 3. seqq. Quintil. I. O. XI. 2 § 21. Virg. Æn. II. 483. Plin. Epp. II. 17. Plin. H.N. XIV. 1. Paul. Diac. s v. *Atrium* p. 13.

A

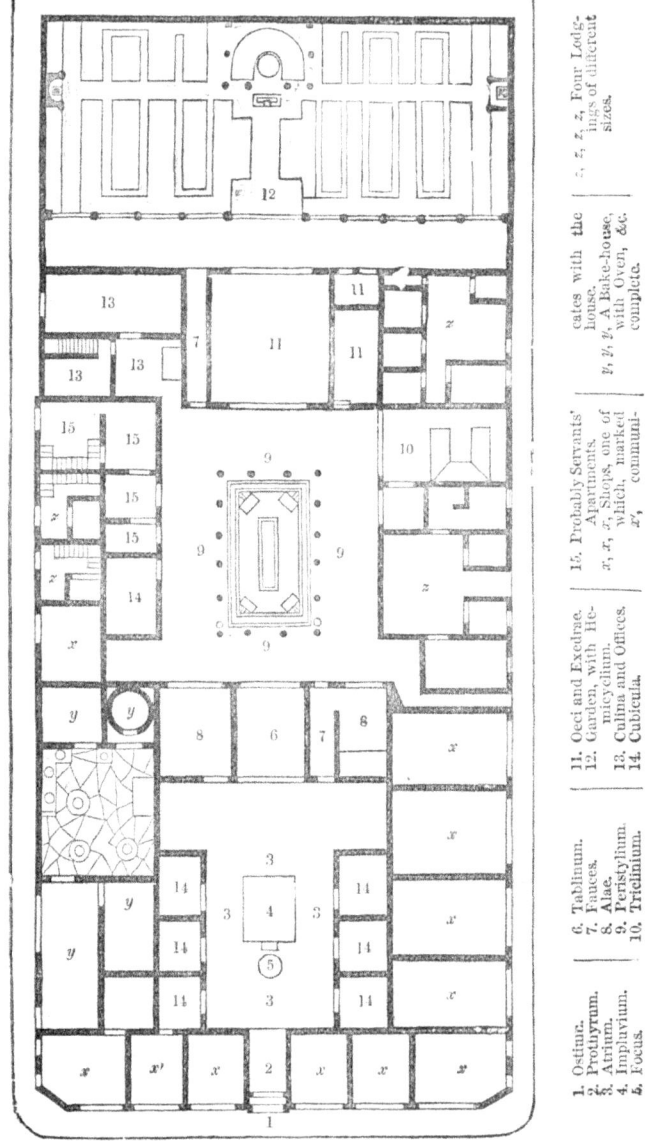

1. Ostium.
2. Prothyrum.
3. Atrium.
4. Impluvium.
5. Focus.
6. Tablinum.
7. Fauces.
8. Alae.
9. Peristylum.
10. Triclinium.
11. Oeci and Exedrae.
12. Garden, with Hemicyclium.
13. Culina and Offices.
14. Cubicula.
15. Probably Servants' Apartments.
x, x, x, Shops, one of which, marked x', communicates with the house.
y, y, y, A Bake-house, with Oven, &c. complete.
z, z, z, Four Lodgings of different sizes.

CHAPTER XV.

AGRICULTURE.[1]

The Romans during the brightest period of their history were passionately devoted to agriculture and the pursuits of a rural life. For many centuries war and the cultivation of the soil were regarded as the only occupations befitting a free-born citizen. Numerous treatises upon farming in general and the various branches of the art were published from time to time, and of these a few have descended to us. The most important is that entitled *De Re Rustica Libri III.*, by the celebrated M. Terentius Varro, the contemporary of Cicero; we have also a longer and more elaborate, but less original production by M. Iunius Columella, who probably flourished under the Emperor Claudius; a compilation in the form of a Farmer's Kalendar by Palladius Rutilius Taurus Æmilianus, a writer of uncertain date and doubtful authority; and a collection of shrewd maxims on various topics connected with the management of a farm and domestic economy by M. Porcius Cato, the Censor. These four, together with a manual, *De Arte Veterinaria*, by a certain Vegetius Renatus, have been frequently published together under the title *Scriptores Rei Rusticae Veteres Latini.* In addition, two books of the *Naturalis Historia* of Pliny, the XVII. and XVIII., are chiefly occupied by matters connected with agriculture, and Virgil has chosen this for the theme of the most perfect and charming didactic poem in existence.

Divisions of the Subject.—*Res Rustica*, to which *Agricultura* is frequently employed as equivalent, may be discussed under two heads.[2]

I. **Agricultura,** in the proper sense of the word, viz., the tillage of the ground.

II. **Pastio,** the management of live stock.

Again, **Agricultura,** in this its proper sense, may be subdivided into—

1. *Agricultura*, in a more restricted sense; comprehending the art of raising the cereal grasses; leguminous plants; vegetables cultivated for their fibre, such as flax; for their oil, such as poppies; or for fodder, such as lucerne.

2. *Cultus Arborum*, arboriculture; comprehending the management of trees in general, but principally fruit trees, and especially the vine and the olive.

3. *Cultus Hortorum*, gardening; comprehending the rearing of flowers, pot herbs (*olera*), and small fruits.

---

[1] The student may consult with profit the well known work, *The Husbandry of the Ancients*, by Adam Dickson, who was minister of Whittingham, in East Lothian, towards the close of the last century, and had great knowledge and experience as a practical farmer. I would beg to refer also to the articles AGRICULTURA, OLEA, VINUM, contributed by me to the *Dictionary of Greek and Roman Antiquities*, edited by Dr. W. Smith. The *Lectures on Roman Husbandry*, published recently by Dr. Daubeny of Oxford, contain interesting matter, and two lively articles on this subject will be found in vols. 87 and 104 of the *Quarterly Review*. Many valuable illustrations are contained in the various commentaries on the Georgics, especially in those of Martyn, and J. H. Voss.

[2] See Varro R. R. I. 2.

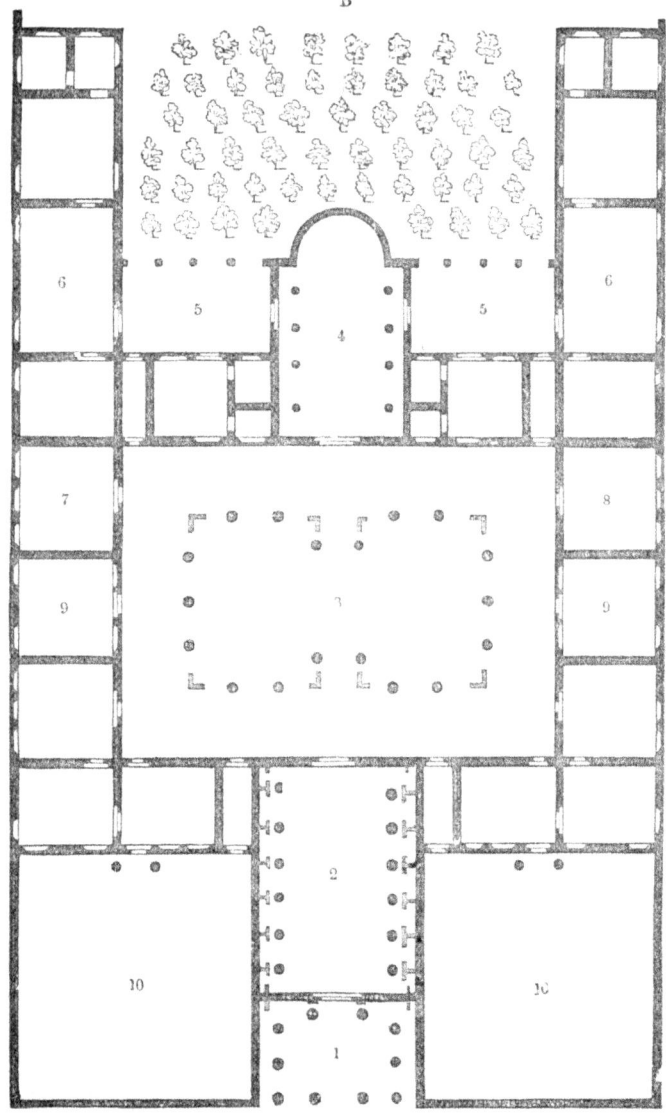

1. Vestibulum.
2. Atrium. [vaedium.
3. Peristylium and Ca-
4. Basilica.
5. Porticus.
6. Triclinia.
7. Bibliotheca.
8. Pinacotheca.
9. Exedrae.
10. Courts.

AGRICULTURE.

So also, **Pastio** may be subdivided into—
1. *Pastio Agrestis* s. *Res Pecuaria*, comprehending the larger and more important domestic animals, such as sheep, oxen, horses, &c.
2. *Pastio Villatica*, comprehending the smaller and less important animals, such as poultry, bees, fish, &c.

These are the divisions of the subject which form the groundwork of the *Georgics:* the first book is devoted to *agricultura* in the restricted sense—

> Quid faciat laetas segetes, quo sidere terram
> Vertere ———

The second to the *Cultus Arborum*—

> Nunc te, Bacche, canam, nec non silvestria tecum
> Virgulta et prolem tarde crescentis olivae.

The third to *Pastio Agrestis*—

> ——— Quae cura boum, qui cultus habendo,
> Sit pecori.

The fourth to that particular department of *Pastio Villatica*, which seemed to afford the greatest scope for poetical ornament, viz., the habits and treatment of bees—

> ——— apibus quanta experientia parcis.

And in the same book there are a few exquisite lines in which (116-148) Virgil excuses himself for not entering at length on the *Cultus Hortorum*.

Following the example of the great poet, we shall make a few remarks on each of the divisions enumerated above, with the exception of gardening, the details belonging to that pursuit being somewhat minute and not frequently alluded to by the classical writers.

I. AGRICULTURA.

Divisions of Agricultura.—Varro[1] treats of *agricultura* proper under four great heads.
1. *Cognitio Fundi*, the natural situation of the farm, the soil, and the climate.
2. *Instrumenta*, the persons, animals, and tools requisite for the cultivation of the farm.
3. *Res quibus arva coluntur*, the various operations to be performed, and the crops which form the object of these operations.
4. *Tempora*, the seasons at which the various operations ought to be performed.

1. *Cognitio Fundi.*

This may be treated of under nine heads.
(1.) *Forma fundi naturalis.* (2.) *Terrae natura.* (3.) *Modus agri.* (4.) *De finibus tuendis.* (5.) *Si regio infesta.* (6.) *Si invectus et avectus idonei.* (7.) *Vecturae.* (8.) *Cultura et natura fundorum confinium.* (9.) *Villa et Stabula.*

(1.) *Forma fundi naturalis*, the natural aspect and character of the locality.[2]

---
[1] Varro R. R. I. 5.
[2] Varro R. R. I. 6, 7. Colum. R. R. I. 2, 3, 4.

(2.) *Terrae natura*, the quality of the soil. These two heads are indicated by Virgil in the lines (G. I. 50)—

> At prius ignotum ferro quam scindimus aequor,
> Ventos et varium coeli praediscere morem
> Cura sit, ac patrios cultus habitusque locorum
> Et quid quaeque ferat regio, et quid quaeque recuset.

While in Bk. II. 177, he enters more at large into the characteristics of different soils, and gives rules for distinguishing them,—

> Nunc locus arvorum ingeniis, quae robora cuique,
> Quis color, et quae sit rebus natura ferendis.

Soils were classified according to their productive powers, their consistency, their chief constituents, their colour, and even their taste. Thus we find land spoken of as—1. *Pinguis* (rich); 2. *Macra—Ieiuna* (poor); 3. *Putris—Soluta* (free); 4. *Spissa—Densa* (stiff); 5. *Humida—Uliginosa* (wet, swampy); 6. *Sicca* (dry); 7. *Argillosa* (Clayey); 8. *Lapidosa* (stony); 9. *Glareosa* (gravelly); 10. *Arenosa* (sandy); 11. *Pulla—Nigra* (black); 12. *Cretosa* (white); 13. *Rubricosa* (red); 14. *Salsa* (salt); 15. *Amara* (bitter); and many others.[1]

(3.) *Modus agri*, the measurement of land and the considerations which regulated the size of a farm. It is sufficient here to state that the land measure in common use among the Romans was the *Jugerum*, which was less than two-thirds and more than three-fifths of an imperial acre.[2]

(4.) *De finibus tuendis*, i. e., fences (*sepes, septa, sepimenta*). The fences in ordinary use were—*a. Sepimentum naturale*, the quickset hedge; *b. Sepimentum agreste*, the wooden paling; *c. Sepimentum militare*, consisting of a ditch (*fossa*) crowned with a bank (*agger*) formed of the earth thrown out; *d. Sepimentum fabrile*, a stone or brick wall, with or without cement.[3]

(5.) *Si regio infesta*, the state of the surrounding country in so far as security of property was concerned, an inquiry by no means unnecessary, for a district might be infested with robbers or exposed to the predatory incursions of hostile tribes.[4]

(6.) *Si Invectus et Arectus idonei*, that is, if there were facilities for purchasing necessaries and for disposing of the products of the farm—good markets at hand for buying and selling.[5]

(7.) *Vecturae*, the accessibility of the farm; whether there were practicable roads or navigable streams.[6]

(8.) *Cultura et Natura fundorum confinium*.

A certain influence was exercised upon the value of a farm by the mode of cultivation adopted in and the natural character of the lands adjacent.[7]

(9.) *Villa et Stabula*, the last and one of the most important topics belonging to the *Cognitio Fundi*, was the consideration of the farm buildings, the dwelling-house, and offices.[8]

The general term comprehending the whole of the farm buildings was *Villa*, and the structure might be discussed under three heads—*a. Villa Urbana*; *b. Villa Rustica*; *c. Villa fructuaria*.

a. Villa Urbana.—This comprehended that portion of the buildings occupied

[1] Varro R. R. I. 7. 8. 9.
[2] Varro R. R. I. 10. 11. Cato R. R. 8.
[3] Varro R. R. I. 14.
[4] Varro R. R. I. 16.
[5] Varro R. R. I. 16.
[6] Varro R. R. I. 16.
[7] Varro R. R. I. 16.
[8] Varro R. R. I. 11. 12. 13. Colum. R. R. I. 6.

by the proprietor. The extent and the decorations depended entirely on his taste and his means, and might embrace anything between the simple cottage of primitive times and the sumptuous palaces of the wealthy in the age of Augustus.

b. Villa Rustica.—This comprehended that portion of the building intended for the accommodation of the *Familia* of slave labourers, and of the domestic animals. The apartments essential for the *familia* were—1. *Culina*, a spacious kitchen where the food of the establishment was cooked and eaten; 2. *Cellae*, sleeping closets for the *Servi Soluti* (see p. 97) and rooms for the *Villicus* and the *Procurator*; 3. *Ergastulum*, a sort of prison, frequently under ground, where the *Servi Vincti* (see p. 97) were confined when within doors. The buildings for the domestic animals were included under the general term *Stabula*, which comprehended *Bubilia* (byres), *Ovilia* (sheep huts), *Equilia* (stables), *Harae* (pig styes), and others.

c. Villa fructuaria.—This comprehended that portion of the buildings intended for storing or preparing the different products of the farm. Such were the *Cella Vinaria* (wine cellar), *Cella Olearia* (oil cellar), *Cella Torcularia* (press room), *Granaria* (granaries), *Foenilia* (hay lofts), *Palearia* (chaff houses), besides a number of apartments for objects which required to be kept dry, included under the general terms *Horrea* and *Apothecae*.

If the farm was of considerable extent the buildings were usually arranged round two courts (*cortes*), and in the centre of each of these was a large tank (*piscina*).

Either within the enclosures of the farm buildings, or immediately adjoining, were erected a mill (*pistrinum*), and a bake-house (*furnum*); the thrashing floor (*area*), to be more particularly described below, was formed, if possible, within sight of the windows, and alongside of it was a huge covered shed called *Nubilarium*, capable of containing the whole grain crop.

2. *Instrumenta.*

The *instrumenta* of a farm were divided into three classes—(1.) *Genus Vocale.* (2.) *Genus Semivocale.* (3.) *Genus Mutum.*[1]

(1.) *Genus Vocale*, i. e., the human beings employed. These might be—
a. Liberi Coloni; b. Mercenarii; c. Servi.

a. Liberi Coloni, small proprietors who cultivated their own lands with their own hands, and with the aid of their families.

b. Mercenarii, free hired labourers. These were but little employed except in the great operations of haymaking (*foenisicium*), the corn harvest (*messis*), and the vintage (*vindemia*), when a number of extra hands were required for a limited period.

The regular work of a large farm was performed almost exclusively by—

c. Servi, slaves, forming the *Familia Rustica*. The *Familia Rustica* was, as we have seen above (p. 97), separated into two divisions—1. *Servi Soluti*, who were not subjected to any personal restraint, and 2. *Servi Vincti*, who worked in fetters (*compede vincti*) when abroad, and who, when within doors, were shut up in a sort of prison called *Ergastulum*.

The slaves on a farm were also divided into gangs, according to the particular duties which they were required to perform, and in large establishments the subdivision of labour was pushed very far. Thus there were *Bubulci* (ox drivers), *Asinarii* (ass drivers), *Armentarii* (neat herds), *Opiliones* (shepherds), *Cap*-

[1] Varro R. R. I. 17.

rarii (goat herds), *Bubulci* (swine herds), *Vinitores* (vine dressers), *Operarii* (ordinary labourers), and very many others.

When the gangs were large and worked together, each had a *Praefectus* or overseer, and in each farm there was a bailiff or superintendent called *Villicus*, who was himself a slave or a freeman. To him was committed the whole charge and general management, and with him a housekeeper called *Villica* was frequently associated. Besides these, when the transactions were numerous and complicated, there was a *Procurator*, or book-keeper, who kept the accounts and took charge of the cash.[1]

(2.) *Genus Semivocale*, i. e., the inferior animals trained to labour. All the ordinary work of a farm, such as ploughing, harrowing, carting, and the like, for which we employ horses, was, in ancient times, performed by oxen trained for the purpose (*boves domiti*), and this practice prevails generally in southern Europe at the present day. Asses were used for turning corn mills, and when fitted with panniers, carried out manure, cleared away the prunings from the vineyard, and went to market (G. I. 273):—

> Saepe oleo tardi costas agitator aselli
> Aut vilibus onerat pomis, lapidemque revertens
> Incusum, aut atrae massam picis, urbe reportat.

Horses and mules were very sparingly employed, except for riding, and for drawing travelling carriages.[2]

(3.) *Genus Mutum*, i. e., tools properly so called. These may be divided into two classes—

a. Those worked by beasts of draught.

b. Those worked by the hand.

In the first class we may notice—(1.) *Aratrum*. (2.) *Irpex*. (3.) *Crates*. (4.) *Plaustrum*. (5.) *Tribulum*. (6.) *Trahea*.

In the second class—(7.) *Rastrum*. (8.) *Ligo*. (9.) *Marra*. (10.) *Pala*. (11.) *Bipalium*. (12.) *Rutrum*. (13.) *Pastinum*. (14.) *Sarculum*. (15.) *Dolabra*. (16.) *Falx*. (17.) *Vannus*.

Aratrum.—Numerous allusions to the most important implement of agriculture are to be found in ancient writers, but the most distinct and connected description of the different parts of the plough is contained in a well known passage of Virgil's 1st Georgic, v. 169—

> Continuo in silvis magna vi flexa domatur
> In burim et curvi formam accipit ulmus aratri.
> Huic ab stirpe pedes temo protentus in octo,
> Binae aures, duplici aptantur dentalia dorso.
> Caeditur et tilia ante jugo levis, altaque fagus
> Stivae[3] quae currus a tergo torqueat imos.

The interpreters of these lines unfortunately differ so widely from each other, that any young scholar who reads and compares the various explanations proposed, is likely to become bewildered. Without attempting to examine and refute a multitude of conflicting opinions, many of which are altogether preposterous, we shall endeavour to show that the text of Virgil exactly describes the simple instrument still used in many parts of southern Italy, of Greece, and of

---

[1] Varro R. R. I. 17. 18. Colum. R. R. I. 7. 8. 9.
[2] Varro R. R. I. 19. 20.
[3] We have adopted the emendation of Martyn for the common reading *stivaque quae*, which, although susceptible of explanation, is very awkward.

Asia. A representation of one of these is subjoined from a rude sketch by the author, taken from a plough which he saw at work, a few years ago, in the neighbourhood of Benevento, and it corresponds closely with the representations found upon many ancient monuments.

Before describing the different parts in detail, we must premise that Virgil, in the passage quoted above, mentions those portions only of the plough which were made of wood; and to this day, in light friable soils, ploughs made of wood exclusively, without any iron share, are still employed.

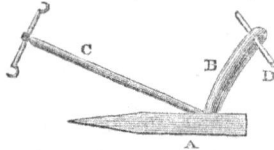

1. *Dentalia*, the *share-beam*, marked A in the figure. This was a strong, straight beam, terminating in a double cutting edge, tapered to a sharp point. It presented two similar and symmetrical sides (*duplici dentalia dorso*); and hence the plural, *dentalia*, was commonly employed, as in the case of such words as *frena* and *habenae*, although the singular, *dentale*, is also found.[1] Over the wooden *Dentale* or *Dentalia*, an iron share was sometimes slipped, as appears from the words of Cato[2]—*Vomis indutilis optimus erit*—and sometimes an iron point was attached. Thus Pliny,[3] when describing different kinds of shares—*Tertium in solo facili, nec toto porrectum dentali, sed exigua cuspide in rostro*—i. e., the *dentale* was merely tipped with iron, not fully shod. The *Vomis* is mentioned by Virgil in line 162:—

Vomis et inflexi primum grave robur aratri.

But in the passage now before us he confines himself, as already noticed, to the wooden parts. *Dens* is used to denote the sharp-pointed extremity which pierces the soil, without reference to the absence or presence of a *Vomis*.

2. *Buris*, marked B. This was a piece of strong crooked timber, forming the plough-handle or plough-tail; the ancient plough differing from the modern in this essential point, that it had one handle only, instead of two. The shape of the *Buris* gave rise to the epithet *curvus*, applied here and elsewhere to the *Aratrum*.

3. *Temo*, the pole, marked C, with the *Iugum* attached. With regard to these there is no doubt or controversy.

4. *Stiva*. The real nature and object of the *Stiva* has proved a source of much unsatisfactory discussion; but a careful examination of the representations of ploughs exhibited upon ancient monuments, will enable us to remove every difficulty.

It is obvious that, so long as the soil was light and free, the ploughman would have no difficulty in guiding the plough by the single handle, or *Buris*; but when the soil was stiff, and it became necessary to drive the plough deep, it would be almost impossible to regulate the progress of the share by means of the *Buris*, especially when it was very short, as appears to have been frequently the case. Hence the necessity, in such cases, for the cross bar, marked D in the figure, inserted near the upper extremity of the *Buris*, which, acting as a powerful lever, would give the labourer complete command over the *dentalia*;

---

[1] Freund asserts in his Lexicon, that *dentale* is not met with in the singular until we come down to Servius (Virg. G. I. 172), and Isidorus (20. 14. 2), but it occurs in a passage in Pliny (H. N. xviii. 18) quoted below.
[2] R. R. 135.
[3] H. N. XVIII. 18.

and when he leaned heavily upon it, he would be enabled to drive the share as deep as he found expedient.

The power of turning the whole frame of the machine from side to side is specially mentioned by Virgil as the use of the *Stiva*—

> Stivae, quae currus a tergo torqueat imos;

and hence, a ploughman, when leaning heavily on the plough, is represented as pressing upon the *Stiva*. Thus Ovid (*Met.* VIII. 218.)—

> Aut pastor baculo, stivave innixus arator;

and again (*Fast.* IV. 825.)—

> Inde premens stivam designat moenia aratro;

while Columella (I. 9.) says of a tall ploughman—*Arando stivae paene rectus inntitur*.

If, then, we had no explanation of the different parts of the plough except that afforded by Virgil, we might rest satisfied that the bar D (see fig. in last page) corresponds to the *Stiva*, since it answers all the conditions. But there is a passage in Varro *De Lingua Latina*,[1] in which he enumerates the different parts of the plough, and which we cannot reconcile with this view:—ARATRUM, *quod aruit terram eius ferrum*. DENS, *quod eo mordetur terra*. *Supra id regula quae stat*, STIVA *ab stando: et in ea transversa regula* MANICULA, *quod manu bubulci tenetur*. *Qui quasi temo est inter boves*, BURA *a bubus*. *alii hoc a curvo* URVOM *appellant*. *Sub iugo medio cavum, quod bura extrema addita oppilatur, vocatur* COUS *a cavo*. IUGUM et IUMENTUM *ab iunctu*.

Here we find the *Stiva* described as a straight piece of wood, standing perpendicular to the share beam, and furnished with a *Manicula*, or handle; and the *Bura* is defined as *quasi temo inter boves*, and no separate *Temo* is mentioned. It is clear, therefore, that Varro is describing a plough different in form and arrangements from that of 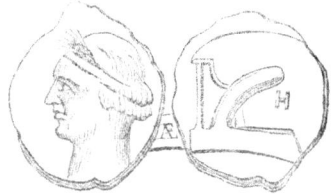 Virgil; but the annexed figure, taken from a coin of Centuripae, in the Hunterian collection, will make everything clear.

Here the curved *Buris* is turned in the opposite direction from that in the first figure; it bends away from the ploughman, and is in reality, as Varro states, *quasi temo inter boves*, to which the yoke might be attached. But in this case the *Buris* could no longer be held by the ploughman; and the straight pole, or *Stiva*, with its *Manicula*, both of which are plainly depicted, became necessary. When the *Buris* was grasped by the ploughman, then the cross bar D (see last page), answered every purpose; and this is, in all probability, the *Stiva* of Virgil, who makes no mention of a *Manicula*.

5. *Aures*. Mould-Boards. Two of these, which were not required in ordinary ploughing, were attached to the plough when it was wished to rib (*lirare*) the land, as will be explained more fully when we treat of the operation of ploughing. The ordinary modern plough has one mould-board permanently attached; but double mould-board ploughs have been recently introduced in turnip-husbandry.

---

[1] Lib. V. § 134. ed. Müller.

A plough with the mould-boards attached was termed *Aratrum auritum*, as opposed to the *Aratrum simplex*.[1]

6. *Culter.* In addition to the parts named by Virgil, Pliny[2] mentions the *Culter*, which he reckons as a kind of share; but it is manifest from his words that it was quite distinct from the *Vomer*. It was employed in breaking up very stiff lea before the first regular ploughing was given, and was, in all probability, essentially the same with the modern Coulter:—*Culter vocatur, praedensam, prius quam proscindatur, terram secans, futurisque sulcis vestigia praescribens incisuris, quas resupinus in arando mordeat vomer*.

7. *Ralla* s. *Rallum.* This appendage to the plough is described by Pliny alone; it was a small spade, or scraper, attached to a long handle, and used for cleaning the share when clogged with earth:—*Purget vomerem subinde stimulus cuspidatus rallo.*[3] (Plin. l. c.) What is now termed the *plough-staff* is employed for the same purpose.

The three essential parts of the plough—the *Buris*, the *Dentalia*, and the *Temo*—are mentioned by Hesiod,[4] under the names of γυης, ἔλυμα, and ἱστοβοευς, respectively; and in another passage he speaks of the ὀρπηξ ἐχετλης, which must be the *Stiva* or *Manicula*.[5] Hesiod, moreover, distinguishes between the ἄροτρον αὐτογυον—in which the *Buris*, *Dentalia*, and *Temo* were composed of a single piece of timber—and the ἄροτρον πηκτον, in which the different parts were nailed together.[6]

Irpex s. *Hirpex* s. *Urpex*, was a plank armed with numerous teeth, and dragged by oxen over the surface of the ground, for the purpose of tearing up weeds. The description given by Varro[7] is quite distinct—IRPICES *regula compluribus dentibus, quam item ut plaustrum boves trahunt ut eruant quae in terra serpunt*.[8] It answered the same end as what is now termed a *Grubber*.

Crates is a general term applied to textures of rods, twigs, straw, sedge, reeds, fern, &c.[9] Such were employed for a great variety of rural purposes. Thus *Crates vimineae*[10] were dragged over ploughed land for the purpose of breaking down the clods; and *Crates dentatae*,[11] answering in all respects to a modern harrow, were used in Gaul for covering up the seed. *Crates stercorariae*[12] were panniers in which manure was carried out to the field; *Crates ficariae*[13] were used in drying figs; when grapes were made into raisins, they were spread out upon *crates*;[14] and when *crates* were formed of strong materials, they were used for fences or pens, like our *hurdles*—*Claudensque textis cratibus laetum pecus*. (Hor. Epod. II. 45.)

Plaustrum s. **Plostrum** dim. **Plostellum.**—This term is equivalent to the Greek ἅμαξα, and includes carts, waggons, and wheeled vehicles of every description employed for agricultural purposes. The wheels, like those in the

---

[1] Pallad. I. 43.
[2] H. N. XVIII. 18.
[3] Edd. vary in the form given to this word. In some we find *rallo*; in others, *ralla*; in others *rulla*.
[4] Opera et Dies v. 427. seqq.
[5] v. 467. In this passage ἔνδρυον is generally supposed to be the *Temo*, and μεσάβοος the *Jugum*. The Greek word for the iron share, or *Vomer*, is ὕνις. (Plut. Rom. 11.)
[6] A figure of an ἄροτρον αὐτογυον, as still used in Mysia, will be found in *Travels in Asia Minor*, by Charles Fellowes, p. 71.—J. H. Voss, in his translation of Virgil's *Georgics* (Altona, 1800), has given a plate, with representations of twenty-five varieties of ancient and modern ploughs, which serve to illustrate this subject.
[7] Varro L. L. V. § 136. ed. Müller. Comp. Paul. Diac. s. v. *irpices*, p. 105. ed. Müller.
[8] See also Cato R. R. 10. Serv. ad Virg. G. I. 95.
[9] So Virgil, Aen. XI. 64. *Haud segnes alii crates et molle feretrum=Arbuteis texunt virgis et vimine querno*; and Columell. R. R. XII. 15.—*Crates pastorales culmo vel carice vel filice textae*.
[10] Virg. G. I. 95. [11] Plin. H. N. XVIII. 18. [12] Cato R. R. 10. Varr. R. R. 1. 22.
[13] Cato R. R. 48. [14] Columell. R. R. XII. 16.

toy-carts of children, were generally composed of discs of solid timber, and were called *tympana* (G. II. 444):—

Hinc radios trivere rotis, hinc tympana plaustris;

such may be still seen in the secluded districts of southern Italy, in Greece, Asia Minor, and India.

The number of wheels was usually two; indeed, Isidorus defines the *Plaustrum* to be *vehiculum duarum rotarum;* but four-wheeled carts were certainly in use, since they appear on various ancient monuments, although they may have been distinguished by a different name. Cato[1] notices *plostra maiora;* but there is no ground for the conclusion that these had four wheels.[2]

The *Plostellum Punicum* will be noticed immediately.

Tribulum. Plostellum Punicum. Thrashing-Machines.—The *Tribulum* was a framework of heavy planks, the under side of which was studded all over with iron teeth, or sharp stones. This was dragged by a team of horses or oxen over the corn when spread out upon the thrashing floor; and it rubbed out a portion of the grain while it turned the straw over and over; so that the whole was thoroughly trodden by the animals. In the *Plostellum Punicum* the toothed planks were mounted upon wheels. Varro[3] describes both the form and use of these implements so distinctly as to require no comment—*E spicis in aream excuti grana: quod fit apud alios iumentis iunctis, ac* TRIBULO: *id fit e tabula lapidibus aut ferro asperata, quo imposito auriga, aut pondere grandi trahitur iumentis iunctis, ut discutiat e spica grana: aut ex assibus dentatis cum orbiculis, quod vocant* PLOSTELLUM PUNICUM. A representation of a *Tribulum*, as still used in Mysia, answering exactly to the description of Varro, will be found in Fellowes' *Travels in Asia Minor*, p. 70 (1839).[4]

Trahea s. Traha.—A sort of sledge, may be regarded as a variety of the *Tribulum*, in conjunction with which it is mentioned by Virgil[5]—

Tribulaque traheaeque et iniquo pondere rastri.

The words of Columella[6] leave no doubt as to the purpose for which it was employed—*At si competit, ut in area teratur frumentum, nihil dubium est, quin equis melius quam bubus ea res conficiatur: et, si pauca iuga sunt, adiicere Tribulam et Traham possis.*

Rastrum,—in the plural usually **Rastri,**—is the general term for any toothed implement used for stirring the ground. Thus Varro[7]—RASTRI, *quibus dentatis penitus eradunt terram atque eruunt.* The diminutive *Rastelli* corresponds closely to our *hand-rakes,*—RASTELLI, *ut irpices, serrae leves; ita qui homo in pratis, per fenisecta eo festucas corradit, quo ab rasu rastelli*

---

[1] R. R. 10. Comp. Varr. R. R. I. 22.
[2] The subject of ancient *Plaustra* has been exhausted by SCHEFFER. *De Re Vehiculari veterum* II. c. 19 (Fracof. 1671), and GINZROT, *Die Wägen und Fahrwerke der Griechen und Römer*, cap. XII. seqq. (München, 1817). The cut given above, representing a dung-cart, is copied from the last mentioned work. Tab. VII. fig. 1. and is taken from a Roman bas-relief.
[3] Varro R. R. I. 52.
[4] See also Varro L. L. V. § 18. where Müller reads *Trivolum*. Colum. R. R. II. 21. Plin. H. N. XVIII. 30. Serv. ad Virg. G. I. 164. Scheffer, *De Re Vehiculari*, I. 7.
[5] G. I. 164.
[6] R. R. II. 21.
[7] L. L. V. § 136, ed. Müller. Comp. Virg. Aen. VII. 725, IX. 608. G. III. 534.

dicti,[1]—and again,—*tum de pratis stipulam rastellis eradi, atque addere foenisiciae cumulum* (R. R. I. 49).

One of the most important purposes to which *Rastri* were applied was crushing clods. So Virgil,[2]—

> Multum adeo rastris glebas qui frangit inertes
> Vimineasque trahit crates, iuvat arva, . . .

and Pliny,[3]—*Aratione per transversum iterata, occatio sequitur, ubi res poscit, crate vel rastro.* Such instruments were necessarily large and heavy; and hence the expression,—*iniquo pondere rastri.*[4] One form of the *Rastrum* in very common use, consisted of two long thick iron teeth, set nearly at right angles to a short strong wooden shaft. This was termed emphatically,—

Bidens,[5] was used for a great variety of purposes, and is still the favourite tool of the vineyard labourer, retaining in Italy its ancient name,—*Bidente*. Cato includes *Rastri Quadridentes* among the *instrumenta* required for the olive garden and vineyard.[6] When the *Rastrum* assumed the form of a rake, it was occasionally, as among ourselves, made entirely of wood; Columella specially enjoins that the seed of lucerne (*medica*) should be covered up *ligneis rastris*, or, as he calls them in a subsequent chapter,—*ligneis rastellis.*[7]

Ligo.—The *Ligo*, like the *Bidens*, was used for loosening and turning up the soil; and like the *Rastrum*, for breaking down tenacious clods. After examining and comparing the passages referred to below, we must arrive at the conclusion that it could not have been either a *spade*, as some, or a *hatchet*, as other scholars have imagined, but must, in all probability, have been a *pick-axe*, an instrument which will answer all the conditions.[8]

Marra.—All that we can say with regard to this implement is, that it was applied to the same purposes as the *Ligo*, and that it had a broad iron blade. Thus Columella (X. 71.)—

> Tu gravibus rastris cunctantia perfode terga,
> Tu penitus *latis* eradere viscera *marris*
> Ne dubita ———

and again, V. 87.—

> Aequora dulcis humi repetat mucrone bidentis,
> Mox bene cum glebis vivacis cespitis herbam
> Contundat marrae seu fracti dente ligonis.

Hence the *Marra* was, very probably, a *one-bladed mattock*, an instrument which is constantly seen in the hands of the field labourer in the south of Europe, and still retains its ancient name, being called *Marra* in Italy, and *Marre de vigneron* in France. Pliny, in the passage quoted above, when

---

[1] Varro l. c. These words are evidently corrupt, but the general meaning is clear.
[2] G. I. 94.
[3] H. N. XVIII. 20.
[4] Virg. G. I. 164.
[5] Lucret. V. 209. Tibull. I. i. 29. I. x. 49. II. iii. 6. Virg. G. II. 400. Ov. Fast. IV. 927. Iuv. S. III. 228. It was probably identical with the Greek δίκελλα.
[6] Cato R. R. 10. 11.
[7] Col. R. R. II. 11. 13.
[8] The passages which seem to indicate the form of the *Ligo* are,—Colum. R. R. X. 89. Ov. E. P. I. viii. 59. Amorr. III. x. 31. Stat. Theb. III. 589. The following merely point out the uses to which it was applied,—Hor. Od. III. vi. 38. Epod. V. 30. Epp. I. xiv. 27. Mart. IV. lxiv. 32. Iuv. S. VII. 33. XI. 89. Pallad. R. R. I. 43. simply names *ligones* in his list of *instrumenta*.

treating of the *Bipalium*, mentions the *Marra* in such terms as to confirm the view we have taken.[1]

Pala.—This was a *pointed spade* or *shovel*. The actual upturning and stirring of the soil was performed chiefly by the plough, the *ligo* and the *bidens*, and the *pala* is mentioned specially in connection with swampy land and soft garden mould.[2] That it was pointed at the extremity, appears from the words of Pliny, when he is enumerating the different kinds of shares; one of which he describes as having a *cuspis in mucronem fastigiata*, and then adds—*cuspis effigiem palae habet*.[3] Cato ranks the *pala* among iron implements (*ferramenta*),[4] but it was sometimes made of hardwood, tipped or edged with iron—

    Tum mihi ferrato versetur robore palae
    Dulcis humus[6] . . . .

and sometimes of wood alone (*palae ligneae*),[6] in which case it was used for turning over and winnowing corn, and was in this form probably identical with the *Ventilabrum*,[7] the πτυον of the Greeks.

Bipalium.—Occasionally, for deep digging or trenching, a *Pala* of great size and strength was employed, and in this shape was termed *Bipalium*. The ordinary length of the iron blade must have been two feet and upwards; for Columella says[8]—*satis erit, non alto bipalio, id est, minus duos pedes ferramento, novale converti*.

The above is the account of the *Bipalium* given in the most approved works on Archaeology; but there is a passage in Pliny[9] which, if there be no error in the text, seems to prove that he at least gave this name to the double iron prong of the *Bidens*—*Solum apricum et quam amplissimum in seminario sive in cinea, bidente pastinari debet ternos pedes bipalio alto: marra reici quaternum pedum ferramento*.[10]

Rutrum also must have been some kind of spade or shovel, judging from the purposes to which it was applied. Thus it was used for stirring and tempering plaster, stucco,[11] and mixtures of various kinds;[12] while Ovid represents Celer as killing Remus with a *Rutrum*, when the latter leaped over the newly-cut trench which marked the circuit of the infant city—

    Nec mora transiluit, rutro Celer occupat ausum,
    Ille premit duram sanguinolentus humum.[13]

Rutellum, apparently the diminutive from the above, must have been what is now termed a corn *strike*, i. e., a cylindrical piece of wood, with which the grain in a measure is scraped level with the brim.[14]

---

[1] There is, however, another passage in Pliny, H. N. XVIII. 16. in which he speaks of cutting lucerne, when three years old, close to the ground with "*marris*," which it is difficult to reconcile with our idea of a common mattock. Iuvenal XV. 167. mentions *marrae* in general terms along with *sarcula*, *rastra*. and the *vomer*, and so again III. 311.
[2] Plin. H. N. XVIII. 6. Comp. XVII. 17. Colum. X. 45. In digging a ditch the earth would be first loosened by the *ligo* or mattock, and then thrown out with the shovel; hence, Cincinnatus is represented (Liv. III. 26.) as having been four'd *fossam fodiens palae innixus*, where, however, *palae* is a conjectural emendation for *palo*, and some edd. read *bipalio*.
[3] H. N. XVIII. 18.   [4] R. R. 10. 11.   [5] Colum. X. 45.
[6] Cato R. R. 11.   [7] Col. R. R. II. 10.
[8] R. R. XI. 3. See also V. 6. *bipalio pastinabimus*. Cato R. R. 6. 45. 151. Varro R. R. L 37. Plin. H. N. XVIII. 26.
[9] H. N. XVII. 21.
[10] Most edd. have *fermento*, which is unintelligible.
[11] Pallad. R. R. I. 15. Vitruv. VII. 3. Plin. H. N. XXXVI. 23.
[12] Cato R. R. 37. 128. Comp. 10. 11. Varro L. L. V. § 134. ed. Müll.
[13] Ov. F. IV. 843. Comp. Varro ap. Non. s. v. *Rutrum*, p. 18.
[14] Lucil ap. Non. l. c.

Pastinum.—The verb *pastino* and the substantive *pastinatio* are used by the agricultural writers to denote the operation of deep digging or trenching, which seems to have been usually performed with the *bidens* or the *bipalium*.[1] But the instrument called *Pastinum* was not, as we might have supposed, a spade or pickaxe, but *a two-pronged dibble* for setting young plants. Thus Columella—PASTINUM *vocant agricolae ferramentum bifurcum, quo semina vanguntur*.[2]

Palladius uses *pastinum* sometimes as equivalent to *pastinatio*, and sometimes in the sense of ground that has been trenched, *i. e.*, *solum pastinatum*.[3]

Sarculum s. Sarculus.—The chief use of the *Sarculum* was to loosen the soil and destroy the weeds around the roots of the growing corn, which was sowed in such a manner as to spring up in regular rows or drills, the operation being called *sarritio*. Although we have no distinct account of the form of this instrument, we can scarcely doubt that it resembled our common hoe, which is used for a similar purpose in turnip husbandry, and is also applied, like the *Sarculum*, to many other purposes connected with stirring and pulverizing the ground. Columella describes very graphically the process of "earthing up" young vegetables in a garden with the *Sarculum*.[4]

Palladius[5] distinguishes between *Sarculos simplices* and *Sarculos bicornes*. What the latter may have been, it is hard to discover, unless we suppose with Dickson that it was a double-bladed hoe, constructed in such a manner that one-half would go on each side of a row of corn, and heap up the earth towards the plants.

Dolabra dim. **Dolabella.**—This was a strong broad chisel set straight upon a long wooden handle.[6] It was extensively employed in the construction of field works, and in various other military operations, and was one of the chief tools of the carpenter, while the use to which it was applied in agriculture is fully explained by Columella,[7]—*Nec minus dolabra quam vomere bubulcus utatur: et praefractas stirpes, summasque radices, quibus ager arbusto consitus implicatur, omnes refodiat ac persequatur*. The *dolabra*, or *dolabella*, likewise answered the purpose of a small spade in the hands of the gardener and the vine-dresser.[8] Sometimes an axe had, as is well known, a double blade, in which form it was called *Bipennis*, and sometimes instead of the second blade a *dolabra* was attached. Such an instrument was termed *Securis dolabrata*.[9]

Falx dim. **Falcula**, was the general name for any cutting instrument with a curved edge, and included the Scythe of the mower (*F. foenaria*), the Sickle of the reaper (*F. messoria—stramentaria*), the Bill of the hedger and the forester (*F. silvatica—arborea—ruscaria—lumaria—sirpicula*), and the Pruning-knife of the gar-

---

[1] *e. g.*, Colum. R. R. III. 13. Plin. H. N. XVII. 21.
[2] Colum. R. R. III. 18.
[3] Pallad. R. R. II. 10. III. 9. The operation of *Pastinatio* is mentioned very frequently in connection with the preparation of land for the formation of a vineyard. See Colum. R. R. IV. 13. 15. 16.
[4] Cato R. R. 10. Colum. II. 11. X. 91. Plin. H. N. XVIII. 19.
[5] R. R. I. 43.
[6] The different modifications and uses of the *Dolabra* have been fully described and illustrated by Mr. James Yates, in a paper contained in the 6th volume of the *Archaeological Journal*. See also his excellent article "Dolabra," in the *Dictionary of Greek and Roman Antiquities*, edited by Doctor Smith, as it stands in the *first* edition of that work, for in the second edition it is much curtailed.
[7] R. R. II. 2. Comp. Pallad. R. R. II. 3.
[8] Pallad. R. R. III. 21. Colum. R. R. IV. 24.
[9] Pallad. R. R. I. 43. who opposes it to the *Securis simplex*.

dener and the vine-dresser (*F. putatoria—vinitoria s. vineatica*).[1] Columella describes minutely the somewhat complicated form of the *Falx Vinitoria*, which will be understood from the annexed cut, which is copied from a representation found in several MSS. of that writer.[2]

Vannus, called by Virgil *mystica vannus Iacchi*,[3] was certainly an instrument for winnowing corn,—*ipsae autem spicae melius fustibus tunduntur vannisque expurgantur*,[4] and was probably identical with the Greek λικνον. Our only information with regard to its form is derived from the words of Servius, who calls it *cribrum areale*, from which we conclude that it was a kind of sieve,—and shallow baskets of this shape are to be seen in various representations of Bacchanalian ceremonies, containing the sacred utensils, and borne on the heads of attendants, who were hence termed λικνοφοροι.

3. Res.

The most important operations performed by the farmer were,—(1.) *Aratio* (ploughing). (2.) *Occatio* (harrowing). (3.) *Satio — Sementis* (sowing). (4.) *Sarritio et Runcatio* (hoeing and weeding). (5.) *Messio* (reaping). (6.) *Tritura et Ventilatio* (thrashing and winnowing). (7.) *Conditio* (storing).

(1.) *Aratio*; (2.) *Occatio*; (3.) *Satio*.[5] — The number of ploughings requisite in order to render the land fit for the reception of seed, depends upon so many contingencies—the nature of the soil, the condition of the soil, the crop desired—that no rule could ever be laid down of universal application. But, according to Roman practice, land, when about to receive a crop, was seldom ploughed less than twice, or more than four times. When a lea field (*ager novalis*) was broken up, the ploughman, when he gave the first ploughing, was said *proscindere*—when he gave the second, *iterare*, or *offringere*, because this was usually a cross ploughing (G. I. 97.)—

> Et qui proscisso quae suscitat aequore terga
> Rursus in obliquum verso perrumpit aratro,

—When he gave the third, *tertiare*.

If the soil was stiff, after each ploughing, the clods (*glebae inertes*) were broken down with heavy hand-rakes (*rastris*) or by dragging hurdles (*crates*) over the surface, and these were sometimes toothed (*crates dentatae*). This operation was termed *Occatio*, and resembled in every respect *harrowing*,— (G. I. 94.)—

> Multum adeo rastris glebas qui frangit inertes,
> Vimineasque trahit crates, iuvat arva. . . .

When the soil was completely pulverized and presented a perfectly smooth surface, which was generally achieved by the second or third ploughing and harrowing, the seed corn was cast upon the ground, a pair of mould-boards (*binae aures*) were attached to the share beam (*dentalia*), and the seed was ploughed in, the land being by this operation *ribbed* or raised in ridges, as in potato or turnip husbandry. In giving this last ploughing, the husbandman was said

---

[1] Cato R. R. 10, 11. Varro R. R. I. 22. L. L. V. § 137. ed. Müll. Pallad. R. R. I. 43.
[2] Colum. R. R. IV. 25.
[3] Virg. Georg. I. 166. and note of Servius.
[4] Colum. R. R. II. 21.
[5] Colum. II. 2. 4. 8. 9. 10. 11. 13. XI. 2. 3. Plin. H. N. XVIII. 17. 19. 20. 24. 26. Varr. R. R. I. 1. 29. Cato R. R. 61.

lirare s. *in liram redigere*, the elevated ridge of earth was called *porca*, the depression between each two *porcae* was called *lira* or *sulcus*.

Sometimes, however, the land was prepared for sowing by ploughing it in ridges before sowing, then casting the seed into the furrows, and covering it up by harrows as among ourselves. This was regarded as inferior husbandry, for it was held that the soil ought to be completely pulverized before the seed was committed to the ground; that this, however, was not always the case is evident from the lines (G. I. 104.)—

> Quid dicam, iacto qui semine, comminus arva
> Insequitur cumulosque ruit male pinguis arenae.

(4.) *Sarritio et Runcatio.*[1]—It will be understood from what has been said above with regard to the mode of covering up the seed, that the young plants would spring in regular rows, leaving a considerable space between the drills, so that two operations, little resorted to by the modern farmer in the case of corn crops, could be performed with safety and facility. These were hand hoeing, called *sarritio*, executed with an instrument called *sarculum*, the object being to loosen the soil and admit air and moisture to the young plants; and weeding, called *runcatio*, which was performed at a subsequent stage in the growth of the crop—*subiungenda deinde est sarritioni runcatio*—and both operations were repeated as often as circumstances seemed to demand.

Hand hoeing and weeding were among the ordinary and regular operations performed upon the corn crops, but there were others resorted to occasionally only and to meet particular emergencies—thus, when the young corn was too rank, the over luxuriance was checked by depasturing it, as enjoined by Virgil (G. I. 111.)—

> Quid qui ne gravidis procumbat culmus aristis
> Luxuriem segetum tenera depascit in herba,

—when the crop was parched by excessive drought, the husbandman betook himself to irrigation, as described in the charming lines (G. I. 106.)—

> Deinde satis fluvium inducit rivosque sequentes, &c.,

this being different, however, from the systematic irrigation which formed part of the established culture in some districts.

(5.) *Messio.*[2]—Mention is made by Varro of three different modes of reaping corn (*frumenti tria genera sunt messionis*) adopted in different parts of Italy. According to one method, the stem was shorn close to the ground with a reaping hook (*falx*), and the ears were then cut off from the straw, and carried away in baskets (*corbes*); according to the second, the ears alone were cut off with a small saw, fitted into a crooked wooden handle; according to the third, the stem was divided midway between the ear and the root. When either the second or the third method was followed, the straw left standing was subsequently mown.

(6.) (7.) *Tritura—Ventilatio—Conditio.*[3]—The mode of thrashing corn followed by the ancient Romans is still retained in southern Italy, in Greece, and in the East, and is frequently alluded to in Scripture. A small plot of ground, generally of a circular form, was marked out in the immediate vicinity of the *Villa*; it was surrounded with a low wall, the surface was either levelled,

[1] Colum. R. R. II. 12. 13. Plin. H. N. XVIII. 21. 26. Cato R. R. 37. Varr. R. R. I. 18. 30. 36.
[2] Varro R. R. I. 50. Colum. R. R. II. 21. Plin. H. N. XVIII. 30.
[3] Varro R. R. I. 13. 51. 52. 53. 57. Colum. R. R. I. 6. II. 20. Cato R. R. 91. 129. Plin. H. N. XVIII. 30.

or raised slightly in the centre, was made perfectly smooth, and hardened into a sort of concrete by the addition of chalk and other materials—the space thus prepared was called *Area* (G. I. 178.)—

> Area cum primis ingenti aequanda cylindro
> Et vertenda manu, et creta solidanda tenaci
> Ne subeant herbae, neu pulvere victa fatiscat.

To this enclosure the ears of corn, either cut close off, or with a portion of the straw attached, were conveyed and spread out, and the grain was then trodden or rubbed out (*terere*) by oxen or horses driven round and round. In order that the ears might be turned over, and every portion subjected in turn to the treading action of the feet, heavy beams of wood, with iron spikes attached, called *Tribula* and *Traheae* were dragged backwards and forwards by some of the animals. The corn was then winnowed by tossing it in the air by a wooden shovel called *ventilabrum*, or by agitating it in a sieve called *vannus*, and when thoroughly cleaned, was stored up in carefully constructed granaries (*granaria—horrea*). Sometimes, however, when the ears of corn were cut close off from the straw, they were conveyed to the barn (*horreum*), and there the grain was beaten out with flails (*baculis excutere—fustibus tundere*).[1]

4. *Tempora*.[2]

The seasons at which the different operations were performed necessarily varied greatly according to circumstances. Thus, rich strong land was ploughed early in spring, and again before the summer solstice, while dry poor soil was not ploughed at all until autumn. Virgil gives the precept distinctly, and adds the reasons (G. I. 63.)—

> ——————————— Ergo age terrae
> Pingue solum primis extemplo a mensibus anni
> Fortes invertant tauri, glebasque iacentes
> Pulverulenta coquat maturis solibus aestas.
> At si non fuerit tellus fecunda, sub ipsum
> Arcturum sat erit tenui suspendere sulco :
> Illic, officiant laetis ne frugibus herbae,
> Hic, sterilem exiguus ne deserat humor arenam.

So also different crops were sown at different seasons. Wheat, as among ourselves, might be sown twice a-year, towards the close of autumn, and in spring, the latter being called *trimestris satio*, because the grain was reaped about three months after it was sown. Virgil speaks of the autumn sowing only, and says that the farmer ought not to commence before the latter end of October (G. I. 219.)—

> At si triticeam in messem robustaque farra
> Exercebis humum, solisque instabis aristis,
> Ante tibi Eoae Atlantides abscondantur
> Debita quam sulcis committas semina, &c.

---

[1] Colum. R. R. II. 21.
[2] The Eleventh Book of Columella is almost entirely occupied by an exposition of the seasons of the year in which the different operations of Agriculture ought to be performed,—*Itaque praecipiemus quid quoque mense faciendum sit, sic temporibus accommodantes opera ruris, ut permiserit status coeli: cuius varietatem mutationemque, si ex hoc commentario fuerit praemonitus villicus, aut nunquam decipietur, aut certe non frequenter*, c. 2. Varro also devotes ten chapters (R. R. I. 27. . . . . 36.) to the same topic, dividing the year into eight *intervalla*, and the whole work of Palladius, as noticed above, is thrown into the form of a *Kalendarium Rusticum*, a book being devoted to each month. See also Plin. H. N. XVIII. 25. 26. 27. 28. 29.

In like manner the poet tells us that *hordeum* (barley), *linum* (flax), *papavera* (poppies), *vicia* (the vetch), and *faselus* (the kidney-bean), ought to be sown about the beginning of November, but *faba* (the bean), *medica* (lucerne), and *milium* (millet), in spring. Even here the practice varied in different parts of Italy, for Pliny remarks upon bean sowing that Virgil describes the usage of his native province on the Po, while in central and southern Italy beans were commonly sown in autumn.

Under the head of *Tempora* would fall the consideration of days propitious for work (*felices operum*) and those on which it was unlucky to commence any undertaking (G. I. 276.)—

>Ipsa dies alios alio dedit ordine Luna
>Felices operum—Quintam fuge, &c.

—moreover certain tasks could be performed without impiety even on days consecrated to the gods (G. I. 268.)—

>Quippe etiam festis quaedam exercere diebus
>Fas et iura sinunt. . . .

—some occupations could be prosecuted in bad weather (G. I. 259.)—

>Frigidus agricolam si quando continet imber
>Multa, &c.

—some even in winter (G. I. 291.)—

>Et quidam seros hiberni ad luminis ignes
>Pervigilat. . . .

—nay, particular hours of the day were regarded as peculiarly appropriate to certain toils. Thus grass and stubble were best cut during the night or in the early morning when the ground was still wet with dew—

>Multa adeo gelida melius se nocte dedere,

while ploughing, sowing, reaping, and thrashing succeeded best during the noontide heat (G. I. 297.)—

>At rubicunda Ceres medio succiditur aestu
>Et medio tostas aestu terit area fruges.
>Nudus ara, sere nudus. . . . .

Under the head of *Tempora* would fall also, in ancient times, that knowledge of astronomy which taught the rustic to determine the different epochs of the year by observing the position of some conspicuous stars and constellations with regard to the sun (G. I. 257.)—

>Nec frustra signorum obitus speculamur et ortus,

and also that familiarity with certain natural appearances which enables those who have resided long in any particular locality to predict changes in the weather. These prognostics were termed by the Greeks Διοσημεια, and the poem of Aratus bearing that title has been closely followed by Virgil in several passages of the first *Georgic*.

Crops.—We may now briefly enumerate the chief crops cultivated by the Romans, the objects of the various operations detailed above.

1. Corn Crops (*frumenta*).—Of these the most important was wheat, and of this cereal two distinct species were in common use, *Far* and *Triticum*.

Far, said to have been the grain first cultivated in Italy, is the species known to botanists as *Triticum Spelta*, or *Spelt Wheat*, and is still raised on high and poor soils in central Europe. It is much coarser than common wheat, and the husk adheres so closely to the grain that it cannot be separated by thrashing, but must be removed by a process similar to that applied to oats and barley before they are ground into meal. This operation was designated by the verb *pinsere*, the place where it was performed as *pistrinum*, and the workman as *pistor*, words which, strictly speaking, are distinguished from *molere* and its derivatives. But in ancient times the grain was husked, ground, and baked in the same place and by the same person, and hence *pistrinum* frequently denotes a *mill* or a *bakehouse*, and *pistor* usually signifies a *baker*.

Triticum seems to have been specifically the same with the wheat cultivated by ourselves, and, like it, admitted of many varieties, the most common of which were *Siligo*, *Robur*, *Ador*, and *Semen Trimestre*—the last we may identify with our spring wheat.

Hordeum (barley) also was cultivated largely, and, to a more limited extent, *Milium* (millet) and *Secale* (rye). *Avena* (the oat) does not succeed in a climate so hot as that of Italy, and, when sown, was probably cut green for forage.

2. Leguminous Crops (*Legumina*).—Of these the most important were— *Faba* (the bean); *Pisum* (the pea); *Faselus* (the kidney bean); *Vicia* (the vetch); *Lens* s. *Lenticula* (the lentile); *Cicer* (the chick pea); *Lupinus* (the lupine).

3. Forage Crops (*Pabula*).—Of these the most important were—*Foenum* (hay); *Medica* (lucerne); *Ervum* (tares). It was common to sow together various kinds of grain, tares, and vetches, and to cut the whole when green, such a combination being called *farrago*.

To this class belong *Napus* (rape), and *Rapum* (the turnip), which were extensively cultivated in Gaul.

4. Crops cultivated for their fibre.—Of these the chief were *Linum* (flax), and *Cannabis* (hemp).

5. Crops cultivated for the sake of other crops.—To this class belonged *Arundo* (the reed), extensively used for the support of vines, and *Salix* (the osier) employed for withes and baskets.

Papavera (poppies), which were raised for the sake of the oil which they yielded, cannot be conveniently ranked under any of the above heads.

Manuring—Fallows—Rotation of Crops, &c.—Land will not continue to produce crops for an indefinite number of years in succession, unless means are taken to stimulate and recruit its powers. This may be effected in two ways.

1. By repose. 2. By the application of manure (*stercoratio*), combined with a change of crops.

The usual practice among the Romans was to allow corn land to lie fallow every alternate year. This is evident from the precepts of Virgil, who enjoins the farmer to plough rich land early in spring, and to sow late in autumn, thus implying that the ground remained unproductive during the interval. This system of *Summer Fallows*, as it is called, prevailed extensively in England until a recent period, but has now been in a great measure superseded by improved modes of culture.

Some land, however, was naturally so rich that it was cropped every year, and hence was called *Ager restibilis;* but in this case it was necessary to apply manure liberally. On the other hand, *Novale,* or *Ager Novalis,* is the term commonly used to designate land which was allowed to repose for a year, and then broken up afresh—*Novale est quod alternis annis seritur.* Again, *Vervactum,* which properly signifies land ploughed in spring—*quod vere semel aratum est, a temporis argumento* VERVACTUM *vocatur*—is also opposed to *Ager restibilis,* because land ploughed in spring was, generally speaking, not sown until the following autumn, and therefore rested for a season.[1]

The ancient agriculturist was fully alive to the importance of collecting as much manure (*stercus*) as possible.—*Sterquilinium magnum stude ut habeas: stercus sedula conserva,* are the words of Cato, and minute directions are given for preparing and applying it. Varro recommends the formation of two dung-hills (*Sterquilinia*), or one large dunghill in two divisions, close to the farm-house (*secundum villam*), one for old and well-rotted dung ready for use, the other as a receptacle for all fresh additions.[2]

But however rich land may be, and however highly manured, if the same kind of crop is sown for several years in succession upon the same ground, it rapidly degenerates; and hence the necessity, well known to the ancients, of what is now called a *Rotation,* that is, of varying the crops, so that corn, leguminous plants, and forage shall succeed each other in a certain cycle.

The passage in Virgil (G. I. 71.-83.) in which he touches upon this theme is somewhat obscure, and has been variously interpreted, but the true meaning seems to be as follows :—

1. The exhausted energies of the soil may be recruited by a summer fallow—by allowing the ground to remain uncropped every other year (*alternis annis cessare*), 71. 72.

2. But if the extent of the farm is not sufficient to admit of this, the same object may be attained by varying the crop in such a manner that corn (*farra*) shall be succeeded by green crops, such as vetches, beans, and lupines, 73.-76.

3. However, flax, poppies, and oats must be excluded from the rotation, for, although they are not corn crops, they scourge (*urunt*) the ground, and, therefore, cannot be employed to recruit it, 77. 78.

4. But, if you keep flax, &c., out of your rotation, it will be easy work for the land, although you crop it every year, provided you vary the crop (*alternis enim facilis labor*[3]), and give the ground plenty of rich manure, for, by a change of crops the land does, as it were, find repose, and thus, although not yielding corn, is not altogether unproductive.

---

[1] Cato R. R. 27. 35. Varro R. R. I. 29. 44. L. L. V. § 39. ed. Müll. Colum. R. R. II. 9. 10. XI. 2. § 32. Plin. H. N. XVIII. 19. 21. 23. *Ager novalis,* or *Novale solum,* are sometimes used to denote *land newly brought into cultivation;* and hence *land in a state of nature,* pasture that has never been ploughed.
[2] Cato R. R. 5. 37. Varro R. R I. 13. 38. Colum. R. R. II. 15. Plin. H. N. XVII. 9.
[3] The main difficulty of the passage lies in the word *alternis.* In line 71, all agree in understanding *alternis* to mean *alternis annis,* and to refer to a summer fallow : but in line 79, *Sed tamen alternis facilis labor,* taken in connection with what follows, and especially with

Sic quoque mutatis requiescunt foetibus arva,

it would appear that *alternis* must denote the alternation of a green crop with a corn crop.

Cultus Arborum.

Propagation of Trees.—Virgil (G. II. 9.) enters upon this portion of his subject by describing the different ways in which trees are propagated—

> Principio arboribus varia est natura creandis,

and of these he enumerates nine, three natural and six artificial.[1]

Natural Methods. (*Hos natura modos primum dedit.*)—1. Some trees spring up and cover the ground spontaneously (*sponte sua*), the soil producing them, apparently, without seed. Such are broom (*humiles genistae*), osiers (*molle siler*), and natural copse (*frutices*). 2. Others spring from seed which has been visibly dropped (*posito de semine*). 3. Others are multiplied by suckers (*Pullulat ab radice aliis densissima silva*).

Artificial Methods. (*Quos ipse via sibi reperit usus.*)—1. Tearing away the suckers (*plantae*) and planting them out in regular trenches—

> Hic plantas tenero abscidens de corpore matrum
> Deposuit sulcis ——

2. Cutting off portions of the root (*stirpes*[2]) and burying them in the ground either split across (*quadrifidas sudes*), or sharpened to a point (*acuto robore vallos*). 3. By layers (*pressos propaginis arcus*). 4. By slips or cuttings (*nil radicis egent aliae*, &c.) 5. By planting pieces of the solid wood, as in the propagation of the olive—

> Quin et caudicibus sectis, mirabile dictu,
> Traditur e sicco radix oleagina ligno.

6. By grafting or budding (*inserere—insitio—oculos imponere*).

Without dwelling longer upon trees in general, we may at once pass on to the consideration of those two which were of paramount importance to the Italian agriculturist—*the vine* and *the olive*.

Cultivation of the Vine.[3]—When a farmer was about to form a vineyard, the first inquiry was whether, taking into account the circumstances of the locality, it would be advisable to select a level spot or sloping ground (G. II. 273.)—

> Collibus an plano melius sit ponere vitem
> Quaere prius. . . .

It was well known that a larger quantity of grapes could be obtained from rich low-lying land, but that the quality of the wine grown upon light hilly soil was superior—*fere autem omni statu locorum campestria largius vinum, sed iucundius afferunt collina* (Colum. III. 2.) The site having been fixed, the next care was to select those kinds of vine which were best suited to the place, no easy task, for the varieties known to the ancients were so numerous that Virgil, after enumerating a few, exclaims that it would be more easy to count the waves or the sands on the sea shore, than to examine all the different kinds and rehearse their names (G. II. 103, comp. Colum. III. 2.)

---

[1] Comp. Varro R. R. I. 39, 40. Plin. H. N. XVII. 10.
[2] Many scholars believe that *stirpes* here mean *portions of thick branches*.
[3] Columella devotes nearly the whole contents of four books (III. IV. V. VI.) to the cultivation of the vine, entering into the most minute details. Varro touches very lightly on the subject, R. R. I. 8, 25, 26. Pliny dwells much upon the vine in H. N. XVII, especially in chapters 21, 22, 23. See also Cato, R. R. 28, 29, 32, 33, 41, 43, 49, 157.

Propagation of the Vine.—Several methods are mentioned by ancient writers, and Virgil seems specially to approve of that by layers (G. II. 62.)—

> Sed truncis oleae melius, propagine vites
> Respondent ——

but the one generally adopted was that by *malleoli*. The *malleolus* was a young shoot cut from the vine with a small knob of the wood of the preceding year projecting on each side, so as to present the form of a little hammer, and hence the name. Columella describes it most distinctly (III. 6.)—MALLEOLUS *autem novellus est palmes, innatus prioris anni flagello, cognominatusque a similitudine rei, quod in ea parte quae deciditur ex vetere sarmento prominens utrinque* MALLEOLI *speciem praebet.* The *malleoli* were planted out in a nursery (*seminarium vitiarium*), the soil of which was prepared for their reception by repeated diggings, and those who were most careful selected for this purpose a spot resembling, as closely as might be, in quality and exposure, the ground to which they were ultimately to be transferred (G. II. 268.)—

> Mutatam ignorent subito ne semina matrem.

At the end of three years the *malleoli*, having in the meantime been properly pruned, had formed vigorous roots: hence they were now termed *Viviradices*, and were ready to be transplanted.

The *vivaridices* were planted out in the vineyard which had been prepared for their reception in one of three modes (Plin. H. N. XVII. 35.) 1. *In pastinato, i. e.*, when the whole surface had been deeply trenched, and the soil completely pulverized by repeated manipulations, this was regarded as the best mode. 2. *In sulco, i. e.*, in trenches. 3. *In scrobe, i. e.*, in pits.

In any case, the young plants (*semina*) stood in parallel rows (*ordines*), those in each row were placed at equal distances from each other, and the distance between each of the parallel rows was equal to the distance between each plant in the row; so that each vine had exactly the same amount of free space all round. The distance between each vine varied in different localities, according to the quality of the soil—

> . . . . Si pinguis agros metabere campi,
> Densa sere, in denso non segnior ubere Bacchus;
> Sin tumulis adclive solum collisque supinos
> Indulge ordinibus¹—

According to Pliny, the distance in the richest land was not less than four, and in the poorest not more than eight feet; but others allow an interval of ten feet.

Down the middle of the vineyard ran a road called *Limes decumanus*, or simply *Decumanus*, eighteen feet broad, so as to admit of two carts passing each other; a series of narrower paths called *semitae* or *viae* were formed, some parallel, and others at right angles to the *decumanus*, the distance between the *semitae* being always the same. In this manner, the whole vineyard was divided into square plots of equal size, which were termed *antes*, *horti*, or *hortuli*, each *hortus* containing one hundred plants. The circumstance that the *viae* or *semitae* were all either at right angles or parallel to the *decumanus*, is indicated by Virgil, when he says—

> . . . . nec secius omnis in unguem
> Arboribus positis secto via limite quadret.

---

[1] Columella, however, says exactly the reverse, R. R. III. 15.

The vines were sometimes set simply in ordinary rows—

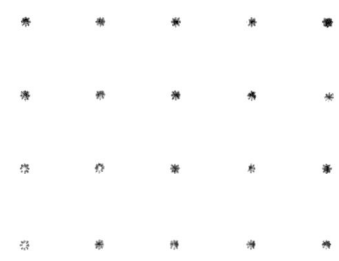

and sometimes arranged in the form called a *quincunx*[1]—

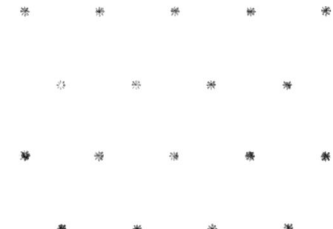

Supports for the Vines.—On the manner in which the vines were supported depended the technical distinction between an *Arbustum* and a *Vinea* or *Vinetum* proper.

In an *arbustum* (i. e., *arborisetum*), the vines were supported by growing trees planted for this purpose in rows at regular intervals, the ground between the rows being frequently cultivated for other crops. The trees most commonly employed were the elm (*ulmisque adiungere vites*) and the poplar. The union between the fragile, yielding, fruitful vine and the sturdy stock by which it was sustained, was frequently compared, both by poets and prose writers, to the marriage state; hence the celebrated simile in Catullus LXII. 49 seqq.—

> Ut vidua in nudo vitis quae nascitur arvo
>
> At si forte eadem est ulmo coniuncta marito,

and the expression of Horace when describing the pursuits of a rural life (Epod. II. 9.)—

> Ergo aut adulta vitium propagine
> Altas maritat populos.

Sometimes the trees in an *arbustum* were not allowed to rise higher than fifteen or twenty feet, which is the general practice in many parts of northern Italy at

---

[1] See on the whole of this subject, Plin. H. N. XVII. 11. 22. XVIII. 34. Colum. R. R. III. 13. 15. 20. IV. 18. 20. X. 376. Virg. G. II. 273. seqq. 417.

present, but frequently were permitted to attain to their full height, as is common to this day in Campania. In the latter case, the branches were pruned in such a manner as to present a series of storeys or stages called *tabulata*, and to these Virgil alludes (G. II. 361.; comp. Colum. V. 6.)—

. . . Summasque sequi tabulata per ulmos.

In the *Vinea* or *Vinetum* proper the vines were either left to trail upon the ground, partially supporting themselves (*sparsis per terram palmitibus aut per se rite subrecta*—Plin. XXXV. 6.), as we now see them in some parts of Provence, or they were supported (*vites pedatae*) by props (*adminicula— pedamenta*), which were either entire sticks (*pali*), or pieces of cleft timber (*ridicae*.) Again, the vine was either attached to a single upright support (*adminiculum sine iugo*), as in all the finest vineyards of modern France, or to two uprights and a cross piece (*pedatae simplici iugo*), or they were trained upon a sort of trellis formed by four uprights set in the angles of a square, and connected by cross pieces at top, so as to form a kind of roof (*compluviatae quadruplici iugo*), both of the last mentioned arrangements being still very common in Italy. The cross pieces which formed the connection at top, were either poles (*perticae*), or ropes (*funiculi*), or strands of hair (*crines*).

Different operations performed on the Vine.—Both when in the *Seminarium* and after it had been transplanted to the *Vinea*, the young vine was repeatedly cut down nearly to the ground, in order that the roots might acquire vigour, and was not allowed to bear fruit until the seventh year—*antequam septimum annum a sarculo compleat*—Plin. H. N. XVII. 35.), but when the vineyard was in full bearing, the ordinary operations performed each year were four—
1. *Pastinatio.* 2. *Pampinatio.* 3. *Putatio.* 4. *Ablaqueatio.*

1. *Pastinatio, i. e.*, trenching. The whole vineyard was dug three or four times at least each year (G. II. 398.)—

. . . . Omne quotannis
Terque quaterque solum scindendum, glebaque versis
Aeternum frangenda bidentibus. . . . .

the instrument usually employed being the *Bidens*, which is still in common use for the same purpose, although the plough was occasionally resorted to.

2. *Pampinatio*, i. e., leaf-plucking.—A portion of the vine leaves were removed by the hand—*omne levandum fronde nemus*—twice each year; once in spring before the plant began to blossom, and again in autumn after the grapes were formed, in order to admit the sun freely to the fruit.

3. *Putatio*, i. e., pruning.—The superfluous shoots (*sarmenta*) were usually pruned off after the conclusion of the vintage; the knife employed, called *Falx Vinitoria*, was of a peculiar form, and has been minutely described by Columella, IV. 2.; and represented above, p. 480.

4. *Ablaqueatio.*—This operation was performed late in October, and consisted in digging round the vine so as to expose the upper portion of the roots; those which approached within eighteen inches of the surface were lopped off, the remainder were left open to the weather for a longer or shorter period according to the climate, and, before the hole was filled up, a little manure was occasionally thrown in.

With regard to the vintage (*vindemia*), the treatment of the grapes, and the process of making and preserving wine, we have already spoken, p. 437.[1]

[1] See Cato R. R. 28. 29. 31. 42.—46. 51. 64.—68. 93. 100. 117.—119. Varro R.R. I. 24. 55. 60. 64. 66. Colum. R. R. III. 17. VI. 6. 7. Plin. H. N. XVII. 18.

Culture of the Olive.—While the vine demanded constant watchfulness and unceasing toil, the management of the olive was so easy that, comparatively, it might be said to require no cultivation (G. II. 420.)—

> Contra, non ulla est oleis cultura. . . .

The operation of *Ablaqueatio*, the same as that described above in the case of the vine, performed each autumn—the occasional loosening of the soil in the olive-yard, either with the *Bidens* or the plough—and pruning at long intervals, were sufficient to keep the plant in health, and to secure abundant crops—thus Columella, V. 9.— *Quinetiam compluribus interpositis annis olivetum putandum est: nam veteris proverbii meminisse convenit, eum qui aret olivetum, rogare fructum; qui stercoret, exorare; qui caedat, cogere.*

Propagation of the Olive.—The mode generally adopted was curious. A *seminarium* having been carefully prepared, young, long, healthy, fruitful branches, about the thickness of a man's wrist, were detached from a full grown tree. These branches were cut transversely into sections eighteen inches in length, which are called *trunci* by Virgil (G. II. 63.), and *taleae* by Columella. The extremities of the *taleae* were smeared over with a mixture of dung and ashes, and then planted in the *seminarium* to such a depth that the top of the *talea* should be three inches under the surface, care being taken at the same time that the extremity of the *talea* which was uppermost in the parent branch should be uppermost in the ground. At the end of five years, the plants, having been regularly cleaned and pruned, had become little trees (*arbusculae*), and were fit to be transplanted out in the *Olivetum*. (Colum. V. 9.)

There was another mode of propagating the olive known to Virgil, which consisted in cutting up the trunk of an old olive tree into small billets, for these, if planted out, would germinate (G. II. 30.) This practice is still occasionally followed in Italy, where the stock is divided into pieces, resembling a mushroom in shape and size, from which circumstance they are called *novoli*.

Gathering the Olives.—The olive harvest (*oleitas*) usually took place in December. The olives were first crushed in a sort of mill (*mola olearia*) and then subjected to the action of the oil press (*trapetum—teritur Sicyonia bacca trapetis*[1]). With regard to the oil (*Olivum, Oleum*) thus obtained, nothing need be said, but there was another product called *amurca*, the nature of which is frequently misunderstood in consequence of the somewhat inconsistent explanations of lexicographers, who render the word *lees of oil*, or *scum of oil*. In fact, the pulp of the olive (*caro*), when expressed, yields two distinct fluids, oil, and a dark coloured watery fluid heavier than the oil. This dark coloured watery fluid is the *amurca* of the Romans, the ἀμοργή of the Greeks, and, although not an article of food, was used by the ancients for a great variety of purposes, many of which are enumerated by Pliny (H. N. XV. 8. XXIII. 3. Comp. Virg. G. I. 194. III. 448).

II. Pastio s. Res Pastoricia s. Res Pecuaria.

Technically, *Agricultura* is opposed to *Pastio*; *Colonus* to *Pastor*; and descending to subdivisions *Segetes* to *Prata*; *Arator* to *Opilio*; *Boves domiti* to *Armentum*; *Bubulcus* to *Armentarius*.

---

[1] The *Mola Olearia* and the *Trapetum* were combined in one machine, which has been elaborately described by Cato (R. R. 20. 21. 22.) in a passage which scholars have vainly striven to comprehend and explain.

Pastio includes everything connected with providing and managing stock.
The division of the general term *Pastio* into *Pastio Agrestis* and *Pastio Villatica* we have already explained.

1. *Pastio Agrestis.*[1]

The different kinds of domestic animals comprehended under this head were—
1. *Oves* (sheep); 2. *Caprae* (goats); 3. *Sues* (swine); 4. *Boves* (kine);
5. *Asini* (asses); 6. *Equi* (horses); 7. *Muli* (mules); to which were added
—8. *Canes* (dogs); 9. *Pastores* (shepherds and herdsmen).

Providing Stock.[2]—The matters to be inquired into when providing a stock of domestic animals (*in pecore parando*) were four—1. The age (*qua aetate*); 2. The breed (*quo seminio*); 3. The points (*qua forma*); 4. The legal forms of purchase and warranty (*stipulatio*).

Managing Stock.[3]—Suitable stock having been provided, the matters to be considered in reference to management were five—1. Feeding (*pastio*); 2. Breeding (*foetura*), extending *a conceptu ad partum;* 3. Rearing the young stock (*nutricatus*); 4. Preserving the stock in health, and applying the proper remedies in disease (*sanitas*); 5. Determining the proper numbers (*numerus*), that is, the total number of animals to be kept; the number of each kind; the proper size of each flock and herd; the relative proportion of males and females, of full grown and of young animals; the amount of surplus stock (*reiiculae—delectus quotannis habendus et reiiculae reiiciundae*, Varro R. R. II. 5.) to be got rid of; and the selection of young animals to be reared for supplying vacancies, a process technically expressed by the verb *submittere*, e. g., Varro R. R. II. 3.—*Hoedi trimestres cum sint facti, tum submittuntur et in grege incipiunt esse;* and Virgil G. III. 159.—

Et, quos aut pecori malint submittere habendo.

A complete treatise upon *Pastio* would embrace full information on each of the above nine points in reference to each class of animals separately, and in addition, in treating of sheep and goats, it would be necessary to enter into some details with regard to shearing (*tonsura*) and cleaning wool and hair, and a separate chapter would be required upon dairy produce (*de lacte et caseo*), a subject on which, under the title τυροποιΐα, much was written by the Greeks.

Before entering upon any details, we must call attention to a circumstance connected with the management of large flocks and herds in Italy, which arose out of the physical conformation of the country, consisting as it does of extensive level plains, dry and parched in summer, but yielding abundant herbage after the rains of October, these plains being intersected throughout the whole length of the peninsula by a lofty and rugged mountain range. These mountains are, in many districts, covered with dense forests, and afford abundant pasture and shelter from the sun during the summer months. Accordingly, as soon as the heats set in, all the flocks and herds, except those employed in agricultural toil, and those for which there was accommodation in the buildings of the farm, were, and still are, driven from the arid expanse of Apulia to the

---

[1] The Second Book of Varro de R. R. and the Seventh and Eighth of Columella are devoted to *Pastio Agrestis.*
[2] Varro R. R. II. 1.
[3] Varro R. R. II. 1.

Lucanian and Calabrian hills, and from the Tuscan Maremma and the Campagna of Rome to the Samnite and Sabine ranges, returning again to the milder climate of the low country at the end of autumn. The communications between the high and low lands were kept open by drove roads (*calles*),[1] which now, as in ancient times, are thronged twice a-year by endless troops of oxen, sheep, and goats, accompanied by the herdsmen and their families. These mountain pastures were, for the most part, the property of the state, and were farmed out to large contractors (*publicani*), by whom again they were sub-let to the owners of stock, the sum charged being in proportion to the number of animals.

This being premised, we may now say a very few words upon each of the classes of animals enumerated above.

Sheep.[2]—The general terms are—*Oves, Ovillum pecus, Pecus lanare;* specially, *Aries* is the ram, *Ovis* the ewe, *Vervex* the wether, *Agnus* s. *Agna* the lamb, *Ovile* the sheepfold, *Opilio* the shepherd.

A distinction was made between the finer and more delicate sheep, which being kept upon the farm the whole year round, were termed *Greges Villatici*, and the more numerous flocks which passed the winter in the low grounds, and were driven to the forests and mountains in summer—*Greges qui in saltibus pascuntur*.

Again, sheep were divided into *Oves Hirtae* and *Oves Pellitae*. The *Oves hirtae* were those whose wool was of an ordinary quality, and required no protection: the *Oves pellitae* were those which, in consequence of the fineness of their wool, were covered with skin jackets (*pellibus integuntur*) in order that the fleece might be kept perfectly smooth and clean, and thus be more easily washed, prepared, and dyed—*ne lana inquinetur quominus vel infici recte possit, vel lavari et parari.* The sheep reared in the neighbourhood of Tarentum belonged to this variety, and to these Horace alludes in the well known lines—

> Dulce pellitis ovibus Galesi
> Flumen, et regnata petam
> Rura Phalanto.

Suitable *Stabula*, or covered pens, were provided, in which the sheep and goats found refuge during the cold of winter, and the greatest care was taken that these buildings should have a warm exposure, and be kept clean and dry. The general management of the flocks during winter, and the system followed in pasturing them during the heat of summer, are most accurately described by Virgil (G. III. 295. seqq.) in a passage which has been closely followed by Columella (VII. 3.)

Sheep Shearing.[3]—This operation, called *Tonsura Ovium*, was performed between the vernal equinox and the solstice, after the sheep had begun to sweat, and during the heat of the day (*cum sudare inceperunt oves*), for wool, when impregnated with the natural moisture of the animal (*lana sucida*), was heavier, softer, and of a better colour. The fleeces, when detached and rolled up, were called *vellera* or *velumina*, terms from which Varro infers that originally the fleeces were plucked, not shorn, from the animal, a system which, he adds, was still followed by some persons. *Oves hirtae*, as soon as shorn, were smeared with wine and oil, to which some added white wax and lard (*adeps suillus*); in

---

[1] Varro R. R. II. 10. Comp. Cic. pro Sext. 5. Liv. XXII. 14. Tacit. Ann. IV. 27. Suet. Iul. 19.
[2] Varro R. R. II. 2. Colum. R. R. VIII. 2—5.
[3] Varro R. R. II. 11

the case of *Oves pellitae* the inside of the jacket was smeared with the same mixture, and then it was replaced.

Goats.[1]—The general terms are—*Capellae, Grex Caprinus·* specially, *Hircus* is the buck goat; *Capra, Capella,* the Nanny goat; *Hoedus,* the kid; *Caprile,* the goat fold; *Caprarius,* the goat herd.

The management and feeding of goats was much the same as that of sheep, except that the former were more hardy, and while sheep preferred open pastures, goats took delight in woody regions where they could obtain abundance of *virgulta,* which formed their favourite food.

Goats were shorn for the sake of their hair, which was employed in the manufacture of a coarse kind of cloth used by soldiers and sailors (G. III. 311.)—

> Nec minus interea barbas incanaque menta
> Cinyphii tondent hirci, saetasque comantes,
> Usum in castrorum et miseris velamina nautis.

Cloth of this kind was termed *Cilicium,* from having been first fabricated in Phrygia and Cilicia, and Martial (XIV. 140.) mentions *Udones Cilicii,* which must have been socks or overshoes made of this material.

Swine.[2]—The general terms are—*Sues, Suillum genus, Suillum pecus:* specially, *Verres* is the boar; *Sus,* the sow; *Scrofa,* the breeding sow; *Maialis,* the castrated male; *Porci,* the young pigs, which, when sucking, were called *Lactentes;* when ten days old, being then regarded as pure and fit for sacrifice, *Sacres;* when first weaned, *Nefrendes* and *Delici; Hara,* the pig-stye; *Subulcus,* the swine herd; *Suilla Carro, Succidia,* pork; *Pernae,* hams; *Petasones, Taniacae, Tomacinae,* flitches and gammons of bacon; *Tomacula,* pork sausages.

Kine.[3]—The general terms were—*Boves, Bubulum genus, Armenticium pecus:* specially, *Taurus,* the bull; *Vacca,* the cow; *Forda,* a cow in calf; *Taura,* a barren cow; *Bos,* the castrated male; *Vitulus, Vitula,* the calf. Four degrees of age were distinguished—1. *Vitulus, Vitula.* 2. *Iuvencus, Iuvenca.* 3. *Taurus, Vacca.* 4. *Vetuli. Bubile* is the cattle shed.

Virgil (G. III. 157.) bids the farmer divide his calves into three classes— 1. Those intended to form a portion of the herd. 2. Those reserved for sacrifice. 3. Those destined for agricultural labour (*boves domiti*).

Since nearly all the heavy work of the farm was performed by oxen, it was necessary to set apart a considerable number for that purpose, and these from an early age were regularly trained according to the system minutely described in the lines which immediately follow those referred to above. In the same book (G. III. 51.) we find the points of the breeding cow carefully specified.

Horses.[4]—The general terms are—*Equi, Pecus equinum:* specially, *Equus admissarius* is the stallion; *Equa,* the mare; *Canterius,* the gelding; *Equulus, Pullus,* the colt; *Equile,* the stable. *Equiso, Equarius, Agaso,* are words all of which occur in the sense of a groom or horse-keeper, but are scarcely to be found in the agricultural writers.

In purchasing, rearing, feeding, and training horses, it was absolutely necessary to have regard to the purpose for which the animal was ultimately destined; whether for war (*ad rem militarem*), for riding or draught (*ad vecturam*), for racing (*ad cursuram*), or for breeding (*ad admissuram*).

---

[1] Varro R. R. II. 3.   Colum. R. R. 6. 7.
[2] Varro R. R. II. 4.   Colum. R. R. VIII. 9. 10. 11.
[3] Varro R. R. II. 5.   Colum. R. R. VII. 1—25.
[4] Varro R. R. II. 7.   Colum. R. R. VII, 26—34.

Hence the *belli peritus* made choice of a particular kind of steed, and managed him in a particular manner, and so the *quadrigarius*, the *desultor*, and he who wished *rectarios facere*. It is almost unnecessary to call attention to the magnificent lines in which Virgil describes the high bred colt (G. III. 75.)

Asses.[1]—The general and special terms are—*Asinus, Asellus, Asina, Pullus Asininus*.

We have already mentioned the purposes for which asses were employed by the farmer. Large herds were chiefly in the hands of merchants who used pack-asses (*aselli dossuarii*) for conveying agricultural produce to the coast or to distant markets.

The asses of Arcadia were the most famous in Greece; those of Reate bore off the palm in Italy, and sometimes brought immense prices. Varro (R. R. II. 1.) mentions one which, in his recollection, had been sold for 60,000 sesterces, about £500, and says that a team of four had been bought at Rome for 400,000 sesterces, upwards of £3,300.

Mules.[2]—*Mulus* and *Mula* are the general terms for the hybrid progeny of the horse and the ass, but, strictly speaking, a distinction was drawn between the *Mulus* and the *Hinnus*.

The *Mulus* was produced by the union of a mare (*equa*) with a male ass (*asinus admissarius*).

The *Hinnus* by the union of a she-ass (*asina*) with a stallion (*equus admissarius*).

Dogs.[3]—The general term for dogs of both sexes is *Canes*, and for the whelps, *Catuli*.

Dogs were divided into two classes (*genera*)—

1. Sporting dogs—*unum (genus) venaticum et pertinet ad feras bestias et silvestres*.

2. Sheep dogs—*alterum, quod custodiae causa paratur et pertinet ad pastorem*.

It must be remembered, that while the sheep dog of this country is employed only for guiding the movements of the flocks, those of the Alps, the Appenines, the Pyrenees, and the mountains of Greece, are required to protect them from wolves, and therefore always were and are much larger, stronger, and more fierce than those with which we are familiar. The breeds most valued by the ancients were—the Spartan (*Lacones*), the Epirotan (*Epirotici, Molossi*), and the Calabrian (*Sallentini*).

Shepherds.[4]—*Pastores* is the general term comprehending all who tended the domestic animals not employed in labour. They were divided into two classes—1. Those who remained always upon the farm (*qui in fundo versantur*); and 2. Those who took charge of the flocks and herds which were driven to the mountains in summer (*qui in callibus versantur*). While youths, and even women, might perform the tasks allotted to the first class, the second class was composed of strong men in the vigour of manhood, capable of enduring the hardships and dangers incident to a wild, rough life among the hills. They were furnished with arms in order to repel the attacks of wild beasts and robbers, lived in temporary huts (*in casis repentinis*), and carried about with them all the utensils and implements required for themselves and their flocks (*omnia instru-*

---

[1] Varro R. R. II. 6. Colum. R. R. VIII. 1.
[2] Varro R. R. II. 8. Colum. R. R. VII. 35, 36, 37.
[3] Varro R. R. II. 9. Colum. R. R. VIII. 12, 13.
[4] Varro R. R. II. 10.

menta quae pecori et pastoribus opus sunt), being attended in their journeys by a certain number of beasts of burden (*iumenta dossuaria*), and also by some active, hardy women, who collected fuel, prepared the food, and kept guard over the huts when the men were absent. The whole troop was under the command of an overseer called *magister pecoris*, a person qualified by character, knowledge, experience, and education, to direct and control the proceedings of the party, and to keep the accounts (*rationes dominicas pecuarias conficere*).

Dairy Produce.[1]—This was confined to milk (*lac*) and cheese (*caseus*). It is very singular that butter (*butyrum*), although not altogether unknown, was so little used that it is not even mentioned by any of the agricultural writers except Pliny, who calls it (XXXVIII. 9.) *barbararum gentium lautissimus cibus.* See also H. N. XI. 41.

Milk was esteemed the most nourishing of all liquid food—*omnium rerum quas cibi causa capimus liquentium maxime alibile.* The first place in this respect was occupied by ewe milk (*lac ovillum*), the second by goats' milk (*caprinum*); the most purifying (*quod maxime perpurget*) was held to be mares' milk (*equinum*), next, asses' milk (*asininum*), third, cows' milk (*bubulum*), and fourth, goats' milk (*caprinum*).

Cheese was made, as among ourselves, by the addition of rennet (*coagulum*) to milk; the rennet procured from the leveret (*coagulum leporinum*) or the kid (*hoedinum*) being regarded as superior to that from the lamb (*agninum*). Rennet from the calf is not mentioned at all by Varro. The milky sap of the fig tree (*de fici ramo lac*) and vinegar (*acetum*), were also used for separating the curd from the whey (*serum*). Cheeses made from cows' milk (*casei bubuli*) were considered as the most nourishing, and at the same time as the most difficult of digestion; next in order were ewe milk cheeses (*ovilli*); while those made of goats' milk (*caprini*) were the least nourishing and the most easily digested.

2. *Pastio Villatica.*[2]

Under this was included the management of all animals, wild or tame, which could be fed at all seasons within the precincts of the farm buildings, or in enclosures immediately adjacent—*res quae in villa circumve eam ali ac pasci possint.* Originally this kind of stock consisted of some common poultry, rabbits, and bees; but towards the close of the Republic this department received great development, and many persons derived a larger revenue from their *Villaticae Pastiones* than from the farm itself. Varro claims to have been the first to draw up an independent systematic treatise upon this topic, to which he devotes the third book of his *De Re Rustica.*

Villaticae Pastiones were distributed under three heads—

1. *Ornithones.* 2. *Leporaria.* 3. *Piscinae.*

Aviaries.[3]—*Ornithones*, in the most extended acceptation of the term, included all receptacles for birds, whether wild or tame, land fowl or water fowl; in a more restricted sense, *ornithones* were huge aviaries in which thousands of wild birds were confined.

The old Roman farmer had his *aviaria* (before the introduction of the Greek word) consisting merely of a court-yard for chickens (*cohors in plano*), and a

---

[1] Varro R. R. II. 11. Colum. R. R. VIII. 8.
[2] The Third Book of Varro de R. R. and the Ninth and Tenth of Columella are devoted to *Pastio Villatica.* The whole of the Tenth Book of Columella, with the exception of the first chapter, is occupied with details regarding bees.
[3] Varro R. R. III. 4—11. Colum. R. R. IX. 1—15.

dove-cot (*columbarium*) for pigeons, but by degrees many varieties of poultry were introduced, and appropriate accommodation provided for each kind. We may enumerate—(1.) *Gallinae*, of which there were three species—*a. Villaticae*, common barn-door fowls; *b. Rusticae*, seldom tame, and therefore kept in coops (*in caveis*), which may possibly have been pheasants; and *c. Africanae*, generally supposed to have been guinea fowls. (2.) *Pavones*, peacocks. These were little known until towards the end of the Republic, and when Varro wrote brought a high price. A pea-hen's egg was at that time worth five denarii, *i. e.*, upwards of three shillings, and a full-grown young bird sold for fifty denarii, *i. e.*, about a guinea and a-half. We may also mention—(3.) *Columbae*, pigeons, of which there were several species. (4.) *Turtures*, turtle-doves. (5.) *Anseres*, geese; and (6.) *Anates*, ducks.

In the *Ornithon* proper, which was an enormous cage (see Varro R. R. III. 5.) were shut up vast numbers of thrushes (*turdi*), quails (*coturnices*), beccaficoes (*ficedulae*), millet-fowl (*miliariae*), and other birds of passage, of which immense flocks visit Italy every year. These were caught alive by fowlers (*aucupes*) kept for the purpose, and when shut up, were carefully fattened until ready for the market. Varro mentions one ornithon out of which 5,000 thrushes were sold in a single season at three denarii (*i. e.*, two shillings) a-head, amounting to the sum of 60,000 sesterces, or about £500 sterling.

Leporaria.[1]—So called because originally, being of very limited extent, they were intended for hares (*lepores*) or rabbits (*cuniculi*) only. At a later period the more general term *Vivaria*, which we may translate *preserves*, was introduced, when it became common to enclose a large space of ground in the neighbourhood of the villa with a lofty wall, and to keep in this park various wild animals, such as stags (*cervi*), roe-deer (*capreae*), and wild boars (*apri*), which were fed for the table, and sometimes hunted for sport.

Besides these, the *leporarium* frequently contained *Gliraria*, which were large jars (*dolia*) for a species of dormouse (*glis*); *Cochlearia*, places for fattening edible snails (*cochleae*); and *Alvearia*, for bees, which in the early ages used to find shelter under the eaves of the mansion (*subter subgrundas*).

Piscinae, *ponds*.[2]—Fresh water ponds (*piscinae dulces*) were frequently, even in primitive times, attached to the villa, and entailed little or no expense. But in the age of Varro, salt water ponds (*piscinae maritimae*) came into fashion, and the taste soon became a passion with many of the more wealthy. These were constructed in connection with the marine villas on the Campanian coast, and large sums were lavished in forming, stocking, and maintaining them —*aedificantur magno*—*implentur magno*—*aluntur magno*. Hirrus, a contemporary of Cicero, one of those whom he contemptuously nicknames *piscinarii*, obtained 6,000,000 of sesterces (about £50,000) for a very ordinary villa, on account of the quantity of fish in his salt ponds, and he is said to have given the loan of several thousand *muraenae* to Caesar, in order to furnish forth his triumphal banquets. (Plin. H. N. XVII. 81. Varro R. R. III. 17.)

[1] Varro R. R. III. 12—16. Colum. R. R. IX. 1—16
[2] Varro R. R. III. 17. Colum. R. R. VIII. 16. 17.

INDEX.

	Page
A	108, 299
Abacus	422, 443
Abdicare se Magistratu	180
Abdicatio	179
Ablegmina	342
Abolla	454
Abrogatio Imperii	182
Absens Creari	176
Absolutio	281
Absolvo	108, 299
Accensi	70, 198, 383
Accensi Velati	70
Accepti Latio	270, 273
Acceptum ferre, &c.	270
Accumbere Mensae	440
Accusare Rei Capitalis	83
Acerra	343
Acetabulum	411
Acetum	439
Acies	388
Acroama	447
Actio Communi dividundo	274
—— Damni iniuria dati	274
—— Emti	271
—— Familiae erciscundae	276
—— Finium regundorum	274
—— Furti	273
—— Furti oblati	273
—— Iniuriarum	274
—— Mandati	272
—— Noxalis	310
—— Prima	299
—— Secunda	299
—— Venditi	271
Actionem Dare	280
—— Edere	280
Actiones, Definition and Classification of	267, 208
Actiones Arbitrariae	268, 276
—— ex Fide bona	268, 276
—— Extraordinariae	275
—— in Personam	268
—— in Rem	268
—— Legitimae	277
—— Ordinariae	276
—— Rei uxoriae	258
—— Stricti Iuris	268, 276
Actionis Postulatio	280
Actor	98, 267, 277, 315
Actus	258, 409
—— Minimus	410
—— Quadratus	410
Ad Murciae	39
—— Murcim	39
Adfines	264, 267
Adiudicatio	254
Adlectio	118
Administration of Justice	275, 315
Addicere	258
—— Bona	276
Addictus	269
Adoptio	118, 267
Adoption in the Comitia Curiata	117
Adscriptitii	70
Adspergillum	343
Adstipulator	270
Adfinitas	267
Admissiones primae, &c.	431
Adversaria	270
Adversarius	277
Advocatus	312
Aedes Castoris	18
—— Cereris	39
—— Deum Penatium	14, 23
Aedes Divi Iulii	13
—— Herculis Musarum	44
—— Larum Permarinum	48
—— Privatae	462
—— Rotunda Herculis	39
—— Vectilianae	35
—— Vestae	14, 42
Aedicula	325
—— Concordiae	14
Aediles	155–160
—— Cereales	159
—— Curules	156
—— Plebeii	156
Aegyptus (Provincia)	193
Ænea	5
Aequimelium	39, 40
Aerarium	28, 155, 163
Aerarii	82, 169
Aes	411
—— Equestre	72, 73
—— Hordearium	72, 73
—— Militare	235
Aesculapius	323
Aestimatio Litis	300
Aestivum Aurum	445
Aetas Quaestoria	174
—— Senatoria	215
Ager Campanus	225, 231
—— Effatus	5
—— Hostilis	44
—— Publicus	158, 225, 232
—— Publicus, in the Provinces	189
—— Scripturarius	234
—— Vaticanus	3
Agere Conventus	188
—— cum Tribunis	221
Agger	396, 400

2 K

INDEX.

	Page
Agger Servii Tulii	6
Agitatores	350
Agmen	387
Agnati	255, 264, 265
Agnomen	61
Agonalia	320
Agone?	342
Agrarian Laws	225–231
Agri Censui censendo	167
Aius Locutius	22
Ala	384–386
Alabastron	446
Alae	465
Alarii	385
Alba Linea	348, 350
Albogalerus	333
Album Senatorium	213, 167
—— Iudicum	294
Alea	446
Aleatores	444
Alia Omnia	219
Alio Die	112
Aliptes	434
Alites	111
Altare	325
Alveus (in the bath)	434
—— (in a ship)	403
Amica	250
Amitini (ae)	267
Ambarvale Sacrum	331
Ambarvalia	319
Ambire—Ambitio	178
Ambitus	178, 398
Amictus	453, 455
Amiculum	456
Amphitheatrum Tauri	48
Amphitheatres	356
Amphora (measure)	410
Amphorae	438
Ampliatio	299
Amplius	299
Ampulla	446
Ancilla	94
Ancora	403
Ancoralia	403
Angustus Clavus	75
Animadversio Censoria	168
Anio Novus	57
—— Vetus	56
Anna Perenna	322
Annales Maximi	328
Annuli	455
Annulus Aureus	75, 221
—— Pronubus	423
Annus Bissextus	364
Annus Confusionis	373
Anquina	405
Anquirere	288
Anquisitio	288
Antemeridianum Tempus	428
Antennae	406
Antepilani	383, 384
Antesignani	384
Antestari	280
Antipolis	5
Antiquare Rogationem	106
Antiquo	108
Antlia	403
Antrum Caci	32
Anubis	323
Aperire Caput	180
Apex	333, 344
Aplustre	405
Apodyterium	434
Apollo	318

	Page
Apotheca	438
Apotheosis of the Emperors	210
Apparitores	199
Aprilis	362, 367
Aqua Appia — Marcia — Tepula — Iulia — Virgo — Alsietina s. Augusta — Claudia — Anio Vetus — Anio Novus	55–57
Aqua Crabra	3
—— Petronia	48
—— Mercurii	35
Aquae et Ignis Interdictio	84, 304, 309, 310
Aqueducts	54–58
Aquila Legionis	392
Ara	325
—— Consi	39
—— Evandri	32
—— Febris	37
—— Iani Curiatii	37
—— Iovis Elicii	32
—— Iovis Inventoris	32
—— Iunonis Iugae	40
—— Iunonis Sororiae	37
—— Malae Fortunae	37
—— Martis	48
—— Maxima	39, 322, 323
—— Saturni	28
Arae Fontis	49
Aratores	288
Arbiter Bibendi	443
Arbitri	276
Arbitrium	276
Archimimus	426
Arcula Turaria	343
Arculae	457
Arcus Argentarius	41
—— Claudii	43
—— Constantini	36
—— Dolabellae	35
—— M. Aurelii	43
—— S. Severi	27
—— Titi	30
—— Traiani	23
Area Capitolina	29
—— Capitolina	26
—— Circi	348
—— Concordiae	27
—— (Dwelling-house)	463
—— Fori Traiani	23
—— Vulcani	14
Arena	348, 356
Argentariae (Tabernae)	18, 159
Argentarii	271
Argentifodinae	234
Argiletum	3, 462
Aries	400
Armamenta	403
Armaria	462
Armillae	395, 396
Armilustrium	32
Army, Constitution of	377
Arra	271
Arrogatio	117, 128, 267
Artemon	405
Arundo	457, 459
Arx	25
—— Tarpeia	25
As, (weight)	408
— (coin)	412
— applied to measures of capacity	411
— applied to measures of surface	410

	Page
As, applied to measures of length	410
Asiani	238, 239
Assa voce	447
Assidui	71
Assurgere	180
Asylum	25
Athletae	350
Atellanae	352
Atramentum	459
Atrati	426, 457
Atrium (Dwelling House)	463
—— Fori Traiani	23
—— Libertatis	33
—— Regium	15
—— Vestae	15
Attack and Defence of Fortified Places	399
Auctoramentum	359
Auctorati	359
Augures	328
Augusta	207
Augustales	210
Augustus (Mensis)	362
—— (as a title)	206
Aulaeum	356
Aurigae	350
Annona Salaria	234
Aurelii Gradus	17
Aurelium Tribunal	17
Aureus (coin)	417
Aurifodinae	234
Aurora	322
Aurum Coronarium	188, 192
—— Vicesimarium	236
Auspex	423
Auspicia	110
—— in connection with Comitia	111
—— Maiora	184
—— Minora	184
Authenticae (Constitutiones)	246
Auxilia	378
Auxiliares	378
Auxilium Tribunicium	142
Aventinus, Mons	2, 32
Averruncus	320
Avis	329
Axamenta	333
Axicia	455
Bacchanalia	320
Bail	281
Balinea—Balnea	435
Balineum—Balneum	435
Balistae	400
Baptisterium	434
Barbari	85
Barbitos	449
Basilica of St. Peter	49
—— Aemilia	19
—— Constantiniana	31
—— Fulvia	19
—— Iulia	20
—— Neptuni	47
—— Opimia	19
—— Paulli	19
—— Porcia	19
—— Sempronia	19
—— Traiani	23
—— Ulpia	23
Basilicae	19, 280
Baths	433
Bellona	319

INDEX.

	Page		Page		Page
Bes a. Bessis	408	Capitale Crimen	83	Centuriae...........382, 384,	385
Bestiarii	360	Capite Censi...........70, 378,	385	——— Cornicinum	70
Bestiis obiicere	311	Capitis Deminutio	83	——— Equitum	71
Betrothment	423	——— Sacratio	309	——— Fabrum	70
Bibliotheca	464	Capitolinus, Mons	25	——— Iuniorum	69
——— Octaviae	45	Capitolium	25	——— Iure Vocatae	119
——— Ulpia	23	——— Vetus	38	——— Primo Vocatae	119
Bigarii	350	Capsae	422	——— Seniorum	96
Bigae	349	Capsarii	422	——— (of Servius)	69
Bigati	415	Capulus	426	Centuriam Conficere	178
Binae Centesimae	420	Caput (money)	419	Centuries and Tribes incorporated	120
Biremes	405	——— Sacrae Viae	21	Centuriones...........382,	386
Bissextum	364	——— (Political)	83	Centussis	408
Bombyx	457	——— Tralaticium	243	Cera Prima	460
Bona Dea	319	Carbasa	404	Ceres—Cerealia...318, 319, 320, 347
Bona Vi rapta.........273,	274	Carbasus	457	
Bonus Eventus	320	Carcer	310	Cermalus............2,	29
Books...... 461,	462	——— Lautumiarum	3	Ceroliensis,............3,	35
Book-binding.........461,	462	——— Mamertinus	28	Ceruchi	405
Britannicus	211	Carceres............348,	349	Cerussa	457
Bridges	50	Carchesium	406	Cessio (In Iure)	258
Bruna	428	Carenum	439	Chaplets	444
Bulla.................340,	421	Carina	403	Charta	459
Business in Comitia Centuriata	120	Carinae.................2,	36	——— Augusta	459
		Carmenta—Carmentalia	323	——— Claudia	459
——— Curiata	117	Carpere Lanam	457	——— Emporetica	459
——— Tributa	124	Carptor	442	——— Hieratica	459
Bustum	426	Casa Romuli	29	——— Liviana	459
Buxus	448	Casus Venerius	444	Chelys	449
Byssus	457	Castella	96	Choraula	449
		Castello di S. Angelo	49	Chordae	449
C	108, 299	Castor	321	Chorus	354
Cadi	438	Castra............396,	399	Church of S. Balbina	32
Coena Auguralis	330	——— Praetoria	380	——— of S. Giovanni in Laterano	35
Caerites	82	Cataphracti	385	
Caesar, as a title	207	Catapultae	400	——— of S. Lorenzo	36
Calamus	459	Catasta	96	——— of S. Maria in Aracœli	25
Calamistrum	455	Catellae	457	
Calantica	456	Catervarii	360	——— of S. Maria Liberatrice	15
Calare...............127,	128	Cati Fons	48	
Calatores	127	Causa Capitalis	83	——— of S. Maria degli Angeli	38
Calcatorium	438	Causae Coniectio	281	
Calcei...............450,	454	——— Collectio	281	——— of S. Maria Maggiore	73
Calices Gemmati	443	Causia............358,	450	
Calceus Senatorius	221	Causidicus	313	——— of S. Maria ad Martyres	47
Calculi	422	Cavaedium	463	
Caldarium............434,	435	Cavalry of the Legion	384	——— of S. Maria del Sole	42
Calendae............363,	368	Cavea	353	——— of S. Maria Egiziaca	42
Calendar, the........362,	376	Cedere	258	——— of S. Pietro in Vincoli	36
Calendaria	270	Celeres	72	
Calices	443	Cella	325	——— of S. Sabba	32
Caliga	401	——— Frigidaria	434	——— of S. Stefano delle Carrozze	42
Caligula	402	——— Ostiarii	463	
Catumnia,	314	——— Penuaria	465	Ciboria	443
Calx	348	——— Vinaria..... 438,	465	Cinerarii	456
Camenae	323	Cenotaphium	427	Cinctus............452,	455
Camillus............341,	424	Censere—Censeri	167	——— Gabinus............4,	452
Campagna di Roma	1	Censio	167	
Campus Agrippae	43	Censor Perpetuus	171	Cingula	452
——— Esquilinus	37	——— (as an imperial title,)...........171,	205	Cingulum............423, 452,	455
——— Flaminius	43			Ciniflones	456
——— Martialis	35	Censores............164—171		Cippi Pomoeri	4
——— Martius.......1, 42,	46	Censoriae Leges.........170,	272	Circumvallare	401
——— Sceleratus......38,	335	Censum agere, habere, &c.	166	Circumvallatio	401
Candidates for the higher magistracies.........176—179		Census	166	Circus Agonalis	48
		——— Senatorius	215	——— Flaminius......42, 43,	348
Candidati	177	——— Equester.... .72, 74,	215	——— Maximus........3, 39,	347
——— Principis, s. Imperatoris, s. Caesaris, s. Augusti,	164, 169	Centesima Rerum Venalium	237	——— Neronis	348
				——— (General form)	347
		Centesimatio	396	Cispius, Mons............2,	36
Canis (in dice)	444	Centumviri	276	Cistae S. Cistellae	108
Canthari	444	Centumvirale Iudicium	277	Citatio	295
Capere...............334,	336	Centumviralis Hasta	277	Cithara	449
Capillatus	455	Centuria (Land measure)	410	Cities on the Seven Hills older than Rome,	5
Capita aut Navia	444	——— Praerogativa..119	122		

INDEX.

	Page
City of Romulus	5
— in the Age of Augustus,	9
Cives Facti	81
—— Nati	81
—— Optimo Iure	81
—— Romanae	81
—— Romani	79
Civil Suits	275—284
——, Parties	277
——, Form of Process	279
——, Proceedings in Iure	280
——, Proceeding in Indicio	281
Civitas	81
—— sine Suffragio	82
Civitates Foederatae	190
—— Immunes	190
—— Liberae	190, 192
Clamor Supremus	425
Clarigatio	332
Classes of Servius	69
Classiarii	406
Classici	71, 406
Classis	69, 406
Claustra	348
Clavus	404
—— Angustus	75
—— Latus	75
Clepsydrae	429
Clientela	63
Clientes	63
—— of later times	66
Clivus Capitolinus	27
—— Publicius	33
—— Sacer	21
—— Urbius	3
—— Victoriae	30
Cloaca Maxima	3, 58
Cloacina	318
Cloacinae Sacrum	17
Clypeus	69
—— (in the bath)	434
Coae Vestes	457
Cochlearia	442
Coci	437
Codeta Maior	49
—— Minor	49
Codex Gregorianus	245
—— Hermogenianus	245
—— Iustinianus	246
—— Theodosianus	245
Codices s. Codicilli	460
—— Expensi et Accepti	270
Coelius Minor	34
—— Mons	34
Coeliolus	2, 34
Coemptionator	252
Coena	436
—— Aditialis	330
—— (Arrangements)	441
—— Feralis	427
—— Funeris	427
—— Nuptialis	424
Coemptio	251
Cognati	265
Cognatio	265, 267
Cognitor	277, 280
Cognomen	61
Cohors	384, 385, 386
—— Praetoria	189, 389
Cohortes Alariae	385
—— Urbanae	390
—— Vigilum	390
Coins	411

	Page
Coitio	178
Colare (Vinum)	439
Collection of the Revenue	238
Collis Quirinalis	38
Collega Consulis	153, 184
—— in the Empire	211
Collegia Sacerdotum	326
Collegium Tribunorum	141
Collis Agonus	38
—— Dianae	32
—— Hortulorum	2, 38
—— Quirinalis	2, 38
—— Viminalis	2, 37
Coloniae	88, 90
—— in the Provinces	190
—— Civium Romanorum	89
—— Latinae	89
—— Maritimae	89
—— Militares	90
Colosseum	36
Colum Vinarium	439
Columbarium	427
Columna Antoniniana	48
—— Bellica	44
—— Maenia	17
—— Rostrata	17
—— Traiani	23
Columnae	462
Colus	458
Comitia	104—130
——, abrupt termination of	114
—— Aedilicia — Censoria — Consularia — Praetoria, &c.	106
—— (Auspicia)	111
—— Calata	105, 127
—— Centuriata	105, 118, 123
—— Curiata	105, 115—118
——, different kinds of	105
——, Hour of Meeting	114
—— (in general)	104—115
——, Manner of Voting	107
——, Notice of	113
——, Presiding Magistrate	106, 107
——, Quorum	110
—— Tributa	105, 123—127
—— under the Empire	128—130
Comitialis Morbus	114
Comitiatus	104
—— Maximus	118, 286, 287
Comitium	12—16, 116, 280
Commissatio	436
Commoda	594
Commodatum	269
Communi dividundo Formula	259
Comperendinatio	280, 299
Compitalia	69
Compluvium	464
Compotatio	444
Computation of Money	417
Conciliabula	93
Concamerata Sudatio	434
Concilium	105
—— Plebis	123
Concio	104, 105
Concionari	105
Conciones	104, 105
Conclamatus	425

	Page
Concubia Nox	429
Concubina	250
Concubinatus	250
Condemnatio	281
Condemno	108, 299
Condere Lustrum	170, 375
Conditio	423
Condition of Slaves	95
Conducere	170, 271, 272
Conductor	272
Confarreatio	251
Congiarium	411
Congius	411
Connubium	152, 250
Conquisitio	380
Conquisitores	380
Consanguinei	264
Consecration of the Emperors	210
Conserere Manum	283
Consilium	289, 291
—— Principis	223
Consobrini	267
Constitution of Servius	69
Constitutiones Principum	245
Consul sine Collega	133
Consularis Potestas	205
—— Exercitus	387
Consulatum Continuare	182
Consules	132—140
—— Designati	139
—— Honorarii	139
—— Minores	139
—— Ordinarii	133, 138
—— Suffecti	133, 138
Consulship under the Empire	138, 205
Consus—Consualia	323, 346
Contemplari	325
Conticinium	429
Contubernium	95, 250
Conventio	105
—— in Manum	251
Conventus	188
Convivium Publicum	345
Cooptatio	118, 142, 326, 329, 337
Copper Coinage	412
Corbes	438
Cornu	449
Cornua	404, 461
Cornus	29
Corollae	444
Coroliarium	445, 447
Corona Castrensis	395
—— Cingere	400
—— Civica	395
—— Muralis	395
—— Navalis	395
—— Obsidionalis	395
—— Rostrata	395
—— Vallaris	395
Coronae	395, 444
—— Aegyptiae	445
—— Hibernae	445
—— Pactiles	445
—— Plectiles	445
—— Sutiles	445
Corpus Iuris Civilis	246
Cortex	438
Corvi	407
Coryphaeus	354
Costae	403
Cothurnus	356
Cotoriae	284
Cotyla	411

INDEX. 501

	Page
Creditor	268
Crepida	454
Crepusculum	429
Creta	348
Cretifodinae	234
Criminal Iurisdiction of the Kings	284
—— of the Senate	286
—— of the Comitia	287
—— of Quaesitores	288
Criminal Trials	284—315
Crimen Capitale	83
—— de Residuis	308
Crotala	449
Cruralia	453
Crustae	443
Cubicula	465
Cubital	454
Cubitus	409
Cucullus	450
Culeus	411
Culina	465
Culter	343, 455
Cultrarii	341
Cululli	443
Cumerus	424
Cunei	354, 356
Cuniculi	400
Cupae	438
Cupra	317
Curatores	255, 256
—— Annonae	157, 158
—— Ludorum solennium	157, 159
—— Regionum	201
—— Urbis	157, 201
—— Viarum	201
Curia Calabra s. Kalabra 26, 128
—— Hostilia	14
—— Iulia	15
—— Octaviae	45
—— Pompeii	44
—— Saliorum	29
Curiae	61
—— Veteres	29
Curiales	61
Curio Maximus	61, 116, 332
Curiones	61, 332
Curricula	349
Cursus	350, 432
Curulis Sella	67
Custodes	109, 399
Custodia Libera	310
Custodiae	399
Customhouse dues	235
Custos Urbis	132, 171
Cyathus	411, 442
Cybele	323
Cymbala	449
Cypress wood	462
Dactyliotheca	455
Damnum Iniuria datum	273, 274
Dare Actionem	276, 280
—— Facere Praestare	268
—— Iudices	276
—— Praedes Litis et Vindiciarum	282
Datatim Ludere	433
Dating, Method of	363
Day, Divisions of	428
Days, Classification of	365
Decedere de Via	180
December	362, 367

	Page
Decempeda	409
Decemviri Sacrorum	330
—— Legibus Scribendis	150—152
—— Stlitibus iudicandis	197, 276
Decima Manumissionum	236
Decimatio	396
Decreta Principum	245
—— Augurum	329
Decretum Praetoris	283
—— Ultimum	149, 216
Decumae	233
Decumani	238
Decuria	384
Decuriae Apparitorum	199
—— Iudicum	293, 294
—— Scribarum	199
—— of Slaves	97
Decuriare populum	178
Decurio	61, 71, 384
Decussis	408
Deditio Noxae	310
Deducere nubentem	424
Deductores—Deducere	178
Defaecare (Vinum)	439
Deferre Nomen	295
Defrutum	439
Delatores	295
Delectus	379
Delibare	343
Delphini	348, 350
Delubrum	325
Delator	268
Demensum	99
Deminutio Capitis	83
Denarius	415
—— Aureus	417
Denuntiare Testimonium	297
Deportatio	84
Depositum	269
Desultores	349
Designati (Magistratus)	179
Designator	425
Detestatio Sacrorum	128
Detergere	406
Deunx	408
Deus, as a title of the Emperors	209
Dextans	408
Dextera Ala	387
Dials	429
Diana	318
Diarium	99
Dicere Dictatorem	146
—— Ius	276
Dictata	422
Dictator	146—149
—— abolition of the office	149
Diem dicere	288
Diespiter	317
Dies Atri	366
—— Bissextus	364
—— Comitiales	114, 366
—— Fasti	244, 276, 280, 365
—— Nefasti	365
—— Intercisi	365
—— Festi	346, 365
—— Profesti	365
—— Lustricus	421
Diffarreatio	252
Diffundere (Vinum)	438
Digesta	246
Digitus	409

	Page
Dignitas—Dignitates	181
Dignitates Tribunitiae	140
Dii Cabiri	321
—— Consentes	317, 319
—— Indigetes	322
—— Novensiles	321
—— Selecti	320
Dimachaeri	360
Diptychi	460
Dirae	323
Diribitores	108
Diribitorium	46
Dis Pater	321
Discessio	219
Disci Iactus	350
Discidium	252
Discumbere Mensae	440
Discus	432
Ditis	321
Dius Fidius	322
Diva Triformis	318
—— Palatua	323
Divinatio	295, 328
Divisores	108, 179
Divorce	252
Divortium	252
Divus, applied to the Emperors	209
Do, Dico, Addico	276
Dodrans	408
Dolabra	343
Dolia	438
Dollola	39
Dolon	404
Domestic Gods	321
Dominium	257
—— Legitimum	257
—— Quiritarium	251
Dominus et Deus	210
Dominus, as a title of the Emperors	209
Dominus	95, 101
Domitianus (Mensis)	363
Domus Agrippae	30
—— M. Antonii	30
—— Aquilii	38
—— Aurea	30
—— Catilinae	30
—— Ciceronis	30
—— Crassi	30
—— Fulvii Flacci	29
—— Hortensii	30
—— Lateranorum	35
—— Livii Drusi	30
—— Mamurrae	35
—— Messalae	30
—— Pompeii M.	36
—— Pomponii Attici	38
—— M. Scauri	30
—— Tarquinii Prisci	29
—— Tiberiana	30
—— Transitoria	30
—— Tulli Hostilii	35
—— Vacci	29
—— (Aedes Privatae)	162
Donaria	339
Donativum	411
Dormitoria	465
Dos	253
—— Adventitia	253, 254
—— Profectitia	253, 254
—— Receptitia	254
Dotalia pacta	253
Dowry, Law of	253, 254
Drachma	409

INDEX.

	Page
Drama, Roman	352
Dress of Men	450
—— of Women	455
Drinking Customs	442
—— Vessels	442
Ducere Uxorem	424
Duella	408
Duodevicesimani	381
Dupondius	408
Duplicatio	280
Duumviri Perduellionis	160
—— Sacrorum	330
—— Viis extra Urbem purgandis	197
Edere Actionem	280
Editio Iudicum	290
Editor Spectaculi	342, 360, 361
Edicta Magistratuum	243
—— Praetorum	243
—— Principum	245
Edictum Perpetuum	243
—— Repentinum	243
Education	421
Egeriae Vallis	34
Elaiothesium	434
Elementa	422
Emblemata	443
Emeritus	392
Emporium	4, 33
Emperors, The, and their Titles	202—212
Emptio et Venditio	271
Encampments	396
Endromis	454
Epibatae	406
Epidromos	404
Epithalamium	421
Epulae—Epulum	344
Epulones	330
Epulum Iovis 317, 344, 345, 441
Equestrian Order under the Emperors	73
Equester Ordo	71
Equi Desultorii	349
—— Singulares	349
Equiria	35, 319, 346
Equitatus	378
Equitatio	350
Equiti Equum adimere	169
Equites, Choosing of	73
—— Equo privato	71, 73
—— Equo publico	71
—— Illustres	76, 223
—— Insignia of	75
—— Number in Legion	381
—— (Publicani)	238
—— Ordo Equester	71
—— Rise and progress	71
—— Splendidi	76
Equitum Probatio	73
—— Recognitio	73
—— Transvectio	73
Equo Publico merere	72
Equus October	319
—— Publicus	72
Erciscundae Familiae Formula	259
Ergastulum	97
Eruptio	251
Eruptiones	401
Esquiliae	2, 36
Esquilinus Mons	2, 36
Essedarii	360
Etruscum Aurum	421

	Page
Euripus	347, 351
Exauctoratio	392
Exaugurare	337
Exceptio	280
Exercitus Urbanus	121
Excubiae	399
Exedrae	465
Exercises	432
Exercitationes	432
Expeditae Cohortes	386
Expediti Milites	386
Expulsim Ludere	433
Expensi Latio	270, 273
Expensum ferre, &c.	270
Expugnatio	399
Exsequiae	425
Exsilium	84
Extispices	331
Extraordinarii	385, 398
Fabii s. Fabiani	335
Fabulae	352
Facinus Capitale	83
Factio Albata	350
—— Aurata	350
—— Prasina	350
—— Purpurea	250
—— Russata	350
—— Veneta	350
—— Testamenti	259
Factiones Circi	350
Factionarii	380
Familia Rustica	97
Fagutal	8, 37
Falacer Pater	323
Falae	348, 350
Falsum	307
Familia of Slaves	94
Familia Urbana	97
Familiae	61
Famosi Libelli	274
Famuli	94
Fanaticus	324
Fanum	324, 325
Far	437
Farina	323, 437
Farreus Panis	251
Fas	324
Fasces	134, 155
—— submittere	180
Fasciae s. Fasciolae	453
Fasti	366
—— Calendares	367
—— Consulares	367
—— Capitolini	367
—— Triumphales	367
Fata	323
Fatua	319
Fatum	324
Fauces	465
Faunus—Fauna—Faunalia	322
Favilla	426
Fax Prima	429
Februarius	362, 368, 369
Felix, as a title	209
Feminalia	452, 453
Feneratores	158
Fenus	419
—— Unciarium	420
Feralia	323
Feretum	342
Ferculа	352, 441
Ferentarii	76, 386
Feretrum	426
Feriae	346

	Page
Feriae Conceptivae	365
—— Imperativae	365
—— Latinae	171, 317, 346
—— Privatae	365
—— Publicae	365
—— Sementivae	319
—— Stativae	365
Feronia	323
Festa Stultorum	322
Festuca	282
Fetiales	83, 331
Fibulae	395
Fimbriatae Tunicae	452
Ficus Ruminalis	13, 29
Fidepromissores	281
Fides	449
Fideiussores	281
Figura	405
Fila	449
Fiscinae	438
Fiscus	155, 192
Fistula	449
Flamen Curialis	61
—— Dialis	332
—— Martialis	332
—— Quirinalis	332
Flamines	332
Flaminica	333
Flammeum	424
Flavius Cn.	280, 372, 244
Flexumines	72
Flora—Floralia	320, 346, 347
Focalia	454
Foci penetrales	464
Focus	464
Fodinae	224
Foliatum	447
Follis s. Folliculus	433
Folium	446
Food	437
Fora	93
—— in general	11
—— of the Empire	22
Foreign Deities	323
Fori	403
Fornae Literarum	422
Formula Censendi	167
Formula Petitoria	283
Formulae	277, 278
—— in Ius conceptae	279
—— in Factum conceptae	279
Fornax—Fornacalia	322
Fornix Fabianus	16
Forull	462
Forum Augusti	3, 22
—— Boarium	4, 39
—— Iulium	3, 22
—— Nervae	3, 23
—— Olitorium	43
—— Pacis	30
—— Palladium	23
—— Pervium	23
—— Romanum	3, 11—21
—— Romanum, Plan	10
—— Traiani	3, 23
—— Transitorium	23
—— Vespasiani	30
Fossa	396
Founding a City, Ceremonies	4
Fratres Arvales	331
—— Patrueles	267
—— Pileati	321
Frigidarium	434, 435

INDEX.

	Page		Page		Page
Fritillus	443	Haruspices	331	Ianus Summus	17
Frontes	461	Haruspicina	331	Iduare	369
Fructus	226	Hasta	383	Idus	363, 368
Frumentarii	158	—— Coelibaris	424	Ientaculum	436
Frumentum in Cellam	189	—— a symbol of Dominium		Ignobiles	67
Fullones	457		277	Ignominia	84, 169
Fumarium	438	Hastae Velitares	384	Ilicet	342
Fundi, Populi	92	Hastati 382, 383, 384, 388		Imperator	202
Funditores	378, 386	Hebdomas	365	Imperium	117, 134, 181
Funeral Rites	425	Heirs	261	—— Maius	184
Funes	404	—— Classification of	261	—— Minus	184
Funus Censorium	427	Hemicyclia	465	—— Proconsulare of	
—— Indictivum	427	Hemina	411	the Emperors	205
—— Publicum	427	Hera	317	—— of Proconsuls	
Fur Manifestus	273	Hercules	322	and Propractors	183
Furcifer	100	—— Romanus	210	Impluvium	464
Furiae	323	Heres Institutus	261	Imus (Lectus)	440
Furti per Lancem et Licium Conceptio	273	Heredes Extranei 261, 262		Inauguratio 326, 329, 337	
		—— Necessarii	261	Inaures	457
Furtum — Furtum Manifestum — Furtum nec Manifestum	273	—— Sui	261	Incendium	304
		—— Scripti	263	Index	469
		Heredium	410	Indigetes	322
Fustuarium	396	Hereditatem Cernere—Adire	261	Inducere Locationem	239
				Indusium	452
Gabinus Cinctus	452	High Roads	52	Indutus	453
Gaesa	383	Hister s. Histrio	352, 356	Infamia	84
Galea	69, 384	Hoc Habet	361	Infancy	421
Galerus	456	Holy Places	324	Infantry of the Legion	381
Gallicus Tumultus	386	Holy Things	324	Inferiae	342, 428
Gallicinium	429	Homicidium	304	Inferior Magistrates	195, 200
Games of Chance	443	Honorem gerere	172	Infima Nova Via	22
Games Sacred, Classification	346	Honore deicere	178	Infra Classem	71
		Honores	172	Infula	341
Gates of the Servian City	7	Hoplomachi	360	Ingenui	80
Gausape	442	Hora	428	Inheritance, Division of	262
Germalus	2, 13, 29	Horaria	429	Iniuria	273
Gemoniae Scalae	28	Horreum	438	In Iure Cessio	258
Gener	267	Horologia	429	Inlicium Vocare	105
Genius	321	Horta	323	In Ordinem cogi	181
Gens Togata	450	Horti Agrippinae	49	Inscriptio	295
Gentes	61	—— Caesaris	49	Insigne	405
Gentiles	61, 264	—— Domitiae	49	Insignia of Aediles	156
Gentilitia Sacra	117	—— Luculliani	38	—— Augurs	329
Germanicus	210	—— Maecenatiani	37	—— Censors	166
—— (Mensis)	363	—— Neronis	49	—— Consuls	137
Glarea Sternere	53	—— Sallustiani	38	—— Dictator	149
Gladius	384	Hostiae	340	—— Flamines	333
Gladiators	358–361	Hospes	85	—— Kings	132
Glos	267	—— Publicus	87	—— Praetors	154
Gods worshipped by the Romans	316–324	Hospitium	85	—— Quaestors	163
		Hostiae Iniuges	341	—— Senators	221
Gold Coinage	417	—— Lactentes	340	—— Tribuni Militum Consulari Potestate	153
Gossipium	457	—— Maiores	340		
Gradus	353, 354, 356, 409	Hostis	85	—— Tribuni Plebis	415
—— Aurelii	17	Houses	462	Instita	456
—— Cognationis, Table	266	Hydraula	449	Institor	431
Gradivus	319	Hymenaeus	424	Institutiones of Gaius	246
Graecostasis	14	Hypocaustum	434	—— Iustinian	246
—— Imperii	20			Insula	463
Graecostadium	20	Iactus Venerius	448	—— Lycaonia	48
Grammaticus	422	Iaculatio	250, 432	—— Tiberina	2, 46, 48
Grammatistes	422	Iaculatores	378, 386	Insularius	463
Graphium	460	Iana	320	Intempesta Nox	429
Gratulatio	338	Iani	7, 17	Intentio	280
Gregorian Calendar	373	Ianiculum	2, 8, 49	Inter Caesa et Porrecta	342
Gremium	53	Ianitor	463	Inter duos Lucos	25
Gubernator	406	Ianua	463	Inter duos Pontes	48
Gubernaculum	404	Ianuarius	362, 368, 369	Intercalation of Julian Year	364
Gustus s. Gustatio	441	Ianus	320		
Guttus	343	—— Bifrons	20	—— of Lunar Year	370
Gymnasia	433	—— Geminus	20	Intercedere	141
		—— Inus	17	Interdictum Exhibitorium — Prohibitorium — Restitutorium	283
Habet	361	—— Medius	17		
Halteres	432	—— Quadrifrons	38, 41		
Harpagones	407	—— Quirinus	20	Interest of Money	418

INDEX.

	Page
Intercessio	142
—— Collegae	221
Interpretes	179
Interrex	131, 136
Interrogatio	295
Intervallum	396
Intestate, Law of Succession	263
Intonsus	455
Intusium	452
Inuus	322
Involucre	455
Iovino	317
Iovis	317, 319
Irrogare Poenam	288
Iseum	47
Isis	323
Isola di S. Bartolomeo	48
Italia (Provincia)	193
Iter	256
Iudex	276
—— Quaestionis	291, 292, 294
—— Tutelaris	155
Judges in Civil Suits	275
Iudicia	275, 293
—— Privata	275–284
—— Publica	284–315
Iudices	133
—— Editiii	297, 309
—— in Civil Suits	270
—— in Criminal Trials	291
—— in the Quaestiones Perpetuae	292–294
—— Selecti	294
Iudicis Datio	280
—— Postulatio	278
Iudicium Acceptum	280
—— Capitis	83
—— Desertum	281
—— Hastae	277
—— Ordinatum	281
—— Proferre	281
Iudicum Decuriae	294
—— Editio	296
—— Reiectio	296
—— Sortitio	296
—— Subsortitio	296
Iuga	463
Iugerum	410
Iugum	458
Julian Era	364
—— Year	362
Iulius (Mensis)	362
Iunius (Mensis)	362, 367
Iuno	317
Iupiter	317
—— Hospitalis	86
—— Indiges	322
—— Latiaris	394
Iura Publica	80
—— Privata	80
—— in Re	257
Iurare in Acta Principis	222
Iurati	297
Iuris-Auctores	244
—— Consulti	244
—— Periti	244
—— Peritorum Auctoritas	244
Iursidictio	275
—— inter Cives	153
—— Peregrinos	153
Ius	241
—— Aelianum	244
—— Augurium	329

	Page
Ius Civile	242, 245
—— Civitatis	80
—— Commercii	81
—— Connubii	81, 250
—— Consuetudinis	243
—— Flavianum	244
—— Gentilitium	264
—— Gentium	242
—— Honorum	81
—— Honorarium	243
—— Imaginum	67
—— Intercessionis	142
—— Latii	87
—— Naturale	242
—— non Scriptum	243
—— Postliminii	83
—— Praetorium	243
—— Provocationis	81, 285
—— Quiritium	81
—— Sacrum	328
—— Suffragii	81
—— tertiae, quartae, &c. Relationis	223
Iusta facere	427
Iustus Equitatus	384
Iuturnae Lacus	18
K	315
Kings	131, 132
Labrum	434
Lacerna	454
Laconicum	434
Lacus Iuturnae	18
—— Servilius	20
—— Torcularius	438
Laena	333, 454
Lagenae	448
Lala	318
Lances	344
Lanista	359
Lapicidinae	434
Lapis Alabastrites	446
—— Manalis	34
Laquearii	360
Lara—Larunda—Larentia	323
Lararium	465
Larentalia	323
Lares	321
—— Praestites	321
Latini	80, 87, 250
—— Iuniani	103
Latinitas	87
Latinum Nomen	94
Latio Accepti	270, 273
—— Expensi	270, 273
Latium—Latio donari	87
Latus Clavus	75
Latrina	465
Latrones	444
Latrunculi	444
Laudatio Funebris	426
—— Solemnis	426
Laudatores	297
Lauretum	32
Lautumiae	3
Lautolae	21
Laws of the Twelve Tables	151, 242
Laverna	323
Lectisternium	344
Lecti Triclinares	440
Lectio Senatus	213
Lectus Funebris	425
Lectus Genialis	425, 464

	Page
Legacies, different modes of bequeathing	261
Legare per Damnationem	262
—— per Praeceptionem	263
—— per Vindicationem	262
—— Sinendi Modo	262
Legata	262
Legatarii	262
Legati	186, 187, 387
—— Caesaris s. Augusti	192
Legatio Libera	222
Legem Abrogare—Ferre, &c.	107
Leges Agrariae	225–231
—— Censoriae	169, 239
—— Centuriatae	120, 243
—— Curiatae	116, 128, 243
—— Iudiciariae	291
—— Regiae	242
—— Sacratae	141, 309
—— Tabellariae	108
—— Tributae	125, 243
—— XII. Tabularum	151, 242
Legio	380–387
—— Classica	406
Legionarii	380
Legiones	378, 380
Legis Actiones	244, 277
—— per Iudicis Postulationem	278
—— per Manus Iniectionem	278
—— per Pignoris Captionem	278
—— Sacramento	278
Lemures—Lemuria	323
Lemnisci	445
Letters	461
Levir	267
Levis Armatura	386
Levying Soldiers	379
Lex	106
—— Acilia de Repetundis	307
—— Acilia Calpurnia de Ambitu	308
—— Aelia s. Aelia et Fufia	113
—— Aelia Sentia	102
—— Aebutia de Formulis	278
—— Aemilia	165, 186
—— Annua	243
—— Antonia Iudiciaria	293
—— Appuleia Agraria	231
—— Appuleia de Maiestate	302
—— Aquillia	95, 186, 274
—— Atia	326, 329
—— Atilia	255
—— Atinia	143
—— Aternia Tarpeia	286, 311
—— Aurelia Iudiciaria	293
—— Baebia de Numero Praetorum	154
—— Caecilia Didia	113, 177, 365
—— Calpurnia de Repetundis	290, 306
—— Canuleia	81
—— Canuleia de Connubio	152, 250
—— Cassia Agraria	229
—— Cassia Tabellaria	108, 298
—— Censui censendo	167
—— Cincia Muneralis	313
—— Claudia	214
—— Clodia	171
—— Coelia Tabellaria	108

INDEX.

Lex Cornelia Baebia de Ambitu... 308
—— Cornelia de Falsis.... 307
—— Cornelia de Iniuriis.. 274
—— Cornelia de Magistratibus... 175
—— Cornelia de Maiestate 302
—— Cornelia de Provinciis 191
—— Cornelia de Repetundis... 307
—— Cornelia de Sacerdotiis 326, 329
—— Cornelia de Sicariis 304, 305
—— Cornelia de Tribunis Plebis... 145
—— Cornelia Fulvia de Ambitu... 308
—— Cornelia Iudiciaria 290, 291, 293
—— Curiata de Imperio.. 117
—— Domitia... 104, 325, 326
—— Duillia de Provocatione... 285
—— Fabia de Ambitu.... 308
—— Fufia... 113
—— Falcidia... 263
—— Flaminia Agraria... 230
—— Furia... 263
—— Furia Caninia... 102
—— Gabinia Tabellaria... 108
—— Hortensia.... 114, 124, 243
—— Icilia... 144
—— Iulia de Sociis... 68, 89, 92
—— Iulia de Provinciis 187, 192
—— Iulia Agraria... 231
—— Iulia de Formulis... 278
—— Iulia Iudiciaria... 293
—— Iulia de Maiestate... 302
—— Iulia de Peculata... 307
—— Iulia de Vi... 303
—— Iulia de Repetundis... 307
—— Iulia de Ambitu... 309
—— et Papia Poppaea 249, 253, 255
—— Iunia Norbana... 103
—— de Repetundis. 307
—— Licinia...81, 116, 136, 149, 152
—— Licinia Iunia... 114
—— Licinia Agraria... 229
—— Linicia de Sodalitiis.. 297
—— Licinia de Ambitu.. 309
—— Livia Iudiciaria... 293
—— Lutatia de Vi... 303
—— Marcia... 166
—— Maria de Ambitu... 308
—— Naturae... 242
—— Ogulnia... 326, 329
—— Ovinia... 213
—— Papia... 334
—— Papiria Tabellaria.... 108
—— Petronia... 95, 314
—— Plautia Papiria de Sociis... 68, 89, 92
—— Plautia Iudiciaria... 293
—— Plautia de Vi... 303
—— Poetelia... 83, 270
—— Poetelia Papiria... 310
—— Pompeia de iure magistratuum... 177
—— Pompeia Iudiciaria... 293
—— Pompeia de Vi... 303

Lex Pompeia de Parricidio 305
—— Pompeia de Ambitu... 309
—— Porcia de Provocatione... 286
—— Porcia de Repetundis. 306
—— Publilia..116, 119, 124, 157, 165, 243
—— Publilia de Magistratibus Plebeiis... 141
—— Pupia... 114
—— Remmia... 315
—— Roscia Theatralis..75, 354
—— Rupilia... 186
—— Sempronia Iudiciaria.. 74, 216, 289, 292
—— Sempronia de Provinciis Consularibus... 191
—— Sempronia Agraria... 230
—— Servilia Agraria... 231
—— Servilia Iudiciaria.... 293
—— Servilia de Repetundis 307
—— Sulpicia de Sociis.... 68
—— Tallonis... 274
—— Thoria Agraria... 281
—— Trebonia... 142
—— Valeria de Provocatione... 81, 134, 135, 285
—— Valeria Horatia..124, 148, 217, 243
—— Valeria Horatia de Provocatione... 285
—— Varia de Maiestate... 302
—— Vatinia... 186
—— Villia Annalis... 173
—— Voconia... 263
Libare... 343
Libelli Famosi... 274
Libellus Munerarius... 361
Liber... 460
Liber Pater... 320
Libera... 320
Liberalia... 320
Liberi... 80
Liberi Iusti... 250
Libertas Iusta... 101
Libertini..80, 173, 250, 378, 385
—— Names of... 101
—— Social Condition 102
—— Political Condition... 102
Libertinus... 101
Libertus... 101
—— Orcinus... 101
Libertina... 325, 425
Libitinarii... 425
Libra... 408
Librarii... 462
Libri Lintei... 458
—— Pontificales... 328
—— Sibyllini... 330
Libripens... 258, 259
Libum... 342
Licia... 458
Lictor Curiatus... 116, 117
—— Proximus... 134
Lictores... 134, 198
—— Atri... 426
—— Paludati... 401
Lignarii... 33
Ligula... 411
Ligulae... 442, 454
Linteo... 458
Lintea... 404, 434
Linteariis... 458
Lintei libri... 458

Linteum... 455
Linum... 458
Liquare (Vinum)... 439
Lis Vindiciarum... 282
Literae Laureatae... 394
Literator... 422
Litis Contestatio... 280
—— Aestimatio... 300
Lituus... 112, 329
Local Tribes... 68
Locare... 170, 271, 272
—— aliquid faciendum. 272
—— utendum... 272
Locatio et Conductio ..271, 273
Locationem Inducere... 239
Locator... 272
Locus Consularis... 441
Loculi... 422, 426
Loculamenta... 462
Locupletes... 71
Lora... 438
—— Rubra... 461
—— Patricia... 221
Lorarii... 99
Lorica... 384
Loricati... 385
Losna... 318
Lower Forum... 12, 16—21
Lua Mater... 321
Luceres... 71
—— s. Lucerenses... 61
Lucta... 350, 432
Lucumo... 61
Lucus... 325
—— Camenarum... 34
—— Esquilinus... 37
—— Fagutalis... 37
—— Furinae... 49
—— Iunonis Lucinae... 37
—— Mefitis... 37
—— Poetelius... 37
Ludere Pila... 432
—— Par Impar... 444
Ludi Apollinares..154, 318—347
—— Cereales... 347
—— Circenses... 346, 347
—— Conceptivi... 346
—— Funebres... 346, 359, 427
—— Gladiatorii... 359
—— Imperativi... 346
—— Literarum... 421
—— Magni... 318, 346, 347
—— Magister... 422
—— Megalenses... 347
—— Piscatorii... 154
—— Romani.157, 318, 346, 347
—— Scenici... 346, 252
—— Stati... 346
—— Seculares... 375, 376
—— Votivi... 346
Ludio... 352
Ludus Duodecim Scriptorum... 414
—— Latrunculorum... 444
—— Literarius... 421
—— Troiae... 351
Luna... 318, 319
Lumina prima... 429
Lunula... 221
Lupercal... 29, 322, 335
Lupercalia... 322, 338
Luperci... 335
Lupercus... 29
Lustrare Agros... 331
Lustrum... 170, 374

INDEX.

	Page
Lympha	320
Lyra	449
Machinae	380, 402
Macrocollum	459
Macte	342
Maeniana	17
Magister Collegii	329
—— Equitum	150
—— Navis	406
—— Pagi	69
—— Populi	146
—— Societatis	239
—— Vici	69
Magistrates of Coloniae	89
—— Election of	172
—— General Remarks on the higher	172—184
—— Inferior under the Empire	201
—— Inferior under the Republic	195
—— of Municipia	91
—— New, under the Empire	199—201
—— of Praefecturae	92
—— Qualification as to age	173
—— Qualification as to birth	173
—— Qualification as to Re-election	175
Magistratum deponere	180
Magistratus	79, 80, 172
—— Ordinarii— Extraordinarii—Curules —Non Curules—Patricii —Plebeii — Majores— Minores	183, 184
—— Designati	179
—— Vitio creati	179
Magistri Vicorum	169, 201
Maia	319
Majestatem minuere	302
Majestas	302
Major Consul	135
Majora Auspicia	184
Majores Flamines	362
Majus	319, 362, 367
Majus Imperium	184
Mala Carmina	274
Malus	404
Matutinus Pater	320
Mamers	319
Mamertinus Carcer	28
Mamillare	456
Manceps	239, 272
Mancipatio	258, 260
Mancipio dare—accipere	258
Mancipium	94
Mandare	272
Mandata Principum	245
Mandatarius	272
Mandatum	271, 272
Mane	428
Manes	323
Mangones	96
Mania	321, 323
Manicatae Tunicae	452
Manipulus	382—384
Manum Conserere	282
Manumissio	100
—— per Censum	101
—— inter Amicos	103
—— Justa	101
—— per Epistolam	103

	Page
Manumissio per Mensam	103
—— per Testamentum	101
—— per Vindictam	100
Manumission, Informal	103
—— by the State	103
—— of Slaves	100
Mansiones	53
Mantelia	442
Manus	249
—— Ferreae	407
—— Injectio	269, 278
Mappa	349
Mappae	442
Mars s. Mavers	319
—— Gradivus	333
—— Silvanus	319
Marriage	249—252
—— Ceremonies	423
—— in May	423
Marspiter	319
Mater Matuta	322
Materfamilias	251
Matrona	251
Matronalia	317
Matrimonii Dissolutio	252
Matrimonium Injustum	250
—— Justum	250
Mausoleum Augusti	47
Meals	436
Medicamina Faciei	457
Medius (Lectus)	440
Megalesia	157, 323
Membrana	459
Mensa	440
Mensae Secundae	442
Mensarii	271
Menses	362, 367, 368, 37
Mensis Intercalaris	372
Menstruum	99
Mercatores	238
Mercurius	319
Merenda	437
Meridiani	360
Meridiei Inclinatio	428
Meridies	428
Merum	442
Meta Sudans	36
Metae	348, 389
Metalla	284
Meton, Cycle of	370
Metatores	386
Micare (Digitis)	444
Mile, Roman, compared with English	410
Military Affairs	397—402
—— Pay	391
—— Standards	392
Milites	444
Militia Equestris	76
Mille Passuum	409
Milliaria	53
Milliarium Aureum	18
Mini	352, 356
Minerva	317, 320
Minerval	422
Ministers of Religion	326—337
Minor Coelius	2
Minor Campus	346
Minora Auspicia	184
Minores Flamines	332
—— Magistratus	195
Minus Imperium	184
Mirmillones	360
Missilia	358
Missio	392

	Page
Missus	349, 440
Mitrae	451
Modius	409, 461
Modus Lydius	449
—— Dorius	449
—— Phrygius	449
Mola Salsa	342
Monaulos	448
Moneta	416
Monilia	456
Monocrota	405
Mons Albanus	1
—— Aventinus	2, 32
—— Augustus	34
—— Coelius	2, 34
—— Capitolinus	2, 25
—— Cispius	2, 36
—— Esquilinus	2, 36
—— Oppius	2, 37
—— Palatinus	2, 28
—— Pincius	2, 38
—— Querquetulanus	2, 34
—— Sacer	141
—— Saturnius	5
—— Tarpeius	25
—— Testaceus	83
—— Vaticanus	3, 49
Monte Testaccio	33
Month, divisions of	363
Months, Julian Year	362
—— Year of Romulus	367
—— Numa	368, 372
Monumentum Catuli	26
—— Marii	26
Morbus Comitialis	114
Moriones	447
Morra	444
Mors	309
Morum Regimen	166, 168
Mourning Dress	457
Mucia Prata	49
Mulciber	319
Mulcta	310
Mulleus	221
Mulsum	439
Mundus Muliebris	457
Munera Gladiatoria	346, 358
Municipes	90
Municipia	90—92
—— in the Provinces	190
Munus	360
Murrhina (Vasa)	443
Musculi	400
Music	447
Musical Instruments	448
Mustum	438, 439
—— Lixivium	438
—— Pressum	438
—— Tortivum	438
Mutare Vestem	75
Mutui Datio	268
N. L.	108, 299
Naeniae	426
Names	61—63
—— of Libertini	101
—— of Slaves	95
—— of Women	63
Nani	447
Nardus	446
Nardinum	447
Natatio	351
—— s. Natatorium	434
Nauclerus	406
Naumachia	351

INDEX. 507

	Page
Nautae	406
Nautea	403
Navales Socii	406
Navalia	47
Naval Affairs	402—407
—— Warfare	406
Navarchus	406
Naves	403
—— Longae	405
—— Practoriae	406
—— Turritae	406
Nefas	324
Negotiatores	431
Nemus Caesarum	49
Nemoralia	318
Neptunalia	319
Neptunus	319
Neria s. Nerlene	319
Nervi	449
Nethuns	319
Nexi	269
Nexu Solutus	270
Nexu Vinctus	269
Nexum	269
Nexum ire	269
Nexus	269
Night, Divisions of	428
Nobiles	67
Noctis Mediae Inclinatio	429
Nominis Delatio	295
Nomen	61
—— Facere—Scribere	270
—— Latinum	94, 378
—— (Mercantile)	270
—— Transcriptitium	270
Nomenclator	178
Nominis Receptio	295
Non Liquet	108, 299
Nonae	363, 368
Notice of Comitia	113
Notatio Censoria	168
Notio Censoria	168
Nova Nupta	423
—— Via	22
Novellae (Constitutiones Iustinian)	246
—— (Constit. Imp. Leon,)	246
—— Constitutiones (Cod. Theod.)	245
Novae (Tabernae)	18
Novacula	458
Noverca	267
November	362, 367
Novi Homines	67
Nox Intempesta	429
Nox Concubia	429
Noxae Deditio	310
Nubere	425
Nummi Familiarum	416
Nuntium Mittere	423
Nundinae	364
Nuptiae cum Conventione	251
—— Iniustae	250
—— Iustae	250
—— sine Conventione	251
Nuntiatio	112, 113
Nurus	267
Oath of Office for Magistrates	180
Obelisks in the Circus	348
Obligationes, Definition and Classification	268
—— ex Consensu	271
—— ex Delicto	273, 275

	Page
Obligationes, ex Contractu	268—272
—— Litteris	270
—— quasi ex Delicto	274
—— quasi ex Contractu	274
—— Re	268
—— Verbis	269
Obmovere	342
Obnuntiatio	112, 113
Obolus	409
Obsecrare	324
Obsignatores	298
Obsignare	461
Obsidio	399, 401
Obsidione Cingere	401
Ocrea	384
Octodecim Centuriae Equitum	69, 72, 73
October	362, 367
Octavae	233
Octussis	408
Octaviae Opera	45
Octaeteris	370
Odd and Even	444
Oeci	465
Official Dresses	454
Officers of Legion	386
Omen	328
Onychites s. Onyx	440
Opalia	319
Operae (Publicanorum)	239
Opisphorae	404
Opifex	431
Opisthographus	460
Oppidum	348
Oppida	93
Oppius, Mons	2, 37
Oppugnatio	399
Ops	319
Optimates	67
Optio	384
Optiones	386
Orae	404
Orchestra	221, 354
Orciniana Sponda	426
Orcus	321
Ordines Remorum	405
Ordinarii	360
Ordo	384
—— Equester	71, 74
—— Magistratuum	174
—— Publicanorum	238
—— Scribarum	198
—— Senatorius	223
Organization of Legion	381
Origin of Roman People	60
Ornamenta Aedilitia	140
—— Consularia	139
—— Practoria	140
—— Quaestoria	140
Oscines	111
Osiris	323
Ostia	348
Ostiarius	463
Ostium	463
Ova	348, 350
Ovatio	395
Ovilia	46, 108
Pactum Dotale	253, 254
Paedagogus	422
Paenula	454
Paganalia	69, 319

	Page
Pagi	68
Pagina	459
Palaestrae	433
Palatium	2, 28
Palazzo Caffarelli	25
Paludamentum	460
Pales—Palilia	322
Palimpsestus	460
Palla	453, 456
Pallas	317
Pallium	451
Palmae	352
Palmipes	409
Palmulae	405
Palmus	409
—— Maior	410
Paludamentum	401
Paludatus	401
Paludes Pomptinae	1
Palus Capreae	48
Pan	322
Pandectae	246
Pantheon	47
Pantomimi	352
Papyrus	459
Parcae	323
Parens Patriae	208
Parentales Dies	428
Parentalia	428
Parentare	428
Parma	384
Parrici Quaestores	289, 304
Parricida	304
Parricide, Punishment of	305
Parricidium	300, 304
Parties in Civil Suits	277
Pascua	232
Passus	409
Pastores	234
Patagium	456
Patella	343
Pater Patratus	83, 332
Pater Patriae	208
Patera	343
Paterae	443
Patres	63
—— Conscripti	77
—— Maiorum Gentium	77
—— Minorum Gentium	77
—— Patricii	77
Patria Potestas	247
Patricii	63
Patrimi et Matrimi	251
Patrons and Clients	64
Patroni	63
Patroni (legal)	277
Patronus	101
Patronus and Libertus	101
Patronus (pleader)	312
Paxillus	405
Pay of the soldiers	391
Pecten	449—455
Pectorale	384
Pecuaria	411
Pecuarii	158, 234, 238
Peculatus	307
Peculium	95
—— Castrense	259
Pecuniae Residuae	308
Pedarii Senatores	220
Pedes	404
Peditatus	378
Pedites, Number in Legion	381
Pedibus in Sententiam Ire	219
Pellex	250
Penates	321

INDEX.

Pensum... 458
Penetralia... 464
Perduellio... 309
Peregrini,... 80, 85, 250
——— Dediticii... 85
Peregrina Iurisdictio... 153
Perfumes... 445
——— mixed with wine 446
Pergamena... 459
Period of Military Service 392
Peristylium... 464
Perscribere ab Argentario 271
Personae, Alieni Iuris... 247
——— Classification of 247
——— in Mancipio... 256
——— in Manu... 249
——— in Potestate Parentum... 247
——— in Tutela... 254
——— Sui Iuris... 247
Pertica... 409
Pes... 404
—— (measure)... 409
Petasus... 450
Petere... 179
Petitio... 179
Petitor... 267, 277, 315
Petitores... 179
Phalanx... 382
Phalangae... 402
Phalerae... 395
Phialae... 443
Philosophus... 422
Philyra... 443, 461
Philyrae... 459
Phinnus... 443
Phoebus... 818
Phuphluns... 320
Piazza di Pescheria... 46
——— Navona... 48
Picariae... 234
Pignoris Captio... 278
Pignus... 269
Pila... 432
—— Trigonalis... 433
—— Paganica... 432
Pilae... 462
Pilani... 384
Pileus... 401, 450
Pilum... 384
Pinacotheca... 465
Pinarii... 336
Piscatorii Ludi... 49
Piscina... 434
——— Publica... 34
Pistores... 437
Pistrinum... 465
Pitch and Toss... 444
Pius, as a title... 209
Plagula... 459
Planipedes... 356
Planipediae... 356
Pleaders in Courts of Law 311
—313
Plebs, amalgamated with Clientes... 66
—— of later times... 66
—— origin of... 65
Plebes s. Plebis, origin of... 64
Plebeian Gentes... 66
Plebiscita... 123, 243
Plectrum... 449
Pleaders, Remuneration... 312
Pleading, Time allowed... 312
Plutei... 400

Poculum... 442
Podium... 356, 358
Poena Capitalis... 83
Pollex... 409
Pollinctor... 425
Polluctum... 342
Pollux... 321
Pomeridianum Tempus... 428
Pomoerium... 4
Pomona... 322
Pompa Circi... 352
——— Funebris... 426
——— Nuptialis... 424
Pons Aelius... 51
——— Aemilius... 51
——— Aurelius... 52
——— Cestius... 51
——— Fabricius... 51
——— Gratianus... 51
——— Lapideus... 51
——— Lepidi... 51
——— Milvius... 52
——— Neronianus... 52
——— Probi... 52
——— Pontes, Ponticulus (in voting)... 108
——— Sublicius... 8, 50
Ponte S. Angelo... 51
——— S. Bartolomeo... 51
——— Molle... 52
——— Quattro Capi... 51
——— Rotto... 51
——— Sisto... 52
Pontes... 50, 403
Pontifex Maximus... 326, 327
——— under the Empire... 206
Pontifices... 326—328
——— Minores... 327
Popae... 341
Populares... 67
Populi Fundi... 92
Populus Romanus... 69
——— et Plebs... 65
Porca Praecidanea... 428
Porta Capena... 7, 33
——— Carmentalis... 7
——— Coelimontana... 7
——— Collina... 7, 335
——— Decumana... 397
——— Esquilina... 7
——— Flaminia... 43
——— Flumentalis... 7
——— Fontinalis... 7
——— Ianualis... 20
——— Lavernalis... 7
——— Mugionis s. Mugonia 5
——— Naevia... 7
——— Navalis... 7
——— Palatii... 5
——— Praetoria... 397
——— Principalis Dextra... 397
——— Sinistra... 397
——— Querquetulana s. Querquetularia... 7
——— Ratumena... 7
——— Rauduscularia... 7
——— Romana s. Romanula 5
——— Salutaris... 8
——— Sanqualis... 8
——— Scelerata... 7
——— Trigemina... 7
——— Triumphalis... 8, 393
——— Viminalis... 7
Porticus ad Nationes... 44

Porticus Aemilia... 33
——— Argonautarum... 47
——— Catuli... 29
——— Corinthia... 44
——— Europae... 43
——— Metelli... 45
——— Octavia... 44, 45
——— Polae... 43
——— Pompeii... 44
——— Vipsania... 43
Portitores... 238
Portoria... 235
Portunus... 314
Posidonium... 47
Possessio... 226
Possessor... 226
Possidere... 226
Postliminium... 83
Potestas... 134, 181
——— (Tribunicia)... 204
Potitii... 336
Praecinctiones... 354, 356
Praecones... 198
Praedes... 281
Praefecti... 187
——— Aerarii... 164
——— Morum... 171
——— Sociorum... 386
Praefectus Aegypti... 193
——— Alae... 384
——— Annonae s. Rei Frumentariae... 158, 200
——— Augustalis... 193
——— Classis... 406
——— Navis... 406
——— Praetorio... 200, 390
——— Urbi... 132
——— Urbis s. Urbi... 171
——— Vigilum 160, 200, 399
Praepetes... 111
Praeficae... 426
Praefecturae... 92
Praefericulum... 313
Praeiudicia... 244
Praeire Verba... 333
Praemia... 391
Praemio Legis... 176
Praenomen... 421
Praerogativa... 119
Praesecta... 342
Praesens Profiteri... 177
Praescriptum Puerile... 212
Praesides Provinciarum... 193
Praeterire... 214
Praeteriti Senatores... 169, 214
Praetextatus... 337, 428
Praetoriani... 389
Praevaricatio... 314
Praetorship under the Empire... 155
Praetor Peregrinus... 153
Praetores... 133, 153—155
Praetoriae Cohortes... 389
Praetores, in Criminal Trials... 291
——— Aerarii... 164
Praetor Candidatus... 179
Praetor Tutelaris... 155
Praetor Urbanus... 153
Praetor de Fideicommissis 155
Praetorium... 396
Prandium... 436
Prata Flaminia... 1, 43
—— Quinctia... 3
—— Mucia... 49

INDEX.

	Page
Poena Capitalis	80
Postulatio	295
Prayers	338
Precationes	338
Preces	338
Prehensio	134, 144
Prelum	438
Prensare	178
Prensio	181
Prescription	259
President in Comitia, his functions	106
Priapus	323
Priests, Age, Precedence, &c.	337
Priests, General Remarks on	336, 337
Primani	381
Primigenius Sulcus	4
Primipilus	387, 393
Princeps	208
—— Iuventutis	76, 208
—— Senatus	208, 214
Principes	383–385, 388
Principia	384, 397
Principium in the Comitia Tributa	126
Principium in the Comitia Curiata	115
Privatus	194
Privigna	267
Privignus	267
Pro Consule rem gerere	182
—— Imperio agere	181
—— Magistratu agere	181
—— Potestate agere	181
Processus Consularis	137
Procincta Classis	259
Proconsul	182, 187, 193, 194, 195
—— as an imperial title	205
Proconsulare Imperium	182, 183, 195
—— Imperium of the Emperors	205
Procubitores	383
Procuratio Aedium sacrarum	158
Procurator	98, 277, 272, 280
Procuratores Caesaris	192
Prodictator	149
Profanus	324
Professional Business	431
Profiteri	177, 179
—— ad Publicanum	234
Proletarii	70, 378, 385
Prolusio	361
Promulgare Rogationem	106
Promulsis	441
Pronubae	424
Propagatio Imperii	182
Property, Right of	257
—— Modes of acquiring	258
Propes	404
Propino	443
Propraetor	182, 187, 195
Propugnacula	406
Proquaestor	182
Prora	403
Prorogatio Imperii	182
Proserpina	320
Prosicìae	342
Prothyrum	463
Protropum	435

	Page
Provinces, Landed Property	189
—— Constitution of	186
—— List of, under Republic	90
—— of the Magistrates	184—195
—— Taxation	189
—— under the Empire	192
Provincia, Aquaria	162
—— Signification	184, 186
—— Urbana	153
Provinciae Consulares	185, 186, 191
—— Imperatoriae	192, 193
—— Praetoriae	186, 191
—— Senatoriae	192, 193
Provincial Governors	186. 187, 188
Provinciam Dare extra Ordinem	185
Provincias Sortiri, &c.	185
Provocatores	360
Psaltriae	447
Public Lands	225—231
Publicani	238
Publicum	232
—— Quadragesimae	235
Pugilatus	350, 432
Pugilares	460
—— Eborei	460
—— Membranei	460
Pugna	351
Puer	94
Pueri Symphoniaci	447
Pullati	457
Pulli	111
Pulmentum	437
Puls	437
Pulvini	440
Pulvinaria	344
Punctum	109
Punishments	309
Pupae	340
Pupilli	255
Puppis	403
Purpurissum	457
Puteal Libonis	12
—— Scribonianum	12
Pyra	426
Pyrgus	443
Quadragesima	235, 237
—— Litium	237
Quadrans (at the bath)	433, 436
—— (weight)	408
—— (coin)	412—433, 436
Quadrantal	410
Quadrigae	349
Quadrigarii	350
Quadrigati	415
Quadriremes	405
Quaesitores	160
Quaestio	289
—— (Torture)	297
Quaestor Candidatus	164, 179
—— Principis	164
Quaestores	132, 160—164
—— Aerarii	160, 289
—— Caesaris	164
—— Classici	161
—— Consulis	164
—— (Judicial)	289

	Page
Quaestores Parricidii	160, 289
—— Provinciarum	164
—— Urbani	161
Quaestorii Ludi	164
Quaestorium	398
Quaestiones Perpetuae	290–309
Quaestorship under the Empire	163
Quartarius	411
Quaterne Centesimae	420
Quatuordecim ordines	75, 355
Quatuorviri Viis in Urbe purgandis	97
Quercus Civilis	359
Quinae Mercedes	420
Quinarius	515
Quincunx	408
Quincuplices	460
Quinctilii s. Quinctiliani	385
Quindecemviri Sacrorum	330
Quinquagesima	237
Quinquagesima Mancipiorum Venalium	237
Quinquatria	422
Quinquatrus s. Quinquatria	317
Quinquatrus Minusculae	317
Quinque Tabernae	18
Quinqueremes	405
Quinquertium	350
Quintanae	369
Quintilis	362, 367
Quirinus	419, 322
Quiritare	61
Quirites	60
Quorum in Comitia	110
—— of Senate	221
Radere	445
Radius	458
Ramnes s. Ramnenses	61, 71
Ramnenses Priores	72
—— Posteriores	72
Rapina	273, 274
Raptim Ludere	433
Rationes Conficere	270
—— ad Aerarium referre	192
Receptitia Bona	253
Recuperatores	277
Redimere	170
Redemtor	170, 272
Redemtores	238
Re-election of Magistrates	176
Referre ad Senatum	218
Reges	131, 132
Regia	14, 331
Regifugium	372
Regilla	423
Regimen Morum	166, 168
Regina	331
Regio Collina	8, 68
—— Esquilina	8, 68
—— Palatina	8, 68
—— Suburana	8, 68
—— Transtiberina	3, 49
Regiones of Augustus	9
—— of Servius	8, 68
—— Rusticae	68
—— Urbanae	68
Regis Sacrificuli Domus	21
Reiectio Iudicum	296
Relatio	218
Relationship, Table of Degrees	266
Relegatio	84

INDEX.

	Page
Religio	324
Religion of Rome	316
Remex	465
Remi	465
Remigium	465
Remoria s. Remuria	32
Remulcum	465
Renuntiare Magistratum	179
Renuntiatio	252
Repagula	348, 349
Repetundae	306
Repotia	425
Replicatio	280
Repositoria	442
Republic	195—199
Repudium	252, 423
Res, Classification of	256
—— Iudicatae	244
—— Mancipi	257
—— Nec Mancipi	257
Rescripta Principum	245
Resecrare	324
Reserved Seats in Circus	347
—————— in Theatre	354
Resignare	461
Responsa Augurum	329
Responsa Prudentium	244
Restipulatio	270, 283
Restipulator	270
Retentio	254
Retiarii	360
Reticulum	456
—————— Luteum	424
Retinacula	404
Reus	315, 267, 277
Revenue, Sources	233
—————— from Land	233
—————— Mode of Collecting	238
—————— Total Amount	239
Revenues	232—240
Rewards, Military	393
Rex Sacrificus s. Sacrificulus	153, 331
Rex Sacrorum	153, 331
Rex as a title of the Emperors	210
Rhetor	422
Ricae s. Riculae	456
Ricinium	456
Robigus—Robigalia	320
Rogare Legem—Rogare Magistratus, &c.	166
Rogatio	166
Rogatores	109
Rogus	426
Roma Quadrata	5
Roman People, origin of	60
Roman Law	241—275
Roman Law, Systems	245
Romani Cives, their rights	80
Romulus	322
Rorarii	70, 383
Rostra	13
—— Iulia	13
Rostrum	406
Rudentes	404
Rudes	359
Rudus	35
Ruminalis Ficus	29
Rupes Tarpeia	25
Saburra	403
Saccare (Vinum)	439
Saccus Nivarius	439
—— Vinarius	439

	Page
Sacellum	324, 405
—— Deae Carnae	34
—— Dianae	34
—— Ditis	28
—— Iovis Fagutalis	37
—— Larum	22
—— Minervae Captae	34
—— Pudicitiae Patriciae	39
—— Streniae	21
Sacer	309, 324
—— Clivus	21
Sacerdos	324
Sacerdotes Summorum Collegiorum	326
Sacra Privata	117
—— Via	21
Sacramento adigere	379
Sacramentum	278, 283, 324, 379
Sacrare	324
Sacrarium	324
Sacratio Capitis	309
Sacred Utensils	343
Sacred Banquets	344
Sacrificia	340
Sacrilegium	307
Sancrosancta Potestas	141, 156
Sacrosanctus	309
Sacrum	324
Sagittarii	378, 386
Sagum	401, 451
Saltaria Carmina	333
Saliares Dapes	334
Salii	333
—— Agonales	334
—— Collini	334
—— Palatini	334
Salinae	32, 231
Saltatrices	447
Saltus	350, 410, 432
Salutatio	429, 430
Sambuca	449
Sambacistriae	447
Samnites	360
Sanctus	324
Sapa	439
Sarta Tecta exigere	170, 272
Satura	220
Saturnalia	321, 422
Saturnia	5
Saturnus	320
Saxum Rubrum	33
—— Tarpeium	25
Scalae	354, 356
—— Gemoniae	28
Scalmus	405
Scalprum Librarium	459
Scapus	59
Scena	353, 354
—— Ductilis	354
—— Versatilis	354
Scheda	459
Schola Octaviae	45
Sciaterica	429
Scorpiones	400
Scribae	197
—— ab Aerario	198
Scribendo Adesse	220
Scribere ab Argentario	271
—— Milites	379
Scrinia	462
Scriptura	234
Scripturarii	238
Scripturarius ager	234
Scrupulum	408

	Page
Scutum	383, 384
Securis	134, 343
Secespita	343
Secundani	381
Sectatores	178
Secular Games	375, 376
Seculum	375
Senatores	360
Sella Curulis	67
Sellisternium	345, 441
Semestre Imperium	118
Semisextula	408
Semis s. Semissis	405
Semis (coin)	412
Semimodius	411
Semo Sancus	322
Semones	322
Semuncia	408
Senaculum	14
Senate	213—224
—— Manner of choosing	213
—— Meetings	217
—— Mode of Summoning	217
—— Mode of conducting business	218
—— Numbers of	78
—— Origin of	77
—— Place of Meeting	218
—— Power and Duties	215
—— Qualifications of Members	214
—— Quorum	221
—— Relation to Magistrates	217
—— under the Kings	215
—— under the Republic	216—222
—— under the Empire	222—224
Senatores Pedarii	220
Senatores Praeteriti	169
Senators not allowed to trade	214
Senators, Number under Empire	223
Senatum Consulere	219
—— Legere	167
—— Numerare	221
—— Vocare s. Cogere	217
Senatus	16, 63, 80
—— Auctoritas	220
—— Consultum	220, 243
—— Consultum Turpilianum	7
—— Frequens	21
—— Infrequens	218
Seniores	444
Sententiam Dicere	219
—— Dividere	220
Sentina	403
Sepia	460
Seplasia	447
Septa	46, 168
—— Iulia	46
—— Agrippiana	46
Septem Tabernae	81
Septemviri Epulones	330
Septimanae	369
Septimontium	8
Septizonium	30
Septunx	408
Sepulcrum	427
Sequestres	179
Serapeum	47

INDEX.

	Page
Serapis	323
Sericum	457
Serrati	415
Serta	341, 444
Servants of the Magistrates	197
Servare de Coelo	112
Serlae	438
Servi	80, 94—100, 250
—— Ordinarii	98
—— Publici	103
—— Soluti	97
—— Vincti	97, 99
—— Vulgares	98
Servian Walls	6
Serviles Nuptiae	250
Servilius Lacus	20
Servitus	310
Servitutes	257
—— —— Praediorum Urbanorum	257
—— —— Praediorum Rusticorum	257
—— —— Praediales	257
Sescunx	408
Sesquipes	409
Sestertia	418
Sestertii	419
Sestertio	419
Sestertium	418
Sestertius	415
—— Value of	418
Sesuncia	408
Sethlans	319
Seven Hills of Rome	1
Sex Centuriae Equitum	72
—— Suffragia	72
Sexprimi	198
Sextans (weight)	408
—— (Coin)	412
Sextarius	411
Sextilis	362, 367
Sextula	408
Ships	402, 407
Sicarii	305
Sicilicus	408
Signa	392
Signifer	402
Signum	396
Silentium	112
Silice Sternere	53
Silicernium	427
Siliqua	408
Silvanus	322
Silver Coinage	415
Simpulum	343
Simpuvium	343
Sindon	457
Sinistra Ala	387
Sinus	415
Siparium	356
Sistrum	450
Site of Rome	1
Sitella	108, 109, 299
Slave Dealers	96
Slaves	94—100
—— as Witnesses	297
—— Classification of	97
—— Dress and Food	99
—— Manumission	100
—— Number of	97
—— Price of	96
—— Punishments	99
Sobrinus (a) Propior	672
Sobrini (ae)	267

	Page
Socci Lutei	424
Socer	267
Societates	431
—— Publicanorum	298, 259
Socii	94, 272, 378, 385
—— Navales	406
—— (Publicani)	238
Soccus	356
Societatis Auctor	239
—— —— Magister	239
Societas	271, 272
Socrus	267
Sodales Augustales	210, 336
—— Claudiales	336
—— Flaviales	336
—— Hadrianales	336
—— Titiales	336
—— Titii	336
Sodalitates—Sodalitia	178, 309
Sol	319
Solaria	429
Soldier, the Roman	378
Soleae	450, 454
Solennitas Consularis	140
Solis Ortus	428
—— Occasus	428
Solitaurilia	341
Solstitium	428
Soluti legibus	176
Solvere ab Argentario	271
Soranus	323
Sordidati	75
Sorores Patruelea	267
Sors	419
—— Peregrina	153, 186
—— Urbana	153, 186
Sortitio Iudicum	296
Sparsiones	358
Spectio	113
Speculum	455, 457
Sphaeristerium	433
Spina	348, 350
—— Alba	424
Spinning	458
Spolia	395
—— Opima	395
Spoliarium	361
Spondeo	270
Sponsalia	423
Sponsio	283
—— Poenalis	283
—— Praeiudicialis	283
Sponsores	281
Sponsus—Sponsa	423
Sportula	66, 429, 430
Spurii	250
Stagna Neronis	36
Stamen	458
Standards	392
Stationes	399
Statue of Cloelia	22
—— of Horatius Cocles	14
—— of Marsyas	17
Statues in the Forum	17
Status	83
—— Permutatio	83
Statumen	53
Statumina	403
Stilus	460
Stipendia Splendidae Militiae	76
Stipendium	391
Stips s. Stipes	411
Stipulatio	270, 283

	Page
Stipulator	270
Stola	456
Strada del Corso	43
Streniae Sacellum	21, 36
Strigil	434
Stropha	405
Strophium	456
Structor	442
Struppus	408
Subucula	452
Subsellia	145, 280
Subscriptio	295
—— Censoria	168
Subscriptores	295, 312, 313
Subsortitio Iudicum	296
Subtemen	458
Suburra	3
Succession, Law of	263
—— to the Empire	211
Sudatorium	434
Suffragatores	178
Suffragia Diribere — Dirimere—Describere	108
Suffragium inire—ferre, &c.	106
Sulcus Primigenius	4
Summa Nova Via	22
—— Sacra Via	21
Summanus	321
Summus (Lectus)	440
Sun-dials	429
Suovetaurilia	171, 341
Suppara	404
Supparus	453
—— s. Supparum	457
Supplicatio	338, 345, 394
Suscipere liberos	421
Suspensurae Caldariorum	434
Symphoniae	447
Syngraphae s. Syngrapha	271
Synthesis	454
Tabellariae Leges	108
Tabellarii	461
Tabellas Diribere	108
Tabernaculum	112, 325
—— in Augury	112
Tabernae Argentariae	19
—— Librariae	462
—— Novae	18
—— (Quinque)	18
—— (Septem)	18
—— Veteres	18
Tabernola	3
Tablinum	465
Tabula	460
—— Lusoria	443
—— Sestia	18
—— Valeria	18
Tabulae Caeritum	82
—— Censoriae	166
—— Ceratae	459, 460
—— Testamenti	460
—— (in evidence)	298
Tabularium	28, 163
Tabulas conficere	270
Tabulata	400, 403
Taedae	424
Taenia	405
Talares Tunicae	452
Tali	443
Teaching	422
Tellus	319
Templum	112, 325
—— Aesculapii	48
—— Apollinis	43

INDEX.

Templum Apollinis Palatini 29
—— Bellonae.......... 43
—— Bonae Deae..... 33
—— Capere.......... 112
—— Castoris et Pollucis................. 44
—— Censurae...... 167
—— Cereris, Liberi et Liberae............... 39
—— Concordiae...... 27
—— Dianae.......... 32
—— Dei Fidii 48
—— Dianae et Iunonis Reginae........ 44
—— Divae Faustinae 14
—— Divi Claudii ... 35
—— Traiani.... 23
—— Fauni 48
—— Felicitatis...... 14
—— Fidis............ 26
—— Florae........38, 39
—— Fortis Fortunae.. 49
—— Fortunae Equestris.................. 44
—— Fortunae Primigeniae................ 38
—— Fortunae Virilis 39, 42
—— Herculis Custodis 44
—— Honoris et Virtutis..............26, 33
—— Iani 20
—— Iani Quadrifrontis................... 23
—— Iovis............ 48
—— Iovis Capitolini.. 25
—— Iovis Custodis .. 27
—— Iovis Feretrii ... 26
—— Iovis, Iunonis et Minervae............25, 38
—— Iovis Statoris ... 46
—— Iovis Tonantis.. 27
—— Isidis........... 35
—— Iunonis 46
—— Iunonis Monetae 27
—— Iunonis Matutae 43
—— Iunonis Reginae 33
—— Iunonis Sospitae 43
—— Iuturnae........ 48
—— Inventatis 39
—— Libertatis 33
—— Lunae 33
—— Magnae Matris.. 29
—— Martis 34, 44
—— Matris Matutae.. 39
—— Mentis.......... 26
—— Mercurii 39
—— Minervae...16, 23, 33
—— Neptuni......44, 47
—— Pacis 31
—— Pietatis........ 44
—— Quirini........ 38
—— Salutis 38
—— Saturni 28
—— Semonis Sanci.. 48
—— Solis........39, 43
—— Spei 43
—— Summani 39
—— Telluris....... 36
—— Tiberini....... 48
—— Martis Ultoris..22, 27
—— Veiovis 27
—— Victoriae...... 29
—— Veneris 39

Templum Veneris Erycinae 26, 38
—— Veneris Genetricis 22
—— Veneris et Romae 31
Tenebrae Primae 429
Tepidarium 434, 435
Terentum 48
Tergiversatio 313
Terminus—Terminalia ... 322, 369, 372
Terra Mater 319
Terreus Murus........... 36
Tertiani 381
Teruncius............... 408
Tessera 399
—— Hospitalis........ 86
Tesserae 413
Tesserarii 399
Testamenta 259, 265
Testamenti Nuncupatio... 260
Testamentum in Procinctu 259
Testamentum per Aes et Libram 260
Testator................ 260
Testes (Criminal Trials)... 297
Testimonia (Criminal Trials) 297
Testimonia Publica........ 298
Testudo 400, 449
Thalamus Nuptialis 424
Thalassio 424
Theatres............... 353
Theatrum Balbi 44
—— Marcelli 44
—— Pompeii...... 44
Thensae 352
Thermae 435
—— Agrippae 47
—— Alexandrinae... 48
—— Diocletiani..... 38
—— Titi........... 36
Thermopolia 389
Thesan 323
Thorax................. 384
—— Laneus........... 452
Threces................ 360
Tibia................... 448
Tibiae Dextrae........448, 449
—— Doriae......448, 449
—— Impares 448, 449
—— Ludicrae.....448, 449
—— Lydiae......448, 449
—— Pares........448, 449
—— Phrygiae 448, 449
—— Sacrificae....448, 449
—— Sinistrae.....448, 449
—— Incentivae...448, 449
—— Succentivae..448, 449
Tibialia 452, 453
Tibicen................. 448
Tigillum Sororium........ 37
Tina s. Tinia 317
Tirocinium Fori 422
Tirones 359
Tities s. Titienses....... 61, 71
Titii Sodales............ 336
Titulus 438
Toga 450, 451
—— Candida 177
—— Liberior.......... 422
—— Picta 393, 455
—— Praetexta 75, 329, 421, 422, 455
—— Pura............. 422
—— Virilis............ 422

Tollere liberos 421
Tondere per Pectinem.... 455
—— Strictim 455
Tonsae 405
Tonsores 455
Tonstrina 455
Topography of Rome ....1—59
Torcular—Torcularium 438
Toreumata.............. 443
Tormenta............380, 400
Torques 395
Trabea 329
Traditio 259
Tralaticium Caput........ 243
Trama 458
Transcriptio 271
Transductio ad Plebem ... 118
Transtra............... 463
Trapezitae 271
Tres Maximae........... 335
Tressis................ 408
Tria Fora.............. 23
—— Verba............ 276
Trials, Criminal ......284—315
—— Civil ......275—286
Triarii..........383, 384, 388
Tribes, Original 61
—— Local 68
Tribes and Centuries Incorporated 120
Tribonianus............. 246
Tribules................ 61
Tribum Conficere........ 178
Tribunal.............12, 280
—— Aurelium 17
Tribunes of the Plebs under the Empire........... 145
Tribuni Aerarii ... 239, 293
—— Laticlavii........ 386
—— Militares Consulari Potestate.........152, 153
—— Militum........ 386
—— Plebis. 141, 145
Tribunicia Potestas........ 204
Tribunus, ... 61
—— Celerum.......73, 132
—— Plebis Candidatus 179
Tributum.............164, 235
Tribus Iure Vocatae 126
—— Praerogativa 126
—— Rusticae........ 68
—— Urbanae......... 68
Triclinia 465
Triclinium 440
Triens (weight) 408
—— (coin) 412
Trientalia 413
Trigae 319
Trigon 433
Trinundinum........113, 365
Triplices 460
Triplicatio............. 280
Triptychi.............. 460
Tripudium Solistimum... 112
Tripus 343
Triremes.............. 405
Triumphalia Ornamenta . 394
Triumphus 393
Triumviri Capitales 17, 196
Triumviri s. Quinqueviri Mensarii............. 198
—— Monetales...... 197
—— Nocturni....... 196
Trochus............... 432
Trossuli................ 72

INDEX. 513

	Page
Trullae	443
Tuba	449
Tullianum	28
Tumultus	380
Tunica	450, 452
—— Augusticlavia	75
—— Interior s. Intima	456
—— Laticlavia	75, 221
—— Molesta	311
—— Palmata	393, 455
—— Recta	423
Turan	318
Turibulum	343
Turricula	443
Turma	384
Turmae Equitum	71
Turms	319
Turres	400, 406
Turris Maecenatiana	37
Tutela	254, 405
Tutores	255, 256
—— Tutores Atiliani— Dativi—Legitimi—Optivi	255
Tympana	449
U. R.	108
Ulna	410
Umbo	451
Umbracula	358
Uncia (weight)	408, 409
—— (coin)	412
Unguenta	446
Unguentarii	447
Umbilici	461
Uniones	444
Urbana Iurisdictio	153
Urceoli Ministratorii	442
Urna	108, 109, 411
Ustrina	426
Usus (Marriage)	252
—— s. Usucapio	259
Ususfructus	251, 258
Usurae	419
—— Centesimae	420
—— Semisses, &c.	999
Uti Rogas	108
Utricularius	449
Uxor	251, 424
Vacci Prata	29
Vacuna	323
Vadari	281
Vades	281, 288
Vadimonium	281
—— Deserere	281
Valli	396
Vallis Egeriae	34
—— Murcia	3, 39, 347
—— Quirini	37
Vallum	396
Vappa	439
Vasa Unguentaria	446
Vasarium	187
Vectigal Mancipiorum- Venalium	237
—— Rerum Venalium	236
Vectigalia	232
—— Conducere	238
—— Locare	238

	Page
Vectigalia Redimere	238
Vedius	321
Velovis	321
Vela	357
Velabrum	3, 39, 40
Velia	2, 60
Velites	383, 384
Venalis	94
Venalitii	66
Venatio	351
—— Direptionis	351
Venefici	305
Veneficia	306
Ventralia	454
Venus	318, 320
—— (in dice)	443
Verna	94
Vernae	99, 250
Versura	420
Versus	410
Vertumnus	322
Vespera	429
Vesperna	436
Vesta—Vestalia	318
Vestales	334
Vestalis Maxima	335
Vestem Mutare	75
Vestes Bombycinae	457
—— Coae	457
—— Holosericae	457
—— Subsericae	457
Vestibulum	463
Vestis Serica	457
Veteres (Tabernae)	18
Veto	143
Vexilla	383, 390, 392
Vexillarii	390
Vexillarius	392
Vexillum	383, 405
Via	258
—— Appia—Latina—Praenestina—Gabina—Collatina—Tiburtina—Sublacensis—Nomentana—Salaria—Flaminia—Cassia—Claudia—Valeria	
—— Ostiensis	53, 54
—— Flaminia	43
—— Lata	42, 43
—— Nova	22
—— Quintana	398
—— Sacra	21
—— di S. Vitale	37
Viae—Viae Militares	52—54
Viatores	143
Vicarii	98
Vicarius	95
Vicesimani	381
Vicesimarium Aurum	236
Vicessis	408
Vici	69, 93
Vicus Cyprius	3
—— Frumentarius	33
—— Ingarius	439, 40
—— Largus	37
—— Patricius	3
—— Sandalius	462
—— Sceleratus	3

	Page
Vicus Tuscus	4, 39, 40
Victimae	340
Victimarii	341
Victoriati	416
Vigesima Hereditatium	239
—— Manumissionum	236
Vigiles	399
Vigilia Prima, &c.	429
Vigiliae	399, 429
Villa Publica	46, 167
Villicus	98
Vinalia	318
Vincula	310
Vindex	269, 280
Vindicare	258, 282
Vindiciae	282
Vindicias dare	282
Vindicta	282
Vineae	400
Vinum	438
—— de Cupa	438
—— Diachytum	439
—— Doliare	438
—— Passum	439
—— (varieties)	440
Viridis Pannus	350
Vis	303
—— Civilis	282
—— Quotidiana	282
Visceratio	427
Vitia	341
Vitricus	267
Vocatio	134, 143, 181
—— in Ius	280
Volones	103
Volsellae	455
Volturnus	323
Vomitoria	354
Voting in Comitia	107—110
Votiva Tabella	338, 346
Votum	338
Vulcanal	14
Vulcanalia	319
Vulcanus	319
Walls of Aurelian	9
—— Honorius	11
—— Probus	15
—— Romulus	1
—— Servius Tullius	5, 59
Weaving	999
Week, Roman	365
Weights	408
Wills	259—265
Wines	437—439
—— mixed with Perfumes	446
Worship of the Gods	337
Writing Materials	999
Xylinum	457
Year of the Decemvirs	372
—— Julian	362
—— of Numa	368, 372
—— of Romulus	367
Zona	456

2 T.

INDEX TO CHAP. XV.—AGRICULTURE.

	Page		Page		Page
Ablaqueatio	489, 490	Lana sucida	492	Rastrum	476
Ador	484	Legumina	484	Res	469
Ager novalis	485	Lens	484	—— Pastoricia	490
—— restibilis	485	Leporaria	496	—— Pecuaria	469, 490
Agricultura	468, 495	Ligo	477	Restibilis ager	485
Alvearia	496	Linum	484	Ridicae	489
Amurca	490	Lira	481	Robur	484
Aratio	480	Lirare	481	Rotation of crops	484, 485
Arator	490	Litres	487	Runcatio	481
Aratrum	472	Lupinus	484	Rutellum	498
Arbustum	488	Malleoli	487	Rutrum	478
Area	482	Manicula	474	Salix	484
Armentarius	490	Manuring	484, 485	Sanitas	491
Armentum	490	Marra	477	Sarculum	479
Arundo	484	Medica	484	Sarritio	481
Asini	494	Messio	481	Satio	480
Aures	474	Milium	484	—— Trimestris	482
Avena	484	Mola Olearia	490	Secale	484
Aviaries	495	Muli	494	Securis Dolabrata	479
Baculis excutere	482	Napus	484	Segetes	490
Bidens	477	Novalis ager	485	Semen Trimestre	484
Bipalium	478	Nutricatus	491	Seminarium vitiarium	487
Boves	493	Occatio	480	Semitae	487
—— domiti	490	Oculos inserere	486	Serum	495
Bubulcus	490	Offringere	480	Siligo	484
Buris	473	Olea	490	Stercus	485
Butyrum	495	Oleitas	490	Sterquilinium	485
Canes	494	Oleum	490	Stirpes	486
Cannabis	484	Olive, cultivation of	490	Stipulatio	491
Capellae	493	Olivum	490	Stiva	473
Caseus	495	Opilio	499	Stock, managing	491
Cicer	484	Ordo	487	—— providing	491
Cochlearia	496	Ornithones	495	Sudes	486
Cognitio Fundi	469	Oves	492	Sues	493
Colonus	490	—— Hirtae	492	Sulcus	481
Conditio	481	—— Pellitae	492	Tabulata	489
Crates	475	Pabula	484	Taleae	490
Crops	483	Pala	478	Temo	473
Culter	475	Pali	489	Tempora	469, 482
Cultus Arborum	468, 486	Pampinatio	489	Terere	482
—— Hortorum	468	Papavera	484	Tonsura Ovium	492
Dairy Produce	495	Pastinatio	489	Traha, Trahea	476, 482
Decumanus	487	Pastinum	479	Trapetum	490
Dentalia—Dentale	473	Pastio	468, 469, 490	Tribulum	476, 482
Dolabra	479	Pastio Agrestis	469, 490, 491	Triticum	484
Equi	493	—— Villatica	469, 495	Tritura	481
Ervum	484	Pastor	490	Trunci	490
Faba	484	Pastores	494	Urpex	475
Fallows	484, 485	Pedamenta	489	Urvom	474
Falx	479	Perticae	489	Valli	486
Far	484	Piscinae	496	Vannus	480
Farrago	484	Pisum	484	Ventilabrum	482
Faselus	484	Plantae	486	Ventilatio	481
Foenum	484	Plaustrum	475	Vervactum	485
Foetura	491	Plostellum Poenicum	476	Viae	487
Frumenta	484	Porca	481	Vicia	484
Fustibus tundere	482	Prata	490	Villa et Stabula	469
Gliraria	496	Propagation of the olive	490	—— Fructuaria	471
Greges villatici	492	Propagation of the vine	487	—— Rustica	471
Hirpex	475	Propagation of trees	486	—— Urbana	470
Hordeum	484	Propago	486	Vine, cultivation of	486-489
Inserere	486	Props for vines	488	Vinea	488, 489
Insitio	486	Proscindere	480	Vinetum	489
Instrumenta	469, 471	Quincunx	488	Vites compluviatae	489
Irpex	475	Ralla	475	—— pedatae	489
Iterare	480	Rallum	475	Vivaria	496
Iugum	473, 489	Rapum	484	Viviradices	487
Lac	495	Rastelli	476	Vomer—Vomis	473

www.ingramcontent.com/pod-product-compliance
Lightning Source LLC
Chambersburg PA
CBHW071219290426
44108CB00013B/1230